A note about the cover: Academic writing is a *recursive* process. As you write, you circle back to rethink your assumptions, expand your understanding, and add support to your ideas. The artwork on the cover of *From Inquiry to Academic Writing* reflects the looping nature of this process.

FROM INQUIRY TO ACADEMIC WRITING

A Text and Reader

FROM INQUIRY TO ACADEMIC WRITING

A Text and Reader

FOURTH EDITION

Stuart Greene
University of Notre Dame

April Lidinsky
Indiana University South Bend

 bedford/st.martin's
Macmillan Learning

Boston | New York

For Bedford/St. Martin's

Vice President, Editorial, Macmillan Learning Humanities: Edwin Hill
Senior Program Director for English: Leasa Burton
Program Manager: John E. Sullivan III
Executive Marketing Manager: Joy Fisher Williams
Director of Content Development: Jane Knetzger
Senior Developmental Editor: Mara Weible
Associate Editor: Stephanie Thomas
Editorial Assistant: Aubrea Bailis
Senior Content Project Manager: Ryan Sullivan
Senior Workflow Project Manager: Lisa McDowell
Production Supervisor: Robert Cherry
Media Project Manager: Rand Thomas
Editorial Services: Lumina Datamatics, Inc.
Composition: Lumina Datamatics, Inc.
Photo Editor: Angela Boehler
Photo Researcher: Richard Fox, Lumina Datamatics, Inc.
Permissions Manager: Kalina Ingham
Senior Art Director: Anna Palchik
Cover Design: William Boardman
Cover Art: Mina De La O/Getty Images
Printing and Binding: LSC Communications

Manufactured in the United States of America.

2 1 0 9 8 7
f e d c b a

For information, write: Bedford/St. Martin's, 75 Arlington Street, Boston, MA 02116

ISBN 978-1-319-07123-3

Acknowledgments

Text acknowledgments and copyrights appear at the back of the book on pages 811–15, which constitute an extension of the copyright page. Art acknowledgments and copyrights appear on the same page as the art selections they cover.

Preface for Instructors

Academic writing can be a challenging hurdle for students entering college. They must learn new habits of writing, reading, and even thinking. That's where *From Inquiry to Academic Writing* comes in. It addresses the challenges of academic writing, offering a clear, methodical approach to meeting those challenges. Our students, and many others, have told us that our approach demystifies academic writing, while helping them to see that its skills carry over to civic participation and life issues beyond their college years.

Specifically, *From Inquiry to Academic Writing: A Text and Reader* is a composition rhetoric and thematic anthology that introduces students to college-level inquiry, analysis, and argument. It is based on a first-year composition course in which we guide students to produce essays that use evidence and sources in increasingly complex ways. In this book, as in our classes, we present academic writing as a collaborative conversation, undertaken to pursue new knowledge. We teach students to see that academic writing is a social act that involves working responsibly with the ideas of others. At the same time, we encourage students to see themselves as makers of knowledge who use sources to advance arguments about important academic and cultural issues.

This fourth edition encompasses an even greater range of academic habits and skills than the third, with more support for synthesis and analysis. The anthology features enhanced and updated multidisciplinary themes. Overall, nearly half the readings are new and explore issues that have become more prominent in academia and public life over the past few years. This edition of *From Inquiry to Academic Writing* is available with LaunchPad, including the complete text and interactive materials in a flexible course space that you can tailor to the needs of your course and students. Read on for details about what's new to the text and to the reader.

A CLOSER LOOK AT THE RHETORIC TEXT

The chapters in the rhetoric begin with academic thinking and proceed through academic reading and research, integrating academic writing throughout. Yet Chapters 1–13 are freestanding enough to be taught in any order that suits your course. What unites them is our constant emphasis on the recursive nature of these skills and the centrality of the writing process. We punctuate every chapter with short readings and activities that prompt students to practice what we teach.

Chapter 1 is an overview of academic writing as a process motivated by inquiry, and it introduces academic habits of mind. Chapter 2 encourages students to practice writerly reading—the rhetorical analysis of other writers' decisions — to learn appropriate strategies for their own writing. Chapter 3 is new and provides students with opportunities to practice basic skills of summary and paraphrase, while learning to write themselves into an academic conversation that entails representing others' ideas accurately. While Chapters 2–6 address the essentials of getting started on writing, from how to mark a text to forming questions and developing a working thesis, we recognize that this process is rarely linear and that it benefits from conversation with invested readers. Chapters 6 and 7 help students develop and support their theses by providing strategies for finding and working with sources. Chapter 8 focuses on synthesis and includes a new set of readings encouraging students to see their everyday lives in and out of school through the lens of civic engagement. Chapter 9 again links writerly reading with readerly writing—this time with writing that reflects rhetorical appeals and strategies of structure and development. Chapter 10 provides new support for visual analysis, including strategies to help students effectively analyze visual rhetoric and incorporate maps, photographs, tables, and graphs to support and enrich their writing. Chapter 11 provides students with strategies for writing introductions and conclusions.

Chapter 12 presents revision in the context of peer groups. The responses of classmates can help students determine when they might need to read additional material to shape more effective research questions, or when they might need more evidence to support an argument. Our supporting materials for peer workshops foster productive group interaction at every stage of the peer review process. Finally, in Chapter 13, we provide students with updated strategies for conducting original research and working with human subjects. This material builds upon earlier chapters about using personal experience and writing a researched argument.

Although the process of developing an academic argument can be unruly, the structured, step-by-step pedagogy in the rhetoric text supports students during each stage of the process. Several readings are followed by

"Reading as a Writer" questions that send students back into the reading to respond to the rhetorical moves writers make. "Steps to" boxes summarize the major points about each stage of thinking, reading, and writing, offering quick references that bring key information into focus for review. "Practice Sequences" ask students to try out and build on the strategies we have explained or demonstrated. We also provide templates, formulas, and worksheets that students may use to organize information as they read and write.

Your students should feel further supported and encouraged by the abundance of student writing (annotated to highlight the rhetorical moves students make) that we use as examples in the rhetoric text, side by side with examples of professional writing.

WHAT'S NEW IN THE RHETORIC CHAPTERS?

Among many smaller revisions, we made the following additions in response to numerous comments by instructors:

- **New emphasis on reflection.** Chapter 1 now offers a series of key reflection prompts to help students take control of their own learning.
- **More support for critical reading and analysis, including multimodal texts.** Chapter 4, on analyzing arguments, helps students read critically and detect causal and definition claims. The new Chapter 10 guides students through analyzing the variety of visuals they encounter in multimodal texts and helps them apply that thinking to their own multimodal projects.
- **New advice on summarizing, now earlier in the book.** The authors discuss summary in a new Chapter 3 — earlier and in more detail than before — to give students a head start with this foundational academic skill.
- **Extended coverage of synthesizing sources.** Chapter 8 uses new readings focused on civic engagement to help students grasp the process and value of successfully synthesizing sources.

A CLOSER LOOK AT THE THEMATIC READER

The thematic reader chapters (Chapters 14–19) are organized into interdisciplinary issues and include both popular and scholarly selections that reflect the kinds of reading and writing college students are expected to do in other college classes. The reading and writing strategies in the first part of the book and the guidelines in the headnotes and questions after the readings help students digest and analyze the selections. Moreover, our students are usually exhilarated by what they discover in the readings — the kind of "big thinking" they came to college to experience.

As you would expect in a book that emphasizes cross-curricular writing, many of the readings come from journals and publications intended for scholarly audiences and thus model what would traditionally be considered academic writing. Among these are selections from the work of Agustín Fuentes, C. J. Pascoe, and Melissa Avdeeff, scholars whose texts are influential among their peers in academe. Other selections are drawn from thought-provoking and engaging books on recent best-seller lists, the kind of books that become popular and sometimes required reading on college campuses. The authors of these books — Sherry Turkle, Carol Dweck, Robert Reich, and Michael Pollan, to name a few — use the same kinds of strategies of research and analysis as academic writers, and like academic writers they use those skills to take on big ideas, frame them in interesting new ways, and offer striking examples that present them provocatively to readers. Still other readings — by Barbara Ehrenreich and William Powers, for instance — are brief and accessible, chosen to draw students into the conversation of ideas that longer selections unpack and extend in greater detail.

While these readings are at some level researched essays — texts that build on ideas others have written — they also provide students with a wide range of rhetorical styles to use as models. Some readings take a journalistic approach and some occasionally dip into autobiographical details, with authors using personal anecdotes to explain their interest in an issue or illustrate an example, while other readings take a more formal tone, relying on research and expertise to build their arguments. We chose these selections in part because of the many different strategies they use to make many different kinds of connections — from the personal to the scholarly, from individual experiences to larger social patterns. This multileveled inquiry is at the heart of the thinking and writing we invite students to learn in this book.

We have divided the selections in the reader into six chapters, each focused on an issue broadly associated with a particular discipline:

Chapter 14, "Education," contains readings that ask, "What does it mean to be educated? Who has access to a good education, and why?" The authors in this chapter ask us to question what it means to get a "real" education in college, despite a culture of distraction. We are also invited to think critically and carefully about the structural inequalities that keep so many children from accessing meaningful education, and to envision solutions that are both personal and political.

Chapter 15, "Sociology," plunges into questions about how shifting cultural understandings of race, class, and gender influence us. The authors in this chapter suggest models for making sense of those three interrelated concerns that shape our daily lives, whether we are conscious of them or not. Concepts such as "system of privilege," "fag discourse," and the "path of least resistance" offer arresting perspectives on this complex arena of ideas.

Chapter 16, "Media Studies," explores the question "What can we learn from what entertains us?" with probing readings on popular culture, from Jean Kilbourne's classic analysis of fashion advertisements to contemporary examinations of Disney Pixar films and Instagram, BuzzFeed, and YouTube. Too often students are reluctant to think critically about popular entertainment, but these readings provide the provocations and tools to do so.

Chapter 17, "Psychology and Biology," takes a broad view in response to the question of how our physical and cultural selves intersect. These selections reveal how cultural assumptions occlude our vision of where nature ends and nurture begins, from understandings of our own potential, to addictive behaviors, to attitudes toward our own and others' perceived identities.

Chapter 18, "Sustainability and Environmental Studies," explores the issue of how our decisions affect our environment. For example, Anna Lappé connects our eating habits to global climate problems, and Michael Pollan makes the case that small personal efforts can have a cumulative positive effect on the environment—an argument challenged by Derrick Jensen and Stephanie McMillan in an excerpt from their graphic text *As the World Burns: 50 Simple Things You Can Do to Stay in Denial.* Andrew Hoffman and McKay Jenkins offer rhetorical advice and evidence for optimism, despite the often gloomy news.

Chapter 19, "Economics," addresses topics that will feel close to home, including the impact of student loans, the phenomenon of the "working poor," and the variety of factors consumers face when making decisions about renting an apartment, considering a career path, or deciding which shirt to buy. In other words, this chapter is pressingly about everyday life and the multifaceted ways we think about "value," "worth," and who we are as consumers and producers.

Every selection in the thematic reader is introduced by a headnote that provides biographical and contextual information, as well as some tactics for students (and instructors) to engage the text actively on first and subsequent readings. Furthermore, every reading is followed by two types of questions, "Reading as a Writer: Analyzing Rhetorical Choices," which asks students to consider the stylistic decisions a writer makes in crafting the piece, and "Writing as a Reader: Entering the Conversation of Ideas," which uses each essay as a launching point for further inquiry, research, and discovery about an issue raised in the text. The questions and assignments in the reader support students by reinforcing the skills and strategies presented in the rhetoric.

The book concludes with an Appendix that introduces the basics of documentation in current MLA and APA styles.

WHAT'S NEW IN THE THEMATIC READER?

- **Many new readings on arresting topics.** While we retained the most popular readings from the third edition, each chapter offers new and relevant texts to choose from, and many of them encourage and model interdisciplinary cultural analysis on popular topics that students will find eye-opening and personally engaging. For example, Sara Goldrick-Rab's analysis of the student loan crisis provides a historical context and offers solutions to a worrying problem. Other new authors debate the "addictive" aspect of screen culture and invite students to understand the psychology of failure and choice-making in potentially life-changing ways.

- **A new Thematic Table of Contents.** More ways to work with the readings appear in the Thematic Table of Contents, which places readings in conversations across chapters and disciplines. Students will have an opportunity to revisit texts through inventive themes and issues that encourage interdisciplinary analysis and flexible thinking, skills that are essential to university thinking and beyond.

- **A new interdisciplinary theme.** At the suggestion of many adopters of the third edition, we have shifted the focus of our "Business and Marketing" chapter and recast it as "Economics." In new readings, Sara Goldrick-Rab argues that making college affordable benefits everyone, and Robert Reich explains how policy shifts have decreased unemployment "while increasing the number of poor people who have jobs."

AVAILABLE IN STANDALONE E-BOOK FORMATS

From Inquiry to Academic Writing is available as an e-Book in a variety of electronic formats. Online at a value price, e-Books are available from a variety of vendors. You can find more information at **macmillanlearning.com/ebooks** or contact your Bedford/St. Martin's representative for more details.

THE TEXT IS AVAILABLE SEPARATELY

If you are interested in assigning only the rhetoric chapters, they are available without the thematic chapters as *From Inquiry to Academic Writing: A Practical Guide*, Fourth Edition.

AN INSTRUCTOR'S MANUAL IS AVAILABLE FOR DOWNLOAD

We have prepared an instructor's manual, *Resources for Teaching From Inquiry to Academic Writing: A Text and Reader*, Fourth Edition. The first part of the manual addresses every step of the process of academic writing we set forth in the rhetoric text, with additional comments on the readings integrated in the text chapters. Not only do we discuss many of the issues involved in taking our rhetorical approach to academic argument— problems and questions students and instructors may have—but we also suggest background readings on the research informing our approach. The second part of the manual provides concrete strategies for teaching the selections in the thematic reader, and is based on our own experiences working with these readings. We also suggest possible responses to the questions that follow the readings in Part 2. The instructor's manual can be downloaded from **macmillanlearning.com**. Visit the instructor resources tab for *From Inquiry to Academic Writing*.

ACKNOWLEDGMENTS

We would first like to thank the many reviewers who commented on the proposal, the manuscript, and the first edition, as well as the reviewers of the second and third editions in both their full and compact iterations. Invariably their comments were useful, and frequently helpful and cheering as well. The list of reviewers includes Andrea Acker, Seton Hill University; Angela Adams, Loyola University–Chicago; Steve Adkison, Idaho State University; Kay Ames, University of Mount Olive; Teresa Fernandez Arab, University of Kansas; Jonathan Arnett, Kennesaw State University; Brian Artese, Kennesaw State University; Yesho Atil, Asheville-Buncombe Technical Community College; Anthony Atkins, University of North Carolina, Wilmington; Paula Bacon, Pace University–Pleasantville; Susan Bailor, Front Range Community College; Mary Ellen Bertolini, Middlebury College; Laurel Bollinger, University of Alabama–Huntsville; Rebecca Boncal, John Tyler Community College; Margaret Bonesteel, Syracuse University; Elizabeth Brewer, Central Connecticut State University; James Brill, University of California, Chico; Laurie Britt-Smith, St. Louis University; Christina Riley Brown, Mercyhurst University; Siobhan Brownson, Winthrop University; William Brugger, Brigham Young University Idaho; Lise Buranen, California State University–Los Angeles; Keely Byars-Nichols, University of Mount Olive; Robin Caine, Montclair State University; Bettina Caluori, Mercer County Community College; Jeffrey Cebulski, Kennesaw State University; Kathleen Chriest, Mercyhurst University; Marie Coffey, San Antonio College; Carolyn Cole, Oklahoma Baptist University; Tami Comstock-Peavy, Arapahoe Community College; Emily Cosper, Delgado Community College; Karen Cox, City College of San Francisco; Donna Craine, Front Range Community College; Ryan Crider, Missouri State University; Virginia Crisco, California State University–Fresno; Bonnie Cross, Community College of Allegheny; Calum Cunningham, Fanshawe College–London; Sarah Dangelantonio, Franklin Pierce University; Alexis Davis, University of Mount Olive; J. Madison Davis, University of Oklahoma–Norman; Anne DeMarzio, University of Scranton; Erin Denney, Community College of San Francisco; Jason DePolo, North

Carolina A&T State University; Brock Dethier, Utah State University; Clark Draney, College of Southern Idaho; Eugenia C. Eberhart, Garden City Community College; Lisa Egan, Brown University; Ed Eleazer, Francis Marion University; Brant Ellsworth, Penn State Harrisburg; Larry Eson, Front Range Community College; Jennifer Fletcher, University of Phoenix; Elaine Fredericksen, University of Texas–El Paso; Hannah Furrow, University of Michigan–Flint; Christine A. Geyer, Cazenovia University; Zan Goncalves, Franklin Pierce University; Rhoda Greenstone, Long Beach City College; Rima Gulshan, George Mason University; Sinceree Gunn, University of Alabama–Huntsville; Clinton Hale, Blinn College; Juli E. Hale, King College; Jane Hammons, University of California, Berkeley; Amy Hankins, Blue River Community College; Ann Hartney, Fort Lewis College; Beth Hedengren, Brigham Young University; Tara Hembrough, Southern Illinois University, Carbondale; Virginia Scott Hendrickson, Missouri State University; Zachery Hickman, University of Miami; Wilbur Higgins, University of Massachusetts Dartmouth; Monica Hogan, Johnson County Community College; Shelli Homer, University of Missouri–Columbia; Jean Incampo, Gateway Community College; Karen Keaton Jackson, North Carolina Central University; Dennis Jerz, Seton Hill University; T. Christine Jesperson, Western State College of Colorado; Margaret Johnson, Idaho State University; Therese Jones, Lewis University; Laura Katsaros, Monmouth University; Michael Kaufmann, Indiana University–Purdue and University Fort Wayne; Trevor Kearns, Greenfield Community College; Howard Kerner, Polk Community College; Lynn Kilpatrick, Salt Lake Community College; Jeff Klausman, Whatcom Community College; Marcel Kristel, Ohlone College; Tamara Kuzmenkov, Tacoma Community College; Michelle LaFrance, UMass Dartmouth; Thomas Lapointe, Bergen Community College; Erin Lebacqz, University of New Mexico; Lindsay Lewan, Arapahoe Community College; April Lewandowski, Front Range Community College–Westminster; Meredith Love-Steinmetz, Francis Marion University; Robert Lundergan, Fullerton College; Renee Major, Louisiana State University; Diane L. Maldonado, Point Park University; Michael Manis, Indiana University; Brenna Manuel, Franklin Pierce University; Gina Maranto, University of Miami; Loren Loving Marquez, Salisbury University; Carola Mattord, Kennesaw State University; Mark McBeth, John Jay College; Megan McGee-Yinger, Pennsylvania State University–Harrisburg; Timothy McGinn, Northwest Arkansas Community College; Craig Medvecky, Loyola University; Erica Messenger, Bowling Green State University–Main; Keri Mikulski, Rowan University; Alyce Miller, Indiana University; Deborah Miller, University of Georgia; Lamata Mitchell, Rock Valley College; Robert Mohrenne, University of Central Florida; Whitney Myers, University of New Mexico; Nela Navarro, Rutgers University; Erin Nelson, Blinn College; Teddy Norris, St. Charles Community College; Lolly J. Ockerstrom, Park University; Judy Olson, California State University, Los Angeles; Jill Onega, University of Alabama–Huntsville; Jill Parrott,

Eastern Kentucky University; Robert Peltier, Trinity College; Valeries L. Perry, Lewis University; Jeanette Pierce, San Antonio College; Christian Pyle, Eastern Kentucky University; Mary Jo Reiff, University of Tennessee; Tonya Ritola, Georgia Gwinnett College; Mary Roma, New York University; Claudia Rubner, Mercer County Community College; David Ryan, University of San Francisco; Amanda McGuire Rzicznek, Bowling Green State University; Daniel Schenker, University of Alabama–Huntsville; Roy Stamper, North Carolina State University; Jeannine Stanko, Community College of Allegheny; Scott Stevens, Western Washington University; Sarah Stone, University of California–Berkeley; Joseph Sullivan, Marietta College; Mark Todd, Western State Colorado University; Gretchen Treadwell, Fort Lewis College; Tisha Turk, University of Minnesota, Morris; Raymond M. Vince, University of Tampa; Tonya Warden, East Tennessee State University; Charles Warren, Salem State College; Patricia Webb, Arizona State University; Susan Garrett Weiss, Goucher College; Worth Weller, Indiana University–Purdue University–Fort Wayne; Jackie White, Lewis University; Edward Whitelock, Gordon State College; Audrey Wick, Blinn College; and Rodney Zink, Pennsylvania State University.

We are also grateful to the many people at Bedford/St. Martin's, starting with Edwin Hill, vice president, editorial, Macmillan Learning Humanities; senior program director for English Leasa Burton; and program manager John Sullivan. Since the first edition, senior executive editor Steve Scipione has been a terrific collaborator, reading our work carefully and offering sage advice every step of the way. We are especially grateful to Mara Weible, senior editor, who has guided us through the fourth edition. Executive media editor Adam Whitehurst and associate editor Stephanie Thomas were invaluable advisors who helped us develop the new LaunchPad. We are grateful to executive marketing manager Joy Fisher Williams for her wise and imaginative marketing efforts, assisted by Andie Aiken. The talented production department steered the manuscript through a demanding schedule to create the book you hold. We thank Elise Kaiser, Michael Granger, Lisa McDowell, and especially Ryan Sullivan, the book's accommodating and masterly production editor. Kalina Ingham, Angie Boehler, Richard Fox, and Arthur Johnson negotiated the complicated process of permissions acquisition. Thanks also to William Boardman for the striking cover design.

Stuart Greene writes: I wish to thank the many students and faculty with whom I have worked over the years. Specifically, I would like to thank Kelly Kinney, Stephen Fox, Rebecca Nowacek, and Katherine Weese, who served as my assistant directors in the past and who taught me a great deal about the teaching of writing. I would also like to thank Robert Kachur, who contributed a great deal to our early iterations of this book. And I will always appreciate the many discussions I have had with John Duffy during these many years, and with Connie Mick, a tireless and innovative teacher of writing. Susan Ohmer provided much insight into my understanding of media and student culture. A special thanks to Mike Palmquist, with whom I taught writing as "conversation" over thirty years ago and who gave this book direction. Finally, thanks to Denise Della Rossa, who has listened to me rehearse these ideas for years. I dedicate this book to her.

April Lidinsky writes: I am grateful for the superb pedagogical mentorship I received from Lou Kelly at the University of Iowa. I thank Kurt Spellmeyer, Hugh English, and Ron Christ at Rutgers, the State University of New Jersey, for my training in both hermeneutical and rhetorical approaches to teaching writing. My colleagues and graduate student instructors at the University of Notre Dame, especially Julie Bruneau, Connie Mick, Marion C. Rohrleitner, Misty Schieberle, and Scott T. Smith, inspired early versions of this text. Thanks to Joshua Wells, Mara Weible, and Ollie Lidinsky-Smith for their suggestions for readings for this fourth edition. My students continue to challenge and sharpen my teaching and especially my own learning. Finally, I am indebted to my parents, JoElla Hunter and Tom Lidinsky, for their model of lifelong reading and learning, and to Ken Smith, Ollie Lidinsky-Smith, and Miriam Lidinsky-Smith for ensuring every day is filled with wit and wisdom.

WE'RE ALL IN. AS ALWAYS.

Bedford/St. Martin's is as passionately committed to the discipline of English as ever, working hard to provide support and services that make it easier for you to teach your course your way.

Find **community support** at the Bedford/St. Martin's English Community (**community.macmillan.com**), where you can follow our *Bits* blog for new teaching ideas, download titles from our professional resource series, and review projects in the pipeline.

Choose **curriculum solutions** that offer flexible custom options, combining our carefully developed print and digital resources, acclaimed works from Macmillan's trade imprints, and your own course or program materials to provide the exact resources your students need.

Rely on **outstanding service** from your Bedford/St. Martin's sales representative and editorial team. Contact us or visit **macmillanlearning .com** to learn more about any of the options below.

■ LaunchPad for *From Inquiry to Academic Writing*: Where Students Learn

LaunchPad provides engaging content and new ways to get the most out of your book. Get an interactive e-Book combined with assessment tools in a fully customizable course space; then assign and mix our resources with yours.

- LaunchPad for *From Inquiry to Academic Writing* includes **reading comprehension quizzes** and interactive **"Reading as a Writer"** prompts and **"Practice Sequences."**
- **Diagnostics** provide opportunities to assess areas for improvement and assign additional exercises based on students' needs. Visual reports show performance by topic, class, and student as well as improvement over time.
- **Pre-built units**—including readings, videos, quizzes, and more—are easy to adapt and assign by adding your own materials and mixing them with our high-quality multimedia content and ready-made assessment options, such as **LearningCurve** adaptive quizzing and Exercise Central.
- Use LaunchPad on its own or **integrate it** with your school's learning management system so that your class is always on the same page.

LaunchPad for *From Inquiry to Academic Writing* can be purchased on its own or packaged with the print book at a significant discount. An activation code is required. To order LaunchPad for *From Inquiry to Academic Writing* with the print book, use ISBN 978-1-319-14722-8. For more information, go to **launchpadworks.com**.

■ Choose from Alternative Formats of *From Inquiry to Academic Writing*

Bedford/St. Martin's offers a range of formats. Choose what works best for you and your students. For details on our e-Book partners, visit **macmillanlearning.com/ebooks**.

■ Select Value Packages

Add value to your text by packaging any Bedford/St. Martin's resource, such as *Writer's Help 2.0* or *LaunchPad Solo for Readers and Writers*, with *From Inquiry to Academic Writing* at a significant discount. Contact your sales representative for more information.

LaunchPad Solo for Readers and Writers allows students to work on what they need help with the most. At home or in class, students learn at their own pace, with instruction tailored to each student's unique needs. *LaunchPad Solo for Readers and Writers* features:

- **Pre-built units that support a learning arc.**   Each easy-to-assign unit is comprised of a pre-test check, multimedia instruction and assessment, and a post-test that assesses what students have learned about critical reading, writing process, using sources, grammar, style, and mechanics. Dedicated units also offer help for multilingual writers.

- **Diagnostics that help establish a baseline for instruction.**   Assign diagnostics to identify areas of strength and areas for improvement and to help students plan a course of study. Use visual reports to track performance by topic, class, and student as well as improvement over time.

- **A video introduction to many topics.**   Introductions offer an overview of the unit's topic, and many include a brief, accessible video to illustrate the concepts at hand.

- **Twenty-five reading selections with comprehension quizzes.**   Assign a range of classic and contemporary essays, each of which includes a label indicating Lexile level to help you scaffold instruction in critical reading.

- **Adaptive quizzing for targeted learning.**   Most of the units include LearningCurve, game-like adaptive quizzing that focuses on the areas in which each student needs the most help.

- **Additional reading comprehension quizzes.**   *From Inquiry to Academic Writing* includes multiple-choice quizzes, which help you quickly gauge your students' understanding of the assigned reading. These are available in *LaunchPad Solo for Readers and Writers*.

Order ISBN 978-1-319-19246-4 to package *LaunchPad Solo for Readers and Writers* with *From Inquiry to Academic Writing* at a significant discount.

Students who rent or buy a used book can purchase access and instructors may request free access at **macmillanlearning.com/readwrite**.

Writer's Help 2.0 is a powerful online writing resource that helps students find answers, whether they are searching for writing advice on their own or as part of an assignment.

- **Smart search.** Built on research with more than 1,600 student writers, the smart search in *Writer's Help 2.0* provides reliable results even when students use novice terms, such as *flow* and *unstuck*.

- **Trusted content from our best-selling handbooks.** Choose *Writer's Help 2.0, Hacker Version*, or *Writer's Help 2.0, Lunsford Version*, and ensure that students have clear advice and examples for all of their writing questions.

- **Diagnostics that help establish a baseline for instruction.** Assign diagnostics to identify areas of strength and areas for improvement and to help students plan a course of study. Use visual reports to track performance by topic, class, and student as well as improvement over time.

- **Adaptive exercises that engage students.** *Writer's Help 2.0* includes LearningCurve, game-like online quizzing that adapts to what students already know and helps them focus on what they need to learn.

- **Reading comprehension quizzes.** *From Inquiry to Academic Writing* includes multiple-choice quizzes, which help you quickly gauge your students' understanding of the assigned reading. These are available in *Writer's Help 2.0*.

Student access is packaged with *From Inquiry to Academic Writing* at a significant discount. Order ISBN 978-1-319-19244-0 to package the text with *Writer's Help 2.0, Hacker Version*, or ISBN 978-1-319-19251-8 to package the text with *Writer's Help 2.0, Lunsford Version*, to ensure your students have easy access to online writing support. Students who rent or buy a used book can purchase access and instructors may request free access at **macmillanlearning.com/writershelp2**.

INSTRUCTOR RESOURCES

You have a lot to do in your course. We want to make it easy for you to find the support you need—and to get it quickly.

Resources for Teaching From Inquiry to Academic Writing: A Text and Reader, **Fourth Edition,** is available as a PDF that can be downloaded from **macmillanlearning.com**. Visit the instructor resources tab for *From Inquiry to Academic Writing*. In addition to chapter overviews and teaching tips, the instructor's manual includes sample syllabi, commentaries on all the readings, and classroom activities.

Brief Contents

Contents

1 Starting with Inquiry

Habits of Mind of Academic Writers   1

6   From Formulating to Developing a Thesis   141

7   From Finding to Evaluating Sources   165

8 From Synthesis to Researched Argument 187

9   From Ethos to Logos

Appealing to Your Readers   247

Entering the Conversation of Ideas   401

14 Education

What does it mean to be educated? Who has access to a good education, and why?   403

Sociology

How does studying human social behaviors help us understand ourselves and the world? 453

16 Media Studies

What can we learn from what entertains us? 494

17 Psychology and Biology

18 Sustainability and Environmental Studies

How do our decisions affect our environment? 666

19 Economics

How do economics shape our self-understandings and possibilities? What kinds of choices do we have?   741

Thematic Table of Contents

Communication Challenges and Breakthroughs
How does the framing of a contentious issue affect the outcome?

Overcoming Adversity
What can we learn from personal and social struggles?

Representing Ourselves
What can we learn from the ways we present ourselves to others?

Screen Culture

"Real" or not, how do our screens shape the ways we see the world and ourselves?

Reading Bodies

How is the body a site of reflection of and resistance to social values?

The Power of Visual Arguments
How do images persuade us?

Individual and Group Identities
What can we learn when we see ourselves as insiders or outsiders?

Staying Connected
What might happen if we get off the fast track?

Stories We Tell Ourselves

What truths do we tell when we tell stories about our lives?

Our Wallets, Ourselves

What power do we have as consumers, and how does the dollar hold power over us?

Conversations about Gender

How do gender categories constrain and enable aspects of ourselves?

Conversations about "Race"

How does an identity category with no biological meaning shape peoples' experiences so profoundly?

Conversations about "Class"

How does economic class affect our experiences in a country that tells stories of "equal opportunity"?

How This Book Supports WPA Outcomes for First-Year Composition

Note: This chart aligns with the latest WPA Outcomes Statement, ratified in July 2014.

WPA OUTCOMES	RELEVANT FEATURES OF *FROM INQUIRY TO ACADEMIC WRITING: A TEXT AND READER*, FOURTH EDITION
Rhetorical Knowledge	
Learn and use key rhetorical concepts through analyzing & composing a variety of texts.	A full range of rhetorical concepts is presented throughout the text. For example, see: • the treatment of rhetorical analysis in Chapter 2, "From Reading as a Writer to Writing as a Reader" • the treatment of argument in Chapter 4, "From Identifying Claims to Analyzing Arguments" • the treatment of rhetorical appeals in Chapter 9, "From Ethos to Logos"
Gain experience reading and composing in several genres to understand how genre conventions shape and are shaped by readers' and writers' practices and purposes.	A wide range of genres is represented in the text and the reader for analysis and composition. • See the literacy narratives that conclude Chapter 1 and the Practice Sequence that follows (pp. 19–37). • Chapter 2 presents rhetorical context as a tool for analysis. • Throughout the text chapters, all student essays are annotated to indicate particular practices for particular purposes. • The reader chapters feature a range of texts from many academic and popular sources, each introduced by headnotes and followed by "Reading as a Writer" questions that prompt students to consider context and conventions.

WPA Outcomes	Relevant Features of *From Inquiry to Academic Writing: A Text and Reader*, Fourth Edition
Develop facility in responding to a variety of situations and contexts, calling for purposeful shifts in voice, tone, level of formality, design, medium, and/or structure.	Throughout the text chapters, students are instructed to attend to situations and contexts and given strategies for recognizing and responding to them in their composing. For example: • Chapter 6 shows how to establish a context for a thesis. • Chapter 9 shows analysis and modulation of appeals, and Chapter 10 includes examples of visual appeals. • Numerous texts in Chapters 14–19 model the uses of charts, diagrams, and graphs for evidence in different disciplines.
Understand and use a variety of technologies to address a range of audiences.	The range of texts and technologies in the print text and available through LaunchPad help students understand and analyze different technologies they can use in their own composing. • Chapter 10 provides new coverage of visual and multimodal analysis, along with new texts for students to analyze.
Match the capacities of different environments (e.g., print & electronic) to varying rhetorical situations.	The rhetorical and analytical instruction in the text chapters (Chapters 1–13) helps students match the capacities of different composing technologies to different rhetorical situations in the reader chapters (Chapters 14–19), including both print and multimodal examples.
Critical Thinking, Reading, and Composing	
Use composing and reading for inquiry, learning, thinking, and communicating in various rhetorical contexts.	• Chapter 1 sets the stage for academic writing as a form of inquiry. • Chapters 2–5 show critical reading in action. • Chapters 6 and 8 show how to generate texts and compositions from reading in various rhetorical contexts.
Read a diverse range of texts, attending especially to relationships between assertion and evidence, to patterns of organization, to interplay between verbal and nonverbal elements, and how these features function for different audiences and situations.	• Chapter 4 offers instruction in identifying claims and assertions and relating them to evidence. • Chapter 6 presents thesis statements as ways of developing claims and using evidence depending on the situation. • Chapter 11 shows how to shape a composition via different patterns of organization. • Chapters 14–19 present a wide range of diverse texts that demonstrate relationships between assertion and evidence, patterns of organization, the interplay between verbal and nonverbal elements, and how these features function for different audiences and situations.

WPA OUTCOMES	RELEVANT FEATURES OF *FROM INQUIRY TO ACADEMIC WRITING: A TEXT AND READER*, FOURTH EDITION
Locate and evaluate primary and secondary research materials, including journal articles, essays, books, databases, & informal Internet sources.	• Chapter 7, "From Finding to Evaluating Sources," presents instruction in locating and evaluating primary and secondary research materials, including journal articles, essays, books, databases, and informal Internet sources. • Chapter 13, "Other Methods of Inquiry," helps students do primary research via interviews and focus groups.
Use strategies—such as interpretation, synthesis, response, critique, and design/redesign—to compose texts that integrate the writer's ideas with those from appropriate sources.	• Chapter 8, "From Synthesis to Researched Argument," helps students compose texts that integrate the writer's ideas with those from appropriate sources. • "Writing as a Reader" assignments after every selection in Chapters 14–19 ask students to put various texts in conversation and join those conversations.
Processes	
Develop a writing project through multiple drafts.	• Chapters 1–13 provide instruction in the various stages of developing writing projects. • Within chapters, the "Practice Sequences" often present compound activities for chapter-specific writing projects, such as comparing arguments in Chapter 4 (pp. 112–13) and developing a synthesis in Chapter 8 (p. 218).
Develop flexible strategies for reading, drafting, reviewing, collaboration, revising, rewriting, rereading, and editing.	• Chapters 2 and 4 offer flexible strategies for rhetorical reading and inventive reading, such as reading to extend the ideas of others. • Chapters 11 and 12 feature concrete strategies on drafting, collaborating, revising, and editing.
Use composing processes and tools as a means to discover and reconsider ideas.	• Throughout the text chapters, the importance of rereading and rewriting to discover and reconsider ideas is emphasized. • Chapter 6 teaches the importance of revising a thesis in light of new evidence.
Experience the collaborative and social aspects of writing processes.	• The habits of mind of academic writing set forth in Chapter 1 emphasize the importance of collaboration and the idea of academic writing as conversation. • Chapter 12, "From Revising to Editing: Working with Peer Groups," presents collaboration and revision as essential components of academic writing.
Learn to give and act on productive feedback to works in progress.	Chapter 12 includes sample documents and worksheets for the various stages of productive feedback readers can give writings.

WPA OUTCOMES	RELEVANT FEATURES OF *FROM INQUIRY TO ACADEMIC WRITING: A TEXT AND READER*, FOURTH EDITION
Adapt composing processes for a variety of technologies and modalities.	Chapter 10's coverage of visual analysis fosters an awareness of how rhetorical concepts function across various technologies and modalities.
Reflect on the development of composing practices and how those practices influence their work.	"Writing as a Reader" assignments often encourage students to reflect on their composing practices and how those practices influence their work.

Knowledge of Conventions

Develop knowledge of linguistic structures, including grammar, punctuation, and spelling, through practice in composing and revising.	Chapters 11 and 12, on drafting, revising, and editing, help students develop knowledge of linguistic structures, including grammar, punctuation, and spelling.
Understand why genre conventions for structure, paragraphing, tone, and mechanics vary.	• The overarching emphasis on rhetorical context and situation in the text chapters fosters critical thinking about genre conventions. • The headnotes and "Reading as a Writer" questions that surround the selections in the reader chapters (Chapters 14–19) make students aware of genre conventions, encouraging meta-aware thinking.
Gain experience negotiating variations in genre conventions.	Critical reading of the variety of formats and genres represented by the multidisciplinary selections in the text and reader chapters imparts experience negotiating variations in genre conventions.
Learn common formats and/or design features for different kinds of texts.	• Annotated texts such as the student essays in the text chapters impart awareness of common formats and/or design features for difference kinds of texts. • The Appendix on documentation styles gives specific instruction in formats and design. • The range of multidisciplinary readings in Chapters 14–19 foregrounds a variety of formats used in the humanities, social sciences, and sciences.
Explore the concepts of intellectual property (such as fair use and copyright) that motivate documentation conventions.	• A "Practice Sequence" in Chapter 8 concerns critical thinking about copyright and intellectual property (p. 246). • The Appendix on documenting sources (specifically MLA and APA formats) raises issues of different documentation conventions.
Practice applying citation conventions systematically in their own work.	The Appendix enables students to apply citation conventions of MLA and APA styles systematically in their own work.

FROM INQUIRY TO ACADEMIC WRITING

A Text and Reader

Starting with Inquiry
Habits of Mind of Academic Writers

WHAT IS ACADEMIC WRITING?

In the strictest sense, *academic writing* is what scholars do to communicate with other scholars in their fields of study, their *disciplines*. It's the research report a biologist writes, the interpretive essay a literary scholar composes, the media analysis a film scholar produces. At the same time, *academic writing* is what you have to learn so that you can participate in the different disciplinary conversations that take place in your courses. You have to learn to *think* like an academic, *read* like an academic, *do research* like an academic, and *write* like an academic—even if you have no plans to continue your education and become a scholar yourself. Learning these skills is what this book is about.

Fair warning: It isn't easy. Initially you may be perplexed by the vocabulary and sentence structure of many of the academic essays you read. Scholars use specialized language to capture the complexity of an issue or to introduce specific ideas from their discipline. Every discipline has its own vocabulary. You probably can think of words and phrases that are not used every day but that are necessary, nevertheless, to express certain ideas precisely. For example, consider the terms *centrifugal force*, *Oedipus complex*, and *onomatopoeia*. These terms carry with them a history of study; when you learn to use them, you also are learning to use the ideas they represent. Such terms help us describe the world specifically rather than generally; they help us better understand how things work and how to make better decisions about what matters to us.

Sentence structure presents another challenge. The sentences in academic writing are often longer and more intricate than the sentences in popular magazines. Academics strive to go beyond what is quick, obvious, and general. They ask questions based on studying a subject from multiple points of view, to make surprising connections that would not occur to someone who has not studied the subject carefully. It follows that academic writers are accustomed to extensive reading that prepares them to examine an issue, knowledgeably, from many different perspectives, and to make interesting intellectual use of what they discover in their research. To become an adept academic writer, you have to learn these practices as well.

Academic writing will challenge you, no doubt. But hang in there. Any initial difficulty you have with academic writing will pay off when you discover new ways of looking at the world and of making sense of it. Moreover, the habits of mind and core skills of academic writing are highly valued in the world outside the academy.

Basically, academic writing entails making an **argument**—a text that is crafted to persuade an audience—often in the service of changing people's minds and behaviors. When you write an academic essay, you have to

- define a situation that calls for some response in writing;
- demonstrate the timeliness of your argument;
- establish a personal investment;
- appeal to readers whose minds you want to change by understanding what they think, believe, and value;
- support your argument with good reasons; and
- anticipate and address readers' reasons for disagreeing with you, while encouraging them to adopt your position.

Academic argument is not about shouting down an opponent. Instead, it is the careful expression of an idea or perspective based on reasoning and the insights gathered from a close examination of the arguments others have made on the issue.

Making academic arguments is also a social act, like joining a conversation. When we sit down to write an argument intended to persuade someone to do or to believe something, we are never really the first to broach the topic about which we are writing. Thus, learning how to write a researched argument is a process of learning how to enter conversations that are already going on in written form. This idea of writing as dialogue—not only between author and reader but between the text and everything that has been said or written about its subject beforehand—is crucial. Writing is a process of balancing our goals with the history of similar kinds of communication, particularly others' arguments that have been made on the same subject. The conversations that have already been going on about a subject are the subject's historical context.

WHAT ARE THE HABITS OF MIND OF ACADEMIC WRITERS?

The chapters in the first part of this book introduce you to the habits of mind and core skills of academic writing. By **habits of mind**, we mean the patterns of thought that lead you to question assumptions and opinions, explore alternative opinions, anticipate opposing arguments, compare one type of experience to another, and identify the causes and consequences of ideas and events. These forms of **critical thinking** demand an inquiring mind that welcomes complexities and seeks out and weighs many different points of view, a mind willing to enter complex conversations both in and out of the academy. We discuss academic habits of mind in the rest of Chapter 1 and refer to them throughout this book.

Such habits of mind are especially important today, when we are bombarded with appeals to buy this or that product and with information that may or may not be true. For example, in "106 Science Claims and a Truckful of Baloney" (*The Best American Science and Nature Writing*, 2005), William Speed Weed illustrates the extent to which the claims of science vie for our attention alongside the claims of advertising. He notes that advertisers often package their claims as science, but wonders whether a box of Cheerios really can reduce cholesterol.

As readers, we have a responsibility to test the claims of both science and advertising in order to decide what to believe and act upon. Weed found that "very few of the 100 claims" he evaluated "proved completely true" and that "a good number were patently false." Testing the truth of claims—learning to consider information carefully and critically and to weigh competing points of view before making our own judgments—gives us power over our own lives.

The habits of mind and practices valued by academic writers are probably ones you already share. You are behaving "academically" when you comparison shop, a process that entails learning about the product in the media and on the Internet and then looking at the choices firsthand before you decide which one you will purchase. You employ these same habits of mind when you deliberate over casting a vote in an election. You inform yourself about the issues that are most pressing; you learn about the candidates' positions on these issues; you consider other arguments for and against both issues and candidates; and you weigh those arguments and your own understanding to determine which candidate you will support.

Fundamentally, academic habits of mind are *analytical*. When you consider a variety of factors before making a shopping choice—the quality and functionality of the item you plan to buy, how it meets your needs, how it compares to similar items—you are conducting an **analysis**. That is, you are pausing to examine the reasons why you should buy something, instead of simply handing over your cash and saying, "I want one of those."

To a certain extent, analysis involves breaking something down into its various parts and then reflecting on how the parts do or don't work together. For example, when you deliberate over your vote, you may consult one of those charts that newspapers often run around election time: A list of candidates appears across the top of the chart, and a list of issues appears on the side. With a chart from a credible news source in hand, you can scan the columns to see where each candidate stands on the issues, and you can scan the rows to see how the candidates compare on a particular issue. The newspaper editors have performed a preliminary analysis for you. They've asked, "Who are the candidates?" "What are the issues?" and "Where does each candidate stand on the issues?"; and they have presented the answers to you in a format that can help you make your decision.

But you still have to perform your own analysis of the information before you cast your ballot. Suppose no candidate holds your position on every issue. Whom do you vote for? Which issues are most important to you? Or suppose two candidates hold your position on every issue. Which one do you vote for? What characteristics or experience are you looking for in an elected official? And you may want to investigate further by visiting the candidates' Web sites or by talking with your friends to gather their thoughts on the election.

As you can see, analysis involves more than simply disassembling or dissecting something. It is a process of continually asking questions and looking for answers. Analysis reflects, in the best sense of the word, a *skeptical* habit of mind, an unwillingness to settle for obvious answers in the quest to understand why things are the way they are and how they might be different.

This book will help you develop the questioning, evaluating, and conversational skills you already have into strategies that will improve your ability to make careful, informed judgments about the often conflicting and confusing information you are confronted with every day. With these strategies, you will be in a position to use your writing skills to create change where you feel it is most needed.

The first steps in developing these skills are to recognize the key academic habits of mind and then to refine your practice of them. We explore five key habits of mind in the rest of this chapter:

1. inquiring,
2. seeking and valuing complexity,
3. understanding that academic writing is a conversation,
4. understanding that writing is a process, and
5. reflecting.

ACADEMIC WRITERS MAKE INQUIRIES

Academic writers usually study a body of information so closely and from so many different perspectives that they can ask questions that may not occur to people who are just scanning the information. That is, academic writers learn to make **inquiries**. Every piece of academic writing begins with a question about the way the world works, and the best questions lead to rich, complex insights that others can learn from and build on.

You will find that the ability to ask good questions is equally valuable in your daily life. Asking thoughtful questions about politics, popular culture, work, or anything else — questions like, What exactly did that candidate mean by "Family values are values for all of us," anyway? What is lost and gained by bringing Tolkien's *Lord of the Rings* trilogy to the screen? What does it take to move ahead in this company? — is the first step in understanding how the world works and how it can be changed.

Inquiry typically begins with **observation**, a careful noting of phenomena or behaviors that puzzle you or challenge your beliefs and values (in a text or in the real world). Observers attempt to understand phenomena by **asking questions** (Why does this exist? Why is this happening? Do things have to be this way?) and **examining alternatives** (Maybe this doesn't need to exist. Maybe this could happen another way instead.).

For example, Steven Pearlstein, a professor of public affairs at George Mason University, *observes* that only a small percentage of the students he teaches are enrolled as majors in the humanities. This prompts him to *ask* why this is the case, particularly because students express their appreciation for the opportunity to read popular works of history. In his essay "Meet the Parents Who Won't Let Their Children Study Literature," he also points out that faculty at other universities, including Harvard, share his concern that fewer and fewer students are majoring in English or history. He wonders why this is the case and finds that parents, the media, and politicians all advise students to steer clear of the liberal arts. He wonders further why parents in particular would adopt such a view, and he *examines different explanations* such as parents' anxieties over debt, the trends toward professionalism, and parents' own interests. Parents, he concludes, want to see a "direct line" between what their children study and a job. This, Pearlstein argues, is unfortunate since the available data show that students completing a major in the humanities have many job opportunities. In the end, he *asks* what happens to students who major in fields to please their parents and who lack the motivation to study what they are passionate about. For that matter, what will happen if fewer and fewer students learn "discipline, persistence, and how to research, analyze, communicate clearly and think logically"?

In her reading on the American civil rights movement of the 1950s and 1960s, one of our students *observed* that the difficulties many immigrant groups experienced when they first arrived in the United States are not acknowledged as struggles for civil rights. This student of Asian descent *wondered why* the difficulties Asians faced in assimilating into American culture are not seen as analogous to the efforts of African Americans to gain civil rights (Why are things this way?). In doing so, she *asked* a number of relevant questions: What do we leave out when we tell stories about ourselves? Why reduce the struggle for civil rights to black-and-white terms? How can we represent the multiple struggles of people who have contributed to building our nation? Then she *examined alternatives* — different ways of presenting the history of a nation that prides itself on justice and the protection of its people's civil rights (Maybe this doesn't need to exist. Maybe this could happen another way.). The academic writing you will read — and write yourself — starts with questions and seeks to find rich answers.

Steps to Inquiry

1 Observe. Note phenomena or behaviors that puzzle you or challenge your beliefs and values.

2 Ask questions. Consider why things are the way they are.

3 Examine alternatives. Explore how things could be different.

A Practice Sequence: Inquiry Activities

The activities below will help you practice the strategies of observing, asking questions, and examining alternatives.

1 Find an advertisement for a political campaign, and write down anything about what you observe in the ad that puzzles you or that challenges your beliefs and values. Next, write down questions you might have (Do things have to be this way?). Finally, write down other ways you think the ad could persuade you to vote for this particular candidate (Maybe this could happen another way instead.).

2 Locate and analyze data about the students at your school. For example, you might research the available majors and determine which departments have the highest and lowest enrollments. (Some schools have fact books that can be accessed online; and typically the registrar maintains a database with this information.) Is there anything that puzzles you? Write down any questions you have (Why are things the way they are?). What alternative explanations can you provide to account for differences in the popularity of the subjects students major in?

ACADEMIC WRITERS SEEK AND VALUE COMPLEXITY

Seeking and valuing complexity are what inquiry is all about. As you read academic arguments (for example, about school choice), observe how the media work to influence your opinions (for example, in political ads), or analyze data (for example, about candidates in an election), you will explore reasons why things are the way they are and how they might be different. When you do so, we encourage you not to settle for simple either/or reasons. Instead, look for multiple explanations.

When we rely on **binary thinking** — imagining there are only two sides to an issue — we tend to ignore information that does not fall tidily into one side or the other. Real-world questions (How has the Internet changed our sense of what it means to be a writer? What are the global repercussions of fast-food production and consumption? How do we make sense of terrorism?) don't have easy for-or-against answers. Remember that an **issue** is open to dispute and can be explored and debated. Issue-based questions, then, need to be approached with a mind open to complex possibilities. (We say more about identifying issues and formulating issue-based questions in Chapter 5.)

If we take as an example the issue of terrorism, we would discover that scholars of religion, economics, ethics, and politics tend to ask very different questions about terrorism and to propose very different approaches for addressing this worldwide problem. This doesn't mean that one approach is right and the others are wrong; it means that complex issues are likely to have multiple explanations, rather than a simple choice between A and B.

In her attempt to explain the popularity of hip-hop culture, Bronwen Low, a professor of education, provides a window on the steps we can take to examine the complexity of a topic. In the introductory chapters of her book, *Slam School: Learning Through Conflict in the Hip Hop and Spoken Word Classroom,* she begins with the observation that hip-hop "is the single-most influential cultural force shaping contemporary urban youth culture in the United States, and its international reach is growing." She then defines what she means by hip-hop culture, distinguishing it from "rapping," and helps readers understand hip-hop culture as encompassing graffiti art and "a whole culture of style," including "fashion" and "sensibility." Motivated by a sense of curiosity, if not puzzlement, Low asks questions that guide her inquiry: What is it that makes hip-hop culture so compelling to young people across such a wide spectrum of race, culture, and gender? Further, how can social, cultural, and literary critics better understand the evolution of new forms of language and performance, such as spoken-word poetry, in "youth-driven popular culture"? Notice that she indicates that she will frame her inquiry using the multiple perspectives of social, cultural, and literary critics. In turn, Low explains that she began to answer these questions by giving herself a "hip-hop education." She attended spoken-word poetry festivals ("slams") across the United States, listened to the music, and read both "academic theory and journalism" to see what others had to say about "poetry's relevance and coolness to youth."

In still another example, one of our students was curious about why her younger brother struggled in school and wondered if boys learn differently than girls. She began her inquiry by reading an article on education, "It's a Boy Thing (or Is It?)," and realized that researchers have begun to study the question that she was curious about. However, rather than presenting a clear-cut answer, the author of this article, Sara Mead, pointed out that researchers have generated a number of conflicting opinions. Mead's article motivated our student to deepen her inquiry by examining different perspectives in the disciplines of cognitive theory, education, counseling psychology, and sociology. She was able to refine her question based on an issue that puzzled her: If educators are aware that boys have difficulty in school despite receiving more attention than girls receive, how can research explain what seems like a persistent gap between the achievement of boys and girls? In looking at this issue-based question, the student opened herself up to complexity by resisting simple answers to a question that others had not resolved.

Steps to Seeking and Valuing Complexity

1 **Reflect on what you observe.** Clarify your initial interest in a phenomenon or behavior by focusing on its particular details. Then reflect on what is most interesting and least interesting to you about these details, and why.

2 **Examine issues from multiple points of view.** Imagine more than two sides to the issue, and recognize that there may well be other points of view, too.

3 **Ask issue-based questions.** Try to put into words questions that will help you explore why things are the way they are.

A Practice Sequence: Seeking and Valuing Complexity

These activities build on the previous exercises we asked you to complete.

1 Look again at the political ad you selected earlier. Think about other perspectives that would complicate your understanding of how the ad might persuade voters.

2 Imagine other perspectives on the data you found on the students in your school. Let's say, for example, that you've looked at data on student majors. How did you explain the popularity of certain majors and the unpopularity of others? How do you think other students would explain these discrepancies? What explanations would faculty members offer?

ACADEMIC WRITERS SEE WRITING AS A CONVERSATION

Another habit of mind at the heart of academic writing is the understanding that ideas always build on and respond to other ideas, just as they do in the best kind of conversations. Academic conversations are quite similar to those you have through e-mail and social media: You are responding to something someone else has written (or said) and are writing back in anticipation of future responses.

Academic writing also places a high value on the belief that good, thoughtful ideas come from conversations with others, *many* others. As your exposure to other viewpoints increases, as you take more and different points of view into consideration and build on them, your own ideas will develop more fully and fairly. You already know that to get a full picture of something, often you have to ask for multiple perspectives. When you want to find out what "really" happened at an event when your friends are telling you different stories, you listen to all of them and then evaluate the evidence to draw conclusions you can stand behind—just as academic writers do.

Theologian Martin Marty starts a conversation about hospitality in his book *When Faiths Collide* (2004). *Hospitality* is a word he uses to describe a human behavior that has the potential to bring about real understanding among people who do not share a common faith or culture. As Marty points out, finding common ground is an especially important and timely concern "in a world where strangers meet strangers with gunfire, barrier walls, spiritually land-mined paths, and the spirit of revenge." He believes that people need opportunities to share their stories, their values, and their beliefs; in doing so, they feel less threatened by ideas they do not understand or identify with.

Yet Marty anticipates the possibility that the notion of hospitality will be met with skepticism or incomprehension by those who find the term "dainty." Current usage of the term—as in "hospitality suites" and "hospitality industries"—differs from historical usage, particularly biblical usage. To counter the incredulity or incomprehension of those who do not immediately understand his use of the term *hospitality*, Marty gives his readers entrée to a conversation with other scholars who understand the complexity and power of the kind of hospitality shown by people who welcome a stranger into their world. The stranger he has in mind may simply be the person who moves in next door, but that person could also be an immigrant, an exile, or a refugee.

Marty brings another scholar, Darrell Fasching, into the conversation to explain that hospitality entails welcoming "the stranger . . . [which] inevitably involves us in a sympathetic passing over into the other's life and stories" (cited in Marty, p. 132). And John Koenig, another scholar Marty cites, traces the biblical sources of the term in an effort to show the value of understanding those we fear. That understanding, Marty argues, might lead to peace among warring factions. The conversation Marty begins on the page helps us see that his views on bringing about peace have their source in other people's ideas. In turn, the fact that he draws on multiple sources gives strength to Marty's argument.

The characteristics that make for effective oral conversation are also in play in effective academic conversation: empathy, respect, and a willingness to exchange and revise ideas. **Empathy** is the ability to understand the perspectives that shape what people think, believe, and value. To express both empathy and respect for the positions of all people involved in the conversation, academic writers try to understand the conditions under which each opinion might be true and then to represent the strengths of that position accurately.

For example, imagine that your firm commitment to protecting the environment is challenged by those who see the value of developing land rich with oil and other resources. In challenging their position, it would serve you well to understand their motives, both economic (lower gas prices, new jobs that will create a demand for new houses) and political (less dependence on foreign oil). If you can demonstrate your knowledge of these factors, those committed to developing resources in protected areas will listen to you. To convey empathy and respect while presenting your own point of view, you might introduce your argument this way:

> Although it is important to develop untapped resources in remote areas of the United States both to lower gas prices and create new jobs and to eliminate our dependence on other countries' resources, it is in everyone's interest to use alternative sources of power and protect our natural resources.

As you demonstrate your knowledge and a sense of shared values, you could also describe the conditions under which you might change your own position.

People engaging in productive conversation try to create change by listening and responding to one another rather than dominating one another. Instead of trying to win an argument, they focus on reaching a mutual understanding. This does not mean that effective communicators do not take strong positions; more often than not they do. However, they are more likely to achieve their goals by persuading others instead of ignoring them and their points of view. Similarly, writers come to every issue with an agenda. But they realize that they may have to compromise on certain points to carry those that mean the most to them. They understand that their perceptions and opinions may be flawed or limited, and they are willing to revise them when valid new perspectives are introduced.

In an academic community, ideas develop through give and take, through a conversation that builds on what has come before and grows stronger from multiple perspectives. You will find this dynamic at work in your classes when you discuss your ideas: You will build on other people's insights, and they will build on yours. As a habit of mind, paying attention to academic conversations can improve the thinking and writing you do in every class you take.

Steps to Joining an Academic Conversation

1 **Be receptive to the ideas of others.** Listen carefully and empathetically to what others have to say.

2 **Be respectful of the ideas of others.** When you refer to the opinions of others, represent them fairly and use an evenhanded tone. Avoid sounding scornful or dismissive.

3 **Engage with the ideas of others.** Try to understand how people have arrived at their feelings and beliefs.

4 **Be flexible in your thinking about the ideas of others.** Be willing to exchange ideas and to revise your own opinions.

A Practice Sequence: Joining an Academic Conversation

The following excerpt is taken from Thomas Patterson's *The Vanishing Voter* (2002), an examination of voter apathy. Read the excerpt and then complete the exercises that follow.

> Does a diminished appetite for voting affect the health of American politics? Is society harmed when the voting rate is low or in decline? As the *Chicago Tribune* said in an editorial, it may be "humiliating" that the United States, the oldest continuous democracy, has nearly the lowest voting rate in the world. But does it have any practical significance? . . .
>
> The increasing number of nonvoters could be a danger to democracy. Although high participation by itself does not trigger radical change, a flood of new voters into the electorate could possibly do it. It's difficult to imagine a crisis big and divisive enough to prompt millions of new voters to suddenly flock to the polls, especially in light of Americans' aversion to political extremism. Nevertheless, citizens who are outside the electorate are less attached to the existing system. As the sociologist Seymour Martin Lipset observed, a society of nonvoters "is potentially more explosive than one in which most citizens are regularly involved in activities which give them some sense of participation in decisions which affect their lives."
>
> Voting can strengthen citizenship in other ways, too. When people vote, they are more attentive to politics and are better informed about issues affecting them. Voting also deepens community involvement, as

the philosopher John Stuart Mill theorized a century ago. Studies indicate that voters are more active in community affairs than nonvoters are. Of course, this association says more about the type of person who votes as opposed to the effect of voting. But recent evidence, as Harvard University's Robert Putnam notes, "suggests that the act of voting itself encourages volunteering and other forms of government citizenship."

1   In this excerpt, Patterson presents two arguments: that increasing voter apathy is a danger to democracy and that voting strengthens citizenship. With which of these arguments do you sympathize more? Why? Can you imagine reasons that another person might not agree with you? Write them down. Now do the same exercise with the argument you find less compelling.

2   Your instructor will divide the class into four groups and assign each group a position—pro or con—on one of Patterson's arguments. Brainstorm with the members of your group to come up with examples or reasons why your group's position is valid. Make a list of those examples or reasons, and be prepared to present them to the class.

3   Your instructor will now break up the groups into new groups, each with at least one representative of the original groups. In turn with the other members of your new group, take a few moments to articulate your position and the reasons for it. Remember to be civil and as persuasive as possible.

4   Finally, with the other members of your new group, talk about the merits of the various points of view. Try to find common ground ("I understand what you are saying; in fact, it's not unlike the point I was making about . . ."). The point of this discussion is not to pronounce a winner (who made the best case for his or her perspective) but to explore common ground, exchange and revise ideas, and imagine compromises.

ACADEMIC WRITERS UNDERSTAND THAT WRITING IS A PROCESS

Academic writing is a process of defining issues, formulating questions, and developing sound arguments. This view of writing counters a number of popular myths: that writing depends on inspiration, that writing should happen quickly, that learning to write in one context prepares you to write in other contexts, and that revision is the same as editing. The writing process addresses these myths. First, choosing an idea that matters to you is one way to make your writing matter. And there's a better chance that writing you care about will contribute in a meaningful way to the conversation going on about a given issue in the academic community. Second, writers who invest time in developing and revising their ideas will improve the quality of both their ideas and their language—their ability to be specific and express complexity.

There are three main stages to the writing process: collecting information, drafting, and revising. We introduce them here and expand on them throughout this book.

■ Collect Information and Material

Always begin the process of writing an essay by collecting *in writing* the material—the information, ideas, and evidence—from which you will shape your own argument. Once you have read and marked the pages of a text, you have begun the process of building your own argument. The important point here is that you start to put your ideas on paper. Good writing comes from returning to your ideas on your own and with your classmates, reconsidering them, and revising them as your thinking develops. This is not something you can do with any specificity unless you have written down your ideas. The following box shows the steps for gathering information from your reading, the first stage in the process of writing an academic essay. (In Chapter 2, these steps are illustrated and discussed in more detail.)

Steps to Collecting Information and Material

1 **Mark your texts as you read.** Note key terms; ask questions in the margins; indicate connections to other texts.

2 **List quotations you find interesting and provocative.** You might even write short notes to yourself about what you find significant about the quotations.

3 **List your own ideas in response to the reading or readings.** Include what you've observed about the way the author or authors make their arguments.

4 **Sketch out the similarities and differences among the authors whose work you plan to use in your essay.** Where would they agree or disagree? How would each respond to the others' arguments and evidence?

■ Draft, and Draft Again

The next stage in the writing process begins when you are ready to think about your focus and how to arrange the ideas you have gathered in the collecting stage. Writers often find that writing a first draft is an act of discovery, that their ultimate focus emerges during this initial drafting process. Sometimes it is only at the end of a four-page draft that a writer says, "Aha! This is what I really want to talk about in this essay!" Later revisions of an essay, then, are not simply editing or cleaning up the grammar of a first draft. Instead, they truly involve *re*vision, seeing the first draft again to establish the clearest possible argument and the most persuasive evidence. This means that you do not have to stick with the way a draft turns out the first time. You can—and must!—be willing to rewrite a substantial amount of a first draft if the focus of the argument changes, or if in the process of writing new ideas emerge that enrich the essay. This is why it's important not to agonize over wording in a first draft: It's difficult to toss out a paragraph you've sweated over for hours. Use the first draft to get your ideas down on paper so that you and your peers can discuss what you see there, with the knowledge that you (like your peers) will need to stay open to the possibility of changing an aspect of your focus or argument.

Steps to Drafting

1 **Look through the materials** you have collected to see what interests you most and what you have the most to say about.

2 **Identify what is at issue** and what is open to dispute.

3 **Formulate a question** that your essay will respond to.

4 **Select the material you will include,** and decide what is outside your focus.

5 **Consider the types of readers** who might be most interested in what you have to say.

6 **Gather more material** once you've decided on your purpose—what you want to teach your readers.

7 **Formulate a working thesis** that conveys the point you want to make.

8 **Consider possible arguments** against your position and your response to them.

■ Revise Significantly

The final stage, revising, might involve several different drafts as you continue to sharpen your insights and the organization of what you have written. As we discuss in Chapter 12, you and your peers will be reading one another's drafts, offering feedback as you move from the larger issues to the smaller ones. It should be clear by now that academic writing is done in a community of thinkers: That is, people read other people's drafts and make suggestions for further clarification, further development of ideas, and sometimes further research. This is quite different from simply editing someone's writing for grammatical errors and typos. Instead, drafting and revising with real readers, as we discuss in Chapter 12, allow you to participate in the collaborative spirit of the academy, in which knowledge making is a group activity that comes out of the conversation of ideas. Importantly, this process approach to writing in the company of real readers mirrors the conversation of ideas carried on in the pages of academic books and journals.

Steps to Revising

1 **Draft and revise the introduction and conclusion.**

2 **Clarify any obscure or confusing passages** your peers have pointed out.

3 **Provide details and textual evidence** where your peers have asked for new or more information.

4 **Make sure you have included opposing points of view** and have addressed them fairly.

5 **Consider reorganization.**

6 **Make sure that every paragraph contributes clearly to your thesis or main claim** and that you have included signposts along the way, phrases that help a reader understand your purpose ("Here I turn to an example from current movies to show how this issue is alive and well in pop culture.").

7 **Consider using strategies you have found effective in other reading** you have done for class (repeating words or phrases for effect, asking rhetorical questions, varying your sentence length).

ACADEMIC WRITERS REFLECT

Reflection entails pausing and taking note of what you are doing—finding answers to complex questions about why unemployment persists or solving a problem to ensure that schools can be safe places where all kids can learn—and observing yourself for a moment. For example, as you are skimming articles to find answers to questions or searching for possible solutions, it's valuable to *monitor* what you feel you are learning, particularly if you are accustomed to doing research in an online environment where it's easy to get distracted. Monitoring entails asking yourself a few questions: What did I just read? Did I comprehend the writer's argument? Do I need to go back and reread the argument? It's equally useful to *evaluate* what you are learning and what you still want or need to know to ensure that you discuss an issue in complex ways that avoid binary thinking. Try to *formulate strategies*, based on your own self-assessment, to address any challenges, such as comprehending a technical argument. What other sources of information can you consult? Whom can you ask for additional help? Finally, *apply what you learn about your own learning* by compiling a repertoire of strategies that can guide you in the reading, writing, and problem solving that you are doing in different classes.

Reflection is essentially having an awareness of our own thought processes. What do I want to accomplish? Is this the right question to ask? What other questions could I be asking? Where should I look for answers? What steps should I take? Why? Educator Jackie Gerstein developed the following cycle of questions for taking control of our own learning:

- Was I resourceful in terms of finding information, resources, and materials?
- Did I ask other people for feedback and information; to collaborate?
- Did I share my work and findings with others?
- Did I learn something new?
- Did I try to either make something better or create something new, rather than just copy something that already exists?
- Did I approach learning as an open-ended process, open to new and all possibilities?
- Did I accept failure as part of the process and use it to inform my learning?

—Jackie Gerstein

Gerstein is insistent when she explains, "If we don't create a process of reflecting . . . then we are leaving learning up to chance."

Reflection in writing can focus on different types of knowledge: (1) the *content* of an issue, such as how economic resources are distributed in different neighborhoods and schools or trade policies that affect employment; (2) the *strategies* one might use to write an essay to persuade readers that immigration policies do not affect opportunities in employment as much as trade policies do; (3) the *procedures* for developing an argument, such as using stories of people affected by unemployment or the failures of providing safe environments for kids in and out of school; and (4) the *conditions* under which certain kinds of strategies might work in one context or another. That is, stories might be a powerful way to raise an issue for a class in sociology or education, but some hard data might be more appropriate in developing a persuasive argument in economics. Making decisions like this one emphasizes the role of reflection—monitoring, evaluating, developing strategies, and taking control over your own learning.

Finally, reflection is an important habit of mind because the act of thinking and questioning encourages us to critically examine our own lived experiences. In his memoir *Between the World and Me*, Ta-Nehisi Coates writes about a moment in his life when he first became literate, and he explains in the following passage how literacy—reading and writing—opened up a world that he wanted to know more about. Here Coates, recipient of a MacArthur Foundation "Genius Grant," addresses his son, as he does throughout his memoir, to tell a story of a time when his mother would make him write when he was in trouble. For us, the story he conveys is about the power of reflection that comes from writing—the significance of writing to make thinking visible, to ask questions that prompt Coates to consider his actions in the present, and to envision future actions based on what he has learned.

> Your grandmother taught me to read when I was only four. She also taught me to write, by which I mean not simply organizing a set of sentences into a series of paragraphs, but organizing them as a means of investigation. When I was in trouble at school (which was quite often) she would make me write about it. The writing had to answer a series of questions: *Why did I feel the need to talk at the same time as my teacher? Why did I not believe that my teacher was entitled to respect? How would I want someone to behave while I was talking? What would I do the next time I felt the urge to talk to my friends during a lesson?* [Our emphasis].

Coates admits that his mother's assignment never really taught him to "curb" his behavior, but these early lessons were a powerful source of learning to "interrogate" the world. Reflecting on the past, present, and future drew Coates into "consciousness," as he puts it. "Your grandmother was not teaching me how to behave in class. She was teaching me how to ruthlessly interrogate the subject that elicited the most sympathy and rationalizing—myself."

Researchers are consistent in describing the importance of encouraging us to think critically on our own lived experiences before we begin to think about how we can participate in a project, take action, and create meaningful change in our surroundings. The following steps can help you pause and make sure learning is actually happening.

Steps to Reflection

1. **Monitor.** Pause and ask yourself some questions: Did I comprehend the writer's argument? Do I need to go back and reread the argument?

2. **Evaluate.** Assess what you are learning and what you still want or need to know to ensure that you discuss an issue in complex ways that avoid binary thinking.

3 **Formulate strategies.** Identify some next steps, based on your own self-assessment, for addressing any challenges, such as comprehending a technical argument, solving a problem you have formulated, or answering a question you have posed. What other sources of information can you consult? Whom can you ask for additional help?

4 **Apply what you learn about your own learning.** Write down some of the challenges you have faced in writing — formulating a question, collecting materials, drafting, or revising, for example. How have you dealt with those challenges? How would you apply what you have learned to completing other academic writing assignments?

A Practice Sequence: Reflection Activities

The activities that follow will give you an opportunity to practice monitoring your work, evaluating what you are learning, formulating strategies, and documenting how you will apply what you learned.

1   Reflect upon and write about the steps you are taking to collect information for what you are writing, to draft your essay, and to revise your work.

- Pause and consider the approach you are taking and whether this is the best way to fulfill your goals as a writer and reach your audience.

- Assess what you are learning about taking a process approach to writing.

- Formulate some next steps for your writing.

- What have you learned so far about writing that you can apply to this and other kinds of academic tasks? That is, if you have faced some uncertainties, what did you do to address these moments? Did you talk to others in your writing group? Were they helpful? Or did you seek other forms of help to get what you needed?

2   Earlier we suggested that you might find a political advertisement or data about majors at your school to analyze. Choose one of these two areas of inquiry.

- As you try to find information, monitor the steps you are taking by pausing for a moment. How is the process going for you? Are you getting what you need? Why or why not?

- Assess what you are learning from your search for relevant information and data.

- Formulate next steps if you are having trouble finding what you want.

- Write down what you have learned about locating information and what you still need to know in order to find relevant, timely information in an efficient way.

The five academic habits of mind we have discussed throughout this chapter—making inquiries, seeking and valuing complexity, understanding writing as a conversation, understanding writing as a process, and reflecting—are fundamental patterns of thought you will need to cultivate as an academic writer. The core skills we discuss through the rest of the book build on these habits of mind.

Moreover, the kind of writing we describe in this chapter may challenge some models of writing that you learned in high school, particularly the five-paragraph essay. The five-paragraph essay is a **genre**, or kind, of writing that offers writers a conventional formula for transmitting information to readers. Such a formula can be useful, but it is generally too limiting for academic conversations. By contrast, academic writing is a genre responsive to the role that readers play in guiding writing and the writing process. That is, academic writing is about shaping and adapting information for the purpose of influencing how readers think about a given issue, not simply placing information in a conventional organizational pattern. We expect academic readers to critically analyze what we have written and anticipate writers' efforts to address their concerns. Therefore, as writers, we need to acknowledge different points of view, make concessions, recognize the limitations of what we argue, and provide counterarguments. Reading necessarily plays a prominent role in the many forms of writing that you do, but not necessarily as a process of simply gathering information. Instead, as James Crosswhite suggests in his book *The Rhetoric of Reason*, reading "means making judgments about which of the many voices and encounters can be brought together into productive conversation."

BECOMING ACADEMIC: THREE NARRATIVES

In the following passages, three writers describe their early experiences as readers. A well-known journalist and writer, Ta-Nehisi Coates reflects upon his growing sense of curiosity at Howard University, which he refers to as Mecca, the site where he is motivated to learn about the history of black people and where he learns to formulate questions to help him better understand who he is as an individual. The passage we include here is taken from his award-winning book *Between the World and Me*, and is addressed to his son. Coates makes many references to authors he has read and public figures he admires. We invite you to do some research to learn about who these people are and their significance in the ways Coates writes about his education. Richard Rodriguez and Gerald Graff are well known outside the academy. In this excerpt from *Hunger of Memory*, Rodriguez describes what it was like growing up as a bookish bilingual "scholarship boy" in a Spanish-speaking household. In the other excerpt, from *Beyond the Culture Wars*, Graff narrates how he disliked reading books, especially literature and history books, well into his undergraduate years as an English major. Both of their narratives turn around moments of recognition triggered by exposure to the ideas of others. As you read the selections, consider these questions:

- Where are the turning points in each narrative? What are the most important things the writers seem to learn?

- What incidents or insights did you find most interesting in the narratives? Why?

- What seem to be the key ideas in each narrative? Do these ideas strike you as being potentially useful in your own work as a thinker and writer?

- Do you find that the writers exhibit academic habits of mind (making inquiries, seeking and valuing complexity, seeing writing as a kind of conversation, and reflecting)? If so, where?

TA-NEHISI COATES

Between the World and Me

A journalist, educator, and writer, Ta-Nehisi Coates received the 2015 National Book Award for *Between the World and Me*, from which the following excerpt is taken. He has also written a memoir, *The Beautiful Struggle: A Father, Two Sons, and an Unlikely Road to Manhood*, and he is a regular contributor to *The Atlantic*, where he writes about culture, politics, race, and the persistence of racial inequality in the United States. His writings have appeared in the *Washington Post*, *The New York Times Magazine*, *Time*, and the *Village Voice*. Most recently, he has been working on an eleven-issue series of *Black Panther* for Marvel. When the Black Panther character debuted in an issue of *Fantastic Four* in 1966, he was the first black superhero in mainstream American comics.

When I came to Howard, Chancellor Williams's *Destruction of*   1
Black Civilization was my Bible. Williams himself had taught at Howard. I read him when I was sixteen, and his work offered a grand theory of multi-millennial European plunder. The theory relived me of certain troubling questions—this is the point of nationalism—and it

gave me my Tolstoy. I read about Queen Nzinga, who ruled in Central Africa in the sixteenth century, resisting the Portuguese. I read about her negotiating with the Dutch. When the Dutch ambassador tried to humiliate her by refusing her a seat, Nzinga had shown her power by ordering one of her advisers to all fours to make a human chair of her body. That was the kind of power I sought, and the story of our own royalty became for me weapon. My working theory then held all black people as kings in exile, a nation of original men severed from our original names and our majestic Nubian culture. Surely this was the message I took from gazing out on the Yard. Had any people, anywhere, ever been as sprawling and beautiful as us?

I needed more books. At Howard University, one of the greatest collections of books could be found in the Moorland-Spingarn Research Center, where your grandfather once worked. Moorland held archives, papers, collections, and virtually any book ever written by or about black people. For the most significant portion of my time at The Mecca, I followed a simple ritual. I would walk into the Moorland reading room and fill out three call slips for three different works. I would take a seat at one of these long tables. I would draw out my pen and one of my black-and-white composition books. I would open the books and read, while filling my composition books with notes on my reading, new vocabulary words, and sentences of my own invention. I would arrive in the morning and request, three call slips at a time, the works of every writer I had heard spoken of in classrooms or out on the Yard: Larry Neal, Eric Williams, George Padmore, Sonia Sanchez, Stanley Crouch, Harold Cruse, Manning Marable, Addison Gayle, Carolyn Rodgers, Etheridge Knight, Sterling Brown. I remember believing that the key to all life lay in articulating the precise difference between "the Black Aesthetic" and "Negritude." How, specifically, did Europe underdevelop Africa? I must know. And if the Eighteenth Dynasty pharaohs were alive today, would they live in Harlem? I had to inhale all the pages. 2

I went into this investigation imagining history to be a unified narrative, free of debate, which, once uncovered, would simply verify everything I had always suspected. The smokescreen would lift. And the villains who manipulated the schools and the streets would be unmasked. But there was so much to know—so much geography to cover—Africa, the Caribbean, the Americas, the United States. And all of these areas had histories, sprawling literary canons, fieldwork, ethnographies. Where should I begin? 3

The trouble came almost immediately. I did not find a coherent tradition marching lockstep but instead factions, and factions within factions. Hurston battled Hughes, Du Bois warred with Garvey, Harold Cruse fought everyone. I felt myself at the bridge of a great ship that I could not control because C.L.R. James was a great wave and Basil 4

Davidson was a swirling eddy, tossing me about. Things I believed merely a week earlier, ideas I had taken from one book, could be smashed to splinters by another. Had we retained any of our African inheritance? Frazier says it was all destroyed, and this destruction evidences the terribleness of our capturers. Herskovitz says it lives on, and this evidences the resilience of our African spirit. By my second year, it was natural for me to spend a typical day mediating between Frederick Douglass's integration into America and Martin Delany's escape into nationalism. Perhaps they were somehow both right. I had come looking for a parade, for a military review of champions marching in ranks. Instead I was left with a brawl of ancestors, a herd of dissenters, sometimes marching together but just as often marching away from each other.

I would take breaks from my reading, walk out to the vendors who   5
lined the streets, eat lunch on the Yard. I would imagine Malcolm, his body bound in a cell, studying the books, trading his human eyes for the power of flight. And I too felt bound by my ignorance, by the questions that I had not yet understood to be more than just means, by my lack of understanding, and by Howard itself. It was still a school, after all. I wanted to pursue things, to know things, but I could not match the means of knowing that came naturally to me with the expectations of professors. The pursuit of knowing was freedom to me, the right to declare your own curiosities and follow them through all manner of books. I was made for the library, not the classroom. The classroom was a jail of other people's interests. The library was open, unending, free. Slowly, I was discovering myself. The best parts of Malcolm pointed the way. Malcolm, always changing, always evolving toward some truth that was ultimately outside the boundaries of his life, of his body. I felt myself in motion, still directed toward the total possession of my body, but by some other route which I could not before then have imagined.

I was not searching alone. I met your uncle Ben at The Mecca. He   6
was, like me, from one of those cities where everyday life was so different than the Dream that it demanded an explanation. He came, like me, to The Mecca in search of the nature and origin of the breach. I shared with him a healthy skepticism and a deep belief that we could somehow read our way out. Ladies loved him, and what a place to be loved—for it was said, and we certainly believed it to be true, that nowhere on the Earth could one find a more beautiful assembly of women than on Howard University's Yard. And somehow even this was part of the search—the physical beauty of the black body was all our beauty, historical and cultural, incarnate. Your uncle Ben became a fellow traveler for life, and I discovered that there was something particular about journeying out with black people who knew the length of the road because they had traveled it too.

I would walk out into the city and find other searchers at lectures, book signings, and poetry readings. I was still writing bad poetry. I read this bad poetry at open mics in local cafes populated mostly by other poets who also felt the insecurity of their bodies. All of these poets were older and wiser than me, and many of them were well read, and they brought this wisdom to bear on me and my work. What did I mean, *specifically*, by the loss of my body? And if every black body was precious, a one of one, if Malcolm was correct and you must preserve your life, how could I see these precious lives as simply a collective mass, as the amorphous residue of plunder? How could I privilege the spectrum of dark energy over each particular ray of light? These were notes on how to write, and thus notes on how to think. The Dream thrives on generalization, on limiting the number of possible questions, on privileging immediate answers. The Dream is the enemy of all art, courageous thinking, and honest writing. And it became clear that this was not just for the dreams concocted by Americans to justify themselves but also for the dreams that I had conjured to replace them. I had thought that I must mirror the outside world, create a carbon copy of white claims to civilization. It was beginning to occur to me to question the logic of the claim itself. I had forgotten my own self-interrogations pushed upon me by my mother, or rather I had not yet apprehended their deeper, lifelong meaning. I was only beginning to learn to be wary of my own humanity, of my own hurt and anger—I didn't yet realize that the boot on your neck is just as likely to make you delusional as it is to ennoble.

The art I was coming to love lived in this void, in the not yet knowable, in the pain, in the question. The older poets introduced me to artists who pulled their energy from the void—Bubber Miley, Otis Redding, Sam and Dave, C. K. Williams, Carolyn Forché. The older poets were Ethelbert Miller, Kenneth Carroll, Brian Gilmore. It is important that I tell you their names, that you know that I have never achieved anything alone. I remember sitting with Joel Dias-Porter, who had not gone to Howard but whom I found at The Mecca, reviewing every line of Robert Hayden's "Middle Passage." And I was stunned by how much Hayden managed to say without, seemingly, saying anything at all—he could bring forth joy and agony without literally writing the words, which formed as pictures and not slogans. Hayden imagined the enslaved, during the Middle Passage, from the perspective of the enslavers—a mind-trip for me, in and of itself; why should the enslaver be allowed to speak? But Hayden's poems did not speak. They conjured:

> You cannot stare that hatred down
> or chain the fear that stalks the watches

I was not in any slave ship. Or perhaps I was, because so much of what I'd felt in Baltimore, the sharp hatred, the immortal wish, and the timeless will, I saw in Hayden's work. And that was what I heard in Malcolm, but never like this—quiet, pure, and unadorned. I was learning the craft of poetry, which really was an intensive version of what my mother had taught me all those years ago—the craft of writing as the art of thinking. Poetry aims for an economy of truth—loose and useless words must be discarded, and I found that these loose and useless words were not separate from loose and useless thoughts. Poetry was not simply the transcription of notions—beautiful writing rarely is. I wanted to learn to write, which was ultimately, still, as my mother had taught me, a confrontation with my own innocence, my own rationalizations. Poetry was the processing of my thoughts until the slag of justification fell away and I was left with the cold steel truths of life.

These truths I heard in the works of other poets around the city. They were made of small hard things—aunts and uncles, smoke breaks after sex, girls on stoops drinking from mason jars. These truths carried the black body beyond slogans and gave it color and texture and thus reflected the spectrum I saw out on the Yard more than all of my alliterative talk of guns or revolutions or paeans to the lost dynasties of African antiquity. After these readings, I followed as the poets would stand out on U Street or repair to a café and argue about everything—books, politics, boxing. And their arguments reinforced the discordant tradition I'd found in Moorland, and I began to see discord, argument, chaos, perhaps even fear, as a kind of power. I was learning to live in the disquiet I felt in Moorland-Spingarn, in the mess of my mind. The gnawing discomfort, the chaos, the intellectual vertigo was not an alarm. It was a beacon. *10*

RICHARD RODRIGUEZ

Scholarship Boy

Richard Rodriguez was born into a Mexican immigrant family in San Francisco, California, and spoke only Spanish until age six. He had a formidable education, receiving a BA from Stanford University and an MA from Columbia University; studying for a PhD at the University of California, Berkeley; and attending the Warburg Institute in London on a Fulbright fellowship. Instead of pursuing a career in academia, he became a journalist. He is perhaps best known for his contributions to PBS's *The NewsHour with Jim Lehrer* and for his controversial opposition to affirmative action and bilingual education. His books include *Hunger of Memory: The Education of Richard Rodriguez* (1981), *Mexico's Children* (1990), *Days of Obligation: An Argument with My Mexican Father* (1992), and *Brown: The Last Discovery of America* (2002).

I stand in the ghetto classroom—"the guest speaker"—attempting to lecture on the mystery of the sounds of our words to rows of diffident students. "Don't you hear it? Listen! The music of our words. '*Sumer is i-cumen in.* . . .' And songs on the car radio. We need Aretha Franklin's voice to fill plain words with music—her life." In the face of their empty stares, I try to create an enthusiasm. But the girls in the back row turn to watch some boy passing outside. There are flutters of smiles, waves. And someone's mouth elongates heavy, silent words through the barrier of glass. Silent words—the lips straining to shape each voiceless syllable: "*Meet meee late errr.*" By the door, the instructor smiles at me, apparently hoping that I will be able to spark some enthusiasm in the class. But only one student seems to be listening. A girl, maybe fourteen. In this gray room her eyes shine with ambition. She keeps nodding and nodding at all that I say; she even takes notes. And each time I ask a question, she jerks up and down in her desk like a marionette, while her hand waves over the bowed heads of her classmates. It is myself (as a boy) I see as she faces me now (a man in my thirties).

The boy who first entered a classroom barely able to speak English, twenty years later concluded his studies in the stately quiet of the reading room in the British Museum. Thus with one sentence I can summarize my academic career. It will be harder to summarize what sort of life connects the boy to the man.

With every award, each graduation from one level of education to the next, people I'd meet would congratulate me. Their refrain always the same: "Your parents must be very proud." Sometimes then they'd ask me how I managed it—my "success." (How?) After a while, I had several quick answers to give in reply. I'd admit, for one thing, that I went to an excellent grammar school. (My earliest teachers, the nuns, made my success their ambition.) And my brother and both my sisters were very good students. (They often brought home the shiny school trophies I came to want.) And my mother and father always encouraged me. (At every graduation they were behind the stunning flash of the camera when I turned to look at the crowd.)

As important as these factors were, however, they account inadequately for my academic advance. Nor do they suggest what an odd success I managed. For although I was a very good student, I was also a very bad student. I was a "scholarship boy," a certain kind of scholarship boy. Always successful, I was always unconfident. Exhilarated by my progress. Sad. I became the prized student—anxious and eager to learn. Too eager, too anxious—an imitative and unoriginal pupil. My brother and two sisters enjoyed the advantages I did, and they grew to be as successful as I, but none of them ever seemed so anxious about their schooling. A second-grade student, I was the one who came home and corrected the "simple" grammatical mistakes of our parents. ("Two negatives make a positive.") Proudly I announced—to my family's startled silence—that a teacher had said I was losing all trace of a Spanish accent. I was oddly annoyed when I was unable to get parental help with a homework assignment. The night my father tried to help me with an arithmetic exercise, he kept reading the instructions, each time more deliberately, until I pried the textbook out of his hands, saying, "I'll try to figure it out some more by myself."

When I reached the third grade, I outgrew such behavior. I became   5 more tactful, careful to keep separate the two very different worlds of my day. But then, with ever-increasing intensity, I devoted myself to my studies. I became bookish, puzzling to all my family. Ambition set me apart. When my brother saw me struggling home with stacks of library books, he would laugh, shouting: "Hey, Four Eyes!" My father opened a closet one day and was startled to find me inside, reading a novel. My mother would find me reading when I was supposed to be asleep or helping around the house or playing outside. In a voice angry or worried or just curious, she'd ask: "What do you see in your books?" It became the family's joke. When I was called and wouldn't reply, someone would say I must be hiding under my bed with a book.

(How did I manage my success?)   6

What I am about to say to you has taken me more than twenty years   7 to admit: *A primary reason for my success in the classroom was that I couldn't forget that schooling was changing me and separating me from the life I enjoyed before becoming a student.* That simple realization! For years I never spoke to anyone about it. Never mentioned a thing to my family or my teachers or classmates. From a very early age, I understood enough, just enough about my classroom experiences to keep what I knew repressed, hidden beneath layers of embarrassment. Not until my last months as a graduate student, nearly thirty years old, was it possible for me to think much about the reasons for my academic success. Only then. At the end of my schooling, I needed to determine how far I had moved from my past. The adult finally confronted, and now must publicly say, what the child shuddered from knowing and could never admit to himself or to those many faces that smiled at his every success. ("Your parents must be very proud. . . .")

At the end, in the British Museum (too distracted to finish my disser-   8 tation) for weeks I read, speed-read, books by modern educational theorists, only to find infrequent and slight mention of students like me. (Much more is written about the more typical case, the lower-class student who barely is helped by his schooling.) Then one day, leafing through Richard Hoggart's *The Uses of Literacy*, I found, in his description of the scholarship boy, myself. For the first time I realized that there were other students like me, and so I was able to frame the meaning of my academic success, its consequent price—the loss.

Hoggart's description is distinguished, at least initially, by deep understanding. What he grasps very well is that the scholarship boy must move between environments, his home and the classroom, which are at cultural extremes, opposed. With his family, the boy has the intense pleasure of intimacy, the family's consolation in feeling public alienation. Lavish emotions texture home life. *Then*, at school, the instruction bids him to trust lonely reason primarily. Immediate needs set the pace of his parents' lives. From his mother and father the boy learns to trust spontaneity and nonrational ways of knowing. *Then*, at school, there is mental calm. Teachers emphasize the value of a reflectiveness that opens a space between thinking and immediate action.

Years of schooling must pass before the boy will be able to sketch the cultural differences in his day as abstractly as this. But he senses those differences early. Perhaps as early as the night he brings home an assignment from school and finds the house too noisy for study.

> He has to be more and more alone, if he is going to "get on." He will have, probably unconsciously, to oppose the ethos of the hearth, the intense gregariousness of the working-class family group. Since everything centers upon the living-room, there is unlikely to be a room of his own; the bedrooms are cold and inhospitable, and to warm them or the front room, if there is one, would not only be expensive, but would require an imaginative leap—out of the tradition—which most families are not capable of making. There is a corner of the living-room table. On the other side Mother is ironing, the wireless is on, someone is singing a snatch of song or Father says intermittently whatever comes into his head. The boy has to cut himself off mentally, so as to do his homework, as well as he can.[1]

The next day, the lesson is as apparent at school. There are even rows of desks. Discussion is ordered. The boy must rehearse his thoughts and raise his hand before speaking out in a loud voice to an audience of classmates. And there is time enough, and silence, to think about ideas (big ideas) never considered at home by his parents.

Not for the working-class child alone is adjustment to the classroom difficult. Good schooling requires that any student alter early childhood habits. But the working-class child is usually least prepared for the change. And, unlike many middle-class children, he goes home and sees in his parents a way of life not only different but starkly opposed to that of the classroom. (He enters the house and hears his parents talking in ways his teachers discourage.)

---

[1] All quotations in this selection are from Richard Hoggart, *The Uses of Literacy* (London: Chatto and Windus, 1957), chapter 10.

Without extraordinary determination and the great assistance of others—at home and at school—there is little chance for success. Typically most working-class children are barely changed by the classroom. The exception succeeds. The relative few become scholarship students. Of these, Richard Hoggart estimates, most manage a fairly graceful transition. Somehow they learn to live in the two very different worlds of their day. There are some others, however, those Hoggart pejoratively terms "scholarship boys," for whom success comes with special anxiety. Scholarship boy: good student, troubled son. The child is "moderately endowed," intellectually mediocre, Hoggart supposes—though it may be more pertinent to note the special qualities of temperament in the child. High-strung child. Brooding. Sensitive. Haunted by the knowledge that one *chooses* to become a student. (Education is not an inevitable or natural step in growing up.) Here is a child who cannot forget that his academic success distances him from a life he loved, even from his own memory of himself.

Initially, he wavers, balances allegiance. ("The boy is himself [until he reaches, say, the upper forms] very much of *both* the worlds of home and school. He is enormously obedient to the dictates of the world of school, but emotionally still strongly wants to continue as part of the family circle.") Gradually, necessarily, the balance is lost. The boy needs to spend more and more time studying, each night enclosing himself in the silence permitted and required by intense concentration. He takes his first step toward academic success, away from his family.

From the very first days, through the years following, it will be with his parents—the figures of lost authority, the persons toward whom he feels deepest love—that the change will be most powerfully measured. A separation will unravel between them. Advancing in his studies, the boy notices that his mother and father have not changed as much as he. Rather, when he sees them, they often remind him of the person he once was and the life he earlier shared with them. He realizes what some Romantics also know when they praise the working class for the capacity for human closeness, qualities of passion and spontaneity, that the rest of us experience in like measure only in the earliest part of our youth. For the Romantic, this doesn't make working-class life childish. Working-class life challenges precisely because it is an *adult* way of life.

The scholarship boy reaches a different conclusion. He cannot afford to admire his parents. (How could he and still pursue such a contrary life?) He permits himself embarrassment at their lack of education. And to evade nostalgia for the life he has lost, he concentrates on the benefits education will bestow upon him. He becomes especially ambitious. Without the support of old certainties and consolations, almost mechanically, he assumes the procedures and doctrines of the classroom. The kind of allegiance the young student might have given his

12

13

14

15

mother and father only days earlier, he transfers to the teacher, the new figure of authority. "[The scholarship boy] tends to make a father-figure of his form-master," Hoggart observes.

But Hoggart's calm prose only makes me recall the urgency with which I came to idolize my grammar school teachers. I began by imitating their accents, using their diction, trusting their every direction. The very first facts they dispensed, I grasped with awe. Any book they told me to read, I read—then waited for them to tell me which books I enjoyed. Their every casual opinion I came to adopt and to trumpet when I returned home. I stayed after school "to help"—to get my teacher's undivided attention. It was the nun's encouragement that mattered most to me. (She understood exactly what—my parents never seemed to appraise so well—all my achievements entailed.) Memory gently caressed each word of praise bestowed in the classroom so that compliments teachers paid me years ago come quickly to mind even today.

16

The enthusiasm I felt in second-grade classes I flaunted before both my parents. The docile, obedient student came home a shrill and precocious son who insisted on correcting and teaching his parents with the remark: "My teacher told us. . . ."

17

I intended to hurt my mother and father. I was still angry at them for having encouraged me toward classroom English. But gradually this anger was exhausted, replaced by guilt as school grew more and more attractive to me. I grew increasingly successful, a talkative student. My hand was raised in the classroom; I yearned to answer any question. At home, life was less noisy than it had been. (I spoke to classmates and teachers more often each day than to family members.) Quiet at home, I sat with my papers for hours each night. I never forgot that schooling had irretrievably changed my family's life. That knowledge, however, did not weaken ambition. Instead, it strengthened resolve. Those times I remembered the loss of my past with regret, I quickly reminded myself of all the things my teachers could give me. (They could make me an educated man.) I tightened my grip on pencil and books. I evaded nostalgia. Tried hard to forget. But one does not forget by trying to forget. One only remembers. I remembered too well that education had changed my family's life. I would not have become a scholarship boy had I not so often remembered.

18

Once she was sure that her children knew English, my mother would tell us, "You should keep up your Spanish." Voices playfully groaned in response. "¡*Pochos*!" my mother would tease. I listened silently.

19

After a while, I grew more calm at home. I developed tact. A fourth-grade student, I was no longer the show-off in front of my parents. I became a conventionally dutiful son, politely affectionate, cheerful enough, even—for reasons beyond choosing—my father's favorite. And much about my family life was easy then, comfortable, happy in the

20

rhythm of our living together: hearing my father getting ready for work; eating the breakfast my mother had made me; looking up from a novel to hear my brother or one of my sisters playing with friends in the backyard; in winter, coming upon the house all lighted up after dark.

But withheld from my mother and father was any mention of what most mattered to me: the extraordinary experience of first-learning. Late afternoon: In the midst of preparing dinner, my mother would come up behind me while I was trying to read. Her head just over mine, her breath warmly scented with food. "What are you reading?" Or, "Tell me all about your new courses." I would barely respond, "Just the usual things, nothing special." (A half smile, then silence. Her head moving back in the silence. Silence! Instead of the flood of intimate sounds that had once flowed smoothly between us, there was this silence.) After dinner, I would rush to a bedroom with papers and books. As often as possible, I resisted parental pleas to "save lights" by coming to the kitchen to work. I kept so much, so often, to myself. Sad. Enthusiastic. Troubled by the excitement of coming upon new ideas. Eager. Fascinated by the promising texture of a brand-new book. I hoarded the pleasures of learning. Alone for hours. Enthralled. Nervous. I rarely looked away from my books—or back on my memories. Nights when relatives visited and the front rooms were warmed by Spanish sounds, I slipped quietly out of the house.   21

It mattered that education was changing me. It never ceased to matter. My brother and sisters would giggle at our mother's mispronounced words. They'd correct her gently. My mother laughed girlishly one night, trying not to pronounce *sheep* as *ship*. From a distance I listened sullenly. From that distance, pretending not to notice on another occasion, I saw my father looking at the title pages of my library books. That was the scene on my mind when I walked home with a fourth-grade companion and heard him say that his parents read to him every night. (A strange-sounding book—*Winnie the Pooh*.) Immediately, I wanted to know, "What is it like?" My companion, however, thought I wanted to know about the plot of the book. Another day, my mother surprised me by asking for a "nice" book to read. "Something not too hard you think I might like." Carefully I chose one, Willa Cather's *My Ántonia*. But when, several weeks later, I happened to see it next to her bed unread except for the first few pages, I was furious and suddenly wanted to cry. I grabbed up the book and took it back to my room and placed it in its place, alphabetically on my shelf.   22

"Your parents must be very proud of you." People began to say that to me about the time I was in sixth grade. To answer affirmatively, I'd smile. Shyly I'd smile, never betraying my sense of the irony: I was not proud of my mother and father. I was embarrassed by their lack   23 of education. It was not that I ever thought they were stupid, though stupidly I took for granted their enormous native intelligence. Simply, what mattered to me was that they were not like my teachers.

But, "Why didn't you tell us about the award?" my mother demanded, her frown weakened by pride. At the grammar school ceremony several weeks after, her eyes were brighter than the trophy I'd won. Pushing back the hair from my forehead, she whispered that I had "shown" the *gringos*. A few minutes later, I heard my father speak to my teacher and felt ashamed of his labored, accented words. Then guilty for the shame. I felt such contrary feelings. (There is no simple roadmap through the heart of the scholarship boy.) My teacher was so soft-spoken and her words were edged sharp and clean. I admired her until it seemed to me that she spoke too carefully. Sensing that she was condescending to them, I became nervous. Resentful. Protective. I tried to move my parents away. "You both must be very proud of Richard," the nun said. They responded quickly. (They were proud.) "We are proud of all our children." Then this afterthought: "They sure didn't get their brains from us." They all laughed. I smiled.

24

GERALD GRAFF

Disliking Books

Gerald Graff received his BA in English from the University of Chicago and his PhD in English and American literature from Stanford University. In his distinguished academic career, he has taught at numerous universities and is currently a professor of English and education at the University of Illinois at Chicago. He is probably best known for his pedagogical theories, especially "teaching the controversies," an approach he argues for most famously in his book *Beyond the Culture Wars: How Teaching the Conflicts Can Revitalize American Education* (1993), from which this excerpt is taken. His other well-known books include *Literature Against Itself: Literary Ideas in Modern Society* (1979), *Professing Literature: An Institutional History* (1987), and *Clueless in Academe: How Schooling Obscures the Life of the Mind* (2003).

■ ■ ■

I like to think I have a certain advantage as a teacher of literature because when I was growing up I disliked and feared books. My youthful aversion to books showed a fine impartiality, extending across the whole spectrum of literature, history, philosophy, science, and what by then (the late 1940s) had come to be called social studies. But had I

1

been forced to choose, I would have singled out literature and history as the reading I disliked most. Science at least had some discernible practical use, and you could have fun solving the problems in the textbooks with their clear-cut answers. Literature and history had no apparent application to my experience, and any boy in my school who had cultivated them—I can't recall one who did—would have marked himself as a sissy.

As a middle-class Jew growing up in an ethnically mixed Chicago neighborhood, I was already in danger of being beaten up daily by rougher working-class boys. Becoming a bookworm would have only given them a decisive reason for beating me up. Reading and studying were more permissible for girls, but they, too, had to be careful not to get too intellectual, lest they acquire the stigma of being "stuck up."

In *Lives on the Boundary*, a remarkable autobiography of the making of an English teacher, Mike Rose describes how the "pain and confusion" of his working-class youth made "school and knowledge" seem a saving alternative. Rose writes of feeling "freed, as if I were untying fetters," by his encounters with certain college teachers, who helped him recognize that "an engagement with ideas could foster competence and lead me out into the world."[1] Coming at things from my middle-class perspective, however, I took for granted a freedom that school, knowledge, and engagement with ideas seemed only to threaten.

My father, a literate man, was frustrated by my refusal to read anything besides comic books, sports magazines, and the John R. Tunis and Clair Bee sports novels. I recall his once confining me to my room until I finished a book on the voyages of Magellan, but try as I might, I could do no better than stare bleakly at the pages. I could not, as we would later say, "relate to" Magellan or to any of the other books my father brought home—detective stories, tales of war and heroism, adventure stories with adolescent heroes (the *Hardy Boys*, *Hans Brinker*, or *The Silver Skates*), stories of scientific discovery (Paul de Kruif's *Microbe Hunters*), books on current events. Nothing worked.

It was understood, however, that boys of my background would go to college and that once there we would get serious and buckle down. For some, "getting serious" meant prelaw, premed, or a major in business to prepare for taking over the family business. My family did not own a business, and law and medicine did not interest me, so I drifted by default into the nebulous but conveniently noncommittal territory of the liberal arts. I majored in English.

At this point the fear of being beaten up if I were caught having anything to do with books was replaced by the fear of flunking out of college if I did not learn to deal with them. But though I dutifully did my

---

[1] Mike Rose, *Lives on the Boundary* (New York: Free Press, 1989), pp. 46–47.

homework and made good grades (first at the University of Illinois, Chicago branch, then at the University of Chicago, from which I graduated in 1959), I continued to find "serious" reading painfully difficult and alien. My most vivid recollections of college reading are of assigned classics I failed to finish: *The Iliad* (in the Richmond Lattimore translation); *The Autobiography of Benvenuto Cellini*, a major disappointment after the paperback jacket's promise of "a lusty classic of Renaissance ribaldry"; E. M. Forster's *Passage to India*, sixty agonizing pages of which I managed to slog through before giving up. Even Hemingway, Steinbeck, and Fitzgerald, whose contemporary world was said to be "close to my own experience," left me cold. I saw little there that did resemble my experience.

Even when I had done the assigned reading, I was often tongue-tied and embarrassed when called on. What was unclear to me was what I was supposed to *say* about literary works, and why. Had I been born a decade or two earlier, I might have come to college with the rudiments of a literate vocabulary for talking about culture that some people older than I acquired through family, high school, or church. As it was, "cultured" phrases seemed effete and sterile to me. When I was able to produce the kind of talk that was required in class, the intellectualism of it came out sounding stilted and hollow in my mouth. If *Cliffs Notes* and other such crib sheets for the distressed had yet come into existence, with their ready-to-copy summaries of widely taught literary works, I would have been an excellent customer. (As it was, I did avail myself of the primitive version then in existence called *Masterplots*.) 7

What first made literature, history, and other intellectual pursuits seem attractive to me was exposure to critical debates. There was no single conversion experience, but a gradual transformation over several years, extending into my first teaching positions, at the University of New Mexico and then Northwestern University. But one of the first sparks I remember was a controversy over *Adventures of Huckleberry Finn* that arose in a course during my junior year in college. On first attempt, Twain's novel was just another assigned classic that I was too bored to finish. I could see little connection between my Chicago upbringing and Huck's pre–Civil War adventures with a runaway slave on a raft up the Mississippi. 8

My interest was aroused, however, when our instructor mentioned that the critics had disagreed over the merits of the last part of the novel. He quoted Ernest Hemingway's remark that "if you read [the novel] you must stop where the nigger Jim is stolen by the boys. This is the real end. The rest is cheating." According to this school of thought, the remainder of the book trivializes the quest for Jim's freedom that has motivated the story up to that point. This happens first when Jim becomes an object of Tom Sawyer's slapstick humor, then when it is 9 revealed that unbeknownst to Huck, the reader, and himself, Jim has already been freed by his benevolent owner, so that the risk we have assumed Jim and Huck to be under all along has been really no risk at all.

Like the critics, our class divided over the question: Did Twain's end- *10* ing vitiate the book's profound critique of racism, as Hemingway's charge of cheating implied? Cheating in my experience up to then was something students did, an unthinkable act for a famous author. It was a revelation to me that famous authors were capable not only of mistakes but of ones that even lowly undergraduates might be able to point out. When I chose to write my term paper on the dispute over the ending, my instructor suggested I look at several critics on the opposing sides, T. S. Eliot and Lionel Trilling, who defended the ending, and Leo Marx, who sided with Hemingway.

Reading the critics was like picking up where the class discussion had *11* left off, and I gained confidence from recognizing that my classmates and I had had thoughts that, however stumbling our expression of them, were not too far from the thoughts of famous published critics. I went back to the novel again and to my surprise found myself rereading it with an excitement I had never felt before with a serious book. Having the controversy over the ending in mind, I now had some issues *to watch out for* as I read, issues that reshaped the way I read the earlier chapters as well as the later ones and focused my attention. And having issues to watch out for made it possible not only to concentrate, as I had not been able to do earlier, but to put myself in the text—to read with a sense of personal engagement that I had not felt before. Reading the novel with the voices of the critics running through my mind, I found myself think-ing of things that I might say about what I was reading, things that may have belonged partly to the critics but also now belonged to me. It was as if having a stock of things to look for and to say about a literary work had somehow made it possible for me to read one.

One of the critics had argued that what was at issue in the debate *12* over *Huckleberry Finn* was not just the novel's value but its cultural significance: If *Huckleberry Finn* was contradictory or confused in its attitude toward race, then what did that say about the culture that had received the novel as one of its representative cultural documents and had made Twain a folk hero? This critic had also made the intriguing observation—I found out only later it was a critical commonplace at that time—that judgments about the novel's aesthetic value could not be separated from judgments about its moral substance. I recall taking in both this critic's arguments and the cadence of the phrases in which they were couched; perhaps it would not be so bad after all to become the sort of person who talked about "cultural contradictions" and the "inseparability of form and content." Perhaps even mere literary-critical talk could give you a certain power in the real world. As the possibility dawned on me that reading and intellectual discussion might actually have something to do with my real life, I became less embarrassed about using the intellectual formulas.

The Standard Story

It was through exposure to such critical reading and discussion over a period of time that I came to catch the literary bug, eventually choosing the vocation of teaching. This was not the way it is supposed to happen. In the standard story of academic vocation that we like to tell ourselves, the germ is first planted by an early experience of literature itself. The future teacher is initially inspired by some primary experience of a great book and only subsequently acquires the secondary, derivative skills of critical discussion. A teacher may be involved in instilling this inspiration, but a teacher who seemingly effaces himself or herself before the text. Any premature or excessive acquaintance with secondary critical discourse, and certainly with its sectarian debates, is thought to be a corrupting danger, causing one to lose touch with the primary passion for literature. . . .

The standard story ascribes innocence to the primary experience of literature and sees the secondary experience of professional criticism as corrupting. In my case, however, things had evidently worked the other way around: I had to be corrupted first in order to experience innocence. It was only when I was introduced to a critical debate about *Huckleberry Finn* that my helplessness in the face of the novel abated and I could experience a personal reaction to it. Getting into immediate contact with the text was for me a curiously triangular business; I could not do it directly but needed a conversation of other readers to give me the issues and terms that made it possible to respond.

As I think back on it now, it was as if the critical conversation I needed had up to then been withheld from me, on the ground that it could only interfere with my direct access to literature itself. The assumption was that leaving me alone with literary texts themselves, uncontaminated by the interpretations and theories of professional critics, would enable me to get on the closest possible terms with those texts. But being alone with the texts only left me feeling bored and helpless, since I had no language with which to make them mine. On the one hand, I was being asked to speak a foreign language—literary criticism—while on the other hand, I was being protected from that language, presumably for my own safety.

The moral I draw from this experience is that our ability to read well depends more than we think on our ability to *talk well* about what we read. Our assumptions about what is "primary" and "secondary" in the reading process blind us to what actually goes on. Many literate people learned certain ways of talking about books so long ago that they have forgotten they ever had to learn them. These people therefore fail to understand the reading problems of the struggling students who have still not acquired a critical vocabulary.

How typical my case was is hard to say, but many of the students I teach seem to have grown up as the same sort of nonintellectual, non-bookish person I was, and they seem to view literature with some of the same aversions, fears, and anxieties. That is why I like to think it is an advantage for a teacher to know what it feels like to grow up being indifferent to literature and intimidated by criticism and what it feels like to overcome a resistance to talking like an intellectual.   *17*

A Practice Sequence: Composing a Literacy Narrative

A *literacy narrative*—a firsthand, personal account about reading or composing—is a well-established genre that is popular both inside and outside the academy. Coates's, Rodriguez's, and Graff's, autobiographical stories dealing with aspects of how they became literate and their relationship with reading and writing are literacy narratives. Coates's narrative is part of *Between the World and Me*, a memoir that examines racial identity and the politics of race in the United States. Rodriguez's narrative is part of *Hunger of Memory: The Education of Richard Rodriguez*, a memoir that explores the politics of language in American culture. Graff's narrative is embedded in his *Beyond the Culture Wars: How Teaching the Conflicts Can Revitalize American Education*, which, as the subtitle suggests, presents arguments and proposals for altering educational practices.

We would like you to write your own literacy narrative. The following practice sequence suggests some strategies for doing so.

1   Reflect on your experiences as a reader. Spend some time jotting down answers to these questions (not necessarily in this order) or to other related questions that occur to you as you write.

- Can you recall the time when you first began to read?
- What are the main types of reading you do? Why?
- How would you describe or characterize yourself as a reader?
- Is there one moment or event that encapsulates who you are as a reader?
- What are your favorite books, authors, and types of books? Why are they favorites?

- In what ways has reading changed you for the better? For the worse?

- What is the most important thing you've learned from reading?

- Have you ever learned something important from reading, only to discover later that it wasn't true or sufficient? Explain.

2 Write your literacy narrative, focusing on at least one turning point, at least one moment of recognition or lesson learned. Write no fewer than two pages but no more than five pages. See where your story arc takes you. What do you conclude about your own "growing into literacy"?

3 Then start a conversation about literacy. Talk with some other people about their experiences. You might talk with some classmates—and not necessarily those in your writing class—about their memories of becoming literate. You might interview some people you grew up with—a parent, a sibling, a best friend—about their memories of you as a reader and writer and about their own memories of becoming literate. Compare their memories to your own. Did you all have similar experiences? How were they different? Do you see things the same way? Then write down your impressions and what you think you may have learned.

4 Recast your literacy narrative, incorporating some of the insights you gathered from other people. How does your original narrative change? What new things now have to be accounted for?

5 Like Graff, who takes his own experience as a starting point for proposing new educational policies, can you imagine your insights having larger implications? Explain. Do you think what you've learned from reading Coates's, Rodriguez's, and Graff's literacy narratives has implications for the ways reading is taught in school?

2

From Reading as a Writer to Writing as a Reader

Reading for class and then writing an essay might seem to be separate tasks, but reading is the first step in the writing process. In this chapter we present methods that will help you read more effectively and move from reading to writing your own college essays. These methods will lead you to understand a writer's purpose in responding to a situation, the motivation for asserting a claim in an essay and entering a particular conversation with a particular audience.

Much if not all of the writing you do in college will be based on what you have read. This is the case, for example, when you summarize a philosopher's theory, analyze the significance of an experiment in psychology, or, perhaps, synthesize different and conflicting points of view in making an argument about race and academic achievement in sociology.

As we maintain throughout this book, writing and reading are inextricably linked to each other. Good academic writers are also good critical readers: They leave their mark on what they read, identifying issues, making judgments about the truth of what writers tell them, and evaluating the adequacy of the evidence in support of an argument. This is where writing and inquiry begin: understanding our own position relative to the scholarly conversations we want to enter. Moreover, critical readers try to understand the strategies that writers use to persuade readers to agree with them. At times, these are strategies that we can adapt in advancing our arguments.

READING AS AN ACT OF COMPOSING: ANNOTATING

Leaving your mark on the page—**annotating**—is your first act of composing. When you mark the pages of a text, you are reading critically, engaging with the ideas of others, questioning and testing those ideas, and inquiring into their significance. **Critical reading** is sometimes called *active reading* to distinguish it from memorization, when you just read for the main idea so that you can "spit it back out on a test." When you read actively and critically, you bring your knowledge, experiences, and interests to a text, so that you can respond to the writer, continuing the conversation the writer has begun.

Experienced college readers don't try to memorize a text or assume they must understand it completely before they respond to it. Instead they read strategically, looking for the writer's claims, for the writer's key ideas and terms, and for connections with key ideas and terms in other texts. They also read to discern what conversation the writer has entered, and how the writer's argument is connected to those he or she makes reference to.

When you annotate a text, your notes in the margins might address the following questions:

- What arguments is this author responding to?
- Is the issue relevant or significant?
- How do I know that what the author says is true?
- Is the author's evidence legitimate? Sufficient?
- Can I think of an exception to the author's argument?
- What would the counterarguments be?

Good readers ask the same kinds of questions of every text they read, considering not just *what* a writer says (the content), but *how* he or she says it given the writer's purpose and audience.

The marks you leave on a page might indicate your own ideas and questions, patterns you see emerging, links to other texts, even your gut response to the writer's argument—agreement, dismay, enthusiasm, confusion. They reveal your own thought processes as you read and signal that you are entering the conversation. In effect, they are traces of your own responding voice.

Developing your own system of marking or annotating pages can help you feel confident when you sit down with a new reading for your classes. Based on our students' experiences, we offer this practical tip: Although wide-tipped highlighters have their place in some classes, it is more useful to read with a pen or pencil in your hand, so that you can do more than draw a bar of color through words or sentences you find important. Experienced readers write their responses to a text in the margins, using personal codes (boxing key words, for example), writing out definitions of words they have looked up, drawing lines to connect ideas on facing pages, or writing notes to themselves ("Connect this to Edmundson on consumer culture"; "Hirsch would disagree big time—see his ideas on memorization in primary grades"; "You call THIS evidence?!"). These notes help you get started on your own writing assignments.

Annotating your readings benefits you twice. First, it is easier to participate in class discussions if you have already marked passages that are important, confusing, or linked to specific passages in other texts you have read. It's a sure way to avoid that sinking feeling you get when you return to pages you read the night before but now can't remember at all. Second, by marking key ideas in a text, noting your ideas about them, and making connections to key ideas in other texts, you have begun the process of writing an essay. When you start writing the first draft of your essay, you can quote the passages you have already marked and explain what you find significant about them based on the notes you have already made to yourself. You can make the connections to other texts in the paragraphs of your own essay that you have already begun to make on the pages of your textbook. If you mark your texts effectively, you'll never be at a loss when you sit down to write the first draft of an essay.

Let's take a look at how one of our students marked several paragraphs of Douglas Massey and Nancy Denton's *American Apartheid: Segregation and the Making of the Underclass* (1993). In the excerpt below, the student underlines what she believes is important information and begins to create an outline of the authors' main points.

1. racist attitudes

2. private behaviors

3. & institutional practices lead to ghettos (authors' claim?)

Ghetto = "multistory, high-density housing projects." Post-1950

I remember this happening where I grew up, but I didn't know the government was responsible. Is this what happened in There Are No Children Here?

Authors say situation of "spatial isolation" remains despite court decisions. Does it?

The spatial isolation of black Americans was achieved by a conjunction of <u>racist attitudes</u>, <u>private behaviors</u>, and <u>institutional practices</u> that disenfranchised blacks from urban <u>housing markets and led to the creation of the ghetto</u>. Discrimination in employment exacerbated black poverty and limited the economic potential for integration, and black residential mobility was systematically blocked by pervasive discrimination and white avoidance of neighborhoods containing blacks. <u>The walls of the ghetto were buttressed after 1950</u> by government programs that promoted slum clearance and <u>relocated displaced ghetto residents into multi-story, high-density housing projects</u>.   1

In theory, this self-reinforcing cycle of prejudice, discrimination, and segregation was broken during the 1960s by a growing rejection of racist sentiments by whites and a series of court decisions and federal laws that banned discrimination in public life. (1) <u>The Civil Rights Act of 1964 outlawed racial discrimination in employment</u>, (2) the <u>Fair Housing Act of 1968 banned discrimination in housing</u>, and (3) the <u>*Gautreaux* and *Shannon* court decisions prohibited public authorities from placing housing projects</u> exclusively in black neighborhoods. Despite these changes, however, the <u>nation's largest black communities remained as segregated as ever in 1980</u>. Indeed, many urban areas displayed a pattern of intense racial isolation that could only be described as <u>hypersegregation</u>.   2

Although the racial climate of the United States improved outwardly during the 1970s, <u>racism still restricted the residential freedom of black Americans</u>; it just did so in less blatant ways. In the aftermath of the civil rights revolution, few whites voiced openly racist sentiments; realtors no longer refused outright to rent or sell to blacks; and few local governments went on record to oppose public housing projects because they would contain blacks. This lack of overt racism, however, did not mean that prejudice and discrimination had ended.

Subtler racism, not on public record.

Lack of enforcement of Civil Rights Act? Fair Housing Act? Gautreaux and Shannon? Why? Why not?

Notice how the student's annotations help her understand the argument the authors make.

1. She numbers the three key factors (racist attitudes, private behaviors, and institutional practices) that influenced the formation of ghettos in the United States.

2. She identifies the situation that motivates the authors' analysis: the extent to which "the spatial isolation of black Americans" still exists despite laws and court decisions designed to end residential segregation.

3. She makes connections to her own experience and to another book she has read.

By understanding the authors' arguments and making these connections, the student begins the writing process. She also sets the stage for her own research, for examining the authors' claim that residential segregation still exists.

READING AS A WRITER: ANALYZING A TEXT RHETORICALLY

When you study how writers influence readers through language, you are analyzing the **rhetoric** (available means of persuasion) of what you read. When you identify a writer's purpose for responding to a situation by composing an essay that puts forth claims meant to sway a particular audience, you are performing a rhetorical analysis. Such an analysis entails identifying the features of an argument to better understand how the argument works to persuade a reader:

- how the writer sees the situation that calls for a response in writing
- the writer's purpose for writing
- intended audience
- kinds of claims
- types of evidence

We discuss each of these elements as we analyze the following preface from E. D. Hirsch's book *Cultural Literacy: What Every American Needs to Know* (1987). Formerly a professor of English, Hirsch has long been interested in educational reform. That interest developed from his (and others') perception that today's students do not know as much as students did in the past. Although Hirsch wrote the book decades ago, many observers still believe that the contemporary problems of illiteracy and poverty can be traced to a lack of cultural literacy.

Read the preface. You may want to mark it with your own questions and responses, and then consider them in light of our analysis (following the preface) of Hirsch's rhetorical situation, purpose, claims, and audience.

E. D. HIRSCH JR.

Preface to *Cultural Literacy*

E. D. Hirsch Jr., a retired English professor, is the author of many acclaimed books, including *The Schools We Need and Why We Don't Have Them* (1996) and *The Knowledge Deficit* (2006). His book *Cultural Literacy* was a best seller in 1987 and had a profound effect on the focus of education in the late 1980s and 1990s.

▧ ▧ ▧

Rousseau points out the facility with which children lend themselves to our false methods: . . ."The apparent ease with which children learn is their ruin."

—JOHN DEWEY

There is no matter what children should learn first, any more than what leg you should put into your breeches first. Sir, you may stand disputing which is best to put in first, but in the meantime your backside is bare. Sir, while you stand considering which of two things you should teach your child first, another boy has learn't 'em both.

—SAMUEL JOHNSON

To be culturally literate is to possess the basic information needed to thrive in the modern world. The breadth of that information is great, extending over the major domains of human activity from sports to science. It is by no means confined to "culture" narrowly understood as an acquaintance with the arts. Nor is it confined to one social class. Quite the contrary. Cultural literacy constitutes the only sure avenue of opportunity for disadvantaged children, the only reliable way of combating the social determinism that now condemns them to remain in the same social and educational condition as their parents. That children from poor and illiterate homes tend to remain poor and illiterate is an unacceptable failure of our schools, one which has occurred not because our teachers are inept but chiefly because they are compelled

1

to teach a fragmented curriculum based on faulty educational theories. Some say that our schools by themselves are powerless to change the cycle of poverty and illiteracy. I do not agree. They *can* break the cycle, but only if they themselves break fundamentally with some of the theories and practices that education professors and school administrators have followed over the past fifty years.

Although the chief beneficiaries of the educational reforms advocated in this book will be disadvantaged children, these same reforms will also enhance the literacy of children from middle-class homes. The educational goal advocated is that of mature literacy for *all* our citizens.

The connection between mature literacy and cultural literacy may already be familiar to those who have closely followed recent discussions of education. Shortly after the publication of my essay "Cultural Literacy," Dr. William Bennett, then chairman of the National Endowment for the Humanities and subsequently secretary of education in President Ronald Reagan's second administration, championed its ideas. This endorsement from an influential person of conservative views gave my ideas some currency, but such an endorsement was not likely to recommend the concept to liberal thinkers, and in fact the idea of cultural literacy has been attacked by some liberals on the assumption that I must be advocating a list of great books that every child in the land should be forced to read.

But those who examine the Appendix to this book will be able to judge for themselves how thoroughly mistaken such an assumption is. Very few specific titles appear on the list, and they usually appear as words, not works, because they represent writings that culturally literate people have read about but haven't read. *Das Kapital* is a good example. Cultural literacy is represented not by a *prescriptive* list of books but rather by a *descriptive* list of the information actually possessed by literate Americans. My aim in this book is to contribute to making that information the possession of all Americans.

The importance of such widely shared information can best be understood if I explain briefly how the idea of cultural literacy relates to currently prevailing theories of education. The theories that have dominated American education for the past fifty years stem ultimately from Jean Jacques Rousseau, who believed that we should encourage the natural development of young children and not impose adult ideas upon them before they can truly understand them. Rousseau's conception of education as a process of natural development was an abstract generalization meant to apply to all children in any time or place: to French children of the eighteenth century or to Japanese or American children of the twentieth century. He thought that a child's intellectual and social skills would develop naturally without regard to the specific content of education. His content-neutral conception of educational development has long been triumphant in American schools of education and has long dominated the "developmental," content-neutral curricula of our elementary schools.

In the first decades of this century, Rousseau's ideas powerfully influenced the educational conceptions of John Dewey, the writer who has the most deeply affected modern American educational theory and practice. Dewey's clearest and, in his time, most widely read book on education, *Schools of Tomorrow*, acknowledges Rousseau as the chief source of his educational principles. The first chapter of Dewey's book carries the telling title "Education as Natural Development" and is sprinkled with quotations from Rousseau. In it Dewey strongly seconds Rousseau's opposition to the mere accumulation of information.   6

> Development emphasizes the need of intimate and extensive personal acquaintance with a small number of typical situations with a view to mastering the way of dealing with the problems of experience, not the piling up of information.

Believing that a few direct experiences would suffice to develop the skills that children require, Dewey assumed that early education need not be tied to specific content. He mistook a half-truth for the whole. He placed too much faith in children's ability to learn general skills from a few typical experiences and too hastily rejected "the piling up of information." Only by piling up specific, communally shared information can children learn to participate in complex cooperative activities with other members of their community.   7

This old truth, recently rediscovered, requires a countervailing theory of education that once again stresses the importance of specific information in early and late schooling. The corrective theory might be described as an anthropological theory of education, because it is based on the anthropological observation that all human communities are founded upon specific shared information. Americans are different from Germans, who in turn are different from Japanese, because each group possesses specifically different cultural knowledge. In an anthropological perspective, the basic goal of education in a human community is acculturation, the transmission to children of the specific information shared by the adults of the group or polis.   8

Plato, that other great educational theorist, believed that the specific contents transmitted to children are by far the most important elements of education. In *The Republic* he makes Socrates ask rhetorically, "Shall we carelessly allow children to hear any casual tales which may be devised by casual persons, and to receive into their minds ideas for the most part the very opposite of those which we shall wish them to have when they are grown up?" Plato offered good reasons for being concerned with the specific contents of schooling, one of them ethical: "For great is the issue at stake, greater than appears—whether a person is to be good or bad."   9

Time has shown that there is much truth in the durable educational *10* theories of both Rousseau and Plato. But even the greatest thinkers, being human, see mainly in one direction at a time, and no thinkers, however profound, can foresee the future implications of their ideas when they are translated into social policy. The great test of social ideas is the crucible of history, which, after a time, usually discloses a one-sidedness in the best of human generalizations. History, not superior wisdom, shows us that neither the content-neutral curriculum of Rousseau and Dewey nor the narrowly specified curriculum of Plato is adequate to the needs of a modern nation.

Plato rightly believed that it is natural for children to learn an adult *11* culture, but too confidently assumed that philosophy could devise the one best culture. (Nonetheless, we should concede to Plato that within our culture we have an obligation to choose and promote our best traditions.) On the other side, Rousseau and Dewey wrongly believed that adult culture is "unnatural" to young children. Rousseau, Dewey, and their present-day disciples have not shown an adequate appreciation of the need for transmission of specific cultural information.

In contrast to the theories of Plato and Rousseau, an anthropologi- *12* cal theory of education accepts the naturalness as well as the relativity of human cultures. It deems it neither wrong nor unnatural to teach young children adult information before they fully understand it. The anthropological view stresses the universal fact that a human group must have effective communications to function effectively, that effective communications require shared culture, and that shared culture requires transmission of specific information to children. Literacy, an essential aim of education in the modern world, is no autonomous, empty skill but depends upon literate culture. Like any other aspect of acculturation, literacy requires the early and continued transmission of specific information. Dewey was deeply mistaken to disdain "accumulating information in the form of symbols." Only by accumulating shared symbols, and the shared information that the symbols represent, can we learn to communicate effectively with one another in our national community.

Now let's take a look at the steps for doing a rhetorical analysis.

■ Identify the Situation

The **situation** is what moves a writer to write. To understand what motivated Hirsch to write, we need look no further than the situation he identifies in the first paragraph of the preface: "the social determinism that now condemns [disadvantaged children] to remain in the same social and educational condition as their parents." Hirsch wants to make sure his readers are aware of the problem so that they will be motivated to read his argument (and take action). He presents as an urgent problem the situation of disadvantaged children, an indication of what is at stake for the writer and for the readers of the argument. For Hirsch, this situation needs to change.

The urgency of a writer's argument is not always triggered by a single situation; often it is multifaceted. Again in the first paragraph, Hirsch identifies a second concern when he states that poverty and illiteracy reflect "an unacceptable failure of our schools, one which has occurred not because our teachers are inept but chiefly because they are compelled to teach a fragmented curriculum based on faulty educational theories." When he introduces a second problem, Hirsch helps us see the interconnected and complex nature of the situations authors confront in academic writing.

■ Identify the Writer's Purpose

The **purpose** for writing an essay may be to respond to a particular situation; it also can be what a writer is trying to accomplish. Specifically, what does the writer want readers to do? Does the writer want us to think about an issue, to change our opinions? Does the writer want to make us aware of a problem that we may not have recognized? Does the writer advocate for some type of change? Or is some combination of all three at work?

Hirsch's main purpose is to promote educational reforms that will produce a higher degree of literacy for all citizens. He begins his argument with a broad statement about the importance of cultural literacy: "Cultural literacy constitutes the only sure avenue of opportunity for disadvantaged children, the only reliable way of combating the social determinism that now condemns them to remain in the same social and educational condition as their parents" (para. 1). As his argument unfolds, his purpose continues to unfold as well. He identifies the schools as a source of the problem and suggests how they must change to promote literacy:

> Some say that our schools by themselves are powerless to change the cycle of poverty and illiteracy. I do not agree. They *can* break the cycle, but only if they themselves break fundamentally with some of the theories and practices that education professors and school administrators have followed over the past fifty years. (para. 1)

The "educational goal," Hirsch declares at the end of paragraph 2, is "mature literacy for *all* our citizens." To reach that goal, he insists, education must break with the past. In paragraphs 5 through 11, he cites the influence of Jean-Jacques Rousseau, John Dewey, and Plato, tracing what he sees as the educational legacies of the past. Finally, in the last paragraph of the excerpt, Hirsch describes an "anthropological view, . . . the universal fact that a human group must have effective communications to function effectively, that effective communications require shared culture, and that shared culture requires transmission of specific information to children." It is here, Hirsch argues, in the "transmission of specific information to children," that schools must do a better job.

■ Identify the Writer's Claims

Claims are assertions that authors must justify and support with evidence and good reasons. The **thesis**, or **main claim**, is the controlling idea that crystallizes a writer's main point, helping readers track the idea as it develops throughout the essay. A writer's purpose clearly influences the way he or she crafts the main claim of an argument, the way he or she presents all assertions and evidence.

Hirsch's main claim is that "cultural literacy constitutes the only sure avenue of opportunity for disadvantaged children, the only reliable way of combating the social determinism that now condemns them to remain in the same social and educational condition as their parents" (para. 1). Notice that his thesis also points to a solution: making cultural literacy the core of public school curricula. Here we distinguish the main claim, or thesis, from the other claims or assertions that Hirsch makes. For example, at the very outset, Hirsch states that "to be culturally literate is to possess the basic information needed to thrive in the modern world." Although this is an assertion that requires support, it is a **minor claim**; it does not shape what Hirsch writes in the remainder of his essay. His main claim, or thesis, is really his call for reform.

■ Identify the Writer's Audience

A writer's language can help us identify his or her **audience**, the readers whose opinions and actions the writer hopes to influence or change. In Hirsch's text, words and phrases like *social determinism, cycle of poverty and illiteracy, educational reforms, prescriptive,* and *anthropological* indicate that Hirsch believes his audience is well educated. References to Plato, Socrates, Rousseau, and Dewey also indicate the level of knowledge Hirsch expects of his readers.

Finally, the way the preface unfolds suggests that Hirsch is writing for an audience that is familiar with a certain **genre**, or type, of writing: the formal argument. Notice how the author begins with a statement of the situation and then asserts his position. The very fact that he includes a preface speaks to the formality of his argument. Hirsch's language, his references, and the structure of the document all suggest that he is very much in conversation with people who are experienced and well-educated readers.

More specifically, the audience Hirsch invokes is made up of people who are concerned about illiteracy in the United States and the kind of social determinism that appears to condemn the educationally disadvantaged to poverty. Hirsch also acknowledges directly "those who have closely followed recent discussions of education," including the conservative William Bennett and liberal thinkers who might be provoked by Bennett's advocacy of Hirsch's ideas (para. 3). Moreover, Hirsch appears to assume that his readers have achieved "mature literacy," even if they are not actually "culturally literate." He is writing for an audience that not only is well educated but also is deeply interested in issues of education as they relate to social policy.

Steps to Analyzing a Text Rhetorically

1 **Identify the situation.** What motivates the writer to write?

2 **Identify the writer's purpose.** What does the writer want readers to do or think about?

3 **Identify the writer's claims.** What is the writer's main claim? What minor claims does he or she make?

4 **Identify the writer's audience.** What do you know about the writer's audience? What does the writer's language imply about the readers? What about the writer's references? The structure of the essay?

Hirsch's writings on cultural literacy have inspired and provoked many responses to the conversation he initiated decades ago. Eugene F. Provenzo's book *Critical Literacy: What Every American Needs to Know*, published in 2005, is a fairly recent one. Provenzo examines the source of Hirsch's ideas, his critiques of scholars like John Dewey, the extent to which Hirsch's argument is based on sound research, and the implications of Hirsch's notion of cultural literacy for teaching and learning. Despite its age, Hirsch's book remains relevant in discussions about the purpose of education, demonstrating how certain works become touchstones and the ways academic and cultural conversations can be sustained over time.

A Practice Sequence: Analyzing a Text Rhetorically

To practice the strategies of rhetorical analysis, read "Hirsch's Desire for a National Curriculum," an excerpt from Eugene F. Provenzo's book, using these questions as a guide:

- What motivates Provenzo as a writer?
- What does he want readers to think about?

- What is Provenzo's main point?
- Given the language Provenzo uses, who do you think his main audience is?

EUGENE F. PROVENZO JR.

Hirsch's Desire for a National Curriculum

Eugene F. Provenzo Jr. is a professor in the Department of Teaching and Learning in the School of Education at the University of Miami in Coral Gables, Florida. His career as a researcher has been interdisciplinary in nature. Throughout his work, his primary focus has been on education as a social and cultural phenomenon. One of his prime concerns has been the role of the teacher in American society. He is also interested in the impact of computers on contemporary children, education, and culture. He is author or coauthor of numerous books, including *Teaching, Learning, and Schooling: A Twenty-First Century Perspective* (2001); *Internet and Online Research for Teachers* (Third Edition, 2004); and *Observing in Schools: A Guide for Students in Teacher Education* (2005).

To a large extent, Hirsch, in his efforts as an educational reformer, wants to establish a national curriculum.   *1*

> Our elementary schools are not only dominated by the content-neutral ideas of Rousseau and Dewey, they are also governed by approximately sixteen thousand independent school districts. We have viewed this dispersion of educational authority as an insurmountable obstacle to altering the fragmentation of the school curriculum even when we have questioned that fragmentation. We have permitted school policies that have shrunk the body of information that Americans share and these policies have caused our national literacy to decline.

This is an interesting argument when interpreted in a conservative political context. While calling for greater local control, Hirsch and other conservatives call for a curriculum that is controlled not at the state and local level, but at the national level by the federal government.

Putting contradictions like this aside, the question arises as to whether or not Hirsch even has a viable curriculum. In an early review of Hirsch's *Cultural Literacy*, Hazel Whitman Hertzberg criticized the book and its list of 5,000 things every American needs to know for its fragmentation. As she explained: *2*

Hirsch's remedy for curricular fragmentation looks suspiciously like more fragmentation. Outside of the dubious claim that his list represents what literate people know, there is nothing that holds it together besides its arrangement in alphabetical order. Subject-matter organization is ignored. It is not hard to imagine how Hirsch's proposal would have been greeted by educational neoconservatives had it been made by one of those professors of education who he charges are responsible for the current state of cultural illiteracy.

Hertzberg wonders what Hirsch's "hodgepodge of miscellaneous, arbitrary, and often trivial information" would look like if it were put into a coherent curriculum.

In 1988 Hirsch did in fact establish the Core Knowledge Foundation,   3
which had as its purpose the design of a national curriculum. Called the "Core Knowledge Sequence," the sequence offered a curriculum in six content areas: history, geography, mathematics, science, language arts, and fine arts. Hirsch's curriculum was intended to represent approximately half of the total curriculum for K–6 schools. Subsequent curriculum revisions include a curriculum for grades seven and eight as well as one at the preschool level.

Several hundred schools across the United States currently use   4
Hirsch's model. A national conference is held each year, which draws several thousand people. In books like *What Your First Grader Needs to Know* (1991) as well as *A First Dictionary of Cultural Literacy: What Our Children Need to Know* (1989) and *The Dictionary of Cultural Literacy* (1993), along with the Core Knowledge Sequence, one finds a fairly conservative but generally useful curriculum that conforms to much of the content already found in local school systems around the country.

Hirsch seems not to recognize that there indeed is a national curricu-   5
lum, one whose standards are set by local communities through their acceptance and rejection of textbooks and by national accreditation groups ranging from the National Council of Teachers of Mathematics to the National Council for Social Studies Teachers and the National Council of Teachers of English. One need only look at standards in different subject areas in school districts across the country to realize the extent to which there is indeed a national curriculum.

Whether the current curriculum in use in the schools across the   6
country is adequate is of course open to debate. Creating any curriculum is by definition a deeply political act, and is, or should be, subject to considerable negotiation and discussion at any level. But to act as though there is not a de facto national curriculum is simply inaccurate. First graders in most school districts across the country learn about

the weather and the seasons, along with more basic skills like adding and subtracting. Students do not learn to divide before they learn how to add or multiply. Local and state history is almost universally introduced for the first time in either third or fourth grade. It is reintroduced in most states at the seventh or eighth grade levels. Algebra is typically taught in the ninth grade. Traditions, developmental patterns of students, textbook content, and national subject standards combine to create a fairly uniform national curriculum.

Hirsch's complaint that there is no national curriculum is not 7 motivated by a desire to establish one but rather a desire to establish a curriculum that reflects his cultural and ideological orientation. It is a sophisticated assault on more inclusive and diverse models of curriculum and culture—one that represents a major battle in the culture wars of the last twenty years in the United States.

WRITING AS A READER: COMPOSING A RHETORICAL ANALYSIS

One of our favorite exercises is to ask students to choose a single paragraph or a brief section from a text they have read and to write a rhetorical analysis. We first ask our students to identify the writer's key claims and ideas to orient them to the main points they want to make in their analysis. We then ask our students to consider such features as the situation that calls for a response in writing and the writer's purpose, intended audience, kinds of claims, and types of evidence. In their rhetorical analyses, we encourage our students to analyze the ways writers develop their ideas and the extent to which these strategies succeed. That is, we ask our students to consider how writers express their ideas, develop their points of view, respond to a given situation, and use evidence to persuade readers. Once you are able to identify *how* writers make arguments, look critically at what works and what doesn't in making a persuasive argument; then you will be able to make use of their strategies in your own writing.

For example, one of our students wrote a rhetorical analysis of an excerpt from David Tyack's book on education, *Seeking Common Ground: Public Schools in a Diverse Society* (2004). In his book, Tyack examines the extent to which the purpose of education in American schools has developed out of and reflected the political, economic, and moral concerns of the nation. His analysis begins with the emergence of public schools in the nineteenth century and demonstrates a sense of continuity in twenty-first-century education, particularly in light of contemporary debates around national standards, teacher evaluation, social justice, equity, civic engagement, and the common good. This continuity is best represented in the quest for a common denominator of political and moral truths, often evidenced in textbooks that point to the progress of history and American democracy, the focus on great men who understood the grandeur of America's destiny, and the importance of individual character in building a strong nation founded on shared values. For Tyack, history textbooks have served as a significant source of civic education — that is, "what adults thought children should learn about the past" — and assimilation. However, the search for common values in official histories (what he calls "stone monuments") has not been without dissent, given their focus on white, male, Protestant ideology. Tyack also writes about the ways in which educators have dealt with questions of social and educational diversity, particularly race, immigration and ethnicity, and gender; efforts to establish models of educational governance to meet the needs of a pluralistic society; and the implications of opening public education to a free market.

Note that in the following passage, Tyack assesses the state of American history textbooks by citing a number of writers, sometimes generally and at other times more specifically, to address ways to solve the problems he identifies (for example, Patricia Nelson Limerick's proposal for a "pluralistic model of history").

As you read the Tyack passage, take notes on the rhetorical situation, purpose, main claim, audience, and language. You may want to underline passages or circle words and phrases where the writer makes the following points explicit:

- the situation that motivates his writing,
- the purpose of his analysis and argument,
- his main claim or thesis, and
- who he believes his audience is.

DAVID TYACK

Whither History Textbooks?

David Tyack was the Vida Jacks Professor of Education and Professor of History, Emeritus, at Stanford University. In addition to writing *Seeking Common Ground*, he authored *The One Best System: A History of American Urban Education* (1974) and coauthored *Tinkering Toward Utopia: A Century of Public School Reform* (1997), *Law and the Shaping of Public Education, 1785–1954* (1991), *Learning Together: A History of Coeducation in American Public Schools* (1992), and *Public Schools in Hard Times: The Great Depression and Recent Years* (1984).

A history textbook today is hardly the republican catechism that
Noah Webster appended to his famous speller. It is more like
pieces of a sprawling novel with diverse characters and fascinating
subplots waiting for an author to weave them into a broader narrative. Now a noisy confusion reigns about what stories the textbooks
should tell. Special-interest groups of the right and left pressure
publishers to include or drop topics, especially in big states such as
California or Texas. Worries abound about old truths betrayed and
new truths ignored. Many groups want to vet or veto what children
learn, and it is unclear what roles teachers, parents, ethnic groups,
religious activists, historians, and others should play. Tempers rise.
In New York debates over a multicultural curriculum, Catherine
Cornbleth and Dexter Waugh observed, "both sides engaged in a
rhetoric of crisis, doom, and salvation."

In the United States, unlike most other nations, private agencies—
publishing companies—create and sell textbooks. Thus commerce
plays an important part in deciding which historical truths shall be
official. To be sure, public agencies usually decide which textbooks to
adopt (about half of the states delegate text adoption to local districts,
and the rest use some form of state adoption). For all the conventional-
ity of the product, the actual production and sale of textbooks is still
a risky business. It's very expensive to create and print textbooks, and
the market (the various agencies that actually decide which to adopt)
is somewhat unpredictable. In addition, at any time some citizens are
likely to protest whatever messages the texts send. Textbook adoption
can be a free-for-all.

Thus it is not surprising that textbooks still beget textbooks. To control
risk, companies find it wise to copy successes. Old icons (Washington)
remain, but publishers respond to new demands by multiplying new
state-approved truths. It has been easier to add those ubiquitous side-
bars to the master narrative than to rethink it, easier to incorporate new
content into a safe and profitable formula than to create new accounts.
American history textbooks are enormous—888 pages, on average—in
part because publishers seek to neutralize or anticipate criticisms by
adding topics. The result is often not comprehensive coverage but a
bloated book devoid of style or coherence.

The traditional American fear of centralized power, salient today
in debates over national standards and tests, has resulted in a strange
patchwork of agencies and associations—textbook companies, state
and local governments, lobby groups of many persuasions, individuals
who want to play Grand Inquisitor—to choose and monitor the public
truths taught in the texts. One of the most rapid ways of changing what
students learn in American schools is to transform the textbooks, but
the present Rube Goldberg system of creating and selecting textbooks

makes such a change very difficult (though fine history textbooks have on occasion appeared).

What are some strategies to cope with the cross-cutting demands on history textbooks? Three possible ones are these: muddling through with modest improvements; turning over the task of writing textbooks to experts; or devising texts that depart from the model of state-approved truths and embrace instead the taking of multiple perspectives. Each of these has some advantages and faults that are worth contemplating. 5

Muddling through may seem sensible to people who believe that there is a vast gap between superheated policy talk about the defects of textbooks and the everyday reality teachers face in classrooms. Is all the debate over bad textbooks a dust-devil masquerading as a tornado? For many teachers, the big challenge is to prepare students for high-stakes tests they must take for graduation, and textbooks are a key resource in that task. 6

Teachers tend to find the status quo in textbooks more bearable than do the critics. When a sample of classroom teachers was asked their opinion of the textbooks they used, they generally said that the books are good and getting better. Teachers rely heavily on textbooks in their instruction, employing them for about 70 percent of class time. 7

A commonsense argument for muddling through, with gradual improvement of textbooks, is that pedagogical reforms rarely work well if they are imposed on teachers. Study after study has shown that teachers tend to avoid controversy in teaching American history (indeed, being "nonpartisan" is still judged a virtue, as it was in the past). And parents and school board members, like teachers, have their own ideas about what is "real history." Too sharp a turn in the historical highway might topple reform. So some teachers argue that the best way to improve education is to keep the old icons and welcome the newcomers in the textbooks. And hope that the students in fact *do read* the textbooks! Common sense — that's the way to cope amid all the confusion. 8

An alternate approach to reform of textbooks is to set good state or local standards for history courses and turn the writing of textbooks over to experts — an approach used in many nations and sometimes advocated in the United States today. Muddling through just maintains the status quo and guarantees incoherence in textbooks and hence in learning. In the current politics and commerce of text publishing, "truth" becomes whatever the special interests (left or right) pressure textbook companies to say. Current textbooks are often victims of commercial timidity, veto groups, and elephantiasis (888 pages!). 9

What is missing, proponents of this view argue, is a clear set of national standards about what students should know and a vivid and cogent text that engages students in learning. Those who call for 10 expertise suggest that history is too important *not* to be left to the historians.

But this response to the faults of history texts presents its own problems. Calling in the experts doesn't eliminate disputes; PhDs love to differ among themselves. Teachers are adept at sabotaging reforms dropped on them from above. And amid all the commercialism and special interests now rife in the process of selecting textbooks, the public still deserves some say in deciding what American students learn about the past, expert or not.   *11*

Patricia Nelson Limerick, professor of history at the University of Colorado, suggests a pluralistic model of history that contrasts with both muddling through and textbooks by experts. She recently suggested that the Little Bighorn Battlefield, where Sioux and Cheyenne fought George Armstrong Custer, needed not two monuments, one in honor of the Indians and one to recognize Custer and his soldiers, but "a different kind of memorial—one in which no point of view dominates." She imagines visitors walking among memorials to the warriors and Custer, but also to the enlisted men dragooned into the slaughter, to Custer's widow, to the families of the white soldiers, and to the children and wives of the Indian warriors.   *12*

Such perspective-taking lies at the core of historical understanding of a socially diverse nation. Pluralistic history can enhance ethnic self-respect and empathy for other groups. Parallel to the monuments Limerick proposes, texts for a pluralistic civic education might have not one master narrative but several, capturing separate identities and experiences.   *13*

But the history of Americans in their separate groups would be partial without looking as well at their lives in interaction. Our society is pluralistic in character, and so should be the history we teach to young citizens. But alongside that *pluribus* citizens have also sought an *unum*, a set of shared political aspirations and institutions. One reason there have been so many textbook wars is that group after group has, in turn, sought to become part of a common story told about our past. The *unum* and the *pluribus* have been in inescapable tension, constantly evolving as Americans struggled to find common ground and to respect their differences.   *14*

AN ANNOTATED STUDENT RHETORICAL ANALYSIS

Now read our student's rhetorical analysis about David Tyack's discussion of history textbooks in "Whither History Textbooks?" We have annotated the student's analysis to point out how he identifies the author's situation, purpose, argument, and audience.

Collie 1

Quentin Collie

A Rhetorical Analysis of
"Whither History Textbooks?"

The student provides an overview of the author's argument.

In my analysis, I will focus on "Whither History Textbooks?"   1
which serves as a conclusion to David Tyack's chapter on American
history textbooks in his book *Seeking Common Ground.* In this
section, Tyack explains the state of history textbooks in American
schools today, the causes and influences that result in what he sees
as a problem with trying to cover too many topics without much
depth, and possible ways in which history textbooks can be changed
and improved. In advocating for a pluralistic account of history,
Tyack use specific words and phrases that convey his impatience
with American history textbooks and presents a number of options
to make his discussion appear fair.

The student explains the author's argument in more detail and, specifically, the source of what the author sees as a problem in teaching history. This is the situation that calls for some response in writing: that textbooks have become "heavy" and "boring." The student then describes three possible approaches that the author takes to address the problem he identifies in teaching history in school.

Tyack points out that today's textbooks are, for the most   2
part, bulky and disjointed. Many storylines and historic figures
are pieced together without any all-encompassing narrative flow
or style. Textbooks have come to take this form because of two
significant influences. On one hand, nearly every interest group
argues for certain events, figures, or issues to be included in the
history curriculum. On the other hand, in a more economical sense,
textbooks that present the traditional and generic American narrative
have been the most successful. As a result, textbook authors and
producers attempt to intersperse the variety of new pieces into the
original American narrative. This results in the heavy and boring
textbooks that students use in the classroom today. Tyack offers
three possibilities for how to navigate through the demands and
difficulties involved in history textbook production: continuing the
use of current textbooks with moderate additions and improvements,
delegating the writing of textbooks to experts, and embracing a new
style of textbook which emphasizes the multiple perspectives of
Americans.

In this particular section of the book, Tyack's purpose seems   3
to be a call for change. In describing the current types of textbooks,
he implies his personal stance through his word choice. Tyack's
use of vivid imagery throughout this part of his book allows him to
delve into the textbook problem by appealing to the emotions of

Collie 2

The student underscores the author's purpose. He then shows how language reflects the author's point of view. In addition, the student helps us see that the situation the author responds to is not only about how textbooks are written, but how educators choose to adopt textbooks.

the reader. For instance, Tyack explains that the average American history textbook is 888 pages long and laments this length as the reason that most of today's history books are "bloated" and "devoid of style or coherence" (para. 3). He also alludes to anarchy when he claims that "textbook adoption can be a free-for-all" (para. 2), establishing his skeptical perspective on the decision processes of textbook writers as well as of those who buy them. Another way Tyack explains his views on the methodology behind buying and selling textbooks is through an allusion to a "Rube Goldberg system" (para. 4) in his description of how textbooks are created and sold. This reference implies that our current method has become unnecessarily complex and has rendered making changes in history textbooks difficult or impossible.

He points out the author's strategy for developing the argument, one that forces knowledgeable readers to draw their own conclusions.

Tyack does not advocate for just any change, but, rather, a particular change and ideal type of textbook. He does not make an outright statement of support for a particular plan. Instead, he presents an examination of possibilities that leads the audience to decide which one option is superior. The possibilities include using the same format with slight changes, having experts write the textbooks, and departing from the regular model of textbooks to include new truths and multiple perspectives. He makes a point to state that each option has both pros and cons to be considered.

4

The student points to the author's concession that not everyone agrees that the quality of textbook writing is a problem. The student again demonstrates how word choice conveys an author's point of view and that the author does not find this first solution tenable.

Tyack writes that teachers, in general, do not have a large problem with the current types of textbooks, and pedagogical reforms rarely work if imposed on teachers. This evidence argues in favor of using the same types of textbooks. The discussion of this particular option, however, ends with its success resting on a "hope that the students in fact *do read* the textbooks!" (para. 8). This statement carries a tone of sarcasm, leaving the reader with a feeling that Tyack believes that students will not read this type of textbook, so this particular plan of action is not likely to improve the schools. In addition, Tyack's exact phrasing for this possibility is "muddling through with modest improvements" (para. 5). From word choice alone, the reader can see that Tyack discredits this idea. The verb *muddle* is associated with things being confused, messed up, and unclear, so his choice of this word implies that he thinks using the current format for textbooks results in teachers and students having

5

Collie 3

a confused and incorrect view of American history. Eventually, he concludes that "muddling through just maintains the status quo and guarantees incoherence in textbooks and hence learning" (para. 9).

He presents the author's second possible solution to the problem but explains why the author is not sympathetic to that position.

His next suggested approach is using textbooks written by experts. This option could set clear national standards about what students should be learning about history by those most informed. This option, however, also has its faults as Tyack argues that the experts differ in their opinions. Furthermore, the public does deserve some input about material to be taught to its children, which this option would take away.

6

Although it would seem that the author lets readers draw their own conclusions, the student explains how Tyack uses research to give credence to this last solution to the problem.

Tyack's final option is "a pluralistic model of history that contrasts with both muddling through and textbooks by experts" (para. 12). Tyack argues that "such perspective-taking lies at the core of historical understanding of a socially diverse nation. Pluralistic history can enhance ethnic self-respect and empathy for other groups" (para. 13). Tyack supports this point of view with quotations from a professor of history, which gives credibility to this option. In addition, Tyack does not discuss any possible difficulties in pursuing this type of textbook, even though he stated earlier that each option has both benefits and faults. In this, Tyack appears to be considering multiple possibilities for textbook reform, but, at the same time, he dismisses two of the options and advocates for a particular course of action through his writing strategy.

7

WRITING A RHETORICAL ANALYSIS

By now you should have a strong sense of what is involved in rhetorical analysis. You should be ready to take the next steps: performing a rhetorical analysis of your own and then sharing your analysis and the strategies you've learned with your classmates.

Read the next text, "The Flight from Conversation" by Sherry Turkle, annotating it to help you identify her situation, purpose, thesis, and audience. As you read, also make a separate set of annotations—possibly with a different color pen or pencil, circled, or keyed with asterisks—in which you comment on or evaluate the effectiveness of her essay. What do you like or dislike about it? Why? Does Turkle persuade you to accept her point of view? What impressions do you have of her as a person? Would you like to be in a conversation with her?

SHERRY TURKLE

The Flight from Conversation

Sherry Turkle—the Abby Rockefeller Mauzé Professor of the Social Studies of Science and Technology in the Program in Science, Technology, and Society at the Massachusetts Institute of Technology—is a licensed clinical psychologist with a joint doctorate in sociology and personality psychology from Harvard University. Director of the MIT Initiative on Technology and Self, she is the author or editor of many books, including *The Second Self: Computers and the Human Spirit* (1984), *Life on the Screen: Identity in the Age of the Internet* (1995), *Simulation and Its Discontents* (2009), and *Alone Together: Why We Expect More from Technology and Less from Each Other* (2011). "The Flight from Conversation" appeared in the April 12, 2012, issue of *The New York Times Magazine*.

We live in a technological universe in which we are always communicating. And yet we have sacrificed conversation for mere connection. 1

At home, families sit together, texting and reading e-mail. At work 2 executives text during board meetings. We text (and shop and go on Facebook) during classes and when we're on dates. My students tell me about an important new skill: It involves maintaining eye contact with someone while you text someone else; it's hard, but it can be done.

Over the past fifteen years, I've studied technologies of mobile con- 3 nection and talked to hundreds of people of all ages and circumstances about their plugged-in lives. I've learned that the little devices most of us carry around are so powerful that they change not only what we do, but also who we are.

We've become accustomed to a new way of being "alone together." 4 Technology-enabled, we are able to be with one another, and also elsewhere, connected to wherever we want to be. We want to customize our lives. We want to move in and out of where we are because the thing we value most is control over where we focus our attention. We have gotten used to the idea of being in a tribe of one, loyal to our own party.

Our colleagues want to go to that board meeting but pay attention 5 only to what interests them. To some this seems like a good idea, but we can end up hiding from one another, even as we are constantly connected to one another.

A businessman laments that he no longer has colleagues at work. He 6 doesn't stop by to talk; he doesn't call. He says that he doesn't want to interrupt them. He says they're "too busy on their e-mail." But then he pauses and corrects himself. "I'm not telling the truth. I'm the one who doesn't want to be interrupted. I think I should. But I'd rather just do things on my BlackBerry."

A 16-year-old boy who relies on texting for almost everything says 7 almost wistfully, "Someday, someday, but certainly not now, I'd like to learn how to have a conversation."

In today's workplace, young people who have grown up fearing con- 8 versation show up on the job wearing earphones. Walking through a college library or the campus of a high-tech start-up, one sees the same thing: We are together, but each of us is in our own bubble, furiously connected to keyboards and tiny touch screens. A senior partner at a Boston law firm describes a scene in his office. Young associates lay out their suite of technologies: laptops, iPods, and multiple phones. And then they put their earphones on. "Big ones. Like pilots. They turn their desks into cockpits." With the young lawyers in their cockpits, the office is quiet, a quiet that does not ask to be broken.

In the silence of connection, people are comforted by being in touch 9 with a lot of people—carefully kept at bay. We can't get enough of one another if we can use technology to keep one another at distances we can control: not too close, not too far, just right. I think of it as a Goldilocks effect.

Texting and e-mail and posting let us present the self we want to be. 10 This means we can edit. And if we wish to, we can delete. Or retouch: the voice, the flesh, the face, the body. Not too much, not too little—just right.

Human relationships are rich; they're messy and demanding. We 11 have learned the habit of cleaning them up with technology. And the move from conversation to connection is part of this. But it's a process in which we shortchange ourselves. Worse, it seems that over time we stop caring, we forget that there is a difference.

We are tempted to think that our little "sips" of online connec- 12 tion add up to a big gulp of real conversation. But they don't. E-mail, Twitter, Facebook, all of these have their places—in politics, commerce, romance, and friendship. But no matter how valuable, they do not substitute for conversation.

Connecting in sips may work for gathering discrete bits of informa- 13 tion or for saying, "I am thinking about you." Or even for saying, "I love you." But connecting in sips doesn't work as well when it comes to understanding and knowing one another. In conversation we tend to one another. (The word itself is kinetic; it's derived from words that mean to move, together.) We can attend to tone and nuance. In conversation, we are called upon to see things from another's point of view.

Face-to-face conversation unfolds slowly. It teaches patience. When 14 we communicate on our digital devices, we learn different habits. As we ramp up the volume and velocity of online connections, we start to expect faster answers. To get these, we ask one another simpler questions; we dumb down our communications, even on the most important matters. It is as though we have all put ourselves on cable news. Shakespeare might have said, "We are consum'd with that which we were nourish'd by."

And we use conversation with others to learn to converse with ourselves. So our flight from conversation can mean diminished chances to learn skills of self-reflection. These days, social media continually asks us what's "on our mind," but we have little motivation to say something truly self-reflective. Self-reflection in conversation requires trust. It's hard to do anything with 3,000 Facebook friends except connect.

15

As we get used to being shortchanged on conversation and to getting by with less, we seem almost willing to dispense with people altogether. Serious people muse about the future of computer programs as psychiatrists. A high school sophomore confides to me that he wishes he could talk to an artificial intelligence program instead of his dad about dating; he says the AI would have so much more in its database. Indeed, many people tell me they hope that as Siri, the digital assistant on Apple's iPhone, becomes more advanced, "she" will be more and more like a best friend—one who will listen when others won't.

16

During the years I have spent researching people and their relationships with technology, I have often heard the sentiment "No one is listening to me." I believe this feeling helps explain why it is so appealing to have a Facebook page or a Twitter feed—each provides so many automatic listeners. And it helps explain why—against all reason—so many of us are willing to talk to machines that seem to care about us. Researchers around the world are busy inventing sociable robots, designed to be companions to the elderly, to children, to all of us.

17

One of the most haunting experiences during my research came when I brought one of these robots, designed in the shape of a baby seal, to an elder-care facility, and an older woman began to talk to it about the loss of her child. The robot seemed to be looking into her eyes. It seemed to be following the conversation. The woman was comforted.

18

And so many people found this amazing. Like the sophomore who wants advice about dating from artificial intelligence and those who look forward to computer psychiatry, this enthusiasm speaks to how much we have confused conversation with connection and collectively seem to have embraced a new kind of delusion that accepts the simulation of compassion as sufficient unto the day. And why would we want to talk about love and loss with a machine that has no experience of the arc of human life? Have we so lost confidence that we will be there for one another?

19

We expect more from technology and less from one another, and seem increasingly drawn to technologies that provide the illusion

20

of companionship without the demands of relationship. Always-on/always-on-you devices provide three powerful fantasies: that we will always be heard; that we can put our attention wherever we want it to be; and that we never have to be alone. Indeed our new devices have turned being alone into a problem that can be solved.

When people are alone, even for a few moments, they fidget and reach for a device. Here connection works like a symptom, not a cure, and our constant, reflexive impulse to connect shapes a new way of being. *21*

Think of it as "I share, therefore I am." We use technology to define ourselves by sharing our thoughts and feelings as we're having them. We used to think, "I have a feeling; I want to make a call." Now our impulse is, "I want to have a feeling; I need to send a text." *22*

So, in order to feel more, and to feel more like ourselves, we connect. But in our rush to connect, we flee from solitude, our ability to be separate and gather ourselves. Lacking the capacity for solitude, we turn to other people but don't experience them as they are. It is as though we use them, need them as spare parts to support our increasingly fragile selves. *23*

We think constant connection will make us feel less lonely. The opposite is true. If we are unable to be alone, we are far more likely to be lonely. If we don't teach our children to be alone, they will know only how to be lonely. *24*

I am a partisan for conversation. To make room for it, I see some first, deliberate steps. At home, we can create sacred spaces: the kitchen, the dining room. We can make our cars "device-free zones." We can demonstrate the value of conversation to our children. And we can do the same thing at work. There we are so busy communicating that we often don't have time to talk to one another about what really matters. Employees asked for casual Fridays; perhaps managers should introduce conversational Thursdays. Most of all, we need to remember — in between texts and e-mails and Facebook posts — to listen to one another, even to the boring bits, because it is often in unedited moments, moments in which we hesitate and stutter and go silent, that we reveal ourselves to one another. *25*

I spend the summers at a cottage on Cape Cod, and for decades I walked the same dunes that Thoreau once walked. Not too long ago, people walked with their heads up, looking at the water, the sky, the sand and at one another, talking. Now they often walk with their heads down, typing. Even when they are with friends, partners, children, everyone is on their own devices. *26*

So I say, look up, look at one another, and let's start the conversation. *27*

A Practice Sequence: Writing a Rhetorical Analysis

1   Write a brief rhetorical analysis of Sherry Turkle's essay, referring to your notes and citing passages where she indicates her situation, purpose, main claim, and audience.

2   An option for group work: As a class, divide into three or more groups. Groups should answer the following questions in response to Turkle's essay:

> *Group 1*: Identify the situation(s) motivating Turkle to write. Then evaluate: How well does her argument function as a conversation with other authors who have written on the same topic?

> *Group 2*: Analyze the audience's identity, perspectives, and conventional expectations. Then evaluate: How well does the argument function as a conversation with the audience?

> *Group 3*: Analyze the writer's purpose. Then evaluate: Do you believe Turkle achieves her purpose in this essay? Why or why not?

Then, as a class, share your observations:

- To what extent does the author's ability as a conversationalist— that is, her ability to enter into a conversation with other authors and her audience—affect your evaluation of whether she achieves her purpose in this essay?

- If you were to meet this writer, what suggestions or advice would you give her for making her argument more persuasive?

3

From Writing Summaries and Paraphrases to Writing Yourself into Academic Conversations

Reading like a writer and writing like a reader help you understand how texts work rhetorically. When you start to use those texts to build your own arguments, there are certain strategies for working with the words and ideas of others that you will have to learn. Often you can quote the words of an author directly; but just as often you will restate (paraphrase) and condense (summarize) the arguments of others to educate your reader about the issues in a particular academic conversation. Indeed, many academic essays begin with a **literature review**—a roundup that summarizes important arguments and perspectives in such a conversation—as a prelude to the writer setting forth his or her own arguments on an issue. In this chapter, we will present methods of paraphrase and summary. Learning to paraphrase and summarize helps you understand texts and convey that understanding to other participants in the conversation.

SUMMARIES, PARAPHRASES, AND QUOTATIONS

In contrast to quotations, which involve using another writer's exact words, paraphrases and summaries are both restatements of another writer's ideas in your own words, but they differ in length and scope:

- A paraphrase is frequently about the same length as the original passage.

- A summary generally condenses a significantly longer text, conveying the argument not only of a few sentences but also of entire paragraphs, essays, or books.

In your own writing, you might paraphrase a few sentences or even a few paragraphs, but you certainly would not paraphrase a whole essay (much less a whole book). In constructing your arguments, however, you will often have to summarize the main points of the lengthy texts with which you are in conversation.

Both paraphrasing and summarizing are means to inquiry. That is, the act of recasting someone else's words or ideas into your own language, to suit your argument and reach your readers, forces you to think critically: What does this passage really mean? What is most important about it for my argument? How can I best present it to my readers? It requires making choices, not least of which is determining the best way to present the information—through paraphrase, summary, or direct quotation. In general, the following rules apply:

- *Paraphrase* when all the information in the passage is important, but the language is not key to your discussion, or if it may be difficult for your readers to understand.

- *Summarize* when you need to present only the key ideas of a passage (or an essay or a book) to advance your argument.

- *Quote* when the passage is so effective—so clear, so concise, so authoritative, so memorable—that you would be hard-pressed to improve on it.

WRITING A PARAPHRASE

A **paraphrase** is a restatement of all the information in a passage in your own words, using your own sentence structure and composed with your own audience in mind to advance your argument.

- When you paraphrase a passage, start by identifying key words and phrases, and think of other ways to state them. You may have to reread what led up to the passage to remind yourself of the context. For example, did the writer define terms earlier that he or she uses in the passage and now expects you to know?

- Continue by experimenting with word order and sentence structure, combining and recombining phrases to convey what the writer says without replicating his or her style. As you consider how best to state the writer's idea in your own words, you should come to a much better understanding of what the writer is saying. By thinking critically, then, you are clarifying the passage for yourself as much as for your readers.

Let's look at a paraphrase of a passage from science fiction writer and scholar James Gunn's essay "Harry Potter as Schooldays Novel"*:

ORIGINAL PASSAGE

The situation and portrayal of Harry as an ordinary child with an extraordinary talent make him interesting. He elicits our sympathy at every turn. He plays a Cinderella-like role as the abused child of mean-spirited foster parents who favor other, less-worthy children, and also fits another fantasy role, that of changeling. Millions of children have nursed the notion that they cannot be the offspring of such unremarkable parents; in the Harry Potter books, the metaphor is often literal truth.

PARAPHRASE

According to James Gunn, the circumstances and depiction of Harry Potter as a normal boy with special abilities captivate us by playing on our empathy. Gunn observes that, like Cinderella, Harry is scorned by his guardians, who treat him far worse than they treat his less-admirable peers. And like another fairy-tale figure, the changeling, Harry embodies the fantasies of children who refuse to believe that they were born of their undistinguished parents (146).

In this paraphrase, the writer uses his own words to express key terms (*circumstances and depiction* for "situation and portrayal," *guardians* for "foster parents") and rearranges the structure of the original sentences. But the paraphrase is about the same length as the original and says essentially the same things as Gunn's original.

Now, compare the paraphrase with this summary:

SUMMARY

James Gunn observes that Harry Potter's character is compelling because readers empathize with Harry's fairy tale–like plight as an orphan whose gifts are ignored by his foster parents (146).

The summary condenses the passage, conveying Gunn's main point without restating the details. Notice how both the paraphrase and the summary indicate that the ideas are James Gunn's, not the writer's — "According to James Gunn," "James Gunn observes" — and signal, with page references, where Gunn's ideas end. *It is essential that you acknowledge your sources*, a subject we come back to in our discussion of plagiarism on page 228. The

---

*Gunn's essay appears in *Mapping the World of Harry Potter: An Unauthorized Exploration of the Bestselling Fantasy Series of All Time*, edited by Mercedes Lackey (Dallas: BenBella, 2006).

point we want to make here is that borrowing from the work of others is not always intentional. Many students stumble into plagiarism, especially when they are attempting to paraphrase. Remember that it's not enough to change the words in a paraphrase; you must also change the structure of the sentences and cite your source.

You may be wondering: "If paraphrasing is so tricky, why bother? What does it add? I can see how the summary of Gunn's paragraph presents information more concisely and efficiently than the original, but the paraphrase doesn't seem to be all that different from the source and doesn't seem to add anything to it. Why not simply quote the original or summarize it?"

Good questions. The answer is that you paraphrase when the ideas in a passage are important but the language is not key to your discussion or it may be difficult for readers to understand. When academics write for their peers, they draw on the specialized vocabulary of their disciplines to make their arguments. By paraphrasing, you may be helping your readers, providing a translation of sorts for those who do not speak the language.

Consider this paragraph by George Lipsitz from his academic book *Time Passages: Collective Memory and American Popular Culture* (1990), and compare the paraphrase that follows it:

ORIGINAL PASSAGE

The transformations in behavior and collective memory fueled by the contradictions of the nineteenth century have passed through three major stages in the United States. The first involved the establishment and codification of commercialized leisure from the invention of the telegraph to the 1890s. The second involved the transition from Victorian to consumer-hedonist values between 1890 and 1945. The third and most important stage, from World War II to the present, involved extraordinary expansion in both the distribution of consumer purchasing power and in both the reach and scope of electronic mass media. The dislocations of urban renewal, suburbanization, and deindustrialization accelerated the demise of tradition in America, while the worldwide pace of change undermined stability elsewhere. The period from World War II to the present marks the final triumph of commercialized leisure, and with it an augmented crisis over the loss of connection to the past.

PARAPHRASE

Historian George Lipsitz argues that Americans' sense of the past is rooted in cultural changes dating from the 1800s and has evolved through three stages. In the first stage, technological innovations of the nineteenth century gave rise to widespread commercial entertainment. In the second stage, dating from the 1890s to about 1945, attitudes toward the consumption of goods and services changed. Since 1945, in the third stage, increased consumer spending and the growth of the mass media have led to a crisis in which Americans find themselves cut off from their traditions and the memories that give meaning to them (12).

Notice that the paraphrase is not a word-for-word translation of the original. Instead, the writer has made choices that resulted in a slightly briefer and more accessible restatement of Lipsitz's thinking. (Although this paraphrase is shorter than the original passage, a paraphrase can also be a little longer than the original if extra words are needed to help readers understand the original.)

Notice too that several specialized terms and phrases from the original passage—the "codification of commercialized leisure," "the transition from Victorian to consumer-hedonist values," "the dislocations of urban renewal, suburbanization, and deindustrialization"—have disappeared. The writer not only looked up these terms and phrases in the dictionary but also reread the several pages that preceded the original passage to understand what Lipsitz meant by them.

The paraphrase is not meant to be an improvement on the original passage—in fact, historians would most likely prefer what Lipsitz wrote—but it may help readers who do not share Lipsitz's expertise understand his point without distorting his argument.

Now compare this summary to the paraphrase:

SUMMARY

Historian George Lipsitz argues that technological, social, and economic changes dating from the nineteenth century have culminated in what he calls a "crisis over the loss of connection to the past," in which Americans find themselves cut off from the memories of their traditions (12).

Which is better, the paraphrase or the summary? Neither is better or worse in and of itself. Their correctness and appropriateness depend on how the restatements are used in a given argument. That is, the decision to paraphrase or summarize depends entirely on the information you need to convey. Would the details in the paraphrase strengthen your argument? Or is a summary sufficient? In this case, if you plan to focus your argument on the causes of America's loss of cultural memory (the rise of commercial entertainment, changes in spending habits, globalization), then a paraphrase might be more helpful. But if you plan to define *loss of cultural memory*, then a summary may provide enough context for the next stage of your argument.

Steps to Writing a Paraphrase

1 **Decide whether to paraphrase.** If your readers don't need all the information in the passage, consider summarizing it or presenting the key points as part of a summary of a longer passage. If a passage is clear, concise, and memorable as originally written, consider quoting instead of paraphrasing. Otherwise, and especially if the original was written for an academic audience, you may want to paraphrase the original to make its substance more accessible to your readers.

2 **Understand the passage.** Start by identifying key words, phrases, and ideas. If necessary, reread the pages leading up to the passage, to place it in context.

3 **Draft your paraphrase.** Replace key words and phrases with synonyms and alternative phrases (possibly gleaned from the context provided by the surrounding text). Experiment with word order and sentence structure until the paraphrase captures your understanding of the passage, in your own language, for your readers.

4 **Acknowledge your source.** Protect yourself from a charge of plagiarism and give credit for ideas you borrow.

A Practice Sequence: Writing a Paraphrase

1 In one of the sources you've located in your research, find a sentence of some length and complexity, and paraphrase it. Share the original and your paraphrase of it with a classmate, and discuss the effectiveness of your restatement. Is the meaning clear to your reader? Is the paraphrase written in your own language, using your own sentence structure?

2 Repeat the activity using a short paragraph from the same source. You and your classmate may want to attempt to paraphrase the same paragraph and then compare results. What differences do you detect?

WRITING A SUMMARY

As you have seen, a **summary** condenses a body of information, presenting the key ideas and acknowledging the source. A common activity or assignment in a composition class is to *summarize* a text. You may be asked to read a text, reduce it to its main points, and convey them, without any details or examples, in a written summary. The goal of this assignment is to sharpen your reading and thinking skills as you learn to distinguish between main ideas and supporting details. Being able to distill information in this manner is crucial to critical thinking.

However, summarizing is not an active way to make an argument. While summaries do provide a common ground of information for your readers, you must shape that information to support the purposes of your researched argument with details that clarify, illustrate, or support their main ideas for your readers.

We suggest a method of summarizing that involves

1. describing the author's key claims,

2. selecting examples to illustrate the author's argument,

3. presenting the gist of the author's argument, and

4. contextualizing what you summarize.

We demonstrate these steps for writing a summary following Clive Thompson's article "On the New Literacy."

CLIVE THOMPSON

On the New Literacy

A print journalist at *New York Magazine*, Clive Thompson started his blog, Collision Detection, in September 2002, when he was beginning his year as a Knight Fellow in Science Journalism at MIT. Collision Detection has become one of the most well-regarded blogs on technology and culture. The blog receives approximately 3,000 to 4,000 hits a day. His piece on literacy appeared in *Wired* magazine in 2009.

As the school year begins, be ready to hear pundits fretting once again about how kids today can't write—and technology is to blame. Facebook encourages narcissistic blabbering, video and PowerPoint have replaced carefully crafted essays, and texting has dehydrated language into "bleak, bald, sad shorthand" (as University College of London English professor John Sutherland has moaned). An age of illiteracy is at hand, right?

Andrea Lunsford isn't so sure. Lunsford is a professor of writing and rhetoric at Stanford University, where she has organized a mammoth project called the Stanford Study of Writing to scrutinize college students' prose. From 2001 to 2006, she collected 14,672 student writing samples—everything from in-class assignments, formal essays, and journal entries to e-mails, blog posts, and chat sessions. Her conclusions are stirring.

"I think we're in the midst of a literacy revolution the likes of which we haven't seen since Greek civilization," she says. For Lunsford, technology isn't killing our ability to write. It's reviving it—and pushing our literacy in bold new directions.

The first thing she found is that young people today write far more than any generation before them. That's because so much socializing takes place online, and it almost always involves text. Of all the writing that the Stanford students did, a stunning 38 percent of it took place out of the classroom—life writing, as Lunsford calls it. Those Twitter updates and lists of 25 things about yourself add up.

It's almost hard to remember how big a paradigm shift this is. Before the Internet came along, most Americans never wrote anything, ever, that wasn't a school assignment. Unless they got a job that required producing text (like in law, advertising, or media), they'd leave school and virtually never construct a paragraph again.

But is this explosion of prose good, on a technical level? Yes. Lunsford's team found that the students were remarkably adept at what rhetoricians call *kairos*—assessing their audience and adapting their tone and technique to best get their point across. The modern world of online writing, particularly in chat and on discussion threads, is conversational and public, which makes it closer to the Greek tradition of argument than the asynchronous letter and essay writing of 50 years ago.

The fact that students today almost always write for an audience (something virtually no one in my generation did) gives them a different sense of what constitutes good writing. In interviews, they defined good prose as something that had an effect on the world. For them, writing is about persuading and organizing and debating, even if it's over something as quotidian as what movie to go see. The Stanford students were almost always less enthusiastic about their in-class writing because it had no audience but the professor: It didn't serve any purpose other than to get them a grade. As for those texting short-forms and smileys defiling *serious* academic writing? Another myth. When Lunsford examined the work of first-year students, she didn't find a single example of texting speak in an academic paper.

Of course, good teaching is always going to be crucial, as is the mastering of formal academic prose. But it's also becoming clear that online media are pushing literacy into cool directions. The brevity of texting and status updating teaches young people to deploy haiku-like concision. At the same time, the proliferation of new forms of online pop-cultural exegesis—from sprawling TV-show recaps to 15,000-word videogame walkthroughs—has given them a chance to write enormously long and complex pieces of prose, often while working collaboratively with others.

> We think of writing as either good or bad. What today's young people   9
> know is that knowing who you're writing for and why you're writing
> might be the most crucial factor of all.

■ Describe the Key Claims of the Text

As you read through a text with the purpose of summarizing it, you want
to identify how the writer develops his or her argument. You can do this by
what we call "chunking," grouping related material together into the argument's key claims. Here are two strategies to try.

Notice how paragraphs begin and end.   Often, focusing on the first and last
sentences of paragraphs will alert you to the shape and direction of an
author's argument. It is especially helpful if the paragraphs are lengthy
and full of supporting information, as much academic writing is.

Because of his particular journalistic forum, *Wired* magazine, the
paragraphs Thompson writes are generally rather short, but it's still
worth taking a closer look at the first and last sentences of his opening
paragraphs:

> *Paragraph 1:* As the school year begins, be ready to hear pundits fretting
> once again about how kids today can't write—and technology is to blame.
> Facebook encourages narcissistic blabbering, video and PowerPoint have
> replaced carefully crafted essays, and texting has dehydrated language
> into "bleak, bald, sad shorthand" (as University College of London
> English professor John Sutherland has moaned). An age of illiteracy is at
> hand, right?

> *Paragraph 2:* Andrea Lunsford isn't so sure. Lunsford is a professor of
> writing and rhetoric at Stanford University, where she has organized a
> mammoth project called the Stanford Study of Writing to scrutinize college
> students' prose. From 2001 to 2006, she collected 14,672 student writing
> samples—everything from in-class assignments, formal essays, and jour-
> nal entries to e-mails, blog posts, and chat sessions. Her conclusions are
> stirring.

Right away you can see that Thompson has introduced a topic in each
paragraph—pundits' criticism of students' use of electronic media in the
first, and a national study designed to examine students' literacy in the
second—and has indicated a connection between them. In fact, Thompson
is explicit in doing so. He asks a question at the end of the first paragraph
and then raises doubts as to the legitimacy of critics' denunciation of young
people's reliance on blogs and posts to communicate. How will Thompson
elaborate on this connection? What major points does he develop?

Notice the author's point of view and use of transitions.   Another strategy for identifying major points is to pay attention to descriptive words and transitions. For example, Thompson uses a rhetorical question ("An age of illiteracy is at hand, right?") and then offers a tentative answer ("Andrea Lunsford isn't so sure") that places some doubt in readers' minds.

Notice, too, the words that Thompson uses to characterize the argument in the first paragraph, which he appears to challenge in the second paragraph. Specifically, he describes these critics as "pundits," a word that traditionally refers to an expert or knowledgeable individual. However, the notion of a pundit, someone who often appears on popular talk shows, has also been used negatively. Thompson's description of pundits "fretting," wringing their hands in worry that literacy levels are declining, underscores this negative association of what it means to be a pundit. Finally, Thompson indicates that he does not identify with those who describe students as engaging in "narcissistic blabbering." This is clear when he characterizes the professor as having "moaned."

Once you identify an author's point of view, you will start noticing contrasts and oppositions in the argument—instances where the words are less positive, or neutral, or even negative—which are often signaled by how the writer uses transitions.

For example, Thompson begins with his own concession to critics' arguments when he acknowledges in paragraph 8 that educators should expect students to "[master] formal academic prose." However, he follows this concession with the transition word "but" to signal his own stance in the debate he frames in the first two paragraphs: "online media are pushing literacy into cool directions." Thompson also recognizes that students who write on blogs tend to write short, abbreviated texts. Still, he qualifies his concern with another transition, "at the same time." This transition serves to introduce Thompson's strongest claim: New media have given students "a chance to write enormously long and complex pieces of prose, often while working collaboratively with others."

These strategies can help you recognize the main points of an essay and explain them in a few sentences. For example, you could describe Thompson's key claims in this way:

1. Electronic media give students opportunities to write more than in previous generations, and students have learned to adapt what they are writing in order to have some tangible effect on what people think and how they act.

2. Arguably, reliance on blogging and posting on Twitter and Facebook can foster some bad habits in writing.

3. But at least one major study demonstrates that the benefits of using the new media outweigh the disadvantages. This study indicates that students write lengthy, complex pieces that contribute to creating significant social networks and collaborations.

■ Select Examples to Illustrate the Author's Argument

A summary should be succinct, which means you should limit the number of examples or illustrations you use. As you distill the major points of the argument, try to choose one or two examples to illustrate each major point. Here are the examples (in italics) you might use to support Thompson's main points:

1. Electronic media give students opportunities to write more than in previous generations, and students have learned to adapt what they are writing in order to have some tangible effect on what people think and how they act. *Examples from the Stanford study: Students "defined good prose as something that had an effect on the world. For them, writing is about persuading and organizing and debating"* (para. 7).

2. Arguably, reliance on blogging and posting on Twitter and Facebook can foster some bad habits in writing. *Examples of these bad habits include critics' charges of "narcissistic blabbering," "bleak, bald, sad shorthand," and "dehydrated language"* (para. 1). *Thompson's description of texting's "haiku-like concision"* (para. 8) *seems to combine praise (haiku can be wonderful poetry) with criticism (it can be obscure and unintelligible).*

3. But at least one major study demonstrates that the benefits of using the new media outweigh the disadvantages. *Examples include Thompson's point that the writing in the new media constitutes a "paradigm shift"* (para. 5). *Andrea Lunsford observes that students are "remarkably adept at what rhetoricians call* kairos—*assessing their audience and adapting their tone and technique to best get their point across"* (para. 6).

A single concrete example may be sufficient to clarify the point you want to make about an author's argument. Throughout the essay, Thompson derives examples from the Stanford study to support his argument in the final two paragraphs. The most concrete, specific example of how the new media benefit students as writers appears in paragraph 6, where the primary research of the Stanford study describes students' acquisition of important rhetorical skills of developing writing that is opportune (*kairos*) and purposeful. This one example may be sufficient for the purposes of summarizing Thompson's essay.

■ Present the Gist of the Author's Argument

When you present the **gist** of an argument, you are expressing the author's central idea in a sentence or two. The gist is not quite the same thing as the author's thesis statement. Instead, it is your formulation of the author's main idea, composed for the needs of your own argument.

Thompson's observations in paragraph 8 represent his thesis: "But it's also becoming clear that online media are pushing literacy into cool directions. . . . [T]he proliferation of new forms of online pop-cultural exegesis—from sprawling TV-show recaps to 15,000-word videogame walkthroughs—has given [students] a chance to write enormously long and complex pieces of prose, often while working collaboratively with others." In this paragraph, Thompson clearly expresses his central ideas in two sentences, while also conceding some of the critics' concerns. However, in formulating the gist of his argument, you want to do more than paraphrase Thompson. You want to use his position to support your own. For example, suppose you want to qualify the disapproval that some educators have expressed in drawing their conclusions about the new media. You would want to mention Thompson's own concessions when you describe the gist of his argument:

GIST

In his essay "On the New Literacy," Clive Thompson, while acknowledging some academic criticism of new media, argues that these media give students opportunities to write more than in previous generations and that students have learned to adapt what they are writing in order to have some tangible effect on what people think and how they act.

Notice that this gist could not have been written based only on Thompson's thesis statement. It reflects knowledge of Thompson's major points, his examples, and his concessions.

■ Contextualize What You Summarize

Your summary should help readers understand the context of the conversation:

- Who is the author?
- What is the author's expertise?
- What is the title of the work?
- Where did the work appear?
- What was the occasion of the work's publication? What prompted the author to write the work?
- What are the issues?
- Who else is taking part in the conversation, and what are their perspectives on the issues?

Again, because a summary must be concise, you must make decisions about how much of the conversation your readers need to know. If your assignment is to practice summarizing, it may be sufficient to include only information about the author and the source. However, if you are using the summary to build your own argument, you may need to provide more context. Your practice summary of Thompson's essay should mention that

Key Claim(s)	Examples	Gist	Context
1. Electronic media prompt more student writing than ever before, and students use their writing to make a difference.	The Stanford study: Students "defined good prose as something that had an effect on the world" (para. 7).	In his essay "On the New Literacy," Clive Thompson, while acknowledging some academic criticism of new media, argues that these media give students opportunities to write more than in previous generations and that students have learned to adapt what they are writing in order to have some tangible effect on what people think and how they act.	Thompson is a journalist who has written widely on issues in higher education. His essay "On the New Literacy" appeared in *Wired* in August 2009 (http://www.wired.com/techbiz/people/magazine/17-09/st_thompson). Under consideration is the debate that he frames in his opening paragraphs.
2. Arguably, reliance on blogging and posting can foster some bad writing habits.	Complaints of "bleak, bald, sad shorthand" and "narcissistic blabbering" (para. 1); texting can be obscure.		
3. But one major study shows the benefits of new media on student writing.	A "paradigm shift" (para. 5) to fluency in multiple formats and skill in assessing and persuading audiences.		

FIGURE 3.1   Worksheet for Writing a Summary

he is a journalist and should cite the title of and page references to his essay. You also may want to include information about Thompson's audience, publication information, and what led to the work's publication. Was it published in response to another essay or book, or to commemorate an important event?

We compiled our notes on Thompson's essay (key claims, examples, gist, context) in a worksheet (Figure 3.1). All of our notes in the worksheet constitute a type of prewriting, our preparation for writing the summary. Creating a worksheet like this can help you track your thoughts as you plan to write a summary.

Here is our summary of Thompson's essay:

The gist of Thompson's argument.

This concession helps to balance enthusiasm based on a single study.

Thompson's main point with example.

In his essay "On the New Literacy," Clive Thompson, while acknowledging some academic criticism of new media, argues that these media give students opportunities to write more than in previous generations and that students have learned to adapt what they are writing in order to have some tangible effect on what people think and how they act. Arguably, reliance on blogging and posting on Twitter and Facebook can foster some bad habits in writing. But at least one major study demonstrates that the benefits of using the new media outweigh the disadvantages. Students write lengthy, complex pieces that contribute to creating significant social networks and collaborations.

Steps to Writing a Summary

1 **Describe the key claims of the text.** To understand the shape and direction of the argument, study how paragraphs begin and end, and pay attention to the author's point of view and use of transitions. Then combine what you have learned into a few sentences describing the key claims.

2 **Select examples to illustrate the author's argument.** Find one or two examples to support each key claim. You may need only one example when you write your summary.

3 **Present the gist of the author's argument.** Describe the author's central idea in your own language with an eye to where you expect your argument to go.

4 **Contextualize what you summarize.** Cue your readers into the conversation. Who is the author? Where and when did the text appear? Why did the author write? Who else is in the conversation?

A Practice Sequence: Writing a Summary

1   Summarize a text that you have been studying for research or for one of your other classes. You may want to limit yourself to an excerpt of just a few paragraphs or a few pages. Follow the four steps we've described, using a summary worksheet for notes, and write a summary of the text. Then share the excerpt and your summary of it with two of your peers. Be prepared to justify your choices in composing the summary. Do your peers agree that your summary captures what is important in the original?

2   With a classmate, choose a brief text of about three pages. Each of you should use the method we describe above to write a summary of the text. Exchange your summaries and worksheets, and discuss the effectiveness of your summaries. Each of you should be prepared to discuss your choice of key claims and examples and your wording of the gist. Did you set forth the context effectively?

WRITING YOURSELF INTO ACADEMIC CONVERSATIONS

In her essay "The Flight from Conversation" (see p. 59), Sherry Turkle reflects upon her research on mobile technology and what she sees as the unfortunate trend toward "sacrificing conversation for mere connection."

You are probably familiar with the experience of walking into a coffee shop or the library on campus and seeing friends sitting across from one another but engaged with laptops or phones instead of with each other. "Alone together," as Turkle puts it, and she laments the "diminished chances to learn skills of self-reflection," a habit of mind that we agree is vital to academic writing and thinking. Thus, she blames technology that encourages broad and shallow connection without real face-to-face engagement. But as we also suggest, much academic conversation occurs on the page and screen, involving the exchange of ideas through writing. The philosopher Kenneth Burke uses this metaphor of an ongoing parlor conversation to capture the spirit of academic writing:

> Imagine that you enter a parlor. You come late. When you arrive, others have long preceded you, and they are engaged in a heated discussion, a discussion too heated for them to pause and tell you exactly what it is about. In fact, the discussion had already begun long before any of them got there, so that no one present is qualified to retrace for you all the steps that had gone before. You listen for a while, until you decide that you have caught the tenor of the argument; then you put in your oar. Someone answers; you answer him; another comes to your defense; another aligns himself against you, to either the embarrassment or gratification of your opponent, depending upon the quality of your ally's assistance. However, the discussion is interminable. The hour grows late, you must depart. And you do depart, with the discussion still vigorously in progress.*

Now that you have learned some important skills of rhetorical analysis and summary, then, it is important to think about ways to write yourself into academic conversations. Doing so will depend on three strategies:

- which previously stated arguments you share;
- which previously stated argument you want to refute; and
- what new opinions and supporting information you are going to bring to the conversation.

You may, for example, affirm others for raising important issues about the environment, employment opportunities, or the tendency of new technologies to limit community building and democratic deliberation. Then again, as you consider the arguments of others, you may feel that they have not given sufficient thought or emphasis to ideas that you think are important. In the end, you can write yourself into the conversation by explaining that writers have ignored a related issue entirely. So you are looking for gaps in others' arguments—something we discuss in more detail in the chapters that follow—an opening that provides an opportunity to provide a unique perspective in the conversation of ideas.

---

*Kenneth Burke, *The Philosophy of Literary Form* (Berkeley: University of California Press, 1941, pp. 110–11).

Steps to Writing Yourself into an Academic Conversation

- **Retrace the conversation**, including the relevance of the topic and situation, for readers by briefly discussing an author's key claims and ideas. This discussion can be as brief as a sentence or two and include a quotation for each author you cite.
- **Respond to the ideas of others** by helping readers understand the context in which another's claims make sense. "I get this if I see it this way."
- **Discuss possible implications** by putting problems aside and asking, "Do their claims make sense?"
- **Introduce conflicting points of view** and raise possible criticisms to indicate something the authors whose ideas you discuss may have overlooked.
- **Formulate your own claim** to assert what you think.
- **Ensure that your own purpose as a writer is clear to readers.**

A Practice Sequence: Writing Yourself into an Academic Conversation

1   We would like you to read an excerpt from Tom Standage's book *Writing on the Wall*, follow the steps to writing yourself into the conversation, and write a short, one-page argument. In doing so, retrace the conversation by explaining Standage's argument in ways that demonstrate your understanding of it. In turn, formulate your own position by explaining whether you believe that Standage has represented the issue well. Is there an opening in his argument that enables you to offer a perspective that he has perhaps ignored or overlooked?

2   An option for group work:

- As a group, discuss Sherry Turkle's argument in Chapter 2 that mobile technology has led to sacrificing conversation for mere connection—that we are "alone together." List the reasons why her argument makes sense and reasons why your group might take issue with her perspective. What do you feel she might have ignored or overlooked?
- Next, compare Turkle's argument with Standage's point of view in which he challenges Turkle's assertion that new technologies encourage "flight from conversation."
- Finally, each member of the group should write an argument that takes into account the conversation that Turkle and Standage have initiated with their efforts to make sense of how mobile technology has affected our lives.

TOM STANDAGE

History Retweets Itself

A writer and journalist from England with a degree from Oxford University, Tom Standage has published six books, including *The Victorian Internet* and *Writing on the Wall*, from which the excerpt that follows is taken. He has published articles on science, technology, and business in the *New York Times*, *Wired*, and the *Daily Telegraph*. He has also worked as a science and technology writer for the *Guardian* and deputy editor at *The Economist*.

❖ ❖ ❖

Social media, whether in the form of the printing press or the Internet, can be a force for freedom and openness, simply because oppressive regimes often rely on manipulating their citizens' view of the world, and a more open media environment makes that harder to accomplish. But the other side of the scales is not empty; this benefit must be weighed against the fact that social media can make repression easier, too. As Morozov notes, the Internet "penetrates and reshapes all walks of political life, not just the ones conducive to democratization." Anyone who hopes that the Internet will spread Western-style liberal democracy must bear in mind that the same digital tools have also been embraced by campaigners with very different aims, such as Hezbollah in Lebanon and ultra-right-wing nationalist groups in Russia. The test case in this argument is China, which now has more Internet users than any other country—more than in North America and Europe combined. Weibo and other online forums have given Chinese Internet users unprecedented freedom to express their views. Yet the swift and ruthless censoring of blog posts and weibo messages criticizing senior officials or calling for real-world demonstrations shows that widespread Internet adoption need not necessarily threaten the regime. Indeed, the ability to monitor the Internet may make it easier for the government to keep the lid on dissent. 1

A rather more mundane but widely expressed concern about social media is that the ease with which anyone can now publish his or her views online, whether on Twitter, on blogs, or in comment threads, has led to a coarsening of public discourse. Racism, sexism, bigotry, incivility, and ignorance abound in many online discussion forums. Twitter allows anyone to send threats or abuse directly to other users. No wonder the Internet is often likened to a sewer by politicians, clergymen, and newspaper columnists. 2

Yet the history of media shows that this is just the modern incarnation of the timeless complaint of the intellectual elite, every time 3 technology makes publishing easier, that the wrong sort of people will use it to publish the wrong sorts of things. In the early sixteenth century, Erasmus complained that printers "fill the world with pamphlets and books that are foolish, ignorant, malignant, libelous, mad, impious and subversive; and such is the flood that even things that might have done some good lose all their goodness." Worse, these "swarms of new books" were "hurtful to scholarship" because they lured readers away from the classics, which is what Erasmus felt people ought to have been reading.

Printers had, however, quickly realized that there was a far larger *4* audience, and more money to be made, printing pamphlets and contemporary works rather than new editions of classical works. Similarly, in England, the Worshipful Company of Stationers bemoaned the explosion of unlicensed pamphlets that appeared after the collapse of press controls in 1641, complaining that "every ignorant person that takes advantage of a loose presse may publish the fancies of every idle brain as so manyfestly appeareth by the swarmes of scandalous and irksome pamphletts that are cryed about the streetes." The Company was hoping to be granted a renewed monopoly on printing, which had previously allowed it to control what was printed, and therefore what people read. Its grumbling is not dissimilar to that of professional journalists bemoaning the rise of pajama-clad bloggers, invading their turf and challenging the status quo.

Those in authority always squawk, it seems, when access to publish- *5* ing is broadened. Greater freedom of expression, as John Milton noted in *Areopagitica*, means that bad ideas will proliferate as well as good ones, but it also means that bad ideas are more likely to be challenged. Better to provide an outlet for bigotry and prejudice, so they can be argued against and addressed, than to pretend that such views, and the people who hold them, do not exist. In a world where almost anyone can publish his or her views, the alternative, which is to restrict freedom of expression, is surely worse. As Milton's contemporary Henry Robinson put it in 1644, "It were better that many false doctrines were published, especially with a good intention and out of weaknesse only, than that one sound truth should be forcibly smothered or wilfully concealed; and by the incongruities and absurdities which accompany erroneous and unsound doctrines, the truth appears still more glorious, and wins others to the love thereof." One man's coarsening of discourse is another man's democratization of publishing. The genie is out of the bottle. Let truth and falsehood grapple!

Whatever you think about the standards of online discussions, there *6* is no doubt that people are spending a lot of time engaging in them. This raises another concern: that social media is a distracting waste of time that diverts people from more worthwhile pursuits, such as work and study. Surveys carried out in 2009 found that more than half of British and American companies had banned workers from using Twitter, Facebook, and other social sites. Many employers also block access to LinkedIn, a social-networking site for business users, because they worry that it allows employees to spend their time networking and advertising themselves to other potential employers. Simply put, companies readily equate social networking with social notworking.

This too is a familiar worry. Coffeehouses, the social-media platforms of their day, inspired similar reactions in the seventeenth century. They were denounced in the 1670s as "a vast loss of time grown out of a pure novelty" and "great enemies to diligence and industry." But the mixing of people and ideas that occurred in coffeehouses, where patrons from many walks of life would gather to discuss the latest pamphlets, led to innovations in science, commerce, and finance. By providing an environment in which unexpected connections could be made, coffeehouses proved to be hotbeds of collaborative innovation.   *7*

Similarly, a growing number of companies have concluded that social networking does have a role to play in the workplace, if done in the right way. They have set up "enterprise social networks," which create a private, Facebook-like social network to facilitate communication among employees and, in some cases, with workers at client and supplier companies, too. This sort of approach seems to have several benefits: its similarity to Facebook means little or no training is required; sharing documents and communicating via discussion threads is more efficient than using e-mail; it is easier to discover employees' hidden knowledge and talents; and it makes it easier for far-flung teams to collaborate.   *8*

A study by McKinsey and Company, a management consulting firm, found that the use of social networking within companies could increase the productivity of skilled knowledge workers by 20 to 25 percent and that the adoption of the technology in four industries (consumer goods, financial services, professional services, and advanced manufacturing) could create economic benefits worth between $900 billion and $1.3 trillion a year. Such predictions should always be taken with a very large dose of salt, but McKinsey found that 70 percent of companies were already using social technologies to some extent; and more than 90 percent said they were already benefitting as a result. Far from being a waste of time, then, Facebook-like social networks may in fact be the future of business software.   *9*

Even if it has value in the office, however, is there a danger that social media is harming our personal lives? Some observers worry that social media is in fact antisocial, because it encourages people to commune with people they barely know online to the detriment of real-life relationships with family and friends. "Does virtual intimacy degrade our   *10* experience of the other kind and, indeed, of all encounters, of any kind?" writes Sherry Turkle, an academic at MIT, in her book *Alone Together*. She worries that "relentless connection leads to a new solitude. We turn to new technology to fill the void, but as technology ramps up, our emotional lives ramp down." Similarly, William Powers, author of *Hamlet's BlackBerry*, laments the way that his family would rather chat with their online friends than with each other. "The digital crowd has a way of elbowing its way into everything, to the point where a family can't sit in a room together for half an hour without somebody, or everybody, peeling off," he writes. His proposed solution: an "Unplugged Sunday" when the use of computers and smartphones is banned.

It is clear that the desire to be connected to one's distant friends, 11 using whatever technology is available, is timeless. Cicero particularly valued the way letters connected him to his friends in the months after the death of his beloved daughter Tullia in 45 B.C. And he relished the contact his daily letters with his friend Atticus provided, even when they contained little information. "Write to me . . . every day," he wrote to Atticus. "When you have nothing to say, why, say just that!" Concerns about unhealthy dependence on new media technologies also have a long history: recall Plato's objections to writing in the *Phaedrus*, and Seneca's derision of his fellow Romans as they rushed to the docks to get their mail. By the seventeenth century, satirists were lampooning news junkies and the hunger with which they sought out the latest corantos.

From Roman letter-writers to manuscript poetry-sharing networks 12 to news-sharing clergymen in the American colonies, the exchange of media has long been used to reinforce social connections. The same is true today. Zeynep Tufekci, a media theorist at Princeton University, suggests that the popularity of social media stems from its ability to reconnect people in a world of suburbanization, long working hours, and families scattered around the globe by migration. Social media, she argues, is also a welcome antidote to the lonely, one-way medium of television. People who use social media can stay in contact with people they would otherwise lose touch with and make contact with like-minded individuals they might otherwise have never met. "Social media is enhancing human connectivity as people can converse in ways that were once not possible," Tufekci argues. A study published in 2011 by researchers at the University of Pennsylvania concluded that "it is incorrect to maintain that the Internet benefits distant relationships at the expense of local ties. The Internet affords personal connections at extreme distances but also provides the opportunity for new and supplemental local interaction." Another analysis, conducted in 2009 by researchers at the University of Toronto and involving four thousand Canadians, found that 35 percent felt that technology made them feel closer and more connected to other family members, and only 7 percent said that technology made them feel less connected. Tellingly, 51% of respondents said it made no difference, which suggests that many people no longer make a distinction between online and offline worlds, but regard them as an integrated whole.

New technologies are often regarded with suspicion. Turkle worries   *13* about the "flight from conversation," citing teenagers who would rather send a text than make a phone call. And on Unplugged Sunday, Powers and his family engage in communal pursuits that include watching television together. It seems odd to venerate the older technologies of the telephone and the television, though, given that they were once condemned for being anti-social in the same way social media is denounced today. ("Does the telephone make men more active or more lazy? Does it break up home life and the old practice of visiting friends?" asked a survey carried out in San Francisco in 1926.) There is always an adjustment period when new technologies appear, as societies work out the appropriate etiquette for their use and technologies are modified in response. During this transitional phase, which takes years or even decades, technologies are often criticized for disrupting existing ways of doing things. But the technology that is demonized today may end up being regarded as wholesome and traditional tomorrow, by which time another apparently dangerous new invention will be causing the same concerns.

What clues can history provide about the future evolution of social   *14* media? Even though Facebook, Twitter, and other social platforms provide a way for people to share information by sharing along social connections, they still resemble old-fashioned media companies such as newspapers and broadcasters in two ways: they are centralized (even though the distribution of information is carried out by the users, rather than the platform owners) and they rely on advertising for the majority of their revenue. Centralization grants enormous power to the owners of social platforms, giving them the ability to suspend or delete users' accounts and censor information if they choose to do so—or are compelled to do so by governments. Relying on advertising revenue, meanwhile, means platform owners must keep both advertisers and users happy, even though their interests do not always align. As they try to keep users within the bounds of their particular platforms, to maximize their audience for advertising, the companies that operate social networks have started to impose restrictions on what their customers can do and on how easily information can be moved from one social platform to another. In their early days, it makes sense for new social platforms to be as open as possible, to attract a large number of users. Having done so, however, such platforms often try to fence their users into "walled gardens" as they start trying to make money.

The contrast between big social platforms on the one hand, and   *15* e-mail and the web on the other, is striking. Both e-mail and web publishing work in an entirely open, decentralized way. The servers that store and deliver e-mail and the programs used to read and write messages are all expected to work seamlessly with each other, and for the most part they do. The same is true of web servers, which store and deliver pages, and the web browsers used to display pages and navigate between them. Anyone who wants to set up a new e-mail or web server can add it to the Internet's existing ecosystem of such servers. If you are setting up a new blog or website, there are also plenty of companies to choose from who will host it for you, and you can move from one to another if you are unsatisfied with their service. None of this is true for social networking, however, which takes place inside huge, proprietary silos owned by private companies. Moving your photos, your list of friends, or your archive of posts from one service to another is difficult at best, and impossible at worst. It may be that healthy competition among those companies, and a reluctance to alienate their hundreds of millions of users by becoming too closed, will enable the big social platforms to continue in this semi-open state for many years to come.

But another possibility is that today's social platforms represent a   *16* transitional stage, like AOL and CompuServe in the 1990s. They were proprietary, centralized services that introduced millions of people to the wonders of the Internet, but they were eventually swept aside by the open web. Similarly, perhaps the core features of social networking and social media—maintaining lists of friends, and exchanging information with them—will move to an open, decentralized model. Such a model is possible for e-mail and web publishing because of the existence of agreed technical standards on how e-mail messages and web pages ought to be encoded and transmitted. Several such standards have already been proposed for decentralized or distributed social networks, though none has yet gained much traction. There will be technical difficulties synchronizing friend lists, maintaining privacy and security, and delivering updates quickly across millions of users, all of which give centralized social networks a clear advantage at the moment. But every time a major social network is involved in a privacy violation, an unpopular change in the terms of service, or a spat over censorship, a few more adventurous users decide to give one of the various decentralized social networks a try. "I think it's important to design new systems that work in a distributed way," says Tim Berners-Lee. "We must make systems in which people can collaborate together, but do it in a way that's decentralized, so it's not based on one central hub."

A decentralized social platform could be based around personal   *17* silos of data over which users would have direct control. This approach would also address concerns that the new online public sphere that has been brought into being by social media is largely in the hands of private companies who are beholden to advertisers and shareholders rather than users. But there is another way for Facebook, Twitter, and other platforms to make themselves more accountable to users and less dependent on advertisers: to start charging users for some or all services. Many Internet services operate on a model in which a small percentage of paying customers subsidize a much larger number of nonpaying users. Social platforms could charge for things such as providing detailed analytics to commercial users of their platforms, more customization options for user profiles, or an advertising-free service. App.net, a subscription-funded Twitter-like service launched in September 2012, prides itself on being an "ad-free social network" that is based on "selling our product, not our users." This ensures, the company says, that its financial incentives are aligned with those of its members. Whether or not its particular model proves to have broad appeal, the future of social media is likely to see new models based on decentralized architectures and paying customers being added to the mix.

But whatever form social media takes in the future, one thing is clear: it is not going away. As this book has argued, social media is not new. It has been around for centuries. Today, blogs are the new pamphlets. Microblogs and online social networks are the new coffeehouses. Media-sharing sites are the new commonplace books. They are all shared, social platforms that enable ideas to travel from one person to another, rippling through networks of people connected by social bonds, rather than having to squeeze through the privileged bottleneck of broadcast media. The rebirth of social media in the Internet age represents a profound shift—and a return, in many respects, to the way things used to be.

18

From Identifying Claims to Analyzing Arguments

A **claim** is an assertion of fact or belief that needs to be supported with **evidence**—the information that backs up a claim. A main claim, or **thesis**, summarizes the writer's position on a situation and answers the question(s) the writer addresses. It also encompasses the minor claims, along with their supporting evidence, that the writer makes throughout the argument.

As readers, we need to identify a writer's main claim, or thesis, because it helps us organize our own understanding of the writer's argument. It acts as a signpost that tells us, "This is what the essay is about," "This is what I want you to pay attention to," and "This is how I want you to think, change, or act."

When you evaluate a claim, whether it is an argument's main claim or a minor claim, it is helpful to identify the type of claim it is: a claim of fact, a claim of value, or a claim of policy. You also need to evaluate the reasons for the claim and the evidence that supports it. Because academic argument should acknowledge multiple points of view, you should also be prepared to identify what, if any, concessions a writer offers his or her readers, and what counterarguments he or she anticipates from others in the conversation.

IDENTIFYING TYPES OF CLAIMS

To illustrate how to identify a writer's claims, let's take a look at a text written by an educator in the field of business ethics, Dana Radcliffe, that examines the relationship between social media and democracy.

The text is followed by our analysis of the types of claims (fact, value, and policy) and then, in the next section, of the nature of arguments (use of evidence, concessions, and counterarguments) the author presents.

DANA RADCLIFFE

Dashed Hopes: Why Aren't Social Media Delivering Democracy?

Dana Radcliffe has taught business ethics at the Samuel Curtis Johnson Graduate School of Management at Cornell University since 2000. As an adjunct at Syracuse University, he teaches ethics courses in the Maxwell School of Citizenship and Public Affairs and the College of Engineering and Computer Science. As a blogger for the *Huffington Post*, he has written about ethics in business, politics, and public policy. Professor Radcliffe earned a PhD from Syracuse University, an MBA from the University of California, Los Angeles, an MPhil in philosophy from Yale University, and a BA in philosophy from Fort Hays State University. This essay is a version of remarks presented to a session of the Pacific Council on International Policy, October 10, 2015. It follows up on his 2011 blog post "Can Social Media Undermine Democracy?"

▧　▧　▧

1   Four years ago, in the months following the Arab Spring,[1] hopes ran high that the growing use of social media would bring a flowering of democracy throughout the world. Facebook and Twitter had helped dissidents drive tyrants from power in Tunisia, Egypt, and Libya. In established democracies, citizens' groups—most notably, the Tea Party in the U.S.—were influencing politics by leveraging social media. Indeed, a *Forbes* cover story on the power of social media concluded that "the world is becoming more democratic and reflective of the will of ordinary people."

2   Sadly, such optimism proved ill-founded. Now, in 2015, popular government seems to be receding globally. With the qualified exception of Tunisia, the Arab Spring did not transform dictatorships into democracies, and democratic governments seem unable to find consensus solutions to many pressing policy questions. What happened? Why haven't social media made the world more democratic?

3   In seeking an answer, we can begin with [the] nature of democracy itself. Because a country's citizens have competing interests and values, their effectively governing themselves through elections of leaders

---

[1] *Editor's note:* Arab Spring was a revolutionary wave of demonstrations, protests, and civil wars that began on December 17, 2010. Most insurgencies occurred in Syria, Libya, and Yemen, with uprisings in other countries, including Saudi Arabia, Iraq, Algeria, Kuwait, and Morocco.

and other democratic processes requires *deliberation*. It requires that citizens and their representatives discuss and debate what the government should or should not do, defending their views by appealing to shared principles and purposes. As one scholar, Daniel Gayo-Avello, recently observed, "Deliberation is crucial in modern democracy . . . Proper democratic deliberation assumes that citizens are equal participants, opposing viewpoints are not only accepted but encouraged, and that the main goal is to achieve 'rationally motivated consensus.'" Political philosophers Amy Gutmann and Dennis Thompson, in their influential *Democracy and Disagreement* (Belknap, 1996), point out that "the demand for deliberation has been a familiar theme in the American constitutional tradition. It is integral to the ideal of republican government as the founders understood it. James Madison judged the design of political institutions in part by how well they furthered deliberation."

To be sure, "deliberative democracy" is an ideal to which existing democratic systems only roughly approximate. Nevertheless, the concept provides a plausible standard for evaluating democracies. Moreover, it reminds us that the health of a democracy depends in large part on its fostering deliberation that leads to policies whose legitimacy most citizens accept. Hence, the impact of social media on democratic deliberation may help explain why they have not brought about a new global era of democracy. 4

The issue here is the political power of social media, and it entails three key questions: What power do they confer? Who possesses that power? How do those who have the power use it? 5

First, the power of social media is evident. Functionally, it is the ability to communicate, instantaneously, with a large number of people. Politically, it is the power to inform or misinform, to engage or manipulate, to mobilize or control. In general, it is the power to affect, directly and on a vast scale, the political beliefs and actions of citizens. 6

Second, when the government controls social media, this power is in its hands. When the government does not control social media, its political power belongs to citizens who can access them and is exercised by groups of like-minded individuals who use them to organize and coordinate political activities. 7

Third, as for how the political power of social media is wielded by those who possess them, recent history gives us some salient examples: 8

- Protesters using them in organizing mass demonstrations against oppressive governments during the Arab Spring;
- the Chinese government's allowing critics of public officials and policies to "vent" online but tightly censoring calls for collective action;

- the Russian government's employing its immense digital propaganda machine to convince many Europeans that the CIA shot down the Malaysian airliner over Ukraine;
- the Islamic State's utilizing social media to recruit disaffected Muslim youths from around the world;
- in 2008, the Obama campaign's innovative application of social media to raise record amounts of money from small donors and customize its messages to different demographics;
- the use of social media by an impassioned minority of Americans angry at "big government" to form and advance the Tea Party movement.

In all these cases, social media were—or are—used as *political weapons*. Of course, I am not implying moral equivalence in these examples. My point is that the political power of social media has been used most effectively in *adversarial* contexts—in circumstances of *struggle* or *competition*. In those cases, the regime, organization, or group holding the power uses it against individuals, groups, or institutions whose interests or goals conflict with theirs. Consequently, whether they are revolutionaries, totalitarian governments, candidates for office, or special interests, political partisans using social media as tactical weapons are not concerned about *deliberation*. 9

Who, then, cares about promoting democratic deliberation? It is citizens and leaders who understand that democratic processes necessitate deliberative disagreement and, in the legislative process, negotiation and compromise. However, when these advocates of democracy look to social media to establish and strengthen democratic processes, they encounter a basic problem: social media appear unsuited to serve as forums of political deliberation. Research into online behavior suggests several reasons: 10

- Users tend not to seek opportunities to engage in serious political dialogue with people whose views differ from their own. Rather, as social media expert Curtis Hougland notes, "people choose to reinforce their existing political opinions through their actions online."
- A recent Pew Research Center report offers evidence that people are much less willing to post their political views on social media when they believe their followers would disagree with them.
- Daniel Gayo-Avello has found that "when political discussions occur they are not rational and democratic deliberations . . . [because] political information in social media generally lacks quality and strong arguments, is usually incoherent and highly opinionated."

To these I would add some intuitions of mine: *11*

- When people who have strong political opinions avoid engaging opponents in reasoned debate but have them bolstered by social media followers, they tend to become more rigid in those views—and so, are even less interested in democratic deliberation.

- As a result, political partisans connected through social media tend to oppose legislative compromises on their pet issues, demanding that elected representatives they support "stand on principle," regardless of political realities or the common good.

- Finally, perhaps because using social media is, physically, a solitary activity, it tends not to cultivate civic virtues—such as respect for opponents—that Gutmann and Thompson argue are critical to democratic deliberation.

In short, with regard to political discussion, current use of social   *12*
media favors affinity over engagement, expression over debate, silence over disagreement, dogmatism over compromise, and—toward opponents—disdain over respect. This, I believe, is largely why we have so far been unable to move beyond the use of social media as political weapons to make them instruments of deliberative democracy.

■ Identify Claims of Fact

Claims of fact are assertions (or arguments) that seek to define or classify something or establish *that a problem or condition has existed, exists, or will exist*. Claims of fact are made by individuals who believe that something is true; but claims are never simply facts, and some claims are more objective, and so easier to verify, than others.

For example, "It's raining in Portland today" is a "factual" claim of fact; it's easily verified. But consider the argument some make that the steel and automotive industries in the United States have depleted our natural resources and left us at a crisis point. This is an assertion that a condition exists. A careful reader must examine the basis for this kind of claim: Are we truly facing a crisis? And if so, are the steel and automotive industries truly responsible? A number of politicians counter this claim of fact by insisting that if the government were to harness the vast natural resources in Alaska, there would be no "crisis." This is also a claim of fact, in this case an assertion that a condition will exist in the future. Again, it is based on evidence, evidence gathered from various sources that indicates sufficient resources in Alaska to keep up with our increasing demands for resources and to allay a potential crisis.

Our point is that most claims of fact are debatable and challenge us to provide evidence to verify our arguments. They may be based on factual information, but they are not necessarily true. Most claims of fact present **interpretations** of evidence derived from **inferences**. That is, a writer will examine evidence (for example, about the quantity of natural resources in Alaska and the rate that industries harness those resources and process them into goods), draw a conclusion based on reasoning (an inference), and offer an explanation based on that conclusion (an interpretation).

So, for example, an academic writer will study the evidence on the quantity of natural resources in Alaska and the rate that industries harness those resources and process them into goods; only after the writer makes an informed decision on whether Alaska's resources are sufficient to keep pace with the demand for them will he or she take a position on the issue.

Claims that seek to define or classify are also claims of fact. For example, researchers have sought to define a range of behaviors such as autism that actually resist simple definition. After all, autism exists along a behavioral spectrum attributed variably to genetics and environment. Psychologists have indeed tried to define autism using a diagnostic tool to characterize behaviors associated with communication and social interaction. However, definitions of autism have changed over time, reflecting changing criteria for assessing human behavior and the perspective one takes. So do we in fact have a "crisis" in the over diagnosis of autistic behaviors as some have claimed? For that matter, who gets to decide what counts as a crisis?

Let's now come to Radcliffe's claim of fact that social media services have not fulfilled the promise of fostering a more democratic world, nor have they promoted (as the *Forbes* article asserts) "the will of ordinary people." Despite a few exceptions in which social media services have empowered democratic change, Radcliffe's review of the global political climate forces readers to reconsider claims that connect social media and the growth of democracy. Do social media services actually have a causal relationship with the Arab Spring—the wave of insurrections across the Middle East that triggered subsequent shifts to democracy? Radcliffe takes issue with this apparently factual **causal claim**. But the careful reader will want to see how Radcliffe goes about challenging others' claims to support his own claim of fact that "such optimism proved ill-founded." Note how he asks questions to propel his argument ("What happened? Why haven't social media made the world more democratic?") and provides a claim of definition. Radcliffe's **definitional claim** serves as an important rhetorical strategy for making an argument about what democracy is and the conditions that exist to support democratic principles. After all, how can others maintain that social media services such as Twitter and Facebook foster the spread of democracy if they have not defined a key term like "democracy"? This is especially true if a primary component of democracy is what Radcliffe describes as a "deliberative process."

We invite you to examine Radcliffe's primary claim and the evidence he uses to challenge a prevailing argument in the media and to support his own view that a true democracy "requires that citizens and their representatives discuss and debate what the government should or should not do, defending their views by appealing to shared principles and purposes." Does he convincingly present his argument that others overstate the effect of social media because, at least implicitly, they fail to adequately define democracy and the democratic process? That is, do you accept his definition as the standard—or at least a plausible standard rooted in a **factual claim**—upon which to measure others' arguments? Do social media services confer power? If so, who uses such power, and how do they use it? Finally, to what extent do social media services act as adequate forums for deliberation?

▪ Identify Claims of Value

A claim of fact is different from a **claim of value**, which *expresses an evaluation of a problem or condition that has existed, exists, or will exist*. Is a condition good or bad? Is it important or inconsequential?

For example, an argument that developing the wilderness in Alaska would irreversibly mar the beauty of the land indicates that the writer values the beauty of the land over the possible benefits of development. A claim of value presents a judgment, which is sometimes signaled by a value-laden word like *ugly, beautiful*, or *immoral*, but may also be conveyed more subtly by the writer's tone and attitude.

Radcliffe makes a claim of value when he concludes by stating "with regard to political discussion, current use of social media favors affinity over engagement, expression over debate, silence over disagreement, dogmatism over compromise, and—toward opponents—disdain over respect." This statement follows from Radcliffe's initial observation that use of social media does not support the "reflective . . . will of ordinary people," and from the evidence presents that social media services can be detrimental to the will of people when controlled by oppressive leaders. He writes, "When people who have strong political opinions avoid engaging opponents in reasoned debate but have them bolstered by social media followers, they tend to become more rigid in those views. . . . As a result, political partisans connected through social media tend to oppose legislative compromises on their pet issues . . . regardless of political realities or the common good." Radcliffe underscores these observations in the final paragraph: "This, I believe, is largely why we have so far been unable to move beyond the use of social media as political weapons to make them instruments of deliberative democracy." This may seem like a claim of fact, but Radcliffe's claim is based on interpretation of the evidence he presents and the definition he establishes as the standard on which to judge whether a country is democratic. Whether you are persuaded by Radcliffe's claim depends on the evidence and reasons he uses for support. We discuss the nature of evidence and what constitutes "good" reasons later in this chapter.

▪ Identify Claims of Policy

A **claim of policy** is an argument for what should be the case, *that a condition should exist*. It is a call for change or a solution to a problem.

Two recent controversies on college campuses center on claims of policy. One has activists arguing that universities and colleges should have a policy that all workers on campus earn a living wage. The other has activists arguing that universities and colleges should have a policy that prevents them from investing in countries where the government ignores human rights. Claims of policy are often signaled by words like *should* and *must*: "For public universities to live up to their democratic mission, they *must* provide all their workers with a living wage."

In "Ten Ways Social Media Can Improve Campaign Engagement and Reinvigorate American Democracy," political scientist Darrell West describes how social media can "reinvigorate American democracy." West develops an argument that echoes Dana Radcliffe's claim that social media services do not foster or promote democratic practices, much less the kind of civic engagement that others (such as the author of the *Forbes* article Radcliffe cites) suggest. Although West makes a **claim of fact** when he observes that "Despite social networking's track record for generating democratic engagement . . . it has proven difficult to sustain political interest and activism online over time and move electronic engagement from campaigns to governance," he is most concerned with fostering policies that increase interest in the political process.

West describes a meeting of experts at the Brookings Institute, where participants share ways to encourage grassroots efforts to create change and govern at local, state, and national levels. One participant, political consultant Mindy Finn, argues that political advocacy "should take advantage of [social] networks to set the agenda and drive civic discussions," explaining that advocacy should "involve everything from the questions that get asked during debates to the manner in which journalists cover the election." Finn appears less interested in the deliberative process that preoccupies Radcliffe and embraces the role that social media can play in motivating citizenship and engagement. Another participant, professor of government Diana Owens, suggests that universities "[should] take on the responsibility as a matter of policy to increase civic education for political action." A policy claim points readers to a set of actions they can take in the future, and West's participants all declare policies they would like to see pursued.

Not all writers make their claims as explicitly as these authors do, and it is possible that claims of fact may seem like interpretive claims, as they are based on the inferences we draw from evidence. Thus, it is the writer's task to make a distinction between a claim of fact and interpretation with sufficient evidence. But you should be able to identify the different types of claims. Moreover, you should keep in mind what the situation is and what kind of argument can best address what you see as a problem. Ask yourself: Does the situation involve a question of fact? Does the situation involve a question of value? Does the situation require a change in policy? Or is some combination at work?

Steps to Identifying Claims

1 **Ask:** Does the argument assert that a problem or condition has existed, exists, or will exist? Does the argument seek to establish that a definition is true and can serve as a standard for making relevant judgments? Does the argument ask you to accept the premise that one thing has caused another? If so, it's claim of fact.

2 **Ask:** Does the argument express an evaluation of a problem or condition that has existed, exists, or will exist? If so, it's a claim of value.

3 **Ask:** Does the argument call for change, and is it directed at some future action? If so, it's a claim of policy.

A Practice Sequence: Identifying Claims

What follows is a series of claims. Identify each one as a claim of fact, value, or policy. Be prepared to justify your categorizations.

1 Taxing the use of fossil fuels will end the energy crisis.

2 We should reform the welfare system to ensure that people who receive support from the government also work.

3 Images of violence in the media create a culture of violence in schools.

4 The increase in homelessness is a deplorable situation that contradicts the whole idea of democracy.

5 Distributing property taxes more equitably is the one sure way to end poverty and illiteracy.

6 Individual votes don't really count.

7 Despite the 20 percent increase in the number of females in the workforce over the past forty years, women are still not treated equitably.

8 Affirmative action is a policy that has outlived its usefulness.

9 There are a disproportionate number of black males in American prisons.

10 The media are biased, which means we cannot count on newspapers or television news for the truth.

ANALYZING ARGUMENTS

Analyzing an argument involves identifying the writer's main and minor claims and then examining (1) the reasons and evidence given in support of each claim, (2) the writer's concessions, and (3) the writer's attempts to handle counterarguments.

▪ Analyze the Reasons Used to Support a Claim

Stating a claim is one thing; supporting that claim is another. As a critical reader, you need to evaluate whether a writer has provided *good reasons* to support his or her position. Specifically, you will need to decide whether the support for a claim is recent, relevant, reliable, and accurate. As a writer, you will need to use the same criteria when you support your claims.

Is the source recent?   Knowledgeable readers of your written arguments not only will be aware of classic studies that you should cite as "intellectual touchstones"; they will also expect you to cite recent evidence, evidence published within five years of when you are writing.

Of course, older research can be valuable. For example, in a paper about molecular biology, you might very well cite James Watson and Francis Crick's groundbreaking 1953 study in which they describe the structure of DNA. That study is an intellectual touchstone that changed the life sciences in a fundamental way.

Or if you were writing about educational reform, you might very well mention E. D. Hirsch's 1987 book *Cultural Literacy*. Hirsch's book did not change the way people think about curricular reform as profoundly as Watson and Crick's study changed the way scientists think about biology, but his term *cultural literacy* continues to serve as useful shorthand for a particular way of thinking about curricular reform that remains influential to this day.

Although citing Hirsch is an effective way to suggest you have studied the history of an educational problem, it will not convince your readers that there is a crisis in education today. To establish that, you would need to use as evidence studies published over the past few years to show, for example, that there has been a steady decline in test scores since Hirsch wrote his book. And you would need to support your claim that curricular reform is the one sure way to bring an end to illiteracy and poverty with data that are much more current than those available to Hirsch in the 1980s. No one would accept the judgment that our schools are in crisis if your most recent citation is decades old.

Is the source relevant?   Evidence that is relevant must have real bearing on your issue. It also depends greatly on what your readers expect. For example, suppose two of your friends complain that they were unable to sell their condominiums for the price they asked. You can claim there is a crisis in the housing market, but your argument won't convince most readers if your only evidence is personal anecdote.

Such *anecdotal evidence* may alert you to a possible topic and help you connect with your readers, but you will need to test the **relevance** of your friends' experience — Is it pertinent? Is it typical of a larger situation or condition? — if you want your readers to take your argument seriously. For example, you might scan real estate listings to see what the asking prices are for properties comparable to your friends' properties. By comparing listings, you are defining the grounds for your argument. If your friends are disappointed that their one-bedroom condominiums sold for less than a three-bedroom condominium with deeded parking in the same neighborhood, it may well be that their expectations were too high.

In other words, if you aren't comparing like things, your argument is going to be seriously flawed. If your friends' definition of what constitutes a "reasonable price" differs dramatically from everyone else's, their experience is probably irrelevant to the larger question of whether the local housing market is depressed.

Is the source reliable?   You also need to evaluate whether the data you use to support your argument are reliable. After all, some researchers present findings based on a very small sample of people that can also be rather selective.

For example, a researcher might argue that 67 percent of the people he cited believe that school and residential integration are important concerns. But how many people did this person interview? More important, who responded to the researcher's questions? A reliable claim cannot be based on a few of the researcher's friends.

Let's return to the real estate example. You have confirmed that your friends listed their condominiums at prices that were not out of line with the market. Now what? You need to seek out reliable sources to continue testing your argument. For example, you might search the real estate or business section of your local newspaper to see if there are any recent stories about a softening of the market; and you might talk with several local real estate agents to get their opinions on the subject.

In consulting local newspapers and local agents, you are looking for **authoritative sources** against which to test your anecdotal evidence — the confirmation of experts who report on, study, evaluate, and have an informed opinion on local real estate. Local real estate agents are a source of **expert testimony**, firsthand confirmation of the information you have discovered. You would probably not want to rely on the testimony of a single real estate agent, who may have a bias; instead, talk with several agents to see if a consensus emerges.

Is the source accurate?   To determine the accuracy of a study that you want to use to support your argument, you have to do a little digging to find out who else has made a similar claim. For instance, if you want to cite authoritative research that compares the dropout rate for white students with the rate for students of color, you could look at research conducted by the Civil Rights Project. Of course, you don't need to stop your search there. You could also check the resources available through the National Center for Education Statistics. You want to show your readers that you have done a relatively thorough search to make your argument as persuasive as possible.

The accuracy of **statistics**—factual information presented numerically or graphically (for example, in a pie or bar chart)—is difficult to verify. To a certain extent, then, their veracity has to be taken on faith. Often the best you can do is assure yourself that the source of your statistical information is authoritative and reliable—government and major research universities generally are "safe" sources—and that whoever is interpreting the statistical information is not distorting it.

Returning again to our real estate example, let's say you've read a newspaper article that cites statistical information about the condition of the local real estate market (for example, the average price of property and volume of sales this year in comparison to last year). Presumably the author of the article is an expert, but he or she may be interpreting rather than simply reporting on the statistics.

To reassure yourself one way or the other, you may want to check the sources of the author's statistics—go right to your source's sources—which a responsible author will cite. That will allow you to look over the raw data and come to your own conclusions. A further step you could take would be to discuss the article with other experts—local real estate agents—to find out what they think of the article and the information it presents.

Now, let's go back to Dana Radcliffe's essay. How does he develop his assertion that social media services do not foster democratic principles of deliberation or help participants engage in serious dialogue about views different from their own? For that matter, how does Radcliffe arrive at the conclusion—or claim—that "social media appear unsuited to serve as forums of political deliberation?" Radcliffe first establishes what he sees as a plausible standard for defining deliberation as a key principle underlying a democratic society. He bolsters his argument by citing two well-known political philosophers, Amy Gutmann and Dennis Thompson, whose influential *Democracy and Disagreement* (Belknap, 1996) he quotes: "They point out that the demand for deliberation has been a familiar theme in the American constitutional tradition. It is integral to the ideal of republican government as the founders understood it. James Madison judged the design of political institutions in part by how well they furthered deliberation." Importantly, Gutmann and Thompson cite former president and founding father James Madison to identify deliberation as a significant component of democracy and a standard with which to measure the extent to which a society promotes democratic principles.

Radcliffe then makes a series of observations about events that have occurred across the world since the Arab Spring. He points out that the Chinese government seems to allow "critics of public officials and policies to 'vent' online but tightly censors calls for collective action." He also suggests that the Islamic State uses "social media to recruit disaffected Muslim youths from around the world," and as you will note, he uses additional examples to illustrate the extent to which social media services have been "used as *political weapons*." As readers, we may take for granted that Radcliffe's observations are based in "fact," but Radcliffe does not actually cite sources of his "data" to show that "the regime, organization, or group holding the power uses it against individuals, groups, or institutions whose interests or goals conflict with theirs." You would be right to question the basis of such a claim.

In advancing his claim that social media does not support democratic engagement, Radcliffe relies on authoritative sources to explain the behavior of those who use social media. He cites a recent Pew Research Center report, which "offers evidence that people are much less willing to post their political views on social media when they believe their followers would disagree with them." The Pew Research Center describes itself as a "nonpartisan, non-advocacy group" whose aim is to stimulate citizen involvement in community issues and conduct research on public opinion on social and political issues. Radcliffe also cites Daniel Gayo-Avello, who concludes that "when political discussions occur they are not rational and democratic deliberations . . . [because] political information in social media generally lacks quality and strong arguments [and] is usually incoherent and highly opinionated." A professor of computer science at the University of Oviedo in Spain who conducts social media research, Gayo-Avello serves as a credible source of data to support Radcliffe's claim. However, as critical readers, we should inquire into the nature of authors' claims, the source of evidence, and the accuracy of the information authors rely on to advance their claims.

■ Identify Concessions

Part of the strategy of developing a main claim supported with good reasons is to offer a **concession**, an acknowledgment that readers may not agree with every point the writer is making. A concession is a writer's way of saying, "Okay, I can see that there may be another way of looking at the issue or another way to interpret the evidence used to support the argument I am making."

For instance, you may not want your energy costs to go up, but after examining the reasons why it may be necessary to increase taxes on gasoline—to lower usage and conserve fossil fuels—you might concede that a tax increase on gasoline could be useful. The willingness to make concessions is valued in academic writing because it acknowledges both complexity and the importance of multiple perspectives. It also acknowledges the fact that information can always be interpreted in different ways.

Dana Radcliffe makes a concession when he acknowledges that not every reader will define democracy as he does, with an emphasis on deliberation. "Who, then, cares about promoting democratic deliberation?" He maintains that much is at stake for readers who identify with the value he attaches to deliberation as a core principle of democracy: "It is citizens and leaders who understand that democratic processes necessitate deliberative disagreement and, in the legislative process, negotiation and compromise."

Often a writer will signal concessions with phrases like the following:

- "It is true that . . ."
- "I agree with X that Y is an important factor to consider."
- "Some studies have convincingly shown that . . ."

Generally, the writer will then go on to address the concession, explaining how it needs to be modified or abandoned in the light of new evidence or the writer's perspective on the issue.

■ Identify Counterarguments

As the term suggests, a **counterargument** is an argument raised in response to another argument. You want to be aware of and acknowledge what your readers may object to in your argument. Anticipating readers' objections is an important part of developing a conversational argument.

For example, if you were arguing in support of universal health care, you would have to acknowledge that the approach departs dramatically from the traditional role the federal government has played in providing health insurance. That is, most people's access to health insurance has depended on their individual ability to afford and purchase this kind of insurance. You would have to anticipate how readers would respond to your proposal, especially readers who do not feel that the federal government should ever play a role in what has typically been an individual responsibility.

Anticipating readers' objections demonstrates that you understand the complexity of the issue and are willing at least to entertain different and conflicting opinions.

In Dana Radcliffe's essay on social media and democracy, he implicitly concedes that not all readers will care about promoting deliberative democracy; he acknowledges a possible counterargument by citing a *Forbes* article, the author of which contends that "the world is becoming more democratic and reflective of the will of ordinary people." Of course, this is the point that Radcliffe takes issue with, one that clearly resonates for others. Radcliffe remains mindful of critical readers when he reiterates the counterargument that challenges his very definition of whether a nation promotes democracy. "To be sure, 'deliberative democracy' is an ideal to which existing democratic systems only roughly approximate. Nevertheless, the concept provides a plausible standard for evaluating democracies." That is, he recognizes that his definition is the "ideal" and that few governments in practice actually reflect this ideal. But he is invested in such an idea and returns to his original premise: "Nevertheless, the concept provides a plausible standard for evaluating democracies. Moreover, it reminds us that the health of a democracy depends in large part on its fostering deliberation that leads to policies whose legitimacy most citizens accept."

In an argument that is more conversational than confrontational, writers establish areas of common ground, both to convey different views that are understood and to acknowledge the conditions under which those different views are valid. Writers do this by making concessions and anticipating and responding to counterarguments.

This conversational approach is what many people call a **Rogerian approach to argument**, based on psychologist Carl Rogers's approach to psychotherapy. The objective of a Rogerian strategy is to reduce listeners' sense of threat so that they are open to alternatives. For academic writers, it involves four steps:

1. Conveying to readers that their different views are understood.
2. Acknowledging conditions under which readers' views are valid.
3. Helping readers see that the writer shares common ground with them.
4. Creating mutually acceptable solutions to agreed-on problems.

The structure of an argument, according to the Rogerian approach, grows out of the give-and-take of conversation between two people and the topic under discussion. In a written conversation, the give-and-take of face-to-face conversation takes the form of anticipating readers' counterarguments and uses language that is both empathetic and respectful, to put the readers at ease.

AN ANNOTATED STUDENT ARGUMENT

We have annotated the following essay to show the variety of claims the student writer uses, as well as some of the other argumentative moves he performs. The assignment was to write an argument out of personal experience and observation about the cultural impact of a technological innovation. Marques Camp chose to write about the Kindle, an electronic reading device developed by the online retailer Amazon that allows users to download books for a fee. The user cannot share the download electronically with other users. Camp touches on a number of issues reflected in his claims.

As you read the essay, imagine how you would respond to his various claims. Which do you agree with, which do you disagree with, and why? What evidence would you present to support or counter his claims? Do you detect a main claim? Do you think his overall essay develops and supports it?

Camp 1

Marques Camp
Professor Fells
English 1020
January 28, 20—
   The End of the World May Be Nigh, and It's the Kindle's Fault

"Libraries will in the end become cities."
— Gottfried Wilhelm Leibniz, German polymath

The student presents a claim of fact that others have made.

   The future of written human history will come, as they will have us believe, in the form of the Amazon Kindle and its millions of titles, ready to change the way people read, ready to revolutionize the way people see the world.

1

He lays the basis for a counterargument by questioning whether this is a real threat at all, citing some technological precedents.

   The Kindle is a signpost for our times, a major checkpoint in our long and adventurous journey from the world of printed paper to the twenty-first-century world of digitalization. We first saw this paradigm shift with newspapers, where weekly columns were taken over by daily blog posts, where 48-point sans-serif headlines transformed into 12-point Web links. We then moved on into television, where Must-See TV was replaced with On-Demand TV, where consumers no longer sat around in the living room with their families during prime time but rather watched the latest episode of their favorite show commercial-free from the comfortable and convenient confines of their laptop, able to fast-forward, rewind, and pause with a delightful and devilish sense of programming omnipotence. We are now seeing it, slowly but surely, slay the giant that we never thought could be slain: the world of books.

2

In this paragraph, he makes a claim of fact about unequal access to technological innovation and offers a concession to what many see as the value of the Kindle.

   Contrary to popular belief, easier access to a wider quantity of literature is not a universal revolution. The Kindle speaks to the world that measures quantity by the number of cable television channels it has, speed by the connectivity of its wireless networks, and distance by the number of miles a family travels for vacation. Yes, the Kindle is the new paradigm for universal access and literary connectivity. But it is much like a college degree in the sense that it is merely a gateway to a wealth of opportunity. The problem, however, is gaining access to this gateway in the first place.

3

Camp 2

He supports
his claim of
fact with
evidence based
on experience:
that sharing
books provides
something
technology
cannot offer.

Books often pass from hand to hand, from friend to friend, 4
from generation to generation, many times with the mutual
understanding that remuneration is not necessary — merely the
promise of hope that the new reader is as touched and enlightened
by the book as the previous one. This transfer serves more than a
utilitarian function; symbolically, it represents the passage of hope, of
knowledge, of responsibility.

Evidence from
observation: not
everyone has
access to new
technologies,
but people
will always
have access
to books.

The book, in many cases, represents the only sort of hope for 5
the poorest among us, the great equalizer in a world full of financial
and intellectual capital and highly concentrated access to this capital.
The wonderful quality of the book is that its intellectual value is very
rarely proportional to its financial value; people often consider their
most valuable book to be one they happened to pick up one day for
free.

An evaluative
claim — that
the widening
gap between
rich and poor
is danger-
ous — adds
another layer to
the argument.

The proliferation of the Kindle technology, however, 6
will result in a wider disconnect between the elite and the non-
elite — as the old saying goes, the rich will get richer and the poor
will get poorer. Unfortunately for the poor, this is no financial
disconnect — this is a widening of the gap in the world of ideas. And
this is, perhaps, the most dangerous gap of all.

A further
evaluative
claim — that
new tech-
nological
devices offer
little hope to
"victims" of
illiteracy — is
followed by a
claim of fact
that books
inspire people
to create
change in
the world.

The Kindle Revolution, ironically, may end up contributing to 7
the very disease that is antithetical to its implied function: illiteracy.
Make no mistake, the Kindle was not designed with the poor in mind.
For those in most need of the printed word, for those who are the most
vulnerable victims of the illiteracy threat, the pricey Kindle offers little
in the way of hope. One book for a poor person is all he or she needs
to be inspired and change the world; with the Kindle, that one book
is consolidated and digitized, transformed from a tangible piece of
hope and the future into a mere collection of words in the theoretically
infinite dimension of cyberspace. A "book" on the Kindle is a book
wedged among many other books, separated by nothing more than title,
devoid of essence, devoid of uniqueness, devoid of personality, devoid
of its unique position in space — precisely what makes a book a "book,"
as opposed to a mere collection of words. It is no longer singular, no
longer serendipitous, no longer distinguishable.

The e-book cannot, like a bound book, pass through multiple 8
hands and eventually settle itself on the right person, ready

Camp 3

An evaluative claim in which the author observes that technology can make reading passive. Then a claim of fact: that the experience of reading can be transformative.

to be unleashed as a tool to change the world. Due to the restrictions on sharing and reselling e-books with the Kindle, the very nature of reading books transforms from highly communal to individualistic, from highly active to somewhat passive. The Kindle will lead to the mystification of books, wherein they become less unique capsules of thoughts and ideas and experiences and more utility-oriented modes of information-giving. What many Kindle advocates fail to realize is that oftentimes, the transformative quality of books resides less in the actual words comprising the book and more in the actual experience of reading.

There is also something to be said for the utter corporeality of books that lies at the heart of Leibniz's metaphor. Libraries are physical testaments to all that we have learned and recorded during human history. The sheer size of libraries and the sheer number of volumes residing in them tell us, in a spatial sense, of all the theoretical knowledge we have accumulated in the course of our existence, and all the power we have to further shape and define the world we live in. The Kindle and other digital literary technologies are threatening the very connection between the world of ideas and the material world, threatening to take our literal measures of progress and hide them away in the vast database of words and ideas, available only to those with money to spare and a credit card for further purchases.

9

The student offers a final evaluative claim, observing that the Kindle threatens to mask the relationship between ideas and the world.

His concluding claim falls just short of making a proposal — but he does suggest that those in positions of power must ensure the proliferation of books.

If libraries will indeed become cities, then we need to carefully begin to lay the foundations, book on top of book on top of book, and we are going to have to ensure that we have enough manpower to do it.

10

Steps to Analyzing an Argument

1. **Identify the type of claim.** Is it a claim of fact? Value? Policy?

2. **Analyze the reasons used to support the claim.** Are they recent? Relevant? Reliable? Accurate?

3. **Identify concessions.** Is there another argument that even the author acknowledges is legitimate?

4. **Identify counterarguments.** What arguments contradict or challenge the author's position?

A Practice Sequence: Analyzing an Argument

Use the criteria in the "Steps to Analyzing an Argument" box to analyze the following blog post by Susan D. Blum. What types of claim does she advance? What seems to be her main claim? Do you find her reasons recent, relevant, reliable, and accurate? What sort of concessions does she make? What counterarguments would you raise?

SUSAN D. BLUM

The United States of (Non)Reading: The End of Civilization or a New Era?

Susan D. Blum is a professor of anthropology at the University of Notre Dame whose wide areas of professional interest and expertise include Asian studies and education. She has written or edited many publications, including *Portraits of "Primitives": Ordering Human Kinds in the Chinese Nation* (2001), *My Word! Plagiarism and College Culture* (2009), and *Making Sense of Language: Readings in Culture and Communication* (2009; 2013). She also writes the Learning versus Schooling blog for the *Huffington Post*, where this essay was posted on October 8, 2013.

■ ▩ ▩

Just the other day one of my undergraduate assistants reported a friend's boast that he had not read anything for school since fifth grade. A student at an excellent university, successful, "clever," "smart," he can write papers, take exams, participate in class or online discussions. Why would he have to read? *1*

Students sometimes don't buy the class books. Professors are shocked. *2*

Several years ago a student told me that she regarded all assigned reading as "recommended," even if the professors labeled it "required." Were professors so dumb that they didn't know that? *3*

The idea of assigned reading, as the core activity of college students, is old. Students don't see it as central; faculty do. *4*

And though I used to, and sometimes still do, spend a lot of energy lamenting this, by taking a broader view of the nature of reading and writing, I have come to understand it and even to some extent accept it. *5*

Student avoidance of reading is not an entirely new problem. When I was in graduate school, in the 1980s, one of my most indelible memories was of a new classmate, straight out of a first-rate college, *6*

complaining in our anthropology theory class that we had to keep finding out what other people thought. When was it time for us to convey
our viewpoints? Why all that reading?

Some college course evaluations ask students what percentage of the   7
reading they did. Some report they did as much as 90 percent. Some as
little as 25 percent.

In a systematic study of college students' reading, Kylie Baier and   8
four colleagues reported that students mostly (40 percent) read for
exams. Almost 19 percent don't read for class. In terms of time, 94 percent of students spend less than two hours on any given reading for
class; 62 percent spend less than an hour. Thirty-two percent believe
they could get an A without reading; 89 percent believe they could get
at least a C.

Among many other educational crises, there is a perceived crisis   9
given that "students are increasingly reading less and less."

When faculty enter new institutions, they often ask colleagues: 10
How much reading should I assign? Some departments offer guidelines about the number of pages: Assign twenty-five pages for each
meeting of first-year classes, but no more than one hundred pages a
week for any course. This has always struck me as strange, given that
a page of a novel and a page of a double-column textbook have completely different amounts of text, and take different kinds of attention
and time. In response to this faculty challenge, Steve Volk—named
the Carnegie Professor of the Year in 2011, so he knows something
about teaching—wrote on the Web site of Oberlin College's Center for
Teaching Innovation and Excellence that there is no magic formula for
numbers of pages. He suggests instead that faculty consider "What do
you want the reading to do?"

But it is not only college teachers who worry about how much   11
people are reading. There is a widespread belief that Americans in
general read less and less. This perception builds on public conversations about the lack of reading. In 2007 a National Endowment for the
Arts study concluded that adults' reading habits were in severe decline.
Only 57 percent of adults read a book voluntarily in 2002, down from
61 percent in 1992.

This was supposed to have all sorts of terrible consequences: educa-   12
tional, of course, but also economic, social, moral, you name it.

Reversing the cup-half-empty conclusion, a 2013 study showed that   13
more than half read books for pleasure—just not what the NEA defines
(or would if the Government were functioning) as "literature."

And the Pew interpretation was that if reading for work and school is   14
added to "voluntary reading," then almost all people read "books" at some
point during the year: 79 percent of 18 to 24 year-olds, and 90 percent of
16 to 17 year-olds.

It is undeniable that people are reading (looking at) writing all *15* the time. It may not be in physical books, however. And just this week, *USA Today* argued that digital devices increase book reading (on the devices).

David Carr wrote in 2008 about the decline in attention—not only *16* in our students. Attention spans, focus, mindfulness . . . all these are shrinking. Technology plays a role in this, as many of us spend much of our lives looking at short items. *The Onion*, the humor website, puts most of its efforts into its headlines. Blogs should be at most one thousand words, but three hundred is better. (This one is too long.)

So if students are sipping text constantly on their devices, and *17* suddenly they are asked to consume what sounds like an insurmountable mountain of pages in some other form—and for what!?—they are likely to avoid it entirely.

"Flipping the classroom" has attempted to seek some kind of *18* accountability from students for their reading, so that they have to engage in one way or another with their material prior to assembling for the precious moment of face-to-face interaction. This requires reading—but reading with a goal. Students often like to do that, as a kind of scavenger hunt for what is useful and important. Just having them read for background ideas seems to be fading.

Actually, I have stopped worrying constantly about this. Students *19* are reading. The public is reading. They may not sit for hours, still and attentive, and focus on one item. They may confuse their facts. They may miss a complex argument.

Don't misunderstand. I worship reading. When I travel for three *20* days, in addition to all my devices I bring six books and five (print) magazines. Yet I cannot concentrate the way I used to. So those less devoted. . . . Should we cut them off from the world, isolate them in soundproof rooms with no WiFi, and force them to read a book?

Writing has evolved, and will evolve. And with it reading changes. *21* From clay tablets designed to record debts to bronze proclamations of kings and emperors, from bamboo strips recording rituals to complex philosophical arguments on paper, from paintings for the royal afterlife to paperback novels, from stone tablets proclaiming a new moral code to infinitesimal elements on a shiny handheld device—from its origins, writing has transformed, and will continue to change. It is not entirely that the medium is the message, but the medium affects the message. Since humans are the ones doing the writing, we get the writing that suits our purposes.

We are all getting a front-row seat to a sudden change in medium, *22* and therefore in writing and reading. What a quick and shocking ride this is!

Read all about it! *23*

ANALYZING AND COMPARING ARGUMENTS

As an academic writer, you will often need to compare disparate claims and evidence from multiple arguments addressing the same topic. Rarely, however, will those arguments be simplistic pro/con pairs meant to represent two opposing sides to an issue. Certainly the news media thrive on such black-and-white conflict, but academic writers seek greater complexity and do not expect to find simple answers. Analyzing and comparing essays on the same topic or issue will often reveal the ways writers work with similar evidence to come up with different, and not necessarily opposed, arguments.

The next two selections are arguments about grade inflation. Both are brief, and we recommend you read through them as a prelude to the activity in analyzing and comparing arguments that follows them. As you read, try to note their claims, the reasons used to support them, concessions, and counterarguments.

STUART ROJSTACZER

Grade Inflation Gone Wild

A former professor of geophysics at Duke University with a PhD in applied earth sciences, Stuart Rojstaczer has written or coauthored many geological studies in his career as a scientist. He has also published a book, Gone for Good: Tales of University Life after the Golden Age (1999), and numerous articles on higher education and grading. He is the creator of gradeinflation.com, where he posts a variety of charts and graphs chronicling his data about grade inflation. This op-ed piece appeared in the Christian Science Monitor *on March 24, 2009.*

▪ ▪ ▪

About six years ago, I was sitting in the student union of a small   *1*
liberal arts college when I saw a graph on the cover of the student newspaper that showed the history of grades given at that institution in the past 30 years.

Grades were up. Way up.   *2*

I'm a scientist by training and I love numbers. So when I looked at   *3*
that graph, I wondered, "How many colleges and universities have data like this that I can find?" The answer is that a lot of schools have data like this hidden somewhere. Back then, I found more than 80 colleges and universities with data on grades, mostly by poking around the Web. Then I created a website (gradeinflation.com) so that others could find this data. I learned that grades started to shoot up nationwide in the 1960s, leveled off in the 1970s, and then started rising again in

the 1980s. Private schools had much higher grades than public schools, but virtually everyone was experiencing grade inflation.

What about today? 4

Grades continue to go up regardless of the quality of education. 5 At a time when many are raising questions about the quality of U.S. higher education, the average GPA at public schools is 3.0, with many flagship state schools having average GPAs higher than 3.2. At a private college, the average is now 3.3. At some schools, it tops 3.5 and even 3.6. "A" is average at those schools! At elite Brown University, two-thirds of all letter grades given are now A's.

These changes in grading have had a profound influence on college 6 life and learning. When students walk into a classroom knowing that they can go through the motions and get a B+ or better, that's what they tend to do, give minimal effort. Our college classrooms are filled with students who do not prepare for class. Many study less than 10 hours a week—that's less than half the hours they spent studying 40 years ago. Paradoxically, students are spending more and more money for an education that seems to deliver less and less content.

With so few hours filled with learning, boredom sets in and stu- 7 dents have to find something to pass the time. Instead of learning, they drink. A recent survey of more than 30,000 first-year students across the country showed that nearly half were spending more hours drinking than they were studying. If we continue along this path, we'll end up with a generation of poorly educated college graduates who have used their four years principally to develop an addiction to alcohol.

There are many who say that grade inflation is a complicated issue 8 with no easy fix. But there are solutions. At about the same time that I started to collect data on rising grades, Princeton University began to actually do something about its grade-inflation problem. Its guidelines have the effect of now limiting A's on average to 35 percent of students in a class. Those guidelines have worked. Grades are going back down at Princeton and academic rigor is making a comeback. A similar successful effort has taken place at Wellesley College in Massachusetts. And through a concerted effort on the part of faculty and leadership, grades at Reed College in Oregon have stayed essentially constant for 20 years.

Princeton, Wellesley, and Reed provide evidence that the effort to 9 keep grade inflation in check is not impossible. This effort takes two major steps. First, school officials must admit that there is a problem. Then they must implement policies or guidelines that truly restore excellence.

I asked Dean Nancy Malkiel at Princeton why so few schools seem to 10 be following Princeton's lead. "Because it's hard work," she answered.

"Because you have to persuade the faculty that it's important to do the work."

Making a switch will take hard work, but the effort is worthwhile. *11* The alternative is a student body that barely studies and drinks out of boredom. That's not acceptable. Colleges and universities must roll up their sleeves, bring down inflated grades, and encourage real learning. It's not an impossible task. There are successful examples that can be followed. I'm looking forward to the day when we can return to being proud of the education that our nation's colleges and universities provide.

PHIL PRIMACK

Doesn't Anybody Get a C Anymore?

Phil Primack is a journalist, editor, and policy analyst who teaches journalism at Tufts University, where he is a senior fellow at the Jonathan M. Tisch College of Citizenship and Public Service. His articles have appeared in many regional and national publications, including the *New York Times*, the *Boston Globe*, and *Columbia Journalism Review*. The following piece appeared in the *Boston Globe* on October 5, 2008.

■ ▓ ▓

The student deserved a B-minus. Maybe even a C-plus, I had decided. *1* One paper was especially weak; another was late. But then I began to rationalize. The student had been generally prepared and contributed to class discussion, so I relented and gave what I thought was a very generous B. At least I wouldn't get a complaint about this grade, I figured. Then came the e-mail.

Why such a "low grade," the indignant student wrote. *2*

"Low grade"? Back when I attended Tufts in the late 1960s, a B in cer- *3* tain courses was something I could only dream about. But grade inflation, the steady rise in grade point averages that began in the 1960s, now leaves many students regarding even the once-acceptable B—which has always stood for "good"—as a transcript wrecker, and a C—that is, "average"—as unmitigated disaster. More and more academic leaders may lament grade inflation, but precious few have been willing to act against it, leaving their professors all alone in the minefield between giving marks that reflect true merit and facing the wrath of students for whom entitlement begins with the letter A.

Grade inflation "is a huge problem," says former U.S. senator *4* Hank Brown, who tried to make it a priority issue as president of the

University of Colorado in 2006. "Under the current system at a lot of schools, there is no way to recognize the difference between an out-standing job and a good job. Grade inflation hides laziness on the part of the students, and as long as it exists, even faculty who want to do a good job [in grading] don't feel they can."

That's because many professors fear that "tough grading" will trig-ger poor student evaluations or worse, which in turn can jeopardize the academic career track. "In my early years, students would say they liked my class, but the grades were low and the work level high," says retired Duke University professor Stuart Rojstaczer. "I had to get with the pro-gram and reduce my own expectations of workload and increase grades in order to have students leave my class with a positive impression to give to other students so they would attend [next year]. I was teaching worse, but the student response was much more positive."

Harvard University is the poster campus for academic prestige—and for grade inflation, even though some of its top officials have warned about grade creep. About 15 percent of Harvard students got a B-plus or better in 1950, according to one study. In 2007, more than half of all Harvard grades were in the A range. Harvard declined to release more current data or officially comment for this article. At the University of Massachusetts at Amherst, the average GPA in 2007 was 3.19 (on a four-point scale), up from 3.02 a decade earlier. That "modest increase" simply reflects better students, UMass spokesman Ed Blaguszewski says in an e-mail. "Since our students have been increasingly well-prepared . . . it makes sense that their UMass grades have crept up. Essentially, the profile of the population has changed over time, so we don't consider this to be grade inflation."

That's certainly the most common argument to explain away grade inflation—smarter students naturally get higher grades. But is it that simple? Privately, many faculty members and administrators say col-leges are unwilling to challenge and possibly offend students and their hovering, tuition-paying parents with some tough grade love. And with-out institutional backing, individual faculty members simply yield to whining students.

But not everywhere. The most cited—and extreme—case of taking on grade inflation is at Princeton University, which in 2004 directed that A's account for less than 35 percent of undergraduate course grades. From 2004 to 2007, A's (A-plus, A, A-minus) accounted for 40.6 percent of undergraduate course grades, down from 47 percent in the period 2001 to 2004.

Closer to home, Wellesley College calls for the average grade in basic undergraduate courses to be no higher than a B-plus (3.33 GPA). "It's not that we're trying to get grades down, but we're trying to get grades to mean something," says associate dean of the college Adele Wolfson, who teaches chemistry. Wellesley's GPA, which stood at 3.47 in 2002 and was 3.4 when the policy was implemented two years later, fell to 3.3 this year, mainly because of more B grades and fewer A's. "The A has really become the mark of excellence," she says, "which is what it should be."

The problem, says Rojstaczer, is that such policies are the excep- *10* tions, and that grade inflation will be reduced only through consistent prodding and action by top officials. "In truth, some university leaders are embarrassed that grading is so lax, but they are loath to make any changes," he says in an e-mail. "Grade inflation in academia is like the alcoholic brother you pretend is doing just fine. When someone calls your brother a drunk, you get angry and defend him, although privately you worry. That's where we are with grade inflation: public denial and private concern."

A Practice Sequence: Analyzing and Comparing Arguments

1   To practice these strategies, first break up into small groups to discuss four different concerns surrounding grade inflation:

Group 1: Define what you think grade inflation is.

Group 2: Discuss whether you think grade inflation is a problem at the university or college you attend. What evidence can you provide to suggest that it is or is not a problem?

Group 3: Why should students or faculty be concerned with grade inflation? What's at stake?

Group 4: How would you respond if the administration at your university or college decided to limit the number of A's that faculty could give students?

Reassemble as a class and briefly report on the discussions.

2   Analyze Stuart Rojstaczer's argument in "Grade Inflation Gone Wild," addressing the following questions:

• What evidence does Rojstaczer use to indicate that there is a problem?

• How would you characterize this evidence (for example, scientific, anecdotal), and to what extent are you persuaded by the evidence he provides to suggest that grade inflation has a profound effect on "life and learning"?

• To what extent does he persuade you that a change in policy is necessary or that such a change would make a difference?

3 Now compare Phil Primack's and Stuart Rojstaczer's strategies for developing an argument.

- How does Primack establish that there is a problem? To what extent is his approach as persuasive as Rojstaczer's?

- What strategies would you identify in either argument as strategies that you might employ to develop your own argument?

- To what extent are you persuaded by the counterargument that Primack introduces?

- What do you think Primack wants you to do or think about in his analysis?

- In the end, does Primack add anything to your understanding of the problem of whether your college or university should introduce a policy to limit grade inflation?

4 As an alternative assignment, write a three-page essay in which you compare the arguments student Marques Camp and Professor Susan D. Blum make about the state of reading today. Consider their main claims and how they support them. Explain which argument you find more persuasive, and why. Feel free to draw on your own experience and make use of personal anecdotes to make your case.

5

From Identifying Issues to Forming Questions

Remember that inquiry is central to the process of composing. As you move from reading texts to writing them, you will discover that writing grows out of answering these questions:

- What are the concerns of the authors I've been reading?
- What situations motivate them to write?
- What frames or contexts do these writers use to construct their arguments?
- What is my argument in response to their writing?
- What is at stake in my argument?
- Who will be interested in reading what I have to say?
- How can I connect with both sympathetic and antagonistic readers?
- What kinds of evidence will persuade my readers?
- What objections are they likely to raise?

To answer these questions, you must read in the role of writer, with an eye toward

- *identifying an issue* (an idea or a statement that is open to dispute) that compels you to respond in writing,
- *understanding the situation* (the factors that give rise to the issue and shape your response), and
- *formulating a question* (what you intend to answer in response to the issue).

TABLE 5.1   A Series of Situations with Related Issues and Questions

SITUATION	ISSUE	QUESTION
Different state legislatures are passing legislation to prevent Spanish-speaking students from using their own language in schools.	Most research on learning contradicts the idea that students should be prevented from using their own language in the process of learning a new language.	Under what conditions should students be allowed to use their own language while they learn English?
A manufacturing company has plans to move to your city with the promise of creating new jobs in a period of high unemployment.	You feel that this company will compromise the quality of life for the surrounding community because the manufacturing process will pollute the air.	What would persuade the city to prevent this company from moving in, even though the company will provide much-needed jobs?
Your school has made an agreement with a local company to supply vending machines that sell drinks and food. The school plans to use its share of the profits to improve the library and purchase a new scoreboard for the football field.	You see that the school has much to gain from this arrangement, but you also know that obesity is a growing problem at the school.	Is there another way for the school to generate needed revenue without putting students' health at risk?
An increasing number of homeless people are seeking shelter on your college campus.	Campus security has stepped up its efforts to remove the homeless, even though the shelters off campus are overcrowded.	How can you persuade the school to shelter the homeless and to provide funds to support the needs of the homeless in your city?

In Table 5.1, we identify a series of situations and one of the issues and questions that derive from each of them. Notice that the question you ask defines the area of inquiry as you read; it also can help you formulate your working thesis, the statement that answers your question. (We say more about developing a thesis in Chapter 6.) In this chapter, in addition to further discussing the importance of situation, we look at how you can identify issues and formulate questions to guide your reading and writing.

IDENTIFYING ISSUES

In this section we present several steps to identifying an issue. You don't have to follow them in this particular order, and you may find yourself going back and forth among them as you try to bring an issue into focus.

Keep in mind that issues do not simply exist in the world well formed. Instead, writers construct what they see as issues from the situations they observe. For example, consider legislation to limit downloads from the Internet. If such legislation conflicts with your own practices and sense of freedom, you may have begun to identify an issue: the clash of values over what constitutes fair use and what does not. Be aware that others may not understand your issue and that in your writing you will have to explain carefully what is at stake.

▪ Draw on Your Personal Experience

You may have been taught that formal writing is objective, that you must keep a dispassionate distance from your subject, and that you should not use *I* in a college-level paper. The fact is, however, that our personal experiences influence how we read, what we pay attention to, and what inferences we draw. It makes sense, then, to begin with you—where you are and what you think and believe.

We all use personal experience to make arguments in our everyday lives. In an academic context, the challenge is to use personal experience to argue a point, to illustrate something, or to illuminate a connection between theories and the sense we make of our daily experience. You don't want simply to tell your story. You want your story to strengthen your argument.

For example, in *Cultural Literacy*, E. D. Hirsch personalizes his interest in reversing the cycle of illiteracy in America's cities. To establish the nature of the problem in the situation he describes, he cites research showing that student performance on standardized tests in the United States is falling. But he also reflects on his own teaching in the 1970s, when he first perceived "the widening knowledge gap [that] caused me to recognize the connection between specific background knowledge and mature literacy." And he injects anecdotal evidence from conversations with his son, a teacher. Those stories heighten readers' awareness that school-aged children do not know much about literature, history, or government. (For example, his son mentions a student who challenged his claim that Latin is a "dead language" by demanding, "What do they speak in Latin America?")

Hirsch's use of his son's testimony makes him vulnerable to criticism, as readers might question whether Hirsch can legitimately use his son's experience to make generalizations about education. But in fact, Hirsch is using personal testimony—his own and his son's—to augment and put a human face on the research he cites. He presents his issue, that schools must teach cultural literacy, both as something personal and as something with which we should all be concerned. The personal note helps readers see Hirsch as someone who has long been concerned with education and who has even raised a son who is an educator.

▪ Identify What Is Open to Dispute

An issue is something that is open to dispute. Sometimes the way to clarify an issue is to think of it as a *fundamental tension* between two or more conflicting points of view. If you can identify conflicting points of view, an issue may become clear.

Consider E. D. Hirsch, who believes that the best approach to educational reform is to change the curriculum in schools. His position: A curriculum based on cultural literacy is the one sure way to reverse the cycle of poverty and illiteracy in urban areas.

What is the issue? Hirsch's issue emerges in the presence of an alternative position. Jonathan Kozol, a social activist who has written extensively about educational reform, believes that policymakers need to address reform by providing the necessary resources that all students need to learn. Kozol points out that students in many inner-city schools are reading outdated textbooks and that the dilapidated conditions in these schools—windows that won't close, for example—make it impossible for students to learn.

In tension are two different views of the reform that can reverse illiteracy: Hirsch's view that educational reform should occur through curricular changes, and Kozol's view that educational reform demands socioeconomic resources.

▪ Resist Binary Thinking

As you begin to define what is at issue, try to tease out complexities that may not be immediately apparent. That is, try to resist the either/or mindset that signals binary thinking.

If you considered only what Hirsch and Kozol have to say, it would be easy to characterize the problems facing our schools as either curricular or socioeconomic. But it may be that the real issue combines these arguments with a third or even a fourth, that neither curricular nor socioeconomic changes by themselves can resolve the problems with American schools.

After reading essays by both Hirsch and Kozol, one of our students pointed out that both Hirsch's focus on curriculum and Kozol's socioeconomic focus ignore another concern. She went on to describe her school experience in racial terms. In the excerpt below, notice how this writer uses personal experience (in a new school, she is not treated as she had expected to be treated) to formulate an issue.

> Moving from Colorado Springs to Tallahassee, I was immediately struck by the differences apparent in local home life, school life, and community unity, or lack thereof. Ripped from my sheltered world at a small Catholic school characterized by racial harmony, I was thrown into a large public school where outward prejudice from classmates and teachers and "race wars" were common and tolerated. . . .
>
> In a school where students and teachers had free rein to abuse anyone different from them, I was constantly abused. As the only black student in English honors, I was commonly belittled in front of my "peers" by my teacher. If I developed courage enough to ask a question, I was always answered with the use of improper grammar and such words as "ain't" as my teacher attempted to simplify the material to "my level" and to give me what he called "a little learning." After discussing several

subjects, he often turned to me, singling me out of a sea of white faces, and asked, "Do *you* understand, Mila?" When asking my opinion of a subject, he frequently questioned, "What do *your* people think about this?" Although he insisted on including such readings as Martin Luther King's "I Have a Dream" speech in the curriculum, the speech's themes of tolerance and equity did not accompany his lesson.

Through her reading, this student discovered that few prominent scholars have confronted the issue of racism in schools directly. Although she grants that curricular reform and increased funding may be necessary to improve education, she argues that scholars also need to address race in their studies of teaching and learning.

Our point is that issues may be more complex than you first think they are. For this student, the issue wasn't one of two positions—reform the curriculum or provide more funding. Instead, it combined a number of different positions, including race ("prejudice" and "race wars") and the relationship between student and teacher ("Do *you* understand, Mila?") in a classroom.

In this passage, the writer uses her experience to challenge binary thinking. Like the student writer, you should examine issues from different perspectives, avoiding either/or propositions that oversimplify the world.

■ Build on and Extend the Ideas of Others

Academic writing builds on and extends the ideas of others. As an academic writer, you will find that by extending other people's ideas, you will extend your own. You may begin in a familiar place, but as you read more and pursue connections to other readings, you may well end up at an unexpected destination.

For example, one of our students was troubled when he read Melissa Stormont-Spurgin's description of homeless children. The student uses details from her work (giving credit, of course) in his own:

> The children . . . went to school after less than three hours of sleep. They wore the same wrinkled clothes that they had worn the day before. What will their teachers think when they fall asleep in class? How will they get food for lunch? What will their peers think? What could these homeless children talk about with their peers? They have had to grow up too fast. Their worries are not the same as other children's worries. They are worried about their next meal and where they will seek shelter. Their needs, however, are the same. They need a home and all of the securities that come with it. They also need an education (Stormont-Spurgin 156).

Initially the student was troubled by his own access to quality schools, and the contrast between his life and the lives of the children Stormont-Spurgin describes. Initially, then, his issue was the fundamental tension between his own privileged status, something he had taken for granted, and the struggle that homeless children face every day.

However, as he read further and grew to understand homelessness as a concern in a number of studies, he connected his personal response to a larger conversation about democracy, fairness, and education:

> Melissa Stormont-Spurgin, an author of several articles on educational studies, addresses a very real and important, yet avoided issue in education today. Statistics show that a very high percentage of children who are born into homeless families will remain homeless, or in poverty, for the rest of their lives. How can this be, if everyone actually does have the same educational opportunities? There must be significant educational disadvantages for children without homes. In a democratic society, I feel that we must pay close attention to these disadvantages and do everything in our power to replace them with equality.

Ultimately, the student refined his sense of what was at issue: *Although all people should have access to public education in a democratic society, not everyone has the opportunity to attend quality schools in order to achieve personal success.* In turn, his definition of the issue began to shape his argument:

> Parents, teachers, homeless shelters, and the citizens of the United States who fund [homeless] shelters must address the educational needs of homeless children, while steering them away from any more financial or psychological struggles. Without this emphasis on education, the current trend upward in the number of homeless families will inevitably continue in the future of American society.

The student shifted away from a personal issue—the difference between his status and that of homeless children—to an issue of clashing values: the principle of egalitarian democracy on the one hand and the reality of citizens in a democracy living in abject poverty on the other. When he started to read about homeless children, he could not have made the claim he ends up making, that policymakers must make education a basic human right.

This student offers us an important lesson about the role of inquiry and the value of resisting easy answers. He has built on and extended his own ideas—and the ideas of others—after repeating the process of reading, raising questions, writing, and seeing problems a number of times.

■ Read to Discover a Writer's Frame

A more specialized strategy of building on and extending the ideas of others involves reading to discover a writer's **frame**, the perspective through which a writer presents his or her arguments. Writers want us to see the world a certain way, so they frame their arguments much the same way photographers and artists frame their pictures.

For example, if you were to take a picture of friends in front of the football stadium on campus, you would focus on what you would most like to remember—your friends' faces—blurring the images of the people walking behind your friends. Setting up the picture, or framing it, might require using light and shade to make some details stand out more than others. Writers do the same with language.

E. D. Hirsch uses the concept of *cultural literacy* to frame his argument for curricular reform. For Hirsch, the term is a benchmark, a standard: People who are culturally literate are familiar with the body of information that every educated citizen should know. Hirsch's implication, of course, is that people who are not culturally literate are not well educated. But that is not necessarily true. In fact, a number of educators insist that literacy is simply a means to an end—reading to complete an assignment, for example, or to understand the ramifications of a decision—not an end in itself. By defining and using *cultural literacy* as the goal of education, Hirsch is framing his argument; he is bringing his ideas into focus.

When writers use framing strategies, they also call attention to the specific conversations that set up the situation for their arguments. Framing often entails quoting specific theories and ideas from other authors and then using those quotations as a perspective, or lens, through which to examine other material. In his memoir *Hunger of Memory: The Education of Richard Rodriguez* (1982), Richard Rodriguez uses this method to examine his situation as a nonnative speaker of English desperate to enter the mainstream culture, even if it means sacrificing his identity as the son of Mexican immigrants. Reflecting on his life as a student, Rodriguez comes across Richard Hoggart's book *The Uses of Literacy* (1957). Hoggart's description of "the scholarship boy" presents a lens through which Rodriguez can see his own experience. Hoggart writes:

> With his family, the boy has the intense pleasure of intimacy, the family's consolation in feeling public alienation. Lavish emotions texture home life. *Then*, at school, the instruction bids him to trust lonely reason primarily. Immediate needs set the pace of his parents' lives. From his mother and father the boy learns to trust spontaneity and nonrational ways of knowing. *Then*, at school, there is mental calm. Teachers emphasize the value of a reflectiveness that opens a space between thinking and immediate action.
>
> Years of schooling must pass before the boy will be able to sketch the cultural differences in his day as abstractly as this. But he senses those differences early. Perhaps as early as the night he brings home an assignment from school and finds the house too noisy for study. He has to be more and more alone, if he is going to "get on." He will have, probably unconsciously, to oppose the ethos of the hearth, the intense gregariousness of the working-class family group. . . . The boy has to cut himself off mentally, so as to do his homework, as well as he can.

Here is Rodriguez's response to Hoggart's description of the scholarship boy:

> For weeks I read, speed-read, books by modern educational theorists, only to find infrequent and slight mention of students like me. . . . Then one day, leafing through Richard Hoggart's *The Uses of Literacy*, I found, in his description of the scholarship boy, myself. For the first time I realized that

there were other students like me, and so I was able to frame the meaning of my academic success, its consequent price—the loss.

Notice how Rodriguez introduces ideas from Hoggart "to frame" his own ideas: "I found, in his description of the scholarship boy, myself. For the first time I realized that there were other students like me, and so I was able to frame the meaning of my academic success, its consequent price—the loss." Hoggart's scholarship boy enables Rodriguez to revisit his own experience with a new perspective. Hoggart's words and idea advance Rodriguez's understanding of the problem he identifies in his life: his inability to find solace at home and within his working-class roots. Hoggart's description of the scholarship boy's moving between cultural extremes—spontaneity at home and reflection at school—helps Rodriguez bring his own youthful discontent into focus.

Rodriguez's response to Hoggart's text shows how another writer's lens can help frame an issue. If you were using Hoggart's term *scholarship boy* as a lens through which to clarify an issue in education, you might ask how the term illuminates new aspects of another writer's examples or your own. And then you might ask, "To what extent does Hirsch's cultural literacy throw a more positive light on what Rodriguez and Hoggart describe?" or "How do my experiences challenge, extend, or complicate the scholarship-boy concept?"

■ Consider the Constraints of the Situation

In identifying an issue, you have to understand the situation that gives rise to the issue, including the contexts in which it is raised and debated. One of the contexts is the *audience*. In thinking about your issue, you must consider the extent to which your potential readers are involved in the dialogue you want to enter, and what they know and need to know. In a sense, audience functions as both context and **constraint**, a factor that narrows the choices you can make in responding to an issue. An understanding of your potential readers will help you choose the depth of your discussion; it will also determine the kind of evidence you can present and the language you can use.

Another constraint on your response to an issue is the form that response takes. For example, if you decide to make an issue of government-imposed limits on what you can download from the Internet, your response in writing might take the form of an editorial or a letter to a legislator. In this situation, length is an obvious constraint: Newspapers limit the word count of editorials, and the best letters to legislators tend to be brief and very selective about the evidence they cite. A few personal examples and a few statistics may be all you can include to support your claim about the issue. By contrast, if you were making your case in an academic journal, a very different set of constraints would apply. You would have more space for illustrations and support, for example.

Finally, the situation itself can function as a major constraint. For instance, suppose your topic is the decline of educational standards. It's difficult to imagine any writer making the case for accelerating that decline, or any audience being receptive to the idea that a decline in standards is a good thing.

Steps to Identifying Issues

1 **Draw on your personal experience.** Start with your own sense of what's important, what puzzles you, or what you are curious about. Then build your argument by moving on to other sources to support your point of view.

2 **Identify what is open to dispute.** Identify a phenomenon or some idea in a written argument that challenges what you think or believe.

3 **Resist binary thinking.** Think about the issue from multiple perspectives.

4 **Build on and extend the ideas of others.** As you read, be open to new ways of looking at the issue. The issue you finally write about may be very different from what you set out to write about.

5 **Read to discover a writer's frame.** What theories or ideas shape the writer's focus? How can these theories or ideas help you frame your argument?

6 **Consider the constraints of the situation.** Craft your argument to meet the needs of and constraints imposed by your audience and form.

IDENTIFYING ISSUES IN AN ESSAY

In the following editorial, published in 2002 in *Newsweek*, writer Anna Quindlen addresses her concern that middle-class parents overschedule their children's lives. She calls attention to the ways leisure time helped her develop as a writer and urges parents to consider the extent to which children's creativity depends on having some downtime. They don't always have to have their time scheduled. As you read Quindlen's "Doing Nothing Is Something," note what words and phrases Quindlen uses to identify the situation and to indicate who her audience is. Identify her main claim as one of fact, value, or policy. Finally, answer the questions that follow the selection to see if you can discern how she locates, defines, and advances her issue.

ANNA QUINDLEN

Doing Nothing Is Something

Anna Quindlen is a best-selling author of novels and children's books, but she is perhaps most widely known for her nonfiction and commentary on current events and contemporary life. She won a Pulitzer Prize in 1992 for her "Public and Private" column in the *New York Times*, and for ten years wrote a biweekly column for *Newsweek*. Some of her novels are *Object Lessons* (1991), *Blessings* (2002), and *Every Last One* (2010). Her nonfiction works and collections include *Living Out Loud* (1988), *Thinking Out Loud* (1994), *Loud and Clear* (2004), and *Good Dog. Stay.* (2007).

S ummer is coming soon. I can feel it in the softening of the air, but I can see it, too, in the textbooks on my children's desks. The number of uncut pages at the back grows smaller and smaller. The loose-leaf is ragged at the edges, the binder plastic ripped at the corners. An old remembered glee rises inside me. Summer is coming. Uniform skirts in mothballs. Pencils with their points left broken. Open windows. Day trips to the beach. Pickup games. *1*

Hanging out. How boring it was. *2*

Of course, it was the making of me, as a human being and a writer. Downtime is where we become ourselves, looking into the middle distance, kicking at the curb, lying on the grass, or sitting on the stoop and staring at the tedious blue of the summer sky. I don't believe you can write poetry, or compose music, or become an actor without downtime, and plenty of it, a hiatus that passes for boredom but is really the quiet moving of the wheels inside that fuel creativity. *3*

And that, to me, is one of the saddest things about the lives of American children today. Soccer leagues, acting classes, tutors—the calendar of the average middle-class kid is so over the top that soon Palm handhelds will be sold in Toys "R" Us. Our children are as overscheduled as we are, and that is saying something. *4*

This has become so bad that parents have arranged to schedule times for unscheduled time. Earlier this year the privileged suburb of Ridgewood, New Jersey, announced a Family Night, when there would be no homework, no athletic practices, and no after-school events. This was terribly exciting until I realized that this was not one night a week, but one single night. There is even a free-time movement, and Web site: familylife1st.org. Among the frequently asked questions provided online: "What would families do with family time if they took it back?" *5*

Let me make a suggestion for the kids involved: How about nothing? It is not simply that it is pathetic to consider the lives of children who don't have a moment between piano and dance and homework to talk about their day or just search for split ends, an enormously satisfying *6* leisure-time activity of my youth. There is also ample psychological research suggesting that what we might call "doing nothing" is when human beings actually do their best thinking, and when creativity comes to call. Perhaps we are creating an entire generation of people whose ability to think outside the box, as the current parlance of business has it, is being systematically stunted by scheduling.

A study by the University of Michigan quantified the downtime deficit; in the last twenty years American kids have lost about four unstructured hours a week. There has even arisen a global Right to Play movement: in the Third World it is often about child labor, but in the United States it is about the sheer labor of being a perpetually busy child. In Omaha, Nebraska, a group of parents recently lobbied for additional recess. Hooray, and yikes.   7

How did this happen? Adults did it. There is a culture of adult distrust that suggests that a kid who is not playing softball or attending science-enrichment programs—or both—is huffing or boosting cars: If kids are left alone, they will not stare into the middle distance and consider the meaning of life and how come your nose in pictures never looks the way you think it should, but instead will get into trouble. There is also the culture of cutthroat and unquestioning competition that leads even the parents of preschoolers to gab about prestigious colleges without a trace of irony: This suggests that any class in which you do not enroll your first grader will put him at a disadvantage in, say, law school.   8

Finally, there is a culture of workplace presence (as opposed to productivity). Try as we might to suggest that all these enrichment activities are for the good of the kid, there is ample evidence that they are really for the convenience of parents with way too little leisure time of their own. Stories about the resignation of presidential aide Karen Hughes unfailingly reported her dedication to family time by noting that she arranged to get home at 5:30 one night a week to have dinner with her son. If one weekday dinner out of five is considered laudable, what does that say about what's become commonplace?   9

Summer is coming. It used to be a time apart for kids, a respite from the clock and the copybook, the organized day. Every once in a while, either guilty or overwhelmed or tired of listening to me keen about my monumental boredom, my mother would send me to some rinky-dink park program that consisted almost entirely of three-legged races and making things out of Popsicle sticks. Now, instead, there are music camps, sports camps, fat camps, probably thin camps. I mourn hanging out in the backyard. I mourn playing Wiffle ball in the street without a sponsor and matching shirts. I mourn drawing in the dirt with a stick.   10

Maybe that kind of summer is gone for good. Maybe this is the leading edge of a new way of living that not only has no room for contemplation but is contemptuous of it. But if downtime cannot be squeezed during the school year into the life of frantic and often joyless activity with   11 which our children are saddled while their parents pursue frantic and often joyless activity of their own, what about summer? Do most adults really want to stand in line for Space Mountain or sit in traffic to get to a shore house that doesn't have enough saucepans? Might it be even more enriching for their children to stay at home and do nothing? For those who say they will only watch TV or play on the computer, a piece of technical advice: The cable box can be unhooked, the modem removed. Perhaps it is not too late for American kids to be given the gift of enforced boredom for at least a week or two, staring into space, bored out of their gourds, exploring the inside of their own heads. "To contemplate is to toil, to think is to do," said Victor Hugo. "Go outside and play," said Prudence Quindlen. Both of them were right.

Reading as a Writer

1. What evidence of Quindlen's personal responses and experiences can you identify?
2. What phenomenon has prompted her to reflect on what she thinks and believes? How has she made it into an issue?
3. Where does she indicate that she has considered the issue from multiple perspectives and is placing her ideas in conversation with those of others?
4. What sort of lens does she seem to be using to frame her argument?
5. What constraints (such as the format of an editorial) seem to be in play in the essay?

A Practice Sequence: Identifying Issues

This sequence of activities will give you practice in identifying and clarifying issues based on your own choice of reading and collaboration with your classmates.

1   Draw on your personal experience. Reflect on your own responses to what you have been reading in this class or in other classes, or issues that writers have posed in the media. What concerns you most? Choose a story that supports or challenges the claims people are making in what you have read or listened to. What questions do you have? Make some notes in response to these questions, explaining your personal stake in the issues and questions you formulate.

2   Identify what is open to dispute. Take what you have written and formulate your ideas as an issue, using the structure we used in our example of Hirsch's and Kozol's competing arguments:

   • Part 1: Your view of a given topic
   • Part 2: At least one view that is in tension with your own

If you need to, read further to understand what others have to say about this issue.

3 Resist binary thinking. Share your statement of the issue with one or more peers and ask them if they see other ways to formulate the issue that you may not have thought about. What objections, if any, do they make to your statement in part 1? Write these objections down in part 2 so that you begin to look at the issue from multiple perspectives.

4 Build on and extend the ideas of others. Now that you have formulated an issue from different perspectives, explaining your personal stake in the issue, connect what you think to a broader conversation in what you are reading. Then try making a claim using this structure: "Although some people would argue _____, I think that _____."

5 Read to discover a writer's frame. As an experiment in trying out multiple perspectives, revise the claim you make in exercise 4 by introducing the frame, or lens, through which you want readers to understand your argument. You can employ the same sentence structure. For example, here is a claim framed in terms of race: "Although people should have access to public education, recent policies have worsened racial inequalities in public schools." In contrast, here is a claim that focuses on economics: "Although people should have access to public education, the unequal distribution of tax money has created what some would call an 'economy of education.'" The lens may come from reading you have done in other courses or from conversations with your classmates, and you may want to attribute the lens to a particular author or classmate: "Although some people would argue_____, I use E. D. Hirsch's notion of cultural literacy to show_____."

6 Consider the constraints of the situation. Building on these exercises, develop an argument in the form of an editorial for your local newspaper. This means that you will need to limit your argument to about 250 words. You also will need to consider the extent to which your potential readers are involved in the conversation. What do they know? What do they need to know? What kind of evidence do you need to use to persuade readers?

FORMULATING ISSUE-BASED QUESTIONS

As we have said, when you identify an issue, you need to understand it in the context of its situation. Ideally, the situation and the issue will be both relevant and recent, making the task of connecting to your audience that much easier when you write about the issue. For example, the student writer who was concerned about long-standing issues of homelessness and lack of educational opportunity connected to his readers by citing recent statistics and giving the problem of homelessness a face: "The children . . . went to school after less than three hours of sleep. They wore the same wrinkled clothes that they had worn the day before." If your issue does not immediately fulfill the criteria of relevance and timeliness, you need to take that into consideration as you continue your reading and research on the issue. Ask yourself, "What is on people's minds these days?" "What do they need to know about?" Think about why the issue matters to you, and imagine why it might matter to others. By the time you write, you should be prepared to make the issue relevant for your readers.

In addition to understanding the situation and defining the issue that you feel is most relevant and timely, you can formulate an issue-based question that can help you think through what you might be interested in writing about. This question should be specific enough to guide inquiry into what others have written. An issue-based question can also help you accomplish the following:

- clarify what you know about the issue and what you still need to know;
- guide your inquiry with a clear focus;
- organize your inquiry around a specific issue;
- develop an argument (rather than simply collecting information) by asking *How?*, *Why?*, *Should?*, or *To what extent is this true (or not true)?*;
- consider who your audience is;
- determine what resources you have, so that you can ask a question that you will be able to answer with the resources available to you.

A good question develops out of an issue, some fundamental tension that you identify within a conversation. In "Doing Nothing Is Something," Anna Quindlen identifies a problem that middle-class parents need to know about: that overscheduling their children's lives may limit their children's potential for developing their creativity. As she explores the reasons why children do not have sufficient downtime, she raises a question that encourages parents to consider what would happen if they gave their children time to do nothing: "Might it be even more enriching for their children to stay at home and do nothing?" (para. 11). Through identifying what is at issue, you should begin to understand for whom it is an issue—for whom you are answering the question. In turn, the answer to your question will help you craft your thesis.

In the following section, we trace the steps one of our students took to formulate an issue-based question on the broad topic of language diversity. Although we present the steps in sequence, be aware that they are guidelines only: The steps often overlap, and there is a good deal of room for rethinking and refining along the way.

■ Refine Your Topic

Generally speaking, a **topic** is the subject you want to write about. For example, homelessness, tests, and violence are all topics. So are urban homelessness, standardized tests, and video game violence. And so are homelessness in New York City, aptitude tests versus achievement tests, and mayhem in the video game *Grand Theft Auto*. As our list suggests, even a specific topic needs refining into an issue before it can be explored effectively in writing.

The topic our student wanted to focus on was language diversity, a subject her linguistics class had been discussing. She was fascinated by the extraordinary range of languages spoken in the United States, not just by immigrant groups but by native speakers whose dialects and varieties of English are considered nonstandard. She herself had relatives for whom English was not a first language. She began refining her topic by putting her thoughts into words:

> I want to describe the experience of being raised in a home where non–Standard English is spoken.

> I'd like to know the benefits and liabilities of growing up bilingual.

> I am curious to know what it's like to live in a community of nonnative speakers of English while trying to make a living in a country where the dominant language is English.

Although she had yet to identify an issue, her attempts to articulate what interested her about the topic were moving her toward the situation of people in the United States who don't speak Standard English or don't have English as their first language.

■ Explain Your Interest in the Topic

At this point, the student encountered E. D. Hirsch's *Cultural Literacy* in her reading, which had both a provocative and a clarifying effect on her thinking. She began to build on and extend Hirsch's ideas. Reacting to Hirsch's assumption that students should acquire the same base of knowledge and write in Standard Written English, her first, somewhat mischievous thought was, "I wonder what Hirsch would think about cultural literacy being taught in a bilingual classroom?" But then her thinking took another turn, and she began to contemplate the effect of Hirsch's cultural-literacy agenda on speakers whose English is not standard or for whom English is not a first language. She used a demographic fact that she had learned in her linguistics class in her explanation of her interest in the topic: "I'm curious about the consequences of limiting language diversity when the presence of ethnic minorities in our educational system is growing."

■ Identify an Issue

The more she thought about Hirsch's ideas, and the more she read about language diversity, the more concerned our student grew. It seemed to her that Hirsch's interest in producing students who all share the same base of knowledge and all write in Standard Written English was in tension with her sense that this kind of approach places a burden on people whose first language is not English. That tension clarified the issue for her. In identifying the issue, she wrote:

> Hirsch's book actually sets some priorities, most notably through his list of words and phrases that form the foundations of what it means to be "American." However, this list certainly overlooks several crucial influences in American culture. Most oversights generally come at the expense of the minority populations.

These two concerns—with inclusion and with exclusion—helped focus the student's inquiry.

■ Formulate Your Topic as a Question

To further define her inquiry, the student formulated her topic as a question that pointed toward an argument: "To what extent can E. D. Hirsch's notion of 'cultural literacy' coexist with our country's principles of democracy and inclusion?" Notice that her choice of the phrase *To what extent* implies that both goals do not go hand in hand. If she had asked, "Can common culture coexist with pluralism?" her phrasing would imply that a yes or no answer would suffice, possibly foreclosing avenues of inquiry and certainly ignoring the complexity of the issue.

Instead, despite her misgivings about the implications of Hirsch's agenda, the student suspended judgment, opening the way to genuine inquiry. She acknowledged the usefulness and value of sharing a common language and conceded that Hirsch's points were well taken. She wrote:

> Some sort of unification is necessary. Language, . . . on the most fundamental level of human interaction, demands some compromise and chosen guidelines. . . . How can we learn from one another if we cannot even say hello to each other?

Suspending judgment led her to recognize the complexity of the issue, and her willingness to examine the issue from different perspectives indicated the empathy that is a central component of developing a conversational argument.

■ Acknowledge Your Audience

This student's question ("To what extent can E. D. Hirsch's notion of 'cultural literacy' coexist with our country's principles of democracy and inclusion?") also acknowledged an audience. By invoking cultural literacy, she assumed an audience of readers who are familiar with Hirsch's ideas, probably including policymakers and educational administrators. In gesturing toward democracy, she cast her net very wide: Most Americans probably admire the "principles of democracy." But in specifying inclusion as a democratic principle, she wisely linked all Americans who believe in democratic principles, including the parents of schoolchildren, with all people who have reason to feel excluded by Hirsch's ideas, especially nonnative speakers of English, among them immigrants from Mexico and speakers of African American Vernacular English. Thus, this student was acknowledging an audience of policymakers, administrators, parents (both mainstream and marginalized), and those who knew about and perhaps supported cultural literacy.

Steps to Formulating an Issue-Based Question

1 **Refine your topic.** Examine your topic from different perspectives. For example, what are the causes of homelessness? What are its consequences?

2 **Explain your interest in the topic.** Explore the source of your interest in this topic and what you want to learn.

3 **Identify an issue.** Determine what is open to dispute.

4 **Formulate your topic as a question.** Use your question to focus your inquiry.

5 **Acknowledge your audience.** Reflect on what readers may know about the issue, why they may be interested, and what you would like to teach them.

A Practice Sequence: Formulating an Issue-Based Question

As you start developing your own issue-based question, it might be useful to practice a five-step process that begins with a topic, a word or phrase that describes the focus of your interests. Here, apply the process to the one-word topic *homelessness*.

1   Expand your topic into a phrase. "I am interested in the *consequences* of homelessness," "I want to *describe* what it means to be homeless," or "I am interested in discussing the *cause* of homelessness."

2   Explain your interest in this topic. "I am interested in the consequences of homelessness because homelessness challenges democratic principles of fairness."

3 Identify an issue. "The persistence of homelessness contradicts my belief in social justice."

4 Formulate your topic as a question. "To what extent can we allow homelessness to persist in a democratic nation that prides itself on providing equal opportunity to all?"

5 Acknowledge your audience. "I am interested in the consequences of homelessness because I want people who believe in democracy to understand that we need to work harder to make sure that everyone has access to food, shelter, and employment."

The answer to the question you formulate in step 4 should lead to an assertion, your main claim, or *thesis*. For example, you could state your main claim this way: "Although homelessness persists as a widespread problem in our nation, we must develop policies that eliminate homelessness, ensuring that everyone has access to food, shelter, and employment. This is especially important in a democracy that embraces social justice and equality."

The thesis introduces a problem and makes an assertion that you will need to support: "We must develop policies that eliminate homelessness, ensuring that everyone has access to food, shelter, and employment." What is at issue? Not everyone would agree that policies must be implemented to solve the problem. In fact, many would argue that homelessness is an individual problem, that individuals must take responsibility for lifting themselves out of poverty, homelessness, and unemployment. Of course, you would need to read quite a bit to reach this final stage of formulating your thesis.

Try using the five-step process we describe above to formulate your own topic as a question, or try formulating the following topics as questions:

- violence in video games
- recycling
- the popularity of a cultural phenomenon (a book, a film, a performer, an icon)
- standardized tests
- professional sports injuries
- town-gown relationships
- media representation and gender
- government and religion
- vegetarianism

AN ACADEMIC ESSAY FOR ANALYSIS

The following essay by William Deresiewicz provides an intriguing academic extension of the topic that Anna Quindlen writes about (p. 123): the need for the young to have solitary, unscheduled time. His essay illustrates many of the strategies we have discussed thus far: raising questions, stating a thesis by placing an argument in the stream of a broader conversation, using evidence to support his claims. As you read Deresiewicz's essay, you might use the following questions as a guide:

- What is Deresiewicz's thesis? Would you characterize his claim as one of fact? Value?
- What types of evidence does he use to support his claim?
- What do Deresiewicz's vocabulary and citations indicate about his target audience?
- What does Deresiewicz want his readers to do or think about?

WILLIAM DERESIEWICZ

The End of Solitude

William Deresiewicz taught English at Yale University from 1998 to 2008. He is now a contributing writer at *The Nation* and was nominated for a 2009 National Magazine Award for his reviews and criticism. His essay "The End of Solitude" appeared in *The Chronicle of Higher Education* in January 2009 and represents one of many debates about literacy that scholars have waged concerning the benefits and limits of new technologies. Deresiewicz observes that technology fulfills a human impulse to be known, to be connected with others. Posting on social media enables us to be visible and helps validate who we are as individuals. However, he worries that this instinct to be connected also has an adverse effect: We lose a sense of solitude and the space he believes we all need to have in order to understand who we are, what we believe, and what we value. He worries, too, that a new generation does not see the point of solitude because so many young people equate solitude with loneliness.

■   ■   ■

What does the contemporary self want? The camera has created a culture of celebrity; the computer is creating a culture of connectivity. As the two technologies converge — broadband tipping the Web from text to image, social-networking sites spreading the mesh of interconnection ever wider — the two cultures betray a common impulse. Celebrity and connectivity are both ways of becoming known. This is what the contemporary self wants. It wants to be recognized, wants to be connected: It wants to be visible. If not to the millions, on *Survivor* or *Oprah*, then to the hundreds, on Twitter or Facebook. This is the quality that validates us, this is how we become real to ourselves—by being seen by others. The great contemporary terror is anonymity. If Lionel Trilling was right, if the property that grounded the self, in Romanticism, was sincerity, and in modernism it was authenticity, then in postmodernism it is visibility.

So we live exclusively in relation to others, and what disappears from our lives is solitude. Technology is taking away our privacy and our concentration, but it is also taking away our ability to be alone. Though I shouldn't say taking away. We are doing this to ourselves; we are discarding these riches as fast as we can. I was told by one of her older relatives that a teenager I know had sent 3,000 text messages one recent month. That's 100 a day, or about one every 10 waking minutes, morning, noon, and night, weekdays and weekends, class time, lunch time, homework time, and toothbrushing time. So on average, she's never alone for more than 10 minutes at once. Which means, she's never alone. 2

I once asked my students about the place that solitude has in their lives. One of them admitted that she finds the prospect of being alone so unsettling that she'll sit with a friend even when she has a paper to write. Another said, why would anyone want to be alone? 3

To that remarkable question, history offers a number of answers. Man may be a social animal, but solitude has traditionally been a societal value. In particular, the act of being alone has been understood as an essential dimension of religious experience, albeit one restricted to a self-selected few. Through the solitude of rare spirits, the collective renews its relationship with divinity. The prophet and the hermit, the sadhu and the yogi, pursue their vision quests, invite their trances, in desert or forest or cave. For the still, small voice speaks only in silence. Social life is a bustle of petty concerns, a jostle of quotidian interests, and religious institutions are no exception. You cannot hear God when people are chattering at you, and the divine word, their pretensions notwithstanding, demurs at descending on the monarch and the priest. Communal experience is the human norm, but the solitary encounter with God is the egregious act that refreshes that norm. (Egregious, for no man is a prophet in his own land. Tiresias was reviled before he was vindicated, Teresa interrogated before she was canonized.) Religious solitude is a kind of self-correcting social mechanism, a way of burning out the underbrush of moral habit and spiritual custom. The seer returns with new tablets or new dances, his face bright with the old truth. 4

Like other religious values, solitude was democratized by the Reformation and secularized by Romanticism. In Marilynne Robinson's interpretation, Calvinism created the modern self by focusing the soul inward, leaving it to encounter God, like a prophet of old, in "profound isolation." To her enumeration of Calvin, Marguerite de Navarre, and 5

Milton as pioneering early-modern selves we can add Montaigne, Hamlet, and even Don Quixote. The last figure alerts us to reading's essential role in this transformation, the printing press serving an analogous function in the sixteenth and subsequent centuries to that of television and the Internet in our own. Reading, as Robinson puts it, "is an act of great inwardness and subjectivity." "The soul encountered itself in response to a text, first Genesis or Matthew and then *Paradise Lost* or *Leaves of Grass*." With Protestantism and printing, the quest for the divine voice became available to, even incumbent upon, everyone.

But it is with Romanticism that solitude achieved its greatest   *6* cultural salience, becoming both literal and literary. Protestant solitude is still only figurative. Rousseau and Wordsworth made it physical. The self was now encountered not in God but in Nature, and to encounter Nature one had to go to it. And go to it with a special sensibility: The poet displaced the saint as social seer and cultural model. But because Romanticism also inherited the eighteenth-century idea of social sympathy, Romantic solitude existed in a dialectical relationship with sociability—if less for Rousseau and still less for Thoreau, the most famous solitary of all, then certainly for Wordsworth, Melville, Whitman, and many others. For Emerson, "the soul environs itself with friends, that it may enter into a grander self-acquaintance or solitude; and it goes alone, for a season, that it may exalt its conversation or society." The Romantic practice of solitude is neatly captured by Trilling's "sincerity": the belief that the self is validated by a congruity of public appearance and private essence, one that stabilizes its relationship with both itself and others. Especially, as Emerson suggests, one beloved other. Hence the famous Romantic friendship pairs: Goethe and Schiller, Wordsworth and Coleridge, Hawthorne and Melville.

Modernism decoupled this dialectic. Its notion of solitude was   *7* harsher, more adversarial, more isolating. As a model of the self and its interactions, Hume's social sympathy gave way to Pater's thick wall of personality and Freud's narcissism—the sense that the soul, self-enclosed and inaccessible to others, can't choose but be alone. With exceptions, like Woolf, the modernists fought shy of friendship. Joyce and Proust disparaged it; D. H. Lawrence was wary of it; the modernist friendship pairs— Conrad and Ford, Eliot and Pound, Hemingway and Fitzgerald—were altogether cooler than their Romantic counterparts. The world was now understood as an assault on the self, and with good reason.

The Romantic ideal of solitude developed in part as a reaction   *8* to the emergence of the modern city. In modernism, the city is not only more menacing than ever, it has become inescapable, a labyrinth: Eliot's London, Joyce's Dublin. The mob, the human mass, presses in. Hell is other people. The soul is forced back into itself—hence the development of a more austere, more embattled form of self-validation, Trilling's "authenticity," where the essential relationship is only with oneself. (Just as there are few good friendships in modernism, so are there few good marriages.) Solitude becomes, more than ever, the arena of heroic self-discovery, a voyage through interior realms made vast and terrifying by Nietzschean and Freudian insights. To achieve authenticity is to look upon these visions without flinching; Trilling's exemplar here is Kurtz. Protestant self-examination becomes Freudian analysis, and the culture hero, once a prophet of God and then a poet of Nature, is now a novelist of self—a Dostoyevsky, a Joyce, a Proust.

But we no longer live in the modernist city, and our great fear is not submersion by the mass but isolation from the herd. Urbanization gave way to suburbanization, and with it the universal threat of loneliness. What technologies of transportation exacerbated—we could live farther and farther apart—technologies of communication redressed—we could bring ourselves closer and closer together. Or at least, so we have imagined. The first of these technologies, the first simulacrum of proximity, was the telephone. "Reach out and touch someone." But through the 1970s and 1980s, our isolation grew. Suburbs, sprawling ever farther, became exurbs. Families grew smaller or splintered apart, mothers left the home to work. The electronic hearth became the television in every room. Even in childhood, certainly in adolescence, we were each trapped inside our own cocoon. Soaring crime rates, and even more sharply escalating rates of moral panic, pulled children off the streets. The idea that you could go outside and run around the neighborhood with your friends, once unquestionable, has now become unthinkable. The child who grew up between the world wars as part of an extended family within a tight-knit urban community became the grandparent of a kid who sat alone in front of a big television, in a big house, on a big lot. We were lost in space.

Under those circumstances, the Internet arrived as an incalculable blessing. We should never forget that. It has allowed isolated people to communicate with one another and marginalized people to find one another. The busy parent can stay in touch with far-flung friends. The gay teenager no longer has to feel like a freak. But as the Internet's dimensionality has grown, it has quickly become too much of a good thing. Ten years ago we were writing e-mail messages on desktop computers and transmitting them over dial-up connections. Now we are sending text messages on our cell phones, posting pictures on our Facebook pages, and following complete strangers on Twitter. A constant stream of mediated contact, virtual, notional, or simulated, keeps us wired in to the electronic hive—though contact, or at least two-way contact, seems increasingly beside the point. The goal now,

9

10

it seems, is simply to become known, to turn oneself into a sort of miniature celebrity. How many friends do I have on Facebook? How many people are reading my blog? How many Google hits does my name generate? Visibility secures our self-esteem, becoming a substitute, twice removed, for genuine connection. Not long ago, it was easy to feel lonely. Now, it is impossible to be alone.

As a result, we are losing both sides of the Romantic dialectic.   *11* What does friendship mean when you have 532 "friends"? How does it enhance my sense of closeness when my Facebook News Feed tells me that Sally Smith (whom I haven't seen since high school, and wasn't all that friendly with even then) "is making coffee and staring off into space"? My students told me they have little time for intimacy. And of course, they have no time at all for solitude.

But at least friendship, if not intimacy, is still something they want.   *12* As jarring as the new dispensation may be for people in their 30s and 40s, the real problem is that it has become completely natural for people in their teens and 20s. Young people today seem to have no desire for solitude, have never heard of it, can't imagine why it would be worth having. In fact, their use of technology—or to be fair, our use of technology—seems to involve a constant effort to stave off the possibility of solitude, a continuous attempt, as we sit alone at our computers, to maintain the imaginative presence of others. As long ago as 1952, Trilling wrote about "the modern fear of being cut off from the social group even for a moment." Now we have equipped ourselves with the means to prevent that fear from ever being realized. Which does not mean that we have put it to rest. Quite the contrary. Remember my student, who couldn't even write a paper by herself. The more we keep aloneness at bay, the less are we able to deal with it and the more terrifying it gets.

There is an analogy, it seems to me, with the previous generation's   *13* experience of boredom. The two emotions, loneliness and boredom, are closely allied. They are also both characteristically modern. The *Oxford English Dictionary*'s earliest citations of either word, at least in the contemporary sense, date from the nineteenth century. Suburbanization, by eliminating the stimulation as well as the sociability of urban or traditional village life, exacerbated the tendency to both. But the great age of boredom, I believe, came in with television, precisely because television was designed to palliate that feeling. Boredom is not a necessary consequence of having nothing to do, it is only the negative experience of that state. Television, by obviating the need to learn how to make use of one's lack of occupation, precludes one from ever discovering how to enjoy it. In fact, it renders that condition fearsome, its prospect intolerable. You are terrified of being bored—so you turn on the television.

I speak from experience. I grew up in the 1960s and 1970s, the *14* age of television. I was trained to be bored; boredom was cultivated within me like a precious crop. (It has been said that consumer society wants to condition us to feel bored, since boredom creates a market for stimulation.) It took me years to discover—and my nervous system will never fully adjust to this idea; I still have to fight against boredom, am permanently damaged in this respect—that having nothing to do doesn't have to be a bad thing. The alternative to boredom is what Whitman called idleness: a passive receptivity to the world.

So it is with the current generation's experience of being alone. *15* That is precisely the recognition implicit in the idea of solitude, which is to loneliness what idleness is to boredom. Loneliness is not the absence of company, it is grief over that absence. The lost sheep is lonely; the shepherd is not lonely. But the Internet is as powerful a machine for the production of loneliness as television is for the manufacture of boredom. If six hours of television a day creates the aptitude for boredom, the inability to sit still, a hundred text messages a day creates the aptitude for loneliness, the inability to be by yourself. Some degree of boredom and loneliness is to be expected, especially among young people, given the way our human environment has been attenuated. But technology amplifies those tendencies. You could call your schoolmates when I was a teenager, but you couldn't call them 100 times a day. You could get together with your friends when I was in college, but you couldn't always get together with them when you wanted to, for the simple reason that you couldn't always find them. If boredom is the great emotion of the TV generation, loneliness is the great emotion of the Web generation. We lost the ability to be still, our capacity for idleness. They have lost the ability to be alone, their capacity for solitude.

And losing solitude, what have they lost? First, the propensity for *16* introspection, that examination of the self that the Puritans, and the Romantics, and the modernists (and Socrates, for that matter) placed at the center of spiritual life—of wisdom, of conduct. Thoreau called it fishing "in the Walden Pond of [our] own natures," "bait[ing our] hooks with darkness." Lost, too, is the related propensity for sustained reading. The Internet brought text back into a televisual world, but it brought it back on terms dictated by that world—that is, by its remapping of our attention spans. Reading now means skipping and skimming; five minutes on the same Web page is considered an eternity. This is not reading as Marilynne Robinson described it: the encounter with a second self in the silence of mental solitude.

But we no longer believe in the solitary mind. If the Romantics had *17* Hume and the modernists had Freud, the current psychological model—

and this should come as no surprise—is that of the networked or social mind. Evolutionary psychology tells us that our brains developed to interpret complex social signals. According to David Brooks, that reliable index of the social-scientific zeitgeist, cognitive scientists tell us that "our decision-making is powerfully influenced by social context"; neuroscientists, that we have "permeable minds" that function in part through a process of "deep imitation"; psychologists, that "we are organized by our attachments"; sociologists, that our behavior is affected by "the power of social networks." The ultimate implication is that there is no mental space that is not social (contemporary social science dovetailing here with postmodern critical theory). One of the most striking things about the way young people relate to one another today is that they no longer seem to believe in the existence of Thoreau's "darkness."

The MySpace page, with its shrieking typography and clamorous   18
imagery, has replaced the journal and the letter as a way of creating and communicating one's sense of self. The suggestion is not only that such communication is to be made to the world at large rather than to oneself or one's intimates, or graphically rather than verbally, or performatively rather than narratively or analytically, but also that it can be made completely. Today's young people seem to feel that they can make themselves fully known to one another. They seem to lack a sense of their own depths, and of the value of keeping them hidden.

If they didn't, they would understand that solitude enables us to   19
secure the integrity of the self as well as to explore it. Few have shown this more beautifully than Woolf. In the middle of *Mrs. Dalloway*, between her navigation of the streets and her orchestration of the party, between the urban jostle and the social bustle, Clarissa goes up, "like a nun withdrawing," to her attic room. Like a nun: She returns to a state that she herself thinks of as a kind of virginity. This does not mean she's a prude. Virginity is classically the outward sign of spiritual inviolability, of a self untouched by the world, a soul that has preserved its integrity by refusing to descend into the chaos and self-division of sexual and social relations. It is the mark of the saint and the monk, of Hippolytus and Antigone and Joan of Arc. Solitude is both the social image of that state and the means by which we can approximate it. And the supreme image in *Mrs. Dalloway* of the dignity of solitude itself is the old woman whom Clarissa catches sight of through her window. "Here was one room," she thinks, "there another." We are not merely social beings. We are each also separate, each solitary, each alone in our own room, each miraculously our unique selves and mysteriously enclosed in that selfhood.

To remember this, to hold oneself apart from society, is to begin   20
to think one's way beyond it. Solitude, Emerson said, "is to genius

the stern friend." "He who should inspire and lead his race must be defended from traveling with the souls of other men, from living, breathing, reading, and writing in the daily, time-worn yoke of their opinions." One must protect oneself from the momentum of intellectual and moral consensus—especially, Emerson added, during youth. "God is alone," Thoreau said, "but the Devil, he is far from being alone; he sees a great deal of company; he is legion." The university was to be praised, Emerson believed, if only because it provided its charges with "a separate chamber and fire"—the physical space of solitude. Today, of course, universities do everything they can to keep their students from being alone, lest they perpetrate self-destructive acts, and also, perhaps, unfashionable thoughts. But no real excellence, personal or social, artistic, philosophical, scientific, or moral, can arise without solitude. "The saint and poet seek privacy," Emerson said, "to ends the most public and universal." We are back to the seer, seeking signposts for the future in splendid isolation.

Solitude isn't easy, and isn't for everyone. It has undoubtedly never been the province of more than a few. "I believe," Thoreau said, "that men are generally still a little afraid of the dark." Teresa and Tiresias will always be the exceptions, or to speak in more relevant terms, the young people—and they still exist—who prefer to loaf and invite their soul, who step to the beat of a different drummer. But if solitude disappears as a social value and social idea, will even the exceptions remain possible? Still, one is powerless to reverse the drift of the culture. One can only save oneself—and whatever else happens, one can still always do that. But it takes a willingness to be unpopular. 21

The last thing to say about solitude is that it isn't very polite. Thoreau knew that the "doubleness" that solitude cultivates, the ability to stand back and observe life dispassionately, is apt to make us a little unpleasant to our fellows, to say nothing of the offense implicit in avoiding their company. But then, he didn't worry overmuch about being genial. He didn't even like having to talk to people three times a day, at meals; one can only imagine what he would have made of text-messaging. We, however, have made of geniality—the weak smile, the polite interest, the fake invitation—a cardinal virtue. Friendship may be slipping from our grasp, but our friendliness is universal. Not for nothing does "gregarious" mean "part of the herd." But Thoreau understood that securing one's self-possession was worth a few wounded feelings. He may have put his neighbors off, but at least he was sure of himself. Those who would find solitude must not be afraid to stand alone. 22

Writing as a Reader

1. Recast Deresiewicz's essay as Anna Quindlen might in her *Newsweek* column. Obviously, her *Newsweek* column is much shorter (an important constraint). She also writes for a more general audience than Deresiewicz, and her tone is quite different. To strengthen your sense of her approach, you may want to browse some of Quindlen's other essays in editions of *Newsweek* or in some of her essay collections listed in the headnote on page 123.

2. Recast Deresiewicz's essay in terms of a writer you read regularly—for example, a columnist in your local newspaper or a blogger in some online venue. Use your imagination. What is the audience, and how will you have to present the issue to engage and persuade them?

From Formulating to Developing a Thesis

A cademic writing explores complex issues that grow out of relevant, timely conversations in which something is at stake. An academic writer reads as a writer to understand the issues, situations, and questions that lead other writers to make claims. Readers expect academic writers to take a clear, specific, logical stand on an issue, and they evaluate how writers support their claims and anticipate counterarguments. The logical stand is the **thesis**, an assertion that academic writers make at the beginning of what they write and then support with evidence throughout their essay. The illustrations and examples that a writer includes must relate to and support the thesis. Thus, a thesis encompasses all of the information writers use to further their arguments; it is not simply a single assertion at the beginning of an essay.

One of our students aptly described the thesis using the metaphor of a shish kebab: The thesis runs through every paragraph, holding the paragraphs together, just as a skewer runs through and holds the ingredients of a shish kebab together. Moreover, the thesis serves as a signpost throughout an essay, reminding readers what the argument is and why the writer has included evidence—examples, illustrations, quotations—relevant to that argument.

An academic thesis

- makes an assertion that is clearly defined, focused, and supported.
- reflects an awareness of the conversation from which the writer has taken up the issue.
- is placed at the beginning of the essay.

- runs through every paragraph like the skewer in a shish kebab.
- acknowledges points of view that differ from the writer's own, reflecting the complexity of the issue.
- demonstrates an awareness of the readers' assumptions and anticipates possible counterarguments.
- conveys a significant fresh perspective.

It is a myth that writers first come up with a thesis and then write their essays. The reality is that writers use issue-based questions to read, learn, and develop a thesis throughout the process of writing. Through revising and discussing their ideas, writers hone their thesis, making sure that it threads through every paragraph of the final draft. The position writers ultimately take in writing—their thesis—comes at the end of the writing process, after not one draft but many.

WORKING VERSUS DEFINITIVE THESES

Writers are continually challenged by the need to establish their purpose and to make a clear and specific assertion of it. To reach that assertion, you must first engage in a prolonged process of inquiry, aided by a well-formulated question. The question serves as a tool for inquiry that will help you formulate your **working thesis**, your first attempt at an assertion of your position. A working thesis is valuable in the early stages of writing because it helps you read selectively, in the same way that your issue-based question guides your inquiry. Reading raises questions, helping you see what you know and need to know, and challenging you to read on.

Never accept your working thesis as your final position. Instead, continue testing your assertion as you read and write, and modify your working thesis as necessary. A more definitive thesis will come once you are satisfied that you have examined the issue from multiple perspectives.

For example, one of our students wanted to study representations of femininity in the media. In particular, she focused on why the Barbie doll has become an icon of femininity despite what many cultural critics consider Barbie's "outrageous and ultimately unattainable physical characteristics." Our student's working thesis suggested she would develop an argument about the need for change:

> The harmful implications of ongoing exposure to these unattainable ideals, such as low self-esteem, eating disorders, unhealthy body image, and acceptance of violence, make urgent the need for change.

The student assumed that her research would lead her to argue that Barbie's unattainable proportions have a damaging effect on women's self-image and that something needs to be done about it. However, as she read scholarly research to support her tentative thesis, she realized that a more compelling project would be less Barbie-centric. Instead, she chose to examine the broader phenomenon of how the idea of femininity is created and reinforced by society. That is, her personal interest in Barbie was supplanted by her discoveries about cultural norms of beauty and the power they have to influence self-perception and behavior. In her final draft, this was her definitive thesis:

> Although evidence may be provided to argue that gender is an innate characteristic, I will show that it is actually the result of one's actions, which are then labeled *masculine* or *feminine* according to society's definitions of ideal gender. Furthermore, I will discuss the communication of such definitions through the media, specifically in music videos, on TV, and in magazines, and the harmful implications of being exposed to these ideals.

Instead of arguing for change, the student chose to show her readers how they were being manipulated, leaving it to them to decide what actions they might want to take.

DEVELOPING A WORKING THESIS: FOUR MODELS

What are some ways to develop a working thesis? We suggest four models that may help you organize the information you gather in response to the question guiding your inquiry.

■ The Correcting-Misinterpretations Model

This model is used to correct writers whose arguments you believe have misconstrued one or more important aspects of an issue. The thesis typically takes the form of a factual claim. Consider this example and the words we have underlined:

> <u>Although scholars have addressed curriculum</u> to explain low achievement in schools, <u>they have failed to fully appreciate the impact of limited resources</u> to fund up-to-date textbooks, quality teachers, and computers. Therefore, reform in schools must focus on economic need as well as curriculum.

The clause beginning with "Although" lays out the assumption that many scholars make, that curriculum explains low educational achievement; the clause beginning with "they have failed" identifies the error those scholars have made by ignoring the economic reasons for low achievement in schools. Notice that the structure of the sentence reinforces the author's position. He explains what he sees as the faulty assumption in a subordinate clause and reserves the main clause for his own position. The two clauses indicate that different authors hold conflicting opinions. Note that the writer could have used a phrase such as "they [scholars] have *understated* the impact of limited resources" as a way to reframe the problem in his thesis. In crafting your thesis, choose words that signal to readers that you are correcting others' ideas, or even misinterpretations, without being dismissive. One more thing: Although it is a common myth that a thesis can be phrased in a single sentence (a legacy of the five-paragraph theme, we suspect), this example shows that a thesis can be written in two (or more) sentences.

■ The Filling-the-Gap Model

The gap model points to what other writers may have overlooked or ignored in discussing a given issue. The gap model typically makes a claim of value. Consider this student's argument that discussions of cultural diversity in the United States are often framed in terms of black and white. Our underlining indicates the gap the writer has identified:

> If America is truly a "melting pot" of cultures, as it is often called, then why is it that stories and events seem only to be in black and white? Why is it that when history courses are taught about the period of the civil rights movement, only the memoirs of African Americans are read, like those of Melba Pattillo Beals and Ida Mae Holland? Where are the works of Maxine Hong Kingston, who tells the story of alienation and segregation in schools through the eyes of a Chinese child? African Americans were denied the right to vote, and many other citizenship rights; but Chinese Americans were denied even the opportunity to become citizens. I am not diminishing the issue of discrimination against African Americans, or belittling the struggles they went through. I simply want to call attention to discrimination against other minority groups and their often-overlooked struggles to achieve equality.

In the student's thesis, the gap in people's knowledge stems from their limited understanding of history. They need to understand that many minority groups were denied their rights.

A variation on the gap model also occurs when a writer suggests that although something might appear to be the case, a closer look reveals something different. For example: "Although it would *appear* that women have achieved equality in the workplace, their paychecks suggest that this is not true."

One of our students examined two poems by the same author that appeared to contradict each other. She noticed a gap others had not seen:

> In both "The Albatross" and "Beauty," Charles Baudelaire chooses to explore the plight of the poet. Interestingly, despite their common author, the two poems' portrayals of the poet's struggles appear contradictory. "The Albatross" seems to give a somewhat sympathetic glimpse into the exile of the poet — the "winged voyager" so awkward in the ordinary world. "Beauty" takes what appears to be a less forgiving stance: The poet here is docile, simply a mirror. Although both pieces depict the poet's struggles, a closer examination demonstrates how the portrayals differ.

In stating her thesis, the student indicates that although readers might expect Baudelaire's images of poets to be similar, a closer examination of his words would prove them wrong.

■ The Modifying-What-Others-Have-Said Model

The modification model of thesis writing assumes that mutual understanding is possible. For example, in proposing a change in policy, one student asserts:

> Although scholars have claimed that the only sure way to reverse the cycle of homelessness in America is to provide an adequate education, we need to build on this work, providing school-to-work programs that ensure graduates have access to employment.

Here the writer seeks to modify other writers' claims, suggesting that education alone does not solve the problem of homelessness. The challenge he sets for himself is to understand the complexity of the problem by building on and extending the ideas of others. In effect, he is in a constructive conversation with those whose work he wants to build on, helping readers see that he shares common ground with the other writers and that he hopes to find a mutually acceptable solution to the agreed-on problem.

■ The Hypothesis-Testing Model

The hypothesis-testing model begins with the assumption that writers may have good reasons for supporting their arguments, but that there are also a number of legitimate reasons that explain why something is, or is not, the case. The questions motivating your research will often lead you to a number of possible answers, but none are necessarily more correct than others. That is, the evidence is based on a hypothesis that researchers will continue to test by examining individual cases through an inductive method until the evidence refutes that hypothesis.

For example, over the last decade, researchers have generated a number of hypotheses to explain the causes of climate change. Some have argued that climate change, or global warming, can be explained by natural causes, that change is a cyclical process. Those who adopt such a view might use evidence to demonstrate that oceans produce heat and that change can be attributed to a steady increase in heat production over time. Others have persuasively shown that humans have caused global warming by burning fossil fuels that increase the amount of carbon in the air, which creates what scientists call the "greenhouse effect." Each assertion is based on a set of inferences from observation and the data available to test each hypothesis. Moreover, the truth value of any assertion is based on the probability that global warming can be attributed to any one cause or explanation.

The hypothesis-testing model assumes that the questions you raise will likely lead you to multiple answers that compete for your attention. The following is one way to formulate such an argument in which you examine rival hypotheses before coming to a conclusion.

> Some people explain *this* by suggesting *that*, but a close analysis of the problem reveals several compelling, but competing explanations.

You may not find a definitive explanation, so you will need to sort through the evidence you find, develop an argument, and acknowledge the reasonable counterarguments that critical readers will raise. In the end, you are not really proving that something is the case, such as the causes of global warming, but you are helping readers understand what you see as the best case given the available evidence.

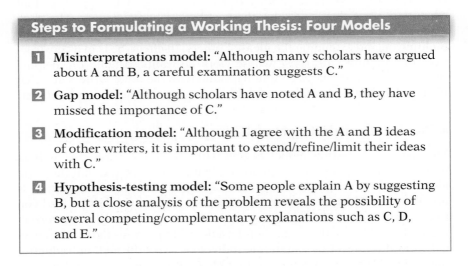

Steps to Formulating a Working Thesis: Four Models

1 **Misinterpretations model:** "Although many scholars have argued about A and B, a careful examination suggests C."

2 **Gap model:** "Although scholars have noted A and B, they have missed the importance of C."

3 **Modification model:** "Although I agree with the A and B ideas of other writers, it is important to extend/refine/limit their ideas with C."

4 **Hypothesis-testing model:** "Some people explain A by suggesting B, but a close analysis of the problem reveals the possibility of several competing/complementary explanations such as C, D, and E."

A Practice Sequence: Identifying Types of Theses

Below is a series of working theses. Read each one and then identify the model—misinterpretations, gap, modification, or hypothesis-testing—that it represents.

1 A number of studies indicate that violence on television has a detrimental effect on adolescent behavior. However, few researchers have examined key environmental factors like peer

pressure, music, and home life. In fact, I would argue that many researchers have oversimplified the problem.

2   Although research indicates that an increasing number of African American and Hispanic students are dropping out of high school, researchers have failed to fully grasp the reasons why this has occurred.

3   I want to argue that studies supporting single-sex education are relatively sound. However, we don't really know the long-term effects of single-sex education, particularly on young women's career paths.

4   Although recent studies of voting patterns in the United States indicate that young people between the ages of 18 and 24 are apathetic, I want to suggest that not all of the reasons these studies provide are valid.

5   Indeed, it's not surprising that students are majoring in fields that will enable them to get a job after graduation. But students may not be as pragmatic as we think. Many students choose majors because they feel that learning is an important end in itself.

6   Some reformers have assumed that increasing competition will force public schools to improve the quality of education, but it seems that a number of recent initiatives can be used to explain why students have begun to flourish in math and reading, particularly in the primary grades.

7   It is clear that cities need to clean up the dilapidated housing projects that were built over half a century ago; but few, if any, studies have examined the effects of doing so on the life chances of those people who are being displaced.

8   In addition to its efforts to advance the cause of social justice in the new global economy, the university must make a commitment to ending poverty on the edge of campus.

9   Although the writer offers evidence to explain the sources of illiteracy in America, he overstates his case when he ignores other factors, among them history, culture, and economic well-being. Therefore, I will argue that we place the discussion in a broader context.

10   More and more policymakers argue that English should be the national language in the United States. Although I agree that English is important, we should not limit people's right to maintain their own linguistic and cultural identity.

ESTABLISHING A CONTEXT FOR A THESIS

In addition to defining the purpose and focus of an essay, a thesis must set up a **context** for the writer's claim. The process of establishing a background for understanding an issue typically involves four steps:

1. Establish that the topic of conversation, the issue, is current and relevant—that it is on people's minds or should be.

2. Briefly summarize what others have said to show that you are familiar with the topic or issue.

3. Explain what you see as the problem—a misinterpretation, a gap, or a modification that needs to be made in how others have addressed the topic or issue—perhaps by raising the questions you believe need to be answered.

4. State your thesis, suggesting that your view on the issue may present readers with something new to think about as it builds on and extends what others have argued.

You need not follow these steps in this order as long as your readers come away from the first part of your essay knowing why you are discussing a given issue and what your argument is.

AN ANNOTATED STUDENT INTRODUCTION: PROVIDING A CONTEXT FOR A THESIS

We trace these four steps below in our analysis of the opening paragraphs of a student's essay. Motivating his argument is his sense that contemporary writers and educators may not fully grasp the issues that limit the opportunities for low-income youth to attend college. His own family struggled financially, and he argues that a fuller appreciation of the problem can help educators partner with families to advise youth in more informed ways.

O'Neill 1

Colin O'Neill

Money Matters:

Framing the College Access Debate

The student establishes the timeliness and relevance of an issue that challenges widely held assumptions about the value of attending college.

College is expensive. And with prices continuing to rise each year, there are those who are beginning to question whether or not college is a worthy investment. In a recent *Newsweek* article, journalist Megan McArdle (2012) asserts that the process of obtaining a college degree has morphed into a "national neurosis"

1

O'Neill 2

and calls upon Americans to question whether college is necessary for lifelong success. McArdle joins a chorus of voices calling upon a reevaluation of the current educational pipeline at a time when the number of American students who are ill-prepared to face the rigors of a college curriculum has increased. Some writers suggest that a renaissance of vocational education may, in fact, begin to compensate for the disparate nature of American education. Based on research conducted by Bozick and DeLuca (2011), it is clear that these opinions are grounded in reality.

He begins to summarize what others have said to demonstrate his familiarity with the conversation in popular media and scholarship.

Of nearly 3,000 surveyed "college non-enrollees," roughly 50 percent attributed their withdrawal from the education system to either the high cost of college education or the desire to look for work and embark along their chosen career path. However, for those like me, who believe strongly that higher education is a right that ought to be available to all students, McArdle's and others' assertions add to the list of physical and social barriers that keep students of poorer backgrounds from pursuing their educational aspirations. The ability to pay for college may not be the only consideration keeping students from exploring higher education. Instead, researchers have overlooked the extent to which knowledge (or the lack of it) of college costs and awareness of different financing options (such as grants, scholarships, and loans) may preemptively alter the way in which children envision themselves within the college experience.

The student identifies what he sees as a problem signaled by words like "however," "overlooked," and "instead" and begins to formulate his own argument.

He points out a misconception that he wants to correct.

2

In many cities where the median household income often hovers slightly above $30,000, college is, according to some educators, a pipedream to which nearly every family aspires, but most are not convinced this goal will ever become a reality (United States Census Bureau). Indeed, with the average cost of a college education rising to upwards of $20,000, it is unclear whether this dream will, in fact, come true. Although parents have a strong desire to send their kids to college, the financial numbers do not seem to add up. While educators have tended to leave parents responsible for educating their children on the financial realities of higher education, researchers such as Elliot, Sherraden, Johnson, and Guo (2010) make the case that awareness of college costs makes its way into the worldview of students as young as second grade. In light of this work, it becomes important to note that the large price tag of a college

The student cites research to further define the problem and show that he is aware of the very real barriers that affect college access for low-income youth.

3

O'Neill 3

degree may have implications that spread far beyond a particular family's capacity to fund their children's education. As the recent research of Bozick and DeLuca (2011) suggests, the cost of college is changing and challenging the way students begin to examine the purpose and necessity of college education. College costs are diminishing one's access to college in more ways than restricting their ability to foot the bill. For low-income students and their families, for whom every day is filled with financial burdens of all sorts, high college costs are changing the way they perceive college as an institution.

He uses research to understand further a problem that others may have overlooked or ignored.

The correlation between the college choice process and students' perceptions of the cost of higher education is not an unexamined phenomenon. Many researchers have looked at the ways in which the cost of a college education affects the ways low-income students begin to foster a relationship with the college system. The existing body of research, however, has tended to focus solely on high school students, students who are mere months away from beginning the college search process. According to Cabrera and La Nasa (2000), the college choice process actually begins much earlier, commencing between the time a child enters middle school and embarks upon his or her high school journey. It is this process that ultimately dictates the level of college access a particular student does or does not have. Therefore, my study will focus primarily on what Cabrera and La Nasa (2000) termed the "predisposition" stage. Between grades seven and nine, predisposition draws upon parental encouragement, socioeconomic status, and "information about college." Along the trajectory set in place by Cabrera and La Nasa (2000), these factors have a profound influence on the search and choice stages of the college-access process. Recognizing the interrelational nature of these different stages, that is, both how they are different and how each one builds upon the other, is key to navigating the ill-defined nature of the pre-collegiate experience.

Citing a key study, the student underscores a gap in the research, again signaled by "however."

He adopts a frame through which to think about the issue and narrow his focus.

4

He begins to offer a solution to a problem researchers have not fully appreciated.

Given the findings of prior research, it is important to push back the discussion about college affordability and college access to examine how the notion of cost impacts the fragile, emerging relationship that middle school students are just beginning to develop. To recognize how students begin to understand college

5

O'Neill 4

and develop college aspirations, then, I conducted interviews with middle school children to assess how early awareness of college costs plays a role in shaping families' decisions about the need, desire for, and accessibility of higher education. By doing so, I have tried to fill a gap left behind by previous research and add to the wider discussion of college affordability and its overall impact on college access amongst students of all ages. Although educators may argue that American education ought to revert to an old, draconian system of vocational education, preparing low-income students to enter technical fields, I argue that it is important to create programs that encourage parents, teachers, and students to think early about the costs of college and the possibilities that exist to help children pursue a college degree.

The student explains that the purpose of his research is to fill the gap he identifies above and correct a misunderstanding.

Here he makes a policy-related claim that challenges a conflicting point of view.

■ Establish That the Issue Is Current and Relevant

Ideally, you should convey to readers that the issue you are discussing is both current (what's on people's minds) and relevant (of sufficient importance to have generated some discussion and written conversation). In the first two sentences of the first paragraph, O'Neill explains that the increase in college costs has not only become a focus of national attention, evidenced in the *Newsweek* article he cites, but has motivated writers to question whether the cost to low-income families is a worthwhile investment. In the next sentence, he explains that the author of this article, Megan McArdle, is not alone in challenging some widely held assumptions about the value of attending college. In fact, O'Neill indicates that McArdle "joins a chorus of voices calling upon a reevaluation of the current educational pipeline at a time when the number of American students who are ill-prepared to face the rigors of a college curriculum has increased." Thus, O'Neill demonstrates that the issue he focuses on is part of a lively conversation and debate that has captured the imagination of many writers at the time he was writing about college access.

■ Briefly Present What Others Have Said

It is important to introduce who has said what in the conversation you are entering. After all, you are joining that conversation to make your contribution, and those who are in that conversation expect you to have done your homework and acknowledge those who have already made important contributions.

In the first few sentences of his introduction, O'Neill sets the stage for his review of research by citing McArdle's *Newsweek* article. Although he takes issue with McArdle, he is careful to explain her argument. In addition, he refers to research in the final sentence of the first paragraph to suggest the extent to which her argument may be "grounded in reality." Indeed, in the second paragraph, he cites a study that reports on the significant number of students surveyed who dropped out of college, nearly half attributing their decision to the high costs of pursuing a college degree. However, O'Neill, who makes clear that he believes everyone has a "right" to an education, uses his review to reframe the issue, calling attention to the way McArdle and others have "overlooked the extent to which knowledge (or the lack of it) of college costs and awareness of different financing options (such as grants, scholarships, and loans) may preemptively alter the way in which children envision themselves within the college experience." In turn, O'Neill highlights research that focuses on parents' and children's perceptions of college access as a way to challenge those writers who call for a "reevaluation of the current educational pipeline."

By pointing out what journalists and researchers may have overlooked in discussing the college-going prospects of low-income youth, O'Neill is doing more than listing the sources he has read. He is establishing that a problem, or issue, exists. Moreover, his review gives readers intellectual touchstones, the scholars (e.g., Cabrera and La Nasa [2000]) who need to be cited in any academic conversation about college access. A review is not a catchall for anyone writing on a topic. Instead it should represent a writer's choice of the most relevant participants in the conversation. O'Neill's choice of sources and his presentation of them convey that he is knowledgeable about his subject. (Of course, it is his readers' responsibility to read further to determine whether he has reviewed the most relevant work and has presented the ideas of others accurately. If he has, readers will trust him, whether or not they end up agreeing with him on the issue.)

▪ Explain What You See as the Problem

If a review indicates a problem, as O'Neill's review does, the problem can often be couched in terms of the models we discussed earlier: misinterpretations, gaps, modification, or hypothesis testing. In paragraph 4, O'Neill identifies what he sees as a gap in how journalists and researchers approach the cost of attending college and the question of "whether college is necessary to lifelong success." He suggests that such a view is the consequence of a gap in knowledge (notice our underlining):

> The existing body of research, however, has tended to focus solely on high school students, students who are mere months away from beginning the college search process. According to Cabrera and La Nasa (2000), the college choice process actually begins much earlier, commencing between the time a child enters middle school and embarks upon his or her high school journey.

While O'Neill acknowledges the value of others' writing, his review of research culminates with his assertion that it is important to understand the problem of college costs with greater depth and precision. After all, researchers and journalists have overlooked or ignored important sources of information. At stake for O'Neill is that limiting low-income youth's access to higher education challenges a more equitable view that all children deserve a chance to have a successful life. Moreover, at the end of paragraph 3, he shifts the burden from parents, alone, to educators who clearly influence the "way students begin to examine the purpose and necessity of college education."

▪ State Your Thesis

An effective thesis statement helps readers see the reasoning behind a writer's claim; it also signals what readers should look for in the remainder of the essay. O'Neill closes paragraph 5 with a statement that speaks to both the purpose and the substance of what he writes:

> Although educators may argue that American education ought to revert to an old, draconian system of vocational education, preparing low-income students to enter technical fields, I argue that it is important to create programs that encourage parents, teachers, and students to think early about the costs of college and the possibilities that exist to help children pursue a college degree.

In your own writing, you can make use of the strategies that O'Neill uses in his essay. Words like *although, however, but, instead,* and *yet* can set up the problem you identify. Here is a variation on what O'Neill writes: "One might argue that vocational programs may provide a reasonable alternative to meeting the needs of low-income students for whom college seems unaffordable and out of reach; however [but, yet], such an approach ignores the range of possibilities that exist for changing policies to ensure that all children have access to a college education."

Steps to Establishing a Context for a Thesis

1 **Establish that the issue is current and relevant.** Point out the extent to which others have recognized the problem, issue, or question that you are writing about.

2 **Briefly present what others have said.** Explain how others have addressed the problem, issue, or question you are focusing on.

3 **Explain what you see as the problem.** Identify what is open to dispute.

4 **State your thesis.** Help readers see your purpose and how you intend to achieve it — by correcting a misconception, filling a gap, modifying a claim others have accepted, or stating an hypothesis.

■ Analyze the Context of a Thesis

In "Teaching Toward Possibility," educator Kris Gutiérrez argues that teaching should focus on student learning and provide students with multiple tools from different disciplines to ensure that students engage in what she describes as "deep learning." She also explains that culture plays a key role in learning, particularly for students from nondominant groups. However, she reframes the notion of culture as a set of practices, as a verb, which she distinguishes from inert conceptions of culture based on individuals' membership in a particular ethnic community. Her essay, published in 2011, is addressed to educators, teachers, and policy makers. As you read the following excerpt, you may feel puzzled by some of Gutiérrez's vocabulary and perhaps even excluded from the conversation at times. Our purpose in reprinting this excerpt is to show through our annotations how Gutiérrez has applied the strategies we have been discussing in this chapter. As you read, make your own annotations, and then try to answer the questions—which may involve careful rereading—that we pose after the selection. In particular, watch for signpost words or phrases that signal the ideas the writer is challenging.

KRIS GUTIÉRREZ

From Teaching Toward Possibility: Building Cultural Supports for Robust Learning

The author establishes the relevance and timeliness of the issue.

Consider the potential learning power of a unit on environmental inequities or environment racism for middle or high school students in which students are provided the opportunity to examine the issue deeply and broadly. We did just this over a number of years in rigorous summer programs for high school students from migrant farm worker backgrounds. Students learned environmental science, learned traditional information about the environment, learned about the history of the area of study, as well as the history of environmental issues in their local and immediate communities. This way of learning required interdisciplinary reading, including reading across genres, points of view, and across historical time and space. These learning practices enticed students to want to learn more, to research, and to make connections across relevant ideas and their varied meanings within and across academic

This is particularly relevant for an audience of teachers who want to know how to motivate students whose backgrounds they may be unfamiliar with.

1

and home communities. In short, instruction was coherent, historicized, textured, layered, and deeply supported in ways that allowed students to access and engage with rigorous texts and high status knowledge, as well as work in and through the contradictions and tensions inherent in knowledge production and authentic science/learning issues.

In the following section, I draw on the case of teaching science to migrant students mentioned above to elaborate a challenge to reductive approaches to teaching and learning that offer the "quick-fix" and provide "off the shelf" solutions to education; that is, those relying on silver bullet solutions to solve complex educational problems or using theory and research uncritically or without sufficient understanding because it is fashionable to do so. One such quick-fix approach is found in learning styles approaches to learning, particularly cultural learning styles conceptions in which regularities in cultural communities are characterized as static and unchanging and general traits of individuals are attributable categorically to ethnic group membership.

Gutiérrez further establishes the relevance of teaching non-dominant students and seeks to correct a misconception about the nature of teaching, learning, and culture.

In my work (Gutiérrez, 2002; Gutiérrez & Rogoff, 2003), I have argued the importance of moving beyond such narrow assumptions of cultural communities by focusing both on regularity and variance in a community's practices (as well as those of individuals). Employing a cultural-historical-activity theoretical approach to learning and development (Cole & Engeström, 2003; Engeström, 1987; Leontiev, 1981) is one productive means toward challenging static and ahistorical understandings of cultural communities and their practices, as this view focuses attention on variations in individual and group histories of engagement in cultural practices. Variations, then, are best understood as proclivities of people who have particular histories of engagement with specific cultural activities, not as traits of individuals or collections of individuals. In other words, individual and group experience in activities—not their traits—become the focus.

She cites her own work to support her argument and then reviews relevant studies to challenge approaches to teaching and learning that fail to conceptualize the notion of culture adequately.

Gutiérrez reframes the way educators should view culture, and this new frame is the lens through which she develops her argument.

2

3

Through this new conception of culture, Gutiérrez defines what she sees as a gap in what educators know and need to know. She attributes this gap to what educators have ignored and cites additional research to make her point.

Within this view, it becomes easier to understand the limitations of learning styles approaches in which individuals from one group might be characterized as "holistic learners"—where individuals from another group may be characterized as learning analytically or individuals may be divided into cooperative versus individualist learners on the basis of membership in a particular cultural group. Such methods ignore or minimize variation and focus on perceived or over-generalized regularities. Further, learning styles pedagogical practices have been used to distinguish the learning styles of "minority" group members and to explain "minority" student failure (see Foley, 1997; Kavale & Forness, 1987; Irvine & York, 1995 for reviews). Of consequence, addressing learning styles as traits linked to membership in cultural communities also seems to be a common way to prepare teachers about diversity (Guild, 1994; Matthews, 1991). Understandably, teaching to a difference that can be labeled (e.g., learning modalities) may be appealing to teachers who have limited resources, support, or training to meet the challenges of new student populations. However, attribution of learning style or difference based on group membership can serve to buttress persistent deficit model orientations to teaching students from nondominant communities; without acknowledging both the regularity and variance makes it harder to understand the relation of individual learning and the practices of cultural communities, which in turn can hinder effective assistance to student learning (Gutiérrez & Rogoff, 2003).

Her use of "however" distinguishes what she sees as a prevailing school of thought and what she believes should be the case. Educators' misconceptions about culture are the source of the problem she identifies.

Gutiérrez reaffirms the issue between two competing ideas.

The key issue here is that learning styles approaches are grounded in reductive notions of culture that conflate race/ethnicity with culture—a practice that often leads to one-size-fits-all approaches and understandings of the learning process of students from non-dominant communities. Consider familiar statements such as "My Latino students learn this way" or "I need to teach to the cultural background of my African American students" and even, "Asian students

4

5

The lens of culture that she has adopted helps us understand the nature of the misconception that she identifies and solve a problem in educating students from nondominant groups. This last sentence is her main claim.

are good at math." Such generalizations are based on the assumption that people hold uniform cultural practices based on their membership in a particular community. Culture from this perspective is something you can observe from people's phenotype, physical characteristics, national origin, or language. Culture, then, is best considered a verb or said differently, culture is better understood as people's practices or how people live culturally (Moll, 1998). This more dynamic and instrumental role of culture should help us avoid the tendency to conflate culture with race and ethnicity and assumptions about people's cultural practices.

To avoid conflating race/ethnicity with culture, I often remind researchers and educators to invoke the "100-percent Piñata rule"—that is, 100-percent of Mexicans do not hit piñatas 100-percent of the time. While piñatas may in fact be a prevalent cultural artifact in many Mexican and Mexican-descent communities (and now across many household and communities in the Southwest), we would not make generalizations about their use and would expect variation in piñata practices, their meaning, value, and use. Thus, while cultural artifacts mediate human activity, they have varying functions in use and in practice, just as there is regularity and variance in any cultural community and its practices.

6

She restates her claim about culture.

Reading as a Writer

1. What specific places can you point to in the selection that illustrate what is at issue for Gutiérrez?

2. How does she use her review to set up her argument?

3. What specific words and phrases does she use to establish what she sees as the problem? Is she correcting misinterpretations, filling a gap, or modifying what others have said?

4. What would you say is Gutiérrez's thesis? What specifics can you point to in the text to support your answer?

5. What would you say are the arguments Gutiérrez wants you to avoid? Again, what specific details can you point to in the text to support your answer?

A Practice Sequence: Building a Thesis

We would like you to practice some of the strategies we have covered in this chapter. If you have already started working on an essay, exercises 1 through 4 present an opportunity to take stock of your progress, a chance to sort through what you've discovered, identify what you still need to discover, and move toward refining your thesis. Jot down your answer to each of the questions below and make lists of what you know and what you need to learn.

1   Have you established that your issue is current and relevant, that it is or should be on people's minds? What information would you need to do so?

2   Can you summarize briefly what others have said in the past to show that you are familiar with how others have addressed the issue? List some of the key texts you have read and the key points they make.

3   Have you identified any misunderstandings or gaps in how others have addressed the issue? Describe them. Do you have any ideas or information that would address these misunderstandings or help fill these gaps? Where might you find the information you need? Can you think of any sources you should reread to learn more? (For example, have you looked at the works cited or bibliographies in the texts you've already read?)

4   At this point, what is your take on the issue? Try drafting a working thesis statement that will present readers with something new to think about, building on and extending what others have argued. In drafting your thesis statement, try out the models discussed in this chapter and see if one is an especially good fit:

- *Misinterpretations model:* "Although many scholars have argued about A and B, a careful examination suggests C."

- *Gap model:* "Although scholars have noted A and B, they have missed the importance of C."

- *Modification model:* "Although I agree with A and B ideas of other writers, it is important to extend/refine/limit their ideas with C."

- *Hypothesis-testing model:* "Some people explain A by suggesting B, but a close analysis of the problem reveals the possibility of several competing/complementary explanations such as C, D, and E."

5 If you haven't chosen a topic yet, try a group exercise. Sit down with a few of your classmates and choose one of the following topics to brainstorm about as a group. Choose a topic that everyone in the group finds interesting, and work through exercises 1 through 4 in this practice sequence. Here are some suggestions:

- the moral obligation to vote
- the causes or consequences of poverty
- the limits of academic freedom
- equity in education
- the popularity of _____
- gender stereotypes in the media
- linguistic diversity
- the uses of a liberal education
- journalism and truth
- government access to personal information

AN ANNOTATED STUDENT ESSAY: STATING AND SUPPORTING A THESIS

We have annotated the following student essay to illustrate the strategies we have discussed in this chapter for stating a thesis that responds to a relevant, timely problem in a given context. The assignment was to write an argument focusing on literacy, based on research. Veronica Stafford chose to write about her peers' habit of texting and the ways in which this type of social interaction affects their intellectual development. Stafford develops a thesis that provides a corrective to a misconception that she sees in the ongoing conversations about texting. Her approach is a variation on the strategy in which writers correct a misinterpretation. In turn, you will see that she makes claims of fact and evaluation in making an argument for changing her peers' penchant for texting.

As you read the essay, reflect on your own experiences: Do you think the issue she raises is both timely and relevant? How well do you think she places her ideas in conversation with others? How would you respond to her various claims? Which do you agree with and disagree with, and why? What evidence would you present to support or counter her claims? Do you think she offers a reasonable corrective to what she believes is a misconception about texting?

Stafford 1

Veronica Stafford

Professor Wilson

English 1102

April 20 —

Texting and Literacy

As students walk to class each day, most do not notice the other people around them. Rather than talking with others, they are texting their friends in the next building, in their dorm, or back home. Although social networking is the most common use for text messages, they are not used solely for socializing. While texting is a quick and easy way to keep up with friends, it threatens other aspects of our lives. When students spend time texting rather than focusing on those other important aspects, texting becomes detrimental. Students' enjoyment of reading, their schoolwork, and their relationships with others are all negatively affected by text messaging.

Due to the mass appeal of text messaging, students pass their free time chatting through their cell phones rather than enjoying a great book. Texting is so widespread because 25 percent of students under age eight, 89 percent of students ages eleven to thirteen, and over 95 percent of students over age fifteen have a cell phone ("Mobile Phones"). On average, 75.6 million text messages are sent in a day, with 54 percent of the population texting more than five times per day ("Mobile Phones"). In contrast to the time they spend texting, fifteen- to twenty-four-year-olds read a mere seven minutes per day for fun and only 1.25 hours a week (NEA 10), which is less than half the time that seventh-grade students spend texting: 2.82 hours a week (Bryant et al.). While more than half of the population texts every day, almost as many (43 percent) have not read a single book in the past year (NEA 7). It seems there is a direct correlation between reading and texting because, as text messaging increases in popularity, reading decreases. The National Endowment for the Arts surveyed eighteen- to twenty-four-year-olds and discovered that the enjoyment of reading in this age group is declining the fastest. Inversely, it is the group that sends the most text messages: 142 billion a year (NEA 10). From 1992 to 2002, 2.1 million potential readers, aged eighteen to twenty-four years old, were lost (NEA 27). As proved by the direct correlation, reading does not have

The student identifies an issue, or problem, and states her thesis as an evaluative claim that attempts to correct a misconception.

She summarizes research, placing the conversation in a larger context. Her citations also indicate that the problem she identifies is relevant and timely.

She uses evidence to support her thesis — that we take for granted a mode of communication that actually threatens the development of literacy.

1

2

Stafford 2

the same appeal because of texting. Students prefer to spend time in the technological world rather than sitting with a book.

She refines her thesis, first stating what people assume is true and then offering a corrective in the second part of her thesis.

However, reading well is essential to being successful academically. Although some argue that text messages force students to think quickly and allow them to formulate brief responses to questions, their habit is actually stifling creativity. When a group of twenty students was given a chance to write responses to open-ended questions, the students who owned cell phones with text messaging wrote much less. They also had more grammatical errors, such as leaving apostrophes out of contractions and substituting the letter "r" for the word "are"

She also makes a secondary claim related to her thesis.

(Ward). Because of text messages, students perceive writing as a fun way to communicate with friends and not as a way to strongly voice an opinion. Students no longer think of writing as academic, but rather they consider it social. For instance, in Scotland, a thirteen-year-old student wrote this in a school essay about her summer vacation: "My smmr hols wr CWOT. B4 we used 2 go to NY 2C my bro, & 3 kids FTF ILNY, its gr8 . . ." (Ward). She used writing that would appear in a text message for

And she elaborates on this claim to point out one of the detrimental effects of texting.

a friend rather than in a report for school. Furthermore, students who text become so accustomed to reading this type of shorthand lingo that they often overlook it in their own writing (O'Connor). This means that teachers have to spend even longer correcting these bad habits. Regardless, Lily Huang, a writer for *Newsweek*, believes that text messages increase literacy because a student must first know how to spell a word to abbreviate it in texting.

The student presents a possible counter-argument from a published writer and then restates her thesis in an effort to correct a misconception.

However, texting affects not only the way that students write, but also the way in which they think about language. As a critic of Huang's article writes, "Habitual use of shorthand isn't just about choppy English, but choppy thinking" (Muffie). Writers who text will have trouble thinking creatively, and will especially have trouble composing intricate works like poetry because of the abridged way of thinking to which they are accustomed.

Outside of school, students' interactions with one another are similarly altered. Three in five teens would argue with a friend and one in three would break up with someone through a text message ("Technology Has Tremendous Impact"). Text messaging is now the most popular way for students to arrange to meet with friends, have a quick conversation, contact

Stafford 3

a friend when bored, or invite friends to a party ("Technology Has Tremendous Impact"). Eight out of ten teens would rather text than call ("Mobile Phones"). Although it is true that text messaging has made conversations much simpler and faster, it has not improved communication. Texting may make it more convenient to stay in contact with friends, but it does not ensure that the contact is as beneficial as talking in person.

She restates an evaluative claim that runs through the essay like the skewer we discussed earlier.

Text messages do not incorporate all of the body language and vocal inflections that a face-to-face conversation does. These nonverbal cues are essential to fully comprehending what is being communicated. Only 7 percent of a message is verbal. When the message is not communicated face-to-face, 93 percent of that message is lost ("Importance of Nonverbal"), and this nonverbal message is crucial to maintaining close relationships. According to Don McKay, a contributor to healthinfosource.com, the most important aspect of lasting friendships is effective communication. Friends must be able to convey emotions and empathize with others (McKay). However, friends who communicate solely through text messages will miss out on any truly personal interaction because they can never see the other person's posture, body language, or gestures.

She provides current research to support her thesis.

All of the negative effects of text messaging additionally deteriorate literacy. The enjoyment of reading leads to avid readers who eagerly absorb written words. A devotion to schoolwork encourages students to read so that they may be informed about important topics. Through book clubs and conversations about great literature, even relationships can foster a love for reading. However, text messaging is detracting from all three. In today's society, literacy is important. Schools focus on teaching English at an early age because of the active role that it forces students to take (Le Guin). While students can passively text message their friends, they need to focus on reading to enjoy it. In order to really immerse themselves in the story, they need to use a higher level of thinking than that of texting. This learning is what causes avid readers to become so successful. Those who read for fun when they are young score better on standardized tests, are admitted to more selective universities, and are able to secure the most competitive jobs (NEA 69). The decline in literacy caused by text messaging

She concludes by restating her premise about the value of reading and her evaluation of texting as a form of communication that erodes what she considers the very definition of literacy.

She also concludes with a claim in which she proposes that students need to elevate the way they read and write.

5

could inevitably cost a student a selective job. If students spent less time texting and more time reading, it could give them an advantage over their peers. Imagine a scenario between classes without any students' eyes to the ground. Imagine that Notre Dame students are not texting acquaintances hours away. Perhaps instead they are all carrying a pen and notebook and writing a letter to their friends. Maybe they are conversing with those around them. Instead of spending time every week text messaging, they are reading. When those other students text "lol," it no longer is an abbreviation for "laugh out loud," but for "loss of literacy."

Works Cited

Bryant, J. Alison, et al. "IMing, Text Messaging, and Adolescent Social Networks." *Journal of Computer-Mediated Communication*, vol. 11, no. 2, Jan. 2006, pp. 577–92.

Huang, Lily. "Technology: Textese May be the Death of English." *Newsweek*, 1 Aug. 2008, www.newsweek.com/ technology-textese-may-be-death-english-87727.

"The Importance of Nonverbal Communication." *EruptingMind Self Improvement Tips*, 2008, www.eruptingmind.com/ the-importance-of-nonverbal-communication/.

Le Guin, Ursula K. "Staying Awake: Notes on the Alleged Decline of Reading." *Harper's Magazine*, Feb. 2008, harpers.org/ archive/2008/02/staying-awake/.

McKay, Don. "Communication and Friendship." *EzineArticles*, 22 Feb. 2006, ezinearticles.com/?Communication-And -Friendship&id=150491.

"Mobile Phones, Texting, and Literacy." *National Literacy Trust*, 2008, www.literacytrust.org.uk/news/mobile_phones _texting_and_literacy.

Muffie. Comment on "Technology: Textese May be the Death of English," by Lily Huang. *Newsweek*, 18 Aug. 2008, www.newsweek.com/technology-textese-may-be-death -english-87727.

Stafford 5

O'Connor, Amanda. "Instant Messaging: Friend or Foe of
 Student Writing?" *New Horizons for Learning,* Johns Hopkins
 School of Education, Mar. 2005, education.jhu.edu/PD/
 newhorizons/strategies/topics/literacy/articles/
 instant-messaging/.

"Technology Has Tremendous Impact on How Teens
 Communicate." *Cellular-news*, 19 Feb. 2007,
 www.cellular-news.com/story/22146.php.

To Read or Not To Read: A Question of National Consequence.
 National Endowment for the Arts, Nov. 2007, www.arts.gov/
 publications/read-or-not-read-question-national
 -consequence-0.

Ward, Lucy. "Texting 'Is No Bar to Literacy.'" *The Guardian*,
 23 Dec. 2004, www.theguardian.com/technology/2004/
 dec/23/schools.mobilephones.

7

From Finding to Evaluating Sources

In this chapter, we look at strategies for expanding the base of sources you work with to support your argument. The habits and skills of close reading and analysis that we have discussed and that you have practiced are essential for evaluating the sources you find. Once you find sources, you will need to assess the claims the writers make, the extent to which they provide evidence in support of those claims, and the recency, relevance, accuracy, and reliability of the evidence. The specific strategies we discuss here are those you will use to find and evaluate the sources you locate in your library's electronic catalog or on the Internet. These strategies are core skills for developing a researched academic argument.

Finding sources is not difficult; finding and identifying reliable, relevant sources is challenging. You know how simple it is to look up a subject in an encyclopedia or to use a search engine like Google to discover basic information on a subject or topic. Unfortunately, this kind of research will take you only so far. What if the information you find doesn't really address your question? True, we have emphasized the importance of thinking about an issue from multiple perspectives—and finding multiple perspectives is easy when you search the Internet. But how do you know whether a perspective is authoritative or trustworthy or even legitimate? Without knowing how to find and identify good sources, you can waste a lot of time reading material that will not contribute to your essay. Our goal is to help you use your time wisely to collect the sources you need to support your argument.

IDENTIFYING SOURCES

We assume that by the time you visit the library or search the Internet to find sources, you are not flying blind. At the very least you will have chosen a topic you want to explore (something in general you want to write about), possibly will have identified an issue (a question or problem about the topic that is arguable), and perhaps will even have a working thesis (a main claim that you want to test against other sources).

Let's say, for example, that you are interested in the topic of nutrition and obesity. Perhaps you have begun to formulate an issue: Trends show that obesity is increasing at a time when published reports are also showing that the food industry may have been complicit by engineering processed foods with high fat, sugar, and salt content. In fact, these reports point to the lack of nutritional value of processed foods. The issue might be between what you see as an unfortunate trend that affects the health of a growing population of children and adults in the United States and the extent to which food manufacturers contribute to the problem. You may have begun to formulate a question about who is responsible for addressing this problem. Should individuals be more responsible for making good choices? Should food manufacturers monitor themselves and be more responsible to consumers? Should the government intervene to ensure that processed foods provide adequate nutrients and less fat, sugar, and salt? The closer you are to identifying an issue or question, the more purposeful your research will be and the more you will be able to home in on the materials that will be most useful. As you read, your research will help you refine your idea, formulate a question, and develop a working thesis.

However, a working thesis is just a place to begin. As you digest all of the perspectives that your research yields, your interest in the topic or issue may shift significantly. Maybe you'll end up writing about the extent to which the government should have a role, any role, in regulating the food industry rather than about obesity. Perhaps you become interested in trends in food distribution and end up writing about what some call the "locavore" movement. Be open to revising your ideas and confronting the complexities inherent in any topic. Pursue what interests you and what is timely and relevant to your readers. The question, then, is what are you trying to learn and demonstrate?

If you are unsure about where to start, we provide a list of standard resources for conducting research in Table 7.1. For example, you could begin by looking up abstracts, a tool researchers use to get a brief snapshot of the field and summaries of potentially relevant articles. You can simply do a Google search, type in "abstracts," and add the topic that interests you ("abstracts in health sciences"). You can also look up book reviews to see how others might have responded to a book from which you first learned about the problems of obesity, nutrition, food production, and the like. More specialized searches will take you to databases available on a given library's Web site.

TABLE 7.1   Standard Resources for Conducting Research

Source	Type of Information	Purpose	Limitations	Examples
Abstract	Brief summary of a text and the bibliographic information needed to locate the complete text	To help researchers decide whether they want to read the entire source	May be too brief to fully assess the value of a source	*Biological Abstracts* *Historical Abstracts* *New Testament Abstracts* *Reference Sources in History: An Introductory Guide*
Bibliography	List of works, usually by subject and author, with full publication information	For an overview of what has been published in a field and who the principal researchers in the field are	Difficult to distinguish the best sources and the most prominent researchers	Bibliography of the History of Art *MLA International Bibliography*
Biography	Story of an individual's life and the historical, cultural, or social context in which he or she lived	For background on a person of importance	Lengthy and reflects the author's bias	Biography and Genealogy Master Index Biography Resource Center Biography.com Literature Resource Center *Oxford Dictionary of National Biography*
Book review	Description and usually an evaluation of a recently published book	To help readers stay current with research and thought in their field and to evaluate scholarship	Reflects the reviewer's bias	ALA *Booklist* *Book Review Digest* Book Review Index *Bowker Books in Print*
Database	Large collection of citations and abstracts from books, journals, and digests, often updated daily	To give researchers access to a wide range of current sources	Lacks evaluative information	EBSCOhost Education Resources Information Center (ERIC) Humanities International Index Index to Scientific & Technical Proceedings United Nations Bibliographic Information System
Data, statistics	Measurements derived from studies or surveys	To help researchers identify important trends (e.g., in voting, housing, residential segregation)	Requires a great deal of scrutiny and interpretation	American FactFinder American National Election Studies Current Index to Statistics Current Population Survey *U.S. Census Bureau National Data Book*

(continued on next page)

TABLE 7.1   *(continued)*

Source	Type of Information	Purpose	Limitations	Examples
Dictionary	Alphabetical list of words and their definitions	To explain key terms and how they are used		*Merriam-Webster's Collegiate Dictionary* *Oxford English Dictionary* *The Oxford Dictionary of Current English*
Encyclopedia	Concise articles about people, places, concepts, and things	A starting point for very basic information	Lack of in-depth information	*The CQ Researcher* Encyclopedia Brittanica Online *McGraw-Hill Encyclopedia of Science & Technology*
Internet search engine	Web site that locates online information by keyword or search term	For quickly locating a broad array of current resources	Reliability of information open to question	Google Google Scholar
Newspaper, other news sources	Up-to-date information	To locate timely information	May reflect reporter's or medium's bias	America's Historical Newspapers LexisNexis Academic Newspaper Source ProQuest Historical Newspapers World News Connection
Thesaurus	Alphabetical list of words and their synonyms	For alternative search terms		*Roget's II: The New Thesaurus* *Pro Quest Thesaurus*

■ Consult Experts Who Can Guide Your Research

Before you embark on a systematic hunt for sources, you may want to consult with experts who can help guide your research. The following experts are nearer to hand and more approachable than you may think.

Your writing instructor.   Your first and best expert is likely to be your writing instructor, who can help you define the limits of your research and the kinds of sources that would prove most helpful. Your writing instructor can probably advise you on whether your topic is too broad or too narrow, help you identify your issue, and perhaps even point you to specific reference works or readings you should consult. He or she can also help you figure out whether you should concentrate mainly on popular or scholarly sources (for more about popular and scholarly sources, see pp. 170–73).

Librarians at your campus or local library.   In all likelihood, there is no better repository of research material than your campus or local library, and
no better guide to those resources than the librarians who work there.
Their job is to help you find what you need (although it's up to you to
make the most of what you find). Librarians can give you a map or tour of
the library and provide you with booklets or other handouts that instruct
you in the specific resources available and their uses. They can explain the
catalog system and reference system. And, time allowing, most librarians
are willing to give you personal help in finding and using specific sources,
from books and journals to indexes and databases.

Experts in other fields.   Perhaps the idea for your paper originated outside
your writing course, in response to a reading assigned in, say, your psychology or economics course. If so, you may want to discuss your topic
or issue with the instructor in that course, who can probably point you
to other readings or journals you should consult. If your topic originated
outside the classroom, you can still seek out an expert in the appropriate
field. If so, you may want to read the advice on interviewing we present in
Chapter 13.

Manuals, handbooks, and dedicated Web sites.   These resources exist in
abundance, for general research as well as for discipline-specific research.
They are especially helpful in identifying a wide range of authoritative
search tools and resources, although they also offer practical advice on
how to use and cite them. Indeed, your writing instructor may assign one
of these manuals or handbooks, or recommend a Web site, at the beginning of the course. If not, he or she can probably point you to the one that
is best suited to your research.

■ Develop a Working Knowledge of Standard Sources

As you start your hunt for sources, it helps to know broadly what kinds of
sources are available and what they can help you accomplish. Table 7.1
lists a number of the resources you are likely to rely on when you are
looking for material, the purpose and limitations of each type of resource,
and some well-known examples. Although it may not help you pinpoint
specific resources that are most appropriate for your research, the table
does provide a basis for finding sources in any discipline. And familiar-
izing yourself with the types of resources here should make your conversations with the experts more productive.

■ Distinguish between Primary and Secondary Sources

As you define the research task before you, you will need to understand
the difference between primary and secondary sources and figure out

which you will need to answer your question. Your instructor may specify which he or she prefers, but chances are you will have to make the decision yourself. A **primary source** is a firsthand, or eyewitness, account, the kind of account you find in letters or newspapers or research reports in which the researcher explains his or her impressions of a particular phenomenon. A **secondary source** is an analysis of information reported in a primary source.

If you were exploring issues of language diversity and the English-only movement, you would draw on both primary and secondary sources. You would be interested in researchers' firsthand (primary) accounts of language learning and use by diverse learners for examples of the challenges nonnative speakers face in learning a standard language. And you would also want to know from secondary sources what others think about whether national unity and individuality can and should coexist in communities and homes as well as in schools. You will find that you are often expected to use both primary and secondary sources in your research.

■ Distinguish between Popular and Scholarly Sources

To determine the type of information to use, you also need to decide whether you should look for popular or scholarly books and articles. **Popular sources** of information—newspapers like *USA Today* and *The Chronicle of Higher Education*, and large-circulation magazines like *Time Magazine* and *Field & Stream*—are written for a general audience. This is not to say that popular sources cannot be specialized: *The Chronicle of Higher Education* is read mostly by academics; *Field & Stream*, by people who love the outdoors. But they are written so that any educated reader can understand them. **Scholarly sources**, by contrast, are written for experts in a particular field. *The New England Journal of Medicine* may be read by people who are not physicians, but they are not the journal's primary audience. In a manner of speaking, these readers are eavesdropping on the journal's conversation of ideas; they are not expected to contribute to it (and in fact would be hard pressed to do so). The articles in scholarly journals undergo **peer review**. That is, they do not get published until they have been carefully evaluated by the author's peers, other experts in the academic conversation being conducted in the journal. Reviewers may comment at length about an article's level of research and writing, and an author may have to revise an article several times before it sees print. And if the reviewers cannot reach a consensus that the research makes an important contribution to the academic conversation, the article will not be published.

When you begin your research, you may find that popular sources provide helpful information about a topic or an issue—the results of a national poll, for example. Later, however, you will want to use scholarly sources to advance your argument. You can see from Table 7.2 that popular magazines and scholarly journals can be distinguished by a number of characteristics. Does the source contain advertisements? If so, what kinds of advertisements? For commercial products? Or for academic events and resources? How do the advertisements appear? If you find ads and glossy pictures and illustrations, you are probably looking at a popular magazine. This is in contrast to the tables, charts, and diagrams you are likely to find in an education, psychology, or microbiology journal. Given your experience with rhetorical analyses, you should also be able to determine the makeup of your audience—specialists or nonspecialists—and the level of language you need to use in your writing.

Again, as you define your task for yourself, it is important to consider why you would use one source or another. Do you want facts? Opinions? News reports? Research studies? Analyses? Personal reflections? The extent to which the information can help you make your argument will serve as your basis for determining whether a source of information is of value.

TABLE 7.2   Popular Magazines versus Scholarly Journals

CRITERIA	POPULAR MAGAZINES	SCHOLARLY JOURNALS
Advertisements	Numerous full-page color ads	Few if any ads
Appearance	Eye-catching; glossy; pictures and illustrations	Plain; black-and-white graphics, tables, charts, and diagrams
Audience	General	Professors, researchers, and college students
Author	Journalists	Professionals in an academic field or discipline
Bibliography	Brief acknowledgment of sources in text, usually without complete citation information	Extensive bibliography at the end of each article; footnotes and other documentation
Content	General articles to inform, update, or introduce a contemporary issue	Research projects, methodology, and theory
Examples	*Newsweek, National Review, PC World, Psychology Today*	*International Journal of Applied Engineering Research, New England Journal of Medicine*
Language	Nontechnical, simple vocabulary	Specialized vocabulary
Publisher	Commercial publisher	Professional organization, university, research institute, or scholarly press

Information from materials at the Hesburgh Library, University of Notre Dame.

Steps to Identifying Sources

1   **Consult experts who can guide your research.** Talk to people who can help you formulate issues and questions.

2   **Develop a working knowledge of standard sources.** Identify the different kinds of information that different types of sources provide.

3   **Distinguish between primary and secondary sources.** Decide what type of information can best help you answer your research question.

4   **Distinguish between popular and scholarly sources.** Determine what kind of information will persuade your readers.

A Practice Sequence: Identifying Sources

We would now like you to practice using some of the strategies we have discussed so far: talking with experts, deciding what sources of information you should use, and determining what types of information can best help you develop your paper and persuade your readers. We assume you have chosen a topic for your paper, identified an issue, and perhaps formulated a working thesis. If not, think back to some of the topics mentioned in earlier chapters. Have any of them piqued your interest? If not, here are five very broad topics you might work with:

- higher education student loans
- the media and gender
- global health
- science and religion
- immigration

Once you've decided on a topic, talk to experts and decide which types of sources you should use: primary or secondary, popular or scholarly. Consult with your classmates to evaluate the strengths and weaknesses of different sources of information and the appropriateness of using different types of information. Here are the steps to follow:

1   Talk to a librarian about the sources you might use to get information about your topic (for example, databases, abstracts, or bibliographies). Be sure to take notes.

2   Talk to an expert who can provide you with some ideas about current issues in the field of interest. Be sure to take detailed notes.

3 Decide whether you should use primary or secondary sources or some combination of the two. What type of information would help you develop your argument?

4 Decide whether you should use popular or scholarly sources or whether some of each would be appropriate. What type of information would your readers find compelling?

SEARCHING FOR SOURCES

Once you've decided on the types of sources you want to use—primary or secondary, popular or scholarly—you can take steps to locate the information you need. You might begin with a tour of your university or local library, so that you know where the library keeps newspapers, government documents, books, journals, and other sources of information. Notice where the reference desk is: This is where you should head to ask a librarian for help if you get stuck. You also want to find a computer where you can log on to your library's catalog to start your search. Once you have located your sources in the library, you can begin to look through them for the information you need.

You may be tempted to rely on the Internet and a search engine like Google. But keep in mind that the information you retrieve from the Internet may not be trustworthy: Anyone can post his or her thoughts on a Web site. Of course, you can also find excellent scholarly sources on the Internet. (For example, Johns Hopkins University Press manages Project MUSE, a collection of 300-plus academic journals that can be accessed online through institutional subscription.) School libraries also offer efficient access to government records and other sources essential to scholarly writing.

Let's say you are about to start researching a paper on language diversity and the English-only movement. When you log on to the library's site, you find a menu of choices: Catalog, Electronic Resources, Virtual Reference Desk, and Services & Collections. (The wording may vary slightly from library to library, but the means of locating information will be the same.) When you click on Catalog, another menu of search choices appears: Keyword, Title, Author, and Subject (Figure 7.1). The hunt is on.

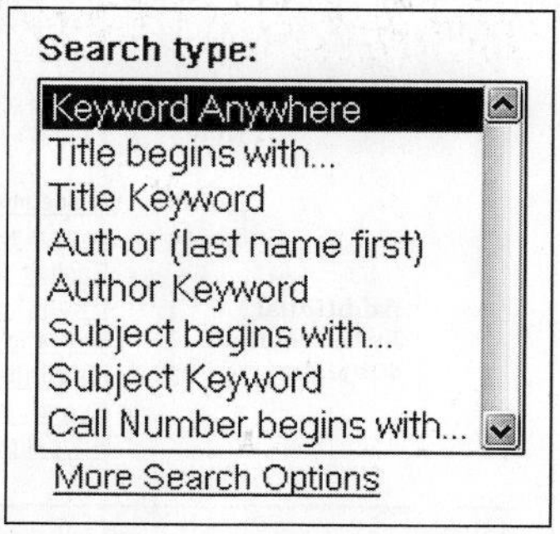

Search type:

Keyword Anywhere
Title begins with...
Title Keyword
Author (last name first)
Author Keyword
Subject begins with...
Subject Keyword
Call Number begins with...

More Search Options

■ Perform a Keyword Search

A **keyword** is essentially your topic: It defines the topic of your search. To run a keyword search, you can look up information by

FIGURE 7.1 Menu of Basic Search Strategies

author, title, or subject. You would search by author to locate all the works a particular author has written on a subject. So, for example, if you know that Paul Lang is an expert on the consequences of the English-only movement, you might begin with an author search. You can use the title search to locate all works with a key term or phrase in the title. The search results are likely to include a number of irrelevant titles, but you should end up with a list of authors, titles, and subject headings to guide another search.

A search by subject is particularly helpful as you begin your research, while you are still formulating your thesis. You want to start by think-ing of as many words as possible that relate to your topic. (A thesaurus can help you come up with different words you can use in a keyword search.) Suppose you type in the phrase "English only." A number of different sources appear on the screen, but the most promising is Paul Lang's book *The English Language Debate: One Nation, One Language?* You click on this record, and another screen appears with some valu-able pieces of information, including the call number (which tells you where in the library you can find the book) and an indication that the book has a bibliography, something you can make use of once you find the book (Figure 7.2). Notice that the subject listings — *Language policy, English language–Political aspects, English-only movement, Bilingual education* — also give you additional keywords to use in finding relevant information. The lesson here is that it is important to generate keywords to get initial information and then to look at that information carefully for

Full View of Record

Record 12 out of 18

Source {
Author : Lang, Paul (Paul C.)
Title : The English language debate : one nation, one language? / Paul Lang.
Published : Springfield, N.J. : Enslow Publishers, c1995.
112 p. : ill. ; 24 cm.
}

ND Has : All items
Hesburgh Library General Collection
P 119.32 .U6 E55 1995   [Call number

Indicates book has a bibliography
Notes : Includes bibliographical references (p. 107-109) and index.

Series : Multicultural issues
Subjects : Language policy – United States – Juvenile literature.
English language – Political aspects – United States – Juvenile literature.
Additional list of related subjects {
English-only movement – United States – Juvenile literature.
Education, Bilingual – United States – Juvenile literature.
English-only movement.
English language – Political aspects.
Education, Bilingual.
}

Done

FIGURE 7.2 Full-View Bibliographic Entry

more keywords and to determine if the source has a bibliography. Even if this particular source isn't relevant, it may lead you to other sources that are.

■ Try Browsing

Browse is a headings search; it appears in the menu of choices in Figure 7.1 as "Subject begins with…" This type of search allows you to scroll through an alphabetical index. Some of the indexes available are the Author Index, the Title Index, and the Library of Congress Subject Headings, a subject index. Browse

- displays an alphabetical list of entries;
- shows the number of records for each entry;
- indicates whether there are cross-references for each entry.

What appears in the window is "Browse List: Choose a field, enter a phrase and click the 'go' button." Figure 7.3 shows the results of a preliminary browse when the words "English-only" are entered. Notice that a list of headings or titles appears on the screen. This is not a list of books, and not all of the entries are relevant. But you can use the list to determine which headings are relevant to your topic, issue, or question.

For your paper on the English-only movement, the first two headings seem relevant: *English-only debate and English-only movement*. A further click would reveal the title of a relevant book and a new list of subject headings (Figure 7.4) that differs from those of your initial search. This list gives you a new bibliography from which you can gather new leads and a list of subject headings to investigate.

Browse List: Subjects

No. of Recs	Entry
	English one-act plays - [LC Authority Record] See: One-act plays, English
	English-only debate - [LC Authority Record] See: English-only movement
4	English-only movement - [LC Authority Record]
1	English-only movement — California — Case studies
1	English-only movement — Colorado
4	English-only movement — United States
1	English-only movement — United States — Juvenile literature
	English-only question - [LC Authority Record] See: English-only movement
1	English — Ontario — Correspondence
1	English oration

FIGURE 7.3   Preliminary Browse of "English-only" Subject Heading

#	Year	Author	Title
1 ☐	2006	United States.	**English as the official language : hearing before the Subcommittee on Education Reform of the Co** \<Book\> Click for ONLINE ACCESS (Text version:) Documents Center Owned: 1 Checked Out: 0 Display full record
2 ☐	1996	United States.	**S. 356—Language of Government Act of 1995 : hearings before the Committee on Governmental Affai** \<Book\> Documents Center Display full record
3 ☐	1996	United States.	**Hearing on English as the common language : hearing before the Subcommittee on Early Childhood,** \<Book\> Documents Center Display full record
4 ☐	1995	United States.	**Hearing on English as a common language : hearing before the Subcommittee on Early Childhood, Yo** \<Book\> Documents Center Display full record

Done

FIGURE 7.4   Results of Browsing Deeper: A New List of Sources

We suggest that you do a keyword search first and then a browse search to home in on a subject. Especially when you don't know the exact subject, you can do a quick keyword search, retrieve many sets of results, and then begin looking at the subjects that correspond to each title. Once you find a subject that fits your needs, you can click on the direct subject (found in each bibliographic record) and execute a new search that will yield more relevant results.

■ Perform a Journal or Newspaper Title Search

Finally, you can search by journal or newspaper title. For this kind of search, you will need exact information. You can take the name of a journal, magazine, or newspaper cited in your keyword or browse search. The journal or newspaper title search will tell you if your library subscribes to the publication and in what format—print, microform or microfilm, or electronic.

Suppose you want to continue your search for information on the English-only movement by looking for articles in the *New York Times*. You would run a basic search under the category "Periodicals": "Periodical Title begins with . . ." That would give you access to a limited number of articles that focused on the debate surrounding the English-only movement. To find more recent articles, you could go to the *New York Times* Web site (nytimes.com), where you could find many potentially useful listings. Newspaper articles will lack the depth and complexity of more scholarly studies, but they are undeniably useful in helping you establish the timeliness and relevance of your research. You can usually preview the articles because the Web site will include a few sentences describing the content of each article. If a site requires that you subscribe or pay a nominal fee before viewing the full text of an article, check to see if you already have free access through your school's library.

Steps to Searching for Sources

1 **Perform a keyword search.** Choose a word or phrase that best describes your topic.

2 **Try browsing.** Search an alphabetical list by subject.

3 **Perform a journal or newspaper title search.** Find relevant citations by limiting your search with the exact title of a journal or newspaper.

A Practice Sequence: Searching for Sources

If you tried the practice sequence on identifying sources (pp. 172–73), explore your topic further by practicing the types of searches discussed in this section: a keyword search; a browse; and a journal or newspaper title search (or a subject search).

EVALUATING LIBRARY SOURCES

The information you encounter will vary in terms of its relevance and overall quality. You will want to evaluate this information as systematically as possible to be sure that you are using the most appropriate sources to develop your argument. Once you have obtained at least some of the sources you located by searching your library's catalog, you should evaluate the material as you read it. In particular, you want to evaluate the following information for each article or book:

- the author's background and credentials (What is the author's educational background? What has he or she written about in the past? Is this person an expert in the field?)
- the author's purpose
- the topic of discussion
- the audience the author invokes and whether you are a member of that audience
- the nature of the conversation (How have others addressed the problem?)
- what the author identifies as a misinterpretation or a gap in knowledge, an argument that needs modifying, or a hypothesis
- what the author's own view is

- how the author supports his or her argument (that is, with primary or secondary sources, with popular or scholarly articles, with facts or opinions)
- the accuracy of the author's evidence (Can you find similar information elsewhere?)

If your topic is current, chances are your searches are going to turn up a large number of possible sources. How do you go about choosing which sources to rely on in your writing? Of course, if time were not an issue, you could read them all from start to finish. But in the real world, assignments come with due dates. To decide whether a library source merits a close reading and evaluation, begin by skimming each book or article. **Skimming**—briefly examining the material to get a sense of the information it offers—involves four steps:

1. Read the introductory sections.
2. Examine the table of contents and index.
3. Check the notes and bibliographic references.
4. Skim for the argument.

■ Read the Introductory Sections

Turn to the introductory sections of the text first. Many authors use a preface or an introduction to explain the themes they focus on in a book. An **abstract** serves a similar purpose, but article abstracts are usually only 250 words long. In the introductory sections, writers typically describe the issue that motivated them to write and indicate whether they believe the work corrects a misconception, fills a gap, or builds on and extends the research of others. For example, in the preface to her book *Learning and Not Learning English: Latino Students in American Schools* (2001), Guadalupe Valdés explains that even after two years of language instruction, many students remain at a low level of language competence. In this passage, Valdés makes clear the purpose of her work:

> This book examines the learning of English in American schools by immigrant children. It focuses on the realities that such youngsters face in trying to acquire English in settings in which they interact exclusively with other non-English-speaking youngsters the entire school day. It is designed to fill a gap in the existing literature on non-English-background youngsters by offering a glimpse of the challenges and difficulties faced by four middle-school students enrolled in the United States for the first time when they were 12 or 13 years old. It is my purpose here to use these youngsters' lives and experiences as a lens through which to examine the policy and instructional dilemmas that now surround the education of immigrant children in this country. (p. 2)

If you were looking for sources for a paper on the English-only movement, in particular the consequences of that movement for young students, you might very well find Valdés's words compelling and decide the book is worth a closer reading.

▪ Examine the Table of Contents and Index

After reading the introductory sections, you will find it useful to analyze the **table of contents** to see how much emphasis the writer gives to topics that are relevant to your own research. For example, the table of contents to *Learning and Not Learning English* includes several headings that may relate to your interest: "Educating English-Language Learners," "Challenges and Realities," "Implications for Policy and Practice," and the "Politics of Teaching English." You also should turn to the back of the book to examine the **index**, an alphabetical list of the important and recurring concepts in a book, and the page numbers on which they appear. An index also would include the names of authors cited in the book. In the index to Valdés's book, you would find references to "English-language abilities and instruction" with specific page numbers where you can read what the author has to say on this subject. You would also find references to "English-only instruction," "equal educational opportunities," and "sheltered instruction."

▪ Check the Notes and Bibliographic References

Especially in the initial stages of your writing, you should look closely at writers' notes and bibliographies to discern who they feel are the important voices in the field. Frequent citation of a particular researcher's work may indicate that the individual is considered to be an expert in the field you are studying. Notes usually provide brief references to people, concepts, or context; the bibliography includes a long list of related works. Mining Valdés's bibliography, you would find such titles as "Perspectives on Official English," "Language Policy in Schools," "Not Only English," "Language and Power," and "The Cultural Politics of English."

▪ Skim for the Argument

Skimming a book or an article entails briefly looking over the elements we have discussed so far: the preface or abstract, the table of contents and the index, and the notes and bibliography. Skimming also can mean reading chapter titles, headings, and the first sentence of each paragraph to determine the relevance of a book or an article.

Skimming the first chapter of *Learning and Not Learning English*, you would find several topic sentences that reveal the writer's purpose:

"In this book, then, I examine and describe different expressions that both learning and not-learning English took among four youngsters."

"In the chapters that follow . . ."

"What I hope to suggest . . ."

These are the types of phrases you should look for to get a sense of what the author is trying to accomplish and whether the author's work will be of use to you.

If, after you've taken these steps, a source still seems promising, you should reflect on whether it might help you answer your research question. Keep in mind the critical reading skills you've learned and see if you can discern the author's overall situation, purpose, claims, and audience. Assess the evidence used to support the claims—is it recent, relevant, accurate, reliable? What kinds of evidence does the author use? Primary or secondary? Popular or scholarly? What kind of data, facts, or statistical evidence? Note whether facts or opinions seem to predominate. Ultimately you have to determine whether to set the source aside or commit yourself to a thorough understanding of its argument and all the note taking and critical thinking that will entail.

Steps to Evaluating Library Sources

1 **Read the introductory sections.** Get an overview of the author's argument.

2 **Examine the table of contents and index.** Consider the most relevant chapters to your topic and the list of relevant subjects.

3 **Check the notes and bibliographic references.** Identify other writers an author refers to and the titles of both books and articles (are the names and titles cited in many other works?).

4 **Skim for the argument.** Read chapter titles, headings, and topic sentences to determine the source's relevance to your research. Go deeper to assess the type and quality of evidence the author uses. Note whether the author uses credible evidence to support the argument.

A Practice Sequence: Evaluating Library Sources

For this exercise, we would like you to choose a specific book or article to examine to practice these strategies. If you are far along on your own research, use a book or an article you have identified as potentially useful.

1   Read the introductory sections. What issue is the author responding to? What is the author's purpose? To correct a misconception? To fill a gap? To build on or extend the work of others? To address a hypothesis?

2   Examine the table of contents and index. What key words or phrases are related to your own research? Which topics does the author focus on? Are you intending to give these topics similar emphasis? (Will you give more or less emphasis?)

3   Check the notes and bibliographic references. Make a list of the sources you think you want to look up for your own research. Do certain sources seem more important than others?

4   Skim for the argument. What is the author's focus? Is it relevant to your own topic, issue, question, working thesis? What kinds of evidence does the author use? Does the author use primary or secondary sources? Popular or scholarly articles? Statistics? Facts or opinions? Do you want to commit yourself to grappling with the author's argument?

EVALUATING INTERNET SOURCES

Without question, the Internet has revolutionized how research is conducted. It has been a particular boon to experienced researchers who have a clear sense of what they are looking for, giving them access to more information more quickly than ever before. But the Internet is rife with pitfalls for inexperienced researchers. That is, sites that appear accurate and reliable may prove not to be. The sources you find on the Internet outside your school library's catalog pose problems because anyone can post anything he or she wants. Although Internet sources can be useful, particularly because they are often current, you must take steps to evaluate them before using information from them.

■ Evaluate the Author of the Site

If an author's name appears on a Web site, ask the following: Who is this person? What credentials and professional affiliations qualify this person to make a legitimate argument in the field being investigated?

One of our students googled "English only" and clicked on the first result, "Language Policy—English Only Movement," which eventually led her to James Crawford's Language Policy Web Site & Emporium. On the site, Crawford explains that he is "a writer and lecturer—formerly the Washington editor of *Education Week*—who specializes in the politics of language."* He notes that "since 1985, I have been reporting on the English Only movement, English Plus, bilingual education, Native American

---

Education Week has been published since 1981 by Editorial Projects in Education, a nonprofit organization that was founded with the help of a Carnegie grant. The publication covers issues related to primary and secondary education. If you are not familiar with a publication and are uncertain about its legitimacy, you can always ask your instructor, a librarian, or another expert to vouch for its reliability.

language revitalization, and language rights in the U.S.A." Between 2004 and 2006, he also served as executive director of the National Association for Bilingual Education. Perhaps most important, Crawford has authored four books and a number of articles and has testified before Congress on "Official English Legislation." From this biographical sketch, the student inferred that Crawford is credentialed to write about the English-only movement.

Less certain, however, are the credentials of the writer who penned an article titled "Should the National Anthem Be Sung in English Only?" which appeared on another Web site our student visited. Why? Because the writer's name never appears on the site. An anonymous posting is the first clue that you want to move on to a more legitimate source of information.

■ Evaluate the Organization That Supports the Site

You have probably noticed that Internet addresses usually end with a domain name extension: .edu, .gov, .org, or .com. The .edu extension means the site is associated with a university or college, which gives it credibility. The same holds true for .gov, which indicates a government agency. Both types of sites have a regulatory body that oversees their content. The extension .org indicates a nonprofit organization; .com, a commercial organization. You will need to approach these Web sites with a degree of skepticism because you cannot be sure that they are as carefully monitored by a credentialed regulatory body. (In fact, even .edu sites may turn out to be postings by a student at a college or university.)

Our student was intrigued by James Crawford's site because he appears to be a credible source on the English-only movement. She was less sure about the reference to the Institute for Language and Education Policy. Is the institute a regulatory body that oversees what appears on the site? How long has the institute existed? Who belongs to the institute? Who sits on its board of directors? As a critical thinker, the student had to ask these questions.

■ Evaluate the Purpose of the Site

Information is never objective, so whenever you evaluate a book, an article, or a Web site, you should consider the point of view the writer or sponsor is taking. It's especially important to ask if there is a particular bias among members of the group that sponsors the site. Can you tell what the sponsors of the site advocate? Are they hoping to sell or promote a product, or to influence opinion?

Not all Web sites provide easy answers to these questions. However, James Crawford's Language Policy Web Site & Emporium is quite explicit. In fact, Crawford writes that "the site is designed to encourage discussion of language policy issues, expose misguided school 'reforms,'" and, among other goals, "promote [his] own publications." (Notice "Emporium" in the name of the site.) He is candid about his self-interest, which does raise a question about his degree of objectivity.

What about a site like Wikipedia ("The Free Encyclopedia")? The site appears to exist to convey basic information. Although the popularity of Wikipedia recommends it as a basic resource, you should approach the site with caution because it is not clear whether and how the information posted on the site is regulated. It is prudent to confirm information from Wikipedia by checking on sites that are regulated more transparently rather than take Wikipedia as an authoritative source.

■ Evaluate the Information on the Site

In addition to assessing the purpose of a Web site like Wikipedia, you need to evaluate the extent to which the information is recent, accurate, and consistent with information you find in print sources and clearly regulated Web sites. For example, clicking on "The modern English-only movement" on Wikipedia takes you to a timeline of sorts with a number of links to other sites. But again, what is the source of this information? What is included? What is left out? You should check further into some of these links, reading the sources cited and keeping in mind the four criteria for evaluating a claim—recency, relevance, reliability, and accuracy. In general, it is wise to treat Wikipedia as only a potential starting point. Most instructors don't allow students to cite Wikipedia entries as sources, but looking at relevant entries may lead you to trustworthy sources. Because you cannot be certain that Internet sources are reviewed or monitored, you need to be scrupulous about examining the claims they make: How much and what kind of evidence supports the author's (or site's) argument? Can you offer counterarguments?

In the last analysis, it comes down to whether the information you find stands up to the criteria you've learned to apply as a critical reader and writer. If not, move on to other sources. In a Web-based world of information, there is no shortage of material, but you have to train yourself not to settle for the information that is most readily available if you cannot determine that it is credible.

Steps to Evaluating Internet Sources

1 **Evaluate the author of the site.** Determine whether the author is an expert.

2 **Evaluate the organization that supports the site.** Find out what the organization stands for and the extent of its credibility.

3 **Evaluate the purpose of the site.** What interests are represented on the site? What is the site trying to do? Provide access to legitimate statistics and information? Advance an argument? Spread propaganda?

4 **Evaluate the information on the site.** Identify the type of information on the site and the extent to which the information is recent, relevant, reliable, and accurate.

A Practice Sequence: Evaluating Internet Sources

For this exercise, we would like you to work in groups on a common topic. The class can choose its own topic or use one of the topics we suggest on page 172. Then google the topic and agree on a Web site to analyze:

Group 1: Evaluate the author of the site.

Group 2: Evaluate the organization that supports the site.

Group 3: Evaluate the purpose of the site.

Group 4: Evaluate the information on the site.

Next, each group should share its evaluation. The goal is to determine the extent to which you believe you could use the information on this site in writing an academic essay.

WRITING AN ANNOTATED BIBLIOGRAPHY

In this chapter, we have suggested some strategies that you can use to locate information to help you learn more about a topic, issue, or question and to assess the extent to which this information can help you develop a legitimate, credible, and well-supported argument. As you read, it is important to write down the citation, or bibliographic information, of each source, including the author's name, date of publication, the title of an article or book, the journal title where an article appears, page numbers, and publishing information for a book.

Collecting the basic information about each source is useful, but we also suggest that you write an annotated bibliography to record your preliminary evaluation of the information you find. In writing an annotation, you should include the key ideas and claims from each source. You can also identify where you see gaps, misconceptions, and areas that you can build upon in developing your own argument. That is, in addition to stating what a given source is about, you can address the following questions: What is the issue the author responds to? What is the author's purpose? To what extent is the argument persuasive? Does it overlook any issues that are important? Finally, you can explain the relevance of this work to your own research, given your own purpose for writing and what you want to demonstrate.

You can limit each annotation to a few sentences in which you present the author's key claims and ideas, briefly analyze the author's argument, and then explain how you will use that information in your own researched argument. The annotation below provides one such example, using APA format for the citation.

> Loftstrom, M., & Tyler, J. H. (2009). Finishing high school: Alternative pathways and dropout recovery. *The Future of Children, 19*(1), 77–103. Retrieved from http://www.jstor.org/stable/27795036

> This article provides a good history and analysis of the present dropout problem facing our nation. Researchers examine the discrepancy in statewide high school completion requirements that have led to debates about reality of dropout rates. The authors also examine social and economic consequences of failure to complete high school and the inadequacy of a GED certificate as a replacement for a high school diploma. The researchers conclude by examining some dropout prevention programs and by calling for more research in this area. In doing so, they identify a gap that my research at an alternative high school can help to fill, especially my interviews with students currently enrolled in the program and those who have dropped out.

Steps to Writing an Annotated Bibliography

1 **Present key ideas.** Describe in just a few sentences what this research is about and what you have learned.

2 **Analyze.** Explain the situation the author responds to, the purpose of the research, possible gaps in reasoning or misconceptions, and adequacy of evidence.

3 **Determine relevance.** Discuss how you might use this research in developing your own argument. As background for your own work? To explain how you fill a gap or correct a misconception? Will you build upon and extend this work?

A Practice Sequence: Writing an Annotated Bibliography

Write an annotation of a book, book chapter, or article that you have read for your research. Follow the steps in the previous box by first discussing the content of what you have read and analyzing the author's argument. Then determine the relevance of this research to your own work. If you have not chosen a topic yet, we invite you to write an annotation of a book, book chapter, or article related to any of the following broad topics:

- higher education student loans
- the media and gender
- global health
- science and religion
- immigration

8

From Synthesis to Researched Argument

A **synthesis** is a discussion that forges connections between the arguments of two or more authors. Like a summary (discussed in Chapter 3), a synthesis requires you to understand the key claims of each author's argument, including his or her use of supporting examples and evidence. Also like a summary, a synthesis requires you to present a central idea, a *gist*, to your readers. But in contrast to a summary, which explains the context of a source, a synthesis creates a context for your own argument. That is, when you write a synthesis comparing two or more sources, you demonstrate that you are aware of the larger conversation about the issue and begin to claim your own place in that conversation.

Comparing different points of view prompts you to ask why they differ. It also makes you more aware of *counterarguments*—passages where claims conflict ("writer X says this, but writer Y asserts just the opposite") or at least differ ("writer X interprets this information this way, while writer Y sees it differently"). And it starts you formulating your own counterarguments: "Neither X nor Y has taken this into account. What if they had?"

Keep in mind that the purpose of a synthesis is not merely to list the similarities and differences you find in different sources or to assert your agreement with one source as opposed to others. Instead, it sets up your argument. Once you discover connections among texts, you have to decide what those connections mean to you and your readers. What bearing do they have on your own thinking? How can you make use of them in your argument?

WRITING A SYNTHESIS

To compose an effective synthesis, you must (1) make connections among ideas in different texts, (2) decide what those connections mean, and (3) formulate the gist of what you've read, much like you did when you wrote a summary. The difference is that in a synthesis, your gist should be a succinct statement that brings into focus not the central idea of one text but the relationship among different ideas in multiple texts.

To help you grasp strategies of writing a synthesis, read the following essays from activist Paul Rogat Loeb, who writes about building community through grassroots activism; educators Anne Colby and Thomas Ehrlich, whose work with the Carnegie Foundation for Teaching and Learning focuses on the reasons why young people, especially undergraduates, need to be more civically engaged in their communities; and Laurie Ouellette, a professor of communication studies who writes about media and the recent trend toward the media's efforts to do good works in local communities at a time when the federal government in the United States has cut social programs and continues to rely on private entities to support families in need. We have annotated these readings not only to comment on the ideas that these authors have put forth, but also to model some of the ways that you might annotate texts as a useful first step in writing a synthesis.

PAUL ROGAT LOEB

Making Our Lives Count
(from *Soul of a Citizen*)

Paul Rogat Loeb is an American social and political activist. A graduate of Stanford University, he has published widely in both newspapers and journals. *Hope in Hard Times* is one of several books that he has written and depicts ordinary Americans involved in grassroots peace activism, while *Soul of a Citizen* seeks to inspire civic engagement activism. His book *The Impossible Will Take a Little While*, an anthology of the achievements of activists in history who faced enormous obstacles, was named the #4 political book of 2004 by the History Channel and the American Book Association and won the Nautilus Book Award for the best social change book that year.

Souls are like athletes that need opponents worthy of them if they are to be tried and extended and pushed to the full use of their powers.

—THOMAS MERTON

***

"Heart," "spark," "spirit"—whatever word we use for the mysterious force that animates us, its full potential cannot be realized in isolation. Indeed, according to developmental psychologists, individual growth is possible only through interaction with the human and natural world, and through experiences that challenge us. "Souls are like athletes," wrote the Trappist monk Thomas Merton, "that need opponents worthy of them if they are to be tried and extended and pushed to the full use of their powers."

Cites research to emphasize the value of human interaction.

Many of us may already know the value of stretching our souls in personal life. We know the virtue of learning to voice our needs, fight for our choices, and recover from psychological intimidation. This process may require acknowledging painful truths, withstanding conflict, standing firm on what seems like shaky ground. We may need to question familiar habits, overcome self-doubt, and begin to separate who we really are from the roles we've been taught. Jungian analysts like James Hillman would say that by taking these steps we reconnect with what the Greeks called the *daimon,* the "acorn" of character at the core of our being. Psychiatrist M. Scott Peck described spiritual healing as "an ongoing process of becoming increasingly conscious."

Acknowledges that many of us are aware of the value of voicing our own needs and taking care of ourselves, and sets up the argument about community building.

We are slower to attempt such transformations in the public sphere. Self-assertion there requires us not only to modify our outlook and behavior but also to confront a bewildering and often disorienting maze of institutions and individuals, powers and principalities. So we stay silent in the face of common choices that we know are unwise or morally troubling. We keep our opinions to ourselves, because we doubt our voices will be heard, mistrust our right to speak,

Expresses concern that we may be less likely to think about our well-being as connected to others in the public sphere. Also identifies with those who may be reluctant to be assertive in the public sphere because they fear their voices won't be heard.

1

2

3

or fear the consequences if we do speak out. We feel we lack essential political skills. Like … Rosa Parks before her first NAACP meeting, we simply do not know we have it in us.

Elaborates on his point that human connection is necessary. Uses an anecdote to show how getting involved with others helps us better understand who we are as individuals.

Yet coming out of one's cocoon in the public 4
sphere is just as necessary to self-realization as it is in the private. I once told a young Puerto Rican activist about the notion, common among many of his fellow students, that they'd lose their identity by getting involved—find themselves "swallowed up" by the movements they joined. He laughed and said the reverse was true. "You learn things you never knew about yourself. You get pushed to your limits. You meet people who make you think and push you further. You don't lose your identity. You begin to find out who you really are. I feel sad for people who will never have this experience."

Reiterates his point that interacting with others teaches us about who we are and what we value. Cites the work of a scholar who studies Buddhism and a doctor who believes her work in low-income communities has helped her be a better version of herself.

You begin to find out who you really are. The 5
implication is clear enough: We become human only in the company of other human beings. And this involves both opening our hearts and giving voice to our deepest convictions. The biblical vision of *shalom* describes this process with its concept of "right relationships" with our fellow humans, and with all of God's creation. The turning point for the Buddha, writes James Hillman, came only "when he left his protected palace gardens to enter the street. There the sick, the dead, the poor, and the old drew his soul down into the question of how to live life in the world." As Hillman stresses, the Buddha became who he was precisely by leaving the cloistered life. A doctor I know works in a low-income clinic because, she says, "seeing the struggles of others helps me be true to myself. It helps me find out how people in very different circumstances live out their humanity." Community involvement, in other words, is the mirror that best reflects our individual choices, our strengths and weaknesses, our accomplishments and failures. It allows our lives to count for something.

Community involvement helps us see that we matter.

The Cost of Silence

Offers an illustration to support the value of activism but also shows that speaking out for what we value can have its costs.

Twenty years after Harvard Law School hired him as its first fulltime African American professor, Derrick Bell took an unpaid protest leave, refusing to teach until the school hired a minority woman to its faculty. It was not a decision made in haste. Bell had long campaigned for this. But each time a new position opened, the Law School somehow could find not a single minority female candidate in the world who was worthy enough to hire. The school's resistance continued despite Bell's stand. After three years, the school forced him to resign. His conscience had cost him a tenured job at the most prestigious law school in America.

What might seem like failure can actually be a factor that bolsters our commitment to make a difference.

Yet Bell didn't feel defeated. Quite the opposite. His public stance had preserved his core identity and integrity. "It is the determination to protect our sense of who we are," he writes, "that leads us to risk criticism, alienation, and serious loss while most others, similarly harmed, remain silent."

Helps readers understand that remaining silent about issues that matter can be more costly than failed action.

What Bell means is that silence is more costly than speaking out, because it requires the ultimate sacrifice—the erosion of our spirit. The toll we pay for stifling our emotions in personal life is fairly obvious. Swallowed words act like caustic acids, eating at our gut. If the condition persists and the sentiments are sufficiently intense, we grow numb, detached, dead to the world around us. When, however, we take steps to redress our private losses and sorrows, we often feel a renewed sense of strength and joy, of reconnecting with life.

One cost to remaining silent is that we are no longer true to ourselves and we lose our ability to be whole human beings.

A similar process occurs when we want to address public issues but stay silent. It takes energy to mute our voices while the environment is ravaged, greed runs rampant, and families sleep in the streets. It takes energy to distort our words and actions because we fear the consequences of speaking out. It takes energy, in other words, to sustain what the psychiatrist Robert Jay Lifton calls "the broken connection," splitting our

6

7

8

9

lives from our values. Like autistic children, we can blank out the voices of our fellow human beings. But if we do, we risk the decay of our humanity. When we shrink from the world, our souls shrink, too.

Cites additional research to explain how serving our communities with others can have an effect on us physically, not just psychologically, and contribute to our health and well-being.

Social involvement reverses this process, releas-   10
ing our choked-off energy, overcoming the psychic paralysis that so many of us feel, reintegrating mind and heart, body and soul, so that we can speak in one voice—our own—and mean what we say. There's even a physical corollary to this integration. In *The Healing Power of Doing Good*, Allan Luks describes various studies that confirm what he calls the "helper's high." People who volunteer in their communities experience significantly greater physical pleasure and well-being in the process of their work, a general sense of increased energy, and in some cases an easing of chronic pain. A Harvard School of Public Health study found that African Americans who challenged repeated discrimination had lower blood pressure than those who did not. So taking stands for what we believe may help us save more than our souls.

Cites further evidence to explain the importance of acting on our convictions.

Sociologist Parker Palmer describes the result-   11
ing unleashing of truth, vision, and strength in the lives of people like Rosa Parks, Vaclav Havel, Nelson Mandela, and Dorothy Day, who've acted on their deepest beliefs. "These people," he wrote, "have understood that no punishment could be worse than the one we inflict on ourselves by living a divided life." And nothing could be more powerful than the decision to heal that rift, "to stop acting differently on the outside from what they knew to be true inside."

Learned Helplessness

Laments the extent to which American culture seems to work against the idea of activism, community work, and human agency—the ability to envision change and the capacity to act on our convictions in meaningful ways.

America's predominant culture insists that little we   12
do can matter. It teaches us not to get involved in shaping the world we'll pass on to our children. It encourages us to leave such important decisions to others—whether they be corporate and government leaders, or social activists whose lifestyles seem impossibly selfless or foreign. Sadly, and ironically, in

a country born of a democratic political revolution, to be American in recent years is too often to be apolitical. For many, civic withdrawal has become the norm. The 2008 presidential campaign challenged this trend by inspiring vast numbers of previously disengaged citizens to volunteer in ways that shifted not only the presidential race, but also close races for the Senate, the House, and state governorships. But even then over a third of potentially eligible Americans ended up staying home. And despite all the passionate volunteers, far more citizens did little beyond casting their vote. Absent a highly contested election, it's easier still to sit on the sidelines and simply hope our leaders will take care of things.

Argues that we need to adopt a view of democratic engagement that our Founding Fathers offered.

Overcoming our instinctive civic withdrawal re- 13 quires courage. It requires learning the skills and developing the confidence to participate.... It also requires creating a renewed definition of ourselves as citizens—something closer to the nation of active stakeholders that leaders like Thomas Jefferson had in mind.

The importance of citizens' direct participation in 14 a democracy was expressed thousands of years ago, by the ancient Greeks. In fact, they used the word "idiot" for people incapable of involving themselves in civic life. Now, the very word "political" has become so debased in our culture that we use it to describe either trivial office power plays or leaders who serve largely personal ambitions. We've lost sight of its original roots in the Greek notion of the *polis*: the democratic sphere in which citizens, acting in concert, determine the character and direction of their society. "All persons alike," wrote Aristotle, should share "in the government to the utmost."

Uses a play to illustrate the extent to which it is not enough to focus on problems without taking action.

Reclaiming this political voice requires more than 15 just identifying problems, which itself can feed our sense of overload. I think of an Arthur Miller play, *Broken Glass*, whose heroine obsesses while Hitler steadily consolidates his power. From her safe home in Brooklyn, she reads newspaper articles about *Kristallnacht:* synagogues smashed and looted; old men forced to scrub streets with toothbrushes while storm troopers laugh at them; and finally, children shipped off to the camps in cattle cars. Her concern contrasts with the approach of her family and friends, who insist, despite the mounting evidence, that such horrors are exaggerated. Yet she does nothing to address the situation publicly, except to grow more anxious. Eventually she becomes psychosomatically paralyzed.

The approach Miller's protagonist takes toward the horrors of Nazism echoes that of far too many people who spend hours following every twist and turn of the twenty-four-hour news cycle, yet never take action that might address them. It also resembles the condition of learned helplessness. People who suffer from severe depression, psychologist Martin Seligman found, do so less as a result of particular unpleasant experiences than because of their "explanatory style"—the story they tell themselves about how the world works. Depressed people have become convinced that the causes of their difficulties are permanent and pervasive, inextricably linked to their personal failings. There's nothing to be done because nothing can be done. This master narrative of their lives excuses inaction; it provides a rationale for remaining helpless. In contrast, individuals who function with high effectiveness tend to believe that the problems they face result from factors that are specific, temporary, and therefore changeable. The story they live by empowers them.

The story we tell ourselves about the world can either lead us to a feeling of helplessness or a sense of empowerment — that there are things we can do to create change.

This is not to say that change is easy, nor that everyone is in an equal position to bring it about. Some individuals and groups in America possess far more material and organizational resources than others. This reflects our deep social and economic inequities. But as *Tikkun* magazine founder Rabbi Michael Lerner has observed, we often fail to use the resources we do have, which may be of a different kind. "Most of us," Lerner says, "have been subjected to a set of experiences in our childhood and adult lives that makes us feel that we do not deserve to have power." Consequently, we can't imagine changing the direction of

16

17

our society. We decide that things are worse than they actually are—a condition Lerner refers to as "surplus powerlessness."...

The illusion of powerlessness can just as easily afflict the fortunate among us. I know many people who are confident and successful in their work and have loving personal relationships, yet can hardly conceive of trying to work toward a more humane society. Materially comfortable and professionally accomplished, they could make important social contributions. Instead they restrict their search for meaning and integrity to their private lives. Their sense of shared fate extends only to their immediate families and friends. Despite their many advantages, they, too, have been taught an "explanatory style" that precludes participation in public life, except to promote the most narrow self-interest.

Whatever our situations, we all face a choice. We can ignore the problems that lie just beyond our front doors; we can allow decisions to be made in our names that lead to a meaner and more desperate world. We can yell at the TV newscasters and complain about how bad things are, using our bitterness as a hedge against involvement. Or we can work, as well as we can, to shape a more generous common future.

Points out that some of the most well-off people are driven by self-interest when they might use their wealth to make important "social contributions."

Leaves us with a clear decision about whether or not we allow others to make choices for us or to take on the responsibility of working for the common good.

18

19

ANNE COLBY AND THOMAS EHRLICH, WITH ELIZABETH BEAUMONT AND JASON STEPHENS
Undergraduate Education and the Development of Moral and Civic Responsibility

At the time that the two primary authors published this essay, they worked at the Carnegie Foundation for the Advancement of Teaching, a U.S.-based education policy and research center founded by Andrew Carnegie in 1905. The foundation embraces a commitment to developing networks of ideas, individuals, and institutions to advance teaching and learning. Anne Colby holds a PhD in psychology from Columbia and currently serves as a consulting professor at Stanford University. Prior to that, she was director of the Henry Murray Research Center at Harvard University. With Thomas Ehrlich, she published *Educating for Democracy: Preparing Undergraduates* for *Responsible Political Engagement* and won the 2013 Frederic W. Ness Book Award for their book *Rethinking Undergraduate Business Education: Liberal Learning for the Profession*. Thomas Ehrlich is a consulting professor at the Stanford Graduate School of Education. He is a graduate of Harvard College and Harvard Law School and holds five honorary degrees. Professor Ehrlich has previously served as president of Indiana University, provost of the University of Pennsylvania, and dean of Stanford Law School. His most recent book (2013) is *Civic Work, Civic Lessons: Two Generations Reflect on Public Service*.

■ ■ ■

Shares a concern that Loeb expresses about trends toward increased individualism and lack of civic engagement. Especially interested in reaching out to undergraduates, whereas Loeb addresses a more general audience.

We are among those increasingly concerned about two related trends in contemporary American culture—excessive individualism and moral relativism on the one hand and popular disdain for civic engagement, particularly political involvement, on the other. In our view, undergraduate years are an important time for developing in students moral and civic responsibility that can help reverse these trends. This essay describes our work-in-progress, under the auspices of the Carnegie Foundation for the Advancement of Teaching, to analyze the American undergraduate scene in terms of efforts to promote students' moral and civic responsibility and to encourage our colleges and universities to strengthen those efforts.

Stresses the responsibility that universities and colleges have to encourage students to be involved.

As concerned with morality as with civic engagement, which is a departure from Loeb. Maintains that moral and civic responsibility are inextricably linked.

Some people who have written about these issues have focused exclusively on civic responsibility, avoiding the more controversial area of morality (e.g., Barber, 1998). We include moral as well as civic responsibility in the scope of our project, because we believe the two are inseparable. Our democratic principles, including tolerance and respect for others, procedural impartiality, and concern for both the rights of the individual and the welfare of the group, are all grounded in moral principles. Likewise, the problems that the civically engaged citizen must confront always include strong moral themes—for example, fair access to resources such as housing, the moral obligation to consider future generations in making environmental policy, and the conflicting claims of multiple stakeholders in community decision-making. None of these issues can be adequately resolved

Elaborates on how moral principles are tied to democratic principles. Contends that decision making relies on having a "strong moral compass."

1

2

Educators must commit themselves to teaching civic responsibility and morality.

without a consideration of moral questions. A person can become civically and politically active without good judgment and a strong moral compass, but it is hardly wise to promote that kind of involvement. Because civic responsibility is inescapably threaded with moral values, we believe that higher education must aspire to foster both moral and civic maturity and must confront educationally the many links between them.

Defines moral engagement in broad terms to promote thoughtful reflection and call upon institutions of higher education to foster moral engagement.

What do we mean by "moral" and by "civic"? We consider "moral," in its broadest sense, to include matters of values both personal and public. As we use the term, "morality" is not confined to a specific sphere of life or action, nor is it necessarily tied to religion. In advocating moral engagement, we are not promoting any particular moral or meta-ethical viewpoint. Rather, we are interested in fostering more thoughtful moral reflection generally and the adoption of viewpoints and commitments that emerge from reasoned consideration. We believe that higher education should encourage and facilitate the development of students' capacities to examine complex situations in which competing values are often at stake, to employ both substantive knowledge and moral reasoning to evaluate the problems and values involved, to develop their own judgments about those issues, and then to act on their judgments.

3

Defines civic engagement as a necessary means for sustaining a democracy that encompasses both thoughtful reflection and subsequent action.

We consider "civic" to range over all social spheres beyond the family, from neighborhoods and local communities to state, national, and cross-national arenas. Political engagement is a particular subset of civic engagement that is required for sustaining American democracy. We are not promoting a single type of civic or political engagement, but instead urging that the effective operation of social systems and the successful achievement of collective goals demand the time, attention, understanding, and action of all citizens. Institutions of higher education have both the opportunity and obligation to cultivate in their graduates an appreciation for the responsibilities and rewards of civic engagement, as well as to

4

foster the capacities necessary for thoughtful participation in public discourse and effective participation in social enterprises.

In general terms, we believe that a morally and civically responsible individual recognizes himself or herself as a member of a larger social fabric and therefore considers social problems to be at least partly his or her own; such an individual is willing to see the moral and civic dimensions of issues, to make and justify informed moral and civic judgments, and to take action when appropriate. 5

We believe that moral and civic development is enhanced by mutually interdependent sets of knowledge, virtues, and skills. Because they are interdependent, no simple listing of attributes is adequate. Such a listing may imply that the elements involved have precise definitions and parameters that might be gained through a single course or even from reading a few books. We have come to understand through studying various colleges and universities that this is not the case. Instead, enriching the moral and civic responsibility of all members of the campus community is best achieved through the cumulative, interactive effect of numerous curricular and extracurricular programs, within an environment of sustained institutional commitment to these overarching goals.... 6

Included in the core knowledge we consider integral to moral and civic learning is knowledge of basic ethical concepts and principles, such as justice and equity, and how they have been interpreted by various seminal thinkers. Also included is a comprehension of the diversity of American society and global cultures, and an understanding of both the institutions and processes of American and international civic, political, and economic affairs. Finally, deep substantive knowledge of the particular issues in which one is engaged is critical. 7

This core of knowledge cannot be separated from the virtues and skills that a morally and civically responsible individual should strive to attain. The virtues and skills we have in mind are not distinct to moral and civic learning but are necessary for active 8

The teaching of civic and moral engagement should occur in different fields of study and programs supported by a national organization such as the Carnegie Foundation for the Advancement of Teaching.

Avoids defining values that can inform judgment, but offers a description of core knowledge and concepts that educators should impart to their students.

Core knowledge of key issues and an understanding of civic, political, and economic concerns should go hand in hand with moral and civic learning.

engagement in many personal and professional realms. Among the core virtues is the willingness to engage in critical self-examination and to form reasoned commitments, balanced by open-mindedness and a willingness to listen to and take seriously the ideas of others. Moral and civic responsibility also requires honesty in dealings with others, and in holding oneself accountable for one's action and inactions.

Elaborates upon the idea of community building that Loeb introduces, particularly empathy, trust, and compassion.

Without a basis of trust, and habits of cooperation, no community can operate effectively. Empathy and compassion are also needed, not only for relating to those in one's immediate social sphere, but for relating to those in the larger society as well. Willingness to form moral and civic commitments and to act on those is a core virtue that puts the others into practice.

Finally, the core skills of moral and civic responsibility are essential for applying core knowledge and virtues, transforming informed judgments into

Maintains that to act requires applying core knowledge and values, in contrast to Loeb, who uses evidence from sociology, health, and psychology to inspire people to become civically and politically engaged.

action. They include the abilities to recognize the moral and civic dimensions of issues and to take a stand on those issues. But they also include skills that apply to much broader arenas of thought and behavior, such as abilities to communicate clearly orally and in writing, to collect, organize, and analyze information, to think critically and to justify positions with reasoned arguments, to see issues from the perspectives of others and to collaborate with others. They also include the ability and willingness to lead, to build a consensus, and to move a group forward under conditions of mutual respect.

9

LAURIE OUELLETTE

Citizen Brand: ABC and the Do Good Turn in US Television

Laurie Ouellette is a professor of communication studies at the University of Minnesota. The author of *Lifestyle TV* and coauthor of *Better Living through Reality TV: Television and Post-Welfare Citizenship*, she has published extensively about public broadcasting, TV history, fashion and style, self-help culture, and social media.

The greatest moments in life are not concerned with self-ish achievement, but rather with the things we do for other people.

—WALT DISNEY

***

Better Communities and Corporate Citizens

Introduces the idea of corporate sponsorship of community involvement and raises the question of what has motivated this kind of initiative to involve viewers, actors, and the like.

In 2002, ABC launched its long-running Better Community public outreach campaign, with a mission of advancing the television network's standing as a corporate citizen through "community outreach efforts that serve the public interest, inform and inspire." ... Encompassing announcements urging TV viewers to perform community service, as well as an online guide to volunteering and a slate of popular entertainment programs showcasing corporate and personal humanitarianism, the campaign positioned ABC as a socially responsible corporate citizen. More than this, it constituted ABC as a gateway to a Better Community comprising network stars, nonprofit partners, commercial sponsors, and socially conscious TV viewers who—much more than other television consumers—contribute resources (time and money) to the well-being of the communities in which they live. Why would ABC pursue what it claimed to be the "comprehensive and recognizable public service initiative" on US television in the wake of deregulatory policies? To make sense of the Better Community initiative—and the television industry's investment in civic empowerment more broadly—it is useful to trace the burgeoning and deeply intertwined currency of communitarian discourse and corporate social responsibility.

Uses the term "civic empowerment," which is different from Loeb, as well as Colby and her colleagues. Also introduces the word "communitarian" to the conversation.

1

Offers some historical perspective and describes some of the economic reforms in government that have placed more responsibility on private citizens, among others, to support children and families living in poverty.

The Better Community campaign appeared in the midst of the reinvention of government in the US, an assemblage of reforms encompassing public sector downsizing, the encouragement of public–private partnerships, the outsourcing of many government services to commercial firms, and the dismantling of welfare programs.... ABC translated a bipartisan call for private initiative and personal responsibility as empowering alternatives to big government into

2

TV stations like ABC interpreted the call for more private and personal responsibility as a way to promote volunteerism and their own interests. Community activism would replace social welfare programs, while the government fostered a free, unregulated economic market.

fifteen-second public service announcements that doubled as station promotions, and advertising stuffed entertainment revolving around corporate giving and volunteerism. The campaign embraced the entre-preneurial zeal guiding political reform, but it also inserted the ABC television network and its viewers into communitarian solutions to the underside of unfettered capitalism. Like other examples of do good television, the Better Community campaign exempli-fies an enterprising turn in governing and at the same time seeks to help overcome the consequences of a pure market logic in the civic realm.

Corporate social responsibility seems separate from political interests while still support-ing democracy, but corporate involve-ment has its roots in efforts by both former presidents Bush and Clinton to find alternatives to welfare programs.

Community is an especially popular corporate civic objective due to its positive currency and safe distance from unruly political activism or controversy. The turn to community, which is also a dominant theme in do good television, is also closely intertwined with communitarian political discourses and strategies of governing. Communitarianism is an applied political philosophy that endorses market capitalism and lim-ited public powers but calls for additional changes to ensure the civic functionality of democratic societies. It advocates the nourishing of voluntary associations as a buffer between the downsized welfare state and the competitive self-interest found in the commercial marketplace.... Both the Clinton and Bush adminis-trations adopted communitarian models of "govern-ing through community," from the designation of community empowerment zones as an alternative to public housing programs (Clinton) to the creation of

Observes that an ethic of communitarianism derives from policy, in contrast to the moral argument that Colby and her col-leagues describe or the humanitarian principles that Loeb explains. Communitarianism has become necessary in the absence of government-supported programs.

the Office of Faith-Based and Community Initiatives to "nourish dispersed religious and civil alternatives to public welfare programs" and a USA Freedom Corps Volunteer Network to mobilize citizens into "armies of compassion" (Bush). Bush also entrusted the new President's Council on National and Com-munity Service, composed of leaders from business, entertainment, sports, the nonprofit sector, educa-tion, and media, to help the White House cultivate a stronger ethic of service and responsibility in the US. While there were crucial differences between Clinton

3

and Bush, the point to be made here is that community has become an objective of governing across political regimes. This matters for our purposes for two reasons: First, good communities (like good citizens) are not born but made—constituted through policies, political discourses, and cultural technologies such as television. Second, as Nikolas Rose persuasively contends, community has become "another word for citizenship" that stresses civic duties rather than collective entitlements. Rose sees the uptake of communitarianism as a substitute for a diminishing social contract—an intervention that softens the "harshest dimensions of neo-capitalist restructuring" by encouraging citizens to serve associations (neighborhoods, localities, social networks, families) that are "decidedly private and which more or less absolve the state of responsibility for society."...

In the US, communitarianism is closely associated with prominent scholar and political consultant Amitai Etzioni.... In his many books, speeches, and ongoing work with the Institute for Communitarian Studies at George Washington University, Etzioni promotes an understanding of community as a counterbalance to a model of society created in the image of the "marketplace, in which self-serving individuals compete with one another."... Communities, he contends, also offset the need for public oversight by reinforcing a voluntary moral order rooted in "traditional values" of respectability, responsibility, and independence. Conceived as dispersed, self-managed ethical zones, community poses an alternative not only to the welfare state but also to the model of democracy associated with broadcast regulation and earlier interpretations of the public interest in television. As Rose points out, community as conceived by Etzioni and other influential thinkers offers a way to "regenerate society" that comes not from "law, information, reason, or deliberative democracy" but from moral "dialogue and action" within voluntary associations....

4

Traces the term "communitarianism" to one scholar who developed a model of communitarian values that seems to mirror those of Colby and her colleagues, given their similar emphasis on "moral dialogue and action."

While Etzioni naturalizes the space of community, he concedes that citizens *must be trained* to "participate in communitarian society." Even those who have "acquired virtue" will require ongoing guidance, "for if left to their own devices... [they] gradually lose much of their commitment to values."...

Cites Putnam's study reported in Bowling Alone and reiterates concerns of others about the decline of volunteerism and civic engagement. This decline seems connected, according to another scholar, Rose, to a number of social problems.

What Rose calls technologies of community have proliferated since the 1990s, offering tutelage and instruction. This is partly a response to widely circulating reports of declining volunteerism, everyday philanthropy, and civic engagement in the US. Robert Putnam's influential study *Bowling Alone* lamented the collapse of voluntary associations, indicating that few contemporary Americans demonstrate the civic propensities that Alexis de Tocqueville credited with the "capacity to make democracy work."... By the mid-1990s, barely one American in three reported any charitable giving in the previous month, and fewer than two in five claimed even "occasional religious giving," according to Putnam's study.... These trends paralleled an equally sharp reduction in participation in community institutions, from lodges to parent-teacher associations.... As Rose points out, the "decline of community" ascribed to these trends was also held responsible for a slew of civic problems, from "drugs, crime and alienation, to family breakdown and the loss of good neighborliness."... For Putnam (who penned Bush's 2001 inaugural speech), any attempt to reinvent government also needed to "revitalize" community and its subjects.

While communitarianism gained currency, corporate social responsibility was also actively encouraged as a dimension of governmental reform. Both Clinton and Bush called on the corporate sector to partner in social programs and fill gaps left by the divested welfare state. As Andrew Barry argues, the market's willingness to take on responsibility for ethical problems is not surprising. In an era when "direct state control has declined," he explains, corporations are increasingly expected to "perform the job of government at

Introduces the term "cause marketing," which combines the ideas of corporate social responsibility and profit. This concept highlights the role that businesses have taken on in the context of economic reform and the responsibility of businesses to make money. It seems that corporate social responsibility is a key to financial success.

a distance."... Yet, the rise of cause marketing, corporate philanthropy, and other manifestations of what Barry calls ethical capitalism are only viable to the extent that they are also profitable. The age of paternalistic philanthropy, exemplified by Andrew Carnegie's view of wealth as a "sacred trust, which its possessor was bound to administer for the good of the community," passed some time ago.... In 1970, Milton Friedman, a leading figure of the Chicago school of neoliberalism, unapologetically declared in the *New York Times*, "The social responsibility of business is to increase profits."... Nonetheless, corporations have increasingly embraced objectives (fundraising for cures, promoting recycling, citizenship training) that blur boundaries between public and private, governing and profiteering. According to business historian David Vogel, this development is not only the outcome of public sector downsizing and government at a distance. As the entrepreneurial spirit was reforming the welfare state, many corporations were discovering a lucrative "market for virtue." Today, says Vogel, corporate social responsibility is approached not as an unprofitable duty but as the key to successful profit maximization....

Cites one scholar who reiterates a concern the author shares: corporate social responsibility has become a means for creating wealth rather than a virtuous act of being involved in "ethical issues" and "civic affairs."

In his genealogy of corporate social responsibility, Vogel argues that contemporary advocates of ethical capitalism have basically accepted "Friedman's position that the primary responsibility of companies is to create wealth for their shareholders"—with an important twist: in order for companies to maximize profit, he explains, the prevailing assumption is that "they must now act virtuously." In other words, social responsibility is enacted less as a paternalistic duty than as a competitive business strategy. "Never before has the claim that corporate virtue can and should be profitable enjoyed so much currency or influence," Vogel writes.... The new tendency to approach social responsibility as an instrument of profitability is the outcome of the neoliberal reforms, including deregulation and expanded entrepreneurialism, that Friedman and his colleagues promoted, and that spawned a

7

perceived need for greater corporate involvement in ethical issues and civic affairs....

Points out that the trend toward "citizen branding" represents this shift in emphasis away from civic engagement for its own sake toward profitability. Doing so has entailed masking the profit motive to project an image of a company committed to doing good work in the community.

The concept of the citizen brand, which has revolutionized marketing in recent years, takes this a step further by placing corporations and consumer culture at the center of governing and citizenship. In his book *Citizen Brand: 10 Commandments Transforming Brand Culture in a Consumer Democracy* (2002), Mark Gobé argues that corporations that wish to increase profits will have to distance themselves from the greed and exploitation associated with deregulated global capitalism. One way of doing so, he suggests, is to integrate do good activities into business plans and branding strategies so that an image of trust and ethics can be built on a "real dedication to being part of human solutions around the world."... In his manual *Citizen Brands: Putting Society at the Heart of Your Business* (2003), Michael Willmott agrees that citizenship must "be a part of branding" and explains how the public interest can be harnessed as a form of market intelligence.... As one example, he suggests that public support for community (bolstered by the policies and discourses discussed earlier) can be appropriated as an objective of corporate citizenship and channeled into "economic success."...

The Better Community campaign exemplifies the ethical turn in capitalism, presented not as an obligation (which might imply public oversight) but as ABC's *choice* to advance an empowering civic agenda. ABC is positioned at the center of communitarian strategies for activating citizens and buffering the consequences of privatization and welfare reform. Public outreach entails channeling the demands being placed on individuals and communities into the ethical value of the ABC network. It is not coincidental that the Better Community project is overseen entirely by ABC Corporate Initiatives, for its approach to doing good is much more compatible with new directions in marketing and branding than were earlier (unrealized) public service ideals emphasizing rational debate and an informed citizenry.

8

9

Citizen Disney and the Rebranding of ABC

Disney, overseeing the rebranding of ABC, represents the trend the author has described — taking on the role of responsible corporate citizen and promoting the role of the good citizen.

The Disney Corporation, the parent corporation of   *10*
ABC, is a prime example of the multilayered use of community as a technology of governing, a strategic business practice, and a branding strategy. The Disney Corporation, the largest media conglomerate in the world, characterizes itself as a good neighbor visibly committed to social responsibility (exemplified by employee volunteer programs and corporate giving) and humanitarian causes — particularly community and the environment. Disney has diffused these commitments across its corporate holdings, including film studios, theme parks, television networks, and cable channels.... The Disney-owned ESPN channel incorporates volunteerism and community service into its operations, enticing employees and "sports enthusiasts" at home to make a difference by volunteering on behalf of nonprofit organizations. The (now defunct) SOAPNet partnered with volunteer events in Hollywood and sponsored community outreach programs in public schools, using soap opera clips to promote family, responsibility, and communication skills. The Disney-ABC Television Group, which oversees the Disney Channel and ABC, is also dedicated to "serving and inspiring individuals and communities through a variety of public service initiatives and outreach programs." Disney-ABC claims that it "proudly supports non-profit organizations in their endeavors to make the world a better place," while its television channels — with their capacity to reach millions of people — provide "ideal platforms to inspire viewers to drive positive change in their

Attributes Disney's investment in humanitarian endeavors to changes in federal policies. While writers such as Putnam and Etzioni might lament the fragmentation of community, media is also now responsible for increased civic engagement and community building.

communities." ...

Disney's investment in community and volunteerism is related to the reinvention of government. Disney was a corporate partner in the Bush White House's efforts to encourage volunteerism as a solution to postwelfare needs and problems. Disney also sponsored the National Conference on Volunteering and Service organized by the Corporation for National Community Service, the Points of Light   *11*

Foundation, and the USA Freedom Corps. At the 2005 meeting, leaders from government and the corporate sector met to devise strategies for developing volunteer service (a term used to describe everything from corporate giving to bake sales) to meet America's "pressing social needs." The responsibilities bestowed upon corporations and individual citizens were evident by the keynote speeches: US Department of Health and Human Services secretary Mike Leavitt lectured on the importance of "economic goodness" and the closing remarks were delivered by Mark Victor Hansen, best-selling author of the Christian self-help book *Chicken Soup for the Soul*.... It is telling, but not surprising, that culture industries and popular media figured heavily in the brainstorming session. Although communitarians (including Etzioni and Putnam) condemn mass media as a factor in the decline of community, television and the web are also recognized as useful instruments for retraining citizens and rebuilding voluntary associations independently of big government. ABC's Better Community campaign is one such technology, operating at a distance from the state to constitute responsibility for post-welfare society as a corporate and community affair.

ABC has inserted itself into the communitarian space between the uncaring market and so-called welfare dependency. The question remains: If corporate social responsibility is now practiced as a profit-making endeavor, as Vogel suggests, how does the Better Community campaign fuel ABC's and Disney's coffers? To understand how valuable commitments to ethical business and community building have become for the cultural industries, it is worth juxtaposing the current approach to public service with the "all-business" mentality unleashed by broadcast deregulation. While Disney has always billed itself as an all-American company committed to traditional values, the media mergers and takeovers of the 1980s led all conglomerates to an intensified focus on the bottom line. Within an increasingly competitive

Despite the benefits of citizen branding, the author again reminds us that we cannot ignore the profit motive of companies that have fulfilled a role once played by the federal government in what is now a postwelfare state. To what extent are these roles in conflict with one another?

12

industrial climate, former Disney CEO Michael Eisner confessed in a 1981 memo, "We have no obligation to make history; we have no obligation to make art; we have no obligation to make a statement; to make money is our only objective." ... Sounding a lot like Milton Friedman a decade earlier, Eisner acknowledged that the company's primary, indeed sole, purpose was to maximize profits for shareholders. As late as 1997, the ABC television network (recently purchased by Disney) owned up to a similar sentiment with its TV is Good branding campaign. Mocking any notion that television should serve a purpose higher than producing wealth, the spots proudly positioned ABC as a venue for the hedonistic consumption of trivial entertainment. Pitting TV viewers seeking pleasure and escape against the concerns of do good reformers, the advertisements offered tongue-in-cheek advice such as "Life is short. Watch TV" and "Don't worry, you've got billions of brain cells."

ABC's attempt to brand the right to consume television with no redeeming attributes was short-lived. In 2002, the network switched gears dramatically with what it called the most visible public service campaign on television. Branded as ABC—A Better Community, the campaign generated more than 100 public service announcements to date, in which ABC stars urge TV viewers to "make a difference" in their communities. Early in the campaign, the talent read quotations by famous historical figures in order to situate ABC within a recognizable genealogy of ethical activity and public service. Interspersed with pitches for automobiles, mouthwash, and diet soda were reminders that: *"You make a living by what you get, but you make a life by what you give"* (Winston Churchill); *"Everyone has the power for greatness ... because greatness is determined by service"* (Dr. Martin Luther King Jr.); *"No man can sincerely help another without helping himself"* (Ralph Waldo Emerson); *"The best way to find yourself ... is to lose yourself in the service of others"* (Mahatma Gandhi); and *"The greatest moments in life are not concerned with selfish*

13

Describes how ABC and Disney rebranded themselves with public service announcements and connecting their work in media with public service.

achievement, but rather with the things we do for other people" (Walt Disney).

Visually framed by the ABC Better Community logo, accompanied by inspirational music and ending with a call to action (including a visit to the ABC website), the spots linked ABC to an iconic pantheon of civic leadership. Within the logic of the campaign, the political differences between entrepreneurs like Disney and activists like King were insignificant; what mattered was their shared commitment to doing good—a moral disposition to which the ABC audience should aspire. Once ABC had established its ethical credibility, the inspirational passages were dropped and well-known ABC stars such as George Lopez (*The George Lopez Show*), Nicollette Sheridan (*Desperate Housewives*), and Evangeline Lilly (*Lost*) urged TV viewers to take specific actions, like becoming a mentor or cleaning up a neighborhood park. The stars took over as civic tutors in the new promotions, guiding the conduct of individuals while also constituting ABC as a Better Community on the basis of values presumably shared by executives, talent, and audiences. While the initial spots had selectively linked civic progress to the legacy of political figures like King, the announcements that followed disassociated good citizenship from any reminder of grassroots activism or critique. What was radical about the campaign, however, was its aggressive attempt to move TV viewers away from their sets, into civic life. Breaking commercial television's associations with leisure, domesticity, and passive consumption, it recast the ABC audience as an active community of unselfish, civically responsible people. The imagined viewer was addressed as an ethical subject who, with gentle reminders and practical advice, could make a difference in the world outside commercial television. In this way the public service campaign provides what Etzioni calls the training required to "restrain impulses," "delay gratification," and balance "pleasure and living up to one's moral commitments."...

Takes a critical stance toward ABC's rebranding that associated their calls for public service with Martin Luther King's leadership during the civil rights movement. Ignoring differences enabled ABC to project an image that is problematic but clearly served ABC's goals.

Acknowledges the extent to which this strategy was able to position ABC as an ethical corporation and viewers as responsible citizens.

In 2006, ABC re-launched the Better Community *15*
initiative with much fanfare. The renewed commitment to community service provided the occasion
for a new round of publicity kicked off by a special
announcement from actress Geena Davis. Davis,
who portrayed the first female president of the
US on ABC's (now-canceled) drama *Commander-in-
Chief*, addressed the audience during a special network showing of *The Ten Commandments*. Drawing

Illustrates the way
media corporations
can use celebrities
to add credibility to
their message, even
when the reference is
a fictional character
on TV.

civic credibility from her television character and a
moral compass from the biblical film, she reiterated
the ABC network's unique contributions to community service and volunteerism. Davis also reminded
viewers of their crucial role in realizing the network's
mission by making a difference in the communities
in which they live. Here as before, the Better Community was doubly constituted as an imagined community whose membership involved consuming ABC,
and as the outcome of suggested civic actions. Carried out across multiple sites, these actions supported
the communitarian turn in government while also
providing coveted ethical value to the ABC brand.

The profitability of corporate social responsibil- *16*
ity and community is realized in the generation of
brand identity and value. The stakes are high for a
mass television network in the age of cultural fragmentation and niche marketing. As one handbook
on the television business explains, "In a world with
dozens and eventually hundreds of television channels, those with the most clearly differentiated brands
would be the ones most likely to succeed." ... ABC

Adds one more term,
"brand community,"
to describe
corporations' efforts
to distinguish their
product from others
in an increasingly
competitive
market and foster
the development
of a community
that shares their
values — in this case,
the shared sense of
ethical responsibility.

combines the concept of the citizen brand with the
brand community to differentiate the network's compassion and civic relevance. "Brand community" is
a relatively new term used by market researchers to
describe a "specialized, non-geographically bound
community, based on a structured set of social relationships among admirers of a brand." ... Like other
communities, brand communities are believed to possess "a shared consciousness, rituals and traditions,
and a sense of moral responsibility." ... The Better

Community campaign envisions the mass audience as a brand community composed of ABC viewers, each of whom exercises ethical dispositions and capacities within existing institutions (schools, hospitals, charities) and spaces (neighborhoods, parks, municipalities). Although this ethical activity takes place outside television culture, it can only be realized through the ABC brand, which activates and rewards action with affirmation and belonging. ABC operates as what Celia Lury calls a branded interface—not only to the consumption of television but to the duties and practices of contemporary citizenship.... TV is no longer good in the self-interested sense evoked by the earlier ABC campaign. ABC is the gateway for civic obligations in the double service of the "community" and the Better Community brand.

■ Make Connections among Different Texts

The texts by Loeb, Colby and her colleagues, and Ouellette all deal with some aspect of civic engagement, activism, and community building. The authors write about efforts to motivate people to work with one another to foster the health of communities based on moral or humanistic principles or to take up the call to compensate for changing economic policies. The texts are very much in conversation with one another, as the authors focus on relevant experiences and research to convey what they see as the value of civic and political engagement. However, each author offers a slightly different perspective that forces readers to ask if morality has a place in the ways we conceptualize civic engagement, the role that colleges and universities should play in promoting civic engagement in the undergraduate curriculum, or the extent to which corporations' commitment to community building is in conflict with their profit motives.

- Loeb urges readers to value the human connection that results from working together for the common good of a community and uses research to convey the psychological and physiological benefits of doing so. He also brings into focus the consequences of silence and the disconnect that can occur when we see injustice and fail to act.

- Colby and her colleagues share Loeb's perceptions about the value of community engagement but argue that teaching moral principles and core knowledge can have the positive effect of serving as a compass or guide for action. Though the authors are reluctant to identify specific values that they believe students should learn, they are particularly interested in the education of undergraduates and see the importance of helping students develop the ability to make informed judgments.

- Ouellette takes a different approach when she uses ABC as a case example to document the ways corporations have taken on the responsibility of serving families in need with changes in economic policy. In telling this story, she affirms the value of building community and shows that media can foster community; however, she also seems to question the profit-making motive that underlies the branding of corporations as civically engaged.

■ Decide What Those Connections Mean

Having annotated the selections, we filled out the worksheet in Figure 8.1, making notes in the grid to help us see the three texts in relation to one another. Our worksheet included columns for

- author and source information,
- the gist of each author's argument,
- supporting examples and illustrations,
- counterarguments, and
- our own thoughts.

A worksheet like this one can help you concentrate on similarities and differences in the texts to determine what the connections among texts mean. Of course, you can design your own worksheet as well, tailoring it to your needs and preferences. If you want to take very detailed notes about your authors and sources, for example, you may want to have separate columns for each.

Once you start making connections, including points of agreement and disagreement, you can start identifying counterarguments in the reading—that perhaps educators should not be inclined to teach morality in their classes and that the human connection that Loeb describes will serve as a sufficient motive for acting on behalf of the common good in a given community. Perhaps we need to look more critically at a corporation's interest in communities where their executives do not live, work, go to school, and shop. Identifying questions and even counterarguments can give you a sense of what is at issue for each author and what is at stake. And how can we test the claims that experts make about how policies have affected the health and well-being of communities where many children and families may be feeling the consequences of policies designed to shift the responsibility from the federal government to private corporations and private agencies? What causes the fragmentation that concerns some of the authors cited in these essays? What are the best ways to build community? For that matter, how effective have media corporations been in fostering the health of communities and a shared sense of responsibility?

■ Formulate the Gist of What You've Read

Remember that your gist should bring into focus the relationship among different ideas in multiple texts. Looking at the information juxtaposed on the worksheet (Figure 8.1), you can begin to construct the gist of your synthesis:

- Paul Loeb cites studies and uses his own experiences to motivate readers to be more civically engaged in their communities, to resist focusing on their own interests, and to enter into relationships with others to fulfill what it means to be human. He addresses those readers who may be discouraged by others who would silence or ignore their voices and commit themselves to speaking out about the issues that concern them. He points out the consequences of remaining silent and explains that we should not be discouraged by our "failed" attempts to create change.

- Anne Colby and her colleagues share a common concern that Loeb expresses about trends toward increased individualism and lack of civic engagement. The authors are especially interested in reaching out to undergraduates and speak to the need to equip young people with the kinds of tools that would enable them to translate what they are learning into actions they can take as civic-minded, politically engaged citizens. One of those tools is judgment, and the best way to teach judgment is by imparting values and core knowledge that can serve as a moral compass and guide action.

- Ouellette broadens the discussion of civic engagement and political action by looking at the branding of corporations as socially responsible "citizens." Her analysis explains the extent to which presidents Clinton and then Bush reached out to businesses to provide initiatives to support children and families in need given changes in federal economic policies.

How do you formulate this information into a gist? You can use a transition word such as *although* or *however* to connect ideas that different authors bring together while conveying their differences. Thus, a gist of these essays might read:

GIST OF A SYNTHESIS

As a response to increased fragmentation of American society, Paul Loeb and Anne Colby and her colleagues underscore the reasons individuals need to be more involved in both civic and political engagement. They help highlight the ways human interaction makes us more fully human and the extent to which community engagement fulfills the Founding Fathers' vision of democracy. However, Laurie Ouellette broadens readers' understanding of why it is necessary to be more involved. She focuses on changes in economic policy in the United States that have shifted funding for families and children with the greatest needs to private entities and corporations.

Author and Source	Gist of Argument	Examples/Illustrations	Counterarguments/Challenging Assumptions	What I Think
Paul Rogat Loeb "Making Our Lives Count" from *Soul of a Citizen*	Argues that connecting to others through civic participation and working for the common good is what makes us more fully human.	Uses research from psychology, public health, and sociology, as well as personal stories to explain the value of community involvement. He also describes a number of negative effects of failing to be engaged and living with the disconnect between our convictions and our decision not to act on those convictions.	If there is a counterargument, it is implied when Loeb anticipates readers who have been silenced and feel their points of view do not matter. These readers are skeptical of the benefits of engagement.	The examples serve as compelling reasons to be involved, but I also understand why others feel that their voices might not be heard or taken seriously. This is often the case, but remaining silent can also be difficult. I also appreciate his point about failure. What might seem like failure can actually be a factor that bolsters our commitment to make a difference.
Anne Colby and Thomas Ehrlich with Elizabeth Beaumont and Jason Stephens "Undergraduate Education and the Development of Moral and Civic Responsibility"	Shares the concern Loeb raises—that there is a growing trend away from being civically and politically engaged. The authors add that moral principles are inextricably tied to democratic principles of rights, respect, tolerance, and community.	Limits the argument to the authors' own conceptions of civic and moral engagement, as well as the kind of core knowledge that is necessary to translate judgments into actions that people can take in a participant democracy.	Recognizes the extent to which the focus on moral engagement sets the authors' ideas apart from others like Loeb who try to motivate people to be civically engaged. It is implicit that others may feel uncomfortable with an argument that includes moral engagement, and the authors are careful to explain that they do not have a specific set of values in mind. Still, the counterargument may very well be that educators should not blur the line between the subject they teach and values.	I agree that universities should take more responsibility for the communities they are a part of. Classes in political science might address both theories of government and action—not just voting but community involvement. I am not sure I agree that professors should teach values.

Author and Source	Gist of Argument	Examples/Illustrations	Counterarguments/Challenging Assumptions	What I Think
Laurie Ouellette "Citizen Brand: ABC and the Do Good Turn in US Television"	Examines the reasons corporate social responsibility has emerged in recent years, emphasizing shifts in government policies that placed greater responsibility on the private sector for supporting children and families living in poverty. Argues that initiatives like "The Better Community" campaign are not altogether altruistic and serve corporate interests in creating wealth for their stakeholders.	Uses case examples of ABC's Better Community public outreach campaign and ABC's parent company to illustrate roles that corporations have taken on. On the one hand, they have taken on the mantle of social responsibility, and on the other hand, they use social responsibility as a marketing tool to create profits.	Acknowledges the value of ABC's strategy of positioning itself as a socially conscious corporation. However, looks critically at efforts that associate the leadership of figures such as Martin Luther King and the grassroots movement of the Civil Rights struggle with civic-minded projects that ABC has promoted. Also questions whose interests are served when corporations promote civic engagement as a profit-making venture.	I hadn't really thought about the economic factors that have prompted corporations to be more invested in community development. I am a little skeptical of the role that corporations can or should play in communities and worry that their motives blur, serving a community as a good in itself and doing so to make money.

FIGURE 8.1 Worksheet for Writing a Synthesis

Having drafted the gist, we returned to our notes on the worksheet to complete the synthesis, presenting examples and using transitions to signal the relationships among the texts and their ideas. Here is our brief synthesis of the three texts:

The gist of our synthesis.

As a response to increased fragmentation of society, Paul Loeb and Anne Colby and her colleagues underscore the reasons why individuals need to be more involved in both political and civic engagement. They help highlight the ways human interaction makes us more fully human and the extent to which community engagement fulfills the Founding Fathers' vision of democracy. Loeb's research in psychology, public health, and sociology also demonstrates the ways that community engagement contributes to our own sense of well-being. Colby and her colleagues share Loeb's outlook, but they add that moral principles are inextricably tied to democratic principles of rights, respect, tolerance, and community. They also argue that individuals need tools to make decisions, especially a core knowledge of key issues and a moral compass to serve as a guide to action that is aimed at the common good. Still, they recognize the extent to which their focus on moral engagement sets their ideas apart from others like Loeb who try to motivate people to be civically engaged. It is implicit that others may feel uncomfortable with an argument that includes moral engagement, and the authors are careful to explain that they do not have a specific set of values in mind.

Transition: There is an alternative reason individuals should be civically and politically engaged.

Evidence demonstrates that the urgency of a changing economy is a strong factor in motivating individuals to get involved, especially when sponsored by corporations that have been given the responsibility to fulfill what was an obligation of the federal government.

However, Laurie Ouellette broadens readers' understanding of why it is necessary to be more involved. This is especially true when she focuses her analysis on changes in economic policy in the United States that have shifted funding for families and children with the greatest needs to private entities and corporations. In pointing to this shift in policy, she shows how corporations such as Disney have rebranded themselves as socially responsible, marketing themselves in a way that appeals to viewers who share a view of themselves as altruistic. Thus, Ouellette helps show that there are reasons beyond the humanizing principles that Loeb advances and the kinds of values that Colby and her colleagues believe are inextricably tied to teaching and learning in institutions of higher education. That is, communities may appear to be more fragmented than ever before, but the urgency created by government social welfare programs serves as a pragmatic call to service that we cannot ignore.

1

2

One formulation of an argument that emerges from the three texts. The transition "yet" and the questions posed set up the direction of what is to follow.

While some may argue that corporations act out of self-interest in branding themselves as socially responsible, evidence indicates that the media may be more successful at motivating individuals to be involved than other means. Yet in considering the reasons why it is important to be an engaged citizen, whether as individuals or as a corporation, Ouellette, among others, forces us to ask whose interests are served when any of us becomes invested in communities where we do not live, work, shop, or go to school. Despite the benefits of citizen branding, Ouellette reminds us that we cannot ignore the profit motive of companies that have fulfilled a role once played by the federal government in what is now a postwelfare state. To what extent, if at all, are these roles in conflict with one another? For that matter, what values should guide investments and personal responsibility in reaching out to communities with the greatest needs?

Writing a synthesis, like writing a summary, is principally a strategy for framing your own argument. It's one thing to synthesize what you read and convey to your readers how various points in a conversation intersect and diverge. It's quite another to write yourself into the conversation. This entails thinking critically about what you are reading, raising questions, conducting further research, and taking a stance based on your own understanding of what you have read, what you believe and value, and the available evidence.

Steps to Writing a Synthesis

1 **Make connections between and among different texts.** Annotate the texts you are working with, with an eye to comparing them. As you would for a summary, note major points in the texts, choose relevant examples, and formulate the gist of each text.

2 **Decide what those connections mean.** Fill out a worksheet to compare your notes on the different texts, track counterarguments, and record your thoughts. Decide what the similarities and differences mean to you and what they might mean to your readers.

3 **Formulate the gist of what you've read.** Identify an overarching idea that brings together the ideas you've noted, and write a synthesis that forges connections and makes use of the examples you've noted. Use transitions to signal the direction of your synthesis.

A Practice Sequence: Writing a Synthesis

1   To practice the strategies for synthesizing that we describe in this chapter, read the following three essays, which focus on the role that online media play in conveying information to diverse groups of readers or viewers. As you discuss the strategies the authors use to develop their arguments, consider these questions:

  - How would you explain the popularity of blogs, Twitter, and YouTube?
  - What themes have the writers focused on as they have sought to enter the conversation surrounding the use of electronic media?
  - To what extent do you think the criticisms of media presented by the authors are legitimate?
  - Do blogs, Twitter, and YouTube pose a threat to traditional journalism?
  - Do you think that blogs, Twitter, and YouTube add anything to print journalism? If so, what?

2   To stimulate a conversation, or a debate, we suggest that you break up into four different groups:

  > *Group 1:* Print journalism
  > *Group 2:* Blogs
  > *Group 3:* Twitter
  > *Group 4:* YouTube

  Students in each group should prepare an argument indicating the strengths and limitations of the particular mode of communication that they represent. In preparing the argument, be sure to acknowledge what other modes of communication might add to the ways we learn about news and opinions. One student from each group will present this argument to the other groups.

3   Based on the discussion you have had in exercise 1 and/or exercise 2, write a synthesis of the three essays using the steps we have outlined in this chapter.

  - Summarize each essay.
  - Explain the ways in which the authors' arguments are similar or different, using examples and illustrations to demonstrate the similarities and differences.
  - Formulate an overall gist that synthesizes the points each author makes.

DAN KENNEDY

Political Blogs: Teaching Us Lessons about Community

Dan Kennedy, an assistant professor of journalism at Northeastern University, writes on media issues for *The Guardian* and for *CommonWealth* magazine. His blog, Media Nation, is online at dankennedy.net.

The rise of blogging as both a supplement and a challenge to traditional journalism has coincided with an explosion of opinion mongering. Blogs—and the role they play in how Americans consume and respond to information—are increasingly visible during our political season, when our ideological divide is most apparent. From nakedly partisan sites such as Daily Kos on the left and Little Green Footballs on the right, to more nuanced but nevertheless ideological enterprises such as Talking Points Memo, it sometimes seems there is no room in blogworld for straight, neutral journalism.

The usual reasons given for this are that reporting is difficult and expensive and that few bloggers know how to research a story, develop and interview sources, and assemble the pieces into a coherent, factual narrative. Far easier, so this line of thinking goes, for bloggers to sit in their pajamas and blast their semi-informed opinions out to the world.

There is some truth to this, although embracing this view wholeheartedly requires us to overlook the many journalists who are now writing blogs, as well as the many bloggers who are producing journalism to a greater or lesser degree. But we make a mistake when we look at the opinion-oriented nature of blogs and ask whether bloggers are capable of being "objective," to use a hoary and now all but meaningless word. The better question to ask is why opinion-oriented blogs are so popular—and what lessons the traditional media can learn from them without giving up their journalistic souls.

Perhaps what's happening is that the best and more popular blogs provide a sense of community that used to be the lifeblood of traditional news organizations and, especially, of newspapers. Recently I reread part of Jay Rosen's book, *What Are Journalists For?*, his 1999 postmortem on the public journalism movement. What struck me was Rosen's description of public journalism's origins, which were grounded in an attempt to recreate a sense of community so that people might discover a reason to read newspapers. "Eventually I came to the conclusion ... that journalism's purpose was to see the public into fuller existence," Rosen writes. "Informing people followed that."

Rosen's thesis—that journalism could only be revived by reawak-   5
ening the civic impulse—is paralleled by Robert Putnam's 2000 book,
Bowling Alone, in which he found that people who sign petitions, attend
public meetings, and participate in religious and social organizations are more likely to be newspaper readers than those who do not.
"Newspaper readers are older, more educated, and more rooted in their
communities than is the average American," Putnam writes.

Unfortunately for the newspaper business, the traditional idea of   6
community, based mainly on geography, remains as moribund today
as it was when Rosen and Putnam were analyzing its pathologies. But
if old-fashioned communities are on the decline, the human impulse to
form communities is not. And the Internet, as it turns out, is an ideal
medium for fostering a new type of community in which people have
never met, and may not even know each other's real names, but share
certain views and opinions about the way the world works. It's interesting that Rosen has become a leading exponent of journalism tied
to these communities, both through his PressThink blog and through
NewAssignment.net, which fosters collaborations between professional
and citizen journalists.

Attitude First, Facts Second

This trend toward online community-building has given us a mediascape   7
in which many people—especially those most interested in politics and
public affairs—want the news delivered to them in the context of their
attitudes and beliefs. That doesn't mean they want to be fed a diet of
self-reinforcing agit-prop (although some do). It does mean they see
their news consumption as something that takes place within their
community, to be fit into a preexisting framework of ideas that may be
challenged but that must be acknowledged.

Earlier this year John Lloyd, a contributing editor for the *Financial*   8
Times, talked about the decline of just-the-facts journalism on *Open*
Source, a Web-based radio program hosted by the veteran journalist
Christopher Lydon. It has become increasingly difficult, Lloyd said, to
report facts that are not tied to an ideological point of view. The emerging paradigm, he explained, may be "that you can only get facts through
by attaching them to a very strong left-wing, right-wing, Christian, athe-
ist position. Only then, only if you establish your bona fides within this
particular community, will they be open to facts."

No less a blogging enthusiast than Markos Moulitsas, founder of   9
Daily Kos, has observed that political blogs are a nonentity in Britain,
where the newspapers themselves cater to a wide range of different
opinions. "You look at the media in Britain, it's vibrant and it's exciting

and it's fun, because they're all ideologically tinged," Moulitsas said at an appearance in Boston last fall. "And that's a good thing, because people buy them and understand that their viewpoints are going to be represented."

The notion that journalism must be tied to an ideological community may seem disheartening to traditionalists. In practice, though, journalism based on communities of shared interests and beliefs can be every bit as valuable as the old model of objectivity, if approached with rigor and respect for the truth. *10*

Last year, for instance, Talking Points Memo (TPM) and its related blogs helped break the story of how the U.S. Department of Justice had fired eight U.S. attorneys for what appeared to be politically motivated reasons, a scandal that led to the resignation of Attorney General Alberto Gonzales. TPM's reporting was based in part on information dug up and passed along by its liberal readership. The founder and editor, Joshua Micah Marshall, received a George Polk Award, but it belonged as much to the community he had assembled as it did to him personally. *11*

Of course, we still need neutral, non-opinionated journalism to help us make sense of the world around us. TPM's coverage of the U.S. attorneys scandal was outstanding, but it was also dismissive of arguments that it was much ado about nothing, or that previous administrations had done the same or worse. Liberals or conservatives who get all of their news from ideologically friendly sources don't have much incentive to change their minds. *12*

Connecting to Communities of Shared Interests

Even news outlets that excel at traditional, "objective" journalism do so within the context of a community. Some might not find liberal bias in the news pages of the *New York Times*, as the paper's conservative critics would contend, but there's little doubt that the *Times* serves a community of well-educated, affluent, culturally liberal readers whose preferences and tastes must be taken into account. Not to be a journalistic relativist, but all news needs to be evaluated within the context in which it was produced, even an old-fashioned, inverted-pyramid-style dispatch from the wires. Who was interviewed? Who wasn't? Why? These are questions that must be asked regardless of the source. *13*

We might now be coming full circle as placeblogs—chatty, conversational blogs that serve a particular geographic community—become more prevalent. Lisa Williams, founder of H2Otown, a blog that serves her community of Watertown, Massachusetts, believes that such forums could help foster the sense of community that is a necessary *14* precondition to newspaper readership. Williams also runs a project called Placeblogger.com, which tracks local blogs around the world.

"The news creates a shared pool of stories that gives us a way to talk   15
to people who aren't family or close friends or people who we will never meet—in short, our fellow citizens," Williams says by e-mail. "The truth is, people still want those neighbor-to-neighbor contacts, but the traditional ways of doing it don't fit into the lives that people are actually living today. Your core audience is tired, sitting on the couch with their laptop, and watching *Lost* with one eye. Give them someone to sit with."

Critics of blogs have been looking at the wrong thing. While tradi-   16
tionalists disparage bloggers for their indulgence of opinion and hyperbole, they overlook the sense of community and conversation that blogs have fostered around the news. What bloggers do well, and what news organizations do poorly or not at all, is give their readers someone to sit with. News consumers—the public, citizens, us—still want the truth. But we also want to share it and talk about it with our like-minded neighbors and friends. The challenge for journalism is not that we'll lose our objectivity; it's that we won't find a way to rebuild a sense of community.

JOHN DICKERSON

Don't Fear Twitter

John Dickerson is a political columnist for *Slate* magazine and chief Washington correspondent for CBS News. Before joining *Slate*, Dickerson covered politics for *Time* magazine, including four years as the magazine's White House correspondent. Dickerson has also written for the *New York Times* and *Washington Post* and is a regular panelist on *Washington Week in Review*. This essay first appeared in the Summer 2008 issue of *Nieman Reports*.

◾ ◾ ◾

If I were cleverer, this piece on Twitter and journalism would fit in   1
Twitter's 140-character limitation. The beauty of Twitter when properly used—by both the reader and the writer—is that everyone knows what it is. No reader expects more from Twitter than it offers, and no one writing tries to shove more than necessary into a Twitter entry, which is sometimes called a Tweet, but not by me, thank you.

Not many people know what Twitter is, though, so I'm going to go on   2
for a few hundred words. Twitter is a Web site that allows you to share your thoughts instantly and on any topic with other people in the Twitter network as long as you do so in tight little entries of 140 characters

or less. If you're wondering how much you can write with that space limitation, this sentence that you're reading right now hits that mark perfectly.

For some, journalism is already getting smaller. Newspapers are 3 shrinking. Serious news is being pushed aside in favor of entertainment and fluff stories. To many journalists and guardians of the trade, the idea that any journalist would willingly embrace a smaller space is horrifying and dumb. One journalism professor drew himself up to his full height and denounced Twitter journalism—or microjournalism, as someone unfortunately called it—as the ultimate absurd reduction of journalism. (I think he may have dislodged his monocle, he was waving his quill pen so violently.) Venerable CBS newsman Roger Mudd had a far lighter touch when he joked to me that he could barely say the word "texting" when he and I were talking about the idea of delivering a couple of sentences and calling it journalism.

We can all agree that journalism shouldn't get any smaller, but 4 Twitter doesn't threaten the traditions of our craft. It adds, rather than subtracts, from what we do.

As I spend nearly all of my time on the road these days reporting on 5 the presidential campaigns, Twitter is the perfect place for all of those asides I've scribbled in the hundreds of notebooks I have in my garage from the campaigns and stories I've covered over the years. Inside each of those notebooks are little pieces of color I've picked up along the way. Sometimes these snippets are too off-topic or too inconsequential to work into a story. Sometimes they are the little notions or sideways thoughts that become the lead of a piece or the kicker. All of them now have found a home on Twitter.

As journalists we take people places they can't go. Twitter offers a 6 little snapshot way to do this. It's informal and approachable and great for conveying a little moment from an event. Here's an entry from a McCain rally during the Republican primaries: "Weare, NH: Audience man to McCain: 'I heard that Hershey is moving plants to Mexico and I'll be damned if I'm going to eat Mexican chocolate.'" In Scranton covering Barack Obama I sent this: "Obama: 'What's John McCain's problem?' Audience member: 'He's too old.' Obama: 'No, no that's not the problem. There are a lot of wise people. . . .'" With so many Democrats making an issue of McCain's age, here was the candidate in the moment seeming to suggest that critique was unfair.

Occasionally, just occasionally, reporters can convey a piece of news 7 that fits into 140 characters without context. If Twitter had been around when the planes hit the World Trade Center, it would have been a perfect way for anyone who witnessed it to convey at that moment what they'd seen or heard. With Twitter, we can also pull back the curtain on our lives a little and show readers what it's like to cover a campaign. ("Wanna be a reporter? On long bus rides learn to sleep in your own hand.")

The risk for journalism, of course, is that people spend all day 8 Twittering and reading other people's Twitter entries and don't engage with the news in any other way. This seems a pretty small worry. If written the right way, Twitter entries build a community of readers who find their way to longer articles because they are lured by these moment-by-moment observations. As a reader, I've found that I'm exposed to a wider variety of news because I read articles suggested to me by the wide variety of people I follow on Twitter. I'm also exposed to some keen political observers and sharp writers who have never practiced journalism.

Twitter is not the next great thing in journalism. No one should try 9 to make Twitter do more than it can and no reader should expect too much from a 140-character entry. As for the critics, their worries about Twitter and journalism seem like the kind of obtuse behavior that would make a perfect observational Twitter entry: "A man at the front of the restaurant is screaming at a waiter and gesticulating wildly. The snacks on the bar aren't a four-course meal!"

STEVE GROVE

YouTube: The Flattening of Politics

Steve Grove is director of Google News Lab, and formerly directed all news, political programming, and citizen journalism for YouTube. He has been quoted as saying that he regards himself less as an editor than as a curator of the Web site's "chaotic sea of content." A native of Northfield, Minnesota, he worked as a journalist at the *Boston Globe* and ABC News before moving to YouTube.

■ ■ ■

For a little over a year, I've served as YouTube's news and political 1 director—perhaps a perplexing title in the eyes of many journalists. Such wonderment might be expected since YouTube gained its early notoriety as a place with videos of dogs on skateboards or kids falling off of trampolines. But these days, in the ten hours of video uploaded to YouTube every minute of every day (yes—every minute of every day), an increasing amount of the content is news and political video. And with YouTube's global reach and ease of use, it's changing the way that politics—and its coverage—is happening.

Each of the sixteen one-time presidential candidates had YouTube 2 channels; seven announced their candidacies on YouTube. Their staffs uploaded thousands of videos that were viewed tens of millions of times. By early March of this year, the Obama campaign was uploading two to three videos to YouTube every day. And thousands of advocacy groups and nonprofit organizations use YouTube to get their election messages into the conversation. For us, the most exciting aspect is that ordinary people continue to use YouTube to distribute their own political content; these range from "gotcha" videos they've taken at campaign rallies to questions for the candidates, from homemade political commercials to video mash-ups of mainstream media coverage.

What this means is that average citizens are able to fuel a new meritocracy for political coverage, one unburdened by the gatekeeping "middleman." Another way of putting it is that YouTube is now the world's largest town hall for political discussion, where voters connect with candidates—and the news media—in ways that were never before possible. 3

In this new media environment, politics is no longer bound by traditional barriers of time and space. It doesn't matter what time it is, or where someone is located—as long as they have the means to connect through the Web, they can engage in the discussion. This was highlighted in a pair of presidential debates we produced with CNN during this election cycle during which voters asked questions of the candidates via YouTube videos they'd submitted online. In many ways, those events simply brought to the attention of a wider audience the sort of exchanges that take place on YouTube all the time.... 4

News Organizations and YouTube

Just because candidates and voters find all sorts of ways to connect directly on YouTube does not mean there isn't room for the mainstream media, too. In fact, many news organizations have launched YouTube channels, including the Associated Press, the *New York Times*, the BBC, CBS, and the *Wall Street Journal*. 5

Why would a mainstream media company upload their news content to YouTube? 6

Simply put, it's where eyeballs are going. Research from the Pew Internet & American Life project found that 37 percent of adult Internet users have watched online video news, and well over half of online adults have used the Internet to watch video of any kind. Each day on YouTube hundreds of millions of videos are viewed at the same time that television viewership is decreasing in many markets. If a mainstream news organization wants its political reporting seen, YouTube offers visibility without a cost. The ones that have been doing this for a while rely on a strategy of building audiences on YouTube and then 7 trying to drive viewers back to their Web sites for a deeper dive into the content. And these organizations can earn revenue as well by running ads against their video content on YouTube.

In many ways, YouTube's news ecosystem has the potential to offer much more to a traditional media outlet. Here are some examples: 8

1. **Interactivity:** YouTube provides an automatic focus group for news content. How? YouTube wasn't built as merely a "series of tubes" to distribute online video. It is also an interactive platform. Users comment on, reply to, rank, and share videos with one another and form communities around content that they like. If news organizations want to see how a particular piece of content will resonate with audiences, they have an automatic focus group waiting on YouTube. And that focus group isn't just young people: 20 percent of YouTube users are over age 55—which is the same percentage that is under 18. This means the YouTube audience roughly mirrors the national population.

2. **Partner with audiences:** YouTube provides news media organizations new ways to engage with audiences and involve them in the programming. Modeled on the presidential debates we cohosted last year, YouTube has created similar partnerships, such as one with the BBC around the mayoral election in London and with a large public broadcaster in Spain for their recent presidential election. Also on the campaign trail, we worked along with Hearst affiliate WMUR-TV in New Hampshire to solicit videos from voters during that primary. Hundreds of videos flooded in from across the state. The best were broadcast on that TV station, which highlighted this symbiotic relationship: On the Web, online video bubbles the more interesting content to the top and then TV amplifies it on a new scale. We did similar arrangements with news organizations in Iowa, Pennsylvania, and on Super Tuesday, as news organizations leveraged the power of voter-generated content. What the news organizations discover is that they gain audience share by offering a level of audience engagement—with opportunities for active as well as passive experiences.

For news media organizations, audience engagement is much easier to achieve by using platforms like YouTube than it is to do on their own. And we just made it easier: Our open API (application programming interface), nicknamed "YouTube Everywhere"—just launched a few months ago—allows other companies to integrate our upload functionality into their online platforms. It's like having a mini YouTube on your Web site and, once it's there, news organizations   9 can encourage—and publish—video responses and comments on the reporting they do.

Finally, reporters use YouTube as source material for their stories. *10* With hundreds of thousands of video cameras in use today, there is a much greater chance than ever before that events will be captured—by someone—as they unfold. No need for driving the satellite truck to the scene if someone is already there and sending in video of the event via their cell phone. It's at such intersections of new and old media that YouTube demonstrates its value. It could be argued, in fact, that the YouTube platform is the new frontier in newsgathering. On the election trail, virtually every appearance by every candidate is captured on video—by someone—and that means the issues being talked about are covered more robustly by more people who can steer the public discussion in new ways. The phenomenon is, of course, global, as we witnessed last fall in Burma (Myanmar) after the government shut down news media outlets during waves of civic protests. In time, YouTube was the only way to track the violence being exercised by the government on monks who'd taken to the streets. Videos of this were seen worldwide on YouTube, creating global awareness of this situation—even in the absence of journalists on the scene.

Citizen journalism on YouTube—and other Internet sources—is *11* often criticized because it is produced by amateurs and therefore lacks a degree of trustworthiness. Critics add that because platforms like YouTube are fragmenting today's media environment, traditional newsrooms are being depleted of journalists, and thus the denominator for quality news coverage is getting lower and lower. I share this concern about what is happening in the news media today, but I think there are a couple of things worth remembering when it comes to news content on YouTube.

Trusting What We See

When it comes to determining the trustworthiness of news content on *12* YouTube, it's important to have some context. People tend to know what they're getting on YouTube, since content is clearly labeled by username as to where it originated. A viewer knows if the video they're watching is coming from "jellybean109" or "thenewyorktimes." Users also know that YouTube is an open platform and that no one verifies the truth of content better than the consumer. The wisdom of the crowd on YouTube is far more likely to pick apart a shoddy piece of "journalism" than it is to elevate something that is simply untrue. In fact, because video is ubiquitous and so much more revealing and compelling than text, YouTube can provide a critical fact-checking platform in today's media environment. And in some ways, it offers a backstop for accuracy since a journalist can't afford to get the story wrong; if they do, it's likely that someone else who was there got it right—and posted it to YouTube.

Scrutiny cuts both ways. Journalists are needed today for the work   *13* they do as much as they ever have been. While the wisdom of crowds might provide a new form of fact checking, and the ubiquity of technology might provide a more robust view of the news, citizens desperately need the Fourth Estate to provide depth, context, and analysis that only comes with experience and the sharpening of the craft. Without the work of journalists, the citizens—the electorate—lose a critical voice in the process of civic decision making.

This is the media ecosystem in which we live in this election cycle.   *14* Candidates and voters speak directly to one another, unfiltered. News organizations use the Internet to connect with and leverage audiences in new ways. Activists, issue groups, campaigns, and voters all advocate for, learn about, and discuss issues on the same level platform. YouTube has become a major force in this new media environment by offering new opportunities and new challenges. For those who have embraced them—and their numbers grow rapidly every day—the opportunity to influence the discussion is great. For those who haven't, they ignore the opportunity at their own peril.

AVOIDING PLAGIARISM

Whether you paraphrase, summarize, or synthesize, it is essential that you acknowledge your sources. Academic writing requires you to use and document sources appropriately, making clear to readers the boundaries between your words and ideas and those of other writers. Setting boundaries can be a challenge because so much of academic writing involves interweaving the ideas of others into your own argument. Still, you must acknowledge your sources. It's only fair. Imagine how you would feel if you were reading a text and discovered that the writer had incorporated a passage from one of your papers, something you had slaved over, without giving you credit. You would see yourself as a victim of plagiarism, and you would be justified in feeling very angry indeed.

In fact, **plagiarism**—the unacknowledged use of another's work, passed off as one's own—is a serious breach of academic integrity, and colleges and universities deal with it severely. If you are caught plagiarizing in your work for a class, you can expect to fail that class and you may even be expelled from your college or university. Furthermore, although a failing grade on a paper or in a course, honestly come by, is unlikely to deter an employer from hiring you, the stigma of plagiarism can come back to haunt you when you apply for a job. Any violation of the principles set forth in Table 8.1 could have serious consequences for your academic and professional career.

TABLE 8.1   Principles Governing Plagiarism

1. All written work submitted for any purpose is accepted as your own work. This means it must not have been written, even in part, by another person.

2. The wording of any written work you submit is assumed to be your own. This means you must not submit work that has been copied, wholly or partially, from a book, an article, an essay, a newspaper, another student's paper or notebook, or any other source. Another writer's phrases, sentences, or paragraphs can be included only if they are presented as quotations and the source acknowledged.

3. The ideas expressed in a paper or report are assumed to originate with you, the writer. Written work that paraphrases a source without acknowledgment must not be submitted for credit. Ideas from the work of others can be incorporated in your work as starting points, governing issues, illustrations, and the like, but in every instance the source must be cited.

4. Remember that any online materials you use to gather information for a paper are also governed by the rules for avoiding plagiarism. You need to cite electronic sources as well as printed and other sources.

5. You may correct and revise your writing with the aid of reference books. You also may discuss your writing with your peers in a writing group or with peer tutors at your campus writing center. However, you may not submit writing that has been revised substantially by another person.

Even if you know what plagiarism is and wouldn't intentionally plagiarize, watch out for unintentional plagiarism. Again, paraphrasing can be especially tricky: Attempting to restate a passage without using the original words and sentence structure is, to a certain extent, an invitation to plagiarism. If you remember that your paper is *your* argument, and understand that any paraphrasing, summarizing, or synthesizing should reflect *your* voice and style, you will be less likely to have problems with plagiarism. Your paper should sound like you. And, again, the surest way to protect yourself is to cite your sources and carefully check your work.

Steps to Avoiding Plagiarism

1   **Always cite the source.** Signal that you are paraphrasing, summarizing, or synthesizing by identifying your source at the outset—"According to Laurie Ouellette," "Paul Loeb argues," "Anne Colby and her colleagues ... point out." And if possible, indicate the end of the paraphrase, summary, or synthesis with relevant page references to the source. If you cite a source several times in your paper, don't assume that your first citation has you covered; acknowledge the source as often as you use it.

2   **Provide a full citation in your bibliography.** It's not enough to cite a source in your paper; you must also provide a full citation for every source you use in the list of sources at the end of your paper.

INTEGRATING QUOTATIONS INTO YOUR WRITING

When you integrate quotations into your writing, bear in mind a piece of advice we've given you about writing the rest of your paper: Take your readers by the hand and lead them step by step. When you quote other authors to develop your argument—using their words to support your thinking or to address a counterargument—discuss and analyze the words you quote, showing readers how the specific language of each quotation contributes to the larger point you are making in your essay. When you integrate quotations, then, there are three basic things you want to do: (1) Take an active stance, (2) explain the quotations, and (3) attach short quotations to your own sentences.

■ Take an Active Stance

Critical reading requires that you adopt an active stance toward what you read—that you raise questions in response to a text. You should be no less active when you are using other authors' texts to develop your own argument.

Taking an active stance when you are quoting means knowing when to quote. Don't quote when a paraphrase or summary will convey the information from a source more effectively. More important, you have to make fair and wise decisions about what and how much you should quote to make your argument.

- You want to show that you understand the writer's argument, and you want to make evenhanded use of it in your own argument. It's not fair (or wise) to quote selectively—choosing only passages that support your argument—when you know you are distorting the argument of the writer you are quoting.

- Remember that your ideas and argument—your thesis—are what is most important to the readers and what justifies a quotation's being included at all. It's not wise (or fair to yourself) to flesh out your paper with an overwhelming number of quotations that could make readers think that you do not know your topic well or do not have your own ideas. Don't allow quotations to take over your paragraphs.

Above all, taking an active stance when you quote means taking control of your writing. You want to establish your own argument and guide your readers through it, allowing sources to contribute to but not dictate its direction. You are responsible for plotting and pacing your essay. Always keep in mind that your thesis is the skewer that runs through every paragraph, holding all of the ideas together. When you use quotations, then, you must organize them to enrich, substantiate, illustrate, and help support your central claim or thesis.

■ Explain the Quotations

When you quote an author to support or advance your argument, make sure that readers know exactly what they should learn from the quotation.

Read the excerpt below from one student's early draft of an argument that focuses on the value of service learning in high schools. The student reviews several relevant studies—but then simply drops in a quotation, expecting readers to know what they should pay attention to in it.

> Other research emphasizes community service as an integral and integrated part of moral identity. In this understanding, community service activities are not isolated events but are woven into the context of students' everyday lives (Yates, 1995); the personal, the moral, and the civic become "inseparable" (Colby, Ehrlich, Beaumont, & Stephens, 2003, p. 15). In their study of minority high schoolers at an urban Catholic school who volunteered at a soup kitchen for the homeless as part of a class assignment, Youniss and Yates (1999) found that the students underwent significant identity changes, coming to perceive themselves as lifelong activists. The researchers' findings are worth quoting at length here because they depict the dramatic nature of the students' changed viewpoints. Youniss and Yates wrote,
>
> > Many students abandoned an initially negative view of homeless people and a disinterest in homelessness by gaining appreciation of the humanity of homeless people and by showing concern for homelessness in relation to poverty, job training, low-cost housing, prison reform, drug and alcohol rehabilitation, care for the mentally ill, quality urban education, and welfare policy. Several students also altered perceptions of themselves from politically impotent teenagers to involved citizens who now and in the future could use their talent and power to correct social problems. They projected articulated pictures of themselves as adult citizens who could affect housing policies, education for minorities, and government programs within a clear framework of social justice. (p. 362)

The student's introduction to the quoted passage provided a rationale for quoting Youniss and Yates at length, but it did not help her readers see how the research related to her argument. The student needed to frame the quotation for her readers. Instead of introducing the quotation by saying "Youniss and Yates wrote," she should have made clear that the study supports the argument that community service can create change. A more appropriate frame for the quotation might have been a summary like this one:

Frames the quoted material, explaining it in the context of the student's argument.
One particular study underscores my argument that service can motivate change, particularly when that change begins within the students who are involved in service. Youniss and Yates (1999) wrote that over the course of their research,

the students developed both an "appreciation of the humanity of homeless people" and a sense that they would someday be able to "use their talent and power to correct social problems" (p. 362).

In the following example, notice that the student writer uses Derrick Bell's text to say something about how the effects of desegregation have been muted by political manipulation.* The writer shapes what he wants readers to focus on, leaving nothing to chance.

> The effectiveness with which the meaning of *Brown v. Board of Education* has been manipulated, Derrick Bell argued, is also evidenced by the way in which such thinking has actually been embraced by minority groups. Bell claimed that a black school board member's asking "But of what value is it to teach black children to read in all-black schools?" indicates this unthinking acceptance that whiteness is an essential ingredient to effective schooling for blacks. Bell continued:
>
>> The assumption that even the attaining of academic skills is worthless unless those skills are acquired in the presence of white students illustrates dramatically how a legal precedent, namely the Supreme Court's decision in Brown v. Board of Education, has been so constricted even by advocates that its goal — equal educational opportunity — is rendered inaccessible, even unwanted, unless it can be obtained through racial balancing of the school population. (p. 255)
>
> Bell's argument is extremely compelling, particularly when one considers the extent to which "racial balancing" has come to be defined in terms of large white majority populations and small nonwhite minority populations.

Notice that the student's last sentence helps readers understand what the quoted material suggests and why it's important by embedding and extending Bell's notion of racial balancing into his explanation.

In sum, you should always explain the information that you quote so that your readers can see how the quotation relates to your own argument. ("Take your readers by the hand ...") As you read other people's writing, keep an eye open to the ways writers introduce and explain the sources they use to build their arguments.

■ Attach Short Quotations to Your Sentences

The quotations we discussed above are **block quotations,** lengthy quotations of more than five lines that are set off from the text of a paper with indention. Make shorter quotations part of your own sentences so that your readers can easily follow along and understand how the quotations connect to your argument. How do you make a quotation part of your own sentences? There are two main methods:

---

*This quotation is from Derrick Bell's *Silent Covenants: Brown v. Board of Education and the Unfulfilled Hopes for Racial Reform* (New York: Oxford UP, 2005).

- Integrate quotations within the grammar of your writing.
- Attach quotations with punctuation.

If possible, use both to make your integration of quotations more interesting and varied.

Integrate quotations within the grammar of a sentence.   When you integrate a quotation into a sentence, the quotation must make grammatical sense and read as if it is part of the sentence:

> Fine, Weiss, and Powell (1998) expanded upon what others call "equal status contact theory" by using a "framework that draws on three traditionally independent literatures — those on community, difference, and democracy" (p. 37).

If you add words to the quotation, use square brackets around them to let readers know that the words are not original to the quotation:

> Smith and Wellner (2002) asserted that they "are not alone [in believing] that the facts have been incorrectly interpreted by Mancini" (p. 24).

If you omit any words in the middle of a quotation, use an **ellipsis,** three periods with spaces between them, to indicate the omission:

> Riquelme argues that "Eliot tries ... to provide a definition by negations, which he also turns into positive terms that are meant to correct misconceptions" (p. 156).

If you omit a sentence or more, make sure to put a period before the ellipsis points:

> Eagleton writes, "What Eliot was in fact assaulting was the whole ideology of middle-class liberalism.... Eliot's own solution is an extreme right-wing authoritarianism: men and women must sacrifice their petty 'personalities' and opinions to an impersonal order" (p. 39).

Whatever you add (using square brackets) or omit (using ellipses), the sentence must read grammatically. And, of course, your additions and omissions must not distort the author's meaning.

> Leah is also that little girl who "stares at her old street and look[s] at the abandoned houses and cracked up sidewalks."

Attach quotations with punctuation.   You also can attach a quotation to a sentence by using punctuation. For example, this passage attaches the run-in quotation with a colon:

> For these researchers, there needs to be recognition of differences in a way that will include and accept all students. Specifically, they raised this key question: "Within multiracial settings, when are young people invited to discuss, voice, critique, and re-view the very notions of race that feel so fixed, so hierarchical, so damaging, and so accepted in the broader culture?" (p. 132).

In conclusion, if you don't connect quotations to your argument, your readers may not understand why you've included them. You need to explain a significant point that each quotation reveals as you introduce or end it. This strategy helps readers know what to pay attention to in a quotation, particularly if the quotation is lengthy.

Steps to Integrating Quotations into Your Writing

1 **Take an active stance.** Your sources should contribute to your argument, not dictate its direction.

2 **Explain the quotations.** Explain what you quote so your readers understand how each quotation relates to your argument.

3 **Attach short quotations to your sentences.** Integrate short quotations within the grammar of your own sentences, or attach them with appropriate punctuation.

A Practice Sequence: Integrating Quotations

1   Using several of the sources you are working with in developing your paper, try integrating quotations into your essay. Be sure you are controlling your sources. Carefully read the paragraphs where you've used quotations. Will your readers clearly understand why the quotations are there—the points the quotations support? Do the sentences with quotations read smoothly? Are they grammatically correct?

2   Working in a small group, agree on a substantial paragraph or passage (from this book or some other source) to write about. Each member should read the passage and take a position on the ideas, and then draft a page that quotes the passage using both strategies for integrating these quotations. Compare what you've written, examining similarities and differences in the use of quotations.

AN ANNOTATED STUDENT RESEARCHED ARGUMENT: SYNTHESIZING SOURCES

The student who wrote the essay "A Greener Approach to Groceries: Community-Based Agriculture in LaSalle Square" did so in a first-year writing class that gave students the opportunity to volunteer in the local community. For this assignment, students were asked to explore debates about community and citizenship in contemporary America and to focus their research and writing on a social justice–related issue of their choice. The context of the course guided their inquiry as all the students in the course explored community service as a way to engage meaningfully and to develop relationships in the community.

We have annotated her essay to show the ways that she summarized and paraphrased research to show the urgency of the problem of food insecurity that exists around the world and to offer possible solutions. Notice how she synthesizes her sources, taking an active stance in using what she has read to advance her own argument.

Paul 1

Nancy Paul
Professor McLaughlin
English 2102
May 11, 20—

A Greener Approach to Groceries:
Community-Based Agriculture in LaSalle Square

In our post–9/11 society, there is incessant concern for the security of our future. Billions of dollars are spent tightening borders, installing nuclear detectors, and adjudicating safety measures so that the citizens of the United States can grow and prosper without fear. Unfortunately, for some urban poor, the threat from terrorism is minuscule compared to the cruelty of their immediate environment. Far from the sands of the Afghan plains and encapsulated in the midst of inner-city deterioration, many find themselves in gray-lot deserts devoid of vegetation and reliable food sources. Abandoned by corporate supermarkets, millions of Americans are maimed by a "food insecurity" — the nutritional poverty that cripples them developmentally, physically, and psychologically.

The student's thesis

The midwestern city that surrounds our university has a food-desert sitting just west of the famously lush campus. Known as LaSalle Square, it was once home to the lucrative Bendix plant and has featured both a Target and a Kroger supermarket in recent years. But previous economic development decisions have driven both stores to the outskirts of town, and without a local supplier, the only food available in the neighborhood is prepackaged and sold at the few small convenience stores. This available food is virtually devoid

She calls attention to both the immediacy and urgency of the problem

1

2

of nutrition and inhibits the ability of the poor to prosper and thrive. Thus, an aging strip mall, industrial site, and approximately three acres of an empty grass lot between the buildings anchor — and unfortunately define — the neighborhood.

She proposes a possible solution.

While there are multiple ways of providing food to the destitute, I am proposing a co-op of community gardens built on the grassy space in LaSalle Square and on smaller sites within the neighborhood, supplemented by extra crops from Michiana farmers, which would supply fresh fruit and vegetables to be sold or distributed to the poor. Together the co-op could meet the nutritional needs of the people, provide plenty of nutritious food, not cost South Bend any additional money, and contribute to neighborhood revitalization, yielding concrete increases in property

She places her solution in a larger context to indicate its viability.

values. Far from being a pipe dream, LaSalle Square already hosted an Urban Garden Market this fall, so a co-op would simply build upon the already recognized need and desire for healthy food in the area. Similar coalitions around the world are harnessing the power of community to remedy food insecurity without the aid of corporate enterprise, and South Bend is perfectly situated to reproduce and possibly exceed their successes.

Many, myself previously included, believe that the large-volume, cheap industrialization of food and the welfare system have obliterated hunger in the United States. Supermarkets like Wal-Mart and Kroger seem ubiquitous in our communities, and it is difficult to imagine anyone being beyond their influence. However, profit-driven corporate business plans do not mix well with low-income, high-crime populations, and the gap between the two is growing wider. This polarization, combined with the vitamin deficiency of our high-fructose corn syrup society, has created food deserts in already struggling communities where malnutrition is the enemy *inconnu* of the urban poor.

More context

LaSalle Square's food insecurity is typical of many urban areas. The grocery stores that used to serve the neighborhood have relocated to more attractive real estate on the outskirts of the city, and only local convenience stores, stocking basic necessary items and tobacco products, remain profitable. Linda Wolfson, a member of the steering committee for the LaSalle Square Redevelopment Plan, notes that if the community was fiscally healthy, it would be reasonable

to expect the inhabitants to simply drive the six miles to the strip
mall district, but unfortunately many are marginally employed and
do not have access to cars. For them, it is economically irresponsible
to spend the extra money to get to the supermarket, and so they
feed their families on the cheap soda, chips, and processed food

Synthesizing helps illustrate the extent of the problem and bolster her view that the poor suffer the most from the problem she identifies (Garnett; Smith; Brown and Carter).

that are readily available at the convenience store. Especially since
high-calorie, low-nutrient, packaged food tends to be denser, urban
mothers find that it helps their children feel full (Garnett). Sadly, a
health investigation released in 2006 concluded that by the age of
three, more than one-third of urban children are obese, due in large
part to the consumption of low-quality food obtained from corner
stores (Smith). A recent analysis of urban stores in Detroit found that
only 19 percent offer the healthy food array suggested by the FDA
food pyramid (Brown and Carter 5). The food that is offered contains
25 percent less nutrient density, and consequently, underprivileged
socioeconomic populations consume significantly lower levels of the
micronutrients that form the foundation for proper protein and brain

Here she paraphrases findings.

development. In a recent study of poor households, it was found that
two-thirds of children were nutritionally poor and that more than
25 percent of women were deficient in iron, vitamin A, vitamin C,
vitamin B6, thiamin, and riboflavin (Garnett). Of course, some may
challenge the relevance of these vitamins and nutrients since they
are not something the average person consciously incorporates into
his or her diet on a daily basis. Yet modern research, examining
the severely homogenous diets of the poor, has found severe
developmental consequences associated with the lack of nutritional
substance. For those afflicted, these deficiencies are not simply
inconvenient, but actually exacerbate their plight and hinder their
progress toward a sustainable lifestyle.

    The human body is a complex system that cannot be
sustained merely on the simple sugars and processed carbohydrates
that comprise most cheap and filling foodstuffs, and research
shows a relationship between nutritional deficiencies and a host of
cognitive and developmental impairments that are prevalent in the
undernourished families from urban America. Standardized tests of
impoverished siblings, one of whom received nutritional supplements
and the other who did not, showed cognitive gains in the well-

6

Paul 4

Again she both summarizes and cites a relevant study to advance her argument.

nourished child as well as increased motor skills and greater interest in social interactions when compared to the other child. In the highly formative toddler years, undernutrition can inhibit the myelination of nerve fibers, which is responsible for neurotransmitting and proper brain function. Collaborators Emily Tanner from the University of Oxford and Matia Finn-Stevenson from Yale University published a comprehensive analysis of the link between nutrition and brain development in 2002. Their analysis, which they linked to social policy, indicated that a shortage of legumes and leafy green vegetables, which are nearly impossible to find in corner stores, is the leading cause of the iron-deficiency anemia afflicting 25 percent of urban children. This extreme form of anemia is characterized by impaired neurotransmission, weaker memory, and reduced attention span (Tanner and Finn-Stevenson 186). For those who do not have access to the vitamins, minerals, and micronutrients found in fruits and vegetables, these maladies are not distant risks, but constant, inescapable threats.

In light of these severe consequences of undernutrition, the term "food insecurity" encapsulates the condition wherein the economically disadvantaged are vulnerable simply because their bodies are unable to receive adequate fuel for optimal functioning. Just as one cannot expect a dry, parched plant to bloom and pollinate a garden, by constraining the development of individuals, food insecurity also constrains the development of the neighborhoods in which the individuals contribute. For the health of a city and its communities, all roadblocks to progress must be removed, and food insecurity must be cut out at its roots so that individuals have the resources for advancement.

As socially conscious citizens and local governments have recognized the prevalence and danger of food insecurity in inner cities, there have been attempts at a remedy. Obviously, the easiest solution is simply to introduce a grocery store that would provide a variety of quality, healthful foods. However, for big-box supermarkets driven by the bottom line, urban areas are less than desirable business locales from a standpoint of both profitability and maintenance. It is simply irrational for a supermarket to invest in an urban area with less revenue potential, size constraints, an

7

8

Paul 5

unattractive locale, and an increased threat of theft and defacement when it is so easy to turn a profit in spacious and peaceful suburbia (Eisenhauer 131). Supermarkets must have significant incentive, beyond humanitarian ends, if they are to take the financial risk of entering a poor, urban marketplace.

She takes an active stance in citing initiatives that could be applied more effectively to alleviate the problem of food insecurity.

Certain cities are using the power of Tax Increment Financing (TIF) districts to encourage supermarkets to invest in urban centers. Under these redevelopment laws, tax revenues from retail development or other commercial enterprises are devoted, for a specified number of years, to infrastructural improvement of the district ("TIF Reform"). This approach has been effective in enticing new businesses; in fact, the exterior growth around South Bend is the result of a TIF district established in the late 1980s. LaSalle Square is currently part of a TIF district, but there is discussion as to how the TIF monies should best be applied (Wolfson). It may be possible to use the power of the TIF to encourage another large retailer such as Kroger to establish a presence in the square, but a smaller enterprise may be a better option. Experts indicate that for the destitute and

She paraphrases a researcher's findings.

food-insecure, reliance on a corporate entity is not optimal. Elizabeth Eisenhauer, a researcher from the State University of New York, investigated the interplay between supermarkets and the urban poor; she concluded that large big-box stores lack a commitment to the communities they serve and can be relied on only when it is clear they will make a profit, which may or may not happen when TIF benefits expire (131). Even when a portion of proceeds is used in the community, the majority of the cash flow from a supermarket is going to a corporate headquarters elsewhere, not directly supporting the surrounding neighborhood. Likewise, while some employees may be local, the highest-salary management positions are generally given to outsiders, making the stores and their employees set apart, rather than integrated into the neighborhood (Eisenhauer 130). Certainly a supermarket in an urban area will greatly contribute to the reduction of food insecurity, but it is not the only available option, and the city of South Bend is ripe for alternative solutions. The city is primed for a cooperative effort that could shift the paradigm for urban renewal from a quick, corporate solution, to a long-term enterprise built on community contributions and under local control.

Paul 6

She cites a number of examples as evidence to demonstrate the viability of the solution she offers.

Around the globe, many destitute urban areas have found the   *10*
means to reverse nutritional poverty through a literal and figurative
grassroots effort. In an effort to avoid packaged, convenience store
food, neighbors in the Bronx, San Francisco, Los Angeles, London,
and most successfully in Philadelphia, have been planting their own
crops right in the heart of the city (Brown and Carter 3-4). Truly
farming the food desert, coalitions that link community gardens,
local farmers, and urban markets are providing healthy, sustainable
food sources without a supermarket. Interestingly, in the process,
such coalitions are generating jobs, increasing property value, and, in
some cases, actually reversing the effects of poverty. The city of South
Bend, uniquely situated in the breadbasket of the United States, is
in the perfect position to launch a "greening" effort, modeled after
the successes in other parts of the world, which would both solve the
problem of food insecurity of LaSalle Square and invigorate the local
economy.

While modern Americans have the tendency to think that food   *11*
production should be, and always has been, industrialized, countries
around the world, especially economically disadvantaged nations, are

The use of multiple sources would make her case even stronger than using just one source of information, in this case Brown and Carter.

exemplifying the possibilities of local gardening efforts. Far removed
from industrial farms, Cubans grow half their vegetables within
the city; vacant land in Russian cities produces 80 percent of the
nation's vegetables, and specifically in Moscow, 65 percent of families
contribute to food production. Singapore has 10,000 urban farmers,
and nearly half of the residents of Vancouver grow food in their
gardens (Brown and Carter 10). These habits are not simply a novelty;
rather, populations that garden tend to be healthier, eating six out of
the fourteen vegetable categories more regularly than nongardeners
and also consuming fewer sweet and sugary foods per capita (Brown
and Carter 13). These data, compiled by the North American Urban
Agriculture Committee, were synthesized from the *Journal of Public
Health Policy* and the *Journal of Nutrition Education* and show the
interrelatedness of nutritional access and availability to healthy
personal choices. While these trends toward healthful lifestyles and
gardening have been gaining ground slowly in the United States, when
food insecurity and poverty take their toll, cities are finding that urban
agriculture is an increasingly attractive and profitable alternative.

Paul 7

American communities have shown that creativity and
collaboration can be quite effective at reversing food insecurity. The
Garden Project of the Greater Lansing Food Bank has successfully
combined gardening and Midwest access to local farms to bring
food security to urban residents and senior citizens. Their eighteen
community gardens and volunteers provide fresh fruits and
vegetables year-round to low-income families, food pantries, the

*She synthe-
sizes different
sources to make
her point.*

elderly, and social service organizations. Completely bypassing the
commercial market, the Garden Project has trained 500 families
to grow their own food in backyard plots so that they can always
have healthy food in the midst of the city (Brown and Carter 1).
The gardens are supplemented by a process known as "gleaning," in
which volunteers harvest extra crops from local farmers that would
otherwise go to waste, and deliver it to residents of subsidized
housing ("Gleaning"). In 2008 alone, the Garden Project actively
involved 2,500 individual gardeners and was able to provide over
250,000 pounds of produce from gleaning alone, plus the yields
of the community plots that were used directly by the gardeners
("GLFB Facts"). This Lansing coalition serves over 5,000 individuals
per month, yet only 4,400 reside under the poverty line in the
LaSalle Square area (*City-Data.com*). If half of the inhabitants of
LaSalle Square became engaged in the gardening effort, a similar
collaboration could meet the needs of the region, and greater
participation could yield an excess.

Similar efforts have demonstrated not only that inner-city
food production is achievable but also that it can be cost-effective
and self-sufficient, unlike a food bank. Frustrated by the inner-city
downturn she describes as "an overgrown dog toilet," industrious
London entrepreneur Julie Brown created a community gardening
company aimed at providing unmechanized, local, sustainable food.

*In this paragraph,
she summarizes
research to
address the
possible counter-
argument.*

The company, Growing Communities, uses organic box gardens and
small farms to supply more than 400 homes with weekly deliveries of
organic fruits and vegetables. After a ten-year investment in local
farmers and mini-gardens within the city, Growing Communities is
now financially independent and generates over $400,000 per year
(Willis 53). Compelled by both capitalism and social concern, Brown's
efforts have shown that community-supported agriculture not

12

13

Paul 8

only is possible but can be profitable as well! Our own community agriculture program should not be an entrepreneurial endeavor, but Brown's work in London indicates that it need not be a financial burden to the city either. Rather, the co-op would be financially self-sufficient, with the potential to generate revenues and fiscal growth in the city.

There are environmental factors that make South Bend an   *14*
even better place to launch a profitable community agriculture program than London. Chiefly, South Bend has many more farms in the immediate vicinity than Ms. Brown could ever have dreamed of in the U.K. While Brown was limited to twenty-five local farms within 100 miles of the city, South Bend has over fifty farms within 25 miles of LaSalle Square (*Local Harvest*). Offering a broader production base creates more potential for profits by decreasing transportation time and increasing product, thereby making it easier for a coalition to become financially self-sufficient in a shorter time frame than Ms. Brown's ten-year plan.

She again cites research to address the counter-argument.

Urban Philadelphia has led the way in demonstrating the   *15*
profitability of community solutions to food insecurity through an offshoot of the Pennsylvania Horticultural Society (PHS) known as Philadelphia Greens. Since the 1970s, this coalition has reclaimed parks, planted trees, and created community gardens, both to revitalize the neighborhood and to serve the nutritionally and economically poor. Through a process that plants trees, builds wooden fences, and gardens the more than 1,000 vacant lots of Philadelphia, PHS combines housing projects and reclaimed space to "green" and reinvigorate the neighborhood ("The Effects"). Since LaSalle Square is essentially a large empty grassy area at the moment, a community agricultural co-op should turn this vacant lot and others in the neighborhood into community gardens, which would work in tandem with the gleaning from local farms. Similar to the Philadelphia project, these gardens would simultaneously yield produce and improve the appearance of the neighborhood.

One PHS project, in the New Kensington neighborhood of   *16*
north Philadelphia, was the subject of a recent socioeconomic study conducted by the University of Pennsylvania's renowned Wharton School of Business. In the New Kensington area, PHS recently planted

Paul 9

480 new trees, cleaned 145 side yards, developed 217 vacant lots, and established 15 new community gardens. The effort was a model of the collaborative strategy between PHS and the local community development corporation, making it the ideal subject of the Wharton

She summarizes a study and then paraphrases.

study. The findings, published in 2004, showed significant increases in property values around the PHS greening projects and were the first step in quantifying the fiscal returns of neighborhood greening beyond the qualitative benefits of remedying food insecurity. After analyzing the sales records of thousands of New Kensington homes between 1980 and 2003, the study reported that PHS greening had led to a $4 million gain in property value from tree plantings alone and a $12 million gain from vacant lot improvements. Simply greening a vacant lot increased nearby property values by as much as 30 percent ("Seeing Green"). While a supermarket might modestly improve property values for those immediately near the store, community greening involves multiple plots across an area, benefiting many more people and properties. The Wharton study showed that community greening would provide increases in the value of any property near a green space, up to multiple millions of dollars. The New Kensington neighborhood covers 1.4 square miles, which is approximately the size of LaSalle Square, so while the overall property values are lower simply because South Bend is a smaller city, the gains might be proportional (*City-Data.com*). It is reasonable to believe that cleaning up LaSalle Square and planting gardens would quantitatively benefit the fiscal situation of the city and increase assets of the homeowners while subsequently improving the quality of life over many acres.

Certainly there are challenges to the sort of dynamical, community-based solution that I am proposing. Such an agricultural co-op hinges on the participation of the people it serves and cannot be successful without the dedicated support of the neighborhood. It could be noted that lower-income economic groups are less socially involved than their higher-income counterparts, and some might believe that they are unlikely to contribute to, or care about, a greening effort. Yet I believe that there is a distinction between political involvement and neighborhood interaction. Middle-class Americans are conscious of gas prices and the fluctuations of the

17

Paul 10

stock market that affect their job security and ability to provide for their families; yet the unemployed poor without cars must rely on their neighborhoods to eke out a living. Their sustenance comes not from a salary, but from odd jobs, welfare, and the munificence of fate. The battle to put food on the table is more familiar to the poor than foreign conflict and is one that they fight every day. Therefore, while the poor are less inclined to vote or worry about governmental affairs because of the difficulties associated simply with daily living, they are acutely aware of their immediate surroundings and how those surroundings challenge or contribute to their success. This position makes them uniquely inclined to invest in the betterment of their surroundings since it can have a dramatic effect on their personal lives. The real success of the sustainable food movement may come from harnessing the power of urban communities that can derive great, immediate, and lasting benefit from neighborhood revitalization.

In this paragraph, she takes an active stance in using research to alleviate fears that the local community would have to start from scratch with limited expertise.

It has been argued that urban growers, especially from lower socioeconomic classes, do not have the expertise or knowledge base to generate successful yields that will ensure food security. Fortunately, agriculture is Indiana's fourth-largest industry, and the state boasts over 63,000 farms ("A Look"). In addition to the many inhabitants of LaSalle Square who have a background in agriculture, there is a wealth of knowledge about proper planting methods available from the farmers around the local area. Many of these farmers have already shown a willingness to help by selling or donating their produce to the local Urban Market. Additionally, national urban agriculture nonprofit groups, such as Master Gardening and Cooperative Extension, offer free public education to cities beginning community agriculture programs, and some will even perform on-site training (Brown and Carter 16). By harnessing the assets of local, gratuitous knowledge and supplementing that knowledge with national support groups, South Bend has multiple resources available to train and encourage its burgeoning urban farmers.

18

The economic and nutritional gains of the people would only be heightened by the personal well-being that is born of interpersonal collaboration that crosses racial and social

19

boundaries. Such an effort is ambitious; it will indeed require the time and talents of many people who care about the health of their community. But the local community is rich with the necessary seeds for such a project, which may, in time, blossom and grow to feed its people.

Works Cited

Brown, Katherine H., and Anne Carter. *Urban Agriculture and Community Food Security in the United States: Farming from the City Center to the Urban Fringe*. Community Food Security Coalition, Oct. 2003.

City-Data.com. Advameg, 16 Apr. 2008, www.city-data.com/city/South-Bend-Indiana.html.

"The Effects of Neighborhood Greening." *Pennsylvania Horticultural Society*, Jan. 2001, phsonline.org/programs/effects-of-neighborhood-greening.

Eisenhauer, Elizabeth. "In Poor Health: Supermarket Redlining and Urban Nutrition." *GeoJournal*, vol. 53, no. 2, Feb. 2001, pp. 125–33.

Garnett, Tara. "Farming the City." *The Ecologist*, vol. 26, no. 6, Nov./Dec. 1996, p. 299.

"Gleaning." *Greater Lansing Food Bank*, greaterlansingfoodbank.org/programs/programs-home/the-garden-project/gleaning/. Accessed 15 Apr. 20—.

"GLFB Facts." *Greater Lansing Food Bank*, greaterlansingfoodbank.org/our-impact/fact-sheet/. Accessed 15 Apr. 20—.

LocalHarvest. Local Harvest, 2008, www.localharvest.org/south-bend-in.

"A Look at Indiana Agriculture." *National Agriculture in the Classroom*, www.agclassroom.org/kids/ag_facts.htm. Accessed 18 Apr. 20—.

Paul 13

"Seeing Green: Study Finds Greening Is a Good Investment."
    Pennsylvania Horticultural Society, 2005, phsonline.org/
    programs/seeing-green.
Smith, Stephen. "Obesity Battle Starts Young for Urban Poor." *The
    Boston Globe*, 29 Dec. 2006, archive.boston.com/news/nation/
    articles/2006/12/29/obesity_battle_starts_young_for_urban
    _poor/.
Tanner, Emily M., and Matia Finn-Stevenson. "Nutrition and Brain
    Development: Social Policy Implications." *American Journal of
    Orthopsychiatry*, vol. 72, no. 2, Apr. 2002, pp. 182–93.
"TIF Reform." *New Rules Project*, Institute for Local Self-Reliance,
    2008, ilsr.org/rule/tif-reform/.
Willis, Ben. "Julie Brown of Growing Communities." *The Ecologist*,
    vol. 38, no. 5, June 2008, pp. 58–61.
Wolfson, Linda. Personal interview, 20 Apr. 20—.

A Practice Sequence: Thinking about Copyright

1   Now that you have read about steps to avoiding plagiarism
    (pp. 228–29) and Nancy Paul's essay on community gardens
    (p. 235) we would like you to examine the idea of copyright. That
    is, who owns the rights to images that the organizers of a commu-
    nity garden use to market their idea? What if you wanted to use
    that image in a paper? Or what if you wanted to use a published
    ad in your own paper? Under what circumstances would you be
    able to use that ad for your own purposes?

2   After conducting your own inquiry into copyright, what would
    you conclude about the need to document the use of images,
    ideas, and text? Are the guidelines clear or are there some ambig-
    uous areas for what to cite and how? What advice would you give
    your peers?

From Ethos to Logos
Appealing to Your Readers

Your understanding of your readers influences how you see a particular situation, define an issue, explain the ongoing conversation surrounding that issue, and formulate a question. You may need to read widely to understand how different writers have dealt with the issue you address. And you will need to anticipate how others might respond to your argument—whether they will be sympathetic or antagonistic—and to compose your essay so that readers will "listen" whether or not they agree with you.

To achieve these goals, you will no doubt use reason in the form of evidence to sway readers. But you can also use other means of persuasion. That is, you can use your own character, by presenting yourself as someone who is knowledgeable, fair, and just, and you can appeal to your readers' emotions. Although you may believe that reason alone should provide the means for changing people's minds, people's emotions also color the way they see the world.

Your audience is more than your immediate reader—your instructor or a peer. Your audience encompasses those you cite in writing about an issue and those you anticipate responding to your argument. This is true no matter what you write about, whether it be an interpretation of the novels of a particular author, an analysis of the cultural work of horror films, the ethics of treating boys and girls differently in schools, or the moral issues surrounding homelessness in America.

In this chapter we discuss different ways of engaging your readers, centering on three kinds of appeals: **ethos**, appeals from character; **pathos**, appeals to emotion; and **logos**, appeals to reason. *Ethos, pathos,* and *logos* are terms derived from ancient Greek writers, but they are still of great value today when considering how to persuade your audience. Readers

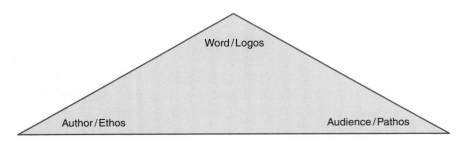

FIGURE 9.1   The Rhetorical Triangle

will judge your writing on whether or not you present an argument that is fair and just, one that creates a sense of goodwill. All three appeals rely on these qualities.

Figure 9.1, the **rhetorical triangle**, visually represents the interrelationship among ethos, pathos, and logos. Who we think our readers are (pathos: which of their emotions do we appeal to?) influences decisions about the ways we should represent ourselves to them (ethos: how can we come across as fair, credible, and just?). In turn, we use certain patterns of argument (logos: how do we arrange our words to make our case?) that reflect our interpretation of the situation to which we respond and that we believe will persuade readers to accept our point of view. Effective communication touches on each of the three points of the triangle. Your task as a writer is to determine the proper balance of these different appeals in your argument, based on your thesis, the circumstances, and your audience.

CONNECTING WITH READERS: A SAMPLE ARGUMENT

To see how an author connects with his audience, read the following excerpt from James W. Loewen's book *Lies My Teacher Told Me: Everything Your American History Textbook Got Wrong*. As you read the excerpt, note Loewen's main points and select key examples that illustrate his argument. As a class, test the claims he makes: To what extent do you believe that what Loewen argues is true? This may entail recalling your own experiences in high school history classes or locating one or more of the books that Loewen mentions.

JAMES W. LOEWEN

The Land of Opportunity

In addition to *Lies My Teacher Told Me* (1995, 2007), James Loewen, who holds a PhD in sociology, has written several other books, including *Lies across America: What Our Historic Sites Get Wrong* (1999) and *Sundown Towns: A Hidden Dimension of American Racism* (2005). As the titles of these books suggest, Loewen is a writer who questions the assumptions about history that many people take for granted. This is especially true of the following excerpt, from a chapter in which Loewen challenges a common American belief—that everyone has an equal chance in what he calls the "land of opportunity"—by arguing that we live in a class system that privileges some people and raises barriers for others. History textbook writers, he points out, are guilty of complicity in this class system because they leave a great deal of history out of their textbooks.

High school students have eyes, ears, and television sets (all too many have their own TV sets), so they know a lot about relative privilege in America. They measure their family's social position against that of other families, and their community's position against other communities. Middle-class students, especially, know little about how the American class structure works, however, and nothing at all about how it has changed over time. These students do not leave high school merely ignorant of the workings of the class structure; they come out as terrible sociologists. "Why are people poor?" I have asked first-year college students. Or, if their own class position is one of relative privilege, "Why is your family well-off?" The answers I've received, to characterize them charitably, are half-formed and naïve. The students blame the poor for not being successful. They have no understanding of the ways that opportunity is not equal in America and no notion that social structure pushes people around, influencing the ideas they hold and the lives they fashion.

High school history textbooks can take some of the credit for this state of affairs. Some textbooks do cover certain high points of labor history, such as the 1894 Pullman strike near Chicago that President Cleveland broke with federal troops, or the 1911 Triangle Shirtwaist fire that killed 146 women in New York City, but the most recent event mentioned in most books is the Taft-Hartley Act of sixty years ago. No book mentions any of the major strikes that labor lost in the late twentieth century, such as the 1985 Hormel meatpackers' strike in Austin, Minnesota, or the 1991 Caterpillar strike in Decatur, Illinois—defeats that signify labor's diminished power today. Nor do most textbooks describe any continuing issues facing labor, such as the growth of multinational corporations and their exporting of jobs overseas. With such omissions, textbook authors can construe labor history as something that happened long ago, like slavery, and that, like slavery, was corrected long ago. It logically follows that unions now appear anachronistic. The idea that they might be necessary for workers to have a voice in the workplace goes unstated.

These books' poor treatment of labor history is magnificent compared to their treatment of social class. *Nothing* that textbooks discuss—not even strikes—is ever anchored in any analysis of social class.[1] This amounts to delivering the footnotes instead of the lecture! Half of the eighteen high school American history textbooks I examined contain no index listing at all for *social class, social stratification, class structure, income distribution, inequality,* or any conceivably related topic. Not one book lists *upper class* or *lower class*. Three list *middle class*, but only to assure students that America is a middle-class country. "Except for slaves, most of the colonists were members of the 'middling ranks,'" says *Land of Promise*, and nails home the point that we are a middle-class country by asking students to "describe three 'middle-class' values that united free Americans of all classes." Several of the textbooks note the explosion of middle-class suburbs after World War II. Talking about the middle class is hardly equivalent to discussing social stratification, however. On the contrary, as Gregory Mantsios has pointed out, "such references appear to be acceptable precisely because they mute class differences."[2]

Stressing how middle-class we all are is increasingly problematic today, because the proportion of households earning between 75 percent and 125 percent of the median income has fallen steadily since 1967. The Reagan-Bush administrations accelerated this shrinkage of the middle class, and most families who left its ranks fell rather than rose.[3] As late as 1970, family incomes in the United States were only slightly less equal than in Canada. By 2000, inequality here was much greater than Canada's; the United States was becoming more like Mexico, a very stratified society.[4] The Bush II administration, with its tax cuts aimed openly at the wealthy, continued to increase the gap between the haves and have-nots. This is the kind of historical trend one would think history books would take as appropriate subject matter, but only five of the eighteen books in my sample provide any analysis of social stratification in the United States. Even these fragmentary analyses are set mostly in colonial America. Boorstin and Kelley, unusual in actually including *social class* in its index, lists only *social classes in 1790* and *social classes in early America*. These turn out to be two references to the same paragraph, which tells us that England "was a land of rigid social classes," while here in America "social classes were much more fluid." "One great difference between colonial and European society was that the colonists had more social mobility," echoes *The American Tradition*. Never mind that the most violent class conflicts in American history—Bacon's Rebellion and Shays's Rebellion—took place in and just after colonial times. Textbooks still say that colonial society was relatively classless and marked by upward mobility.

And things have only gotten rosier since. "By 1815," *The Challenge of Freedom* assures us, two classes had withered away and "America was a country of middle class people and of middle class goals." This book returns repeatedly, every fifty years or so, to the theme of how open opportunity is in America. The stress on upward mobility is striking. There is almost nothing in any of these textbooks about class inequalities or barriers of any kind to social mobility. "What conditions made it possible for poor white immigrants to become richer in the colonies?" *Land of Promise* asks. "What conditions made/make it difficult?" goes unasked. Boorstin and Kelley close their sole discussion of social class (in 1790, described above) with the happy sentence, "As the careers of American Presidents would soon show, here a person might rise by hard work, intelligence, skill, and perhaps a little luck, from the lowest positions to the highest."

If only that were so! Social class is probably the single most important variable in society. From womb to tomb, it correlates with almost all other social characteristics of people that we can measure. Affluent expectant mothers are more likely to get prenatal care, receive current medical advice, and enjoy general health, fitness, and nutrition. Many poor and working-class mothers-to-be first contact the medical profession in the last month, sometimes the last hours, of their pregnancies. Rich babies come out healthier and weighing more than poor babies. The infants go home to very different situations. Poor babies are more likely to have high levels of poisonous lead in their environments and their bodies. Rich babies get more time and verbal interaction with their parents and higher quality day care when not with their parents. When they enter kindergarten, and through the twelve years that follow, rich children benefit from suburban schools that spend two to three times as much money per student as schools in inner cities or impoverished rural areas. Poor children are taught in classes that are often 50 percent larger than the classes of affluent children. Differences such as these help account for the higher school-dropout rate among poor children.

Even when poor children are fortunate enough to attend the same school as rich children, they encounter teachers who expect only children of affluent families to know the right answers. Social science research shows that teachers are often surprised and even distressed when poor children excel. Teachers and counselors believe they can predict who is "college material." Since many working-class children give off the wrong signals, even in first grade, they end up in the "general education" track in high school. "If you are the child of low-income parents, the chances are good that you will receive limited and often careless attention from adults in your high school," in the words of Theodore Sizer's bestselling study of American high schools, *Horace's Compromise*. "If you are the child of upper-middle-income parents, the chances are good that you will receive substantial and careful attention."[5] Researcher Reba Page has provided vivid accounts of how high school American history courses use rote learning to turn off lower-class students.[6] Thus schools have put into practice Woodrow Wilson's rec-ommendation: "We want one class of persons to have a liberal educa-tion, and we want another class of persons, a very much larger class of necessity in every society, to forgo the privilege of a liberal education and fit themselves to perform specific difficult manual tasks."[7]

As if this unequal home and school life were not enough, rich teenag-ers then enroll in the Princeton Review or other coaching sessions for the Scholastic Aptitude Test. Even without coaching, affluent children are advantaged because their background is similar to that of the test makers, so they are comfortable with the vocabulary and subtle sub-cultural assumptions of the test. To no one's surprise, social class cor-relates strongly with SAT scores.

All these are among the reasons that social class predicts the rate of college attendance and the type of college chosen more effectively than does any other factor, including intellectual ability, however measured. After college, most affluent children get white-collar jobs, most working-class children get blue-collar jobs, and the class differ-ences continue. As adults, rich people are more likely to have hired an attorney and to be a member of formal organizations that increase their civic power. Poor people are more likely to watch TV. Because affluent families can save some money while poor families must spend what they make, wealth differences are ten times larger than income differences. Therefore most poor and working-class families cannot accumulate the down payment required to buy a house, which in turn shuts them out from our most important tax shelter, the write-off of home mortgage interest. Working-class parents cannot afford to live in elite subdivisions or hire high-quality day care, so the process of educational inequality replicates itself in the next generation. Finally, affluent Americans also have longer life expectancies than lower- and working-class people, the largest single cause of which is better access to health care. Echoing the results of Helen Keller's study of blindness, research has determined that poor health is not distributed randomly about the social structure but is concentrated in the lower class. Social Security then become a huge transfer system, using monies contrib-uted by all Americans to pay benefits disproportionately to longer-lived affluent Americans.

Ultimately social class determines how people think about social class. When asked if poverty in America is the fault of the poor or the fault of the system, 57 percent of business leaders blamed the poor; just 9 percent blamed the system. Labor leaders showed sharply reversed choices: only 15 percent said the poor were at fault while 56 percent blamed the system. (Some people replied "don't know" or chose a middle position.) The largest single difference between our two main political parties lies in how their members think about social class: 55 percent of Republicans blamed the poor for their poverty, while only 13 percent blamed the system for it; 68 percent of Democrats, on the other hand, blamed the system, while only 5 percent blamed the poor.[8]

Few of these statements are news, I know, which is why I have not bothered to document most of them, but the majority of high school students do not know or understand these ideas. Moreover, the processes have changed over time, for the class structure in America today is not the same as it was in 1890, let alone in colonial America. Yet in the most recent *American Pageant*, for example, social class goes unmentioned in the twentieth century. Many teachers compound the problem by avoiding talking about social class in the twenty-first. A study of history and social studies teachers "revealed that they had a much broader knowledge of the economy, both academically and experientially, than they admitted in class." Teachers "expressed fear that students might find out about the injustices and inadequacies of their economic and political institutions."[9] By never blaming the system, American history courses thus present Republican history.

Notes

1. Jean Anyon, "Ideology and United States History Textbooks," *Harvard Educational Review* 49, no. 3 (8/1979): 373.

2. Gregory Mantsios, "Class in America: Myths and Realities," in Paula S. Rothernberg, ed., *Racism and Sexism: An Integrated Study* (New York: St. Martin's, 1988), 56.

3. Ibid., 60; Kevin Phillips, *The Politics of Rich and Poor* (New York: Random House, 1990); Robert Heilbroner, "Lifting the Silent Depression," *New York Review of Books*, 10/24/1991, 6; and Sylvia Nasar, "The Rich Get Richer," *New York Times*, 8/16/1992. Stephen J. Rose, *Social Stratification in the United States* (New York: New Press, 2007), is a posterbook that shows graphically the shrinkage of the middle class between 1979 and 2004.

4. "Income Disparity Since World War II—The Gini Index," in "Gini co-efficient," en.wikipedia.org/wiki/Gini_coefficient, 9/2006.

5. Sizer quoted in Walter Karp, "Why Johnny Can't Think," *Harper's*, 6/1985, 73.

6. Reba Page, "The Lower-Track Students' View of Curriculum," (Washington, D.C.: American Education Research Association, 1987).

7. Woodrow Wilson quoted in Lewis H. Lapham, "Notebook," *Harper's*, 7/1991, 10.

8. Survey data from about 1979 reported in Sidney Verba and Gary Orren, *Equality in America* (Cambridge: Harvard University Press, 1985), 72–75.

9. Linda McNeil, "Defensive Teaching and Classroom Control," in Michael W. Apple and Lois Weis, eds., *Ideology and Practice in Schooling* (Philadelphia: Temple University Press, 1983), 116.

Reading as a Writer

1. List what you think are Loewen's main points. What appeals does he seem to draw on most when he makes those points: appeals based on his own character (ethos), on the emotions of his reader (pathos), or on the reasonableness of his evidence (logos)? Are the appeals obvious or difficult to tease out? Does he combine them? Discuss your answers with your classmates.

2. Identify what you think is the main claim of Loewen's argument, and choose key examples to support your answer. Compare your chosen claim and examples to those chosen by your classmates. Do they differ significantly? Can you agree on Loewen's gist and his key examples?

3. As a class, test the claims Loewen makes by thinking about your own experiences in high school history classes. Do you remember finding out that something you were taught from an American history textbook was not true? Did you discover on your own what you considered to be misrepresentations in or important omissions from your textbook? If so, did these misrepresentations or omissions tend to support or contradict the claims about history textbooks that Loewen makes?

APPEALING TO ETHOS

Although we like to believe that our decisions and beliefs are based on reason and logic, in fact they are often based on what amounts to character judgments. That is, if a person you trust makes a reasonable argument for one choice, and a person you distrust makes a reasonable argument for another choice, you are more likely to be swayed by the argument of the person you trust. Similarly, the audience for your argument will be more disposed to agree with you if its members believe you are a fair, just person who is knowledgeable and has good judgment. Even the most well-developed argument will fall short if you do not leave this kind of impression on your readers. Thus, it is not surprising that ethos may be the most important component of your argument.

There are three strategies for evoking a sense of ethos:

1. Establish that you have good judgment.
2. Convey to readers that you are knowledgeable.
3. Show that you understand the complexity of the issue.

These strategies are interrelated: A writer who demonstrates good judgment is more often than not someone who is both knowledgeable about an issue and who acknowledges the complexity of it by weighing the strengths *and* weaknesses of different arguments. However, keep in mind that these characteristics do not exist apart from what readers think and believe.

■ Establish That You Have Good Judgment

Most readers of academic writing expect writers to demonstrate good judgment by identifying a problem that readers agree is worth addressing. In turn, good judgment gives writers credibility.

Loewen crafts his introduction to capture the attention of educators as well as concerned citizens when he claims that students leave high school unaware of class structure and as a consequence "have no understanding of the ways that opportunity is not equal in America and no notion that social structure pushes people around, influencing the ideas they hold and the lives they fashion" (para. 1). Loewen does not blame students, or even instructors, for this lack of awareness. Instead, he writes, "textbooks can take some of the credit for this state of affairs" (para. 2) because, among other shortcomings, they leave out important events in "labor history" and relegate issues facing labor to the past.

Whether an educator—or a general reader for that matter—will ultimately agree with Loewen's case is, at this point, up for grabs, but certainly the possibility that high schools in general, and history textbooks in particular, are failing students by leaving them vulnerable to class-based manipulation would be recognized as a problem by readers who believe America should be a society that offers equal opportunity for all. At this point, Loewen's readers are likely to agree that the problem of omission he identifies may be significant if its consequences are as serious as he believes them to be.

Writers also establish good judgment by conveying to readers that they are fair-minded and just and have the best interests of readers in mind. Loewen is particularly concerned that students understand the persistence of poverty and inequality in the United States and the historical circumstances of the poor, which they cannot do unless textbook writers take a more inclusive approach to addressing labor history, especially "the growth of multinational corporations and their exporting of jobs overseas" (para. 2). It's not fair to deny this important information to students, and it's not fair to the poor to leave them out of official histories of the United

States. Loewen further demonstrates that he is fair and just when he calls attention in paragraph 6 to the inequality between rich and poor children in schools, a problem that persists despite our forebears' belief that class would not determine the fate of citizens of the United States.

■ Convey to Readers That You Are Knowledgeable

Being thoughtful about a subject goes hand in hand with being knowledgeable about the subject. Loewen demonstrates his knowledge of class issues and their absence from textbooks in a number of ways (not the least of which is his awareness that a problem exists — many people, including educators, may not be aware of this problem).

In paragraph 3, Loewen makes a bold claim: "*Nothing* that textbooks discuss — not even strikes — is ever anchored in any analysis of social class." As readers, we cannot help wondering: How does the author know this? How will he support this claim? Loewen anticipates these questions by demonstrating that he has studied the subject through a systematic examination of American history textbooks. He observes that half of the eighteen textbooks he examined "contain no index listing at all for *social class, social stratification, class structure, income distribution, inequality*, or any conceivably related topic" and that "not one book lists *upper class* or *lower class*." Loewen also demonstrates his grasp of class issues in American history, from the "violent class conflicts" that "took place in and just after colonial times" (para. 4), which contradict textbook writers' assertions that class conflicts did not exist during this period, to the more recent conflicts in the 1980s and early 1990s (paras. 2 and 4).

Moreover, Loewen backs up his own study of textbooks with references to a number of studies from the social sciences to illustrate that "social class is probably the single most important variable in society" (para. 6). Witness the statistics and findings he cites in paragraphs 6 through 10. The breadth of Loewen's historical knowledge and the range of his reading should convince readers that he is knowledgeable, and his trenchant analysis contributes to the authority he brings to the issue and to his credibility.

■ Show That You Understand the Complexity of a Given Issue

Recognizing the complexity of an issue helps readers see the extent to which authors know that any issue can be understood in a number of different ways. Loewen acknowledges that most of the history he recounts is not "news" (para. 11) to his educated readers, who by implication "know" and "understand" his references to historical events and trends. What may be news to his readers, he explains, is the extent to which class structure in the United States has changed over time. With the steady erosion of middle-class households since 1967, "class inequalities" and "barriers . . . to social mobility" (para. 5) are limiting more and more Americans' access to even the most fundamental of opportunities in a democratic society—health care and education.

Still, even though Loewen has introduced new thinking about the nature of class in the United States and has demonstrated a provocative play of mind by examining an overlooked body of data (high school history textbooks) that may influence the way class is perceived in America, there are still levels of complexity he hasn't addressed explicitly. Most important, perhaps, is the question of why history textbooks continue to ignore issues of class when there is so much research that indicates its importance in shaping the events history textbooks purport to explain.

Steps to Appealing to Ethos

1 **Establish that you have good judgment.** Identify an issue your readers will agree is worth addressing, and demonstrate that you are fair-minded and have the best interests of your readers in mind when you address it.

2 **Convey to readers that you are knowledgeable.** Support your claims with credible evidence that shows you have read widely on, thought about, and understand the issue.

3 **Show that you understand the complexity of the issue.** Demonstrate that you understand the variety of viewpoints your readers may bring—or may not be able to bring—to the issue.

APPEALING TO PATHOS

An appeal to pathos recognizes that people are moved to action by their emotions as well as by reasonable arguments. In fact, pathos is a vital part of argument that can predispose readers one way or another. Do you want to arouse readers' sympathy? Anger? Passion? You can do that by knowing what readers value.

Appeals to pathos are typically indirect. You can appeal to pathos by using examples or illustrations that you believe will arouse the appropriate emotions and by presenting them using an appropriate tone.

To acknowledge that writers play on readers' emotions is not to endorse manipulative writing. Rather, it is to acknowledge that effective writers use all available means of persuasion to move readers to agree with them. After all, if your thoughtful reading and careful research have led you to believe that you must weigh in with a useful insight on an important issue, it stands to reason that you would want your argument to convince your readers to believe as strongly in what you assert as you do.

For example, if you genuinely believe that the conditions some families are living in are abysmal and unfair, you want your readers to believe it too. And an effective way to persuade them to believe as you do, in addition to convincing them of the reasonableness of your argument and of your own good character and judgment, is to establish a kind of emotional common ground in your writing — the common ground of pathos.

▪ Show That You Know What Your Readers Value

Let's consider some of the ways James Loewen signals that he knows what his readers value.

In the first place, Loewen assumes that readers feel the same way he does: Educated people should know that the United States has a class structure despite the democratic principles that the nation was founded on. He also expects readers to identify with his unwillingness to accept the injustice that results from that class structure. He believes that women living in poverty should have access to appropriate health care, that children living in poverty should have a chance to attend college, and that certain classes of people should not be written off to, as Woodrow Wilson recommended, "perform specific difficult manual tasks" (para. 7).

Time and again, Loewen cites examples that reveal that the poor are discriminated against by the class structure in the United States not for lack of ability, lack of desire, lack of ambition, or lack of morality, but for no better reason than lack of money — and that such discrimination has been going on for a long time. He expects that his readers also will find such discrimination an unacceptable affront to their values of fair play and democracy and that they will experience the same sense of outrage that he does.

▪ Use Illustrations and Examples That Appeal to Readers' Emotions

You can appeal to readers' emotions indirectly through the illustrations and examples you use to support your argument.

For instance, in paragraph 2, Loewen contends that textbook writers share responsibility for high school students' not knowing about the continued relevance of class issues in American life. Loewen's readers — parents, educators, historians — may very well be angered by the omissions he points out. Certainly he would expect them to be angry when they read about the effects of economic class on the health care expectant mothers and then their children receive (para. 6) and on their children's access to quality education (paras. 6–8). In citing the fact that social class "correlates strongly with SAT scores" (para. 8) and so "predicts the rate of college attendance and the type of college chosen" (para. 9), Loewen forces his readers to acknowledge that the educational playing field is far from level.

Finally, he calls attention to the fact that accumulated wealth accounts for deep class divisions in our society—that the inability to save prevents the poor from hiring legal counsel, purchasing a home, or taking advantage of tax shelters. The result, Loewen observes, is that "educational inequality replicates itself in the next generation" (para. 9).

Together, these examples strengthen both Loewen's argument and what he hopes will be readers' outrage that history textbooks do not address class issues. Without that information, Americans cannot fully understand or act to change the existing class structure.

■ Consider How Your Tone May Affect Your Audience

The **tone** of your writing is your use of language that communicates your attitude toward yourself, your material, and your readers. Of course, your tone is important in everything you write, but it is particularly crucial when you are appealing to pathos.

When you are appealing to your readers' emotions, it is tempting to use loaded, exaggerated, and even intemperate language to convey how you feel (and hope your readers will feel) about an issue. Consider these sentences: "The Republican Party has devised the most ignominious means of filling the pockets of corporations." "These wretched children suffer heartrending agonies that can barely be imagined, much less described." "The ethereal beauty of the Brandenburg concertos thrill one to the deepest core of one's being." All of these sentences express strong and probably sincere beliefs and emotions, but some readers might find them overwrought and coercive and question the writer's reasonableness.

Similarly, some writers rely on irony or sarcasm to set the tone of their work. **Irony** is the use of language to say one thing while meaning quite another. **Sarcasm** is the use of heavy-handed irony to ridicule or attack someone or something. Although irony and sarcasm can make for vivid and entertaining writing, they also can backfire and end up alienating readers. The sentence "Liberals will be pleased to hear that the new budget will be making liberal use of their hard-earned dollars" may entertain some readers with its irony and wordplay, but others may assume that the writer's attitude toward liberals is likely to result in an unfairly slanted argument. And the sentence "In my opinion, there's no reason why Christians and Muslims shouldn't rejoice together over the common ground of their both being deluded about the existence of a God" may please some readers, but it risks alienating those who are uncomfortable with breezy comments about religious beliefs. Again, think of your readers and what they value, and weigh the benefits of a clever sentence against its potential to detract from your argument or offend your audience.

You often find colorful wording and irony in op-ed and opinion pieces, where a writer may not have the space to build a compelling argument using evidence and has to resort to shortcuts to readers' emotions. However, in academic writing, where the careful accumulation and presentation of evidence and telling examples are highly valued, the frequent use of loaded language, exaggeration, and sarcasm is looked on with distrust.

Consider Loewen's excerpt. Although his outrage comes through clearly, he never resorts to hectoring. For example, in paragraph 1, he writes that students are "ignorant of the workings of the class structure" and that their opinions are "half-formed and naïve." But he does not imply that students are ignoramuses or that their opinions are foolish. What they lack, he contends, is understanding. They need to be taught something about class structure that they are not now being taught. And paragraph 1 is about as close to name-calling as Loewen comes. Even textbook writers, who are the target of his anger, are not vilified.

Loewen does occasionally make use of irony, for example in paragraph 4, where he points out inconsistencies and omissions in textbooks: "Never mind that the most violent class conflicts in American history—Bacon's Rebellion and Shays's Rebellion—took place in and just after colonial times. Textbooks still say that colonial society was relatively classless and marked by upward mobility. And things have only gotten rosier since." But he doesn't resort to ridicule. Instead, he relies on examples and illustrations to connect with his readers' sense of values and appeal to their emotions.

Steps to Appealing to Pathos

1 **Show that you know what your readers value.** Start from your own values and imagine what assumptions and principles would appeal to your readers. What common ground can you imagine between your values and theirs? How will it need to be adjusted for different kinds of readers?

2 **Use illustrations and examples that appeal to readers' emotions.** Again, start from your own emotional position. What examples and illustrations resonate most with you? How can you present them to have the most emotional impact on your readers? How would you adjust them for different kinds of readers?

3 **Consider how your tone may affect your audience.** Be wary of using loaded, exaggerated, and intemperate language that may put off your readers; and be careful in your use of irony and sarcasm.

A Practice Sequence: Appealing to Ethos and Pathos

Discuss the language and strategies the writers use in the following passages to connect with their audience, in particular their appeals to both ethos and pathos. After reading each excerpt, discuss who you think the implied audience is and whether you think the strategies the writers use to connect with their readers are effective or not.

1   Almost a half century after the U.S. Supreme Court concluded that Southern school segregation was unconstitutional and "inherently unequal," new statistics from the 1998–99 school year show that segregation continued to intensify throughout the 1990s, a period in which there were three major Supreme Court decisions authorizing a return to segregated neighborhood schools and limiting the reach and duration of desegregation orders. For African American students, this trend is particularly apparent in the South, where most blacks live and where the 2000 Census shows a continuing return from the North. From 1988 to 1998, most of the progress of the previous two decades in increasing integration in the region was lost. The South is still much more integrated than it was before the civil rights revolution, but it is moving backward at an accelerating rate.

> — GARY ORFIELD, "Schools More Separate: Consequences of a Decade of Resegregation"

2   When the judgment day comes for every high school student — that day when a final transcript is issued and sent to the finest institutions, with every sin of class selection written as with a burning chisel on stone — on that day a great cry will go up throughout the land, and there will be weeping, wailing, gnashing of teeth, and considerable grumbling against guidance counselors, and the cry of a certain senior might be, "WHY did no one tell me that Introduction to Social Poker wasn't a solid academic class?" At another, perhaps less wealthy school, a frustrated and under-nurtured sculptress will wonder, "Why can't I read, and why don't I care?" The reason for both of these oversights, as they may eventually discover, is that the idea of the elective course has been seriously mauled, mistreated, and abused under the current middle-class high school system. A significant amount of the blame for producing students who are stunted, both cognitively and morally, can be traced back to this pervasive fact. Elective courses, as shoddily planned and poorly funded as they may be, constitute the only formation that many students get in their own special types of intelligences. Following the model of Howard Gardner, these may

be spatial, musical, or something else. A lack of stimulation to a student's own intelligence directly causes a lack of identification with the intelligence of others. Instead of becoming moderately interested in a subject by noticing the pleasure other people receive from it, the student will be bitter, jealous, and without empathy. These are the common ingredients in many types of tragedy, violent or benign. Schools must take responsibility for speaking in some way to each of the general types of intelligences. Failure to do so will result in students who lack skills, and also the inspiration to comfort, admire, emulate, and aid their fellow humans.

"All tasks that really call upon the power of attention are interesting for the same reason and to an almost equal degree," wrote Simone Weil in her *Reflections on Love and Faith*, her editor having defined attention as "a suspension of one's own self as a center of the world and making oneself available to the reality of another being." In Parker Palmer's *The Courage to Teach*, modern scientific theorist David Bohm describes "a holistic underlying implicate order whose information unfolds into the explicate order of particular fields." Rilke's euphemism for this "holistic . . . implicate order," which Palmer borrows, is "the grace of great things." Weil's term would be "God." However, both agree that eventual perception of this singular grace, or God, is accessible through education of a specific sort, and for both it is doubtless the most necessary experience of a lifetime. Realizing that this contention is raining down from different theorists, and keeping in mind that the most necessary experience of a lifetime should not be wholly irrelevant to the school system, educators should therefore reach the conclusion that this is a matter worth looking into. I assert that the most fruitful and practical results of their attention will be a wider range of electives coupled with a new acknowledgment and handling of them, one that treats each one seriously.

—ERIN MEYERS,
"The Educational Smorgasbord as Saving Grace"

APPEALING TO LOGOS: USING REASON AND EVIDENCE TO FIT THE SITUATION

To make an argument persuasive, you need to be in dialogue with your readers, using your own character (ethos) to demonstrate that you are a reasonable, credible, and fair person and to appeal to your readers' emotions (pathos), particularly their sense of right and wrong. Both types of appeal go hand in hand with appeals to logos, using converging pieces of evidence—statistics, facts, observations—to advance your claim. Remember that the type of evidence you use is determined by the issue, problem, situation, and readers' expectations. As an author, you should try to anticipate and address readers' beliefs and values. Ethos and pathos are concerned with the content of your argument; logos addresses both form and content.

An argument begins with one or more premises and ends with a conclusion. A **premise** is an assumption that you expect your readers to agree with, a statement that is either true or false—for example, "Alaska is cold in the winter"—that is offered in support of a claim. That claim is the **conclusion** you want your readers to draw from your premises. The conclusion is also a sentence that is either true or false.

For instance, Loewen's major premise is that class is a key factor in Americans' access to health care, education, and wealth. Loewen also offers a second, more specific premise: that textbook writers provide little discussion of the ways class matters. Loewen crafts his argument to help readers draw the following conclusion: "We live in a class system that runs counter to the democratic principles that underlie the founding of the United States, and history textbooks must tell this story. Without this knowledge, citizens will be uninformed."

Whether readers accept this as true depends on how Loewen moves from his initial premises to reach his conclusion—that is, whether we draw the same kinds of inferences, or reasoned judgments, that he does. He must do so in a way that meets readers' expectations of what constitutes relevant and persuasive evidence and guides them one step at a time toward his conclusion.

There are two main forms of argument: deductive and inductive. A **deductive argument** is an argument in which the premises support (or appear to support) the conclusion. If you join two premises to produce a conclusion that is taken to be true, you are stating a **syllogism**. This is the classic example of deductive reasoning through a syllogism:

1. All men are mortal. (First premise)
2. Socrates is a man. (Second premise)
3. Therefore, Socrates is mortal. (Conclusion)

In a deductive argument, it is impossible for both premises to be true and the conclusion to be false. That is, the truth of the premises means that the conclusion must also be true.

By contrast, an **inductive argument** relies on evidence and observation to reach a conclusion. Although readers may accept a writer's premises as true, it is possible for them to reject the writer's conclusion.

Let's consider this for a moment in the context of Loewen's argument. Loewen introduces the premise that class matters, then offers the more specific premise that textbook writers leave class issues out of their narratives of American history, and finally draws the conclusion that citizens need to be informed of this body of knowledge in order to create change:

1. Although class is a key factor in Americans' access to health care, education, and wealth, students know very little about the social structure in the United States.

2. In their textbooks, textbook writers do not address the issue of class, an issue that people need to know about.

3. Therefore, if people had this knowledge, they would understand that poverty cannot be blamed on the poor.

Notice that Loewen's premises are not necessarily true. For example, readers could challenge the premise that "textbook writers do not address issues of class." After all, Loewen examined just eighteen textbooks. What if he had examined a different set of textbooks? Would he have drawn the same conclusion? And even if Loewen's evidence convinces us that the two premises are true, we do not have to accept that the conclusion is true.

The conclusion in an inductive argument is never definitive. That is the nature of any argument that deals with human emotions and actions. Moreover, we have seen throughout history that people tend to disagree much more on the terms of an argument than on its form. Do we agree that Israel's leaders practice apartheid? (What do we mean by *apartheid* in this case?) Do we agree with the need to grant women reproductive rights? (When does life begin?) Do we agree that all people should be treated equally? (Would equality mean equal access to resources or to outcomes?)

Deductive arguments are conclusive. In a deductive argument, the premises are universal truths—laws of nature, if you will—and the conclusion must follow from those premises. That is, a^2 plus b^2 always equals c^2, and humans are always mortal.

By contrast, an inductive argument is never conclusive. The premises may or may not be true; and even if they are true, the conclusion may be false. We might accept that class matters and that high school history textbooks don't address the issue of class structure in the United States; but we still would not know that students who have studied social stratification in America will necessarily understand the nature of poverty. It may be that social class is only one reason for poverty; or it may be that textbooks are only one source of information about social stratification in the United States, that textbook omissions are simply not as serious as Loewen claims. That the premises of an argument are true establishes only that the conclusion is probably true and, perhaps, true only for some readers.

Inductive argument is the basis of academic writing; it is also the basis of any appeal to logos. The process of constructing an inductive argument involves three steps:

1. State the premises of your argument.
2. Use credible evidence to show readers that your argument has merit.
3. Demonstrate that the conclusion follows from the premises.

In following these three steps, you will want to determine the truth of your premises, help readers understand whether or not the inferences you draw are justified, and use word signals to help readers fully grasp the connections between your premises and your conclusion.

■ State the Premises of Your Argument

Stating a premise establishes what you have found to be true and what you want to persuade readers to accept as truth as well. Let's return to Loewen, who asserts his premise at the very outset of the excerpt: "Middle-class students . . . know little about how the American class structure works . . . and nothing at all about how it has changed over time." Loewen elaborates on this initial premise a few sentences later, arguing that students "have no understanding of the ways that opportunity is not equal in America and no notion that the social structure pushes people around, influencing the ideas they hold and the lives they fashion."

Implicit here is the point that class matters. Loewen makes this point explicit several paragraphs later, where he states that "social class is probably the single most important variable in society" (para. 6). He states his second, more specific premise in paragraph 2: "High school history textbooks can take some of the credit for this state of affairs." The burden of demonstrating that these premises are true is on Loewen. If readers find that either of the premises is not true, it will be difficult, if not impossible, for them to accept his conclusion that with more knowledge, people will understand that poverty is not the fault of the poor (para. 10).

■ Use Credible Evidence

The validity of your argument depends on whether the inferences you draw are justified, and whether you can expect a reasonable person to draw the same conclusion from those premises. Loewen has to demonstrate throughout (1) that students do not have much, if any, knowledge about the class structure that exists in the United States and (2) that textbook writers are in large part to blame for this lack of knowledge. He also must help readers understand how this lack of knowledge contributes to (3) his conclusion that greater knowledge would lead Americans to understand that poor people are not responsible for poverty. He can help readers with the order in which he states his premises and by choosing the type and amount of evidence that will enable readers to draw the inferences that he does.

Interestingly, Loewen seems to assume that one group of readers—educators—will accept his first premise as true. He does not elaborate on what students know or do not know. Instead, he moves right to his second premise, which involves first acknowledging what high school history textbooks typically cover, then identifying what he believes are the important events that textbook writers exclude, and ultimately asserting that textbook discussions of events in labor history are never "anchored in any analysis of social class" (para. 3). He supports this point with his own study of eighteen textbooks (paras. 3–5) before returning to his premise that "social class is probably the single most important variable in society" (para. 6). What follows is a series of observations about the rich and references to researchers' findings on inequality (paras. 7–9). Finally, he asserts that "social class determines how people think about social class" (para. 10), implying that fuller knowledge would lead business leaders and conservative voters to think differently about the source of poverty. The question to explore is whether or not Loewen supports this conclusion.

■ Demonstrate That the Conclusion Follows from the Premises

Authors signal their conclusion with words like *consequently, finally, in sum, in the end, subsequently, therefore, thus, ultimately,* and *as a result.* Here is how this looks in the structure of Loewen's argument:

1. Although class is a key factor in Americans' access to health care, education, and wealth, students know very little about the social structure in the United States.

2. In their textbooks, textbook writers do not address the issue of class, an issue that people need to know about.

3. Ultimately, if people had this knowledge, they would understand that poverty cannot be blamed on the poor.

We've reprinted much of paragraph 9 of Loewen's excerpt below. Notice how Loewen pulls together what he has been discussing. He again underscores the importance of class and achievement ("All these are among the reasons"). And he points out that access to certain types of colleges puts people in a position to accumulate and sustain wealth. Of course, this is not true of the poor "because affluent families can save some money while poor families must spend what they make." This causal relationship ("Because") heightens readers' awareness of the class structure that exists in the United States.

> All these are among the reasons that social class predicts the rate of college attendance and the type of college chosen more effectively than does any other factor, including intellectual ability, however measured. After college,

most affluent children get white-collar jobs, most working-class children get blue-collar jobs, and the class differences continue. As adults, rich people are more likely to have hired an attorney and to be a member of formal organizations that increase their civic power. Poor people are more likely to watch TV. Because affluent families can save some money while poor families must spend what they make, wealth differences are ten times larger than income differences. Therefore most poor and working-class families cannot accumulate the down payment required to buy a house, which in turn shuts them out from our most important tax shelter, the write-off of home mortgage interest. Working-class parents cannot afford to live in elite subdivisions or hire high-quality day care, so the process of educational inequality replicates itself in the next generation. Finally, affluent Americans also have longer life expectancies than lower- and working-class people, the largest single cause of which is better access to health care. . . .

Once Loewen establishes this causal relationship, he concludes ("Therefore," "Finally") with the argument that poverty persists from one generation to the next.

In paragraph 10, Loewen uses the transition word *ultimately* to make the point that social class matters, so much so that it limits the ways in which people see the world, that it even "determines how people think about social class." (We discuss how to write conclusions in Chapter 11.)

Steps to Appealing to Logos

1. **State the premises of your argument.** Establish what you have found to be true and what you want readers to accept as well.

2. **Use credible evidence.** Lead your readers from one premise to the next, making sure your evidence is sufficient and convincing and your inferences are logical and correct.

3. **Demonstrate that the conclusion follows from the premises.** In particular, use the right words to signal to your readers how the evidence and inferences lead to your conclusion.

RECOGNIZING LOGICAL FALLACIES

We turn now to **logical fallacies,** flaws in the chain of reasoning that lead to a conclusion that does not necessarily follow from the premises, or evidence. Logical fallacies are common in inductive arguments for two reasons: Inductive arguments rely on reasoning about probability, not certainty; and they derive from human beliefs and values, not facts or laws of nature.

Here we list fifteen logical fallacies. In examining them, think about how to guard against the sometimes-faulty logic behind statements you might hear from politicians, advertisers, and the like. That should help you examine the premises on which you base your own assumptions and the logic you use to help readers reach the same conclusions you do.

1. *Erroneous Appeal to Authority.* An authority is someone with expertise in a given subject. An *erroneous authority* is an author who claims to be an authority but is not, or someone an author cites as an authority who is not. In this type of fallacy, the claim might be true, but the fact that an unqualified person is making the claim means there is no reason for readers to accept the claim as true.

Because the issue here is the legitimacy of authority, your concern should be to prove to yourself and your readers that you or the people you are citing have expertise in the subject. An awareness of this type of fallacy has become increasingly important as celebrities offer support for candidates running for office or act as spokespeople for curbing global warming or some other cause. The candidate may be the best person for the office, and there may be very good reasons to control global warming; but we need to question the legitimacy of a nonexpert endorsement.

2. *Ad Hominem.* An ad hominem argument focuses on the person making a claim instead of on the claim itself. (*Ad hominem* is Latin for "to the person.") In most cases, an ad hominem argument does not have a bearing on the truth or the quality of a claim.

Keep in mind that it is always important to address the claim or the reasoning behind it, rather than the person making the claim. "Of course Senator Wiley supports oil drilling in Alaska—he's in the pocket of the oil companies!" is an example of an ad hominem argument. Senator Wiley may have good reasons for supporting oil drilling in Alaska that have nothing to do with his alleged attachment to the oil industry. However, if an individual's character is relevant to the argument, then an ad hominem argument can be valid. If Senator Wiley has been found guilty of accepting bribes from an oil company, it makes sense to question both his credibility and his claims.

3. *Shifting the Issue.* This type of fallacy occurs when an author draws attention away from the issue instead of offering evidence that will enable people to draw their own conclusions about the soundness of an argument. Consider this example:

> Affirmative action proponents accuse me of opposing equal opportunity in the workforce. I think my positions on military expenditures, education, and public health speak for themselves.

The author of this statement does not provide a chain of reasoning that would enable readers to judge his or her stance on the issue of affirmative action.

4. *Either/Or Fallacy.* At times, an author will take two extreme positions to force readers to make a choice between two seemingly contradictory positions. For example:

> Either you support the war, or you are against it.

Although the author has set up an either/or condition, in reality one position does not exclude the other. People can support the troops involved in a war, for example, even if they don't support the reasons for starting the war.

5. *Sweeping Generalizations.* When an author attempts to draw a conclusion without providing sufficient evidence to support the conclusion or examining possible counterarguments, he or she may be making sweeping generalizations. Consider this example:

> Despite the women's movement in the 1960s and 1970s, women still do not receive equal pay for equal work. Obviously, any attempt to change the status quo for women is doomed to failure.

As is the case with many fallacies, the author's position may be reasonable, but we cannot accept the argument at face value. Reading critically entails testing assumptions like this one—that any attempt to create change is doomed to failure because women do not receive equal pay for equal work. We could ask, for example, whether inequities persist in the public sector. And we could point to other areas where the women's movement has had measurable success. Title IX, for example, has reduced the dropout rate among teenage girls; it has also increased the rate at which women earn college and graduate degrees.

6. *Bandwagon.* When an author urges readers to accept an idea because a significant number of people support it, he or she is making a bandwagon argument. This is a fairly common mode of argument in advertising; for example, a commercial might attempt to persuade us to buy a certain product because it's popular.

> Because Harvard, Stanford, and Berkeley have all added a multicultural component to their graduation requirements, other institutions should do so as well.

The growing popularity of an idea is not sufficient reason to accept that it is valid.

7. *Begging the Question.* This fallacy entails advancing a circular argument that asks readers to accept a premise that is also the conclusion readers are expected to draw:

> We could improve the undergraduate experience with coed dorms because both men and women benefit from living with members of the opposite gender.

Here readers are being asked to accept that the conclusion is true despite the fact that the premises—men benefit from living with women, and women benefit from living with men—are essentially the same as the conclusion. Without evidence that a shift in dorm policy could improve on the undergraduate experience, we cannot accept the conclusion as true. Indeed, the conclusion does not necessarily follow from the premise.

8. *False Analogy.* Authors (and others) often try to persuade us that something is true by using a comparison. This approach is not in and of itself a problem, as long as the comparison is reasonable. For example:

> It is ridiculous to have a Gay and Lesbian Program and a Department of African American Culture. We don't have a Straight Studies Program or a Department of Caucasian Culture.

Here the author is urging readers to rethink the need for two academic departments by saying that the school doesn't have two other departments. That, of course, is not a reason for or against the new departments. What's needed is an analysis that compares the costs (economic and otherwise) of starting up and operating the new departments versus the contributions (economic and otherwise) of the new departments.

9. *Technical Jargon.* If you've ever had a salesperson try to persuade you to purchase a television or an entertainment system with capabilities you absolutely *must* have—even if you didn't understand a word the salesperson was saying about alternating currents and circuit splicers—then you're familiar with this type of fallacy. We found this passage in a student's paper:

> You should use this drug because it has been clinically proven that it inhibits the reuptake of serotonin and enhances the dopamine levels of the body's neurotransmitters.

The student's argument may very well be true, but he hasn't presented any substantive evidence to demonstrate that the premises are true and that the conclusion follows from the premises.

10. *Confusing Cause and Effect.* It is challenging to establish that one factor causes another. For example, how can we know for certain that economic class predicts, or is a factor in, academic achievement? How do we know that a new president's policies are the cause of a country's economic well-being? Authors often assume cause and effect when two factors are simply associated with each other:

> The current recession came right after the president was elected.

This fallacy states a fact, but it does not prove that the president's election caused the recession.

11. *Appeal to Fear.* One type of logical fallacy makes an appeal to readers' irrational fears and prejudices, preventing them from dealing squarely with a given issue and often confusing cause and effect:

> We should use whatever means possible to avoid further attack.

The reasoning here is something like this: "If we are soft on defense, we will never end the threat of terrorism." But we need to consider whether there is indeed a threat, and, if so, whether the presence of a threat should lead to action, and, if so, whether that action should include "whatever means possible." (Think of companies that sell alarm systems by pointing to people's vulnerability to harm and property damage.)

12. *Fallacy of Division.* A fallacy of division suggests that what is true of the whole must also be true of its parts:

> Conservatives have always voted against raising the minimum wage, against stem cell research, and for defense spending. Therefore, we can assume that conservative Senator Harrison will vote this way.

The author is urging readers to accept the premise without providing evidence of how the senator has actually voted on the three issues.

13. *Hasty Generalization.* This fallacy is committed when a person draws a conclusion about a group based on a sample that is too small to be representative. Consider this statement:

> Seventy-five percent of the seniors surveyed at the university study just 10 hours a week. We can conclude, then, that students at the university are not studying enough.

What you need to know is how many students were actually surveyed. Seventy-five percent may seem high, but not if the researcher surveyed just 400 of the 2,400 graduating seniors. This sample of students from a total population of 9,600 students at the university is too small to draw the conclusion that students in general are not studying enough.

14. *The Straw Man Argument.* A straw man fallacy makes a generalization about what a group believes without actually citing a specific writer or work:

> Democrats are more interested in running away than in trying to win the war on terrorism.

Here the fallacy is that the author simply ignores someone's actual position and substitutes a distorted, exaggerated, or misrepresented version of that position. This kind of fallacy often goes hand in hand with assuming that what is true of the group is true of the individual, what we call the fallacy of division.

15. *Fallacy of the Middle Ground.* The fallacy of the middle ground assumes that the middle position between two extreme positions must be correct. Although the middle ground may be true, the author must justify this position with evidence.

> E. D. Hirsch argues that cultural literacy is the only sure way to increase test scores, and Jonathan Kozol believes schools will improve only if state legislators increase funding; but I would argue that school reform will occur if we change the curriculum and provide more funding.

This fallacy draws its power from the fact that a moderate or middle position is often the correct one. Again, however, the claim that the moderate or middle position is correct must be supported by legitimate reasoning.

ANALYZING THE APPEALS IN A RESEARCHED ARGUMENT

Now that you have studied the variety of appeals you can make to connect with your audience, we would like you to read an article on urban health problems by Meredith Minkler and analyze her strategies for appealing to her readers. The article is long and carefully argued, so we suggest you take detailed notes about her use of appeals to ethos, pathos, and logos as you read. You may want to refer to the Practice Sequence questions on page 286 to help focus your reading. Ideally, you should work through the text with your classmates, in groups of three or four, appointing one student to record and share each group's analysis of Minkler's argument.

MEREDITH MINKLER

Community-Based Research Partnerships: Challenges and Opportunities

Meredith Minkler is a professor of health and social behavior at the School of Public Health, University of California, Berkeley. She is an activist and researcher whose work explores community partnerships, community organizing, and community-based participatory research. With more than one hundred books and articles to her credit, she is coeditor of the influential *Community Based Participatory Research for Health* (2003). The following article appeared in *The Journal of Urban Health* in 2005.

Abstract
The complexity of many urban health problems often makes them ill suited to traditional research approaches and interventions. The resultant frustration, together with community calls for genuine partnership in the research process, has highlighted the importance of an alternative paradigm. Community-based participatory research (CBPR) is presented as a promising collaborative approach that combines systematic inquiry, participation, and action to address urban health problems. Following a brief review of its basic tenets and

historical roots, key ways in which CBPR adds value to urban health research are introduced and illustrated. Case study examples from diverse international settings are used to illustrate some of the difficult ethical challenges that may arise in the course of CBPR partnership approaches. The concepts of partnership synergy and cultural humility, together with protocols such as Green et al.'s guidelines for appraising CBPR projects, are highlighted as useful tools for urban health researchers seeking to apply this collaborative approach and to deal effectively with the difficult ethical challenges it can present.

Keywords

Community-based participatory research, Ethical issues in research, Participatory action research, Partnership, Urban health.

Introduction

The complexity of urban health problems has often made them poorly suited to traditional "outside expert"–driven research and intervention approaches.[1] Together with community demands for authentic partnerships in research that are locally relevant and "community based" rather than merely "community placed," this frustration has led to a burgeoning of interest in an alternative research paradigm.[1,2] Community-based participatory research (CBPR) is an overarching term that increasingly is used to encompass a variety of approaches to research that have as their centerpiece three interrelated elements: participation, research, and action.[3] As defined by Green et al.[4] for the Royal Society of Canada, CBPR may concisely be described as "systematic investigation with the participation of those affected by an issue for purposes of education and action or affecting social change." The approach further has been characterized as

> [A] collaborative process that equitably involves all partners in the research process and recognizes the unique strengths that each brings. CBPR begins with a research topic of importance to the community with the aim of combining knowledge and action for social change to improve community health and eliminate health disparities.[5,6]

This article briefly describes CBPR's roots and core principles and summarizes the value added by this approach to urban health research. Drawing on examples from a variety of urban health settings nationally and internationally, it discusses and illustrates several of the key challenges faced in applying this partnership approach to inquiry and action. The article concludes by suggesting that despite such challenges and the labor-intensive nature of this approach, CBPR offers an exceptional opportunity for partnering with communities in ways that can enhance both the quality of research and its potential for helping address some of our most intractable urban health problems.

Historical Roots and Core Principles

The roots of CBPR may be traced in part to the action research school developed by the social psychologist Kurt Lewin[7] in the 1940s, with its emphasis on the active involvement in the research of those affected by the problem being studied through a cyclical process of fact finding, action, and reflection. But CBPR is most deeply grounded in the more revolutionary approaches to research that emerged, often independently from one another, from work with oppressed communities in South America, Asia, and Africa in the 1970s.[3,8,9] Brazilian adult educator Paulo Freire[9] provided critical grounding for CBPR in his development of a dialogical method accenting co-learning and action based on critical reflection. Freire,[9] Fals-Borda,[10] and other developing countries' scholars developed their alternative approaches to inquiry as a direct counter to the often "colonizing" nature of research to which oppressed communities were subjected, with feminist and postcolonialist scholars adding further conceptual richness.[11,12]

Among the tenets of participatory action approaches to research outlined by McTaggart[13] are that it is a political process, involves lay people in theory-making, is committed to improving social practice by changing it, and establishes "self-critical communities." As Israel et al.[6] adds, other core principles are that CBPR "involves systems development and local community capacity development," is "a co-learning process" to which community members and outside researchers contribute equally, and "achieves a balance between research and action." CBPR reflects a profound belief in "partnership synergy." As described by Lasker et al.[14]:

> [T]he synergy that partners seek to achieve through collaboration is more than a mere exchange of resources. By combining the individual perspectives, resources, and skills of the partners, the group creates something new and valuable together—something that is greater than the sum of its parts.

Moreover, CBPR embodies a deep commitment to what Tervalon and Murray-Garcia[15] have called cultural humility. As they point out, although we can never become truly competent in another's culture, we can demonstrate a "lifelong commitment to self evaluation and self-critique," to redress power imbalances and "develop and maintain mutually respectful and dynamic partnerships with communities."[15] Although the term *cultural humility* was coined primarily in reference to race and ethnicity, it also is of value in helping us understand and address the impacts of professional cultures (which tend to be highly influenced by white, western, patriarchal belief systems), as these help shape interactions between outside researchers and their community partners.[15]

CBPR is not a method per se but an orientation to research that may employ any of a number of qualitative and quantitative methodologies. As Cornwall and Jewkes[16] note, what is distinctive about CBPR is "the attitudes of researchers, which in turn determine how, by and for whom research is conceptualized and conducted [and] the corresponding location of power at every stage of the research process." The accent placed by CBPR on individual, organizational, and community empowerment also is a hallmark of this approach to research.

6

With the increasing emphasis on partnership approaches to improving urban health, CBPR is experiencing a rebirth of interest and unprecedented new opportunities for both scholarly recognition and financial support. In the United States, for example, the Institute of Medicine[17] recently named "community-based participatory research" as one of eight new areas in which all schools of public health should be offering training.

7

Although the renewed interest in CBPR provides a welcome contrast to more traditional top-down research approaches, it also increases the dangers of co-optation as this label is loosely applied to include research and intervention efforts in search of funding that do not truly meet the criteria for this approach. The sections below illustrate some of the value added to urban research when authentic partnership approaches are taken seriously and then briefly highlight some of the ethical challenges such work may entail.

8

The Value Added to Urban Health Research by a CBPR Approach

CBPR can enrich and improve the quality and outcomes of urban health research in a variety of ways. On the basis of the work of many scholars and institutions,[4,6,8,18] and as summarized by the National Institutes of Health (http://grants.nih.gov/grants/guide/pa-files/PAR-05-026.html), some of its primary contributions may be characterized and illustrated as follows.

9

CBPR Can Support the Development of Research Questions That Reflect Health Issues of Real Concern to Community Members

Ideally, CBPR begins with a research topic or question that comes from the local community, as when the nongovernmental organization (NGO) Alternatives for Community and Environment (ACE) in the low-income Roxbury section of Boston, reached out to Harvard University's School of Public Health and other potential partners to

10

study and address the high rates of asthma in their neighborhood. Collaborative studies using air-monitoring and other approaches yielded data supporting the hypothesis that Roxbury was indeed a hot spot for pollution contributing to asthma. This in turn paved the way for a variety of policy and community education actions and outcomes.[19]

Although having a community partner such as ACE identify an issue *11* and catalyze a research partnership may be the ideal, it is often the privileged outside researcher who initiates a CBPR project. In these instances too, however, a genuine commitment to high-level community involvement in issue selection, with NGOs and formal and informal community leaders engaged as equal partners, can help ensure that the research topic decided upon really is of major concern to the local population.

CBPR Can Improve Our Ability to Achieve Informed Consent, and to Address Issues of "Costs and Benefits" on the Community, and Not Simply the Individual Level[20]

With its accent on equitable community involvement in all stages of *12* the research process,[6] CBPR often finds creative means of ensuring informed consent. The "One Hand, One Heart" study in urban and rural Tibet, which included a randomized controlled clinical trial of an indigenous medicine to prevent maternal hemorrhaging, actively involved local midwives and other community partners on the research team who played a key role in helping find locally translatable concepts to improve informed consent. Their help in early ethnographic work thus revealed that the concept of disclosing risk was highly problematic, because such disclosure was believed to disturb the wind element responsible for emotions, potentially leading to emotional upset and other adverse outcomes. By reframing risk disclosure as "safety issues," needed information could be conveyed in a far more culturally acceptable manner.[21]

CBPR also offers an important potential opening for extending *13* the gaze of our ethical review processes such that we examine and address risks and benefits for the community. In Toronto, Travers and Flicker[20] have pioneered in developing such guidelines, pointing out the importance of having us ask such questions as "Will the methods used be sensitive and appropriate to various communities?" "What training or capacity building opportunities will you build in?" and "How will you balance scientific rigor and accessibility?" The strong philosophical fit between questions such as these and CBPR's commitments to equitable partnership and community capacity building reflect another source of value added to urban health research through this approach.

CBPR Can Improve Cultural Sensitivity and the Reliability and Validity of Measurement Tools through High-Quality Community Participation in Designing and Testing Study Instruments

Particularly in survey research, community advisory boards (CABs) and other partnership structures can improve measurement instruments by making sure that questions are worded in ways that will elicit valid and reliable responses. In a study of urban grandparents raising grandchildren due to the crack cocaine epidemic, the author and her colleagues used validated instruments, such as those for depressive symptomatology. However, they also learned from CAB members how to word other questions about sensitive topics. Rather than asking a standard (and disliked) question about income, for example, the CAB encouraged us to rephrase the question as "How much money is available to help you in raising this child?" When this alternate wording was used, a wealth of detailed income data was obtained, which improved our understanding of the challenges faced by this population.[22]

CBPR Can Uncover Lay Knowledge Critical to Enhancing Understanding of Sensitive Urban Health Problems

Through the cultural humility and partnership synergy involved in deeply valuing lay knowledge and working in partnership with community residents, CBPR can uncover hidden contributors to health and social problems. The high rates of HIV/AIDS in India and the often sensitive nature of this subject among young men led the Deepak Charitable Trust to develop a research committee for a study in the industrial area of Nandesari, in Gujarat, comprised of several male village health workers and other young men from the area. Working closely with a medical anthropologist, the research committee planned the research, including developing a sampling plan and the phrasing of culturally sensitive questions. Their insider knowledge helped reveal that AIDS itself was not perceived as a major problem by the young men in this area. Instead, men who were engaging in high-risk behaviors wanted to find sex partners at least partly to avoid "thinning of the semen" and sexual dysfunction and fatigue, which were believed to be long-term consequences of masturbation and nocturnal emissions. These fears appeared to be contributing to high rates of unprotected intercourse with sex workers at the area's many truck stops and with other sex partners.[23] This insider knowledge both strengthened the research and led to subsequent interventions to help dispel such misinformation.

By Increasing Community Trust and Ownership, CBPR Can Improve Recruitment and Retention Efforts

In a participatory epidemiology project on diabetes in an urban Aboriginal community in Melbourne, Australia, a marked increase in

14

15

16

recruitment was experienced following the hiring of a community codi-rector and the changing of the project's name to one chosen by the local community.[24] Similarly, a 69 percent response rate achieved in a CBPR study of the health and working conditions of the largely immigrant hotel room cleaner population (many of them undocumented) in several of San Francisco's major tourist hotels was heavily attributed to the hiring and training of a core group of twenty-five room cleaners as key project staff. That high response rate, together with the high quality of data collected, made a substantial contribution when results later were presented and used to help negotiate a new contract.[25]

CBPR Can Help Increase Accuracy and Cultural Sensitivity in the Interpretation of Findings

Even highly engaged community members of the research team may not wish to be involved in the labor-intensive data analysis phase of a research project,[26] nor do all methodological approaches lend themselves to such involvement. Yet when applicable and desired, community involvement in data analysis can make real contributions to our understanding of the themes and findings that emerge. In a U.S. study of and with people with disabilities on the contentious topic of death with dignity legislation in their community, the author and an "insider/outsider" member of the research team met on alternate Saturdays with a subcommittee of the CAB to engage in joint data analysis. Using redacted transcripts, and applying lessons learned in qualitative data interpretation, the diverse CAB members came up with far richer codes and themes than outside researchers could have achieved alone.[27]

17

CBPR Can Increase the Relevance of Intervention Approaches and Thus the Likelihood of Success

One of the strengths of CBPR is its commitment to action as part of the research process. But without strong community input, researchers not infrequently design interventions that are ill suited to the local context in which they are applied. In the Gujarat case study mentioned above, partnership with local community members helped in the design of culturally relevant interventions, such as street theater performed by locally recruited youth at *melas* (or fairs), and the dissemination of study findings through the fifteen local credit and savings groups that often provided platforms for discussing reproductive health and related issues. Both these approaches provided critical means of information dissemination on this culturally and emotionally charged topic.[23]

18

Ethical and Other Challenges in Community-Based Participatory Research

Engaging in urban health research with diverse community partners can indeed enrich both the quality and the outcomes of such studies.

19

At the same time, CBPR is fraught with ethical and related challenges, several of which are now highlighted.

"Community Driven" Issue Selection

A key feature of CBPR involves its commitment to ensuring that the research topic comes from the community. Yet many such projects "paradoxically . . . would not occur without the initiative of someone outside the community who has the time, skill, and commitment, and who almost inevitably is a member of a privileged and educated group."[28] In such instances, outside researchers must pay serious attention to community understandings of what the real issue or topic of concern is.

In South Africa, for example, high rates of cervical cancer in the Black and Colored populations led Mosavel et al.[29] to propose an investigation of this problem. In response to community feedback, however, they quickly broadened their initial topic to "cervical health," a concept which "acknowledged the fact that women's health in South Africa extends well beyond the risk of developing cervical cancer, and includes HIV-AIDS and STDs, sexual violence, and multiple other social problems." In other instances, the outside researcher as an initiator of a potential CBPR project needs to determine whether the topic he or she has identified really is of concern to the local community—and whether outsider involvement is welcome. The Oakland, California–based Grandmother Caregiver Study mentioned above grew out of the interests of my colleague and me in studying the strengths of as well as the health and social problems faced by the growing number of urban African American grandmothers who were raising grandchildren in the context of a major drug epidemic. As privileged white women, however, we had to determine first whether this was a topic of local concern and, if so, whether there might be a role for us in working with the community to help study and address it. We began by enlisting the support of an older African American colleague with deep ties in the community, who engaged with us in a frank discussion with two prominent African American NGOs. It was only after getting their strong support for proceeding that we wrote a grant, with funds for these organizations, which in turn helped us pull together an outstanding CAB that was actively involved in many stages of the project.[21,26]

We were lucky in this case that a topic we as outsiders identified turned out to represent a deep concern in the local community. Yet not infrequently "the community" is in fact deeply divided over an issue. Indeed, as Yoshihama and Carr[30] have argued, "communities are not places that researchers enter but are instead a set of negotiations that inherently entail multiple and often conflicting interests." In such situations, outside researchers can play a useful role in helping community partners think through who "the community" in fact is in relation to a proposed project and the pros and cons of undertaking the project to begin with. The holding of town hall meetings and other forums may then be useful in helping achieve consensus on an issue that is truly of, by, and for the community, however it is defined.[26]

Insider–Outsider Tensions

Urban health researchers in many parts of the world have written poignantly about the power dynamics and other sources of insider–outsider tensions and misunderstandings in CBPR and related partnership efforts. Ugalde[31] points out how in Latin America participants may be exploited as cheap sources of labor or may become alienated from their communities because of their participation. In her work with Native American and other marginalized groups in New Mexico, Wallerstein[32] further illustrates how even outsiders who pride ourselves on being trusted community friends and allies often fail to appreciate the extent of the power that is embedded in our own, often multiple sources of privilege, and how it can affect both process and outcomes in such research. *23*

One major source of insider–outsider tensions involves the differential reward structures for partners in CBPR. For although a major aim of such research is to benefit the local community, the outside researchers typically stand to gain the most from such collaborations, bringing in grants, getting new publications, and so forth. The common expectation that community partners will work for little or no pay and the fact that receipt of compensation may take months if the funds are coming through a ministry of health or a university are also sources of understandable resentment.[6,26] *24*

To address these and other sources of insider–outsider tensions in work with indigenous communities in both urban and rural areas, researchers in New Zealand,[33] Australia,[34] the United States,[35] and Canada[36] have worked with their community partners to develop ethical guidelines for their collaborative work, including protocols that address *25*

1. negotiating with political and spiritual leaders in the community to obtain their input and their approval for the proposed research,

2. ensuring equitable benefits to participants (e.g., appropriate training and hiring of community members) in return for their contributions and resources,

3. developing agreements about the ownership and publication of findings, and the early review of findings by key community leaders.

Although such protocols cannot begin to address all of the conflicts that may arise in CBPR, they can play a critical role in helping pave the way for the continued dialogue and negotiation that must be an integral part of the process. *26*

Constraints on Community Involvement

Outside researchers committed to a CBPR approach not infrequently express frustration at the difficulty moving from the goal of heavy community partner involvement in the research process to the reality. As Diaz and Simmons[37] found in their Reproductive Health Project in Brazil, despite a strong commitment to involving the most marginalized and vulnerable classes (in this case, women who were users of the public sector services being studied), such individuals often "are least likely to be in a position to donate their time and energy." Further, and even when outside researchers are careful to provide child care and transportation, there are differential costs of participation by gender.[30]

Still another set of challenges may arise when community desires with respect to research design and methods clash with what outsider researchers consider to be "good science." In an oft-cited CBPR study with a local Mohawk community in Québec, Chataway[38] describes how community members at first strongly objected to the idea of using a questionnaire approach which they saw as "putting their thoughts in boxes." Through respectful listening on both sides, the value of such an approach was realized and a more qualitative methodology developed, through which community members would then be actively involved in helping analyze and interpret the quantitative findings that emerged. As such case studies illustrate, CBPR does not condone an abandonment of one's own scientific standards and knowledge base. But it does advocate a genuine co-learning process through which lay and professional ways of knowing both are valued and examined for what they can contribute.[26]

Dilemmas in the Sharing and Release of Findings

A crucial step in CBPR involves returning data to the community and enabling community leaders and participants to have an authentic role in deciding how that data will be used. As Travers and Flicker[20] suggest, ethical research review processes that ask questions such as "Are there built-in mechanisms for how unflattering results will be dealt with?" should be employed at the front end of our CBPR projects. In addition to the formal IRB process they propose, which offers a critical next step for the field, CBPR partners can look to a variety of formal or informal research protocols and particularly to the detailed guidelines for health promotion research developed by Green et al.,[4,39] which help partnerships decide in advance how potentially difficult issues concerning the sharing and release of findings and other matters will be handled.

Challenges in the Action Dimensions of CBPR

Numerous ethical challenges lastly may arise in relation to the critical action component of CBPR. In some instances, community partners may wish to move quickly into action, whereas academic and other outside research partners may want to "put the [brakes] on" until findings have been published or other steps brought to fruition. In other cases, the nature of funding (e.g., from a government body) may constrain action on the policy level that is prohibited or discouraged by the funder. And in still other instances, including the Brazilian Reproductive Health Project[37] cited above, community members may not wish to be associated with a CBPR project that appears connected to a broader political agenda.

Participation in the action phase of CBPR projects may sometimes present risks to community participants, as when immigrant hotel room cleaners in the San Francisco study took part in a Labor Day sit-in and in some cases faced arrest.[25] And for both professionally trained researchers and their community partners, actions that involve challenging powerful corporate or other entrenched interests may have negative consequences for those involved. At the same time, CBPR's fundamental commitment to action and to redressing power imbalances makes this aspect of the work a particularly important contributor to urban health improvement through research.

31

Conclusion

Difficult ethical challenges may confront urban health researchers who engage in CBPR. Yet this approach can greatly enrich the quality of our research, helping ensure that we address issues of genuine community concern and use methods and approaches that are culturally sensitive and that improve the validity and reliability of our findings. Moreover, through its commitment to action as an integral part of the research process, CBPR can help in translating findings as we work with community partners to help address some of our most intractable urban health problems.

32

Acknowledgement

Many current and former community and academic partners have contributed to my understanding of the advantages and pitfalls of collaborative urban health research and I am deeply grateful. Particular thanks are extended to Nina Wallerstein, Kathleen M. Roe, Barbara Israel, Lawrence W. Green, and Ronald Labonte, who have greatly stimulated my own thinking and scholarship in this area. I am grateful to former students, Rima Shaw and Caroline Bell, as well as other individuals who have shared some of the cases drawn upon in this paper. My gratitude is extended to Claire Murphy for assistance with manuscript preparation.

33

References

1. Minkler M, Wallerstein N. Community Based Participatory Research for Health. San Francisco, CA: Jossey-Bass; 2003.

2. Green LW, Mercer SL. Can public health researchers and agencies reconcile the push from funding bodies and the pull from communities? *Am J Public Health.* 2001;91:1926–1929.

3. Hall BL. From margins to center: the development and purpose of participatory action research. *Am Sociol.* 1992;23:15–28.

4. Green LW, George A, Daniel M, et al. *Study of Participatory Research in Health Promotion.* Ottawa, Ontario: Royal Society of Canada; 1995.

5. Community Health Scholars Program. *The Community Health Scholars Program: Stories of Impact.* Ann Arbor, MI; 2002.

6. Israel BA, Schulz AJ, Parker EA, Becker AB. Review of community-based research: assessing partnership approaches to improve public health. *Annu Rev Public Health.* 1998;19:173–202.

7. Lewin K. Action research and minority problems. *J Soc Issues.* 1946;2:34–46.

8. Brown LD, Tandon R. Ideology and political economy in inquiry: action research and participatory research. *J Appl Behav Sci.* 1983; 19:277–294.

9. Freire P. *Pedagogy of the Oppressed.* New York, NY: Seabury Press; 1970.

10. Fals-Borda O. The application of participatory action-research in Latin America. *Int Sociol.* 1987;2:329–347.

11. Maguire P. *Doing Participatory Research: A Feminist Approach.* Amherst, MA: Center for International Education; 1987.

12. Duran E, Duran B. *Native American Postcolonial Psychology.* Albany, NY: State University of New York Press; 1995.

13. McTaggart R. Sixteen tenets of participatory action research. In: Wadsworth Y, ed. *Everyday Evaluation on the Run.* Sydney, Australia: Allen & Unwin; 1997:79.

14. Lasker RD, Weiss ES, Miller R. Partnership synergy: a practical framework for studying and strengthening the collaborative advantage. *Milbank Q.* 2001;79:179–205, III–IV.

15. Tervalon M, Murray-Garcia J. Cultural humility vs. cultural competence: a critical distinction in defining physician training outcomes in medical education. *J Health Care Poor Underserved.* 1998;9:117–125.

16. Cornwall A, Jewkes R. What is participatory research? *Soc Sci Med*. 1995;41:1667–1676.

17. Gebbie K, Rosenstock L, Hernandez LM. *Who Will Keep the Public Healthy? Educating Public Health Professionals for the 21st Century*. Washington, DC: Institute of Medicine; 2002.

18. O'Fallon LR, Dearry A. Community-based participatory research as a tool to advance environmental health sciences. *Environ Health Perspect*. 2002;110:155–159.

19. Loh P, Sugerman-Brozan J. Environmental justice organizing for environmental health: case study on asthma and diesel exhaust in Roxbury, Massachusetts. *Environ Health Perspect*. 2002;584: 110–124.

20. Travers R, Flicker S. Ethical issues in community based research. In: *Urban Health Community-Based Research Series Workshop*. Wellesley, MA; 2004.

21. Bell C. *One HEART (Health Education and Research in Tibet) Community Based Participatory Research on Top of the World*. Unpublished manuscript, University of California, Berkeley, School of Public Health; 2004.

22. Roe KM, Minkler M, Saunders FF. Combining research, advocacy and education: the methods of the Grandparent Caregiving Study. *Health Educ Q*. 1995;22:458–475.

23. Shah R. *A Retrospective Analysis of an HIV Prevention Program for Men in Gujarat, India*. Unpublished manuscript, University of California, Berkeley, School of Public Health; 2004.

24. Thompson SJ. Participatory epidemiology: methods of the Living With Diabetes Project. *Intl Q Community Health Educ*. 2000;19: 3–18.

25. Lee P, Krause N, Goetchius C. Participatory action research with hotel room cleaners: from collaborative study to the bargaining table. In: Minkler M, Wallerstein N, eds. *Community Based Participatory Research for Health*. San Francisco, CA: Jossey-Bass; 2003: 390–404.

26. Minkler M. Ethical challenges for the "outside" researcher in community based participatory research. *Health Educ Behav*. 2004;31: 684–701.

27. Fadem P, Minkler M, Perry M, et al. Ethical challenges in community based participatory research: a case study from the San Francisco Bay Area disability community. In: Minkler M, Wallerstein N, eds. *Community Based Participatory Research for Health*. San Francisco, CA: Jossey-Bass; 2003.

28. Reason P. *Participation in Human Inquiry.* London, UK: Sage; 1994.

29. Mosavel M, Simon C, van Stade D, Buchbinder M. *Community Based Participatory Research (CBPR) in South Africa: Engaging Multiple Constituents to Shape the Research Question.* Unpublished manuscript; 2004.

30. Yoshihama M, Carr ES. Community participation reconsidered: feminist participatory action research with Hmong women. *J Community Pract.* 2002;10:85–103.

31. Ugalde A. Ideological dimensions of community participation in Latin American health programs. *Soc Sci Med.* 1985;21:41–53.

32. Wallerstein N. Power between evaluator and community: research relationships within New Mexico's healthier communities. *Soc Sci Med.* 1999;49:39–53.

33. Cram F. Rangahau Maori: Tona tika, tona pono: The validity and integrity of Maori research. In: Tolich M, ed. *Research Ethics in Aotearoa New Zealand.* Longman, Auckland: Pearson Education; 2001:35–52.

34. Anderson I. Ethics and health research in Aboriginal communities. In: Daly J, ed. *Ethical Intersections: Health Research, Methods and Researcher Responsibility.* St. Leonards, New South Wales: Allen & Unwin; 1996:153–165.

35. Turning Point, National Association of County and City Health Officials. Thirteen policy principles for advancing collaborative activity among and between tribal communities and surrounding jurisdictions. In: Minkler M, Wallerstein N, eds. *Community Based Participatory Research for Health.* San Francisco, CA: Jossey-Bass; 2003:436, Appendix E.

36. Stuart CA. Care and concern: an ethical journey in participatory action research. *Can J Couns.* 1998;32:298–314.

37. Diaz M, Simmons R. When is research participatory? Reflections on a Reproductive Health Project in Brazil. *J Women's Health.* 1999;8:175–184.

38. Chataway CJ. Examination of the constraints of mutual inquiry in a participatory action research project. *J Soc Issues.* 1997;53:747–765.

39. Green LW, George MA, Daniel M, et al. Guidelines for participatory research in health promotion. In: Minkler M, Wallerstein N, eds. *Community Based Participatory Research for Health.* San Francisco, CA: Jossey-Bass; 2003:419, Appendix C.

A Practice Sequence: Analyzing the Appeals in a Researched Argument

1   Make a list of the major premises that inform Minkler's argument, and examine the evidence she uses to support them. To what extent do you find her evidence credible? Do you generally agree or disagree with the conclusions she draws? Be prepared to explain your responses to your class or peer group.

2   Note instances where Minkler appeals to ethos, pathos, and logos. How would you describe the ways she makes these three types of appeals? How does she present herself? What does she seem to assume? How does she help you understand the chain of reasoning by which she moves from premises to conclusion?

3   Working in groups of three or four, compose a letter to Minkler in which you take issue with her argument. This does not mean your group has to disagree with her entire argument, although of course you may. Rather, present your group's own contribution to the conversation in which she is participating. You may want to ask her to further explain one or more of her points, or suggest what she might be leaving out, or add your own take or evidence to her argument. As a group, you will have to agree on your focus. In the letter, include a summary of Minkler's argument or the part of it on which your group is focusing. Pay close attention to your own strategies for appealing to her — how you present yourselves, how you appeal to her values and emotions, and how you present your reasons for your own premises and conclusion.

From Image to Text

This chapter focuses on visual rhetoric—that is, the ways images communicate meaning and act upon us as we begin to interpret those images. As you analyze the advertisements in this chapter, for example, it will be important to reflect upon the ways the designers of these ads merge images and text to affect how you feel about issues such as gender, hunger, accommodations for those with disabilities, the role of the environment in our lives, and the like. How do these images make us feel? How do these images do the work of reframing the world as we know it and what we value? Do they make us want to do something to support a cause or challenge an injustice?

We encourage you to "read" these images as you would any text in the role of a writer. After all, in a world that increasingly uses images to affect what we think and believe, you will want to design your own multimodal texts—texts that combine what you have written with photographs, maps, tables, and graphs. Integrating visuals can help you convey a sense of immediacy, if not urgency, in an effort to move readers to understand what you think is important, to emphasize patterns and trends that might otherwise get lost in the data you use, and to appeal to readers' own lived experiences. Images provide readers with what one educator describes as "a vivid presence" that words alone are sometimes too abstract to convey. Actively reading the visuals around you will help you effectively produce and use visuals in your own work.

Pause for a moment to consider the types and forms of argumentation that might benefit from being presented visually as you think about your own work. Visuals can make us aware of the gravity of a given issue and convey the force, strength, and urgency of an issue. But how can an image, for example, encourage an emotional response in readers and motivate them to act? You will want to think about the following questions in developing a visual argument.

- What is your purpose for including an image, such as a chart, map, graph, or photograph? What trends or patterns do you want to emphasize?

- What story does the image help you tell?

- How does this image complement or highlight your written argument?

- How do you want readers to respond to this image? What ideas should they associate with an image? What emotions do you want to evoke?

- What sort of caption should you include to help readers understand the context and meaning of the chart, map, graph, or photograph?

These kinds of questions place rhetoric at the center of your decisions about how to present your argument—whether and in what ways images can help you fulfill your goals as a writer by telling a story about what matters and motivating readers to reframe the ways they see the world and perhaps act to create change.

ANALYZING VISUAL RHETORIC: ADVERTISEMENTS

This section focuses on ways of analyzing visual images as texts, what we have referred to throughout this book as rhetorical analysis or rhetorical reading of how writers construct arguments. In this case, we discuss the ways we can, in our role as readers and writers, begin to understand how images tell stories by conveying values (*ethos*), evoking very specific emotions (*pathos*) in readers, and appealing to readers' sense of reason (*logos*). Images prompt readers to fill in information given their own values, beliefs, and knowledge. Therefore, it might be best to think of images as constructions as opposed to representations of the world. This is to say that most images, especially photographs, are at best generative because they spark our own imagination and cannot really capture the complexity of day-to-day experiences. We fill in that complexity within the context of our own frames of reference.

Imagine, for example, a public service announcement or ad (PSA) that places an image of the earth at the center with minimal text that simply states, "It may not be much, but it's all we got." Some people might associate such an image with the celebration of Earth Day, conservation, sustainability, and climate change. Such associations will influence the conclusions readers draw about what this PSA means and what the ad is asking of its audience. Other readers may make associations that tell a different story—one that the designers of the PSA had not intended or anticipated. Thus it is important to keep in mind the benefits of using images and some of the limitations to convey an argument.

To examine the strategies you can use to understand how images and texts convey meaning, we would like you to analyze a PSA from Feeding America (Figure 10.1), distributed by the Ad Council, a nonprofit institution founded in 1942 for the purpose of bringing attention to social issues. The long, horizontal advertisement shows a blurry group of children in the background playing street hockey. In the foreground to the right is a bright red alarm bell attached to a wooden telephone pole. The text reads, "School may be out for summer but lunch is always in session." A sentence in smaller text below it reads, "If your kids rely on free school meals, call your Feeding America member food bank or visit FeedingAmerica .org/SummerMeals." Examine the advertisement and answer the questions that follow it.

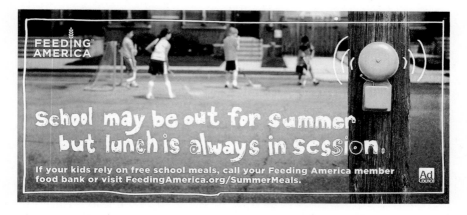

FIGURE 10.1   Feeding America PSA

1. In writing, reflect on the story that the ad is telling us about kids, spaces where kids can be themselves and play, and food insecurity. What does the Ad Council want us to think about this story and what we might do? What appeals does the ad seem to draw on most: appeals based on our cultural relationship to children (*ethos*), on our emotional reaction to the idea of hungry children (*pathos*), or on the ways text and image work together to convey an argument (*logos*)? To what extent do these appeals overlap so that it might be difficult to tease out the differences among *ethos*, *pathos*, and *logos*?

2. Formulate what you think is the ad's argument, whether it's stated explicitly or not. What inferences do you make about the ad's argument when considering its use of text and images? What specific details seem to support the conclusions you draw? Compare your

ideas with those of your classmates. Do they differ significantly? Can you agree on what the argument is?

3. As a class, discuss the extent to which you believe that the following assumptions in the ad are true: When school is in session, policies are in place to ensure federally funded schools feed children in need. Less certain is the extent to which children in need receive sufficient nutrition during the summer when school is out.

Let's begin with the assumption that everything in a public service announcement or ad appears for a specific reason in a particular place to direct your attention in a specific sequence. The economy of the genre and its constraints dictate that the message come across quickly in a limited space.

■ Notice Where the Ad Appears

Analyzing an ad begins with noting where the ad appears. In this case, the Ad Council posted the Feeding America ad on billboards in a wide range of cities across the United States. An ad on a billboard will reach many people whose assumptions about hunger in America will vary, as will their education, age, faith, ethnicity, race, gender, and sexual orientation. Therefore, it's worthwhile to consider how an ad about hunger will connect with such a wide range of possible viewers who will interpret the ad in different ways, create images of children at play given their own experiences, and draw inferences based on their assumptions about hunger in America. The inferences readers draw will not only influence their interpretations but the extent to which they feel compelled to act, if at all. It is also worth considering the Ad Council's choice to post the ad in urban areas, as opposed to rural towns in the United States. Does the Ad Council assume there are greater hunger issues in urban areas? Is this a fair assumption? And equally important, can we assume that the people who should have access to the information on the ad will actually see it and get the support they need?

Imagine for a moment that the ad had appeared in a print issue of *Time* magazine, one of the most widely read magazines in the United States. As a news magazine, not an entertainment magazine such as *People*, *Time* aims to reach a broad, educated, even affluent readership interested in keeping up with current events. Producers of ads always have a target audience in mind when they design and place an ad. They assume that the audience shares certain beliefs and values, and that the ad will move the audience to think and act in particular ways.

As you compare the effects of posting an ad on a billboard versus placing an ad in a widely read magazine, you will inevitably discuss how a particular advertisement will travel from one medium to another. Certainly this Feeding America ad could appear in other popular news magazines such as *Newsweek*. How effective would it be in a weekly tabloid? A fashion magazine? Or someplace more public, such as in a bus terminal or waiting area in a public service office?

■ Identify and Reflect on What Draws Your Attention

Identify what draws your eye when you look at the ad, and think about why that element seems more important or affecting than others. Is it larger or more colorful than other elements? Is it foregrounded? What makes it stand out? Most viewers likely focus first on the central image of four children playing street hockey on a summer day. Does the photograph of children playing evoke your own childhood memories? Is this a familiar scene, one that helps you identify with this particular moment in children's lived experiences? Is there something startling, perhaps even shocking about the situation depicted in the photograph and what the text seems to suggest about hunger in America? Something puzzling that holds your attention? Something about the use of color, the size of the image or text, or the font that catches your eye?

Although the ad was designed to spark our imagination and humanize the problem of hunger in America, the blurred images of individual children also invite us to provide our own images based on our memories, experiences, and relationships. We acknowledge it is reasonable to blur children's faces to protect their identity, but we wonder if it matters that the ad does not specify race and ethnicity. Who are these children? What are they like? How does this reluctance to show race and ethnicity affect or even challenge our assumptions about who is poor in America? Who would personally identify with these children?

We may find ourselves puzzling over the alarm bell in the foreground to the right. (In the full-color ad, the alarm bell is bright red and demands our attention.) If the image of the children provides us with a sense of immediacy in telling a story about growing up, the bell seems to disrupt a sense that this carefree moment will last. What specifically does the designer of the ad want us to understand by juxtaposing children playing during the summer with an image that for many of us represents school? Is there a sense of urgency in the ad that we might easily overlook without this additional image of the bell alongside a scene of children at play? It's difficult to grasp the significance of these juxtapositions without further inquiry, in this case without looking at the text in the foreground of the ad. We assume that the designer intends for readers to look there next, because the writing is large and distinctive—like children's chalk writing on the sidewalk. Finally, our eyes are drawn to the Feeding America logo, and it prompts us to ask *What is Feeding America, and what values does it espouse?*

 LaunchPad
macmillan learning   To view this ad in full color, visit LaunchPad for *From Inquiry to Academic Writing*.

■ Consider the Ethos of the Ad

The next step is to evaluate the ethos of the creator or sponsor of the ad. What does the ad say about how the sponsor or creator wishes to be perceived? If you don't recognize a sponsor's logo or brand, it's important to ask, *What is the sponsor's mission? To sell a product or promote a practice? What values does the sponsor espouse? Is the creator or sponsor a nonprofit or commercial enterprise?* You need to know the answers to these questions to assess any underlying bias and to determine how willing you are to believe what the ad promotes. In this case, you might find it helpful to go to the Feeding America Web site (listed in the ad) or to do a simple Internet search to see whether the organization has been discussed by others writing about hunger. Has Feeding America done significant work in the area of hunger? What kind of community organization is it? Is it a reputable organization that benefits those it advocates for? Is there evidence that the organization's past ad campaigns have been successful?

■ Analyze the Pathos in the Ad

Next, analyze the *pathos* in the ad—how images and words appeal to your emotions. An appeal to pathos is meant to evoke emotions such as empathy (which might prompt us to identify with an image) or outrage (which might spur us to act in a certain way). In this case, the image of children playing outdoors with friends on a neighborhood street is likely to appeal to many of us, evoking as it does idyllic childhood memories. Its nostalgic appeal invites us into an apparently calm, innocent world of peaceful play and encourages us to sympathize with the children pictured and described.

■ Understand the Logos of the Ad

We should also consider the composition of the ad as a whole. What is the logic of the ad? What is its appeal to reason? How do the images and text work together to persuade us? What is the takeaway message?

The text in the Feeding America ad helps clarify the meaning of the central images of the children and the alarm bell. The alarm bell ties the image in the background to the foregrounded text: "School may be out for summer, but lunch is always in session." Food insecurity is a problem every day for children in need. But where do these children get their food when school is not in session?

Hunger is not readily visible to many of us. Images of playfulness, even childlike innocence, can mask the deprivation that any of the people surrounding us may experience in their own lives. The text makes the appeal in the ad explicit. Those living in hunger are all around us.

The smaller text answers the question of where children in need can receive the nutrition they require. Children who are eligible for free lunch during the school year are also eligible to receive free meals during the summer.

Translating the discrete images and text into a coherent argument requires inductive reasoning, moving from specific pieces of evidence to a major premise. We would conclude that the argument in the ad goes something like this:

1. Hunger in America is a reality in the lives of many children and families.

2. Food insecurity exists for children year round—whether school is in session or not.

3. Feeding America can help children and families gain access to the nutrition they require.

There are other ways to formulate the argument, and we invite you to discuss these alternatives as a class. Our main point, though, is that visual images present claims to us as viewers in much the same ways as any written text does. Having the tools of visual rhetoric can help you discern how images and text work together to produce an argument.

Steps to Visual Analysis

1 **Notice where the ad appears.** What does the publication space tell you about the ad's target audience? To what extent does the placement of the ad in a magazine or newspaper or on a billboard determine the potential audience of the ad?

2 **Identify and reflect on what draws your attention.** Where does your eye go? To an image, some words, some odd juxtaposition? What elements seem to be given prominence and how? Do color, foregrounding, size, font choice, or other methods of visual emphasis make some elements seem more important than others? Is there something startling or shocking about the images or words—or about the situation depicted? Something puzzling that holds your attention?

3 **Consider the *ethos* of the ad.** Evaluate the legitimacy, or *ethos*, of the ad's creator or sponsor. For example, what do you know about the corporation or institution behind the ad? What values does it espouse? To what extent do you share its values? Is the creator or sponsor a nonprofit or commercial enterprise?

4   Analyze the *pathos* in the ad. How do the images and words appeal to your emotions? What do the images or words make you feel or think about?

5   Understand the *logos* of the ad. What is the logic of the ad? Taken together, what do the cluster of images and words convey? How are the different images and words related to the claim that the ad is making?

A Practice Sequence: Analyzing the Rhetoric of an Advertisement

To practice these strategies, we would like you to analyze the following PSA designed by the American Disability Association (Figure 10.2). First, evaluate the *ethos*, or values, that the PSA tries to project by encouraging us to reframe the experience of climbing stairs to get from one place to another. Some of us may very well take for granted the task of climbing stairs to get to class, to reach a professor's office where there isn't a ramp to ease entry into the building, or reach our seat on a bus to get to work. Those who designed the PSA prompt us to consider that a relatively simple task may seem insurmountable to people with physical disabilities. It would be helpful to do some research into the work of the American Disability Association, especially the work it has done to advocate for people with disabilities. In doing this research, write a brief summary of the company's values. Do you share those values? Do you consider yourself part of the ad's target audience? Why? Is there information available to suggest that the American Disability Association has had success in prior ad campaigns?

Second, reflect on and write about what the images and text make you feel about your own experiences with accessing public spaces. If you don't typically experience physical barriers, in what ways do you identify with those who do not have access to the spaces that you take for granted? Do you find the comparison to scaling Everest effective? If you have struggled with access in spaces without accommodations for physical disabilities, how do you feel about the ad's presentation of that struggle? Is this an adequate representation of the problem, one that might help gain allies in an effort to remedy the problem of access that many people face?

Third, work in small groups to identify the logic of the narrative that the images and words convey. What do you see as the main premise of the ad? What is its goal? How did you arrive at your conclusion? Report your group's findings to the class. Be sure to present the evidence to support your claim.

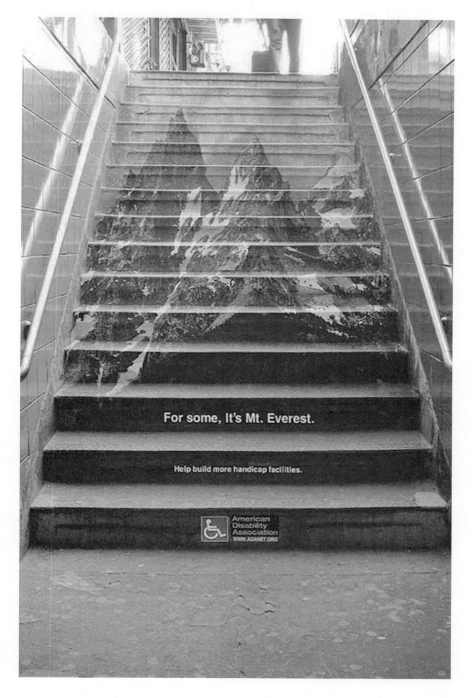

FIGURE 10.2   American Disability Association PSA

■ Further Ads for Analysis: Figures 10.3 and 10.4

FIGURE 10.3
UN Women PSA

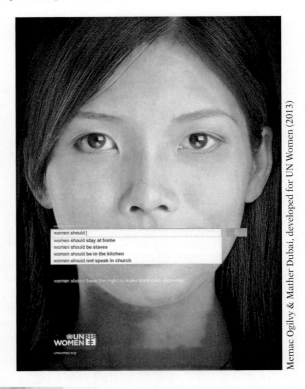

Memac Ogilvy & Mather Dubai, developed for UN Women (2013)

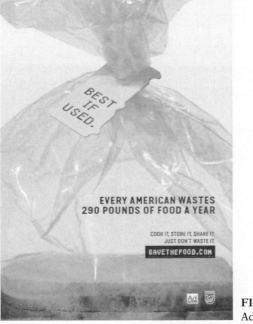

FIGURE 10.4
Ad Council Food Waste PSA

ANALYZING VISUAL RHETORIC: MAPS, PHOTOGRAPHS, TABLES OR CHARTS, AND GRAPHS

Thus far, we have focused on the ways an image can enhance an argument by creating a sense of immediacy (the day-to-day lives of children), urgency (children we see every day may experience the stress of going hungry), and importance (we need to prevent child hunger). An image sparks our imagination, evokes memories, and in many cases adds a human dimension to a problem that in the abstract may not seem to affect us very much. But visualizing the physical challenges that some people face in ascending the stairs to get to a subway platform or the neglect we see when young people face hunger can change the way we feel. We can be more empathic and identify with others. Thus it is important as you write to consider the purpose of what you are trying to accomplish and to use all of the means of persuasion available to you in constructing an argument that moves readers to understand a problem, grasp its immediacy, reframe how they see the world, and perhaps act with a sense of conviction to change the world for the better.

In this section, then, we extend our conversation of integrating images and text to other visuals that can help you support your argument. As always, your purpose, audience, and context are central to the ways you develop an argument. After all, how you establish an argument depends on which conversation you want to enter, who is part of the conversation, and what you want to accomplish. An image of children may be an effective means of conveying a sense of urgency to readers about hunger in America, but using a map can demonstrate to readers where in the United States there is the greatest concentration of children living in poverty and facing the consequences of food insecurity—not knowing when they will get their next meal. A map can offer a different kind of visual representation of a problem that people need to know about or that policy makers need to solve. It can tell a story of where food insecurity exists, how prevalent it is, and perhaps how food insecurity correlates with other problems in different regions of the country, including lack of employment opportunities and residential segregation among different racial and ethnic groups. With numerical data in the form of tables and graphs, you can create a powerful narrative that conveys the sense of immediacy, urgency, and importance that we have described in analyzing an advertisement. Using all of these tools is also what we mean by using the resources available to you—that is, all of the available means of persuasion. At the same time, you'll want to consider the best way to communicate your ideas to make an effective argument.

In the readings that follow, consider the following: the author's purpose, how the author uses maps and other images to frame an argument; what the author assumes about readers' knowledge and values; the source of the data; whether the use of visuals helps establish the importance, urgency, and immediacy of the problem the author identifies; and the extent to which the author integrates visuals into the written argument. These are concerns that you should focus on in reading and interpreting any kind of image, whether it's a map, photograph, table, or graph.

■ Using Maps to Make a Point

Let's now look at a specific use of a map in a 2015 article from the *Washington Post* that examines the relationship between poverty and access to public education. In this case, you might ask if the two maps serve the author well in advancing her purpose or whether she could have represented the problem she identifies in another, perhaps more effective way.

EMILY BADGER

Mapped: The Places Where Most Public School Children Are Poor

Formerly a staff writer at *The Atlantic Cities*, Emily Badger is a regular contributor to the *Washington Post* and writes about politics, race, and urban neighborhoods.

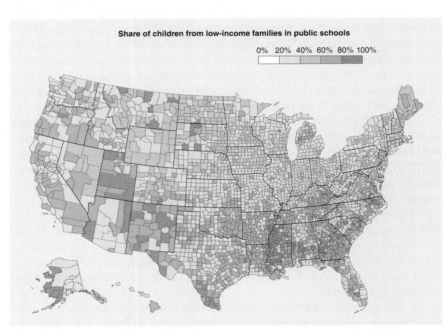

Map: "Share of Children from Low-Income Families in Public Schools," originally from Reed Jordan, "A Closer Look at Income and Race Concentration in Public Schools," Urban Institute, May 13, 2015, http://www.urban.org/features/closer-look-income-and-race-concentration-public-schools

Earlier this year, the Southern Education Foundation reported that America's public schools had reached a dispiriting milestone: A majority of children attending them are now low-income. As the *Post*'s Lyndsey Layton noted at the time, we haven't seen such demographics in public schools at any point over the past half-century. And they mean that teachers must increasingly prioritize combating the effects of poverty—ensuring children feel safe, fed and well-clothed—before the learning even begins.

This picture of poverty in the classroom, however, varies widely across the country, between North and South, and between urban counties and nearby suburban ones. The Urban Institute on Wednesday released interactive maps showing that the concentration of poor children in public schools is remarkably high in some of these places relative to others—and that these geographic disparities are magnified for children of color.

The above map shows the share of children in public schools in each county who come from low-income families (low-income is defined here as households making at or below 185 percent of the federal poverty line, the cutoff for free and reduced-price lunch programs). Particularly striking is the "belt of rural poverty" across the South, as the Urban Institute puts it.

The share of low-income children is also high in several metropolitan areas: in Dallas County (73 percent), in Cook County around Chicago (66 percent), in the District of Columbia (61 percent). In several Lakota counties in South Dakota, the number of public school children who come from low-income families approaches 100 percent.

This concentration of poverty, which reflects underlying patterns in where the rich and poor live, also means that a poor child in America is much more likely than a middle-class or wealthier child to attend a high-poverty school. About 40 percent of low-income children attend public schools where 75 percent of the other students are low-income, too. The same is true of just 6 percent of non-poor kids. "This is concentrated disadvantage," writes Urban Institute researcher Reed

1

2

3

4

5

Identifies a problem that educators have never faced before.

Identifies the source of data in the map that frames the argument and introduces the idea that poverty affects children of color more than others.

Integrates reference to the map into the argument.

Offers more specific data that the map does not fully present in its emphasis on high-poverty areas marked in dark blue. Note the way the author uses color-coded key for identifying low- and high-poverty families.

Amplifies the argument with statistical data from a reliable source and establishes the importance, urgency, and immediacy of the patterns she identifies.

Jordan, "the children who need the most are concentrated in schools least likely to have the resources to meet those needs."

Across the country, black children are also about six times more likely to attend high-poverty schools than white children. In many counties in the rural South, nearly all of the black children attend high-poverty schools.

Leads up to a key point that frames the way readers will look at the map that follows.

6

Disparities in the level of school poverty that white and black children experience often vary as well within the same region. Jordan again:

7

> In some metropolitan areas, the racial concentration of school poverty is so severe that black and white students effectively attend two different school systems: one for middle- and upper-middle-income white students, and the other for poor students and students of color.

This happens, for example, in Cook County around Chicago. There, 75 percent of black students attend high-poverty schools. For white children, the share is less than 10 percent.

Reaffirms the value of the maps as a way to visualize the problem and create goals that might inform policy.

These maps reflect the importance of better integrating schools, creating environments in which poor children learn alongside upper-income peers. But that's a goal that will be hard to achieve if we don't talk as well about the housing patterns and policies that helped create these maps.

8

Share of black children in high-poverty schools

0% 20% 40% 60% 80% 100%

Urban Institute

Map: "Share of Black Children in High-Poverty Schools," originally from Reed Jordan, "A Closer Look at Income and Race Concentration in Public Schools," Urban Institute, May 13, 2015, http://www.urban.org/features/closer-look-income-and-race-concentration-public-schools

■ Using Photographs to Provide Context or Stir Emotions

Of all visuals that appear in multimodal texts, photographs might be the most common. They can serve a wide range of functions in the text and are frequently used to provide context or encourage a particular emotional response — or both. Take online news articles, for example. Most of them, regardless of the topic, include a visual. If the article discusses a statement made by a politician, a photo of the politician usually appears with the writing. This photo provides a visual context for the writer's subject — the politician — but rarely does it capture the exact moment in which the politician made the statement being discussed. The text will usually include a photo that instead reveals something about how the writer wants the politician to be perceived. If the writer questions the validity of the politician's statement, the chosen photo may show the politician wearing a combative or smug expression, for example. These kinds of photos are usually not the subject of overt discussion, but they do connect to the subject and influence most readers' perceptions of the text.

Sometimes photos are at the center of a writer's text. For example, a writer questioning whether the 2017 Women's March in Washington, DC, was inclusive might analyze a photo of the crowd that seems to capture the prevailing mix of genders, races, and ages of the participants. Or in covering the blight of foreclosed, uninhabited homes in low-income neighborhoods in Chicago, a writer might include a photo of one such boarded-up house to characterize the problem and the neighborhood and maybe generate compassion for those living in adjacent properties.

When you encounter photographs in your reading, we encourage you to analyze the photograph by reflecting on your own emotional response to what is depicted and any memories that the photograph helps spark. To what extent does it reflect a world that you know or help reframe what you know and have experienced? What purpose does the photograph serve in the text? That is, what story does the photograph help the author tell? How effective is it in establishing a sense of importance, immediacy, and urgency?

■ Using Tables to Capture the Issue and Present Findings

We now turn to the ways writers use tables as a formal structure to help readers understand the kinds of patterns that complex data represent. Tables tend to be used to present statistics and serve as a starting point for analysis and discussion. You will see that it is a good rule of thumb to summarize and highlight key points in the text you write rather than try to include all of the information that you will include in a table. It's also important to explain what you think readers should pay attention to in a table and offer some context. Don't just include a table without explanation.

In what follows, we provide an excerpt from a 2001 article in which researchers Susan B. Neuman and Donna Celano examine the educational resources that children and their families have access to in two low-income neighborhoods and two middle-class neighborhoods. The excerpt we include describes the methods the researchers used to collect data and some of the results they found. We limit our discussion of results to the quantity and quality of literacy resources available to children.

We encourage you to analyze the way the authors choose to visually represent their findings alongside their discussion of the availability of reading materials for adolescents and adults, where they found these resources, and the differences between quantity and quality of resources in low- and high-income neighborhoods. How effective is their use of tables in establishing a sense of importance, immediacy, and urgency? How do the tables help the authors fulfill their purpose? What story do they tell? And finally, note how the authors have designed the table and used labels to identify the information provided in a given table. Is the information clear? Do the authors integrate the discussion of what is in the tables into the text?

SUSAN B. NEUMAN AND DONNA CELANO

Access to Print in Low-Income and Middle-Income Communities: An Ecological Study of Four Neighborhoods

A former U.S. Assistant Secretary of Elementary and Secondary Education, Dr. Susan B. Neuman is an educator, researcher, and education policy-maker in early childhood and literacy development. Now a professor of education at the University of Michigan, she is director of the Michigan Research Program on Ready to Learn. She has published widely, including her most recent book with Professor Donna Celano, *Giving Our Children a Fighting Chance*. Dr. Celano is a faculty member in the Communication Department at La Salle University, Philadelphia, and has published in *Reading Research Quarterly*, *Phi Delta Kappan*, *Education Week*, and *Educational Leadership*.

■ ■ ■

Our multicultural research team included a project investigator, a project coordinator, and six applied urban anthropology doctoral students. Together, we devised a research strategy to examine literacy resources and opportunities in each community. This strategy recognized that any one variable, or

States the purpose of their study: to identify literacy resources and opportunities from different perspectives (not defined by any one variable or place). The discussion of methods provides some context for analyzing how the authors examine the amount and kinds of literacy materials available in low-income and middle-income neighborhoods.

Identifies why the research team looked at the specific factors that influence how children learn.

The authors describe the kinds of reading materials that children in low-income and middle-income neighborhoods have access to.

measure in and of itself, could not explain variations in print access and opportunity. Rather, we hypothesized that each measure operated within a web of relationships, acting simultaneously and in ways that intersected with one another. Initial data collection and analysis were followed by additional data collection and analysis throughout the year.

The research team devised a theory of community influences that might have an impact on children's early literacy development (Connell, Kubisch, Schorr, & Weiss, 1995). On the basis of accumulated evidence from early literacy research, the theory implies that children learn about literacy through contact, experiences, and observations of written language use in their everyday lives (Goodman, 1986; Neuman & Roskos, 1997; Teale & Sulzby, 1989). Children construct an understanding of how print works through their independent explorations of print and signs, interactions around books and other print resources, and participation with others engaged in purposeful literacy activities. Accordingly, community access was operationally defined as (a) the quantity and selection of children's books that parents could conceivably purchase in the neighborhood, (b) the environmental print (signs, labels, and logos) in the business area that children might begin to identify, (c) the public areas where children might observe people reading, (d) the quantity and quality of books in the child-care centers they would most likely attend, (e) the quantity and quality of books in the local elementary school libraries, and (f) the collections in the local public library. Although each of these influences most likely plays some role, together they might play a powerful role in children's development as literacy learners.

Survey of reading materials. Using the census boundaries, research assistants walked each block throughout a neighborhood, stopping at every store (i.e., bookstore, grocery store, bodega) likely to have reading resources for purchase: newspapers, magazines, children's books, and teen and adult books. Total number of titles, descriptions of the types of materials,

2

3

and age distribution for the materials were placed on a spreadsheet. To the degree possible, we also counted newspaper boxes, honor boxes, and newspaper stands by type of newspapers. For the purposes of this study, information on children's resources was then plotted on maps to provide information on proximity to resources across the neighborhood....

The authors explain where these different kinds of reading materials are accessible — if they are accessible at all.

Books in child-care centers. Because increasing numbers of children spend most of their day not around their neighborhood, but in child-care centers within the area in which they live (Children's Defense Fund, 1999), our next step was to focus on access to books in childcare centers. Considering that independent access to books is likely to be particularly important for 3- and 4-year-old children, we randomly selected two classrooms in six not-for-profit child-care centers in each neighborhood (i.e., 48 classrooms).... For the purposes of this study, only two areas of the literacy environment were examined. Children's book displays were rated for availability, according to a scale of 1 (no books accessible to children) to 7 (books available in library corner and other interest areas around the room). Quality was rated from 1 (no attractive books displayed) to 7 (variety of genre and a wide range of age-appropriate selections).... 4

School libraries. We next visited the local school libraries. Many young children were likely to attend prekindergarten and kindergarten in elementary schools and later go on to the middle schools in the neighborhood. We concentrated on public schools, but included several parochial and private ones if they seemed to draw large numbers of children from the local area. Visiting a total of 24 schools, we examined (a) their resources (i.e., number and condition of available books — book count was estimated by multiplying the number of books on a shelf times the number of shelves, and condition was estimated by publication date and condition of the cover on a random selection of books); (b) staffing (i.e., librarian's training and years of work experience); and (c) children's access (i.e., number of days the library 5 was open per week, and whether children could visit independently or needed to go at designated times). Differences in quantity and quality of books and book access were then compared across communities.

Public libraries. Our final analysis focused on the public library branches in each neighborhood.... We limited our analysis to the size of the collection, average number of books per child and adult in the catchment area, and hours of library service for each branch. 6

Results

The authors highlight the extent to which middle-class families have far more access to reading materials than do low-income families and their children.

Results of the data were consistent. There were minor differences in access to print between neighborhoods of similar income, but major and striking differences at almost all levels between neighborhoods of different income. These data indicate that children from middle-income neighborhoods were likely to be deluged with a wide variety of reading materials. However, children from poor neighborhoods would have to aggressively and persistently seek them out.... 7

A summary of what the authors found in the four neighborhoods listed at the top in Table 2. On the left side of the table is a list of what the authors examined and which they described earlier in their method for collecting data. Use of a table helps the authors selectively discuss the data presented and emphasize the clear differences in access between low- and middle-class families.

Survey of print resources. Table 2 describes the number of stores in each area that carried children's books and magazines. In Chestnut Hill and Roxborough, 11 and 13 places respectively sold print materials for children. There were seven bookstores with special sections for children in Chestnut Hill and three bookstores, with a large children's selection in one, in Roxborough. In contrast, Kingsessing and Kensington, with a far greater density of children, had 4 places in each community that carried children's print materials. No bookstores were found in either neighborhood. 8

Note that the researchers underscore what they want readers to understand from the table. They stress the "scarcity" of materials they think all children should have access to.

As shown in Table 2, drugstores were the most common source of print materials for children. Young adult materials, defined as chapter books, or magazines more suitable to middle-grade children in all areas were scarce. Apart from the bookstores and a couple of convenience stores in the middle-income areas, these materials were largely absent in any business establishment. 9

Four additional tables further analyze data presented in the summary table. The authors integrate the tables by discussing findings in the text, while offering readers the argument they make about this "disturbing picture."

Looking more closely in each area, Tables 3a through 3d describe an even more disturbing picture and equation. To provide some evidence of choice (not quality), we counted the number of *different* children's titles in each store. Detailing the type of store, number of children's titles, and general type of reading material (e.g., magazines, books, comics), massive differences were reported in print access across community—not only in number, but in type of materials available. Children in Chestnut Hill, for example, had access to literally thousands of book, magazine, and comic-book titles. Roxborough children, though with access to far fewer, still had substantial numbers of book titles to choose from, whereas children in Kensington had only hundreds and in Kingsessing even fewer. No young adult titles were available in either of the two lower-income neighborhoods.   *10*

The authors summarize what we find in Tables 3a, b, c, and d. Again, the researchers can be selective in what they write about so as not to overwhelm readers because all of the data appears in the tables they provide.

These data indicate that the equation was dramatically skewed in favor of children from middle-income communities. There were about 13 titles for every 1 child in Chestnut Hill, and 1 book title for about every 3 children in Roxborough. Compare this situation with the low-income communities: There was 1 title for about every 20 children in Kensington and 1, all of which were coloring book titles, for about every 300 children in Kingsessing.   *11*

Consequently, even though living in the same city, children's access to print resources was widely differential. In these low-income neighborhoods, children would find it difficult, if not impossible, to purchase a book of any quality in local stores; in the middle-income neighborhoods, children would find it hard to escape them. Such differential access might account for differential print exposure as recorded in research by Stanovich and his colleagues (Stanovich & Cunningham, 1993; Stanovich & West, 1989).   *12*

Table 2 Number of Places Selling Children's
Reading Resources

STORES	KENSINGTON	KINGSESSING	ROXBOROUGH	CHESTNUT HILL
Children's resources				
Bookstores	0	0	1	3
Drugstores	2	1	5	2
Grocery stores	0	1	3	1
Bargain stores	1	1	2	0
Corner stores	1	0	0	0
Other stores	0	1	1	1
Children's stores	0	0	1	4
Total	4	4	13	11
Young adult				
Bookstores	0	0	1	1
Drugstores	0	0	1	0
Grocery stores	0	0	0	0
Bargain stores	0	0	0	0
Corner stores	0	0	0	0
Other stores	0	0	1	0
Total	0	0	3	1

Table 3a Reading Resources in Kensington

STORE NAME	TYPE	CHILDREN'S TITLES	YOUNG ADULT TITLES	TYPE
Rite Aid	Drugstore	112	0	Book/magazines (picture, puzzle, comics, activity)
Rite Aid	Drugstore	142	0	Book/magazines (picture, puzzle, comics, activity)
Chico's Cut Rate	Bargain store	95	0	Magazines (comics)
Maria's Candy	Corner store	9	0	Magazines (comics, puzzles)
Total		358	0	

Tables: Republished with permission from John Wiley & Sons, Inc., from "Access to Print in Low-Income and Middle-Income Communities: An Ecological Study of Four Neighborhoods," by Susan B. Neuman and Donna Celano, *Reading Research Quarterly* 36.1 (January/February/March 2001), pp. 8–26; permission conveyed through Copyright Clearance Center, Inc.

Table 3b   Reading Resources in Kingsessing

Store Name	Type	Children's Titles	Young Adult Titles	Type
Pharmacy	Drugstore	15	0	Magazines
Thriftway	Grocery store	5	0	Magazines
Dollar Store	Bargain store	30	0	Books (coloring)
Newstand	Other	5	0	Magazines
Total		55	0	

Table 3c   Reading Resources in Roxborough

Store Name	Type	Children's Titles	Young Adult Titles	Type
Encore Books	Bookstore	1,000	500	Books
CVS	Drugstore	18	0	Books
Rite Aid	Drugstore	34	0	Books/magazines
Eckerd	Drugstore	69	0	Books
Eckerd	Drugstore	55	0	Books/magazines (coloring/activity, easy crossword)
CVS	Drugstore	27	30	Books (picture, coloring/activity, popular teen fiction)
Superfresh	Grocery store	20	0	Books (Golden books, coloring/activity)
Superfresh	Grocery store	27	0	Books/magazines (Disney, Read & Listen, coloring/activity, comics)
Acme	Grocery store	14	0	Books (bargain)
Dollar Store	Bargain store	35	0	Books (toddler, picture, coloring)
Dollar Store	Bargain store	31	0	Books/magazines (picture, activity, Disney, comics)
World Wide Aquarium	Other store	30	0	Books ("family style" books about pets)
Family Toy Warehouse	Children's store	237	30	Books (toddler, picture, workbooks, Golden books, coloring/activity)
Total		1597	560	

Tables: Republished with permission from John Wiley & Sons, Inc., from "Access to Print in Low-Income and Middle-Income Communities: An Ecological Study of Four Neighborhoods," by Susan B. Neuman and Donna Celano, *Reading Research Quarterly* 36.1 (January/February/March 2001), pp. 8–26; permission conveyed through Copyright Clearance Center, Inc.

Table 3d Reading Resources in Chestnut Hill

Store Name	Type	Children's Titles	Young Adult Titles	Type
Borders	Bookstore	14,000	Unspecified	Books
Christian Literature Crusade	Bookstore	640	0	Books (toddler, picture, coloring)
Philadelphia Print Shop	Bookstore	1	0	Books (coloring)
CVS	Drugstore	7	0	Books (coloring)
Eckerd	Drugstore	34	0	Books (toddler, workbooks, coloring/activity)
Superfresh	Grocery store	6	0	Books/magazines
Chris's Store	Children's store	10	0	Unspecified
Benders	Children's store	1,000	0	Unspecified
O'Doodles	Children's store	115	0	Books (toddler, picture, educational coloring, family style art)
Mes Enfants	Toy store	120	0	Books (toddler, picture)
Performing Art Store	Other	520	0	Books (scripts, scores, toddler, stories, multicultural, dance, biography)
Total		16,453	0	

▪ Using Graphs to Present Findings

One final way of presenting data is to use a graph, as Neuman and Celano do to provide a quick summary that gives readers a snapshot of key findings.

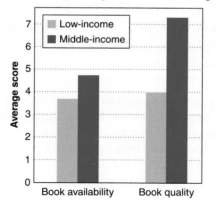

FIGURE 10.5 Book Availability and Book Quality in Preschool Classrooms

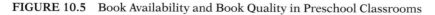

Table and figure: Republished with permission from John Wiley & Sons, Inc., from "Access to Print in Low-Income and Middle-Income Communities: An Ecological Study of Four Neighborhoods," by Susan B. Neuman and Donna Celano, *Reading Research Quarterly* 36.1 (January/February/March 2001), pp. 8–26; permission conveyed through Copyright Clearance Center, Inc.

They use a bar graph, but you can also use pie charts, scatter plots, and line graphs to emphasize patterns and trends.

Interestingly, Neuman and Celano use tables more frequently to summarize the differences between the types and quantity of literacy resources that low- and middle-income families have access to. Some of the results they present are quite dramatic, especially when we become aware of the tens of thousands of titles in middle-income neighborhoods and the scarcity of books in low-income neighborhoods. They could have easily compiled what they found in a graph like the one on page 309. Why do you think they chose to use a table to represent trends but then use a graph to describe the availability of books in preschools? What differences would you call attention to in using a table versus a graph? What effect do these two different kinds of images have on you? To what extent does the purpose for writing determine the choice? To what extent does either one convey importance, immediacy, or urgency better than the other?

Steps to Using Visuals in Writing an Argument

1   **Identify.** Consider what you want to accomplish—your purpose—in using a visual or a series of visuals. What is the story you want to tell? Are you reframing readers' experiences, sparking their imagination, presenting data, or motivating readers to act?

2   **Analyze.** Conduct some research to understand an audience's values and knowledge base. How might readers respond to your choice of visuals?

3   **Evaluate.** Assess the extent to which a visual will add clarity or create a sense of importance, urgency, and immediacy.

4   **Question.** Examine the source of the data in a map, photograph, table, or graph. Are the data accurate or biased in any way? Does the source of data reveal anything?

5   **Integrate.** Discuss and analyze any visuals you include. Be sure that readers understand the relationship between the text you write and the image(s) you present. What conclusions can readers draw from your maps, photographs, tables, or graphs?

A Practice Sequence: Using Visuals to Enhance an Argument

1   With your own writing in mind, write down how you would follow the steps for integrating visuals in a written argument.

- **Identify** your purpose. What is the story you want to tell?
- **Analyze** your audience's values and knowledge base to determine how they might react to different kinds of media.
- **Evaluate** which kind of visuals will provide support or clarity or create a sense of importance, urgency, and immediacy.
- **Question** the source of the data you want to use. Does the source of data reveal anything?
- **Integrate** the text you have written and the visual(s) you include. What conclusions can readers draw from your discussion of visuals?

2   As a class or in small groups, discuss the strategies that authors use to integrate visuals and discussion in the readings in this section.

- When does using a map make sense? What about a photograph, table, or graph?
- Are there instances when the authors might have combined strategies to fulfill their purpose as writers?
- What are some best practices for integrating visuals that help readers understand the importance, immediacy, and urgency of an argument?

3   Analyze the following editorial as a class or in small groups. The writer collaborated with three other students in an effort to prevent a library from closing in the city where they live and attend a school. The authors were limited to just 700 words and could not include visuals to amplify their argument.

- To what extent could a map have helped readers understand the resources that children and families have access to?
- What would including a photograph add to the story the students wanted to tell?
- Could the writers have added a table with census data or even a graph to advance their argument? Why or why not?

Jindra 1

Nathan Jindra*

Neighbors Need LaSalle Branch

I am writing on behalf of a group of 11 middle and high   *1*
school students who participated in the Neighborhood Resource
Corporation Youth Leadership Workshop, with an enthusiasm for
bettering the community. We read with interest the *Tribune* article
"Report: Business tax cut to cost county $31.6M," published in
January of this year.

The story talked about Governor Pence's efforts to spur   *2*
economic development in the state and the impact that eliminating
the business personal property tax could have on local governments.
A total loss to St. Joseph County could be up to $31.6 million
in 2015 and $8 million in South Bend alone. The effects can be
devastating to public education, transportation, parks, and libraries.
We are concerned about all of these, but especially the consequences
that tax cuts will have on local libraries. To save money for the
library system, Donald Napoli, library director, said he would consider
closing the LaSalle Branch, which could save $500,000 a year.

We have met monthly for the past 10 months, and we   *3*
have been studying and learning about libraries and their place in
communities. Looking at the article, we had some shared concerns,
particularly the fact that the data only looked at book circulation
and not other library uses. It is important to note that libraries have
other functions in addition to circulating books, such as Internet
use, gathering spaces, and safe environments for learning. Also, in
our modern society, not just in South Bend, the use of electronic
media is growing rapidly. This is resulting in fewer books being
circulated and checked out. It doesn't seem fair to close the LaSalle
Branch based just on book circulation.

The LaSalle Library Branch is in a neighborhood that   *4*
needs it the most. According to ZipSkinny.com, 13 percent of the
neighborhood is at or below the poverty line, and 50 percent of
residents make $34,000 or less a year. In addition, 20 percent of the
neighborhood consists of school-age children, many of whom use the
library regularly. A member of our council uses this library frequently
and says it provides a good space where she can complete her
schoolwork. She will be attending a four-year college in Indianapolis

next year. With school cuts being made more and more, closing this library would leave many kids without resources for learning as the other nearest libraries are three miles away. This is a long walk for young children and bicycling is really not an option given the busy roads nearby. Closing the library seems like a counterintuitive way to ensure a successful future for our community. Why take something away from those who need it most?

School resources are a great asset to libraries, but they are not the only one. Libraries are used as shelter in winter and summer when the weather can be extreme. Youth and adults alike use libraries as community centers and much more. Offering programs that community members want is a great way to encourage library use. More programs could include tutoring sessions, activity days, camp, and read-alouds for small children. These could also be alternate sources of revenue. Instead of cutting back on public resources, trying to find other sources of income could be very beneficial for the whole community.

5

As a community, we need to know more about the people who are using this library. How can we support our community? Are the choices we are making benefiting everyone, or just some? These are points we need to take into consideration. As a council, we feel until all these questions are thoughtfully answered, there has been insufficient planning for the removal of a community asset. We hope the library board and others will take these thoughts into consideration and plan accordingly. As the president of the American Library Association put it so well, "Teens need these kinds of places to find their voices."

6

*The author wishes to thank Kai Brown, Indonesia Brown, and Julia McKenna for their help in writing this article.

From Introductions to Conclusions
Drafting an Essay

In this chapter, we describe strategies for crafting introductions that set up your argument. We then describe the characteristics of well-formulated paragraphs that will help you build your argument. Finally, we provide you with some strategies for writing conclusions that reinforce what is new about your argument, what is at stake, and what readers should do with the knowledge you convey.

DRAFTING INTRODUCTIONS

The introduction is where you set up your argument. It's where you identify a widely held assumption, challenge that assumption, and state your thesis. Writers use a number of strategies to set up their arguments. In this section we look at five of them:

- Moving from a general topic to a specific thesis (inverted-triangle introduction)
- Introducing the topic with a story (narrative introduction)
- Beginning with a question (interrogative introduction)
- Capturing readers' attention with something unexpected (paradoxical introduction)
- Identifying a gap in knowledge (minding-the-gap introduction)

Remember that an introduction need not be limited to a single paragraph. It may take several paragraphs to effectively set up your argument.

Keep in mind that you have to make these strategies your own. That is, we can suggest models, but you must make them work for your own argument. You must imagine your readers and what will engage them. What tone do you want to take? Playful? Serious? Formal? Urgent? The attitude you want to convey will depend on your purpose, your argument, and the needs of your audience.

■ The Inverted-Triangle Introduction

An **inverted-triangle introduction**, like an upside-down triangle, is broad at the top and pointed at the base. It begins with a general statement of the topic and then narrows its focus, ending with the point of the paragraph (and the triangle), the writer's thesis. We can see this strategy at work in the following introduction from a student's essay. The student writer (1) begins with a broad description of the problem she will address, (2) then focuses on a set of widely held but troublesome assumptions, and (3) finally, presents her thesis in response to what she sees as a pervasive problem.

The student begins with a general set of assumptions about education that she believes people readily accept.

⌐In today's world, many believe that education's sole purpose is to communicate information for students to store and draw on as necessary. By storing this information, students hope to perform well on tests. Good test scores assure good grades. Good grades eventually lead to acceptances into good colleges, which ⌐ultimately guarantee good jobs. Many teachers and students, convinced that education exists as a tool to secure good jobs,

She then cites author bell hooks, to identify an approach that makes use of these assumptions — the "banking system" of education, a term hooks borrows from educator Paulo Freire.

rely on the *banking system*. In her essay "Teaching to Transgress," bell hooks defines the *banking system* as an "approach to learning that is rooted in the notion that all students need to do is consume information fed to them by a professor and be able ⌐to memorize and store it" (185). Through the banking system, students focus solely on facts, missing the important themes and life lessons available in classes and school materials. The banking system misdirects the fundamental goals of education. Education's true purpose is to prepare students for the real world

The student then points to the banking system as the problem. This sets up her thesis about the "true purpose" of education.

by allowing them access to pertinent life knowledge available in their studies. Education should then entice students to apply this pertinent life knowledge to daily life struggles through praxis. In addition to her definition of the banking system, hooks offers the idea of praxis from the work of Paulo Freire. When incorporated into education, *praxis*, or "action and reflection upon the world ⌐in order to change it" (185), offers an advantageous educational tool that enhances the true purpose of education and overcomes the banking system.

The strategy of writing an introduction as an inverted triangle entails first identifying an idea, an argument, or a concept that people appear to accept as true; next, pointing out the problems with that idea, argument, or concept; and then, in a few sentences, setting out a thesis—how those problems can be resolved.

■ The Narrative Introduction

Opening with a short **narrative**, or story, is a strategy many writers use successfully to draw readers into a topic. A narrative introduction relates a sequence of events and can be especially effective if you think you need to coax indifferent or reluctant readers into taking an interest in the topic. Of course, a narrative introduction delays the declaration of your argument, so it's wise to choose a short story that clearly connects to your argument, and get to the thesis as quickly as possible (within a few paragraphs) before your readers start wondering "What's the point of this story?"

Notice how the student writer uses a narrative introduction to her argument in her essay titled "Throwing a Punch at Gender Roles: How Women's Boxing Empowers Women."

The student's entire first paragraph is a narrative that takes us into the world of women's boxing and foreshadows her thesis.

Glancing at my watch, I ran into the gym, noting to myself that being late to the first day of boxing practice was not the right way to make a good first impression. I flew down the stairs into the basement, to the room the boxers have lovingly dubbed "The Pit." What greeted me when I got there was more than I could ever have imagined. Picture a room filled with boxing gloves of all sizes covering an entire wall, a mirror covering another, a boxing ring in a corner, and an awesome collection of framed newspaper and magazine articles chronicling the boxers whose pictures were hanging on every wall. Now picture that room with seventy-plus girls on the floor doing push-ups, sweat dripping down their faces. I was immediately struck by the discipline this sport would take from me, but I had no idea I would take so much more from it.

With her narrative as a backdrop, the student identifies a problem, using the transition word "yet" to mark her challenge to the conditions she observes in the university's women's boxing program.

The university offers the only nonmilitary-based college-level women's boxing program in America, and it also offers women the chance to push their physical limits in a regulated environment. Yet the program is plagued with disappointments. I have experienced for myself the stereotypes female boxers face and have dealt with the harsh reality that boxing is still widely recognized as only a men's sport. This paper will show that the women's boxing program at Notre Dame serves as a much-needed outlet for females to come face-to-face with

The writer then states her thesis (what her paper "will show"): Despite the problems of stereotyping, women's boxing offers women significant opportunities for growth.

aspects of themselves they would not typically get a chance to explore. It will also examine how viewing this sport as a positive opportunity for women at ND indicates that there is growing hope that very soon more activities similar to women's boxing may be better received by society in general. I will accomplish these goals by analyzing scholarly journals, old *Observer* [the school newspaper] articles, and survey questions answered by the captains of the 20-- women's boxing team of ND.

The student writer uses a visually descriptive narrative to introduce us to the world of women's college boxing; then, in the second paragraph, she steers us toward the purpose of the paper and the methods she will use to develop her argument about what women's boxing offers to young women and to the changing world of sports.

■ The Interrogative Introduction

An **interrogative introduction** invites readers into the conversation of your essay by asking one or more questions, which the essay goes on to answer. You want to think of a question that will pique your readers' interest, enticing them to read on to discover how your insights shed light on the issue. Notice the question Daphne Spain, a professor of urban and environmental planning, uses to open her essay "Spatial Segregation and Gender Stratification in the Workplace."

Spain sets up her argument by asking a question and then tentatively answering it with a reference to a published study.

In the third sentence, she states her thesis — that men and women have very little contact in the workplace.

Finally, she outlines the effects that this lack of contact has on women.

To what extent do women and men who work in different occupations also work in different space? Baran and Teegarden propose that occupational segregation in the insurance industry is "tantamount to spatial segregation by gender" since managers are overwhelmingly male and clerical staff are predominantly female. This essay examines the spatial conditions of women's work and men's work and proposes that working women and men come into daily contact with one another very infrequently. Further, women's jobs can be classified as "open floor," but men's jobs are more likely to be "closed door." That is, women work in a more public environment with less control of their space than men. This lack of spatial control both reflects and contributes to women's lower occupational status by limiting opportunities for the transfer of knowledge from men to women.

By the end of this introductory paragraph, Spain has explained some of the terms she will use in her essay (*open floor* and *closed door*) and has offered in her final sentence a clear statement of her thesis.

In "Harry Potter and the Technology of Magic," literature scholar Elizabeth Teare begins by contextualizing the Harry Potter publishing phenomenon. Then she raises a question about what fueled this success story.

In her first four sentences, Teare describes something she is curious about and she hopes readers will be curious about — the popularity of the Harry Potter books.

The July/August 2001 issue of *Book* lists J. K. Rowling as one of the ten most influential people in publishing. She shares space on this list with John Grisham and Oprah Winfrey, along with less famous but equally powerful insiders in the book industry. What these industry leaders have in common is an almost magical power to make books succeed in the marketplace, and this magic, in addition to that performed with wands, Rowling's novels appear to practice. Opening weekend sales charted like those of a blockbuster movie (not to mention the blockbuster movie itself), the reconstruction of the venerable *New York Times* bestseller lists, the creation of a new nation's worth of web sites in the territory of cyberspace, and of course the legendary inspiration of tens of millions of child readers — the Harry Potter books have transformed both the technologies of reading and the way

In the fifth sentence, Teare asks the question she will try to answer in the rest of the essay.

we understand those technologies. What is it that makes these books — about a lonely boy whose first act on learning he is a wizard is to go shopping for a wand — not only an international phenomenon among children and parents and teachers but also a topic of compelling interest to literary, social, and cultural critics? I will argue that the stories the

Finally, in the last sentence, Teare offers a partial answer to her question — her thesis.

books tell, as well as the stories we're telling about them, enact both our fantasies and our fears of children's literature and publishing in the context of twenty-first-century commercial and technological culture.

In the final two sentences of the introduction, Teare raises her question about the root of this "international phenomenon" and then offers her thesis. By the end of the opening paragraph, then, the reader knows exactly what question is driving Teare's essay and the answer she proposes to explain throughout the essay.

■ The Paradoxical Introduction

A **paradoxical introduction** appeals to readers' curiosity by pointing out an aspect of the topic that runs counter to their expectations. Just as an interrogative introduction draws readers in by asking a question, a paradoxical introduction draws readers in by saying, in effect, "Here's something completely surprising and unlikely about this issue, but my essay will go on to show you how it is true." In this passage from "'Holding Back': Negotiating a Glass Ceiling on Women's Muscular Strength," sociologist Shari L. Dworkin points to a paradox in our commonsense understanding of bodies as the product of biology, not culture.

In the first sentence, Dworkin quotes from a study to identify the thinking that she is going to challenge.

Current work in gender studies points to how "when examined closely, much of what we take for granted about gender and its causes and effects either does not hold up, or can be explained differently." These arguments become especially contentious when confronting nature/culture debates on gendered *bodies*. After all, "common

Notice how Dworkin signals her own position "However" relative to commonly held assumptions.

sense" frequently tells us that flesh and blood bodies are about biology. However, bodies are also shaped and constrained through cumulative social practices, structures of opportunity, wider cultural meanings, and more.

Dworkin ends by stating her thesis, noting a paradox that will surprise readers.

Paradoxically, then, when we think that we are "really seeing" naturally sexed bodies, perhaps we are seeing the effect of internalizing gender ideologies—carrying out social practices—and this constructs our vision of "sexed" bodies.

Dworkin's strategy in the first three sentences is to describe common practice, the understanding that bodies are biological. Then, in the sentences beginning "However" and "Paradoxically," she advances the surprising idea that our bodies—not just the clothes we wear, for example—carry cultural gender markers. Her essay then goes on to examine women's weight lifting and the complex motives driving many women to create a body that is perceived as muscular but not masculine.

■ The Minding-the-Gap Introduction

This type of introduction takes its name from the British train system, the voice on the loudspeaker that intones "Mind the gap!" at every stop, to call riders' attention to the gap between the train car and the platform. In a **minding-the-gap introduction**, a writer calls readers' attention to a gap in the research on an issue and then uses the rest of the essay to fill in the "gap." A minding-the-gap introduction says, in effect, "Wait a minute. There's something missing from this conversation, and my research and ideas will fill in this gap."

For example, in the introductory paragraphs to their book *Men's Lives*, Michael S. Kimmel and Michael A. Messner explain how the book is different from other books that discuss men's lives, and how it serves a different purpose.

The authors begin with an assumption and then challenge it. A transition word "but" signals the challenge.

This is a book about men. But, unlike other books about men, which line countless library shelves, this is a book about men as men. It is a book in which men's experiences are not taken for granted as we explore the "real" and significant accomplishments of men, but a book in which those experiences are treated as significant and important in themselves.

The authors follow with a question that provokes readers' interest and points to the gap they summarize in the last sentence.

But what does it mean to examine men "as men"? Most courses in a college curriculum are about men, aren't they?

But these courses routinely deal with men only in their public roles, so we come to know and understand men as scientists, politicians, military figures, writers, and philosophers. Rarely, if ever, are men understood through the prism of gender.

Kimmel and Messner use these opening paragraphs to highlight both what they find problematic about the existing literature on men and to introduce readers to their own approach.

Steps to Drafting Introductions: Five Strategies

1 **Use an inverted triangle.** Begin with a broad situation, concept, or idea, and narrow the focus to your thesis.

2 **Begin with a narrative.** Capture readers' imagination and interest with a story that sets the stage for your argument.

3 **Ask a question that you will answer.** Provoke readers' interest with a question, and then use your thesis to answer the question.

4 **Present a paradox.** Begin with an assumption that readers accept as true, and formulate a thesis that not only challenges that assumption but may very well seem paradoxical.

5 **Mind the gap.** Identify what readers know and then what they don't know (or what you believe they need to know).

A Practice Sequence: Drafting an Introduction

1   Write or rewrite your introduction (which, as you've seen, may involve more than one paragraph), using one of the five drafting strategies discussed in this chapter. Then share your introduction with one of your peers and ask the following questions:

- To what extent did the strategy compel you to want to read further?

- To what extent is my thesis clear?

- How effectively do I draw a distinction between what I believe others assume to be true and my own approach?
- Is there another way that I might have made my introduction more compelling?

After listening to the responses, try a second strategy and then ask your peer which introduction is more effective.

2 If you do not have your own introduction to work on, revise the introduction below from a student's essay, combining two of the five drafting strategies we've discussed in this chapter.

> News correspondent Pauline Frederick once commented, "When a man gets up to speak people listen then look. When a woman gets up, people look; then, if they like what they see, they listen." Ironically, the harsh reality of this statement is given life by the ongoing controversy over America's most recognizable and sometimes notorious toy, Barbie. Celebrating her fortieth birthday this year, Barbie has become this nation's most beleaguered soldier (a woman no less) of idolatry who has been to the front lines and back more times than the average "Joe." This doll, a piece of plastic, a toy, incurs both criticism and praise spanning both ends of the ideological spectrum. Barbie's curvaceous and basically unrealistic body piques the ire of both liberals and conservatives, each contending that Barbie stands for the distinct view of the other. One hundred and eighty degrees south, others praise Barbie's (curves and all) ability to unlock youthful imagination and potential. M. G. Lord explains Barbie best: "To study Barbie, one sometimes has to hold seemingly contradictory ideas in one's head at the same time.... The doll functions like a Rorschach test: people project wildly dissimilar and often opposing meanings on it.... And her meaning, like her face, has not been static over time." In spite of the extreme polarity, a sole unconscious consensus manifests itself about Barbie. Barbie is "the icon" of womanhood and the twentieth century. She is the American dream. Barbie is "us." The question is always the same: What message does Barbie send? Barbie is a toy. She is the image of what we see.

DEVELOPING PARAGRAPHS

In your introduction, you set forth your thesis. Then, in subsequent paragraphs, you have to develop your argument. Remember our metaphor: If your thesis, or main claim, is the skewer that runs through each paragraph in your essay, then these paragraphs are the "meat" of your argument. The paragraphs that follow your introduction carry the burden of evidence in your argument. After all, a claim cannot stand on its own without supporting evidence. Generally speaking, each paragraph should include a topic sentence that brings the main idea of the paragraph into focus, be unified around the main idea of the topic sentence, and adequately develop the idea. At the same time, a paragraph does not stand on its own; as part of your overall argument, it can refer to what you've said earlier, gesture toward where you are heading, and connect to the larger conversation to which you are contributing.

We now ask you to read an excerpt from "Reinventing 'America': Call for a New National Identity," by Elizabeth Martínez, and answer some questions about how you think the author develops her argument, paragraph by paragraph. Then we discuss her work in the context of the three key elements of paragraphs: *topic sentences*, *unity*, and *adequate development*. As you read, pay attention to how, sentence by sentence, Martínez develops her paragraphs. We also ask that you consider how she makes her argument provocative, impassioned, and urgent for her audience.

ELIZABETH MARTÍNEZ

From Reinventing "America": Call for a New National Identity

Elizabeth Martínez is a Chicana activist who since 1960 has worked in and documented different movements for change, including the civil rights, women's, and Chicano movements. She is the author of six books and numerous articles. Her best-known work is *500 Years of Chicano History in Pictures* (1991), which became the basis of a two-part video she scripted and codirected. Her latest book is *De Colores Means All of Us: Latina Views for a Multi-Colored Century* (1998). In "Reinventing 'America,'" Martínez argues that Americans' willingness to accept a "myth" as "the basis for [the] nation's self-defined identity" has brought the country to a crisis.

For some fifteen years, starting in 1940, 85 percent of all U.S. elemen- *1* tary schools used the Dick and Jane series to teach children how to read. The series starred Dick, Jane, their white middle-class parents, their dog Spot, and their life together in a home with a white picket fence.

"Look, Jane, look! See Spot run!" chirped the two kids. It was a house *2* full of glorious family values, where Mom cooked while Daddy went to work in a suit and mowed the lawn on weekends. The Dick and Jane books also taught that you should do your job and help others. All this affirmed an equation of middle-class whiteness with virtue.

In the mid-1990s, museums, libraries, and eighty Public Broadcast- *3* ing Service (PBS) stations across the country had exhibits and programs commemorating the series. At one museum, an attendant commented,

"When you hear someone crying, you know they are looking at the Dick and Jane books." It seems nostalgia runs rampant among many Euro-Americans: a nostalgia for the days of unchallenged White Supremacy—both moral and material—when life was "simple."

We've seen that nostalgia before in the nation's history. But today it signifies a problem reaching a new intensity. It suggests a national identity crisis that promises to bring in its wake an unprecedented nervous breakdown for the dominant society's psyche.

Nowhere is this more apparent than in California, which has long been on the cutting edge of the nation's present and future reality. Warning sirens have sounded repeatedly in the 1990s, such as the fierce battle over new history textbooks for public schools, Proposition 187's ugly denial of human rights to immigrants, the 1996 assault on affirmative action that culminated in Proposition 209, and the 1997 move to abolish bilingual education. Attempts to copycat these reactionary measures have been seen in other states.

The attack on affirmative action isn't really about affirmative action. Essentially it is another tactic in today's war on the gains of the 1960s, a tactic rooted in Anglo resentment and fear. A major source of that fear: the fact that California will almost surely have a majority of people of color in twenty to thirty years at most, with the nation as a whole not far behind.

Check out the February 3, 1992, issue of *Sports Illustrated* with its double-spread ad for *Time* magazine. The ad showed hundreds of new-born babies in their hospital cribs, all of them Black or brown except for a rare white face here and there. The headline says, "Hey, whitey! It's your turn at the back of the bus!" The ad then tells you, read *Time* magazine to keep up with today's hot issues. That manipulative image could have been published today; its implication of shifting power appears to be the recurrent nightmare of too many potential Anglo allies.

Euro-American anxiety often focuses on the sense of a vanishing national identity. Behind the attacks on immigrants, affirmative action, and multiculturalism, behind the demand for "English Only" laws and the rejection of bilingual education, lies the question: with all these new people, languages, and cultures, what will it mean to be an American? If that question once seemed, to many people, to have an obvious, universally applicable answer, today new definitions must be found. But too often Americans, with supposed scholars in the lead, refuse to face that need and instead nurse a nostalgia for some bygone clarity. They remain trapped in denial.

An array of such ostriches, heads in the sand, began flapping their feathers noisily with the publication of Allan Bloom's 1987 best-selling book, *The Closing of the American Mind.* Bloom bemoaned the decline of our "common values" as a society, meaning the decline of Euro-American cultural centricity (shall we just call it cultural imperialism?). Since then we have seen constant sniping at "diversity" goals across the land. The assault has often focused on how U.S. history is taught. And with reason, for this country's identity rests on a particular narrative about the historical origins of the United States as a nation.

The Great White Origin Myth

Every society has an origin narrative that explains that society to itself and the world with a set of stories and symbols. The origin myth, as scholar-activist Roxanne Dunbar Ortiz has termed it, defines how a society understands its place in the world and its history. The myth provides the basis for a nation's self-defined identity. Most origin narratives can be called myths because they usually present only the most flattering view of a nation's history; they are not distinguished by honesty.   *10*

Ours begins with Columbus "discovering" a hemisphere where some 80 million people already lived but didn't really count (in what became the United States, they were just buffalo-chasing "savages" with no grasp of real estate values and therefore doomed to perish). It continues with the brave Pilgrims, a revolution by independence-loving colonists against a decadent English aristocracy, and the birth of an energetic young republic that promised democracy and equality (that is, to white male landowners). In the 1840s, the new nation expanded its size by almost one-third, thanks to a victory over that backward land of little brown people called Mexico. Such has been the basic account of how the nation called the United States of America came into being as presently configured.   *11*

The myth's omissions are grotesque. It ignores three major pillars of our nationhood: genocide, enslavement, and imperialist expansion (such nasty words, who wants to hear them? — but that's the problem). The massive extermination of indigenous peoples provided our land base; the enslavement of African labor made our economic growth possible; and the seizure of half of Mexico by war (or threat of renewed war) extended this nation's boundaries north to the Pacific and south to the Rio Grande. Such are the foundation stones of the United States, within an economic system that made this country the first in world history to be born capitalist....   *12*

Racism as Linchpin of the U.S. National Identity

A crucial embellishment of the origin myth and key element of the national identity has been the myth of the frontier, analyzed in Richard Slotkin's *Gunfighter Nation*, the last volume of a fascinating trilogy. He   *13* describes Theodore Roosevelt's belief that the West was won thanks to American arms, "the means by which progress and nationality will be achieved." That success, Roosevelt continued, "depends on the heroism of men who impose on the course of events the latent virtues of their 'race.'" Roosevelt saw conflict on the frontier producing a series of virile "fighters and breeders" who would eventually generate a new leadership class. Militarism thus went hand in hand with the racialization of history's protagonists. . . .

The frontier myth embodied the nineteenth-century concept of Manifest Destiny, a doctrine that served to justify expansionist violence by means of intrinsic racial superiority. Manifest Destiny was Yankee conquest as the inevitable result of a confrontation between enterprise and progress (white) versus passivity and backwardness (Indian, Mexican). "Manifest" meant "God-given," and the whole doctrine is profoundly rooted in religious conviction going back to the earliest colonial times. In his short, powerful book *Manifest Destiny: American Expansion and the Empire of Right*, Professor Anders Stephanson tells how the Puritans reinvented the Jewish notion of chosenness and applied it to this hemisphere so that territorial expansion became God's will. . . . *14*

Manifest Destiny Dies Hard

The concept of Manifest Destiny, with its assertion of racial superiority sustained by military power, has defined U.S. identity for 150 years. . . . *15*

Today's origin myth and the resulting concept of national identity make for an intellectual prison where it is dangerous to ask big questions about this society's superiority. When otherwise decent people are trapped in such a powerful desire not to feel guilty, self-deception becomes unavoidable. To cease our present falsification of collective memory should, and could, open the doors of that prison. When together we cease equating whiteness with Americanness, a new day can dawn. As David Roediger, the social historian, has said, "[Whiteness] is the empty and therefore terrifying attempt to build an identity on what one isn't, and on whom one can hold back." *16*

Redefining the U.S. origin narrative, and with it this country's national identity, could prove liberating for our collective psyche. It does not mean Euro-Americans should wallow individually in guilt. It does mean accepting collective responsibility to deal with the implications of our real origin. A few apologies, for example, might be a step in the right direction. In 1997, the idea was floated in Congress to apologize for slavery; it encountered opposition from all sides. But to reject the notion because corrective action, not an apology, is needed misses the point. Having defined itself as the all-time best country in the world, the United States fiercely denies the need to make a *17* serious official apology for anything.... To press for any serious, official apology does imply a new origin narrative, a new self-image, an ideological sea-change.

Accepting the implications of a different narrative could also shed   *18* light on today's struggles. In the affirmative-action struggle, for example, opponents have said that that policy is no longer needed because racism ended with the Civil Rights Movement. But if we look at slavery as a fundamental pillar of this nation, going back centuries, it becomes obvious that racism could not have been ended by thirty years of mild reforms. If we see how the myth of the frontier idealized the white male adventurer as the central hero of national history, with the woman as sunbonneted helpmate, then we might better understand the dehumanized ways in which women have continued to be treated. A more truthful origin narrative could also help break down divisions among peoples of color by revealing common experiences and histories of cooperation.

Reading as a Writer

1. To what extent does the narrative Martínez begins with make you want to read further?
2. How does she connect this narrative to the rest of her argument?
3. How does she use repetition to create unity in her essay?
4. What assumptions does Martínez challenge?
5. How does she use questions to engage her readers?

■ Use Topic Sentences to Focus Your Paragraphs

The **topic sentence** states the main point of a paragraph. It should

- provide a partial answer to the question motivating the writer.
- act as an extension of the writer's thesis and the question motivating the writer's argument.
- serve as a guidepost, telling readers what the paragraph is about.
- help create unity and coherence both within the paragraph and within the essay.

Elizabeth Martínez begins by describing how elementary schools in the 1940s and 1950s used the Dick and Jane series not only to teach reading but also to foster a particular set of values — values that she believes do not serve all children enrolled in America's schools. In paragraph 4, she states her thesis, explaining that nostalgia in the United States has created "a national identity crisis that promises to bring in its wake an unprecedented nervous breakdown for the dominant society's psyche." This is a point that builds on an observation she makes in paragraph 3: "It seems nostalgia runs rampant among many Euro-Americans: a nostalgia for the days of unchallenged White Supremacy—both moral and material—when life was 'simple.'" Martínez often returns to this notion of nostalgia for a past that seems "simple" to explain what she sees as an impending crisis.

Consider the first sentence of paragraph 5 as a topic sentence. With Martínez's key points in mind, notice how she uses the sentence to make her thesis more specific. Notice too, how she ties in the crisis and breakdown she alludes to in paragraph 4. Essentially, Martínez tells her readers that they can see these problems at play in California, an indicator of "the nation's present and future reality."

> *Nowhere is this more apparent than in California, which has long been on the cutting edge of the nation's present and future reality.* Warning sirens have sounded repeatedly in the 1990s, such as the fierce battle over new history textbooks for public schools, Proposition 187's ugly denial of human rights to immigrants, the 1996 assault on affirmative action that culminated in Proposition 209, and the 1997 move to abolish bilingual education. *Attempts to copycat these reactionary measures have been seen in other states.*

The final sentence of paragraph 5 sets up the remainder of the essay.

As readers, we expect each subsequent paragraph to respond in some way to the issue Martínez has raised. She meets that expectation by formulating a topic sentence that appears at the beginning of the paragraph. The topic sentence is what helps create unity and coherence in the essay.

▪ Create Unity in Your Paragraphs

Each paragraph in an essay should focus on the subject suggested by the topic sentence. If a paragraph begins with one focus or major point of discussion, it should not end with another. Several strategies can contribute to the unity of each paragraph.

Use details that follow logically from your topic sentence and maintain a single focus — a focus that is clearly an extension of your thesis.   For example, in paragraph 5, Martínez's topic sentence ("Nowhere is this more apparent than in California, which has long been on the cutting edge of the nation's present and future reality") helps to create unity because it refers back to her thesis (*this* refers to the "national identity crisis" mentioned in paragraph 4) and limits the focus of what she includes in the paragraph to "the fierce battle over new history textbooks" and recent pieces of legislation in California that follow directly from and support the claim of the topic sentence.

Repeat key words to guide your readers. A second strategy for creating unity is to repeat (or use synonyms for) key words within a given paragraph. You can see this at work in paragraph 12 (notice the words we've underscored), where Martínez explains that America's origin narrative omits significant details:

> The myth's omissions are grotesque. It ignores three major pillars of our nationhood: <u>genocide</u>, <u>enslavement</u>, and <u>imperialist expansion</u> (such nasty words, who wants to hear them?—but that's the problem). The massive <u>extermination</u> of indigenous peoples provided our land base; the <u>enslavement</u> of African labor made our economic growth possible; and the <u>seizure</u> of half of Mexico by war (or threat of renewed war) extended this nation's boundaries north to the Pacific and south to the Rio Grande. Such are the foundation stones of the United States, within an economic system that made this country the first in world history to be born capitalist....

Specifically, Martínez tells us that the origin narrative ignores "three major pillars of our nationhood: genocide, enslavement, and imperialist expansion." She then substitutes *extermination* for "genocide," repeats *enslavement*, and substitutes *seizure* for "imperialist expansion." By connecting words in a paragraph, as Martínez does here, you help readers understand that the details you provide are all relevant to the point you want to make.

Use transition words to link ideas from different sentences. A third strategy for creating unity within paragraphs is to establish a clear relationship among different ideas by using **transition words** or phrases. Transition words or phrases signal to your readers the direction your ideas are taking. Table 11.1 lists common transition words and phrases grouped by function—that is, for adding a new idea, presenting a contrasting idea, or drawing a conclusion about an idea.

Martínez uses transition words and phrases throughout the excerpt here. In several places, she uses the word *but* to make a contrast—to draw a distinction between an idea that many people accept as true and an alternative idea that she wants to pursue. Notice in paragraph 17 how she signals the importance of an official apology for slavery—and by implication genocide and the seizure of land from Mexico:

> ... A few apologies, for example, might be a step in the right direction. In 1997, the idea was floated in Congress to apologize for slavery; it encountered opposition from all sides. <u>But</u> to reject the notion because corrective action, not an apology, is needed misses the point. Having defined itself as the all-time best country in the world, the United States fiercely denies the need to make a serious official apology for anything.... To press for any serious, official apology does imply a new origin narrative, a new self-image, an ideological sea-change.

Similarly, in the last paragraph, Martínez counters the argument that affirmative action is not necessary because racism no longer exists:

TABLE 11.1   Common Transition Words and Phrases

Adding an Idea	Presenting a Contrasting Idea	Drawing a Logical Conclusion
also, and, further, moreover, in addition to, in support of, similarly	although, alternatively, as an alternative, but, by way of contrast, despite, even though, however, in contrast to, nevertheless, nonetheless, rather than, yet	as a result, because of, consequently, finally, in sum, in the end, subsequently, therefore, thus

. . . In the affirmative-action struggle, for example, opponents have said that that policy is no longer needed because racism ended with the Civil Rights Movement. <u>But</u> if we look at slavery as a fundamental pillar of this nation, going back centuries, it becomes obvious that racism could not have been ended by thirty years of mild reforms. . . .

There are a number of ways to rephrase what Martínez is saying in paragraph 18. We could substitute *however* for "but." Or we could combine the two sentences into one to point to the relationship between the two competing ideas: *Although some people oppose affirmative action, believing that racism no longer exists, I would argue that racism remains a fundamental pillar of this nation.* Or we could pull together Martínez's different points to draw a logical conclusion using a transition word like *therefore.* Martínez observes that our country is in crisis as a result of increased immigration. *Therefore, we need to reassess our conceptions of national identity to account for the diversity that increased immigration has created.* We can substitute any of the transition words in Table 11.1 for drawing a logical conclusion.

The list of transition words and phrases in Table 11.1 is hardly exhaustive, but it gives you a sense of the ways to connect ideas so that readers understand how your ideas are related. Are they similar ideas? Do they build on or support one another? Are you challenging accepted ideas? Or are you drawing a logical connection from a number of different ideas?

■ Use Critical Strategies to Develop Your Paragraphs

To develop a paragraph, you can use a range of strategies, depending on what you want to accomplish and what you believe your readers will find persuasive. Among these strategies are using examples and illustrations; citing data (facts, statistics, evidence, details); analyzing texts; telling a story or an anecdote; defining terms; making comparisons; and examining causes and evaluating consequences.

Use examples and illustrations.   Examples make abstract ideas concrete through illustration. Using examples is probably the most common way to develop a piece of writing. Of course, Martínez's essay is full of examples.

In fact, she begins with an example of a series of books—the Dick and Jane books—to show how a generation of schoolchildren were exposed to white middle-class values. She also uses examples in paragraph 5, where she lists several pieces of legislation (Propositions 187 and 209) to develop the claim in her topic sentence.

Cite data.   **Data** are factual pieces of information. They function in an essay as the bases of propositions. In the first few paragraphs of the excerpt, Martínez cites statistics ("85 percent of all U.S. elementary schools used the Dick and Jane series to teach children how to read") and facts ("In the mid-1990s, museums, libraries, and eighty Public Broadcasting Service . . . stations across the country had exhibits and programs commemorating the series") to back up her claim about the popularity of the Dick and Jane series and the nostalgia the books evoke.

Analyze texts.   Analysis is the process of breaking something down into its elements to understand how they work together. When you analyze a text, you point out parts of the text that have particular significance to your argument and explain what they mean. By *texts*, we mean both verbal and visual texts. In paragraph 7, Martínez analyzes a visual text, an advertisement that appeared in *Sports Illustrated*, to reveal "its implication of shifting power"—a demographic power shift from Anglos to people of color.

Provide narratives or anecdotes.   Put simply, a narrative is an account of something that happened. More technically, a narrative relates a sequence of events that are connected in time; and an **anecdote** is a short narrative that recounts a particular incident. An anecdote, like an example, can bring an abstraction into focus. Consider Martínez's third paragraph, where the anecdote about the museum attendant brings her point about racially charged nostalgia among white Americans into memorable focus: The tears of the museum-goers indicate just how profound their nostalgia is.

By contrast, a longer narrative, in setting out its sequence of events, often opens up possibilities for analysis. Why did these events occur? Why did they occur in this sequence? What might they lead to? What are the implications? What is missing?

In paragraph 11, for example, Martínez relates several key events in the origin myth of America. Then, in the next paragraph, she explains what is omitted from the myth, or narrative, and builds her argument about the implications and consequences of those omissions.

Define terms.   A definition is an explanation of what something is and, by implication, what it is not. The simplest kind of definition is a synonym, but for the purpose of developing your argument, a one-word definition is rarely enough.

When you define your terms, you are setting forth meanings that you want your readers to agree on, so that you can continue to build your argument on the foundation of that agreement. You may have to stipulate that your definition is part of a larger whole to develop your argument. For example: "Nostalgia is a bittersweet longing for things of the past; but for the purposes of my essay, I focus on white middle-class nostalgia, which combines a longing for a past that never existed with a hostile anxiety about the present."

In paragraph 10, Martínez defines the term *origin narrative* — a myth that explains "how a society understands its place in the world and its history . . . the basis for a nation's self-defined identity." The "Great White Origin Myth" is an important concept in her developing argument about a national crisis of identity.

Make comparisons. Technically, a **comparison** shows the similarities between two or more things, and a **contrast** shows the differences. In practice, however, it is very difficult, if not impossible, to develop a comparison that does not make use of contrast. Therefore, we use the term *comparison* to describe the strategy of comparing *and* contrasting.

Doubtless you have written paragraphs or even whole essays that take as a starting point a version of this sentence: "X and Y are similar in some respects and different in others." This neutral formulation is seldom helpful when you are developing an argument. Usually, in making your comparison — in setting forth the points of similarity and difference — you have to take an evaluative or argumentative stance.

Note the comparison in this passage:

> Although there are similarities between the current nostalgias for Dick and Jane books and for rhythm and blues music of the same era — in both cases, the object of nostalgia can move people to tears — the nostalgias spring from emotional responses that are quite different and even contradictory. I will argue that the Dick and Jane books evoke a longing for a past that is colored by a fear of the present, a longing for a time when white middle-class values were dominant and unquestioned. By contrast, the nostalgia for R&B music may indicate a yearning for a past when multicultural musicians provided white folks with a sweaty release on the dance floor from those very same white-bread values of the time.

The writer does more than list similarities and differences; she offers an analysis of what they mean and is prepared to argue for her interpretation.

Certainly Elizabeth Martínez takes an evaluative stance when she compares versions of American history in paragraphs 11 and 12. In paragraph 11, she angrily relates the sanitized story of American history, setting up a contrast in paragraph 12 with the story that does not appear in history textbooks, a story of "genocide, enslavement, and imperialist expansion." Her evaluative stance comes through clearly: She finds the first version repugnant and harmful, its omissions "grotesque."

Examine causes and evaluate consequences. In any academic discipline, questions of cause and consequence are central. Whether you are analyzing the latest election results in a political science course, reading about the causes of the Vietnam War in a history course, or speculating about the long-term consequences of climate change in a science course, questions of why things happened, happen, or will happen are inescapable.

Examining causes and consequences usually involves identifying a phenomenon and asking questions about it until you gather enough information to begin analyzing the relationships among its parts and deciding which are most significant. You can then begin to set forth your own analysis of what happened and why.

Of course, this kind of analysis is rarely straightforward, and any phenomenon worthy of academic study is bound to generate a variety of conversations about its causes and consequences. In your own thinking and research, avoid jumping to conclusions and continue to sift evidence until plausible connections present themselves. Be prepared to revise your thinking—perhaps several times—in light of new evidence.

In your writing, you also want to avoid oversimplifying. A claim like this—"The answer to curbing unemployment in the United States is to restrict immigration"—does not take into account corporate outsourcing of jobs overseas or the many other possible causes of unemployment. At the very least, you may need to explain the basis and specifics of your analysis and qualify your claim: "Recent studies of patterns of immigration and unemployment in the United States suggest that unrestricted immigration is a major factor in the loss of blue-collar job opportunities in the Southwest." Certainly this sentence is less forceful and provocative than the other one, but it does suggest that you have done significant and focused research and respect the complexity of the issue.

Throughout her essay, Martínez analyzes causes and consequences. In paragraph 8, for example, she speculates that the cause of "attacks on immigrants, affirmative action, and multiculturalism" is "Euro-American anxiety," "the sense of a vanishing national identity." In paragraph 13, she concludes that a *consequence* of Theodore Roosevelt's beliefs about race and war was a "militarism [that] went hand in hand with the racialization of history's protagonists." In paragraph 16, the topic sentence itself is a statement about causes and consequences: "Today's origin myth and the resulting concept of national identity make for an intellectual prison where it is dangerous to ask big questions about this society's superiority."

Having shown where and how Martínez uses critical strategies to develop her paragraphs, we must hasten to add that these critical strategies usually work in combination. Although you can easily develop an entire paragraph (or even an entire essay) using comparison, it is almost impossible to do so without relying on one or more of the other strategies. What if you need to tell an anecdote about the two authors you are comparing? What if you have to cite data about different rates of economic growth to clarify the main claim of your comparison? What if you are comparing different causes and consequences?

Our point is that the strategies described here are methods for exploring your issue in writing. How you make use of them, individually or in combination, depends on which can help you best communicate your argument to your readers.

Steps to Developing Paragraphs

1 **Use topic sentences to focus your paragraphs.** Remember that a topic sentence partially answers the question motivating you to write; acts as an extension of your thesis; indicates to your readers what the paragraph is about; and helps create unity both within the paragraph and within the essay.

2 **Create unity in your paragraphs.** The details in your paragraph should follow logically from your topic sentence and maintain a single focus, one tied clearly to your thesis. Repetition and transition words also help create unity in paragraphs.

3 **Use critical strategies to develop your paragraphs.** Use examples and illustrations; cite data; analyze texts; tell stories or anecdotes; define terms; make comparisons; and examine causes and evaluate consequences.

A Practice Sequence: Working with Paragraphs

We would like you to work in pairs on paragraphing. The objective of this exercise is to gauge the effectiveness of your topic sentences and the degree to which your paragraphs are unified and fully developed.

Make a copy of your essay and cut it up into paragraphs. Shuffle the paragraphs to be sure they are no longer in the original order, and then exchange cut-up drafts with your partner. The challenge is to put your partner's essay back together again. When you both have finished, compare your reorderings with the original drafts. Were you able to reproduce the original organization exactly? If not, do the variations make sense? If one or the other of you had trouble putting the essay back together, talk about the adequacy of your topic sentences, ways to revise topic sentences in keeping with the details in a given paragraph, and strategies for making paragraphs more unified and coherent.

DRAFTING CONCLUSIONS

In writing a conclusion to your essay, you are making a final appeal to your audience. You want to convince readers that what you have written is a relevant, meaningful interpretation of a shared issue. You also want to remind them that your argument is reasonable. Rather than summarize all of the points you've made in the essay—assume your readers have carefully read what you've written—pull together the key components of your argument in the service of answering the question "So what?" Establish why your argument is important: What will happen if things stay the same? What will happen if things change? How effective your conclusion is depends on whether or not readers feel that you have adequately addressed "So what?"—that you have made clear what is significant and of value.

In building on the specific details of your argument, you can also place what you have written in a broader context. (What are the sociological implications of your argument? How far-reaching are they? Are there political implications? Economic implications?) Finally, explain again how your ideas contribute something new to the conversation by building on, extending, or even challenging what others have argued.

In her concluding paragraph, Elizabeth Martínez brings together her main points, puts her essay in a broader context, indicates what's new in her argument, and answers the question "So what?":

> Accepting the implications of a different narrative could also shed light on today's struggles. In the affirmative-action struggle, for example, opponents have said that that policy is no longer needed because racism ended with the Civil Rights Movement. But if we look at slavery as a fundamental pillar of this nation, going back centuries, it becomes obvious that racism could not have been ended by thirty years of mild reforms. If we see how the myth of the frontier idealized the white male adventurer as the central hero of national history, with the woman as sunbonneted helpmate, then we might better understand the dehumanized ways in which women have continued to be treated. A more truthful origin narrative could also help break down divisions among peoples of color by revealing common experiences and histories of cooperation.

Let's examine this concluding paragraph:

1. Although Martínez refers back to important events and ideas she has discussed, she does not merely summarize. Instead, she suggests the implications of those important events and ideas in her first sentence (the topic sentence), which crystallizes the main point of her essay: Americans need a different origin narrative.

2. Then she puts those implications in the broader context of contemporary racial and gender issues.

3. She signals what's new in her argument with the word *if* (*if we look at slavery in a new way*; *if we look at the frontier myth in a new way*).

4. Finally, her answers to why this issue matters culminate in the last sentence. This last sentence connects and extends the claim of her topic sentence, by asserting that a "more truthful origin narrative" could help heal divisions among peoples of color who have been misrepresented by the old origin myth. Clearly, she believes the implications of her argument matter: A new national identity has the potential to heal a country in crisis, a country on the verge of a "nervous breakdown" (para. 4).

Martínez also does something else in the last sentence of the concluding paragraph: She looks to the future, suggesting what the future implications of her argument could be. Looking to the future is one of five strategies for shaping a conclusion. The others we discuss are echoing the introduction, challenging the reader, posing questions, and concluding with a quotation. Each of these strategies appeals to readers in different ways; therefore, we suggest you try them all out in writing your own conclusions. Also, remember that some of these strategies can be combined. For example, you can write a conclusion that challenges readers, poses a question, looks to the future, and ends with a quotation.

■ Echo the Introduction

Echoing the introduction in your conclusion helps readers come full circle. It helps them see how you have developed your idea from beginning to end. In the following example, the student writer begins with a voice speaking from behind an Islamic veil, revealing the ways that Western culture misunderstands the symbolic value of wearing the veil. The writer repeats this visual image in her conclusion, quoting from the Koran: "Speak to them from behind a curtain."

Notice that the author begins with "a voice from behind the shrouds of an Islamic veil" and then echoes this quotation in her conclusion: "Speak to them from behind a curtain."

Introduction: A voice from behind the shrouds of an Islamic veil exclaims: "I often wonder whether people see me as a radical, fundamentalist Muslim terrorist packing an AK-47 assault rifle inside my jean jacket. Or maybe they see me as the poster girl for oppressed womanhood everywhere." In American culture where shameless public exposure, particularly of females, epitomizes ultimate freedom, the head-to-toe covering of a Muslim woman seems inherently oppressive. Driven by an autonomous national attitude, the inhabitants of the "land of the free" are quick to equate the veil with indisputable persecution. Yet Muslim women reveal the enslaving hijab as a symbolic display of the Islamic ideals — honor, modesty, and stability. Because of an unfair American assessment, the aura of hijab mystery cannot be removed until the customs and ethics of Muslim culture are genuinely explored. It is this form of enigmatic seclusion that forms the feminist controversy between Western liberals, who perceive the veil as an inhibiting factor against free will, and Islamic disciples, who conceptualize the veil as a sacred symbol of utmost morality.

Conclusion: For those who improperly judge an alien religion, the veil becomes a symbol of oppression and devastation, instead of a representation of pride and piety. Despite Western images, the hijab is a daily revitalization and reminder of the Islamic societal and religious ideals, thereby upholding the conduct and attitudes of the Muslim community. Americans share these ideals yet fail to recognize them in the context of a different culture. By sincerely exploring the custom of Islamic veiling, one will realize the vital role the hijab plays in shaping Muslim culture by sheltering women, and consequently society, from the perils that erupt from indecency. The principles implored in the Koran of modesty, honor, and stability construct a unifying and moral view of the Islamic Middle Eastern society when properly investigated. As it was transcribed from Allah, "Speak to them from behind a curtain. This is purer for your hearts and their hearts."

Notice how the conclusion echoes the introduction in its reference to a voice speaking from behind a curtain.

▪ Challenge the Reader

By issuing a challenge to your readers, you create a sense of urgency, provoking them to act to change the status quo. In this example, the student writer explains the unacceptable consequences of preventing young women from educating themselves about AIDS and the spread of a disease that has already reached epidemic proportions.

Here the author cites a final piece of research to emphasize the extent of the problem.

Here she begins her explicit challenge to readers about what they have to do to protect themselves or their students from infection.

The changes in AIDS education that I am suggesting are necessary and relatively simple to make. Although the current curriculum in high school health classes is helpful and informative, it simply does not pertain to young women as much as it should. AIDS is killing women at an alarming rate, and many people do not realize this. According to Daniel DeNoon, AIDS is one of the six leading causes of death among women aged 18 to 45, and women "bear the brunt of the worldwide AIDS epidemic." For this reason, DeNoon argues, women are one of the most important new populations that are contracting HIV at a high rate. I challenge young women to be more well-informed about AIDS and their link to the disease; otherwise, many new cases may develop. As the epidemic continues to spread, women need to realize that they can stop the spread of the disease and protect themselves from infection and a number of related complications. It is the responsibility of health educators to present this to young women and inform them of the powerful choices that they can make.

■ Look to the Future

Looking to the future is particularly relevant when you are asking readers to take action. To move readers to action, you must establish the persistence of a problem and the consequences of letting a situation continue unchanged. In the concluding paragraph below, the student author points out a number of things that teachers need to do to involve parents in their children's education. She identifies a range of options before identifying what she believes is perhaps the most important action teachers can take.

The second through fifth sentences present an array of options.

First and foremost, teachers must recognize the ways in which some parents are positively contributing to their children's academic endeavors. Teachers must recognize nontraditional methods of participation as legitimate and work toward supporting parents in these tasks. For instance, teachers might send home suggestions for local after-school tutoring programs. Teachers must also try to make urban parents feel welcome and respected in their school. Teachers might call parents to ask their opinion about a certain difficulty their child is having, or invite them to talk about something of interest to them. One parent, for instance, spoke highly of the previous superintendent who had let him use his work as a film producer to help with a show for students during homeroom. If teachers can develop innovative ways to utilize parents' talents and interests rather than just inviting them to be passively involved in an already-in-place curriculum, more parents might respond. Perhaps, most importantly, if teachers want parents to be involved in students' educations, they must make the parents feel as though their opinions and concerns have real weight. When parents such as those interviewed for this study voice concerns and questions over their child's progress, it is imperative that teachers acknowledge and answer them.

In the last two sentences, the writer looks to the future with her recommendations.

■ Pose Questions

Posing questions stimulates readers to think about the implications of your argument and to apply what you argue to other situations. This is the case in the following paragraph, in which the student writer focuses on immigration and then shifts readers' attention to racism and the possibility of hate crimes. It's useful to extrapolate from your argument, to raise questions that test whether what you write can be applied to different situations. These questions can help readers understand what is at issue.

The first question.

Other speculative questions follow from possible responses to the writer's first question.

Also, my research may apply to a broader spectrum of sociological topics. There has been recent discussion about the increasing trend of immigration. Much of this discussion has involved the distribution of resources to immigrants. Should immigrants have equal access to certain economic and educational resources in America? The decision is split. But it will be interesting to see how this debate will play out. If immigrants are granted more resources, will certain Americans mobilize against the distribution of these resources? Will we see another rise in racist groups such as the Ku Klux Klan in order to prevent immigrants from obtaining more resources? My research can also be used to understand global conflict or war. In general, groups mobilize when their established resources are threatened by an external force. Moreover, groups use framing processes to justify their collective action to others.

■ Conclude with a Quotation

A quotation can strengthen your argument, indicating that others in positions of power and authority support your stance. A quotation also can add poignancy to your argument, as it does in the following excerpt, in which the quotation amplifies the idea that people use Barbie to advance their own interests.

The question still remains, what does Barbie mean? Is she the spokeswoman for the empowerment of women, or rather is she performing the dirty work of conservative patriarchy? I do not think we will ever know the answer. Rather, Barbie is the undeniable "American Icon." She is a toy, and she is what we want her to be. A test performed by Albert M. Magro at Fairmont State College titled "Why Barbie Is Perceived as Beautiful" shows that Barbie is the epitome of what we as humans find beautiful. The test sought to find human preferences on evolutionary changes in the human body. Subjects were shown a series of photos comparing different human body parts, such as the size and shape of the eyes, and asked to decide which feature they preferred: the primitive or derived (more evolved traits). The test revealed that the subjects preferred the derived body traits. It is these preferred evolutionary features that are utilized on the body of Barbie. Barbie is truly an extension of what we are and

The writer quotes an authority to amplify the idea that individually and collectively, we project significance on toys.

what we perceive. Juel Best concludes his discourse on Barbie with these words: "Toys do not embody violence or sexism or occult meanings. People must assign toys their meanings." Barbie is whoever we make her out to be. Barbie grabs hold of our imaginations and lets us go wild.

Steps to Drafting Conclusions: Five Strategies

1 **Pull together the main claims of your essay.** Don't simply repeat points you make in the paper. Instead, show readers how the points you make fit together.

2 **Answer the question "So what?"** Show your readers why your stand on the issue is significant.

3 **Place your argument in a larger context.** Discuss the specifics of your argument, but also indicate its broader implications.

4 **Show readers what is new.** As you synthesize the key points of your argument, explain how what you argue builds on, extends, or challenges the thinking of others.

5 **Decide on the best strategy for writing your conclusion.** Will you echo the introduction? Challenge the reader? Look to the future? Pose questions? Conclude with a quotation? Choose the best strategy or strategies to appeal to your readers.

A Practice Sequence: Drafting a Conclusion

1 Write your conclusion, using one of the strategies described in this section. Then share your conclusion with a classmate. Ask this person to address the following questions:

   • Did I pull together the key points of the argument?

   • Did I answer "So what?" adequately?

   • Are the implications I want readers to draw from the essay clear?

   After listening to the responses, try a second strategy, and then ask your classmate which conclusion is more effective.

2 If you do not have a conclusion of your own, analyze each example conclusion above to see how well each appears to (1) pull together the main claim of the essay, (2) answer "So what?" (3) place the argument in a larger context, and (4) show readers what is new.

ANALYZING STRATEGIES FOR WRITING: FROM INTRODUCTIONS TO CONCLUSIONS

Now that you have studied the various strategies for writing introductions, developing your ideas in subsequent paragraphs, and drafting conclusions, read Barbara Ehrenreich's essay, "Cultural Baggage," and analyze the strategies she uses for developing her argument about diversity. It may help to refer to the practice sequences for drafting introductions (p. 320) and conclusions (p. 339), as well as Steps to Developing Paragraphs (p. 333). Ideally, you should work with your classmates, in groups of three or four, assigning one person to record your ideas and share with the whole class.

Alternatively, you could put the essays by Ehrenreich and Elizabeth Martínez "in conversation" with one another. How do Martínez and Ehrenreich define the issues around diversity? What is at stake for them in the arguments they develop? What things need to change? How would you compare the way each uses stories and personal anecdotes to develop her ideas? Would you say that either writer is a more effective "conversationalist" or more successful in fulfilling her purpose?

BARBARA EHRENREICH

Cultural Baggage

Barbara Ehrenreich is a social critic, activist, and political essayist. Her book *Nickel and Dimed: On (Not) Getting By in America* (2001) describes her attempt to live on low-wage jobs; it became a national best seller in the United States. Her book, *Bait and Switch: The (Futile) Pursuit of the American Dream* (2005), explores the shadowy world of the white-collar unemployed. Recent books of cultural analysis by Ehrenreich include *Bright-Sided: How the Relentless Promotion of Positive Thinking Has Undermined America* and *This Land Is Their Land: Reports from a Divided Nation* (both published in 2009). Ehrenreich has also written for *Mother Jones, The Atlantic, Ms., The New Republic, In These Times,* Salon.com, and other publications. "Cultural Baggage" was originally published in the *New York Times Magazine* in 1992. Her most recent book is *Living with a Wild God,* a memoir that she published in 2014.

An acquaintance was telling me about the joys of rediscovering her   *1* ethnic and religious heritage. "I know exactly what my ancestors were doing 2,000 years ago," she said, eyes gleaming with enthusiasm, "and *I can do the same things now.*" Then she leaned forward and inquired politely, "And what is your ethnic background, if I may ask?"

"None," I said, that being the first word in line to get out of my mouth. Well, not "none," I backtracked. Scottish, English, Irish—that was something, I supposed. Too much Irish to qualify as a WASP; too much of the hated English to warrant a "Kiss Me, I'm Irish" button; plus there are a number of dead ends in the family tree due to adoptions, missing records, failing memories, and the like. I was blushing by this time. Did "none" mean I was rejecting my heritage out of Anglo-Celtic self-hate? Or was I revealing a hidden ethnic chauvinism in which the Britannically derived serve as a kind of neutral standard compared with the ethnic "others"?

Throughout the 1960s and 70s, I watched one group after another— African Americans, Latinos, Native Americans—stand up and proudly reclaim their roots while I just sank back ever deeper into my seat. All this excitement over ethnicity stemmed, I uneasily sensed, from a past in which *their* ancestors had been trampled upon by *my* ancestors, or at least by people who looked very much like them. In addition, it had begun to seem almost un-American not to have some sort of hyphen at hand, linking one to more venerable times and locales.

But the truth is, I was raised with none. We'd eaten ethnic foods in my childhood home, but these were all borrowed, like the pasties, or Cornish meat pies, my father had picked up from his fellow miners in Butte, Montana. If my mother had one rule, it was militant ecumenism in all manners of food and experience. "Try new things," she would say, meaning anything from sweetbreads to clams, with an emphasis on the "new."

As a child, I briefly nourished a craving for tradition and roots. I immersed myself in the works of Sir Walter Scott. I pretended to believe that the bagpipe was a musical instrument. I was fascinated to learn from a grandmother that we were descended from certain Highland clans and longed for a pleated skirt in one of their distinctive tartans.

But in *Ivanhoe*, it was the dark-eyed "Jewess" Rebecca I identified with, not the flaxen-haired bimbo Rowena. As for clans: Why not call them "tribes," those bands of half-clad peasants and warriors whose idea of cuisine was stuffed sheep gut washed down with whiskey? And then there was the sting of Disraeli's remark—which I came across in my early teens—to the effect that his ancestors had been leading orderly, literate lives when my ancestors were still rampaging through the Highlands daubing themselves with blue paint.

Motherhood put the screws on me, ethnicity-wise. I had hoped that by marrying a man of Eastern European Jewish ancestry I would acquire for my descendants the ethnic genes that my own forebears so sadly lacked. At one point, I even subjected the children to a seder of my own design, including a little talk about the flight from Egypt and its relevance to modern social issues. But the kids insisted on buttering their matzos and snickering through my talk. "Give me a break, Mom," the older one said. "You don't even believe in God."

After the tiny pagans had been put to bed, I sat down to brood over Elijah's wine. What had I been thinking? The kids knew that their Jewish grandparents were secular folks who didn't hold seders themselves. And if ethnicity eluded me, how could I expect it to take root in my children, who are not only Scottish English Irish, but Hungarian Polish Russian to boot?   8

But, then, on the fumes of Manischewitz, a great insight took form in my mind. It was true, as the kids said, that I didn't "believe in God." But this could be taken as something very different from an accusation—a reminder of a genuine heritage. My parents had not believed in God either, nor had my grandparents or any other progenitors going back to the great-great level. They had become disillusioned with Christianity generations ago—just as, on the in-law side, my children's other ancestors had shaken their Orthodox Judaism. This insight did not exactly furnish me with an "identity," but it was at least something to work with: We are the kind of people, I realized—whatever our distant ancestors' religions—who do *not* believe, who do not carry on traditions, who do not do things just because someone has done them before.   9

The epiphany went on: I recalled that my mother never introduced a procedure for cooking or cleaning by telling me, "Grandma did it this way." What did Grandma know, living in the days before vacuum cleaners and disposable toilet mops? In my parents' general view, new things were better than old, and the very fact that some ritual had been performed in the past was a good reason for abandoning it now. Because what was the past, as our forebears knew it? Nothing but poverty, superstition, and grief. "Think for yourself," Dad used to say. "Always ask why."   10

In fact, this may have been the ideal cultural heritage for my particular ethnic strain—bounced as it was from the Highlands of Scotland across the sea, out to the Rockies, down into the mines, and finally spewed out into high-tech, suburban America. What better philosophy, for a race of migrants, than "Think for yourself"? What better maxim, for a people whose whole world was rudely inverted every thirty years or so, than "Try new things"?   11

The more tradition-minded, the newly enthusiastic celebrants of Purim and Kwanzaa and Solstice, may see little point to survival if the survivors carry no cultural freight—religion, for example, or ethnic tradition. To which I would say that skepticism, curiosity, and wide-eyed ecumenical tolerance are also worthy elements of the human tradition and are at least as old as such notions as "Serbian" or "Croatian," "Scottish" or "Jewish." I make no claims for my personal line of progenitors except that they remained loyal to the values that may have   12 induced all of our ancestors, long, long ago, to climb down from the trees and make their way into the open plains.

A few weeks ago, I cleared my throat and asked the children, now mostly grown and fearsomely smart, whether they felt any stirrings of ethnic or religious identity, etc., which might have been, ahem, insufficiently nourished at home. "None," they said, adding firmly, "and the world would be a better place if nobody else did, either." My chest swelled with pride, as would my mother's, to know that the race of "none" marches on.

12

From Revising to Editing
Working with Peer Groups

Academic writing is a collaborative enterprise. By reading and commenting on your drafts, your peers can support your work as a writer. And you can support the work of your peers by reading their drafts with a critical but constructive eye.

In this chapter, we set out the differences between revising and editing, discuss the peer editing process in terms of the composition pyramid, present a model peer editing session, and then explain the writer's and reader's responsibilities through early drafts, later drafts, and final drafts, providing opportunities for you to practice peer response on three drafts of a student paper.

REVISING VERSUS EDITING

We make a distinction between revising and editing. By **revising**, we mean making changes to a paper to reflect new thinking or conceptualizing. If a reader finds that the real focus of your essay comes at the end of your draft, you need to revise the paper with this new focus in mind. Revising differs from **editing**, which involves minor changes to what will be the final draft of a paper—replacing a word here and there, correcting misspellings, or substituting dashes for commas to create emphasis, for example.

When you're reading a first or second draft, the niceties of style, spelling, and punctuation are not priorities. After all, if the writer had to change the focus of his or her argument, significant changes to words, phrases, and punctuation would be inevitable. Concentrating on editing errors early on, when the writer is still trying to develop an argument with evidence, organize information logically, and anticipate counterarguments, is inefficient and even counterproductive.

Here are some characteristics of revising and editing that can guide how you read your own writing and comment on the writing of others:

REVISING	EDITING
Treats writing as a work in progress	Treats writing as an almost-finished product
Focuses on new possibilities both within and beyond the text	Addresses obvious errors and deficiencies
Focuses on new questions or goals	Focuses on the draft and does not suggest new avenues for discussion
Considers both purpose and readers' needs	Considers grammar, punctuation, spelling, and style
Encourages further discovery	Polishes up the essay

Again, writing is a process, and revising is an integral part of that process. Your best writing will happen in the context of real readers responding to your drafts. Look at the acknowledgments in any academic book, and you will see many people credited with having improved the book through their comments on drafts and ideas. All academic writers rely on conversations with others to strengthen their work.

THE PEER EDITING PROCESS

We emphasize that the different stages of writing—early, later, and final— call for different work from both readers and writers because writers' needs vary with each successive draft. These stages correspond to what has been called the composition pyramid (Figure 12.1).* The composition

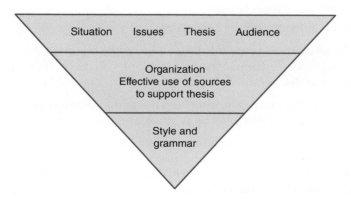

FIGURE 12.1   The Composition Pyramid

*Information from Susannah Brietz-Monta and Anthony Monta.

pyramid represents elements of writing that can help you decide what to pay attention to at different stages of writing.

1. The top of this inverted pyramid corresponds to the early stages of writing. At this point, members of the writing group should identify the situation the writer is responding to (for example, homelessness, inequality, or air pollution), the issue the writer has defined (for example, the economic versus the social costs of homelessness), the thesis or argument the writer advances, and the extent to which the writer addresses a given audience appropriately.

2. The middle portion of the pyramid corresponds to a later stage of the writing process, the point at which members of the group should move on to discuss the writer's organization and use of sources. Is the argument logically organized? Has the writer integrated quotations smoothly into the paper? Is the evidence relevant, recent, and credible?

3. Finally, the bottom of the pyramid corresponds to the final stages of drafting. As the writer's focus shifts to grammar and style, so should the group's. Questions to ask: Is this specific language appropriate to the intended audience? Has the writer presented the argument in ways that will compel readers—even those who disagree—to listen?

Steps in the Peer Editing Process

1. The writer distributes copies of the draft to each member of the writing group. (Ideally, the group should not exceed four students.)

2. The writer distributes a cover letter, setting an agenda for the group.

3. The members read the cover letter.

4. The writer then reads the draft aloud, while members follow along, underlining passages and making notes to prepare themselves to discuss the draft.

5. Members ask questions that help the writer identify concepts that need further elaboration or clarification.

6. Discussion focuses on the strengths and weaknesses of the draft appropriate to the stage of writing and the writer's concerns. (Even in the early stage, readers and the writer should sustain discussion for at least ten minutes before the next student takes a turn as writer.)

PEER GROUPS IN ACTION: A SAMPLE SESSION

Let's take a look at one writing group in action to see the potential of this approach to writing. One student, Rebecca Jegier, worked collaboratively with three other students—Jasmine, Michaela, and Kevin—on a paper about the purpose of education and the extent to which school reforms reflect what she refers to as "a growing culture of impatience." She explained to her group that she struggled to draw a parallel between what she sees as a worn-out factory model of education (students sitting in rows) and the story of Blockbuster, a once-successful movie rental business that failed to respond to customers' changing needs. She also felt that she still needed to sharpen her argument.

Rebecca:	I think we are expected to argue what we think the purpose of education should be and to place our argument in the larger context of how others have defined the purpose historically.
Jasmine:	I am still trying to decide what I think the purpose of education should be. I sort of think that education should prepare people for a job, but we also read that article—you know, the one that said we may not even know what jobs will be available in ten years. The author wrote that schools should prepare people to be creative, innovative, critical thinkers. That other essay explained that school should help people flourish. I haven't decided what that means.
Michaela:	I think the important thing we need to decide is the issue. I agree that schools don't really prepare us to be very creative or innovative. I guess that's the issue.

Rebecca restated her understanding of the assignment before giving Jasmine, Michaela, and Kevin a copy of her draft. This is a valuable starting point because a writer's interpretation of the writing assignment—the task, the purpose, and the audience—helps readers understand why she is taking a particular approach. If readers disagree with the writer's interpretation, they should discuss their differences before the writer shares the draft and determine an appropriate response to the assignment. Rebecca then read her paper aloud while her group members listened and wrote notes to indicate specific words, phrases, and ideas that they wanted to discuss.

AN ANNOTATED STUDENT DRAFT

Here we reprint the main part of Rebecca's draft, with annotations on passages that elicited comments from her peers. Following the draft, we present their discussion in more detail.

Jegier 1

Rebecca Jegier

Student-Centered Learning: Catering to Students' Impatience

In today's world of high-speed Internet and fast food, Americans have gotten used to receiving instant gratification and immediate results. If a Web site takes four seconds or longer to load, an average of one in four Internet users will get fed up with waiting and abandon the page ("Loading time," 2013). In a survey conducted by the Associated Press, the majority of Americans report losing patience after being kept waiting on the telephone for more than five minutes, and half of those surveyed reported that they have refused to return to a business because of long waits (AP, 2006). This paper is about two hundred times as long as the average tweet — how many teenage students would be willing to read it until the end? With the growing culture of impatience, it comes as no surprise that Americans today are frustrated with recent reforms in education and their lack of immediate results. It is also not a surprising issue that American children have trouble staying focused and engaged in today's standardized and "factory-based" education system driven by worksheets and mandated testing. This outdated system has created an environment that is completely contradictory to the interactive, personalized, and relevant world in which students spend most of their lives.

According to Dr. Martin Luther King Jr. (1947), "Intelligence plus character — that is the goal of true education. The complete education gives one not only power of concentration, but worthy objectives upon which to concentrate." In order for education in America to be "complete" and to reach its full potential of empowering students to concentrate and reach their goals, educators and school reformers might very well explore the issue of impatience. In some cases, such as investing in stocks, the unwillingness to be patient can cause people to make a poor trade-off between immediate, although mediocre, results or receiving something much better after a wait; in the example of the stock market, a larger return on investment usually comes with time. In other circumstances, however, impatience can be largely beneficial if it is handled correctly; successful businesses will improve as they make efforts to become more efficient and provide better customer service to those who do not want to wait.

Rebecca's group member, Kevin, says he likes the introduction and agrees with the point that we are all becoming impatient. But he worries that the introduction should state the purpose of education more directly since this is the assignment. Jasmine agrees.

Kevin and Michaela both tell Rebecca that they like this phrase, "the culture of impatience."

They all discuss whether or not this is the argument and if Rebecca could restate her key claim.

Rebecca provides one important way that Americans can think about the purpose of education and tries to connect this perspective to her own ideas about impatience.

She anticipates readers' different interpretations of impatience and whether impatience can also be a good thing.

1

2

Jegier 2

She goes on to explain that school reformers have been impatient, but their approach has been detrimental to learning.

School reformers' impatience belongs in the first category: detrimental and unproductive. Making quality reforms that will be be both effective and enduring is a long-term investment that must be carefully planned instead of hastily implemented. The expectation that coming out with new legislation will immediately change schools for the better is, to put it gently, ludicrous. And it is almost as ridiculous to think that small reforms will be effective when they don't change the underlying problem and allow the system to become relevant to current society.

Rebecca's peer group is intrigued by this analogy and even its relevance. However, Jasmine thinks Rebecca is beginning to lose the focus of her argument.

Take movies, for example. The first Blockbuster store opened in the 1980s, boasting convenience and the ability to customize movie selection to location. By September 2012, however, Blockbuster had filed for bankruptcy and had closed hundreds of stores in a sad attempt to get back on its feet. How did such a successful idea turn into a disaster? The problem with Blockbuster was that it made small improvements to its traditional, formerly successful model and disregarded consumers' changing desires and demands. Netflix had no problem stepping in to fill the gaps with new and innovative methods. In fact, Netflix had been patiently operating and steadily gaining market share for six years before Blockbuster finally came out with its own movie-by-mail service. Albert Einstein once defined insanity as "doing the same thing over and over again and expecting different results." Although schools monopolize the education business, it is still vital for them to adapt and conform to that which is relevant in today's world. Instead of continuing to take a "Blockbuster" attitude towards education — an arguably "insane" route — the U.S. education system needs to examine reforms that have happened in the past as well as reevaluate what its goals are for the children of tomorrow.

In the following three paragraphs, Rebecca shifts the focus from the present to the past, which is part of the assignment, to offer some historical context for contemporary efforts to define the purpose of education.

Ever since education began in America with one-room schoolhouses in the nineteenth century, schools have constantly been adapting to meet the needs of the students and those of the country depending on the time period (Tyack, 2007). As the goals of the country have changed, so have the schools. Initially, Thomas

Jegier 3

Jefferson and Noah Webster wanted children to emerge from school as functioning, self-governing citizens who could contribute to the democracy in a new fragile republic. Later, goals were revised due to changes or events in the world such as immigration, the space race, and the *Brown v. Board of Education* decision. When immigrants began to come to America in the late 1800s, the school system had to adapt to find a way to assimilate immigrants into the established education system. In the 1950s when the Supreme Court delivered its *Brown v. Board of Education* decision, schools had to adapt to desegregation and address the effects of opening their doors to those who formerly had no access to education. In 1957, when the Soviets launched the first satellite and effectively "won" the space race, the United States immediately shifted its focus to math and science classes. These reforms were specific to the time, as well as necessary to the relevant situations of that society, and were eventually effective even though they were not seen in this way at first.

In 1983, the National Commission on Excellence in Education published "A Nation at Risk," a report that pointed out flaws in the U.S. education system — flaws that the nation is still addressing today. It recommended that we should raise the standards of high school graduation requirements and college admissions requirements, as well as increase teacher salaries and raise standards for those who wish to teach, in addition to many other suggestions for reform (National Commission on Excellence in Education, 1983). Since this landmark report was produced, school reformers have repeatedly tried to confront the system head-on.

President George W. Bush's No Child Left Behind Act of 2001 (NCLB) is a commonly cited and criticized reform that requires states to assess all students at select grade levels in order for schools to receive federal funding. Intended to increase the quality of education for everyone by requiring schools to improve their performance, NCLB is limited in that it does not address the root of the problem and places the focus on achievement instead of the teaching and learning process. Although some improvement in test scores has

6

7

Rebecca's group wonders about the point Rebecca makes here, one that implicitly connects to her idea that impatience can be a detriment. This is something Michaela wants Rebecca to say more about.

been reported since its implementation (Dee & Jacob, 2011), frustration with this act has been growing because the tests and the standards sometimes contradict each other and are very often not aligned. NCLB represents an attempt to provide a simple solution for a complex problem. Modern America's "get-rich-quick" attitude toward changes in general and school reforms in particular is a fallacy that must be remedied in order to promote effective reforms in the education system. Although Americans today tend to get frustrated after fifteen minutes of standing in line (AP, 2006), patience is necessary to develop quality reforms that will last in the long term.

Rebecca helps readers think of impatience as a positive trait that she believes educators overlook. Michaela and Kevin also think Rebecca needs to connect this point to what she says about the "culture of impatience."

In contrast to the detrimental effects of citizens' and reformers' impatience with the current state of education, the "impatience" of our children in schools can actually be beneficial to the American education system, if responded to in the correct way. I place the word "impatience" in quotation marks because the pejorative quality of this word does not fully express what is going on in students' minds when they are categorized in this way by teachers, parents, or doctors. The underlying principle lies in their upbringing; kids are used to alleviating their natural curiosity through googling their questions or by texting a more knowledgeable friend who can respond within the hour (if not within the minute!). There is nothing inherently wrong with wanting to receive instant answers and quick results, especially when today's search engines and mobile apps can easily oblige. Similar to the way businesses constantly strive for better customer service, it is the responsibility of the school system to tailor education to its "impatient" (read: curious) students in relevant and timely ways.

Although they agree with this point, Rebecca's group is not sure how this connects with her argument about impatience.

Every child has unique talents and skills that are apparent at very early ages. In the 1980s, Harvard psychologist Howard Gardner proposed the theory of multiple intelligences (MI), which argues that intelligence should not be limited to the traditional "school smarts" that can be measured by Binet's IQ test or by the SAT (Gardner, 1987). In addition to the linguistic and logical-mathematical intelligences that are targeted in most school settings, Gardner

8

9

Jegier 5

proposes that people can be intelligent in other distinct ways. He came up with eight intelligences, including spatial, bodily-kinesthetic, musical, interpersonal, intrapersonal, and naturalist. Besides having different intelligences, students are unique because of their different learning styles (for example, one student might be a visual learner while another learns better from listening to a lecture) and the varying paces which they learn and retain material (Christensen, Horn & Johnson, 2008). This leads us to the question: if all students have different intelligences and learn in different ways, what reasoning do we have to support that standardizing their education would be an effective teaching method for all of them? Is providing the exact same instruction to all students fair, even if such a cookie-cutter method of teaching caters only to those who are "intelligent" in the linguistic and logical-mathematical sense? If the goal is to educate every student, standardization is not an effective way to do it.

Rebecca's group begins with a brief discussion of her introduction and then turns to Rebecca's argument. They ask questions and offer some reflections that they hoped would guide Rebecca toward making a more explicit claim about school reform.

Kevin: I really like your introduction and agree with the idea that we live in a world where we expect instant gratification. I know I get pretty impatient when I have to wait for anything.

Michaela: And you use a great phrase, "a culture of impatience," to describe the problem.

Jasmine: Yes. But isn't the paper supposed to be about the purpose of education? You eventually connect the idea of impatience to the purpose of education, you know, to respond to a generation of students like us who have been brought up on technology. School isn't very responsive to the way we learn. Isn't that what you are arguing?

Rebecca: Okay, I see what you are saying. But I wanted to write an introduction that would capture your attention with something relevant. I'll have to think about that.

Michaela: You do make your argument at the end of the first
            paragraph. Like Jasmine said, you are arguing that schools
            need to be more responsive to kids' needs, who they are, and
            how they learn. I know you are not saying it that way, but is
            that what you mean to say?
Rebecca: I think so, yes.
Kevin: Could you say that?

Kevin begins with a supportive comment that initiates a more specific conversation about the way Rebecca frames her ideas with the phrase, "a culture of impatience." However, Jasmine asks a pointed question that challenges Rebecca and the others in the group to think about the assignment and the role that an introduction should play. In particular, everyone seems to agree that Rebecca's key claim centers on school's lack of responsiveness to a new generation of students who tend to be impatient. The way that Rebecca states this is different from the way Jasmine and Michaela phrase the argument, and Kevin urges her to restate her claim in keeping with their interpretation. In the course of this conversation, then, peer group members provide support, but also question, even challenge, the way that Rebecca frames her argument. Importantly, the questions and advice are specific enough for Rebecca to use what they suggest to change her approach to writing about the purpose of education. Can or should she lead up to her claim with a story that does not directly address the purpose of education? And should she rephrase her claim? If Rebecca took their advice, this would mean revising an evaluative claim that schools are based on a worn-out factory model of education to a policy-driven claim about what school reform should require.

Group members also extended the conversation to helping Rebecca connect the different ideas that she introduces in her paper: school reforms as a negative example of impatience, the comparison she makes to corporations that fail to recognize "a culture of impatience," and recent research on individual learning styles.

Jasmine: So now I get what you are saying about impatience and
            the purpose of school, but now you want to compare this
            to what happened to Blockbuster. The last sentence of your
            paragraph is good, but it takes you a while to make this
            point. In the paragraph above it, you say "Take movies, for
            example. The first Blockbuster store opened in the 1980s,
            boasting convenience and the ability to customize movie
            selection to location." But I think you need to connect your
            two points earlier. Otherwise, I think you are losing focus by
            introducing the example of Blockbuster.
Michaela: I think the same thing happens when you start to talk
            about No Child Left Behind. Your last sentence talks about
            "patience." But you start by summarizing, not making clear
            that there is a connection here.

Kevin (*interrupting*):	Yeah, I think you keep summarizing different ideas and I get lost in how you are connecting everything.
Michaela:	One way to handle this problem is to say something that connects all the dots and not leave your main points until the end of each paragraph. The same thing happens again when you introduce the idea of learning styles.
Rebecca:	Wow, okay. That's a lot. I am going to have to think about all of this.

Rebecca's draft reflects her first attempt to get her ideas down. It's fine for a first draft to explore ideas. When writers formulate a working thesis (or when they fail to do so), readers in a peer group can offer support, noting strengths or pointing to places of greatest interest to sustain the writer's energy for writing. The more specific the advice, the better the writer will be able to translate that advice into action. Rebecca's group helped her generate a plan for taking some next steps by pointing out how she could define the issue and connect different parts of her paper: " . . . say something that connects all the dots and not leave your main points until the end of each paragraph."

A peer group can also ask questions to help a writer set new goals, so that revision is really a process of reenvisioning or reseeing the key concepts in the writer's draft. As a reader, it is useful to paraphrase particular parts of the draft, so that the writer can hear how you have understood what he or she is trying to say. This is what Michaela did when she explained in a questioning sort of way: "You are arguing that schools need to be more responsive to kids' needs, who they are, and how they learn. I know you are not saying it that way, but is that what you mean to say?"

WORKING WITH EARLY DRAFTS

■ Understand the Writer's Responsibilities

When you present an early draft of your essay to your writing group, you want the group to focus on top-level pyramid concerns—situation, issue, thesis, and audience. You should explain this and any other concerns you have in a cover letter. Use the template in Figure 12.2 as a model for what needs explaining in the letter to your readers.

During the session, it's important to be open to suggestions. Although you don't have to incorporate every suggestion your group makes when you revise your draft, be sure you at least understand the members' comments and concerns. If you don't understand what the members are saying about your draft, ask them to clarify or give you an example.

Finally, if you decide not to take someone's suggestion, have a good reason for doing so. If a suggested change means you won't be addressing the terms of the assignment, for example, it's fine to say no.

---

1. What is your question (or assignment)?
2. What is the issue motivating you to write?
3. How have published writers addressed the issue you discuss?
4. What is your working thesis?
5. Who is your audience, and how do you want them to respond?
6. What do you think is working best?
7. What specific aspect of the essay are you least satisfied with at this time?
8. What kind of feedback do you especially want today?

FIGURE 12.2 The Writer's Cover Letter: Early Drafts

■ Understand the Reader's Responsibilities

Your task as a reader is to follow along as the early draft is read, paying special attention to concerns the writer identifies in the cover letter and focusing on the top of the pyramid: situation, issue, thesis, and audience. Take notes directly on the draft, circling or underlining sections you have questions about, so that you can refer to them specifically in the discussion.

When it's your turn to talk, have a conversation about your reactions to the draft—where the draft amused, confused, or persuaded you, for example. Don't just jump in and start telling the writer what he or she should be doing in the paper. Your role as a reader is to give the writer a live audience: Your responses can help the writer decide what parts of the paper are working and what parts need serious revision. There are times, however, when you should play the role of *deferring reader*, putting off certain comments. You don't want to overwhelm the writer with problems no matter how many questions the essay raises.

Offer both positive and negative remarks. Start by pointing out what is working well in the paper, so the writer knows where he or she is on the right track. This also leaves the writer more open to constructive criticism. But don't shy away from telling the writer what should be working better. It's your job as a reader to offer honest and specific responses to the draft, so the writer can develop it into an effective piece of writing. Figure 12.3 lists key questions you should ask as a reader of an early draft.

1. Are the questions and issues that motivate the writer clear?
2. Has the writer effectively described the conversation that published writers are engaged in?
3. What is at issue?
4. What is the writer's thesis?
5. Is the writer addressing the audience's concerns effectively?
6. What passages of the draft are most effective?
7. What passages of the draft are least effective?

FIGURE 12.3   A Reader's Questions: Early Drafts

■ Analyze an Early Draft

Keep these questions in mind as you read the following excerpt from a student's early draft. After reading a number of scholarly articles on the Civil Rights Movement, Tasha Taylor decided to address what she sees as the difference between scholars' understanding of the movement and more popular treatments in textbooks and photographs. She also tries to tie in the larger question of historical memory to her analysis of southern blacks' struggle for equality—what people remember about the past and what they forget. In fact, she begins her essay with a quotation she believes summarizes what she wants to argue ("The struggle of man against power is the struggle of memory against forgetting").

As you read Taylor's essay, take detailed notes, and underline passages that concern you. Then write a paragraph or two explaining what she could do to strengthen the draft. Keep in mind that this is an early draft, so focus on the top level of the pyramid: the situation or assignment, the issue, the thesis, and the audience.

Taylor 1

Tasha Taylor
Professor Winters
English 111
October 23, 20—

Memory through Photography

The struggle of man against power is the struggle of memory against forgetting.

—Milan Kundera

1

Ask the average American what the key components of the civil rights movement are, and most people will probably recall Martin Luther King Jr. speaking of a dream in front of the Lincoln Memorial, Rosa Parks riding a bus, a few court decisions, and perhaps a photograph of Elizabeth Eckford cowering before an angry mob in front of Central High School in Little Rock. Few people are aware A. Philip Randolph planned the march on Washington. Few could describe Rosa Parks's connection to the civil rights movement (for example, the fact that she had been a member of the NAACP since 1943) before her legendary refusal to give up her seat in December 1955, which led to the Montgomery Bus Boycott. Few recognize the years of struggle that existed between the *Brown v. Board of Education* decision and the actual desegregation of schools. Few consider the fate of Elizabeth Eckford after federal troops were sent to protect her and the other members of the Little Rock Nine had left Central High or the months of abuse (physical and emotional) that they endured in the name of integration. What most people know is limited to textbooks they read in school or the captions under photographs that describe where a particular event occurred.

2

Why is it that textbooks exclusively feature the stories of larger than life figures like Martin Luther King? Why is it that we remember things the way we do? Historical events "have little meaning without human interpretation, without our speaking about them within the contexts of our lives and our culture, without giving them names and meanings" (Kolker xix). Each person experiencing the exact same event will carry a different memory from that event. Trying to decipher what memories reveal about each person is a fascinating yet difficult endeavor, because each retelling of a memory and each additional memory alters existing ones.

3

The story that photographs and textbooks tell us does not even begin to describe the depth of the movement or the thousands who risked their lives and the lives of their families to make equality a reality. Embracing this selective memory as a nation prevents understanding and acknowledgment of the harsh reality of other images from the civil rights movement (demonstrators being plowed down by fire hoses, beatings, and the charred bodies of bombing victims) which are key aspects of understanding who we are as a society. The question therefore is why. Why is it that textbook writers and publishers have allowed so much of this history to be skewed and forgotten? How can it be that barely 50 years after these events so many have been forgotten or diluted?

Reading as a Writer

1. What is working well in Taylor's draft?
2. What is Taylor's thesis or argument?
3. To what extent does she connect her analysis of the civil rights movement and historical memory?
4. What parts of her analysis could Taylor explain further? (What do you still need to know?)
5. What would you suggest Taylor do next?

WORKING WITH LATER DRAFTS

■ Understand the Writer's Responsibilities

At a later stage, after you've had the opportunity to take readers' suggestions and do further research, you should be able to state your thesis more definitively than you did in your earlier draft. You also should be able to support your thesis with evidence, anticipating possible counterarguments. Ideally, your readers will still provide constructive criticism, offering their support, as in the first draft, but they will also question and challenge more than before.

Here, too, you want to help readers focus on your main concerns, which you should explain in a cover letter. You may still need to work on one or two top-level pyramid concerns, but your focus will likely be midlevel concerns—organization and the effective use of sources. Use the list of questions in Figure 12.4 to help you write your cover letter.

---

1. What is your research question?

2. What is the issue motivating you to write?

3. What is your thesis?

4. How do you go about identifying a gap in readers' knowledge, modifying other's ideas, or trying to correct readers' misunderstandings?

5. To what extent do you distinguish your argument from the information you quote, summarize, or paraphrase from the sources you have read?

6. To what extent have you organized your ideas in ways that will help readers follow the logic of your argument?

7. To what extent have you anticipated potential counterarguments to your thesis?

8. What do you think is working best?

9. What specific aspect of the essay are you least satisfied with at this time?

FIGURE 12.4   The Writer's Cover Letter: Later Drafts

■ Understand the Reader's Responsibilities

In a later draft, your focus as a reader should be on midlevel concerns in the composition pyramid: places in the writer's text that are confusing, that require better transitions, or that could use sources more effectively. You can challenge writers at this stage of the composing process, perhaps playing the role of *naive reader*, suggesting places in the draft where the writer has left something out or isn't clear. The naive reader's comments tend to take the form of questions: "Do you mean to suggest that everyone who learns to write well succeeds in life? What kind of success are you talking about?" Closely related to the naive reader is the *devil's advocate reader*. This reader's comments also challenge the writer, often taking the form of a question like this: "But why couldn't this be attributed to the effects of socialization rather than heredity?" Figure 12.5 offers questions for reading later drafts.

■ Analyze a Later Draft

Now read the excerpt from Taylor's second draft (pp. 360–62). You will see that she begins with her discussion of historical memory. She also has included an analysis of a book of photographs that Nobel Prize–winning author Toni Morrison compiled. Take notes as you read the draft and write a paragraph in which you describe what you see as some of the strengths of what Taylor has written and what she can do to make other elements stronger. In particular, focus on the middle level of the composition pyramid—on organization and the effective use of sources and evidence to support her thesis.

---

1. To what extent is it clear what questions and issues motivate the writer?

2. What is the writer's thesis?

3. How effectively does the writer establish the conversation—identify a gap in people's knowledge, attempt to modify an existing argument, or try to correct some misunderstanding?

4. How effectively does the writer distinguish between his or her ideas and the ideas he or she summarizes, paraphrases, or quotes?

5. How well does the writer help you follow the logic of his or her argument?

6. To what extent are you persuaded by the writer's argument?

7. To what extent does the writer anticipate possible counterarguments?

8. To what extent does the writer make clear how he or she wants readers to respond?

9. What do you think is working best? Explain by pointing to specific passages in the writer's draft.

10. What specific aspect of the draft is least effective? Explain by pointing to a specific passage in the writer's draft.

FIGURE 12.5   A Reader's Questions: Later Drafts

Taylor 1

Tasha Taylor
Professor Winters
English 111
November 14, 20—

Memory through Photography

> The struggle of man against power is the struggle of
> memory against forgetting.
>
> —Milan Kundera

Memory is such an integral part of what it is to be human, yet
is something so often taken for granted: People assume that their
memories are accurate to protect themselves from the harsh realities
of the atrocities committed by ordinary people. Even the pictures
used to represent the much-celebrated civil rights movement give
us a false sense of security and innocence. For example, the Ku Klux
Klan is most often depicted by covered faces and burning crosses; the
masks allow us to remove ourselves from responsibility. Few could
describe Rosa Parks's connection to the civil rights movement (for
example, the fact that she had been a member of the NAACP since
1943) before her legendary refusal to give up her seat in December
1955, which led to the Montgomery Bus Boycott. Few recognize
the years of struggle that existed between the *Brown v. Board of
Education* decision and the actual desegregation of schools. Few
consider the fate of Elizabeth Eckford after federal troops were sent
to protect her and the other members of the Little Rock Nine had left
Central High or the months of abuse (physical and emotional) that
they endured in the name of integration. What most people know
is limited to textbooks they read in school or the captions under
photographs that describe where a particular event occurred.

It is important, therefore, to analyze what is remembered and
even more importantly to recognize what is forgotten: to question
why it is that it is forgotten, what that says about society today,
how far it has come and how much it has unwittingly fallen back into
old patterns such as prejudice and ignorance. The discrepancies in
cultural memory are due more to a society's desire to remember itself
in the best light and protect itself from the reality of its brutality
and responsibility. Such selective memory only temporarily heals the
wounds of society; lack of awareness does not cause healing.

1

2

Taylor 2

Although there have been many recent moves to increase awareness, they are tainted by unavoidable biases and therefore continue to perpetuate a distorted memory.

Images play a central role in the formation of cultural memory because people can point to photographs and claim them as concrete evidence: "Images entrance us because they provide a powerful illusion of owning reality. If we can photograph reality or paint or copy it, we have exercised an important kind of power" (Kolker 3). A picture of black and white children sitting at a table together is used to reinforce the cultural perception that the problems of racism are over, that it has all been fixed.

In her book *Remember*, Toni Morrison strives to revitalize the memory of school integration through photographs. The book is dedicated to Denise McNair, Carole Robertson, Addie Mae Collins, and Cynthia Wesley, the four girls killed in the 16th Street Baptist Church bombing in 1963. Morrison writes, "Things are better now. Much, much better. But remember why and please remember us" (Morrison 72). The pictures are of black and white children happily eating together, solemnly saluting the flag together, and holding hands. The photographs of the four murdered girls show them peacefully and innocently smiling as if everything really is better now. In reality, according to the United States Bureau of Alcohol, Tobacco and Firearms, between 1995 and 1997 there were 162 incidents of arson or bombing in African American houses of worship. There are a few images of people protesting integration, but they are also consistent with the cultural memory (protesters are shown simply holding signs and yelling, not beating and killing innocent children). Finally, the captions are written in a child's voice. Yet it is not a child's voice at all it is merely a top down view of children that serves to perpetuate a distorted cultural memory.

The photographs used to suggest how things are much, much better now are misleading. For example, the last photograph is of a black girl and a white girl holding hands through a bus window, which was transporting them to an integrated school. The caption reads: "Anything can happen. Anything at all. See?" (71). It is a very powerful image of how the evil of Jim Crow and segregation exists in a distant past and the nation has come together and healed. However, Morrison neglects to point out that the picture

3

4

5

Taylor 3

was taken in Boston, Massachusetts, not the deep south, the heart of racism. Children holding hands in Boston is much less significant than if they were in Birmingham where that action would be concrete evidence of how far we as a nation have come.

Morrison also glorifies Martin Luther King Jr. and Rosa Parks, pointing to them as epitomizing the movement. Unfortunately, she perpetuates the story that one needs to be special or somehow larger than life to affect change. Paul Rogat Loeb writes in *Soul of a Citizen*:

> Once we enshrine our heroes, it becomes hard for mere mortals to measure up in our eyes . . . in our collective amnesia we lose the mechanisms through which grassroots social movements of the past successfully shifted public sentiment and challenged entrenched institutional power. Equally lost are the means by which their participants managed to keep on, sustaining their hope and eventually prevailing in circumstances at least as difficult as those we face today. (Loeb 36, 38)

Placing a select few on pedestals and claiming them as next to divine heroes of the movement does society a disservice; people fail to realize that ordinary people can serve as agents of change.

Morrison's book ignores the thousands of ordinary people who risked their lives for the cause to bring about equality. The caption besides the picture of Rosa Parks in *Remember* reads "because if I ever feel helpless or lonely I just have to remember that all it takes is one person" (Morrison 62). Ironically, Morrison gives credit for the Montgomery Bus Boycott to one person, ignoring the months of planning and dozens of planners involved. Even the photograph presents Rosa Parks in a position of power. It is a low-angle shot up at Parks that makes her appear larger than life and authoritative. The photographs of Martin Luther King Jr. also further the impression of power with a close up shot of his face as he stands above thousands of participants in the March on Washington. Although these photographs were selected to perpetuate the hero illusion, it is more inspiring to remember the ordinary people who took a stand and were able to accomplish extraordinary feats because of their dedication and persistence rather than glorify extraordinary people who were destined for greatness.

6

7

Reading as a Writer

1. What is Taylor's thesis or argument?
2. How well do her transitions help you follow the argument's logic?
3. How effectively does she distinguish between her ideas and the ideas she summarizes, paraphrases, or quotes?
4. To what extent are you persuaded by her argument?
5. What should Taylor do next?

WORKING WITH FINAL DRAFTS

■ Understand the Writer's Responsibilities

Your final draft should require editing, not revising. At this stage, readers should focus on errors in style and grammar in the text, not on the substance of your work. Here, too, indicate your main concerns in a cover letter (Figure 12.6).

---

1. What is your unique perspective on your issue?
2. To what extent do the words and phrases you use reflect who you believe your readers are?
3. Does your style of citation reflect accepted conventions for academic writing?
4. What do you think is working best?
5. What specific aspect of the essay are you least satisfied with at this time?

FIGURE 12.6   The Writer's Cover Letter: Final Drafts

■ Understand the Reader's Responsibilities

Once a writer's ideas are developed and in place, readers should turn their attention to the bottom level of the composition pyramid, to matters of style and grammar. At this stage, details are important: Is this the best word to use? Would this sentence be easier to follow if it were broken into two sentences? Which spelling is correct — *Freedman* or *Friedman*? Are citations handled consistently? Should this question mark precede or follow the quotation mark? The *grammatically correct reader* evaluates and makes judgments about the writer's work. This reader may simply indicate with a mark of some sort that there's a problem in a sentence or paragraph. Figure 12.7 is a list of questions a reader should ask of a final draft.

1. How does the writer go about contributing a unique perspective on the issue?
2. To what extent does the writer use words and phrases that are appropriate for the intended audience?
3. To what extent does the style of citation reflect accepted conventions for academic writing?
4. What do you think is working best?
5. What specific aspect of the essay are you least satisfied with at this time?

FIGURE 12.7 A Reader's Questions: Final Drafts

■ Analyze a Near-Final Draft

Now read Taylor's near-final draft and write a paragraph detailing what she can do to strengthen it. Again, you will see that Taylor has made substantial changes. She compares Morrison's book of photographs to a Spike Lee documentary that she watched with her class. As you read the essay, focus on the bottom level of the composition pyramid: Does the writer use appropriate language? Does she adhere to appropriate conventions for using and citing sources? (See the Appendix for information on MLA and APA formats.)

Taylor 1

Tasha Taylor
Professor Winters
English 111
December 5, 20—

Memory through Photography

Memory is such an integral part of what it is to be human, yet it is something so often taken for granted: people assume that their memories are accurate to protect themselves from the harsh realities of the atrocities committed by ordinary people. Even the pictures used to represent the much-celebrated civil rights movement give us a false sense of security and innocence. For example, the Ku Klux Klan is most often depicted by covered faces and burning crosses; the masks allow us to remove ourselves from responsibility. Few could describe Rosa Parks's connection to the civil

Taylor 2

rights movement before her legendary refusal to give up her seat in December 1955, which led to the Montgomery Bus Boycott (for example, the fact that she had been a member of the NAACP since 1943). Few recognize the years of struggle that existed between the 1954 *Brown v. Board of Education* decision and the actual desegregation of schools. Few consider the fate of Elizabeth Eckford after the federal troops sent to protect her and the other members of the Little Rock Nine had left Central High or the months of abuse (physical and emotional) that they endured in the name of integration. What most people know is limited to the textbooks they read in school or the captions under photographs that describe where a particular event occurred.

It is important, then, to analyze what is remembered, and even more important to recognize what is forgotten: to question why it is that it is forgotten, what that says about society today, how far it has come and how much it has unwittingly fallen back into old patterns of prejudice and ignorance. The discrepancies in cultural memory are due more to society's desire to remember itself in the best light and protect itself from the reality of its brutality and responsibility. Such selective memory only temporarily heals the wounds of society; lack of awareness does not cause healing. Although there have been many recent moves to increase awareness, they are tainted by unavoidable biases and therefore continue to perpetuate a distorted memory.

Images play a central role in the formation of cultural memory because people can point to photographs and claim them as concrete evidence: "Images entrance us because they provide a powerful illusion of owning reality. If we can photograph reality or paint or copy it, we have exercised an important kind of power" (Kolker 3). A picture of black and white children sitting at a table together is used to reinforce the cultural perception that the problems of racism are over, that they have all been fixed.

In her book *Remember*, Toni Morrison strives to revitalize the memory of school integration through photographs. The book is dedicated to Denise McNair, Carole Robertson, Addie Mae Collins, and Cynthia Wesley, the four girls killed in the 16th Street Baptist Church bombing in 1963. Morrison writes: "Things are better now. Much, much better. But remember why and please remember us" (72).

Taylor 3

The pictures are of black and white children happily eating together, solemnly saluting the flag together, and holding hands. The photographs of the four murdered girls show them peacefully and innocently smiling as if everything really is better now. In reality, according to the United States Bureau of Alcohol, Tobacco and Firearms, between 1995 and 1997 there were 162 incidents of arson or bombing in African American houses of worship. There are a few images of people protesting integration, but they are also consistent with the cultural memory (protesters are shown simply holding signs and yelling, not beating and killing innocent children). Finally, the captions are written in a child's voice. Yet it is not a child's voice at all; it is merely a top-down view of children that serves to perpetuate a distorted cultural memory.

The photographs used to suggest how things are much, much better now are misleading. For example, the last photograph, taken through a bus window, is of a black girl and a white girl holding hands; the bus was transporting them to an integrated school. The caption reads: "Anything can happen. Anything at all. See?" (Morrison 71). It is a very powerful image of how the evil of Jim Crow and segregation exists in a distant past and the nation has come together and healed. However, Morrison neglects to point out that the picture was taken in Boston, not in the Deep South, the heart of racism. Children holding hands in Boston is much less significant than if they were in Birmingham, where that action would be concrete evidence of how far we as a nation have come.

Morrison also glorifies Martin Luther King Jr. and Rosa Parks, pointing to them as epitomizing the movement. Unfortunately, she perpetuates the story that one needs to be special or somehow larger than life to effect change. Paul Rogat Loeb writes in *Soul of a Citizen*:

> Once we enshrine our heroes, it becomes hard for mere mortals to measure up in our eyes. . . . In our collective amnesia we lose the mechanisms through which grassroots social movements of the past successfully shifted public sentiment and challenged entrenched institutional power.

5

6

Taylor 4

Equally lost are the means by which their participants
managed to keep on, sustaining their hope and eventually
prevailing in circumstances at least as difficult as those we
face today. (36, 38)

Placing a select few on pedestals and claiming them as
next-to-divine heroes of the movement does society a disservice;
people fail to realize that ordinary people can serve as agents
of change.

Morrison's book ignores the thousands of ordinary people
who risked their lives for the cause to bring about equality. The
caption beside the picture of Rosa Parks in *Remember* reads "Because
if I ever feel helpless or lonely I just have to remember that all it
takes is one person" (Morrison 62). Ironically, Morrison gives credit
for the Montgomery Bus Boycott to one person, ignoring the months
of planning that involved dozens of planners. Even the photograph
presents Rosa Parks in a position of power. It is a low-angle shot up
at Parks that makes her appear larger than life and authoritative. The
photographs of Martin Luther King Jr. also further the impression of
power with a close-up shot of his face as he stands above thousands
of participants in the March on Washington. Although these
photographs were selected to perpetuate the hero illusion, it is more
inspiring to remember the ordinary people who took a stand and were
able to accomplish extraordinary feats because of their dedication
and persistence rather than to glorify extraordinary people who were
destined for greatness.

In contrast, Spike Lee's 1998 documentary titled *4 Little Girls*
is a stirring depiction of the lives and deaths of the girls who died in
the 1963 16th Street Baptist Church bombing. In his film, Spike Lee
looks behind what some would call "societal amnesia" to disclose
the harsh realities of the civil rights movement. Lee interviews
family members and friends of the murdered girls, revealing the
pain and anger that they grapple with more than forty years after
the tragedy. Lee includes not only images of the bombed church but
also the charred and nearly unrecognizable bodies of the murdered
girls. These disturbing images underscore the reality of their deaths
without appearing sensationalist. The film does an exceptional job

7

8

Taylor 5

of reminding the viewer of the suffering and mindless hate that were prevalent during the civil rights movement.

However, the documentary is also biased. For instance, the girls were not little; they were fourteen, not really little girls. Lee chose to describe them as little to elicit emotion and sympathy for their tragic deaths. They were victims. They had not marched through the streets demanding equality; instead, Denise McNair, Carole Robertson, Addie Mae Collins, and Cynthia Wesley were simply attending Sunday school and were ruthlessly murdered. Victimizing Denise, Carole, Addie Mae, and Cynthia is not detrimental to the cultural memory in and of itself. The problem is that the victimization of the four girls is expanded to encompass the entire black community, undermining the power and achievement of the average black citizen. We need to remember the people who struggled to gain employment for blacks in the labor movement of the 1940s and 1950s that initiated the civil rights movement.

One can argue that despite the presence of misleading images in Spike Lee's film and Toni Morrison's book, at least some of the story is preserved. Still, it is easy to fall victim to the cliché: Those who do not remember history are doomed to repeat it. Just because a portion of the story is remembered, it does not mean that society is immune to falling back into its old habits. This cultural amnesia not only perpetuates the injustices of the time but leaves open the possibility that these atrocities can occur again. If people believe the government can simply grant black equality, then they may believe that it can also take it away. In essence memory is about power: "The struggle of man against power is the struggle of memory against forgetting" (Kundera). Those who are remembered hold power over the forgotten. Their legacy is lost and so is their ability to inspire future generations through their memory.

9

10

Taylor 6

Works Cited

4 Little Girls. Directed by Spike Lee, 40 Acres and A Mule Filmworks, 1997.

Kolker, Robert. *Film, Form, and Culture*. McGraw Hill, 1998.

Kundera, Milan. *The Book of Laughter and Forgetting*. Translated by Michael Henry Heim, Penguin Books, 1981.

Loeb, Paul Rogat. *Soul of a Citizen: Living with Conviction in a Cynical Time*. St. Martin's Griffin, 1999.

Morrison, Toni. *Remember: The Journey to School Integration*. Houghton Mifflin, 2004.

United States. Bureau of Alcohol, Tobacco and Firearms. *Arson and Explosives Incidents Report 1994*. US Dept. of the Treasury, 1995.

Reading as a Writer

1. What would you say is Taylor's argument?
2. To what extent does she provide transitions to help you understand how her analysis supports her argument?
3. To what extent does she integrate quotations appropriately into the text of her argument?
4. To what extent does the style of citation reflect accepted conventions for academic writing?
5. If Taylor had more time to revise, what would you suggest she do?

FURTHER SUGGESTIONS FOR PEER EDITING GROUPS

Monitoring your own writing group can help ensure that the group is both providing and receiving the kinds of responses the members need. Here is a list of questions you might ask of one another after a session:

- What topics were discussed?
- Were most questions and comments directed at the level of ideas? Structure? Language?
- Were topics always brought up with a question or a comment?

- Who initiated talk more frequently—the writer or the readers?
- What roles did different group members play?
- Did each author open with specific questions or concerns?
- Did the readers begin by giving specific reactions?

After answering these questions, identify two things that are working well in your group. Then identify two things that you could improve. How would you go about making those improvements?

When we asked our students what they thought contributed to effective conversation in their writing groups, here is what they told us:

- honest and spontaneous expression
- free interaction among members
- high levels of personal involvement
- members' commitment to insight and change
- the sense that self-disclosure is safe and highly valued
- members' willingness to take responsibility for the group's effectiveness
- members' belief that the group is important
- members' belief that they are primary agents of help for one another
- members' focus on communication within the group over other discussions

Other Methods of Inquiry
Interviews and Focus Groups

Sometimes to advance your argument you may need to do original research. By **original research**, we mean using primary sources of evidence you gather yourself. (Another common term for this type of investigation is *field research*.) Remember that primary sources of evidence include firsthand or eyewitness accounts like those found in letters or newspapers, or in research reports in which the researcher explains his or her impressions of a particular phenomenon—for example, gender relations in classroom interactions. (In contrast, a secondary source is an analysis of information contained in primary sources.)

The type of original research we discuss in this chapter relies on people—interviewees and members of focus groups—as primary sources of information. To inquire into gender dynamics in college science classrooms, then, you might conduct interviews with female students to understand their perceptions of how gender affects teaching. Or you might convene a focus group to put a variety of perspectives into play on questions about gendered teaching practices. The pages that follow present strategies for conducting interviews and setting up focus groups that can generate multiple responses to your research questions.

When you conduct research, keep in mind that you are not setting out to prove anything; instead, the process of inquiry will enable you to answer the questions *you* ask, address problems, and move readers to rethink their positions. Good critical readers know that the arguments they produce as writers are influenced by what they choose to discuss and how they construe the evidence they provide.

Although there is really no way to avoid the limitations of writing from one point of view, writers can provide readers with multiple sources of information so that they can make their own judgments about what to believe or not believe. In fact, this is the argument we make on page 371 in studying inequities in education. Relying on a single source of data will inevitably limit your field of vision. Multiple sources of information add complexity and texture to your analysis, conveying to readers the thoroughness of your approach.

WHY DO ORIGINAL RESEARCH?

We can think of four reasons (all of which overlap to some extent) why you might do original research for a writing class.

To increase your ability to read critically. When you do original research, you learn, at a basic and pragmatic level, how the studies you consult in a researched argument come into being. You're on the ground floor of knowledge making.

As a critical reader, you know it's important to ask questions like these: What is the source of the author's claim? Why should I believe the author? What is the source of the author's authority? What are the possible counterarguments? When you are doing original research, you are in the position of that author, with a real stake in establishing your own authority. By coming to understand what it takes to establish your own authority, you are in a better position to evaluate how effectively other researchers establish theirs.

Let's say your research question concerns gender differences in math education. You might read a study that asserts that girls and young women are being shortchanged in math classes, impeding their ability to go into math-related fields. You would want to ask about the nature of the data used to support this claim. If the author of the study states that 56 percent of the female students interviewed said they were discouraged from going into math-related fields, you might wonder where the figure of 56 percent came from. How many girls and young women were interviewed? How was this sample selected? What were the students asked? Questions like these inform your own use of interviews and focus groups.

To increase your own research skills. Doing original research broadens your own range of research methods. By developing a repertoire of research methods, you will be better able to explore questions that may be too complex to answer by examining texts alone. One scholar put it this way: "I couldn't see what a text was doing without looking at the worlds in which these texts served as significant activities."* After all, it is one

---

*C. Bazerman, *Shaping Written Knowledge: The Genre and Activity of the Scientific Article in Science* (Madison: University of Wisconsin Press, 1988), p. 4.

thing to read a research report and understand its purpose, its intended audience, the nature of its claims, and the like. But it is quite another to watch scientists at work and begin to understand how they have come to know what they know. The discovery of DNA, for example, was the result of an arduous process that involved much risk, collaboration, chance, error, and competition. The neat structure of a scientific report could mislead you into thinking that science is a linear process that begins with a question, moves on to an experiment, and ends with an answer. Real research is messier than that. Original research takes us behind the words we read, introducing levels of complexity.

To broaden your scope of inquiry.   Doing original research may also broaden the scope of your inquiry. First, it is useful to use different research methods than the ones you are accustomed to using. Learning to interview and run focus groups, at the very least, can give you insight and practice for nonacademic applications—market research, for example. Second, it can make you aware of how people outside your field address the questions you raise. Consider, for example, the different perspectives an educator, a sociologist, and an economist would bring to the question of educational inequities. An educator might study educational inequities as a curricular problem and therefore analyze the content of different curricula within and across schools. A sociologist might visit students' homes, noting the presence or absence of books or asking parents how they go about preparing their children for school. An economist might examine income levels in both wealthy and impoverished neighborhoods. The point is that each field brings its own perspective to a problem, adding complexity and richness to your own discussion of that problem.

To make a unique contribution to a conversation of ideas.   Finally, doing original research affords you the opportunity to make a unique contribution to a conversation of ideas. Instead of relying exclusively on texts others have written as evidence for your claims, you can offer your own data to address a question or problem, data that others do not have available. For instance, if you wanted to examine claims that primary school teachers pay more attention to boys in class than to girls, you could review the relevant literature and then add to that literature a study that systematically analyzes the ways in which teachers in different classrooms treat boys and girls.

GETTING STARTED: WRITING AN IDEA SHEET

The purpose of writing an **idea sheet** is to help you explore not just what you might want to learn by conducting research but why you are interested in a particular topic, issue, or problem. An idea sheet is a form of exploratory writing that can serve as the basis for a more formal research proposal.

We encourage our students to jot down some ideas about the topic they are interested in, why they find the topic of interest, and why it might be compelling to others. Moreover, we want them to answer the kinds of questions we have addressed throughout this book: What's at stake in conducting this research? What other related ideas compete for our attention and limit our ability to see what you think is important, and why?

To compose an idea sheet, you should follow these steps:

Step One: Explain your topic so that others can understand what you want to study.

Step Two: Detail the personal reasons why you are interested in the topic.

Step Three: Identify what is at issue—what is open to dispute for you.

Step Four: Describe any groups for whom this issue might be significant or important.

Step Five: Formulate an issue-based question.

It is important to discuss an issue in the context of a current situation, so that readers will understand why you are raising a particular issue. As a writer, you will need to familiarize yourself with what people are talking and writing about. What is on people's minds? What is at issue for people? What about for you? What do your readers need to know about? In turn, you will need to help readers understand why they are reading your essay and fulfill their expectations that what you are writing about is both relevant and timely.

Formulating an issue-based question can help you think through what you might be interested in writing about and guide your research. As we suggest in Chapter 5, a good question develops out of an issue, some fundamental tension that you identify within a conversation. Your issue-based question should be specific enough to guide inquiry into what others have written and help you accomplish the following:

- Clarify what you know about the issue and what you still need to know.
- Guide your inquiry with a clear focus.
- Organize your inquiry around a specific issue.
- Develop an argument, rather than simply collecting information by asking "how," "why," "should," or "to what extent is it true or not?"
- Consider who your audience is.
- Determine what resources you have, so that you can ask a question that you will be able answer with the resources available to you.

A STUDENT'S ANNOTATED IDEA SHEET

Grace 1

Dan Grace
Professor Greene
English 320
March 10, 20—

Idea Sheet for Parent/Child Autism Study

The student explains the purpose of his research and begins to explain the method he would use to get the information he is interested in.

I would like to study the parent-child home interaction/ dynamic between an individual with autism and his or her parents in the student's home. I would like to research different intervention programs and interview the parents about their own programs with their child, both home- and school-implemented, as well as observe the parent-child interactions in both school work and natural daily activities such as conversations and meals. I would do this by spending at least fifty hours with the student with autism in his or her home, both individually with him or her and also observing his or her parental interactions. I would like to see how these interactions compare with the research performed in this field.

1

The summer after my freshman year, I worked at a school for children with autism for six weeks. I also worked at a research facility that looked into the effects high vitamin and mineral diets had on individuals with autism. The next summer, and during several breaks in school, I worked at the school for a total of fifteen to twenty weeks. My experiences there have spurred an interest in autism and autism education. I've worked extensively in the classroom setting; however, I've never witnessed the home setting for anyone with autism. Also, I've heard many stories about parents and their different mindsets and levels of involvement with their children, but have never met any parents, except for one at the end of my first summer working at the school. I want to interact with a student outside of the classroom, as well as see the interactions between the student and his or her parents.

2

He explains why he is interested in this subject and this provides a rationale for what he will study.

Children with autism lack the social, emotional, and cognitive (in many cases) skills that healthy individuals possess/have the potential to have. Early intervention is a very important thing in a child with autism's life, since it has been shown that early intervention can significantly help the child's social, emotional, and cognitive development. Early

3

Grace 2

He recognizes the importance of early intervention, but he is not altogether sure what that means in a child's everyday life.

intervention includes the parents as well. It is important for parents to interact with their children early and often, and to work with them to help them develop. Though the individual that I will be working with is already at the end of elementary school, it will still be useful to observe the parent-child interactions, as well as question the parents about what measures were taken early in the child's life.

The student provides a broad context for understanding autism and who else might be interested in this topic.

This topic is important/significant for all those working with children with autism, as well as parents of children with autism. Autism is becoming ever more prevalent in this country, and the world, with more than one in every one hundred children being diagnosed with some form of autism spectrum disorder (ASD). The parents need to know how best to interact with, and better understand, their child.

4

Finally, he formulates the topic as a series of questions that need to be answered.

How can parent-child interaction influence the development of a child with autism? This might be a vague question with many different directions in which to take it, but it is still a pertinent question. How might parental interaction in adolescence affect adolescent development? Why should parents work hard to interact with their children with autism? What are the benefits of early intervention? What are the long-term benefits of early intervention programs? What are the effects of good versus poor parental interaction? These questions need to be answered to fully understand the topic and research question.

5

WRITING A PROPOSAL

A **proposal** is a formal plan that outlines your objectives for conducting a research project, specifies the methods you intend to use, and describes the implications of your work. In its most basic form, a proposal is an argument that provides a rationale for conducting research and persuades readers that the research is worth pursuing. It is also a tool that helps guide you through various stages of the project. The most immediate benefit of writing a proposal is that through the act of writing—by setting forth an outline of your project—your thinking will become more focused and precise. And yet your thinking may change as you read more about your topic.

Typically, a research proposal should include four sections: introduction/purpose, review of relevant research, method, and implications. You may also want to include additional sections with materials that provide concrete support for your proposal—some of the tools that will help you get the job done. You should arrange your plan and use headings so that readers can find information quickly.

■ Describe Your Purpose

In the introduction, you should describe the purpose of your study and establish that the issue you want to study is relevant and timely. Then, briefly summarize how others have treated the issue you are focusing on in order to explain whether you are trying to fill a gap, correct a misconception, build upon and extend others' research, or test a hypothesis. As we point out throughout this book, it is important to help readers understand the context by retracing the conversation. After you provide some context to help readers understand the purpose of your study, you should then formulate the question that is motivating your research.

Finally, you should explain why you are interested in this issue, why it is important, and what is at stake. Ask yourself why others should be interested in your effort to answer the question.

■ Review Relevant Research

Following the introduction, you should provide a review of the relevant research. For a proposal, you should demonstrate that you have a firm grasp of the issue as part of the argument you are making to justify your study. The more effectively you convince readers that you know the issue, the more persuasive your argument. Therefore, you will want to show that you have read widely, that you are aware of the most important studies conducted in your area of research, that you are also aware of current research within the past five years, and that you understand the strengths and limitations of your own approach.

More specifically, you can use your review to accomplish some of the following:

- Define a key term that is central to your study that others may not necessarily agree upon.
- Discuss the history relevant to your research.
- Explain the strengths and limitations of different methodological approaches to answering similar research questions.
- Analyze the different theoretical approaches that authors have used to frame the issue (e.g., psychological, sociological, socioeconomic, racial).
- Identify trends in what researchers are finding or, perhaps, the lack of agreement.
- Point to more comprehensive reviews of research that others have written.

■ Define Your Method

In your method section, you should first explain how you will answer the research question motivating your study using the tools that are available. Some of the tools and strategies you might use include the following:

- conducting interviews or focus groups;
- taking notes;
- recording particular activities;
- doing background, historical, or archival work, and
- observing or coming to terms with your own impressions.

Since this is a proposal for research you will conduct, you should write this section in the future tense. "To answer the question(s) motivating this study, I will conduct interviews and focus groups and take detailed notes. . . ."

Second, describe how you plan to collect your data. Tell readers whether you will audio-record and transcribe interviews and/or focus groups. If you are taking notes, you will want to explain whether you plan to take notes during or after the session. Be sure to explain where you are conducting the interview or focus group. If you are observing classes, meetings, or some event, you will need to explain how often you will observe, for how long, and whether you will be taking notes or transcribing data.

Third, justify why you are using some methods of collecting data and not others. Discuss the appropriateness of these methods given your research question. Given the objectives you have set for yourself and the constraints of doing the research, are some methods better than others? How will the methods you have chosen to use enable you to answer your question(s)?

Finally, you should have some sense of how you will analyze the data you collect. That is, readers will expect that you have done more than simply read your transcripts from interviews and focus groups to form impressions. Therefore, you will want to explain the principles you will use to analyze the data in light of the research question(s) you are asking.

■ Discuss Your Implications

It may seem a little premature to talk about what you hope to find in your study, but it is important to address "So what?" to explain what you believe is the significance of your study. Place your argument in the context of the conversation you want to join, and explain how your study can contribute to that conversation. Write about how your study will build upon, challenge, or extend the studies in your area of research. And finally, identify what you believe will be new about your findings.

■ Include Additional Materials That Support Your Research

Depending on your instructor and the level of formality of your proposal, you may be asked to include additional materials that reveal other dimensions of your research. Those materials may include (1) an annotated bibliography, (2) scripts of the questions you plan to ask in interviews and focus groups, (3) the consent forms you will ask participants to sign, and (4) approval from your university's Institutional Review Board (IRB).

Annotated bibliography. An **annotated bibliography** is a list of sources (arranged alphabetically by author) that you plan to consult and use in your research paper. Typically you provide a citation (author, date, title of source, and publication information) and a short summary of the source. You can present all your sources in one long list or organize them by type of source (books, journals, and so forth). See pages 184–86 in Chapter 7 for a more complete description of how to write an annotated bibliography and an example.

Questions you plan to ask. Including a list (or lists) of the questions you expect to ask those you plan to interview or survey will help focus your thinking. What personal information do you need to know? What information do you need to know about your issue? What opinions and recommendations would be helpful? Each list should include at least five good questions but can include many more. A sample set of questions, focusing on parents of homeless children, appears in Figure 13.1.

Consent forms. Whenever you plan to solicit information in an interview or focus group, you need to get permission from the interviewees or participants to use their comments and contributions in your research paper. The Institutional Review Board on your campus probably has a model for writing a consent form that you can use, but we have included a sample consent form for an interview in Figure 13.2.

IRB approval. Your school's Institutional Review Board ensures that researchers hold high ethical standards in the research they conduct and protect the rights of "human subjects" who participate in a study. It is possible that research conducted for a class will not require IRB approval. You should contact the appropriate office (for example, the Office for Research) on your campus for details and exceptions.

Sample Interview Questions

Parent(s)

1. a. Describe your current living and family situation (parents, siblings, how long homeless, where living, where child attends school).

   b. Describe your child.

   c. Describe your relationship with your child.

2. a. Do you think homelessness is affecting your child's schooling?

   b. If so, tell me how (grades, friends, attendance, transportation).

3. Tell me about enrolling your child in school. What was the process like? Were there any problems? Conditions? Challenges?

4. a. Do you feel that your child's right to an education has been recognized?

   b. Why or why not? Describe any experiences that support your answer.

5. Describe the relationship between your child and his or her teachers.

6. a. What types of support services is your child currently being offered in school and in the community?

   b. How effective are those services?

   c. How supportive of your child's educational and developmental growth do you feel your child's school has been?

   d. What about the Center for the Homeless?

   e. Do you have any recommendations for these sources of help or requests for other types of services for your child that are not currently offered?

7. How do you envision your child's future?

FIGURE 13.1   Sample Interview Questions

■ Establish a Timeline

Draw up a schedule for your research and identify when you expect to complete specific tasks. For example, when will you do the following?

- Submit proposal to Institutional Review Board (if necessary).
- Contact participants and get their commitments.
- Conduct interviews, focus groups, and the like.
- Compile an annotated bibliography.
- Transcribe the data.

Sample Interview Consent Form

You are invited to participate in a study of homelessness and education conducted by Mary Ronan, an undergraduate at the University of Notre Dame, during the next few months. If you decide to participate, you will

1. provide up to two interviews with the researcher
2. allow the researcher to use excerpts from the interviews in publications about research with the understanding that your identity will not be revealed at any time.

Participation is completely voluntary. You may choose to stop participating at any time prior to completion of the project. Should you have any questions at any time, you are welcome to contact the researcher by phone or e-mail. Your decision to participate will have no effect on or prejudice your future relationship with the University of Notre Dame. One possible benefit of participating in the study is that you will have the opportunity to learn about the implications of homelessness on education.

If you are willing to participate in this research, please read and sign the consent form below. You will be given a copy of this form to keep.

CONSENT FORM

I agree to participate in all of the procedures above. I understand that my identity will be protected during the study and that others will not have access to the interviews I provide. I also understand that my name will not be revealed when data from the research are presented in publications. I have read the above and give the researcher, Mary Ronan, permission to use excerpts from transcripts of tapes without identifying me as the writer or speaker.

_____   _____
Date   Signature

_____
[Telephone number]

_____   _____
[E-mail address]

                                         Signature of Researcher

---

FIGURE 13.2   Sample Interview Consent Form

- Analyze the data.
- Draft an introduction, methods, and findings.

Your timeline should include the dates when you expect to finish the proposal, when you will conduct interviews and focus groups, when you expect to have a draft, and when you will complete the project. Be realistic about how long it will actually take to complete the different stages of collecting data and writing. Anticipate that events may prevent things from going exactly as planned. People cannot always meet with you when you would like them to, and you may have to change your own schedule. Therefore, be sure to contact participants well in advance of the time when you would like to speak with them in interviews or focus groups.

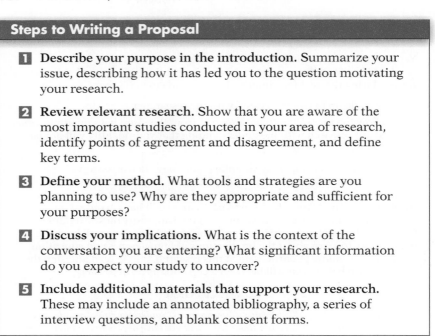

Steps to Writing a Proposal

1 **Describe your purpose in the introduction.** Summarize your issue, describing how it has led you to the question motivating your research.

2 **Review relevant research.** Show that you are aware of the most important studies conducted in your area of research, identify points of agreement and disagreement, and define key terms.

3 **Define your method.** What tools and strategies are you planning to use? Why are they appropriate and sufficient for your purposes?

4 **Discuss your implications.** What is the context of the conversation you are entering? What significant information do you expect your study to uncover?

5 **Include additional materials that support your research.** These may include an annotated bibliography, a series of interview questions, and blank consent forms.

AN ANNOTATED STUDENT PROPOSAL

Our student Laura Hartigan submitted a formal proposal for a study of different types of writing. Hartigan's proposal was exceptionally well prepared, thorough, and thoughtful, and she included a number of additional materials: a script of questions for focus groups with students; sample questions for the teacher and students she planned to interview; and consent forms. We reprint only the main part of her proposal—the part that includes a brief overview of the conversation about different modes of writing, her aims for conducting her study, methods, and implications sections—for you to consider as a model for proposal writing. A more complete example would include a separate review of relevant research. Notice how Hartigan summarizes her issue, explains how it motivated the study she proposes, formulates a set of guiding research questions, and helps readers understand why her research is important, particularly in the implications she draws.

LaunchPad
macmillan learning

Laura Hartigan's completed paper, along with guidelines for a presentation poster, are available with access to LaunchPad for *From Inquiry to Academic Writing.*

Hartigan 1

Laura Hartigan
Professor Greene
English 385
March 28, 20—

Proposal for Research: The Affordances of Multimodal,
Creative, and Academic Writing

The student retraces the recent, and important, conversation about writing and alternative conceptions that challenge some widely held assumptions.

Researchers (Hughes, 2009; Vasudevan, Schultz & Bateman, 2010) have called attention to the unique ways that writing can foster student learning and have for some time now argued that teachers in elementary and high schools should give students more opportunities to write fiction and poetry using image, music, and text to express themselves. Within the last decade, even more alternative modes of writing have gained prominence. Researchers (Hughes, 2009; Hull & Katz, 2006) argue that "multimodal digital storytelling" provides students with ways to help them engage more deeply with their written work. Digital storytelling in particular enables students to examine their experiences by writing personal narratives in which they confront key turning points in their lives and the challenges they face. In turn, they can use images, music, and voice-over to amplify and give meaning to their written stories. Allowing for what researchers call "new literate spaces" creates the opportunity for multiple modes of learning, understanding, and collaboration that challenge the limited ways that students use writing as a mode of learning in school (Hughes, 2009; Hull & Katz, 2006). Students may learn to write persuasive essays, but they also need opportunities to learn about themselves and use their writing as a way to create changes in their lives. Thus researchers urge educators to reform curricular and pedagogical practices to help students use writing to help them develop a sense of identity and ownership of their writing, to see the decision-making power they have as individuals.

She summarizes recent studies and evidence supporting the value of alternative modes of writing. But she also identifies a gap in the argument researchers make.

When they argue that multimodal, digital literacy practices have a place in the standard curriculum, researchers (Hall, 2011; Hughes, 2009; Hull & Katz, 2006; Ranker, 2007; Vasudevan et al., 2010) provide evidence to show how youth grow and develop, become more confident learners, and use what they learn in and out of school. This is particularly true when youth have opportunities to reflect on their lives and use multiple literacies to give meaning to their experience. They can use image, music, and text to confront how

Hartigan 2

things in their lives look and feel, to examine the decisions they have made, and to consider the decisions they might make in confronting hardship, discrimination, and loss. However, most research fails to provide a satisfactory or compelling rationale for why new literacies *should* be used in the classroom (Alvermann, Marshall, McLean, Huddleston, Joaquin, 2012; Binder & Kotsopoulos, 2011; Hull and Katz, 2006; Ranker, 2007) or how the seemingly unique gains could be positively integrated into the standard curriculum. The lack of assessment focusing on how academic and new literacies affect one another reveals a flaw in the conclusions drawn from studies that neglect the realities of teaching in K-12 schools. Increased emphasis on standards, testing, and accountability seem to preclude the kind of focus that new literacies seem to require. Thus, if educators are to allow for "new literate spaces," they need to know how to do so within the standard curriculum.

Recognizing this gap, she explores what she sees as a common problem in a number of studies.

Specifically, few researchers explore students' sense of their literate identity in academic and creative writing or how context matters in how students feel about themselves and their writing. While most researchers (Binder & Kotsopoulos, 2011; Hughes, 2009; Hull & Katz, 2006; Vasudevan et al., 2010) refer to what they call "the mono-literacy landscape" of schools, the limits of literate experience to print, none really compare the opportunities that academic writing gives students versus, say, creative writing before, during, and after the study. That is, focusing only on the value of digital storytelling, for example, or creative writing is not sufficient to effect reform in school. Are there really significant differences between different kinds of writing? What are these differences? Such a gap in research seems to necessitate an inquiry into a student's emergent sense of authorship in different forms of composing, even academic writing in and out of school. Therefore, I propose a study that will provide an analysis of both academic and creative writing in an after-school program that helps children develop as learners through tutoring and enrichment. One implication of my research would be to show why educators might expand the types of literate experiences that students have in school.

In turn, this gap serves as a rationale for conducting her own study. She also points to the possible implications for doing the study she proposes.

3

Having defined the problem, she describes the aims of her study.

In order to investigate the possible differences between multimodal, creative, and standardized academic writing, this proposed study aims to explore (a) the unique opportunities afforded by the

4

Hartigan 3

multiple means of expression inherent in digital storytelling, (b) how and if these opportunities create an alternative space for the growth of empowered literate identities and a sense of agency, (c) the extent to which writing supports a student's development of an authorial voice, and (d) why schools should be concerned with the affordances given to the development of a student's written voice and individual identity by including multimodal digital storytelling in the curriculum. The

She reformulates the four aims of her study as questions to guide her inquiry.

study focuses on analyzing the students' sense of authorship in both their academic and creative assignments. To what extent can standard academic and creative multimodal expression help students develop an authorial identity and the skills they need to flourish in and out of school? Considering the current atmosphere of accountability and federal testing (Hull & Katz, 2006), it is important to ask what role multimodal composing can play in the standard and narrow curriculum.

Method

She describes the approach she will take to answer her questions.

To address the aims of my study, I will conduct interviews and focus groups to examine students' attitudes about writing in and out of school at the Crusoe Community Learning Center (CCLC) in a small midwestern city. Interviews and focus groups will enable me to discover student attitudes and feelings about writing across the in-school and out-of-school contexts in order to develop some insight into how writing can enable or disengage students. I will also take field notes taken by a participant-observer in the afterschool creative writing workshop to develop a picture of the after-school classroom dynamics.

Context

To help orient readers, she explains where her study will take place.

The CCLC is an off-campus educational initiative of a nearby private university in partnership with the surrounding neighborhood residents. Serving around 600 participants in the regular programming, the CCLC also partners with the community schools in the surrounding area with program outreach connecting to nearly 8,000 additional youths throughout the year. Located in a high-traffic, low-income neighborhood, the CCLC's mission centers around promoting hospitality, education, partnership, civic engagement, and sustainability in the surrounding area and all the participants. Organized around operating as a learning center and gathering space, the CCLC fosters relationships with the students, the surrounding residents, and the city's universities in a safe,

5

6

Hartigan 4

collaborative atmosphere. Classes and programming range from English as a New Language (ENL) to financial literacy, entrepreneurship, basic computing, and one-on-one tutoring for area children conducted by college volunteers.

She identifies the specific class that she will focus on in her research and explains why the context for conducting this study makes sense.

The creative writing class and the CCLC's curricular environment will provide an appropriate population and unique space to explore the possible affordances between creative and academic writing. With the after-school programming divided in weekly, day-by-day activities centered on enrichment, academic tutoring, and creative writing, the CCLC's after-school context is inherently connected to the student's school context. Thus the CCLC's efforts to help students with their day-to-day school work and also offer enrichment unique to an after-school program can enrich my understanding of the way students' contexts (in school and after school) influence how they see themselves as writers.

7

Participants

Importantly, she describes who will participate in the study and why she has chosen this particular teacher and class. Note that at this preliminary stage, she offers a brief sketch of the teacher and her credentials. However, she has not yet met the students.

At the CCLC, I will focus on Ms. Smith's class. Ms. Smith is a former fourth-grade teacher serving the center as a full-time AmeriCorps member. As an AmeriCorps member, Ms. Smith works in a federal program funded by the state of Indiana for a full-time forty-hour week at the CCLC. Taking place every Wednesday, the creative writing class centers around brainstorming, drafting, and publishing the student work for display inside the center and on a developing Web log. I have chosen this specific class and student population because it offered the opportunity to talk to students about their school and after-school writing experiences alongside the physical creative artifacts they created in Ms. Smith's class. Due to the participants' weekly experience of academic tutoring and creative class time, the choice was based on the wide range of writing activities that could be probed by the broad, experience-based focus of the question script.

8

Data Collection Procedure and Analysis

She explains the methods she will use to collect the information she needs to answer her research questions. She notes

I will conduct focus groups and interviews with the students in Ms. Smith's class over the course of three weeks. To obtain parental consent in order to conduct the focus groups and subsequent interviews, I will e-mail consent forms requesting each student's participation in my research. I will do so two weeks

9

that she needs the signed informed consent form from each student's parent in the class she is studying. This was stipulated by the Institutional Review Board (IRB).

prior to the study's start in order to provide the necessary time for the forms to be sent home and signed by the parents. (For the complete list of questions, see Appendix A.) Upon receiving confirmation from Ms. Smith that the consent forms had been completed, I can then conduct focus groups and interviews with the participating students.

In keeping with approaches to studies using focus groups and interviews, she plans to transcribe audio recordings. She explains her decision not to take notes during focus groups and interviews.

I will audio-record the focus groups and interviews. Following the end of each session, I will transcribe the recordings. Though I will not take notes during the focus groups and interviews in order to maintain total engagement with the participants, I will type a series of reflections and field notes after the completion of each audio-recorded session. Following the completion of the transcriptions, I will also take more notes to identify the themes that emerge in both interviews with individual children and in the focus groups.

Having explained her approach to collecting data, she now indicates what she will look for in her analysis.

After analyzing student responses, I will construct several categories to explore the CCLC participants' sense of self and authorial identity across contexts: safe spaces, expressing interest and meaningful message, and ownership.

Implications

In conclusion, she points to some possible implications of her research, but first places her proposed study in the broader context of what other researchers are finding. That is, she brings her study full circle to the ongoing conversation that framed her introduction.

Though many unique and compelling findings support a pedagogical shift toward new literacies, researchers (Vasudevan et al., 2010) tend to ignore the impact of a student's outside knowledge, experience, and contexts for writing. Moreover, without clearly understanding the differences and similarities between academic writing and multimodal writing, educators may not see the importance of including alternative modes of literacy in the standard curriculum. Hughes (2009) notes that the multimodal assignments and digital media in her research helped students engage more deeply with language and their own personal sense of command over their written work. The need to explore the changing materiality of texts figures as Hughes's intriguing concern due to its impact on the ways students construct meaning in what they write. Hughes frames performance "as a vehicle for exploration and learning, rather than as a fixed product to be rehearsed and delivered as a final event" (p. 262) that works in tandem with (not in isolation from)

10

11

12

Hartigan 6

She also reminds readers of a significant gap in current research.

literacy practices. Digital media allowed for the students to become what Hughes termed "co-creators," which helped students move beyond simply observing and analyzing poetry as a generally traditional and boring academic topic. However, the shift from print culture to new, performative media has yet to be reflected in classroom culture.

Moreover, after detailing how she will address her research questions above, she justifies the importance of her proposed study.

Sharpening the ideas drawn from the conclusions of Hughes (2009) points to the necessity of documenting the development of a student's voice and presence in multimodal, digital, and academic writing. In essence, research must avoid implying that one form of literacy is somehow more advantageous to the other without also looking at how context influences the ways students feel about themselves and what they write. To address this gap, my study will analyze the differences, and perhaps similarities, in how students develop and perceive their authorial presence and power in both kinds of writing — multimodal and academic — and the influence of context. After all, the mode of writing may not be as significant as the extent to which children feel they have a safe space place to write, where they can take risks without being afraid that their peers and teacher will criticize them. They also need to know that they have ownership of their writing as a means of expression and performance of who they are, who they imagine themselves to be, and what they want for themselves in the future.

13

Hartigan 7

Working Bibliography

Alvermann, D., Marshall, J., McLean, C., Huddleston, A., Joaquin, J., et al. (2012). Adolescents' Web-based literacies, identity construction, and skill development. *Literacy Research and Instruction, 51*(3), 179–195.

Binder, M., & Kotsopoulos, S. (2011). Multimodal literacy narratives: Weaving the threads of young children's identity through the arts. *Journal of Research in Childhood Education, 25*(4), 339–363.

Buckingham, D. (2007). Digital media literacies: Rethinking media education in the age of the Internet. *Research in Comparative and International Education, 2*(1), 43–55.

Hall, T. (2011). Designing from their own social worlds: The digital story of three African American young women. *English Teaching: Practice and Critique, 10*(1), 7–20.

Hughes, J. (2009). New media, new literacies and the adolescent learner. *E-Learning, 6*(3), 259–271.

Hull, G., & Katz, M. (2006). Crafting an agentive self: Case studies of digital storytelling. *Research in the Teaching of English, 41*(1), 43–81.

Ranker, J. (2007). Designing meaning with multiple media sources: A case study of an eight-year-old student's writing processes. *Research in the Teaching of English, 41*(4), 402–434.

Vasudevan, L., Schultz, K., & Bateman, J. (2010). Rethinking composing in a digital age: Authoring literate identities through multimodal storytelling. *Written Communication, 27*(4), 442–468.

INTERVIEWING

An **interview** helps to answer the research question(s) motivating your study by gathering concrete details and stories from various people. In her book *Critical Ethnography: Method, Ethics, and Performance,* D. Soyini Madison offers this advice: "When you first begin to formulate questions, a useful exercise is to reread your research question or problem over several times and then ask yourself, 'If this is what I am to understand, then what is it that I need to know about it to answer the questions or address the problem?' You will then list everything of interest that comes to mind" (p. 31). It's certainly possible to conduct an interview by phone, especially if the interviewee is not local, but a face-to-face conversation, in which you can note physical details and body language, is preferable.

The ways writers incorporate interviews into their writing appears almost seamless, but keep in mind that a finished text hides the process that went into a successful interview. You don't see the planning that occurs. Writers have to make appointments with the people they interview, develop a script or list of questions before the interview, and test the questions beforehand to see if they're likely to lead to the kind of information they're seeking. In other words, the key to a successful interview is preparation. The following information should help you plan your interview and prepare you for writing down your results.

■ Plan the Interview

You'll want to do some preliminary research to identify people who can help you understand more about your topic: What kind of expertise or experience do they have? Then you have to contact them to find out if they are willing to be interviewed. You can send a brief e-mail or letter to initiate a conversation and then follow up with a phone call.

Based on our own experience, it is important to explain the project for participants in plain terms. In fact, when you contact potential participants, we suggest you do so in writing and address the following: Who are you? What are you doing, and why? What will you do with what you find? What are possible benefits and risks? How will you assure confidentiality? How often and how long would you like to meet for interviews?

If you are planning to record the interview—always a wise idea—make sure each individual consents to being recorded. Then make the necessary arrangements. For example, you may need to reserve a room where you can conduct your interview without being disturbed. Try to choose a location that is convenient for the individual(s) you want to interview and familiar, such as a room in a public library.

It's important to set up appointments with people early. To keep on schedule, list the names of people who have agreed to be interviewed:

Interviewee 1:_____   Response? __ yes/no __ date:_____

Interviewee 2:_____   Response? __ yes/no __ date:_____

Interviewee 3:_____   Response? __ yes/no __ date:_____

■ Prepare Your Script

As you prepare the script of questions for your interview, keep coming back to the question motivating your research. To what extent will the questions you want to ask in your interview enable you to answer the broader question motivating your research? That is, what is the story you want to tell in your research? The more specific the questions you ask, the more specific the answers or story that the person you interview will tell.

Build rapport.   In any conversation, you want to build rapport and perhaps establish some common ground. More than getting information from someone, an interview can serve as a means to produce knowledge collaboratively and in ways that are mutually satisfying to you and the people you want to talk to. To create this kind of conversation, you can help the interviewee feel at ease and then move on to the issues you want to learn more about.

Start with nonthreatening questions.   For example, "How long have you been teaching writing?" "When did you start teaching writing in a hybrid classroom?" "What digital tools do you use to teach writing in a hybrid classroom?"

Ask open-ended questions.   Your questions should encourage the person you are interviewing to tell stories that will help you learn about your subject.

This means phrasing questions in ways that avoid simple yes/no answers. For instance, you might ask for an explanation of how children at a homeless center can overcome the obstacles they face as opposed to asking something like this: "Do you think children can overcome the obstacles they face?" Asking for an explanation invites someone to describe the process by which overcoming obstacles is possible. In turn, you can ask specific questions such as the following: "Can you tell me about a specific instance to illustrate the extent to which children can overcome the obstacles they face?" "Can you help me understand what made this possible?"

Avoid leading questions.   It may be tempting to ask leading questions to keep the conversation going in an interview or to fill in something that an individual implies but does not actually say. For example, "Do you think that the food industry has contributed to the problem of obesity?" "So are you saying that the government should formulate policies to regulate the industry?" In each case, the question supplies a possible answer, which is counterproductive. You want to learn from your interviewees, not feed them answers. The questions you ask should allow the person you are interviewing to come to his or her own conclusions. Alternatively, you can ask: "Tell me more about what you are saying about the government's role." Similarly, try not to reinforce or judge the answers that an interviewee gives, such as "That's what I was thinking." "That's great." "You're right." Reinforcing or judging answers may indicate to an interviewee that there is a correct answer to the questions you are asking. Instead, you want this person to explore his or her thoughts in an open, honest way.

Only share experiences occasionally.   Although we have suggested that conducting interviews can be like conversations, you should resist providing your own experiences and stories. Listen to answers and follow up with questions that encourage the person you are interviewing to elaborate.

Rehearse and then revise the script.   After you develop a script of questions, rehearse it with your writing group or a friend who can play the role of the person you want to interview. In doing so, you want to get a sense of how an interviewee is going to respond to your questions. The following questions can serve as a guide for assessing the interview and what you might change:

- What would you point to as an effective exchange?
- What questions helped you get concrete details to tell the story you wanted to tell?
- What would you point to as an example of an exchange that didn't go as well as you had hoped? How would you explain what happened?
- What questions would you rephrase if you were to do the interview again?
- To what extent do you feel that you might have lost some opportunities to follow up?
- Are there follow-up questions you should have asked?

After you answer these questions, revise the script to improve the content, order, and pacing of your questions.

■ Conduct the Interview

On the day before the interview, contact the individual you plan to interview to confirm that he or she remembers the time of the interview and knows how to find the location where the interview will take place. Also, as you prepare for your interview, look over your questions and make sure you know how to use your recording software and device and that your device has sufficient capacity for the interview. Be on time. Have a brief conversation to put the interviewee at ease and then ask this person to read and sign the consent form (see Figure 13.2).

Explain use of technology. Explain why recording the interview is necessary ("Your responses are really important to me. I will take some notes as you talk, but I don't want to miss anything you have to say. As a result, I will record our conversation so I can revisit the important things you tell me").

Describe the interview process. Explain what types of questions you will ask in the interview ("Today, I'm going to ask you questions about school and your family"). In addition, explain why you're interested in knowing this information ("I want to learn more about you and your family so I can understand what techniques for school, family, etc. are helpful for you").

Keep the interview conversational. Use your script as a guide, but be flexible, treating the interview as a conversation. This might mean following the direction that the person you interview takes in answering a question. Listen. Don't interrupt. That is, you might ask what you think is a pointed question and this person might begin to tell a story that may not seem relevant. Let the person finish and patiently return to the questions you would like this person to address. You can also try rephrasing your question(s) to be more specific about the information you need. If you think at some point that the interviewee is implying something of special interest to you, ask for clarification.

Respect silence. If any interviewee is silent for a while after you ask a question, be patient and don't immediately repeat or ask another question. The interviewee may need time to gather his or her thoughts or understand the question. After some time has passed, you can ask this person the question again or ask another question.

Keep track of important questions. Toward the end of the interview, check your script for important questions you may have forgotten to ask. If there are several, try to ask only the most important ones in the time remaining. You can also ask to have a follow-up meeting to ensure that you have gotten the information you need.

Follow up after the interview is over.   Continue getting to know the interviewee. Even though the formal interview is done, you still want this person to feel as though he or she matters to you. Just because this person has completed the interview doesn't mean that his or her relationship with the research project is over.

■ Make Sense of the Interview

Conducting an interview is only part of the challenge; you then have to make sense of what was said. That process involves four steps:

1. *Familiarize yourself with the conversation.* If you recorded the interview, listen to it a couple of times to become really familiar with what was said. Read through your notes several times too.

2. *Transcribe the interview.* Transcribing entails listening carefully to and typing up the audio recording of your interview to help you analyze the conversation. A transcript provides a more manageable way to identify key points in the interview, details that you might miss if you only listened to the interview, and stories that you might recount in your research. Transcribing an interview is an important part of doing this kind of research, but it is time-consuming. If you use transcription software to save time, you will still need to compare your transcript to your recording for accuracy. Therefore, you need to plan accordingly. An hour-long interview usually takes about three hours to transcribe.

3. *Analyze the interview.* Read through the interview again. Look for answers to the questions motivating your research, and look for recurring patterns or themes. Make a list of those ideas relevant to the issues you intend to focus on, especially evidence that might support your argument.

4. *Find one good source.* Using the themes you identify in your analysis as a guide, find one good source that relates to your interview in some way. Maybe your subject's story fits into an educational debate (for example, public versus private education). Or maybe your subject's story counters a common conception about education (that inner-city schools are hopelessly inadequate). You're looking for a source you can link to your interview in an interesting and effective way.

■ Turn Your Interview into an Essay

Try to lay out in paragraphs the material you've collected that addresses the question motivating your research and the focus of your paper. In a first draft, you might take these steps:

1. State your argument, or the purpose of your essay. What do you want to teach your readers?

2. Provide evidence to support your thesis. What examples from your reading, observations, or interviews do you want to offer your readers? How do those examples illuminate your claim?

3. Place quotations from more than one source in as many paragraphs as you can, so that you can play the quotations off against one another. What is significant about the ways you see specific quotations "in conversation" with one another? How do these conversations between quotations help you build your own argument?

4. Consider possible counterarguments to the point you want to make.

5. Help readers understand what is at stake in adopting your position.

Steps to Interviewing

1 **Plan the interview.** After you've identified the people you might like to talk to, contact them to explain your project and set up appointments if they are willing to participate.

2 **Prepare your script.** Draft your questions, rehearse them with your classmates or friends, and then make revisions based on their responses.

3 **Conduct the interview.** Be flexible with your script as you go, making sure to take good notes even if you are recording the interview.

4 **Make sense of the interview.** Review the recording and your notes of the interview, transcribe the interview, analyze the transcript, and connect the conversation to at least one good source.

5 **Turn your interview into an essay.** State your argument, organize your evidence, use quotes to make your point, consider counterarguments, and help your readers understand what's at stake.

USING FOCUS GROUPS

Like interviews, focus groups can provide you with an original source of evidence to complement (or complicate, contradict, or extend) the evidence you find in books and articles. According to Bruce L. Berg in *Qualitative Research Methods for the Social Sciences*, a **focus group** "may be defined as an interview style designed for small groups . . . addressing a particular topic of interest or relevance to the group and the researcher." College administrators often speak with groups of students to understand the nature of a problem—for instance, whether writing instruction is as effective as it should be beyond a first-year writing course, or whether technology is used to best effect in classes across the curriculum. One advantage of a focus group, as opposed to an interview, is that once one person starts talking, others join in. It is generally easier to get a conversation going in a focus group than to get an interview started with a single person.

As a method, focus groups provide a supportive environment for discussing an issue that people may feel less comfortable talking about in an interview. The conversations that emerge in focus groups may also prompt individuals to tell stories that they may not have considered relevant or interesting until they hear others telling their stories. Finally, listening to a focus group discussion can give you a pretty good idea of individuals you may want to interview.

A typical focus group session is guided by a facilitator, or moderator. The moderator's job is much like the interviewer's: to draw out information from the participants on topics of importance to a given investigation. The informal atmosphere of the focus group is intended to encourage participants to speak freely and completely about their behaviors, attitudes, and opinions. Interaction among group members often takes the form of brainstorming, generating a larger number of ideas, issues, topics, and solutions to problems than could be produced through individual conversations.

The following are several basic tasks necessary to orchestrating a focus group.

■ Select Participants for the Focus Group

Focus groups should consist of five to seven participants, in addition to you, the moderator. Think carefully about the range of participants you'll need to gather the information you're hoping to find. Depending on your issue, you might choose participants based on gender, ethnicity, major, year in school, living situation, or some other factor. Do you want a wide range of participants? Or do you want to control the focus of the conversation by looking at just one particular group of people? For instance, if you wanted to find out if technology is serving students' needs, would you talk only to people in the sciences? Or would you want a cross section of disciplines represented? Or if your question is whether colleges and universities should take race and ethnicity into consideration when selecting students from the applicant pool, would you limit participation to the admissions staff? Where should you look for input on the purpose of giving preference to minority students or the advantages of a diverse campus?

■ Plan the Focus Group

Planning is as important for a focus group as it is for an interview. Make specific arrangements with participants about the time and place of the focus group session, and be clear about how much time it will take, usually thirty to forty-five minutes. You should audio-record the session and take notes. Jot down important information during the session, and allow yourself time to make more extensive notes as soon as it is over. You will need

---

Focus Group Consent Form

You are invited to participate in a study of academic writing at the university over the next four years. You were selected from a random sample of all first-year students. If you decide to participate, you will

1. provide the researcher with copies of the writing you complete for every class and the assignment, when available.
2. attend up to four focus group sessions during a given academic year.
3. allow the researcher to use excerpts from the writing you complete and the focus group sessions in publications about research with the understanding that your identity will not be revealed at any time.

In all, out-of-class participation will take no more than four hours during an academic year.

Participation is completely voluntary; you may stop participating at any time prior to completion of the project. Should you have any questions at any time, you are welcome to contact the researcher via phone or e-mail. Your decision to participate or not will have no effect on your grade in any course or prejudice your future relationship with the university. One benefit of participating in the study is that you will have the opportunity to learn important information about writing.

If you are willing to participate in this research, please read and sign the consent form below. You will be given a copy of this form to keep.

CONSENT FORM

I agree to participate in all of the procedures above. I understand that my identity will be protected during the study and that instructors will not have access to the statements I make in focus group sessions. I also understand that my name will not be revealed when data from the research are presented in publications. (Digital files will be kept for five years and then removed from relevant databases.) I have read the above and give the researcher, Stuart Greene, and his coauthors permission to use excerpts from what I write or transcripts of tapes without identifying me as the writer or speaker.

_____   _____
Date   Signature

_____
[Telephone number]

_____
[E-mail address]

                                                        _____
                                                        Signature of Researcher

---

FIGURE 13.3 Sample Consent Form for a Focus Group

to get permission from respondents to use the information they give you and ensure their anonymity. (In your essay, you can refer to participants by letter, number, or some other designation.) Make a sheet with your signature that spells this out clearly, and make sure all your participants sign it before the session. You should include a statement pointing out that people have the right not to participate. We have included sample consent forms in Figures 13.3 and 13.4.

Alternative Focus Group Consent Form

Should colleges and universities take race and ethnicity into consideration when selecting new freshmen from the applicant pool? What is the purpose of giving preference to minority status in admissions? What does a diverse campus offer its students? These are some of the issues I want to discuss in today's focus group. But before we start, let me tell you about the assignment and your involvement.

The focus group is an interview style designed for small groups of five to seven participants. Focus group interviews are guided discussions that address a particular topic of interest or relevance to the group and the researcher. The informality of the focus group structure is intended to encourage participants to speak freely about their behaviors, attitudes, and opinions. For the purposes of my research, focus groups are a way to include multiple perspectives in my paper.

This session will be recorded so that I can prove my research. No names will be used in any drafts or in my final paper; instead, I will use letters (A, B, C) to identify different speakers. Two focus groups — one for minority students at Notre Dame and another for nonminority students — are being held so that I can obtain opinions and viewpoints from both sides of the issue and discuss their similarities and differences in my report. Some things to keep in mind during the session:

- Because I need to transcribe the dialogue, try not to talk over another person.
- Feel free to agree or disagree with a question, statement, or another person's answer.
- Focus on the discussion, not the question.
- Avoid going off on tangents.
- Be open and honest in all your responses.

Thank you for taking the time to be involved in my research. By signing below you give me permission to use the comments you provide for my paper. You understand that in no way will your identity be revealed, except by your minority or nonminority status. If you would like a copy of the results of the focus groups, please include your e-mail address, and the documents will be sent to you.

Name _____

E-mail address _____

Ethnicity _____   Male / Female   Class of _____
                                          (circle one)

FIGURE 13.4   Alternative Sample Consent Form for a Focus Group

■ Prepare Your Script

Many of the guidelines for designing interview questions (see pp. 390–92) apply equally well to focus group questions. So, for example, you might start by establishing common ground or begin with a couple of nonthreatening questions. For variety, and to keep the discussion moving, use open-ended questions. Consider asking participants in the group for definitions, impressions, examples, their ideas of others' perceptions, and the like. Also, you might quote from key passages in the scholarly research you will be using and ask for the group's responses to these "expert" theories. Not only will this be interesting for them; it also will help you organize and integrate your focus group evidence with evidence from library sources in your essay. Ask a wider range of questions than you think you might need so that you can explore side issues if they arise.

■ Conduct the Focus Group

On the day before you conduct the focus group, contact those who have agreed to participate to remind them of when and where it will happen. Show up ahead of time to set up your recording equipment and make sure that the room has sufficient seating for the participants. And don't forget your script. Here are three other guidelines.

Ask questions that draw people out.   During the focus group, be ready to draw out participants with follow-up questions ("Can you offer an example?" "Where do you think this impression comes from?"). Encourage all participants to speak; don't allow one member to dominate the discussion. (You may need to ask a facilitating question like "Do the rest of you agree with X's statement?" or "How would you extend what X has said?" or "Has anyone had a different experience?")

Limit the time of a focus group session.   It's a good idea to limit the session to thirty to forty-five minutes. When deciding how long the session should last, remember that it will take approximately three times longer to transcribe it manually. Even if you use transcription software, you'll need to spend time checking the transcription against the recording for accuracy. You must transcribe the session so that you can read through the participants' comments and quote them accurately.

Notice nonverbal interactions.   Be sure to notice nonverbal interactions and responses in your session, taking notes of body language, reluctance or eagerness to speak, and dynamics among group members that either open up or shut down conversation. These responses should be part of the data you analyze. For this reason, and also because keeping track of multiple speakers in an audio recording can be challenging, video recording may be more effective than audio recording for focus groups. If filming your group is not an option, you will need to take careful notes about interactions during the session.

■ Interpret the Data from the Focus Group

Once you transcribe your focus group session, remember to refer anonymously to your participants in your analysis. You then need to interpret the significance of the way participants talk about issues, as well as the information they relate. Interpret the nonverbal communication in the group as well as the verbal communication.

In making claims based on focus group data, remember that data from focus group interviews are not the same as data from individual interviews. They reflect collective thinking, ideas shared and negotiated by the group. Also, although you might speculate that data from a focus group are indicative of larger trends, be careful about the kinds of claims you make. One first-year student's idea is not necessarily every first-year student's idea.

The principal aim of doing original research is to make a contribution to a conversation using primary material as evidence to support your argument. For instance, when you conduct interviews or focus group discussions, you are collecting information (or data) that can offer a unique perspective. And doing original research also can enable you to test others' claims or assumptions and broaden your scope of inquiry beyond secondary materials. An effective piece of original research still relies on secondary materials, particularly as you find ways to locate what you discover in the context of what other authors have observed and argued. Moreover, there is the value of using multiple sources of information to support your claims — using your observations and the findings of others to say something about your subject. Also important, the research methods you choose depend on the question you ask. A focus on the types of educational opportunities available to the homeless lends itself more to close observation, interviews, and perhaps focus groups.

■ Important Ethical Considerations

Finally, we want to end with an ethical reminder: *Be fair to your sources.* Throughout this chapter, we have included a number of forms on which you can base your own consent forms when you conduct interviews and focus groups. When people give you their consent to use their words, it is incumbent on you—really it is essential—that you represent as faithfully as possible what people have said. As a researcher, you are given a kind of power over the people you interview and write about, using what they tell you for your own purposes. You cannot abuse the trust they place in you when they consent to be part of your research. It is important that they understand why you're doing the research and how your theories and assumptions will likely figure into your interpretation of the information you gather. You must also be aware of how their words will be construed by those who read what you write.

Steps for Conducting a Focus Group

1. **Select participants for the focus group.** Identify the range of your five to seven participants. Are you looking for diverse perspectives or a more specialized group?

2. **Plan the focus group.** Make sure that you have a specified time and place and that your participants are willing to sign consent forms.

3. **Prepare your script.** Prepare a variety of open-ended questions; consider quoting research you are interested in using in your paper to get participants' responses; and try to rehearse and revise.

4. **Conduct the focus group.** Record the session; ask questions that draw people out; limit the time of the session; and notice nonverbal interactions. And don't forget the consent forms.

5. **Interpret the data from the focus group.** Transcribe and analyze the data, including nonverbal communications; draw conclusions, but be careful not to overgeneralize from your small sample.

Entering the Conversation of Ideas

Education

What does it mean to be educated? Who has access to a good education, and why?

© RUCHUDA BOONPLIEN/Shutterstock.com

Students do not always get a chance to step back and reflect on the many elements that shape the educational system—elements that at this very moment affect what you are learning, how you are learning it, and the kind of educated person you will be when you graduate. The readings in this chapter take a range of approaches to two central questions: What does it mean to be educated? Who in the United States has access to a good education, and why?

Mark Edmundson launches the chapter with a provocative question: "Who Are You and What Are You Doing Here? A Word to the Incoming Class." In this lively essay, he challenges new college students to reconsider their ideas of what college is for and proposes that to get a "real education," you may have to work against the comforts of your university, and perhaps even the expectation that landing a specific job is the point of a college degree. Edmundson argues for something more transformative: "The quest at the center of a liberal arts education is not a luxury quest, it's a necessity quest." You will be able to discover whether you agree.

Laura Pappano also examines university life, but she focuses on what happens outside the classroom — in the realm of big-time college sports. Pappano asks why campus identity so often revolves around sports rather than academic accomplishments. (Try to imagine what Mark Edmundson's answer to that question might be.) Whether or not you are a sports fan, the data Pappano offers should make you think carefully about the money in college athletics and the campus traditions that so often interfere with the academic pursuits of both athletes and fans. What is college for?

The other authors in this chapter invite you to consider your earlier educational experiences and to recognize that they unfold in a nation of profound inequalities. Although public education is widely thought to be the most crucial element of a democracy, clearly not all public education in the United States is equal. Two short opinion columns from the *New York Times* offer different perspectives on the income gap and public education: Susan Dynarski's "Why American Schools Are Even More Unequal Than We Thought" and a piece titled "The Good News about Educational Inequality," coauthored by Sean Reardon, Jane Waldfogel, and Daphna Bassok. Both essays consider the long-term effects of childhood poverty on education. After some consideration, you may find that while these pieces examine different data, they might find common ground on solutions.

The final selection in this chapter, by Nikole Hannah-Jones, is a close analysis of the adjoining school districts in Missouri that made national news because of the shooting death of Michael Brown in Ferguson. What does Michael Brown's death have to do with education? Hannah-Jones takes readers on a historical exploration of the myriad political and social shifts in this portion of the country that demonstrate how race and social class so often stack the deck against generations of Americans. The world Hannah-Jones paints may seem far away from the collegiate concerns of grade inflation or tailgating that Edmundson and Pappano write about, but they are certainly connected.

All the writers in this chapter push us to ask what it means in contemporary culture to be educated and who has access to which kinds of education. These readings should help you see your past and present educational experiences through fresh eyes and consider the relationship between education and social power. What do *you* think it should mean to be an educated person in the contemporary United States? Why have we come to accept such profound inequalities in our educational system, and what might create change?

MARK EDMUNDSON

Who Are You and What Are You Doing Here?
A Word to the Incoming Class

Mark Edmundson is an award-winning professor of English at the University of Virginia who writes literary criticism and publishes on a wide range of cultural topics, including the power of profanity, the meanings of football, and the politics of reading and writing. Edmundson has written many popular-press books on the business of teaching and learning. "Who Are You and What Are You Doing Here? A Word to the Incoming Class" is a chapter from *Why Teach? In Defense of a Real Education* (2013). In it, you will hear Edmundson's very distinctive voice, which can be funny as well as sharply critical. He enjoys the role of cultural gadfly and hopes to provoke readers—particularly students—to reconsider their goals.

This essay is written as a "Word to the Incoming Class." As you read, imagine what your response would be if someone spoke these words at your own college orientation. Just a few paragraphs in, Edmundson claims that not only are you going to have to "fight" to get a real education, but you will very likely have to "fight against the institution that you find yourself in." His definition of what a "real education" is emerges throughout the essay. As you read, keep track of his ideas, but also measure them against your own beliefs. What exactly are you hoping to get out of college? Where do you agree and disagree with Edmundson's strongly worded ideas?

Throughout the essay, Edmundson moves between reflections on past conversations with his father before he started his own college career and a current argument that a "real education" means more than getting a job or becoming a "success," if that is measured only in material gains (para. 10). Edmundson has equal criticism for students, professors, and even administrators who, he claims, miss the enormous transformative potential of education. What complaints does he lodge against each of these groups, and how fair is he, given your experience?

Because this is an article for a general readership, Edmundson does not quote other scholars at length or cite them in a bibliography or Works Cited page. However, he does draw on a wide range of literary and cultural references and assumes his readers know what he means when he refers to Foucault (para. 28–29) or Schopenhauer, Burke, Emerson, Dickinson, Blake, Thoreau, and especially Freud. Do you usually look up names and words you don't know? How might your willingness—or unwillingness—to do this "extra" work be connected to Edmundson's argument about "real education"?

Near his conclusion, Edmundson admits, "The whole business is scary, of course," if we take on the challenge of education as the kind of self-transformation he calls for. It may be a challenge to square your own ideals with the realities of supporting yourself as an adult. However, Edmundson argues we should refuse this dichotomy between ideals and practicality: "The quest at the center of a liberal arts education is not a luxury quest, it's a necessity quest" (para. 27). Understanding what he means could change your life.

Welcome and congratulations: Getting to the first day of college is a   *1*
major achievement. You're to be commended, and not just you, but
the parents, grandparents, uncles, and aunts who helped get you here.

It's been said that raising a child effectively takes a village: Well, as you   *2*
may have noticed, our American village is not in very good shape. We've
got guns, drugs, wars, fanatical religions, a slime-based popular culture,
and some politicians who—a little restraint here—aren't what they might
be. Merely to survive in this American village and to win a place in the
entering class has taken a lot of grit on your part. So, yes, congratulations
to all.

You now may think that you've about got it made. Amid the impressive   *3*
college buildings, in company with a high-powered faculty, surrounded by
the best of your generation, all you need is to keep doing what you've done
before: Work hard, get good grades, listen to your teachers, get along with
the people around you, and you'll emerge in four years as an educated
young man or woman. Ready for life.

Do not believe it. It is not true. If you want to get a real education in   *4*
America, you're going to have to fight—and I don't mean just fight against
the drugs and the violence and against the slime-based culture that is still
going to surround you. I mean something a little more disturbing. To get
an education, you're probably going to have to fight against the institution that you find yourself in—no matter how prestigious it may be. (In
fact, the more prestigious the school, the more you'll probably have to
push.) You can get a terrific education in America now—there are aston-
ishing opportunities at almost every college—but the education will not
be presented to you wrapped and bowed. To get it, you'll need to struggle
and strive, to be strong, and occasionally even to piss off some admirable
people.

I came to college with few resources, but one of them was an under-   *5*
standing, however crude, of how I might use my opportunities there. This I
began to develop because of my father, who had never been to college—in
fact, he'd barely gotten out of high school. One night after dinner, he and I
were sitting in our kitchen at 58 Clewley Road in Medford, Massachusetts,
hatching plans about the rest of my life. I was about to go off to college,
a feat no one in my family had accomplished in living memory. "I think I
might want to be prelaw," I told my father. I had no idea what being prelaw was. My father compressed his brow and blew twin streams of smoke,
dragonlike, from his magnificent nose. "Do you want to be a lawyer?" he
asked. My father had some experience with lawyers, and with policemen,
too; he was not well disposed toward either. "I'm not really sure," I told
him, "but lawyers make pretty good money, right?"

My father detonated. (That was not uncommon. He detonated a lot.)   *6*
He told me that I was going to go to college only once, and that while I was
there I had better study what I wanted. He said that when rich kids went
to school, they majored in the subjects that interested them, and that my

younger brother Philip and I were as good as any rich kids. (We were rich kids minus the money.) Wasn't I interested in literature? I confessed that I was. Then I had better study literature, unless I had inside information to the effect that reincarnation wasn't just hype, and I'd be able to attend college thirty or forty times. If I had such info, prelaw would be fine, and maybe even a tour through invertebrate biology could also be tossed in. But until I had the reincarnation stuff from a solid source, I better get to work and pick out some English classes from the course catalog.

"How about the science requirements?" I asked.   7

"Take 'em later," he said. "You never know."   8

My father, Wright Aukenhead Edmundson, Malden High School class   9
of 1948 (by a hair), knew the score. What he told me that evening at the Clewley Road kitchen table was true in itself, and it also contains the germ of an idea about what a university education should be. But apparently almost everyone else—students, teachers, trustees, and parents—see the matter much differently. They have it wrong.

Education has one salient enemy in present-day America, and that 10
enemy is education—university education in particular. To almost everyone, university education is a means to an end. For students, that end is a good job. Students want the credentials that will help them get ahead. They want the certificate that will grant them access to Wall Street, or entrance into law or medical or business school. And how can we blame them? America values power and money, big players with big bucks. When we raise our children, we tell them in multiple ways that what we want most for them is success—material success. To be poor in America is to be a failure. It's to be without decent health care, without basic necessities, often without dignity. Then there are those back-breaking student loans: People leave school as servants, indentured to pay massive bills, so that first job better be a good one. Students come to college with the goal of a diploma in mind—what happens to them in between, especially in classrooms, is often of no deep and determining interest to them.

In college, life is elsewhere. Life is at parties, at clubs, in music, with 11
friends, in sports. Life is what celebrities have. The idea that the courses you take should be the primary objective of going to college is tacitly considered absurd. In terms of their work, students live in the future and not the present; they live with their prospects for success. If universities stopped issuing credentials, half of the clients would be gone by tomorrow morning, with the remainder following fast behind.

The faculty, too, is often absent: Their real lives are also elsewhere. 12
Like most of their students, they aim to get on. The work they are compelled to do to advance—get tenure, promotion, raises, outside offers—is, broadly speaking, scholarly work. No matter what anyone says, this work has precious little to do with the fundamentals of teaching. The proof is that virtually no undergraduate students can read and understand their

professors' scholarly publications. The public senses this disparity and so thinks of the professors' work as being silly or beside the point. Some of it is. But the public also senses that because professors don't pay full-bore attention to teaching, they don't have to work very hard—they've created a massive feather bed for themselves and called it a university.

This is radically false. Ambitious professors, the ones who, like their students, want to get ahead in America, work furiously. Scholarship, even if pretentious and almost unreadable, is nonetheless labor-intense. One can slave for a year or two on a single article for publication in this or that refereed journal. These essays are honest: Their footnotes reflect real reading, real assimilation, and real dedication. Shoddy work—in which the author cheats, cuts corners, copies from others—is quickly detected. The people who do the work have highly developed intellectual powers, and they push themselves hard to reach a certain standard. That the results have almost no practical relevance for students, the public, or even, frequently, other scholars is a central element in the tragicomedy that is often academia. *13*

The students and the professors have made a deal: Neither of them has to throw himself heart and soul into what happens in the classroom. The students write their abstract, overintellectualized essays; the professors grade the students for their capacity to be abstract and overintellectual—and often genuinely smart. For their essays can be brilliant, in a chilly way; they can also be clipped from the Internet, and often are. Whatever the case, no one wants to invest too much in them—for life is elsewhere. The professor saves his energies for the profession, while the student saves his for friends, social life, volunteer work, making connections, and getting in position to clasp hands on the true grail, the first job. *14*

No one in this picture is evil; no one is criminally irresponsible. It's just that smart people are prone to look into matters to see how they might go about buttering their toast. Then they butter their toast. *15*

As for the administrators, their relation to the students often seems based not on love but fear. Administrators fear bad publicity, scandal, and dissatisfaction on the part of their customers. More than anything else, though, they fear lawsuits. Throwing a student out of college for this or that piece of bad behavior is very difficult, almost impossible. The student will sue your eyes out. One kid I knew (and rather liked) threatened on his blog to mince his dear and esteemed professor (me) with a samurai sword for the crime of having taught a boring class. (The class *was* a little boring—I had a damn cold—but the punishment seemed a bit severe.) The dean of students laughed lightly when I suggested that this behavior might be grounds for sending the student on a brief vacation. I was, you might say, discomfited, and showed up to class for a while with my cell phone jiggered to dial 911 with one touch. *16*

Still, this was small potatoes. Colleges are even leery of disciplining guys who have committed sexual assault, or assault plain and simple. *17*

Instead of being punished, these guys frequently stay around, strolling the quad and swilling the libations, an affront (and sometimes a terror) to their victims.

You'll find that cheating is common as well. As far as I can discern, 18 the student ethos goes like this: If the professor is so lazy that he gives the same test every year, it's okay to go ahead and take advantage—you've got better things to do. The Internet is amok with services selling term papers, and those services exist, capitalism being what it is, because people purchase the papers—lots of them. Fraternity files bulge with old tests from a variety of courses. Periodically, the public gets exercised about this situation and there are articles in the national news. But then interest dwindles and matters go back to normal.

One of the reasons professors sometimes look the other way when 19 they sense cheating is that it sends them into a world of sorrow. A friend of mine had the temerity to detect cheating on the part of a kid who was the nephew of a well-placed official in an Arab government complexly aligned with the U.S. Black limousines pulled up in front of his office and disgorged decorously suited negotiators. Did my pal fold? No, he's not the type. But he did not enjoy the process.

What colleges generally want are well-rounded students, civic leaders, 20 people who know what the system demands, how to keep matters light and not push too hard for an education or anything else; people who get their credentials and leave professors alone to do their brilliant work so they may rise and enhance the rankings of the university. Such students leave and become donors and so, in their own turn, contribute immeasurably to the university's standing. They've done a fine job skating on surfaces in high school—the best way to get an across-the-board outstanding record—and now they're on campus to cut a few more figure eights.

In a culture where the major and determining values are monetary, 21 what else could you do? How else would you live if not by getting all you can, succeeding all you can, making all you can?

The idea that a university education really should have no substantial 22 content, should not be about what John Keats was disposed to call "Soul-making," is one that you might think professors and university presidents would be discreet about. Not so. This view informed an address that Richard Brodhead gave to the senior class at Yale before he departed to become president of Duke. Brodhead, an impressive, articulate man, seems to take as his educational touchstone the Duke of Wellington's precept that the Battle of Waterloo was won on the playing fields of Eton. Brodhead suggests that the content of the course isn't really what matters. In five years (or five months, or minutes), the student is likely to have forgotten how to do the problem sets and will only hazily recollect what happens in the ninth book of *Paradise Lost*. The legacy of their college years will be a legacy of difficulties overcome. When they face equally arduous tasks later in life, students will tap their old resources of determination, and they'll win.

All right, there's nothing wrong with this as far as it goes—after all,   *23*
the student who writes a brilliant forty-page thesis in a hard week has
learned more than a little about her inner resources. Maybe it will give
her needed confidence in the future. But doesn't the content of the courses
matter at all?

On the evidence of this talk, no. Trying to figure out whether the stuff   *24*
you're reading is true or false and being open to having your life changed
is a fraught, controversial activity. Doing so requires energy from the professor—which is better spent on other matters. This kind of perspective-
altering teaching and learning can cause the things that administrators
fear above all else: trouble, arguments, bad press, [et cetera]. After the
kid-samurai episode, the chair of my department not unsympathetically
suggested that this was the sort of incident that could happen when you
brought a certain intensity to teaching. At the time I found this remark a
tad detached, but maybe he was right.

So if you want an education, the odds aren't with you: The professors   *25*
are off doing what they call their own work; the other students, who've
doped out the way the place runs, are busy leaving their professors alone
and getting themselves in position for bright and shining futures; the student-services people are trying to keep everyone content, offering plenty of
entertainment and building another state-of-the-art workout facility every
few months. The development office is already scanning you for future
donations.

So why make trouble? Why not just go along? Let the profs roam free   *26*
in the realms of pure thought, let yourselves party in the realms of impure
pleasure, and let the student-services gang assert fewer prohibitions and
newer delights for you. You'll get a good job, you'll have plenty of friends,
you'll have a driveway of your own.

You'll also, if my father and I are right, be truly and righteously   *27*
screwed. The reason for this is simple. The quest at the center of a liberal
arts education is not a luxury quest; it's a necessity quest. If you do not
undertake it, you risk leading a life of desperation—maybe quiet; maybe,
in time, very loud—and I am not exaggerating. For you risk trying to be
someone other than who you are, which, in the long run, is killing.

By the time you come to college, you will have been told who you are   *28*
numberless times. Your parents and friends, your teachers, your counselors, your priests and rabbis and ministers and imams have all had their
say. They've let you know how they size you up, and they've let you know
what they think you should value. They've given you a sharp and pro-
tracted taste of what they feel is good and bad, right and wrong. Much
is on their side. They have confronted you with scriptures—holy books
that, whatever their actual provenance, have given people what they feel
to be wisdom for thousands of years. They've given you family traditions—you've learned the ways of your tribe and community. And, too,
you've been tested, probed, looked at up and down and through. The coach

knows what your athletic prospects are, the guidance office has a sheaf of test scores that relegate you to this or that ability quadrant, and your teachers have got you pegged. You are, as Foucault might say, the intersection of many evaluative and potentially determining discourses: You, boy, you, girl, have been made.

And—contra Foucault—that's not so bad. Embedded in all of the *29* major religions are profound truths. Schopenhauer, who despised belief in transcendent things, nonetheless taught Christianity to be of inexpressible worth. He couldn't believe in the divinity of Jesus or in the afterlife, but to Schopenhauer, a deep pessimist, a religion that had as its central emblem the figure of a man being tortured on a cross couldn't be entirely misleading. To the Christian, Schopenhauer said, pain was at the center of the understanding of life, and that was just as it should be.

One does not need to be as harsh as Schopenhauer to understand the *30* use of religion, even if one does not believe in an otherworldly God. And all those teachers and counselors and friends—and the prognosticating uncles, the dithering aunts, the fathers and mothers with their hopes for your fulfillment, or their fulfillment in you—should not necessarily be cast aside or ignored. Families have their wisdom. The question "Who do they think you are at home?" is never an idle one.

The major conservative thinkers have always been very serious about *31* what goes by the name of common sense. Edmund Burke saw common sense as a loosely made but often profound collective work in which humanity deposited its hard-earned wisdom—the precipitate of joy and tears—over time. You have been raised in proximity to common sense, if you've been raised at all, and common sense is something to respect, though not quite—peace unto the formidable Burke—to revere.

You may be all that the good people who raised you say you are; you *32* may want all they have shown you is worth wanting; you may be someone who is truly your father's son or your mother's daughter. But then again, you may not be.

For the power that is in you, as Emerson suggested, may be new *33* in nature. You may not be the person that your parents take you to be. And—this thought is both more exciting and more dangerous—you may not be the person that you take yourself to be, either. You may not have read yourself aright, and college is the place where you can find out whether you have or not. The reason to read Blake and Dickinson and Freud and Dickens is not to become more cultivated or more articulate or to be someone who, at a cocktail party, is never embarrassed (or can embarrass others). The best reason to read them is to see if they know you better than you know yourself. You may find your own suppressed and rejected thoughts following back to you with an "alienated majesty." Reading the great writers, you may have the experience Longinus associated with the sublime: You feel that you have actually created the text yourself. For somehow your predecessors are more yourself than you are.

This was my own experience reading the two writers who have influ-   *34*
enced me the most, Sigmund Freud and Ralph Waldo Emerson. They gave
words to thoughts and feelings that I had never been able to render myself.
They shone a light onto the world, and what they saw, suddenly I saw, too.
From Emerson I learned to trust my own thoughts, to trust them even
when every voice seems to be on the other side. I need the wherewithal,
as Emerson did, to say what's on my mind and to take the inevitable hits.
Much more I learned from the sage—about character, about loss, about
joy, about writing and its secret sources, but Emerson most centrally
preaches the gospel of self-reliance, and that is what I have tried most to
take from him. I continue to hold in mind one of Emerson's most memorable passages: "Society is a joint-stock company, in which the members
agree, for the better securing of his bread to each shareholder, to surrender
the liberty and culture of the eater. The virtue in most request is confor-
mity. Self-reliance is its aversion. It loves not realities and creators, but
names and customs."

Emerson's greatness lies not only in showing you how powerful names   *35*
and customs can be, but also in demonstrating how exhilarating it is to
buck them. When he came to Harvard to talk about religion, he shocked
the professors and students by challenging the divinity of Jesus and the
truth of his miracles. He wasn't invited back for decades.

From Freud I found a great deal to ponder as well. I don't mean   *36*
Freud the aspiring scientist, but the Freud who was a speculative essayist
and interpreter of the human condition like Emerson. Freud challenges
nearly every significant human ideal. He goes after religion. He says that
it comes down to the longing for the father. He goes after love. He calls it
"the overestimation of the erotic object." He attacks our desire for charismatic popular leaders. We're drawn to them because we hunger for abso-
lute authority. He declares that dreams don't predict the future and that
there's nothing benevolent about them. They're disguised fulfillments of
repressed wishes.

Freud has something challenging and provoking to say about virtually   *37*
every human aspiration. I learned that if I wanted to affirm any consequential ideal, I had to talk my way past Freud. He was—and is—a perpetual challenge and goad.

Never has there been a more shrewd and imaginative cartographer of   *38*
the psyche. His separation of the self into three parts, and his sense of the
fraught, anxious, but often negotiable relations among them (negotiable
when you come to the game with a Freudian knowledge), does a great deal
to help one navigate experience. (Though sometimes—and I owe this to
Emerson—it seems right to let the psyche fall into civil war, accepting bar-
rages of anxiety and grief for this or that good reason.)

The battle is to make such writers one's own, to winnow them out   *39*
and to find their essential truths. We need to see where they fall short and
where they exceed the mark, and then to develop them a little, as the ideas
themselves, one comes to see, actually developed others. (Both Emerson

and Freud live out of Shakespeare—but only a giant can be truly influenced by Shakespeare.) In reading, I continue to look for one thing—to be influenced, to learn something new, to be thrown off my course and onto another, better way.

My father knew that he was dissatisfied with life. He knew that none 40 of the descriptions people had for him quite fit. He understood that he was always out of joint with life as it was. He had talent: My brother and I each got about half the raw ability he possessed, and that's taken us through life well enough. But what to do with that talent—there was the rub for my father. He used to stroll through the house intoning his favorite line from Groucho Marx's ditty "Whatever It Is, I'm Against It." (I recently asked my son, now twenty-one, if he thought I was mistaken in teaching him this particular song when he was six years old. "No!" he said, filling the air with an invisible forest of exclamation points.) But what my father never managed to get was a sense of who he might become. He never had a world of possibilities spread before him, never made sustained contact with the best that has been thought and said. He didn't get to revise his understanding of himself, figure out what he'd do best that might give the world some profit.

My father was a gruff man but also a generous one, so that night at 41 the kitchen table at 58 Clewley Road he made an effort to let me have the chance that had been denied to him by both fate and character. He gave me the chance to see what I was all about, and if it proved to be different from him, proved even to be something he didn't like or entirely comprehend, then he'd deal with it.

Right now, if you're going to get a real education, you may have to be 42 aggressive and assertive.

Your professors will give you some fine books to read, and they'll probably help you understand them. What they won't do, for reasons that perplex me, is ask you if the books contain truths you could live your life by. When you read Plato, you'll probably learn about his metaphysics and his politics and his way of conceiving the soul. But no one will ask you if his ideas are good enough to believe in. No one will ask you, in the words of Emerson's disciple William James, what their "cash value" might be. No one will suggest that you might use Plato as your bible for a week or a year or longer. No one, in short, will ask you to use Plato to help you change your life.

That will be up to you. You must put the question of Plato to yourself. You must ask whether reason should always rule the passions, philosophers should always rule the state, and poets should inevitably be banished from a just commonwealth. You have to ask yourself if wildly expressive music (rock and rap and the rest) deranges the soul in ways that are destructive to its health. You must inquire of yourself if balanced calm is the most desirable human state.

Occasionally—for you will need some help in fleshing out the answers—you may have to prod your professors to see if they will take the text at hand—in this case the divine and disturbing Plato—to be true. And you will have to be tough if the professor mocks you for uttering a sincere question instead of keeping matters easy for all concerned by staying detached and analytical. (Detached analysis has a place, but in the end you've got to speak from the heart and pose the question of truth.) You'll be the one who pesters your teachers. You'll ask your history teacher about whether there is a design to our history, whether we're progressing or declining, or whether, in the words of a fine recent play, *The History Boys*, history's "just one fuckin' thing after another." You'll be the one who challenges your biology teacher about the intellectual conflict between evolutionist and creationist thinking. You'll not only question the statistics teacher about what numbers *can* explain but what they can't.

Because every subject you study is a language, and since you may adopt 46 one of these languages as your own, you'll want to know how to speak it expertly and also how it fails to deal with those concerns for which it has no adequate words. You'll be looking into the reach of every metaphor that every discipline offers, and you'll be trying to see around their corners.

The whole business is scary, of course. What if you arrive at college 47 devoted to premed, sure that nothing will make you and your family happier than life as a physician, only to discover that elementary schoolteaching is where your heart is?

You might learn that you're not meant to be a doctor at all. Of course, 48 given your intellect and discipline, you can still probably be one. You can pound your round peg through the very square hole of medical school, then go off into the profession. And society will help you. Society has a cornucopia of resources to encourage you in doing what society needs done but that you don't much like doing and are not cut out to do. To ease your grief, society offers alcohol, television, drugs, divorce, and buying, buying, buying what you don't need. But all those, too, have their costs.

Education is about finding out what form of work for you is close to 49 being play—work you do so easily that it restores you as you go. Randall Jarrell once said that if he were a rich man, he would pay money to teach poetry to students. (I would, too, for what it's worth.) In saying that, he (like my father) hinted in the direction of a profound and true theory of learning.

Having found what's best for you to do, you may be surprised by how 50 far you rise, how prosperous, even against your own projections, you become. The student who eschews medical school to follow his gift for teaching small children spends his twenties in low-paying but pleasurable and soul-rewarding toil. He's always behind on his student-loan payments; he still lives in a house with four other guys, not all of whom got proper instructions on how to clean a bathroom. He buys shirts from the Salvation Army, has intermittent Internet, and vacations where he can. But lo—he has a gift for teaching. He writes an essay about how to teach, then a book—which no one buys. But he writes another—in part out of a feeling of injured merit, perhaps—and that one they do buy.

Money is still a problem, but in a new sense. The world wants him to *51* write more, lecture, travel more, and will pay him for his efforts, and he likes this a good deal. But he also likes staying around and showing up at school and figuring out how to get this or that little runny-nosed specimen to begin learning how to read. These are the kinds of problems that are worth having, and if you advance, as Thoreau asked us to do, in the general direction of your dreams, you may have them. If you advance in the direction of someone else's dreams—if you want to live someone else's dreams rather than yours—then get a TV for every room, buy yourself a lifetime supply of your favorite quaff, crank up the porn channel, and groove away. But when we expend our energies in rightful ways, Robert Frost observed, we stay whole and vigorous and we don't get weary. "Strongly spent," the poet says, "is synonymous with kept."

■ ■ ■

Reading as a Writer: Analyzing Rhetorical Choices

1. How would you describe Edmundson's ethos (Chapter 9) in this essay? How would you characterize his tone and attitude? Find three passages that you think best illustrate the author's self-representation and discuss how this contributes to or detracts from the argument he makes in this essay.

2. Edmundson names many authors who have shaped his worldview. What do you notice about the writers he lists? Name and discuss some writers who have made a big impact on the way you see the world (and don't forget popular authors like J. K. Rowling or John Green). How diverse is your list? In what ways did these writers contribute to what Edmundson would call your "real education"?

Writing as a Reader: Entering the Conversation of Ideas

1. Edmundson and Nikole Hannah-Jones (pp. 434–52) critique the educational system from very different perspectives, yet both are concerned with the ways the transformative potential of education is often lost for a variety of reasons. Write an essay in which you examine the concept of education as transformation, taking into consideration these authors' claims about the cultural barriers often blocking students from effective education. What is your evaluation of the authors' proposals for change?

2. Consider Mark Edmundson's claims alongside the ideas raised in the following Chapter 4 readings: Stuart Rojstaczer's "Grade Inflation Gone Wild" (pp. 108–10) and Phil Primack's "Doesn't Anybody Get a C Anymore?" (pp. 110–12). Write an essay in which you draw on these authors' complaints and proposals about an improved educational experience to advance your own argument for a "real education" that includes evaluation that you believe is fair and useful.

LAURA PAPPANO

How Big-Time Sports Ate College Life

Laura Pappano is an investigative journalist who writes on education and gender equity issues, including the role of sports culture and the university system. Her writing has appeared in the *New York Times*, the *Boston Globe*, and the *Washington Post*, among many other popular newspapers and magazines. The short paragraphing style in this essay is typical of journalistic writing rather than academic writing. However, Pappano demonstrates many other habits of academic writing, such as supporting her argument with a range of evidence from experts and understanding that most issues grow in complexity the more we analyze them. In this essay, Pappano begins with the premise: "For good or for ill, big-time sports has become the public face of the university, the brand that admissions offices sell, a public-relations machine thanks to ESPN exposure" (para. 8). As the essay unfolds, we learn exactly what she means by the phrase "for good or for ill."

As you read, keep track of the range of evidence Pappano provides to support her claim that the business of college sports has both enhanced universities' profiles (and incomes) and damaged the experience of learning for both student athletes and student fans. What statistics and data does she offer, and how persuasive do you find this evidence? Pappano also offers many anecdotes from college life that you may recognize, including tailgating or valuing good stadium seats over classroom insights (para. 38).

Pappano's depiction of college sports may not be entirely comfortable to read, but that is her point. She asks hard questions that should inspire readers to reconsider the normalization of sports culture in university life. Why does calling yourself a Commodore or a Cornhusker or a Blue Devil (or any other school mascot) matter so much? Why does campus identity so often revolve around sports rather than academic accomplishments? Pappano urges us to question the default setting of sports as the central identity of university life. What would your campus gain, and perhaps lose, if university life revolved around (just imagine!) academic learning and achievement?

■ ■ ■

It was a great day to be a Buckeye. Josh Samuels, a junior from Cincinnati, dates his decision to attend Ohio State to Nov. 10, 2007, and the chill he felt when the band took the field during a football game against Illinois. "I looked over at my brother and I said, 'I'm going here. There is nowhere else I'd rather be.'" (Even though Illinois won, 28–21.)   1

Tim Collins, a junior who is president of Block O, the 2,500-member student fan organization, understands the rush. "It's not something I usually admit to, that I applied to Ohio State 60 percent for the sports. But the more I do tell that to people, they'll say it's a big reason why they came, too."   2

Ohio State boasts 17 members of the American Academy of Arts ₃ and Sciences, three Nobel laureates, eight Pulitzer Prize winners, 35 Guggenheim Fellows and a MacArthur winner. But sports rule.

"It's not, 'Oh, yeah, Ohio State, that wonderful physics department.' ₄ It's football," said Gordon Aubrecht, an Ohio State physics professor.

Last month, Ohio State hired Urban Meyer to coach football for $4 ₅ million a year plus bonuses (playing in the B.C.S. National Championship game nets him an extra $250,000; a graduation rate over 80 percent would be worth $150,000). He has personal use of a private jet.

Dr. Aubrecht says he doesn't have enough money in his own budget ₆ to cover attendance at conferences. "From a business perspective," he can see why Coach Meyer was hired, but he calls the package just more evidence that the "tail is wagging the dog."

Dr. Aubrecht is not just another cranky tenured professor. Hand- ₇ wringing seems to be universal these days over big-time sports, specifically football and men's basketball. Sounding much like his colleague, James J. Duderstadt, former president of the University of Michigan and author of "Intercollegiate Athletics and the American University," said this: "Nine of 10 people don't understand what you are saying when you talk about research universities. But you say 'Michigan' and they understand those striped helmets running under the banner."

For good or ill, big-time sports has become the public face of the uni- ₈ versity, the brand that admissions offices sell, a public-relations machine thanks to ESPN exposure. At the same time, it has not been a good year for college athletics. Child abuse charges against a former Penn State assistant football coach brought down the program's legendary head coach and the university's president. Not long after, allegations of abuse came to light against an assistant basketball coach at Syracuse University. Combine that with the scandals over boosters showering players with cash and perks at Ohio State and, allegedly, the University of Miami and a glaring power gap becomes apparent between the programs and the institutions that house them.

"There is certainly a national conversation going on now that I can't ₉ ever recall taking place," said William E. Kirwan, chancellor of the University of Maryland system and co-director of the Knight Commission on Intercollegiate Athletics. "We've reached a point where big-time intercollegiate athletics is undermining the integrity of our institutions, diverting presidents and institutions from their main purpose."

The damage to reputation was clear in a November survey by Wid- ₁₀ meyer Communications in which 83 percent of 1,000 respondents blamed the "culture of big money" in college sports for Penn State officials' failure to report suspected child abuse to local law enforcement; 40 percent said they would discourage their child from choosing a Division I institution "that places a strong emphasis on sports," and 72 percent said Division I sports has "too much influence over college life."

FIGURE 14.1   Buckeye Nation: Unbridled enthusiasm reigns at Ohio State games.

Has big-time sports hijacked the American campus? The word today is *11* "balance," and the worry is how to achieve it.

The explosion in televised games has spread sports fever well beyond *12* traditional hotbeds like Alabama and Ole Miss. Classes are canceled to accommodate broadcast schedules, and new research suggests that fandom can affect academic performance. Campus life itself revolves around not just going to games but lining up and camping out to get into them.

"It's become so important on the college campus that it's one of the only *13* ways the student body knows how to come together," said Allen Sack, president-elect of the Drake Group, a faculty network that lobbies for academic integrity in college sports. "In China and other parts of the world, there are no gigantic stadiums in the middle of campus. There is a laser focus on education as being the major thing. In the United States, we play football."

Dr. Sack, interim dean of the University of New Haven's college of business, was sipping orange juice at a coffee shop a few blocks from the Yale *14* Bowl. It was a fitting place to meet, given that when the Ivy League was formed in 1954, presidents of the eight member colleges saw where football was headed and sought to stop it. The pact they made, according to a contemporaneous account in *The Harvard Crimson*, aimed to ensure that players would "enjoy the game as participants in a form of recreational competition rather than as professional performers in public spectacles."

There is nothing recreational about Division I football today, points *15* out Dr. Sack, who played for Notre Dame in the 1960s. Since then, athletic departments have kicked the roof off their budgets, looking more like independent franchises than university departments.

It is that point—"this commercial thing" in the middle of academia, as *16* Charles T. Clotfelter, a public policy professor at Duke, put it—that some believe has thrown the system out of kilter. In his recent book "Big-Time Sports in American Universities," Dr. Clotfelter notes that between 1985 and 2010, average salaries at public universities rose 32 percent for full professors, 90 percent for presidents and 650 percent for football coaches.

The same trend is apparent in a 2010 Knight Commission report *17* that found the 10 highest-spending athletic departments spent a median of $98 million in 2009, compared with $69 million just four years earlier. Spending on high-profile sports grew at double to triple the pace of that on academics. For example, Big Ten colleges, including Penn State, spent a median of $111,620 per athlete on athletics and $18,406 per student on academics.

Division I football and basketball, of course, bring in millions of dol- *18* lars a year in ticket sales, booster donations and cable deals. Penn State football is a money-maker: 2010 Department of Education figures show the team spending $19.5 million and bringing in almost $73 million, which helps support 29 varsity sports. Still, only about half of big-time programs end up in the black; many others have to draw from student fees or the general fund to cover expenses. And the gap between top programs and wannabes is only growing with colleges locked into an arms race to attract the best coaches and build the most luxurious venues in hopes of luring top athletes, and donations from happy alumni.

At many Division I big state colleges now, students have pre-game *19* parties, when they are pretty much drunk by 10 am on game day, hours before . . .

College sports doesn't just demand more and more money; it is *20* demanding more attention from fans.

Glen R. Waddell, associate professor of economics at the University *21* of Oregon, wanted to know how much. In a study published last month as part of the National Bureau of Education Research working paper series, Oregon researchers compared student grades with the performance of the Fighting Ducks, winner of this year's Rose Bowl and a crowd pleaser in their Nike uniforms in crazy color combinations and mirrored helmets.

"Here is evidence that suggests that when your football team does *22* well, grades suffer," said Dr. Waddell, who compared transcripts of over 29,700 students from 1999 to 2007 against Oregon's win-loss record. For every three games won, grade-point average for men dropped 0.02, widening the G.P.A. gender gap by 9 percent. Women's grades didn't suffer. In a separate survey of 183 students, the success of the Ducks also seemed to cause slacking off: students reported studying less (24 percent of men, 9 percent of women), consuming more alcohol (28 percent, 20 percent) and partying more (47 percent, 28 percent).

FIGURE 14.2   K-Ville: This is not Occupy Duke. It's annual tenting outside Cameron Indoor Stadium for the best seats at a basketball game.

While acknowledging a need for more research, Dr. Waddell believes 23 the results should give campus leaders pause: fandom can carry an academic price. "No longer can it be the case where we skip right over that inconvenience," he said.

Dr. Clotfelter, too, wanted to examine study habits. He tracked articles 24 downloaded from campus libraries during March Madness, the National Collegiate Athletic Association basketball tournament. Library patrons at universities with teams in the tournament viewed 6 percent fewer articles a day as long as their team was in contention. When a team won an upset or close game, article access fell 19 percent the day after the victory. Neither dip was made up later with increased downloads.

"Big-time sports," Dr. Clotfelter said, "have a real effect on the way 25 people in universities behave."

At Duke, one of the country's top universities, men's basketball sets the 26 rhythms of campus life. Of 600 students who study abroad each year, only 100 do it in the spring. It probably doesn't need to be said, but you don't schedule anything opposite a basketball game. Ever. "If there's a basketball game, you don't hold the meeting, you don't hold the event," said Larry Moneta, vice president for student affairs.

Then there's the annual campout of 1,000 at Krzyzewskiville, the 27 patch of grass named for Coach Mike Krzyzewski outside the hulking Gothic-style gymnasium, to determine the order of the line into the game against the rival University of North Carolina, which the Blue Devils host on March 3. Dr. Moneta several years ago stepped in to ban tents before the first day of classes after winter break (some had started the day after Christmas), but he has mostly "let the students own this." He was pleased when they decided tenting wouldn't start this year until a week later, Jan. 15. Tenters can sleep indoors when it's below 20 degrees or there is "more than two inches of accumulated snow." The rest of the time, students must prove their devotion (extra points for game attendance) and their residency (middle-of-the-night tent checks by "line monitors" signaled by a bullhorn).

Even grad students hold their own campout, with 2,200 spending a   28
weekend in tents and RVs to enter a lottery for season tickets; only 725 get lucky. It's become such a big deal that a law professor said they "have to figure out when that is" so as not to invite law firms to campus for interviews that weekend.

While Dr. Moneta has "concerns about occasional alcohol use and   29
abuse" among K-Ville undergrads (line monitors must intervene if they spot drinking games), he said students manage to camp out "for the most part without any negative effect on academics."

Orin Starn, a Duke professor who is a longtime critic of its partici-   30
pation in Division I athletics, begs to differ. He objects to sports occupying "this gigantic place in the university landscape." He calls basketball "a strain of anti-intellectualism" that claims too much time and attention. But as an anthropologist—he teaches "Anthropology of Sports"—he understands why. "It's like going to the Metropolitan Opera or the New York City Ballet," he said. "It's a chance to see these incredible athletes and this legendary coach."

Dr. Starn put a scholarly spin on it: "Big-time sports have become a   31
modern tribal religion for college students." There are sacred symbols (team logos), a high priest (Coach K) and shared rituals (chants and face painting). "This generation loves pageantry and tradition. School spirit is in right now. Now it's hip to be a joiner and it's hip to be a sports fan." Also, he observed, "these kids have grown up with the idea that sports are really a major part of American society and something they *should* care about."

Duke's game against North Carolina is special, but it doesn't take much   32
to provoke a queue for men's basketball. At 8:50 A.M. one day last month, students gathered at K-Ville. It didn't matter that it was Wednesday, that the game wasn't for 10 hours, that it would rain (even pour), or that Daniel Carp and Matthew Grossman—first in line—had papers due (Mr. Carp on the religious indoctrination of children; Mr. Grossman about Kant and the boundaries of mere reason).

The matchup against Colorado State wasn't even a compelling out-of-   33
conference game. But the point was not just to be at the game but to be first to enter Cameron Indoor Stadium, thereby securing the best seats in the famed student section.

"Every time they swipe my card and I go in, I get this overwhelming 34
enthusiasm. 'I'm here! It's game time!'" Mr. Grossman, a freshman from
Atlanta, explained between bites of a burger topped with crumbled blue
cheese after the game, blue and white paint still adorning his face.

The rise of near-professional college sports has fueled the rise of near- 35
professional fans. Mr. Carp, a freshman from Philadelphia sporting a No. 2
jersey, said that being a fan was integral to college life. "You just learn really
early on how to make going to basketball games part of your everyday routine."

K-Ville is legendary, but similar scenes play out at Oklahoma State, 36
Texas A&M, North Carolina State, the University of Missouri, San Diego
State and Xavier University, where students line up or camp out for days to
get into games. At the University of Kentucky, they camp out for access to
the official start of basketball *practice*.

For a Tuesday night game against Duke in Columbus (for which there 37
were enough seats, according to Mr. Collins, the Block O president), Ohio
State students pitched tents along the outside wall of Schottenstein Center
starting at 5 P.M. on a Sunday.

"I can imagine they may have neglected a class or two on Monday and 38
Tuesday," Mr. Collins said. "But we are here for four years. What will you
remember 10 years from now, that you decided to write that English paper,
or you had front row seats at the Duke game?"

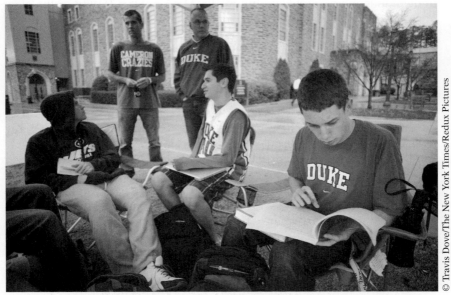

© Travis Dove/The New York Times/Redux Pictures

FIGURE 14.3   Students hold their spot for tickets, and even squeeze in some
studying.

Worry about students making that sort of academic tradeoff led offi- *39* cials at Indiana University, Bloomington, to cut short "Camp Crean" (after Coach Tom Crean) last month when students started lining up four days in advance for the Hoosiers basketball game against Kentucky. "It's the week before finals, and we didn't want the kids camping out and staying up for days when it's going to be in the 20s and — oh, by the way — it's finals," said the university spokesman, Mark Land.

While only "a small number" of students had started camping, Mr. Land *40* noted, "if you get hundreds out there, it's a party atmosphere."

Television has fed the popularity. The more professional big-time college *41* sports has become, the more nonathletes have been drawn in, said Murray Sperber, author of "Beer and Circus: How Big-Time College Sports Has Crippled Undergraduate Education." "Media coverage gets into kids' heads," he said, "and by the time they are ready to choose a college, it becomes a much bigger factor than it was historically."

In the last 10 years, the number of college football and basketball *42* games on ESPN channels rose to 1,320 from 491. This doesn't include games shown by competitors: the Big 10 Network, Fox, CBS/Turner, Versus and NBC. All that programming means big games scheduled during the week and television crews, gridlock and tailgating on campus during the school day.

"How can you have a Wednesday night football game without shutting *43* down the university for a day or two?" asked Dr. Sack of the Drake Group with a twinge of sarcasm. He's not exactly wrong, though. Last semester, the University of Central Florida canceled afternoon classes before the televised game against the University of Tulsa. Mississippi State canceled a day of classes before a Thursday night broadcast of a football game against Louisiana State, creating an online skirmish between Bulldog fans and a blogger who suggested parents should get their tuition back.

Even Boston College bowed, canceling afternoon classes because the *44* football game against Florida State was on ESPN at 8 P.M. Janine Hanrahan, a Boston College senior, was so outraged at missing her political science class, "Immigration, Processes and Policies," that she wrote an opinion piece headlined "B.C.'s Backwards Priorities" in the campus newspaper. "It was an indication that football was superseding academics," she explained. ("We are the national role model," a university spokesman, Jack Dunn, responded. "We are the school everyone calls to say, 'Where do you find the balance?'")

Universities make scheduling sacrifices not just for the lucrative con- *45* tracts but also because few visuals build the brand better than an appearance on ESPN's road show "College GameDay." (In November, it had John L. Hennessey, president of Stanford, out on the Oval at daybreak working the crowd.) The school spirit conveyed by cheering thousands — there were 18,000 on Francis Quadrangle at the University of Missouri, Columbia, on

Oct. 23, 2010, for "GameDay"—is a selling point to students choosing colleges. When Missouri first started recruiting in Chicago a decade ago, few prospective students had ever heard the university's nickname, "Mizzou," according to the admissions director, Barbara Rupp. "Now they know us by 'Mizzou,'" thanks in part to "GameDay." "I can't deny that," she said.

Universities play the sports card, encouraging students to think of 46 themselves as fans. A Vanderbilt admissions blog last fall featured "My Vandy Fanatic Weekend" describing the thrill of attending a basketball game and football game back to back. "One of the things we hear in the admissions office is that students these days who are serious about academics are still interested in sports," said John Gaines, director of undergraduate admissions. Mr. Gaines slipped in that its academic competitor Washington University in St. Louis is only Division III. "We always make sure we throw in a few crowd shots of people wearing black and gold" during presentations. Imagine, he is saying, "calling yourself a Commodore."

Or calling yourself a Cornhusker. A few years ago, the "Big Red Welcome" for new University of Nebraska students began including a special 47 treat: the chance to replicate the football team's famed "tunnel walk," jogging along the snaking red carpet below Memorial Stadium, then crashing through the double doors onto the field (though without the 86,000 fans).

When Kirk Kluver, assistant dean for admissions at Nebraska's College 48 of Law, set up his information table at recruiting fairs last year, a student in Minnesota let him know he would "check out Nebraska now that you are part of the Big 10." He got the same reaction in Arizona. Mr. Kluver said applications last fall were up 20 percent, while law school applications nationally fell 10 percent.

Penn State's new president, Rodney Erickson, announced last month 49 that he wanted to lower the football program's profile. How is unclear. A Penn State spokeswoman declined to make anyone available to discuss the future besides releasing a statement from Dr. Erickson about seeking "balance."

What would balance really look like?   50

Duke officials pride themselves in offering both an excellent education 51 and a stellar sports program.

Six years ago this spring, Duke experienced its own national scandal 52 when three lacrosse players were accused of rape by a stripper hired for a party at the "lacrosse house"—a bungalow since torn down. The charges were found to be false, but the episode prompted university leaders to think hard about the relationship between academics and athletics.

Kevin M. White, the athletic director, now reports directly to the president of Duke. It was part of structural changes to more healthily integrate 53 athletics into university life, said James E. Coleman Jr., a law professor who is chairman of the faculty athletics council and was chairman of the committee that investigated the athletes' behavior. (Vanderbilt made an even stronger move in 2008, disbanding the athletics department and fold-ing it into the student life division.) Sitting in his office on Duke's Durham, N.C., campus, Dr. Coleman set his lunch tray on a mountain of papers and explained the challenges. He calls sports "a public square for universities" but also acknowledges how rising commercialism comes with strings that "have become spider webs."

A 2008 report by the athletics department, "Unrivaled Ambition: A Strategic Plan for Duke Athletics," praises the K-Ville bonding experience and the "identity and cohesion" of the rivalry with U.N.C. as it describes in stressful language the facilities arms race, skyrocketing coach salaries and the downside of television deals. 54

"We no longer determine at what time we will play our games, because they are scheduled by TV executives," it laments, going on to complain about away games at 9 P.M. "Students are required to board a flight at 2 A.M., arriving back at their dorms at 4 or 5 A.M., and then are expected to go to class, study and otherwise act as if it were a normal school day." And: "our amateur student-athletes take the field with a corporate logo displayed on their uniform beside 'Duke.'" 55

"The key thing is to control the things you can control and make sure the athletic program doesn't trump the rest of the university, as it has in some places," Dr. Coleman said. "These presidents have to do more than pay lip service to this notion of balance between athletics and academics." He suggests that elevating academic standards for athletes is one way to assert university—not athletic department—control over programs. 56

He has also tried to foster rapport between faculty members and the ath-letic department. "The difficulty is having faculty understand athletics," he said. "Both sides need to cross lines. Otherwise, it becomes these two silos with no connection." Last month, Dr. Coleman hosted a lunch that brought together Mr. White, athletics staff members and professors on his committee. He's also revamping a program to match faculty members with coaches, and sends them sports-related articles to bone up on issues. 57

Pointed questions about oversight of its athletic program were raised at Penn State's faculty senate meeting last month, and faculty involvement is the subject of a national meeting of the Coalition on Intercollegiate Ath-letics at the University of Tulsa this weekend. John S. Nichols, the group's co-chairman and professor emeritus at Penn State, says professors typi-cally ignore the many issues that swirl around sports and influence the classroom. His list includes decisions about recruiting and admissions, and even conference realignments. Starting in 2013, the Big East will stretch over seven states, meaning not just football and basketball players but all student athletes—and some fans—will be making longer trips to away games. Dr. Nichols says it is time to "put some checks in place" on uncontrolled growth of athletics "or consider a different model." 58

To be sure, efforts to rehabilitate major college sports are not new. Amid much debate, an N.C.A.A. plan to raise scholarship awards by $2,000 59 was being reviewed this month. Some have seen it as the athletes' due, for the money they bring in, and others as pay for play; some colleges have complained they can't afford it.

Many are skeptical that reining in college sports is even possible; the   60
dollars are simply too attractive, the pressures from outside too great. Mr. White said that it was naïve "to think we will ever put the toothpaste back in the tube." He added, "There is an oversized, insatiable interest in sports, and college sports is part of that."

But some decisions are in university hands.   61

Despite Duke's ascent to basketball royalty, Cameron Indoor Stadium—   62
built in 1940, renovated in the 1980s and at 9,300 seats one of the smallest venues for a big-time program—still gives thousands of the best seats to students. At many large programs, courtside seats and luxury boxes go to boosters. But "outsiders with money," Dr. Coleman said, can make demands and change the way the team fits in with a university. "We could easily double the size of our basketball stadium and sell it out," he said. "That will never happen. If it does, you will know Duke has gone over to the dark side."

■ ■ ■

Reading as a Writer: Analyzing Rhetorical Choices

1. Pappano includes images to illustrate her claims. Select two to focus on, and use the visual rhetoric insights in Chapter 10 to analyze what these images mean and how they work in the text. How exactly do the images you choose to analyze support specific aspects of Pappano's argument? How might they offer additional or different information as well?

2. Pappano uses descriptive language throughout this essay, and description is never neutral. Find at least five examples of description that enhance her central argument. What conclusions can you draw about *how* Pappano's descriptions enhance her argument?

Writing as a Reader: Entering the Conversation of Ideas

1. Pappano and Mark Edmundson (pp. 405–15) both examine the ways college campus culture can carry more significance for students sometimes than academic study. In an essay that draws on both authors' analyses of the shortcomings of and potential solutions to this campus dynamic, make an argument of your own about the value of these different aspects of college life.

2. Pappano and Naomi Klein (pp. 768–80 in Economics) are interested in "branding" and its relationship to our identity and feelings of belonging. Write an essay that places these authors in conversation, using Klein's concept of branding to develop Pappano's claims about sports as a significant branding tool for many campuses. Where do you stand on the value or problems with this development? Support your claims with evidence.

SUSAN DYNARSKI

Why American Schools Are Even More Unequal Than We Thought

Susan Dynarski is a professor of education, public policy, and economics at the University of Michigan. Because of her experiences as a first-generation college student, she has focused her writing and teaching on education and social justice issues. Her research topics include financial aid and student debt, how charter schools affect communities, and the relationship between college degrees and the job market. Her work reaches beyond the classroom and academic journals so that it can be used to shape policy; she has even shared her research in a testimonial before Congress. This brief but data-packed guest column for the *New York Times* is a good example of how an expert shapes data for a general audience.

Dynarski opens with a clear statement about the effects of poverty on student achievement. In her second paragraph, though, she makes a classic scholarly move, letting us know the situation is more complex than it seems: "Yet the problem is actually much worse than these statistics show…" (This is a version of the "paradoxical introduction" described in Chapter 11.) The rest of the essay explores the problem of "the crude yardstick for economic hardship" that has had devastating effects on poor children.

As you read, keep track of the variety of evidence Dynarski provides. Mark the paragraphs in which Dynarski offers quantitative data to support her claim that focusing on "disadvantaged" students masks the more serious educational challenges for "persistently disadvantaged" students. How do the numbers she provides help build her case? Make sure you understand how she is using the data; she covers a lot of ground in a small space.

Dynarski makes another classic scholarly move in her conclusion when she asks, "Why does all this matter?" She points to a problem that she believes can be solved, but only if we understand the ways the relationship between poverty and academic achievement has been *mis*understood. What do you think about her conclusion and what it might mean for "persistently disadvantaged" children in a community near you or in your home school district?

■   ■   ■

E ducation is deeply unequal in the United States, with students in poor *1* districts performing at levels several grades below those of children in richer areas.

Yet the problem is actually much worse than these statistics show, *2* because schools, districts and even the federal government have been using a crude yardstick for economic hardship.

A closer look reveals that the standard measure of economic dis- *3* advantage—whether a child is eligible for a free or reduced-price lunch in school—masks the magnitude of the learning gap between the richest and poorest children.

Nearly half of students nationwide are eligible for a subsidized meal *4* in school. Children whose families earn less than 185 percent of the poverty threshold are eligible for a reduced-price lunch, while those below 130 percent get a free lunch. For a family of four, the cutoffs are $32,000 for a free lunch and $45,000 for a reduced-price one. By way of comparison, median household income in the United States was about $54,000 in 2014.

Eligibility for subsidized school meals is clearly a blunt indicator of *5* economic status. But that is the measure that policy makers, educators and researchers rely on when they gauge gaps in academic achievement in schools, districts and states.

The National Assessment of Educational Progress, often called the *6* Nation's Report Card, publishes student scores by eligibility for subsidized meals. Under the federal No Child Left Behind Act and its successor, the Every Student Succeeds Act, districts have reported scores separately for disadvantaged children, with eligibility for subsidized meals serving as the standard measure of disadvantage.

With Katherine Michelmore, a postdoctoral researcher at the University of Michigan, I have analyzed data held by the Michigan Consortium for Educational Research and found that this measure substantially understates the achievement gap. *7*

In Michigan, as in the rest of the country, about half of eighth graders *8* in public schools receive a free or reduced-price lunch. But when we look more closely, we see that just 14 percent have been eligible for subsidized meals every year since kindergarten. These children are the poorest of the poor—the persistently disadvantaged.

The math scores of these poorest children are far lower than predicted *9* by the standard measure of economic disadvantage. The achievement gap between persistently disadvantaged children and those who were never disadvantaged is about a third larger than the gap that is typically measured.

Education researchers often express test score differences in standard *10* deviations, which allows for a consistent measure of gaps across different tests, populations and contexts. Measured using that conventional approach, the gap in math scores between disadvantaged eighth graders and their classmates in Michigan is 0.69 standard deviations. This places disadvantaged children roughly two grades behind their classmates. By contrast, the gap based on persistent disadvantage is much wider: 0.94 standard deviations, or nearly three grades of learning.

In fact, there is a nearly linear, negative relationship between the number of years of economic disadvantage and math scores in eighth grade. These lower scores do not appear to be caused by more years of disadvantage, however. When we look at third-grade scores, nearly all of the *11* eighth-grade score deficit is already in place. By third grade, those children who will end up spending all of primary school eligible for subsidized meals have already fallen far behind their classmates.

What is the explanation? It appears that years spent eligible for subsi- *12* dized school meals serves as a good proxy for the depth of disadvantage. When we look back on the early childhood of persistently disadvantaged eighth graders, we see that by kindergarten they were already far poorer than their classmates.

We can see this with national data. The Early Childhood Longitudinal *13* Study, run by the Department of Education, tracks a sample of children who started kindergarten in 1998. Among children who were eligible for subsidized meals through eighth grade, household income during kindergarten was just $20,000. For those who were only occasionally eligible, it was closer to $47,000, and for those never eligible, $80,000.

These data also show that persistently disadvantaged children are far *14* less likely than other students to live with two parents or have a college-educated mother or father. Just 2 percent of persistently disadvantaged children have a parent with a college degree, compared with 24 percent of the occasionally disadvantaged (and 57 percent of those who were never disadvantaged).

No one ever actively decided that eligibility for subsidized meals was *15* the best way to measure students' economic disadvantage. The metric was widely available and became by default the standard way to distinguish between poorer and richer children. But it was always an imprecise measure, and we can do better at little cost.

Many states now use administrative data on eligibility for means- *16* tested programs such as welfare benefits and food stamps to automatically qualify children for subsidized meals in school. Since these programs have a range of income cutoffs, their eligibility flags can be used to distinguish between children who are extremely poor and those who are nearly middle class. The children whose families persistently receive benefits will be the neediest of all.

Why does all this matter? Many federal, state and local programs dis- *17* tribute money based on the share of a district's students who are eligible for subsidized meals. But schools that have identical shares of students eligible for subsidized meals may differ vastly in the share of students who are deeply poor. The schools with the most disadvantaged children have greater challenges and arguably need more resources.

■ ■ ■

Reading as a Writer: Analyzing Rhetorical Choices

1. A key to understanding Dynarski's point is the distinction she makes between "disadvantaged" and "persistently disadvantaged" students. Find her definitions in the text, and then explain them in your own words.

2. In paragraph 6, Dynarski mentions both the federal No Child Left Behind Act and the Every Student Succeeds Act. Look these laws up and discuss their significance, as well as the problem Dynarski sees in their implementation.

Writing as a Reader: Entering the Conversation of Ideas

1. Dynarski shares an interest in income inequality and the impact on education with the coauthors Sean F. Reardon, Jane Waldfogel, and Daphna Bassok (pp. 430–34). These two essays take very different approaches to the problem, however. In an essay of your own, place these texts in conversation, comparing and evaluating the ways the authors provide claims, data, and conclusions. What conclusions can you draw, based on the material in these brief texts, about the challenges ahead for a more equitable public education system?

2. Dynarski examines precollege educational inequalities and economics that provide the groundwork for the claims Sara Goldrick-Rab (pp. 742–49 in Economics) makes about the crisis in paying for college. Write an essay that connects these essays, using the claims and evidence each author provides to make an argument of your own about the long-term impact of income inequality on access to education and the significance of this impact. What changes do you propose? What will happen if nothing changes? What might happen if changes you propose are implemented?

SEAN F. REARDON, JANE WALDFOGEL, AND DAPHNA BASSOK

The Good News about Educational Inequality

Sean Reardon and Daphna Bassok are professors of education; Jane Waldfogel is a social work professor. You will hear their two areas of expertise in this *New York Times* guest column, which, like the essay by Susan Dynarski, examines the evidence of educational gaps between wealthy and poor children. They begin by acknowledging the drumbeat of bad news about inequality in education. Right away in paragraph 2, however, they cite evidence for "good news" and launch their case—with support—that there is reason to be optimistic about at least one data point: the narrowing gap in readiness for school between poor and wealthy students and also between racial groups. In paragraph 4 they offer the key evidence; be sure you understand what those numbers mean.

Starting in paragraph 7, the authors puzzle through possible interpretations and reasons for the data, which come not just from education reform but from changes in social services and literacy campaigns. Pay attention to the ways the authors weigh one interpretation in paragraph 7 and then challenge the interpretation in the next paragraph. Here, we are seeing the minds of scholars at work as they resist simple conclusions and instead seek to appreciate the complexity of measuring human experiences, given the myriad social contexts and dynamics that affect children's preparation for school.

You may be surprised by their suggestion that changing scientific and cultural attitudes toward early childhood brain development may be one explanation for the narrowed gap between wealthy and poor children. How and why is this the case? What kinds of social programs might be credited with fostering more *Goodnight Moon* time (para. 10) for poor children?

Despite the optimistic frame of this essay, the writers' final three paragraphs assert the limits of their claims. Reread these concluding paragraphs and make note of all the social, economic, and educational changes they believe are necessary for poor children to thrive. Do they leave you with hope or something less than that? What do you think the writers want their readers to do with this information?

⬛ ⬛ ⬛

When inequality is the topic, it can seem as if all the news is bad. *1* Income inequality continues to rise. Economic segregation is growing. Racial gaps in education, employment and health endure. Our society is not particularly fair.

But here is some good news about educational inequality: The enormous gap in academic performance between high- and low-income children has begun to narrow. Children entering kindergarten today are more equally prepared than they were in the late 1990s. *2*

We know this from information collected over the last two decades *3* by the National Center for Education Statistics. In the fall of 1998 and again in 2010, the N.C.E.S. sent early childhood assessors to roughly 1,000 public and private kindergartens across the United States. They sat down one-on-one with 15 to 25 children in each school to measure their reading and math skills. They asked children to identify shapes and colors, to count, to identify letters and to sound out words. They also surveyed parents to learn about the children's experiences before entering kindergarten.

Working with the social scientist Ximena Portilla, we used this data *4* to track changes over time in "school readiness gaps"—the differences in academic skills between low-income and high-income children entering kindergarten. What we found is surprising. From 1998 to 2010, the school readiness gap narrowed by 10 percent in math and 16 percent in reading. The gaps that remain are still vast. But even this modest improvement represents a sharp reversal of the trend over the preceding decades.

It's worth noting that the gap in school readiness narrowed because *5* of relatively rapid improvements in the skills of low-income children, not because the skills of children from high-income families declined. Research one of us did with Scott Latham at the University of Virginia showed that both poor and affluent children entered kindergarten in 2010 with stronger reading and math skills than they did in the late 1990s. School readiness gaps between racial groups have also improved: Both the white-black and white-Hispanic gaps narrowed by roughly 15 percent from 1998 to 2010.

These improvements appear to persist at least into fourth grade. Data *6* from the National Assessment of Educational Progress show that by 2015, when those kindergartners were in fourth grade, their math and reading skills were roughly two-thirds of a grade level higher than those of their counterparts 12 years earlier. This was true for children of all racial and ethnic groups and for poor and nonpoor children alike.

What's behind these surprising developments? One possibility is *7* that school readiness gaps have narrowed because it is easier now for poor families to find high-quality, publicly funded preschool programs for their children. Today 29 percent of 4-year-olds are enrolled in state-funded preschools, up from 14 percent in 2002. Greater availability of affordable preschool programs—particularly if they are high quality—may be part of the reason poor children are starting to catch up to their affluent peers.

It is unlikely, however, that preschool enrollment is the primary expla- *8* nation. Although more poor children today attend preschool than in the 1990s, enrollment rates dipped in 2010, perhaps because of rising unemployment after the Great Recession. And while the quality of the typical preschool program may have improved, as recently as 2004 most poor children attended public preschools that were far inferior to those available in affluent communities.

It may be changes in children's homes that have mattered most. Track- *9* ing the experiences of young children over time, we found that both rich and poor children today have more books and read with their parents more often than they did in the '90s. They are far more likely to have computers, Internet access and computer games focused on reading and math skills. Their parents are more likely to spend time with them, taking them to the library or doing activities at home.

The children of the rich have always had more of these opportuni- *10* ties than poor children. What has changed is that low-income children are now getting more of what the political scientist Robert Putnam calls "'Goodnight Moon' time" than they did in the 1990s. That's excellent news.

But here's the puzzle: In many ways, the lives of rich and poor parents *11* haven't become more equal—far from it. Among families with school-age children, income inequality grew by roughly 10 percent from 1998 to 2010; economic segregation grew by 20 percent. How is it that the school readiness gap is nonetheless narrowing?

We suspect that in part this happened because of the widespread diffu- *12* sion of a single powerful idea: that the first few years of a child's life are the most consequential for cognitive development. This idea is commonplace today, but it wasn't always. Less than a century ago, the historian Julia

Wrigley notes, mainstream magazines routinely advised new mothers that intellectual stimulation of babies was harmful.

Now we know better, the result of decades of scientific research about *13* brain development, poverty and the long-term effects of high-quality preschool programs. But low-income families haven't always had the same information about the unique importance of early childhood. Indeed, part of why the achievement gap grew in the 1980s and 1990s was that rich families rapidly increased their investment of both time and money in their children's cognitive development.

Why are low-income families now adopting these parenting practices? It *14* may be partly a result of public information campaigns like Reach Out and Read, the Too Small to Fail initiative and local efforts in cities like Providence, R.I., which aim to teach parents simple ways to help their children build the vocabulary and cognitive skills that form a foundation for success in school.

In conjunction with public investments in home-visiting programs *15* and high-quality preschool programs, these campaigns represent an effort to ensure that our knowledge about the unique importance of early childhood helps everyone. Like a new medical innovation that is first adopted by the wealthy but then becomes commonplace, the emphasis on public and private investments in young children has helped turn a benefit for the rich into an equalizing force in society.

As encouraging as this new evidence is, we have a long way to go. Poor *16* children still enter kindergarten nearly a year behind their richer peers. Even if school readiness gaps continue to narrow at the rate they did between 1998 and 2010, it would take another 60 to 110 years for them to be completely eliminated.

Changes in parenting are not going to be sufficient to sustain or speed *17* this progress, although more paid leave would help. Economic inequality still constrains poor children's horizons. Low-income and middle-class parents still struggle to find affordable, high-quality preschools. The elementary, middle and high schools that rich and poor students attend differ markedly in resources and quality. And it isn't clear that the recent reductions in school readiness gaps will automatically translate into greater equality in high school, college and beyond.

If we don't do something about these larger problems, the progress *18* we have made toward equality in early childhood may prove only a brief respite from ever-widening educational inequality. "Goodnight Moon," for all its charm and power, is no substitute for comprehensive social policy.

■ ■ ■

Reading as a Writer: Analyzing Rhetorical Choices

1. These three writers come from two different disciplinary backgrounds, education and social work. Reread the essay, and mark in two different colors the portions of the essay that seem drawn from educational research

and insights and those from social work insights. Discuss the rationale for your markings in pairs, small groups, or as a class. If it is difficult to tell which discipline some of their ideas come from, discuss the significance of this observation.

2. These writers mention a few literacy programs in paragraph 14, which they credit with changing parenting patterns and enhancing many low-income children's readiness for school. Do an Internet search for literacy programs in your county. Does the language seem to be pitched to a particular population? Discuss your findings in the context of this essay.

Writing as a Reader: Entering the Conversation of Ideas

1. This essay is directly in conversation with Susan Dynarski's essay in this chapter (pp. 427–29). Write an essay of your own in which you evaluate the claims, evidence, and conclusions in both readings. You might focus on the students' ages in each piece, how the authors define poverty, and the significance you see in their findings. Where is there common ground and contrasting information? What conclusions can you draw?

2. Reardon, Waldfogel, and Bassok are interested in the shifting culture around early childhood education and the longer-term effects this might have on student learning. Carol Dweck (pp. 594–604 in Psychology and Biology) shares an interest in the effect of shifting attitudes and our understanding of human potential. Write an essay that uses information and claims in both readings to make an argument about the significance of cultural attitudes to learning. You should take into consideration the economic inequalities Reardon, Waldfogel, and Bassok include in their essay as you build your own argument.

NIKOLE HANNAH-JONES

School Segregation, the Continuing Tragedy of Ferguson

Nikole Hannah-Jones is an award-winning writer whose reporting has been featured in ProPublica, the *New York Times*, and on NPR and *Face the Nation*, among other news sources. She also helped found the Ida B. Wells Society for Investigative Reporting, which offers mentorship aimed at increasing the number of investigative reporters of color. In this Pro-Publica essay that also ran in the *New York Times Magazine*; Hannah-Jones draws on the circumstances of Michael Brown's life and his tragic shooting death to illustrate the profound educational inequality in his community. His untimely death, she argues, "reveals a more subtle, ongoing racial injustice: the vast disparity in resources and expectations for black children in America's stubbornly segregated educational system" (para. 9).

Hannah-Jones writes in a short paragraph form favored by journalists, as do some of the other writers in this chapter. She also employs many academic rhetorical techniques. For example, you might consider the effect of her narrative introduction (see advice about drafting introductions in Chapter 11), which places readers at Michael Brown's graduation ceremony, only eight days before he was shot by a police officer. The essay's central concern is less the specific experiences of Michael Brown's life and death, however, than it is the profound differences between the Normandy school district where Brown attended the lowest-ranked school system in Missouri and the wealthy, predominantly white Clayton district five miles away ranked in the top 10 percent.

Hannah-Jones reveals that this is not an inevitable inequality. In paragraphs 16 and 17, she points out that Michael Brown's mother, who grew up in the same town, had a far better education than her son did due to desegregating policies that were eventually dismantled. Hannah-Jones offers additional historical context in the section titled "Dred Scott, Desegregation and a Dearth of Progress." The story of all the political decisions that led to the Normandy school district being ranked at the bottom of Missouri's schools by the time Michael Brown enrolled in 2013 is the core of this essay.

Hannah-Jones illustrates her argument about the ways the educational deck is stacked against black students in the Normandy school district with another family's thwarted attempts to improve access to better education for children (in the section titled "Fears, Flight and a Suddenly Black Suburb Left to Crumble"). She also offers two charts of data comparing many aspects of education in Clayton (the nearby wealthy district) and Normandy. In addition, she provides a map of racial percentages in the area. Spend some time with this data, and be ready to explain how they enhance Hannah-Jones's argument.

In the final section, "Little Hope and a Telling Burial," Hannah-Jones answers the question every academic writer should be able to answer: So what? Her response: "Students who spend their careers in segregated schools can look forward to a life on the margins, according to a 2014 study.... They are more likely to be poor. They are more likely to go to jail. They are less likely to graduate from high school, to go to college, and to finish if they go. They are more likely to live in segregated neighborhoods as adults" (para. 116). In other words, educational inequality can inflict generations of damage. Hannah-Jones provides the tragic proof.

O n August 1, five black students in satiny green and red robes and mortar boards waited inside an elementary school classroom, listening for their names to be called as graduates of Normandy High School. The ceremony was held months after the school's main graduation for students who had been short of credits or had opted not to participate earlier. *1*

One of those graduating that day was Michael Brown. He was 18, his mother's oldest son. He was headed to college in the fall. *2*

© Whitney Curtis for ProPublica

Eight days later, Brown was dead—killed in the streets of nearby Fer- *3* guson, Mo., by a white police officer in a shooting that ignited angry pro- tests and another round of painful national debate about race, policing and the often elusive matter of justice.

News reports in the days and weeks after Brown's death often noted *4* his recent graduation and college ambitions, the clear implication that the teen's school achievements only deepened the sorrow over his loss.

But if Brown's educational experience was a success story, it was a *5* damning one.

The Normandy school district from which Brown graduated is among *6* the poorest and most segregated in Missouri. It ranks last in overall aca- demic performance. Its rating on an annual state assessment was so dismal that by the time Brown graduated the district had lost its accreditation.

About half of black male students at Normandy High never graduate. *7* Just one in four graduates enters a four-year college. The college where Brown was headed is a troubled for-profit trade-school that a U.S. Senate report said targeted students for their "vulnerabilities," and that at one time advertised itself to what it internally called the area's "Unemployed, Underpaid, Unsatisfied, Unskilled, Unprepared, Unsupported, Unmoti- vated, Unhappy, Underserved!"

A mere five miles down the road from Normandy is the wealthy county *8* seat where a grand jury recently decided not to indict Darren Wilson, the officer who killed Brown. Success there looks drastically different. The Clayton Public Schools are predominantly white, with almost no poverty to speak of. The district is regularly ranked among the top 10 percent in

FIGURE 14.4 Normandy High School principal Derrick Mitchell has been tasked with turning around a high school where most students read, write, and do math below grade level.

the state. More than 96 percent of students graduate. Fully 84 percent of graduates head to four-year universities.

Brown's tragedy, then, is not limited to his individual potential cut bru- 9 tally short. His schooling also reveals a more subtle, ongoing racial injustice: the vast disparity in resources and expectations for black children in America's stubbornly segregated educational system.

As ProPublica has documented in a series of stories on the reseg- 10 regation of America's schools, hundreds of school districts across the nation have been released from court-enforced integration over the past 15 years. Over that same time period, the number of so-called apartheid schools — schools whose white population is 1 percent or less — has shot up. The achievement gap, greatly narrowed during the height of school desegregation, has widened.

"American schools are disturbingly racially segregated, period," Cath- 11 erine Lhamon, head of the U.S. Education Department's civil rights office, said in an October speech. "We are reserving our expectations for our highest rigor level of courses, the courses we know our kids need to be able to be full and productive members of society, but we are reserving them for a class of kids who are white and who are wealthier."

According to data compiled by the Education Department, black and 12 Latino children are the least likely to be taught by a qualified, experienced teacher, to get access to courses such as chemistry and calculus, and to have access to technology.

The inequalities along racial lines are so profound nationally that in Octo- *13*
ber the department's Office for Civil Rights issued a 37-page letter to school
district superintendents warning that the disparities may be unconstitutional.

What Proficiency Looks Like in Clayton and Normandy

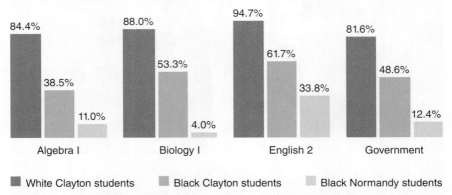

Missouri tracks students' progress toward the state's achievement goals through End-Of-
Course assessment tests. End-Of-Course assessments are grouped by subject, not grade level.
This graphic shows the percentage of students by race and district who scored as "proficient"
or "advanced" in each subject. Scores were not available for white Normandy students as there
were less than 30 students who took the test.
Data from Missouri Department of Elementary and Secondary Education

Few places better reflect the rise and fall of attempts to integrate U.S. *14*
schools than St. Louis and its suburbs.

Decades of public and private housing discrimination made St. Louis *15*
one of the most racially segregated metropolitan areas in the country. Out
of that grew a network of school district boundaries that to this day have
divided large numbers of black students in racially separate schools as
effectively as any Jim Crow law.

In 1983, under federal court order, St. Louis and some of its suburbs *16*
embarked on what would become the grandest and most successful interdistrict school desegregation program in the land, one that, at least for a
time, broke the grim grip of ZIP codes for tens of thousands of black students. As an elementary school student, under this order, Michael Brown's
mother rode the bus from St. Louis to affluent Ladue.

But like so many other desegregation efforts across the country, the *17*
St. Louis plan proved short-lived, largely abandoned after several years
by politicians and others who complained that it was too costly. Jay
Nixon, Missouri's current governor, whose response to Brown's killing has
come under intense scrutiny in recent months, helped lead the effort that
brought the court order to a close.

Since their retreat from desegregation initiatives, many St. Louis *18*
County schools have returned to the world of separate and unequal that
existed before the US. Supreme Court's landmark decision in *Brown v.
Board of Education*.

It could be said that the Normandy school district, where Michael *19* Brown spent the last year and a half of high school, never left. Excluded from the court-ordered integration plan that transformed other school systems in the St. Louis area, Normandy's fiscally and academically disadvantaged schools have essentially been in freefall since the 1980s.

Throughout the region, the educational divide between black chil- *20* dren and white children is stark. In St. Louis County, 44 percent of black children attend schools in districts the state says perform so poorly that it has stripped them of full accreditation. Just 4 percent of white students do.

Yet state education officials say there is little political will to change *21* that.

Instead, they have promised to work to make segregated school dis- *22* tricts equal, the very doctrine the Supreme Court struck down in the *Brown* decision.

"We are failing to properly educate the black child," said Michael Jones, *23* vice president of the Missouri State Board of Education. "Individually, any one person can overcome anything. But we've got masses of children with bad starts in life. They can't win. We ought to be ashamed of that."

Since Aug. 9, the day Michael Brown's lifeless body lay for hours under *24* a hot summer sun, St. Louis County has become synonymous with the country's racial fault lines when it comes to police conduct and the criminalization of black youth. But most black youth will not die at the hands of police.

They will face the future that Brown would have faced if he had lived. *25* That is, to have the outcome of their lives deeply circumscribed by what they learn and experience in their segregated, inferior schools.

Dred Scott, Desegregation and a Dearth of Progress

Missouri is what the locals like to call a Southern state with Northern *26* exposure. It entered the Union through a compromise that determined how much of the country would permit slavery and wound up a slave state surrounded on three sides by free states.

It was in a St. Louis case in 1857 that the U.S. Supreme Court handed *27* down one of its most infamous opinions. The court, in ruling against the enslaved Dred Scott, affirmed that black people were not citizens and "had no rights that the white man was bound to respect."

The spirit of the ruling reverberated for generations in St. Louis, *28* which in the years after the Civil War became the destination for large numbers of former slaves. Indeed, the Mississippi River town became a national leader in how to contain what white real estate agents called the "Negro invasion."

In 1916, after a successful campaign that included placards urging, *29* "Save Your Home! Vote for Segregation!," the city's residents passed a measure requiring that black and white residents live on separate, designated blocks. In doing so, St. Louis became the first city in the country to require housing segregation by popular ballot. The tactic eventually fell to a legal challenge, but white residents found other ways to keep themselves, and their schools, protected from black residents.

One way was to write segregation into the sales contracts of houses. *30* The clauses, known as real estate covenants, ensured the whiteness of neighborhoods by barring the sale of homes to black homebuyers—ever, and across entire sectors of the city. These practices quickly created a clear dividing line in St. Louis that endures to this day: Black people north of Delmar Boulevard; white people south.

In 1948, another landmark St. Louis case led to the U.S. Supreme *31* Court striking down the enforcement of real estate covenants anywhere in the country. The case involved a black resident named J.D. Shelley, who bought a home with a deed restriction and then was sued by a white homeowner, Louis Kraemer, trying to block him from moving into the subdivision.

With legal discrimination under attack in the courts, white residents *32* began abandoning St. Louis altogether. From 1950 to 1970, the city lost

© Whitney Curtis for ProPublica

FIGURE 14.5 Schoemehl pots, concrete sewer pipes filled with dirt named for former St. Louis Mayor Vincent Schoemehl. These barricades, ubiquitous in St. Louis, block off the heavily white neighborhoods along Delmar Boulevard, the city's infamous racial dividing line.

nearly 60 percent of its white population. This white flight was partly underwritten by the federal government, which secured loans reserved only for white homebuyers.

Town after town sprung up along the northern edge of St. Louis, some 33 no larger than a single subdivision. Immediately, many forbade rentals and required homes to be built on large, more expensive lots. These devices helped keep neighborhoods white because black residents tended to be poorer and had difficulty getting home loans after decades of workplace, lending and housing discrimination. Even today, 77 percent of white St. Louis area residents own their homes, compared to 45 percent of black residents, the U.S. Census shows.

Some of the tactics employed by St. Louis suburbs, including zoning, 34 also were knocked down by courts.

But court victories, in the end, mattered little. A century of white effort 35 had lastingly etched the county map: a struggling, heavily black urban core surrounded by a constellation of 90 segregated little towns.

"St. Louis yielded some of the starkest racial dividing lines in any 36 American city, North or South," said Colin Gordon, a University of Iowa professor who traces this history in his book "Mapping Decline: St. Louis and the Fate of the American City." "I like to think of St. Louis not as an outlier, but one in which all the things we're talking about are just more visible."

A Segregation Success, Quickly Abandoned

One legal fight breached—at least temporarily—the St. Louis area's stark 37 boundaries of home and property, and with them the 24 segregated school districts covering those 90 segregated little towns.

In 1954, the year of the *Brown v. Board of Education* Supreme Court 38 decision, St. Louis ran the second-largest segregated school district in the country.

In the face of the ruling, school officials promised to integrate volun- 39 tarily. But they redrew school district lines around distinctly black and white neighborhoods to preserve their segregated schools. Even so, many white families still left, avoiding the chance of integration by simply moving across municipal lines. By 1980, 90 percent of black children in St. Louis still attended predominantly black schools.

With few white students left, it was clear that a desegregation plan 40 that did not include the white suburbs would be futile. In 1981, a federal judge called for a plan to bus black St. Louis children to white suburban schools.

White suburban residents, and their school leaders, revolted. They filed 41 motions in court and penned angry letters to the local newspaper. The judge, William Hungate, responded by threatening to do the one thing the

© Whitney Curtis for ProPublica

FIGURE 14.6 Junior Christopher Higgins, right, works at the chalkboard with other Normandy High School students. Research shows students of all races and incomes do worse in segregated schools.

white suburbs feared more than the bussing plan: Dissolve the carefully constructed school district boundaries and merge all 24 of the discrete districts into a single metro-wide one.

The opposition to the plan to bus children out of St. Louis collapsed. 42 In 1983, St. Louis and its suburbs enacted the largest and most expensive interdistrict school desegregation program in the country.

At its peak, some 15,000 St. Louis public school students a year went to 43 school in 16 heavily white suburban districts. Another 1,300 white students headed the opposite direction to new, integrated magnet schools in St. Louis.

The program had its flaws—chief among them, that it left another 44 15,000 of St. Louis's black students in segregated, inferior schools. And the transition of black urban students into white suburban schools was not always smooth.

But for the transfer students who rode buses out of the city, the plan 45 successfully broke the deeply entrenched connection between race, ZIP code and opportunity. Test scores for 8th and 10th grade transfer students rose. The transfer students were more likely to graduate and go onto college.

In surveys, white students overwhelmingly said they'd benefited from 46 the opportunity to be educated alongside black students. In short order, St. Louis's was heralded by researchers and educators as the nation's most successful metro-wide desegregation program.

But from the moment it started, the St. Louis effort was under assault. *47* It was never popular among the area's white residents. Politicians, Republicans and Democrats alike, vowed to end the program.

Then-state Attorney General John Ashcroft tried first, appealing St. *48* Louis' school desegregation case all the way to the Supreme Court. He was succeeded by Jay Nixon, a Democrat who matched Ashcroft's fervor in seeking to end the program.

"Nixon came from a rural area. His position on school desegregation was *49* more of a Southern Democrat, and it came pretty close to massive resistance," said William Freivogel, director of Southern Illinois University's School of Journalism, who covered the Supreme Court for the *St. Louis Post-Dispatch*

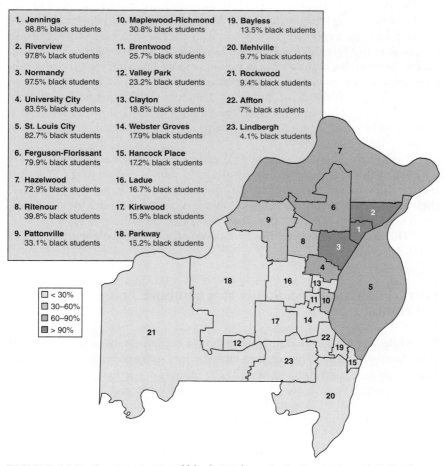

1. **Jennings** 98.8% black students	10. **Maplewood-Richmond** 30.8% black students	19. **Bayless** 13.5% black students
2. **Riverview** 97.8% black students	11. **Brentwood** 25.7% black students	20. **Mehlville** 9.7% black students
3. **Normandy** 97.5% black students	12. **Valley Park** 23.2% black students	21. **Rockwood** 9.4% black students
4. **University City** 83.5% black students	13. **Clayton** 18.8% black students	22. **Affton** 7% black students
5. **St. Louis City** 82.7% black students	14. **Webster Groves** 17.9% black students	23. **Lindbergh** 4.1% black students
6. **Ferguson-Florissant** 79.9% black students	15. **Hancock Place** 17.2% black students	
7. **Hazelwood** 72.9% black students	16. **Ladue** 16.7% black students	
8. **Ritenour** 39.8% black students	17. **Kirkwood** 15.9% black students	
9. **Pattonville** 33.1% black students	18. **Parkway** 15.2% black students	

□ < 30%
□ 30–60%
□ 60–90%
■ > 90%

FIGURE 14.7 Concentration of black Students in St. Louis County School Districts: St. Louis County is etched into 24 racially distinct school districts, with heavily black schools (indicated in blue) clustered in the city of St. Louis and its northern suburbs, and heavily white schools to the west and south.

Data from Missouri Department of Elementary and Secondary Education during the 1980s and early 1990s. "I once wrote that Nixon behaved like a Southern politician standing in the schoolhouse door."

Nixon never expressly opposed the idea of integration. His argument *50* centered on what he considered the astronomical costs of the desegregation plan. The price tag, initially in the hundreds of millions of dollars, would reach $1.7 billion.

Nixon, who would not be interviewed for this article, launched a num- *51* ber of legal challenges and prevailed in 1999 when supporters of the desegregation plan ultimately agreed to make the program voluntary. Nixon had successfully challenged Kansas City's desegregation plan before the U.S. Supreme Court, and some feared he would be similarly successful if the St. Louis case came before the court.

Districts soon began to drop out of the program, and the number of stu- *52* dents participating steadily dwindled. Today, the voluntary program remains in place, still the largest of just eight interdistrict desegregation programs in the country. But it is a shadow of what it once was. Some 4,800 students get to escape the troubles of the St. Louis public schools, but each year, the program receives seven times as many applicants as open spaces.

Amy Stuart Wells is a Columbia's Teachers College professor who co- *53* authored a book, "Stepping Over the Color Line: African-American Students in White Suburban Schools," on the impact of the St. Louis plan on transfer students.

"I don't think many people realized how far ahead St. Louis really *54* was," she said. "There are hundreds of thousands of people in the St. Louis metro area who were affected by this plan, but (the suburbs) did it because they had to and nobody said, 'Look, we're a national model for our country.' There were seeds sewn that could have been so much more.

"This was the epicenter of where people tried to grapple with race, and *55* failed miserably."

Fears, Flight and a Suddenly Black Suburb Left to Crumble

The white flight out of St. Louis left behind a trail of decay, as it did in many *56* large Northern cities. City services lapsed when more affluent residents left. Businesses and jobs migrated as well. The schools in particular suffered.

Not surprisingly, black residents who could afford it looked for a way *57* out, too. They looked to older North St. Louis suburbs, including Normandy. Incorporated in 1945 and covering fewer than two square miles, Normandy became a destination for the city's fleeing white working class.

Nedra Martin's family was among the black strivers who began to *58* make their way to Normandy. Martin, who lives in Normandy today and works for Wal-Mart, said her parents first came to the town in 1975. They both worked government jobs—her dad was a welder for the city, her mom an aide in a state group home.

FIGURE 14.8 Nedra Martin sued the state. Martin said she did it not just for her own child, but "for the parents who are defeated, who feel the same way I feel—that they don't care about our childrens' education."

"My parents raised us to know that we are as good as anybody else," Martin said. 59

But as black families like the Martins moved in, "For Sale" signs went up. White families started moving out, often to emerging outposts even farther from the heart of St. Louis. 60

After 1970, black enrollment in the Normandy schools exploded, more than doubling within eight years to 6,200. By 1978, only St. Louis enrolled more black students than Normandy. 61

Yet Normandy was left out of the metro-wide desegregation order that produced those few years of brighter outcomes for black students between 1983 and 1999. The order capped black enrollment at suburban districts at 25 percent, and Normandy and six other North St. Louis suburbs were already too black. 62

Instead, the Normandy schools buckled under their swift demographic shift, beginning a steep decline. Many of the best teachers followed the white and middle-class exodus. Instruction fell off. The district suffered from a revolving door of leadership, with principals and superintendents seldom sticking around more than a couple of years. Unable to meet minimum requirements for student achievement, the district clung to provisional accreditation for 15 years. 63

But black families had less freedom to simply move away to better school districts than even their poorer white neighbors. Housing 64 discrimination continues to keep black families out of communities with quality schools, according to a 2013 St. Louis housing study.

The most affluent black families in Normandy, then, often opted out 65 of the local school system, paying to send their children to private school. As a result, Normandy's schools ended up considerably poorer and more racially segregated than the communities they serve.

For years, the Normandy school system walked an academic tight- 66 rope. Then, in 2009, the state made matters worse.

New Education Commissioner Chris Nicastro decided that it was time 67 to move on segregated districts that consistently failed their students. The state shuttered Wellston, a desperately poor, 500-student district next to Normandy that held the distinction of being Missouri's only 100 percent-black school system.

One state official had called conditions in Wellston's schools "deplor- 68 able" and "academically abusive."

The issue for state officials was what to do next with Wellston's students. 69

One thing was clear: The students were not going to be absorbed into any 70 of the high-performing, mostly white districts nearby. Jones, the state board of education official, was blunt about why: "You'd have had a civil war."

The Difference Between Clayton and Normandy

Five miles separate the Clayton and Normandy school districts, but much more sets them apart. Here are some characteristics of the two districts from the 2013–2014 school year.

	CLAYTON	NORMANDY
Accreditation status	Accredited	Unaccredited
4-year graduation rate, white students	96.3%	*Too few students to accurately determine*
4-year graduation rate, black students	93.8%	61.4%
Average teacher salary	$71,205	$59,560
Average spending per pupil	$17,851	$15,096
Percentage of high school core classes not taught by "highly qualified" teachers	1.0%	39.7%
Composite ACT score (national average: 21)	25.7	16

SOURCE: Missouri Department of Elementary and Secondary Education

Officials then turned to Normandy, which already enrolled almost 71 5,000 students. Merging two impoverished, struggling systems made sense to almost no one, especially the officials in charge of Normandy's schools.

The state went forward with it anyway. 72

"If you are strictly doing what's best for all kids, you don't merge those 73 two districts," Stanton Lawrence, Normandy's superintendent at the time, said in a recent interview. "Why would you do that? They had written those kids off."

"It Was All Corrupt Politics"

By the time Michael Brown reached his junior year in high school, he had *74*
bounced between local districts and spent most of his career in racially
segregated and economically disadvantaged schools. Behind in credits, he
enrolled at Normandy High in the spring of 2013.

If he had dreams of academic success, he could not have wound up in *75*
a more challenging place to realize them.

The state's 2014 assessment report on Normandy's schools was spec- *76*
tacularly bleak: Zero points awarded for academic achievement in English.
Zero for math, for social studies, for science. Zero for students headed to
college. Zero for attendance. Zero for the percent of students who graduate. Its total score: 10 out of 140.

Out of 520 districts in the state, Normandy, where 98 percent of stu- *77*
dents are black and 9 of 10 were poor in 2013, is marooned at the very
bottom.

Decades of research show that segregated, high-poverty schools are *78*
simply toxic for students of all races and backgrounds. Just last month,
the University of North Carolina at Chapel Hill released a study showing
that black first-graders in segregated schools performed worse than black
students with the same backgrounds (meaning poverty, parental education
and other factors) who attend integrated schools.

© Whitney Curtis for ProPublica

FIGURE 14.9 Out of Missouri's 520 school systems, Normandy is one of just
two that are unaccredited.

But for a moment prior to the start of Brown's senior year, the Nor-   79
mandy district's students were thrown an unlikely lifeline.

Just two years after the merger with Wellston, Normandy's schools   80
were performing so poorly that the state stripped Normandy of its
accreditation altogether. That triggered a state law requiring that any
student there be allowed to transfer to an accredited district nearby.
The law had been challenged by suburban districts uninterested in
absorbing kids from failing schools, but in 2013 the Missouri State
Supreme Court upheld it.

For Nedra Martin, whose honors student daughter, Mah'Ria, was stuck   81
in Normandy's failing schools, the development was the miracle she had
prayed for. Martin could not afford private schools, and her attempts to
enroll her daughter in neighboring white districts had been rebuffed.

Just like that, the court's decision erased the invisible, impenetrable   82
lines of segregation that had trapped her child.

"I was elated," Martin said. "Just elated."   83

Parents in the school districts that would have to take Normandy's stu-   84
dents were not. Normandy had chosen to provide transportation for its
transfers to attend Francis Howell, which was 85 percent white at the time
and some 26 miles away.

When Francis Howell officials held a public forum to address com-   85
munity concerns, more than 2,500 parents packed into the high school
gymnasium.

Would the district install metal detectors? What about the violence   86
their children would be subjected to, an elementary school parent asked.
Wouldn't test scores plummet? The issue wasn't about race, one parent
said, "but trash."

Mah'Ria Martin was sitting in the audience that night with her mother.   87
One of the few brown faces in the audience, the rising 8th grader said she
wiped away tears.

"It made me heartbroken because they were putting us in a box," said   88
Mah'Ria, soft spoken but firm, in recalling the episode. "I was sitting there
thinking, 'Would you want some other parents talking about your kid that
way?'"

In the fall of 2013, nearly 1,000 Normandy students—about a quarter   89
of the district's enrollment—fled to schools in accredited districts. More
than 400, including Mah'Ria, headed to Francis Howell.

Mah'Ria said that she was, in fact, welcomed by students and teach-   90
ers at her new middle school. It was the first time in her life that she'd
attended a district that had the full approval of the state.

She thrived. And she was not alone.   91

Despite the fears, recently released state data shows that, with the   92
exception of one district, test scores in the transfer schools did not drop.

But the success came with a perverse twist. The state required failing   93
districts whose students were allowed to transfer to pay the costs of the

children's education in the adjoining districts. For the whiter, more affluent districts, it was a replay of what had happened during the court-ordered desegregation plan, when transfer students were referred to as "black gold": students the districts had to educate but who cost them nothing.

The millions of dollars in payments to other districts drained Nor- 94 mandy's finances. Within months, the district shuttered an elementary school and laid off 40 percent of its staff. Already deeply troubled, the Normandy schools were headed to insolvency.

"In order to save the district, they killed the district," said John Wright, 95 a longtime St. Louis educator who spent stints as superintendent in both St. Louis and Normandy.

Recognizing the problem of student transfers, the state engineered 96 their end.

This June, when students were on summer break, the state announced 97 that it was taking over the Normandy Public Schools district and reconstituting it as the Normandy Schools Collaborative. As a new educational entity, state officials said, the district got a clean slate. It no longer was unaccredited but operated under a newly created status as a "state oversight district."

The transfer program, the state claimed, no longer applied. One by one, 98 transfer districts announced that Normandy children were no longer welcome.

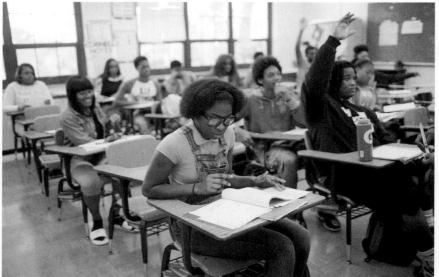

© Whitney Curtis for ProPublica

FIGURE 14.10 Mah'Ria Pruitt-Martin, center, an honors student, transferred out of Normandy last year but returned after the state tried to end student transfers to high-performing districts. In November, her mother pulled Mah'Ria out of the Normandy schools again because she said she saw little improvement.

Martin and her daughter were devastated. "I honestly felt they were   *99* blacklisting our children," Martin said.

Martin and other parents sued, asserting the state had no legal author-   *100* ity to act as it had. St. Louis lawyer Josh Schindler represented the parents.

"These are just families who want their kids to have a good educa-   *101* tion. Decent, hard-working people who want their kids to have a chance," he said in an interview. "This has been a decades-long battle. How are we going to remedy the situation?"

On August 15, after the new school year had begun in some districts,   *102* a state judge granted a temporary injunction that allowed the plaintiffs to enroll their children in the transfer districts.

"Every day a student attends an unaccredited school," the judge wrote,   *103* the child "could suffer harm that cannot be repaired."

The ruling brought a rush of relief to many parents.   *104*

"I cried and just held onto my kid," said Janine Crawford, whose son was   *105* able return to the Pattonville School District. "It meant that he was going to get a decent education. And it meant that I could take a deep breath."

The state is still fighting the ruling, and Francis Howell required all   *106* transfer students to obtain court orders to return.

Martin briefly returned Mah'Ria to the Normandy schools after they   *107* came under state oversight but found them little improved and has since sent her back to Francis Howell. The entire situation has only reinforced her cynicism and despair, she said.

"What about your neighbor? Is it so hard to embrace the children who   *108* clearly need your help right now?" she asked. "The whole way this was handled by the state on down was sheisty and underhanded. They were not thinking about the children."

The state's top education officials admit that the way they've dealt with   *109* Normandy has laid bare racial divisions in St. Louis County and beyond. In an interview, Nicastro, the state superintendent, called it a "low point" in her career, a "blight and commentary about Missouri."

When asked whether black children in Missouri were receiving an   *110* equal education, she paused, then inhaled deeply. "Do I think black chil- dren in Missouri are getting in all cases the same education as their white counterparts?" Nicastro said. "I'd have to say no."

Little Hope and a Telling Burial

On a cold, clear morning in November, with the grand jury still assess-   *111* ing the killing of Michael Brown, a group of black leaders and concerned citizens gathered in a classroom at Harris-Stowe State University in down- town St. Louis. The school was founded in 1829 to train black teachers.

The gathering produced a recommitment to the solution to segrega-   *112* tion floated 30 years before: a single, unified school district for St. Louis and its suburbs.

But there was recognition that the answer would require a long and *113* uphill fight.

"We know what would have been best educationally for these kids—we *114* always know what the best thing to do is. What we lack is the moral courage and political will to do it," said Jones, of the state Board of Education. "If we had treated the civil rights movement the way we've treated the education of black children, we'd still be drinking out of colored drinking fountains."

Separate but equal has not worked, Jones said. Not in St. Louis. Not *115* anywhere else. The school lines that advantage some and deprive others, he said, must be toppled.

Students who spend their careers in segregated schools can look *116* forward to a life on the margins, according to a 2014 study on the long-term impacts of school desegregation by University of California, Berkeley economist Rucker Johnson. They are more likely to be poor. They are more likely to go to jail. They are less likely to graduate from high school, to go to college, and to finish if they go. They are more likely to live in segregated neighborhoods as adults.

Their children are more likely to also attend segregated schools, repeat- *117* ing the cycle.

Even in the fog of her grief, Michael Brown's mother spoke to this *118* struggle. With her son's body laying on the concrete behind police tape,

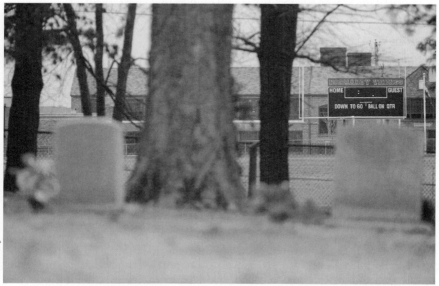

© Whitney Curtis for ProPublica

FIGURE 14.11   Michael Brown is buried in the cemetery that overlooks his old high school.

Lesley McSpadden cried, "Do you know how hard it was for me to get him to stay in school and graduate?

"You know how many black men graduate?" she implored. "Not *119* many."

With a diploma from a district that one report called "catastrophically under- *120* performing," her oldest son had been headed to nearby Vatterott College.

Schools like Vatterott enroll a disproportionate percentage of black *121* students. Those who attend are often saddled with debt they cannot pay back. In 2013, a jury awarded more than $13 million to a single mother who sued Vatterott for misleading enrollment practices.

An executive with Vatterott Educational Centers, Inc. said the company's *122* problems were in the past, and that it had reformed its admissions practices.

Brown never made it to Vatterott. Maybe he would have bucked the *123* odds and found a way to master a trade and make a career.

Today, Brown is buried in the old St. Peter's Cemetery. Right next to *124* Normandy High School.

■ ■ ■

Reading as a Writer: Analyzing Rhetorical Choices

1. What is Jim Crow (para. 15)? Look it up, as well as *Brown v. Board of Education* (para. 18), and share what you find. How do these historical references add to Hannah-Jones's argument?

2. Spend some time with the charts and the map included in this essay. Make sure you understand the information presented in each and its relationship to the rest of the essay. Explain at least one chart to a peer.

Writing as a Reader: Entering the Conversation of Ideas

1. Nikole Hannah-Jones shares a concern with Susan Dynarski (pp. 427–29) and also with Sean F. Reardon, Jane Waldfogel, and Daphna Bassok (pp. 430–33), all of whom examine the impact of economic inequality on children's educations. Perhaps beginning with Hannah-Jones's paragraph 8 as a helpful starting point, bring together these authors' ideas on the multiple aspects of persistent poverty that keep students from accessing meaningful education. Write an essay in which you analyze the ways these authors frame the problems and solutions, and assert your own position about what changes can—or should—be made, while addressing the challenges described in these readings.

2. Hannah-Jones's analysis of racial and economic inequalities is interestingly in conversation with Barbara Ehrenreich's essay (pp. 340–45 in Sociology) about cultural attitudes toward poverty and Ta-Nehisi Coates's essay (pp. 20–24 in Chapter 1) about racial inequalities. Choose one of these authors to place in conversation with Hannah-Jones, and craft an essay that uses insights and evidence from each author to make an argument about the relationship between these social inequalities and education. What is the significance of your findings?

Sociology

How does studying human social behaviors help us understand ourselves and the world?

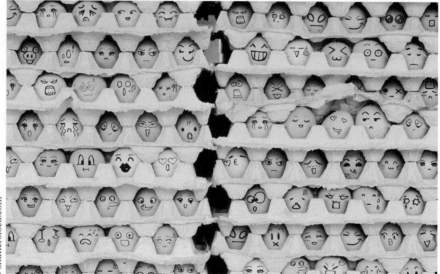

© shutterstock.com

S ociology is the study of human social behaviors, with a particular interest in the origins of these behavior patterns and their significance in the present. As you will see in this chapter's readings, analyzing the world through a sociological lens means finding significance in big assumptions we make about groups of people (often without evidence) or in seemingly insignificant phrases like the schoolyard taunt "Dude, you're a fag."

Sociologists, like other scholars, often ask us to rethink what we *think* we know about the world.

In this chapter, you'll learn from a leading sociologist, Allan G. Johnson, how patterns of privilege — or unearned advantages some groups have over others — can be invisible to those who have the advantages, and devastating to those who do not. Johnson's concept of "systems of privilege" will help you find those patterns in all the other essays in this chapter, whether the writers are discussing racial inequalities, homophobia, or a range of attitudes about poverty. While these are all challenging topics, sociological thinkers are interested in considering solutions to these difficult problems as well. As you read the conclusions in these essays, think about your own experiences of these issues, and test their ideas against your own optimism about changing these social patterns, beliefs, and behaviors.

The writers in this chapter tackle these sometimes overwhelming topics by examining closely the much more mundane aspects of our lives. For example, C. J. Pascoe uses an ethnographic research method to observe and record patterns in high school students' daily interactions. She also interviews teenagers to better understand the many ways the word "fag" is used to negotiate assumptions about gender and sexuality.

Both Claudia Rankine and Allan G. Johnson examine historical and present attitudes about racial difference and reveal the human cost of assumptions about groups of people. To help readers see patterns, they draw on data about arrest records, surveys about stereotypes, and media coverage of the deaths of African Americans that led to the conception of the Black Lives Matter movement. While these writers are examining difficult truths, they are not hopeless; they suggest ways to change these social patterns, too.

Similarly, Barbara Ehrenreich's short journalistic essay in this chapter about the ways we often characterize those who are poor as very different from the rest of "us" and bell hooks's analysis of poverty as a mark of shame help us see how some groups come to be seen as "normal" and even "ideal," while others come to be seen as "others." The effects on the daily lives of those who have social power — and those who do not — are enormous. Sociology's premise is that society is *our* creation. Just as we have created and maintained these behavior patterns — because it is always easier to take the familiar path, the path of least resistance — we can also break new paths for a more just society.

ALLAN G. JOHNSON

What Is a "System of Privilege"?

Allan G. Johnson is a sociologist and public speaker who focuses his research on the ways gender, class, and race assumptions shape our experiences in the world and how we have the power to change those patterns.

His work is motivated by social justice topics. In this piece, he explains a concept scholars have been writing about for decades: privilege. Before you read, you might discuss what you already know or have heard about this term now that it has become more widely used in popular culture.

In this short, pithy essay, Johnson defines privilege and also explains how it works as a system. He lays out his definition in the first sentence. In the first paragraph, he offers an example and supporting data to illustrate privilege in action. Pause after you read the first paragraph and consider what surprises you—if anything—about his example. Why do you think so many people's perceptions and realities are often so far apart?

In the next few paragraphs, Johnson explains some misconceptions about privilege, including the fact that "privilege does not guarantee good outcomes for the privileged group or bad outcomes for everyone else" (para. 3). Instead, systems of privilege "load the odds one way or the other." This insight has profound implications, since it means there is not an even playing field for all people in society. Being born into one social category might give someone unearned social advantages, while being born into another category might give someone else unfair disadvantages.

While Johnson focuses in this essay on examples of white privilege, the concept and patterns of privilege apply to many different social patterns. In paragraph 4, he lays out the three basic principles of systems of privilege: "dominance, identification, and centeredness." Take some time to be sure you understand Johnson's use of these terms, and consider his examples of each in the following paragraphs. Can you think of additional examples of how these principles might maintain unearned privileges (for example, for able-bodied or heterosexual people)?

One of Johnson's key insights is that the unearned advantages that come from social privilege are often invisible to those who experience them. Why is this the case? How does this make it challenging to change patterns of behavior?

Johnson closes, just as he opens, with a statistic-supported example: "Eighty-five percent of people who buy, sell, and use illegal drugs in the U.S. . . . are white, but more than half of the people in jail or prison for drug crimes are people of color" (para. 9). Plainly, understanding and changing systems of privilege is not simply a classroom exercise. Lives, quite literally, are at stake.

■ ■ ■

The concept of privilege refers to any advantage that is unearned, exclusive, and socially conferred. For example, white people are generally assumed to be law-abiding until they show some sign that they are not, while people of color are routinely assumed to be criminals or potential criminals until they show they're not. One way to see this is through a survey in which respondents were asked to close their eyes and picture a drug dealer. When asked to describe what they saw, almost 95 percent mentioned a black person, even though the vast majority of drug dealers in the U.S. are white.

So, when it comes to being randomly stopped and frisked by police, 2
anyone identified as "white" has an advantage they did not earn and
that is exclusive to whites. It is socially conferred in the sense that it
depends on them being perceived in a particular way by the police—as
"white"—before the advantage is given to them in the form of the assumption that they are not criminals.

It's important to note that privilege does not guarantee good out- 3
comes for the privileged group or bad outcomes for everyone else. A white
person, for example, can work hard and have little to show for it, can be
mistreated by the police without cause, be denied a job they're qualified
for. What privilege does is load the odds one way or the other so that the
chance of bad things happening to white people as a category of people
is much lower than for everyone else, and the chance of good things happening is much higher. Privilege is not something a person can *have*, like a
possession, as in "Where's *mine*?" Instead, it is a characteristic of the social
system—like a rule in a game—in which everyone participates.

A system of privilege—a family, a workplace, a society—is organized 4
around three basic principles: dominance, identification, and centeredness.

A system of white privilege, for example, is white-dominated, which 5
means the default is for white people to occupy positions of power. White-
dominance doesn't mean that all white people are powerful, only that the
powerful tend almost always to be white, and when a person of color occu-
pies a position of power, that will be noted as an exception to the rule (as
when Barack Obama is routinely identified as a black President and not
just "the President").

White-identification means that the culture defines "white" people as 6
the standard for human beings in general. People of color, for example,
are routinely identified as "nonwhite," a term that doesn't tell us what they
are, but what they are *not*.

When a category of people is named the standard for human beings 7
in general, the path of least resistance is to see them as superior, there
being no other reason to make them the standard. Several things follow
from this, including seeing the way they do things as simply "human" or
"normal," and giving more credibility to their views than to the views of
"others," in this case people of color. White-identification also encourages
whites to be unaware of themselves *as* white, as if they didn't have a race at
all. It also encourages whites to be unaware of white privilege.

White-centeredness is the tendency to put white people and what they 8
do at the center of attention—the front page of the newspaper or magazine, the main character in the movie.

When you organize a society in this way, the result will be patterns 9
of unearned advantage that are available to whites simply because they
are socially identified as "white." A related consequence is patterns of
oppression centered on people of color. Eighty-five percent of people
who buy, sell, and use illegal drugs in the U.S., for example, are white,
but more than half of the people in jail or prison for drug crimes are

people of color. The white privilege in this example is the practice of the criminal justice system to overlook drug crimes committed by whites, while the corresponding oppressive consequence for people of color is the systematic selection of people of color for arrest, prosecution, and punishment.

■ ■ ■

Reading as a Writer: Analyzing Rhetorical Choices

1. Why does Johnson refer to the dynamic he describes as a "system of privilege"? Locate all the places in this short essay that help you understand why he sees privilege as a system rather than "something a person can *have*" (para. 3).

2. Find the paragraphs in which Johnson uses statistics. What can you say about the placement of these pieces of data? How do they support the central claim of his essay? Refer to the discussion of supporting claims in Chapter 4 as you discuss your responses.

Writing as a Reader: Entering the Conversation of Ideas

1. Johnson's insights about privilege can be put into conversation with Barbara Ehrenreich's analysis of cultural attitudes about poverty in the United States (pp. 482–85). Write an essay in which you use Johnson's terms to analyze the examples in Ehrenreich's essay. What conclusions can you draw about the prevailing attitudes about the poor and the impact this has on those who fall into this category?

2. As a sociologist, Johnson uses different analytical tools than Agustín Fuentes (pp. 629–50 in Psychology and Biology), but both authors are interested in the impact of assumptions we make about "others." In an essay of your own that draws on claims and examples from both authors, make an argument about the cultural significance of assumptions we make about groups of people, often with no evidence. What solutions do these authors provide, and what is your assessment of those solutions?

CLAUDIA RANKINE

The Condition of Black Life Is One of Mourning

Claudia Rankine is an American poet, playwright, editor, and cultural critic who has won numerous awards, including a MacArthur Foundation Award for those "committed to building a more just, verdant, and peaceful world." Her work has been published in major newspapers and magazines, and her 2014 book-length poem, *Citizen: An American Lyric*, has been widely praised as both cultural critique and poetry. Rankine also teaches at Yale University and serves as a chancellor of the Academy of American Poets.

While this essay makes a sociological argument, Rankine uses poetic and creative writing strategies throughout. Consider her choice of a narrative introduction and conclusion, for example (and recall insights in Chapter 11 about drafting these portions of your own essays). In her second paragraph, she uses repetition for rhetorical effect. Read that paragraph aloud, and consider how her word choices support the central ideas in this essay. What effect do these strategies have on you?

Rankine draws on history to contextualize her point that violence against black bodies has been ongoing. Spend some time with paragraph 5, in which she traces a long historical line of events, but through images rather than specific facts or data. To what is she referring in each sentence? What do you make of the final two questions she poses, one of which is a "wrongheaded question" — "What kind of savages are we?" — and one she believes is the correct one — "What kind of country do we live in?"

Finally, as you read (and reread, as careful readers do), think about the meaning of Rankine's title, "The Condition of Black Life Is One of Mourning." The phrase appears in her opening anecdote and reappears in her discussion of the Black Lives Matter movement (see especially para. 14) and appears again in her final paragraph. We often think of mourning as a personal experience, but Rankine is arguing for understanding mourning as a kind of national activism. If you agree with her that one of our national problems is "a lack of feeling for another" (para. 23), how could mourning, as she argues, be a step toward a solution?

A friend recently told me that when she gave birth to her son, before naming him, before even nursing him, her first thought was, I have to get him out of this country. We both laughed. Perhaps our black humor had to do with understanding that getting out was neither an option nor the real desire. This is it, our life. Here we work, hold citizenship, pensions, health insurance, family, friends, and on and on. She couldn't, she didn't leave. Years after his birth, whenever her son steps out of their home, her status as the mother of a living human being remains as precarious as ever. Added to the natural fears of every parent facing the randomness of life is this other knowledge of the ways in which institutional racism works in our country. Ours was the laughter of vulnerability, fear, recognition, and an absurd stuckness.

I asked another friend what it's like being the mother of a black son. "The condition of black life is one of mourning," she said bluntly. For her, mourning lived in real time inside her and her son's reality: At any moment she might lose her reason for living. Though the white liberal imagination likes to feel temporarily bad about black suffering, there really is no mode of empathy that can replicate the daily strain of knowing that as a black person you can be killed for simply being black: no hands in your pockets, no playing music, no sudden movements, no driving your car, no walking at night, no walking in the day, no turning onto this street, no entering this building, no standing your ground, no standing here, no standing there, no talking back, no playing with toy guns, no living while black.

Eleven days after I was born, on September 15, 1963, four black girls ₃ were killed in the bombing of the 16th Street Baptist Church in Birmingham, Alabama. Now, fifty-two years later, six black women and three black men have been shot to death while at a Bible-study meeting at the historic Emanuel African Methodist Episcopal Church in Charleston, South Carolina. They were killed by a homegrown terrorist, self-identified as a white supremacist, who might also be a "disturbed young man" (as various news outlets have described him). It has been reported that a black woman and her five-year-old granddaughter survived the shooting by playing dead. They are two of the three survivors of the attack. The white family of the suspect says that for them this is a difficult time. This is indisputable. But for African American families, this living in a state of mourning and fear remains commonplace.

The spectacle of the shooting suggests an event out of time, as if the ₄ killing of black people with white-supremacist justification interrupts anything other than regular television programming. But Dylann Storm Roof did not create himself from nothing. He has grown up with the rhetoric and orientation of racism. He has seen white men like Benjamin F. Haskell, Thomas Gleason, and Michael Jacques plead guilty to, or be convicted of, burning Macedonia Church of God in Christ in Springfield, Massachusetts, just hours after President Obama was elected. Every racist statement he has made he could have heard all his life. He, along with the rest of us, has been living with slain black bodies.

We live in a country where Americans assimilate corpses in their daily ₅ comings and goings. Dead blacks are a part of normal life here. Dying in ship hulls, tossed into the Atlantic, hanging from trees, beaten, shot in churches, gunned down by the police, or warehoused in prisons: Historically, there is no quotidian without the enslaved, chained, or dead black body to gaze upon or to hear about or to position a self against. When blacks become overwhelmed by our culture's disorder and protest (ultimately to our own detriment, because protest gives the police justification to militarize, as they did in Ferguson), the wrongheaded question that is asked is, What kind of savages are we? Rather than, What kind of country do we live in?

In 1955, when Emmett Till's mutilated and bloated body was recovered ₆ from the Tallahatchie River and placed for burial in a nailed-shut pine box, his mother, Mamie Till Mobley demanded his body be transported from Mississippi, where Till had been visiting relatives, to his home in Chicago. Once the Chicago funeral home received the body, she made a decision that would create a new pathway for how to think about a lynched body. She requested an open coffin and allowed photographs to be taken and published of her dead son's disfigured body.

Mobley's refusal to keep private grief private allowed a body that 7
meant nothing to the criminal-justice system to stand as evidence. By placing both herself and her son's corpse in positions of refusal relative to the
etiquette of grief, she "disidentified" with the tradition of the lynched figure left out in public view as a warning to the black community, thereby
using the lynching tradition against itself. The spectacle of the black body,
in her hands, publicized the injustice mapped onto her son's corpse. "Let
the people see what I see," she said, adding, "I believe that the whole
United States is mourning with me."

It's very unlikely that her belief in a national mourning was fully real- 8
ized, but her desire to make mourning enter our day-to-day world was a
new kind of logic. In refusing to look away from the flesh of our domestic murders, by insisting we look with her upon the dead, she reframed
mourning as a method of acknowledgment that helped energize the civil
rights movement in the 1950s and '60s.

The decision not to release photos of the crime scene in Charleston, 9
perhaps out of deference to the families of the dead, doesn't forestall our
mourning. But in doing so, the bodies that demonstrate all too tragically
that "black skin is not a weapon" (as one protest poster read last year)
are turned into an abstraction. It's one thing to imagine nine black bodies bleeding out on a church floor, and another thing to see it. The lack of
visual evidence remains in contrast to what we saw in Ferguson, where the
police, in their refusal to move Michael Brown's body, perhaps unknow-
ingly continued where Till's mother left off.

After Brown was shot six times, twice in the head, his body was left 10
facedown in the street by the police officers. Whatever their reasoning, by
not moving Brown's corpse for four hours after his shooting, the police
made mourning his death part of what it meant to take in the details of his
story. No one could consider the facts of Michael Brown's interaction with
the Ferguson police officer Darren Wilson without also thinking of the bul-
let-riddled body bleeding on the asphalt. It would be a mistake to presume
that everyone who saw the image mourned Brown, but once exposed to
it, a person had to decide whether his dead black body mattered enough
to be mourned. (Another option, of course, is that it becomes a spectacle
for white pornography: the dead body as an object that satisfies an illicit
desire. Perhaps this is where Dylann Storm Roof stepped in.)

Black Lives Matter, the movement founded by the activists Alicia Garza, 11
Patrisse Cullors, and Opal Tometi, began with the premise that the incom-
mensurable experience of systemic racism creates an unequal playing field.
The American imagination has never been able to fully recover from its
white-supremacist beginnings. Consequently, our laws and attitudes have
been straining against the devaluation of the black body. Despite good intentions, the associations of blackness with inarticulate, bestial criminality persist beneath the appearance of white civility. This assumption both frames
and determines our individual interactions and experiences as citizens.

The American tendency to normalize situations by centralizing white- *12* ness was consciously or unconsciously demonstrated again when certain whites, like the president of Smith College, sought to alter the language of "Black Lives Matter" to "All Lives Matter." What on its surface was intended to be interpreted as a humanist move—"aren't we all just people here? "—didn't take into account a system inured to black corpses in our public spaces. When the judge in the Charleston bond hearing for Dylann Storm Roof called for support of Roof's family, it was also a subtle shift away from valuing the black body in our time of deep despair.

Anti-black racism is in the culture. It's in our laws, in our advertise- *13* ments, in our friendships, in our segregated cities, in our schools, in our Congress, in our scientific experiments, in our language, on the Internet, in our bodies no matter our race, in our communities, and, perhaps most devastatingly, in our justice system. The unarmed, slain black bodies in public spaces turn grief into our everyday feeling that something is wrong everywhere and all the time, even if locally things appear normal. Having coffee, walking the dog, reading the paper, taking the elevator to the office, dropping the kids off at school: All of this good life is surrounded by the ambient feeling that at any given moment, a black person is being killed in the street or in his home by the armed hatred of a fellow American.

The Black Lives Matter movement can be read as an attempt to keep *14* mourning an open dynamic in our culture because black lives exist in a state of precariousness. Mourning then bears both the vulnerability inherent in black lives and the instability regarding a future for those lives. Unlike earlier black-power movements that tried to fight or segregate for self-preservation, Black Lives Matter aligns with the dead, continues the mourning, and refuses the forgetting in front of all of us. If the Rev. Martin Luther King, Jr.'s civil rights movement made demands that altered the course of American lives and backed up those demands with the willingness to give up your life in service of your civil rights, with Black Lives Matter, a more internalized change is being asked for: recognition.

The truth, as I see it, is that if black men and women, black boys and *15* girls, mattered, if we were seen as living, we would not be dying simply because whites don't like us. Our deaths inside a system of racism existed before we were born. The legacy of black bodies as property and subsequently three-fifths human continues to pollute the white imagination. To inhabit our citizenry fully, we have to not only understand this, but also grasp it. In the words of the playwright Lorraine Hansberry, "The problem is we have to find some way with these dialogues to show and to encourage the white liberal to stop being a liberal and become an American radical." And, as my friend the critic and poet Fred Moten has written: "I believe in the world and want to be in it. I want to be in it all the way to the end of it because I believe in another world and I want to be in that." This other world, that world, would presumably be one where black living matters. But we can't get there without fully recognizing what is here.

Dylann Storm Roof's unmediated hatred of black people; Black Lives 16
Matter; citizens' videotaping the killings of blacks; the Ferguson Police
Department leaving Brown's body in the street—all these actions support
Mamie Till Mobley's belief that we need to see or hear the truth. We need
the truth of how the bodies died to interrupt the course of normal life. But
if keeping the dead at the forefront of our consciousness is crucial for our
body politic, what of the families of the dead? How must it feel to a family member for the deceased to be more important as evidence than as an
individual to be buried and laid to rest?

Michael Brown's mother, Lesley McSpadden, was kept away from her 17
son's body because it was evidence. She was denied the rights of a mother,
a sad fact reminiscent of pre-Civil War times, when as a slave she would
have had no legal claim to her offspring. McSpadden learned of her new
identity as a mother of a dead son from bystanders: "There were some girls
down there had recorded the whole thing," she told reporters. One girl, she
said, "showed me a picture on her phone. She said, 'Isn't that your son?' I
just bawled even harder. Just to see that, my son lying there lifeless, for no
apparent reason." Circling the perimeter around her son's body, McSpadden tried to disperse the crowd: "All I want them to do is pick up my baby."

McSpadden, unlike Mamie Till Mobley, seemed to have little desire to 18
expose her son's corpse to the media. Her son was not an orphan body for
everyone to look upon. She wanted him covered and removed from sight.
He belonged to her, her baby. After Brown's corpse was finally taken away,
two weeks passed before his family was able to see him. This loss of control
and authority might explain why after Brown's death, McSpadden was supposedly in the precarious position of accosting vendors selling T-shirts that
demanded justice for Michael Brown that used her son's name. Not only
were the procedures around her son's corpse out of her hands; his name
had been commoditized and assimilated into our modes of capitalism.

Some of McSpadden's neighbors in Ferguson also wanted to create 19
distance between themselves and the public life of Brown's death. They did
not need a constant reminder of the ways black bodies don't matter to law
enforcement officers in their neighborhood. By the request of the community, the original makeshift memorial—with flowers, pictures, notes, and
teddy bears—was finally removed by Brown's father on what would have
been his birthday and replaced by an official plaque installed on the sidewalk next to where' Brown died. The permanent reminder can be engaged
or stepped over, depending on the pedestrian's desires.

In order to be away from the site of the murder of her son, Tamir Rice, 20
Samaria moved out of her Cleveland home and into a homeless shelter.
(Her family eventually relocated her.) "The whole world has seen the same
video like I've seen," she said about Tamir's being shot by a police officer. The video, which was played and replayed in the media, documented
the two seconds it took the police to arrive and shoot; the two seconds
that marked the end of her son's life and that became a document to be

examined by everyone. It's possible this shared scrutiny explains why the police held his twelve-year-old body for six months after his death. Everyone could see what the police would have to explain away. The justice system wasn't able to do it, and a judge found probable cause to charge the officer who shot Rice with murder, while a grand jury declined to indict any of the officers involved. Meanwhile, for Samaria Rice, her unburied son's memory made her neighborhood unbearable.

Regardless of the wishes of these mothers—mothers of men like 21 Brown, John Crawford III, or Eric Garner, and also mothers of women and girls like Rekia Boyd and Aiyana Stanley-Jones, each of whom was killed by the police—their children's deaths will remain within the public discourse. For those who believe the same behavior that got them killed if exhibited by a white man or boy would not have ended his life, the subsequent failure to indict or convict the police officers involved in these various cases requires that public mourning continue and remain present indefinitely. "I want to see a cop shoot a white unarmed teenager in the back," Toni Morrison said in April. She went on to say: "I want to see a white man convicted for raping a black woman. Then when you ask me, 'Is it over?' I will say yes." Morrison is right to suggest that this action would signal change, but the real change needs to be a rerouting of interior belief. It's an individual challenge that needs to happen before any action by a political justice system would signify true societal change.

The Charleston murders alerted us to the reality that a system so 22 steeped in anti-black racism means that on any given day it can be open season on any black person—old or young, man, woman, or child. There exists no equivalent reality for white Americans. We can distance ourselves from this fact until the next horrific killing, but we won't be able to outrun it. History's authority over us is not broken by maintaining a silence about its continued effects.

A sustained state of national mourning for black lives is called for in 23 order to point to the undeniability of their devaluation. The hope is that recognition will break a momentum that laws haven't altered. Susie Jackson; Sharonda Coleman-Singleton; DePayne Middleton-Doctor; Ethel Lee Lance; the Rev. Daniel Lee Simmons, Sr.; the Rev. Clementa C. Pinckney; Cynthia Hurd; Tywanza Sanders; and Myra Thompson were murdered because they were black. It's extraordinary how ordinary our grief sits inside this fact. One friend said, "I am so afraid, every day." Her son's childhood feels impossible, because he will have to be—has to be—so much more careful. Our mourning, this mourning, is in time with our lives. There is no life outside of our reality here. Is this something that can be seen and known by parents of white children? This is the question that nags me. National mourning, as advocated by Black Lives Matter, is a mode of intervention and interruption that might itself be assimilated into the category of public annoyance. This is altogether possible; but also possible is the recognition that it's a lack of feeling for another that is our problem. Grief, then, for these deceased others might align some of us, for the first time, with the living.

■ ■ ■

Reading as a Writer: Analyzing Rhetorical Choices

1. In this essay, Rankine includes the names of many people who have been victims or perpetrators of violence. Circle all the proper names in this essay—including the long list in the final paragraph. As a small-group project, divide the names among several groups, with each group looking up biographical information on their assigned names and then teaching what they have learned to the rest of the class.

2. What do you know about the Black Lives Matter (BLM) movement, mentioned in paragraph 11? Did you know the founders are three women? Read around on the BLM Web site (http://blacklivesmatter.com) and consider the connections you see between Rankine's essay and the BLM principles.

Writing as a Reader: Entering the Conversation of Ideas

1. Rankine's analysis of the specific systems of inequality are interesting to consider in the context of Allan G. Johnson's concepts about privilege (pp. 454–57). In Rankine's essay, you might focus particularly on paragraphs 12 and 13 (on "Black Lives Matter" and "All Lives Matter") and paragraph 15 (on systems of racism). Write an essay in which you bring these writers into conversation with each other, examining how each writer explains the problem and potential solutions. What do you think people need to understand, and how might they learn this information, to address these inequalities?

2. Rankine's essay provides helpful framing for Nikole Hannah-Jones's essay (pp. 434–52 in Education) about the shortcomings of the education system in Ferguson, Missouri. In an essay that uses insights and examples from both pieces, craft an argument of your own that demonstrates how these authors' ideas inform and extend one another, and draw a conclusion, based on your findings, about the relationship between education—inside and outside of formal schooling—and social inequality and change.

C. J. PASCOE

"Dude, You're a Fag": Adolescent Masculinity and the Fag Discourse

C. J. Pascoe is a professor of sociology at the University of Oregon who writes and teaches about youth culture, media, and sexuality. This essay comes from the research for her 2007 book *Dude, You're a Fag: Masculinity and Sexuality in High School*. In this piece, she takes a familiar taunt—"You're a fag"—and examines it through the eyes of a scholar, considering its contexts and meanings. According to Pascoe, "You're a fag" is more than a simple homophobic slur, often used in jest, and so common among schoolkids that it may seem almost meaningless. If we analyze the contexts in which the phrase is used, Pascoe argues, we can understand better how adolescent boys often say it to determine what it means to be masculine. Further, Pascoe points out that this "fag discourse is racialized" (para. 6), used differently in different communities.

Pascoe calls herself a "feminist" scholar, meaning that she is interested in the effects of gender assumptions on the lived experiences of both women and men. While it might seem unlikely for a feminist scholar to be interested in the lives of men, the study of masculinity is a growing field, as scholars examine the ways our cultural assumptions about what it means to be "masculine" often limit boys' and men's lives.

The essay is organized loosely in what is often called the IMRAD style (Introduction, Methods, Research, and Discussion), common to scientific essays and also to many social science essays, like Pascoe's. How does the structure of the essay help you follow Pascoe's argument? While you may find the language in the opening pages a bit challenging, as Pascoe lays out the research others have done in the study of masculinity, try to mark key terms and ideas, and look for the definitions she offers of terms like "the sociology of masculinity" (para. 7), "queer theory" (para. 8), and understandings of gender as something made by culture (para. 10). How do these ideas help her make her larger point?

The Method and Research sections are more descriptive, as Pascoe explains how she gathered data firsthand at a high school. What are the effects of describing the high school and the town this way and including direct quotations from students? Consider your own high school experiences as you think about the challenges of obtaining information through personal interviews and observation.

You may be surprised by Pascoe's conclusion that calling someone a "fag" has little to do with homosexuality. She notes, "Looking at 'fag' as a discourse rather than a static identity reveals that the term can be invested with different meanings in different social spaces" (para. 40). By shifting our focus away from simple assumptions about teen homophobia and toward an analysis of specific social situations in which the term "fag" is used, Pascoe argues that we can see how much is at stake and for whom when adolescent boys evaluate other boys' masculinity. In Pascoe's final paragraph, she suggests implications for future research and notes that the consequences of this kind of teasing can be deadly.

⸰ ⸰ ⸰

"There's a faggot over there! There's a faggot over there! Come look!" yelled Brian, a senior at River High School, to a group of 10-year-old boys. Following Brian, the 10-year-olds dashed down a hallway. At the end of the hallway Brian's friend, Dan, pursed his lips and began sashaying towards the 10-year-olds. He minced towards them, swinging his hips exaggeratedly and wildly waving his arms. To the boys Brian yelled, "Look at the faggot! Watch out! He'll get you!" In response the 10-year-olds raced back down the hallway screaming in terror.

(FROM AUTHOR'S FIELDNOTES)

The relationship between adolescent masculinity and sexuality is *1*
embedded in the specter of the faggot. Faggots represent a penetrated
masculinity in which "to be penetrated is to abdicate power" (Bersani,
1987: 212). Penetrated men symbolize a masculinity devoid of power,
which, in its contradiction, threatens both psychic and social chaos.
It is precisely this specter of penetrated masculinity that functions
as a regulatory mechanism of gender for contemporary American adolescent boys.

Feminist scholars of masculinity have documented the centrality of *2*
homophobic insults to masculinity (Lehne, 1998; Kimmel, 2001) especially in school settings (Wood, 1984; Smith, 1998; Burn, 2000; Plummer,
2001; Kimmel, 2003). They argue that homophobic teasing often characterizes masculinity in adolescence and early adulthood, and that anti-gay
slurs tend to primarily be directed at other gay boys.

This article both expands on and challenges these accounts of rela- *3*
tionships between homophobia and masculinity. Homophobia is indeed
a central mechanism in the making of contemporary American adolescent masculinity. This article both critiques and builds on this finding
by (1) pointing to the limits of an argument that focuses centrally on
homophobia, (2) demonstrating that the fag is not only an identity linked
to homosexual boys[1] but an identity that can temporarily adhere to heterosexual boys as well and (3) highlighting the racialized nature of the fag as
a disciplinary mechanism.

"Homophobia" is too facile a term with which to describe the deployment *4*
of "fag" as an epithet. By calling the use of the word "fag" homophobia—and
letting the argument stop with that point—previous research obscures the
gendered nature of sexualized insults (Plummer, 2001). Invoking homophobia to describe the ways in which boys aggressively tease each other overlooks the powerful relationship between masculinity and this sort of insult.
Instead, it seems incidental in this conventional line of argument that girls
do not harass each other and are not harassed in this same manner.[2] This
framing naturalizes the relationship between masculinity and homophobia,
thus obscuring the centrality of such harassment in the formation of a gendered identity for boys in a way that it is not for girls.

"Fag" is not necessarily a static identity attached to a particular (homo- *5*
sexual) boy. Fag talk and fag imitations serve as a discourse with which
boys discipline themselves and each other through joking relationships.[3]
Any boy can temporarily become a fag in a given social space or interaction. This does not mean that those boys who identify as or are perceived
to be homosexual are not subject to intense harassment. But becoming a
fag has as much to do with failing at the masculine tasks of competence,
heterosexual prowess, and strength or in anyway revealing weakness or
femininity, as it does with a sexual identity. This fluidity of the fag identity
is what makes the specter of the fag such a powerful disciplinary mechanism. It is fluid enough that boys police most of their behaviors out of fear

of having the fag identity permanently adhere and definitive enough so that boys recognize a fag behavior and strive to avoid it.

The fag discourse is racialized. It is invoked differently by and in rela- 6 tion to white boys' bodies than it is by and in relation to African American boys' bodies. While certain behaviors put all boys at risk for becoming temporarily a fag, some behaviors can be enacted by African American boys without putting them at risk of receiving the label. The racialized meanings of the fag discourse suggest that something more than simple homophobia is involved in these sorts of interactions. An analysis of boys' deployments of the specter of the fag should also extend to the ways in which gendered power works through racialized selves. It is not that this gendered homophobia does not exist in African American communities. Indeed, making fun of "Negro faggotry seems to be a rite of passage among contemporary black male rappers and filmmakers" (Riggs, 1991: 253). However, the fact that "white women and men, gay and straight, have more or less colonized cultural debates about sexual representation" (Julien and Mercer, 1991: 167) obscures varied systems of sexualized meanings among different racialized ethnic groups (Almaguer, 1991; King, 2004).

Theoretical Framing

The sociology of masculinity entails a "critical study of men, their 7 behaviors, practices, values and perspectives" (Whitehead and Barrett, 2001: 14). Recent studies of men emphasize the multiplicity of masculinity (Connell, 1995) detailing the ways in which different configurations of gender practice are promoted, challenged or reinforced in given social situations. This research on how men do masculinities has explored gendered practices in a wide range of social institutions, such as families (Coltrane, 2001), schools (Skelton, 1996; Parker, 1996; Mac an Ghaill, 1996; Francis and Skelton, 2001), workplaces (Cooper, 2000), media (Craig, 1992), and sports (Messner, 1989; Edly and Wetherel, 1997; Curry, 2004). Many of these studies have developed specific typologies of masculinities: gay, Black, Chicano, working class, middle class, Asian, gay Black, gay Chicano, white working class, militarized, transnational business, New Man, negotiated, versatile, healthy, toxic, counter, and cool masculinities, to name a few (Messner, 2004). In this sort of model the fag could be (and often has been) framed as a type of subordinated masculinity attached to homosexual adolescent boys' bodies.

Heeding Timothy Carrigan's admonition that an "analysis of mascu- 8 linity needs to be related as well to other currents in feminism" (Carrigan et al., 1987: 64), in this article I integrate queer theory's insights about the relationships between gender, sexuality, identities, and power with the attention to men found in the literature on masculinities. Like the sociology of gender, queer theory destabilizes the assumed naturalness of the social order (Lemert, 1996). Queer theory is a "conceptualization which sees sexual power as embedded in different levels of social life" and interrogates areas of the social world not usually seen as sexuality (Stein and Plummer, 1994). In this sense queer theory calls for sexuality to be looked at not only as a discrete arena of sexual practices and identities, but also as a constitutive element of social life (Warner, 1993; Epstein, 1996).

While the masculinities literature rightly highlights very real inequali-   9
ties between gay and straight men (see for instance Connell, 1995), this emphasis on sexuality as inhered in static identities attached to male bodies, rather than major organizing principles of social life (Sedgwick, 1990), limits scholars' ability to analyze the myriad ways in which sexuality, in part, constitutes gender. This article does not seek to establish that there are homosexual boys and heterosexual boys and the homosexual ones are marginalized. Rather this article explores what happens to theories of gender if we look at a *discourse* of sexualized identities in addition to focusing on seemingly static identity categories inhabited by men. This is not to say that gender is reduced only to sexuality, indeed feminist scholars have demonstrated that gender is embedded in and constitutive of a multitude of social structures—the economy, places of work, families and schools. In the tradition of post-structural feminist theorists of race and gender who look at "border cases" that explode taken-for-granted binaries of race and gender (Smith, 1994), queer theory is another tool which enables an integrated analysis of sexuality, gender and race.

As scholars of gender have demonstrated, gender is accomplished   10
through day-to-day interactions (Fine, 1987; Hochschild, 1989; West and Zimmerman, 1991; Thorne, 1993). In this sense gender is the "activity of managing situated conduct in light of normative conceptions of attitudes and activities appropriate for one's sex category" (West and Zimmerman, 1991:127). Similarly, queer theorist Judith Butler argues that gender is accomplished interactionally through "a set of repeated acts within a highly rigid regulatory frame that congeal over time to produce the appearance of substance, of a natural sort of being" (Butler, 1999: 43). Specifically she argues that gendered beings are created through processes of citation and repudiation of a "constitutive outside" (Butler, 1993: 3) in which is contained all that is cast out of a socially recognizable gender category. The "constitutive outside" is inhabited by abject identities, unrecognizably and unacceptably gendered selves. The interactional accomplishment of gender in a Butlerian model consists, in part, of the continual iteration and repudiation of this abject identity. Gender, in this sense, is "constituted through the force of exclusion and abjection, on which produces a constitutive outside to the subject, an abjected outside, which is, after all, 'inside' the subject as its own founding repudiation" (Butler, 1993: 3). This repudiation creates and reaffirms a "threatening specter" (Butler, 1993: 3) of failed, unrecognizable gender, the existence of which must be continually repudiated through interactional processes.

I argue that the "fag" position is an "abject" position and, as such, is   *11*
a "threatening specter" constituting contemporary American adolescent
masculinity. The fag discourse is the interactional process through which
boys name and repudiate this abjected identity. Rather than analyzing the
fag as an identity for homosexual boys, I examine uses of the discourse that
imply that any boy can become a fag, regardless of his actual desire or self-
perceived sexual orientation. The threat of the abject position infuses the
faggot with regulatory power. This article provides empirical data to illustrate Butler's approach to gender and indicates that it might be a useful
addition to the sociological literature on masculinities through highlighting one of the ways in which a masculine gender identity is accomplished
through interaction.

Method

Research Site

I conducted fieldwork at a suburban high school in north-central California   *12*
which I call River High.[4] River High is a working class, suburban fifty-year-
old high school located in a town called Riverton. With the exception of the
median household income and racial diversity (both of which are elevated
due to Riverton's location in California), the town mirrors national averages in the percentages of white-collar workers, rates of college attendance,
and marriages, and age composition (according to the 2000 census). It is a
politically moderate to conservative, religious community. Most of the students' parents commute to surrounding cities for work.

On average Riverton is a middle-class community. However, students   *13*
at River are likely to refer to the town as two communities: "Old Riverton" and "New Riverton." A busy highway and railroad tracks bisect the
town into these two sections. River High is literally on the "wrong side
of the tracks," in Old Riverton. Exiting the freeway, heading north to Old
Riverton, one sees a mix of 1950s-era ranch-style homes, some with neatly
trimmed lawns and tidy gardens, others with yards strewn with various
car parts, lawn chairs and appliances. Old Riverton is visually bounded by
smoke-puffing factories. On the other side of the freeway New Riverton
is characterized by wide sidewalk-lined streets and new walled-in home
developments. Instead of smokestacks, a forested mountain, home to
a state park, rises majestically in the background. The teens from these
homes attend Hillside High, River's rival.

River High is attended by 2,000 students. River High's racial/ethnic   *14*
breakdown roughly represents California at large: 50 percent white, 9 percent African American, 28 percent Latino and 6 percent Asian (as compared to California's 46, 6, 32, and 11 percent respectively, according to
census data and school records). The students at River High are primarily
working class.

Research

I gathered data using the qualitative method of ethnographic research.   *15*
I spent a year and a half conducting observations, formally interviewing
forty-nine students at River High (thirty-six boys and thirteen girls), one
male student from Hillside High, and conducting countless informal interviews with students, faculty and administrators. I concentrated on one
school because I explore the richness rather than the breadth of data (for
other examples of this method see Willis, 1981; MacLeod, 1987; Eder et al.,
1995; Ferguson, 2000).

I recruited students for interviews by conducting presentations in a   *16*
range of classes and hanging around at lunch, before school, after school
and at various events talking to different groups of students about my
research, which I presented as "writing a book about guys." The interviews
usually took place at school, unless the student had a car, in which case he
or she met me at one of the local fast food restaurants where I treated them
to a meal. Interviews lasted anywhere from half an hour to two hours.

The initial interviews I conducted helped me to map a gendered and   *17*
sexualized geography of the school, from which I chose my observation
sites. I observed a "neutral" site—a senior government classroom, where
sexualized meanings were subdued. I observed three sites that students
marked as "fag" sites—two drama classes and the Gay/Straight Alli-
ance. I also observed two normatively "masculine" sites—auto-shop and
weightlifting.[5] I took daily fieldnotes focusing on how students, faculty
and administrators negotiated, regulated and resisted particular meanings
of gender and sexuality. I attended major school rituals such as Winter
Ball, school rallies, plays, dances, and lunches. I would also occasionally
"ride along" with Mr. Johnson (Mr. J.), the school's security guard, on his
battery-powered golf cart to watch which, how and when students were
disciplined. Observational data provided me with more insight to the
interactional processes of masculinity than simple interviews yielded. If
I had relied only on interview data I would have missed the interactional
processes of masculinity which are central to the fag discourse.

Given the importance of appearance in high school, I gave some   *18*
thought as to how I would present myself, deciding to both blend in and
set myself apart from the students. In order to blend in I wore my standard
graduate student gear—comfortable, baggy cargo pants, a black t-shirt or
sweater, and tennis shoes. To set myself apart I carried a messenger bag
instead of a back-pack, didn't wear makeup, and spoke slightly differently
than the students by using some slang, but refraining from uttering the
ubiquitous "hecka" and "hella."

The boys were fascinated by the fact that a 30-something white "girl"   *19*
(their words) was interested in studying them. While at first many would
make sexualized comments asking me about my dating life or saying that they
were going to "hit on" me, it seemed eventually they began to forget about
me as a potential sexual/romantic partner. Part of this, I think, was related

to my knowledge about "guy" things. For instance, I lift weights on a regular basis and as a result the weightlifting coach introduced me as a "weight-lifter from U.C. Berkeley" telling the students they should ask me for weight-lifting advice. Additionally, my taste in movies and television shows often coincided with theirs. I am an avid fan of the movies "Jackass" and "Fight Club," both of which contain high levels of violence and "bathroom" humor. Finally, I garnered a lot of points among boys because I live off a dangerous street in a nearby city famous for drug deals, gang fights, and frequent gun shots.

What Is a Fag?

"Since you were little boys you've been told, 'hey, don't be a little faggot'," 20 explained Darnell, an African American football player, as we sat on a bench next to the athletic field. Indeed, both the boys and girls I interviewed told me that "fag" was the worst epithet one guy could direct at another. Jeff, a slight white sophomore, explained to me that boys call each other fag because "gay people aren't really liked over here and stuff." Jeremy, a Latino junior, told me that this insult literally reduced a boy to nothing, "To call someone gay or fag is like the lowest thing you can call someone. Because that's like saying that you're nothing."

Most guys explained their or others' dislike of fags by claiming that 21 homophobia is just part of what it means to be a guy. For instance Keith, a white soccer-playing senior, explained, "I think guys are just homophobic." However, it is not just homophobia, it is a *gendered* homophobia. Several students told me that these homophobic insults only applied to boys and not girls. For example, while Jake, a handsome white senior, told me that he didn't like gay people, he quickly added, "Lesbians, okay that's *good*." Similarly Cathy, a popular white cheerleader, told me "Being a lesbian is accepted because guys think 'oh that's cool'." Darnell, after telling me that boys were told not to be faggots, said of lesbians, "They're [guys are] fine with girls. I think it's the guy part that they're like ewwww!" In this sense it is not strictly homophobia, but a gendered homophobia that constitutes adolescent masculinity in the culture of this school. However, it is clear, according to these comments, that lesbians are "good" because of their place in heterosexual male fantasy not necessarily because of some enlightened approach to same-sex relationships. It does however, indicate that using only the term "homophobia" to describe boys' repeated use of the word "fag" might be a bit simplistic and misleading.

Additionally, girls at River High rarely deployed the word "fag" and 22 were never called "fags." I recorded girls uttering "fag" only three times during my research. In one instance, Angela, a Latina cheerleader, teased Jeremy, a well-liked white senior involved in student government, for not ditching school with her, "You wouldn't 'cause you're a faggot." However, girls did not use this word as part of their regular lexicon. The sort of gendered homophobia that constitutes adolescent masculinity does not constitute adolescent femininity. Girls were not called dykes or lesbians in any sort of regular or systematic way. Students did tell me that "slut" was the worst thing a girl could be called. However, my fieldnotes indicate that the word "slut" (or its synonym "ho") appears one time for every eight times the word "fag" appears. Even when it does occur, "slut" is rarely deployed as a direct insult against another girl.

Highlighting the difference between the deployment of "gay" and "fag" 23 as insults brings the gendered nature of this homophobia into focus. For boys and girls at River High "gay" is a fairly common synonym for "stupid." While this word shares the sexual origins of "fag," it does not *consistently* have the skew of gender-loaded meaning. Girls and boys often used "gay" as an adjective referring to inanimate objects and male or female people, whereas they used "fag" as a noun that denotes only un-masculine males. Students used "gay" to describe anything from someone's clothes to a new school rule that the students did not like, as in the following encounter:

> In auto-shop Arnie pulled out a large older version black laptop computer and placed it on his desk. Behind him Nick said "That's a gay laptop! It's five inches thick!"

A laptop can be gay, a movie can be gay or a group of people can be gay. Boys used "gay" and "fag" interchangeably when they refer to other boys, but "fag" does not have the non-gendered attributes that "gay" sometimes invokes.

While its meanings are not the same as "gay," "fag" does have multiple 24 meanings which do not necessarily replace its connotations as a homophobic slur, but rather exist alongside. Some boys took pains to say that "fag" is not about sexuality. Darnell told me "It doesn't even have anything to do with being gay." J. L., a white sophomore at Hillside High (River High's cross-town rival), asserted "Fag, seriously, it has nothing to do with sexual preference at all. You could just be calling somebody an idiot you know?" I asked Ben, a quiet, white sophomore who wore heavy metal t-shirts to auto-shop each day, "What kind of things do guys get called a fag for?" Ben answered "Anything . . . literally, anything. Like you were trying to turn a wrench the wrong way, 'dude, you're a fag.' Even if a piece of meat drops out of your sandwich, 'you fag!'" Each time Ben said "you fag" his voice deepened as if he were imitating a more masculine boy. While Ben might rightly *feel* like a guy could be called a fag for "anything . . . literally, anything," there are actually specific behaviors which, when enacted by most boys, can render him more vulnerable to a fag epithet. In this instance Ben's comment highlights the use of "fag" as a generic insult for incompetence, which in the world of River High, is central to a masculine identity. A boy could get called a fag for exhibiting any sort of behavior defined as non-masculine (although not necessarily behaviors aligned with femininity) in the world of River High: being stupid, incompetent, dancing, caring too much about clothing, being too emotional, or expressing interest (sexual or platonic) in other guys. However, given the extent of its deployment and the laundry list of behaviors that could get a boy in trouble it is no wonder that Ben felt like a boy could be called "fag" for "anything."

One-third (13) of the boys I interviewed told me that, while they may 25 liberally insult each other with the term, they would not actually direct it at a homosexual peer. Jabes, a Filipino senior, told me.

> I actually say it [fag] quite a lot, except for when I'm in the company of an actual homosexual person. Then I try not to say it at all. But when I'm just hanging out with my friends I'll be like, "shut up, I don't want to hear you any more, you stupid fag."

Similarly J. L. compared homosexuality to a disability, saying there is "no way" he'd call an actually gay guy a fag because

> There's people who are the retarded people who nobody wants to associate with. I'll be so nice to those guys and I hate it when people make fun of them. It's like, "bro do you realize that they can't help that?" And then there's gay people. They were born that way.

According to this group of boys, gay is a legitimate, if marginalized, 26 social identity. If a man is gay, there maybe a chance he could be considered masculine by other men (Connell, 1995). David, a handsome white senior dressed smartly in khaki pants and a white button-down shirt, said, "Being gay is just a lifestyle. It's someone you choose to sleep with. You can still throw around a football and be gay." In other words there is a possibility, however slight, that a boy can be gay and masculine. To be a fag is, by definition, the opposite of masculine, whether or not the word is deployed with sexualized or non-sexualized meanings. In explaining this to me, Jamaal, an African American junior, cited the explanation of popular rap artist Eminem.

> Although I don't like Eminem, he had a good definition of it. It's like taking away your title. In an interview they were like, "you're always capping on gays, but then you sing with Elton John." He was like "I don't mean gay as in gay."

This is what Riki Wilchins calls the "Eminem Exception. Eminem 27 explains that he doesn't call people 'faggot' because of their sexual orientation but because they're weak and unmanly" (Wilchins, 2003). This is precisely the way in which this group of boys at River High uses the term "faggot." While it is not necessarily acceptable to be gay, at least a man who is gay can do other things that render him acceptably masculine. A fag, by the very definition of the word, indicated by students' usages at River High, cannot be masculine. This distinction between "fag" as an unmasculine and problematic identity and "gay" as a possibly masculine, although marginalized, sexual identity is not limited to a teenage lexicon, but is reflected in both psychological discourses (Sedgwick, 1995) and gay and lesbian activism.

Becoming a Fag

"The ubiquity of the word faggot speaks to the reach of its discrediting *28*
capacity" (Corbett, 2001: 4). It is almost as if boys cannot help but shout it
out on a regular basis—in the hallway, in class, across campus as a greeting, or as a joke. In my fieldwork I was amazed by the way in which the
word seemed to pop uncontrollably out of boys' mouths in all kinds of situations. To quote just one of many instances from my fieldnotes:

> Two boys walked out of the P.E. locker room and one yelled "fucking faggot!"
> at no one in particular.

This spontaneous yelling out of a variation of fag seemingly apropos of
nothing happened repeatedly among boys throughout the school.

The fag discourse is central to boys' joking relationships. Joking *29*
cements relationships between boys (Kehily and Nayak, 1997; Lyman,
1998) and helps to manage anxiety and discomfort (Freud, 1905). Boys
invoked the specter of the fag in two ways: through humorous imitation
and through lobbing the epithet at one another. Boys at River High imi-
tated the fag by acting out an exaggerated "femininity," and/or by pretending to sexually desire other boys. As indicated by the introductory vignette
in which a predatory "fag" threatens the little boys, boys at River High link
these performative scenarios with a fag identity. They lobbed the fag epithet at each other in a verbal game of hot potato, each careful to deflect the
insult quickly by hurling it toward someone else. These games and imitations make up a fag discourse which highlights the fag not as a static but
rather as a fluid identity which boys constantly struggle to avoid.

In imitative performances the fag discourse functions as a constant *30*
reiteration of the fag's existence, affirming that the fag is out there; at any
moment a boy can become a fag. At the same time these performances
demonstrate that the boy who is invoking the fag is *not* a fag. By invoking
it so often, boys remind themselves and each other that at any point they
can become fags if they are not sufficiently masculine.

> Mr. McNally, disturbed by the noise outside of the classroom, turned to the
> open door saying "We'll shut this unless anyone really wants to watch sweaty
> boys playing basketball." Emir, a tall skinny boy, lisped "I wanna watch the
> boys play!" The rest of the class cracked up at his imitation.

Through imitating a fag, boys assure others that they are not a fag by
immediately becoming masculine again after the performance. They mock
their own performed femininity and/or same-sex desire, assuring themselves and others that such an identity is one deserving of derisive laughter. The fag identity in this instance is fluid, detached from Emir's body. He
can move in and out of this "abject domain" while simultaneously affirming his position as a subject.

Boys also consistently tried to put another in the fag position by lob- *31*
bing the fag epithet at one another.

> Going through the junk-filled car in the auto-shop parking lot, Jay poked his head out and asked "Where are Craig and Brian?" Neil responded with "I think they're over there," pointing, then thrusting his hips and pulling his arms back and forth to indicate that Craig and Brian might be having sex. The boys in auto-shop laughed.

This sort of joke temporarily labels both Craig and Brian as faggots. Because the fag discourse is so familiar, the other boys immediately understand that Neil is indicating that Craig and Brian are having sex. However these are not necessarily identities that stick. Nobody actually thinks Craig and Brian are homosexuals. Rather the fag identity is a fluid one, certainly an identity that no boy wants, but one that a boy can escape, usually by engaging in some sort of discursive contest to turn another boy into a fag. However, fag becomes a hot potato that no boy wants to be left holding. In the following example, which occurred soon after the "sex" joke, Brian lobs the fag epithet at someone else, deflecting it from himself:

> Brian initiated a round of a favorite game in auto-shop, the "cock game." Brian quietly, looking at Josh, said, "Josh loves the cock" then slightly louder, "Josh loves the cock." He continued saying this until he was yelling "JOSH LOVES THE COCK!" The rest of the boys laughed hysterically as Josh slinked away saying "I have a bigger dick than all you mother fuckers!"

These two instances show how the fag can be mapped, momentarily, on to one boy's body and how he, in turn, can attach it to another boy, thus deflecting it from himself. In the first instance Neil makes fun of Craig and Brian for simply hanging out together. In the second instance Brian goes from being a fag to making Josh into a fag, through the "cock game." The "fag" is transferable. Boys move in and out of it by discursively creating another as a fag through joking interactions. They, somewhat ironically, can move in and out of the fag position by transforming themselves, temporarily, into a fag, but this has the effect of reaffirming their masculinity when they return to a heterosexual position after imitating the fag.

These examples demonstrate boys invoking the trope of the fag in a *32* discursive struggle in which the boys indicate that they know what a fag is—and that they are not fags. This joking cements bonds between boys as they assure themselves and each other of their masculinity through repeated repudiations of a non-masculine position of the abject.

Racing the Fag

The fag trope is not deployed consistently or identically across social *33* groups at River High. Differences between white boys' and African American boys' meaning making around clothes and dancing reveal ways in which the fag as the abject position is racialized.

Clean, oversized, carefully put together clothing is central to a hip-hop *34* identity for African American boys who identify with hip-hop culture.[6]

Richard Majors calls this presentation of self a "cool pose" consisting of "unique, expressive and conspicuous styles of demeanor, speech, gesture, clothing, hairstyle, walk, stance and handshake," developed by African American men as a symbolic response to institutionalized racism (Majors, 2001: 211). Pants are usually several sizes too big, hanging low on a boy's waist, usually revealing a pair of boxers beneath. Shirts and sweaters are similarly oversized, often hanging down to a boy's knees. Tags are frequently left on baseball hats worn slightly askew and sit perched high on the head. Meticulously clean, unlaced athletic shoes with rolled up socks under the tongue complete a typical hip-hop outfit.

This amount of attention and care given to clothing for white boys not   35
identified with hip-hop culture (that is, most of the white boys at River High) would certainly cast them into an abject, fag position. White boys are not supposed to appear to care about their clothes or appearance, because only fags care about how they look. Ben illustrates this:

> Ben walked in to the auto-shop classroom from the parking lot where he had been working on a particularly oily engine. Grease stains covered his jeans. He looked down at them, made a face and walked toward me with limp wrists, laughing and lisping in a high pitch, sing-song voice "I got my good pants all dirty!"

Ben draws on indicators of a fag identity, such as limp wrists, as do the boys in the introductory vignette to illustrate that a masculine person certainly would not care about having dirty clothes. In this sense, masculinity, for white boys, becomes the carefully crafted appearance of not caring about appearance, especially in terms of cleanliness.

However, African American boys involved in hip-hop culture talk fre-   36
quently about whether or not their clothes, specifically their shoes, are dirty:

> In drama class both Darnell and Marc compared their white Adidas basketball shoes. Darnell mocked Marc because black scuff marks covered his shoes, asking incredulously "Yours are a week old and they're dirty—I've had mine for a month and they're not dirty!" Both laughed.

Monte, River High's star football player, echoed this concern about dirty shoes when looking at the fancy red shoes he had lent to his cousin the week before, told me he was frustrated because after his cousin used them, the "shoes are hella scuffed up." Clothing, for these boys, does not indicate a fag position, but rather defines membership in a certain cultural and racial group (Perry, 2002).

Dancing is another arena that carries distinctly fag associated mean-   37
ings for white boys and masculine meanings for African American boys who participate in hip-hop culture. White boys often associate dancing with "fag." J. L. told me that guys think "'NSync's gay" because they can dance. 'NSync is an all white male singing group known for their dance moves. At dances white boys frequently held their female dates tightly, locking their

hips together. The boys never danced with one another, unless engaged in a round of "hot potato." White boys often jokingly danced together in order to embarrass each other by making someone else into a fag:

> Lindy danced behind her date, Chris. Chris's friend, Matt, walked up and nudged Lindy aside, imitating her dance moves behind Chris. As Matt rubbed his hands up and down Chris's back, Chris turned around and jumped back startled to see Matt there instead of Lindy. Matt cracked up as Chris turned red.

However dancing does not carry this sort of sexualized gender mean- 38 ing for all boys at River High. For African American boys dancing demonstrates membership in a cultural community (Best, 2000). African American boys frequently danced together in single sex groups, teaching each other the latest dance moves, showing off a particularly difficult move or making each other laugh with humorous dance moves. Students recognized K. J. as the most talented dancer at the school. K. J. is a sophomore of African American and Filipino descent who participated in the hip-hop culture of River High. He continually wore the latest hip-hop fashions. K. J. was extremely popular. Girls hollered his name as they walked down the hall and thrust urgently written love notes folded in complicated designs into his hands as he sauntered to class. For the past two years K. J. won first place in the talent show for dancing. When he danced at assemblies the room reverberated with screamed chants of "Go K.J.! Go K.J.! Go K.J.!" Because dancing for African American boys places them within a tradition of masculinity, they are not at risk of becoming a fag for this particular gendered practice. Nobody called K. J. a fag. In fact in several of my interviews boys of multiple racial/ethnic backgrounds spoke admiringly of K. J.'s dancing abilities.

Implications

These findings confirm previous studies of masculinity and sexuality that 39 position homophobia as central to contemporary definitions of adolescent masculinity. These data extend previous research by unpacking multilayered meanings that boys deploy through their uses of homophobic language and joking rituals. By attending to these meanings I reframe the discussion as one of a fag discourse, rather than simply labeling this sort of behavior as homophobia. The fag is an "abject" position, a position outside of masculinity that actually constitutes masculinity. Thus, masculinity, in part becomes the daily interactional work of repudiating the "threatening specter" of the fag.

The fag extends beyond a static sexual identity attached to a gay boy. 40 Few boys are permanently identified as fags; most move in and out of fag positions. Looking at "fag" as a discourse rather than a static identity reveals that the term can be invested with different meanings in different social spaces. "Fag" may be used as a weapon with which to temporarily assert one's masculinity by denying it to others. Thus "fag" becomes a symbol around which contests of masculinity take place.

The fag epithet, when hurled at other boys, may or may not have 41 explicit sexual meanings, but it always has gendered meanings. When a boy calls another boy a fag, it means he is not a man, not necessarily that he is a homosexual. The boys in this study know that they are not supposed to call homosexual boys "fags" because that is mean. This then, has been the limited *success* of the mainstream gay rights movement. The message absorbed by some of these teenage boys is that "gay men can be masculine, just like you." Instead of challenging gender inequality, this particular discourse of gay rights has reinscribed it. Thus we need to begin to think about how gay men may be in a unique position to challenge gendered as well as sexual norms.

This study indicates that researchers who look at the intersection of 42 sexuality and masculinity need to attend to the ways in which racialized identities may affect how "fag" is deployed and what it means in various social situations. While researchers have addressed the ways in which masculine identities are racialized (Connell, 1995; Ross, 1998; Bucholtz, 1999; Davis, 1999; Price, 1999; Ferguson, 2000; Majors, 2001) they have not paid equal attention to the ways in which "fag" might be a racialized epithet. It is important to look at when, where and with what meaning "the fag" is deployed in order to get at how masculinity is defined, contested, and invested in among adolescent boys.

Research shows that sexualized teasing often leads to deadly results, 43 as evidenced by the spate of school shootings in the 1990s (Kimmel, 2003). Clearly the fag discourse affects not just homosexual teens, but all boys, gay and straight. Further research could investigate these processes in a variety of contexts: varied geographic locations, sexualized groups, classed groups, religious groups, and age groups.

Acknowledgments

The author would like to thank Natalie Boero, Leslie Bell, Meg Jay, and 44 Barrie Thorne for their comments on this article. This work was supported by the Center for the Study of Sexual Culture at University of California, Berkeley.

NOTES

1. While the term "homosexual" is laden with medicalized and normalizing meanings, I use it instead of "gay" because "gay" in the world of River High has multiple meanings apart from sexual practices or identities.
2. Girls do insult one another based on sexualized meanings. But in my own research I found that girls and boys did not harass girls in this manner with the

same frequency that boys harassed each other through engaging in joking about the fag.

3. I use discourse in the Foucauldian sense, to describe truth producing practices, not just text or speech (Foucault, 1978).
4. The names of places and respondents have been changed.
5. Auto-shop was a class in which students learned how to build and repair cars. Many of the students in this course were looking into careers as mechanics.
6. While there are several white and Latino boys at River High who identify with hip-hop culture, hip-hop is identified by the majority of students as an African American cultural style.

REFERENCES

Almaguer, Tomas (1991) "Chicano Men: A Cartography of Homosexual Identity and Behavior," *Differences*. 3:75–100.

Bersani, Leo (1987) "Is the Rectum a Grave?" *October* 43:197–222.

Best, Amy (2000) *Prom Night: Youth, Schools and Popular Culture*. New York: Routledge.

Bucholtz, Mary (1999) "You Da Man: Narrating the Racial Other in the Production of White Masculinity," *Journal of Sociolinguistics*. 3/4: 443–60.

Burn, Shawn M. (2000) "'Heterosexuals' Use of 'Fag' and 'Queer' to Deride One Another: A Contributor to Heterosexism and Stigma," *Journal of Homosexuality*. 40:1–11.

Butler, Judith (1993) *Bodies that Matter*. Routledge: New York.

——. (1999) *Gender Trouble*. New York: Routledge.

Carrigan, Tim, Connell, Bob and Lee, John (1987) "Toward a New Sociology of Masculinity," in Harry Brod (ed.) *The Making of Masculinities: The New Men's Studies*, pp. 188–202. Boston, MA: Allen & Unwin.

Coltrane, Scott (2001) "Selling the Indispensable Father," paper presented at *Pushing the Boundaries Conference: New Conceptualizations of Childhood and Motherhood*, Philadelphia.

Connell, R. W. (1995) *Masculinities*. Berkeley: University of California Press.

Cooper, Marianne (2000) "Being the 'Go-To Guy': Fatherhood, Masculinity and the Organization of Work in Silicon Valley," *Qualitative Sociology*. 23: 379–405.

Corbett, Ken (2001) "Faggot = Loser," *Studies in Gender and Sexuality*. 2:3–28.

Craig, Steve (1992) *Men, Masculinity and the Media*. Newbury Park: Sage.

Curry, Timothy J. (2004) "Fraternal Bonding in the Locker Room: A Profeminist Analysis of Talk About Competition and Women" in Michael Messner and Michael Kimmel (eds.) *Men's Lives*. Boston, MA: Pearson.

Davis, James E. (1999) "Forbidden Fruit, Black Males' Constructions of Transgressive Sexualities in Middle School," in William J. Letts IV and James T. Sears (eds.) *Queering Elementary Education: Advancing the Dialogue About Sexualities and Schooling*, pp. 49 ff. Lanham, MD: Rowan & Litdefield.

Eder, Donna, Evans, Catherine and Parker, Stephen (1995) *School Talk: Gender and Adolescent Culture*. New Brunswick, NJ: Rutgers University Press.

Edly, Nigel and Wetherell, Margaret (1997) "Jockeying for Position: The Construction of Masculine Identities," *Discourse and Society* 8: 203–17.

Epstein, Steven (1996) "A Queer Encounter," in Steven Seidman (ed.) *Queer Theory/ Sociology*, pp. 188–202. Cambridge, MA: Blackwell.

Ferguson, Ann (2000) *Bad Boys: Public Schools in the Making of Black Masculinity*. Ann Arbor: University of Michigan Press.

Fine, Gary (1987) *With the Boys: Little League Baseball and Preadolescent Culture*. Chicago, IL: University of Chicago Press.

Foucault, Michel (1978). *The History of Sexuality, Volume I*. New York: Vintage Books.

Francis, Becky and Skelton, Christine (2001) "Men Teachers and the Construction of Heterosexual Masculinity in the Classroom," *Sex Education* 1: 9–21.

Freud, Sigmund (1905). *The Basic Writings of Sigmund Freud* (translated and edited by A. A. Brill). New York: The Modern Library.

Hochschild, Arlie (1989). *The Second Shift*. New York: Avon.

Julien, Isaac and Mercer, Kobena (1991) "True Confessions: A Discourse on Images of Black Male Sexuality," in Essex Hemphill (ed.) *Brother to Brother: New Writings by Black Gay Men*, pp. 167–73. Boston, MA: Alyson Publications.

Kehily, Mary Jane and Nayak, Anoop (1997) "Lads and Laughter: Humour and the Production of Heterosexual Masculinities," *Gender and Education*. 9: 69–87.

Kimmel, Michael (2001) "Masculinity as Homophobia: Fear, Shame, and Silence in the Construction of Gender Identity," in Stephen Whitehead and Frank Barrett (eds.) *The Masculinities Reader*, pp. 266–87. Cambridge: Polity.

——. (2003) "Adolescent Masculinity, Homophobia, and Violence: Random School Shootings, 1982–2001," *American Behavioral Scientist* 46: 1439–58.

King, D. L. (2004) *Double Lives on the Down Low*. New York: Broadway Books.

Lehne, Gregory (1998) "Homophobia Among Men: Supporting and Defining the Male Role," in Michael Kimmel and Michael Messner (eds.) *Men's Lives*, pp. 237–149. Boston, MA: Allyn and Bacon.

Lemert, Charles (1996) "Series Editor's Preface," in Steven Seidman (ed.) *Queer Theory/Sociology*. Cambridge, MA: Blackwell.

Lyman, Peter (1998) "The Fraternal Bond as a Joking Relationship: A Case Study of the Role of Sexist Jokes in Male Group Bonding," in Michael Kimmel and Michael Messner (eds.) *Men's Lives*, pp. 171–93. Boston, MA: Allyn and Bacon.

Mac an Ghaill, Mairtin (1996) "What about the Boys—School, Class and Crisis Masculinity," *Sociological Review* 44:381–97.

MacLeod, Jay (1987) *Ain't No Makin It: Aspirations and Attainment in a Low Income Neighborhood*. Boulder, CO: Westview Press.

Majors, Richard (2001) "Cool Pose: Black Masculinity and Sports," in Stephen Whitehead and Frank Barrett (eds.). *The Masculinities Reader*, pp. 208–17. Cambridge: Polity.

Messner, Michael (1989) "Sports and the Politics of Inequality," in Michael Kimmel and Michael Messner (eds.) *Men's Lives*. Boston, MA: Allyn and Bacon.

——. (2004) "On Patriarchs and Losers: Rethinking Men's Interests," paper presented at Berkeley *Journal of Sociology* Conference, Berkeley.

Parker, Andrew (1996) "The, Construction of Masculinity Within Boys' Physical Education," *Gender and Education*. 8:141–57.

Perry, Pamela (2002) *Shades of White: White Kids and Racial Identities in High School*. Durham, NC: Duke University Press.

Plummer, David C. (2001) "The Quest for Modern Manhood: Masculine Stereotypes, Peer Culture and the Social Significance of Homophobia," *Journal of Adolescence*. 24:15–23.

Price, Jeremy (1999) "Schooling and Racialized Masculinities: The Diploma, Teachers and Peers in the Lives of Young, African American Men," *Youth and Society*. 31: 224–63.

Riggs, Marlon (1991) "Black Macho Revisited: Reflections of a SNAP! Queen," in Essex Hemphill (ed.) Brother to Brother: *New Writings by Black Gay Men*, pp. 153–260. Boston, MA: Alyson Publications.

Ross, Marlon B. (1998) "In Search of Black Men's Masculinities," *Feminist Studies* 24: 599–626.

Sedgwick, Eve K. (1990) *Epistemology of the Closet*. Berkeley: University of California Press.

——. (1995) "Gosh, Boy George, You Must Be Awfully Secure in Your Masculinity!" in Maurice Berger, Brian Wallis and Simon Watson (eds.) *Constructing Masculinity*, pp. 11–20. New York: Routledge.

Skelton, Christine (1996) "Learning to Be Tough: The Fostering of Maleness in One Primary School," *Gender and Education*. 8:185–97.

Smith, George W. (1998) "The Ideology of 'Fag': The School Experience of Gay Students," *The Sociological Quarterly* 39:309–35.

Smith, Valerie (1994) "Split Affinities: The Case of Interracial Rape," in Anne Herrmann and Abigail Stewart (eds.) *Theorizing Feminism*, pp. 155–70. Boulder, CO: Westview Press.

Stein, Arlene and Plummer, Ken (1994) "'I Can't Even Think Straight': 'Queer' Theory and the Missing Sexual Revolution in Sociology," *Sociological Theory* 12:178 ff.

Thorne, Barrie (1993) *Gender Play: Boys and Girls in School*. New Brunswick, NJ: Rutgers University Press.

Warner, Michael (1993) "Introduction," in Michael Warner (ed.) *Fear of a Queer Planet: Queer Politics and Social Theory*, pp. vii–xxxi. Minneapolis: University of Minnesota Press.

West, Candace and Zimmerman, Don (1991) "Doing Gender," in Judith Lorber (ed.) *The Social Construction of Gender*, pp. 102–21. Newbury Park: Sage.

Whitehead, Stephen and Barrett, Frank (2001) "The Sociology of Masculinity," in Stephen Whitehead and Frank Barrett (eds.) *The Masculinities Reader*, pp. 472–6. Cambridge: Polity.

Wilchins, Riki (2003) "Do You Believe in Fairies?" *The Advocate*, 4 February.

Willis, Paul (1981) *Learning to Labor: How Working Class Kids Get Working Class Jobs*. New York: Columbia University Press.

Wood, Julian (1984) "Groping Toward Sexism: Boy's Sex Talk," in Angela McRobbie and Mica Nava (eds.) *Gender and Generation*. London: Macmillan Publishers.

■ ■ ■

Reading as a Writer: Analyzing Rhetorical Choices

1. After setting up her argument and analyzing a good portion of her data, Pascoe adds another layer to her analysis in the section titled "Racing the Fag." How does the additional analysis of race contribute to Pascoe's central argument? Discuss or write about a few of the examples in this section. What others might you add?

2. Reread the Method section of the essay, and consider how Pascoe uses description. How do the details contribute to her larger argument? How does she explain her strategy in this "qualitative method of ethnographic research" (para. 15)? In pairs or as a class, discuss the strengths and possible weaknesses of her methods, given your own experience of high school dynamics.

Writing as a Reader: Entering the Conversation of Ideas

1. Both Pascoe and Allan G. Johnson (pp. 454–57) examine the thinking patterns people use to categorize and stereotype others. According to these authors, what is at stake, and for whom, in this behavior? Write an essay in which you examine these patterns and each author's analysis of possible solutions. If you like, draw on your own insights of learning (and perhaps resisting) the categorization of others.

2. Pascoe's analysis of adolescent boys is interesting to consider next to Ken Gillam and Shannon R. Wooden's analysis of alternative masculine heroes in Disney/Pixar films (pp. 542–54 in Media Studies). Compose an essay that draws out key insights about the ways we socialize boys into gendered behaviors. What role can the media play in providing a broader range of acceptable male behaviors based on these readings (and, perhaps, based on your experiences and observations)?

BARBARA EHRENREICH

How I Discovered the Truth about Poverty

Barbara Ehrenreich is one of the best-known journalists publishing social commentary in the United States today. She earned a PhD in cell biology but has a voracious appetite for learning and writing about topics far beyond science. She has published and lectured on the state of health care, the history of women as healers, the anxieties of the middle class, and the history of dancing, to name just a few of the topics she's addressed. In addition to the many books she has written, cowritten, and edited, she writes prolifically for newspapers and magazines, including *The New York Times Magazine*, *The Washington Post Magazine*, *The Atlantic*, *The Nation*, and *The New Republic*.

This piece was published in *The Nation* magazine and then republished on AlterNet, an online news source for original and republished journalism. This short, pithy essay is written in a journalistic style, with brief paragraphs and without footnotes. Ehrenreich does, however, draw on sources; this is not simply an opinion piece, as her extended critique of Michael Harrington's book *The Other America* (1962) demonstrates. Why does Ehrenreich consider the phrase from Harrington's book (which he draws from anthropologist Oscar Lewis), "the culture of poverty," to be so problematic? As you read, pay attention to the way Ehrenreich traces the history and uses of that phrase through time. You might even try to paraphrase her ideas about each different political use of the phrase.

Because Ehrenreich moves so quickly through different political figures and examples, it may be a challenge to keep track of her larger point. Try underlining sentences in which she helps us see the big picture she's examining, such as in paragraph 10, where she notes, "Even today, more than a decade later [than Clinton's bill], and four years into a severe economic downturn, as people continue to slide into poverty from the middle classes, the theory maintains its grip. If you're needy, you must be in need of correction, the assumption goes." Where else do you see her moving from examples to her larger point about the way the poor are characterized as "other"?

In her final paragraph, Ehrenreich returns to her opening point about Harrington having "discovered" poverty by noting that it's time for a "new discovery" of poverty that reveals a new truth: "if we look closely enough, we'll have to conclude that poverty is not, after all, a cultural aberration or a character flaw. Poverty is a shortage of money" (para. 14). Given your own experiences and knowledge about attitudes toward the poor and rich, how would you chime in to this conversation?

■ ■ ■

Ｉt's been exactly fifty years since Americans, or at least the non-poor   *1*
among them, "discovered" poverty, thanks to Michael Harrington's engaging book *The Other America*. If this discovery now seems a little overstated, like Columbus's "discovery" of America, it was because the poor,

according to Harrington, were so "hidden" and "invisible" that it took a crusading left-wing journalist to ferret them out.

Harrington's book jolted a nation that then prided itself on its class- 2 lessness and even fretted about the spirit-sapping effects of "too much affluence." He estimated that one-quarter of the population lived in poverty—inner-city blacks, Appalachian whites, farm workers, and elderly Americans among them. We could no longer boast, as President Nixon had done in his "kitchen debate" with Soviet Premier Nikita Khrushchev in Moscow just three years earlier, about the splendors of American capitalism.

At the same time that it delivered its gut punch, *The Other America* 3 also offered a view of poverty that seemed designed to comfort the already comfortable. The poor were different from the rest of us, it argued, radically different, and not just in the sense that they were deprived, disadvantaged, poorly housed, or poorly fed. They *felt* different, too, thought differently, and pursued lifestyles characterized by shortsightedness and intemperance. As Harrington wrote, "There is . . . a language of the poor, a psychology of the poor, a worldview of the poor. To be impoverished is to be an internal alien, to grow up in a culture that is radically different from the one that dominates the society."

Harrington did such a good job of making the poor seem "other" 4 that when I read his book in 1963, I did not recognize my own forbears and extended family in it. All right, some of them did lead disorderly lives by middle-class standards, involving drinking, brawling, and out-of-wedlock babies. But they were also hardworking and in some cases fiercely ambitious—qualities that Harrington seemed to reserve for the economically privileged.

According to him, what distinguished the poor was their unique 5 "culture of poverty," a concept he borrowed from anthropologist Oscar Lewis, who had derived it from his study of Mexican slum-dwellers. The culture of poverty gave *The Other America* a trendy academic twist, but it also gave the book a conflicted double message: "We"—the always presumptively affluent readers—needed to find some way to help the poor, but we also needed to understand that there was *something wrong with them*, something that could not be cured by a straightforward redistribution of wealth. Think of the earnest liberal who encounters a panhandler, is moved to pity by the man's obvious destitution, but refrains from offering a quarter—since the hobo might, after all, spend the money on booze.

In his defense, Harrington did not mean that poverty was *caused* by 6 what he called the "twisted" proclivities of the poor. But he certainly opened the floodgates to that interpretation. In 1965, Daniel Patrick Moynihan—a sometime-liberal and one of Harrington's drinking companions at the famed White Horse Tavern in Greenwich Village—blamed inner-city poverty on what he saw as the shaky structure of the "Negro family," clearing the way for decades of victim-blaming. A few years after The Moynihan

Report, Harvard urbanologist Edward C. Banfield, who was to go on to serve as an advisor to Ronald Reagan, felt free to claim that:

> The lower-class individual lives from moment to moment. . . . Impulse governs his behavior. . . . He is therefore radically improvident: whatever he cannot consume immediately he considers valueless. . . . [He] has a feeble, attenuated sense of self.

In the "hardest cases," Banfield opined, the poor might need to be cared for in "semi-institutions . . . and to accept a certain amount of surveillance and supervision from a semi-social-worker-semi-policeman."

By the Reagan era, the "culture of poverty" had become a cornerstone 7 of conservative ideology: Poverty was caused, not by low wages or a lack of jobs, but by bad attitudes and faulty lifestyles. The poor were dissolute, promiscuous, prone to addiction and crime, unable to "defer gratification," or possibly even set an alarm clock. The last thing they could be trusted with was money. In fact, Charles Murray argued in his 1984 book *Losing Ground*, any attempt to help the poor with their material circumstances would only have the unexpected consequence of deepening their depravity.

So it was in a spirit of righteousness and even compassion that Demo- 8 crats and Republicans joined together to reconfigure social programs to cure, not poverty, but the "culture of poverty." In 1996, the Clinton administration enacted the "One Strike" rule banning anyone who committed a felony from public housing. A few months later, welfare was replaced by Temporary Assistance to Needy Families (TANF), which in its current form makes cash assistance available only to those who have jobs or are able to participate in government-imposed "workfare."

In a further nod to "culture of poverty" theory, the original welfare 9 reform bill appropriated $250 million over five years for "chastity training" for poor single mothers. (This bill, it should be pointed out, was signed by Bill Clinton.)

Even today, more than a decade later and four years into a severe eco- 10 nomic downturn, as people continue to slide into poverty from the middle classes, the theory maintains its grip. If you're needy, you must be in need of correction, the assumption goes, so TANF recipients are routinely instructed in how to improve their attitudes and applicants for a growing number of safety-net programs are subjected to drug testing. Lawmakers in twenty-three states are considering testing people who apply for such programs as job training, food stamps, public housing, welfare, and home heating assistance. And on the theory that the poor are likely to harbor criminal tendencies, applicants for safety net programs are increasingly subjected to fingerprinting and computerized searches for outstanding warrants.

Unemployment, with its ample opportunities for slacking off, is another 11 obviously suspect condition, and last year twelve states considered requiring pee tests as a condition for receiving unemployment benefits. Both Mitt Romney and Newt Gingrich have suggested drug testing as a condition for *all* government benefits, presumably including Social Security. If granny insists on handling her arthritis with marijuana, she may have to starve.

What would Michael Harrington make of the current uses of the "culture of poverty" theory he did so much to popularize? I worked with him in the 1980s, when we were co-chairs of Democratic Socialists of America, and I suspect he'd have the decency to be chagrined, if not mortified. In all the discussions and debates I had with him, he never said a disparaging word about the down-and-out or, for that matter, uttered the phrase "the culture of poverty." Maurice Isserman, Harrington's biographer, told me that he'd probably latched onto it in the first place only because "he didn't want to come off in the book sounding like a stereotypical Marxist agitator stuck-in-the-thirties." *12*

The ruse—if you could call it that—worked. Michael Harrington wasn't red-baited into obscurity. In fact, his book became a bestseller and an inspiration for President Lyndon Johnson's War on Poverty. But he had fatally botched the "discovery" of poverty. What affluent Americans found in his book, and in all the crude conservative diatribes that followed it, was not the poor, but a flattering new way to think about themselves—disciplined, law-abiding, sober, and focused. In other words, not poor. *13*

Fifty years later, a new discovery of poverty is long overdue. This time, we'll have to take account not only of stereotypical Skid Row residents and Appalachians, but of foreclosed-upon suburbanites, laid-off tech workers, and America's ever-growing army of the "working poor." And if we look closely enough, we'll have to conclude that poverty is not, after all, a cultural aberration or a character flaw. Poverty is a shortage of money. *14*

■ ■ ■

Reading as a Writer: Analyzing Rhetorical Choices

1. Reread Ehrenreich's essay, noting all the different places she describes and analyzes Michael Harrington's writing and ideas. Take notes on the different points she makes about him. Why is he such a crucial touchstone for her argument? How do his ideas help her make her larger point?

2. Ehrenreich mentions several turning-point political moments in attitudes toward poverty, some of which might be new to you. Consider dividing the work into different groups to research and report on President Lyndon Johnson's War on Poverty, *The Moynihan Report*, reviews of Charles Murray's 1984 book *Losing Ground*, and President Bill Clinton's One Strike rule. How do your findings contribute to your understanding of Ehrenreich's piece?

Writing as a Reader: Entering the Conversation of Ideas

1. Both Ehrenreich and bell hooks (pp. 486–92) analyze the ways popular understandings of poverty often blame the poor. Place these authors' ideas

in conversation in an essay in which you make an argument about the ways policy making and popular culture often go hand in hand to produce ideas about inequality. What solutions does each author offer, and what do you make of those solutions?

2. Just as Ehrenreich critiques writer Michael Harrington for turning poor people into "others," Robert B. Reich (pp. 749–58 in Economics) examines the ways the "working poor" are often blamed for the very conditions that keep them in poverty. Write an essay in which you analyze the way each author presents the origins of these ideas and their current iterations. What conclusions can you draw about economics and identity in our culture? What solutions would you propose, if any, and why?

BELL HOOKS

Seeing and Making Culture: Representing the Poor

bell hooks is the pen name of Gloria Watkins, a cultural critic, scholar, and prolific writer. She has a wide range of intellectual interests, and her many books on race, gender, politics, and popular culture are taught frequently in both undergraduate and graduate courses. She is well known for her collaborations with prominent scholars such as Cornel West on projects related to activism and spirituality (quoted in this essay). This selection was taken from *Outlaw Culture: Resisting Representations* (1994) and focuses on images of poverty in popular culture and what they tell us about "our" assumptions about "the poor." hooks is interested in social problems, such as the attitudes that so often make being poor a mark of shame in the United States.

Despite bell hooks's publishing success, some scholars have criticized her for refusing to follow the "rules" of academic publishing. For example, although she quotes and engages with numerous scholars in her writing, she does not use footnotes in her work because she believes many readers find them off-putting, and she is interested in making her ideas accessible to readers who are not necessarily academics. As you read, you might pay attention to the many different strategies she uses as a writer to invite readers to think about some challenging ideas—what Americans really think about poverty. Where does she use personal experiences to illustrate her arguments? How does she introduce other scholars into the conversation of her essay? You might mark some of the challenging phrases in this piece, such as some of the quotations by Cornel West in paragraph 1 or anthropologist Carol Stack's ideas about the "ethic of liberal individualism" (para. 11), and work with your peers to make sure you understand these terms, looking up information if necessary. Noticing how exactly hooks moves between personal examples and these scholarly ones in her sentences can help you decide how to make these moves in your own writing.

hooks also cites specific popular culture representations of poverty in this essay, such as *Pretty Woman* and *Menace II Society*. While hooks's essay is as pertinent now as when she published it in 1994, we acknowledge that these references are now a bit dated. As you read this piece, consider more recent representations of poverty in television, film, or even news coverage, and be ready to discuss the ways hooks's ideas help you make sense of those images and the stories that accompany them. What do the examples you come up with tell us about what we believe about poverty and those who are poor?

In this essay, hooks is interested both in illuminating what she considers to be problematic in attitudes toward poverty in the United States, and in proposing solutions. Pay close attention to her closing paragraphs and assess what you think about the solutions she suggests for developing less punishing attitudes toward poverty among people who are poor and those who are not. What values can poverty teach us all?

◼ ◼ ◼

Cultural critics rarely talk about the poor. Most of us use words such as "underclass" or "economically disenfranchised" when we speak about being poor. Poverty has not become one of the new hot topics of radical discourse. When contemporary Left intellectuals talk about capitalism, few if any attempts are made to relate that discourse to the reality of being poor in America. In his collection of essays *Prophetic Thought in Post-modern Times,* black philosopher Cornel West includes a piece entitled "The Black Underclass and Black Philosophers" wherein he suggests that black intellectuals within the "professional-managerial class in U.S. advanced capitalist society" must "engage in a kind of critical self-inventory, a historical situating and positioning of ourselves as persons who reflect on the situation of those more disadvantaged than us even though we may have relatives and friends in the black underclass." West does not speak of poverty or being poor in his essay. And I can remember once in conversation with him referring to my having come from a "poor" background; he corrected me and stated that my family was "working class." I told him that technically we *were* working class, because my father worked as a janitor at the post office, however the fact that there were seven children in our family meant that we often faced economic hardship in ways that made us children at least think of ourselves as poor. Indeed, in the segregated world of our small Kentucky town, we were all raised to think in terms of the haves and the have-nots, rather than in terms of class. We acknowledged the existence of four groups: the poor, who were destitute; the working folks, who were poor because they made just enough to make ends meet; those who worked and had extra money; and the rich. Even though our family was among the working folks, the economic struggle to make ends meet for such a large family always gave us a sense that there was not enough money to take care of the basics. In our house, water was a luxury and using too much could be a cause for punishment. We never talked about being poor. As children we knew we were not supposed to see ourselves as poor but we felt poor.

I began to *see* myself as poor when I went away to college. I never had 2
any money. When I told my parents that I had scholarships and loans to
attend Stanford University, they wanted to know how I would pay for getting there, for buying books, for emergencies. We were not poor, but there
was no money for what was perceived to be an individualistic indulgent
desire; there were cheaper colleges closer to family. When I went to college and could not afford to come home during breaks, I frequently spent
my holidays with the black women who cleaned in the dormitories. Their
world was my world. They, more than other folks at Stanford, knew where
I was coming from. They supported and affirmed my efforts to be educated, to move past and beyond the world they lived in, the world I was
coming from.

To this day, even though I am a well-paid member of what West calls 3
the academic "professional-managerial class," in everyday life, outside
the classroom, I rarely think of myself in relation to class. I mainly think
about the world in terms of who has money to spend and who does not.
Like many technically middle-class folks who are connected in economic
responsibility to kinship structures where they provide varying material
support for others, the issue is always one of money. Many middle-class
black folks have no money because they regularly distribute their earnings
among a larger kinship group where folks are poor and destitute, where
elder parents and relatives who once were working class have retired and
fallen into poverty.

Poverty was no disgrace in our household. We were socialized early 4
on, by grandparents and parents, to assume that nobody's value could be
measured by material standards. Value was connected to integrity, to being
honest and hardworking. One could be hardworking and still be poor. My
mother's mother Baba, who did not read or write, taught us—against the
wishes of our parents—that it was better to be poor than to compromise
one's dignity, that it was better to be poor than to allow another person to
assert power over you in ways that were dehumanizing or cruel.

I went to college believing there was no connection between poverty 5
and personal integrity. Entering a world of class privilege which compelled
me to think critically about my economic background, I was shocked by
representations of the poor learned in classrooms, as well as by the comments of professors and peers that painted an entirely different picture.
They almost always portrayed the poor as shiftless, mindless, lazy, dishonest, and unworthy. Students in the dormitory were quick to assume that
anything missing had been taken by the black and Filipina women who
worked there. Although I went through many periods of shame about my
economic background (even before I educated myself for critical consciousness about class by reading and studying Marx, Gramsci, Memmi,
and the like), I contested stereotypical negative representations of poverty.
I was especially disturbed by the assumption that the poor were without values. Indeed one crucial value that I had learned from Baba, my

grandmother, and other family members was not to believe that "schooling made you smart." One could have degrees and still not be intelligent or honest. I had been taught in a culture of poverty to be intelligent, honest, to work hard, and always to be a person of my word. I had been taught to stand up for what I believed was right, to be brave and courageous. These lessons were the foundation that made it possible for me to succeed, to become the writer I always wanted to be, and to make a living in my job as an academic. They were taught to me by the poor, the disenfranchised, the underclass.

Those lessons were reinforced by liberatory religious traditions that affirmed identification with the poor. Taught to believe that poverty could be the breeding ground of moral integrity, of a recognition of the significance of communion, of sharing resources with others in the black church, I was prepared to embrace the teachings of liberatory theology, which emphasized solidarity with the poor. That solidarity was meant to be expressed not simply through charity, the sharing of privilege, but in the assertion of one's power to change the world so that the poor would have their needs met, would have access to resources, would have justice and beauty in their lives. 6

Contemporary popular culture in the United States rarely represents the poor in ways that display integrity and dignity. Instead, the poor are portrayed through negative stereotypes. When they are lazy and dishonest, they are consumed with longing to be rich, a longing so intense that it renders them dysfunctional. Willing to commit all manner of dehumanizing and brutal acts in the name of material gain, the poor are portrayed as seeing themselves as always and only worthless. Worth is gained only by means of material success. 7

Television shows and films bring the message home that no one can truly feel good about themselves if they are poor. In television sitcoms the working poor are shown to have a healthy measure of self-contempt; they dish it out to one another with a wit and humor that we can all enjoy, irrespective of our class. Yet it is clear that humor masks the longing to change their lot, the desire to "move on up" expressed in the theme song of the sitcom *The Jeffersons*. Films which portray the rags-to-riches tale continue to have major box-office appeal. Most contemporary films portraying black folks—*Harlem Nights, Boomerang, Menace II Society,* to name only a few—have as their primary theme the lust of the poor for material plenty and their willingness to do anything to satisfy that lust. *Pretty Woman* is a perfect example of a film that made huge sums of money portraying the poor in this light. Consumed and enjoyed by audiences of all races and classes, it highlights the drama of the benevolent, ruling-class person (in this case a white man, played by Richard Gere) willingly sharing his resources with a poor white prostitute (played by Julia Roberts). Indeed, many films and television shows portray the ruling class as generous, eager to share, as unattached to their wealth in their interactions with 8 folks who are not materially privileged. These images contrast with the opportunistic avaricious longings of the poor.

Socialized by film and television to identify with the attitudes and val- 9
ues of privileged classes in this society, many people who are poor, or a few paychecks away from poverty, internalize fear and contempt for those who are poor. When materially deprived teenagers kill for tennis shoes or jackets they are not doing so just because they like these items so much. They also hope to escape the stigma of their class by appearing to have the trappings of more privileged classes. Poverty, in their minds and in our society as a whole, is seen as synonymous with depravity, lack, and worthlessness. No one wants to be identified as poor. Teaching literature by African American women writers at a major urban state university to predominantly black students from poor and working-class families, I was bombarded by their questioning as to why the poor black women who were abused in families in the novels we read did not "just leave." It was amazing to me that these students, many of whom were from materially disadvantaged backgrounds, had no realistic sense about the economics of housing or jobs in this society. When I asked that we identify our class backgrounds, only one student—a young single parent—was willing to identify herself as poor. We talked later about the reality that although she was not the only poor person in the class, no one else wanted to identify with being poor for fear this stigma would mark them, shame them in ways that would go beyond our class. Fear of shame-based humiliation is a primary factor leading no one to want to identify themselves as poor. I talked with young black women receiving state aid, who have not worked in years, about the issue of representation. They all agree that they do not want to be identified as poor. In their apartments they have the material possessions that indicate success (a VCR, a color television), even if it means that they do without necessities and plunge into debt to buy these items. Their self-esteem is linked to not being seen as poor.

If to be poor in this society is everywhere represented in the language 10
we use to talk about the poor, in the mass media, as synonymous with being nothing, then it is understandable that the poor learn to be nihilistic. Society is telling them that poverty and nihilism are one and the same. If they cannot escape poverty, then they have no choice but to drown in the image of a life that is valueless. When intellectuals, journalists, or politicians speak about nihilism and the despair of the underclass, they do not link those states to representations of poverty in the mass media. And rarely do they suggest by their rhetoric that one can lead a meaningful, contented, and fulfilled life if one *is* poor. No one talks about our individual and collective accountability to the poor, a responsibility that begins with the politics of representation.

When white female anthropologist Carol Stack looked critically at 11
the lives of black poor people more than twenty years ago and wrote her book *The Culture of Poverty,* she found a value system among them which emphasized the sharing of resources. That value system has long been

eroded in most communities by an ethic of liberal individualism, which affirms that it is morally acceptable not to share. The mass media has been the primary teacher bringing into our lives and our homes the logic of liberal individualism, the idea that you make it by the privatized hoarding of resources, not by sharing them. Of course, liberal individualism works best for the privileged classes. But it has worsened the lot of the poor who once depended on an ethic of communalism to provide affirmation, aid, and support.

To change the devastating impact of poverty on the lives of masses of folks in our society we must change the way resources and wealth are distributed. But we must also change the way the poor are represented. Since many folks will be poor for a long time before those changes are put in place that address their economic needs, it is crucial to construct habits of seeing and being that restore an oppositional value system affirming that one can live a life of dignity and integrity in the midst of poverty. It is precisely this dignity Jonathan Freedman seeks to convey in his book *From Cradle to Grave: The Human Face of Poverty in America,* even though he does not critique capitalism or call for major changes in the distribution of wealth and resources. Yet any efforts to change the face of poverty in the United States must link a shift in representation to a demand for the redistribution of wealth and resources. 12

Progressive intellectuals from privileged classes who are themselves obsessed with gaining material wealth are uncomfortable with the insistence that one can be poor, yet lead a rich and meaningful life. They fear that any suggestion that poverty is acceptable may lead those who have to feel no accountability toward those who have not, even though it is unclear how they reconcile their pursuit with concern for and accountability towards the poor. Their conservative counterparts, who did much to put in place a system of representation that dehumanized the poor, fear that if poverty is seen as having no relation to value, the poor will not passively assume their role as exploited workers. That fear is masked by their insistence that the poor will not seek to work if poverty is deemed acceptable, and that the rest of us will have to support them. (Note the embedded assumption that to be poor means that one is not hardworking.) Of course, there are many more poor women and men refusing menial labor in low-paid jobs than ever before. This refusal is not rooted in laziness but in the assumption that it is not worth it to work a job where one is systematically dehumanized or exploited only to remain poor. Despite these individuals, the vast majority of poor people in our society want to work, even when jobs do not mean that they leave the ranks of the poor. 13

Witnessing that individuals can be poor and lead meaningful lives, I understand intimately the damage that has been done to the poor by a de-humanizing system of representation. I see the difference in self-esteem between my grandparents' and parents' generations and that of my siblings, relatives, friends, and acquaintances who are poor, who suffer from a deep-seated, crippling lack of self-esteem. Ironically, despite the presence 14 of more opportunity than that available to an older generation, low self-esteem makes it impossible for this younger generation to move forward even as it also makes their lives psychically unbearable. That psychic pain is most often relieved by some form of substance abuse. But to change the face of poverty so that it becomes, once again, a site for the formation of values, of dignity and integrity, as any other class positionality in this society, we would need to intervene in existing systems of representation.

Linking this progressive change to radical/revolutionary political *15* movements (such as eco-feminism, for example) that urge all of us to live simply could also establish a point of connection and constructive interaction. The poor have many resources and skills for living. Those folks who are interested in sharing individual plenty as well as working politically for redistribution of wealth can work in conjunction with individuals who are materially disadvantaged to achieve this end. Material plenty is only one resource. Literacy skills are another. It would be exciting to see unemployed folks who lack reading and writing skills have available to them community-based literacy programs. Progressive literacy programs connected to education for critical consciousness could use popular movies as a base to begin learning and discussion. Theaters all across the United States that are not used in the day could be sites for this kind of program where college students and professors could share skills. Since many individuals who are poor, disadvantaged, or destitute are *already* literate, reading groups could be formed to educate for critical consciousness, to help folks rethink how they can organize life both to live well in poverty and to move out of such circumstances. Many of the young women I encounter—black and white—who are poor and receiving state aid (and some of whom are students or would-be students) are intelligent, critical thinkers struggling to transform their circumstances. They are eager to work with folks who can offer guidance, know-how, concrete strategies. Freedman concludes his book with the reminder that

> It takes money, organization, and laws to maintain a social structure but none of it works if there are not opportunities for people to meet and help each other along the way. Social responsibility comes down to something simple—the ability to respond.

Constructively changing ways the poor are represented in every aspect of life is one progressive intervention that can challenge everyone to look at the face of poverty and not turn away.

■ ■ ■

Reading as a Writer: Analyzing Rhetorical Choices

1. bell hooks includes personal anecdotes in this selection. Use a pen or highlighter to mark all the places where she makes use of personal experiences, and discuss with your classmates the relationship you see between these personal experiences and the larger point she is making about perceptions

of poverty in the United States. What do you notice about the structure of this essay? What conclusions can you draw about effective strategies for using personal experiences in scholarly writing?

2. In paragraphs 6, 7, and 8, hooks lays out varying cultural attitudes about the relationship between poverty and personal integrity. What do you notice about the order of the ideas in these paragraphs and the examples she offers? Discuss the way she structures her argument here, and consider how some more recent examples from popular culture would fit with the claims she makes in this section. How do these ideas relate to the solutions she proposes in her final paragraphs?

Writing as a Reader: Entering the Conversation of Ideas

1. hooks, like Allan G. Johnson (pp. 454–57), is committed to understanding the many subtle ways we learn who "counts" in our society and who doesn't. Write an essay in which you apply Johnson's concept of "systems of privilege" to analyze hooks's examples, and draw your own conclusions about the ways privilege works to reinforce economic class stereotypes. Given both authors' insights, how might we change these assumptions? If you like, draw on some examples from your own experience to support your claims.

2. Both hooks and Ann duCille (pp. 781–96 in Economics) are concerned with the ways popular culture often reinforces stereotypes. Using specific examples from current popular culture (books, television, movies, children's toys, etc.), write an essay in which you draw on insights from both authors to analyze the way your examples reinforce common stereotypes, counteract them, or (as is often the case) do both. What do you conclude?

16

Media Studies

What can we learn from what entertains us?

© shutterstock.com

People love to debate the virtues and vices of media culture. Is our obsession with BuzzFeed dumbing us down or making us smarter? Do mainstream advertising and the movie industry reinforce damaging stereotypes or offer more equitable alternatives? Is popular culture worth taking seriously at all? The authors of this chapter's readings believe that far from being too "lite" to take seriously, media culture is the very ground we should be exploring carefully if we wish to make sense of our lives today. These writers discover meanings that may surprise you in the many pastimes, entertainments, and guilty pleasures that tempt us every day. When scholars study what we do for fun—enjoying Instagram, movies, YouTube, and glossy advertising, to name just a few of the pleasures analyzed in these texts—we learn how every cultural artifact, no matter how seemingly insignificant, carries meaning that shapes our lives in often quite significant ways.

In this chapter, you will be invited to consider very different perspectives about the effects of online culture on our identities. Sherry Turkle suggests that there are clear downsides to our "tethered" or "collaborative" selves, particularly on social media, while Mark Hain considers that online communities may be lifesavers. William Powers looks to history to learn how we might most effectively balance connectivity and solitude. Evan Kindley looks forward, suggesting that millennials, in particular, might want to consider what online quiz culture tells us about a hunger for self-definition.

Anyone who has ever enjoyed Instagram, an animated film, or glossy advertising will find provocative examples that invite us to discover layers of meaning in daily distractions. Ken Gillam and Shannon R. Wooden examine unexpected role models for a new kind of masculinity in Pixar films, and Melissa Avdeeff sees Beyoncé's use of social media as another way to craft gender and fan culture. Jean Kilbourne also examines the ways media can reinforce damaging stereotypes that limit the ways we see both women and men. What solutions do these writers offer?

The readings in this chapter acknowledge the positive potential of media culture, but they also help us understand that the past is always with us in our concerns for the present and our hopes for the future. Whether you see media today as the end of culture as we knew it, the same old stuff, or even something entirely new—or perhaps all three—these readings raise provocative questions about the significance of our "just-for-fun" pastimes.

MELISSA AVDEEFF

Beyoncé and Social Media: Authenticity and the Presentation of Self

Melissa Avdeeff is a scholar and lecturer of popular music studies whose research has focused on representations of popularity, images of women in popular music press, and the effects of digital culture on radio, fan identity, and other intersections of technology and music culture. In this scholarly essay, Avdeeff advances a paradoxical claim that the accessible, seemingly "authentic" nature of Instagram actually functions as a highly controlled medium for the mega-star Beyoncé—and perhaps for the rest of us, too. Avdeeff demonstrates how scholars who study popular culture can help us see the important cultural work that is often accomplished in the guise of "entertainment." By examining Beyoncé's use of Instagram, Avdeeff digs deeper to reveal a larger and more interesting truth about our attitudes toward "authenticity" in a digital age.

After explaining her rationale for analyzing Beyoncé's Instagram account (rather than her Facebook or Twitter accounts), Avdeeff uses paragraphs 3 and 4 to explicitly state her thesis. She also introduces the framing theory she uses from sociologist Erving Goffman on the presentation of self. Avdeeff uses the "Filling-the-Gap" model of thesis (see Chapter 6) to describe her contribution to the research on social media and fandom: "An area that has received much less scholarly attention, a problem that I seek to address, is the incorporation, or close examination, of the role of music and musicians within social media use, and, by proxy, the fandoms involved" (para. 4). You might return to this paragraph as you read this essay to ensure you understand how her many examples illuminate this central argument.

As you read, keep your own uses of Instagram in mind, and note the ways Avdeeff addresses aspects like its seeming "authenticity" (para. 5) and its "ephemerality" (para. 10). It may seem paradoxical to claim, as Avdeeff does, that Beyoncé uses Instagram to reveal images for her fans of her "public private self" (para. 8). However, you likely also "curate" (or select) the images you share on social media to promote a particular image of yourself, similar to the way celebrities sell "a product which is essentially themselves" (para. 14). Be sure you can follow Avdeeff's points about the ways Beyoncé's use of Instagram is similar to and different from how other celebrities use social media and the ways musicians may have a particular stake in promotion through digital platforms, given the connection between music-group fandom and identity formation (paras. 7 and 17).

While there is only one Beyoncé, Avdeeff's insights about identity as performance and the ways we use social media to present our "public private selves" may come to mind the next time you pose, snap, and filter with Instagram and then tap Share.

■ ■ ▨

On November 12, 2012, Beyoncé joined Instagram by posting a photo *1* of herself, casually dressed in jeans and a shirt that read "Texans for Obama." She joined without fanfare, but it didn't take long for Beyoncé to become the second most followed account on the site, behind the account for Instagram, itself. As of June 15, 2015, Beyoncé has more than 36.3 million followers on Instagram, followed closely by Kim Kardashian, the self-styled queen of social media, with approximately 34 million followers.

Whereas Kim Kardashian has become synonymous with the selfie—photos that are taken by the poster of themselves—Beyoncé's Instagram account contains very few selfies, and predominantly allows for fans to have a glimpse into her extraordinary life.

Beyoncé's use of social media is outside the norm for contemporary 2 celebrities who are online. Although she has over 14 million followers on Twitter, she does not post on that platform (beyond 8 Tweets that were posted from 2012–2013), and appears to prefer interacting with her fans through Facebook, her personal site, and Instagram. It is widely accepted that those who engage with celebrities through social media expect a certain degree of authenticity in the form of transparency between the celebrity and their posts. Observations of Beyoncé's Facebook feed show that it is largely maintained by a social media manager, as it is fairly obvious that it is not Beyoncé, herself, posting. The authenticity of the posts is under question; therefor, the Facebook feed may function more as a site for news, information, and media, as opposed to a fan/artist relationship that relies on the perception of reciprocity.

This essay will primarily focus on Beyoncé's Instagram use, as it pres- 3 ents an interesting case study of the use of visual-based social media sites in celebrity branding, and a re-negotiation of the fan/artist relationship. This essay explores different approaches to studying celebrity social media use, including Goffman's presentation of self, parasocial interaction, and the circuit of culture, using Beyoncé as a case study. Superficially, Beyoncé's social media relationship with fans appears to be primarily parasocial, but in examining aspects of follower reception, it is demonstrated that her Instagram use actually incorporates a form of reciprocal relationship with fans, as seen in her choice of thematic material, and presentation of identity.

Social media and fandom is a growing area of research. A field is 4 emerging that examines celebrities and their Twitter use, and this research is generally conducted from the perspective of the celebrity, as opposed to the reception of the fans interacting with these accounts (Dobson 2012, Kapidzic and Herring 2015). An area that has received much less scholarly attention, a problem that I seek to address, is the incorporation, or close examination, of the role of music and musicians within social media use, and, by proxy, the fandoms involved. I question whether there is something inherently different about a musician, as opposed to other forms of celebrity, and if these differences are great enough to warrant special treatment. Pop music, a type of music that we can clearly label Beyoncé's music as, is generally agreed upon to be a visual-heavy media. The importance of the visual aspect of the genre is recognized, and has steadily increased in importance since the advent of music videos in 1981. Pop music is clearly not just about the music, and these visual elements are integral to the artist's brand construction. Instagram therefore becomes an important aspect of this identity and brand creation in pop music. Videos remain an important medium of music consumption, especially amongst youths, and the use of social media and Instagram provides not only a behind-the-scenes look into the perceived "authentic" version of the star, but also serves to strengthen the bond between fan and artist through an engagement with visual texts representing, on the one hand, vulnerability, and, in the case of Beyoncé, glamour.

Musician Authenticity on Instagram

A critical discussion of authenticity is prevalent both within the fields of 5 social media and pop music. In discourses surrounding pop music there is an ongoing dichotomy in the mainstream press, and also within the academy to a certain extent, between pop/rock and inauthentic/authentic which has also permeated the use of social media (Frith 1978, Moore 2002). A carefully curated Instagram profile, in some instances, functions to increase perceived authenticity of the star, but on the other hand, functions to mask the authentic self through the curation process. The addition of the Instagram narrative in musicians' branding complicates the authentic/inauthentic dichotomy, as consumers' expectations of Instagram authenticity are not similarly expected in stage or music video performances.

The use of a persona is quite common for pop musicians, whether 6 implicitly stated by the artist, or not. Pop music has long been considered a "carnivalesque" (Railton 2001) medium whereby the artists, and fans, can participate in a temporary period of identity exploration and sexual liberation, largely outside the norms of society. Beyoncé, herself, has utilized the personas of Sasha Fierce and Yonce in order to separate her "authentic" performance of self from her more sexually aggressive stage performances. The persona, or alter ego, allows stars to separate themselves from behaviors that may garner negative reactions in the press, especially for females who are portraying themselves as overtly sexual, which is often outside the accepted societal conventions, no matter how outdated these stereotypes are. While stage and music video personas can challenge societal norms surrounding gender and sexuality conventions, it is the perceived inauthenticity of the persona that allows them to be accepted and consumed by the masses without too much judgment. When an artist presents themselves through social media, however, they are expected to remove themselves from the stage persona in order to present their authentic self to their followers. This has become an unwritten rule within social media use, and one that requires more research and observation.

I argue that the desire for authenticity of pop musicians on Instagram 7 ties into larger notions of music and identity. The idea that music tastes are bound within identity formation adds another layer to the fan/artist relationship. By creating an emotional connection with an artist (persona or otherwise), fans have come to expect a certain degree of authenticity within the relationship that exists on Instagram and other social media platforms. Musical preferences are largely tied to identity formation (Frith 1996), and if consumers feel an emotional and authentic relationship with specific music, it would follow that that relationship would be expected to coincide with the fan's relationship to other aspects of the music's brand, including Instagram.

Perhaps it is the perceived authenticity that is the appeal, as discussed 8 below, of Beyoncé's Instagram photos whereby she is engaged in more private endeavors, such as enjoying time with her daughter or husband. Is this a glimpse into her "authentic" life? Do her fans feel an increased emotional connection to an artist when they can relate on a more personal, albeit mediated, level? David Marshall refers to this as the "public private self" (2010, 44) whereby celebrities present a constructed private version of themselves through social media, which ultimately becomes another version, or layer, in the public presentation of self. With the public private self, according to Marshall, celebrities negotiate their presentation of self through social media in a "recognition of the new notion of a public that implies some sort of further exposer of the individual's life" (2010, 44), enforcing the notion that fans expect a certain degree of interaction and authenticity from the celebrities they follow online. Marshall notes that Twitter has become the primary vehicle for celebrities to demonstrate their public private selves, but it is arguable that Instagram, especially in the way that Beyoncé has used the platform, presents a version of the self that, by utilizing visuals instead of text, removes the possibility for literal misinterpretation. That being said, the intentions behind Beyoncé's Instagram posts are unknown, but if they are considered as both a presentation of self, as well as a form of artwork, they can become subject to subjective interpretation. Marshall's public private self is part of a larger typology of online celebrity presentation of self, which also includes the public self, or the official, industrial version of the self. For Beyoncé, this would be her Facebook account, which largely functions as publicity and promotion. And also the transgressive intimate self, whereby celebrities, often in the heat of the moment, reveal intimate details, or temporary emotion. Beyoncé's strict control over her digital presence negates the presence of a transgressive intimate self (2010, 44–45).

An interview with Beyoncé's digital strategist, Lauren Wirtzer- 9 Seawood, as conducted by Stuart Dredge, has revealed that Beyoncé prefers the visual-based medium to other text-based social media sites, such as Twitter, because it leaves less room for misinterpretation. Instagram functions as a "personal communication" tool for Beyoncé, something "that Beyoncé most of the time uses directly herself: she posts pictures. It's her way of communicating to fans a little bit of what her personal life is like" (Dredge 2013). According to Wirtzer-Seawood, Beyoncé and her digital networking team "don't use Twitter at all. It is a personal choice. I think as an artist, Beyoncé really prefers to communicate in images. It's very hard to say what you want to say in 140 characters" (Dredge 2013). Regardless of how Beyoncé's brand is perceived along the continuum of authenticity, the immense control that Beyoncé exerts over her digital presence represents, on one level, an authenticity of production. The presentation of self is tightly controlled by Beyoncé herself, allowing her to present her public private self, in a carefully curated front stage performance.

Instagramming Beyoncé

As of January 2014, 26 percent of adult internet users, and 21 percent *10* of the entire adult population use Instagram. The Pew Research Centre's research shows that, notably, 53 percent of young adults aged 18–29 use Instagram. The platform has a clear youth preference, as only 11 percent of online adults between the ages of 50–64 use Instagram, and 25 percent of online adults ages 30–49. Since joining Instagram in 2012, Beyoncé has (as of April 18, 2015), posted 991 photos to Instagram. The ephemerality of the platform, however, prevents knowledge of the *actual* amount of photos that have been posted, as photos can be deleted. It is apparent that Beyoncé has deleted many photos from her Instagram feed, as there are photos referenced on older online news sources which do not currently occur in her feed. The ephemerality allows for a continuous curation of identity and brand, taking into account the fact that anything posted on the internet has a certain degree of permanence, as the photos will nevertheless remain online in one form or another. Screen shots of Instagram photos are largely outside the control of the artist, becoming a permanent documentation that, although not posted on "official" sources, are nevertheless a part of the brand of the artist by ultimately contributing to their discourse of identity.

Within the 991 photos, Beyoncé is present in 700 (70.1 percent). Her *11* husband, Jay-Z, is featured in 85 (8.6 percent) of her Instagram photos, and Blue Ivy, their daughter, is present in 38 (3.8 percent). Of the 38 photos of that contain Blue Ivy, only 3 show her face. The choice to originally not show Blue Ivy's face appears to be a conscious effort, most likely to protect the privacy of her daughter (*Huffpost Celebrity* 2013). On February 14, 2015, Beyoncé posted the first full-view face photo of Blue Ivy, alongside herself, in what remains the most "liked" photo in Beyoncé's Instagram feed, with over 1.9 million likes. The photo appears to be a selfie with Beyoncé and her daughter, whereby they have placed small bee ornaments on their faces.

Beyoncé's Instagram photos can be categorized into the following non- *12* mutually-exclusive themes: concert, paparazzi, candid, fashion, throwback, holiday, food, scenery, message, and selfie. Concert photos, which account for 16 percent of her feed, are photos which have been taken during a concert. They appear, for the most part, to be taken by professional photographers. There are no concert selfies. Paparazzi photos are professional photos which appear to have been taken by the paparazzi; they include red carpet photos, photos from premieres, and photos from basketball games.

They account for 6 percent of the feed. Candid photos (20 percent of the feed) are those that show Beyoncé in her potential "authentic" self. Often, these photos are taken when Beyoncé is looking away from the camera, not working, and/or in what could be construed as her version of everyday activities. Fashion photos make up a large percentage of Beyoncé's Instagram feed at 24 percent, reinforcing the notion that pop music branding is all-encompassing, and not dependent solely on the music itself. Beyoncé's focus on fashion may serve to reflect her own involvement with the world of fashion with her label, House of Dereon, but at the same time, her fashion posts do not make mention of specific brands or labels, leaving this information up to the viewers to determine. This category features a fair amount of close-up photos of manicures, jewelry, and full-body shots where the emphasis is clearly on the clothing and Beyoncé's body. Bees are an ongoing theme in Beyoncé's jewelry photos. Photos that are from holidays or travels make up 17 percent of the feed, while scenery shots, those which do not feature any people and are largely scenery-based, make up 14 percent. Statistically, the scenery shots are the least "liked" photos on Beyoncé's Instagram account. Food photos, which are a common theme, in general, on Instagram, occur in 2 percent of Beyoncé's feed. Throwback photos, another common Instagram trope, account for 5 percent. Beyoncé does not often directly address her fans. She rarely captions her Instagram photos, and leaves interpretation largely up to the viewer. That being said, 8 percent of her photos are what I call "message" photos, in that the photos contain a form of text, either typed or hand-written, that presumably address her followers. Often, these message posts are promotion for Beyoncé.com, or hand-written lyrics, motivational quotes, or other forms of self-promotion. As with the scenery photos, these receive less "likes" than photos that show Beyoncé's public private self.

Interestingly, selfies only account for 3 percent of Beyoncé's Instagram 13 feed. This is surprising, as this is the genre that has driven the success of Instagram (Saltz 2014), and is in stark comparison to other celebrities that are highly popular on Instagram, such as Kim Kardashian or Taylor Swift. In reiterating that Beyoncé is a unique case study, it should be noted that she is largely *not* reaching out to an imagined audience for a reciprocal relationship. She is predominantly presenting an opportunity for her audience to glimpse into her highly extraordinary life, as opposed to presenting her extraordinary life as something that is ordinary, and relatable to the average viewer/fan.

Beyoncé and the Presentation of Self

There is much discussion about the presentation of self on social me- 14 dia, through a re-interpretation of Erving Goffman's 1959 book, *The Presentation of Self in Everyday Life*. The dramaturgical model posits that human interaction is filtered through a series of social scripts that prescribe situation-based acceptable forms of behavior. But when we move this interaction to the online realm, and in regards to musician celebrities in particular, it goes beyond the presentation of social scripts, towards a complicated balance between self-branding and a desire to "sell" a product which is essentially themselves. A common theme exists amongst musicians desiring to reveal their "commonness" on Instagram in order to demonstrate similarities between themselves and their fans, presumably to strengthen the consumer bond by incorporating strategic vulnerability. This is common in artists such as Taylor Swift, who regularly posts photos of herself doing everyday activities, such as hanging out with her friends, playing with her cat, and going to the beach. Swift also regularly posts photos of herself with her fans, blurring the boundaries between what is considered a reciprocal relationship, and one that appears as one. With this in mind, Beyoncé's Instagram feed differs from many high-profile musicians. Her photos present a view into life in the 1 percent; highly glamorous, but also built on the foundation of hard work. Labor is represented in the numerous photos of her on stage, in rehearsal, or in the studio. In total, 19.7 percent of her photos have some sort of relation to music and/or the process of creating or performing music. Alice Marwick has found that Instagram users are more likely to "like" photos on Instagram that are aspirational or "reinforce an existing hierarchy of fame, in which the iconography of glamour, luxury, wealth, good looks, and connections is re-inscribed in a visual digital medium" (Marwick 2015, 141). Beyoncé's Instagram feed does not just resemble the "lifestyles of the rich and famous" trope that allows micro-celebrities to become "Instagram famous," rather, she is the epitome of the trope and functions to represent and serve as a model for others seeking online celebrity status. Her glamorous photos do not appear to promote excess for the sake of excess; Beyoncé does not seem to flaunt her wealth and elite lifestyle through Instagram, unlike other Instagram photos that regularly appear on the profile, @richkidsofinstagram. The profile, which originated as a Tumblr account, re-posts photos from wealthy adolescents who flaunt their extravagant lifestyles. The profile of the account reads: "Rich Kids Of Instagram: They have more money than you and this is what they do." Whereas these profiles are, in general, flaunting wealth inequality through inheritance (Marwick 2015), Beyoncé's profile balances photos of extravagance with a demonstration of labor.

Goffman's dramaturgical model of the presentation of self—that we engage in a series of performances, determined by the social situation in which we find ourselves—is quite relevant when discussing the curation that occurs on Instagram, but when we consider the prevalence of the persona within pop music, the issue becomes complicated. As discussed, there is an expectation for female pop musicians to perform under a stage persona, but this can become quite confusing for fans/followers, as they have no concrete evidence to determine what is, and is not, a part of the carefully constructed brand. Photos posted on Instagram serve as a "performative practice" (Marwick and boyd 2011, 140) of celebrity. Marwick and boyd note, in an exploration of celebrity practices on Twitter, that celebrities must "constantly navigate complex identity performances" (2011, 140) and manage the disconnect between the public persona and the "authentic" self. Whereas magazines and paparazzi attempt to disclose celebrities for their "true" selves, Instagram gives that power back to the celebrity, in the form of a carefully curated performance of identity. An ongoing performance of celebrity, through Instagram, is crucial for the maintenance of celebrity in digitally, even for a top-tier performer such as Beyoncé. As Marwick and boyd note, "In the broadcast era, celebrity was something a person *was*; in the Internet era, microcelebrity is something people *do*" (2011, 140). Marwick and boyd often refer to the term microcelebrity as a way to categorize those who are famous online, but I argue that the same holds true for celebrities that are recognizable online and offline, such as Beyoncé. Instagram may allow for new pathways to celebrity status, but it is also a site of fame maintenance.

Where Goffman's theory is most applicable to the discussion surrounding Beyoncé on Instagram, is in the idea of the embodiment of identity; the identity, or persona, by which fans relate to the artist. As musicians disclose personal information through Instagram, they make themselves vulnerable to the public: a vulnerable social performance of identity (Chen 2014). In an investigation of relationship construction through YouTube, Chih-Ping Chen notes that it is this performance of vulnerability that followers identify with. Online relationships and interactions vary vastly from in-person interactions, in that people cannot gauge the reception of their audience and adjust in real time. Instead, artifacts, in this case, photos, are presented to the public and reception comes in the form of "likes" and comments. Hogan refers to social media platforms as exhibition spaces, where photos are presented and processed "when actors are not necessarily present at the same time but still react to each other's data" (Hogan 2010, 344). Therefore, for Hogan, Instagram is still considered a presentation of the self, but outside the time and space constraints of in-person impression management. In examining Beyoncé's Instagram feed, it can be interpreted that, as the curator, she has reacted to the engagement of her followers in order to adapt her impression, outside of real-time engagement. For example, her earlier posts included more "message" photos, but these have subsequently decreased in frequency. These photos received substantially less "likes" than photos from the same time period that featured Beyoncé, or her friends and family. The reduced amount of likes in these earlier message photos cannot solely be attributed to the early adoption of the medium, because fashion photos from the same time period received significantly more likes. To highlight, on November 16, 2012, Beyoncé posted a photo containing a handwritten quote by Anais Nin, "SOME PEOPLE FEEL THE RAIN, OTHERS GET WET," which received approximately 86,600 likes; a fashion photo from two days later received 155,000 likes. Perhaps these message photos decreased in frequency as a reaction to fan engagement and to curate content for maximum appeal. Also from 2012 are a series of photos taken at the Tate Modern Museum. In this series, a photo of the *Slashed Canvas* taken on December 9, 2012, remains the least liked photo in her feed, with approximately 36,8000 likes. This is not to say that almost 37 thousand people liking a photo is trivial, but in comparison to the average amount of likes, which is approximately 532,000, and a median of approximately 491,000, the number is significantly lower....

Conclusion

With the rise of digital media, and digital music dissemination, a de- *17* materialization of consumption has occurred. The dematerialization of musical goods, in the form of MP3s and streaming music platforms such as Spotify, Pandora, and Rdio, has altered the reception and consumption of music. As the physicality of the music playback technology decreases consumers look for new ways to establish a material connection with music, often in the form of playback technologies, such as vinyl and the turntable. In order to find connections to music and musicians, consumers have also looked online, to digital platforms that provide an aspect of music that is not present in the physical copy: the "self" of the artist. This is not to say that fans did not experience emotional relationships with musicians before the advent of social media and Instagram, but the prevalence of these platforms has created a new space where fans and followers can engage on an emotional level with what they perceive to be a more authentic version of the star. Throughout the development of music playback technology, and subsequent digitalization, a tremendous change in listening and consumption habits has followed. Instagram offers a new visual-based platform for music-related materials. Instagram perpetuates the emphasis that is placed on beauty and the body for female pop musicians, which is reflected in Beyoncé's fashion themed photos. On the other hand, her more candid photos provide a glimpse into her everyday life that can be perceived as vulnerable, even if she is not posting them from a position of vulnerability. Beyoncé's obsessive documentation of her everyday life suggests that her extreme awareness of her brand and performance of self leaves little room for vulnerability, although how followers and consumers interpret such visuals may vary. Beyoncé is notorious for being very selective in which interviews she conducts and with whom she talks to in the press, so, often the only way we can access a version of her authentic self is through her Instagram photos. Crossovers exist between her personal life and her music videos, especially in her 2014 self-titled audiovisual album, which includes locations and dramatic reinterpretations of important moments in her life, but it becomes difficult to separate what is *Beyoncé,* and what is a persona, leaving Instagram to help in that understanding. Beyoncé owns her brand, just as she owns her likeness. In the words of Amy Wallace, *GQ* correspondent,

> There ain't no use being hot as fish grease ... if someone else wields the spatula and holds the keys to the cash register. But if you can harness your own power and put it to your own use? Well, then there are no limits. That's what the video camera is all about: owning your own brand, your own face, your own body. Only then, to borrow another Beyoncé lyric, can girls rule the world. And make no mistake, fellas: Queen Bey is comfortable on her throne [Wallace 2013].

Regardless of Beyoncé's personal intentions for using the Instagram platform in an ongoing curation of self, a theme has emerged as a constant in her feed: flawless.

REFERENCES

Bennett, Lance. 2012. "The Personalization of Politics: Political Identity, Social Media, and Changing Patterns of Participation." *Annals* 644.

Chen, Chih-Pin. 2014. "Forming the Digital Self and Parasocial Relationships on YouTube." *Journal of Consumer Culture* 16.1: 1–12.

Dobson, Amy Shields. 2012. "Individuality Is Everything: 'Autonomous' Femininity in MySpace Mottos and Self-Description." *Continuum* 26.3: 371–383.

Dredge, Stuart. 2014. "Here's Why Beyoncé Hasn't Used Twitter Since August 2013." *musically*, November 5. Accessed June 2, 2015. http://musically.com/2014/11/05/beyonce-twitter-facebook-lauren-wirtzer-seawood/.

Du Gay, Paul, Stuart Hall, Linda Janes, Hugh Mackay, and Keith Negus, eds. 1997. *Doing Cultural Studies: The Story of the Walkman*. London: Sage.

Duggan, Maeve, Nicol Ellison, Cliff Lampe, Amanda Lenhart and Mary Madden. 2015. "Social Media Update 2014." *Pew Research Centre*, January 9. Accessed June 15, 2015. http://www.pewinternet.org/2015/01/09/social-media-update-2014/.

Franco, James. 2013. "The Meanings of the Selfie." *New York Times*, December 26. Accessed June 2, 2015. http://www.nytimes.com/2013/12/29/arts/the-meanings-of -the-selfie.html.

Frith, Simon. 1978. *The Sociology of Rock*. London: Constable.

_____. 1996. "Music and Identity." In *Questions of Cultural Identity*, edited by Stuart Hall and Paul du Gay, 108–127. London: Sage.

Goffman, Erving. 1959. *The Presentation of Self in Everyday Life*. Garden City, NY: Doubleday.

Harmsworth, Andrei. 2013. "Beyoncé Knowles Takes Control and 'Bans Photographers from Her Shows and Issues Own Pics.'" *Metro*, April 24. Accessed June 2, 2015. http://metro.co.uk/2013/04/24/beyoncé-knowles-takes-control-and-bans-photographers -from-her-shows-and-issues-own-pics-3664886/.

Hogan, Bernie. 2010. "The Presentation of Self in the Age of Social Media: Distinguishing Performances and Exhibitions Online." *Bulletin of Science, Technology & Society* 30.6: 377.

Horton, Donald, and Richard Wohl. 1956. "Mass Communication and Parasocial Interaction: Observations on Intimacy at a Distance." *Psychiatry* 19: 228.

Huffpost Celebrity. 2013. "Beyoncé Shares Blue Ivy Photo, Still Manages to Keep Her from Prying Eyes." December 20. Accessed June 2, 2015. http://www.huffingtonpost .com/2013/12/10/beyoncé-shares-blue-ivy-photo_n_4420801.html.

Kapidzic, Sanka, and Susan Herring. 2015. "Teens, Gender, and Self-Presentation in Social Media." In *International Encyclopedia of Social and Behavioral Sciences, 2nd Edition*, edited by J.D. Wright. Oxford: Elsevier.

Keats, Emily. 2013. "The Circuit of Culture: A Useful Theoretical Model for Studying Social Media." *Selected Papers of Internet Research* 14.0. Denver.

Marshall, David. 2010. "The Promotion and Presentation of the Self: Celebrity as Marker of Presentational Media." *Celebrity Studies* 1.1: 35–48.

Marwick, Alice. 2015. "Instafame: Luxury Selfies in the Attention Economy." *Public Culture* 1.75: 137–160.

Marwick, Alice, and danah boyd. 2011. "To See and Be Seen: Celebrity Practice on Twitter." *Convergence* 17.2: 139–156.

McRady, Rachel. 2015. "Beyoncé Posts Instagram, Sparks New Pregnancy Rumors: See the Picture!" *Us Weekly*, January 11. Accessed June 2, 2015. http://www.usmagazine .com/celebrity-moms/news/beyoncé-instagram-sparks-pregnancy-rumors-2015111.

Moore, Allen. 2002. "Authenticity as Authentication." *Popular Music* 21.1: 209–223.

O'Reilly, Daragh. 2005. "Cultural Brands/Branding Cultures." *Journal of Marketing Management* 21: 573–588.

Railton, Diane. 2001. "The Gendered Carnival of Pop." *Popular Music* 20.3: 321–331.

Saltz, Jerry. 2014. "Art at Arm's Length: A History of the Selfie." *Vulture*, January 26. Accessed June 2, 2015. http:// www.vulture.com/2014/01/history-of-the-selfie.html.

Spanos, Brittany. 2015. "Beyoncé Fans Attack Kid Rock Online After Derogatory Comments." *Rolling Stone*, February 27. Accessed June 2, 2015. http://www .rollingstone.com/music/news/beyoncé-fans-attack-kid-rock-online-after-derogatory -comments-20150227.

Takeda, Allison. 2013. "Beyoncé Squashes Pregnancy Rumors with Wine-Drinking Picture." *Us Weekly*, May 31. Accessed June 2, 2015. http://www.usmagazine.com/ celebrity-news/news/beyoncé-squashes-pregnancy-rumors-with-wine-drinking -picture-2013315.

Vokes-Dudgeon, Sophie. 2014. "Beyoncé Posts Throwback Pictures with Solange After Jay Z Elevator Fight at Met Gala Party." *Us Weekly*, May 14. Accessed June 2, 2015. http://www.usmagazine.com/celebrity-news/news/beyonce-posts-solange-pictures -instagram-after-jay-z-fight-2014145.

Wallace, Amy. 2013. "Miss Millennium: Beyonce." *GQ*. Accessed June 2, 2015. http:// www.gq.com/story/beyonce-cover-story-interview-gq-february-2013.

■ ■ ■

Reading as a Writer: Analyzing Rhetorical Choices

1. Review the Visual Analysis tools in Chapter 10 and in pairs, in groups, or on your own, analyze some images from Beyoncé's Instagram account. Prepare to discuss the significance of a few images in light of Avdeeff's claims and anything else you draw from Chapter 10's insights.

2. Use a bright color to underline all the references to Goffman in this essay. How are Goffman's ideas important to Avdeeff's argument? What can you say about where she places his ideas to build her point effectively?

Writing as a Reader: Entering the Conversation of Ideas

1. Avdeeff is interested in the function of images in our culture, as is Jean Kilbourne (pp. 554–77). Using the visual rhetoric insights from Chapter 10 and Avdeeff's and Kilbourne's readings, write an essay in which you use a small number of examples from Beyoncé's Instagram account and advertising images to make an argument of your own. You might use your examples to demonstrate how images can shore up or work against a

specific stereotype. Or you might focus on the ways images create a sense of identification and community. Or perhaps there is something else you want to teach your readers about the power of images?

2. Avdeeff argues that celebrities "'Sell' a product that is essentially themselves" (para 14). Naomi Klein (pp. 768–80 in Economics) makes a related point about the connection of branding and consumer identity. Place these authors in conversation with one another in an essay of your own that considers the connection among images, products, identity, and a sense of belonging. Draw on examples from these texts and perhaps additional ones from your personal experience as you make your point.

EVAN KINDLEY

From Quiz Mania

Evan Kindley is a writer, critic, and senior humanities editor at the *Los Angeles Review of Books*, whose work has appeared in *The New Republic* and *The New Yorker*, among other literary and popular journals. His interests include history and popular culture, particularly at the intersections of technology and politics. This piece, "Quiz Mania," is an excerpt from his 2016 book *Questionnaire*. In his opening paragraph, Kindley launches into the absurdity of quiz culture, with a long list of aspects about himself that he has "learned" from online quizzes—from which *Simpsons* character he would be to which philosopher or punk icon best represents him. Before you read, take a few minutes to think about and discuss your own relationship to these alluring quizzes so often shared on social media. Why do we do them?

Like the other authors in this chapter, Kindley urges readers to take our pastimes seriously. Though clicking through a BuzzFeed quiz may seem too ephemeral to count as a pastime, Kindley argues we should reflect on why we're drawn to these self-defining exercises, even if—or especially if—we find them silly. These quizzes, he claims, are part of "monetizing the zeitgeist" (para. 8). What does he mean? (Get in the habit of looking up words that are new to you.)

A central aspect of Kindley's argument is his focus on millennial identity. He begins to develop his point about the ways we participate—willingly—in Big Data gathering by noting that "These quizzes provide a space, at last, where marketers' hunger to define a demographic segment meets individuals' desire to be defined" (para. 15). Note how he connects quiz-taking for fun with companies' increasing use of monitoring and managing workers. Kindley reflects on history in his final paragraphs as he considers where "the art of asking questions" is headed in this data-driven age. What do you make of his predictions?

BuzzFeed-style quizzes are hardly the only way we waste time on the Internet. Kindley challenges us to consider all the ways we might be participating in self-defining that have implications far beyond finding out the quiz answer to "So how big a millennial stereotype are you really?"

I'm quite privileged. I should be a writer. I should live in Portland. I should *1* go to Stanford. I belong in the 1980s. If I were a dog I'd be a Lab. If I were a billionaire tycoon I'd be George Soros. If I were a philosopher I'd be Karl Marx. If I were a punk icon I'd be Patti Smith. Like Saint Jude, I am fierce, kind, and cool as a cucumber. If I were an element I'd be carbon. If I were a character on *The Simpsons* I'd be the Inanimate Carbon Rod. If I were a font I'd be Futura. If I were a design aesthetic I would be the aesthetic void of a college dorm room. The food that best matches my personality is spaghetti and meatballs. My medieval profession would be a witch doctor. If I were a David Bowie I'd be Present Day Bowie. If I were a ghost I'd be an Orb.

What about you? If you've logged on to Facebook in the past two *2* years, you almost certainly witnessed some similarly bizarre existential pronouncements, always accompanied by an invitation to discover and declare your own identity: "Which _____ Are You?" The majority of these quizzes are produced by BuzzFeed, a Manhattan-based company founded in 2006 by the new-media Wunderkind Jonah Peretti; though BuzzFeed has several rivals in the online quiz industry, it towers over the competition in both raw numbers and cultural influence.

The basic format of the typical BuzzFeed quiz is extremely simple. *3* You are asked a series of questions, usually no more than nine or ten, each accompanied by a grid of multiple-choice answers illustrated with colorful images sourced from online image repositories like Photobucket or public message boards like Reddit. (A slight variation on the format allows for a checklist rather than a series of multiple-choice options.) Some of these quizzes deal with matters of concern to any adult human being with a modicum of autonomy over his or her life: "What City Should You Actually Live In?" "What Career Should You Actually Have?" Others cater to niche pop-cultural interests: "How Well Do You Know Your Muppets?" "Which Whit Stillman Character Are You?" Many touch on identity politics or, like *Cosmo's* "Liberation" quizzes, profess a kind of consciousness-raising agenda: "How Privileged Are You?" "How Stereotypically White Are You?" Others are digital versions of carnival guessing games: "Can We Guess Your Age By Your Technology Preferences?" "Can We Guess Your Zodiac Sign Based on Your Favorite Body Shop Butter?" Some quizzes test knowledge, usually of pop culture; others are pegged to hard news or current events, though these attempts at timeliness are often in questionable taste (take a bow, "Which Ousted Arab Spring Ruler Are You?"). Quite a few quizzes are what BuzzFeed calls "branded content," meaning they are paid for by "BuzzFeed Partners"—that is, advertisers—and designed to promote particular products: a "Which Expendable Are You?" quiz tied to the release of *The Expendables 3*, a "Which Barbie Doll Are You?" quiz underwritten by Mattel.

At this point it's a little hard to imagine subject matter that would seem *4* surprising or inappropriate for a BuzzFeed quiz. Indeed, part of the allure of the quizzes stems from their omnivorousness, the way they manage to broach topics, from white supremacy to the "shady tweets" of Zayn Malik from One Direction, that might initially seem either too weighty or too trivial for the form to accommodate.

The most popular BuzzFeed quizzes are aspirational: they imagine 5 a version of yourself more uniquely suited to your environment. As of December 2015, the all-time record-breakers are "What State Do You Actually Belong In?" (42,008,598 page views), "What City Should You Actually Live In?" (20,961,344), and "What Career Should You Actually Have?" (18,778,836). The use of the intensifying adverb "Actually" in all three of these titles registers a sense that the lives the quiz-takers are living are not the true ones. "Just because you were born somewhere doesn't mean you belong there," the brilliant subheadline to "What City Should You Actually Live In?" reads. The quizzes tell you less about who you are than what you should, or could, be. Geography is not destiny; the real is not the actual; "belonging" is a form of longing that may be satisfied by clicking a button and projecting yourself into the warmth of an imagined community. Taking these quizzes you feel, however obscurely, the excitements and satisfactions of lives you could be living, as well as the possibilities inherent in the answers you imagine *other* people providing.

At this point you may well want to object: No one takes these quizzes 6 seriously! This is, broadly, true. BuzzFeed quizzes are explicitly presented as entertainments, not scientific instruments, and many of the people who post their quiz results to social media platforms like Facebook or Twitter preface them with some kind of light-hearted statement of disavowal: *I think this result is wrong, I think this is stupid, I can't believe I'm wasting my time on this fucking quiz when I should be working.*

Of course, from a business point of view, it doesn't matter whether 7 we take BuzzFeed's quizzes seriously or not; what matters is that we take them, and we do. While the numbers have dropped off since the heady days of early 2014, when the combination of novelty and the viral lift from the Facebook algorithm allowed some posts to reach page view counts in the octuple digits, quizzes are still a consistent traffic driver for BuzzFeed. The site currently publishes as many as eighteen per day. As was the case with the Victorian confession album, BuzzFeed quizzes are treated sincerely by some and scornfully by others: to judge by my Facebook feed, at least, hatequizzing appears to be almost as popular a contemporary mode of consumption as hatewatching. But BuzzFeed gets the clicks whether you make fun of them or not, and they're laughing all the way to the next round of venture capital funding.

Quizzes are only one of many examples of BuzzFeed's knack for mone- 8 tizing the zeitgeist. Jonah Peretti, the company's founder and CEO, has made a career out of exploring the intersection of technology, media, and capitalism. In the early 1990s Peretti attended the University of California at Santa Cruz, majoring in environmental studies and taking courses in the school's famously avant-garde History of Consciousness program. "I came out of a university system that was, at that particular moment in the '90s, glorifying postmodern critical theory," Peretti told the journalist Felix Salmon in 2014. "There was a sense that the best way to show you understand something is to write something incomprehensible."[1] In 1996, the year he graduated from Santa Cruz, Peretti published an (actually fairly comprehensible) article in the online journal *Negations* entitled "Capitalism and Schizophrenia: Contemporary Visual Culture and the Acceleration of Identity Formation/Dissolution." "My central contention is that late capitalism not only accelerates the flow of capital, but also accelerates the rate at which subjects assume identities," Peretti wrote. "Identity formation is inextricably linked to the urge to consume, and therefore the acceleration of capitalism necessitates an increase in the rate at which individuals assume and shed identities."[2]

Peretti's essay, which began as a term paper for one of his History of Consciousness classes, is rife with references to postmodern theorists like Deleuze and Guattari, Jameson, Butler, and Lacan. But his basic thesis is not far from the point Susan Douglas makes about the way the women's magazine quizzes of the sixties and seventies "exaggerated [readers'] psychic schizophrenia." Asking questions can orient people in social space, but it can also disorient them. Some queries bolster a sense of identity and personal integrity (*I know the answer to this one; here's what I think*); others unsettle it (*I've never thought about that before; I'm not sure what to say*). What's new in Peretti's formulation, though, is his emphasis on the *acceleration* of this process. In 1996, he attributes this quickening of tempo, somewhat vaguely, to "late capitalism," but today we might be more tempted to pin it on the dizzying pace of social media and Internet publication. It's as if the college-age Peretti already foresaw the world he would help to define.

After Santa Cruz, Peretti went on to do graduate work at the MIT Media Lab, where he studied education and game design. At the same time, he dabbled in "culture jamming," planning and executing high-concept agitprop pranks under the aegis of a loose collective called the Contagious Media Project. In 2001 Peretti ordered a pair of customized Nike sneakers with the word "sweatshop" stitched on them; the company refused to fulfill the order, and Peretti's trolling e-mail exchange with a Nike customer service representative went viral after he forwarded it to ten friends. With his sister, the comedian Chelsea Peretti, he created a website called "Black People Love Us," which satirized the eagerness of white liberals to brag about their black friends. This, too, went viral.

These early stunts piqued Peretti's interest in the way content gets disseminated online, then a relatively new object of inquiry. But the anticapitalist emphasis of his earliest work didn't last long. Like George Gallup and Paul Lazarsfeld before him, Peretti was quickly recruited by advertisers and media executives who anticipated, perhaps before he did, the consequences of his work for their bottom line. Through the sociologist Duncan Watts, an acquaintance from the MIT Lab, he met the media executive Kenneth Lerer, who brought him on to help launch the Huffington Post in 2005. A year later, Peretti launched BuzzFeed. In 2007, he and Watts collaborated on an article for the *Harvard Business Review* entitled "Viral Marketing in the Real World." The techniques that Peretti had honed to critique capitalism were now being used to assist it.

Quizzes were not among BuzzFeed's most popular offerings at first. According to editorial director Summer Anne Burton, they only took off in 2013, when the site's Web development team began to focus on providing editors with "comprehensive quiz tools" and a cleaner, more attractive visual template. A June 2013 quiz called "Which 'Grease' Pink Lady Are You?" (subheadline: "There are worse things you could do than take this quiz") proved, unexpectedly, to be the site's most-shared piece of content at the end of the year. The corporate culture of BuzzFeed is strongly oriented toward replicating accidental successes, and after the *Grease* quiz's success Burton called an editorial staff meeting to discuss the potential for further quizzes. Soon millions of people were coming to the site specifically to take quizzes, and even contributing their own, using a platform called "BuzzFeed Community."³

The evolution of the BuzzFeed quiz recapitulates the history of questionnaires in miniature. Through trial and error, BuzzFeed's editors discovered that personality quizzes worked better than trivia challenges: BuzzFeed's readers seemed to prefer being told who they were to having their knowledge tested, just as Americans generally preferred psychological inventories like the MBTI to intelligence tests like the SAT. They also found that "identity-based" quizzes—keyed not only to racial and ethnic identities but also to online fandoms and neglected demographics—were reliably safe bets. This realization has resulted in micro-targeted quizzes like "What Kind of Goth Are You?"

The common denominator among these various underserved online subcultures is youth. BuzzFeed's content, as everyone knows, is particularly popular among "millennials": a nebulous concept, like all generational categories, but usually defined as encompassing everyone born between the early 1980s and the early 2000s. But "millennial" is not simply a handy term for the site's core demographic: it is also a consistently recurring theme of the quizzes themselves. Cultural reference points tend to center on the 1990s, when the oldest millennials were coming of age. Dewy nostalgia ("Which 'Fresh Prince of Bel Air' Character Are You?") sits easily beside expressions of hip contemporaneity ("Which Song from 'Empire' Describes Your Life?") and state-of-the-art technology consumption ("Let Us Decide Whether You Should Buy the Apple Watch"). Quizzes like "Did You Actually Grow Up in the 90s?" and "Are You More of a 90s Kid or a 00s Kid?" do their best to demarcate these fuzzy borders, encouraging users to place themselves within the smallest generational box possible. This strategy shows no signs of flagging; Matthew Perpetua, BuzzFeed's Director of Quizzes and Games, told me in September 2015 that BuzzFeed's audience is "completely obsessed with age and generation."[4]

The fact that BuzzFeed's young readers enjoy taking quizzes about 15 what marks them generationally is fortuitous, since a large part of the company's standing in the media industry, and its attractiveness to investors and advertisers, is the perception that it has a special relationship to "millennials." Quizzes allow BuzzFeed to test and refine those categories, in ways that resemble nothing so much as a marketing survey. But unlike the subjects of traditional surveys, who are typically cajoled into participating with financial incentives and other perks, people clamor to take BuzzFeed quizzes like "So How Big of a Millennial Stereotype Are You Really?" These quizzes provide a space, at last, where marketers' hunger to define a demographic segment meets individuals' desire to be defined....

... BuzzFeed, like OkCupid before it, has engineered a virtual environment 16 in which people actively *enjoy* answering questions about themselves. The stakes feel vanishingly low; the questions, and answers, are amusing; the ability to immediately share the results with friends, often in a spirit of mock triumph or indignation, adds an irresistible exhibitionistic element. For a lot of us, fucking around and taking quizzes on websites like BuzzFeed is now *part* of the labor process, as routinized as bathroom or cigarette breaks; and this is true whether we work in offices or in Internet-enabled cafes or from our homes.

In the mid-1950s, American white-collar workers took personality 17 tests when they were forced to by their superiors; six decades later, we take and retake them, voluntarily, almost every single day of our lives. This shift in the way we work—or, more precisely, the way we procrastinate—is happening in tandem with the development of new technologies that track employee behaviors in previously unimaginable detail. In "They're Watching You at Work," a 2013 feature story for the *Atlantic*, Don Peck reported that personality testing, which had fallen into disrepute since its high point in the early 1960s for legal as well as scientific reasons, is making a comeback in human resources departments. He described "app-based video games...designed by a team of neuroscientists, psychologists, and data scientists" for the purpose of assessing job candidates; twenty minutes' worth of play was enough to "generate several megabytes of data, exponentially more than what's collected by the SAT or a personality test." A company named Evolv produces "tests [that] allow companies to capture data about everybody who applies for work, and everybody who gets hired—a complete data set from which sample bias, long a major vexation for industrial-organization psychologists, simply disappears." In the near future, as language analysis technology improves, Peck anticipates "programs that [will] automatically trawl through the e-mail traffic of [the] workforce, looking for phrases or communication patterns that can be statistically associated with various measures of success or failure in particular roles." But already the amount of knowledge that sophisticated managers can extract from their employees' "data signatures" is enormous: "Torrents of data are routinely collected by American companies and now sit on corporate servers, or in the cloud, awaiting analysis," Peck writes.[5]

Let's imagine that all of the trends Peck describes continue to accelerate, uncurbed by government regulation or populist backlash. Now imagine that what these perpetually surveilled white-collar workers habitually do, when they're bored, is visit BuzzFeed and take a quiz. The information they provide about themselves will probably seem trivial, ephemeral, and unrelated to whatever it is they do for work. (It may also, of course, be totally inaccurate.) Nonetheless, there is nothing preventing the quiz publisher from logging this data and selling it—perhaps with a detour through a third-party data broker like eXelate, Experian, or BlueKai—back to the bored workers' employers. 18

What could businesses do with this data, once they have it? If it's properly anonymized, they will be unable to use it to punish or reward individual employees, which, for those who fear the social Internet becoming a capitalist panopticon, is some kind of comfort at least. But they will still be able to employ it to rationalize changes in hiring, management, or corporate strategy. It could be used to justify targeted layoffs: not by ratting out individual underachievers (again, assuming the data was kept anonymous) but by constructing types and categories of "desirable" and "undesirable" workers. Peck reports that high-level computer programming skills are strongly correlated with visits to a particular Japanese manga site. If such unexpected correlations are already being used to identify exceptional job candidates, what's to stop companies from taking the next step and using them to filter out "undesirable" ones? 19

The politics of Big Data are still up for grabs, though it's difficult to believe that things won't ultimately tilt in the direction of management rather than labor. Bosses will probably prefer pouring money into data analytics—just as they once did into personality tests—to raising wages. There may be lip service paid, as there was in Isabel Myers's time, to employee morale and "fitting the worker to the job," but the bottom line will be efficiency. Some companies may eschew this kind of optimization for ethical reasons, or because of public disapproval, or because they don't realize its benefits. Others will be priced out of the competition: only the richest will be able to play the game of data to win. 20

There is, for that matter, no reason why the sort of recreational data provision that BuzzFeed is encouraging in our culture couldn't be pressed into the service of something still worse: a revival of eugenics, perhaps, provided the data could be correlated with details on race, ethnicity, or country of origin. Modern-day nativists like Donald Trump (who has publicly endorsed the idea of creating a database of Muslims living in the United States) might well sign on to versions of the agendas advanced by eugenicists like Robert Yerkes and Carl Brigham.[6] It is true that, for the time being, the ideologies espoused by data barons like Peretti, Christian 21

Rudder, and Mark Zuckerberg are (antiunionism aside) fairly progressive. They want to use the awesome capabilities of their proprietary platforms to advance science, expose racism, and promote the free exchange of ideas that is vital to an open society. They want—in a formulation that is by now a Silicon Valley cliché—to make the world a better place. But so did Galton, and Gallup, and Popenoe, and nearly everyone else who, over the course of the past century and a half, has tried to devise new ways to get people to answer questions about themselves, or new purposes to put the answers to. It has not always worked out so well.

The art of asking questions is as liable to misuse as any other art. Infor- 22
mation on what people are like, and what they enjoy, think, or believe, is one of the most powerful props supporting any official ideology. Gallup recognized this back in 1940: it's why he insisted that accuracy in the gauging of public opinion was a crucial part of what separated democracy from dictatorship. Today, the psychological line separating serious inquiries from casual probes has been all but wiped out, while the technological power to collect, sort, and deploy the data that result from these researches grows to gargantuan proportions.

"Here is the voice of The Organization," Whyte wrote in 1956, of work- 23
place personality tests, "and if one wishes to judge what the future would be like were we to intensify organization trends now so evident, let him ponder well what the questions are really driving at."[7] Today Whyte's paranoid style can seem a bit overblown: there is no monolithic Organization, just a tangled network of small-o organizations with shifting, temporarily aligning interests.

Nevertheless, let us ponder: Where is all this headed? What are the 24
new questions driving at?

Think before you answer. This is not a test. 25

NOTES

1. Felix Salmon, "BuzzFeed's Jonah Peretti Goes Long," *Matter* (June 11, 2014), accessed November 21, 2015, https://medium.com/matter/buzzfeeds-jonah-peretti-goes-long -e98cfl3160e7.
2. Jonah Peretti, "Capitalism and Schizophrenia: Contemporary Visual Culture and the Acceleration of Identity Formulation/Dissolution," *Negations* (1996), accessed November 21, 2015, http://www.datawranglers.com/negations/issues/96w/96w _peretti.html.
3. Interview with Summer Anne Burton, conducted by author, June 23, 2014.
4. Interview with Matthew Perpetua, conducted by author, September 4, 2015.
5. Don Peck, "They're Watching You at Work," *The Atlantic* (December 2013), accessed November 21, 2015, http://www.theatlantic.com/magazine/archive/2013/12/theyre -watching-you-at-work/354681/.
6. Jenna Johnson, "Donald Trump would 'certainly' and 'absolutely' create a database of Muslims," *Washington Post* (November 20, 2015), accessed November 29, 2015, https://www.washingtonpost.com/news/post-politics/wp/2015/11/20/donald-trump -would-certainly-and-absolutely-create-a-database-of-muslims/.
7. Whyte, *The Organization Man*, 179.

■ ■ ■

Reading as a Writer: Analyzing Rhetorical Choices

1. Why do you think Kindley includes several paragraphs about the background of BuzzFeed founder Jonah Peretti (paras. 8–11)? How do the details in Peretti's professional history relate to Kindley's argument about the functions of BuzzFeed quizzes?

2. Mark the paragraphs in which Kindley focuses on millennials. How does this generation demonstrate his argument about the intersection of identity formation and consumerism? To what extent do you agree with his claims?

Writing as a Reader: Entering the Conversation of Ideas

1. Kindley and Melissa Avdeeff (pp. 495–506) are both interested in the intersections of technology and identity formation. Where do you stand in this complex and fascinating conversation? Drawing on insights from both authors and perhaps your own experience, write an essay that makes a point about the relationship between technology and identity.

2. The many ways group identity or a sense of community can be fostered online is a fascination for both Kindley and Mark Hain (pp. 525–41). Write an essay of your own that builds on these writers' insights to make a point about the strengths and shortcomings of technology as a communal space.

WILLIAM POWERS

Not So Busy

William Powers studied history and literature as an undergraduate and went on to work as a Senate staff member and then as an investigative journalist and columnist. His writing on the intersections of media and politics has appeared widely, including in *The Washington Post*, *The Atlantic*, and in the column he founded on the media for *The New Republic*.

This reading is a chapter from his book *Hamlet's Blackberry: A Practical Philosophy for Building a Good Life in the Digital Age*. In his second paragraph, Powers sets out his argument, noting that despite the allure of digital connectivity, "If we continue on the current path, over time the costs of this life will erase all the benefits." In this piece he draws on insights from philosophers to propose we rethink our relationship to digital devices so we can "use them to live in a more thoughtful, intentional way" (para 2).

Consider the big questions Powers raises in paragraph 6 about the downfalls of being so "connected," starting with "Why don't I have time to think?" You might even pause to discuss those questions before you read further to reflect on your own senses of what's good—and bad—about technology. Anyone who has ever lost a cell phone or been unexpectedly unable to get a signal can relate to our cultural expectations that being hyperconnected is simply what it means to be human now. Powers wants us to consider whether we can "thrive" in these conditions.

The main body of this piece is structured around his list of seven key historical figures: Plato, Seneca, Gutenberg, Shakespeare, Franklin,

Thoreau, and McLuhan. Take a few moments to look up these people (or divide up the task among your class). What do you notice about this list? As you read, keep track of the key ideas Powers draws from each figure as he builds his case for why we should use technology differently and less. Which of these suggestions speaks to you most and why? Do any seem impossible? If so, why?

Powers makes a point about living meaningfully in the present and stretching your own inner resources in ways that connect to all the other chapters in this reader. Our relationship to technology affects our educations, our media and product consumption, our natural environment, our interactions with others, and our understandings of ourselves. Powers is no technophobe, nor does he self-righteously argue that we should give up technology altogether. He does, however, challenge readers to consider that digital connectivity might have serious costs. Reflecting on history, he argues, could be the key to a thriving future.

■ ■ ■

T hus far into this new era, we've followed a clear-cut approach: we've *1* set out to be as connected as possible, all the time. For most of us, this was not a conscious decision. We did it without really thinking about it, not realizing there was any choice in the matter.

We did have a choice and still do. And because how we live with these *2* devices is a choice, this conundrum is really a philosophical one. It's a matter of the ideas and principles that guide us. If we continue on the current path, over time the costs of this life will erase all the benefits. The answer, therefore, is to adopt a new set of ideas and use them to live in a more thoughtful, intentional way.

There are clues all around us. Whenever I open a gap between myself *3* and my screens, good things happen. I have time and space to think about my life in the digital realm and all the people and information I encounter there. I have a chance to take the outward experiences of the screen back inward. This happened in a small but memorable way the day I called my mother en route to the airport. It was just a routine call, until I put the phone down. Only then did the experience take on unexpected richness and significance.

Such gaps also allow our awareness to return to the physical world. *4* I'm not just a brain, a pair of eyes, and typing fingers. I'm a person with a living body that moves through space and time. In letting screens run my life, I discount the rest of my existence, effectively renouncing my own wholeness. I live a lesser life and give less back to the world. This problem is not just individual and private; it's afflicting all our collective endeavors, in business, schools, and government and at every level of society. We're *living* less and *giving* less, and the world is the worse for it.

This is the moment, while the digital age is still young, to recoup these *5* losses, to bring "all that is human around us," in Google chairman Eric Schmidt's words, back into the equation.

With that aim, in Part II [earlier in Powers's book], I went back into 6 the database of human experience in search of helpful ideas. As the seven philosophers showed, this conundrum is as old as civilization. As human connectedness advances, it always makes life busier, by creating new crowds. And life in the crowd inevitably gives rise to the questions we're asking right now: Why don't I have time to think? What's this lost, restless feeling I can't seem to shake? Where does the crowd end, and where do I begin? What are these tools doing to us, and can we fix it?

The philosophers offered all sort of answers, and a number of themes 7 emerged. The most important was the need to strike a healthy balance between connected and disconnected, crowd and self, the outward life and the inward one.

One might argue that civilization always survives such transitions and 8 moves on, so why worry? Of course we'll survive. The question is whether we'll do more than that. In all the earlier periods we've looked at, there were people who thrived and found happiness and people who didn't. The former found something approximating the happy equilibrium Socrates was seeking when he prayed that his outward and inward selves might "be at one." The latter became hostage to their outwardness and never shook "the restless energy of a hunted mind."

Below is a review of the key points along with more concrete ideas 9 about how they might be applied today. The examples are drawn primarily from my own life and experience, because that's what I know. These are suggestions, not prescriptions. Everyone's circumstances are unique, and there's no best approach to this challenge. The purpose of this exercise is to help you develop strategies of your own. Awareness is half the battle, and *any* effort, no matter how small, counts as progress.

1. Plato

Principle: Distance

In Plato's story, Socrates and his friend put the busyness of Athens behind 10 them just by taking a walk. Physical distance is the oldest method of crowd control. In one obvious sense, today it's much harder to go outside the "walls" of the connected life. Truly disconnected places are increasingly rare. But in another way, it's easier. Take a walk without a digital gadget, and distance is yours. The moment you leave all screens behind, you're outside the walls.

Why isn't this a common practice already? Because taking a mobile 11 along seems so harmless and, indeed, sensible. We have acquired a sense that it's dangerous to venture out without one, as though we could never fend for ourselves. It's *nice* to have your digital friend along with you, just in case.

In subtle but important ways, however, it changes the nature of the 12 experience. Though a smart phone brings convenience and a sense of security, it takes away the possibility of true separateness. It's a psychic leash, and the mind can feel it tugging. That's the problem: we've gotten so used to the tug, it's hard to imagine life without it.

To create the modern equivalent of ancient distance and enjoy the *13* benefits it brings, you have to put screens out of reach. Leave the phone in a drawer and walk out the door. Nothing bad is going to happen, and something good just might. Though your disconnected walk might not produce a Socrates-style rapture, it will yield a new sense of inner freedom. Strolling along a city street surrounded by people bent over screens, just knowing *you're* going "commando" puts a spring in your step.

The same underlying principle can be applied to other everyday expe- *14* riences. Any quick journey out into the world, even the most mundane errand, can double as a miniescape, as long as you have no screen. At the other extreme, try the extended version: an out-of-town holiday. Put on your vacation auto-reply, leave all connective devices at home, and resolve not to check once, even if the opportunity presents itself. Pick a destination, grab a companion, and make a digital escape. If there's a screen at the inn, give it a wide berth.

A few winters ago, *Condé Nast Traveler* magazine[1] sent three report- *15* ers to Moscow, one equipped with a BlackBerry, one with an iPhone, and one with just a hard-copy guidebook. They were given a series of tourist challenges to complete in the frigid metropolis, such as finding a great cheap restaurant and locating a pharmacy open at midnight. The low-tech contestant won. After the article ran, one reader wrote in: "I have traveled successfully around the world armed with nothing more than a dog-eared guidebook and a friendly smile.... As any seasoned traveler will tell you, the kindness of strangers can be relied upon anywhere. Just don't be too absorbed in your BlackBerry to notice."

Meanwhile, distance in the old-fashioned sense hasn't completely lost *16* its meaning. There *are* still places where it's hard or impossible to find a digital connection of any kind, including remote parts of the continental United States. Take every opportunity to enjoy them, because they won't be around forever. In my family, when we're considering vacation possibilities and summer camps, we perk up when we hear there's no mobile phone or Internet service. Though it's increasingly common for airplane flights to have wireless Internet, not all do. If there's a fee for the service, save your money. You'll be getting a much more valuable amenity—distance from your own connectedness—for free.

2. Seneca

Principle: Inner Space

When physical distance either wasn't available or didn't do the trick, *17* Seneca found inner distance. He did so by focusing on one idea or person and tuning out the rest of the world. Today minimizing the crowd is an even more essential skill, and there are more ways to practice it. The first and most obvious is to choose a friend or family member in your physical vicinity and just have a conversation. A focused, undistracted chat, without screens. It's so obvious, it seems absurd to recommend it. But are we *really* talking to each other anymore? If the person you've focused on has a screen, gently ask him or her to put it aside. What you'll be saying, in effect, is: *I want to be with just you.* It's a rarely heard sentiment these days, and it shouldn't be.

Though letter writing is a dying art, there are plenty of other activities 18 that afford the easygoing absorption of the "flow" state. Especially helpful is anything that involves working with the hands, such as splitting wood, knitting, cooking, or tinkering with a car engine or a bicycle.

We can also minimize the crowd right on the screen, and though it 19 won't bring the inner distance that happens offline, it can help. How many Web pages and other windows do you keep open on your screen at a time? Do you shop online while instant messaging while composing e-mails while randomly checking out videos while playing a game on the side? Try the opposite approach: limit yourself to one screen activity at a time, and don't use the screen to wander away from a phone chat. The person on the other end is to you as Lucilius was to Seneca.

Another strategy for reducing time online is to start using *other peo-* 20 *ple* as your search engines. Rather than constantly checking for news and updates, I let friends and family tell me what's happening. What are the headlines? Which movie star is in trouble? What's the latest outrage on the political front? It's more enjoyable listening to the latest developments through the interpretive lens of a person you know, and it saves a lot of trouble.

Somehow, we've gotten it into our heads that the best use of social- 21 networking technologies is to acquire as many friends and contacts as possible, jamming everyone we know into the same virtual space. Thus, that barely remembered "pal" from elementary school who resurfaced a few weeks ago gets to mix and gossip with our current friends from the office—great.

Back when the Internet was a thrilling novelty, there was a natural ten- 22 dency to make the most of it by constantly expanding your social connections. Now that much of the human race is online, it makes sense to move in the other direction. Whenever possible, narrow and refine the crowd. While I was writing this book and trying not to be needlessly distracted, I had just one active social network, dedicated solely to a small group of people (less than two dozen) whom I knew during one brief but important period of my life—*and no one else.* Of course, there are endless ways to form smaller groups within online networks, and you don't want to overdo it. Too many subgroups becomes as complex as too many individuals. But, if used intelligently, this tactic can reduce the digital horde to more manageable slices. Rather than firing up my screen and being confronted by everyone I ever knew, when I went to my micro-network, a more intimate group was always waiting for me. *Ah, here's the old gang.* It was the screen equivalent of a neighborhood pub.

3. Gutenberg

Principle: Technologies of Inwardness

Gutenberg made one of the great tools of inwardness, books, available to 23 more people. Could today's technological innovators pull off an equivalent trick with the devices of this moment? The need for inwardness is as great, if not greater. Yet now all the momentum in technology is in the opposite direction, toward *more* intense connectedness, increasing our exposure to the crowd. "All your applications. All at once" said the ad for one handheld,[2] as if "all at once" were helpful to the mind.

The e-book experience is moving in the same direction. Though often 24 touted as a giant step forward, some e-readers are designed to make the experience of reading more outward. Effectively minicomputers with built-in e-mail and Web browsers, they make it much harder to go inward as a reader. Do we really want to make our books as busy as the rest of our lives?

The Gutenberg principle could be applied to many other digital 25 devices, including the notebook computer. If I want to shut out distractions and really get some work done on my notebook, I turn off the wireless, transforming the computer into a disconnected tool. Unfortunately, on my notebook this is a somewhat cumbersome process involving multiple keys. Digital technologies should acknowledge in their design that it's sometimes good to be disconnected. A small but helpful fix would be to provide a prominent Disconnect button that would allow the user to go back and forth easily between the two zones, connected and not. Today, as in the fifteenth century, everyone needs time away from the crowd. Technology should serve that need.

4. Shakespeare

Principle: Old Tools Ease Overload

In the early print era, handwriting didn't go out of style, it came on strong. 26 As Hamlet's "handheld" shows, old tools can be an effective way to bring the information overload of new ones under control. Today older technologies continue to ground the busy mind.

Paper is the best example. Since the middle of the twentieth century, 27 futurists have been predicting the imminent demise of paper. It hasn't happened, because paper is still a useful tool. It's arguably becoming *more* useful, since it offers exactly what we need and crave, a little disconnect-edness. Read a paper book. Keep a journal or just jot notes in a simple notebook, as I do in my Moleskine. Subscribe to a new magazine. In a mul-titasking world where pure focus is harder and harder to come by, paper's seclusion from the Web is an emerging strength. There's nothing like hold-ing a sheaf of beautifully designed pages in your hands. The whole world slows down, and your mind with it.

Don't assume that the newest tools are the best choice for a given task. 28 One year at Eastertime, our son decided to make a drawing for the fam-ily gathering at my mother's house. Since he wanted to print a copy for everyone, he headed straight for his iMac and a drawing program called Kid Pix. Wait a second, we said. If he did it at the kitchen table by hand with colored markers, he'd have a lot more artistic freedom. Then he could copy it on his color printer. (He'd also be away from Internet temptations, but we didn't mention that.) He thought about it for a moment and agreed that markers are more fun and expressive. It came out beautifully, and he proclaimed, "Kid Pix isn't very good, anyway."

Old tools are plain fun. As virtual life weighs down on us, material 29 objects paradoxically begin to seem light and playful. Vinyl records not only *do* sound better, they're fascinating to handle and ponder. I take yo-yo breaks in my office. Dominoes and marbles have become a draw. Board games can be bliss.

5. Franklin

Principle: Positive Rituals

Ben Franklin brought order to his chaotic life with a ritual based on 30 positive goals. While he was shooting for "moral perfection," we can aim for the more modest goals of clarity and calm. I've already discussed workplace applications of the Franklin approach, but it applies equally to private life, where there are endless possibilities for finding balance through rituals. Rather than just restricting your own screen time, set time limits and rewards. Somehow, when the battery is running down on a laptop, it's much easier not to be distracted from the task at hand. This behavioral fact can be translated into a ritual. Vow to finish all screen tasks by a given time, with a reward if you make it. You'll get more done, reduce your connected time, and earn a bonus.

Another approach is to keep certain hours of the day screen-free. In 31 *The Tyranny of E-mail*,[3] John Freeman recommends not checking your e-mail early in the morning or late at night, practices he rightly notes cre-ate a "workaholic cycle." Of the morning in particular, he writes, "Not checking your e-mail first thing will also reinforce a boundary between your work and your private life, which is essential if you want to be fully present in either place."

Indeed, rituals aimed at offsetting one's digital life don't need to be 32
explicitly *about* digital devices at all. They can be entirely about the positive alternatives. If you've noticed that too many of your evening hours are
given over to the screen, resolve to do something completely different and
appealing with half of those hours—spend more time with your spouse or
partner, study the constellations with a child, or take that Italian cooking
course you've been fantasizing about. Design the ritual around the amount
of time dedicated to the new positive pursuit, rather than how much you're
taking away from the old negative one. Granted, these are just mind tricks,
but it's the mind's own unhelpful tricks that we're trying to combat.

6. Thoreau

Principle: Walden Zones

In the middle of the bustling nineteenth century, and relatively close to 33
the crowd, Thoreau created a zone of inner simplicity and peace. Any
digital home can serve the same purpose, if properly organized, and there
are countless zoning variations. Such spaces don't have to be all about
silence and contemplation, which can suggest (especially to children) that
offline time is boring. Children should learn that the screen isn't the only
place where the action is. If you have a quiet Walden Zone, try to offset
it with a loud one, i.e., a space that's both offline *and* rowdy. These can
also be established outside the house itself. After all, Thoreau's project was
a backyard experiment. Any backyard can be designed as a haven from
digital gadgets, a place where the main event is nature itself. The ultimate
Walden Zone is a tree house.

As technologies converge toward a future in which one screen will 34
offer all varieties of content—from movies to television to social networking to texting—it might be wise to zone different parts of the home for different *kinds* of screen experiences. Many of us already do this in a de facto
way. One room for movies and television-style entertainment best enjoyed
in groups, at a distance from the screen, and separate spaces for the close-
to-the-screen digital experiences we now associate with computers. It's
worth recognizing that these are very distinct activities, which naturally
offset each other—the relaxation of television versus the nervousness of
keyboard tasks—and it can prove useful to maintain the distinction, so
there are clear options within each home.

The Thoreau principle has applications far beyond the private home. 35
There are already Walden Zones in public places—the quiet car on the
train is one, but it's about sound rather than screens. Theaters, museums,
and some restaurants ask patrons to turn off their devices. Though most
schools have been increasing the intensity of their students' connectedness in the last decades, some forward-thinking educators have been creating disconnected environments within their schools for nondigital play
and contemplation. Educator Lowell Monke[4] writes that such spaces "give

children the opportunity to withdraw from the ceaseless noise of high-tech life and do the kinds of things that their childish nature calls them to do." As long as screens continue to proliferate, this countertrend should only build.

Offline coffee shops? No-screen health clubs? Perhaps a revival 36 of the old Prohibition-era "speakeasy" concept in the form of secret, password-only hangouts for digital fugitives.

7. McLuhan

Principle: Lower the Inner Thermostat

McLuhan said that, even in a busy electronic world, each of us can regulate 37 the quality of our experience. Study the maelstrom that is your busy life, and come up with your own creative ways of escape. An acquaintance of mine cooled down his connectedness by getting rid of his smart phone and returning to a basic cell phone, thus removing e-mails and Internet from his mobile existence. It was "an incredible relief," he says, but there was one problem: he's a huge baseball fan, and losing the smart phone meant he couldn't follow his favorite team on the other side of the country as faithfully. Solution: he found a way to listen to the distant radio coverage via his low-end phone. It not only works beautifully, he reports, but also takes him back to the way he listened to games as a boy.

Our efforts to escape the chaos of digital life don't have to be desperate 38 and arduous.... "Accidentally" leave your mobile at home when you go out on the weekend, just to see how everyone reacts when they can't reach you. Have a disconnected party where all devices are confiscated at the door. At a chain supermarket where we often shop, digital screens have been installed everywhere, blaring nonstop ads. Sometimes, when nobody's looking, I reach up and flick one off.

Though McLuhan focused on technology over content, the fact is that 39 choosing your content wisely can be a huge help. For instance, having your mind extended out into the world all day in McLuhanesque fashion takes its toll. Thinking globally is exhausting. One way of reining in the overextended mind is to pay closer attention to *local* media content. Instead of always tracking distant happenings, develop a habit of bringing your awareness back home on a regular basis. Make the screen experience less expansive by choosing one good local news site or blog and following it. Listen to local radio channels. Buy a regional newspaper and take it home. Go out and shoot the breeze with a neighbor. The burgeoning "locavore" movement, which promotes consumption of locally raised food, should have a screen equivalent. Escape the global village for your own village, even if it happens to be one square block of a huge city.

And once you *have* that village, here's an idea: organize get-togethers 40 for trading tips about the tools of modern life. At a "SkillShare" event held in our area, people came together to make the digital era a little more collaborative and humane. A story in the next day's newspaper summed it up: "An eighth-grader taught the Nintendo Wii system, two high school boys lectured on Facebook and cellphone features, while a middle-aged man demonstrated how to cut meat."[5] If *that's* a glimpse of the future, we'll all be fine. . . .

Technology makes the world feel smaller than it really is. There are all *41* kinds of rooms in all kinds of places. Every space is what you make it. But in the end, building a good life isn't about where you are. It's about how you decide to think and live. Place your index finger on your temple and tap twice. It's all in there.

NOTES

1. "Get Smart? Testing the iPhone and the Blackberry Bold," *Condé Nast Traveler*, June 2009. Follow-up letter from Becca Podell published in the August 2009 issue.
2. Online ad for the Palm Pre.
3. John Freeman, *The Tyranny of E-Mail* (New York: Scribner's, 2009), pp. 208–10.
4. Lowell Monke, "Unplugged Schools," *Orion*, September/October 2007, www .orionmagazine.org.
5. K. C. Myers, "Have a Skill? Please Share!" *Cape Cod Times*, October 4, 2009, p. A1.

■ ■ ■

Reading as a Writer: Analyzing Rhetorical Choices

1. Select one of the writers Powers features in his list and weigh the claims against your own experiences. How challenging would it be to make the suggested changes in lifestyle and habits and why?

2. What do you make of the fact that Powers selects only men in his list of historical figures we can learn from? Suggest a few other big thinkers from history (or the present) who might bring diversity to this list, and explain what their ideas might offer people who are reconsidering their use of technology.

Writing as a Reader: Entering the Conversation of Ideas

1. Powers and Sherry Turkle (pp. 578–92) are in conversation about the potential problems of online life. Take your place in this timely conversation by writing an essay in which you assess the shortcomings and advantages of online experiences, drawing on these authors' claims and examples of your own. Ultimately, where do you stand on how technology affects our sense of ourselves and our communities?

2. Powers's ideas have implications for many aspects of our lives. In relation to Powers's claims, consider the readings in Chapter 3 by Clive Thompson (pp. 70–72) and Tom Standage (pp. 80–86) and readings in Chapter 4 by Dana Radcliffe (pp. 88–91) and Susan Blum (pp. 105–7). In an essay of your own about the positive and negative aspects of digital life, draw on Powers's claims and one or two of these other authors to stake your own position in this debate.

MARK HAIN

"We Are Here for You": The It Gets Better Project, Queering Rural Space, and Cultivating Queer Media Literacy

Mark Hain earned his PhD in communications and culture and has published research on video texts and early cinema. This reading is from the anthology *Queering the Countryside: New Frontiers in Rural Queer Studies* (2016). The book addresses the gap in research on the lives of rural people who identify as LGBTQ+ (an acronym for: lesbian, gay, bisexual, transgender, queer/questioning, and other gender identities or sexual orientations beyond cisgender heterosexuality). Gay culture and history often focus on the lives of urban dwellers; this book and this essay instead examine the unique experiences of those who live and find meaning in rural spaces.

Before you read, you might pause to think about or discuss what you know about the many "It Gets Better" videos available on YouTube. You may be surprised to hear there are more than fifty thousand of these videos on the It Gets Better Project station (para. 2). Do you know about the events that prompted this project? While many of those videos are produced by media stars, Hain's interest is in the nonfamous people—particularly rural-dwellers—who share their stories through this medium: "The project therefore not only archives individual stories but also documents an alternative history, telling a collective story of enduring and overcoming adversity, as communicated by a multicultural, multiperspectival, intergenerational and international range of voices" (para. 3). What does each of those adjectives mean in relation to these videos?

This essay is divided into five sections, with headings that explain the purpose of each section or "chunk" of information. As you read, pay attention to this organizational structure, and consider how the ideas and examples in each section are related to the specific heading as well as to the larger purpose of the article. Hain sets out his central argument and his method of providing examples in paragraph 4. You might return to that paragraph as you read to keep connecting Hain's many examples, which include media pop stars like Annie Lennox of the Eurythmics and nonfamous people like Krissy Mahan who have used DIY videos to reach new populations (para. 37).

In Hain's conclusion, he addresses the "so what?" question that every writer should answer in relation to the value of the argument. He invites readers to consider "how media can most productively be exploited by vulnerable individuals" (para. 43), using "exploited" to mean used to its fullest potential. As you read (and reread) this essay, consider how your own relationship to media—produced by both famous people and nonfamous people—has been important to developing your identity and sense of belonging. What "alternative histories" have been important to you and which ones might you write?

Throughout autumn of 2010, a distressingly large number of reports *1*
made national news of teenage boys, either out as gay or perceived
as gay by their peers, who had committed suicide after having been the
targets of sustained anti-gay bullying, in some cases for years. Harassment
and violence against gay youth became the focus of considerable media
attention and purported social concern—for a brief while. The It Gets Better Project, created in September 2011 by advice columnist Dan Savage
and his husband, Terry Miller, was intended as a more lasting response to
the suicides and the circumstances that caused them. Savage and Miller
initiated the project by posting a video of themselves on YouTube, in which
they told their stories of being picked on and bullied during their adolescence, but promising queer youth that "it gets better" and urging them not
to give in to despair.

As its own YouTube channel, the It Gets Better Project now offers view- *2*
ers over fifty thousand video messages of support, as well as opportunities
to add commentary and upload video messages of their own. In total, the
videos have been viewed over fifty million times.[1] While numerous celebrities and politicians, including President Barack Obama, have added their
voices, "everyday" people have contributed most of the videos, including
the most emotionally resonant ones. The project has thus become a forum
for redirecting sorrow, frustration, and rage into well-intentioned messages of hope.

The It Gets Better (IGB) Project has also become an archive of memo- *3*
ries and emotions underrepresented in other media. In her important study
on the intersection of affect and archiving in lesbian public cultures, Ann
Cvetkovich recognizes LGBT people's need to "address trauma through
witnessing and retelling."[2] As so many of the IGB videos attest, emotional
and/or physical trauma appears to be a virtually inescapable component
of life for queer children and adolescents—a trauma that Cvetkovich sees,
in spite of the pain of recollection, as "a point of entry into a vast archive
of feelings, the many forms of love, rage, intimacy, grief, shame, and more
that are part of the vibrancy of queer cultures"[3] and that unify individuals
across contexts of culture, place, and time. Thousands of LGBT people
have told their own stories of mistreatment, struggles with depression, or
suicide attempts through IGB videos, sharing their experiences, good as
well as bad, as a way of encouraging others through difficult life stages.
The project therefore not only archives individual stories but also documents an alternative history, telling a collective story of enduring and overcoming adversity, as communicated by a multicultural, multiperspectival,
intergenerational, and international range of voices. At the same time, it
also records a historical moment in which reevaluation of the past, personal as well as societal, becomes a way of collaboratively negotiating the
present and striving to better the future.

The mass catharsis chronicled by the project externalizes and makes *4*
more visible the internal, individual processes of negotiating difference
that LGBT people undertook long before the advent of new media and

social networking. This essay examines the differences, but more importantly the similarities, in what new and "old" media provide gay and lesbian audiences in terms of identity construction, emotional support, and hope. I will explore how a specifically queer form of media literacy—the exercising of greater control over one's interaction with mediated messages and exerting more agency in the meanings one extracts from media texts—can help gay and lesbian youth in rural environments locate and create queer space, even if only interior space. Looking at the messages explicitly and implicitly conveyed by IGB videos addressed to gay and lesbian youth, I supplement these case studies with my own experiences of popular music sustaining me through difficult times during my adolescence and coming out in 1980s Nebraska. I locate a substantive distinction in how commercial media and user-generated media alter perceptions of celebrity and the "sexual imaginary," the embodied reassurance described by Kath Weston that someone else "like me" is "out there somewhere." The IGB videos created by rural gay men and lesbians for rural gay and lesbian youth emphasize that queer presence, even if hidden, is already *there*, as opposed to the commercial media in which I was vested as a teenager and which further alienated me from my environment. With these matters in mind, my intent is to think through some of the "survival strategies" that may be available to rural gay and lesbian youth whose circumstances do not allow them to leave problematic environments by observing how IGB videos and viewer responses contribute to a repository of coping mechanisms by queering rural spaces and depicting accessible sexual imaginaries.

In many ways, this essay is also an externalization of the self-reflection 5 and impulse towards autoethnography prompted by the It Gets Better Project and the tragic events behind its formation. As the stories and photos of Justin Aaberg, Asher Brown, Raymond Chase, Tyler Clementi, Billy Lucas, Seth Walsh, and the other young people driven to suicide circulated through the media, I, like many, recognized a disconcerting amount of myself in their stories and their faces. That recognition compelled me, again like many, to revisit dark places in my memories. Rather than just dredging up the hurts of the past, personal as well as collective, or losing hope because of the challenge these deaths pose to a sense that things may actually be "getting better" at a societal level, I contend that pondering the questions of "how *we* made it through" may yet give us insight into ways that we might be able to improve the circumstances of young people who are labeled "different" by their communities, peers, and families.

Getting What You Can: Queer Media Literacy

My focus on ways queer youth in rural areas might use media to their 6 benefit is not meant to suggest that popular culture and the media are necessarily the most productive means of alleviating loneliness and anxiety or of attaining a sense of self-worth and hope. Nonetheless, I contend that idiosyncratic engagement with popular cultural artifacts can have positive effects on the lives of young people who are made to feel like outsiders. In times and places where any sense of "gay community" is absent, media texts and consumer cultural products may be the only means by which some young people begin a process of negotiating queer identity. Moreover, social conditions in which queer youth are made to feel excluded or threatened often lead to periods of isolation in which engagement with media may take the place of interaction with peers. In this vacuum of human contact, overinvestment is likely, with media assuming a position of tremendous influence and impact, and the capacity to both help and harm. This alone means that queer use of the media is a topic of pressing concern.

Cultivation of self-fulfilling queer media literacy, however, requires *7* more than using media texts like a life raft in treacherous waters. The crucial matter, I argue, is developing awareness of media uses that include, but also extend beyond, pleasure, solace, identification, or even establishing connections with others, leading instead to explorations and determinations of self-representation. Amateur-created IGB videos in particular model a vital component of this exploration by showing media use as a way of re-presenting, disseminating, and archiving what one deems meaningful — including one's own history and perspectives.

The sincerity and good will of most IGB videos are abundantly appar- *8* ent, yet there are many problematic aspects, especially for rural queer youth. One of the criticisms leveled against the IGB campaign has been its frequent variations on a "just stick it out" theme. While this is not to dismiss the importance of the user-created videos, which offer powerfully affecting words of hope and empowerment that may indeed save lives, it is to endorse at least thinking about something more we might offer young people in crisis than "wait." To thirteen-year-olds like Seth Walsh or Asher Brown, the prospect of five years of "sticking it out" may seem beyond endurance.

Further, a message communicated very clearly in many of these videos *9* reinscribes a familiar belief that part of getting *better* is getting *out* of the narrow-minded rural area, the oppressive small town, the unenlightened "flyover" states, because happiness, acceptance, self-fulfillment, and others like you are to be found only in coastal urban centers.[4] The idea that life for LGBT people is better in cities has been accepted as axiomatic, and for many it may be true. However, the ubiquity of this message can also do a great disservice to LGBT people living in environments consistently represented as hell on earth for queer people.[5] "Escaping" to someplace else is a matter inextricably bound to issues of class, education, family relations and obligations, age, and other factors that may root individuals in rural areas, small towns, or conservative central states. With limited options, the sense of isolation and of feeling trapped can only be compounded by the implication that there must be something wrong with the gay person who does not migrate to the city, further alienating those who are already othered by heteronormativity.

Reflecting broader patterns of neglect by the media, the voices of *10* people in these environments remain underrepresented in IGB videos. Because of the sheer number and variety of these videos, however, they are a particularly informative means for addressing questions about how place, sexuality, and sense of self coalesce in queer use of mass media, including an individual's ability to mine media texts for coping responses. In her valuable study of queer rural youth's engagement with media, Mary L. Gray finds that her informants not only "search online to determine what's 'expected' of queer boys and girls,"[6] but also use media technologies to strategize how to "bring home" performances of queer identity, "anchor them locally, and transform them into experiences of self/senses of identity that can and do happen to youth 'just like them.'"[7] IGB videos provide ample material for this kind of exploration—indeed, it seems to be precisely the intent of most of the noncelebrity videos.

The opportunities afforded by current communications technologies *11* and social networking make acts of self-depiction, "talking back" to the dominant culture, and personalized archiving more apparent, and arguably more accessible to a wider range of participants. Such activity, though, has a long and important place amongst LGBT groups and individuals, as evidenced by the rich but often hidden history of queer lives and cultures—a history that would easily have been lost if people had not taken matters into their own hands to collect, archive, and preserve remembrances and artifacts ignored by institutional entities. Whether tangible or virtual, artifacts, memories, and stories take on a particularly queer cast, I contend, in moments of contextualization and reception that complicate standard assumptions about the past and open history up to reinterpretation and reuse. The engagement with memory and history so prominent in many of the videos prompts consideration of the past's impact on the present, and of older generations of LGBT people's capacity to affect the lives of younger generations. IGB videos have the potential to elicit this kind of consideration, and perhaps some aspect of my own remembrances might, too.

Sweet Dreams (of Somewhere Else): Identity Formation and Popular Culture

Media texts that connect us with historical representations may provide *12* access to a queer usable past, as well as resources for identity work. Historical inquiry, however, is reduced to cold statistics and speculations if it does not maintain some sense of the historical individual. Although we can never know each unique history of how all queer people made their way through adversity and invented their sense of self, we *can* listen to the stories audible all around us and extrapolate how social, political, historical, regional, and mediated influences have established parameters enabling or impeding acts of self-determination.

The time and place of my adolescence had a strong influence on how *13* I understood and apprehensively, falteringly, but eventually accepted what it meant to be gay. I grew up and went to school in a semirural suburb of Omaha. Farmland was within walking and olfactory distance. I am just one generation off the farm myself; my father's large family were farmers in a predominantly Catholic, Czech, and conservative part of Nebraska. From earliest memory, I recall experiences and sensations, both positive and negative, from time spent in the small towns where my parents grew up.

As is the case with too many queer kids of any time or place, my high *14* school years were difficult. Teenagers, as many gay and lesbian youth become painfully aware, seem to have a distressingly acute gaydar, which can manifest in attack. I got harassed, humiliated, tripped, pushed, hit, and—it goes without saying—called "fag" and other slurs. I had bouts of suicidal thoughts, but fears of hurting my parents, eternal damnation, or screwing it up and living on in some even more damaged state stayed my hand more than any sense of hope for the future.

The time and place of coming out to myself also heightened a reliance *15* on popular culture, particularly music, as emotional support. Records, the radio, music videos, and my favorite stars provided a glimpse of a wider, thrillingly weirder world. Rock culture, transmitted through magazines, posters, buttons, T-shirts, and other promotional ephemera almost as much as recordings and videos, was the primary source of queer representation for me, albeit mediated through a thick filter of ambiguity, codedness, and equivocation. Significant scholarly attention has been paid to the larger cultural effects wrought by the AIDS crisis and its prevalence in the media of the 1980s. News reports, made-for-TV movies, and tabloid sensationalism brought homosexuality into average Americans' living rooms. A far less explored matter, however, is the part popular music and music video played in bringing gays into the media spotlight in this period, although often in such a way that homosexuality was equated with gender transgression.

The visual and stylistic images of many 1980s pop stars involved cross- *16* dressing or adoption of an androgynous appearance. In the mainstream press, performers such as Boy George of Culture Club, Annie Lennox of Eurythmics, Grace Jones, Prince, and so-called "hairspray metal" bands like Twisted Sister and Poison, were all labeled "gender benders." While many of these gender bender pop stars were heterosexual, their transgender or gender ambiguous appearance marked them as queer. These stars' teasing suggestion of minority sexuality riled conservative sensibilities, while appearing overly coy and irresponsibly evasive to supporters of gay and lesbian equality. But they could also be a well-spring of fascination and inspiration to people who responded favorably to the music and image of these performers—people such as myself.

I became perhaps overly invested in what my taste in music said about me, not only to others, but also to myself. Already somewhat conscious of living out a gay stereotype, I was particularly drawn to New Wave "divas" such as Siouxsie Sioux, Kate Bush, Lene Lovich, and Nina Hagen—but none more so than Annie Lennox, for whom I harbored something close to mad adoration.[8] Lennox's image and inventive play with gender and identity embodied the fabulous and cosmopolitan, the implacably cool, the sexy yet slightly sinister traits that were so desirable but seemingly unattainable to a gangly fourteen-year-old Nebraskan with untamable cowlicks and oversized glasses.

Adolescence is a crucial period of identity formation, and at a time when little else is within their control, many individuals gain a sense of agency from choosing their likes or dislikes in commercial media. Assertion of choice in one's engagement with cultural products becomes a way of figuring things out, looking at the world, recognizing and rejecting certain ideologies, imagining the self, and locating a sense of self-worth in a time and place where some audiences may be starving for any remotely positive representation of "difference." In a safe yet still meaningful act of identity work, the intensity of my attachment to Lennox increased as I became aware that most of my peers regarded her as a "freak," prompting me to "own" and feel better about my own freakishness.

Pioneering gay media scholar Richard Dyer provides some ideas by which I have attempted to better understand my adolescent fascination with Lennox. According to Dyer, audiences prone to experiencing "a peculiarly intense degree of role/identity conflict and pressure" and a sense of exclusion from the dominant cultural order often form more intense "relationships" with stars. He specifically mentions both adolescent and gay audiences as among those who might find special significance in their attachment to certain stars.[9] Although stars are commodities whose range of meanings marketplace conventions attempt to constrain, queer media literacy involves being able to adapt and repurpose popular culture to fulfill needs and desires ignored or ineptly addressed by the marketplace. Describing stars as inadvertently open signifiers, Dyer regards the polysemy of their images as raw material "that an oppressed group can take up and use to cobble together its own culture."[10] This is significant considering Dyer's argument that stars, as embodiments of social categories such as race, gender, and sexual orientation, are never able to completely erase the ambiguities, instabilities, and contradictions of categorization, which, in turn, furthers their usefulness to marginalized groups.

In many ways, I regard my adolescent devotion to popular music as contributing positively to my emotional stability and sense of self. "My" music was a refuge, a respite from a cultural surround, exemplified for me by John "Cougar" Mellencamp's odious and omnipresent paean to small-town heteronormativity, "Jack and Diane," that seemed intent on invalidating the person I was growing to be. Because commercial media prohibited open acknowledgement of actual homosexuality, however, even with readably gay performers like Boy George, Morrissey or the B-52s, I could not look to pop stars as sites of identification or even sexual imaginaries.

Explaining the role of media in creating the sexual imaginary, Weston *21* notes the greater diversity of media texts within urban areas. Significantly many of these texts that help to create a sense of the sexual imaginary also suggest that life for gays and lesbians is better in urban areas, encouraging the perception that one has to move to the city to "be gay" and putting the lives of gays and lesbians in rural areas further "under erasure."[11] In my case, the fact that so many of the performers to whom I was drawn were British sparked an Anglophilia that, while making the wider world seem exciting and more accepting, further alienated me from my own environment, amplifying the sense it was a place I would never fit in. Thus, while the rock culture in which I was invested played a significant part in queering my private and personal spaces, it was of little use in queering my social space for the better.

Listening to my records in my bedroom, I waited for high school to *22* end, anticipating that things would "get better" at the university—even if it were in Lincoln, Nebraska. The university was indeed a positive change, and my ongoing self-invention was aided by making friends with other young people in various stages of their own coming out processes. Many of my new friends were from small towns and rural areas in Nebraska and South Dakota, and most of them also found music to be a way of imagining a better time and place. For some, who had endured a greater sense of isolation or level of harassment in their hometowns than I, the attachment to certain bands or performers was perhaps even more meaningful. Music also became the means of connecting with others: Eurythmics, Cocteau Twins, Diamanda Galás, and other shared favorites became a way of bonding with a fashion design major from a small South Dakota town, who is still one of my closest friends.

My affective attachment to particular performers has done more than *23* help me connect with peers, though. It has also made me recognize my place in a lineage of gay male fandom of iconic female stars, from Judy Garland, Barbra Streisand, and Diana Ross before my time, to Björk, Christina Aguilera, and Lady Gaga after. My affection for Annie Lennox provides a sense of a queer history and shared culture that further legitimates my feeling that my popular cultural attachments are both personally and culturally meaningful.

Seeing Who's Out There: Rural Production of It Gets Better Videos

Although recounting my teenage use of the media implies a "now versus *24* then" scenario, a thorough inquiry into the use value of media for contemporary rural queer youth demands a more wide-ranging assessment that avoids creating false binaries. Certainly, the use value of the media "then" appears to suffer in contrast with the promise "now" of making connections and alleviating isolation and loneliness, as facilitated by communication technologies and online culture, plus more frequent, overt, and positive representation in the mainstream media.

While this suggests that conditions have indeed gotten better for even those LGBT people in the most constrained of circumstances, I believe there is more value in uncovering the *connections* rather than *differences* with past modes of reception and media use. By avoiding the facile polarization of "old" media and audience practices in the past as lesser, and new media and its myriad current applications as superior, we are better able to identify queer audiences' ingenuity in rearticulating and adapting media use to better fit changing contexts of time, place, technologies, and individual identity constructs. This mode of inquiry also elucidates ways in which the IGB Project's archiving of feelings and memories can forge a connection to a usable past that might inspire new ways of imagining and working towards improved social conditions. 25

For individuals in marginalized social positions, seeing something of oneself, or something pertinent and compelling, in media representations can require a determined assertion of will and motivated repurposing. The proliferation of online self-presentation, including IGB videos, raises intriguing questions about viewer reception of amateur media productions, with their presumably more "authentic" depiction of LGBT realities. In creating arguably more accessible sexual imaginaries, the people appearing in their own videos queer rural space by "representing" gays and lesbians leading sometimes difficult but also fulfilling lives outside urban environments. 26

Through acts of self-representation, the producers of IGB videos perform some of the functions that Dyer theorizes stars do, especially the challenge they pose to restrictive social categorizations. The sheer diversity of people represented creates hundreds of new ways of perceiving and making sense of how race, gender, class, ethnicity, location, age, and other traits intersect with sexuality in the ongoing processes of identity formation and performance. While it would indeed be a stretch to consider these individuals "stars," the risks they take in making their stories, their emotions, and their faces public lend them a microcosmic level of celebrity in online forums. Like stars, they can serve as role models, as points of identification, and as sites of desire, with viewer comments often reading like fan mail. 27

Unlike stars, though, they complicate our vision of an "idealized self," shifting our perception of what constitutes success, beauty, happiness, authenticity, and a life well lived. Unlike the stars that intrigued me in my youth but did little to help me think through affirming ways of being gay, the producers of these videos do not equivocate on matters of gender and sexuality. As Gray discovered, amateur-made online representations of 28 "real" queer peoples' lives resonated more deeply than fictional gay and lesbian characters with rural youth who were formulating queer identities.[12] Further unlike our relation to mass media stars, we have a greater expectation of interaction and belief that individuals we have come to empathize with or admire may respond to our written comments. Rather than presenting stars, IGB videos present people identifiably "us" for a diverse range of viewers, expanding the range of choices of what and from whom to learn far beyond what is available in commercial media.

Most of the IGB videos that I watched and were created by and addressed to people living in rural areas and small towns, follow the format initiated by the Savage and Miller video, describing negative experiences, generally during the high school years, and then talking about how life improved afterwards. The everyday traumas detailed are familiar to many LGBT people who have endured mistreatment, from being shunned, called names, assaulted, and standing by with conflicted feelings while others are being bullied, to negative messages and threats from churches, schools, and family. The producer of one video, from a "really small town," where "if you weren't involved in sports, you were basically a loser," says that his environment caused him to feel "a lot of contempt for myself."[13] Another speaks to the justifiable distrust many queer youth have of adults, saying that on seeking help from a school counselor, he was dismissively told to "toughen up."[14]

In addition to reporting the expected problems of a queer person in rural areas, though, many of the videos' producers also discuss how to make a good life for oneself in these spaces. In her ethnographic study of gays and lesbians living in rural Michigan and Illinois, Emily Kazyak found that most of her informants either wanted to remain in these areas or had returned from urban areas to a place that felt more like home. In fact, one of her interviewees said that it was not until after he moved *away* from a city and back to his small hometown that he was able to determine that "this is who I am and this is what it means for *me* to be gay." As this informant told Kazyak, he felt rural areas offer "more flexibility in terms of how he makes sense of his sexuality."[15]

The individuals she interviewed, Kazyak maintains, distinguish between rural and urban ways of being a gay man or lesbian and understand "rural" in nuanced ways that "provide them with resources to modify cultural narratives that deny the possibility of being gay in the country."[16] By drawing on their "attachments to small town life," her informants have constructed multiple ways of living as gays and lesbians while still being part of their rural communities, in which familiarity, kinship ties, and being perceived as a "good person" may be valued more than sexual difference is condemned. While this does require some circumspection, though not closetedness, her informants told Kazyak that they are more comfortable living their lives in a more private, low-key manner, regarding this as one of the distinctions between rural and urban homosexuality.

Other scholars studying gay and lesbian lives in rural areas have come to similar conclusions about the opportunities as well as the constraints of constructing queer identities in nonurban spaces, in which negotiation of those identities expands ways of being beyond media representations that "genericize" queer identity and politics along an urban model.[17]

Much of the impact of IGB videos derives from such revision of cultural presumptions to recognize and document multiple ways of being gay and lesbian in diverse geographical contexts. Several videos queer rural spaces by acknowledging the presence of not only LGBT individuals but also allies in small towns and farming communities. In one, a woman reminds viewers, "There's more open-minded people, even in a state like South Dakota."[18] In another video, a young man from a small town in Ohio, "where gays arent [sic] accepted at all," tells of being "astonished" when going to a gay pride event and recognizing people he sees "on a daily basis": "I was actually happy to know all these people were around me and I didn't even know it. . . . You just don't know who's around you."[19] {32}

Videos by members of Gay-Straight Alliances (GSAs) in central states are prevalent, although almost all are university-affiliated. For queer youth in rural areas, this could evoke conflicted responses. On the one hand, seeing college students not much older than themselves testifying that life gets better post-high school can convey the message to youth in crisis that positive change is not far off. On the other hand, for younger teens or preadolescents, that change may seem all the farther away, and for young people not interested in or able to attend college, such representations may alienate them further by implying that moving away to pursue higher education is the only "escape." Videos by high school GSAs in small towns and rural areas are far scarcer, but have the potential to resonate with a broader audience in a particularly powerful way. One such example, titled "It Gets Better, Small Town Unity," features eleven members of a GSA "in a small town community, where it isn't accepted very well."[20] In telling their "stories that we want you to hear," these young people from an unnamed town are candid about their circumstances, revealing problems with bullying, parents, depression, and self-cutting, but ultimately emphasizing that their lives have already improved because of the companionship and understanding they have found through joining their GSA. One young woman, acknowledging the difficulties the group faces, remains defiant yet supportive: "We are leaving our mark. We aren't backing down. We are here for you." To underscore this point, another young woman states emphatically: "We all have a voice, and we are making ours heard." {33}

As the video's title implies, the young people onscreen model unity in a manner that conveys hope. Even for young viewers who have no access to GSAs and are experiencing a sense of isolation, videos such as this can perform the function of the sexual imaginary by "being here for you," and demonstrating that other queer youth are "out there," successfully negotiating difference in similarly constrained circumstances. This takes on even {34} greater consequence when considering the observation made by many new media scholars that distinctions between online and offline life have become increasingly artificial, in part because online activities so often precipitate offline realities. In her study of the IGB Project, Amber Muller emphasizes that "virtual and physical realities are forever impacting each other," with unpredictable ramifications. She notes incidents "where makers of It Gets Better videos have become new targets for discrimination and harassment both online and in their real lives."[21] But she also discusses the Make It Better Project, which was established in response to the dearth of practical advice found in IGB videos. Actively striving to "facilitate positive change in the physical world,"[22] the Make It Better Project seeks to "let students, parents, teachers, school administrators, and adult allies know that there are concrete actions they can take right now to make schools safer for all students" and offers advice on how this can be done.[23]

Raising further concerns about the IGB Project's effectiveness, Muller   *35* describes most of the videos as "closed discourse" unable to "engage in dialogue with the different subject positions of the multiple viewers." Her criticisms speak to the largely bourgeois and urban points of view presented in the videos, many of which reinforce the notion that supportive communities exist only in cities or universities. By failing to recognize that these options may not be "viable to all youth," Muller sees them as "making the message of hope … exclusive" to a privileged few.[24]

Almost all of the producers of IGB videos living in rural areas, however,   *36* spoke of finding strength and support from friends and loved ones within their own communities. Billyraymccabe, the maker of a video titled, "It Gets So Much Better … Even If You Are from a Small Town!" tells viewers that although he lives in a conservative part of a conservative state, he nonetheless has friends who "love me for who I am" and reassures viewers, "no matter where you go … you are gonna find people who love you for what you are."[25] Likewise, a video by "a small town farm boy" in "religiously oppressive" Mississippi attests that while his life sometimes can be lonely, he also has friends he can count on to stick up for him.[26] In contrast to video-maker Billyraymccabe, a recent high school graduate from "kind of a closed-minded" small town in Wisconsin tells of the support and understanding he received from teachers at his high school.[27]

Among the videos proffering a sense of hope through positive representations of life as a queer adult in rural areas, one has gained particular   *37* attention and is as interesting for the comments it has generated as for the content of the video itself. At well over twenty-three thousand hits (as of March 2014), "It Gets Better, Rural Dykes!" is by far the most viewed of the videos examined here, and its maker, Krissy Mahan from upstate New York, was included in the book Savage and Miller compiled on the project. Addressing "young lesbians who are not in cities," Mahan writes, "Being a rural dyke has some challenges, but it is really cool, and totally worth sticking around for."[28] While acknowledging that rural life does have its own set of issues, Mahan focuses instead on the positive aspects of country life, especially ones beneficial to people who regard themselves as independent individualists. In the video, she proposes that one of the pluses of rural life is that "you don't have to deal with people all the time," and in her written piece for the book, she remarks on "the long tradition of support for unconventional people in rural areas," which, as supported by Kazyak's study, means that rural gays and lesbians are often evaluated for character traits and abilities completely separate from sexuality or politics. "People are more concerned with what I can do and what skills I have, rather than who I'm involved with," Mahan reports.[29]

Unlike most other IGB videos, Mahan addresses the class issues that 38 are tightly bound to rural life, commenting on the frequent depiction in the media of gays and lesbians as affluent, but making it clear that as "a person who doesn't have a lot of money," she is content with her life and what it has to offer. She upholds the virtues of country life in the comfort and pleasure provided by the natural world, which revitalizes and reminds us "how great it is to be alive."[30] In this view, connection with nature is perceived as vital identity work, completely independent of consumer culture and the media.

The belief that nature has special healing potential and spiritual sig- 39 nificance for queer people has been echoed by many, from participants in lesbian separatist back-to-the-land movements, Radical Faeries, and neo-pagans, to vacationers at gay campgrounds. Reflecting on Tyler Clementi's suicide, Alex Johnson advocates outdoor activities and time alone in nature as a way for bullied queer youth to make "space in which to accept themselves," adding that he himself overcame his "fear of others' hate and meanness" by "connecting with nature ... recognizing that there's a whole world that accepts me for who I am." Based on life histories recorded in his ethnographic study of gay men raised on farms, Will Fellows surmises, "The lack of human diversity in the social experiences" of his informants in their youth "appears to have been offset to some extent by their rich experience of the diversity of the nonhuman world."[31] The isolation that is inherent to farm life, Fellows maintains, meant that some of his informants had more freedom to "invent themselves according to their inclinations and standards."[32] In these view-points, nature allows space for the self-reflection and self-invention that Michel Foucault saw not as "a luxury or a pastime for lesbians and gay men," but as a necessity.[33]

The numerous responses to Mahan's video continue the work of rep- 40 resenting queer rurality and attesting to the presence of LGBT people in small towns and farmland. One commentator affirms Kazyak's findings on gays and lesbians who choose a rural life: "I got to know many (semi) out farm dykes and gay men after coming out in Missouri, and as far as I could tell, they loved their way of life and wouldn't have it any other way."[34] Other commentators go beyond testifying to mere presence, recounting the success gays and lesbians have had in finding a place in rural communities, such as the lesbian couple who run a small town coffee shop: "The main customers are the local farmers (straight men) who go in every morning for coffee and sit around to chat."[35]

As an IGB "star," Mahan also represents another aspect of the sexual imaginary: the object of erotic desire. She herself humorously addresses how rurality evokes the lesbian icon of the stalwart, casually androgynous, ultracapable woman of the land by saying, "everything that's frustrating about right now, being in the country ... rockin' the flannel shirt every now and then, those are gonna be totally hot to somebody."[36] Indeed, her own embodiment of this fantasy image, seated in a barn amidst hay bales, wearing a baseball cap and, yes, flannel, has elicited *many* viewer comments about her desirability, comments that speak to the link between a romanticized impression of country living and the eroticization of distinctly queer, distinctly rural American icons. One commentator states, "I kind of want to move out of the city and be a dyke now,"[37] while another, remarking that Mahan is "totally cute," writes that her video, "almost makes me think I should leave Brooklyn for the boondocks."[38] With the country also the site of gay male desire in iconic figures such as the rugged cowboy, the rough trade trucker, and the tanned-and-muscular naïve farm boy, the rural is just as likely a place to picture the eroticized sexual imaginary as the urban. *41*

Conclusion

IGB videos hold potentially high value for the cultivation of queer media literacy and negotiation of queer identities for those with access to computers, Internet connection, time for online exploration, and enough privacy to explore broadly—things that can be hard to come by for rural queer youth. Seeking ways in which media use is most beneficial to queer youth in crisis therefore requires more than setting up a distinction between passive consumption of "old" media and active production enabled by new media. The production of meaning, affective attachments, and idiosyncratic uses of media are influenced but not determined by technology or media platform. Moreover, locating meaningful coping responses from small, ordinary pleasures and solaces in one's environment may or may not involve engaging with media. *42*

That said, new technologies unarguably introduce many layers of complexity into questions of how media can most productively be exploited by vulnerable individuals. For me, popular music transmitted by various "old" media was a vital part of surviving my difficult adolescent years. This is certainly not something exclusive to alienated queer boys in the Midwest, and gay and lesbian investment in popular culture as a coping strategy is pervasive enough to be a source of humor. The musical short "Shit I Love," by Jake Wilson and Alysha Umphress, frames the song with *43* a narrative in which a guy, referring to himself as "the gayest," is harassed by kids on a city street. Instead of being angry or trying to retaliate, his friend urges him to think of the things that make him happy, kicking off a rap number name-checking everything from kittens and chocolate truffles to pop music stars Britney Spears, Beyoncé, Robyn, and Rihanna. Comic artist Ellen Forney, in her contribution to the IGB book, lists among "high school survival tools" for "quirky misfits, oddballs, and the divinely unconventional" music by queer-oriented bands such as Scissor Sisters, Gossip, the Smiths, and Queen.

Several IGB videos, too, indicate how gays and lesbians in nonurban locations enlist music as a "survival tool." In one video, a man talks about the "little steps" through which one "gains confidence," which for him as a teenager included listening to Destiny's Child while working out with his mother's five-pound plastic weights—a reminiscence that prompts him to quip, "so gay."[39] Two young men in another video wear rock T-shirts, one of which, for the band Joy Division, would have been a signifier of teenage angst and "alternative" tastes even back in my youth.[40] In many of the videos, pop music is used as a backing soundtrack to add emotional weight to the speakers' words, in some cases played so loudly that it interferes with the speakers' intelligibility.

While my own history suggests that popular culture can have some positive influence on queer youth, I can hardly call my teenage "relationship" with my favorite stars completely satisfying. I believe more effective benefits will be found in the words of the nonfamous, in the extraordinary strength, insight, and love to be found right here in the ordinary. One of the most remarkable contributions of the IGB Project is its demonstration of the sociopolitical import of queer historiography and the power generated by listening to individuals telling their stories and speaking for themselves. IGB videos, for producers and viewers alike, satisfy "the emotional need for history" that Cvetkovich proposes is particularly acute with gays and lesbians.[41] Functioning as an archive in these terms, the videos also become what Kate Eichhorn regards as "an apparatus that can be effectively wielded in a reparative manner,"[42] transmuting the hurts of the past into especially powerful ways of communicating encouragement and strength for an improved today as well as tomorrow.

The IGB Project, Savage notes, was driven by the need to create a space for dialogue in which homophobic parents, teachers, and school administrators could no longer prevent adult LGBT people from reaching out to LGBT youth and letting them know the things that we wish we had known as we struggled through adolescence.[43] The archiving of a deeply personal alternative history, along with the deployment of queer media literacy, might help us to realize Foucault's conviction that homosexual subjectivity should not be regarded merely as an expression of individual desires, but as a means to imagining new ways of interacting with others.[44] The unique, vital, but often overlooked ways of inventing and living queer identities in rural spaces, as communicated by an important minority of IGB video producers, hold unlimited possibilities for new ways of being and new forms of interaction that will make rural spaces not merely safe for queer youth, but places to thrive.

NOTES

1. "What Is the It Gets Better Project?" *It Gets Better Project,* n.d., http://www.itgets-better.org/pages/about-it-gets-better-project/ (accessed April 19, 2013).
2. Cvetkovitch, *An Archive of Feelings,* 241.
3. Ibid, 7.
4. One of the most unequivocal examples of this message comes in New York City Mayor Michael Bloomberg's video for the project. Bloomberg directs his words expressly to "gay teens" who feel that they have no hope and are not wanted where they are, telling them emphatically, "New York City wants *you*. New York has always been the place where anyone can go and be who they are supposed to be, regardless of ethnicity, religion, gender, or sexual identity." Although Bloomberg quickly adds that there are "lots of other places in the country and the world" where gay people are welcomed, he says this with far less conviction (http://www.itgetsbetter.org/video/entry/2876/).
5. In his study of gay men who grew up in farming communities, Will Fellows lists the issues that contribute to the impression that rural areas are inhospitable to LGBTQ people: "rigid gender roles, social isolation, ethnic homogeneity, suspicion of the unfamiliar, racism, religious conservatism, sexual prudishness, and limited access to information." He adds, "While none of these conditions is unique to farm culture, they operate in a distinctive synergy in that setting" (*Farm Boys,* ix).
6. Gray, *Out in the Country,* 117.
7. Ibid., 130.
8. I didn't realize quite what a gay stereotype Annie Lennox fandom is until years later, after seeing the 1998 film *Edge of Seventeen* (Moreton), in which the teenaged main character's coming-out process in 1980s suburban Ohio is set against a background of 1980s pop music, represented largely by Lennox.
9. Dyer, *Stars,* 32.
10. Dyer, "In Defense of Disco," 410.
11. Weston, "Get Thee to a Big City," 282.
12. Gray, *Out in the Country,* 121.
13. KindaGayBlog. "It Gets Better: Sam from Small Town, USA," YouTube, August 3, 2011 (accessed May 20, 2013).
14. Billyraymccabe. "It Gets So Much Better … Even If You Are from a Small Town!" YouTube, October 2, 2010 (accessed May 20, 2013).
15. Kazyak, "Disrupting Cultural Selves," 571 (her emphasis).
16. Ibid., 563.
17. Gray, *Out in the Country,* 38.
18. Brittany Buell, "It Gets Better (USD 10% Society)," YouTube, June 20, 2011 (accessed May 20, 2013).
19. Brandon Hostetter, "It Gets Better—Brandon Hostetter," YouTube, September 20, 2012 (accessed June 1, 2013).
20. saggerG, "It Gets Better, Small Town Unity," YouTube, December 15, 2010 (accessed May 20, 2013).
21. Muller, "Virtual Communities and Translation into Physical Reality in the 'It Gets Better' Project," 273.
22. Ibid., 275.
23. "About," *Make It Better Project,* n.d., http://makeitbetterproject.org/about (accessed May 20, 2013).

24. Muller, "Virtual Communities," 275.

25. Billyraymccabe, "It Gets So Much Better."

26. ZydaneJeremiah, "It Gets Better! Cory from MS," YouTube, May 9, 2012 (accessed May 20, 2013).

27. Ross Pearson, "It Gets Better: Ross from Wisconsin," YouTube, August 22, 2011 (accessed May 14, 2013).

28. dykeumentaryi, "It Gets Better, Rural Dykes!" YouTube, October 2, 2010 (accessed May 20, 2013).

29. Mahan, "Rockin' the Flannel Shirt," 71.

30. Ibid., 72.

31. Fellows, *Farm Boys*, 15.

32. Ibid., 16.

33. Halperin, *Saint Foucault*, 81.

34. Vinomazzei, response to dykeumentaryi, "It Gets Better, Rural Dykes!" YouTube, n.d. (accessed May 20, 2013).

35. dja1062, response to dykeumentaryi, "It Gets Better, Rural Dykes!" YouTube, n.d. (accessed May 20, 2013).

36. dykeumentaryi, "It Gets Better, Rural Dykes!"

37. lovedisaster69, response to dykeumentaryi, "It Gets Better, Rural Dykes!" YouTube, n.d. (accessed May 20, 2013).

38. D Avraham, response to dykeumentaryi, "It Gets Better, Rural Dykes!" YouTube, n.d. (accessed May 20, 2013).

39. KindaGayBlog, "It Gets Better."

40. Buell, "It Gets Better (USD 10% Society)."

41. Cvetkovich, *An Archive of Feelings*, 251.

42. Eichhorn, "Archiving the Moment," 26.

43. Savage, "Introduction," 4.

44. Halperin, *Saint Foucault*, 78.

■ ■ ■

Reading as a Writer: Analyzing Rhetorical Choices

1. You might be surprised by Mark Hain's use of the word "queer" in this essay. Look up the history and use of the word to familiarize yourself with how it has been used historically and why some—but not all—people sympathetic to LGBTQ+ causes use the word. Share what you learn with your classmates.

2. Unlike many of our authors, Hain draws on his personal experience in this essay. Locate the paragraphs that include examples from his past, and mark them so they are visible. To what extent do you think they strengthen—or weaken—his overall point? Why?

Writing as a Reader: Entering the Conversation of Ideas

1. Hain has a different perspective on online life than do some of the other authors in this chapter, which is perhaps most evident in his claims in paragraph 34 about the lack of distinction between online and offline lives. Select one of the other authors in this chapter (William Powers, Evan Kindley, and Sherry Turkle are all good possibilities) to place in conversation with Hain. Write an essay in which you assess the claims of your chosen authors and assert your own position in this complex debate about the value of online life.

2. Hain and C. J. Pascoe (pp. 464–81 in Sociology) share an interest in the ways attitudes around sexuality and identity can create a sense of inclusion or isolation. Craft an essay in which you build on these authors' ideas to make an argument about the value of in-person and online communication as tools for social change around identity issues.

KEN GILLAM AND SHANNON R. WOODEN

Post-Princess Models of Gender: The New Man in Disney/Pixar

Ken Gillam directs the composition program at Missouri State University, where he teaches courses on composition theory and pedagogy. Shannon R. Wooden is a professor of English at the same university, where her specialties are British literature, creative writing, literature and science, and adaptations of novels for the screen. This piece is part of the research for their book, *Pixar's Boy Stories: Masculinity in a Postmodern Age*. You may be familiar with the many critiques of Disney princesses, but less has been written about the leading male characters. Gillam and Wooden's work begins to fill this gap in the research.

While every scholarly article is in some way driven by inquiry, Gillam and Wooden make their question explicit in their second paragraph: "Does this nominal feminizing of male also-rans [in *Cars*] (and the simultaneous gendering of success) constitute a meaningful pattern?" The rest of their essay is an answer to this question, elaborating on their thesis that "Pixar consistently promotes a new model of masculinity, one that matures into acceptance of its more traditionally 'feminine' aspects" (para. 2). They argue that the male leads in Pixar films beginning with *Toy Story* in 1995 share a similar storyline of initially striving for an "alpha-male identity," but then, "finally, they achieve (and teach) a kinder, gentler understanding of what it means to be a man" (para. 4). How and where do they define this new kind of masculinity throughout their essay?

As you read, test the authors' argument against the examples and interpretations they offer of films you may know well. You might try to remember your first responses to these Pixar classics as well as what you see as you reflect on them now. Consider their claim that these films share a similar plot, which revolves around a male character: "As these characters begin the film in (or seeking) the tenuous alpha position among fellow characters, each of them is also stripped of this identity—dramatically emasculated—so that he may learn, reform, and emerge again with a different, and arguably more feminine, self-concept" (para. 11). How effectively do their examples from *Toy Story*, *The Incredibles*, and *Cars* support their claim?

In their conclusion, Gillam and Wooden turn their argument in a new direction, looking critically at the Walt Disney Company's enormous audience and calling on the readers to retain "a critical consciousness of the main lessons taught by the cultural monolith of Disney" (para. 24). Slow down and be sure you understand the points the authors make in these densely packed final two paragraphs. What do they claim is at stake in becoming "conscientious cultural critics"? Can childhood movies really make that big an impact? If you think back on your own childhood favorites and how much they meant to you (and perhaps still do), you may have at least the beginning of your own answer.

■ ■ ■

L isping over the Steve McQueen allusion in Pixar's *Cars* (2006), our two-year-old son, Oscar, inadvertently directed us to the definition(s) of masculinity that might be embedded in a children's animated film about NASCAR. The film overtly praises the "good woman" proverbially behind every successful man: The champion car, voiced by Richard Petty, tells his wife, "I wouldn't be nothin' without you, honey." But gender in this twenty-first-century bildungsroman is rather more complex, and Oscar's mispronunciation held the first clue. To him, a member of the film's target audience, the character closing in on the title long held by "The King" is not "Lightning McQueen" but "Lightning the queen"; his chief rival, the always-a-bridesmaid runner-up "Chick" Hicks.

Does this nominal feminizing of male also-rans (and the simultaneous gendering of success) constitute a meaningful pattern? Piqued, we began examining the construction of masculinity in major feature films released by Disney's Pixar studios over the past thirteen years. Indeed, as we argue here, Pixar consistently promotes a new model of masculinity, one that matures into acceptance of its more traditionally "feminine" aspects.

Cultural critics have long been interested in Disney's cinematic products, but the gender critics examining the texts most enthusiastically gobbled up by the under-six set have so far generally focused on their retrograde representations of women. As Elizabeth Bell argues, the animated Disney features through *Beauty and the Beast* feature a "teenaged heroine at the idealized height of puberty's graceful promenade ... [f]emale wickedness ... rendered as middle-aged beauty at its peak of sexuality and authority ... and [f]eminine sacrifice and nurturing ... drawn in pear-shaped, old women past menopause" (108). Some have noted the models of masculinity in the classic animated films, primarily the contrast between the ubermacho Gaston and the sensitive, misunderstood Beast in *Beauty and the Beast*,[1] but the male protagonist of the animated classics, at least through *The Little Mermaid*, remains largely uninterrogated.[2] For most of the early films, this critical omission seems generally appropriate, the various versions of Prince Charming being often too two-dimensional to do more than inadvertently shape the definition of the protagonists' femininity. But if the feminist thought that has shaped our cultural texts for three decades now has been somewhat disappointing in its ability to actually rewrite the princess trope (the spunkiest of the "princesses," Ariel, Belle, Jasmine, and, arguably, even Mulan, remain thin, beautiful, kind, obedient or punished for disobedience, and headed for the altar), it has been surprisingly effective in rewriting the type of masculine power promoted by Disney's products.[3]

Disney's new face, Pixar studios, has released nine films—*Toy Story* (1995) and *Toy Story 2* (1999); *A Bug's Life* (1998); *Finding Nemo* (2003); *Monsters, Inc.* (2001); *The Incredibles* (2004); *Cars* (2006); *Ratatouille* (2007); and now *WALL•E* (2008)—all of which feature interesting male figures in leading positions. Unlike many of the princesses, who remain relatively static even through their own adventures, these male leads are actual protagonists; their characters develop and change over the course of the film, rendering the plot. Ultimately these various developing characters—particularly Buzz and Woody from *Toy Story*, Mr. Incredible from *The Incredibles*, and Lightning McQueen from *Cars*—experience a common narrative trajectory, culminating in a common "New Man" model:[4] they all strive for an alpha-male identity; they face emasculating failures; they find themselves, in large part, through what Eve Sedgwick refers to as "homosocial desire" and a triangulation of this desire with a feminized object (and/or a set of "feminine" values); and, finally, they achieve (and teach) a kinder, gentler understanding of what it means to be a man.

Emasculation of the Alpha Male

A working definition of *alpha male* may be unnecessary; although more traditionally associated with the animal kingdom than the Magic Kingdom, it familiarly evokes ideas of dominance, leadership, and power in human social organizations as well. The phrase "alpha male" may stand for all things stereotypically patriarchal: unquestioned authority, physical power and social dominance, competitiveness for positions of status and leadership, lack of visible or shared emotion, social isolation. An alpha male, like Vann in *Cars*, does not ask for directions; like Doc Hudson in the same film, he does not talk about his feelings. The alpha male's stresses, like Buzz Lightyear's, come from his need to save the galaxy; his strength comes from faith in his ability to do so. These models have worked in Disney for decades. The worst storm at sea is no match for *The Little Mermaid*'s uncomplicated Prince Eric—indeed, any charming prince need only ride in on his steed to save his respective princess. But the postfeminist world is a different place for men, and the post-princess Pixar is a different place for male protagonists.

Newsweek recently described the alpha male's new cinematic and television rival, the "beta male": "The testosterone-pumped, muscle-bound Hollywood hero is rapidly deflating....Taking his place is a new kind of leading man, the kind who's just as happy following as leading, or never getting off the sofa" (Yabroff 64). Indeed, as Susan Jeffords points out, at least since *Beauty and the Beast*, Disney has resisted (even ridiculed) the machismo once de rigueur for leading men (170). Disney cinema, one of the most effective teaching tools America offers its children, is not yet converting its model male protagonist all the way into a slacker, but the New Man model is quite clearly emerging.

Cars, *Toy Story*, and *The Incredibles* present their protagonists as unambiguously alpha in the opening moments of the films. Although Lightning McQueen may be an as-yet incompletely realized alpha when *Cars* begins, not having yet achieved the "King" status of his most successful rival, his ambition and fierce competitiveness still clearly valorize the alpha-male model: "Speed. I am speed ... I eat losers for breakfast," he chants as a prerace mantra. He heroically comes from behind to tie the championship race, distinguishing himself by his physical power and ability, characteristics that catapult him toward the exclusively male culture of sports superstars. The fantasies of his life he indulges after winning the coveted Piston Cup even include flocks of female cars forming a worshipful harem around him. But the film soon diminishes the appeal of this alpha model. Within a few moments of the race's conclusion, we see some of Lightning's less positive macho traits; his inability to name any friends, for example, reveals both his isolation and attempts at emotional stoicism. Lightning McQueen is hardly an unemotional character, as can be seen when he prematurely jumps onto the stage to accept what he assumes to be his victory. For this happy emotional outburst, however, he is immediately disciplined by a snide comment from Chick. From this point until much later in the film, the only emotions he displays are those of frustration and anger. 7

Toy Story's Buzz Lightyear and Sheriff Woody similarly base their worth on a masculine model of competition and power, desiring not only to be the "favorite toy" of their owner, Andy, but to possess the admiration of and authority over the other toys in the playroom. Woody is a natural leader, and his position represents both paternalistic care and patriarchal dominance. In an opening scene, he calls and conducts a "staff meeting" that highlights his unambiguously dominant position in the toy community. Encouraging the toys to pair up so that no one will be lost in the family's impending move, he commands: "A moving buddy. If you don't have one, GET ONE." Buzz's alpha identity comes from a more exalted source than social governance—namely, his belief that he is the one "space ranger" with the power and knowledge needed to save the galaxy; it seems merely natural, then, that the other toys would look up to him, admire his strength, and follow his orders. But as with Lightning McQueen, these depictions of masculine power are soon undercut. Buzz's mere presence exposes Woody's strength as fragile, artificial, even arbitrary, and his "friends," apparently having been drawn to his authority rather than his character, are fair-weather at best. Buzz's authority rings hollow from the very beginning, and his refusal to believe in his own "toyness" is at best silly and at worst dangerous. Like Lightning, Buzz's and Woody's most commonly expressed emotions are anger and frustration, not sadness (Woody's, at having been "replaced") or fear (Buzz's, at having "crash-landed on a strange planet") or even wistful fondness (Woody's, at the loss of Slink's, Bo Peep's, and Rex's loyalty). Once 8 again, the alpha-male position is depicted as fraudulent, precarious, lonely, and devoid of emotional depth.

An old-school superhero, Mr. Incredible opens *The Incredibles* by displaying the tremendous physical strength that enables him to stop speeding trains, crash through buildings, and keep the city safe from criminals. But he too suffers from the emotional isolation of the alpha male. Stopping on the way to his own wedding to interrupt a crime in progress, he is very nearly late to the service, showing up only to say the "I dos." Like his car and toy counterparts, he communicates primarily through verbal assertions of power — angrily dismissing Buddy, his meddlesome aspiring sidekick; bantering with Elastigirl over who gets the pickpocket — and limits to anger and frustration the emotions apparently available to men.

Fraught as it may seem, the alpha position is even more fleeting: In none of these Pixar films does the male protagonist's dominance last long. After Lightning ties, rather than wins, the race and ignores the King's friendly advice to find and trust a good team with which to work, he browbeats his faithful semi, Mack, and ends up lost in "hillbilly hell," a small town off the beaten path of the interstate. His uncontrolled physical might destroys the road, and the resultant legal responsibility — community service — keeps him far from his Piston Cup goals. When Buzz appears as a gift for Andy's birthday, he easily unseats Woody both as Andy's favorite and as the toy community's leader. When Buzz becomes broken, failing to save himself from the clutches of the evil neighbor, Sid, he too must learn a hard lesson about his limited power, his diminished status, and his own relative insignificance in the universe. Mr. Incredible is perhaps most obviously disempowered: Despite his superheroic feats, Mr. Incredible has been unable to keep the city safe from his own clumsy brute force. After a series of lawsuits against "the Supers," who accidentally leave various types of small-time mayhem in their wake, they are all driven underground, into a sort of witness protection program. To add insult to injury, Mr. Incredible's diminutive boss fires him from his job handling insurance claims, and his wife, the former Elastigirl, assumes the "pants" of the family.

Most of these events occur within the first few minutes of the characters' respective films. Only Buzz's downfall happens in the second half. The alpha-male model is thus not only present and challenged in the films but also is, in fact, the very structure on which the plots unfold. Each of these films is about being a man, and they begin with an outdated, two-dimensional alpha prototype to expose its failings and to ridicule its logical extensions: the devastation and humiliation of being defeated in competition, the wrath generated by power unchecked, the paralyzing alienation and fear inherent in being lonely at the top. As these characters begin the film in (or seeking) the tenuous alpha position among fellow characters, each of them is also stripped of this identity — dramatically emasculated — so that he may learn, reform, and emerge again with a different, and arguably more feminine, self-concept.

"Emasculated" is not too strong a term for what happens to these male protagonists; the decline of the alpha-male model is gender coded in all the films. For his community service punishment, Lightning is chained to the giant, snorting, tar-spitting "Bessie" and ordered to repair the damage he has wrought. His own "horsepower" (as Sally cheerfully points out) is used against him when literally put in the service of a nominally feminized figure valued for the more "feminine" orientation of service to the community. If being under the thumb of this humongous "woman" is not emasculating enough, Mater, who sees such subordination to Bessie as a potentially pleasurable thing, names the price, saying, "I'd give my left two lug nuts for something like that!"

Mr. Incredible's downfall is most clearly marked as gendered by his responses to it. As his wife's domestic power and enthusiasm grow increasingly unbearable, and his children's behavior more and more out of his control, he surreptitiously turns to the mysterious, gorgeous "Mirage," who gives him what he needs to feel like a man: superhero work. Overtly depicting her as the "other woman," the film requires Elastigirl to intercept a suggestive-sounding phone call, and to trap her husband in a lie, to be able to work toward healing his decimated masculinity. *13*

In *Toy Story,* the emasculation of the alpha male is the most overt, and arguably the most comic. From the beginning, power is constructed in terms conspicuously gender coded, at least for adult viewers: As they watch the incoming birthday presents, the toys agonize at their sheer size, the longest and most phallic-shaped one striking true fear (and admiration?) into the hearts of the spectators. When Buzz threatens Woody, one toy explains to another that he has "laser envy." Buzz's moment of truth, after seeing himself on Sid's father's television, is the most clearly gendered of all. Realizing for the first time that Woody is right, he is a "toy," he defiantly attempts to fly anyway, landing sprawled on the floor with a broken arm. Sid's little sister promptly finds him, dresses him in a pink apron and hat, and installs him as "Mrs. Nesbit" at her tea party. When Woody tries to wrest him from his despair, Buzz wails, "Don't you get it? I AM MRS. NESBIT. But does the hat look good? Oh, tell me the hat looks good!" Woody's "rock bottom" moment finds him trapped under an overturned milk crate, forcing him to ask Buzz for help and to admit that he "doesn't stand a chance" against Buzz in the contest for Andy's affection, which constitutes "everything that is important to me." He is not figured into a woman, like Buzz is, or subordinated to a woman, like Lightning is, or forced to seek a woman's affirmation of his macho self, like Mr. Incredible is, but he does have to acknowledge his own feminine values, from his need for communal support to his deep, abiding (and, later, maternal) love of a boy. This "feminine" stamp is characteristic of the New Man model toward which these characters narratively journey. *14*

Homosociality, Intimacy, and Emotion

Regarding the "love of a boy," the "mistress" tempting Mr. Incredible away from his wife and family is not Mirage at all but Buddy, the boy he jilted *15* in the opening scenes of the film (whose last name, Pine, further conveys the unrequited nature of their relationship). Privileging his alpha-male emotional isolation, but adored by his wannabe sidekick, Mr. Incredible vehemently protects his desire to "work alone." After spending the next years nursing his rejection and refining his arsenal, Buddy eventually retaliates against Mr. Incredible for rebuffing his advances. Such a model of homosocial tutelage as Buddy proposes at the beginning of the film certainly evokes an ancient (and homosexual) model of masculine identity; Mr. Incredible's rejection quickly and decisively replaces it with a heteronormative one, further supported by Elastigirl's marrying and Mirage's attracting the macho superhero.[5] But it is equally true that the recovery of Mr. Incredible's masculine identity happens primarily through his (albeit antagonistic) relationship with Buddy, suggesting that Eve Sedgwick's notion of a homosocial continuum is more appropriate to an analysis of the film's gender attitudes than speculations about its reactionary heteronormativity, even homophobia.

Same-sex (male) bonds—to temporarily avoid the more loaded term *desire*—are obviously important to each of these films. In fact, in all three, male/male relationships emerge that move the fallen alphas forward in their journeys toward a new masculinity. In each case, the male lead's first and/or primary intimacy—his most immediate transformative relationship—is with one or more male characters. Even before discovering Buddy as his nemesis, Mr. Incredible secretly pairs up with his old pal Frozone, and the two step out on their wives to continue superheroing on the sly; Buddy and Frozone are each, in their ways, more influential on Mr. Incredible's sense of self than his wife or children are. Although Lightning falls in love with Sally and her future vision of Radiator Springs, his almost accidentally having befriended the hapless, warm Mater catalyzes more foundational lessons about the responsibilities of friendship—demanding honesty, sensitivity, and care—than the smell-the-roses lesson Sally represents. He also ends up being mentored and taught a comparable lesson about caring for others by Doc Hudson, who even more explicitly encourages him to resist the alpha path of the Piston Cup world by relating his experiences of being used and then rejected. Woody and Buzz, as rivals-cum-allies, discover the necessary truths about their masculine strength only as they discover how much they need one another. Sedgwick further describes the ways in which the homosocial bond is negotiated through a triangulation of desire; that is, the intimacy emerging "between men" is constructed through an overt and shared desire for a feminized object. Unlike homosocial relationships between women—that is, "the continuum between 'women loving women' and 'women promoting the interests of women'"—male homosocial identity is necessarily homophobic in patriarchal systems, which are structurally homophobic (3). This means the same-sex relationship demands social opportunities for a man to insist on, or prove, his heterosexuality. Citing Rene Girard's *Deceit, Desire, and the Novel,* Sedgwick argues that "in any erotic rivalry, the bond that links the two rivals is as intense and potent as the bond that links either of the rivals to the beloved" (21); women are ultimately symbolically exchangeable "for the primary purpose of cementing the bonds of men with men" (26).

This triangulation of male desire can be seen in *Cars* and *Toy Story* *17* particularly, where the homosocial relationship rather obviously shares a desire for a feminized third. Buzz and Woody compete first, momentarily, for the affection of Bo Peep, who is surprisingly sexualized for a children's movie (purring to Woody an offer to "get someone else to watch the sheep tonight," then rapidly choosing Buzz as her "moving buddy" after his "flying" display). More importantly, they battle for the affection of Andy—a male child alternately depicted as maternal (it is his responsibility to get his baby sister out of her crib) and in need of male protection (Woody exhorts Buzz to "take care of Andy for me!")[6]. *Cars* also features a sexualized romantic heroine; less coquettish than Bo Peep, Sally still fumbles over an invitation to spend the night "not with me, but ..." in the motel she owns. One of Lightning and Mater's moments of "bonding" happens when Mater confronts Lightning, stating his affection for Sally and sharing a parallel story of heterosexual desire. The more principal objects of desire in *Cars*, however, are the (arguably) feminized "Piston Cup" and the Dinoco sponsorship. The sponsor itself is established in romantic terms: With Lightning stuck in Radiator Springs, his agent says Dinoco has had to "woo" Chick instead. Tia and Mia, Lightning's "biggest fans," who transfer their affection to Chick during his absence, offer viewers an even less subtly gendered goal, and Chick uses this to taunt Lightning. It is in the pursuit of these objects, and in competition with Chick and the King, that Lightning first defines himself as a man; the Piston Cup also becomes the object around which he and Doc discover their relationship to one another.

The New Man

With the strength afforded by these homosocial intimacies, the male *18* characters triumph over their respective plots, demonstrating the desirable modifications that Pixar makes to the alpha-male model. To emerge victorious (and in one piece) over the tyrannical neighbor boy, Sid, Buzz and Woody have to cooperate not only with each other but also with the cannibalized toys lurking in the dark places of Sid's bedroom. Incidentally learning a valuable lesson about discrimination based on physical difference (the toys are not monsters at all, despite their frightening appearance), they begin to show sympathy, rather than violence born of their fear, to the victims of Sid's experimentation. They learn how to humble themselves to ask for help from the community. Until Woody's grand plan to escape Sid unfolds, Sid could be an object lesson in the unredeemed alpha-male type: Cruelly almighty over the toy community, he wins at arcade games, bullies his sister, and, with strategically placed fireworks, exerts militaristic might over any toys he can find. Woody's newfound ability to give and receive care empowers him to teach Sid a lesson of caring and sharing that might be microcosmic to the movie as a whole. Sid, of course, screams (like a girl) when confronted with the evidence of his past cruelties, and when viewers last see him, his younger sister is chasing him up the stairs with her doll.

Even with the unceremonious exit of Sid, the adventure is not quite [19] over for Buzz and Woody. Unable to catch up to the moving van as Sid's dog chases him, Woody achieves the pinnacle of the New Man narrative: Armed with a new masculine identity, one that expresses feelings and acknowledges community as a site of power, Woody is able to sacrifice the competition with Buzz for his object of desire. Letting go of the van strap, sacrificing himself (he thinks) to Sid's dog, he plainly expresses a care-taking, nurturing love, and a surrender to the good of the beloved: "Take care of Andy for me," he pleads. Buzz's own moment of truth comes from seizing his power as a toy: holding Woody, he glides into the family's car and back into Andy's care, correcting Woody by proudly repeating his earlier, critical words back to him: "This isn't flying; it's falling with style." Buzz has found the value of being a "toy," the self-fulfillment that comes from being owned and loved. "Being a toy is a lot better than being a space ranger," Woody explains. "You're *his toy*" (emphasis in original).

Mr. Incredible likewise must embrace his own dependence, both [20] physical and emotional. Trapped on the island of Chronos, at the mercy of Syndrome (Buddy's new super-persona), Mr. Incredible needs women — his wife's superpowers and Mirage's guilty intervention—to escape. To overpower the monster Syndrome has unleashed on the city, and to achieve the pinnacle of the New Man model, he must also admit to his emotional dependence on his wife and children. Initially confining them to the safety of a bus, he confesses to Elastigirl that his need to fight the monster alone is not a typically alpha ("I work alone") sort of need but a loving one: "I can't lose you again," he tells her. The robot/monster is defeated, along with any vestiges of the alpha model, as the combined forces of the Incredible family locate a new model of postfeminist strength in the family as a whole. This communal strength is not simply physical but marked by cooperation, selflessness, and intelligence. The children learn that their best contributions protect the others; Mr. Incredible figures out the robot/monster's vulnerability and cleverly uses this against it.

In a parallel motif to Mr. Incredible's inability to control his strength, [21] Buddy/Syndrome finally cannot control his robot/monster; in the defeat, he becomes the newly emasculated alpha male. But like his robot, he learns quickly. His last attempt to injure Mr. Incredible, kidnapping his baby Jack-Jack, strikes at Mr. Incredible's new source of strength and value, his family. The strength of the cooperative family unit is even more clearly displayed in this final rescue: For the shared, parental goal of saving Jack-Jack, Mr. Incredible uses his physical strength and, with her consent, the shape-shifting body of his super-wife. He throws Elastigirl into the air, where she catches their baby and, flattening her body into a parachute, sails gently back to her husband and older children.

Through Lightning McQueen's many relationships with men, as well as his burgeoning romance with Sally, he also learns how to care about others, to focus on the well-being of the community, and to privilege nurture and kindness. It is Doc, not Sally, who explicitly challenges the race car with his selfishness ("When was the last time you cared about something except yourself, hot rod?"). His reformed behavior begins with his generous contributions to the Radiator Springs community. Not only does he provide much-needed cash for the local economy, but he also listens to, praises, and values the residents for their unique offerings to Radiator Springs. He is the chosen auditor for Lizzy's reminiscing about her late husband, contrasting the comic relief typically offered by the senile and deaf Model T with poignancy, if not quite sadness. Repairing the town's neon, he creates a romantic dreamscape from the past, a setting for both courting Sally ("cruising") and, more importantly, winning her respect with his ability to share in her value system. For this role, he is even physically transformed: He hires the body shop proprietor, Ramone, to paint over his sponsors' stickers and his large race number, as if to remove himself almost completely from the Piston Cup world, even as he anticipates being released from his community service and thus being able to return to racing.

Perhaps even more than Buzz, Woody, and Mr. Incredible do, the New Man McQueen shuns the remaining trappings of the alpha role, actually refusing the Piston Cup. If the first three protagonists are ultimately qualified heroes—that is, they still retain their authority and accomplish their various tasks, but with new values and perspectives acquired along the way—Lightning completely and publicly refuses his former object of desire. Early in the final race, he seems to somewhat devalue racing; his daydreams of Sally distract him, tempting him to give up rather than to compete. The plot, however, needs him to dominate the race so his decision at the end will be entirely his own. His friends show up and encourage him to succeed. This is where the other films end: The values of caring, sharing, nurturing, and community being clearly present, the hero is at last able to achieve, improved by having embraced those values. But Lightning, seeing the wrecked King and remembering the words of Doc Hudson, screeches to a stop inches before the finish line. Reversing, he approaches the King, pushes him back on the track, and acknowledges the relative insignificance of the Piston Cup in comparison to his new and improved self. He then declines the Dinoco corporate offer in favor of remaining faithful to his loyal Rust-eze sponsors. Chick Hicks, the only unredeemed alpha male at the end, celebrates his ill-gotten victory and is publicly rejected at the end by both his fans, "the twins," and, in a sense, by the Piston Cup itself, which slides onto the stage and hits him rudely in the side.

Conclusion

The trend of the New Man seems neither insidious nor nefarious, nor is it   24
out of step with the larger cultural movement. It is good, we believe, for
our son to be aware of the many sides of human existence, regardless of
traditional gender stereotypes. However, maintaining a critical consciousness of the many lessons taught by the cultural monolith of Disney remains
imperative. These lessons—their pedagogical aims or results—become
most immediately obvious to us as parents when we watch our son ingest
and express them, when he misunderstands and makes his own sense
of them, and when we can see ways in which his perception of reality is
shaped by them, before our eyes. Without assuming that the values of the
films are inherently evil or representative of an evil "conspiracy to undermine American youth" (Giroux 4), we are still compelled to critically
examine the texts on which our son bases many of his attitudes, behaviors,
and preferences.

Moreover, the impact of Disney, as Henry Giroux has effectively   25
argued, is tremendously more widespread than our household. Citing
Michael Eisner's 1995 "Planetized Entertainment," Giroux claims that 200
million people a year watch Disney videos or films, and in a week, 395 million watch a Disney TV show, 3.8 million subscribe to the Disney Channel,
and 810,000 make a purchase at a Disney store (19). As Benjamin Barber
argued in 1995, "[T]he true tutors of our children are not schoolteachers
or university professors but filmmakers, advertising executives and pop
culture purveyors" (qtd. in Giroux 63). Thus we perform our "pedagogical
intervention[s]" of examining Disney's power to "shap[e] national identity,
gender roles, and childhood values" (Giroux 10). It remains a necessary
and ongoing task, not just for concerned parents, but for all conscientious
cultural critics.

NOTES

1. See Susan Jeffords, "The Curse of Masculinity: Disney's *Beauty and the Beast*" for an
   excellent analysis of that plot's developing the cruel Beast into a man who can love
   and be loved in return: "Will he be able to overcome his beastly temper and terroriz-
   ing attitude in order to learn to love?" (168). But even in this film, she argues, the
   Beast's development is dependent on "other people, especially women," whose job it
   is to tutor him into the new model of masculinity, the "New Man" (169, 170).
2. Two articles demand that we qualify this claim. Indirectly, they support the point
   of this essay by demonstrating a midcentury Disney model of what we call "alpha"
   masculinity. David Payne's "Bambi" parallels that film's coming-of-age plot, ostensibly representing a "natural" world, with the military mindset of the 1940s against
   which the film was drawn. Similarly, Claudia Card, in "Pinocchio," claims that the
   Disneyfied version of the nineteenth-century Carlo Collodi tale replaces the original's model of bravery and honesty with "a macho exercise in heroism [. . . and]
   avoid[ing] humiliation" (66–67).
3. Outside the animated classics, critics have noted a trend toward a postfeminist
   masculinity—one characterized by emotional wellness, sensitivity to family, and

a conscious rejection of the most alpha male values—in Disney-produced films of the 1980s and 1990s. Jeffords gives a sensible account of the changing male lead in films ranging from *Kindergarten Cop* to *Terminator 2.*

4. In Disney criticism, the phrase "New Man" seems to belong to Susan Jeffords's 1995 essay on *Beauty and the Beast,* but it is slowly coming into vogue for describing other postfeminist trends in masculine identity. In popular culture, see Richard Collier's "The New Man: Fact or Fad?" online in *Achilles Heel: The Radical Men's Magazine* 14 (Winter 1992/1993). http://www.achillesheel.freeuk.com/article14_9 .html. For a literary-historical account, see *Writing Men: Literary Masculinities from Frankenstein to the New Man* by Berthold Schoene-Harwood (Columbia UP, 2000).

5. Critics have described the superhero within some framework of queer theory since the 1950s, when Dr. Fredric Wertham's *Seduction of the Innocent* claimed that Batman and Robin were gay (Ameron Ltd, 1954). See Rob Lendrum's "Queering Super-Manhood: Superhero Masculinity, Camp, and Public Relations as a Textual Framework" (*International Journal of Comic Art* 7.1 [2005]: 287–303) and Valerie Palmer-Mehtan and Kellie Hay's "A Superhero for Gays? Gay Masculinity and Green Lantern" (*Journal of American Culture* 28.4 [2005]: 390–404), among myriad nonscholarly pop-cultural sources.

6. Interestingly, Andy and *Toy Story* in general are apparently without (human) male role models. The only father present in the film at all is Sid's, sleeping in front of the television in the middle of the day. Andy's is absent at a dinner out, during a move, and on the following Christmas morning. Andy himself, at play, imagines splintering a nuclear family: when he makes Sheriff Woody catch One-Eyed Black Bart in a criminal act, he says, "Say goodbye to the wife and tater tots . . . you're going to jail."

WORKS CITED

Bell, Elizabeth. "Somatexts at the Disney Shop: Constructing the Pentimentos of Women's Animated Bodies." Bell, *From Mouse to Mermaid* 107–24.

Bell, Elizabeth, Lynda Haas, and Laura Sells, eds. *From Mouse to Mermaid: the Politics of Film, Gender, and Culture.* Bloomington: Indiana UP, 1995.

Card, Claudia. "Pinocchio." Bell, *From Mouse to Mermaid* 62–71.

Cars. Dir. John Lasseter. Walt Disney Pictures/Pixar Animation Studios, 2006.

Collier, Richard. "The New Man: Fact or Fad?" *Achilles Heel: The Radical Men's Magazine* 14 (1992–93). <http://www.achillesheel.freeuk.com/article14_9.html>.

Eisner, Michael. "Planetized Entertainment." *New Perspectives Quarterly* 12.4 (1995): 8.

Giroux, Henry. *The Mouse that Roared: Disney and the End of Innocence.* Oxford, Eng.: Rowman, 1999.

The Incredibles. Dir. Brad Bird. Walt Disney Pictures/Pixar Animation Studios, 2004.

Jeffords, Susan. "The Curse of Masculinity: Disney's *Beauty and the Beast*" Bell, *From Mouse to Mermaid* 161–72.

Lendrum, Rob. "Queering Super-Manhood: Superhero Masculinity, Camp, and Public Relations as a Textual Framework." *International Journal of Comic Art* 7.1 (2005): 287–303.

Palmer-Mehtan, Valerie, and Kellie Hay. "A Superhero for Gays? Gay Masculinity and Green Lantern." *Journal of American Culture* 28.4 (2005): 390–404.

Payne, David. "Bambi." Bell, *From Mouse to Mermaid* 137–47.

Schoene-Harwood, Berthold. *Writing Men: Literary Masculinities from Frankenstein to the New Man.* Columbia: Columbia UP, 2000.

Sedgwick, Eve Kosofsky. *Between Men: English Literature and Male Homosocial Desire.* New York: Columbia UP, 1985.

Toy Story. Dir. John Lasseter. Walt Disney Pictures/Pixar Animation Studios, 1995.

Wertham, Fredric. *Seduction of the Innocent.* New York: Reinhart, 1954.
Yabroff, Jennie. "Betas Rule." *Newsweek* 4 June 2007: 64–65.

■ ■ ■

Reading as a Writer: Analyzing Rhetorical Choices

1. While the topic of this essay comes from popular culture, the language is
    quite scholarly. Circle any words that might be new to you, see what you
    can discern about their meaning from the context, and then look them up.
    For example, you might want to be sure you know the meaning of "bil-
    dungsroman" (para. 1), "patriarchal" (para. 5), "homosocial" (para. 16),
    and "pedagogical" (para. 24), among others. How are these terms impor-
    tant to the authors' argument?

2. You might have some fun applying the authors' argument to Pixar films
    produced after 2008 or to other films made for children. In pairs or groups,
    choose a film to use as a test case, and apply the authors' method of using
    specific examples from the film to analyze whether the lead character's
    gender role changes over the course of the film in the way they claim is
    standard, at least for Pixar films. What happens to the roles of leading
    female characters? What conclusions do you draw?

Writing as a Reader: Entering the Conversation of Ideas

1. Building on insights from Gillam and Wooden and also Jean Kilbourne,
    who writes about visual images and gender norms (pp. 554–77), compose
    an analysis of a film not mentioned in this reading that you believe raises
    interesting issues about gender roles. Be sure to use description and analy-
    sis of specific examples in the film as you make an argument about the
    significance of gender representations in the film.

2. How do Gillam and Wooden's ideas about changing attitudes toward mas-
    culinity intersect with C. J. Pascoe's (pp. 464–81 in Sociology) analysis of
    adolescent masculinity? Write an essay in which you bring together ideas
    from these readings and examples from popular culture that will support
    your claims to make a point about changing—or unchanging—concepts
    of masculinity in the United States.

JEAN KILBOURNE

"Two Ways a Woman Can Get Hurt": Advertising and Violence

Jean Kilbourne, EdD, is an award-winning author and educator who is
best known for her lively campus lectures on the effects of media images
on young people. Her academic interests stem from personal experience.
Although Kilbourne was a superb student when she came of age in the

1960s, she found she was rewarded more for her looks than for her intelligence. Later, after she began working in journalism and education, she noticed the absurd arguments that advertisements often make, many of them insulting to women's intelligence and self-esteem. Once she found her personal and professional interests intersecting, Kilbourne began collecting and analyzing advertisements, eventually shaping them into a lecture series and then a film titled *Killing Us Softly: Advertising's Image of Women* (1979). This film, its three subsequent versions, and other films Kilbourne has produced on anorexia and on tobacco and alcohol addiction, are taught frequently in college classes today. Kilbourne has also published many articles and several books on these topics, including the book from which this essay is excerpted, *Deadly Persuasion: Why Women and Girls Must Fight the Addictive Power of Advertising* (1999).

The first thing you may notice about Kilbourne's essay is that it is filled with advertising images. Before you read, flip through the essay to see if you can get a sense of Kilbourne's argument simply from the advertisements she includes. As you read, keep returning to these images, testing them against Kilbourne's argument and the information she includes from other scholars about violence in our culture (particularly sexualized violence) and the power of the media. Kilbourne's is an important voice among the many media critics who have discussed the ways advertising images normalize—and even make appealing—sexual and violent situations that most often threaten women and children. As you read, pay close attention to the connections Kilbourne makes between the media and social problems. Note the passages you find most and least convincing, and ask yourself why. Getting in the habit of evaluating evidence this way will help you immeasurably when you decide on the kinds of evidence you want to include in your own writing.

Kilbourne is sometimes criticized for being too selective in her choice of images and evidence and too narrow in her analysis. Throughout the essay, you will hear her addressing her critics, anticipating claims that she is simply reading too much into these images or taking advertising too seriously. Often she provides more than one interpretation of an image, for example, saying about the subject of one advertisement, "I suppose this could be a woman awaiting her lover, but it could as easily be a girl being preyed upon" (para. 33). Note the way she builds her claims about images on the research of experts in the fields of anthropology, addiction, gendered violence, and media criticism and also the way she sites newspaper reports of crimes and trends she finds so dangerous.

Given our visually rich media culture, you are likely to find many familiar ideas and images in Kilbourne's essay, and you also are likely to find yourself strongly agreeing or disagreeing—or perhaps both—with her as she builds her case about the "deadly" power of the advertising industry. Even if you do not agree with her on every point, Kilbourne's strategy of analyzing the ways advertising makes dangerous behaviors seem "normal" and even appealing is one all consumers can use to make sense of marketing claims and popular culture.

■   ■   ■

Two Ways A Woman Can Get Hurt.

(Heartbreaker)   (Soap and water shave)

Skintimate® Shave Gel Ultra Protection formula contains 75% moisturizers, including vitamin E, to protect your legs from nicks, cuts and razor burn. So while guys may continue to be a pain, shaving most definitely won't.

SKINTIMATE® SHAVE GEL
LOVE YOUR LEGS

© 1997 S.C. Johnson & Son, Inc. All rights reserved. www.skintimate.com

S ex in advertising is more about disconnection and distance than connection and closeness. It is also more often about power than passion, about violence than violins. The main goal, as in pornography, is usually power over another, either by the physical dominance or preferred status of men or what is seen as the exploitative power of female beauty and female sexuality. Men conquer and women ensnare, always with the essential aid of a product. The woman is rewarded for her sexuality by the man's wealth, as in an ad for Cigarette boats in which the woman says, while lying in a man's embrace clearly after sex, "Does this mean I get a ride in your Cigarette?"

Sex in advertising is porno- graphic because it dehumanizes and objectifies people, especially women, and because it fetishizes products, imbues them with an erotic charge—which dooms us to disappointment since products never can fulfill our sexual desires or meet our emotional needs. The poses and postures of advertising are often borrowed from pornography, as are many of the themes, such as bondage, sadomasochism, and the sexual exploitation of children. When a beer ad uses the image of a man licking the high-heeled

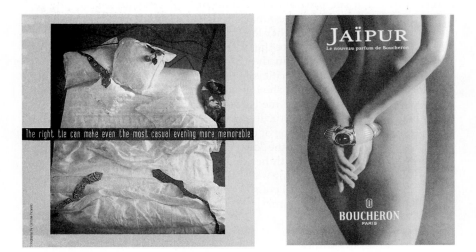

boot of a woman clad in leather, when bondage is used to sell neckties in *The New York Times*, perfume in *The New Yorker*, and watches on city buses, and when a college magazine promotes an S&M Ball, pornography can be considered mainstream.

Most of us know all this by now and I suppose some consider it kinky 3 good fun. Pornography is more dangerously mainstream when its glorification of rape and violence shows up in mass media, in films and television shows, in comedy and music videos, and in advertising. Male violence is subtly encouraged by ads that encourage men to be forceful and dominant, and to value sexual intimacy more than emotional intimacy. "Do you want to be the one she tells her deep, dark secrets to?" asks a three-page ad for men's cologne. "Or do you want to be her deep, dark secret?" The last page advises men, "Don't be such a good boy." There are two identical women looking adoringly at the man in the ad, but he isn't looking at either one of them. Just what is the deep, dark secret? That he's sleeping with both of them? Clearly the way to get beautiful women is to ignore them, perhaps mistreat them.

"Two ways a woman can get hurt," says an ad for shaving gel, featuring a razor and a photo of a handsome man. My first thought is that the man is a batterer or date rapist, but the ad informs us that he is merely a "heartbreaker." The gel will protect the woman so that "while guys may continue to be a pain, shaving most definitely won't." Desirable men are painful—heartbreakers at best. 4

Wouldn't it be wonderful if, realizing the importance of relationships 5 in all of our lives, we could seek to learn relational skills from women and to help men develop these strengths in themselves? In fact, we so often do the opposite. The popular culture usually trivializes these abilities in women, mocks men who have real intimacy with women (it is almost always married men in ads and cartoons who are jerks), and idealizes a template for relationships between men and women that is a recipe for disaster: a template that views sex as more important than anything else,

that ridicules men who are not in control of their women (who are "pussy-whipped"), and that disparages fidelity and commitment (except, of course, to brand names).

Indeed the very worst kind of 6 man for a woman to be in an intimate relationship with, often a truly dangerous man, is the one considered most sexy and desirable in the popular culture. And the men capable of real intimacy (the ones we tell our deep, dark secrets to) constantly have their very masculinity impugned. Advertising often encourages women to be attracted to hostile and indifferent men while encouraging boys to become these men. This is especially dangerous

for those of us who have suffered from "condemned isolation" in childhood: Like heat-seeking missiles, we rush inevitably to mutual destruction.

Men are also encouraged to never take no for an answer. Ad after ad 7 implies that girls and women don't really mean "no" when they say it, that women are only teasing when they resist men's advances. "NO" says an ad showing a man leaning over a woman against a wall. Is she screaming or laughing? Oh, it's an ad for deodorant and the second word, in very small print, is "sweat." Sometimes it's "all in good fun," as in the ad for Possession shirts and shorts featuring a man ripping the clothes off a woman who seems to be having a good time.

And sometimes it is more sinister. A perfume ad running in several 8 teen magazines features a very young woman, with eyes blackened by makeup or perhaps something else, and the copy, "Apply generously to your neck so he can smell the scent as you shake your head 'no.'" In other words, he'll understand that you don't really mean it and he can respond to the scent like any other animal.

Sometimes there seems to be no question but that a man should force 9 a woman to have sex. A chilling newspaper ad for a bar in Georgetown features a closeup of a cocktail and the headline, "If your date won't listen to reason, try a Velvet Hammer." A vodka ad pictures a wolf hiding in a flock of sheep, a hideous grin on its face. We all know what wolves do to sheep. A campaign for Bacardi Black rum features shadowy figures almost obliterated by darkness and captions such as "Some people embrace the night because the rules of the day do not apply." What it doesn't say is that people who are above the rules do enormous harm to other people, as well as to themselves.

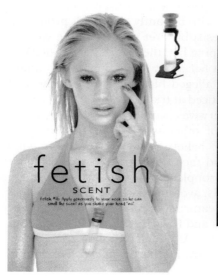

fetish
SCENT

fetish "it: Apply generously to your neck so he can smell the scent as you shake your head 'no.'

IF YOUR DATE WON'T LISTEN TO REASON, TRY A VELVET HAMMER.

Sip exotic cocktails, dine and dance to Swing Era music at Georgetown's top nightspot. 1232 36th St., NW. Reservations, call 342-0009. Free valet parking. Jackets required.

F. SCOTT'S

These ads are particu- *10* larly troublesome, given that between one-third and three-quarters of all cases of sexual assault involve alcohol consumption by the perpetrator, the victim, or both.[1] "Make strangers your friends, and your friends a lot stranger," says one of the ads in a Cuervo campaign that uses colorful cartoon beasts and emphasizes heavy drink-ing. This ad is especially disturbing when we consider the role of alcohol in date rape, as is another ad in the series that says, "The night began with a bottle of Cuervo and ended with a vow of silence." Over half of all reported rapes on college campuses occur when either the victim or the assailant has been drinking.[2] Alcohol's role has different meaning for men and women, however. If a man is drunk when he commits a rape, he is considered less responsible. If a woman is drunk (or has had a drink or two or simply met the man in a bar), she is considered more responsible.

In general, females are still held responsible and hold each other *11* responsible when sex goes wrong—when they become pregnant or are the victims of rape and sexual assault or cause a scandal. Constantly exhorted to be sexy and attractive, they discover when assaulted that that very sexiness is evidence of their guilt, their lack of "innocence." Sometimes the ads play on this by "warning" women of what might happen if they use the product. "Wear it but beware it," says a perfume ad. Beware what exactly? Victoria's Secret tempts young women with blatantly sexual ads promising that their lingerie will make them irresistible. Yet when a young woman accused William Kennedy Smith of raping her, the fact that she wore Victoria's Secret panties was used against her as an indication of her immorality. A jury acquitted Smith, whose alleged history of violence against women was not permitted to be introduced at trial.

It is sadly not surprising that the jury was composed mostly of women. *12* Women are especially cruel judges of other women's sexual behavior, mostly because we are so desperate to believe we are in control of what happens to us. It is too frightening to face the fact that male violence against women is irrational and commonplace. It is reassuring to believe that we can avoid it by being good girls, avoiding dark places, staying out of bars, dressing "innocently." An ad featuring two young women talking intimately at a coffee shop says, "Carla and Rachel considered themselves open-minded and non-judgmental people. Although they did agree Brenda was a tramp." These terrible judgments from other women are an impor-tant part of what keeps all women in line.

If indifference in a man is sexy, then violence is sometimes downright erotic. Not surprisingly, this attitude too shows up in advertising. "Push my buttons," says a young woman, "I'm looking for a man who can totally floor me." Her vulnerability is underscored by the fact that she is in an elevator, often a dangerous place for women. She is young, she is submissive (her eyes are downcast), she is in a dangerous place, and she is dressed provocatively. And she is literally asking for it.

13

14

"Wear it out and make it scream," says a jeans ad portraying a man sliding his hands under a woman's transparent blouse. This could be a seduction, but it could as easily be an attack. Although the ad that ran in the Czech version of *Elle* portraying three men attacking a woman seems unambiguous, the terrifying image is being used to sell jeans *to women*. So someone must think that women would find this image compelling or attractive. Why would we? Perhaps it is simply designed to get our attention, by shocking us and by arousing unconscious anxiety. Or perhaps the intent is more subtle and it is designed to play into the fantasies of domination and even rape that some women use in order to maintain an illusion of being in control (we are the ones having the fantasies, after all, we are the directors).

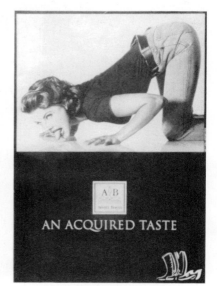

A camera ad features a woman's torso wrapped in plastic, her hands tied behind her back. A smiling woman in a lipstick ad has a padlocked chain around her neck. An ad for MTV shows a vulnerable young woman, her breasts exposed, and the simple copy "Bitch." A perfume ad features a man shadowboxing with what seems to be a woman. 15

Sometimes women are shown dead or in the process of being killed. "Great hair never dies," says an ad featuring a female corpse lying on a bed, her breasts exposed. An ad in the Italian version of *Vogue* shows a man aiming a gun at a nude woman wrapped in plastic, a leather briefcase covering her face. And an ad for Bitch skateboards, for God's sake, shows a cartoon version of a similar scene, this time clearly targeting young people. We believe we are not affected by these images, but most of us experience visceral shock when we pay conscious attention to them. Could they be any less shocking to us on an unconscious level? 16

Most of us become numb to these images, just as we become numb to the daily litany in the news of women being raped, battered, and killed. According to former surgeon general Antonia Novello, battery is the single greatest cause of injury to women in America, more common 17

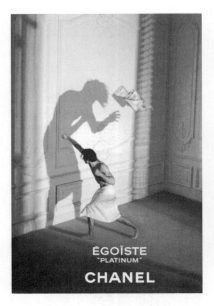

ÉGOÏSTE
"PLATINUM"
CHANEL

La Borsa è la Vita

than automobile accidents, muggings, and stranger rapes combined, and more than one-third of women slain in this country die at the hands of husbands or boyfriends.[3] Throughout the world, the biggest problem for most women is simply surviving at home. The Global Report on Women's Human Rights concluded that "domestic violence is a leading cause of female injury in almost every country in the world and is typically ignored by the state or only erratically punished."[4] Although usually numb to these facts on a conscious level, most

bitch skateboards

women live in a state of subliminal terror, a state that, according to Mary Daly, keeps us divided both from each other and from our most passionate, powerful, and creative selves.[5]

Ads don't directly cause violence, of course. But the violent images 18 contribute to the state of terror. And objectification and disconnection create a climate in which there is widespread and increasing violence. Turning a human being into a thing, an object, is almost always the first step toward justifying violence against that person. It is very difficult, perhaps impossible, to be violent to someone we think of as an equal, someone we have empathy with, but it is very easy to abuse a thing. We see this with racism, with homophobia. The person becomes an object and violence is inevitable. This step is already taken with women. The violence, the abuse, is partly the chilling but logical result of the objectification.

An editorial in *Advertising Age* suggests that even some advertisers are 19 concerned about this: "Clearly it's time to wipe out sexism in beer ads; for the brewers and their agencies to wake up and join the rest of America in realizing that sexism, sexual harassment, and the cultural portrayal of women in advertising are inextricably linked."[6] Alas, this editorial was written in 1991 and nothing has changed.

It is this link with violence that makes the objectification of women 20 a more serious issue than the objectification of men. Our economic system constantly requires the development of new markets. Not surprisingly, men's bodies are the latest territory to be exploited. Although we are growing more used to it, in the beginning the male sex object came as a surprise. In 1994 a "gender bender" television commercial in which a bevy of women office workers gather to watch a construction worker doff his shirt to quaff a Diet Coke led to so much hoopla that you'd have thought women were mugging men on Madison Avenue.[7]

There is no question that men are used as sex objects in ads now as 21 never before. We often see nude women with fully clothed men in ads (as in art), but the reverse was unheard of, until recently. These days some ads do feature clothed and often aggressive women with nude men. And women sometimes blatantly objectify men, as in the Metroliner ad that says, "'She's reading Nietzsche,' Harris noted to himself as he walked towards the café car for a glass of cabernet. And as he passed her seat, Maureen looked up from her book and thought, 'Nice buns.'"

Although these ads are often funny, it 22 is never a good thing for human beings to be objectified. However, there is a world of difference between the objectification of men and that of women. The most important difference is that there is no danger for most men, whereas objectified women are always at risk. In the Diet Coke ad, for instance, the women are physically separated from the shirtless man. He is the one in control. His body is powerful, not passive. Imagine a true role reversal of this ad: A group of businessmen gather to leer at a beautiful woman worker on her break, who removes her shirt before drinking her Diet Coke. This scene would be frightening, not funny, as the Diet Coke ad is. And why is the Diet Coke ad funny? Because we know it doesn't describe any truth. However, the ads featuring images of male violence against women do describe a truth, a truth we are all aware of, on one level or another.

When power is unequal, when one group is oppressed and discrimi- 23 nated against *as a group*, when there is a context of systemic and historical oppression, stereotypes and prejudice have different weight and meaning. As Anna Quindlen said, writing about "reverse racism": "Hatred by the powerful, the majority, has a different weight—and often very different effects—than hatred by the powerless, the minority."[8] When men objectify women, they do so in a cultural context in which women are constantly objectified and in which there are consequences—from economic discrimination to violence—to that objectification.

For men, though, there are no such consequences. Men's bodies are 24 not routinely judged and invaded. Men are not likely to be raped, harassed, or beaten (that is to say, men presumed to be heterosexual are not, and very few men are abused in these ways by women). How many men are frightened to be alone with a woman in an elevator? How many men cross the street when a group of women approach? Jackson Katz, who writes and lectures on male violence, often begins his workshops by asking men to describe the things they do every day to protect themselves from sexual assault. The men are surprised, puzzled, sometimes amused by the question. The women understand the question easily and have no trouble at all coming up with a list of responses. We don't list our full names in the phone directory or on our mailboxes, we try not to be alone after dark, we carry our keys in our hands when we approach our cars, we always look in the back seat before we get in, we are wary of elevators and doorways and bushes, we carry pepper sprays, whistles, Mace.

Nonetheless, the rate of sexual assault in the United States is the high-   25
est of any industrialized nation in the world.[9] According to a 1998 study by the federal government, one in five of us has been the victim of rape or attempted rape, most often before our seventeenth birthday.[10] And more than half of us have been physically assaulted, most often by the men we live with. In fact, three of four women in the study who responded that they had been raped or assaulted as adults said the perpetrator was a current or former husband, a cohabiting partner, or a date. The article reporting the results of this study was buried on page twenty-three of my local newspaper, while the front page dealt with a long story about the New England Patriots football team.

A few summers ago, a Diet Pepsi commercial featured Cindy Crawford   26
being ogled by two boys (they seemed to be about twelve years old) as she got out of her car and bought a Pepsi from a machine. The boys made very suggestive comments, which in the end turned out to be about the Pepsi's can rather than Ms. Crawford's. There was no outcry: The boys' behavior was acceptable and ordinary enough for a soft-drink commercial.

Again, let us imagine the reverse: a sexy man gets out of a car in the   27
countryside and two preteen girls make suggestive comments, seemingly about his body, especially his buns. We would fear for them and rightly so. But the boys already have the right to ogle, to view women's bodies as property to be looked at, commented on, touched, perhaps eventually hit and raped. The boys have also learned that men ogle primarily to impress other men (and to affirm their heterosexuality). If anyone is in potential danger in this ad, it is the woman (regardless of the age of the boys). Men are not seen as *property* in this way by women. Indeed if a woman does whistle at a man or touches his body or even makes direct eye contact, it is still *she* who is at risk and the man who has the power.

"I always lower my eyes to see if a man is worth following,"   28
says the woman in an ad for men's pants. Although the ad is offensive to everyone, the woman is endangering only herself.

"Where women are women   29
and men are roadkill," says an ad for motorcycle clothing featuring an angry-looking African-American

woman. Women are sometimes hostile and angry in ads these days, especially women of color who are often seen as angrier and more threatening
than white women. But, regardless of color, we all know that women are
far more likely than men to end up as roadkill—and, when it happens,
they are blamed for being on the road in the first place.

Even little girls are sometimes held responsible for the violence against   30
them. In 1990 a male Canadian judge accused a three-year-old girl of being
"sexually aggressive" and suspended the sentence of her molester, who was
then free to return to his job of babysitter.[11] The deeply held belief that all
women, regardless of age, are really temptresses in disguise, nymphets,
sexually insatiable and seductive, conveniently transfers all blame and
responsibility onto women.

All women are vulnerable in a cul-   31
ture in which there is such widespread
objectification of women's bodies, such
glorification of disconnection, so much
violence against women, and such blaming of the victim. When everything and
everyone is sexualized, it is the powerless who are most at risk. Young girls, of
course, are especially vulnerable. In the
past twenty years or so, there have been
several trends in fashion and advertising
that could be seen as cultural reactions
to the women's movement, as perhaps
unconscious fear of female power. One
has been the obsession with thinness.
Another has been an increase in images
of violence against women. Most disturbing has been the increasing sexu-
alization of children, especially girls. Sometimes the little girl is made up
and seductively posed. Sometimes the language is suggestive. "Very cherry,"
says the ad featuring a sexy little African-American girl who is wearing a
dress with cherries all over it. A shocking ad in a gun magazine features a
smiling little girl, a toddler, in a bathing suit that is tugged up suggestively
in the rear.[12] The copy beneath the photo says, "short BUTTS from FLEMING
FIREARMS." Other times girls are juxtaposed with grown women, as in the
ad for underpants that says "You already know the feeling."

This is not only an American phenomenon. A growing national obses-   32
sion in Japan with schoolgirls dressed in uniforms is called "Loli-con,"
after Lolita.[13] In Tokyo hundreds of "image clubs" allow Japanese men to
act out their fantasies with make-believe schoolgirls. A magazine called
V-Club featuring pictures of naked elementary-school girls competes with
another called *Anatomical Illustrations of Junior High School Girls*. Masao
Miyamoto, a male psychiatrist, suggests that Japanese men are turning to
girls because they feel threatened by the growing sophistication of older
women.[14]

boy seems embarrassed but he complies. There was a great deal of protest, which brought the issue into national consciousness but which also
gave Klein the publicity and free media coverage he was looking for. He
pulled the ads but, at the same time, projected that his jeans sales would
almost double from $115 million to $220 million that year, partly because
of the free publicity but also because the controversy made his critics seem
like prudes and thus positioned Klein as the daring rebel, a very appealing
image to the majority of his customers.

Having learned from this, in 1999
Klein launched a very brief advertising
campaign featuring very little children
frolicking in their underpants, which
included a controversial billboard in
Times Square.[18] Although in some ways
this campaign was less offensive than the
earlier one and might have gone unnoticed
had the ads come from a department store
catalog rather than from Calvin Klein,
there was the expected protest and Klein
quickly withdrew the ads, again getting a
windfall of media coverage. In my opinion, the real obscenity of this campaign is
the whole idea of people buying designer
underwear for their little ones, especially
in a country in which at least one in five
children doesn't have enough to eat.

37

Although boys are sometimes sexualized in an overt way, they are
more often portrayed as sexually precocious, as in the Pepsi commercial
featuring the young boys ogling Cindy Crawford or the jeans ad portraying
a very little boy looking up a woman's skirt. It may seem that I am reading

38

too much into this ad, but imagine if the genders were reversed. We would fear for a little girl who was unzipping a man's fly in an ad (and we would be shocked, I would hope). Boys are vulnerable to sexual abuse too, but cultural attitudes make it difficult to take this seriously. As a result, boys are less likely to report abuse and to get treatment.

Many boys grow up feeling that they are unmanly if they are not always *39* "ready for action," capable of and interested in sex with any woman who is available. Advertising doesn't cause this attitude, of course, but it contributes to it. A Levi Strauss commercial that ran in Asia features the shock of a schoolboy who discovers that the seductive young woman who has slipped a note into the jeans of an older student is his teacher. And an ad for BIC pens pictures a young boy wearing X-ray glasses while ogling the derriere of an older woman. Again, these ads would be unthinkable if the genders were reversed. It is increasingly difficult in such a toxic environment to see children, boys or girls, as *children.*

In the past few years there has been a proliferation of sexually gro- *40* tesque toys for boys, such as a Spider Man female action figure whose exaggerated breasts have antennae coming out of them and a female Spawn figure with carved skulls for breasts. Meantime even children have easy access to pornography in video games and on the World Wide Web, which includes explicit photographs of women having intercourse with groups of men, with dogs, donkeys, horses, and snakes; photographs of women being raped and tortured; some of these women made up to look like little girls.

It is hard for girls not to learn self-hatred in an environment in which *41* there is such widespread and open contempt for women and girls. In 1997 a company called Senate distributed clothing with inside labels that included, in addition to the usual cleaning instructions, the line "Destroy all girls."[19] A Senate staffer explained that he thought it was "kind of cool." Given all this, it's not surprising that when boys and girls were asked in a recent study to write an essay on what it would be like to be the other

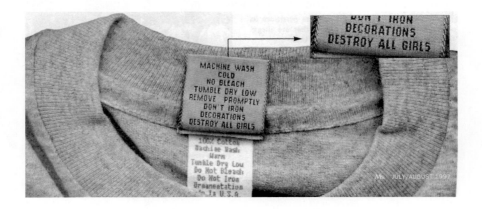

gender, many boys wrote they would rather be dead. Girls had no trouble writing essays about activities, power, freedom, but boys were often stuck, could think of nothing.

It is also not surprising that, in such an environment, sexual harassment is considered normal and ordinary. According to an article in the journal *Eating Disorders*:   42

> In our work with young women, we have heard countless accounts of this contempt being expressed by their male peers: the girls who do not want to walk down a certain hallway in their high school because they are afraid of being publicly rated on a scale of one to ten; the girls who are subjected to barking, grunting, and mooing calls and labels of "dogs, cows, or pigs" when they pass by groups of male students; those who are teased about not measuring up to buxom, bikini-clad [models]; and the girls who are grabbed, pinched, groped, and fondled as they try to make their way through the school corridors.
>
> Harassing words do not slide harmlessly away as the taunting sounds dissipate.... They are slowly absorbed into the child's identity and developing sense of self, becoming an essential part of whom she sees herself to be. Harassment involves the use of words as weapons to inflict pain and assert power. Harassing words are meant to instill fear, heighten bodily discomfort, and diminish the sense of self.[20]

It is probably difficult for those of us who are older to understand   43
how devastating and cruel and pervasive this harassment is, how different from the "teasing" some of us might remember from our own childhoods (not that that didn't hurt and do damage as well). A 1993 report by the American Association of University Women found that 76 percent of female students in grades eight to eleven and 56 percent of male students said they had been sexually harassed in school.[21] One high-school junior described a year of torment at her vocational school: "The boys call me slut, bitch. They call me a 10-timer, because they say I go with 10 guys at the same time. I put up with it because I have no choice. The teachers say it's because the boys think I'm pretty."[22]

High school and junior high school have always been hell for those   44
who were different in any way (gay teens have no doubt suffered the most, although "overweight" girls are a close second), but the harassment is more extreme and more physical these days. Many young men feel they have the right to judge and touch young women and the women often feel they have no choice but to submit. One young woman recalled that "the guys at school routinely swiped their hands across girls' legs to patrol their shaving prowess and then taunt them if they were slacking off. If I were running late, I'd protect myself by faux shaving—just doing the strip between the bottom of my jeans and the top of my cotton socks."[23]

Sexual battery, as well as inappropriate sexual gesturing, touching,   45
and fondling, is increasing not only in high schools but in elementary and middle schools as well.[24] There are reports of sexual assaults by students on other students as young as eight. A fifth-grade boy in Georgia repeatedly

touched the breasts and genitals of one of his fellow students while saying, "I want to get in bed with you" and "I want to feel your boobs."[25] Authorities did nothing, although the girl complained and her grades fell. When her parents found a suicide note she had written, they took the board of education to court.

A high-school senior in an affluent suburban school in the Boston area   46
said she has been dragged by her arms so boys could look up her skirt and that boys have rested their heads on her chest while making lewd comments.[26] Another student in the same school was pinned down on a lunch table while a boy simulated sex on top of her. Neither student reported any of the incidents, for fear of being ostracized by their peers. In another school in the Boston area, a sixteen-year-old girl, who had been digitally raped by a classmate, committed suicide.[27]

According to Nan Stein, a researcher at Wellesley College: 47

> Schools may in fact be training grounds for the insidious cycle of domestic violence. . . . The school's hidden curriculum teaches young women to suffer abuse privately, that resistance is futile. When they witness harassment of others and fail to respond, they absorb a different kind of powerlessness—that they are incapable of standing up to injustice or acting in solidarity with their peers. Similarly, in schools boys receive permission, even training, to become batterers through the practice of sexual harassment.[28]

This pervasive harassment of and contempt for girls and women con-   48
stitute a kind of abuse. We know that addictions for women are rooted in trauma, that girls who are sexually abused are far more likely to become addicted to one substance or another. I contend that all girls growing up in this culture are sexually abused—abused by the pornographic images of female sexuality that surround them from birth, abused by all the violence against women and girls, and abused by the constant harassment and threat of violence. Abuse is a continuum, of course, and I am by no means implying that cultural abuse is as terrible as literally being raped and assaulted. However, it hurts, it does damage, and it sets girls up for addictions and self-destructive behavior. Many girls turn to food, alcohol, cigarettes, and other drugs in a misguided attempt to cope.

As Marian Sandmaier said in *The Invisible Alcoholics: Women and*   49
Alcohol Abuse in America, "In a culture that cuts off women from many of their own possibilities before they barely have had a chance to sense them, that pain belongs to all women. Outlets for coping may vary widely, and may be more or less addictive, more or less self-destructive. But at some level, all women know what it is to lack access to their own power, to live with a piece of themselves unclaimed."[29]

Today, every girl is endangered, not just those who have been physi-   50
cally and sexually abused. If girls from supportive homes with positive role models are at risk, imagine then how vulnerable are the girls who have been violated. No wonder they so often go under for good—ending up in abusive marriages, in prison, on the streets. And those who do are almost

always in the grip of one addiction or another. More than half of women in prison are addicts and most are there for crimes directly related to their addiction.[30] Many who are there for murder killed men who had been battering them for years. Almost all of the women who are homeless or in prisons and mental institutions are the victims of male violence.

Male violence exists within the same cultural and sociopolitical context that contributes to addiction. Both can be fully understood only within this context, way beyond individual psychology and family dynamics. It is a context of systemic violence and oppression, including racism, classism, heterosexism, weightism, and ageism, as well as sexism, all of which are traumatizing in and of themselves. Advertising is only one part of this cultural context, but it is an important part and thus is a part of what traumatizes. 51

All right, you might think, these ads are shocking. They are probably not good for us. But just what is the relationship of all these sexist and violent ads to addiction? Am I blaming advertisers for everything now? No. But I do contend that ads that contribute to a climate of disconnection also contribute to addiction. Ads that objectify women and sexualize children also play a role in the victimization of women and girls that often leads to addiction. When women are shown in positions of powerlessness, submission, and subjugation, the message to men is clear: Women are always available as the targets of aggression and violence, women are inferior to men and thus deserve to be dominated, and women exist to fulfill the needs of men. 52

There is a further connection between images that legitimize male domination of females and addiction. In his classic essay "The Cybernetics of Self" Gregory Bateson describes the fundamental belief of Western culture that we can dominate, control, and have power over almost every aspect of our experience.[31] We can get rid of pain, we can dominate people who threaten us, we can win in any interaction, we can be invulnerable. Bateson theorizes that this belief is fundamentally erroneous and leads to addiction, which he sees as a disordered attempt to get to a more "correct" state of mind, one in which we permit dependency, vulnerability, and mutuality. Bateson argues that we have no culturally sanctioned, nonaddictive way to achieve this state. 53

Claudia Bepko takes Bateson's theory further by arguing that the stage is set for addiction by the overriding belief system maintaining that men have power and women are the objects of that power.[32] This assumption is as erroneous as is the assumption that we can control our emotions. But our entire culture is predicated on this illusion of male dominance, and our institutions are set up in ways that perpetuate it. According to Bepko, being socialized in an erroneous belief system leads to addiction because incongruity may arise between what one believes and how one actually feels. A man who feels he must be dominant but who actually feels vulnerable might use an addictive substance to lessen his feeling of vulnerability 54 or to enhance his sense of dominance. A woman forced to show dependence who really feels powerful might use a drug or other substance either to enhance or disqualify the impulse to be powerful (as the old Jefferson Airplane song says, "One pill makes you larger and one pill makes you small"). Thus gender-role socialization both shapes and is continually challenged by addictive behavior.

Bepko describes what she calls "the yin and yang of addiction." Both   55
men and women become addicted and suffer, but their individual addictions arise from their different positions in the world and have different effects. Men operate within a context in which both autonomy and entitlement to be taken care of are assumed; women within a context in which both dependency on a man and emotional and physical nurturing and caretaking are assumed. The contradictions in these prescriptions obviously create a bind: The male is independent but taken care of and the woman is dependent but the caretaker. Addiction is one response to the pain created by these contradictions.

Although the critical issues are dependency and control, these have   56
radically different meanings and outcomes for women and men. Since money, sexuality, size, strength, and competitive work convey power and status for men, gambling, sexual addictions, and work addiction tend to be predominantly male forms of compulsive behavior (although women are catching up as gender roles change). Women are still socialized to be physically and emotionally nurturing, so eating disorders, obsessive shopping or cleaning, self-mutilation, and compulsive behavior in relationships are common female forms of addictive behavior, as is prescription drug abuse, which reflects the cultural belief that women's emotions need to be subdued and controlled. A man is more likely to engage in addictive behavior that involves having power over others, whereas a woman's attempt at control is often focused on her own body.

It would be foolish to suggest that advertising is *the cause* of violence   57
against women—or of alcoholism or eating disorders or any other major problem. These problems are complex and have many contributing factors. There is no doubt that flagrant sexism and sex role stereotyping abound in all forms of the media. There is abundant information about this. It is far more difficult to document the effects of these stereotypes and images on the individuals and institutions exposed to them because, as I've said, it is difficult to separate media effects from other aspects of the socialization process and almost impossible to find a comparison group (just about everyone in America has been exposed to massive doses of advertising).

But, at the very least, advertising helps to create a climate in which   58
certain attitudes and values flourish, such as the attitude that women are valuable only as objects of men's desire, that real men are always sexually aggressive, that violence is erotic, and that women who are the victims of sexual assault "asked for it." These attitudes have especially terrible consequences for women abused as children, most of whom grow up feeling

like objects and believing they are responsible for their own abuse. These are the very women who are likely to mutilate and starve themselves, to smoke, to become addicted to alcohol and other drugs. As Judith Herman wrote in her classic book *Father-Daughter Incest*:

> These women alone suffered the consequences of their psychological impairment. Almost always, their anger and disappointment were expressed in self-destructive action: in unwanted pregnancies, in submission to rape and beatings, in addiction to alcohol and drugs, in attempted suicide.
>
> ...Consumed with rage, they nevertheless rarely caused trouble to anyone but themselves. In their own flesh, they bore repeated punishment for the crimes committed against them in their childhood.[33]

Addictions are not incidental in the lives of women. Most often they are caused by (or at least related to) disturbances in relationships in childhood, often violent disturbances. They are fueled by a culture that sexualizes children, objectifies, trivializes, and silences women, disparages our interest in and skill at relating, and constantly threatens us with violence. Feeling isolated and disconnected, a girl or a woman reaches out to a substance to numb her pain, to be sure, but also to end her isolation, to relate, to connect. She reaches for alcohol or other drugs, she reaches for cigarettes, she reaches for men who don't love her, or she reaches for food. The advertisers are ready for her.

NOTES

1. Wilsnack, Plaud, Wilsnack, and Klassen, 1997, 262.
2. Abbey, Ross, and McDuffie, 1991. Also Martin, 1992, 230–37.
3. Novello, 1991. Also Blumenthal, 1995.
4. Wright, 1995, A2.
5. Weil, 1999, 21.
6. Brewers can help fight sexism, 1991, 28.
7. Kilbourne, 1994, F13.
8. Quindlen, 1992, E17.
9. Blumenthal, 1995, 2.
10. Tjaden and Thoennes, 1998.
11. Two men and a baby, 1990, 10.
12. Herbert, 1999, WK 17.
13. Schoolgirls as sex toys, 1997, 2E.
14. *Ibid.*
15. Johnson, 1997, 42.
16. Leo, 1994, 27.
17. Sloan, 1996, 27.
18. Associated Press, 1999, February 18.
19. Wire and *Times* staff reports, 1997, D1.
20. Larkin, Rice, and Russell, 1996, 5–26.
21. Daley and Vigue, 1999, A12.
22. Hart, 1998, A12.
23. Mackler, 1998, 56.
24. Daley and Vigue, 1999, A1, A12.
25. Shin, 1999, 32.

26. Daley and Vigue, 1999, A12.
27. Vigue and Abraham, 1999, B6.
28. Stein, 1993, 316–17.
29. Sandmaier, 1980, xviii.
30. Snell, 1991.
31. Bateson, 1972.
32. Bepko, 1989.
33. Herman and Hirschman, 1981, 107–8.

BIBLIOGRAPHY

Abbey, A., Ross, L., and McDuffie, D. (1991). Alcohol's role in sexual assault. In Watson, R., ed. *Addictive behaviors in women*. Totowa, NJ: Humana Press.

Associated Press (1999, February 18). Calvin Klein retreats on ad. *Boston Globe*, A7.

Bateson, G. (1972). The cybernetics of self. In *Steps to an ecology of mind*. New York: Chandler Publishing.

Bepko, C. (1989). Disorders of power: Women and addiction in the family. In McGoldrick, M., Anderson, C. M., and Walsh, F., eds. (1989). *Women in families: A framework for family therapy*. New York: W. W. Norton, 406–26.

Blumenthal, S. J. (1995, July). *Violence against women*. Washington, DC: Department of Health and Human Services.

Brewers can help fight sexism (1991, October 28). *Advertising Age*, 28.

Daley, B., and Vigue, D. I. (1999, February 4). Sex harassment increasing amid students, officials say. *Boston Globe*, A1, A12.

Hart, J. (1998, June 8). Northampton confronts a crime, cruelty. *Boston Globe*, A1, A12.

Herbert, B. (1999, May 2). America's littlest shooters. *New York Times*, WK17.

Herman, J. L., and Hirschman, L. (1981). *Father-daughter incest*. Cambridge, MA: Harvard University Press.

Johnson, J. A. (1997, November 10). JonBenet keeps hold on magazines. *Advertising Age*, 42.

Kilbourne, J. (1994, May 15). 'Gender bender' ads: Same old sexism. *New York Times*, F13.

Larkin, J., Rice, C., and Russell, V. (1996, Spring). Slipping through the cracks: Sexual harassment. *Eating Disorders: The Journal of Treatment and Prevention*, vol. 4, no. 1, 5–26.

Leo, J. (1994, June 13). Selling the woman-child. *U.S. News and World Report*, 27.

Mackler, C. (1998). Memoirs of a (sorta) ex-shaver. In Edut, O., ed. (1998). *Adios, Barbie*. Seattle, WA: Seal Press, 55–61.

Martin, S. (1992). The epidemiology of alcohol-related interpersonal violence. *Alcohol, Health and Research World*, vol. 16, no. 3, 230–37.

Novello, A. (1991, October 18). Quoted by Associated Press, AMA to fight wife-beating. *St. Louis Post Dispatch*, 1, 15.

Quindlen, A. (1992, June 28). All of these you are. *New York Times*, E17.

Sandmaier, M. (1980). *The invisible alcoholics: Women and alcohol abuse in America*. New York: McGraw-Hill.

Schoolgirls as sex toys. (1997, April 16) *New York Times*, 2E.

Shin, A. (1999, April/May). Testing Title IX. *Ms.*, 32.

Sloan, P. (1996, July 8). Underwear ads caught in bind over sex appeal. *Advertising Age*, 27.

Snell, T. L. (1991). *Women in prison*. Washington, DC: U.S. Department of Justice.

Stein, N. (1993). No laughing matter: Sexual harassment in K–12 schools. In Buchwald, E., Fletcher, P. R., and Roth, M. (1993). *Transforming a rape culture*. Minneapolis, MN: Milkweed Editions, 311–31.

Tjaden, R., and Thoennes, N. (1998, November). *Prevalence, incidence, and consequences of violence against women: Findings from the National Violence Against Women Survey.* Washington, DC: U.S. Department of Justice.

Two men and a baby (1990, July/August). *Ms.,* 10.

Vigue, D. I., and Abraham, Y. (1999, February 7). Harassment a daily course for students. *Boston Globe,* B1, B6.

Weil, L. (1999, March). Leaps of faith. *Women's Review of Books,* 21.

Wilsnack, S. C., Plaud, J. J., Wilsnack, R. W., and Klassen, A. D. (1997). Sexuality, gender, and alcohol use. In Wilsnack, R. W., and Wilsnack, S. C., eds. *Gender and alcohol: Individual and social perspectives.* New Brunswick, NJ: Rutgers Center of Alcohol Studies, 262.

Wire and *Times* Staff Reports (1997, May 20). Orange County skate firm's 'destroy all girls' tags won't wash. *Los Angeles Times,* D1.

Wright, R. (1995, September 10). Brutality defines the lives of women around the world. *Boston Globe,* A2.

■ ■ ■

Reading as a Writer: Analyzing Rhetorical Choices

1. Kilbourne spends much of the essay explaining why she finds certain advertisements harmful to women, but she also hints at the damage they do to men. Locate those passages and, in class, discuss how you could develop her argument that men also are harmed by advertising. How would the essay be different if she had included more material on men?

2. Like many writers who analyze the effects of the media, Kilbourne seeks to show how media images influence us, but she does not establish a simplistic "cause and effect" relationship between the images we see and the ways we act. How *does* she explain the relationship between images and ideas/actions? Locate several places in her essay where she explains this relationship, and discuss what you think of the claims she makes.

Writing as a Reader: Entering the Conversation of Ideas

1. Kilbourne and bell hooks (pp. 486–92 in Sociology) use similar strategies of inviting readers to consider familiar images (in advertising or on the screen) through new lenses, considering the ways viewers are positioned to value (or devalue) people on the screen. Choose as a "test case" a film or series of related advertisements to analyze through the lenses of Kilbourne's and hooks's ideas, to see what your test case teaches viewers about gender and class "norms." Consider what these authors say about why it is important to take these images seriously as you draw your own conclusions about your findings.

2. Review Chapter 10's guidelines for analyzing visual rhetoric. Using those insights and Kilbourne's analytic strategies, write an essay in which you analyze a series of advertisements of your choice—in consultation with your instructor—to make a point about the ways they reinforce or resist gender stereotypes. What is the significance of your findings?

SHERRY TURKLE

Growing Up Tethered

Sherry Turkle is a professor in the Program in Science, Technology, and Society at MIT (Massachusetts Institute of Technology), where she also directs the MIT Initiative on Technology and Self. In her research and writing, Turkle focuses on people's subjective experiences with technology, and she has published many books and articles on this rich topic for both scholarly and popular audiences. She is a frequent media commentator on the intersections of technology, media, psychology, and sociology, on NPR, *Nightline*, and *PBS NewsHour*. Turkle gave a TED talk in 2012 titled "Connected, but Alone?", which indicates one of her concerns about the effects of screen culture.

This piece comes from Turkle's 2011 book *Alone Together: Why We Expect More from Technology and Less from Each Other*, from a chapter titled, "Growing Up Tethered." What do her book and chapter titles suggest about her perspective on our use of technology? You might pause after reading the first five paragraphs to reflect on the conversations she reports having with teenagers—and her evaluation. Is it fair to call this generation a "tethered" one? What problems does Turkle find in not being able to separate from one's parents and from one's friends?

As you read, weigh Turkle's description of this new way of being (what she calls the "tethered" or "collaborative self") against her analysis of this media-moderated behavior as either a "pathology" or as just a new norm—or perhaps both. (See paras. 23 to 26 in particular.) Turkle raises some different theories of the self in paragraphs 29 and 30. Slow down and be sure you understand the ideas she attributes to Erik Erikson, Jay Lifton, and her own theory of the narcissistic self. To what extent do her examples and explanations support this claim?

In her sections titled "The Avatar of Me" and "Presentation Anxiety," Turkle offers some extended examples of the ways we self-consciously craft our public personas on social media. Evaluate your own earliest—and then later—experiences with Facebook or other social media services that require a kind of crafting of online identity. We suspect you could have some lively discussions with your classmates (or friends and family outside of your class) about the good and bad and stress-producing aspects of this form of media. How would you respond to Turkle's claims about the benefits versus the deficits of being a "tethered" or "collaborative" self? (And would you respond differently if you were speaking to her *in person* versus via text, tweet, or on another social media platform?)

■ ■ ■

Roman, eighteen, admits that he texts while driving and he is not going to stop. "I know I should, but it's not going to happen. If I get a Facebook message or something posted on my wall . . . I have to see it. I have to." I am speaking with him and ten of his senior classmates at the

Cranston School, a private urban coeducational high school in Connecticut. His friends admonish him, but then several admit to the same behavior. Why do they text while driving? Their reasons are not reasons; they simply express a need to connect. "I interrupt a call even if the new call says 'unknown' as an identifier—I just have to know who it is. So I'll cut off a friend for an 'unknown,'" says Maury. "I need to know who wanted to connect. . . . And if I hear my phone, I have to answer it. I don't have a choice. I have to know who it is, what they are calling for." Marilyn adds, "I keep the sound on when I drive. When a text comes in, I have to look. No matter what. Fortunately, my phone shows me the text as a pop up right up front . . . so I don't have to do too much looking while I'm driving." These young people live in a state of waiting for connection. And they are willing to take risks, to put themselves on the line. Several admit that tethered to their phones, they get into accidents when walking. One chipped a front tooth. Another shows a recent bruise on his arm. "I went right into the handle of the refrigerator."

I ask the group a question: "When was the last time you felt that you *2* didn't want to be interrupted?" I expect to hear many stories. There are none. Silence. "I'm waiting to be interrupted right now," one says. For him, what I would term "interruption" is the beginning of a connection.

Today's young people have grown up with robot pets and on the net- *3* work in a fully tethered life. In their views of robots, they are pioneers, the first generation that does not necessarily take simulation to be second best. As for online life, they see its power—they are, after all risking their lives to check their messages—but they also view it as one might the weather: to be taken for granted, enjoyed, and sometimes endured. They've gotten used to this weather but there are signs of weather fatigue. There are so many performances; it takes energy to keep things up; and it takes time, a lot of time. "Sometimes you don't have time for your friends except if they're online," is a common complaint. And then there are the compulsions of the networked life—the ones that lead to dangerous driving and chipped teeth.

Today's adolescents have no less need than those of previous genera- *4* tions to learn empathic skills, to think about their values and identity, and to manage and express feelings. They need time to discover themselves, time to think. But technology, put in the service of always-on communication and telegraphic speed and brevity, has changed the rules of engagement with all of this. When is downtime, when is stillness? The text-driven world of rapid response does not make self-reflection impossible but does little to cultivate it. When interchanges are reformatted for the small screen and reduced to the emotional shorthand of emoticons, there are necessary simplifications. And what of adolescents' need for secrets, for marking out what is theirs alone?

I wonder about this as I watch cell phones passed around high school *5* cafeterias. Photos and messages are being shared and compared. I cannot help but identify with the people who sent the messages to these wandering phones. Do they all assume that their words and photographs are on public display? Perhaps. Traditionally, the development of intimacy required privacy. Intimacy without privacy reinvents what intimacy means. Separation, too, is being reinvented. Tethered children know they have a parent on tap—a text or a call away.

Degrees of Separation

Mark Twain mythologized the adolescent's search for identity in the Huck   6
Finn story, the on-the-Mississippi moment, a time of escape from an adult world. Of course, the time on the river is emblematic not of a moment but of an ongoing process through which children separate from their parents. That rite of passage is now transformed by technology. In the traditional variant, the child internalizes the adults in his or her world before crossing the threshold of independence. In the modern, technologically tethered variant, parents can be brought along in an intermediate space, such as that created by the cell phone, where everyone important is on speed dial. In this sense, the generations sail down the river together, and adolescents don't face the same pressure to develop the independence we have associated with moving forward into young adulthood.

When parents give children cell phones—most of the teenagers I   7
spoke with were given a phone between the ages of nine and thirteen—the gift typically comes with a contract: Children are expected to answer their parents' calls. This arrangement makes it possible for the child to engage in activities—see friends, attend movies, go shopping, spend time at the beach—that would not be permitted without the phone. Yet, the tethered child does not have the experience of being alone with only him- or herself to count on. For example, there used to be a point for an urban child, an important moment, when there was a first time to navigate the city alone. It was a rite of passage that communicated to children that they were on their own and responsible. If they were frightened, they had to experience those feelings. The cell phone buffers this moment.

Parents want their children to answer their phones, but adolescents   8
need to separate. With a group of seniors at Fillmore, a boys' preparatory school in New York City, the topic of parents and cell phones elicits strong emotions. The young men consider, "If it is always possible to be in touch, when does one have the right to be alone?"

Some of the boys are defiant. For one, "It should be my decision about   9
whether I pick up the phone. People can call me, but I don't have to talk to them." For another, "To stay free from parents, I don't take my cell. Then they can't reach me. My mother tells me to take my cell, but I just don't." Some appeal to history to justify ignoring parents' calls. Harlan, a distinguished student and athlete, thinks he has earned the right to greater independence. He talks about older siblings who grew up before cell phones and enjoyed greater freedom: "My mother makes me take my phone, but I never

answer it when my parents call, and they get mad at me. I don't feel I should have to. Cell phones are recent. In the last ten years, everyone started getting them. Before, you couldn't just call someone whenever. I don't see why I have to answer when my mom calls me. My older sisters didn't have to do that." Harlan's mother, unmoved by this argument from precedent, checks that he has his phone when he leaves for school in the morning; Harlan does not answer her calls. Things are at an unhappy stalemate.

Several boys refer to the "mistake" of having taught their parents *10* how to text and send instant messages (IMs), which they now equate with letting the genie out of the bottle. For one, "I made the mistake of teaching my parents how to text-message recently, so now if I don't call them when they ask me to call, I get an urgent text message." For another, "I taught my parents to IM. They didn't know how. It was the stupidest thing I could do. Now my parents IM me all the time. It is really annoying. My parents are upsetting me. I feel trapped and less independent."

Teenagers argue that they should be allowed time when they are not *11* "on call." Parents say that they, too, feel trapped. For if you know your child is carrying a cell phone, it is frightening to call or text and get no response. "I didn't ask for this new worry," says the mother of two high school girls. Another, a mother of three teenagers, "tries not to call them if it's not important." But if she calls and gets no response, she panics:

> I've sent a text. Nothing back. And I know they have their phones. Intellectually, I know there is little reason to worry. But there is something about this unanswered text. Sometimes, it made me a bit nutty. One time, I kept sending texts, over and over. I envy my mother. We left for school in the morning. We came home. She worked. She came back, say at six. She didn't worry. I end up imploring my children to answer my every message. Not because I feel I have a right to their instant response. Just out of compassion.

Adolescent autonomy is not just about separation from parents. Ado- *12* lescents also need to separate from each other. They experience their friendships as both sustaining and constraining. Connectivity brings complications. Online life provides plenty of room for individual experimentation, but it can be hard to escape from new group demands. It is common for friends to expect that their friends will stay available—a technology-enabled social contract demands continual peer presence. And the tethered self becomes accustomed to its support.

Traditional views of adolescent development take autonomy and strong *13* personal boundaries as reliable signs of a successfully maturing self. In this view of development, we work toward an independent self capable of having a feeling, considering it, and deciding whether to share it. Sharing a feeling is a deliberate act, a movement toward intimacy. This description was always a fiction in several ways. For one thing, the "gold standard" of autonomy validated a style that was culturally "male." Women (and indeed, many men) have an emotional style that defines itself not by boundaries but through relationships.[1] Furthermore, adolescent conversations are by nature exploratory, and this in healthy ways. Just as some writers learn what they think by looking at what they write, the years of identity formation can be a time of learning what you think by hearing what you say to others. But given these caveats, when we think about maturation, the notion of a bounded self has its virtues, if only as a metaphor. It suggests, sensibly, that before we forge successful life partnerships, it is helpful to have a sense of who we are.[2]

But the gold standard tarnishes if a phone is always in hand. You touch   *14* a screen and reach someone presumed ready to respond, someone who also has a phone in hand. Now, technology makes it easy to express emotions while they are being formed. It supports an emotional style in which feelings are not fully experienced until they are communicated. Put otherwise, there is every opportunity to form a thought by sending out for comments.

The Collaborative Self

Julia, sixteen, a sophomore at Branscomb, an urban public high school in   *15* New Jersey, turns texting into a kind of polling. Julia has an outgoing and warm presence, with smiling, always-alert eyes. When a feeling bubbles up, Julia texts it. Where things go next is guided by what she hears next. Julia says,

> If I'm upset, right as I feel upset, I text a couple of my friends . . . just because I know that they'll be there and they can comfort me. If something exciting happens, I know that they'll be there to be excited with me, and stuff like that. So I definitely feel emotions when I'm texting, as I'm texting. . . . Even before I get upset and I know that I have that feeling that I'm gonna start crying, yeah, I'll pull up my friend . . . uh, my phone . . . and say like . . . I'll tell them what I'm feeling, and, like, I need to talk to them, or see them.

"I'll pull up my friend . . . uh, my phone." Julia's language slips tell-   *16* ingly. When Julia thinks about strong feelings, her thoughts go both to her phone and her friends. She mixes together "pulling up" a friend's name on her phone and "pulling out" her phone, but she does not really correct herself so much as imply that the phone is her friend and that friends take on identities through her phone.

After Julia sends out a text, she is uncomfortable until she gets one   *17* back: "I am always looking for a text that says, 'Oh, I'm sorry,' or 'Oh, that's great.'" Without this feedback, she says, "It's hard to calm down." Julia describes how painful it is to text about "feelings" and get no response: "I get mad. Even if I e-mail someone, I want the response, like, right away.[3] I want them to be, like, right there answering me. And sometimes I'm like, 'Uh! Why can't you just answer me?' . . . I wait, like, depending on what it is, I wait like an hour if they don't answer me, and I'll text them again. 'Are you mad? Are you there? Is everything okay?'" Her anxiety is palpable. Julia must have a response. She says of those she texts, "You want them there, because you need them." When they are not there, she moves on with her nascent feelings, but she does not move on alone: "I go to another friend and tell them."

Claudia, seventeen, a junior at Cranston, describes a similar progression. "I start to have some happy feelings as soon as I start to text." As with Julia, things move from "I have a feeling, I want to make a call" to "I want to have a feeling, I need to make a call," or in her case, send a text. What is not being cultivated here is the ability to be alone and reflect on one's emotions in private. On the contrary, teenagers report discomfort when they are without their cell phones.[4] They need to be connected in order to feel like themselves. Put in a more positive way, both Claudia and Julia share feelings as part of discovering them. They cultivate a collaborative self.

Estranged from her father, Julia has lost her close attachments to his relatives and was traumatized by being unable to reach her mother during the day of the September 11 attacks on the Twin Towers. Her story illustrates how digital connectivity—particularly texting—can be used to manage specific anxieties about loss and separation. But what Julia does—her continual texting, her way of feeling her feelings only as she shares them—is not unusual. The particularities of every individual case express personal history, but Julia's individual "symptom" comes close to being a generational style.[5]

Sociologist David Riesman, writing in the mid-1950s, remarked on the American turn from an inner- to an other-directed sense of self.[6] Without a firm inner sense of purpose, people looked to their neighbors for validation. Today, cell phone in hand, other-directedness is raised to a higher power. At the moment of beginning to have a thought or feeling, we can have it validated, almost prevalidated. Exchanges may be brief, but more is not necessarily desired. The necessity is to have someone be there.

Ricki, fifteen, a freshman at Richelieu, a private high school for girls in New York City, describes that necessity: "I have a lot of people on my contact list. If one friend doesn't 'get it,' I call another." This marks a turn to a hyper-other-directedness. This young woman's contact or buddy list has become something like a list of "spare parts" for her fragile adolescent self. When she uses the expression "get it," I think she means "pick up the phone." I check with her if I have gotten this right. She says, "'Get it,' yeah, 'pick up,' but also 'get it,' 'get me.'" Ricki counts on her friends to finish her thoughts. Technology does not cause but encourages a sensibility in which the validation of a feeling becomes part of establishing it, even part of the feeling itself.

I have said that in the psychoanalytic tradition, one speaks about narcissism not to indicate people who love themselves, but a personality so fragile that it needs constant support.[7] It cannot tolerate the complex demands of other people but tries to relate to them by distorting who they are and splitting off what it needs, what it can use. So, the narcissistic self gets on with others by dealing only with their made-to-measure representations. These representations (some analytic traditions refer to them as "part objects," others as "self-objects") are all that the fragile self can handle. We can easily imagine the utility of inanimate companions to such a self because a robot or a computational agent can be sculpted to meet one's needs. But a fragile person can also be supported by selected and limited contact with people (say, the people on a cell phone "favorites" list). In a life of texting and messaging, those on that contact list can be made to appear almost on demand. You can take what you need and move on. And, if not gratified, you can try someone else.

Again, technology, on its own, does not cause this new way of relating   23 to our emotions and other people. But it does make it easy. Over time, a new style of being with each other becomes socially sanctioned. In every era, certain ways of relating come to feel natural. In our time, if we can be continually in touch, needing to be continually in touch does not seem a problem or a pathology but an accommodation to what technology affords. It becomes the norm.

The history of what we think of as psychopathology is dynamic. If in   24 a particular time and place, certain behaviors seem disruptive, they are labeled pathological. In the nineteenth century, for example, sexual repression was considered a good and moral thing, but when women lost sensation or the ability to speak, these troubling symptoms were considered a disease, hysteria. With more outlets for women's sexuality, hysterical symptoms declined, and others took their place. So, the much-prescribed tranquilizers of the 1950s spoke to women's new anxieties when marginalized in the home after a fuller civic participation during World War II.

Now, we have symptoms born of fears of isolation and abandonment.   25 In my study of growing up in the networked culture, I meet many children and teenagers who feel cast off. Some have parents with good intentions who simply work several jobs and have little time for their children. Some have endured divorce—sometimes multiple divorces—and float from one parent to another, not confident of their true home. Those lucky children who have intact families with stable incomes can experience other forms of abandonment. Busy parents are preoccupied, often by what is on their cell phones. When children come home, it is often to a house that is empty until a parent returns from work.

For young people in all of these circumstances, computers and mobile   26 devices offer communities when families are absent. In this context, it is not surprising to find troubling patterns of connection and disconnection: teenagers who will only "speak" online, who rigorously avoid face-to-face encounters, who are in text contact with their parents fifteen or twenty times a day, who deem even a telephone call "too much" exposure and say that they will "text, not talk." But are we to think of these as pathologies? For as social mores change, what once seemed "ill" can come to seem normal. Twenty years ago, as a practicing clinical psychologist, if I had met a college junior who called her mother fifteen times a day, checking in about what shoes to buy and what dress to wear, extolling a new kind of decaffeinated tea, and complaining about the difficulty of a physics problem set, I would have thought her behavior problematic. I would have encouraged her to explore difficulties with separation. I would have assumed that these had to be addressed for her to proceed to successful adulthood. But these days, a college student who texts home fifteen times a day is not unusual.

High school and college students are always texting—while waiting 27 in line at the cafeteria, while eating, while waiting for the campus shuttle. Not surprisingly, many of these texts are to parents. What once we might have seen as a problem becomes how we do things. But a behavior that has become typical may still express the problems that once caused us to see it as pathological. Even a typical behavior may not be in an adolescent's developmental interest.

Consider Leo, a college sophomore far from home, who feels crippling 28 loneliness. He tells me that he "handles" this problem by texting and calling his mother up to twenty times a day. He remarks that this behavior does not make him stand out; everyone he knows is on a phone all day. But even if invisible, he considers his behavior a symptom all the same.

These days, our relationship to the idea of psychological autonomy 29 is evolving. I have said that central to Erik Erikson's thinking about adolescents is the idea that they need a moratorium, a "time out," a relatively consequence-free space for experimentation. But in Erikson's thinking, the self, once mature, is relatively stable. Though embedded in relationships, in the end it is bounded and autonomous.[8] One of Erikson's students, psychiatrist Robert Jay Lifton, has an alternative vision of the mature self. He calls it *protean* and emphasizes its multiple aspects.[9] Thinking of the self as protean accents connection and reinvention. This self, as Lifton puts it, "fluid and many-sided," can embrace and modify ideas and ideologies. It flourishes when provided with things diverse, disconnected, and global.

Publicly, Erikson expressed approval for Lifton's work, but after 30 Erikson's death in 1994, Lifton asked the Erikson family if he might have the books he had personally inscribed and presented to his teacher. The family agreed; the books were returned. In his personal copy of Lifton's *The Protean Self*, Erikson had written extensive marginal notes. When he came to the phrase "protean man," Erikson had scrawled "protean boy?"[10] Erikson could not accept that successful maturation would not result in something solid. By Erikson's standards, the selves formed in the cacophony of online spaces are not protean but juvenile. Now I suggest that the culture in which they develop tempts them into narcissistic ways of relating to the world.

The Avatar of Me

Erikson said that identity play is the work of adolescence. And these days 31 adolescents use the rich materials of online life to do that work. For example, in a game such as The Sims Online (think of this as a very junior version of Second Life), you can create an avatar that expresses aspects of yourself, build a house, and furnish it to your taste. Thus provisioned, you can set about reworking in the virtual aspects of life that may not have gone so well in the real.

Trish, a timid and anxious thirteen-year-old, has been harshly beaten 32 by her alcoholic father. She creates an abusive family on The Sims Online, but in the game her character, also thirteen, is physically and emotionally strong. In simulation, she plays and replays the experience of fighting off her aggressor. A sexually experienced girl of sixteen, Katherine, creates an online innocent. "I want to have a rest," she says. Beyond rest, Katherine tells me she can get "practice at being a different kind of person. That's what Sims is for me. Practice."

Katherine "practices" on the game at breakfast, during school recess, 33 and after dinner. She says she feels comforted by her virtual life. I ask her if her activities in the game have led her to do anything differently in her life away from it. She replies, "Not really," but then goes on to describe how her life is in fact beginning to change: "I'm thinking about breaking up with my boyfriend. I don't want to have sex anymore, but I would like to have a boyfriend. My character on Sims has boyfriends but doesn't have sex. They [the boyfriends of her Sims avatar] help her with her job. I think to start fresh I would have to break up with my boyfriend." Katherine does not completely identify with her online character and refers to her avatar in the third person. Yet, The Sims Online is a place where she can see her life anew.

This kind of identity work can take place wherever you create an 34 avatar. And it can take place on social-networking sites as well, where one's profile becomes an avatar of sorts, a statement not only about who you are but who you want to be. Teenagers make it clear that games, worlds, and social networking (on the surface, rather different) have much in common. They all ask you to compose and project an identity. Audrey, sixteen, a junior at Roosevelt, a suburban public high school near New York City, is explicit about the connection between avatars and profiles. She calls her Facebook profile "my Internet twin" and "the avatar of me."

Mona, a freshman at Roosevelt, has recently joined Facebook. Her 35 parents made her wait until her fourteenth birthday, and I meet her shortly after this long-awaited day. Mona tells me that as soon as she got on the site, "Immediately, I felt power." I ask her what she means. She says, "The first thing I thought was, 'I am going to broadcast the real me.'" But when Mona sat down to write her profile, things were not so straightforward. Whenever one has time to write, edit, and delete, there is room for performance. The "real me" turns out to be elusive. Mona wrote and rewrote her profile. She put it away for two days and tweaked it again. Which pictures to add? Which facts to include? How much of her personal life to reveal? Should she give any sign that things at home were troubled? Or was this a place to look good?

Mona worries that she does not have enough of a social life to make 36 herself sound interesting: "What kind of personal life should I *say* I have?" Similar questions plague other young women in her class. They are starting to have boyfriends. Should they list themselves as single if they are just starting to date someone new? What if they consider themselves in a relationship, but their boyfriends do not? Mona tells me that "it's common sense" to check with a boy before listing yourself as connected to him, but "that could be a very awkward conversation." So there are misunderstandings and recriminations. Facebook at fourteen can be a tearful place. For many, it remains tearful well through college and graduate school. Much that might seem straightforward is fraught. For example, when asked by Facebook to confirm someone as a friend or ignore the request, Helen, a Roosevelt senior, says, "I always feel a bit of panic....Who should I friend? ... I really want to only have my cool friends listed, but I'm nice to a lot of other kids at school. So I include the more unpopular ones, but then I'm unhappy." It is not how she wants to be seen.

In the Victorian era, one controlled whom one saw and to whom one 37 was connected through the ritual of calling cards. Visitors came to call and, not necessarily expecting to be received, left a card. A card left at your home in return meant that the relationship might grow. In its own way, friending on Facebook is reminiscent of this tradition. On Facebook, you send a request to be a friend. The recipient of the request has the option to ignore or friend you. As was the case in the Victorian era, there is an intent to screen. But the Victorians followed socially accepted rules. For example, it was understood that one was most open to people of similar social standing. Facebook is more democratic—which leaves members to make up their own rules, not necessarily understood by those who contact them. Some people make a request to be a Facebook friend in the spirit of "I'm a fan" and are accepted on that basis. Other people friend only people they know. Others friend any friend of a friend, using Facebook as a tool to expand their acquaintanceships. All of this can be exciting or stressful—often both at the same time, because friending has consequences. It means that someone can see what you say about yourself on your profile, the pictures you post, and your friends' postings on your "wall," the shared communication space for you and your friends. Friending someone gives that person implicit permission to try to friend your friends. In fact, the system constantly proposes that they do so.

Early in this project, I was at a conference dinner, sitting next to an 38 author whose publisher insisted that she use Facebook as a way to promote her new book. The idea was to use the site to tell people where she would be speaking and to share the themes of her book with an ever-expanding potential readership. Her publisher hoped this strategy would make her book "go viral." She had expected the Facebook project to feel like business, but instead she described complicated anxieties about not having enough friends, and about envy of her husband, also a writer, who had more friends than she. It also felt wrong to use the word "friends" for all of those she had "friended," since so many of the friended were there for professional reasons alone. She left me with this thought: "This thing took me right back to high school."

I promised her that when I joined Facebook I would record my first   *39*
feelings, while the site was still new to me. My very first feelings now seem
banal: I had to decide between "friending" plan A (this will be a place for
people I actually know) and plan B (I will include people who contact me
because they say they appreciate my work). I tried several weeks on plan A
and then switched to the more inclusive plan B, flattered by the attention
of strangers, justifying my decision in professional terms.

But now that I had invited strangers into my life, would I invite myself   *40*
into the lives of strangers? I would have anticipated not, until I did that
very thing. I saw that one of my favorite authors was a Facebook friend
of a friend. Seized by the idea that I might be this writer's friend, I made
my request, and he accepted me. The image of a cafeteria came to mind,
and I had a seat at his virtual table. But I felt like a gatecrasher. I decided
realistically that I was taking this way too seriously. Facebook is a world
in which fans are "friends." But of course, they are not friends. They have
been "friended." That makes all the difference in the world, and I couldn't
get high school out of my mind.

Presentation Anxiety

What are the truth claims in a Facebook profile? How much can you   *41*
lie? And what is at stake if you do? Nancy, an eighteen-year-old senior at
Roosevelt, answers this question. "On the one hand, low stakes, because no
one is really checking." Then, with a grimace, she says, "No, high stakes.
Everyone is checking." A few minutes later, Nancy comes back to the question: "Only my best friends will know if I lie a little bit, and they will totally
understand." Then she laughs. "All of this, it is, I guess, a bit of stress."[11]

At Cranston, a group of seniors describe that stress. One says,   *42*
"Thirteen to eighteen are the years of profile writing." The years of identity
construction are recast in terms of profile production. These private school
students had to write one profile for their applications to middle school,
another to get into high school, and then another for Facebook. Now they
are beginning to construct personae for college applications. And here,
says Tom, "You have to have a slightly different persona for the different
colleges to which you are applying: one for Dartmouth, a different one,
say, for Wesleyan." For this aficionado of profile writing, every application needs a different approach. "By the time you get to the questions for
the college application, you are a professional profile writer," he says. His
classmate Stan describes his online profiles in great detail. Each serves a
different purpose, but they must overlap, or questions of authenticity will
arise. Creating the illusion of authenticity demands virtuosity. Presenting
a self in these circumstances, with multiple media and multiple goals, is
not easy work. The trick, says Stan, is in "weaving profiles together ... so
that people can see you are not too crazy.... What I learned in high school
was profiles, profiles, profiles, how to make a me."

Early in my study, a college senior warned me not to be fooled by "any- *43* one you interview who tells you that his Facebook page is 'the real me.' It's like being in a play. You make a character." Eric, a college-bound senior at Hadley, a boys' preparatory school in rural New Jersey, describes himself as savvy about how you can "mold a Facebook page." Yet, even he is shocked when he finds evidence of girls using "shrinking" software to appear thinner on their profile photographs. "You can't see that they do it when you look at the little version of the picture, but when you look at a big picture, you can see how the background is distorted." By eighteen, he has become an identity detective. The Facebook profile is a particular source of stress because it is so important to high school social life. Some students feel so in its thrall that they drop out of Facebook, if only for a while, to collect themselves.

Brad, eighteen, a senior at Hadley, is about to take a gap year to do *44* community service before attending a small liberal arts college in the Midwest. His parents are architects; his passion is biology and swimming. Brad wants to be part of the social scene at Hadley, but he doesn't like texting or instant messaging. He is careful to make sure I know he is "no Luddite." He has plenty of good things to say about the Net. He is sure that it makes it easier for insecure people to function. Sometimes the ability to compose his thoughts online "can be reassuring," he says, because there is a chance to "think through, calculate, edit, and make sure you're as clear and concise as possible." But as our conversation continues, Brad switches gears. Even as some are able to better function because they feel in control, online communication also offers an opportunity to ignore other people's feelings. You can avoid eye contact. You can elect not to hear how "hurt or angry they sound in their voice." He says, "Online, people miss your body language, tone of voice. You are not really you." And worst of all, online life has led him to mistrust his friends. He has had his instant messages "recorded" without his knowledge and forwarded on "in a cut-and-paste world."

In fact, when I meet Brad in the spring of his senior year, he tells me *45* he has "dropped out" of online life. "I'm off the Net," he says, "at least for the summer, maybe for my year off until I go to college." He explains that it is hard to drop out because all his friends are on Facebook. A few weeks before our conversation, he had made a step toward rejoining but immediately he felt that he was not doing enough to satisfy its demands. He says that within a day he felt "rude" and couldn't keep up. He felt guilty because he didn't have the time to answer all the people who wrote to him. He says that he couldn't find a way to be "a little bit" on Facebook—it does not easily tolerate a partial buy-in. Just doing the minimum was "pure exhaustion."

In the world of Facebook, Brad says, "your minute movie preferences *46* matter. And what groups you join. Are they the right ones?" Everything is a token, a marker for who you are:

> When you have to represent yourself on Facebook to convey to anyone who doesn't know you what and who you are, it leads to a kind of obsession about minute details about yourself. Like, "Oh, if I like the band State Radio and the

band Spoon, what does it mean if I put State Radio first or Spoon first on my list of favorite musical artists? What will people think about me?" I know for girls, trying to figure out, "Oh, is this picture too revealing to put? Is it prudish if I don't put it?" You have to think carefully for good reason, given how much people will look at your profile and obsess over it. You have to know that everything you put up will be perused very carefully. And that makes it necessary for you to obsess over what you do put up and how you portray yourself.... And when you have to think that much about what you come across as, that's just another way that ... you're thinking of yourself in a bad way.

For Brad, "thinking of yourself in a bad way" means thinking of yourself in reduced terms, in "short smoke signals" that are easy to read. To me, the smoke signals suggest a kind of reduction and betrayal. Social media ask us to represent ourselves in simplified ways. And then, faced with an audience, we feel pressure to conform to these simplifications. On Facebook, Brad represents himself as cool and in the know—both qualities are certainly part of who he is. But he hesitates to show people online other parts of himself (like how much he likes Harry Potter). He spends more and more time perfecting his online Mr. Cool. And he feels pressure to perform him all the time because that is who he is on Facebook. 47

At first Brad thought that both his Facebook profile and his college essays had gotten him into this "bad way" of thinking, in which he reduces himself to fit a stereotype. Writing his Facebook profile felt to him like assembling cultural references to shape how others would see him. The college essay demanded a victory narrative and seemed equally unhelpful: He had to brag, and he wasn't happy. But Brad had a change of heart about the value of writing his college essays. "In the end I learned a lot about how I write and think—what I know how to think about and some things, you know, I really can't think about them well at all." I ask him if Facebook might offer these kinds of opportunities. He is adamant that it does not: "You get reduced to a list of favorite things. 'List your favorite music'—that gives you no liberty at all about how to say it." Brad says that "in a conversation, it might be interesting that on a trip to Europe with my parents, I got interested in the political mural art in Belfast. But on a Facebook page, this is too much information. It would be the kiss of death. Too much, too soon, too weird. And yet ... it is part of who I am, isn't it? ... You are asked to make a lot of lists. You have to worry that you put down the 'right' band or that you *don't* put down some Polish novel that nobody's read." And in the end, for Brad, it is too easy to lose track of what is important: 48

> What does it matter to anyone that I prefer the band Spoon over State Radio? Or State Radio over Cake? But things like Facebook ... make you think that it really does matter.... I look at someone's profile and I say, "Oh, they like these bands." I'm like, "Oh, they're a poser," or "they're really deep, and they're into good music." We all do that, I think. And then I think it doesn't matter, but ...

the thing is, in the world of Facebook it *does* matter. Those minute details *do* matter.

Brad, like many of his peers, worries that if he is modest and doesn't [49] put down all of his interests and accomplishments, he will be passed over. But he also fears that to talk about his strengths will be unseemly. None of these conflicts about self presentation are new to adolescence or to Face-book. What is new is living them out in public, sharing every mistake and false step. Brad, attractive and accomplished, sums it up with the same word Nancy uses: "Stress. That's what it comes down to for me. It's just worry and stressing out about it." Now Brad only wants to see friends in person or talk to them on the telephone. "I can just act how I want to act, and it's a much freer way." But who will answer the phone?

NOTES

1. Carol Gilligan, *In a Different Voice: Psychological Theory and Women's Development* (1982; Cambridge, MA: Harvard University Press, 1993).
2. Erik Erikson, *Identity and the Life Cycle* (1952; New York: W. W. Norton, 1980) and *Childhood and Society* (New York: Norton, 1950).
3. In Julia's world, e-mail is considered "slow" and rarely used because texting has greater immediacy.
4. It is so common to see teenagers (and others) attending to their mobiles rather than what is around them, that it was possible for a fake news story to gain traction in Britain. Taken up by the media, the story went out that there was a trial program to pad lampposts in major cities. Although it was a hoax, I fell for it when it was presented online as news. In fact, in the year prior to the hoax, one in five Britons did walk into a lamppost or other obstruction while attending to a mobile device. This is not surprising because research reported that "62 per cent of Britons concentrate so hard on their mobile phone when texting they lose peripheral vision." See Charlie Sorrel, "Padded Lampposts Cause Fuss in London," *Wired*, March 10, 2008, www.wired.com/gadgetlab/2008/03/padded-lampposts (accessed October 5, 2009).
5. New communications technology makes it easier to serve up people as slivers of self, providing a sense that to get what you need from others you have multiple and inexhaustible options. On the psychology that needs these "slivers," see Paul H. Ornstein, ed., *The Search for Self: Selected Writings of Heinz Kohut (1950–1978)*, vol. 2 (New York: International Universities Press, 1978).
6. David Riesman, Nathan Glazer, and Reuel Denney, *The Lonely Crowd: A Study of the Changing American Character* (1950; New Haven, CT: Yale University Press, 2001).
7. Orenstein, *The Search for Self*. For an earlier work, of a very different time, that linked cultural change and narcissistic personality style, see Christopher Lasch, *The Culture of Narcissism* (New York: Norton, 1979). Lasch said that "pathology represents a heightened version of normality." This formulation is helpful in thinking about the "normal" self in a tethered society and those who suffer more acutely from its discontents. From a psychodynamic perspective, we all suffer from the same things, some of us more acutely than others.
8. See Erik Erikson, *Identity and the Life Cycle and Childhood and Society, Young Man Luther: A Study in Psychoanalysis and History* (New York: W. W. Norton and Company, 1958).
9. Robert Jay Lifton, *The Protean Self. Human Resilience in an Age of Fragmentation* (New York: Basic Books, 1993).

10. Lifton shared this story at a meeting of the Wellfleet Seminar in October 2009, an annual gathering that began as a forum for Erikson and his students as they turned their attention to psychohistory.

11. The performances of everyday life — playing the roles of father, mother, child, wife, husband, life partner, worker — also provide "a bit of stress." There is room for considerable debate about how much online life really shares with our performances of self in "real life." Some look to the sociology of "self-presentation" to argue that online and off, we are always onstage. Erving Goffman, *The Presentation of Self in Everyday Life* (Garden City, NY: Doubleday Anchor, 1959).

■ ■ ■

Reading as a Writer: Analyzing Rhetorical Choices

1. In her opening two sections, Turkle demonstrates that comparison between the past and present is part of her argumentative strategy. As you read through her examples, consider the extent to which she is analyzing or judging (or both) these new strategies and habits of using technology. You might begin, for example, with her claims in paragraph 5: "Intimacy without privacy reinvents what intimacy means. Separation, too, is being reinvented." Try marking places in her opening two sections where she offers examples and places where she evaluates or makes claims about the examples. Where do they overlap?

2. Turkle opens with an example from an interview with an eighteen-year-old, and she uses interviews with teenagers and parents throughout her piece to help make her point. Discuss the effectiveness of this as a way of offering evidence. What are the strengths and limitations of these kinds of examples?

Writing as a Reader: Entering the Conversation of Ideas

1. Turkle's term "the tethered self" contrasts with Mark Hain's (pp. 425–41) relative optimism about the power of online communities. Compose an essay in which you apply these authors' ideas to a specific online community and offer examples as you make an argument about the strengths and/or shortcomings of these communities. Where, ultimately, do you stand on the value of digital connectivity?

2. Consider Turkle's concerns and insights about technology in relation to the readings in Chapter 3 by Clive Thompson (pp. 70–72) and Tom Standage (pp. 80–86) and readings in Chapter 4 by Dana Radcliffe (pp. 88–91) and Susan Blum (pp. 105–7). In an essay of your own about the positive and negative aspects of digital life, draw on claims made by Turkle and one or two of these other authors to stake your own position in this debate.

Psychology and Biology
How do our physical and cultural selves intersect?

© Lightspring/Shutterstock.com

The readings in this chapter invite us to think about the fascinating places where our bodies meet culture. These wide-ranging authors reveal the myriad intersections where biology is shaped by psychological and social expectations of failure, cyber addiction, medical addiction, and beliefs about disabilities and racial differences.

While most of us suspect that the way we see—and feel about— ourselves and others is in part a product of our society, these authors offer fresh perspectives on how this dynamic works, with many eye-opening examples. What we imagine to be "facts" are often not supported by evidence, and the effects of these misunderstandings on people's lives can be dramatic. Conversely, understanding the scientific facts behind our behaviors and attitudes can be life changing.

For example, psychologist Carol Dweck examines the brain science behind those who respond to failure by giving up (a "fixed mindset") and those who instead see failure as an exciting opportunity to learn and grow (a "growth mindset"). Cyberpsychologist Mary Aiken applies scientific analysis of addiction to bear on our often compulsive use of technology and offers insights about breaking the cycle. Bio-anthropologist Agustín Fuentes offers "myth-busting" analysis about race and biology, aiming to demonstrate how often we make the wrong assumptions about what bodies can tell us, and how damaging those assumptions can be.

Some of the authors focus on the ways we alter our bodies and why. For example, Margaret Talbot looks at the significance of "brain-boosting" drugs, which continue to be popular on college campuses, raising the bar for academic performance (particularly when students are also cramming in social activities). William J. Peace extends the conversation about body "norms" into the realm of disability studies and challenges us to reframe our ideas of the disabled body by examining adaptive sports.

These readings will take you from theories and research to your very own body, from your daily practices to the largest questions of what it means to be human. We bet you will have strong responses to these ideas, and we invite you to dive into this raucous conversation.

CAROL DWECK

From Mindset: The New Psychology of Success

Carol Dweck is a psychology professor at Stanford and one of the leading experts in the field of motivation. Beyond her scholarly publications on how and why people succeed, her writing has appeared in the *New York Times*, the *Washington Post*, and many other newspapers and magazines. She lectures all over the world and is frequently interviewed by television news programs. This reading is drawn from her 2006 bestselling book *Mindset: The New Psychology of Success*. Before you read, take a moment to think about your own general response to failure, something all humans experience. You might think of something as common as failing a quiz. How does failure make you feel? What behavioral changes do you usually make—if any—to respond to small or large failures?

Dweck introduces this topic with a narrative example (see Chapter 11) of observing children responding to a challenge with either frustration or excitement. This leads to the inquiry driving her research: "What are the consequences of thinking that your intelligence or personality is something you can develop, as opposed to something that is a fixed, deep-seated trait?" (para. 7). Note that this piece is divided into eight sections, with visuals at the end. As you read, pay attention to the organizational logic of each section and to the ways each (including the visuals) contributes to Dweck's larger point about the difference between a "fixed mindset" and a "growth mindset."

The definitions of "fixed mindset" and "growth mindset" are in the section titled "What Does All This Mean for You? The Two Mindsets." Be sure that you understand these definitions well enough to explain them to someone else. The next section, "A View from the Two Mindsets," offers many examples of these two mindsets in action; as you read those examples, reflect on your own responses to academic challenges. The implications of these two mindsets are explored in the final sections of the reading, where Dweck invites the reader to consider how these mindsets lead to different attitudes about the value of effort and affect how accurately we estimate our abilities.

Dweck concludes with a series of questions designed to engage the reader in self-reflection, inviting you to consider how differently you might approach education—as well as other challenges—with a growth mindset. The *Calvin and Hobbes* comic underscores her point with humor. The final graphic, with contrasting "fixed mindset" and "growth mindset" paths through trying something new, illustrates how Dweck's argument reaches far beyond the classroom. Life is full of challenges. How you handle them, she argues, is something you can change.

When I was a young researcher, just starting out, something happened   *1* that changed my life. I was obsessed with understanding how people cope with failures, and I decided to study it by watching how students grapple with hard problems. So I brought children one at a time to a room in their school, made them comfortable, and then gave them a series of puzzles to solve. The first ones were fairly easy, but the next ones were hard. As the students grunted, perspired, and toiled, I watched their strategies and probed what they were thinking and feeling. I expected differences among children in how they coped with the difficulty, but I saw something I never expected.

Confronted with the hard puzzles, one ten-year-old boy pulled up his 2
chair, rubbed his hands together, smacked his lips, and cried out, "I love
a challenge!" Another, sweating away on these puzzles, looked up with a
pleased expression and said with authority, "You know, I was *hoping* this
would be informative!"

What's wrong with them? I wondered. I always thought you coped with 3
failure or you didn't cope with failure. I never thought anyone *loved* failure. Were these alien children or were they on to something?

Everyone has a role model, someone who pointed the way at a critical 4
moment in their lives. These children were my role models. They obviously knew something I didn't and I was determined to figure it out—to
understand the kind of mindset that could turn a failure into a gift.

What did they know? They knew that human qualities, such as intel- 5
lectual skills, could be cultivated through effort. And that's what they were
doing—getting smarter. Not only weren't they discouraged by failure, they
didn't even think they were failing. They thought they were learning.

I, on the other hand, thought human qualities were carved in stone. 6
You were smart or you weren't, and failure meant you weren't. It was that
simple. If you could arrange successes and avoid failures (at all costs), you
could stay smart. Struggles, mistakes, perseverance were just not part of
this picture.

Whether human qualities are things that can be cultivated or things 7
that are carved in stone is an old issue. What these beliefs mean for you is
a new one: What are the consequences of thinking that your intelligence or
personality is something you can develop, as opposed to something that is
a fixed, deep-seated trait? Let's first look in on the age-old, fiercely waged
debate about human nature and then return to the question of what these
beliefs mean for you.

Why Do People Differ?

Since the dawn of time, people have thought differently, acted differently, 8
and fared differently from each other. It was guaranteed that someone
would ask the question of why people differed—why some people are
smarter or more moral—and whether there was something that made
them permanently different. Experts lined up on both sides. Some claimed
that there was a strong physical basis for these differences, making them
unavoidable and unalterable. Through the ages, these alleged physical
differences have included bumps on the skull (phrenology), the size and
shape of the skull (craniology), and, today, genes.

Others pointed to the strong differences in people's backgrounds, 9
experiences, training, or ways of learning. It may surprise you to know
that a big champion of this view was Alfred Binet, the inventor of the IQ

test. Wasn't the IQ test meant to summarize children's unchangeable intelligence? In fact, no. Binet, a Frenchman working in Paris in the early twentieth century, designed this test to identify children who were not profiting from the Paris public schools, *so that new educational programs could be designed to get them back on track.* Without denying individual differences in children's intellects, he believed that education and practice could bring about fundamental changes in intelligence. Here is a quote from one of his major books, *Modern Ideas About Children,* in which he summarizes his work with hundreds of children with learning difficulties:

> A few modern philosophers . . . assert that an individual's intelligence is a fixed quantity, a quantity which cannot be increased. We must protest and react against this brutal pessimism. . . . With practice, training, and above all, method, we manage to increase our attention, our memory, our judgment and literally to become more intelligent than we were before.

Who's right? Today most experts agree that it's not either-or. It's not 10 nature *or* nurture, genes *or* environment. From conception on, there's a constant give and take between the two. In fact, as Gilbert Gottlieb, an eminent neuroscientist, put it, not only do genes and environment cooperate as we develop, but genes *require* input from the environment to work properly.

At the same time, scientists are learning that people have more capacity for lifelong learning and brain development than they ever thought. Of 11 course, each person has a unique genetic endowment. People may start with different temperaments and different aptitudes, but it is clear that experience, training, and personal effort take them the rest of the way. Robert Sternberg, the present-day guru of intelligence, writes that the major factor in whether people achieve expertise "is not some fixed prior ability, but purposeful engagement." Or, as his forerunner Binet recognized, it's not always the people who start out the smartest who end up the smartest.

What Does All This Mean for You? The Two Mindsets

It's one thing to have pundits spouting their opinions about scientific 12 issues. It's another thing to understand how these views apply to you. For twenty years, my research has shown that *the view you adopt for yourself* profoundly affects the way you lead your life. It can determine whether you become the person you want to be and whether you accomplish the things you value. How does this happen? How can a simple belief have the power to transform your psychology and, as a result, your life?

Believing that your qualities are carved in stone—the *fixed mindset—* 13 creates an urgency to prove yourself over and over. If you have only a certain amount of intelligence, a certain personality, and a certain moral character—well, then you'd better prove that you have a healthy dose of

them. It simply wouldn't do to look or feel deficient in these most basic
characteristics.

Some of us are trained in this mindset from an early age. Even as *14*
a child, I was focused on being smart, but the fixed mindset was really
stamped in by Mrs. Wilson, my sixth-grade teacher. Unlike Alfred Binet,
she believed that people's IQ scores told the whole story of who they were.
We were seated around the room in IQ order, and only the highest-IQ students could be trusted to carry the flag, clap the erasers, or take a note to
the principal. Aside from the daily stomachaches she provoked with her
judgmental stance, she was creating a mindset in which everyone in the
class had one consuming goal—look smart, don't look dumb. Who cared
about or enjoyed learning when our whole being was at stake every time
she gave us a test or called on us in class?

I've seen so many people with this one consuming goal of proving *15*
themselves—in the classroom, in their careers, and in their relationships.
Every situation calls for a confirmation of their intelligence, personality,
or character. Every situation is evaluated: *Will I succeed or fail? Will I look
smart or dumb? Will I be accepted or rejected? Will I feel like a winner or a
loser?*

But doesn't our society value intelligence, personality, and character? *16*
Isn't it normal to want these traits? Yes, but...

There's another mindset in which these traits are not simply a hand *17*
you're dealt and have to live with, always trying to convince yourself and
others that you have a royal flush when you're secretly worried it's a pair
of tens. In this mindset, the hand you're dealt is just the starting point for
development. This *growth mindset* is based on the belief that your basic
qualities are things you can cultivate through your efforts. Although people may differ in every which way—in their initial talents and aptitudes,
interests, or temperaments—everyone can change and grow through
application and experience.

Do people with this mindset believe that anyone can be anything, *18*
that anyone with proper motivation or education can become Einstein or
Beethoven? No, but they believe that a person's true potential is unknown

(and unknowable); that it's impossible to foresee what can be accomplished with years of passion, toil, and training.

Did you know that Darwin and Tolstoy were considered ordinary children? That Ben Hogan, one of the greatest golfers of all time, was completely uncoordinated and graceless as a child? That the photographer Cindy Sherman, who has been on virtually every list of the most important artists of the twentieth century, *failed* her first photography course? That Geraldine Page, one of our greatest actresses, was advised to give it up for lack of talent? ₁₉

You can see how the belief that cherished qualities can be developed creates a passion for learning. Why waste time proving over and over how great you are, when you could be getting better? Why hide deficiencies instead of overcoming them? Why look for friends or partners who will just shore up your self-esteem instead of ones who will also challenge you to grow? And why seek out the tried and true, instead of experiences that will stretch you? The passion for stretching yourself and sticking to it, even (or especially) when it's not going well, is the hallmark of the growth mindset. This is the mindset that allows people to thrive during some of the most challenging times in their lives. ₂₀

A View from the Two Mindsets

To give you a better sense of how the two mindsets work, imagine—as vividly as you can—that you are a young adult having a really bad day: ₂₁

> One day, you go to a class that is really important to you and that you like a lot. The professor returns the midterm papers to the class. You got a C+. You're very disappointed. That evening on the way back to your home, you find that you've gotten a parking ticket. Being really frustrated, you call your best friend to share your experience but are sort of brushed off.

What would you think? What would you feel? What would you do? ₂₂

When I asked people with the fixed mindset, this is what they said: "I'd feel like a reject." "I'm a total failure." "I'm an idiot." "I'm a loser." "I'd feel worthless and dumb—everyone's better than me." "I'm slime." In other words, they'd see what happened as a direct measure of their competence and worth. ₂₃

This is what they'd think about their lives: "My life is pitiful." "I have no life." "Somebody upstairs doesn't like me." "The world is out to get me." "Someone is out to destroy me." "Nobody loves me, everybody hates me." "Life is unfair and all efforts are useless." "Life stinks. I'm stupid. Nothing good ever happens to me." "I'm the most unlucky person on this earth." ₂₄

Excuse me, was there death and destruction, or just a grade, a ticket, and a bad phone call? ₂₅

Are these just people with low self-esteem? Or card-carrying pessi- 26
mists? No. When they aren't coping with failure, they feel just as worthy
and optimistic—and bright and attractive—as people with the growth
mindset.

So how would they cope? "I wouldn't bother to put so much time and 27
effort into doing well in anything." (In other words, don't let anyone measure you again.) "Do nothing." "Stay in bed." "Get drunk." "Eat." "Yell at
someone if I get a chance to." "Eat chocolate." "Listen to music and pout."
"Go into my closet and sit there." "Pick a fight with somebody." "Cry."
"Break something." "What is there to do?"

What is there to do! You know, when I wrote the vignette, I intention- 28
ally made the grade a C+, not an F. It was a midterm rather than a final. It
was a parking ticket, not a car wreck. They were "sort of brushed off," not
rejected outright. Nothing catastrophic or irreversible happened. Yet from
this raw material the fixed mindset created the feeling of utter failure and
paralysis.

When I gave people with the growth mindset the same vignette, here's 29
what they said. They'd think:

"I need to try harder in class, be more careful when parking the car, 30
and wonder if my friend had a bad day."

"The C+ would tell me that I'd have to work a lot harder in the class, 31
but I have the rest of the semester to pull up my grade."

There were many, many more like this, but I think you get the idea. 32
Now, how would they cope? Directly.

"I'd start thinking about studying harder (or studying in a different 33
way) for my next test in that class, I'd pay the ticket, and I'd work things
out with my best friend the next time we speak."

"I'd look at what was wrong on my exam, resolve to do better, pay my 34
parking ticket, and call my friend to tell her I was upset the day before."

"Work hard on my next paper, speak to the teacher, be more care- 35
ful where I park or contest the ticket, and find out what's wrong with my
friend."

You don't have to have one mindset or the other to be upset. Who 36
wouldn't be? Things like a poor grade or a rebuff from a friend or loved
one—these are not fun events. No one was smacking their lips with
relish. Yet those people with the growth mindset were not labeling themselves and throwing up their hands. Even though they felt distressed, they
were ready to take the risks, confront the challenges, and keep working at
them.

So, What's New?

Is this such a novel idea? We have lots of sayings that stress the importance 37
of risk and the power of persistence, such as "Nothing ventured, nothing

gained" and "If at first you don't succeed, try, try again" or "Rome wasn't built in a day." (By the way, I was delighted to learn that the Italians have the same expression.) What is truly amazing is that people with the fixed mindset would not agree. For them, it's "Nothing ventured, nothing lost." "If at first you don't succeed, you probably don't have the ability." "If Rome wasn't built in a day, maybe it wasn't meant to be." In other words, risk and effort are two things that might reveal your inadequacies and show that you were not up to the task. In fact, it's startling to see the degree to which people with the fixed mindset do not believe in effort.

What's also new is that people's ideas about risk and effort grow out 38 of their more basic mindset. It's not just that some people happen to recognize the value of challenging themselves and the importance of effort. Our research has shown that this *comes directly* from the growth mindset. When we teach people the *growth* mindset, with its focus on development, these ideas about challenge and effort follow. Similarly, it's not just that some people happen to dislike challenge and effort. When we (temporarily) put people in a fixed mindset, with its focus on permanent traits, they quickly fear challenge and devalue effort.

We often see books with titles like *The Ten Secrets of the World's Most* 39 *Successful People* crowding the shelves of bookstores, and these books may give many useful tips. But they're usually a list of unconnected pointers, like "Take more risks!" or "Believe in yourself!" While you're left admiring people who can do that, it's never clear how these things fit together or how you could ever become that way. So you're inspired for a few days, but basically the world's most successful people still have their secrets.

Instead, as you begin to understand the fixed and growth mindsets, 40 you will see exactly how one thing leads to another—how a belief that your qualities are carved in stone leads to a host of thoughts and actions, and how a belief that your qualities can be cultivated leads to a host of different thoughts and actions, taking you down an entirely different road. It's what we psychologists call an *Aha!* experience. Not only have I seen this in my research when we teach people a new mindset, but I get letters all the time from people who have read my work.

They recognize themselves: "As I read your article I literally found 41 myself saying over and over again, 'This is me, this is me! They see the connections: "Your article completely blew me away. I felt I had discovered the secret of the universe!" They feel their mindsets reorienting: "I can certainly report a kind of personal revolution happening in my own thinking, and this is an exciting feeling." And they can put this new thinking into practice for themselves *and* others: "Your work has allowed me to transform my work with children and see education through a different lens," or "I just wanted to let you know what an impact—on a personal and practical level—your outstanding research has had for hundreds of students."

Self-Insight; Who Has Accurate Views of Their Assets and Limitations?

Well, maybe the people with the growth mindset don't think they're Ein- 42
stein or Beethoven, but aren't they more likely to have inflated views of
their abilities and try for things they're not capable of? In fact, studies
show that people are terrible at estimating their abilities. Recently, we set
out to see who is most likely to do this. Sure, we found that people greatly
misestimated their performance and their ability. *But it was those with the
fixed mindset who accounted for almost all the inaccuracy.* The people with
the growth mindset were amazingly accurate.

When you think about it, this makes sense. If, like those with the 43
growth mindset, you believe you can develop yourself, then you're open
to accurate information about your current abilities, even if it's unflattering. What's more, if you're oriented toward learning, as they are,
you *need* accurate information about your current abilities in order
to learn effectively. However, if everything is either good news or bad
news about your precious traits—as it is with fixed-mindset people—
distortion almost inevitably enters the picture. Some outcomes are magnified, others are explained away, and before you know it you don't know
yourself at all.

Howard Gardner, in his book *Extraordinary Minds,* concluded that 44
exceptional individuals have "a special talent for identifying their own
strengths and weaknesses." It's interesting that those with the growth
mindset seem to have that talent. . . .

Grow Your Mindset

Which mindset do you have? Answer these questions about intelligence. 45
Read each statement and decide whether you mostly agree with it or disagree with it.

1. Your intelligence is something very basic about you that you can't
   change very much.
2. You can learn new things, but you can't really change how intelligent
   you are.
3. No matter how much intelligence you have, you can always change it
   quite a bit.
4. You can always substantially change how intelligent you are.

Questions 1 and 2 are the fixed-mindset questions. Questions 3 and 4 reflect
the growth mindset. Which mindset did you agree with more? You can be a
mixture, but most people lean toward one or the other.

You also have beliefs about other abilities. You could substitute "artis- 46
tic talent," "sports ability," or "business skill" for "intelligence." Try it.

It's not only your abilities; it's your personal qualities too. Look at 47 these statements about personality and character and decide whether you mostly agree or mostly disagree with each one.

1. You are a certain kind of person, and there is not much that can be done to really change that.
2. No matter what kind of person you are, you can always change substantially.
3. You can do things differently, but the important parts of who you are can't really be changed.
4. You can always change basic things about the kind of person you are.

Here, questions 1 and 3 are the fixed-mindset questions and questions 48 2 and 4 reflect the growth mindset. Which did you agree with more?

Did it differ from your intelligence mindset? It can. Your "intelligence 49 mindset" comes into play when situations involve mental ability.

Your "personality mindset" comes into play in situations that involve 50 your personal qualities—for example, how dependable, cooperative, caring, or socially skilled you are. The fixed mindset makes you concerned with how you'll be judged; the growth mindset makes you concerned with improving.

Here are some more ways to think about mindsets: 51

- Think about someone you know who is steeped in the fixed mindset. Think about how they're always trying to prove themselves and how they're supersensitive about being wrong or making mistakes. Did you ever wonder why they were this way? (Are you this way?) Now you can begin to understand why.

- Think about someone you know who is skilled in the growth mindset—someone who understands that important qualities can be cultivated. Think about the ways they confront obstacles. Think about the things they do to stretch themselves. What are some ways you might like to change or stretch yourself?

- Okay, now imagine you've decided to learn a new language and you've signed up for a class. A few sessions into the course, the instructor calls you to the front of the room and starts throwing questions at you one after another.

Put yourself in a fixed mindset. Your ability is on the line. Can you feel 52 everyone's eyes on you? Can you see the instructor's face evaluating you? Feel the tension, feel your ego bristle and waver. What else are you thinking and feeling?

Now put yourself in a growth mindset. You're a novice—that's why 53 you're here. You're here to learn. The teacher is a resource for learning. Feel the tension leave you; feel your mind open up.

The message is: You can change your mindset. 54

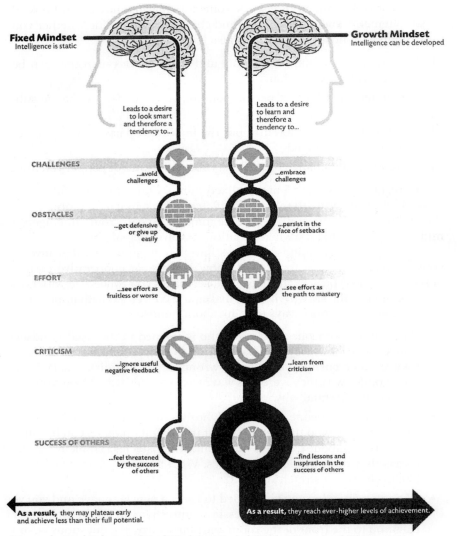

Diagram by Nigel Holmes. In "Fixed Mindset vs. Growth Mindset Figure" and "Chapter 1: The Mindsets" from MINDSET: THE NEW PSYCHOLOGY OF SUCCESS by Carol S. Dweck, Ph.D., copyright © 2006 by Carol S. Dweck, Ph.D. Used by permission of Random House, an imprint and division of Penguin Random House LLC. All rights reserved.

■ ■ ■

Reading as a Writer: Analyzing Rhetorical Choices

1. Dweck mentions several experts in the field of psychology. In pairs or teams, look up information and share your findings on Alfred Binet (para. 9), Gilbert Gottlieb (para. 10), Robert Sternberg (para. 11), and Howard Gardner (para. 44). How are their ideas relevant to Dweck's argument?

2. Draw on the visual rhetoric tools in Chapter 10 to analyze the comic or the graphic at the end of the piece. How does the visual presentation of

the concept enhance Dweck's argument? Connect your response to two specific passages in this reading.

Writing as a Reader: Entering the Conversation of Ideas

1. Dweck argues that we can change our mindset, if we understand the implications of our responses to failure. Mary Aiken (pp. 614–28) considers the ways the digital tools we use for education can foster negative behaviors. Imagine these authors in conversation with one another, challenging one another's claims and perhaps finding some common ground. Now put yourself into this conversation. Write an essay in which you build on these authors' ideas and your own experience and analysis of facing educational challenges in a digital age. Use Chapter 6's models for stating a thesis to help you figure out an approach for your argument.

2. How might Dweck's theory of mindsets help you understand the short narratives on education in Chapter 1 by Ta-Nehisi Coates (pp. 20–24), Richard Rodriguez (pp. 24–31), and Gerald Graff (pp. 31–36)? Choose one or two of those short narratives to consider in light of Dweck's theory, and write an essay in which you apply mindset concepts to the examples depicted in the education narratives. What aspects of those narratives stand out, and what significance do you see in your findings?

MARGARET TALBOT

From Brain Gain: The Underground World of "Neuroenhancing" Drugs

Margaret Talbot is a staff writer at *The New Yorker*, where this article first appeared in 2009. Talbot has also written for *The New Republic* and *The Atlantic Monthly* on a wide range of topics, including changing attitudes toward women's work and family life, the intersection of politics and moral debates, and children's culture. This article on "neuroenhancing" drugs is part of an unfolding conversation among scholars and public intellectuals about the increasingly large role that prescription medication plays in many people's lives. You may be aware of the debates about whether we are "overmedicating" patients for depression or attention deficit disorder. In this article, Talbot takes up a more recent side effect of our medically fascinated culture—the nonmedical use of prescription drugs such as Adderall and Ritalin to enhance academic performance, particularly at the college level. In this piece, Talbot describes stressful dynamics of college life that may be familiar to you—balancing academic demands with other pressures on your time, whether from work or socializing. As you read, compare Talbot's examples to your own experiences and the ways you and your peers struggle to stay on top of the competing demands of contemporary life and college coursework.

Talbot uses an extended example of an anonymous student, "Alex," to make a broader point about the ways many college campuses "have become laboratories for experimentation with neuroenhancement" (para. 2). Pay attention to the strategies Talbot uses to move from her close-up example of Alex to her big-picture analysis of the implications of increasing use among college students of prescription "brain-boosting" drugs. How is one person's decision to use drugs in this way more than a private act, as Talbot claims in paragraph 12? Talbot brings in experts who weigh in on both the negatives and positives of this issue. She also contextualizes this kind of recreational drug use in a long history of people using (or abusing) caffeine and nicotine in order to stay awake and focused at school and at work. What do you make of these comparisons?

If, as Talbot claims, "Every era has its ... defining drug" (para. 26), she invites us to consider the significance of the current use (or abuse) of "brain-boosting" drugs. What do they tell us about what we—and our professors and our employers—expect? What does it take to be competitive right now, and do we agree with the direction we are heading? Talbot offers multiple perspectives on an issue that is likely to be affecting your life right now and will surely affect your future.

A young man I'll call Alex recently graduated from Harvard. As a history major, Alex wrote about a dozen papers a semester. He also ran a student organization, for which he often worked more than forty hours a week; when he wasn't on the job, he had classes. Weeknights were devoted to all the schoolwork that he couldn't finish during the day, and weekend nights were spent drinking with friends and going to dance parties. "Trite as it sounds," he told me, it seemed important to "maybe appreciate my own youth." Since, in essence, this life was impossible, Alex began taking Adderall to make it possible.

Adderall, a stimulant composed of mixed amphetamine salts, is commonly prescribed for children and adults who have been given a diagnosis of attention-deficit hyperactivity disorder. But in recent years Adderall and Ritalin, another stimulant, have been adopted as cognitive enhancers: Drugs that high-functioning, overcommitted people take to become higher-functioning and more overcommitted. (Such use is "off label," meaning that it does not have the approval of either the drug's manufacturer or the Food and Drug Administration.) College campuses have become laboratories for experimentation with neuroenhancement, and Alex was an ingenious experimenter. His brother had received a diagnosis of ADHD, and in his freshman year Alex obtained an Adderall prescription for himself by describing to a doctor symptoms that he knew were typical of the disorder. During his college years, Alex took fifteen milligrams of Adderall most evenings, usually after dinner, guaranteeing that he would maintain intense focus while losing "any ability to sleep for approximately eight to ten hours." In his sophomore year, he persuaded the doctor to add a thirty-milligram "extended release" capsule to his daily regimen.

Alex recalled one week during his junior year when he had four ₃
term papers due. Minutes after waking on Monday morning, around
seven-thirty, he swallowed some "immediate release" Adderall. The drug,
along with a steady stream of caffeine, helped him to concentrate during
classes and meetings, but he noticed some odd effects; at a morning tuto-
rial, he explained to me in an e-mail, "I alternated between speaking too
quickly and thoroughly on some subjects and feeling awkwardly quiet during other points of the discussion." Lunch was a blur: "It's always hard to
eat much when on Adderall." That afternoon, he went to the library, where
he spent "too much time researching a paper rather than actually writing it—a problem, I can assure you, that is common to all intellectually
curious students on stimulants." At eight, he attended a two-hour meeting
"with a group focussed on student mental-health issues." Alex then "took
an extended-release Adderall" and worked productively on the paper all
night. At eight the next morning, he attended a meeting of his organization; he felt like "a zombie," but "was there to insure that the semester's
work didn't go to waste." After that, Alex explained, "I went back to my
room to take advantage of my tired body." He fell asleep until noon, waking "in time to polish my first paper and hand it in."

I met Alex one evening last summer, at an appealingly scruffy bar in ₄
the New England city where he lives. Skinny and bearded, and wearing
faded hipster jeans, he looked like the lead singer in an indie band. He
was ingratiating and articulate and smoked cigarettes with an ironic air of
defiance. Alex was happy enough to talk about his frequent use of Adderall
at Harvard, but he didn't want to see his name in print; he's involved with
an Internet start-up and worried that potential investors might disapprove
of his habit.

After we had ordered beers, he said, "One of the most impressive fea- ₅
tures of being a student is how aware you are of a twenty-four-hour work
cycle. When you conceive of what you have to do for school, it's not in terms
of nine to five but in terms of what you can physically do in a week while
still achieving a variety of goals in a variety of realms—social, romantic,
sexual, extracurricular, résumé-building, academic commitments." Alex
was eager to dispel the notion that students who took Adderall were "academic automatons who are using it in order to be first in their class, or in
order to be an obvious admit to law school or the first accepted at a consulting firm." In fact, he said, "it's often people"—mainly guys—"who are
looking in some way to compensate for activities that are detrimental to
their performance." He explained, "At Harvard, at least, most people are
to some degree realistic about it....I don't think people who take Adderall are aiming to be the top person in the class. I think they're aiming to
be among the best. Or maybe not even among the best. At the most basic
level, they aim to do better than they would have otherwise." He went on,
"Everyone is aware of the fact that if you were up at 3 a.m. writing this
paper it isn't going to be as good as it could have been. The fact that you

were partying all weekend, or spent the last week being high, watching *Lost*—that's going to take a toll."

Alex's sense of who uses stimulants for so-called nonmedical purposes 6 is borne out by two dozen or so scientific studies. In 2005, a team led by Sean Esteban McCabe, a professor at the University of Michigan's Substance Abuse Research Center, reported that in the previous year 4.1 percent of American undergraduates had taken prescription stimulants for off-label use; at one school, the figure was 25 percent. Other researchers have found even higher rates: A 2002 study at a small college found that more than 35 percent of the students had used prescription stimulants nonmedically in the previous year.

Drugs such as Adderall can cause nervousness, headaches, sleepless- 7 ness, and decreased appetite, among other side effects. An FDA warning on Adderall's label notes that "amphetamines have a high potential for abuse" and can lead to dependence. (The label also mentions that adults using Adderall have reported serious cardiac problems, though the role of the drug in those cases is unknown.) Yet college students tend to consider Adderall and Ritalin benign, in part because they are likely to know peers who have taken the drugs since childhood for ADHD. Indeed, McCabe reports, most students who use stimulants for cognitive enhancement obtain them from an acquaintance with a prescription. Usually, the pills are given away, but some students sell them.

According to McCabe's research team, white male undergraduates at 8 highly competitive schools—especially in the Northeast—are the most frequent collegiate users of neuroenhancers. Users are also more likely to belong to a fraternity or a sorority and to have a GPA of 3.0 or lower. They are ten times as likely to report that they have smoked marijuana in the past year, and twenty times as likely to say that they have used cocaine. In other words, they are decent students at schools where, to be a great student, you have to give up a lot more partying than they're willing to give up.

The BoredAt Web sites—which allow college students to chat idly 9 while they're ostensibly studying—are filled with messages about Adderall. Posts like these, from the BoredAtPenn site, are typical: "I have some Adderall—I'm sitting by room 101.10 in a grey shirt and headphones"; "I have Adderall for sale 20mg for $15"; "I took Adderall at 8 p.m., it's 6:30 a.m. and I've barely blinked." On the Columbia site, a poster with an e-mail address from CUNY complains that her friends take Adderall "like candy," adding, "I don't want to be at a disadvantage to everyone else. Is it really that dangerous? Will it fuck me up? My grades weren't that great this year and I could do with a bump." A Columbia student responds, "It's probably not a good idea if you're not prescribed," but offers practical advice anyway: "Keep the dose normal and don't grind them up or snort them." Occasional dissents ("I think there should be random drug testing at every exam") are drowned out by testimonials like this one, from the

BoredAtHarvard site: "I don't want to be a pusher or start people on something bad, but Adderall is AMAZING."

Alex remains enthusiastic about Adderall, but he also has a slightly *10* jaundiced critique of it. "It only works as a cognitive enhancer insofar as you are dedicated to accomplishing the task at hand," he said. "The number of times I've taken Adderall late at night and decided that, rather than starting my paper, hey, I'll organize my entire music library! I've seen people obsessively cleaning their rooms on it." Alex thought that generally the drug helped him to bear down on his work, but it also tended to produce writing with a characteristic flaw. "Often, I've looked back at papers I've written on Adderall, and they're verbose. They're belaboring a point, trying to create this airtight argument, when if you just got to your point in a more direct manner it would be stronger. But with Adderall I'd produce two pages on something that could be said in a couple of sentences." Nevertheless, his Adderall-assisted papers usually earned him at least a B. They got the job done. As Alex put it, "Productivity is a good thing."

Last April, the scientific journal *Nature* published the results of an infor- *11* mal online poll asking whether readers attempted to sharpen "their focus, concentration, or memory" by taking drugs such as Ritalin and Provigil— a newer kind of stimulant, known generically as modafinil, which was developed to treat narcolepsy. One out of five respondents said that they did. A majority of the 1,400 readers who responded said that healthy adults should be permitted to take brain boosters for nonmedical reasons, and 69 percent said that mild side effects were an acceptable risk. Though a majority said that such drugs should not be made available to children who had no diagnosed medical condition, a third admitted that they would feel pressure to give "smart drugs" to their kids if they learned that other parents were doing so....

If Alex, the Harvard student, ... [considers his] use of neuroenhancers a *12* private act, Nicholas Seltzer sees his habit as a pursuit that aligns him with a larger movement for improving humanity. Seltzer has a BA from UC Davis and a master's degree in security policy from George Washington University. But the job that he obtained with these credentials—as a researcher at a defense-oriented think tank, in northern Virginia—has not left him feeling as intellectually alive as he would like. To compensate, he writes papers in his spare time on subjects like "human biological evolution and warfare." He also primes his brain with artificial challenges; even when he goes to the rest room at the office, he takes the opportunity to play memory or logic games on his cell phone. Seltzer, who is thirty, told me that he worried that he "didn't have the mental energy, the endurance, the—I don't know what to properly call this—the *sponginess* that I seem to recall having when I was younger."

Suffice it to say that this is not something you notice when you talk *13* to Seltzer. And though our memory is probably at its peak in our early twenties, few thirty-year-olds are aware of a deficit. But Seltzer is the Washington-wonk equivalent of those models and actors in LA who discern tiny wrinkles long before their agent does. His girlfriend, a technology consultant whom he met in a museum, is nine years younger, and he was already thinking about how his mental fitness would stand up next to hers. He told me, "She's twenty-one, and I want to stay young and vigorous and don't want to be a burden on her later in life." He didn't worry about visible signs of aging, but he wanted to keep his mind "nimble and healthy for as long as possible."

Seltzer considers himself a "transhumanist," in the mold of the Oxford *14* philosopher Nick Bostrom and the futurist writer and inventor Ray Kurzweil. Transhumanists are interested in robots, cryogenics, and living a really, really long time; they consider biological limitations that the rest of us might accept, or even appreciate, as creaky obstacles to be aggressively surmounted. On the Imminst forums—"Imminst" stands for "Immortality Institute"—Seltzer and other members discuss life-extension strategies and the potential benefits of cognitive enhancers. Some of the forum members limit themselves to vitamin and mineral supplements. Others use Adderall or modafinil or, like Seltzer, a drug called piracetam, which was first marketed by a Belgian pharmaceutical company in 1972 and, in recent years, has become available in the United States from retailers that sell supplements. Although not approved for any use by the FDA, piracetam has been used experimentally on stroke patients—to little effect—and on patients with a rare neurological condition called progressive myoclonus epilepsy, for whom it proved helpful in alleviating muscle spasms. Data on piracetam's benefits for healthy people are virtually nonexistent, but many users believe that the drug increases blood flow to the brain.

From the time I first talked to Seltzer, it was clear that although he *15* felt cognitive enhancers were of practical use, they also appealed to him on an aesthetic level. Using neuroenhancers, he said, "is like customizing yourself—customizing your brain." For some people, he went on, it was important to enhance their mood, so they took antidepressants; but for people like him it was more important "to increase mental horsepower." He added, "It's fundamentally a choice you're making about how you want to experience consciousness." Whereas the '90s had been about "the personalization of technology," this decade was about the personalization of the brain—what some enthusiasts have begun to call "mind hacking."

Of course, the idea behind mind-hacking isn't exactly new. Fortifying *16* one's mental stamina with drugs of various kinds has a long history. Sir Francis Bacon consumed everything from tobacco to saffron in the hope of goosing his brain. Balzac reputedly fuelled sixteen-hour bouts of writing with copious servings of coffee, which, he wrote, "chases away sleep, and gives us the capacity to engage a little longer in the exercise of our intellects." Sartre dosed himself with speed in order to finish *Critique of Dialectical Reason*. My college friends and I wrote term papers with the sweaty-palmed assistance of NoDoz tablets. And, before smoking bans, entire office cultures chugged along on a collective nicotine buzz—at least, if *Mad Men* is to be believed. Seltzer and his interlocutors on the Imminst forum are just the latest members of a seasoned cohort, even if they have more complex pharmaceuticals at their disposal.

I eventually met Seltzer in an underground food court not far from *17* the Pentagon. We sat down at a Formica table in the dim light. Seltzer was slim, had a shaved head, and wore metal-frame glasses; matching his fastidious look, he spoke precisely, rarely stumbling over his words. I asked him if he had any ethical worries about smart drugs. After a pause, he said that he might have a concern if somebody popped a neuroenhancer before taking a licensing exam that certified him as, say, a brain surgeon, and then stopped using the drug. Other than that, he couldn't see a problem. He said that he was a firm believer in the idea that "we should have a fair degree of liberty to do with our bodies and our minds as we see fit, so long as it doesn't impinge on the basic rights, liberty, and safety of others." He argued, "Why would you want an upward limit on the intellectual capabilities of a human being? And, if you have a very nationalist viewpoint, why wouldn't you want our country to have the advantage over other countries, particularly in what some people call a knowledge-based economy?" He went on, "Think about the complexity of the intellectual tasks that people need to accomplish today. Just trying to understand what Congress is doing is not a simple thing! The complexity of understanding the gamut of scientific and technical and social issues is difficult. If we had a tool that enabled more people to understand the world at a greater level of sophistication, how can we prejudice ourselves against the notion, simply because we don't like athletes to do it? To me, it doesn't seem like the same question. And it deserves its own debate."

Seltzer had never had a diagnosis of any kind of learning disorder. *18* But he added, "Though I wouldn't say I'm dyslexic, sometimes when I type prose, after I look back and read it, I've frequently left out words or interposed words, and sometimes I have difficulty concentrating." In graduate school, he obtained a prescription for Adderall from a doctor who didn't ask a lot of questions. The drug helped him, especially when his ambitions were relatively low. He recalled, "I had this one paper, on nuclear strategy. The professor didn't look favorably on any kind of creative thinking." On Adderall, he pumped out the paper in an evening. "I just bit my tongue, regurgitated, and got a good-enough grade."

On the other hand, Seltzer recalled that he had taken piracetam to *19* write an essay on "the idea of harmony as a trope in Chinese political discourse"—it was one of the papers he was proudest of. He said, "It was really an intellectual challenge to do. I felt that the piracetam helped me to work within the realm of the abstract, and make the kind of associations that I needed—following this idea of harmony from an ancient religious belief as it was translated throughout the centuries into a very important topic in political discourse."

After a hiatus of several years, Seltzer had recently resumed taking 20 neuroenhancers. In addition to piracetam, he took a stack of supplements that he thought helped his brain functioning: Fish oils, five antioxidants, a product called ChocoMind, and a number of others, all available at the health-food store. He was thinking about adding modafinil, but hadn't yet. For breakfast every morning, he concocted a slurry of oatmeal, berries, soy milk, pomegranate juice, flaxseed, almond meal, raw eggs, and protein powder. The goal behind the recipe was efficiency: To rely on "one goop you could eat or drink that would have everything you need nutritionally for your brain and body." He explained, "Taste was the last thing on my mind; I wanted to be able to keep it down—that was it." (He told me this in the kitchen of his apartment; he lives with a roommate, who walked in while we were talking, listened perplexedly for a moment, then put a frozen pizza in the oven.)

Seltzer's decision to take piracetam was based on his own online 21 reading, which included medical-journal abstracts. He hadn't consulted a doctor. Since settling on a daily regimen of supplements, he had sensed an improvement in his intellectual work and his ability to engage in stimulating conversation. He continued, "I feel I'm better able to articulate my thoughts. I'm sure you've been in the zone—you're having a really exciting debate with somebody, your brain feels alive. I feel that more. But I don't want to say that it's this profound change."

I asked him if piracetam made him feel smarter, or just more alert and 22 confident—a little better equipped to marshal the resources he naturally had. "Maybe," he said. "I'm not sure what being smarter means, entirely. It's a difficult quality to measure. It's the gestalt factor, all these qualities coming together—not only your ability to crunch some numbers, or remember some figures or a sequence of numbers, but also your ability to maintain a certain emotional state that is conducive to productive intellectual work. I do feel I'm more intelligent with the drugs, but I can't give you a number of IQ points."

The effects of piracetam on healthy volunteers have been studied even 23 less than those of Adderall or modafinil. Most peer-reviewed studies focus on its effects on dementia, or on people who have suffered a seizure or a concussion. Many of the studies that look at other neurological effects were performed on rats and mice. Piracetam's mechanisms of action are not understood, though it may increase levels of the neurotransmitter acetylcholine. In 2008, a committee of the British Academy of Medical Sciences noted that many of the clinical trials of piracetam for dementia were methodologically flawed. Another published review of the available studies of the drug concluded that the evidence "does not support the use of piracetam in the treatment of people with dementia or cognitive impairment," but suggested that further investigation might be warranted.

I asked Seltzer if he thought he should wait for scientific ratification of piracetam. He laughed. "I don't want to," he said. "Because it's working."

It makes no sense to ban the use of neuroenhancers. Too many people 24 are already taking them, and the users tend to be educated and privileged people who proceed with just enough caution to avoid getting into trouble. Besides, [University of Pennsylvania neurologist] Anjan Chatterjee is right that there is an apt analogy with plastic surgery. In a consumer society like ours, if people are properly informed about the risks and benefits of neuroenhancers, they can make their own choices about how to alter their minds, just as they can make their own decisions about shaping their bodies.

Still, even if you acknowledge that cosmetic neurology is here to stay, 25 there is something dispiriting about the way the drugs are used—the kind of aspirations they open up, or don't. Jonathan Eisen, an evolutionary biologist at UC Davis, is skeptical of what he mockingly calls "brain doping." During a recent conversation, he spoke about colleagues who take neuroenhancers in order to grind out grant proposals. "It's weird to me that people are taking these drugs to write grants," he said. "I mean, if you came up with some really interesting paper that was *spurred* by taking some really interesting drug—magic mushrooms or something—that would make more sense to me. In the end, you're only as good as the ideas you've come up with."

But it's not the mind-expanding '60s anymore. Every era, it seems, has 26 its own defining drug. Neuroenhancers are perfectly suited for the anxiety of white-collar competition in a floundering economy. And they have a synergistic relationship with our multiplying digital technologies: The more gadgets we own, the more distracted we become, and the more we need help in order to focus. The experience that neuroenhancement offers is not, for the most part, about opening the doors of perception, or about breaking the bonds of the self, or about experiencing a surge of genius. It's about squeezing out an extra few hours to finish those sales figures when you'd really rather collapse into bed; getting a B instead of a B-minus on the final exam in a lecture class where you spent half your time texting; cramming for the GREs at night, because the information-industry job you got after college turned out to be deadening. Neuroenhancers don't offer freedom. Rather, they facilitate a pinched, unromantic, grindingly efficient form of productivity.

This winter, I spoke again with Alex, the Harvard graduate, and 27 found that, after a break of several months, he had gone back to taking Adderall—a small dose every day. He felt that he was learning to use the drug in a more "disciplined" manner. Now, he said, it was less about staying up late to finish work he should have done earlier, and more "about staying focussed on work, which makes me want to work longer hours." What employer would object to that?

■ ■ ■

Reading as a Writer: Analyzing Rhetorical Choices

1. Talbot offers an extended example of the Harvard student "Alex" to illuminate some of the reasons some college students use neuroenhancing drugs. What strengths and weaknesses can you see in using an extended example to illustrate a larger trend? How effectively do you think Talbot ties this example into her larger argument throughout her essay?

2. After reading this piece carefully, list the different perspectives on "brain-boosting" drugs that Talbot lays out in her essay. Does she seem to take sides on this issue? Provide evidence from the text for your responses.

Writing as a Reader: Entering the Conversation of Ideas

1. To what extent do you think Talbot's examples of neuroenhancing drug use are related to the "addictive" quality of being online, as described by Mary Aiken (pp. 614–28)? Use concepts and examples from both readings—and, perhaps, examples from your own experience—to write an essay that makes a point about the competing demands on students. What solutions can you offer for a healthier way to learn and live?

2. Like Talbot, Laura Pappano (pp. 416–26 in Education) is interested in the social dynamics of campus life and the sometimes differing expectations of students and professors about the college experience. Drawing on insights and examples from these authors and your own observations, compose an essay in which you argue for what you think is the most effective balance of college experiences (including, we hope, some time for academic study), and explain your reasoning.

MARY AIKEN

Designed to Addict

Mary Aiken holds a doctorate in forensic cyberpsychology. She has taught at several universities in the United Kingdom based on her expertise in cyber security, cyberstalking, and related cyber threats and addictive behaviors. She has also served as a consultant in a variety of governmental and policy institutes, including the Hague Justice Portal advisory board. Her work inspired the CBS television show *CSI Cyber* (Patricia Arquette's role is modeled after Dr. Aiken). This reading is from Aiken's bestselling 2016 book *The Cyber Effect: A Pioneering Cyberpsychologist Explains How Human Behavior Changes Online.*

While Aiken is a scholar, you will notice that she approaches challenging scientific information with a generalist audience in mind. Rather than taking the tone of a jargon-wielding expert who blames the reader for cyber behaviors, she includes herself in the analysis, using "we" and "us." As you read, notice the ways she pitches her argument carefully, explaining new terms with clear examples and drawing the reader into self-reflection with questions. You may wish to mark every question as you read, to see the pattern throughout this text. Why do you think she uses questions when she does, and how do they affect you?

Aiken uses a narrative introduction (see Chapter 11) designed to horrify readers. How does this set up her argument about the effect of impulsive and compulsive behaviors online? While other authors in this chapter and in our Media Studies chapter (Chapter 16) explore aspects of online behavior, Aiken provides scientific explanations for these addictive behaviors. Be sure to mark the vocabulary that is new to you (for example: *fun failure, affective neuroscience, seeking, addiction, related stimuli, signaling theory, Internet addictive behavior,* and others), and notice the examples she provides to illustrate these concepts. Pay attention, too, to the statistics she provides as evidence of her claim that our Internet behaviors have reached "addictive" levels. What surprises you? What can you say about the statistics you do not find surprising?

We hear about the general dangers of screen culture from every corner of the media these days, but as a scientist, Aiken offers fresh and specific perspective and insights. Understanding the biochemistry behind our behaviors may offer you powerful self-knowledge and tools for your future. It should reassure you that for all the dangers, Aiken believes we can break free of our cyber addictions ... *if* that is what we seek.

Soon after Alexandra Tobias,[1] a twenty-two-year-old mother in Florida, called 911 to report that her three-month-old son, Dylan, had stopped breathing and needed resuscitation, she told investigators that the baby was pushed off the sofa by the family dog and hit his head on the floor. Later, full of regret and sorrow, she confessed to police that she was playing *FarmVille* on her computer and had lost her temper when little Dylan's crying distracted her from the Facebook game. She picked up her baby and began shaking him violently, and his head had hit her computer. At the hospital, he was pronounced dead from head injuries and a broken leg. *1*

At the time of the 2010 incident, *FarmVille*, a wildly popular online game where players become virtual farmers who raise crops and livestock, had 60 million active users. Described in glowing terms as "highly addictive" by its fans, there was eventually a need for FAA (*FarmVille* Addicts Anonymous) support groups, and even an FAA page on Facebook itself. Can we say that Alexandra Tobias was addicted? Is the explanation that simple? Her virtual cattle were doing fine, but her real life was in ruins. *2*

During her trial, she pleaded guilty and showed great remorse, and in a statement said that she hoped to attend college and make something of herself someday. Her own mother had died recently, she said, and Tobias hadn't felt like herself ever since. She received the maximum sentence in Florida for second-degree murder: fifty years. She'll be in jail for most, if not all, of the rest of her life. *3*

As a forensic cyberpsychologist, I am interested in this sad and dis- *4* turbing case for one reason: the role of technology in the escalation of an explosive act of violence. In a nutshell, that is extreme *impulsivity*,[2] an unplanned spontaneous act. And in this case, with devastating consequences.

We are all impulsive to a degree. Some people are by nature more *5* spontaneous than others, more likely to act on a whim without too much thought, whether the behavior is driven by joy or anger. One of the beliefs of our culture is that people reach the end of their lives and wish they'd taken more chances and risks. This may be true for restrained, risk-averse individuals. But extremely impulsive individuals would probably say the opposite: It's not the things they didn't do that they regret. It's the ones they did.

There are risks that reward us and risks that ruin us. The same goes for *6* the hours we spend online. This chapter will discuss many aspects of the Internet that are irresistible—whether it's multiplayer gaming, email check-ing, social-network posting, or bidding on an auction site. Given a host of cyber effects, we may sometimes feel like slaves to our impulses. Why?

The Scale of Impulsiveness

What is impulsivity? It is defined as "a personality trait characterized *7* by the urge to act spontaneously without reflecting on an action and its consequences." The trait of impulsiveness influences several impor-tant psychological processes and behaviors, including self-regulation, risk-taking, and decision-making. It has been found to be a significant component of several clinical conditions, including attention deficit hyperactivity disorder, borderline personality disorder, and the manic phase of bipolar disorder, as well as alcohol and drug abuse and patho-logical gambling.

Researchers studying attention and self-control often assess impul- *8* siveness using personality questionnaires, notably the common Bar-ratt Impulsiveness Scale, which has been used for the past two decades and was updated in 2014 by a group of researchers at Duke University. It's a really fascinating area of interest—and the test, a list of thirty simple statements[3] to be agreed or disagreed with, can be taken in a matter of ten or fifteen minutes. The statements are easy to answer: "I plan tasks carefully," "I am happy-go-lucky," "I am future oriented," "I like puzzles," "I save regularly," and "I am restless at the theater or lectures." You can find the entire test online, but the results need to be assessed by a professional, so taking it on your own, you won't wind up with a final score. Reading over a few of the statements will give you some insight into the three types of impulsivity, which can be physical (difficulty sitting still), cognitive (difficulty concentrating), and sensory (difficulty resisting sensory rewards).

A highly impulsive individual—in all three aspects of impulsivity— 9 tends to be restless, happy-go-lucky, uninterested in planning ahead or saving, not future-oriented. In common parlance, he or she might be described as ADD or ADHD, but it's a bit more complicated than that. When a child is diagnosed with an *executive function disorder,* like ADHD or other attention-related problem, one of the likely aspects of this is something described as suppressed response inhibition,[4] which is generally defined as the inability to suppress an urge to do something, even when environmental contingencies demand it. In other words, the world is telling these children not to do something—"Don't stand up on the bus!"—and telling them why it's a bad idea, but their ability to restrain themselves just isn't there.

A person who is diagnosed as having obsessive-compulsive disorder 10 shares the trait of impulsivity and suppressed response inhibition with ADHD, but he or she finds urges extremely hard to control—and stop. This same trait has been observed in alcoholics, cocaine addicts, heroin- and other substance-dependent patients, as well as smokers. Recent studies have also found impulsivity to be positively correlated with excessive computer game playing and excessive Internet use[5] in general.

Before I go into this subject any deeper, I want to discuss the differ- 11 ence between *impulsive* and *compulsive.* In everyday conversation, we tend to use these two terms almost interchangeably, as if they meant the same thing. But they are actually at opposite ends of a spectrum of behavior. While impulsive behavior is a rash, unplanned act, such as Alexandra Tobias's rage at being interrupted while playing *FarmVille,* compulsive behavior is planned repetitive behavior, like obsessive hand washing or cranking, as discussed in the previous chapter about paraphilia.

Let's describe these in cyber terms. When you constantly pick up your 12 mobile phone to check your Twitter feed, that's compulsive. When you read a nasty tweet and can't restrain yourself from responding with an equally nasty retort (or an even nastier one), that's impulsive.

What makes the Internet so alluring? Why do some individuals strug- 13 gle more than others to pull themselves away from their mobile phones and computer screens?

Fun Failures

Why does anybody buy a Powerball lottery ticket if they know the chances 14 of winning are one in 300 million? For some of the very same reasons that keep people playing any number of beguiling online activities. When we invest time playing *League of Legends* or spend money on the lottery, we know that there's little chance of "hitting it big." Sporadically, though, small rewards do come, and these *intermittent rewards,* as they're called, bring us back again and again.

It's an accepted fact in behavioral psychology that intermittent rein- *15*
forcement is much more effective at motivating people than continuous
rewards. If you are rewarded randomly for an activity, you are likely to
continue doing it—far more likely than if you are rewarded each and every
time. A famous study of pigeons[6] demonstrated this: When pigeons were
consistently rewarded for a certain activity, they did not necessarily continue the activity. But they were much more responsive, and much more
prone to act, when given intermittent reinforcement. Maximum responsiveness was achieved when they were rewarded half the time.

Here's how it works with scratch-off tickets: You are asked, say, to *16*
scratch off six squares on a card and reveal the numbers hidden under-
neath. You will win if you uncover three matching numbers. In terms of
rewards, just the act of scratching off the hidden numbers is a little exciting. A drama is unfolding, and that creates expectancy, which has been
found to deliver a little dopamine to the brain. Dopamine[7] is an organic
chemical released in the brain that helps us regulate movement and emotional responses, and is also associated with pleasurable feelings. More
than 110,000 research papers have been written about dopamine in the
past sixty years. In pursuit of the pleasure it gives us, we do things that
release it. What is fascinating and underresearched is the role of technology in this process.

Most scratch-off cards are designed to lose. But they are also designed *17*
with many matching symbols. Why? You scratch the card, a sequence of
matching symbols begins to appear, and you get excited thinking that you
may win. For a thrilling second, or two, or three, you believe your card
is a winner. In the gambling trade, this tease is called "a heart-stopper,"[8]
because it can give you a surge of excitement, a little buzz of pleasure.
This is classic positive reinforcement. So even when you don't win, that
temporary buzz of excitement is enough to bring you some pleasure and
reinforce card-scratching behavior. And later, the biochemical and psychological memory of that pleasure is enough to keep you in the feedback
loop, and buying more lottery tickets. It's not a huge blast of pleasure,
mind you, but it's just enough.

This is what conditioning is all about. *18*

When any behavior is rewarded with pleasure, you are more likely to *19*
repeat it. The psychology of a casino slot machine works the same way.
Three wheels of the slot machine are spinning—and showing you all those
matching pairs. Two wheels stop. And if the symbols match, it's a heart-
stopper moment. The third wheel stops, and you lose. But somehow, it felt
fun anyway.

In game design this is called "fun failure."[9] Even though you are fail- *20*
ing miserably, you aren't miserable. Why? That biochemical pleasure hit
makes all the difference. And the mere act of anticipating winning is fun.
This is what keeps people buying lottery cards, feeding a slot machine, or
playing *Candy Crush Saga*.

Who hasn't felt the draw of the cyber fun-failure vortex? Who hasn't   *21*
wasted time or money or both online and still managed to feel it was fun?
There is more to it than heart-stoppers. Each type of online activity has its
own attractions, extra built-in rewards that condition users to return.

Why is the mere act of searching online so hypnotically compelling?   *22*
Why are the alerts and notifications on a mobile phone impossible to
ignore? Since my interest is in forensic cyberpsychology—and therefore
I am a bit more focused on pathological behavior than the average person—I have to look at how the various rewards of being online may have a
dark side for some people, and what the implications are for the rest of us.

I Seek, Therefore I Am

If you start simply with psychologist Abraham Maslow's famous "hierar-   *23*
chy of needs"—the needs that demand our attention and motivate human
beings to survive, adapt, and evolve—you'll see them all met online in
one manner or another: from physiological needs to needs for safety, love,
belonging, esteem, self-knowledge, and self-actualization.

Online anonymity offers you a sense of safety. Joining an online com-   *24*
munity, or participating in a multiplayer online game, can give you a sense
of belonging. Getting your Instagram photos or Facebook posts "liked"
meets a need for esteem. But that's just the beginning of social-networking
rewards and pleasures. According to psychiatrist and author Dr. Eva Ritvo
in her article "Facebook and Your Brain," social networking "stimulates
the release of loads of dopamine as well as offering an effective cure to
loneliness. Novelty also triggers these 'feel good' chemicals."[10] Apart from
getting high on likes, posting information about yourself can also deliver
pleasure. About 40 percent of daily speech is normally taken up with self-
disclosure—telling others how we feel or what we think about something—but when we go online the amount of self-disclosure doubles to 80
percent. According to Harvard neuroscientist Diana Tamir, this produces a
brain response similar to the release of dopamine.[11]

Searching online—whether you are hunting down a piece of informa-   *25*
tion, shopping for a pair of shoes, or looking for an old classmate or professional contact—rewards you in another powerful way. Which brings me to
a favorite subject of mine, the fascinating real-world work of Washington
State University neuroscientist Jaak Panksepp, who coined the term *affective neuroscience,* or the biology of arousing feelings or emotions.

Panksepp conducted laboratory experiments on rats and discovered   *26*
what he calls the "seeking" system, something that drives both humans
and animals to seek information that will help them survive. Dopamine-
energized, this mesolimbic seeking system encourages foraging, exploration, investigation, curiosity, craving, and expectancy. In other words,
dopamine fires each time the rat (or human) explores its environment.

Panksepp, who has spent decades mapping the emotional systems of the brain, calls seeking "the granddaddy of the systems." Emily Yoffe in *Slate* explains: "It is the mammalian motivational engine that each day gets us out of the bed, or den, or hole to venture forth into the world."[12] Seeking is so stimulating, according to scientist Temple Grandin, that animals in captivity would prefer to hunt or seek out their food rather than have it delivered to them.

If we think about this in Darwinian terms, Panksepp is essentially   27 arguing that a number of instincts such as seeking, play, anger, lust, panic, grief, and fear are embedded in ancient regions of the human brain or are, as he describes them, evolutionary memories "built into the nervous system at a fundamental level." To Panksepp, these instincts may be considered adaptive traits so fundamental, and so essential to our survival, that they may even constitute what we think of as our "core-self."[13]

I seek, therefore I am?   28

You don't need to sing the joys of seeking and exploring to police detec-   29 tives, investigative journalists, and research scientists. Way before the advent of the Internet, they were experiencing the thrills and rewards of discovery. The drive to seek and explore has kept the human race alive and fed for centuries. But it's Panksepp's work that provides us with a biochemical explanation: The dopamine rewards of seeking and foraging have probably made human beings highly adaptable to new environments. We are rewarded for exploring. One could easily argue that the same reward system, or reinforcement, has made human beings more adaptable to the new environment we are still discovering online.

Addiction is explained in Panksepp's work as an excessive form of   30 seeking. Whether the addict is seeking a hit from cocaine, alcohol, or a Google search, "dopamine is firing, keeping the human being in a constant state of alert expectation." If you think about it, cyberspace is like outer space—infinity in terms of seeking. With our evolutionary memory driving us toward exploring and making sense of this new environment, cyberspace, are we trying to evolve at the speed of technology? And if the biochemical rewards of seeking online are the very ones that can make losing the lottery feel like "fun" to a vast number of the population, what does this mean for individuals who struggle with compulsive gambling or other addictions or ADHD?

Hard to resist. That's how many of us find the Internet. It's always   31 delivering a wild surprise, pulsing with breaking news, statistics, personal messages, and entertainment. The overwhelming evidence points to this: A combination of the fast delivery, exploring opportunities, unexpected information, and intermittent rewards creates a medium that is enticing, exciting, and for some individuals totally irresistible. Now let's add in the design aspects of the apps, ads, games, and social-networking sites—the alerts, push notifications, lights, and other visual triggers that signal us like primitive mating calls.

Check Your Email, Check Your Email, Check Your Email Again. *Now ...*

The Latin word *addictus*[14] was once used to describe the stretch of time an   *32* indentured slave had to serve his or her master. The servant with the sentence was called "the addict."

    We've all observed it firsthand: the otherwise polite and well-mean-   *33* ing friend who chronically checks her phone while you're trying to have a lunch conversation. Does she really mean to be so rude?

    Her connection with you—and the real world—is competing with the   *34* little buzz of pleasure she gets every time she checks her in-box. Most of the emails, texts, or notifications your friend is receiving are not urgent. (Most of her emails are probably advertisements from online retailers!) But she can't stop checking in hopes of getting a personal email from someone she cares about—or exciting news of any kind.

    A 2015 study found that Americans check their phones a total of   *35* 8 billion times a day.[15] As mentioned in the prologue, a study shows that an average adult with a mobile phone connected to the Internet checked his or her phone more than two hundred times a day. That's about every five minutes. In the evening it escalates. When most people are home from work, on average they begin checking their mobile phones once every six minutes. (How many times have you caught yourself picking up your phone mindlessly and checking your email queue again, then realized you just looked at it two minutes before?) Studies differ, but the overall results are similar: Average phone checking per day is surprisingly high.

    Given the dependence on mobile phones, it was only a matter of time   *36* before they were repackaged as wearables and strapped to the wrist—but wouldn't this only escalate the distractibility?

    In terms of controlling compulsive behavior, there are a slew of tests to   *37* take online[16] to scale your own "smartphone addiction." And while these questionnaires are not really scientific, it's worth paying attention if you find yourself starting to feel a little uncomfortable or, worse, nodding in agreement:

- Do you find someone to call as soon as you leave the office or land in a plane? (More important, do you sneak your phone out as soon as the plane has landed and turn it on before the pilot says it's okay? How many can resist that urge?)
- Have you ever been teased because you had your cellphone while working out or doing some other activity?
- Are you unable to resist special offers on the latest cellphone models?
- Do you sometimes believe your phone is ringing, but when you answer it or listen longer, you find it wasn't ringing at all (known as "phantom ringing")?

If you recognize yourself in some of the above compulsive behavior, *38* it might help to understand what makes mobile phones so irresistible. To begin with, they are sleek, well-designed little devils that are portable, they are easy to slip into our handbags and pockets, and they travel with us almost anywhere. (I've heard of swimmers getting waterproof cases for them.) And the mobile phone, like the lottery scratch card, offers an intermittent reward. The surprise of hearing or reading news on our devices gives us a buzz of pleasure, which sets in motion a complex set of reinforcing behaviors: You check your phone to (intermittently) get good or surprising news, which is enough to keep you checking.

Now let's add in what a psychologist would call the *related stimuli* of *39* these digital devices, or the flashing lights and other alerts and notifications that come with each new email or text or Facebook "like," depending on how you've customized your settings. Related stimuli are cues or situations that an addict associates with their addiction. One famous addiction study found that related stimuli associated with drinking alcohol or taking drugs could induce craving, explaining how the sight of a liquor bottle can cause a person to feel the urge to drink. This is the result of classic conditioning, like the lab experiment with the men who became aroused by the slide showing a pair of shoes. In the past, antidrug campaigns often used drug paraphernalia in their posters — syringes, needles, spoons, and piles of white powder, all designed to shock the world into total abstinence. But paradoxically the visual stimuli actually drove some addicts to relapse and led to a fundamental redesign of antidrug campaigns.

Just as substance addicts are constantly fighting urges provoked by *40* related stimuli, the alerts and notifications on a mobile phone can cause its user to have an uncontrollable urge to check his or her device. It isn't so different from the spinning of slot machine wheels or the intense cravings that someone with atypical sexual behavior may have for a fetish object. And while the only noticeable downside for your nice but irritating friend at lunch is that she has alienated you — when will you want to have lunch with her again? — in extreme cases an individual with a serious case of "mobile phone addiction" can become socially isolated and even financially ruined. Depending on where they live and their data plans, compulsive phone users can run up monthly charges that they can't begin to afford.

In the behavioral sciences, a phenomenon called *signaling theory*[17] *41* may help us to understand the irresistibility of mobile phones. Signaling theory, which originated with the study of animal behavior, explains why, for example, peahens choose to mate with peacocks with the biggest tails. Evolutionary psychologists have taken these cues for attention and selection, and have applied signaling theory to understanding human interactions. For instance, a number of research studies have shown that we are likely to be even more afraid of snakes and spiders than we are of large predatory animals such as bears, lions, and tigers. From an evolutionary perspective, this could be because snakes and spiders are difficult to spot, don't make sounds or produce other cues, and are therefore more danger-ous. It made sense that our ancestors would look carefully for poisonous creatures before sticking their hands into overgrown brush or putting their feet into moccasins (still a good idea today). Over time, this fear became an instinctive human reaction.

There are several types of signal cues that communicate and attract— *42* visual, acoustic, chemical, and tactile. The visual signals are limited and require a line of sight. A predatory female firefly lures in males with her flashing body light, and then preys upon them, just like the blinking and flashing of your mobile phone. Vervet monkeys have a language of distinct calls representing different types of threats, not unlike the ringtones or your early morning alarm. The waggle dance of the honeybee is a tactile cue to secure social bonds. Next time your phone vibrates in your pocket, you'll feel its need to bond with you. The scent of a queen bee motivates and attracts her worker drones—and no doubt manufacturers are devel-oping chemical signals for their mobile phones. Just wait until your device starts emitting those irresistible pheromones.

Bria Dunham, in an excellent paper on the role of signaling theory *43* in marketing, asks the question "Why are black iPhones sold with white earbuds?" She wonders if perhaps Apple has a backlog of white earbuds or perhaps white ones are cheaper or easier to produce. Eventually, Dunham settles on a more compelling explanation: White earbuds serve a signal-ing function. Those "telltale white earbuds indicate to passersby that the bearer ascribes to certain notions of coolness and style, engages willingly in some degree of conspicuous consumption, has the necessary resource control to afford a portable Apple device ... that's a lot of information con-tent for less than an ounce of plastic and wire."

In other words, unconsciously we might want to display our phones to *44* signal to others that we are part of the Apple Tribe—and have the requisite status and coolness levels to be accepted. This is herd behavior, of course, and there's just as much of this present in real life, and perhaps even more online.

So you've got your phone to prove (unconsciously) that you belong, and *45* then ... you find that you can't stop checking the darn thing. The problem is great enough that there are now apps created to help compulsive email checkers break these patterns of behavior[18]—or retrain themselves to start feeling "rewarded" by resisting the temptation to check their email in-box. One such technology is BreakFree, an app that will monitor the number of times you pick up your phone, check your email, and search the Web. It offers nonintrusive notifications and will provide you with an "addiction score" every day, every week, and every month—to track your progress. These incentives and rewards help motivate a change in behavior. It's like going on a diet and standing on the scale every night for encouragement.

BreakFree bills itself as a "first of its kind, revolutionary mobile app, *46* aimed at controlling smartphone addiction and helping you maintain a healthy digital lifestyle."

The question is, are you *breaking free* from your compulsion, from   47
yourself, or from the technology? Where does control lie? Who's in charge
of your behavior—you or your new app?

Another app called Checky tracks how often you unlock your iPhone   48
and encourages you to share your stats on Twitter and Facebook. It's a
spin-off from the app Calm, which sells itself with information about
behavioral studies linking compulsive Internet use to ADHD, OCD, and
other serious disorders. In the app description, Calm claims to have been
created by "recovering" phone addict Alex Tew "to help individuals relax
their minds.

> "Like many folks, I am pretty much addicted to my phone," Tew says. "And
> now I know exactly how much: most days I check my phone over 100 times.
> In fact, yesterday I checked my phone 124 times. Today I'm at 76, so far. Hav-
> ing this new awareness makes it easier to control my phone usage. My new
> goal is to check less than 100 times a day."

In psychology, we call this *mindfulness*—adopting Buddhist terminol-   49
ogy to describe the state of mind in which our attention is directed to the
here and now, to what is happening in the moment before us, a way of
being kind to ourselves and validating our own experience. As a way to
stay mindful myself and keep track of my time online, I have set my laptop
computer to call out the time, every hour on the hour, so that even as I'm
working in cyberspace, where time flies, I am reminded every hour of the
temporal real world. It's very helpful for me, but a little unnerving for my
colleagues who are at the other end of a Skype call and have to hear a voice
suddenly call out, *"Eleven o'clock!"*

Some other practical remedies to combat phone distraction—or even   50
compulsive use—are to uninstall some of the beckoning apps on your
phone screen. You can also go to your phone settings and turn off your
notifications, which are how social media sites like Instagram, Twitter, and
WhatsApp keep users checking constantly (because they want you to be
checking constantly). Keeping your phone in "airplane mode" will silence
it—and prevent you from accessing the Internet. Or you could just go cold
turkey every so often and simply turn it off. I went to Bora Bora once and
for the first time was in a country where I could not get cell coverage. For
the first twenty-four hours I went through the predictable phases of mobile
connectivity bereavement: disbelief, anger, panic, and night sweats—followed by exhaustion, then finally *acceptance*. I enjoyed a great five-day
break after that, beautifully cellphone free.

For those who are looking for philosophical or intellectual inspiration,   51
a number of books deal with this new aspect of our lives and offer help
and insights, including Nicholas Carr's *The Shallows*, Sherry Turkle's *Alone
Together*, and William Powers's *Hamlet's BlackBerry*. Since 2006, Powers and his family have taken an "Internet Sabbath," a day or two a week
totally unplugged, which he believes has helped them remain mindful, less
distracted, and in control of their use of technology. Addiction expert and

pioneering psychologist Dr. Kimberly Young also recommends taking a forty-eight-hour "digital detox" every weekend. Plug your device into its charger and leave it there on Saturdays and Sundays. Even Pope Francis calls for an unplugged Christmas.

The conundrum of "connectivity" is only bound to escalate. More *52* mobile phones are sold each year than the year before. For 2017, the number of cellphone users is forecast to reach 4.77 billion.[19] As the "usefulness" of these devices grows, more people will own them—and will be spending more time on them. We use them to read the news, connect with friends, photograph our lives, shop, manage our address books and calendars, and pay our bills. Meanwhile, we aren't just learning how to use new devices, new apps, and new interfaces. We are learning how to live in a totally new environment—cyberspace—unlike any other we've been in before. When people talk about cellphone addiction, what they could be trying to express is something more serious than just compulsive checking of texts or emails. People feel addicted to technology itself.

What Is Internet Addiction?

It is so memorably ironic that one of the great pioneers of computer and *53* online gaming, Dani Berry, remarked: "No one ever said on their deathbed, 'Gee, I wish I had spent more time alone with my computer.'"

Most studies of Internet addictive behavior—and there have been literally hundreds now—build upon the work of Dr. Young, who has been studying compulsive online behavior since 1994 and had the prescience to open the first Internet addiction clinic in the United States the following year. Young's groundbreaking study compared the addiction-like behavior online with compulsion disorders and found many similarities. Her TED Talk on this subject in 2015 offers more interesting insights and warnings about what she calls the dangers of being "too connected."[20] In research papers and psychological journals, this behavior is sometimes called *Internet use disorder* and *Internet addiction.* As neither of these are formal conditions, I will use the broader term, *Internet addictive behavior.*

In everyday language, the word *addiction* is applied to almost anything *55* that a human being can have a craving for—from eating ice cream to singing in the shower. But to meet the clinical criteria for addiction, there must be a biochemical or chemical component. And for an individual to be diagnosed as having an addiction, they have to experience "withdrawal" and demonstrate a developing "tolerance." In other words, there has to be evidence that an individual has an escalating need—wanting to use the Internet more and more. (That's tolerance.) And when the Internet is removed, it causes distress (withdrawal).

A telephone survey conducted by researchers at Stanford University a decade ago showed a rate of 12.5 percent of the U.S. adult population sample reporting they had "at least one problem" due to overuse of the Internet—often email checking, gaming, visiting cybersex sites, or shopping. The cravings they described[21] were similar to drug and alcohol cravings among addicts. As the years have passed, that statistic—12 percent of the population—seems to have remained fairly consistent, but numbers vary depending on who's doing the research, how the questions are asked, and how "addiction" or "misuse" or "excessive use" is defined. And what is considered "normal use" of the Internet can change from country to country. In South Korea, where the issue of Internet addictive behavior has mushroomed into a much-discussed, much-researched, much-diagnosed, and much-treated condition, studies indicate that about 10 percent of Korean teenagers are Internet addicts. In fact, some demonstrate difficulty in living their everyday lives due to the level of their addiction. Slightly higher numbers have been reported in China, with 13.7 percent of Chinese adolescent Internet users meeting the criteria for "addiction."[22] It has been reported that addictions to video games are the fastest-growing forms of Internet addiction, especially in China, Taiwan, and Korea. Interestingly, the highest numbers come from a sample of Italian adolescents[23]—36.7 percent reportedly showed signs of "problematic Internet use."

A study of more than thirteen thousand adolescents in seven European 57 countries[24] in 2014 found that 13.9 percent of the participants demonstrated what was described as *dysfunctional Internet behavior* due to compulsive and frequent use that resulted in problems at home, in school, or in general. In a breakdown of excessive usage, social-networking sites like Facebook gobbled up a lot of their online time, along with watching videos or movies, doing homework, downloading music, sending instant messages, and checking email. Boys were significantly more likely to be at risk for the more serious condition of Internet addictive behavior, with boys from Spain and Romania scoring the highest rates, and boys from Iceland the lowest. The more educated the parents, the less likely the adolescents were to show problems.

The study concluded that about 1 percent of adolescents exhibited 58 Internet addictive behavior and an additional 12.7 percent were at risk. Together, this totaled 13.9 percent who could be said to demonstrate dysfunctional behavior. That means that more than one in ten of these adolescents are at risk.

Along with Kimberly Young, another pioneer in the field of addiction 59 to technology is Dr. David Greenfield, a professor of psychiatry at the University of Connecticut School of Medicine and director of the Center for Internet and Technology Addiction. In 2014, in conjunction with AT&T, Greenfield conducted a telephone survey of one thousand subscribers and concluded that around 90 percent of Americans would "fall in the category of overusing, abusing, or misusing their devices."[25] Greenfield, who is also the author of *Virtual Addiction: Help for Netheads, Cyber Freaks, and Those Who Love Them*, says the incidence of Internet addictive behavior among Americans is around 10 to 12 percent, according to his research.

What are people checking on their phones? The first-quarter results *60* for Facebook in 2016 showed that its users spent an average of fifty minutes a day on the site, which is, according to a *New York Times* article, just a bit less time than most people spend each day eating or drinking.

In Greenfield's survey of phone use alone, 61 percent of respondents *61* said they slept with their mobile phone turned on under their pillow—or on a nightstand next to the bed. More than half described feeling "uncomfortable" when they forget their mobile phone at home or in the car, travel somewhere and are unable to get service, or break the phone. Greenfield's research found that while 98 percent of respondents said that they are aware that texting while driving is dangerous, nearly 75 percent admitted having done it. This is effectively extreme risk-taking, the sort of lack of behavioral control that is usually associated with impulsive and compulsive behavior.

A few years ago, a research colleague of mine proposed to do a study *62* assessing mobile phone addiction. He prepared the research proposal and set about recruiting participants. The idea was that all participants would hand over their mobile phones for a period of time, five or six days, while their levels of anxiety would be measured. Not one person approached was willing to participate in the mobile phone separation-anxiety project—which sort of proves the case.

So what can we do? *63*

Internet addictive behavior expert Kimberly Young recommends three *64* strategies:

1. Check your checking. Stop checking your device constantly.

2. Set time limits. Control your online behavior—and remember, kids will model their behavior on adults.

3. Disconnect to reconnect. Turn off devices at mealtimes—and reconnect with the family.

In other words, it's a revision of Timothy Leary's 1960s mantra, *Turn* *65* *on, tune in, and drop out.*

Turn off, tune in, and reconnect.... *66*

NOTES

1. News4Jax.com, February 1, 2011. Notably it has been reported that the day before the death, Tobias took a personality test on the Internet, which labeled her bipolar: D. Hunt, "Jacksonville Mom Who Killed Baby While Playing FarmVille Gets 50 Years," *The Florida Times-Union,* February 1, 2011.
2. C. G. Coutlee, C. S. Politzer, R. H. Hoyle, and S. A. Huettel (2014), "An Abbreviated Impulsiveness Scale Constructed Through Confirmatory Factor Analysis of the Barratt Impulsiveness Scale Version 11 *Archives of Scientific Psychology* 2: 2.
3. J. H. Patton, M. S. Stanford, and E. S. Barratt (1995), "Factor Structure of the Barratt Impulsiveness Scale," *Journal of Clinical Psychology* 51(6): 768–774.
4. W. Ding et al. (2014), "Trait Impulsivity and Impaired Prefrontal Impulse Inhibition Function in Adolescents with Internet Gaming Addiction Revealed by a Go/No-Go fMRI Study," *Behavioral and Brain Functions* 10: 20.

5. F. Cao and L. Su (2007), "Internet Addiction Among Chinese Adolescents: Prevalence and Psychological Features," *Child: Care, Health and Development* 33(3): 275–81. See also G. J. Meerkerk, R. J. J. M. van den Eijnden, I. H. A. Franken, and H. F. L. Garretsen (2010), "Is Compulsive Internet Use Related to Sensitivity to Reward and Punishment, and Impulsivity?" *Computers in Human Behavior* 26(4): 729–35.

6. D. A. Eckerman and R. N. Lanson (1969), "Variability of Response Location for Pigeons Responding Under Continuous Reinforcement, Intermittent Reinforcement, and Extinction," *Journal of the Experimental Analysis of Behavior* 12(1): 73–80.

7. P. M. Newton, "What Is Dopamine?: The Neurotransmitter's Role in the Brain and Behavior," psychologytoday.com, April 26, 2009.

8. M. Woolf, "That Irresistible Urge to Scratch: Lottery/Instants Fever," *The Independent*, April 15, 1995.

9. M. Breeze, "A Quiet Killer: Why Video Games Are So Addictive," TheNextWeb.com, January 12, 2013.

10. E. Ritvo, "Facebook and Your Brain: The Inside Dope on Facebook," psychologytoday.com, May 24, 2012.

11. D. I. Tamir and J. P. Mitchell (2012), "Disclosing Information About the Self Is Intrinsically Rewarding," *Proceedings of the National Academy of Sciences of the United States of America* 109(21): 8038–43.

12. E. Yoffe, "Seeking: How the Brain Hard-Wires Us to Love Google, Twitter, and Texting. And Why That's Dangerous," Slate.com, August 12, 2009.

13. K. Badt, "Depressed? Your 'SEEKING' System Might Not Be Working: A Conversation with Neuroscientist Jaak Panksepp," huffigtonpost.com, September 17, 2013.

14. R. E. Cytowic, "Ambivalence in Addiction," psychologytoday.com, November 13, 2015.

15. L. Eadicicco, "Americans Check Their Phones 8 Billion Times a Day," Time.com, December 15, 2015.

16. behaviorhealth.bizcalcs.com.

17. B. Dunham (2011), "The Role for Signaling Theory and Receiver Psychology in Marketing," in G. Saad (ed.), *Evolutionary Psychology in the Business Sciences.* (Heidelberg, Germany: Springer), 225–56.

18. K. Montgomery, "To Solve Phone Addiction, App Shows How Many Times You Check Your Phone," Gawker.com, September 16, 2014.

19. Forecast of number of cellphone users worldwide (2013 to 2019) found at www.statista.com.

20. K. Young (2015), "What You Need to Know About Internet Addiction," tedxtalks.ted.com/video/What-You-Need-to-Know-About-Int.

21. E. Aboujaoude et al. (2006), "Potential Markers for Problematic Internet Use: A Telephone Survey of 2,513 Adults," *CNS Spectrums* 11(10): 750–55.

22. See M. H. Hur (2006), "Demographic, Habitual, and Socioeconomic Determinants of Internet Addiction Disorder: an Empirical Study of Korean Teenagers," *Cyberpsychology & Behavior* 9(5): 514–25; J.J. Block (2008), "Issues for DSM-V: Internet Addiction," *American Journal of Psychiatry* 165 (3): 306–7.

23. L. Milani, D. Osualdella, and P. Di Blasio (2009), "Quality of Interpersonal Relationships and Problematic Internet Use in Adolescence," *CyberPsychology & Behavior* 12(6): 681–4.

24. A. Tsitsika et al. (2014), "Internet Addictive Behavior in Adolescence: A Cross-Sectional Study in Seven European Countries," *CyberPsychology, Behavior & Social Networking* 17(8): 528–35.

25. K. Wallace, "10 Signs You Might Be Addicted to Your Smartphone," CNN.com, November 25, 2014.

Reading as a Writer: Analyzing Rhetorical Choices

1. Reread Aiken's text, marking every statistic she includes. (To make these statistics even easier to identify, you may want to use a different color pen or highlighter from what you've used for other annotations.) What surprises you about those numbers, and what does not? Why? Discuss the relationship between the statistics and narrative examples Aiken provides. How do they enhance one another? Which kinds of evidence do you find most persuasive and why?

2. Mark all the specific terminology Aiken includes, and be certain you can explain in your own words the definitions she includes. These might include *impulsive versus compulsive, fun failure, affective neuroscience, addiction, related stimuli, signaling theory,* and the variety of Internet addictive behavior she describes in the "What Is Internet Addiction?" section. Share your findings with your peers.

Writing as a Reader: Entering the Conversation of Ideas

1. Aiken and Margaret Talbot (pp. 605–13), examine patterns of behavior that have similarities and also differences. What strikes you as the most important takeaways of each of their arguments on the nature of being a college student now? Write an essay that brings together what you think are the most useful insights in these readings; make an argument about what you wish college professors understood about being a student. Draw on personal experience as well, if your instructor allows.

2. Aiken is literally in conversation with William Powers (pp. 515–24 in Media Studies) and Sherry Turkle (pp. 578–92 in Media Studies) in paragraph 51. Beyond that paragraph, what do these writers have in common, and where do they differ, about the addictive nature of digital technology? Compose an essay that draws on all three authors (or choose between Powers and Turkle) as you argue for your own perspective on a healthy approach to technology.

AGUSTÍN FUENTES

From The Myth of Race

Agustín Fuentes is a professor of anthropology at the University of Notre Dame, where his research and teaching specialties include the evolution of social organization, primatology, and biological anthropology. Fuentes frequently writes about anthropological and biological issues for a more general audience, too, such as in the book from which we draw this excerpt, *Race, Monogamy, and Other Lies They Told You: Busting Myths about Human Nature* (2012). In the chapter titled "The Myth of Race," Fuentes takes on what he calls the "pernicious myth of race," a popular misconception that "if we can see differences, if we can tell people apart, then there must be real (meaning natural, biological) differences between groups of people" (para. 1). Fuentes cautions us to question what we think we know about the concept of "race" in ways that might shake some of your assumptions to the core. The quick guide to "Testing Core Assumptions about Race" that follows paragraph 5 is a preview of Fuentes's argumentative style. You might discuss these "myth-busting" ideas even before you read the full piece.

Fuentes uses a range of examples to demonstrate his claim that while "humans vary biologically, we can demonstrate that this variation does not cluster into racial groups. What we refer to as human races are not biological units" (para. 7). Explaining the significance of this claim in terms of how we understand the world is his main task, and he goes about it by offering many different kinds of evidence. As you read, keep track of the kinds of evidence he offers and consider which you find most persuasive and why. His analysis of blood types (which begins in para. 12), for example, uses biological language and charts to demonstrate similar data; which is most helpful to you for understanding his point?

After arguing for half this piece that race is a "myth," Fuentes then makes a different kind of point, starting with the section titled "Myth Busting: Race Is Not Biology, but It Still Matters in Our Society." Fuentes considers the language around the election of President Barack Obama, the categories used by the Census Bureau, and a long bulleted list of statistics from the U.S. Department of Labor and the Pew Research Center (starting with para. 27) to build his argument. Again, what evidence do you find most persuasive, and why?

How optimistic is Fuentes that we can change these deeply rooted myths? Given the seriousness of his subject, it might be surprising that Fuentes ends this selection by quoting the band They Might Be Giants. Consider finding and listening to their song "Your Racist Friend" as you read the lyrics and Fuentes's final thoughts. What call to action does Fuentes make? What, specifically, might you do to become a "myth buster"?

■   ■   ■

> The idea of "race" represents one of the most dangerous myths of our time and one of the most tragic. Myths are most effective and dangerous when they remain unrecognized for what they are.
>
> —ASHLEY MONTAGU (ANTHROPOLOGIST)[1]

Ashley Montagu, one of the most prominent anthropologists of the   1
twentieth century, warned about the pernicious myth of race in 1942, and his warning is still relevant today. In his 2010 book, Guy Harrison challenges the biological reality of race:

> Few things are more real than races in the minds of most people. We are different. Anyone can see that. Look at a "black" person and look at an "Asian" person. If a black Kenyan stands next to a white guy from Finland we all can see that they are not the same kinds of people. Obviously they belong to different groups and these groups are called races, right? (Guy Harrison, journalist)[2]

Guy Harrison is calling into question the most common popular perception of human variation—that if we can see differences, if we can
tell people apart, then there must be real (meaning natural) differences
between groups of people.[3] The question of whether humans are divided
into biological races is answered with a resounding academic "no" by the
American Association of Physical Anthropology's (AAPA) statement on the
biological aspects of race:

> Humanity cannot be classified into discrete geographic categories with
> absolute boundaries. Partly as a result of gene flow, the hereditary charac-
> teristics of human populations are in a state of perpetual flux. Distinctive
> local populations are continually coming into and passing out of existence.
> Such populations do not correspond to breeds of domestic animals, which
> have been produced by artificial selection over many generations for specific
> human purposes. There is no necessary concordance between biological
> characteristics and culturally defined groups. On every continent, there are
> diverse populations that differ in language, economy, and culture. There is
> no national, religious, linguistic or cultural group or economic class that
> constitutes a race . . . there is no causal linkage between these physical and
> behavioral traits, and therefore it is not justifiable to attribute cultural charac-
> teristics to genetic inheritance.[4]

However, there are others who answer this question with a resounding
"yes":

> The three-way pattern of race differences is true for growth rates, life span,
> personality, family functioning, criminality, and success in social organiza-
> tion. Black babies mature faster than White babies; Oriental babies mature
> slower than Whites. The same pattern is true for sexual maturity, out of wed-
> lock births, and even child abuse. Around the world, Blacks have the highest
> crime rate, Orientals the least, Whites fall in between. The same pattern is
> true for personality. Blacks are the most outgoing and even have the high-
> est self-esteem. Orientals are the most willing to delay gratification. Whites
> fall in between. Blacks die earliest, Whites next, Orientals last, even when all
> have good medical care. The three-way racial pattern holds up from cradle to
> grave. (J. Phillipe Rushton, psychologist)[5]

How can there be two such different answers to Harrison's question? One
answer states, in dry academic terms, that the popular concept of biological races is not supported by evidence; the other, in straightforward common language, says that there is a three-way pattern of racial differences.
One answer is wrong.

Humans Are Divided into Biological
Races, or Are They?

The myth of human biological races is alive and well in our society. Someone like Phillipe Rushton can make claims about racial patterns, even
though they are incorrect, and have some popular success because the

categories "black" and "white" make sense to us.[6] He uses simple, common language, that resonates with some of the cultural patterns we hear about via the media, in our daily lives, and in some versions of history. Rushton's claims are a mix of popular assumptions presented as if they were biological facts. Nowhere in his book *Race, Evolution and Behavior* does Rushton provide any real data to support his assertion that "Blacks," "Whites," and "Orientals" are true biological groups, but he does selectively draw from social statistics on crime, income, and mortality to make spurious analogies and then leaps to connect these to the different evolutionary histories of human races. On the other hand the AAPA statement on race (as well as a multitude of similar statements, peer-reviewed articles, books, and Web sites) states unequivocally that these types of associates are not supported and that the concept of clear or determinate biological races in humans today is not justifiable given what we know about human evolution and biology.

While most people would not fully agree with Rushton about the impli- 3 cations of racial differences, more than would care to admit it probably do see things in his proposal that seem to fit with common perceptions of human variation in the United States: Blacks as more athletic and overly sexual, Asians as more bookish and reserved, and whites seem to fall in between, more or less the average everyman. This is because many people today see the division of humanity into races as part of human nature. It's time to bust this myth.

This myth involves the assumption that we can define a specific set of 4 traits that consistently differentiates each race from the other with limited overlap between members. This position also assumes that differences in innate behavior, intelligence, sports abilities, aggression, lawlessness, health and physiology, sexuality, and leadership ability exist between these presumed real clusters of humans and that the clusters can be described as the Asian, black, and white races.[7] Nearly everyone holding these beliefs would accept that these clusters do overlap in many ways and that interbreeding between them is always possible and not necessarily negative. However, as the journalist Guy Harrison put it so succinctly (and sarcastically), the majority of people regardless of what they might say in public believe to some degree in the natural reality of human races. This "reality" is an assertion that we can test scientifically.

Buying into at least some of this myth about races also suggests a suite 5 of correlates. One is that since these differences are "natural," we should probably be wary of spending much social and economic capital trying to correct them. Some may also feel that the civil rights movement of the last century and the 2008 election of a black American president indicates that U.S. society has already done as much as is possible to ameliorate racial inequality. From this perspective, focusing on race is not really that important anymore. Finally, many might argue that if race is not a biological entity, then how can the actual, and well-documented, differences in health, sports participation, test scores, and economic achievement between the "races" in the United States be explained? In the same vein, what about ancestry tests? How can a company test our DNA and tell us that we are 40 percent Kenyan or 60 percent Irish? Isn't that about race?

Testing core assumptions about race

To bust the myth of race we have to test the core assumptions and refute them. 6

ASSUMPTION: *Human races are biological units*.

TEST: Is there a set of biological characteristics that naturally divide up humans beings into races? If yes, then the assumption is supported; if no, then it is refuted.

ASSUMPTION: *We live in a (mostly) postracial society*.

TEST: Does our society still use race in assessment, definitions, and daily life? If no, then the assumption is supported; if yes, then it is refuted.

ASSUMPTION: *If race is not a biological category, then racism is not that powerful or important in shaping human lives*.

TEST: Can we demonstrate that racism, without the existence of biological races, is a significant factor affecting human health, well-being, and access to societal goods? If yes, then the assumption is refuted; if no, then it is supported.

ASSUMPTION: *If we can see consistent differences in sports, disease patterns, and other areas tied to physical features between races, these must reflect innate differences between these groups of people.*

TEST: Are these differences consistent over time? Are they due to biological or unique racial characteristics or are they better attributed to other causes? If yes, and they can be linked to biological patterns of human groups, then the assumption is supported; if no, then it is refuted.

If we can refute all four assumptions, the myth is busted.

Myth Busting: Race ≠ Biological Groups

Although humans vary biologically, we can demonstrate that this variation 7
does not cluster into racial groups. What we refer to as human races are not biological units. Many articles, books, and official statements make this point. However, there are very few brief and succinct overviews of human biological diversity as it relates to racial typologies. Reviewing information about blood groups, genetics, and morphological and physiological

variation in the context of evolutionary processes demonstrates unequivocally that there is no way to divide humanity into biological units that correspond to the categories black, white, or Asian, or any other categories.

For close to three hundred years people have been trying to name *8* and classify racial grouping of humans. Carolus Linnaeus, the father of modern taxonomy, made the most important attempt to do so and his classifications still seem very much like current ones.[8] Linnaeus saw the distinction among groups of humans as being rooted in their continental origins (Africa, Asia, Europe, Americas). He saw all humans as belonging to one species, *Homo sapiens*, with a number of subspecies representing the different races.[9] In the tenth edition of his major taxonomy of everything, *Systema Naturae*, published in 1758, Linnaeus proposed four subspecies (races) of *Homo sapiens*: americanus, asiaticus, africanus, and europeanus (he added a fifth category, monstrosous, as a catch-all for wild men and mythical beasts). Unlike his other classifications, which were based on drawings and anatomical analyses of specimens, Linnaeus based his division of humans on what he heard and read about the peoples of the different continents.

> *Homo sapiens americanus* was "red, ill-tempered, subjugated. Hair black, straight, thick; Nostrils wide; Face harsh, Beard scanty. Obstinate, contented, free. Paints himself with red lines. Ruled by custom." *Homo sapiens europeaus* was "white, serious, strong. Hair blond, flowing. Eyes blue. Active, very smart, inventive. Covered by tight clothing. Ruled by laws." *Homo sapiens asiaticus* was "yellow, melancholy, greedy. Hair black. Eyes dark. Severe, haughty, desirous. Covered by loose garments. Ruled by opinion." And last (and obviously least) *Homo sapiens africanus*: "black, impassive, lazy. Hair kinked. Skin silky. Nose flat. Lips thick. Women with genital flap; breasts large. Crafty, slow, foolish. Anoints himself with grease. Ruled by caprice."[10]

These descriptions initiated the still common mistake of mixing presumed cultural differences with biological realities. The anthropologist Jon Marks has repeatedly pointed out that if you read them carefully, Linnaeus's race descriptions sound a lot like those of Rushton's and other modern racialists.

About half a century after Linnaeus the German naturalist Johann *9* Friedrich Blumenbach developed another set of nonscientific human racial classifications, based on geographical definitions and some facets of skull morphology. His classifications included Caucasian, Mongolian, Malayan, American, and Negroid races, which were also referred to as white, yellow, brown, red, and black (based on serious ignorance about skin colors around the planet). Finally, during the mid-twentieth century the physical anthropologist Carleton Coon developed a derivation of Blumenbach's races with a more refined set of skull measurements that is still used by some racial topologists today: the Capoid race (southern and eastern Africa), Caucasian race (western and northern Europeans),

Mongoloid race (Asian and Americans), Negroid (or Congoid) race (all of Africa aside from parts to the south and east), and the Australoid race (Australians). Most importantly Coon proposed that each of these races had a separate evolutionary history and thus a suite of behavioral and other traits that evolved separately.[11]

Despite attempts by researchers over the centuries to divide humans into races based on skull shape, geographic location, and presumed cultural differences, there is absolutely no support for any of these classifications (neither those mentioned above nor the countless others proposed) as actually reflecting the ways in which the human skull, genetic characteristics, or other phenotypes cluster in our species.[12] So what does human biological variation actually look like? *10*

As pointed out in our previous discussion of evolution and genetics in chapter 3, we look at variation in populations. Populations are collections of people that reside in more or less the same place, or in different places but are constantly connected, and mate more with one another than with members of other populations. There are thousands of populations of the species *Homo sapiens* spread across the globe. And in some areas (large international cities like New York, London, or Singapore) individuals from many of those populations congregate. To define a race, then, we need to be able to identify a population or set of populations that has a suite of unique markers that differentiate it from all other such populations and mark it as being affected by slightly different evolutionary forces so as to have altered genetic patterns relative to the rest of the species. Let's look at how we vary biologically between and within populations in our blood, immune system, genetics, body shape and size, skin color, and skull shape. *11*

Blood

For centuries people have looked at blood to tell us about humanity. We know that blood is important (lose enough and you die) and during the last century researchers began to discover that blood itself is made up of a number of different elements, all of which vary a bit! Basically, blood is made up primarily of red blood cells (for oxygen transport), white blood cells (defense against infection), platelets (for clotting), and plasma (the liquid part of blood). There are also a number of other things associated with these main components and even others that use the circulatory system to get to different parts of the body.[13] *12*

Many sets of proteins serve a variety of functions associated with red blood cells. We call these protein sets blood types.[14] The best-known blood type classification is the ABO system, which is often coupled with another system, the Rhesus blood type, noted as positive (Rh+) or negative (Rh−). Today we can track more than fifteen blood type systems whose alleles (forms of genes) are found in variable frequencies across different human populations. *13*

In the ABO gene there are four alleles: A_1, A_2, B, and O. A_1 and A_2 [14] are very similar, and mostly respond identically. The three main alleles, A, B, and O, have a set of relationships with one another, in which A and B are considered dominant to O and codominant to one another.[15] In other words, the eventual phenotype of the genotypes AA and AO is A; that of BB and BO is B; that of OO is O; and that of AB is AB. Across the human species these alleles are found at the following frequencies: 62.5 percent O, 21.5 percent A, and 16 percent B. But if we look at the level of different human populations we see different distributions of these alleles. For example, the frequency of allele B is at, or nearly at, zero in many indigenous populations in South America, southern Africa, northern Siberia, and Australia, and higher than 16 percent in indigenous populations in central Asia (Figure 17.1), central West Africa, northern Russia, and mainland Southeast Asia.[16] Alternatively, the A allele is found at its highest frequencies (more than 40 percent) in the Saami (an indigenous population) of northernmost Europe and in some groups of Australian Aborigines.[17] Are populations that share these similar frequencies of A or B more closely related to one another than to the populations next to them that have different frequencies? No.

Understanding natural selection and gene flow helps us understand [15] the distributions of blood types. Probably the most common allele is O because it is the original allele, while A and B are more recent mutations identical to O but with the addition of an extra sugar group. Also, the different ABO phenotypes confer different slightly different support against diseases. Specific blood types may increase or decrease chances of surviving things like malaria or other blood-based parasites. However, the majority of variation in blood groups comes from the movements of human populations over the past 50,000 years or so. Gene flow is the major evolutionary force acting on distribution of the ABO alleles across human populations. None of these alleles are unique to specific populations, nor are their frequencies. And most importantly, none of the patterns, of ABO (or other blood groups) match up with the black-white-Asian model of dividing humans into racial categories. In fact, the full range of blood variation is found in nearly every single human population. The biology of blood does not support biological race....

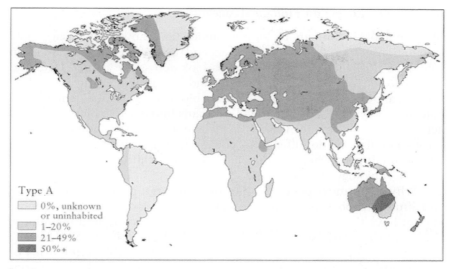

Type A

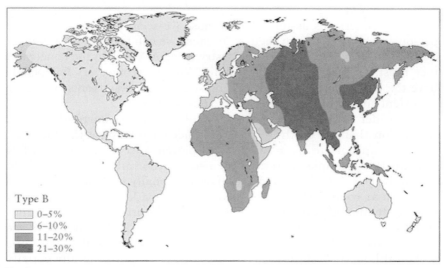

Type B

FIGURE 17.1   Geographical distribution and frequencies of the blood types A and B. Note that they do not follow the big three racial divisions of European, African, and Asian.   Adapted from *Biological Anthropology: Concepts and Connections,* 2nd ed., by Augustín Fuentes. © 2011 McGraw-Hill Education

There is no support for biological races

We can look to human biology to understand how people vary, how *16* populations differ from one another, and how patterns of adaptation and gene flow shape the way humans look across the planet. Data and results from research into body shapes and size, genetics, skin color, skull shapes, and every other aspect of human biological variation demonstrate unequivocally that we cannot divide humans into discrete biological clusters of white, black and Asian. This does not mean that humans do not vary—populations do differ from one another and this variation can be important. It just means that the racial divisions white, black and Asian do not reflect biology: they are cultural constructs.

Why don't most people know this? In large part it is because of *17* our limited exposure to what humans actually look like. Most people do not have the opportunity to travel across the world and see a large subset of the nearly seven billion members of our species. Nor do they have much opportunity to read concise and accessible summaries of thousands of research efforts documenting human biological variation. As previously established in chapter 2, we are who we meet. Our schemata are shaped and our perceptions of reality structured by what we are exposed to. . . .

Many Americans assume that because we seem able to determine a *18* person's race by looking at them or because we can test our DNA and get a percentage of Yoruba or Irish ancestry using AIMs, then the concept of race must have some biological validity. This is wrong; very few people have the background knowledge to make accurate statements regarding the extent and patterns of human biological variation.

Consider an analogy. Nearly all human beings currently accept *19* the notion that the earth is round. We accept it despite the fact that the earth appears to us in our daily experience to be flat. Only a few humans (for example, astronauts or people who sail around the world and arrive back at the same place) have personally seen or experienced the earth as round. The rest of us accept the evidence as scientifically valid even though our personal experience contradicts it. A similar situation holds with the concept of race. Most people do not have the opportunity to see the patterned distribution of humanity across the globe. Although most of us in the United States can generally classify the people we see every day into three to five groups (though not always as easily or reliably as one might think), these groupings might not be valid in other locations. Further, these groupings reflect only a small percentage of the global biological variation in humanity. Thus, as with the shape of the earth, the broader situation is not necessarily obvious from our limited perspectives. If we have the context (broad exposure and the scientific data and understandings reviewed here), we can realize that, although our personal experience and cultural context might seem to show us one thing, the overall pattern of human biological diversity demonstrates something else: that *Homo sapiens* is one species, undivided into races or subspecies. The myth that human races are biological units is busted.

Myth Busting: Race Is Not Biology, but It Still Matters in Our Society

Okay, so if races are not biological units and civil rights has made signifi- 20 cant changes in our society over the last fifty years, then race does not matter, right? Wrong.

> In 2004, fifty years after *Brown v. Board of Education*, the controversies around "race" and racism are raging as brightly as ever. Whether we are talking about the future of affirmative action in elite universities, or what the next U.S. Census form will look like, or what the achievement rates of white males are versus underrepresented students of color, this conversation is by no means finished. (Yolanda Moses, anthropologist)[18]

The point made by Yolanda Moses is that race matters as a social factor in the United States. The concept of race and how it plays out in our society are core factors in structuring our individual schemata and the maintenance of cultural constructs of, and societal expectations for, human behavior. However, in the first and second decades of the twentieth-first century a chorus of voices has emerged arguing that we are moving toward a postracial society, or at least a society where race is no longer as powerful or important as it was for much of the twentieth century.[19] This view contradicts what Moses and the entire American Anthropological Association posit: that race matters as an important cultural component of our society.[20] Although the reality of race and racism as part of our society is not being debated, the relative importance of race is a strong current issue, as noted in a recent poll by ABC News and the *Washington Post*.[21] More than twice as many American blacks identified racism as a "big problem" than did American whites.

Since the 2008 election of Barack Obama as U.S. president, there has 21 been a steady series of debates about the relative role of race and racism in our society—not just about blacks or whites but also about Hispanic/ Latinos and Asians. The improvements in civil rights and the election of a black president do not demonstrate that we are in a (mostly) postracial society. Being black, white, Asian, Latino, or other means something in the United States, and although these categories are not biological units, they are social constructs that are central to many aspects of our society: Race is not biology, but it does matter.

Consider the following question: Why is Barack Obama consid- 22 ered black? He is an individual with one parent born in the United States (who would be considered white) and one parent born in Kenya (who would be considered black). Why, when classifying President Obama, do we call him black or African American and not white or European-American or even better yet Afro-Euro-American? Well, interestingly, this last label is not an option in our classification system; moreover, because of his skin color, hair type, and the fact that one of his parents is black, Obama cannot be white. In the United States we have governmentally crafted definitions of race as well as broadly accepted social definitions. We also practice a form of hypodescent, the notion that racial identity is denoted by physical inheritance and by "blood" from a racial group. But this works in a particular way: The lower ranking group is what defines the descent. So throughout U.S. history (and up to today) "looking" black makes you black, as does any black parentage (even great-grandparents). According to popular opinion, having even one drop of "black blood" in your genealogy makes you black, but having many drops of white blood does not make you white.

Why is this? It is tied to the concept that races are biological units 23 and that some races are better than others; thus biological influence (or contamination) from one race dictates what race you are. This is rooted in misguided notions about genetics and biology, but nonetheless remains, subconsciously, a de facto reality for our society. This is one reason why Barack Obama is considered black and not white.

Another reason has to do with our own government's classification 24 system. The Census Bureau creates and maintains a set of definitions that we use to officially classify people in our society. The official guidelines state that

> The Census Bureau collects race data in accordance with guidelines provided by the U.S. Office of Management and Budget (OMB), and these data are based on self-identification. The race response categories shown on the questionnaire are collapsed into the five minimum race groups identified by the OMB, and the Census Bureau's "Some other race" category. The racial categories included in the following text generally reflect a social definition of race recognized in this country, and not an attempt to define race biologically, anthropologically or genetically. In addition, it is recognized that the categories of the race items include racial and national origin or socio-cultural groups. People may choose to report more than one race to indicate their racial mixture, such as "American Indian" and "White."[22]

Note that there is a specific statement that these are purely social categories and not intending to define race as biological. However, as you will see with the following definitions, this is not totally true. Before the census asks about one's race, it first asks if one is "of Hispanic, Latino, or Spanish origin." These categories are not officially considered racial categories (more on this below). Here are the official definitions of race for the U.S. government:

> Mark the "White" box if this person has origins in any of the original peoples of Europe, the Middle East, or North Africa. This includes people who indicate their race as "White" or report entries such as Irish, German, Italian, Lebanese, Near Easterner, Arab, or Polish.

> Mark the "Black, African Am., or Negro" box if this person has origins in any of the Black racial groups of Africa. This includes people who indicate their race as "Black, African American, or Negro," or provide written entries such as African American, Afro-American, Kenyan, Nigerian, or Haitian.

> Mark the "American Indian or Alaska Native" box if this person has origins in any of the original peoples of North and South America (including Central America) and who maintain tribal affiliation or community attachment. This category includes people who indicate their race as "American Indian or Alaska Native," and/or provide written entries such as Navajo, Blackfeet, Inupiat, Yupik, Canadian Indian, French American Indian, or Spanish American Indian.

> Mark any of the Asian boxes if this person has origins of any of the original peoples of the Far East, Southeast Asia, or the Indian subcontinent including, for example, Cambodia, China, India, Japan, Korea, Malaysia, Pakistan, the Philippine Islands, Thailand, and Vietnam. This includes "Asian Indian," "Chinese," "Filipino," "Korean," "Japanese," "Vietnamese," and "Other Asian."

> Mark the "Asian Indian" box if this person indicates their race as "Asian Indian" or identifies themselves as Bengalese, Bharat, Dravidian, East Indian, or Goanese.

> Mark the "Chinese" box if this person indicates their race as "Chinese" or identifies themselves as Cantonese, or Chinese American. In some census tabulations, written entries of Taiwanese are included with Chinese while in others they are shown separately.

> Mark the "Filipino" box if this person indicates their race as "Filipino" or who reports entries such as Philipino, Philipine, or Filipino American.

> Mark the "Japanese" box if this person indicates their race as "Japanese" or who reports entries such as Nipponese or Japanese American.

> Mark the "Korean" box if this person indicates their race as "Korean" or who provides a response of Korean American.

> Mark the "Vietnamese" box if this person indicates their race as "Vietnamese" or who provides a response of Vietnamese American.

> Mark the "Other Asian" box if this person provides a write-in response of an Asian group, such as Bangladeshi, Bhutanese, Burmese, Cambodian, Hmong,

Laotian, Indochinese, Indonesian, Iwo Jiman, Madagascar, Malaysian, Maldivian, Nepalese, Okinawan, Pakistani, Singaporean, Sri Lankan, Thai, or Other Asian, not specified.

Mark the "Native Hawaiian" box if this person indicates their race as "Native Hawaiian" or identifies themselves as "Part Hawaiian" or "Hawaiian."

Mark the "Guamanian or Chamorro" box if this person indicates their race as such, including written entries of Chamorro or Guam.

Mark the "Samoan" box if this person indicates their race as "Samoan" or who identifies themselves as American Samoan or Western Samoan.

Mark the "Other Pacific Islander" box if this person provides a write-in response of a Pacific Islander group, such as Carolinian, Chuukese (Trukese), Fijian, Kosraean, Melanesian, Micronesian, Northern Mariana Islander, Palauan, Papua New Guinean, Pohnpeian, Polynesian, Solomon Islander, Tahitian, Tokelauan, Tongan, Yapese, or Other Pacific Islander, not specified.

Mark the "Some other race" box if this person is not included in the "White," "Black or African American," "American Indian or Alaska Native," "Asian," and "Native Hawaiian or Other Pacific Islander" race categories described above. Respondents providing entries such as multiracial, mixed, interracial, or a Hispanic, Latino, or Spanish group (for example, Mexican, Puerto Rican, Cuban, or Spanish) in the "Some other race" write-in space are included in this category.

People who are of two or more races may choose to provide two or more races either by checking two or more race response check boxes, by providing multiple responses, or by some combination of check boxes and other responses.[23]

There are a number of relevant factors to be found in these definitions, but one aspect stands out: "black" is treated differently from all the others. If you look closely at the definitions, you will see that "Black, African Am., or Negro" is the only category where the term "racial groups" is used ("if this person has origins in any of the Black racial groups of Africa"). In all of the other main categories the term "original peoples" is used. This marks the black category as a race, a biologized entity, relative to the other categories. Also, note that it is not just any racial groups, but the "Black racial" groups of Africa. Is there any mention of other types of racial groups in Africa (or anywhere else)? No. There is a clear demarcation of "black" as distinct type of category from the other "original peoples" categories. To be sure, the government does explicitly state that "the racial categories included in the following text generally reflect a social definition of race recognized in this country, and not an attempt to define race biologically, anthropologically or genetically." Yet that is exactly what it is doing, indicating with these categories that in the United States race matters and also that there is a hierarchy of races (one that mimics Phillipe Rushton's analyses). There are no reasons given by the

Office of Management and Budget for its use of the terms "racial groups" versus "original peoples," but we can look at the history of naming races from Linnaeus to the modern day to see what is going on here. "Black" is associated with a lower ranking in the hierarchy of races. Race matters. It is worth noting that the U.S. government bureau validates this assertion by stating that it is using the "social definition of race recognized in this country."

Examining the other categories, we also see that these ways of clas- 26 sifying people are clearly nonbiological and in fact emerge largely from events and patterns in U.S. history. The classification of Middle Easterners and Arabs as "white" is certainly left over from a time when the relationship between the United States and the Middle East, especially Muslim countries, was quite different. How many in our society today would define Osama bin Laden, Saddam Hussein, Muammar el-Qaddafi, or anyone from Algeria, Morocco, Iran, or Egypt as "white"? The mandate that to be Native American or American Indian you must hail from the "original peoples of North and South America (including Central America)" and "maintain tribal affiliation or community attachment" stems from the history of treaty signings and manipulation of Indian lands and cultures by the U.S. government. Interestingly, this results in a number of Native Americans without tribal affiliation not being legally classifiable as American Indians. The fact that "Asian" applies to anyone with ancestry in the "Far East, Southeast Asia, or the Indian subcontinent," which is about 70 percent of all humans on the planet and a substantial portion of the overall inhabited landmass, emerges from the limited exposure that the United States has had to the wide range of peoples and populations of Asia. Finally, the "some other race" category is a bit of a catchall (except that you can reinsert Hispanic or Latino as a race at this point) for accounting purposes just in case someone comes up with something else. As part of its normative functioning, the government keeps tabs on the socially defined races (in a very general way) in order to manage the country, which invalidates the assertion that race no longer matters. Race is a core part of the United States.

Let's close this section with a few statistics from the U.S. Department 27 of Labor and the Pew Research Center:[24]

- In tests of housing markets conducted by the U.S. Department of Housing and Urban Development (HUD), black and Hispanic potential renters and buyers are discriminated against (relative to whites) nearly 25 percent of the time.

- Light-skinned immigrants in the United States make more money on average than those with darker complexions, and the chief reason appears to be discrimination.

- Blacks and Hispanics have considerably lower earnings than Asians or whites. In 2009, the median usual weekly earnings of full-time wage and salary workers were $601 for blacks and $541 for Hispanics, compared with $880 for Asians and $757 for whites. The earnings of black men ($621) and Hispanic men ($561) were 65 and 60 percent, respectively, of the earnings of Asian men ($952). The earnings of black women ($582) were 75 percent of the earnings of Asian women ($654), a higher ratio than among black and Asian men. The median earnings for white men and women were 89 and 86 percent of their Asian counterparts in 2009. Median earnings for Hispanic women were $509.

- In 2009, about 90 percent of blacks and Asians (twenty-five years of age and older) in the labor force had received at least a high school diploma, the same proportion as whites. In contrast, about 67 percent of Hispanics had completed high school. Asians were most likely to have graduated from college; 59 percent had a bachelor's degree or higher, compared with 35 percent of whites, 24 percent of blacks, and 16 percent of Hispanics. Although blacks and Hispanics were less likely than whites and Asians to have obtained a college degree, the proportion of college graduates for all groups has increased over time. For all groups, higher levels of education are associated with a greater likelihood of being employed and a lower likelihood of being unemployed. Nonetheless, at nearly every level of education, blacks and Hispanics were more likely to be unemployed in 2009 than Asians or whites.

- The 2008 infant mortality rate per 1,000 births is 5.7 for whites, 13.6 for blacks, 5.6 for Hispanics, and 6.9 for the United States as a whole.

- The 2009 percent of each group living below the poverty level is 11.5 for whites, 32.2 for blacks, 28.4 for Hispanics, 19.4 for other (primarily Asian), and 17.2 for the United States as a whole.

- Percentage of groups without health insurance: 12.2 for whites, 20.9 for blacks, 33.5 for Hispanics, 17.7 for other (primarily Asian), and 17.2 for the United States as a whole.

- The 2009 net worth of U.S. households: white: $113,149, black: $5,677, and Hispanic: $6,325; there is a twentyfold difference between whites and all the others!

I could continue to list statistics, but these are enough to demonstrate 28 the point that, while race is not a biological unit, race as a social reality matters in the United States. The myth that we live mostly in a postracial society and that race does not matter is busted....

What Race Is and What It Is Not

The anthropologist Clarence Gravlee has suggested that we stop saying 29 that race is a myth, and instead accept that parts of it are myths while other aspects are not. He is correct: The myth part about race is that in modern humans there are biological races. The nonmyth part is that in our society the social categories of race are a reality that affects our lives. Thus, white, black, and Asian are not real biological, evolutionary, or natural categories nor do they reflect true divisions in human nature. However, white, black and Asian are real categories in the United States, for historical, political, and social reasons. People get placed in these categories both by themselves and by others. These social race divisions have real effects on the bodies and minds of the people in the United States. Race is not biology, but race affects biology, experience, and social context. Here are some closing thoughts on what race is and what it is not.

Race is not a valid way to talk about human biological variation

Biological anthropologists widely agree about how to describe and interpret variation in the human species. This agreement can be summarized in the following five points that represent our core understanding of biological variation in humanity:[25] *30*

1. There is substantial variation among individuals within populations.
2. Some biological variation is divided up between individuals in different populations and also among larger population groupings.
3. Patterns of within-group and between-group variation have been substantially shaped by culture, language, ecology, and geography.
4. Race is not an accurate or productive way to describe human biological variation.
5. Human variation research has important social, biomedical, and forensic implications.

Race is a social reality that can have lasting biological effects

The work of Clarence Gravlee, Bill Dressler, and others discussed in the preceding sections demonstrate this point: race is not biology but it can affect biology. In a February 2000 editorial, the prestigious, peer-reviewed journal *Nature Genetics* issued the following guideline: *31*

> The laudable objective to find means to improve the health conditions for all or for specific populations must not be compromised by the use of race or ethnicity as pseudo-biological variables. From now on, *Nature Genetics* will therefore require that authors explain why they make use of particular ethnic groups or populations, and how classification was achieved. We will ask reviewers to consider these parameters when judging the merits of a manuscript—we hope that this will raise awareness and inspire more rigorous design of genetic and epidemiological studies.

That is, we may use classifications by race and/or ethnicity when talking about human variation, but we must be clear why and how we are using these categories and about issues of directionality and reality of biological groupings. Race as a concept and racial inequality (racism) as a social reality can affect biology.

Race ≠ ethnicity

Ethnicity is a way of classifying people based on common histories, cul-   32
tural patterns, social ties, language use, symbolic shared identities, and the like. It lays no claim to biology and is used both by those attempting to classify others and by those within the different ethnic groups as a symbol of social unity. Ethnicity is not a natural set of divisions in humanity; it is fluid, changing over time and space. The terms "ethnicity" and "race" are often used interchangeably, even in commercial ancestry testing; this is wrong. This mistaken usage is a holdover from the patterns established by eugenicists trying to identify as biological groups the various national and ethnic groups who were living in, or entering, the United States in the early twentieth century. From that time on the notion of "ethnic" has been used as a technique for establishing "white" as normal and nonethnic, in contrast to the "other." Check out the shampoos and hair care products at your neighborhood drugstore: Most places will have an aisle or section marked "hair care" and another marked "ethnic products" or "ethnic hair care." This is shorthand for "black," or frizzy, hair care products. Think about the common phrase "ethnic food." Does this refer to what is considered to be typical U.S. (or white) food like hamburgers, hotdogs, or meatloaf? No, it means all the other types of foods associated with non-white groups or with subdivisions of southern or eastern European origin, those not considered white in the early parts of the twentieth century, like Jewish, Italian, and Slavic.

The same holds true for commercial ancestry testing. If you submit your   33
DNA sample to one of the many companies that offer such services and your results come back 50 percent Irish, 35 percent German, and 15 percent Yoruba, you might think you were basically "white" but also 15 percent "black." This is a nonsensical statement. The results suggest only that given the limited genetic samples we have to compare your sample with, certain very small parts of your genetic variation seems to fit with the micro-patterns found most commonly in Irish and German samples but there are some small similarities with the patterns found in our Yoruba sample. At best this means that you have mostly western European ancestors, with possibly some West African ancestry mixed in. Or the results might be erroneous given the limited sampling of human populations in the reference samples. Irish/German is not equal to "white" and Yoruba is not equal to "black"; they are simply ethnic labels used to refer to the population samples used in the genetic comparisons. This has nothing to do with "race."

Ethnicity is a valid way to describe social histories and social and 34
symbolic identification, but it is not biology and most definitely is not
race.

Moving Beyond the Myth

If, as a society, we can move beyond the myth of race as describing natural 35
and biological units, then we can better address the inequalities that the
race myth—and its concomitant, the social practices of racism—have created. The myth is strong, even in the face of resounding evidence against
it. However, education and information (and access to them) are the main
tools of myth busting. We will not move past this myth in this generation,
or maybe not even in the next, but it is a possibility for the future of our
society. As more and more of the myth-busting information discussed here
becomes part of our social context, as children develop their schemata in
the context of an accurate, information-rich social network, the effect on
our cultural constructs and societal perceptions can be substantial. Some
of these changes are already under way, but the forces maintaining the
myth of race are many and massive, especially the current pattern of inertia, or maintenance of the status quo, in adults. We may find it very difficult
to change our own views, or once changed, we may find it uncomfortable
to speak up against this myth in many situations. Or, maybe we can try
out the lyrics of the popular song "Your Racist Friend" by the group They
Might Be Giants:[26]

> It was the loveliest party that I've ever attended
> If anything was broken I'm sure it could be mended
> My head can't tolerate this bobbing and pretending
> Listen to some bullet-head and the madness that he's saying
>
> This is where the party ends
> I'll just sit here wondering how you
> Can stand by your racist friend
> I know politics bore you
> But I feel like a hypocrite talking to you
> You and your racist friend

In order to move forward we all have to be active in the discussion 36
about the reality of racism in the United States. We need to confront our
racist friends, family, and society. This chapter contains the basic information and references leading you to more in-depth analyses of the myth of
race and all the details that refute it. Many of our social norms and cultural constructs stand in our way; they support the inertia and patterns
that maintain the myth or at least make it very difficult to challenge it
publicly. However, once we have read this kind of information, we cannot
be hypocrites, we must be myth busters.

NOTES

1. Ashley Montagu (1942), *Man's Most Dangerous Myth: The Fallacy of Race*.
2. Guy Harrison (2010), *Race and Reality: What Everyone Should Know About Our Biological Diversity*, p. 20.
3. Remember the saying in chapter 2, "I would not have seen it if I hadn't believed it."
4. http://physanth.org/association/position-statements/biological-aspects-of-race/?search term=race. This statement is the official stance of the association of scientists (physical or biological anthropologists) who have spent the last 150 years examining human biological variation.
5. This quote is from J. Phillipe Rushton (2000), *Race, Evolution, Behavior: A Life History Perspective*, 2nd ed., p.17. Rushton is a psychologist focused on "proving" the biological basis for race categories. His work has been reviewed, refuted, and rejected by anthropology and biology journals due to its lack of scientific support and his selective use of fringe datasets. He remains active in self-publishing and also still publishes in a few psychology journals. However, his pronouncements about race differences are worth reading as they receive wide attention and are used by many in the lay public (and racist groups) to shore up assertions about a biological basis for race.
6. There have been numerous refutations of Rushton's work. The American Association of Physical Anthropologists refused his membership request on the grounds of his consistent manipulation of information and his continued pushing of racist ideology in spite of countless refutations of his published works. See the rest of this chapter and the Web sites http://www.understandingrace.org/home.html and http://raceandgenomics.ssrc.org for a whole series of examples and articles that deal with the assertions put forward by Ruston and others supporting the reality of biological races in modern humans.
7. Of course, there are five race systems that add Native American and Hispanic, and other systems that add even more. We address this later in the chapter. For this basic introduction we focus on the standard "big three" division.
8. Taxonomy is the science of naming or classifying organisms based on their phenotypes. Linnaeus developed the system of binomial nomenclature (two names) that we use today. His basic system lumps organisms based on similarity to one another. See http://www.ucmp.berkeley.edu/history/linnaeus.html for a brief overview.
9. A subspecies; also referred to as a biological race, is a unit within a species that is taking an evolutionary path different from the overall trajectory of other populations within the species and thus is becoming increasingly differentiated from them at the genetic level. See A. Templeton (1999), Human races: A genetic and evolutionary perspective, *American Anthropologist* 100: 632–50 and R.A. Kittles and K.M. Weiss (2003), Race, genes and ancestry: Implications for defining disease risk, *Annual Reviews in Human Genetics* 4: 33–67 for overviews.
10. This selection (and translation) is from Jon Marks's 1995 excellent overview of Linnaeus and racial taxonomies (p. 50). I leave out *H. s. monstrosous* as this one was not based any actual peoples at all. See J. Marks (1995), *Human Biodiversity: Genes, Race, and History* for a fuller discussion of this topic.
11. Again see J. Marks (1995), *Human Biodiversity: Genes, Race, and History* for a fuller, and extremely engaging, discussion of this.
12. See for example K.M. Weiss (1998), Coming to terms with human variation, *Annual Reviews in Anthropology*, 27: 273–300; S. Molnar (2002), *Human Variation: Races, Types and Ethnic Groups;* J.H. Relethford (2002), Apportionment of global human genetic diversity based on craniometries and skin color, *American Journal of Physical Anthropology*, 118: 393–98; N.G. Jablonski (2004), The evolution of human skin and skin color, *Annual Reviews in Anthropology*, 33: 585–623; C. Ruff (2002), Variation in human body size and shape, *Annual Reviews in Anthropology*, 31: 211–32; and A. Smedley and B. Smedley (2005), Race as biology is fiction, racism as a social problem is real: Anthropological and historical perspectives on the social construction of race, *American*

Psychologist 60(1): 16–26. This is just a small sample of the published, peer-reviewed research and reviews that debunk the race classifications.

13. The circulatory system includes the blood, the blood vessels (arteries, capillaries, and veins), and the heart. This system is the core means of transport for the elements required by the body's tissues for survival.

14. These proteins and their relative compatibility are what set up the problems trying to transfer blood between individuals. In order to be able to transfer blood between humans their blood systems must be very compatible (at least the major ones—ABO and Rh).

15. When talking about alleles, when we say "dominant" we mean that when a dominant allele is paired with a recessive allele in the body only the protein product of the dominant allele is expressed. The recessive allele's protein is not produced, or is produced at very low levels so that the phenotype expressed is that influenced by the dominant alleles. Remember from the last chapter that these alleles are for the same gene and that gene comes in two copies per person.

16. When looking at blood group allele frequencies, it is good to look at indigenous populations or populations that have been in the same location for a long time to see the patterns of allele distribution; if we were to take a random sample from a place like New York City, it would reflect the species-wide averages because of all the gene flow.

17. See S. Molnar (2002), *Human Variation: Races, Types and Ethnic Groups* for a good overview of blood group variation in humans.

18. Yolanda Moses (2004), The continuing power of the concept of "race," *Anthropology and Education Quarterly* 35(1): 146–48.

19. This ranges from commentators on major media outlets (for example see http://www.salon.com/mwt/feature/2010/08/13/dr_laura_the_n_word) to Web sites greeting the postracial society, but at the same time polling indicates that nearly 50 percent of U.S. citizens see racism as a major problem. However, blacks see this as a much greater issue than whites. See the overview of polls related to race in 1999–2009 at http://www.pollingreport.com/race.htm.

20. http://www.aaanet.org/issues/policy-advocacy/AAA-Statement-on-Race.cfm.

21. ABC News/Washington Post poll, January 13–16, 2009.

22. These are directly drawn from the definitions and guidelines for the 2010 census (http://2010.census.gov/partners/pdf/langfiles/qrb_English.pdf). As explained in http://www.understandingrace.org/about/response.html, "the Statistical Policy Division, Office of Information and Regulatory Affairs, of the Office of Management and Budget (OMB) determines federal standards for the. reporting of 'racial' and 'ethnic' statistics. In this capacity, OMB promulgated Directive 15: Race and Ethnic Standards for Federal Statistics and Administrative Reporting in May, 1977, to standardize the collection of racial and ethnic information among federal agencies and to include data on persons of Hispanic origins, as required by Congress. Directive 15 is used in the collection of information on 'racial' and 'ethnic' populations not only by federal agencies, but also, to be consistent with national information, by researchers, business, and industry as well."

23. http://2010.census.gov/partners/pdf/langfiles/qrb_English.pdf.

24. See the following reports and Web sites for data about racial disparities: Labor Force Characteristics by Race and Ethnicity (2009), U.S. Department of Labor U.S. Bureau of Labor Statistics November 2010 Report 1020; http://www.bls.gov/cps/cpsrace2009.pdf; http://www.msnbc.msn.com/id/l6831909; http://www.kaiseredu.org/topics_reflib.asp?id=329&rID=3&parentid=67; and Pew Research Center Report on Social and Demographic trends (2011), http://pewsocialtrends.org/2011/07/26/wealth-gaps-rise-to-record-highs-between-whites-blacks-hispanics.

25. Heather J.H. Edgar and Keith L. Hunley (2009), Race reconciled? How biological anthropologists view human variation, *American Journal of Physical Anthropology* 139: 1–4.

26. They Might Be Giants (1990) from their song "Your Racist Friend" on the album *Flood*.

■ ■ ■

Reading as a Writer: Analyzing Rhetorical Choices

1. Where and how does Fuentes include writers whose ideas differ from his own? Mark those sections and discuss the effectiveness of including those voices as a strategy of advancing his own argument. Where and how does he address readers who might disagree with him? How effectively does he address their concerns?

2. In his section titled "Blood," Fuentes includes data that relies on biological discourse about blood types, and accompanies the data with two charts (Figure 17.1). Discuss the effect of offering this kind of data to a generalist audience. How effectively does this approach help him build a case for his own expertise (his ethos)?

Writing as a Reader: Entering the Conversation of Ideas

1. Place Fuentes's text in conversation with that of Allan G. Johnson (pp. 454–57 in Sociology) to write an essay about the methods by which racial stereotypes and privilege are reinforced and how they can be "busted." Based on the evidence in these texts and perhaps your personal experience, what can you conclude about changing—or unchanging—concepts of race in the United States?

2. While there may be no biological basis for racial difference, Fuentes argues that race "… Still Matters in Our Society." Compose an essay in which you draw on Fuentes's ideas to help explain the specific social dynamics described in texts by Ta-Nehisi Coates (pp. 20–24), Nikole Hannah-Jones (pp. 434–52 in Education), or Claudia Rankine (pp. 457–64 in Sociology). Explain the significance of your findings.

WILLIAM J. PEACE

Slippery Slopes: Media, Disability, and Adaptive Sports

William J. Peace is a multidisciplinary teacher and scholar who writes from an anthropological and sociological perspective about the embodied impact of attitudes toward bodies, body modification, and disabilities. Besides his scholarly publications, he writes the provocatively titled blog *Bad Cripple* (badcripple.blogspot.com). This essay examines the effects of the very narrow media depictions of disability as something to be miraculously and inspirationally "overcome," with very real consequences: "The negative portrayal of disabled people is not only oppressive but also affirms that nondisabled people set the terms of the debate about the meaning of disability" (para. 1). There are a growing number of scholars working in the field of disability studies, and Peace's often-critical voice is well known in this conversation.

Peace claims, "Disabled people have embraced a social model of disability that is based on the belief that disability is a social malady" (para. 3). What do you think this means? As you read, think about your own understanding of "disabilities" and test those ideas against Peace's argument that disability is "a social construct." At the end of paragraph 4, he explains his research methods and overall argument; this is a paragraph to return to after you read the essay. How does he support and explain the claims he sets out here?

In his first subsection, "A Primer on Disability Activism and Disabled Bodies," Peace offers readers a quick background on the history of disability studies. As you learn about the history of this movement, which parallels many other civil rights movements, consider his claims about the challenges of defining the "disabled." Why does such a definition matter when it comes to the law? How does his call for a more "nuanced" view of disability (paras. 12–15) advance the overall argument in this essay?

Peace's extended example of adaptive sports—particularly his own experiences with adaptive skiing—helps illustrate the challenges and possibilities of thinking about disability in new ways. He concludes with a call to action that critiques many scholars in disability studies: "These efforts are critical but contain one flaw I cannot overlook: Disability studies scholars have not done enough to empower the people they study" (para. 27). What actions is he calling for and why? His challenge to engage in "action-oriented scholarship and activism" is a challenge for all of us as we consider what we will *do* with what we learn. How will you—and your classmates—respond?

■ ■ ■

The history and scholarship of mass media have conspicuously ignored the images commonly associated with disability in American society. This is unfortunate because the *media is complicit* in distorting *the cultural perception* of disability (Riley 2005). For decades disabled Americans have grown increasingly appalled, offended, and angry about the way they have been exploited by the media. Dominant images associated with disability are largely negative. Stereotypical portrayals of disability abound, as do feel-good stories. Here I refer to archetypical ninety-second television news segments or 500-word stories in national newspapers that focus on the "remarkable," "heart warming" tale of a disabled person. Disabled athletes in this regard provide the media with endless fodder and great visuals: The paralyzed person, blind person, or amputee who finishes a marathon or performs some other "miraculous" feat. What is celebrated is not the athletic or personal achievement but rather the ability of a disabled person to "overcome" a physical deficit; the more profound and visible the disability, the better the story. The negative portrayal of disabled people is not only oppressive but also affirms that nondisabled people set the terms of the debate about the meaning of disability.

The antiquated images of disability have resonated with the general 2
public and reinforced economic, political, and social oppression experienced by disabled people. Thus the media has contributed to and expanded
the gulf between disabled and non-disabled people. This divide and the
inequities associated with disability are rarely discussed. Thanks to the
Internet, technological advances, laws such as the Americans with Disability Act (ADA), and rapidly aging Baby Boomers, disabled and non-disabled
people are interacting more than at any other time in American history.
The interaction between those with and those without a disability has led
to conflict and misunderstanding. Disabled people have rights, civil rights
guaranteed by the ADA, and are not hesitant to assert them.

Disabled people have embraced a social model of disability that is 3
based on the belief that disability is a social malady. The social model
of disability is at odds with what the average American has been taught
about disability: That the primary problem disabled people have is a physical or cognitive impairment. In contrast, disability scholars assert that a
bodily deficit is used to justify the prejudice, discrimination, and oppression associated with disability. Scholars in the humanities and social sciences such as Simi Linton (1998, 2006), Paul Longmore (2003), Rosemarie
Garland Thomson (1997), and others have firmly established that disability is a social construct. Disability cannot be studied in isolation or on a
case-by-case basis because it is part of the social structure of American
society. This theoretical shift has had a seismic impact on the disability
community and was spearheaded by innovative disability studies scholars. For those with disabilities, the scholarship produced by the aforemen-
tioned scholars provided them with a way of understanding disability that
was empowering. For the first time in American history, people with disabilities understood that the discrimination they encountered was not of
their own making and began to think of themselves as a single, united, and
oppressed minority group.

The media and general public have yet to acknowledge the social 4
model of disability. Thus when disabled people such as myself embrace the
slogan "Disabled and Proud" and assert our civil rights, the average citizen does not know how to respond. The result is a culture clash, disabled
versus nondisabled, one that is being worked out in the media, online, and
in adaptive sport programs across the country. The sporting arena is of
particular interest because the presence of disabled people is unexpected
there. It is assumed that a physical or mental deficit precludes not just an
interest in sports but the ability to participate. Conceptually, the disabled
body from an athletic standpoint is devalued, as are the lives of disabled
people. It is assumed that disabled people should not be skiing, kayaking,
or playing a sport. Instead, they should be focused on an all-out effort to
"fix" their bodies and return to normal (Christopher Reeve's quest for a
cure to spinal cord injury is a perfect example). The fundamental dichotomy between disabled and nondisabled people forms the core of this

chapter. I will detail why adaptive athletic programs are important and how adaptive athletes undermine disability-based prejudice. My research is based on interviews I conducted with adaptive athletes, bloggers, and adaptive sport program co-coordinators in the northeastern United States between 2006 and 2008. I will also draw on my experience as a novice adaptive skier and kayaker.

A Primer on Disability Activism and Disabled Bodies

Disability studies is among the newest fields in American academia. In   5
my estimation, disability scholarship as it is known today began with the publication of the *Body Silent* by Robert Murphy in 1987. I consider this book the Magna Carta for all disabled people. While other scholars such as Irving Zola and Irving Goffman had studied disability for many years, Murphy was the first prestigious scholar based at an Ivy League institution to critically examine disability from a cultural perspective. Murphy did something in the *Body Silent* that no other person had done before: He bared his soul and body and evocatively convinced others that the main problem people with disabilities encounter is not their disability but the social consequences it generates. Given this new perspective, people with disabilities began to "demedicalize" their bodies and push for civil rights legislation while disability studies scholars published ground-breaking books like Nancy Mair's *Waist-High in the World* and Rosemarie Garland Thomson's *Extraordinary Bodies*. The central idea that would emerge from the incipient disability studies field was the belief in a social model of disability. This is the fundamental principle that created and has sustained the disability rights movement. The social model of disability is not complicated: In essence it holds that society disables people with physical and cognitive disabilities. Disability is something imposed on top of a physical impairment that is used to unnecessarily isolate and exclude disabled people from full participation in society.

The origins of disability studies can be found in the 1960s civil rights   6
movement, and the epicenter for disability rights was the San Francisco Bay Area. The efforts of one man, Edward Roberts, known as the "father of the independent movement," stand out. Roberts is remembered for his political prowess and razor-sharp wit. For example, after learning that his doctor had characterized him as a hopeless vegetable, he remarked that if he had to be a vegetable he wanted to be an artichoke—prickly on the outside but with a big heart inside, one that could call on all the other vegetables of the world to unite. Roberts helped lay the foundation for disability pride from which disability studies would emerge. The notion of disability pride is something that is hard for an able-bodied person to grasp. I know this, as do many other disabled people who have been told overtly and covertly that they are inherently defective and incompetent. Family,

friends, and strangers deliver this message as efficiently as a Federal Express package. Roberts was among the first generation of people with a disability to escape institutionalized life and embrace an identity tied to disability. In a letter Roberts sent to Gina Laurie he stated that he was "tired of well-meaning non cripples with their stereotypes of what I can and cannot do directing my life and future. I want cripples to direct their own programs and be able to train others cripples to direct new programs. This is the start of something big—cripple power" (Roberts circa 1970).

For people with disabilities, Roberts became a powerful symbol for all 7 that was wrong with America's perception of disability. He was the Jackie Robinson of the disability rights movement, the single individual around whom others could rally. Like Jackie Robinson, Roberts did not single-handedly end baseless discrimination. He was part of a much larger social movement that produced cataclysmic changes in terms of civil rights. Each civil rights movement was associated with tragic events or charismatic figures: Jerry Rubin was the face of the Students for Democratic Society and encouraged male college students to burn their draft cards. The women's movement burned bras, and Gloria Steinem founded *Ms. Magazine*. The Vietnam War is tied to Lyndon Johnson, the fall of Saigon, and the My Lai Massacre. Martin Luther King Jr. is remembered for his powerful speech "I Have a Dream" and tragic assassination.

What is absent from Americans' general understanding of civil rights 8 is a disability component. Disability rights as civil rights is not a connection people make. Disabled people are an invisible minority and are not considered to be a "distinct and insular minority group." In spite of the fact that I have not walked in over thirty years, I can readily understand why people do not connect disability rights and civil rights. Eighteen years ago the ADA was passed, and since that time the Supreme Court has muddied the meaning of disability in an effort to limit the scope of the law. The definition of disability contained in the ADA was broad by design and was the end product of a generation of lawmaking. The intent of the ADA was to protect the civil rights of all people who were perceived to be disabled. The legislative process to protect the rights of people with disabilities began in 1968 with the Architectural Barriers Act and concluded with the ADA. During this era, 1968 to 1990, fifty acts of Congress were passed designed to protect or enhance the rights of people with a disability (Longmore and Umansky 2001). In spite of all this legislation, the legal definition of disability has not changed since 1973 when it was included as Title V, part of the Rehabilitation Act that barred discrimination against disabled people in programs that receive funding from the federal government. As outlined in the Americans with Disability Act, an "individual with a disability is defined as someone who: (i) has a physical or mental impairment which substantially limits one or more of such person's major life activities, (ii) has a record of such an impairment, or (iii) is regarded as having such an impairment."[1]

Since the ADA was passed, the Supreme Court has used the definition 9
of disability as it relates to the phrases "substantial limitation," "major life
activity," and "regarded as" to narrow the number of people who are considered to be legally disabled. At a theoretical level I understand what the
Supreme Court is trying to do: Identify exactly who is disabled and entitled to protection under the law. However, creating a precise definition of
disability is exceptionally difficult and highlights that disability is a complex construct. There are a multitude of factors involved—social, political, economic, and legal—that make it difficult to identify what all people
with a disability have in common. There is a seemingly endless array of
disabling conditions and no agreement as to what disability means to this
wide cross-section of people. Until we can identify what it means to be disabled, people with disabilities will continue to struggle to defend their civil
rights. Thus the Supreme Court will continue to rule as it has and limit the
scope of the ADA because it perceives disability to be a medical or physical
deficit alone.

In utilizing a medical model of disability, the Supreme Court has 10
ignored the broader ramifications of disability. Here I refer to the fact that
disabled people are as a group uniformly poor, unemployed, and lacking a
basic education. This troika puts disabled people at a distinct disadvantage
before they exit their homes and bars too many from pursuing a rewarding
life. The result is that the Supreme Court has not only narrowed the scope
of the law but also splintered and butchered our understanding of what it
means to be disabled. This has led me to tease my friends that what medical science failed to do—cure my paralyzed body—the Supreme Court
did. In the court's view my disability is "mitigated" by the fact that I use a
wheelchair and all people whose impairments can be alleviated by medication, glasses, or other devices are generally not disabled and so do not
come under the protection of the ADA. In short, the Court determined that
disabled people are not a distinct and insular minority group. Thus people
who are paralyzed, deaf, blind, diabetic, or missing a limb have nothing in
common! This is hard for me to fathom.

Since the Supreme Court narrowed the definition of disability, I do not 11
consider the ADA a mandate that protects the civil rights of disabled people. The ADA was about far more than ramps for wheelchair users, braille
for the blind, and closed captioning for the deaf. The ADA was intended
to protect anyone who experienced discrimination because he or she had
what was perceived to be a disability. According to Silvia Yee of the Disability Rights Education and Defense Fund, the ADA was "built on the conviction that disability prejudice is a fundamental force behind the exclusion
of people with disabilities from a myriad [sic] of social and economic
opportunities." In Yee's estimation there was no question that disability
prejudice existed and that the phenomenon was "not widely understood or
truly accepted among the political and social institutions that are counted
upon to put anti-discrimination laws into practice" (Yee 2007).[2]

Adaptive Sports: Undermining Stigma Associated with the Disabled Body

Too many people fail to realize that the dichotomy between disabled and *12* able-bodied is a fallacy. Life is simply not that definitive. Under the law, I am not disabled. I am a teacher, writer, father, and provider for my son and have been since he was born. Provided I can enter a building or my employer is willing to make a "reasonable accommodation," there is no reason why I cannot work. My ability to work and care for myself is not compromised by my physical deficit: Partial paralysis. Yet when I sit in my wheelchair, a device that supposedly mitigates my disability, I remain the symbolic representation of disability. I am regularly asked, "What happened to you?"—a question that assumes a significant flaw exists. The person asking this question is making a statement about my disability. He or she is telling me that there is something inherently "wrong" with my body. Such a person is also curious or, in some cases, fearful. The tacit understanding is that I am not a fully functioning adult capable of living independently. Even if capable, the only reason I can function "normally" is that I am a remarkable person, one who puts all those other disabled people to shame. All this is called into question when disabled people participate in adaptive sports. It is the only environment in which people with a wide range of disabilities interact not only with one another but with able-bodied people as well.

A nuanced view of disability too often requires personal experience *13* with disability. In part, this is why historian Paul K. Longmore (1995) has argued that the first phase of disability activism centered on civil rights while the second phase has been a quest for a collective identity. In this regard, disability rights scholars have been particularly successful. A cursory glance at the literature published in the last ten years reveals a bevy of exceptionally well-written memoirs and theoretical analyses. For example, Linton's *Claiming Disability* was the first comprehensive account in disability studies that provided the groundwork for terms and concepts in the field and linked them with identity politics. Disability as a cultural identity is well understood by disability studies scholars but has not as yet been incorporated into the multicultural curriculum. Leonard Davis, an influential disability studies scholar, has noted that faculty members who mandate the inclusion of African American, Latino, and Asian American texts and novels do not support the inclusion of works about disability (Davis 2002). In contrast, people outside of academia have embraced this literature and disability culture. Disability culture is created by people with disabilities and is based upon the disability experience. Carol Gill, a disability rights activist, has written that disability culture involves "the pleasure we take in our own community," maintaining that "the assertion of disability pride and the celebration of our culture are a massive assault on ablecentric thinking. It also really rocks people when we so clearly reject the superiority of nondisability" (Gill 1995:98).

I contend that the divide between disabled and nondisabled people is *14* innately tied to the body and individual difference. According to Bérubé, disability "is a category whose constituency is contingency itself" (Bérubé 1998:x). For disabled people it is obvious why nondisabled people resist thinking about disability: The fear of disability itself. It is equally obvious why this fear must be overcome: Nondisabled people perceive disability as inherently negative. Corporal variation is perceived to be deviant; there is a divide between normal and abnormal, disabled and nondisabled. Disabled people know a different reality, one in which "there's no line dividing us. There are shades of ability, varying talents that surface in surprising places. This is true for physical and cognitive disabilities. Most of us, in the course of our lives, discover we have abilities or affinities for some things and lack talent elsewhere, so this idea that a certain class of people lack value or ability to contribute inevitably underestimates and wastes human potential" (Olson 2007).

Like many disabled people, I embrace an identity that is tied to my *15* body. I have been made to feel different, inferior, since I began using a wheelchair thirty years ago and by claiming that I am disabled and proud, I am empowered. A skeptic at heart, I have always craved tangible proof that disability rights have advanced. In part this is why I am critical of disability studies. How can disability rights scholars determine whether progress has been made? The proof I sought became evident two years ago on a ski trip to Vermont. My son had never skied and I had not seen an adaptive sit ski since I was in college. In the late 1970s one adaptive sport, wheelchair basketball, was dominant (I was on my college team). Modern sit skis do not resemble the model I saw in college, and I will never forget the first time I skied in 2006. I had no conception that a veritable technological revolution had taken place. As I looked around I saw an overcrowded room filled with people. Near me I saw people with a host of physical disabilities: amputees, people with cerebral palsy, the blind, and paralyzed people. I also saw many people with cognitive disabilities such as autism, Down Syndrome, and a host of behavioral disorders. Adaptive skiing had come of age, and it was clear that any person who desired could ski.

Adaptive skiing involves the use of specialized equipment that is as *16* diverse as disability itself. Broadly, adaptive skiing can be broken down into basic groups. Two-trackers are adaptive skiers who use archetypical equipment, stiff plastic boots, and two skis along with ski poles. An adaptive skier who can ski in this manner usually has a cognitive impairment such as autism or Down Syndrome. Other two-trackers include visually impaired skiers. Sometimes these skiers wear a bright orange bib that identifies them as "Blind Skier" and they ski with a person whose identical bib identifies him or her as "Blind Guide." The blind skiers I have observed wore this type of bib and skied with a sighted skier who guided them as they skied. Three-tracker adaptive skiers usually have one leg. These skiers ski on one leg and instead of traditional ski poles use poles that have an outrigger or small ski attached to the bottom. The outriggers are used to control speed and direction. They are also used to brake. Four-tracker adaptive skiers ski on two skis and carry two outriggers. A person who has cerebral palsy or walks with a cane or uses crutches is often a four-tracker.

Mono-skiers are the elite of adaptive skiers, and the rigs they use are 17 akin to Ferraris. Prominent mono-skiers such as Kevin Bramble are on the cutting edge of technology in the ski industry and not only participate in the Paralympic Games but also appear in Warren Miller ski films and the popular X-Games broadcast on ESPN. A typical mono-skier is paralyzed in his or her lower extremities, has good torso control, and possesses excellent upper body strength. If the reader has ever seen a seated adaptive skier whiz by, the skier is probably using a mono-ski. A similar device, a bi-ski, exists for those adaptive skiers who cannot master a mono-ski. However, the prestige factor among adaptive athletes is greatly reduced when one uses a bi-ski. The bi-ski is like a mono-ski but has a lower center of gravity and two specially made skis making it easier to master because the two skis actuate independently and the skier is much closer to the ground.

The above clinical description does not convey the effort and knowl- 18 edge needed to ski. It also does not convey the fear I felt when I skied the first time. Skilled volunteers determined the correct rig for a novice such as myself to use. Selecting the appropriate rig is the most important decision an adaptive skier makes. My first season skiing I used a mono-ski. To mono-ski one sits in a small plastic bucket seat that is connected to a single ski with a basic suspension system. To balance and turn one uses two outriggers. What I did not anticipate was exactly how tightly I had to be strapped into the bucket. My body was strapped into the bucket tighter than one's feet in ski boots. The volunteers kept telling me a tight fit was required and the key to success. They also joked that there is no such thing as too tight. I simply tried to focus on being able to breathe. The entire process of getting into the bucket, selecting outriggers, and getting ready takes about an hour for a novice. As I headed outside with two volunteers in tow I was extremely nervous. Having two experienced people at my side helped, but those first few trips up the ski lift and down the slopes were nerve-wracking experiences. By the end of the first season of skiing, I was not only able to enjoy myself but also became aware of what was going on around me. I also learned that I enjoy skiing for many reasons. First, the view from the top of the ski lift was a sight to behold, especially early in the morning. Second, skiing was a physical challenge I could share with my son. It also helped that we each like to go very fast. Third, I liked to socialize with skiers, who struck me as open-minded free spirits. My presence was readily accepted and I felt as though I was an ordinary, nondisabled person. Finally, the bar was packed and the people who helped me ski drank high-quality micro-brewed ale.

Between 2006 and 2008 I skied at least once a month and talked to 19 adaptive skiers and all those affiliated with the adaptive ski programs I participated in. I learned that adaptive sports in general and adaptive skiers in particular were important because they shed light on the dichotomy between the way people who can and cannot walk perceive disability. Among paralyzed people such as myself, a wheelchair and mono-ski are alternate forms of locomotion. Depending upon the environmental setting, they can be a superior or inferior means of movement. At heart a wheelchair and mono-ski are culturally constructed technological devices that empower the human body. As such they affirm how remarkably adaptable the body is. A wheelchair or mono-ski is a type of human adaptation, a process that was recognized by Charles Darwin and tied to disability by Kenny Fries in his memoir *The History of My Shoes* (Fries 2007). Fries wrote about two interconnected stories, one that concerned Darwin and the other about his struggle to understand the meaning of disability. While this may seem to be a tenuous connection, bodily fitness and disability are directly related. The human body is continuously evolving via variation and adaptation, but it is society that determines how a given variation is perceived. In the case of the disabled body, all adaptive athletes know there are advantages to their physical deficit. For instance, Fries found that his shoes, leg braces, and abnormal gate made him a better mountain climber than an able-bodied person. Likewise, when skiing I use the muscle spasms in my torso caused by bumpy terrain to my advantage in terms of balancing on the edges of my skis.

A great deal of stigma is associated with a wheelchair, which can be characterized as a portable social isolation unit (Murphy 1980). In my experience, when I get out of my wheelchair and am active athletically, this diminishes the stigma and isolation associated with disability. The adaptive sport a person with a disability participates in is not as important as the physical activity itself. This is why many disabled people such as myself are drawn to adaptive sports. Physically departing their wheelchair negates negative stereotypes associated with disability. For example, one man told me,

20

> The minute people see a wheelchair they think of all the things that cannot be done. They consider my life a quasi tragedy. The younger and more physically fit the person using a wheelchair is the worse that person's life is thought to be. If you are a guy, they think you can't have sex or push a chair on anything other than a sidewalk. People assume I live in a nursing home. If you are a disabled woman then you cannot give birth or raise a child. This skewed viewpoint is really hard to overcome—people are conditioned and raised to think this way. There is a fundamental philosophical difference between those that walk and those that do not. I see my wheelchair as a powerful means of freedom while those that can walk see it as horrible, a fate worse than death. In some ways this is why I like to get out of my wheelchair as much as possible. I bike, kayak, sail, and ski. When you are doing a sport regardless of what it is, people see you as capable, you do not need to be a Paralympian. When active I am transformed from being thought of as a pathetic human in a wheelchair whose life sucks into an average person. (interview with a disabled male, age thirty-two)

For disabled men and women who have come of age in the post-ADA   *21*
world, there is growing frustration and anger about the law, specifically
the gap between what the ADA is supposed to do and the reality they experience. Many ski lodges I have been to are grossly inaccessible. They have
met the letter of the law; specifically, they have made "reasonable accommodations." However, these accommodations do not mean that ski resorts
seek to be truly inclusive. Discrimination, though increasingly uncommon, exists in part because the bodily image associated with skiing does
not include the presence of disabled people. All ski resorts have a clientele
and an image they project to draw customers. Thus even at resorts where
adaptive skiers abound, corporations do not place great value on adaptive
ski programs. The severely limited number of employees hired to coordinate adaptive programs evidences this. The ski resorts I have been to in
New England are reliant upon well-trained, poorly paid, and overwhelmed
employees. They are also dependent upon a large staff of volunteers. The
adaptive programs I have skied at usually have a staff of less than three
or four full-time employees. The archetypical person who coordinates an
adaptive ski program is a recent college graduate. Stress, long hours, and
substandard pay insure that most adaptive program coordinators do not
work for more than a few ski seasons.

The adaptive skiers I have met are a dedicated group who love the   *22*
physical and social dimension of the sport. It is one of the few activities
that disabled people participate in that permits social networking. Thus it
should be no surprise that adaptive sports and athletic competitions have
played a major role in the disability rights community. Some of the largest
disability-related organizations in this country and abroad can trace their
origins to adaptive sport. In adaptive sports, the Paralympic movement is
easily the largest international competition for people with physical disabilities. Other well-known programs include the Wounded Warrior Project, Disabled Sports USA, Adaptive Sports Association, Special Olympics,
and the American Association of Adaptive Sport Programs, to mention but
a few prominent groups.

Among accomplished adaptive skiers, adult men and women between   *23*
twenty and twenty-five years old, ski resorts are a safe haven, a place to
let loose and not only be among their peers but also develop personal and
professional relationships. One young man told me,

> Skiing is the one place where I am not looked at with pity or scorn by other
> people, especially by older people who just don't get how or even why a para-
> lyzed person would want to ski. What, I wonder, do they expect me to do?
> Sit at home with a lap blanket? When I am out skiing with friends I am just
> another guy out on the slopes. I just happen to be using a mono-ski. I have
> even been asked by nondisabled people if they can rent sit skis. No idiots ask,
> "What happened to you?" which is rude and pisses me off. No one asks a per-
> son who can walk this sort of question. Imagine if I asked someone why they
> were fat or if I went up to a woman and asked her why she had small breasts
> or a big ass. The best part of skiing is that a lot of people, snowboarders for

example, know mono-skiers can really rip it up. I don't like the attitude of snowboarders and hate it when they stop and sit down in the middle of a slope, but to these guys I am cool. The X Games helped a lot in this regard as does the fact a lot of skiers dislike snowboarders. The thing is that when I ski I feel equal to others. I can't tell you how many times I have people yell at me "go for it dude" and I am dumb enough to try and show off. We are all just having fun and I am just another dude sharing the same space. (interview, male, twenty-one)

When I skied I noted that many married couples participated in 24 adaptive programs. The couples I spoke with all felt at ease, that is, their relationship was accepted. For those married or involved in an intimate relationship with a disabled person, such a union is subject to intense public examination. In my experience, it is common for nondisabled people to question why an able-bodied person would consider having a relationship with someone who has an obvious physical deficit. Friends and strangers alike will ask couples intrusive questions that are rude. For example, every nondisabled woman I have been intimately involved with has told me that the first question female friends ask about the relationship is, "Can he have sex?" Apparently the fact that I have a son is not adequate proof of my reproductive ability. Such inappropriate questions place a nondisabled and disabled couple at a distinct disadvantage in that mixed couples are public property, their physical and personal relationship open to scrutiny. Those couples that do not have a disability are exempt from comparable inquiries. One woman who was married to a paralyzed spouse told me,

I love to see my husband play sports. I feel as though we have a mixed marriage—he is paralyzed and I am not. By mixed marriage I think what we experience is like what a married black man and white woman went through in the 1950s—that sort of thing was just not socially acceptable. I hate it when people give me that look of pity or want to put a halo over my head for being married to a man in wheelchair. My husband uses a wheelchair, he is not in a wheelchair. To me, there is a big difference. I lose no matter what—if I get flowers it is not an ordinary event but as though I deserve them 'cause I am married to a disabled guy. The funny thing to me is that I am not into sports at all. He is a much better skier than I am. He has been skiing for ten years and I finally relented and am learning how to snowboard. At the end of the day I am so sore I can barely walk while he is zooming by at a million miles an hour. When people see this, that they know he is a far more skilled athlete, can go on a double diamond while I am still on a bunny hill and holding onto a rope tow as though my life depended upon it makes others think. (interview with female, midtwenties)

The mission statement for most adaptive ski programs focuses on 25 quality-of-life issues and empowerment. For example, New England Disabled Sports at Loon Mountain in Lincoln, New Hampshire, aims to enhance the quality of life of individuals with disabilities through outdoor education. It is believed that participation in outdoor activities in a supportive, boundary-free environment will endow participants with the opportunity to conquer physical challenges that enable them to build self-esteem and confidence. I appreciate the sentiments expressed but know that adaptive skiing is well beyond the economic means of many disabled people. The cost of a mono-ski is prohibitive for many. There are a small number of companies that manufacture adaptive ski equipment. For example, a basic entry-level mono-ski made by Freedom Factory costs $2,600, and two outriggers cost $375. A mono-ski used by a skilled adaptive skier who races can double or triple this amount and often exceeds $5,000. For those who cannot afford to own their own adaptive equipment, all programs rent specialized equipment. Every adaptive program I have participated in has a sliding pay scale and does its best to be inclusive. The cost of adaptive equipment also limits many programs that have tight budgets. The ski season in New England is short, unpredictable, and with the price of gas and lodging, an expensive proposition. Adaptive programs in New England charge disabled skiers between $75 and $110 a day to ski. On average I estimate a weekend of skiing for a disabled person would cost about $500 (this includes gas, an inexpensive motel, food, and ski equipment rental). Adaptive skiing in western states such as Colorado, Utah, and Wyoming is twice as expensive as in New England and restricted to elite skiers.

In spite of the cost, the number of disabled people participating in   26
adaptive sports has increased significantly in the last decade. Although no federal laws such as Title IX, which has helped female athletes, exist, disabled people who cannot afford to ski can find other easily adaptable sports such as kayaking. Disabled kayakers such as myself can afford not only to purchase a reasonably good kayak but also to inexpensively modify it with dry cell foam and duct tape that costs no more than $50. For instance, my kayak cost $500, and required ancillary equipment such as a life vest, paddle, and roof rack brought the total up to about $1,000. This amount is the equivalent of two weekends of skiing or a deposit on a mono-ski. The cost of renting a kayak for one day is half the price of a mono-ski. A disabled person with a limited budget is more likely to be able to afford to purchase or rent a kayak. Kayaking offers disabled people the same feeling of empowerment that skiing does. One kayaker told me economics were a major factor in his decision to paddle instead of ski.

> It took me two minutes to figure out skiing was too expensive. Kayaking is my sport. I am pretty new to kayaking but can get places where I could never dream of being when using my wheelchair. For example, I recently camped on an island in Long Island Sound. Being on the water is relaxing and after using a wheelchair for most of my life it is a different movement. But the best part of kayaking is the feeling of equality. When on the water I am just another kayaker—no one knows I use a wheelchair. I am not Mr. Cripple, a living symbol of how life can go wrong. Shit, why are people so stupid when it comes to disability? No other place in American society offers me the sense of equality as when I am out on the water. I truly feel liberated when I am in my boat. Sometimes when I paddle I really wish I did not have to return to the dock

and get back in my wheelchair and the hassles associated with it. (interview with male, forty-five years old)

Conclusion

In this chapter I have constantly referred to the disability rights movement 27 and a number of influential disability studies scholars. While I have tried not to be biased, it must be apparent that I am drawn to the disability rights movement. There are two reasons for this: First, in spite of the important contributions disability studies scholars have made, in my estimation the field has lost its soul. I do not question the dedication, effort, and contributions made by disability studies scholars. There is no doubt their work is important and intellectually rigorous. I am also aware that the place of disability studies in academia is by no means secure. Opposition to disability studies within academia is an ongoing problem because some scholars perceive disability as degrading or as watering down the integrity of identities. Given this, disability scholars have focused on the important job of securing a place in higher education where disability is perceived to be a form of human diversity as well as an intellectual endeavor. These efforts are critical but contain one flaw I cannot overlook: Disability studies scholars have not done enough to empower the people they study. People with disabilities are the most overlooked, disenfranchised, and stigmatized minority group in American society. Given this reality, I think every disability studies scholar must make a practical contribution to the lives of the disabled people they study. Jim Charlton in *Nothing about Us without Us* (2002) has chronicled the history and legacy of exclusion familiar to disabled people past and present, and this is exactly the sort of oppression disability scholars must work to end.

Second, thanks to the Internet, people with disabilities are communi- 28 cating daily if not hourly and are not as isolated as they once were. People with disabilities have embraced the Internet with gusto and have formed a vibrant cyber community. Disability studies scholars have also embraced the Internet, but their communication and scholarship is restricted and exclusionary. This is a significant problem. For example, the journal of the Society for Disability Studies, *Disability Studies Quarterly*, can only be read by members. Membership costs $95 a year. This is far too costly when one considers that dozens of disability-related blogs and web sites exist that are free to all who can access the Internet. The exclusive nature of disability studies scholarship is particularly unfortunate. I worry about those who could benefit the most from disability studies but are unable to read the work intended to empower them. In my estimation this highlights how far disability studies has distanced itself from the disability rights movement. Disability studies is more than an intellectual endeavor. I know this, as do many disability scholars who are not only engaged scholars but activists as well. It is imperative for all academics, activists, universities, independent living centers, bloggers, and cultural institutions to work together and demonstrate the relevance of post-secondary education. This type of action-oriented scholarship and activism can only enhance the quality of life for all people—those with and those without disabilities.

NOTES

1. This definition is from Title I of the 1990 Americans with Disabilities Act. Retrieved August 2008 from the U.S. Department of Justice Americans with Disabilities Act, ADA homepage. Available at http://www.eeoc.gov/types/ada.html.
2. Both quotations in this paragraph are from the Disability Rights Education and Defense Fund web site, which is available at http://www.dredf.org/publications/civil_rights_to_ human_rights.pdf.

REFERENCES

Bérubé, Michael. 1998. "Foreword: Pressing the Claim." In *Claiming Disability*, edited by Simi Linton. New York: NYU Press. Pp. vii-xii.
Davis, Leonard. 2002. *Bending over Backwards: Disability, Dismodernism, and Other Difficult Positions*. New York: NYU Press.
Fries, Kenny. 2007. *The History of My Shoes*. New York: Carroll Graf.
Gill, Carol. 1995. "The Pleasure We Take in Our Community." *Disability Rag*, September/October.
Linton, Simi. 1998. *Claiming Disability: Knowledge and Identity*. New York: NYU Press.
———. 2006. *My Body Politic: A Memoir*. Ann Arbor: University of Michigan Press.
Longmore, Paul K. 1995. "The Second Phase: From Disability Rights to Disability Culture." *Disability Rag*, September/October.
———. 2003. *Why I Burned My Book and Other Essays on Disability*. Philadelphia: Temple University Press.
Longmore, Paul K., and Lauri Umansky. 2001. *The New Disability History*. New York: NYU Press.
Mairs, Nancy. 1997. *Waist-High in the World: A Life among the Nondisabled*. Boston: Beacon Press.
Murphy, Robert. 1980. *Body Silent*. New York: Norton.
Olson, Kay. 2007. "Updated: CNN, Developmental Disability, and Institutionalization." The Gimp Parade, August 1 (http://www.thegimpparade.com).
Thomson, Rosemarie Garland. 1997. *Extraordinary Bodies: Figuring Physical Disability in American Culture and Literature*. New York: Columbia University Press.
Riley, Charles A. 2005. *Disability and the Media: Prescriptions for Change*. Hanover, NH: University Press of New England.
Roberts, Edward. Ca. 1970. Letter to Gina Laurie, University of California, Bancroft Library Special Collections.
Yee, Sylvia. 2007. "From Civil Rights to Human Rights." Disability Rights Education and Defense Fund, available at http://dredf.org/publications/Civil_rights_to_human _rights.pdf.

■ ■ ■

Reading as a Writer: Analyzing Rhetorical Choices

1. While Peace draws information from interviews and contextualizes this data in research from the field of disability studies, he also includes himself and his experiences as a disabled person as sources of information

here. What effect does this have on his piece, particularly when you think about strategies of persuasion through ethos, pathos, and logos?

2. How might you summarize the attitude toward disability that Peace argues against and that which he argues for? What examples stand out to you without looking back at your text?

Writing as a Reader: Entering the Conversation of Ideas

1. Peace is interested in the stories that the media tell about disability, just as bell hooks (pp. 486–92 in Sociology) is concerned with the media images we most often see of the poor. Drawing on both authors' insights about media representations and their effects, compose an essay in which you draw larger conclusions about the ways the media can be used to uphold or undo stereotypes. Include a specific, brief media example or two, if you like, to help you make your point.

2. Like Peace, Jean Kilbourne (pp. 554–77 in Media Studies) makes an argument about the ways expectations of bodies change based on historical and cultural context. While Kilbourne focuses on women's bodies, you can apply her insights to men's bodies as well. Compose an essay in which you consider the significance of changing expectations for male bodies, drawing on these readings and some media examples of your choosing that provide evidence for your claims.

Sustainability and Environmental Studies

How do our decisions affect our environment?

Shutterstock/18042011

I n this chapter, you plunge into high-stakes arguments and very personal conversations about our individual relationships to the planet. In the face of climate change and dwindling resources, you have certainly heard the cacophony of voices on television, in the movies, and in newspapers and magazines addressing these frightening global problems with "green" or "sustainable" solutions. What do these terms mean? More importantly, what do they mean for *you* as you go about your daily activities of getting from one place to the next, eating meals, buying things, learning, and occasionally cleaning your living space?

While "environmental studies" may sound mostly scientific, as you will see, thinkers in many different disciplines are challenging us to reconsider our relationship to the environment in eye-opening and innovative ways. For example, groundbreaking scientist and author Rachel Carson draws us into the environmental debate with a story that feels like a fairy tale—or, really, a nightmare—about the need to change our behaviors. Other authors try different approaches to persuade us to care about climate change, from scientist and mother Sandra Steingraber urging that we "Despair Not," to Derrick Jensen and Stephanie McMillan using the graphic novel format to invite us to question many of the "easy" ways we have heard of to "save the Earth." You will also hear scientist Andrew J. Hoffman's measured consideration of the many ways to enter the debate, keeping in mind why it is so challenging to get people to change their worldview. Carolyn Merchant picks up on the conversation about our desire to "buy nature," often at great cost to producers and ourselves.

Other writers focus on the politics of food in a growing chorus of thinkers whose ideas are captured in Anna Lappé's title "The Climate Crisis at the End of Our Fork." What is the connection between your supper plate and our planet? Lappé offers statistics about the food industry's enormous contributions to global warming, as well as solutions you might consider. Well-known food writer Michael Pollan reminds us, as do many of the authors in this chapter, that the answers to our environmental problems must go beyond scientific and technological solutions. What can we gain not only by changing what we eat but by altering what Pollan calls our "cheap-energy minds"? Journalist McKay Jenkins offers portraits of "enlightened local farmers" who aim to bring mindful food production to more consumers.

These writers share the rhetorical challenge of inviting readers to think creatively and more knowledgeably about an issue that is weighted with bad news. What approaches, examples, facts, and personal anecdotes will inspire you to think, make connections, and act? How might you try these strategies in your own conversation and writing?

RACHEL CARSON

A Fable for Tomorrow

Rachel Carson was a marine biologist and nature writer whose most famous work, *Silent Spring* (1962), is credited with bringing environmental concerns to the attention of the general American public. Her focus on the damage of the then-popular insecticide DDT led to strong opposition of her work by chemical companies but successfully changed the national pesticide policies. She died of breast cancer in 1964, but her work continues at the Silent Spring Institute, a multidisciplinary hub for research on the relationship between the environment and breast cancer.

"A Fable for Tomorrow" is the first chapter of *Silent Spring*. What do you notice from the opening words, "There was once . . ."? Why might Carson, as a scientist, use this rhetorical approach to introduce readers to a very difficult topic? As you read, you might circle the words that are designed to evoke emotion. In her carefully crafted description of "a town in the heart of America," Carson uses pathos (see Chapter 9) to persuade us to feel the tragedy of a once-healthy landscape being destroyed. In paragraph 3, she writes of a "strange blight," like an "evil spell" that brings sickness and death, as well as the absence of birdsong—the "spring without voices"—that gives her book the title *Silent Spring*.

While Carson writes of this desolate change as if it is a "strange" mystery, she reveals the truth in paragraph 8: "No witchcraft, no enemy action had silenced the rebirth of new life in this stricken world. The people had done it themselves." This shocking truth leads to the rest of this classic book (which we hope you will read one day), meant to inspire change through teaching the public about the science behind the environmental movement. First, though, Carson hooks us with a story. What do you think about this approach?

Tここに was once a town in the heart of America where all life seemed to *1*
live in harmony with its surroundings. The town lay in the midst of a checkerboard of prosperous farms, with fields of grain and hillsides of orchards where, in spring, white clouds of bloom drifted above the green fields. In autumn, oak and maple and birch set up a blaze of color that flamed and flickered across a backdrop of pines. Then foxes barked in the hills and deer silently crossed the fields, half hidden in the mists of the fall mornings.

Along the roads, laurel, viburnum and alder, great ferns and wildflow- *2*
ers delighted the traveler's eye through much of the year. Even in winter the roadsides were places of beauty, where countless birds came to feed on the berries and on the seed heads of the dried weeds rising above the snow. The countryside was, in fact, famous for the abundance and variety of its bird life, and when the flood of migrants was pouring through in spring and fall people traveled from great distances to observe them. Others came to fish the streams, which flowed clear and cold out of the hills and contained shady pools where trout lay. So it had been from the days many years ago when the first settlers raised their houses, sank their wells, and built their barns.

Then a strange blight crept over the area and everything began to *3*
change. Some evil spell had settled on the community: mysterious maladies swept the flocks of chickens; the cattle and sheep sickened and died. Everywhere was a shadow of death. The farmers spoke of much illness among their families. In the town the doctors had become more and more puzzled by new kinds of sickness appearing among their patients. There

had been several sudden and unexplained deaths, not only among adults but even among children, who would be stricken suddenly while at play and die within a few hours.

There was a strange stillness. The birds, for example—where had they *4* gone? Many people spoke of them, puzzled and disturbed. The feeding stations in the backyards were deserted. The few birds seen anywhere were moribund; they trembled violently and could not fly. It was a spring without voices. On the mornings that had once throbbed with the dawn chorus of robins, catbirds, doves, jays, wrens, and scores of other bird voices there was now no sound; only silence lay over the fields and woods and marsh.

On the farms the hens brooded, but no chicks hatched. The farmers *5* complained that they were unable to raise any pigs—the litters were small and the young survived only a few days. The apple trees were coming into bloom but no bees droned among the blossoms, so there was no pollination and there would be no fruit.

The roadsides, once so attractive, were now lined with browned *6* and withered vegetation as though swept by fire. These, too, were silent, deserted by all living things. Even the streams were now lifeless. Anglers no longer visited them, for all the fish had died.

In the gutters under the eaves and between the shingles of the roofs, *7* a white granular powder still showed a few patches; some weeks before it had fallen like snow upon the roofs and the lawns, the fields and streams.

No witchcraft, no enemy action had silenced the rebirth of new life in *8* this stricken world. The people had done it themselves.

This town does not actually exist, but it might easily have a thousand *9* counterparts in America or elsewhere in the world. I know of no community that has experienced all the misfortunes I describe. Yet every one of these disasters has actually happened somewhere, and many real communities have already suffered a substantial number of them. A grim specter has crept upon us almost unnoticed, and this imagined tragedy may easily become a stark reality we all shall know.

What has already silenced the voices of spring in countless towns in *10* America? This book is an attempt to explain.

■ ■ ■

Reading as a Writer: Analyzing Rhetorical Choices

1. Carson titles this "A Fable for Tomorrow." What is a fable? Look it up, and prepare to discuss how this brief reading works as a fable and why it is a fable "for Tomorrow." Point to specific passages in your discussion.

2. Referring directly to the discussion of pathos in Chapter 9, explain how Carson uses this rhetorical strategy in this piece, referring to specific examples in the text. To what extent do you think this is an effective strategy and why?

Writing as a Reader: Entering the Conversation of Ideas

1. Carson's storytelling approach is useful to consider in light of the differ-
    ent strategies offered by Sandra Steingraber (pp. 670–76) and Andrew J.
    Hoffman (pp. 693–701). Refer to ideas in Chapters 4 and 9 on argumen-
    tation and persuasion as you analyze their claims and evidence. Write
    an essay in which you use examples from these texts to make a point
    about effective strategies for teaching a generalist audience about climate
    change.

2. Compared to Carson's essay, Derrick Jensen and Stephanie McMillan's
    graphic novel seems to take an oppositional approach to discussing cli-
    mate change. These authors might have more in common than seems
    apparent, however. Spend some time examining the rhetorical approaches
    and effects of these texts. Write an essay in which you evaluate how these
    texts affect you as a reader, and draw some conclusions about effective
    persuasive tactics on contentious issues.

SANDRA STEINGRABER

Despair Not

Sandra Steingraber is an ecologist who began her work in the science lab
and then expanded her work to write for general audiences about the relationship between environmental and human health. A cancer survivor, she
writes frequently of environmental links to cancer, as in her landmark 1997
book, *Living Downstream: An Ecologist's Personal Investigation of Cancer
and the Environment*. Steingraber is also a poet and blogger and writes frequent columns such as this one in the online journal *In These Times* for
their series about whether or not we should "despair" about the issue of climate change. Steingraber's title makes her perspective clear: "Despair Not."

Given readers' expectations that she is writing about climate change, her
opening paragraphs might come as a surprise. What is the effect of beginning this conversation with a description of the murder of an abolitionist in
1837? How does she connect the response to this murder—the increase in
antislavery activity—with the contemporary environmental crisis?

Steingraber claims there are "two branches" to the environmental crisis, "although they share a common cause." As you read, follow the ways
she distinguishes between these two "branches" and the ways she connects
them, in part through her ethos as a scientist and as a mother. What is the
effect of her decision to highlight her relationship to her son (and the experience of sewing his "polar bear" Halloween costume) before leading into
the data-rich list under "New Morbidities of Childhood"?

Despite her title, Steingraber is not exactly a cheerful optimist when it
comes to the issue of climate change. What will you do with the information she offers here? Given this data, why do you think she might still say we
should "despair not"? This is a conversation we need to have for ourselves,
and, if you are persuaded at all by her claims, for the next generations, too.

What will we say when our grandchildren ask us the names of the *1* departed? Or, by then, will the loss of favorite animals be the least of our worries?

In Alton, Ill., downstream from Peoria, the Illinois River town where *2* I grew up, the abolitionist Elijah Lovejoy was pumped full of bullets on a dark November night by a mob intent on silencing the man once and for all. On this evening, they succeeded.

By dawn, Elijah was dead, and his printing press—the means by *3* which he distributed his radical ideas—lay at the bottom of the Mississippi River. The year was 1837. The Rev. Lovejoy, a Presbyterian minister who attended Princeton Theological Seminary, was buried on this thirty-fifth birthday.

But the story doesn't end there. *4*

Almost immediately, membership in antislavery societies across the *5* nation swelled. Vowing to carry on the work of his fallen friend, Edward Beecher, president of Illinois College in Jacksonville, threw himself into abolitionist efforts and, in so doing, inspired his sister, Harriet Beecher Stowe, who went on to write the most famous abolitionist treatise of all: *Uncle Tom's Cabin*. Meanwhile, Elijah's brother, Owen Lovejoy, turned his own house into a station along the Underground Railroad. Owen went on to win a seat in Congress and, along the way, befriended a young Illinois politician by the name of Abraham Lincoln.

These facts impressed me as a child. *6*

When I read Reverend Lovejoy's biography as a grown-up and mother, *7* I found other things impressive. Such as the fact that, at the time of his assassination, Elijah had a young family. And yet, in the weeks before his death—when it became clear that the mob pursuing him was growing bolder by the hour—he did not desist from speaking out against slavery. So Elijah declared in one of his final speeches:

> While all around me is violence and tumult, all is peace within. . . . I sleep sweetly and undisturbed, except when awakened by the brickbats of the mob.

Truly? With a pregnant wife in the bed next to him and a one-year-old *8* son in the next room? He wasn't worried?

A letter to his mother in Maine tells a more nuanced story: *9*

> Still I cannot but feel that it is harder to "fight valiantly for the truth" when I risk not only my own comfort, ease, and reputation, and even life, but also that of another beloved one.

And then there's this poignant aside: *10*

> I have a family who are dependent on me. . . . And this is it that adds the bitterest ingredient to the cup of sorrow I am called to drink.

Here's something else that I've noticed while reading his words. To the *11* slave owners and murderous thugs, Elijah spoke calmly. He reserved his fierce language for the members of the community who gladly lived in the free state of Illinois but wished to remain above the fray: the ones who added their signatures to a resolution asking him to cease publication of his newspaper and leave town, but would not sign a resolution that urged protection of law against mob rule; the ones who agreed that slavery was a homicidal abomination but who feared that emancipation without recompense to slave owners for loss of property would be socially destabilizing; the ones who believed themselves upstandingly moral but who chose to remain silent about the great moral crisis of the day.

Two Crises, One Cause

In the spirit of Elijah Lovejoy—the man who is the namesake of my nine-year-old son—the time has come for outspoken, full-throated heroism in the face of the great moral issue of our own day: the environmental crisis—an unfolding calamity whose main victims are our own children and grandchildren.   *12*

In fact, the environmental crisis is actually two crises, although they share a common cause. You could view it as a tree with two main branches: One branch represents what is happening to our planet through the atmospheric accumulation of heat-trapping gases (most notably, carbon dioxide and methane). The second branch represents what is happening to us through the accumulation of inherently toxic chemical pollutants in our bodies.   *13*

Follow the first branch and you find droughts, floods, acidifying oceans, dissolving coral reefs, and faltering plankton stocks (the oceans' plankton provides half of our atmospheric oxygen supply). Follow the second branch and you find pesticides in children's urine, lungs stunted by air pollutants, abbreviated pregnancies, altered hormone levels, and lower scores on cognitive tests.   *14*

The trunk of this tree is an economic dependency on fossil fuels, primarily coal (plant fossils) and petroleum and natural gas (animal fossils). When we light them on fire, we threaten the global ecosystem. When we use them as feedstocks for making stuff, we create substances—pesticides, solvents, plastics—that can tinker with our subcellular machinery and various signaling pathways that make it run.   *15*

Biologist Rachel Carson first called our attention to these manifold dangers in her 1962 book, *Silent Spring*. She wrote, "Future generations are unlikely to condone our lack of prudent concern for the integrity of the natural world that supports all life." Since then, the scientific evidence for the disintegration of our world has become irrefutable, and members of the future generations to whom she was referring are now occupying our homes.   *16*

They are our kids.   *17*

I mean this in the most basic ways. When my son Elijah, at age 4, asked to be a polar bear for Halloween, I sewed a polar bear costume—and I did so with the full knowledge that his costume might outlast the species. No other generation of mothers before mine has ever borne such   *18* knowledge—nor wondered if we should share this terrible news with our children. Or not. It's a novel situation. Indeed, according to the most recent assessment, one in every four mammal species (and one in every three marine animals) is now threatened with extinction, including that icon of Halloween itself: the little brown bat. Thus, animal costumes whose real-life correspondents have been wiped from Earth may well become commonplace.

This leads me to wonder: What will we say when our grandchildren   *19* ask us the names of the departed? When bats, bees, butterflies, whales, polar bears and elephants disappear, will children still read books about them? Will they want to dress up as vanished species? Or, by then, will the loss of favorite animals be the least of their worries?

"New Morbidities of Childhood"

Chronic childhood diseases linked to toxic chemical exposures are rising   *20* in prevalence. Here are a few of the current trends:

- One in eight U.S. children is born prematurely. Preterm birth is the leading cause of death in the first months of life and the leading cause of disability. Its price tag is $26 billion per year in medical costs, special services, and lost productivity. Preterm birth has demonstrable links to air pollution, especially maternal exposure to fine particles and combustion byproducts of the type released from coal-burning power plants.

- One in eleven U.S. children has asthma, the most common chronic childhood disease and a leading cause of school absenteeism. Asthma symptoms have been linked to certain ingredients in plastic (phthalates) as well as outdoor air pollution, including traffic exhaust. The annual cost of childhood asthma is estimated at $18 billion. Its incidence has doubled since 1980.

- One in ten U.S. children has a learning disability, and nearly one in ten has attention deficit/hyperactivity disorder. All together, special education services now consume 22 percent of U.S. school spending—about $77.3 billion per year at last count. Neurodevelopmental disorders have significant associations with exposures to air pollution, organophosphate pesticides like diazinon, and the heavy metals lead, mercury, and arsenic, among others.

- One in 110 children has autism or is on the autism spectrum. Annual costs are $35 billion. Causes are unknown, but exposure to chemical agents in early pregnancy is one of several suspected contributors.

- One in ten U.S. white girls and one in five U.S. black girls begin breast development before the age of eight. On average, breast development begins nearly two years earlier (age 9) than it did in the early 1960s (age 11). A risk factor for breast cancer in adulthood, early puberty in girls is associated with increasing body fat as well as exposure to some hormonally active chemical agents known as "estrogen mimickers." We have no cost estimates for the shortened childhoods of girls.

All together, asthma, behavioral problems, intellectual impairments and preterm birth are among the "new morbidities of childhood." So concludes a 2006 federally funded investigation of pediatric environmental health. Ironically, by becoming so familiar a presence among children, these disorders now appear almost normal or inevitable. And yet, with an entirely different chemical regulatory system, farm bill, and energy policy, their prevalence might be much reduced.

The fact that we do not identify and abolish hormone-disrupting, 21 brain-damaging chemicals to which children are routinely exposed raises profound ethical questions. The authors of the pediatric health investigation, published in *Environmental Health Perspectives*, put it this way:

> In the absence of toxicity testing, we are inadvertently employing pregnant women and children as uninformed subjects to warn us of new environmental toxicants. . . . Paradoxically, because industry is not obligated to supply the data on developmental neurotoxicity, the costs of human disease, research, and prevention are socialized whereas the profits are privatized.

In the absence of federal policies that protect child development and 22 the ecology of the planet on which our children's lives depend, we parents have to serve as our own regulatory agencies and departments of interior.

Already manically busy, we are encouraged by popular media reports 23 to read labels, consult Web sites, vet the contents of birthday party goody bags, shrink our carbon footprints, mix our own nontoxic cleaning products, challenge our school districts to embrace pesticide-free soccer fields, and limit the number of ounces of mercury-laced tuna fish consumed by each child per week.

"Well-Informed Futility"

Thoughtful but overwhelmed parents correctly perceive a disconnect between 24 the enormity of the problem and the ability of individual acts of vigilance and self-sacrifice to fix it. Awareness without corresponding political change leads to paralyzing despair. And so, eventually, we begin to discount or ignore the latest evidence of harm. We feel helpless in the face of our knowledge, and we're not sure we want to know anything more. The apt term for this is "well-informed futility syndrome."

"Well-informed futility" refers to a particular kind of learned helpless- 25 ness. It's a term that was coined in 1973 by psychologist Gerhart Wiebe, who was writing in an age when television had brought war into the living rooms of Americans for the first time. Wiebe noticed that a steady onslaught of information about a problem over which people feel little sense of personal agency gives rise to a sense of futility. Ironically, the more we know about such a problem, the more we are filled with a paralyzing sense of futility. That sense, in turn, forestalls action. And yet, action is the cure for paralysis.

Just down the street from well-informed futility resides denial. Accord- 26 ing to contemporary risk communication expert Peter Sandman, we all instinctively avoid information that triggers intolerable emotions—such as intolerable fear or intolerable guilt. In the face of knowledge too upsetting to bear, there is nothing to do but look away.

Well-informed futility and its inattentive neighbor, denial, especially 27 flourish, says Sandman, when there are discontinuities in the messages we receive, as when we are told that a problem (mass extinctions, melting icecaps) is dire but the proposed solutions (buy new light bulbs) seem trivial. If the problem were really so dire, wouldn't we all be asked to respond with actions of equivalent magnitude? So . . . maybe the problem isn't so dire.

It is such discontinuity that provides the exit doors. And soon enough, 28 we retreat into silent paralysis rather than stand up for *abolition now*.

The Antidote to Despair

Action is the antidote to despair, and by action I do not mean shopping dif- 29 ferently. Indeed, the notion that toxicity should be a consumer choice must be soundly rejected. Instead, we must seek the higher ground of human rights, and from that vantage explore systemic solutions to the ongoing chemical contamination of our children and our biosphere.

The domestic routines of family life with young children—however 30 isolated and detached from public life they seem—are inextricably bound to the most urgent public health issues of our time:

- Risks for asthma are related to transportation and energy policies.
- Bedtime snacks are linked to global systems of agricultural subsidies.
- The highly explosive raw materials used for manufacturing my kitchen floor pose demonstrable threats to national security.
- Sunburn at the beach is linked to the stability of the ozone layer, which, in turn, is threatened by particular pesticides used in the production of tomatoes and strawberries.
- The capture of a rabid bat in the kids' bedroom demonstrates the precautionary principle in action as enlightened public health policy. The proposal to extract natural gas from the Marcellus Shale that lies below my rural county in upstate New York demonstrates the abandonment of that same principle.

From understanding the inter-relatedness of situations like these, two 31 epiphanies emerge.

ONE: Ultimately the environmental crisis is a parenting crisis. It undermines my ability to carry out my two fundamental duties: to protect my children from harm and to plan for their future.

Current environmental policies must be realigned to safeguard the healthy development of children and sustain the planetary life-support systems on which their lives depend.

> **TWO:** Such a realignment necessitates emancipation from our terrible addiction to fossil fuels in all their toxic forms.

Happily, the best science shows us that we can do so. Mark Jacobson and Mark Delucchi, in their 2009 *Scientific American* article, "A Path to Sustainable Energy by 2030," explain how in the course of the next twenty years, we could entirely meet our energy requirements with renewable, non-carbon-based sources, if we cut our energy consumption by half. With the willingness to make deep cuts in consumption, the whole fossil-fuel freedom project becomes doable. And this is a place where a thousand molehills really do a mountain make.

According to Paul Stern, the director of the Committee on the Human Dimensions of Global Climate Change at the National Research Council, in the United States, individuals' homes and vehicles are responsible for 38 percent of carbon dioxide emissions. Therefore, we don't have to wait around for political change before making immediate and radical transformations in our own lives and spheres of influence. 32

We should not despair. We can break the spell. We can prepare the way. In other words, as Elijah Lovejoy exhorted his fellow citizens when encouraging them to imagine a U.S. economy no longer dependent on the unpaid labor of people held as property: It's time to "come up to the rescue, and let it be known whether the spirit of freedom yet presides." 33

■ ■ ■

Reading as a Writer: Analyzing Rhetorical Choices

1. Steingraber argues by analogy in this piece, claiming that just as slavery was the moral crisis of the nineteenth century, so the environment is the moral crisis of our day. What evidence does she provide for this claim? How does she link the personal and family lives of people to the larger issue in each case? What do you conclude about the effectiveness of this argumentative strategy?

2. What do you know about Carson? The first chapter of her book *Silent Spring* is included in this chapter (pp. 667–69). Read it (it is brief) and the headnote, and perhaps look online for other facts about Carson's remarkable life. How do her accomplishments fit into Steingraber's argument about how we should address the environmental crisis?

Writing as a Reader: Entering the Conversation of Ideas

1. Both Steingraber and Robert B. Reich (pp. 749–58 in Economics) use appeals to history in their essays. What does this historical background add to their arguments about contentious issues (climate change and

attitudes toward the poor, respectively)? Compose an essay in which you consider the effectiveness of these specific uses of history and draw larger conclusions about the role history can (or should?) play in our analysis of contemporary issues.

2. Like many of the writers in this chapter, Steingraber struggles with balancing pessimism and optimism while writing about the environment. After all, there is reason for pessimism, given the grim news about a range of environmental crises. However, without at least a little optimism, it is hard to find reasons to act. Other writers who foreground this balancing act are Derrick Jensen and Stephanie McMillan (pp. 677–92) and Michael Pollan (pp. 715–21). Compose an essay in which you analyze the ways these three texts use optimism and pessimism to make their points, taking care to cite examples and analyze them. What larger conclusions can you draw about effective methods of motivating readers to act on difficult issues like environmental crises?

DERRICK JENSEN AND STEPHANIE McMILLAN

As the World Burns: 50 Simple Things You Can Do to Stay in Denial

Derrick Jensen and Stephanie McMillan are writers and graphic artists who have published individually and who teamed up to write the book-length comic satire *As the World Burns: 50 Simple Things You Can Do to Stay in Denial* (2007). This reading is a section of this satiric graphic novel, which makes a challenging—and somewhat uncomfortable—argument: All the little things we do to help the environment may be making us feel better about ourselves but may not be helping the planet as much as we like to think.

Jensen and McMillan use sarcasm to get across their somewhat counterintuitive argument, as is apparent in the opening exchange between a pigtailed do-gooder who recycles a can (seemingly a good thing to do, yes?) and the one-eyed rabbit who reveals that her approach does not address the much larger corporate structures that harm the health of the planet and individuals.

What follows is a series of scenarios of "easy" ways to "save the Earth" that will be familiar to most of us—and are likely to be actions we have taken and felt pretty good about. In the witty interplay between two characters, you will hear strategies and statistics that sound persuasive in the mouth of the optimistic environmentalist . . . until the dark-clad character reveals how little these "easy" solutions accomplish, given the enormity of environmental problems. Pay attention to the way each character uses facts to make a point, and also pay attention to your own reactions to this rhetorical approach. How do the images underscore the emotions of this argument?

Jensen and McMillan do not let readers off the hook very easily here, but does this piece suggest that we should simply give up on trying to "save the Earth"? Jensen and McMillan argue that if we really want to work toward better environmental policies, we should know the full facts, the full picture. We would do better, they argue through their graphics, to focus less on changing light bulbs and more on changing corporations' policies and legislation. This is not an "easy" solution to our environmental problems, but it is also not giving up. How does that make you feel?

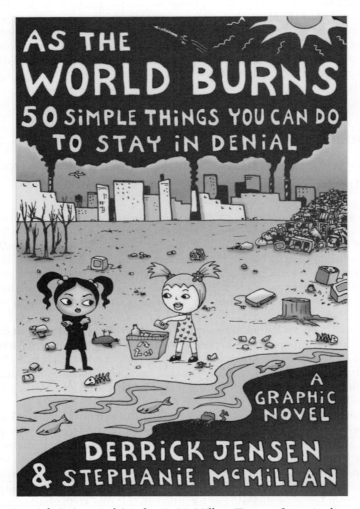

Derrick Jensen and Stephanie McMillan. Excerpt from *As the World Burns: 50 Simple Things You Can Do to Stay in Denial.* Copyright © 2007. Reprinted with the permission of The Permissions Company, Inc., on behalf of Seven Stories Press, www.sevenstories.com.

And then they'll add the cans to millions of other used cans and melt them down using coal-burning plants that spew toxins into the air,
and then use all that metal to make more cans, using still more energy.
So you can drink more soda.
And the melting and re-forming will take somewhat less energy than making all totally new cans.
So as a FABULOUS BONUS...
You can watch three episodes of "Survivor," or even Six "Brady Bunch" reruns with the energy that's saved.
Therefore using the same amount of energy as before, but gaining three hours of brainwashing! What a brilliant scheme!
You're a real party-pooper, you know that?

Another important one is to avoid products with a lot of packaging.
I can still buy things, right? I just avoid the ones with packaging...
That's it exactly! You can save 1,200 pounds of carbon dioxide if you cut down your garbage by 10 percent!
The next one is to adjust your thermostat. Moving your thermostat down just two degrees in winter and up two degrees in summer could save about 2,000 pounds of CO_2 a year.

Reading as a Writer: Analyzing Rhetorical Choices

1. How do the drawings underscore the meaning in this text? For example, what do you make of the one-eyed rabbit in the opening sequence? What difference would it make if the characters were older? How does body language illustrate each character's perspective?

2. There are a lot of statistics in this text. How are they used to make the argument? Given all the numbers that the characters throw at one another, what is the overall point the authors seem to make about the way data are often used in claims about the environment?

Writing as a Reader: Entering the Conversation of Ideas

1. Jensen and McMillan take a different approach to the climate crisis than Michael Pollan (pp. 715–21), who argues that people should go "personally green" by planting gardens and making different daily choices. Write an essay in which you play these authors' ideas off one another, considering similarities and differences in the ways they understand environmental problems and propose solutions. Evaluate the strengths and weaknesses of their claims given the evidence they provide. Where do they overlap, if at all, in their vision of how we should—or can—act to "save the Earth"?

2. Like Jensen and McMillan, Carolyn Merchant (pp. 732–39) seeks to awaken consumers to the harsh reality that it will not be easy to slow (much less reverse) the damage people have caused to our environment. Compose an essay that places these writers in conversation, considering the claims they make and the evidence they provide. Include in your analysis the extent to which you think so much "bad news" might either paralyze readers into inaction, or awaken them to advocate for the environment. What do you conclude about effective arguments by environmentalists?

ANDREW J. HOFFMAN

The Full Scope

Andrew J. Hoffman is a professor of environmental studies and sustainability whose research focuses on the cultural, institutional, and political contexts of environmental debates. He is the education director of the Graham Sustainability Institute at the University of Michigan. This reading is a chapter from his book *How Culture Shapes the Climate Change Debate* (2015). As you can tell from the title, Hoffman's focus here is less on the science of climate change than on the "competing worldview and cultural beliefs of people who must accept the science, even when it challenges those beliefs" (para. 18).

You might linger a bit over the epigraph—the quotation at the start of the chapter—by Stephen Jay Gould (look him up if that name is new to you). What's the effect of Hoffman starting with these words and then plunging into a description of himself playing golf? Hoffman builds his ethos (see Chapter 9) strategically here, revealing different aspects of himself. After you have read the first two paragraphs, pause to reflect on the issues he has raised about making arguments and appealing to readers. (Chapters 4 and 9 will aid your reflections.)

Despite the contentious aspect of many debates about climate change, Hoffman proposes three approaches to a "consensus-building path" (para. 6) that will engage a majority of citizens. Mark his three strategies clearly as you read (paras. 5–10), and think about real people in your life and how they might respond to these approaches. (Persuasion, after all, is about convincing real people of the value of your claims.) As a scientist, Hoffman provides plenty of evidence (paras. 12–13) that in this Anthropocene epoch (look it up!) we need to talk about our changing world, recognizing that it is as challenging as it was for Enlightenment thinkers to help people shift their world views (para. 15).

Hoffman argues that history offers us models for changing "hearts and minds" (para. 3) and that we must do so through empathy for rather than demonization of those with whom we disagree. What is your theory of change? How can you most effectively enact it? Hoffman offers you some tools.

■ ■ ■

We have become, by the power of a glorious evolutionary accident called intelligence, the stewards of life's continuity on earth. We did not ask for this role, but we cannot abjure it. We may not be suited to it, but here we are.

— STEPHEN JAY GOULD

I play in a casual summer golf league that is as much about beer-drinking banter as it is about hitting a golf ball. We don't generally talk about work. But one day, Greg, a fellow golfer, asked me, "Hey, Andy, what do you do for a living, anyway?" I told him that I was a professor and that I studied environmental issues. He asked, "Do you mean like climate change? That's not real, is it?" I told him that the science was quite compelling and that the issue was real. His next question was, "Are you a Democrat or Republican?" I told him that I was an independent. He replied, "So what do you think about Al Gore?" I told him that I thought Al Gore had called needed attention to the issue but that, unfortunately, perceptions of his partisan identity also helped to polarize the issue.

I think about that conversation often. Greg was not challenging my ideas; he was questioning my motives. He was trying to find out if he could trust me enough to listen to what I had to say, to figure out if I was part of his cultural community, his tribe. And I can imagine the hesitation he may have had in broaching this topic. Would I get condescending and give him a science lecture, challenging his lack of deep knowledge on the issue while asserting my own? Or would I begin to judge him and his lifestyle, critiquing his choice of car, house, vacation habits, or any one of the multitude of "unsustainable" activities that we all undertake? Or might I begin to pontificate on the politics of the issue, complaining of the partisan split on the issue and the corporate influence on our political system? These are all plausible and unpleasant scenarios that lead people to avoid this topic.

These conversations come up often enough—you've probably had 3
one—that it is worth asking, What are we trying to get out of these discussions? Are we trying to change "hearts and minds," or are we trying to
make a point? Do we want to allow people a face-saving way to come to
their own conclusions, or do we want to win, forcing them to acquiesce?
The only solution that is sustainable in the long term, as explained by the
research presented in this book, is to engage people in a way that draws
them towards an understanding they can embrace, not forcing them to
renounce a set of beliefs we have deemed inappropriate. We cannot scold,
lecture, or treat people with disrespect if we are to gain their trust; and
trust is at the center of an effective theory of change. That trust will not be
gained by bludgeoning those we engage. It can only be won through the
art of persuasion and a recognition of the political landscape in which the
cultural debate is taking place. A theory of change must include an understanding of the processes that are available for creating change and the
true scope of the cultural challenge before us.

Recognize the Political Landscape

When I say climate change, what do you hear? As described earlier, some 4
hear scientific consensus and the need for a carbon price. Others hear
more government, extreme environmentalists, restrictions on freedom,
restraints on the free market, and even a challenge to their notion of
God. These are real concerns and they may all be triggered by this one
idea. Solutions will only be found by recognizing this complex fabric and
being able to speak to its full scope. Offered here are three central points
to this recognition and the social movements that will be necessary to
address it.

Focus on the middle. Within the public debate over climate change, we fix 5
a disproportionate amount of attention on the extremes. On the one side,
it's all a hoax, humans have no impact on climate, and nothing is happening. On the other side, it's an imminent crisis, human activity explains all
climate change, and it will devastate life on earth as we know it. To fixate
on these positions is to focus more on the competing worldviews that distort the scientific debate and engage in the pessimistic path, where competing sides are simply trying to win.

Instead, messaging on climate change must be focused on the 6
consensus-based path and aimed at those who are open to discussion.[1]
Attention must center less on "the small minority of active deniers" and
more on "the vulnerability of the majority to their influence."[2] The debate
must engage the middle of the Six Americas—the Cautious, Disengaged,
and Doubtful segments.[3] In the words of Tony Leiserowitz of the YPCCC,
"the proper model for thinking about the climate debate is not a boxing
match, but a jury trial. We can never convince the die-hard skeptics, just

like a prosecutor will never convince the defense lawyer, and doesn't try. Rather, we should focus on convincing the silent jury of the mass public." To reach that middle, Cara Pike of the Social Capital Project argues for more capacity-building among the Alarmed and using them as a lever or motivator that will have a ripple effect through the rest of society.[4]

Employ the radical flank. The ability of moderate, consensus-oriented 7 change agents to operate is influenced by the presence of radical, conflict-oriented groups and actions through what is called the "radical flank effect."[5] All members and ideas of a social movement are viewed in contrast to others, and extreme positions can make other ideas and organizations seem more reasonable to movement opponents.[6] For example, when Martin Luther King Jr. first began speaking his message, it was perceived as too radical for the majority of white America. But when Malcolm X entered the debate, he pulled the radical flank further out and made King's message look more moderate by comparison.[7] Capturing this sentiment, Russell Train, second administrator of the EPA, once quipped, "Thank God for the David Browers of the world. They make the rest of us seem reasonable."[8]

So when writer and activist Bill McKibben founded 350.org, he 8 deserved tremendous credit both for creating a social movement where others could not, and for helping to pull the radical flank further out on the political spectrum. McKibben created a movement out of a specific constituency (young people), framing an issue that affects them personally (their future will be altered), giving them a common enemy (fossil fuel companies), and establishing a tangible goal (divestment). The group scored a major victory in May 2014 when Stanford University became the first major university to divest its $18.7 billion endowment of stock in coalmining companies. Many pundits dismissed the move as having no impact on the economics of coal. But that is not where the real impact of this move lies. It changed the debate over climate change by staking a position on the radical flank. Similarly, when Farmers Insurance filed a class action against nearly two hundred communities in the Chicago area for failing to prepare for flooding by arguing that the towns should have known that climate change would lead to this outcome,[9] pundits argued that Farmers would lose the case. But the real effect, again, is staking out the radical flank. With these two actions, and others like them, the debate over climate change evolves and the revolutionary change described by Thomas Kuhn becomes increasingly possible.

The question then becomes, what kinds of anomalous events will pre- 9 cipitate a period of revolutionary change that will drive broad-scale cultural change? Or more to the point, how can events be utilized to drive the change that is necessary? Returning to Rahm Emanuel's quip, how can we be sure to "never waste a good crisis"?

Never waste a good crisis. The Third National Climate Assessment in 2014 *10* made its point quite clear: the effects of climate change have already begun.[10] The first decade of the twenty-first century was the hottest decade on record. As a result, extreme weather events in the United States have become both more frequent and more intense, with an increase in both extended heat waves and extreme rainfall events. And there has been a large decrease in the number of extreme cold waves. Nationally, the freeze-free season (the number of days with temperatures above 32 degrees Fahrenheit) increased by two weeks over the last century. The West and North experienced the greatest warming, while parts of the Southeast, Great Plains, and Midwest did not experience a statistically significant warming trend.[11] These changes are driving changes in public opinion polls; people react to weather as something salient and personal.[12]

Scientists can tell us that by the end of the century, heavy downpour *11* events that once occurred every twenty years are expected at a frequency of every four to fifteen years depending on the region; wetter areas (such as the Northeast) are expected to get even wetter, increasing the chance of severe flooding. The number of consecutive days with less than 0.1 inch of rain is expected to increase across much of the Southwest, taxing areas already prone to water shortages.[13] Cities already prone to heat waves can expect the events to become more frequent, longer, and more intense over the next several decades. Rising sea levels will magnify storm-surge flooding and shoreline erosion, placing additional stress on coastal communities and habitats.[14] The intensity of tropical cyclones is a particular cause for concern for the eastern United States, as climate simulations find that a 1-degree Celsius rise in global temperature will translate to a twofold to sevenfold increase in the probability of Katrina-magnitude hurricane events.[15]

But these are objective and gradual trends. What kinds of discrete, *12* personally salient, and evocative events might precipitate cultural change? What will drive our awareness that we are living in a "new normal"? One answer is that the impacts of climate change must be monetized. According to the NOAA's National Climatic Data Center, 2012 was the second costliest year since 1980, with a total of more than $110 billion in damages throughout the year due, in large part, to eleven weather and climate disaster events, each with losses exceeding one billion dollars in damages. The year 2005 still stands as the most expensive: four devastating landfalling hurricanes inflicted damages of $160 billion.[16] Munich Re reports that worldwide, natural catastrophes have both increased and become more erratic in number and costs since 1980.[17] Looking to the future, a 2014 Government Accountability Office report warned that the energy infrastructure in the United States is at risk of diminished water supplies, warming temperatures, and damage from severe weather.[18]

As the costs of increased storm damage enter the market and costs *13* begin to rise for both business and the consumer, people will be increasingly open to the reality of climate change. People in some coastal areas saw sharp increases in their property insurance rates following Hurricane Katrina. Some insurance companies have withdrawn or restricted policies in other coastal areas, such as Cape Cod, in the wake of Hurricane Sandy. Energy Corporation, a large utility, filed for bankruptcy after incurring the costs of infrastructure damage from Hurricanes Katrina and Rita. These changes send ripples through the economy. A disruptive shift in the market might take the form of three Hurricane Sandy–sized events in the same year. This would have calamitous effects on insurance markets and force a national debate over what has changed. The shift in public consciousness would be dramatic. In the end, it is only this kind of event, one that affects the affluent 20 percent of the world's population who consume 86 percent of the world's resources, that will drive deep cultural change.

The Full Scope of the Issue

Climate change is part of a large-scale shift that is taking place in human *14* history. That larger shift is called the Anthropocene, a new geologic epoch in which human activities have a significant impact on the earth's ecosystems. While this term has yet to acquire formal, geological recognition, the notion is an acknowledgment that we are now occupying a place in the ecosystem that is without historic precedent. The Anthropocene began with the industrial revolution of the eighteenth century, but became more acute in what is called the "Great Acceleration" around 1950 onwards. According to Paul Crutzen, the Nobel Prize laureate and chemist who, with Eugene Stoermer, first proposed the term in 2000, the epoch is marked by the reality that "human activity has transformed between a third and a half of the land surface of the planet; Many of the world's major rivers have been dammed or diverted; Fertilizer plants produce more nitrogen that is fixed naturally by all terrestrial ecosystems; Humans use more than half of the world's readily accessible freshwater runoff."[19] Carbon dioxide levels are above 400 parts per million and rising; we are introducing synthetic chemicals to terrestrial and aquatic ecosystems at levels that cause dead zones and chromosomal abnormalities. Consider for a moment that there are measurable levels of ibuprofen in the Mediterranean Sea and scientists are even more concerned over the impact of birth control pills and antidepressants in aquatic ecosystems. These chemicals are altering the flora and fauna in the environment and finding their way back to human populations through municipal water systems that cannot handle them. Think about these facts for a minute. How does this change your sense of who we are as humans and how we relate to the world around us?

The answer to this question is synonymous with the new reality cre- *15* ated by climate change. Whether we like it or not, we have taken a role in the operation of many of the earth's systems. This brings a fundamental shift in how we think about ourselves and the world we occupy. Recognizing this emerging reality commences a cultural shift akin to the

Enlightenment of the seventeenth and eighteenth centuries. The Enlightenment marked a disruptive period in which knowledge was advanced through the scientific method rather than tradition, superstition, and religion. Placing climate change on this scale helps to understand the truly disruptive aspect it presents. The scientific method is no longer singularly adequate for understanding the world as it now exists.

Further, it illuminates the great challenge that is required in communicating the details of its science. People cannot really learn about climate change through personal experience. While extreme weather patterns have increased the social consensus on the issue, a real appreciation of climate change requires an understanding of large-scale systems through "big data" models. And both the models and an appreciation for how they work are generally unavailable to the average individual. John Sterman, system dynamics professor at MIT, points out that people would need to be taught about complex dynamic systems and the ways in which feedback loops, time delays, accumulations, and nonlinearities operate within those systems if they were ever to understand the climate change issue.[20]

The Ultimate Goal

In May 2014, the U.S. government released the third National Climate Assessment, which presented grave warnings that "climate change, once considered an issue for a distant future, has moved firmly into the present" and included an assessment of the effects of climate change on important sectors such as health, water, energy, and agriculture, as well as impacts on urban areas, rural communities, and indigenous peoples. As to be expected, a rhetorical war immediately followed the release of the report, which was interpreted as either a serious warning or seriously flawed. In an editorial, the *New York Times* wrote that "apart from the disinformation sowed by politicians content with the status quo, the main reason neither Congress nor much of the American public cares about global warming is that, as problems go, it seems remote. Anyone who reads the latest National Climate Assessment, released on Tuesday, cannot possibly think that way any longer."[21]

The premise of this statement is a faulty one. This has been the central message of this book. More science, though important, will not by itself change people's minds and create the collective will to act. Those who disbelieve the science will not be compelled by yet another scientific report. The debate over climate change is not about greenhouse gases and climate models alone. It is about the competing worldviews and cultural beliefs of people who must accept the science, even when it challenges those beliefs. When engaging the debate, we must think not only of the science of climate change, but also about the sociopolitical processes and tactics necessary to get people to hear it.

When you find yourself engaged in a debate over climate change with [19] an uncle over the holiday dinner table, think carefully about your theory of change. Rather than immediately presenting more data to secure victory, you might do well to consider where your relative is coming from. How will you gain his trust? What segment of the Six Americas might he fit into? Does he fully understand the science? What other issues is climate change triggering for him—big government, the liberal agenda, distrust of scientists, belief in God? How will you address any distrust he may have for the message, messengers, process, or solutions proposed? What messengers might you invoke to make your arguments? Does he understand the state of scientific consensus that exists? What kinds of broker frames might best appeal to him—national security, health, economic competitiveness? Can you frame a few proposed solutions in a way that appeals to his sense of a desired future?

These are the questions to ask before instinctively providing more [20] data to make your case. Through all of these considerations you might find ways to draw your uncle into a middle ground where all-out domination and capitulation are not the only acceptable outcomes. And if your answers to these questions lead you to determine that you cannot gain your uncle's trust or that he is in the Dismissive segment of the Six Americas spectrum and interested only in the pessimistic, win–lose path of debate, perhaps it would be best to enjoy your family dinner and talk about football instead. Know your theory of change and enact it.

NOTES

1. Maibach, E., A. Leiserowitz, C. Roser-Renouf, & C. Mertz. 2011. "Identifying like-minded audiences for global warming public engagement campaigns: An audience segmentation analysis and tool development." *PLoS ONE.* DOI: 10.1371/journal .pone.0017571
2. Hamilton, 2010. See Chapter 2, Note 4.
3. Leiserowitz, Maibach, Roser-Renouf, Feinberg, & Rosenthal, 2014. See Chapter 1, Note 38.
4. Balbus, 2012. See Chapter 4, Note 41.
5. Haines, H. 1984. "Black radicalization and the funding of civil rights: 1957–1970." *Social Problems* 32(1): 31–43.
6. Hoffman, A. 2009. "Shades of green." *Stanford Social Innovation Review* (Spring): 40–49.
7. Haines, 1984. See Note 5.
8. U.S. EPA. 1993. *US EPA oral history interview no. 2: Russell Train.* Washington, DC: U.S. Government Printing Office.
9. Rosenberg, M. 2014. "Climate change lawsuits filed against some 200 US communities." *Christian Science Monitor,* May 17.
10. U.S. Climate Change Research Program. 2014. *Climate change impacts in the United States.* Washington, DC: U.S. National Climate Assessment.
11. Kunkel, K., et al. 2013. *Regional climate trends and scenarios for the US National Climate Assessment. Part 9: Climate of the contiguous United States.* Washington, DC: National Oceanic and Atmospheric Administration.
12. Borick & Rabe, 2012. See Chapter 1, Note 11.

13. Kunkel, et al., 2013. See Note 11.

14. Pachauri, R. et al. 2008. *Climate change 2007: Synthesis report*. Washington, DC: Intergovernmental Panel on Climate Change.

15. Grinsted, A., et al. 2013. "Projected Atlantic hurricane surge threat from rising temperatures." *Proceedings of the National Academy of Sciences*, February 11.

16. National Climatic Data Center. 2013. *NCDC releases 2012 billion-dollar weather and climate disasters information*. Washington, DC: National Oceanic and Atmospheric Administration.

17. Munich Re. 2014. NatCat Service: Download center for statistics on natural catastrophes. http://www.munichre.com/en/reinsurance/business/non-life/natcatservice/index.html

18. Patel, S. 2014. "GAO report: Power sector is clearly exposed to climate change risks." *Power,* March 7.

19. Crutzen, P., & E. Stoermer. 2000. "The Anthropocene,'" *Global Change Newsletter* 41: 17–18.

20. Sterman, J. 2011. "Communicating climate change risks in a skeptical world." *Climatic Change* 108(4): 811–26.

21. Editorial. 2014. "Climate disruptions, close to home." *New York Times,* May 7.

■ ■ ■

Reading as a Writer: Analyzing Rhetorical Choices

1. Mark and be ready to discuss Hoffman's three strategies of addressing climate change. Draw on ideas in Chapters 4 and 9 on argumentation and persuasion as you consider the effectiveness of these strategies. What other contentious issues might benefit from these approaches?

2. While Hoffman deliberately writes about making science accessible to the general public, he does use some vocabulary that might be new to you. Be sure you look up any words you do not know, and include "Anthropocene," even if you have heard it before. How might the term be received by audiences who believe (or not) in climate change?

Writing as a Reader: Entering the Conversation of Ideas

1. Given his focus on persuasive strategies, it is easy to imagine that Hoffman would have a lot to say about the approaches other climate writers take on the issue. What might he say about the rhetorical approaches of Rachel Carson (pp. 667–69), Derrick Jensen and Stephanie McMillan (pp. 677–92), or Michael Pollan (pp. 715–21)? Select two texts to analyze through Hoffman's frameworks, and write an essay in which you evaluate the authors' approaches and draw conclusions about effective argumentation.

2. Hoffman acknowledges that the financial cost of climate change may be one of the ways to persuade skeptics that we cannot ignore changes in our environment. To what extent do his ideas about "monetizing" (para. 12) the climate-change debate overlap with Carolyn Merchant's discussion (pp. 732–39) of the problematic way nature is often "sold" to us? Write an essay that places these authors in conversation about the relationship between money and environmental debates. Where might they agree and disagree about problems and solutions, and where do you stand in this complex debate?

ANNA LAPPÉ

The Climate Crisis at the End of Our Fork

Anna Lappé is a best-selling author, public speaker, and founder (along with her mother, the food activist Frances Moore Lappé) of the Small Planet Institute, an international network of scholars, activists, and educators who are interested in the intersections of hunger and poverty. Lappé is a frequent guest writer for the *New York Times*, *Gourmet*, *O: The Oprah Magazine*, and *Body + Soul*, to name a few of the many publications that have featured her writing on food politics. This piece with the same name was published in the anthology *Food Inc.: A Participant Guide: How Industrial Food Is Making Us Sicker, Fatter, and Poorer—and What You Can Do about It* (2009), edited by Karl Weber. The book is a companion to the documentary film *Food, Inc.*, about the ecological and health effects of the industrialization of the food chain.

In this piece, Lappé opens by describing the gasping response of the audience at a talk at which a climate-change scholar discussed the enormous impact of the food system on global warming. She throws at readers the same surprising information she learned at this talk, that "the global system for producing and distributing food accounts for roughly *one-third* of the human-caused global warming effect . . . [and] the livestock sector alone is responsible for 18 percent of the world's total global warming effect—more than the emissions produced by every plane, train, and steamer ship on the planet" (para. 5, author's emphasis). This statistic launches her argument that if the food sector is a critical part of the global-warming problem, it is also critical to the solution. Lappé wants readers to see that changing the food system is as crucial as—or even more crucial than—any other ecological solutions we commonly think of, such as changing light bulbs or driving more efficient cars.

As you read, pay close attention to the evidence Lappé offers, in her text and in her copious footnotes. What do you think are the most persuasive examples and statistics she offers to make her point about the problem and how much is at stake? How does she use evidence to propose solutions in her final section?

Lappé is part of a rapidly expanding group of scholars, writers, and activists who are interested in all aspects of food politics. Unlike some forms of consumption, which we can avoid—like smoking, for example—we all need to eat to survive. What will we spear on the end of our fork when we take our next bite of food? Lappé argues that our answer will affect not only our bodies, but the fate of the planet.

＊ ＊ ＊

We could hear audible gasps from the two dozen New York state farmers gathered at the Glynwood Center on a cold December day in 2007 when NASA scientist Cynthia Rosenzweig, one of the world's leading experts on climate change and agriculture, explained the slide glowing on the screen in front of us.

The Glynwood Center, an education nonprofit and farm set on ₂ 225 acres in the Hudson Valley, had brought Rosenzweig to speak to area farmers about the possible impact of climate change on the region. Pointing to an arrow swooping south from New York, Rosenzweig said: "If we don't drastically reduce greenhouse gas emissions by 2080, farming in New York could feel like farming in Georgia."

"It was all projections before. It's not projections now—it's observa- ₃ tional science," said Rosenzweig. We are already seeing major impacts of climate change on agriculture: droughts leading to crop loss and salinization of soils, flooding causing waterlogged soils, longer growing seasons leading to new and more pest pressures, and erratic weather shifting harvesting seasons, explained Rosenzweig.

When people think about climate change and food, many first think ₄ of the aspect of the equation that Rosenzweig focused on that day—the impact of climate change on farming. But when it comes to how the food system impacts global warming, most draw a blank.

Challenged to name the human factors that promote climate change, ₅ we typically picture industrial smokestacks or oil-thirsty planes and automobiles, not Pop-Tarts or pork chops. Yet the global system for producing and distributing food accounts for roughly *one-third* of the human-caused global warming effect. According to the United Nation's seminal report, *Livestock's Long Shadow*, the livestock sector alone is responsible for 18 percent of the world's total global warming effect—more than the emissions produced by every plane, train, and steamer ship on the planet.[1]

Asked what we can do as individuals to help solve the climate change ₆ crisis, most of us could recite these eco-mantras from memory: Change our light bulbs! Drive less! Choose energy-efficient appliances! Asked what we can do as a nation, most of us would probably mention promoting renewable energy and ending our addiction to fossil fuels. Few among us would mention changing the way we produce our food or the dietary choices we make.

Unfortunately, the dominant story line about climate change—its big- ₇ gest drivers and the key solutions—diverts us from understanding how other sectors, particularly the food sector, are critical parts of the *problem*, but even more importantly can be vital strategies for *solutions*.

If the role of our food system in global warming comes as news to ₈ you, it's understandable. Many of us have gotten the bulk of our information about global warming from Al Gore's wake-up call *An Inconvenient Truth*, the 2006 Oscar-winning documentary that became the fourth-highest grossing nonfiction film in American history.[2] In addition to the record-breaking doc, Gore's train-the-trainer program, which coaches educators on sharing his slideshow, has further spread his central message about the threat posed by human-made climate change. But Gore's program offers little information about the connection between climate change and the food on your plate.

Mainstream newspapers in the United States haven't done a much bet-   *9*
ter job of covering the topic. Researchers at Johns Hopkins University analyzed climate change coverage in sixteen leading U.S. newspapers from
September 2005 through January 2008. Of the 4,582 articles published on
climate change during that period, only 2.4 percent addressed the role of
the food production system, and most of those only peripherally. In fact,
just half of 1 percent of all climate change articles had "a substantial focus"
on food and agriculture.[3] Internationally, the focus hasn't been much different. Until recently, much of the attention from the international climate
change community and national coordinating bodies was also mostly
focused on polluting industries and the burning of fossil fuels, not on the
food sector.

This is finally starting to change. In the second half of 2008, writers   *10*
from *O: The Oprah Magazine* to the *Los Angeles Times* started to cover the
topic, increasing the public's awareness of the food and climate change
connection. In September 2008, Dr. Rajendra Pachauri, the Indian economist serving his second term as chair of the United Nations Intergovernmental Panel on Climate Change, made a bold statement about the
connection between our diet and global warming. Choosing to eat less
meat, or eliminating meat entirely, is one of the most important personal
choices we can make to address climate change, said Pachauri.[4] "In terms
of immediacy of action and the feasibility of bringing about reductions in
a short period of time, it clearly is the most attractive opportunity," said
Pachauri. "Give up meat for one day [a week] initially, and decrease it from
there."[5]

Why does our food system play such a significant role in the global   *11*
warming effect? There are many reasons, including the emissions created by industrial farming processes, such as fertilizer production, and
the carbon emissions produced by trucks, ships, and planes as they
transport foods across nations and around the world. Among the main
sources of the food system's impact on climate are land use changes,
especially the expansion of palm oil production, and effects caused by
contemporary agricultural practices, including the emissions produced
by livestock.

The Land Use Connection

Let's look at land use first. A full 18 percent of the world's global warming   *12*
effect is associated with "land use changes," mostly from the food system.[6] The biggest factors are the destruction of vital rainforests through
burning and clearing and the elimination of wetlands and peat bogs to
expand pasture for cattle, feed crops for livestock, and oil palm plantations, especially in a handful of countries, Brazil and Indonesia chief
among them.[7]

What do Quaker Granola Bars and Girl Scout Cookies have to do with the climate crisis?[8] These processed foods—along with other popular products, including cosmetics, soaps, shampoo, even fabric softeners—share a common ingredient, one with enormous climate implications: palm oil.[9] As the taste for processed foods skyrockets, so does the demand for palm oil, production of which has more that doubled in the last decade.[10] Today, palm oil is the most widely traded vegetable oil in the world, with major growth in the world's top two importing countries, India and China.[11] 13

As oil palm plantations expand on rainforests and peat lands in Southeast Asia, the natural swamp forests that formerly filled those lands are cut down and drained, and the peat-filled soils release carbon dioxide and methane into the atmosphere. (Methane is a key greenhouse gas with twenty-three times the global warming impact of carbon dioxide.) In a recent study, researchers estimate that producing one ton of palm oil can create fifteen to seventy tons of carbon dioxide over a twenty-five year period.[12] 14

Three of the world's biggest agribusiness companies are major players in the palm oil market, which is concentrated in two countries—Malaysia and Indonesia—where in 2007, 43 percent and 44 percent of the world's total palm oil was produced, respectively.[13] Wilmar, an affiliate of the multinational giant Archer Daniels Midland, is the largest palm oil producer in the world;[14] soy behemoth Bunge is a major importer of palm oil into the United States (although at the moment it doesn't own or operate any of its own facilities);[15] and grain-trading Cargill owns palm plantations throughout Indonesia and Malaysia.[16] These three companies and others producing palm oil claim that guidelines from the Roundtable on Sustainable Palm Oil (RSPO), established in 2004 by industry and international nonprofits, ensure sustainable production that minimizes the destruction of forest and peat bogs as well as deleterious effect on the global climate.[17] 15

However, some environmental and human rights groups argue that loopholes in the Roundtable's regulations still leave too much wiggle room. Says Greenpeace, "The existing standards developed by the RSPO will not prevent forest and peat land destruction, and a number of RSPO members are taking no steps to avoid the worst practices of the palm oil industry."[18] 16

We also know from new data that palm plantation expansion on peat land is not slowing. According to Dr. Susan Page from the University of Leicester, deforestation rates on peat lands have been increasing for twenty years, with one-quarter of all deforestation in Southeast Asia occurring on peat lands in 2005 alone.[19] 17

The other side of the land use story is deforestation driven by the increased production of livestock, expanding pasture lands and cropland for feed. In Latin America, for instance, nearly three-quarters of formerly forested land is now occupied by pastures; feed crops for livestock cover much of the remainder.[20] Globally, one-third of the world's arable land is dedicated to feed crop production.[21] Poorly managed pastures lead to overgrazing, compaction, and erosion, which release stored carbon into 18 the atmosphere. With livestock now occupying 26 percent of the planet's ice-free land, the impact of this poor land management is significant.[22]

Raising livestock in confinement and feeding them diets of grains *19* and other feedstock—including animal waste by-products—is a relatively recent phenomenon. In the postwar period, intensification of animal production was seen as the path to productivity. As livestock were confined in high stocking densities often far from where their feed was grown, a highly inefficient and environmentally costly system was born.

As a British Government Panel on Sustainable Development said in *20* 1997, "Farming methods in the last half century have changed rapidly as a result of policies which have favored food production at the expense of the conservation of biodiversity and the protection of the landscape."[23] Despite these environmental costs, confined animal feeding operations (CAFOs) spread in the 1960s and 1970s into Europe and Japan and what was then the Soviet Union. Today, CAFOs are becoming increasingly common in East Asia, Latin America, and West Asia.

As the largest U.S.-based multinational meat companies, includ *21* ing Tyson, Cargill, and Smithfield, set their sights overseas, the production of industrial meat globally is growing.[24] In addition, the increasing supply of meat in developing countries flooded with advertising for Western-style eating habits is leading to a potential doubling in demand for industrial livestock production, and therefore feed crops, from 1997–1999 to 2030.[25]

Although the shift from traditional ways of raising livestock to *22* industrial-scale confinement operations is often defended in the name of "efficiency," it's a spurious claim. As a way of producing edible proteins, feedlot livestock production is inherently inefficient. While ruminants such as cattle naturally convert inedible-to-humans grasses into high-grade proteins, under industrial production, grain-fed cattle pass along to humans only a fraction of the protein they consume.[26] Debates about this conversion rate abound. The U.S. Department of Agriculture estimates that it takes seven pounds of grain to produce one pound of beef.[27] However, journalist Paul Roberts, author of *The End of Food*, argues that the true conversion rate is much higher. While feedlot cattle need at least ten pounds of feed to gain one pound of live weight, Roberts states, nearly two-thirds of this weight gain is for inedible parts, such as bones, other organs, and hide. The true conversion ratio, Roberts estimates, is twenty pounds of grain to produce a single pound of beef, 7.3 pounds for pigs, and 3.5 pounds for poultry.[28]

The inefficiency of turning to grain-fed livestock as a major compo *23* nent of the human diet is devastating in itself, especially in a world where nearly one billion people still go hungry. But now we know there is a climate cost as well. The more consolidation in the livestock industry— where small-scale farmers are pushed out and replaced by large-scale confinement operations—the more land will be turned over to feed production. This production is dependent on fossil fuel—intensive farming, from synthesizing the human-made nitrogen fertilizer to using fossil fuel-based chemicals on feed crops. Each of these production steps cost in emissions contributing to the escalating greenhouse effect undermining our planet's ecological balance.

The Agriculture Connection

One reason we may have been slow to recognize the impact of the food system on climate change may be a certain "carbon bias." While carbon dioxide is the most abundant human-made greenhouse gas in the atmosphere, making up 77 percent of the total human-caused global warming effect, methane and nitrous oxide contribute nearly all the rest.[29] (Other greenhouse gases are also relevant to the global warming effect, but are currently present in much smaller quantities and have a less significant impact.)[30] Agriculture is responsible for most of the human-made methane and nitrous oxide in the atmosphere, which contribute 13.5 percent of total greenhouse gas emissions, primarily from animal waste mismanagement, fertilizer overuse, the natural effects of ruminant digestion, and to a small degree rice production[31] (1.5 percent of total emissions come from methane produced during rice cultivation).[32] *24*

Though livestock only contribute 9 percent or carbon dioxide emissions, the sector is responsible for 37 percent of methane and 65 percent of nitrous oxide.[33] Here again, recent changes in agricultural practices are a significant factor. For centuries, livestock have been a vital part of sustainable food systems, providing muscle for farm work and meat as a vital protein source. Historically, properly grazed livestock produced numerous benefits to the land: Hooves aerate soil, allowing more oxygen in the ground, which helps plant growth; their hoof action also presses grass seed into the earth, fostering plant growth, too; and, of course, their manure provides natural fertilizer. Indeed, new self-described "carbon farmers" are developing best management practices to manage cattle grazing to reduce compaction and overgrazing and, mimicking traditional grazing patterns, increasing carbon sequestration in the soil.[34] *25*

But modern livestock production has steered away from these traditional practices toward the industrial-style production described above and to highly destructive overgrazing. In sustainable systems tapping nature's wisdom, there is no such thing as waste: Manure is part of a holistic cycle and serves to fertilize the same lands where the animals that produce it live. In CAFOs, there is simply too much waste to cycle back through the system. Instead, waste is stored in manure "lagoons," as they're euphemistically called. Without sufficient oxygenation, this waste emits methane and nitrous oxide gas. As a consequence of industrial livestock production, the United States scores at the top of the world for methane emissions from manure. Swine production is king in terms of methane emissions, responsible for half of the globe's total.[35] *26*

The sheer numbers of livestock exacerbate the problem. In 1965, eight 27 billion livestock animals were alive on the planet at any given moment; ten billion were slaughtered every year. Today, thanks in part to CAFOs that spur faster growth and shorter lifespan, twenty billion livestock animals are alive at any moment, while nearly fifty-five billion are slaughtered annually.[36]

Ruminants, such as cattle, buffalo, sheep, and goats, are among 28 the main agricultural sources of methane. They can't help it; it's in their nature. Ruminants digest through microbial, or enteric, fermentation, which produces methane that is then released by the animals, mainly through belching. While this process enables ruminants to digest fibrous grasses that we humans can't convert into digestible form, it also contributes to livestock's climate change impact. (Enteric fermentation accounts for 25 percent of the total emissions from the livestock sector; land use changes account for another 35.4 percent; manure accounts for 30.5 percent.)[37]

In addition to the ruminants' digestive process, emissions from live- 29 stock can be traced back to the production of the crops they consume. Globally, 33 percent of the world's cereal harvest and 90 percent of the world's soy harvest are now being raised for animal feed.[38] Feed crop farmers are heavily dependent on fossil fuels, used to power the on-farm machinery as well as used in the production of the petroleum-based chemicals to protect against pests, stave off weeds, and foster soil fertility on large-scale monoculture fields. In addition, these crops use up immense quantities of fertilizer. In the United States and Canada, half of all synthetic fertilizer is used for feed crops.[39] In the United Kingdom, the total is nearly 70 percent.[40] To produce this fertilizer requires tons of natural gas; on average 1.5 tons of oil equivalents are used up to make one ton of fertilizer.[41] Yet in the United States, only about half of the nitrogen fertilizer applied to corn is even used by the crop.[42] This needless waste is all the more alarming because nitrogen fertilizer contributes roughly three-quarters of the country's nitrous oxide emissions.

Erosion and deterioration of soils on industrial farms is another factor 30 in the food sector's global warming toll. As industrial farms diminish natural soil fertility and disturb soil through tillage, soil carbon is released into the atmosphere.[43] Because industrialized agriculture also relies on huge amounts of water for irrigation, these farms will be more vulnerable as climate change increases drought frequency and intensity and decreases water availability. Globally, 70 percent of the world's available freshwater is being diverted to irrigation-intensive agriculture.[44]

The Waste and Transportation Connection

The sources of food system emissions on which we've focused so far— 31 including land use changes and agricultural production—are responsible for nearly one-third of the total human-made global warming effect. That's already quite a lot, but other sectors include emissions from the food chain, including transportation, waste, and manufacturing.

For example, 3.6 percent of global greenhouse gas emissions come from waste, including landfills, wastewater, and other waste.[45] The food production system contributes its share to this total. After all, where does most of our uneaten food and food ready for harvest that never even makes it to our plates end up? Landfills. Solid waste, including food scraps, produces greenhouse gas emissions from anaerobic decomposition, which produces methane, and from carbon dioxide as a by-product of incineration and waste transportation.[46] 32

An additional 13.1 percent of the emissions that contribute to the global warming effect come from transportation, toting everything from people to pork chops.[47] The factory farming industry, in particular, demands energy-intensive shipping. CAFOs, for example, transport feed and live animals to feedlots and then to slaughter. Then the meat must be shipped to retail distribution centers and to the stores where it is sold to us consumers. 33

Americans, in particular, import and export a lot of meat. In 2007, the United States exported 1.4 billion pounds of beef and veal (5.4 percent of our total production of beef)[48] and imported 3.1 billion pounds of the same.[49] One could argue that a lot of that transport is unnecessary from a consumer point of view and damaging from an environmental point of view. 34

Globally, international trade in meat is rapidly accelerating. As recently as 1995, Brazil was exporting less than half-a-million dollars' worth of beef. A little more than a decade later, the Brazilian Beef Industry and Exporters Association estimates the value of beef exports could reach $5.2 billion and expects revenues of $15 billion from beef exports by 2013.[50] 35

All of these billions of pounds of meat being shipped around the world add significantly to the carbon emissions from transportation. So do the Chilean grapes shipped to California, the Australian dairy destined for Japan, or the Twinkies toted across the country—all the meat and dairy, drinks, and processed foods shipped worldwide in today's globalized food market. 36

The Organic Solution

The globalized and industrialized food system has not only negative health consequences—think of all those Twinkies, that factory-farmed meat, and that chemically raised produce—but a climate change toll as well. But the news is not all bad. Once we gaze directly at the connection between food, farming, and global warming, we see plenty of cause for hope. 37

First, unlike many other climate change conundrums, we already know many of the steps we can take now to reduce carbon emissions from 38 the food sector. For instance, we know that compared with industrial farms, small-scale organic and sustained farms can significantly reduce the sector's emissions. Small-scale sustainable agriculture relies on people power, not heavy machinery, and depends on working with biological methods, not human-made chemicals, to increase soil fertility and handle pests. As a result, small-scale sustained farms use much fewer fossil fuels and have been found to emit between one-half and two-thirds less carbon dioxide for every acre of production.[51]

We also are just beginning to see results from long-term studies show-   39
ing how organic farms create healthy soil, which has greater capacity to store carbon, creating those all-important "carbon sinks."[52] By one estimate, converting 10,000 medium-sized farms to organic would store as much carbon in the soil as we would save in emissions if we took one million cars off the road.[53]

We're closer than ever to global consensus about the direction in which   40
we need to head. In April 2008, a report on agriculture initiated by the World Bank, in partnership with the United Nations and representatives from the private sector, NGOs, and scientific institutions from around the world, declared that diverse, small-holder sustainable agriculture can play a vital role in reducing the environment impacts of the agriculture sector.

The result of four years of work by hundreds of scientists and review-   41
ers,[54] the International Assessment of Agriculture Science and Technology for Development (IAASTD) calls for supporting agroecological systems; enhancing agricultural biodiversity; promoting small-scale farms; and encouraging the sustainable management of livestock, forest, and fisheries, as well as supporting "biological substitutes for agrochemicals" and "reducing the dependency of the agricultural sector on fossil fuels."[55] A civil society statement timed with the report's release declared that the IAASTD represents the beginning of a "new era of agriculture" and offers "a sobering account of the failure of industrial farming."[56] Said Greenpeace, the IAASTD report recommends a "significant departure from the destructive chemical-dependent, one-size-fits-all model of industrial agriculture."[57]

(Not everyone involved in the process was happy with the final report,   42
which was signed by fifty-seven governments.[58] Chemical giant and agricultural biotechnology leaders Syngenta and Monsanto, for instance, refused to sign on to the final document. No public statements were given at the time.[59] But in an interview, Syngenta's Martin Clough told me, "When it became pretty evident that the breadth of technologies were not getting equal airtime, then I think the view was that there was no point in participating. It's important to represent the technological options and it's equally important to say that they get fair play. That wasn't happening."[60])

Despite the chemical industry holdouts, there is also consensus   43
that sustainable farming practices create more resilient farms, better able to withstand the weather extremes of drought and flooding already afflicting many regions as a result of climate change. In other words,

mitigation *is* adaptation. Because organic farms, by their design, build healthy soil, organic soils are better able to absorb water, making them more stable during floods, droughts, and extreme weather changes. In one specific example, conventional rice farmers in a region in Japan were nearly wiped out by an unusually cold summer, while organic farmers in the same region still yielded 60 to 80 percent of their typical production levels.[61]

In ongoing studies by the Pennsylvania-based Rodale Institute, organic crops outperformed nonorganic crops in times of drought, yielding 35 to 100 percent more in drought years than conventional crops.[62] Visiting a Wisconsin organic farmer just after the major Midwest flooding of the summer of 2008, I could see the deep ravines in the surrounding corn fields caused by the recent flooding, while I spent the afternoon walking through a visibly unscathed biodiverse organic farm.   44

Encouraging sustainable agriculture will not only help us reduce emissions and adapt to the future climate chaos, it will have other beneficial ripples: addressing hunger and poverty, improving public health, and preserving biodiversity. In one study comparing organic and conventional agriculture in Europe, Canada, New Zealand, and the United States, researchers found that organic farming increased biodiversity at "every level of the food chain," from birds and mammals, to flora, all the way down to the bacteria in the soil.[63]   45

Finally, we know that shifting toward sustainable production need not mean sacrificing production. In one of the largest studies of sustainable agriculture, covering 286 projects in fifty-seven countries and including 12.6 million farmers, researchers from the University of Essex found a yield increase of 79 percent when farmers shifted to sustainable farming across a wide variety of systems and crop types.[64] Harvests of some crops such as maize, potatoes, and beans increased 100 percent.[65]   46

Here's the other great plus: we all have to eat, so we can each do our part to encourage the shift to organic, sustainable farming every time we make a choice about our food, from our local market, to our local restaurants, to our local food policies.   47

I was recently talking with Helene York, director of the Bon Appétit Management Company Foundation, an arm of the Bon Appétit catering company, which serves eighty million meals a year at 400 venues across the country. York has been at the forefront of educating consumers and chefs about the impacts of our culinary choices on climate change, including leading the charge of the foundation's "Low Carbon Diet," which has dramatically reduced greenhouse gas emissions associated with their food. She summed up the challenge of awakening people to the food and climate change connection this way: "When you're sitting in front of a steaming plate of macaroni and cheese, you're not imagining plumes of greenhouse gases. You're thinking, dinner."   48

But the truth is those plumes of gases are there nonetheless, in the *49*
background of how our dinners are produced, processed, and shipped
to our plates. Thankfully, more and more of us eaters and policymakers are considering the climate crisis at the end of our fork and what
we can do to support the organic, local, sustainable food production
that's better for the planet, more pleasing to the palate, and healthier
for people too.

NOTES

1. Henning, Steinfeld et al., *Livestock's Long Shadow: Environmental Issues and Options* (Rome: Food and Agriculture Organization of the United Nations, 2006). While livestock is responsible for 18 percent of total emissions, transportation is responsible for a total of 13 percent of the global warming effect.
2. Film stats from Box Office Mojo. Available online at http://www.boxofficemojo.com/movies/?page=main&id=inconvenienttruth.htm.
3. R. A. Neff, I. L. Chan, and K. A. Smith, "Yesterday's Dinner, Tomorrow's Weather, Today's News?: US Newspaper Coverage of Food System Contributions to Climate Change," *Public Health Nutrition* (2008).
4. Rajendra Pachauri, "Global Warning—The Impact of Meat Production and Consumption on Climate Change," paper presented at the Compassion in World Farming, London, September 8, 2008.
5. Ibid.
6. N. H. Stern, *The Economics of Climate Change: The Stern Review* (Cambridge: Cambridge University Press, 2007), 539.
7. Ibid.
8. Ingredients for Quaker Granola Bar available online: https://www.wegmans.com/webapp/wcs/stores/servlet/ProductDisplay?langId=&storeId=10052&productId=359351&catalogId=10002&krypto=QJrbAudPd0vzXUGByeatog%3D%3D&ddkey=http:Product Display.
9. Marc Gunther, "Eco-Police Find New Target: Oreos," *Money*, August 21, 2008. Available online at http://money.cnn.com/2008/08/21/news/companies/palm_oil.fortune/index.htm?postversion=2008082112.
10. Ibid.
11. USDA FAS, "Indonesia: Palm Oil Production Prospects Continue to Grow," December 31, 2007. Total area for Indonesia palm oil in 2006 is estimated at 6.07 million hectares according to information from the Indonesia Palm Oil Board (IPOB). Available online at http://www.pecad.fas.usda.gov/highlights/2007/12/Indonesia_palmoil/.
12. "New Data Analysis Conclusive About Release of CO_2 When Natural Swamp Forest Is Converted to Oil Palm Plantation," CARBOPEAT Press Release, December 3, 2007. Dr. Sue Page or Dr. Chris Banks (CARBOPEAT Project Office), Department of Geography, University of Leicester, UK.
13. USDA FAS.
14. "Palm Oil Firm Wilmar Harming Indonesia Forests-Group," Reuters, July 3, 2007. Available at http://www.alertnet.org/thenews/newsdesk/SIN344348.htm.
15. Bunge Corporate Web site. Online at http://www.bunge.com/about-bunge/promoting_sustainability.html.
16. See information at Cargill-Malaysia's website, http://www.cargill.com.my/, and Cargill-Indonesia, http://www.cargill.com/news/issues/palm_current.htm.
17. See, for instance, Cargill's position statement: http://www.cargill.com/news/issues/palm_roundtable.htm#TopOfPage. Bunge: http://www.bunge.com/about-bunge/promoting_sustainability.html.

18. Greenpeace. See, for instance, http://www.greenpeace.org.uk/forests/faq-palm-oil -forests-and-climate-change.
19. "New Data Analysis . . ." For more information, see "Carbon-Climate-Human Interactions in Tropical Peatlands: Vulnerabilities, Risks & Mitigation Measures."
20. Steinfield *et al.*, xxi.
21. Ibid., xxi.
22. Ibid.
23. British Government Panel on Sustainable Development, *Third Report*, 1997. Department of the Environment.
24. From company annual reports, Tyson and Smithfield, 2007.
25. Steinfield *et al.*, 45.
26. For further discussion, see Paul Roberts, *The End of Food* (Boston: Houghton Mifflin, 2008), 293. See also Frances Moore Lappé, *Diet for a Small Planet*, 20th anniversary ed. (New York: Ballantine Books, 1991).
27. Conversion ratios from USDA, from Allen Baker, Feed Situation and Outlook staff, ERS, USDA, Washington, D.C.
28. Roberts, quoting "Legume Versus Fertilizer Sources of Nitrogen: Ecological Trade-offs and Human Need," *Agriculture, Ecosystems, and Environment* 102 (2004): 293.
29. World GHG Emissions Flow Chart, World Resources Institute, Washington, D.C. Based on data from 2000. All calculations are based on CO_2 equivalents, using hundred-year global warming potentials from the IPCC (1996). Land use change includes both emissions and absorptions. Available online at http://cait.wri.org/figures.php?page=WorldFlowChart.
30. According to the IPCC, greenhouse gases relevant to radiative forcing include the following (parts per million [ppm] and parts per trillion [ppt] are based on 1998 levels): carbon dioxide (CO_2), 365 ppm; methane (CH_4), 1,745 ppb; nitrous oxide (N_2O), 314 ppb; tetrafluoromethane (CF_2), 80 ppt; hexafluoromethane (C_2F_6), 3 ppt; sulfur hexafluoride (SF_6), 4.2 ppt; trifluoromenthane (CHF_3), 14 ppt; 1,1,1,2-tetrafluoroethane ($C_2H_2F_4$), 7.5 ppt; 1,1-Difluoroethane ($C_2H_4F_2$), 0.5 ppt.
31. IPCC, *Climate Change 2007: Fourth Assessment Report of the Intergovernmental Panel on Climate Change* (New York: Cambridge University Press, 2007). Graphic 13.5.
32. World GHG Emissions Flow Chart, World Resources Institute.
33. Steinfeld et al., 79. See also, for instance, http://www.fao.org/ag/magazine/0612spl.htm.
34. See, for example, Carbon Farmers of Australia. http://www.carbonfarmersofaustralia .com.au.
35. Steinfeld et al.
36. United Nations FAO, quoting Anthony Weis, *The Global Food Economy: The Battle for the Future of Farming* (London: Zed Books, 2007), 19.
37. J. McMichael et al., "Food, Livestock Production, Energy, Climate Change, and Health," *The Lancet* 370 (2007):1253–63.
38. Pachauri.
39. Steinfeld et al.
40. Ibid.
41. CNN, "All About: Food and Fossil Fuels," March 17, 2008, cnn.com. Available online at http://edition.cnn.com/2008/WORLD/asiapcf/03/16/eco.food.miles/; author communication with Professor Jonathan Lynch, University of Pennsylvania.
42. Author communication with Lynch.
43. Stern.
44. See, for instance, Niles Eldredge, *Life on Earth: An Encyclopedia of Biodiversity, Ecology, and Evolution* (Santa Barbara, Calif.: ABC-CLIO, 2002). Online at http://www.landinstitute.org/vnews/display.v/ART/2002/08/23/439bd36c9acf1.
45. World GHG Emissions Flow Chart, World Resources Institute.
46. For more detail, see Environmental Protection Agency, "General Information on the Link Between Solid Waste and Greenhouse Gas Emissions." Available online at http://www.epa.gov/climatechange/wycd/waste/generalinfo.html#ql.

47. IPCC. See Figure 1, Chapter 2.
48. Most recent data available from USDA/ERS, U.S. Cattle and Beef Industry, 2002–2007. Available online at http://www.ers.usda.gov/news/BSECoverage.htm.
49. Pounds noted here are measured by commercial carcass weight. U.S. Red Meat and Poultry Forecasts. Source: World Agricultural Supply and Demand Estimates and Supporting Materials. From USDA/ERS. See also http://www.ers.usda.gov/Browse/TradeInternationalMarkets/.
50. Data from Brazilian Beef Industry and Exporters Association. Cited in "Brazilian Beef Break Records in September," October 3, 2008, The Beef Site. Available online at http://www.thebeefsite.com/news/24565/brazilian-beef-break-records-in-september.
51. IPCC.
52. http://www.rodaleinstitute.org.
53. See, for instance, studies from the Rodale Institute, found here: http://www.newfarm.org/depts/NFfield_trials/1003/carbonsequest.shtml.
54. Editorial, "Deserting the Hungry?" *Nature* 451 (17 January 2008):223–24; dio:l0.1038/451223b; published online January 16, 2008. Available at http://www.nature.com/nature/journal/v451 /n7176/full/451223b.html.
55. Executive Summary, 9. IAASTD, "Summary Report," paper presented at the International Assessment of Agricultural Science and Technology for Development, Johannesburg, South Africa, April 2008.
56. "Civil Society Statement from Johannesburg, South Africa: A New Era of Agriculture Begins Today," April 12, 2008. Available online at http://www.agassessment.org/docs/Civil_Society_Statement_on_I AASTD-28Apr08.pdf.
57. Greenpeace Press Release, "Urgent Changes Needed in Global Farming Practices to Avoid Environmental Destruction," April 15, 2008.
58. Fifty-seven governments approved the Executive Summary of the Synthesis Report. An additional three governments—Australia, Canada, and the United States of America—did not fully approve the Executive Summary of the Synthesis Report, and their reservations are entered in the Annex. From the Executive Summary of IAASTD, "Summary Report."
59. *Nature*, 223–24.
60. Author interview with Martin Clough, head of biotech R & D and president of Syngenta Biotechnology, Inc., based in North Carolina; and Anne Birch, director with Corporate Affairs, Syngenta, September 9, 2008.
61. Nadia El-Hage Scialabba and Caroline Hattam, "General Concepts and Issues in Organic Agriculture," in *Organic Agriculture, Environment and Food Security*, ed. Environment and Natural Resources Service Sustainable Development Department (Rome: Food and Agriculture Organization of the United Nations, 2002), chapter 1. Available online at http://www.fao.org/docrep/005/y4137e/y4137e01.htm#P0_3.
62. "Organic Crops Perform up to 100 Percent Better in Drought and Flood Years," November 7, 2003, Rodale Institute. Online at www.newfarm.org.
63. D. G. Hole et al., "Does Organic Farming Benefit Biodiversity?," *Biological Conservation* 122 (2005):113–30, quoting James Randerson, "Organic Farming Boosts Biodiversity," *New Scientist*, October 11, 2004. Note: *New Scientist* emphasizes that neither of the two groups of researchers—from the government agency, English Nature, and from the Royal Society for the Protection of Birds—" has a vested interest in organic farming."
64. Jules Pretty, *Agroecological Approaches to Agricultural Development* (Essex: University of Essex, 2006).
65. Ibid.

Reading as a Writer: Analyzing Rhetorical Choices

1. Lappé offers many different forms of evidence in this piece. Mark at least three different places in the text and three different endnotes where you think the evidence is especially compelling. Explain the strengths you see in these examples. What conclusions can you draw about providing evidence in your own persuasive writing?

2. Like Al Gore, Lappé tells us some fairly "inconvenient truths" about our daily food habits. How does she coax readers into seeing that there is a problem? What solutions does she offer? Locate some specific places where you see her addressing how challenging it can be to acknowledge the connection between our eating habits and the health of the planet. How and where does she try to bring skeptics to her side? How effective do you think she is and why?

Writing as a Reader: Entering the Conversation of Ideas

1. Lappé and McKay Jenkins (pp. 722–31) bring us the backstory of food production. To what extent do these writers' ideas about producing and consuming food overlap? Write an essay in which you place these writers in conversation, using their ideas and examples to help you build an argument about what consumers should know about how their food was raised and why.

2. Lappé, like Michael Pollan (pp. 715–21), urges us to see the connections between our supper plates and the planet. Compose an essay that draws on the ideas and examples in both texts to build your own argument about the problems in the ways most Americans eat and possible solutions. Develop your evidence with some additional research about food consumption in the United States, if you like.

MICHAEL POLLAN

Why Bother?

When it comes to the politics of food, Michael Pollan is one of the best-known American public intellectuals on the topic. He is also a professor of journalism at the University of California, Berkeley. Pollan's lively critiques of modern agribusiness and the harms our industrial food chain cause our environment and ourselves have appeared in dozens of top-ranked news and literary magazines, including the *New York Times Magazine* and *Harper's Magazine*. His research and writing and dynamic public lectures are interdisciplinary, bringing together history, the sciences, cultural studies, anthropology, sociology, and environmental justice (to name a few) in his focus on food—the ways we think about it and the ways we do not think about it. His most recent books, *In Defense of Food: An Eater's Manifesto* (2009), *Food Rules: An Eater's Manual* (2009), and *Cooked: A Natural History of Transformation* (2014), are all designed to make readers far more mindful about what we put into our mouths. Pollan reveals to us the ways every bite of food is connected to politics and practices that we might find unsavory if we knew about them.

This is an excerpt of a longer essay that ran in the *New York Times Magazine* (2008). Pollan opens with a question that many of us have asked when faced with the overwhelming problem of climate change: Can small differences in our daily lives really make a difference to our planet's health? In this essay, Pollan works through the doubts many of us have that our personal attempts to "go green" will matter very much when, for example, we see neighbors driving gas guzzlers or power mowers. For Pollan, the "why bother" question is answered partially by the writing of Wendell Berry, a farmer and writer who for more than thirty years has been arguing that the crisis in our relationship to the land is a "disease of the modern character" in which we have become accustomed to specialists solving our problems and therefore no longer see our role in the big picture of personal and planetary health (para. 9).

Drawing on Berry's insights and his own interest in industrial food production as a key contributor to global warming, Pollan offers a very concrete solution: Plant a garden. (If you don't have a yard, Pollan very practically suggests trying to grow some of your food in a planter or buying into a community garden.) Pollan acknowledges that this can seem like too small a gesture in the face of climate change, but he argues that growing even a little of your own food is "one of the most powerful things an individual can do—to reduce your carbon footprint, to be sure, but more important, to reduce your sense of dependence and dividedness: to change the cheap-energy mind" (para. 18).

Pollan reframes climate change as a call for *personal* change, noting that if we cultivate the ground in a garden, we will be cultivating different "habits of mind" (para. 21). He is part of a growing chorus of scholars who connect our cheap and unhealthy food supply to our increasingly unhealthy planet. Pollan's point is that the solution—changing the way we eat—will be delicious and make us feel better. In the face of so much "feel-bad" news about global warming, you might be hungry for his perspective.

▨ ▨ ▨

W hy bother? That really is the big question facing us as individuals 1 hoping to do something about climate change, and it's not an easy one to answer. I don't know about you, but for me the most upsetting moment in *An Inconvenient Truth* came long after Al Gore scared the hell out of me, constructing an utterly convincing case that the very survival of life on earth as we know it is threatened by climate change. No, the really dark moment came during the closing credits, when we are asked to . . . change our light bulbs. That's when it got really depressing. The immense disproportion between the magnitude of the problem Gore had described and the puniness of what he was asking us to do about it was enough to sink your heart.

But the drop-in-the-bucket issue is not the only problem lurking 2 behind the "why bother" question. Let's say I do bother, big time. I turn my life upside-down, start biking to work, plant a big garden, turn down the thermostat so low I need the Jimmy Carter signature cardigan, forsake the clothes dryer for a laundry line across the yard, trade in the station wagon for a hybrid, get off the beef, go completely local. I could theoretically do all that, but what would be the point when I know full well that halfway around the world there lives my evil twin, some carbon-footprint *doppelgänger* in Shanghai or Chongqing who has just bought his first car (Chinese car ownership is where ours was back in 1918), is eager to swallow every bite of meat I forswear and who's positively itching to replace every last pound of CO_2 I'm struggling no longer to emit. So what exactly would I have to show for all my trouble? . . .

There are so many stories we can tell ourselves to justify doing nothing, but perhaps the most insidious is that, whatever we do manage to do, it will be too little too late. Climate change is upon us, and it has arrived well ahead of schedule. Scientists' projections that seemed dire a decade ago turn out to have been unduly optimistic: the warming and the melting is occurring much faster than the models predicted. Now truly terrifying feedback loops threaten to boost the rate of change exponentially, as the shift from white ice to blue water in the Arctic absorbs more sunlight and warming soils everywhere become more biologically active, causing them to release their vast stores of carbon into the air. Have you looked into the eyes of a climate scientist recently? They look really scared. 3

So do you still want to talk about planting gardens? 4

I do. 5

Whatever we can do as individuals to change the way we live at this suddenly very late date does seem utterly inadequate to the challenge. It's hard to argue with Michael Specter, in a recent *New Yorker* piece on carbon footprints, when he says: "Personal choices, no matter how virtuous [N.B.!], cannot do enough. It will also take laws and money." So it will. Yet it is no less accurate or hardheaded to say that laws and money cannot do enough, either; that it will also take profound changes in the way we live. Why? Because the climate-change crisis is at its very bottom a crisis of lifestyle—of character, even. The Big Problem is nothing more or less than the sum total of countless little everyday choices, most of them made by us (consumer spending represents 70 percent of our economy), and most of the rest of them made in the name of our needs and desires and preferences. 6

For us to wait for legislation or technology to solve the problem of how we're living our lives suggests we're not really serious about changing—something our politicians cannot fail to notice. They will not move until we do. Indeed, to look to leaders and experts, to laws and money and grand schemes, to save us from our predicament represents precisely the sort of thinking—passive, delegated, dependent for solutions on specialists—that helped get us into this mess in the first place. It's hard to believe that the same sort of thinking could now get us out of it. 7

Thirty years ago, Wendell Berry, the Kentucky farmer and writer, put forward a blunt analysis of precisely this mentality. He argued that the 8 environmental crisis of the 1970s—an era innocent of climate change; what we would give to have back *that* environmental crisis!—was at its heart a crisis of character and would have to be addressed first at that level: at home, as it were. He was impatient with people who wrote checks to environmental organizations while thoughtlessly squandering fossil fuel in their everyday lives—the 1970s equivalent of people buying carbon offsets to atone for their Tahoes and Durangos. Nothing was likely to change until we healed the "split between what we think and what we do." For Berry, the "why bother" question came down to a moral imperative: "Once our personal connection to what is wrong becomes clear, then we have to choose: we can go on as before, recognizing our dishonesty and living with it the best we can, or we can begin the effort to change the way we think and live."

For Berry, the deep problem standing behind all the other problems 9 of industrial civilization is "specialization," which he regards as the "disease of the modern character." Our society assigns us a tiny number of roles: we're producers (of one thing) at work, consumers of a great many other things the rest of the time, and then once a year or so we vote as citizens. Virtually all of our needs and desires we delegate to specialists of one kind or another—our meals to agribusiness, health to the doctor, education to the teacher, entertainment to the media, care for the environment to the environmentalist, political action to the politician.

As Adam Smith and many others have pointed out, this division of 10 labor has given us many of the blessings of civilization. Specialization is what allows me to sit at a computer thinking about climate change. Yet this same division of labor obscures the lines of connection—and responsibility—linking our everyday acts to their real-world consequences, making it easy for me to overlook the coal-fired power plant that is lighting my screen, or the mountaintop in Kentucky that had to be destroyed to provide the coal to that plant, or the streams running crimson with heavy metals as a result.

Of course, what made this sort of specialization possible in the first 11 place was cheap energy. . . . Cheap energy, which gives us climate change, fosters precisely the mentality that makes dealing with climate change in our own lives seem impossibly difficult. Specialists ourselves, we can no longer imagine anyone but an expert, or anything but a new technology or law, solving our problems. . . .

The "cheap-energy mind," as Wendell Berry called it, is the mind that 12 asks, "Why bother?" because it is helpless to imagine—much less attempt—a different sort of life, one less divided, less reliant. Since the cheap-energy mind translates everything into money, its proxy, it prefers to put its faith in market-based solutions—carbon taxes and pollution-trading schemes. If we could just get the incentives right, it believes, the economy will properly value everything that matters and nudge our self-interest down the proper channels. The best we can hope for is a greener version of the old invisible hand. Visible hands it has no use for.

But while some such grand scheme may well be necessary, it's doubtful *13* that it will be sufficient or that it will be politically sustainable before we've demonstrated to ourselves that change is possible. Merely to give, to spend, even to vote, is not to do, and there is so much that needs to be done— without further delay. In the judgment of James Hansen, the NASA climate scientist who began sounding the alarm on global warming 20 years ago, we have only 10 years left to start cutting—not just slowing—the amount of carbon we're emitting or face a "different planet." Hansen said this more than two years ago, however; two years have gone by, and nothing of consequence has been done. So: eight years left to go and a great deal left to do.

Which brings us back to the "why bother" question and how we might *14* better answer it. The reasons not to bother are many and compelling, at least to the cheap-energy mind. But let me offer a few admittedly tentative reasons that we might put on the other side of the scale:

If you do bother, you will set an example for other people. If enough *15* other people bother, each one influencing yet another in a chain reaction of behavioral change, markets for all manner of green products and alternative technologies will prosper and expand. (Just look at the market for hybrid cars.) Consciousness will be raised, perhaps even changed: new moral imperatives and new taboos might take root in the culture. . . .

Going personally green is a bet, nothing more or less, though it's one we *16* probably all should make, even if the odds of it paying off aren't great. Sometimes you have to act as if acting will make a difference, even when you can't prove that it will. . . .

So what would be a comparable bet that the individual might make in *17* the case of the environmental crisis? [Vaclav] Havel himself has suggested that people begin to "conduct themselves as if they were to live on this earth forever and be answerable for its condition one day." Fair enough, but let me propose a slightly less abstract and daunting wager. The idea is to find one thing to do in your life that doesn't involve spending or voting, that may or may not virally rock the world but is real and particular (as well as symbolic) and that, come what may, will offer its own rewards. Maybe you decide to give up meat, an act that would reduce your carbon footprint by as much as a quarter. Or you could try this: determine to observe the Sabbath. For one day a week, abstain completely from economic activity: no shopping, no driving, no electronics.

But the act I want to talk about is growing some—even just a little— *18* of your own food. Rip out your lawn, if you have one, and if you don't—if you live in a high-rise, or have a yard shrouded in shade—look into getting a plot in a community garden. Measured against the Problem We Face, planting a garden sounds pretty benign, I know, but in fact it's one of the most powerful things an individual can do—to reduce your carbon footprint, sure, but more important, to reduce your sense of dependence and dividedness: to change the cheap-energy mind.

A great many things happen when you plant a vegetable garden, *19* some of them directly related to climate change, others indirect but related nevertheless. Growing food, we forget, comprises the original solar technology: calories produced by means of photosynthesis. Years ago the cheap-energy mind discovered that more food could be produced with less effort by replacing sunlight with fossil-fuel fertilizers and pesticides, with a result that the typical calorie of food energy in your diet now requires about 10 calories of fossil-fuel energy to produce. It's estimated that the way we feed ourselves (or rather, allow ourselves to be fed) accounts for about a fifth of the greenhouse gas for which each of us is responsible.

Yet the sun still shines down on your yard, and photosynthesis still *20* works so abundantly that in a thoughtfully organized vegetable garden (one planted from seed, nourished by compost from the kitchen and involving not too many drives to the garden center), you can grow the proverbial free lunch—CO_2-free and dollar-free. This is the most-local food you can possibly eat (not to mention the freshest, tastiest and most nutritious), with a carbon footprint so faint that even the New Zealand lamb council dares not challenge it. And while we're counting carbon, consider too your compost pile, which shrinks the heap of garbage your household needs trucked away even as it feeds your vegetables and sequesters carbon in your soil. What else? Well, you will probably notice that you're getting a pretty good workout there in your garden, burning calories without having to get into the car to drive to the gym. (It is one of the absurdities of the modern division of labor that, having replaced physical labor with fossil fuel, we now have to burn even more fossil fuel to keep our unemployed bodies in shape.) Also, by engaging both body and mind, time spent in the garden is time (and energy) subtracted from electronic forms of entertainment.

. . . Still more valuable are the habits of mind that growing a little of *21* your own food can yield. You quickly learn that you need not be dependent on specialists to provide for yourself—that your body is still good for something and may actually be enlisted in its own support. If the experts are right, if both oil and time are running out, these are skills and habits of mind we're all very soon going to need. We may also need the food. Could gardens provide it? Well, during World War II, victory gardens supplied as much as 40 percent of the produce Americans ate.

But there are sweeter reasons to plant that garden, to bother. At least in *22* this one corner of your yard and life, you will have begun to heal the split between what you think and what you do, to commingle your identities as consumer and producer and citizen. Chances are, your garden will re-engage you with your neighbors, for you will have produce to give away and the need to borrow their tools. You will have reduced the power of the cheap-energy mind by personally overcoming its most debilitating weakness: its helplessness and the fact that it can't do much of anything that doesn't involve division or subtraction. The garden's season-long transit from seed to ripe fruit—*will you get a load of that zucchini?!*—suggests that the operations of addition and multiplication still obtain, that the abundance of nature is not exhausted. The single greatest lesson the garden teaches is that our relationship to the planet need not be zero-sum, and that as long as the sun still shines and people still can plan and plant, think and do, we can, if we bother to try, find ways to provide for ourselves without diminishing the world.

■ ■ ■

Reading as a Writer: Analyzing Rhetorical Choices

1. Pollan's title is an indicator that he understands it can be hard to believe our personal actions can have an effect on the environment. Throughout the essay, he addresses this skepticism in various ways. Mark the places where you see him addressing skeptical readers and evaluate how effective you find his strategies for inviting readers to see this issue from his perspective.

2. Pollan draws on the ideas of Wendell Berry, a farmer and well-known environmentalist writer, to develop his argument here. Mark the places where he explicitly mentions Berry. How, exactly, do Berry's concepts help Pollan make his own point in this essay?

Writing as a Reader: Entering the Conversation of Ideas

1. Pollan and authors Derrick Jensen and Stephanie McMillan (pp. 677–92) argue that to make an impact on climate change, citizens have to do more than tweak their daily behaviors; they have to change their values and understand their relationship to the world differently. Compose an essay in which you draw on the insights and examples in both texts to make your own argument about the ways we could and should live more healthful lives for ourselves and the planet. Be sure to anticipate and address counterarguments to your proposals. (If change were easy, more of us would do it, after all.)

2. Pollan and other writers in this chapter argue that changing our dietary habits can improve our health and the health of the planet. Compose an essay in which you place Pollan in conversation with either Anna Lappé (pp. 702–14) or McKay Jenkins (pp. 722–31). Use key ideas and examples from the two authors to build an argument about which changes you think are most pressing, given the evidence you have learned in these pieces. What challenges do you see, and how do you suggest addressing them?

McKAY JENKINS

Can GMOs Be Sustainable?

McKay Jenkins is a professor of English and journalism and environmental humanities and is also the author of numerous books about environmental debates intended for the general public. The titles of his recent publications reveal his interests and rhetorical approach: *Food Fight: GMOs and the Future of the American Diet* (2017); *ContamiNation* (2016), about the synthetic chemicals damaging us in our daily lives; and *Poison Spring* (2014), coauthored by E. G. Vallianatos, about the surprising connections between the Environmental Protection Agency and the chemical industry.

In this excerpt from *Food Fight*, Jenkins takes a nuanced approach to the debate about GMOs (genetically modified organisms). What do you know about GMOs, and what is your attitude about them? Pause to consider this before reading the rest of this essay. Jenkins aims to offer examples from the small-scale farm industry that might complicate your perspective, no matter what your initial attitudes.

Jenkins's essay looks in detail at "sweet spot" farmers (described in para. 5) who are making their living at a scale between farmers' market farmers and giant agribusiness. As you read these profiles of farmers, keep track of what surprises you (including, perhaps, their gender). These "enlightened local farmers" (para. 12) aim to balance their use of technology and sustainable farming practices and offer explanations of their decisions about which products and techniques to use. The critiques they level against the romanticization of the "organic" movement (para. 37) and the marketing of companies like Chipotle and Whole Foods might make you rethink what you thought you knew about the word "natural" or the meanings of "sustainable" agribusiness.

The science and business behind the food industry—at any scale—is in part about persuasion and marketing. Jenkins offers us, as consumers, plenty to chew on.

▪ ▪ ▪

No matter where you stand on GMOs, it seems reasonable to ask if   *1*
our food system hasn't somehow become too big to fail. If industrial farming is the real culprit in our national eating disorder, perhaps a solution can be found simply by scaling back. Not in the interest of purity, or in pursuit of utopian visions of food. Not to get rid of GMOs, or even to (completely) rid the world of pesticides. Perhaps it's enough to have food produced on a smaller scale, by farmers who take excellent care of their land.

To get to Jennie Schmidt's farm, you drive east across the Chesapeake   *2*
Bay Bridge, then hook a left and head north through an endless tapestry of some of the most fertile land on the Eastern Seaboard. Her Maryland farm is just beyond a shooting range, out along Sudlersville Cemetery Road. When I arrived on a cold February day, the Schmidts' dog Dozer met me

out front. Jennie apologized for the carpet guys who were replacing the wall-to-wall carpeting that had been covering the floors of their modest home for thirty-seven years.

The Schmidts work 2,000 acres. It's not a huge operation, by Iowa standards, but consider this: Last year the Schmidts produced 12 million pounds of Roma tomatoes, enough to fill twenty tractor trailers every day for two weeks. Over the years, the Schmidts have experimented with sweet corn, sweet peas, and lima beans, but given the risks—the Eastern Shore gets forty-five inches of rain a year, much of it during spring growing season—they have settled on their current mix: Tomatoes and green beans for the vegetable market. Soft red wheat, which they ship to a processor in Pennsylvania to make into crackers and pretzels. Twenty-two acres of grapes for local vineyards.   *3*

And 1,500 acres of soybeans and corn, a good deal of it grown from GM seeds.   *4*

As third-generation farmers, the Schmidts have found a sweet spot between small-scale farms that survive by supplying farmers' markets, and industrial-scale operations that must invest millions into their own harvesting and canning infrastructure. Jennie Schmidt calls her farm a "supermarket farm," but not because most of her crops go into the vegetable aisle. They don't. She and her husband, Hans, grow for canneries, which turn their tomatoes into "value added" products like salsa and tomato sauce. Tomatoes harvested at her farm in August are trucked to Pennsylvania and are in jars or cans less than forty-eight hours after they are picked.   *5*

Sitting as it does in the middle of the Eastern Shore—a lobe of beautifully fertile land stretching from near Wilmington, Delaware, all the way to the bridge to Virginia Beach—the Schmidt farm has had to adapt to the industrial agriculture that has grown up alongside it. Long considered to have some of the most productive soil on the Atlantic coast, the Eastern Shore is also situated near some of the biggest food markets in the world.   *6*

"I'm not a 'farmers' market farmer,'" Jennie Schmidt told me. "If I took 12 million pounds of tomatoes to a farmers' market, we'd flood the market. It wouldn't work. We get better income from vegetables than from grain production. But we have the markets for diverse crops. Where in Iowa are they going to sell cannery-grade tomatoes? A hundred miles from a farm in Iowa, you're still in the middle of nowhere. Here, in less than a hundred miles, we can be in Washington, D.C., Baltimore, or Philadelphia. We can be in New York City in three hours. Without the cannery and trucking infrastructure, we wouldn't even be in vegetables."   *7*

The Schmidts' farm, while not enormous, still sits at the very center of the industrial food system, and not just because of their tomatoes and the trucking infrastructure. Their corn and soybeans go straight into the maw of giant agribusinesses, overseen and orchestrated by some of the largest and most influential companies in the world. The Schmidts' GM seeds are engineered by companies like DuPont Pioneer, and they use chemical herbicides (like glyphosate) first designed by companies like Monsanto.   *8*

And their harvested beans are sold to companies like Perdue, which, in addition to being one of the world's largest chicken producers, is also one of the country's largest grain companies. It has to be: the company has to feed most of the 569 million chickens that grow on the Eastern Shore alone.

But the Schmidts also win awards for environmental stewardship. [9] They practice a wide range of soil conservation techniques that would please even the crankiest environmentalist. Rather than strip their fields bare after a harvest, they leave withered plants to serve as "green manure." They rotate crops. They use integrated pest management. Because they spray their weeds, the Schmidts don't have to till their soil, which means they can reduce their carbon footprint—both by driving their tractor less and by leaving carbon in the soil, where it belongs. They plant cover crops, which both hold their soil in place for future crops and prevent erosion. This prevents both soil and the nutrient phosphorous that attaches to it from running off into the Chesapeake Bay. To avoid StarLink-style contamination of their soybeans, they flush out their combines and grain elevators whenever they harvest to make sure none of the GM beans intended for the chicken feed market get into the seeds grown for the tofu market.

"The truth is, you will never get to zero," Jennie said. "You can't get rid [10] of every soybean in your combine. But there are those of us who take the time to meet that level of due diligence. Our tofu beans don't get labeled by the Non-GMO Project, but they get tested, and they are non-GMO. If they find half of 1 percent, they get sold on the Perdue market. If we can't verify that they are non-GMO, they don't get sold that way. Most people don't think we pay that level of attention. They think we're just blowing smoke, which is sad."

Given this level of scrupulous attention to soil health, conservation, [11] and best weed- and pest-control practices, the Schmidts' farm has been certified by the state for its "agricultural stewardship," meaning it has met high standards for preserving soil and water quality.

The Schmidt farm—industrial but local, pro-GMO but pro-sustain- [12] ability—offers a glimpse at a kind of middle way farming that employs technology at a scale that minimizes many of the ills associated with corporate agriculture. Their approach doesn't answer all questions, like whether we really need to be raising 569 million chickens on some of Maryland's best farmland, or whether we need to be eating so many chicken nuggets in the first place. But until we tackle those larger questions, farms like the Schmidts' suggest that the secret to better food production may lie not with enlightened global agribusinesses, but with enlightened local farmers.

Providing the Crops That Industry Demands

Jennie Schmidt received her bachelor's degree in nutrition and food sci- [13] ence, with a minor in international agriculture. She spent a couple of years with 4-H, teaching agricultural techniques to schools in Botswana. She later returned to graduate school for a master's degree in human nutrition; her thesis looked at food and biotechnology just as the GMO industry was finding its legs. Today, she is the only woman on the board of the Maryland Grain Producers Utilization Board, and now the first female president of the U.S. Wheat Foods Council. She is also past president of the Maryland Grape Growers Association and past chair of the Maryland Farm Bureau's Specialty Crop Committee.

Now that her husband, Hans, has been appointed Maryland's assis- *14* tant secretary of agriculture, Jennie relies more than ever on help from her in-laws and her brother-in-law. Still, Jennie herself has to do a lot more than just manage the family's twenty-two-acre vineyard, oversee the farm's crew, and keep the books. She also maintains a blog, *The Foodie Farmer*, on which she spends a lot of time trying to disabuse people of their fears over GMOs. Given the intensity (and in Jennie's opinion, the ignorance) of opinions on the topic, Jennie got into the GMO debate reluctantly. "I just started writing about biotech this last year," Jennie told me. "I didn't want to bring that into my home. When you criticize a farmer for what they do or don't do, you're criticizing their home. In the blogosphere, it gets very personal."

The Schmidts' neighbors, who run a 350-acre farm across the way, sell *15* their vegetables to local supermarket chains like Giant and Whole Foods. They run a farm stand. When people think about "local farmers," it is the Schmidts' neighbors they have in their heads, not the Schmidts. This is a source of constant irritation.

"On Facebook, whenever a friend says, 'Support your local farmer,' *16* I always chime in and say, 'You know, if you buy canned tomato products, I was one of the significant growers,'" Schmidt said. "That's the disconnect— our faces are not on those products. People don't know who we are."

This "disconnect" between consumers and farmers lies at the very *17* root of the GMO debate, Jennie Schmidt says. Forget about gene sequenc- ing—plenty of people don't even understand that potatoes and carrots come out of the ground.

Jennie's father-in-law, who still lives across the road, started farming *18* in the 1930s, about ten years after the introduction of hybrid corn, which dramatically boosted the yields growers could get from their fields. Eighty years later, GMOs offer Schmidt Farms a similar boost. Using Bt corn, the Schmidts now get 221 bushels of corn per acre—more than 35 bushels (and $100) per acre more than they get for non-GM corn. It would be hard to persuade a farmer to give up such advantages, and indeed, it is this margin—more corn grown on the same acreage—that has made farmers enthusiastic about GMOs since they were first introduced thirty years ago.

In recent years, the Schmidts have started planting a new GM soy- *19* bean engineered by DuPont Pioneer called the Plenish. In addition to being good chicken feed, the Plenish beans, when processed for their oil, create a second market, for fast-food frying oil. Oil made from Plenish soybeans has zero grams of trans fat and 20 percent less saturated fat than hydrogenated vegetable oil, and is high in oleic acid. The oil is also "shelf stable," and so is especially useful in the creation of processed foods that sometimes sit on store shelves for weeks or months. Perdue can use the soybeans to feed its chickens and then process the soybean oil to sell to the fast-food industry, which sees GM soybean oil as the future of fried food.

"High oleic soy can help reduce lots of health problems, because if you don't have high oleic oil, what you need to do is hydrogenate the oil to be suitable for frying and other cooking, and when you hydrogenate oils you end up with something that's conducive to cardiovascular disease," Paul Anderson from the Danforth Center told me. "High oleic doesn't have the instability that requires hydrogenation. It's very beneficial." 20

The Plenish beans have clearly been a boon for the Schmidts: they clear $263 per acre for these beans, compared with $124 for feed beans and just $62 for the beans they grow for direct human consumption, like the tofu market. 21

In other words, GM seeds are good for the Schmidts. And because the grains they grow help form a significant block in the foundation of the country's industrial food system, from its chicken nuggets to its french fries, the GM seeds are also good for the many food industries that use them. With GM products like the Plenish bean, fast food and processed food will be a bit less unhealthy. To those overseeing this industrial food system, this is a good thing. 22

"We've had folks ask us, 'Why didn't the industry get started with a biotech product like this?'" Russ Sanders, the director of food and industry markets for Pioneer, has said. "We think it's a great opportunity to help illustrate the positive aspects of biotech that go beyond farmer benefits." 23

Clearly, the companies that both provide the seeds and buy the beans from the Schmidts think the system is working. In the fall of 2014, DuPont Pioneer and Perdue AgriBusiness announced that Perdue would more than double—to about 50,000—the acreage contracted to Eastern Shore and Pennsylvania farmers for growing Plenish beans "with the intention of marketing the high oleic soybean oil by the food industry in 2015." Nationwide, the United Soybean Board has set a goal of 18 million acres of high-oleic soybeans by 2023, which would make the beans the fourth largest crop in the United States, behind corn, conventional soybeans, and wheat. 24

The move to expand Plenish beans in the Mid-Atlantic was hailed as "an important milestone for Pioneer in its efforts to bring product innovation to the food industry and complements solutions offered by DuPont Nutrition & Health to address the world's challenges in food." 25

"We're always looking for ways to bring new market opportunities to our grower customers," a Perdue AgriBusiness vice president said. "By working with DuPont Pioneer on the production of Plenish high oleic soybeans on the Eastern Shore, we're hoping to generate additional profit opportunities and long-term industry growth. 26

So here we are again: GMOs have always been pitched as "good" for 27 farmers, and for farmers like the Schmidts, this is plainly true. They are also clearly good for the companies that make them. But are the foods these grains produce good for the rest of us? Processed foods fried in high-oleic-acid soybeans, after all, are still processed fried foods. Beyond this, are tens (or hundreds) of thousands of acres planted with these new seeds good for the environment?

Jennie Schmidt can't control the first question, but she can control the 28 second. She has no interest in telling people what they should or should not eat. If the market demands Roma tomatoes, she will grow them. If the market demands high-oleic-acid soybeans, she will grow them. And she will do it in as sustainable a way as she can. And to her mind, GMOs help with this.

Jennie and Hans first started using GM seeds in 1998, and like many 29 GM farmers, they maintain that the crops—which are designed to withstand the herbicide glyphosate—have allowed them to dramatically reduce their use of harsher pesticides, like atrazine. "We've been farming with GMOs for seventeen years and have seen a real benefit," Jennie told me. "A real reduction in the volume of pesticides for Roundup Ready crops. Using Bt corn has also eliminated a lot of insecticide use. We're using softer chemicals and using less of them."

The Schmidts consider their farm synergistic, in that it uses techniques 30 from all three forms of agriculture: organic, conventional, and biotech. Because they plant GM crops and use synthetic pesticides, the Schmidts farm cannot be certified as "organic." The Schmidts still use some atrazine on their corn, to suppress weeds, and—given the forty-five inches of rain that falls during the growing season—they have to spray their vegetables with fungicides "just to deal with mold," Jennie said.

"There is no 'one' system that is 'best,'" Jennie wrote. "There is no 'one' 31 way of doing things that should be done carte blanche by every farmer, everywhere. There is no 'cookie-cutter' system that should be applied to every farm. What we farmers should be doing is maximizing the synergies of all best management practices that meld together the best for our soils while preserving our inputs and natural resources."

Jennie Schmidt speaks with honesty and precision about all parts of 32 the growing process on *The Foodie Farmer*. She explains the difference between spraying and dousing, noting (right down to the ounces per acre) exactly what kind and how much fungicide she and Hans apply to their fields. In one post, she showed her readers a photograph of a paper towel she laid down alongside a row of grapevines just before she drove by with her tractor-mounted sprayer. After passing over the towel with the sprayer, she snapped another photo. The towel is speckled, but far from drenched.

"Because this is spraying and not dousing, I do not need to soak the 33 paper towel," she wrote. "The plants do not get 'doused.' The is no dripping off of chemical solution. They do not need to be soaked in herbicide to achieve good weed control. There is no saturation. There is no dousing."

This is precisely the kind of transparency that activists tried (in vain) to ³⁴ wring from the big companies on Kauai and Maui. The gamble for farmers like the Schmidts is that consumers will be willing to buy produce grown with chemicals—or with GMOs—as long as they trust that their farmer is both skilled and forthcoming about the work that goes into growing their food. For the Schmidts, this approach clearly seems to be working.

Besides, Jennie told me, it's not like the "natural" pesticides used by ³⁵ organic farmers are benign. The Schmidts have had as many as 100 acres of certified organic fields in the past, and even then (and even today) they still used "organic" fungicides like sulfur and copper sulfate that are, in the strictest sense, toxic.

"The copper and sulfur we use on our grapes are 'natural,' but they ³⁶ are still very toxic," Jennie told me, noting that nicotine, which tobacco plants generate to protect themselves from insects, is also a "natural" pesticide. "If 'natural' were safe, then smoking would be good for us," she said. "I would love a GMO grape. Sulfur is not a fun product to work with."

Especially for a farmer who has experience working organically, ³⁷ Schmidt has very little patience for the way some companies market the "organic movement." She now considers the label "organic" to be little more than a cynical marketing ploy that ends up making food more expensive than it needs to be and—worse—pits one kind of farmer against another.

Take Chipotle. In 2015, the fast-food burrito franchise received both ³⁸ praise and rebukes for announcing that it would provide GMO-free ingredients in its many restaurants. This was initially hailed as a victory by anti-GMO forces, until they learned that Chipotle would continue to sell both soda (made with GM corn syrup) and meat (raised on GM corn and soybeans). Pro-GM farmers and scientists were equally appalled, but for far different reasons.

Chipotle's campaign creates "a disservice to American farmers," the ³⁹ Danforth Center's Jim Carrington told me. "It creates the impression that there's evil farming and happy idyllic farming, and they source their meat from happy farms. That's simply marketing. Science has shown that the feelings they are marketing are not grounded in reality.

"In general, people who have not come from a farm have notions of ⁴⁰ farming and agriculture that are romantic," Carrington said. "The wholesome farm with happy cows and all that. But the organic industry is a very advanced and well-organized industry that has grown in part by having a villain, and the villain is conventional agriculture. Organic claims to be much better than conventional and commands a price premium. It's a very lucrative premium and is in part defended by marketing campaigns, blogging campaigns, websites, and many other ways with the intent of seeing the organic industry increase in size. There is money to be made."

Indeed, like virtually every farmer I spoke with—organic, conven- ⁴¹ tional, or GMO—Jennie Schmidt practically spat when I asked her about the marketing campaigns that tout a food company's "values." She laughed bitterly when I asked her about the posters in Whole Foods that inevitably portray farmers as beautifully tanned models with a bunch of carrots in one hand and a smiling baby in the other.

"When Whole Foods or Chipotle runs these ad campaigns saying they *42* only use food from 'farmers with values,' it's just like, 'Really? You have to throw everybody under the bus to further your own marketing campaign?'" Schmidt told me. "Painting everyone as bad except for the people they do business with? That's really frustrating. That's led a number of us to become more vocal and more transparent. We have to say, 'That's not true for me.'" . . .

Organic? Sustainable? Or Regenerative?

. . . Bryan Snyder [is] head of the Pennsylvania Association for Sustain- *43* able Agriculture and one of the country's leading voices for farming done with the health of the planet in mind. Snyder wonders whether produce grown by farmers like Jennie Schmidt . . . might be given its own label: not "GMO" or "organic," but "sustainable." Marking food as "sustainable" would reward farmers for preserving topsoil, for example, or building soil quality through the use of nitrogen fixers, cover crops, or composting—even if they used GM seeds.

"People accept that 'organic' is never going to include GMO, but the *44* question is whether the term 'sustainable' can include GMO," Snyder said. "The problem is, none of these things are simple. Compared to 'organic,' 'sustainable' offers a bigger tent that includes more than organic produce. No-till agriculture would qualify, and no-till farmers mostly use GMO seeds. We might have to consider a world with GMOs, to save soil and build soil quality. Instead of labeling foods with a skull and crossbones, they'd rather have a 'sustainable' label that is a positive thing, even though it may have GMOs in it. That idea is not completely without merit."

GMOs themselves will never cause a fraction of the problems caused *45* by the industrial food system itself. "We are going to waste a lot of time and energy on whether GMOs are helpful or harmful to people, when that's not the most important question," Snyder said. "The most important question is what kind of *system* do they generate and support? The most effective criticisms of GMOs are about the peripheral realities of this system. It used to be that farmers always retained a percentage of their crop for seeds for the next year. They did this for thousands of years. Now, in the last couple of decades, almost none do that."

These ideas also sit nicely with Blake Meyers, the University of Dela- *46* ware geneticist, who thinks GMOs may one day be a key component in sustainable agriculture. "I buy and eat organic food, and I don't like chemical residue on my food," Meyers told me. "So the question is, why should you not have organically grown GM crops? So far the USDA has said you can't have GMOs and label them organic, but I would prefer to get rid of all the chemistry and confer the desirable traits with genetics. Petroleum won't be with us forever. I'm perfectly okay with transgenics: imagine if we could create a wonder crop that requires genetic modification but is grown organically, free of chemical inputs, and resists drought, resists pests, and outcompetes weeds. I'd be okay with that."

Some of the critics of GMOs "are the same people who spray copper   47
or sulfur on their plants and say it's okay because it's 'organic,'" Meyers said. "They apply Bt to their crops, but God forbid you take the same genes they're eating in the bacteria and insert them into the plant. Ultimately, our agriculture has got to be sustainable, or we're not going to be here long term. GM will be a large part of that. Fifty years from now, we'll see that spraying anything on plants created a huge amount of waste and pollution. We'll see that 90 percent of the chemicals washed off, ending up in our soil and water. If you eliminate that waste, if you can use GMOs to replace these inputs, achieving similar yields, without all the chemical inputs, you've done a world of good."

There are legitimate worries, of course, that a comparatively loose term   48
like "sustainable" could be distorted and abused—"greenwashed"—by industrial farms in ways that a strict, legally precise term like "organic" cannot. The word "sustainable" has been "overused, misused, and it has been shamelessly co-opted by corporations for the purpose of greenwashing," write veteran food activists André Leu and Ronnie Cummins. Indeed, they note, the word is featured prominently on Monsanto's website, where the company boasts of a "commitment to sustainable agriculture—pledging to produce more, conserve more, and improve farmers' lives by 2030."

"Industrial agriculture today, with its factory farms, waste lagoons, anti-   49
biotics and growth hormones, GMOs, toxic pesticides and prolific use of synthetic fertilizers, doesn't come close to 'not using up or destroying natural resources,'" Leu and Cummins write. Instead of "sustainable," they would like to see foods affixed with one of two labels: "degenerative" or "regenerative." Consumers could then choose food produced by chemical-intensive, monoculture-based industrial systems that "destabilize the climate, and degrade soil, water, biodiversity, health and local economies," Leu and Cummins write. Or they could choose food produced using organic regenerative practices that rejuvenate the soil, grasslands, and forests; replenish water; promote food sovereignty; and restore public health and prosperity—"all while cooling the planet by drawing down billions of tons of excess carbon from the atmosphere and storing it in the soil where it belongs."

Such rhetoric—powerful, convincing, and justifiable as it may be—is   50
plainly directed at giant corporate farms, and the global food companies they serve. The question for midsize farmers like Jennie Schmidt . . . is: Can they operate inside this system in a way that is more benign? And can GMOs be a part of this? As with everything else in the American food system, there are no simple solutions: as enlightened as [farmers like] Jennie Schmidt . . . may be, they are still plugged into a larger food system that uses enormous amounts of chemicals on vast swaths of land to create huge quantities of unhealthy food. But it's a start.

To Jennie Schmidt, this global food system—with all its downsides— *51*
will continue to evolve because people will continue to enjoy foods they
can't grow themselves.

"I'm not going to give up coffee or chocolate," she told me. "I love the *52*
fact that we have so many food choices. Yes, there are downsides, but
there are lots of upsides to it too. I like the fact that in February I can go to
Millington, Maryland—two miles away is the closest grocery store—and
get fresh produce. Think about what we'd have to do to grow that produce
around here, in winter, in hoop houses, and at what cost? When you have
to use so much propane to heat the hoop house, that can be more energy-
intensive than getting it from Mexico.

"My concern with people's resistance to the technology of GMOs is that *53*
the next generation of products, and the next round of benefits for folks
in developing countries—for traits they need to resist certain diseases or
yield—don't come about because they are not *allowed* to, because there has
been so much pushback," Schmidt said. "All of plant breeding, whether
it's traditional or GMO, has benefits, and my concern is that science will
be stifled because there has been so much resistance to it. Think of what
we could do if we could get rid of food allergies from soy or peanuts. If you
could silence the protein that causes peanut allergies, that would be a big
deal. I'm afraid we're going to throw the baby out with the bathwater."

■ ■ ■

Reading as a Writer: Analyzing Rhetorical Choices

1. Spend some time researching and learning about GMOs and the range of
   perspectives in this debate. What is at stake and for whom? Where do you
   stand? Discuss your findings and perspectives with your classmates.

2. How do the farmers featured in Jenkins's essay explain their reasoning for
   choosing the products and techniques they use? Refer to ideas in Chapters 4
   and 9 on argumentation and persuasion as you analyze their claims and
   evidence. What significance do you see in your findings?

Writing as a Reader: Entering the Conversation of Ideas

1. Jenkins offers a perspective on the food industry that is different from that
   presented by Michael Pollan (pp. 715–21) and Anna Lappé (pp. 702–14).
   Place these authors in conversation, and consider how each of them contributes to an understanding of aspects of the food system. Compose an
   essay that brings these insights together to make an argument about what
   you, as a consumer, believe other consumers should know about our food
   system and why.

2. The farmers in Jenkins's essay critique the marketing of Chipotle and
   Whole Foods (paras. 38–42). Do some research about these businesses,
   and consider them in light of Naomi Klein's argument about the power of
   branding (pp. 768–80 in Economics). Write an essay that draws on your
   research and these authors' ideas to advance your own perspective on the
   significance of transparency, branding, and consumers' rights.

CAROLYN MERCHANT

Eden Commodified

Carolyn Merchant is a professor of environmental history, philosophy, and ethics in the Department of Conservation and Resource Studies at the University of California, Berkeley. She has published widely and won many awards for her work on the interrelationships between these areas of study in her pursuit to explain better the long-term effects of human behaviors on the environment. This reading comes from her book *Reinventing Eden: The Fate of Nature in Western Culture* (2003, republished in 2013).

Merchant opens with a detailed description of a contemporary mall as a kind of Garden of Eden, with "pleasures and temptations" that will be familiar to anyone who has wandered through a shopping mall with indoor gardens, fountains, and enticingly arrayed treats to purchase and consume. By paragraph 4, though, her argument begins to emerge more fully: "Malls are designed to be morally uplifting places. Sanitized surroundings, central surveillance systems, noise restrictions, and strict behavioral rules regulate the undesirable, homeless, and criminal elements of society, while socializing both young and old into the acceptable consumer culture of the new twenty-first century." You might pause to discuss what she might mean by this list even before you read the whole essay. What examples from your own experience might illustrate—or challenge—this depiction of a typical mall?

Merchant moves from her rich descriptions of the "malling" of the United States (and the world) to her analysis of biotechnology. How, exactly, does she make this somewhat unexpected connection? Consider what you already know about GMOs (genetically modified organisms), and weigh the examples that Merchant offers here. Which do you find surprising?

Throughout this piece, Merchant weaves together our fascination with the idea of an Edenic nature with our consumerist desires for convenience and "perfection." As she moves back and forth between these two aspects of her argument, consider additionally what this changing technology might mean for workers in these industries and for you as a consumer (both as a purchaser of products and as someone who literally eats the fruits of biotechnology). Merchant's endnotes (especially note 17) help us think about costs of our desires that are not always apparent when we head out, optimistically, to shop.

■   ■   ■

Cora had been in the mall since early morning. Donning her pink jogging suit, she joined twelve other seniors who set out each day to circle the inner mall. As she passed each shop she gazed longingly at the orlon dresses, silk Parisian scarves, blue-steel tennis rackets, DVDs, television sets, cafe lattés, and orange smoothies. Her limited retirement budget prevented her from purchasing more than one little "luxury" a month, but she reveled in her daydreams. After her aerobic fitness exercises ended, she finished her bagel and coffee in the garden café and wandered through the big department stores checking for new fall styles and jotting down ideas for Christmas. How lucky I am, she thought. This beautiful world, right across the street from my house, is an Eden on Earth.

—CAROLYN MERCHANT, 1998

The modern version of the Garden of Eden is the enclosed shopping mall. Surrounded by a desert of parking lots, malls comprise gardens of shops covered by glass domes, accessed by spiral staircases and escalators reaching upward toward heaven. Today's malls feature life-sized trees, trellises decorated with flowers, stone grottoes, birds, animals, and even indoor beaches that simulate nature as a cultivated, benign garden. The "river that went out of the Eden to water the garden" is reclaimed in meandering tree-lined streams and ponds filled with bright orange goldfish. The commodified Eden is the Recovery Narrative's epitome in the modern world.

This garden in the city re-creates the pleasures and temptations of the original Eden, where people can peacefully harvest the fruits of earth with gold grown by the market. Within manicured spaces of trees, flowers, and fountains, we can shop for nature at the Nature Company, purchase "natural" clothing at Esprit, sample organic foods and "rainforest crunch" in kitchen gardens, buy twenty-first-century products at The Sharper Image, and play virtual reality games in which SimEve is reinvented in cyberspace. The spaces and commodities of the shopping mall epitomize consumer capitalism's vision of Recovery from the Fall of Adam and Eve.[1]

Consumer's Nature

Canada's West Edmonton Mall, the first of a generation of megamalls, is eight city blocks long by four blocks wide and covers 5.2 million square feet. It sports an indoor surfing beach with adjustable wave heights, an amusement park, an ice-skating rink, a twenty-screen movie theater, and eight hundred stores. Cul-de-sacs within the mall replicate New Orleans's Bourbon Street and Paris's boulevards. It has a 360-room hotel, with theme rooms inspired by places such as Polynesia, Hollywood, and Victorian England, along with rooms based on transportation forms such as sports cars, pickup trucks, and horse-drawn carriages. People from around the world celebrate honeymoons, anniversaries, and birthdays in the hotel, while those with recreational vehicles may spend an entire summer camped in the parking lot to maximize shopping access.[2]

Malls are places of light, hope, and promise—transitions to new worlds. People are reinvented and redeemed by the mall. Said one ecstatic visitor, "I *am* the mall. . . . This place is heaven." In the film *Dawn of the Dead*, the apocalypse has come and the survivors have gathered in a shopping mall as the best place to make their last stand. Malls are designed to be morally uplifting places. Sanitized surroundings, central surveillance systems, noise restrictions, and strict behavioral rules regulate the undesirable, homeless, and criminal elements of society, while socializing both young and old into the acceptable consumer culture of the new twenty-first century. Like the enclosed gardens of the Middle Ages, they are redemptive places of ecstasy. Like the eighteenth-century gardens of the nobility, they are displays of power, surprise, and desire. Like the public parks of the nineteenth century, they uplift, temper, and socialize the masses.[3]

Malls have replaced orange groves, cornfields, and pine forests. Arti- 5 ficial nature has redeemed natural nature. Nature is captured in the West Edmonton Mall in a palm-lined beach, an artificial lagoon, an underwater seascape, performing dolphins, caged birds, and tame Siberian tigers. Sunlit gardens, tree-lined paths, meandering streams, and tropical flowers adorn courtyard restaurants. Nature in the mall is a dense text to be read by the visitors. It exemplifies not only human control over nonhuman nature, but the reinvention of nature itself as Edenic space. It portrays original innocence and delight in nature, calming the consumer as she contemplates elements for purchase and duplication in the home. Just as the mall keeps out the socially undesirable, it rejects the naturally undesirable—weeds, pests, and garbage.[4]

Outside of Minneapolis is the Mall of America, which aspires to the 6 iconic and totemic status of the Grand Canyon, and in which four hundred trees are planted in interior gardens. At the mall's center is Knott's Camp Snoopy, a seven-acre theme park that "brings the outdoors indoors." "Inspired by Minnesota's natural habitat—forests, meadows, river banks, and marshes," it feels, smells, and sounds like a perpetual summer of 70-degree temperatures in the Minnesota woods. But those alien year-around temperatures forced Camp Snoopy to substitute 256 tons of non-Minnesota figs, azaleas, oleanders, jasmine, hibiscus, and olive trees from the tropics. Although marketers for Camp Snoopy assert that the park's mealy bugs, aphids, and spider mites are controlled through the use of integrated pest management methods (such as lady beetles), the staff actually spend nights spraying with pesticides to minimize insect damage.[5]

The Mall of America declares itself "the most environmentally con- 7 scious shopping center in the industry," and claims to recycle up to 80 percent of its refuse, as a "dedication to Mother Earth." Yet Rich Doering of Browning-Ferris Industries, the contractor responsible for dealing with the 700 tons of garbage produced at the mall each month, says that only about one-third of the stores' waste is actually recycled and very little of the shoppers' trash: "The venture is unprofitable to Browning-Ferris, which would find it far cheaper to recycle the mall's refuse somewhere other than in its basement."[6]

Mall culture has diversified to take advantage of changing economic *8* times and consumer habits. The malling of America has become the malling of the world, reconstituting the Shakespearean dictum as, "All the world's a mall and all the men and women merely shoppers." Streets are blocked off to become pedestrian malls. Lifestyle malls target achievers, emulators, and belongers, while class-conscious malls focus on lower income and ethnic consumers. Specialty malls cater to New Age, new chic, and cool commodity shoppers. Boutiques, antiques, museum shops, art galleries, cultural centers, history theme parks, Renaissance fairs, piazzas, and discount malls are featured in a profusion of difference within unity. Even "hip teens" for whom malls are "totally uncool" reinvent the East Village streets of New York City, Goodwill, and Salvation Army stores, and warehouse "labs" as "anti-mall Meccas." Malls, they claim, are all look-alikes, are not teen savvy, are designed for parents and kids, and have too many suffocating antinoise, antismoking, and anti-skateboarding rules.[7]

As a way of life, consumer culture reclaims pleasure, innocence, tran- *9* quility, youth, and even nature itself as a garden. It replicates "the most enchanting dream which has ever consoled mankind, the myth of a Golden Age in which man lived on the fruits of the earth, peacefully, piously, and with primitive simplicity." As Joseph Addison put it in the eighteenth century, "I look upon the pleasure which we take in a Garden, as one of the most innocent Delights in Human . . . Life. A Garden was the Habitation of our first Parents before the Fall. . . . [The] satisfaction which a Man takes in these Works of Nature, [is] a laudable, if not a virtuous Habit of Mind."

Biotechnology

Just as the mall re-creates the Garden of Eden, biotechnology re-creates *10* the tree of life at the center of the garden. While mechanistic science deciphered the book of nature, biotechnology decodes the book of life. It "improves" on nature's heritage, correcting "her" mistakes by removing genetic flaws, cloning genetically perfect organisms, and banking designer genes for future human brains and bodies. From genetically engineered apples to "Flavr-Savr" tomatoes, the fruits of the original, evolved garden are being redesigned so that the salinated, irrigated desert can continue to blossom as the rose. In the recovered Garden of Eden, fruits will ripen faster, have fewer seeds, need less water, require fewer pesticides, contain less saturated fat, and have longer shelf lives. The human temptation to engineer nature is reaching too close to the powers of God warn the Jeremiahs. Still, the progressive engineers who design the technologies that allow the Recovery of Eden to accelerate see only hope in the new fabrications.[8]

Biotechnology, the Recovery Narrative's newest chapter, illustrates the *11* reading of nature's bible in sentences, books, and libraries comprising genetic sequences. Information encoded in the DNA of each species can be manipulated to create new books in the library of nature.[9] It assumes:

- DNA is composed of the four bases adenine, thymine, cytosine, and guanine that are the molecular "letters" that form the words needed to create the many hundred-word sentences that comprise the gene—the "universal building block of life."

- Genes are discrete bits of information assembled into "books" of chromosomal messages, "libraries" of bacterial clones, and databanks to be edited, revised, and reorganized.

- Because the gene is the fundamental building block of life, a gene will maintain its identity through change when inserted into the matter of another species and yet continue to function as it did in the original.

- Individual genes can be studied and analyzed in models before being assembled into new combinations.

- Genetically engineered organisms can be introduced into new environmental contexts with little or no risk since the laboratory and the fields are one and continuous.

In the "garden of unearthly delights," genetically engineered food is created by taking genes from one life form and implanting them in another. The process ensures "summertime tastes" year around with "vine-ripened" flavors. Companies such as Calgene, Monsanto, Upjohn, Pioneer, and DeKalb are pioneering efforts to improve the genes of cantaloupes and squash to resist viruses, corn that requires fewer herbicides, potatoes with higher starch content, bell peppers that stay fresh longer, and rice with higher protein value. Calgene's tomatoes have a gene that reverses the action of the enzyme that causes decay, eliminating the need to pick green tomatoes for shipment followed by rapid ripening—degreening—with ethylene gas.[10]

Calgene's "MacGregor" tomato (so named for its warm Farmer   12 MacGregor and Peter Rabbit feeling) was engineered by inserting a copy of the "rotting" gene backwards, allowing the tomato to stay in the field a few days longer and be picked pink, or vine-ripe, rather than green. The process of implanting this "antisense" gene was patented, so that in the future the company could collect royalties, not only on bioengineered tomatoes, but on any other crop altered by the same technique. The vertically integrated company controlled the entire process, from planting to processing and distributing the tomatoes. The bioengineered tomato, approved by the U.S. Food and Drug Administration (FDA) in early 1994, was the first step toward realizing huge profits on the new DNA technology. Unfortunately for investors, the Farmer MacGregor lacked the taste of a garden ripened tomato and Calgene lost value in the marketplace.[11]

Farmers prepare fields for engineered tomatoes by covering them with   13 black plastic to prevent weed growth and soil erosion. Computer-regulated, plastic drip-irrigation pipes ensure that correct amounts of water at proper times are released to the seedlings. The tomatoes are grown using techniques of sustainable agriculture. Correct amounts of nitrogen are applied to the fields and deep drainage ditches collect the runoff to prevent it from damaging the surrounding environment. Cover crops and fallowing improve soil quality and integrated pest management (IPM) techniques control pests through the use of beneficial insects and minimal pesticides. In the packing house the tomatoes are labeled with a brand-name sticker and boxed stem-side up so the customer will see the fruit in its prime, reminding her or him of its Edenic summer freshness and taste.[12]

14 Corn is another crop that biotechnology companies such as Monsanto are engineering as new marketplace commodities. Genetically modified varieties can be made resistant to pests, salinization, and drought. A problem arises, however, over the question of genetic pollution—a potential clash between genes versus ecosystems and genetics versus ecology. In some cases, engineered genes (transgenes) may cross over into other corn plants, via pollen from the modified plant that mixes with unmodified plants, thus "contaminating" them with engineered genes. In this way the evolutionary diversity of corn in its center of origin (Mexico) might become polluted with new genetically engineered varieties not heretofore found in nature. Such a situation apparently has occurred in Mexico and could be of concern for other crop cradles (such as rice, barley, wheat, potatoes, and so on) which have been sources of diversity for plant breeders responding to catastrophic diseases (such as the Irish potato blight). In the case of "polluted plants," the transgenes do not decline over time, but instead replicate their genetic information repeatedly.[13]

15 In the reinvented Eden, animals too would be modified for greater productivity, increasing their share in the commodities markets. Dairy cows produce more milk with less fat when cows are injected with a bovine growth hormone, such as Posilac, marketed by Monsanto Chemicals after FDA approval in November 1993. More milk per cow means more profit for the dairy farmer and for Monsanto. Monsanto's promotional video tells farmers that "Posilac is the single most tested product in history . . . You'll want to inject Posilac in every eligible cow, as every cow not treated is a lost income opportunity." Observes critic Robin Mather, "There are dozens of cows in every [video] segment, but no one ever touches them—except to inject them. Cows are shown eating in long rows stretching to the camera's horizon; cows are shown in milking parlors. . . . There are cows in barns, but not cows in pastures. That's not how cows are 'managed' these days."[14]

16 Chickens are harder to engineer than cattle or fruit crops because the embryo is encased in the hard eggshell. Nevertheless bioengineers work toward genetically engineered chickens that will resist influenza and salmonella, while also attempting to breed docile chickens that will show less aggressiveness in the close quarters of today's vast poultry houses. Scientists aim to manipulate chicken DNA so that the birds produce more lean white meat, less dark meat, and less fat. If a poultry company could patent its new chicken, it could own it as well as the eggs it produces.[15]

While bioengineered domesticated animals may be controlled to *17* some degree, transgenic wild animals are not so easily managed. Transgenic salmon are created by introducing genes from ocean pout fish that promote growth in the salmon. Such "Frankenfish" seem to biotechnologists to be the answer to feeding growing populations with healthy food, without depleting ocean supplies. Environmentalists, on the other hand, fear that transgenic fish might escape their ocean breeding pens, mate with wild fish and contaminate the wild salmon gene pool. In fact, one study showed that not only did wild salmon prefer to mate with transgenic fish, but that the offspring died young, raising fears that the wild fish would die out.[16]

Biotechnology contributes the science and technology needed for *18* consumer capitalism's vision of Recovery from the Fall. Not only does bioengineering reinvent the products of fallen nature to make them more perfect, it redeems human labor by introducing new labor-saving technologies. Tomato planting is done by automatic drill and picking by the tomato harvester; dairy cows are milked by automatic carousel milkers; chickens are stunned by electric shock, killed by a spinning blade, plucked by "rubber fingers," and mechanically eviscerated. Now computer-driven robots are being designed to pick apples from the trees, saving Eve the task of reaching for the fruit, but not of tasting it.[17]

NOTES

1. Richard Keller Simon, "The Formal Garden in the Age of Consumer Culture: A Reading of the Twentieth-Century Shopping Mall," in *Mapping American Culture*, ed. Wayne Franklin and Michael Steiner (Iowa City. University of Iowa Press, 1992), 124–25, 231–50.
2. Margaret Crawford, "The World in a Shopping Mall," in *Variations on a Theme Park*, ed. Michael Sorkin (New York: Hill and Wang, 1992), 3–30.
3. David Guterson, "Enclosed, Encyclopedic, Endured: One Week at the Mall of America," in *A Forest of Voices: Reading and Writing the Environment*, ed. Chris Anderson and Lex Runciman (Mountain View, Calif.: Mayfield, 1995), 124–36; see esp. 126, 128, quotation on 126; Crawford, "The World in a Shopping Mall," 27; Simon, "The Formal Garden in the Age of Consumer Culture," 244.
4. Crawford, "The World in a Shopping Mall," 7; Simon, "The Formal Garden in the Age of Consumer Culture," 238; Guterson, "Enclosed, Encyclopedic, Endured," 132–34.
5. Guterson, "Enclosed, Encyclopedic, Endured," 133–34.
6. Ibid., 132.
7. Crawford, "The World in a Shopping Mall," 9, 28–30; Bruce Horovitz, "Malls are Like, Totally Uncool, Say Hip Teens," *USA Today*, May 1, 1996, 1–2.
8. Philip Elmer-Dewitt, "Fried Gene Tomatoes," *Time*, May 30, 1994, 54–55.
9. Francesca Lyman, "Are We Redesigning Nature in Our Own Image? An Interview with Jeremy Rifkin," *Environmental Action*, April 1983, 20–25; P. J. Regal, "Models of Genetically Engineered Organisms and their Ecological Impact," in *Ecology of Biological Invasions in North America and Hawaii*, ed. Harold Mooney (New York: Springer-Verlag, 1986); Marc Lappé, *Broken Code: The Exploitation of DNA* (San Francisco, Calif.: Sierra Club Books, 1984); Marc Lappé and Britt Bailey, *Against the Grain: Biotechnology and the Corporate Takeover of Your Food* (Monroe, Maine: Common Courage Press, 1998); Jon Beckwith, *Making Genes, Making Waves* (Cambridge, Mass.: Harvard University Press), 2002.

10. Robin Mather, *A Garden of Unearthly Delights: Bioengineering and the Future of Food* (New York: E. P. Dutton, 1995), 25–49; Elmer-Demitt, "Fried Gene Tomatoes," 54, 55.

11. Mather, *Garden of Unearthly Delights*, 27–30, 42; Herb Greenberg, "Calgene's Biotech Bounty Disappears From Grocers' Shelves," *San Francisco Chronicle*, Jan. 17, 1995, B1, B3.

12. Mather, *Garden of Unearthly Delights*, 31–33, 44–46.

13. Michael Pollan, "Genetic Pollution of Corn in Mexico," *New York Times*, Dec. 9, 2001.

14. Mather, *Garden of Unearthly Delights*, 84–94, quotations on 90, 91–92.

15. Ibid., 121–22.

16. Jane Kay, "Frankenfish Spawning Controversy," *San Francisco Chronicle*, April 29, 2002, A4.

17. Mather, *Garden of Unearthly Delights*, 35, 80, 131–33; Claude Gele, "L'Agriculture manque de robots," *Sciences and Techniques* 26 (1986): 22–29 and cover illustration. Such technology, which delivers perfect fruit, pure milk, and lean meat to the supermarket, masks the labor of the field and processing plant. Much of that labor now comes from Mexico, legally or illegally, via the tomato, chicken, and pork trails. Men and women work on their feet all day grading, packing, and inspecting tomatoes. Men who inject cows, mix feed, and clean milking equipment often labor under bitterly cold or hot, humid conditions. Women who catch and correct chickens missed by the eviscerating machinery work under cold, moist conditions that may cause illnesses leading to job loss. Yet for industry, the problems are offset by the advantages. (Mather, *Garden of Unearthly Delights*, 43–45, 80–82, 132–33.)

■ ■ ■

Reading as a Writer: Analyzing Rhetorical Choices

1. Merchant uses description to do more than depict the places we shop; she uses description to build her point of view. Return to the early paragraphs of her essay in which she describes malls, and mark the passages in which you can hear her argument emerging in her choice of details and in her language. What do you conclude about the effectiveness of using description in the service of argument?

2. Merchant includes plenty of science in her discussion and analysis of biotechnology. What effect does this information have on her overall argument? Consider looking up some recent information about GMOs. What varying perspectives do you find, and from which sources? Share your insights with a partner, small group, or the class.

Writing as a Reader: Entering the Conversation of Ideas

1. McKay Jenkins (pp. 722–31) writes about farmers who share Merchant's concerns about "greenwashing" products, designed to make customers feel environmentally virtuous about commodities that may not actually be good for the earth. How do these writers extend, complement, and perhaps complicate one another's ideas? Write an essay in which you bring together the ideas of these auth ors and your own conclusions about the significance of the trend of "selling nature," given our current environmental problems.

2. Merchant and Ann duCille (pp. 781–96 in Economics) are interested in the complicated relationship between marketing and social justice issues (environmental awareness and diversity). Take some time to review how each author critiques what exactly is being "sold" in the marketing approaches they analyze. Compose an essay in which you use insights from these authors to make an argument about a marketing campaign of your choosing that is interesting to consider through the lenses of marketing and a social justice issue. Ultimately, do you think business can be or should be an engine to drive forward social progress and, if so, why and how?

Economics

How do economics shape our self-understandings and possibilities? What kinds of choices do we have?

© YinYang/Getty Images

E conomics may sound like a forbidding topic, but this chapter should demonstrate that this social science, which examines the ways we consume goods and services, is probably something you already think about a lot. Any time you worry about student loans, rent an apartment, consider a career path, or decide which shirt to buy, you are engaging in an economic deliberation. In other words, this chapter is pressingly about your everyday life, and the multifaceted ways we think about "value," "worth," and who we are as consumers and producers.

Sara Goldrick-Rab takes on the student financial aid crisis, perhaps one of the most immediate concerns for many of you. Her analysis of the current system's failures and her bold proposals for change may offer you hope, or at least help you discern where you stand in this unfolding conversation about college affordability. Robert B. Reich addresses economic inequalities in the workplace, a topic that is also related to access to a college education. He asks how it has come to be that policies have "reduced the number of poor people who are jobless, while increasing the number of poor people who have jobs." Like Goldrick-Rab, Reich urges us to reflect on our values and sense of fairness as we consider our relationship to economic inequalities. There is plenty of food for thought in these pieces.

Taking a different approach, Richard H. Thaler, Cass R. Sunstein, and John P. Balz—the founders of the term "choice architecture"—offer insight into the ways we make decisions about many of our consumer interactions, whether or not we are aware of the "nudges" companies provide. How did you choose your college, your lunch, or the shirt you put on this morning? You may be surprised, or at least enlightened, by the structures that shape our seemingly free choices. Naomi Klein focuses on the shift from mere advertising to "branding," which goes far beyond selling products to selling experiences and lifestyles. Finally, Ann duCille uses an extended analysis of the marketing of multicultural Barbies to demonstrate how problematic and limited "our" understanding of diversity is—and why it is so unsettling that we continue to sell these ideas to our children.

The diverse perspectives these authors bring to the practices, effects, and costs (to our wallets and to ourselves) of the current market should inspire you to think carefully about how free you are—or are not—to act according to your values when you invest in yourself, your education, your community, and the world.

SARA GOLDRICK-RAB

From Paying the Price

Sara Goldrick-Rab describes herself as a "scholar-activist" whose interdisciplinary work focuses on increasing college access and success, particularly for marginalized populations. She is also a professor of higher education policy and sociology and founder of the Wisconsin HOPE Lab, a hub for research on college affordability. She has worked with policymakers and published widely on this topic and is a frequent guest on talk shows, including *The Daily Show with Trevor Noah*. This reading is from her acclaimed book *Paying the Price: College Costs, Financial Aid, and the Betrayal of the American Dream* (2016).

Goldrick-Rab establishes her ethos (see Chapter 9) in her first paragraph, noting, "For fifteen years, I have listened to financial aid administrators, deans of students, student affairs practitioners, and college presidents describe the problems of undergraduates on their campuses" (para. 1). Goldrick-Rab's experience supports her claim that despite "good intentions," many campus administrators fail to address the fundamental problems with student financial aid. This essay takes a corrective stance, providing historical context from the 1970s that explains all the policy, market, and cultural changes that have led to college being financially out of reach for so many.

As you read, pay attention to all the facts and statistics Goldrick-Rab provides to support her claim that "Everyone will benefit from a better-educated, more productive American workforce" (para. 10). Why is this the case, according to her? Goldrick-Rab anticipates the opposition in paragraph 11, raising questions and responding to critics of her position (see the discussion of identifying counterarguments in Chapter 4). In paragraph 13, she begins to propose solutions for the problems she has identified. Keep track of her proposals, and be ready to evaluate and discuss them with your peers. Goldrick-Rab is calling for some profound changes in the ways we see college education. Do you agree?

This reading will likely hit close to home; if you have not struggled with college costs, someone you know surely has. Goldrick-Rab argues that small tweaks to the existing system are not enough. Draw on your personal experiences as you read, considering what you know about the complexity of financing college and paying back loans. Goldrick-Rab offers her view of the problem and solutions. Where do you stand in this timely debate?

❋ ❋ ❋

Despite its good intentions, our current financial aid system is failing today's students. For fifteen years, I have listened to financial aid administrators, deans of students, student affairs practitioners, and college presidents describe the problems of undergraduates on their campuses. They talk about their personal experiences of college and those of their friends to craft a picture of struggle met with fortitude, success gained through hard work, and the achievement of what looked impossible. In their day, college looked affordable—and in their eyes, it can look affordable still. *1*

The people who tell me these stories have genuine empathy for students. When they talk to me they look worried, sometimes pained, always concerned. Their eyes convey a sense of wishing for better behavior, sensible decision making, and an easier process that wasn't always so complicated. But fundamentally, at some basic level, they tend to agree that the system itself is fine—it can work, if only students work it. If today's students only had a certain moral fiber, like the students of yesteryear, they would be fine. *2*

Other people I encounter, whether at community meetings, on airplanes, or the staff of state and federal legislators from both sides of the *3* aisle, are frustrated. When I mention my research on financial aid, many parents say, "We save, work hard, and pay a lot of money to attend college and still we can't cover the bills—and the school takes our hard-earned dollars and gives it to someone else. It's unfair." The redistribution of funds from the rich to the poor in order to finance programs is a common approach, and at least in theory, sometimes these individuals support it. But the kind of anger expressed in the above quote comes from the sense that when it comes to affording college they aren't "rich" but rather middle class. And it's hard to watch your daughter's college roommate receive a Pell Grant while your child is offered only loans.

We have to learn from the experiences of both Pell recipients and the middle-class families left out of that program. Today's undergraduates are experiencing college very differently than those in previous decades. It is no longer the case that, if students from low-income families work hard, college will be affordable (recall that the average net price for a year at community college equals 40% of their annual family income). At the same time, it is out of reach for middle-class families as well (for whom a year at a public institution ranges from 16% to 25% of their annual family income).[1] When nearly 75 percent of American families find college unaffordable, and the means-tested financial aid system fails to do its job even for the poorest, it is time for a change. . . . *4*

First Degree for Free

Education pays substantial dividends, both for individuals and families, as well as for communities. . . . *5*

The effects of higher education accrue across generations, not merely within cohorts. We have long understood this, building national prosperity in the twentieth century by making high school free. Yes, individuals reap economic benefits from attending high school, and wealthy kids attending good public schools reap many more benefits than low-income kids attending crummy ones. But we don't insist that individuals pay their way for high school because we recognize how important it is that everyone has an opportunity to finish high school. We do our best to ensure that money does not get in the way. *6*

Decades ago, many Americans got a pretty good deal. With family support, some work, and perhaps a modest Pell Grant, college prices were such that those who did go could usually make ends meet. And they entered a labor market where a college degree conferred a bonus but was not required. There were a fairly large number of good-paying jobs available to people who were not college graduates. *7*

That world is gone. Young people from all families and older workers in need of new skills want to attend college, and they plan on enrolling, even if it means ending up with debt and no degree, at risk of defaulting on loans.[2] Lower-income individuals, people of color, and women know that *8* there's no economic security in their futures without at least some sort of college credential. Research confirms this: Ron Haskins has called a college education a "powerful" intervention like no other.[3]

In the 1970s, targeting financial aid to only the poorest individuals made sense—after all, most people didn't want to attend college, it wasn't required, and college prices were low enough that the Pell Grant largely covered the bills.[4] Today, that same model fails: the vast majority of the populace wants access to affordable, high-quality public higher education, it is required, and costs are so high that grants and scholarships provide only a meager discount restricted to only a fraction of students with financial need.[5] Means-tested financial aid, administered via a massive bureaucracy, leaves out the very poorest—who cannot navigate the system—and squeezes the middle class, who are offered only loans.[6]

America can't afford to ignore the calls for a broad, inclusive system of public higher education that helps families obtain economic security.[7] Of course, a universal, free system will have progressive effects—tearing down the price and bureaucratic barriers will matter most to the poorest people, who have made very little progress accessing college under the current system. But the benefits will be broadly shared. Completion rates for working- and middle-class students will rise as their costs of college are more fully covered.[8] Accreditation reform and greater accountability will accompany this shift to ensure quality and a high return on public investment. Everyone will benefit from a better-educated, more productive American workforce.

What about downsides? For example, will the movement of more students into higher education diminish the quality of undergraduates or the returns to their degrees? It is very unlikely. In a recent study that examines change in student quality over the last thirty years, economist Robert Archibald and his colleagues conclude: "Existing federal policies that have reduced the financial obstacles to college attendance have not caused lower completion rates. Reforms that stimulate further increases in college attendance, either by improving information about the net cost of attendance or by reducing the net cost, are not necessarily self-defeating given the remaining potential to move high-quality students into 4-year programs. In addition, state policies that reduce the net cost of attendance for students who have achieved some performance thresholds could complement federal assistance."[9]

When the movement for free public high school began in the 1800s, many opposed it, calling it "a contrivance of the rich to rob the poor."[10] They were wrong—when high school became free, families from all walks of life came to get educated.[11] Some argue that the United States can't afford to make college free. The truth is, we can't afford not to.

We should follow an incremental approach that begins by making the associate degree free to all students who pursue it.[12] This is the initial entry point to college, and all public institutions should award it. Many students start at four-year institutions, last four semesters, and leave with nothing in hand. It is important that these institutions reward that effort with an associate degree and that we establish that degree as the new "first degree." We should begin, as Federal Reserve Board chairman Ben Bernanke said, with the community colleges: "We must move beyond the view that education is something that takes place only in K-through-12 schools and four-year colleges, as important as those are. Education and skills must be provided flexibly and to people of any age."[13]

Then we can work on making the first degree free at any public college or university.[14] We need to work toward the time when "public colleges and universities" have the same meaning as public K–12 schools, or public parks, or public roads: goods paid for by all, intended for universal free use by all who wish to use them for their intended purposes. Students like those in this book would be greatly helped by a complete overhaul of the financing system for public colleges and universities. As many have said, "Programs for poor people make for poor programs."[15] A more inclusive financing system will also likely be a more sustainable one.   *14*

But money should not come without assurances. We can do much more to support the public sector so that its quality is high and its costs are reasonable. Neither do we have the same relationship with nor should we intrude on private colleges and universities. We have provided trillions of dollars in resources to both private nonprofit and private for-profit colleges and universities for decades and still can't guarantee that they are either accessible or affordable. But when it comes to working with public colleges and universities to update their approaches to student services, identifying effective practices to teaching and learning, and finding ways to increase capacity, we have plenty of experience and road maps to guide us.[16]   *15*

While there is a long way to go in public higher education, there has been progress. Governors and legislatures have gained control over tuition increases at their state's colleges and universities time and again.[17] Some have allocated additional appropriations to prevent increases, and this works to ensure that the institutions do not raise tuition while also ensuring they have the resources needed to support students. Community colleges across the country have shown a willingness to engage their states in thoughtful discussions about how best to fund their work and, in exchange, have received increases in state support.[18] In fact, today most states are *not* cutting public higher education.[19] They are reinvesting.   *16*

That is because there is a substantial public benefit to high rates of college attendance. It is far more difficult to quantify than the returns to individuals (expressed in terms of boosted wages) but that does not mean that it is smaller.[20] Listen to economist Walter McMahon, author of *Higher Learning, Greater Good:* "The private non-market benefits are estimated more comprehensively . . . their value is about $9,883 per year after graduation for each year of college degree. This turns out to be approximately equal to the benefits from each year of college to annual earnings ($9,967).   *17*

This alone means that half of the private benefits of college to students and their families are being overlooked."[21] Twelve years of education does not go as far as it once did, and after a century of technological advancements and upskilling, it is reasonable to expect that some post–high school education is beneficial. States know that they cannot attract employers or grow their economies without an educated workforce.

But their efforts to do this are being undermined by the clear and growing risk that too many people encounter when pursuing that first degree. A year or two of college credits without a degree means not only wasted time but also significant debt. Those who are being left behind today are the people who decide that risk is too great.

The main barrier to college entry is price. By eliminating the price of admission, we can send a powerful message: there is no harm in trying. And for people who do try . . . by eliminating their need to work while in college, we improve their chances of success. If they don't make it, very little harm to students will be done—they can look back and assess what happened, but they will not be doing it while paying monthly bills to a debt collection agency for that failure. . . .

Sixty percent of Americans aged twenty-five to sixty-four do not hold a college credential. But 22 percent of them—32.6 million Americans—have tried to get one.[22] They left college frustrated, often saying it had something to do with money.[23] The ladder people must climb to get to graduation has eroded, and a critical rung—affordability—is almost completely broken. We have to repair it. Doing nothing will be far more expensive than making an upfront investment now.

The first step in addressing the college affordability crisis is taking the problem seriously. Money matters. Lack of financial resources is keeping students from succeeding. Suggesting that low-income students merely need to learn how to live more frugally is usually a misplaced recommendation—and an offensive one, to boot. As Oscar Wilde wrote, "To recommend thrift to the poor is both grotesque and insulting. It is like advising a man who is starving to eat less."[24]

Researchers need to do their part to help illuminate how and why price is a barrier to education. As these new models of financing emerge, they need to be evaluated not only for the impacts they achieve but also for how they affect the college experiences and lives of individual students. To help ensure that this work gets done, I recently founded the Wisconsin HOPE Lab, an applied research shop staffed by talented researchers committed to rigorous studies that can be directly translated into action. This sort of research, conducted in communities across the nation, must inform public policies if we are to find better ways forward.

Forty-five million young people will turn eighteen in America in the next ten years. Will the children of the wealthy leave college with elite networks, the sons and daughters of the middle class with degrees they can use, and the next generation of low-income Americans with mainly debt and despair?

The new economics of college is undermining the fundamental con- 24
nection between education and democracy that has helped our nation
thrive. More than a century ago, American policymakers realized that
the wealth of your family or the resources of your community should not
determine access to K–12 schooling.[25] In time, every state, and the nation
as a whole, shouldered the responsibility of educating all children through
high school. In 1973, U.S. senator Claiborne Pell and his generation made
noble strides to expand college access, helping America build the largest
middle class the world has ever known. With economic inequality on the
rise, and low-income and middle-class Americans under pressure, this
generation must meet the challenge of making one of the best ways out of
poverty and into the middle class—a college education—affordable for all.

NOTES

1. Goldrick-Rab and Kendall, *F2CO Redefining College Affordability*, 7.
2. Ingles and Dalton, *High School Longitudinal Study of 2009*, 5; and Looney and Yan-
   nelis, "A Crisis in Student Loans?" 12–16.
3. Haskins, "Education and Economic Mobility," 6.
4. Goldrick-Rab and Kendall, *F2CO Redefining College Affordability*, 6.
5. Ibid., 5-14; and Oreopoulos and Petronijevic, "Making College Worth It," 41–65.
6. Bettinger et al., "The Role of Application Assistance and Information in College
   Decisions," 1205–42.
7. *Chattanooga Times Free Press*, "Gov. Haslam Urges High School Seniors to Apply
   for Tennessee Promise"; and Dynarski, "Rising Inequality in Postsecondary Education."
8. See Goldrick-Rab et al., "Reducing Income Inequality in Higher Education."
9. Archibald, Feldman, and McHenry, "A Quality-Preserving Increase in Four-Year
   College Attendance," 295.
10. Philbrick, *City School Systems in the United States*, 105.
11. Goldin and Katz, *The Race between Education and Technology*, 158–66.
12. I am advocating for "incremental universalism," a phrase borrowed from Sanford
    Schram, to whom I am indebted for great inspiration. See Schram, *After Welfare*.
13. Bernanke, "National and Regional Economic Overview."
14. There are many proposals for how to do this, including a proposal from 2016 presi-
    dential candidate Bernie Sanders. Here are two: Goldrick-Rab and Kendall, *F2CO
    Redefining College Affordability*; and Samuels, *Why Public Higher Education Should
    Be Free*.
15. Schram, *After Welfare*, 24; Skocpol, "Sustainable Social Policy"; and Wilson, *When
    Work Disappears*, 156–57.
16. Some of the best insights into how to improve public higher education are found
    in the following volumes: Bailey, Jaggers, and Jenkins, *Redesigning America's Com-
    munity Colleges*; Crow and Dabars, *Designing the New American University*; Folbre,
    Saving State U; Kuh et al., *Using Evidence of Student Learning to Improve Higher
    Education*; and Newfield, *Unmaking the Public University*.
17. Associated Press, "Commissioner: New Funding Saves Big College Tuition Hike";
    Indiana University Newsroom, "Indiana University to Freeze Undergraduate Tui-
    tion for Hoosier Residents Attending IU Bloomington"; and Fain, "Boom Budget in
    California."
18. National Council on State Legislatures, "Performance-Based Funding for Higher
    Education"; and Fingerhut and Kazis, *Tying Funding to Community College Outcomes*.
19. Woodhouse, "Funding Woes"; and Bidwell, "The 'New Normal' of Higher Ed
    Funding."

20. For further reading, see Behrman and Stacey, *The Social Benefits of Education;* Johnson, "Are Public Subsidies to Higher Education Regressive?"; and Wolfe and Haveman, "Social and Nonmarket Benefits from Education in an Advanced Economy."
21. Jaschik, "Higher Learning, Greater Good."
22. Lumina Foundation, *A Stronger America through Higher Education,* 2.
23. Johnson et al., *With Their Whole Lives Ahead of Them,* 1–52.
24. Wilde, "The Soul of Man under Socialism," 4.
25. For further reading, see Reese, *The Origins of the American High School.*

■　■　■

Reading as a Writer: Analyzing Rhetorical Choices

1. Goldrick-Rab structures her writing into naming the problems she sees in student financial aid and then offering solutions. Use two different colors of ink to mark problems and solutions, and prepare to discuss her claims. Based on your experience (and perhaps research), does she leave out problems or solutions?

2. Look up the history of Pell grants and also the Wisconsin HOPE Lab, both easily found in Internet searches. How does this additional information enhance your understanding of Goldrick-Rab's argument about what should change in our approach to student financial aid? Discuss with your classmates.

Writing as a Reader: Entering the Conversation of Ideas

1. Both Goldrick-Rab and Robert B. Reich (pp. 749–58) begin their essays with paradoxical statements and go on to explain the history and policies that have led to problems in the present. Where do their ideas about social mobility, education, and inequality overlap? Compose an essay in which you build on these authors' insights to make a point about the relationship between these concepts. Why should students care?

2. Goldrick-Rab examines the daunting economic challenges to college students, and Nikole Hannah-Jones (pp. 434–52 in Education) reveals the economic inequalities that can affect students before they even reach college. Write an essay in which you place these authors in conversation to consider how their ideas create a broader picture of economic inequality and the impact on students. What would a fair solution look like, according to these authors and to you?

ROBERT B. REICH

The Rise of the Working Poor

Robert B. Reich is a professor of public policy and economics at the University of California at Berkley. Besides serving as Secretary of Labor for President Bill Clinton, he is a prolific author who has a very public presence on social media, with an active blog and widely shared posts on Facebook, Twitter, and Tumblr. His documentary *Inequality for All* explores themes in this reading, which is drawn from Reich's book *Saving Capitalism for the Many, Not the Few* (2015). While this selection, like all of Reich's writing for the public, is intended to make economic concepts accessible to noneconomists, you may find yourself rereading paragraphs and looking up words. In fact, doing this demonstrates that you are reading as a careful academic writer should.

Reich uses a paradoxical introduction (see Chapter 11): "The standard assumption that work determines worth—and validates one's personal virtue and social responsibility—is further confounded by a substantial increase in the number of people working full-time who are still poor, and a simultaneous surge in the comparatively smaller ranks of people who do not work at all but are rich" (para. 1). What do you make of this fact? The rest of the reading is an explanation of why this has come to be the case and the implications for the "working poor," an important phrase for Reich (para. 2).

Reich provides a quick economic history of the policy shifts that have led to this situation of so many U.S. workers living in poverty. Keep track of all the reasons Reich offers, from outsourcing work (para. 4) to suppressing the minimum wage (paras. 4–10) to welfare reform (para. 12), which have "reduced the number of poor people who are jobless, while increasing the number of poor people who have jobs" (para. 13). All these changes, Reich argues, have added up to fewer opportunities for the poor to climb into the middle class. The parallel effect on increasing educational inequalities is an additional thread through Reich's argument (paras. 17–23).

As a numbers expert, Reich supports his claims with statistics. Consider marking all of the statistics in a different color so that you can see where he uses them in relation to each of his points. You may even want to see if you can gather some updated statistics (about the minimum wage or other information of interest to you). Clearly, Reich's position is not neutral. If you find yourself agreeing with him that the current situation is unfair, be ready to explain why. If you disagree with him, also be ready to explain why. Numbers tell one kind of story, but it is up to us to decide what those numbers mean.

■ ■ ■

The standard assumption that work determines worth—and validates *1* one's personal virtue and social responsibility—is further confounded by a substantial increase in the number of people working full-time who are still poor, and a simultaneous surge in the comparatively smaller ranks of people who do not work at all but are rich. It is difficult to hold firm to the belief that people are "worth" what they earn when more and more people who are working full-time do not earn enough to lift themselves and their families out of poverty, while another group of people at the opposite end of the income spectrum have so much wealth—much of it inherited—that they can live comfortably off the income it generates without ever breaking a sweat.

Until quite recently, poverty was largely confined to those who did *2* not work—widows and children, the elderly, the disabled and seriously ill, and those who had lost their jobs. Public safety nets and private charities were created to help them. It was rare for a full-time worker to be in poverty because . . . the economy generated a plethora of middle-class jobs that paid reasonably well and were inherently secure. This is no longer the case. Some politicians cling to the view, as expressed, for example, by Speaker of the House John Boehner in 2014, when he said the poor have "this idea" that "I really don't have to work. I don't really want to do this. I think I'd rather just sit around."[1] The reality is that America's poor work diligently,[2] often more than forty hours a week, sometimes in two or more jobs. Yet they and their families remain poor.

There are several reasons for the growth of America's working poor. *3* First, wages at the bottom have continued to drop, adjusted for inflation. By 2013, the ranks of the working poor had swelled to forty-seven million people in the United States, one out of every seven Americans. One-fourth of all American workers were in jobs paying below what a full-time, full-year worker needed in order to support a family of four above the federally defined poverty line.[3] The downward trend of low wages continued even in the so-called recovery following the Great Recession. Between 2010 and 2013, average incomes for the bottom fifth dropped 8 percent, and their average wealth declined 21 percent.[4] According to a study by Oxfam America,[5] more than half of America's forty-six million users of food pantries and other charitable food programs in 2013 had jobs or were members of working families.

It is doubtful that all these working people came to be "worth" that *4* much less, except in the tautological sense that their pay dropped. In reality, the decline has had a great deal to do with their lack of economic and political power. CEOs seeking profits in a lackluster economy have continued to slash labor costs, often by outsourcing the work, substituting automated machines, or forcing workers to accept lower wages. This process has pushed many previously middle-class workers into local service jobs that pay less than the jobs they once had. Low-paying industries such as retail and fast food accounted for 22 percent of the jobs lost in the Great Recession.[6] But they generated 44 percent of the jobs added between the end of the recession and 2013, according to a report from the National Employment Law Project.[7] Employers in these industries tend to be virulently anti-union and have fought successfully against any efforts to organize their workers.

Meanwhile, the real value of the federal minimum wage has been *5* steadily eroded by inflation. Congress (to be more precise, Republicans in Congress) has chosen not to raise it to compensate for this decline. The National Restaurant Association and the National Retail Federation, along with the largest fast-food chains and retailers that support them, have lobbied against any increase in the federal minimum wage, which is tantamount to allowing it to erode even further. By 2014, its real value ($7.25 an hour) was below the level to which it had been raised in 1996,[8] when, as secretary of labor, I had led the political fight to raise it. Had the minimum wage retained the value it had in 1968, it would be $10.86 an hour.[9] And, of course, by 2014 the nation's economy was far larger than it was then, and far more productive.

Some have claimed, nonetheless, that any attempt to restore the real   6 value of the minimum wage will cause employers to fire workers at the lowest rungs, because such workers would no longer be "worth" the cost. In June 2014, at a conference for the Republicans' largest donors hosted by Charles and David Koch at the luxurious St. Regis Monarch Beach Resort in Dana Point, California, Richard Fink, the Kochs' in-house economist, sounded off against the minimum wage. "The big danger of minimum wage isn't the fact that some people are being paid more than their value-added," he said. "It's the five hundred thousand people that will not have a job because of minimum wage."[10] Fink warned that such a large group of disillusioned and unemployed people would become "the main recruiting ground for totalitarianism, for fascism."[11] The conference-goers presumably nodded in sober agreement before getting back to their foie gras.

The mythology that a minimum-wage increase (or, in real terms,   7 restoring it to its 1968 level) would cause employers to reduce employment is a common trope. A corollary is that getting rid of the minimum wage altogether and allowing employers to pay what employees are "worth" will reduce or even eliminate unemployment. As former congresswoman Michele Bachmann once put it, if the minimum wage were repealed "we could potentially virtually wipe out unemployment completely because we would be able to offer jobs at whatever level."[12] Theoretically, Bachmann is correct. But her point is irrelevant. It is no great feat for an economy to create a large number of very-low-wage jobs. Slavery, after all, was a full-employment system.

In fact, evidence suggests that few if any jobs would be lost if the min-   8 imum wage were to be increased at least to its 1968 level, adjusted for inflation. Unlike industrial jobs, minimum-wage retail service jobs cannot be outsourced abroad. Nor are these workers likely to be replaced by automated machinery and computers, because the service they provide is personal and direct: Someone has to be on hand to help customers or dole out the food. In addition, and significantly, the gains from a higher minimum wage extend well beyond those who receive it directly. More money in the pockets of low-wage workers means more sales in the places where they live, which in turn creates faster growth and more jobs. Research by Arindrajit Dube, T. William Lester, and Michael Reich[13] confirms this. They examined employment in several hundred pairs of adjacent counties lying on opposite sides of state borders, each with different minimum wages (one at the federal minimum, the other at a higher minimum enacted by a state) and found no statistically significant increase in unemployment in the higher-minimum-wage counties, even after four years. (Other researchers who found contrary results failed to control for counties where unemployment was already growing before the minimum wage had been increased.)[14] Dube, Lester, and Reich also found that employee turnover was lower where the minimum wage was higher,[15] presumably saving employers money on recruiting and training new workers.

Most workers earning the minimum wage are no longer teenagers   *9* seeking additional spending money. According to the Bureau of Labor Statistics, the median age of fast-food workers in 2014 was twenty-eight, and the median age of women in those jobs, who constituted two-thirds of such workers, was thirty-two. The median age of workers in big-box retail establishments was over thirty. More than a quarter of them have children. These workers are typically major breadwinners for their families, accounting for at least half their family's earnings.

Needless to say, a higher minimum wage would also reduce the neces-   *10* sity for other taxpayers to pay for the Medicaid, food stamps, and additional assistance these workers and their families need in order to cope with poverty. A study by my colleagues at the University of California, Berkeley and researchers at the University of Illinois at Urbana-Champaign found that in 2012, 52 percent of fast-food workers were dependent on some form of public assistance, and they received almost $7 billion in support from federal and state governments.[16] That sum is in effect a subsidy the rest of American taxpayers pay the fast-food industry for the industry's failure to pay its workers enough to live on.

Whatever wage gains these workers receive are rarely passed on to con-   *11* sumers in the form of higher prices. That is because big-box retailers and fast-food chains compete intensely for customers and have no choice but to keep their prices low. It is notable, for example, that in Denmark, where McDonald's workers over the age of eighteen earn the equivalent of twenty dollars an hour, Big Macs cost only thirty-five cents more than they do in the United States.[17] Any wage gains low-paid workers receive will more than likely come out of profits—which, in turn, will slightly reduce returns to shareholders and the compensation packages of top executives. I do not find this especially troubling. According to the National Employment Law Project,[18] most low-wage workers are employed by large corporations that, by 2013, were enjoying healthy profits. Three-quarters of these employers (the fifty biggest employers of low-wage workers) were generating higher profits than they did before the recession.[19] Between 2000 and 2013, the compensation of the CEOs of fast-food companies quadrupled, in constant dollars, to an average of $24 million a year.[20] Walmart, too, pays its executives handsomely. In 2012, Walmart's CEO received $20.7 million.[21] Not incidentally, the wealth of the Walton family—which still owns the lion's share of Walmart stock—by then exceeded the wealth of the bottom 40 percent of American families combined, according to an analysis by the Economic Policy Institute.[22]

● ● ●

Another reason for the rise in the number of working poor is a basic shift   *12*
in the criteria used by the government to determine eligibility for government assistance. As I noted, assistance used to be targeted to the nonem-
ployed. Now, those who are out of work receive very little. By 2014, only
26 percent of jobless Americans were receiving any kind of jobless benefit.[23] Typically, recipients of public assistance must be working in order to
qualify. Bill Clinton's welfare reform of 1996 pushed the poor off welfare
and into work, but the work available to them has provided low wages
and offered few ladders into the middle class. The Earned Income Tax
Credit, a wage subsidy, has been expanded. But here, too, having a job is a
prerequisite. Although it's not necessary to have a job in order to get food
stamps, it turns out that a large and growing share of food stamp recipients are employed as well. (The share of recipients with earnings has risen
from 19 percent in 1980 to 31 percent in 2012.[24] And since about a third of
food stamp recipients cannot work because they're elderly or disabled, far
more than 31 percent of those able to work are employed.)

Overall, the new work requirements have not reduced the number or   *13*
percentage of Americans in poverty. The poverty rate in 2013 was 14.5 percent,[25] well above its levels of 11.3 percent in 2000 and 12.5 percent in
2007. In effect, the new work requirements have merely reduced the number of poor people who are jobless, while increasing the number of poor
people who have jobs.

An additional and perhaps more fundamental explanation for the increasing   *14*
numbers of working poor is found in what has happened to the rest of America. Some would rather deny such a connection and assume the shrinking
middle class and redistribution of income and wealth to the top have no
bearing on what has happened to those at the bottom. The question we
ought to be asking, according to Harvard economist Greg Mankiw, is "How
do we help people at the bottom, rather than thwart people at the top?"[26]

Yet the issues are inseparable. As more of the gains have gone to the   *15*
top, the middle class has lost the purchasing power necessary for ensuring
that the economy grows as quickly as it did as recently as the early 2000s.
Once the middle class exhausted all its methods for maintaining spending
in the face of flat or declining wages[27]—with wives and mothers surging
into paid work in the 1970s and 1980s, everyone putting in longer hours in
the 1990s, and households falling ever deeper into debt before 2008—the
middle class as a whole was unable to spend more. The inevitable consequence has been fewer jobs and slower growth. Both have hit the poor
especially hard. Those at the bottom are the first to be fired, last to be
hired, and most likely to bear the brunt of declining wages and benefits.

As the income ladder has lengthened and many of its middle rungs   *16*
have disappeared, moreover, the challenge of moving upward has become
more daunting. A smaller middle class yields fewer opportunities for joining it. Shortly after World War II, a child born into poverty had a somewhat better than fifty-fifty chance of becoming middle class by the time

he or she was an adult.[28] Today, 43 percent of children born into poverty in the United States will remain in poverty for their entire lives.[29]

Some continue to believe that the poor remain poor because they lack   17
ambition. But what they really lack is opportunity and the political power to get the resources needed to realize that opportunity. It begins with inadequate child care and extends through primary and secondary schools, which helps explain the growing achievement gap between lower- and higher-income children. Thirty years ago, the average gap on SAT-type tests between children of families in the richest 10 percent and bottom 10 percent was about 90 points on an 800-point scale.[30] By 2014 it was 125 points. The gap in the mathematical abilities of American kids, by income, is one of the widest among the sixty-five countries participating in the Program for International Student Assessment. On their reading skills, children from high-income families score 110 points higher, on average, than those from poor families.[31]

The achievement gap between poor kids and wealthy kids isn't mainly   18
about race.[32] In fact, the racial achievement gap has been narrowing. It's a reflection of the nation's widening gulf between poor and wealthy families, of how schools in poor and rich communities are financed, and of the nation's increasing residential segregation by income. According to the Pew Research Center's analysis of the 2010 census tract and household income data,[33] residential segregation by income has grown over the past three decades across the United States.

This matters, because a large portion of the money to support public   19
schools comes from local property taxes. The federal government provides only about 10 percent of all funding, and the states provide 45 percent, on average.[34] The rest is raised locally. Most states do try to give more money to poor districts,[35] but most also cut way back on their spending during the recession and haven't nearly made up for the cutbacks. Meanwhile, real estate markets in lower-income communities remain weak, so local tax revenues are down. As we segregate by income into different communities, schools in lower-income areas have fewer resources than ever. The result is widening disparities in funding per pupil,[36] to the direct disadvantage of poor kids.

The wealthiest, highest-spending districts are now providing about twice   20
as much funding per student as are the lowest-spending districts, according to a federal advisory commission report.[37] In some states, such as California, the ratio is greater than three to one. What are called "public schools" in many of America's wealthy communities aren't really public at all. In effect, they're private schools, whose tuition is hidden away in the purchase price of upscale homes there, and in the corresponding property taxes.

Even where courts have required richer school districts to subsi-   21
dize poorer ones, large inequalities remain. Rather than pay extra taxes that would go to poorer districts, many parents in upscale communities have quietly shifted their financial support to tax-deductible parents'

foundations designed to enhance their own schools. About 12 percent of the more than fourteen thousand school districts across America are funded in part by such foundations. They're paying for everything from a new school auditorium (Bowie, Maryland) to a high-tech weather station and language arts program (Newton, Massachusetts). "Parents' foundations," observed *The Wall Street Journal*, "are visible evidence of parents' efforts to reconnect their money to their kids"[38]—and not, it should have been noted, to kids in another community, who are likely to be poorer.

As a result of all this, the United States is one of only three out of thirty-four advanced nations surveyed by the Organization for Economic Cooperation and Development (OECD) whose schools serving higher-income children have more funding per pupil and lower student-teacher ratios than do schools serving poor students (the two others are Turkey and Israel).[39] Other advanced nations do it differently. Their national governments provide 54 percent of funding, on average,[40] and local taxes account for less than half the portion they do in America. And they target a disproportionate share of national funding to poorer communities. As Andreas Schleicher, who runs the OECD's international education assessments, told *The New York Times*, "The vast majority of OECD countries either invest equally into every student or disproportionately more into disadvantaged students. The U.S. is one of the few countries doing the opposite."[41]   22

Money isn't everything, obviously. But how can we pretend it doesn't count? Money buys the most experienced teachers, less-crowded classrooms, high-quality teaching materials, and after-school programs. Yet we seem to be doing everything except getting more money to the schools that most need it. We're requiring all schools to meet high standards, requiring students to take more and more tests, and judging teachers by their students' test scores. But until we recognize that we're systematically hobbling schools serving disadvantaged kids, we're unlikely to make much headway.   23

In all these ways, poverty among those who work and their political powerlessness are intimately connected.   24

NOTES

1. See Paul Krugman, "Those Lazy Jobless," *New York Times*, September 21, 2014.
2. U.S. Bureau of Labor Statistics, *A Profile of the Working Poor, 2010*, U.S. Bureau of Labor Statistics website, March 2012.
3. Rebecca Thiess, *The Future of Work: Trends and Challenges for Low-Wage Workers*, Briefing Paper #341, Economic Policy Institute website, April 27, 2012, p. 4.
4. Jesse Bricker, Lisa J. Dettling, Alice Henriques, Joanne W. Hsu, et al., "Changes in U.S. Family Finances from 2010 to 2013: Evidence from the Survey of Consumer Finances," *Federal Reserve Bulletin* 100, no. 4 (September 2014): 9, 12.
5. Oxfam America, *From Paycheck to Pantry: Hunger in Working America*, Oxfam America website, p. 3.
6. National Employment Law Project, *The Low-Wage Recovery: Industry Employment and Wages Four Years into the Recovery*, Data Brief, National Employment Law Project website, April 2014, p. 1.
7. Ibid.

8. U.S. Department of Labor, "History of Federal Minimum Wage Rates Under the Fair Labor Standards Act, 1938–2009," U.S. Department of Labor website. Figures were adjusted for inflation using the CPI.

9. Ibid.

10. Elias Isquith, "Koch Brothers' Top Political Strategist: The Minimum Wage Leads to Fascism!" *Salon,* September 3, 2014.

11. Ibid.

12. Antoine Gara, "Would Killing the Minimum Wage Help?" *Bloomberg Businessweek,* June 30, 2011.

13. Arindrajit Dube, T. William Lester, and Michael Reich, *Minimum Wage Effects Across State Borders: Estimates Using Contiguous Counties,* IRLE Working Paper No. 157-07, Institute for Research on Labor and Employment website, November 2010.

14. Ibid.

15. Arindrajit Dube, T. William Lester, and Michael Reich, *Minimum Wage Shocks, Employment Flows and Labor Market Frictions,* IRLE Working Paper No. 149-13, Institute for Research on Labor and Employment website, October 2014.

16. Sylvia Allegretto, Marc Doussard, Dave Graham-Squire, Ken Jacobs, et al., *Fast Food, Poverty Wages: The Public Cost of Low-Wage Jobs in the Fast-Food Industry,* U.C. Berkeley Labor Center website, October 15, 2013, p. 1.

17. William Finnegan, "Dignity: Fast-Food Workers and a New Form of Labor Activism," *New Yorker,* September 15, 2014.

18. National Employment Law Project, "Big Business, Corporate Profits, and the Minimum Wage," National Employment Law Project website, July 2012, p. 1.

19. Ibid.

20. Catherine Ruetschlin, *Fast Food Failure: How CEO-to-Worker Pay Disparity Undermines the Industry and the Overall Economy,* Demos website, 2014, p. 2.

21. Jessica Wohl, "Wal-Mart CEO's Pay Jumps 14.1 Percent to $20.7 Million," Reuters, April 22, 2013.

22. Josh Bivens, "Inequality, Exhibit A: Walmart and the Wealth of American Families," *The Economic Policy Institute Blog,* July 17, 2012.

23. Josh Bivens, "Poverty Reduction Stalled by Policy, Once Again: Unemployment Insurance Edition," *The Economic Policy Institute Blog,* September 16, 2014.

24. See Dorothy Rosenbaum, *The Relationship Between SNAP and Work Among Low-Income Households,* Center on Budget and Policy Priorities website, January 2013.

25. Office of the Assistant Secretary for Planning and Evaluation, "Information on Poverty and Income Statistics: A Summary of 2014 Current Population Survey Data," ASPE Issue Brief, U.S. Department of Health and Human Services website, September 16, 2014, p. 3.

26. "Piketty v. Mankiw on Economic Challenges and Inequality," *On Point with Tom Ashbrook,* radio broadcast, April 29, 2014.

27. For a full discussion of middle-class coping mechanisms, see Robert B. Reich, *Supercapitalism: The Transformation of Business, Democracy, and Everyday Life* (New York: Alfred A. Knopf, 2007).

28. See Daniel Aaronson and Bhashkar Mazumder, "Intergenerational Economic Mobility in the U.S., 1940 to 2000," *Journal of Human Resources* 43, no. 1 (2005): 139–72.

29. Pew Charitable Trusts, "Moving On Up: Why Do Some Americans Leave the Bottom of the Economic Ladder, but Not Others?" Pew Charitable Trusts website, November 2013, p. 1.

30. Sean F. Reardon, "No Rich Child Left Behind," *New York Times,* April 27, 2013.

31. Program for International Student Assessment, "Reading Literacy: School Poverty Indicator," National Center for Education Statistics website, 2012.

32. Kelsey Hill, Daniel Moser, R. Sam Shannon, and Timothy St, Louis, *Narrowing the Racial Achievement Gap: Policy Success at the State Level,* University of Wisconsin-Madison, Robert M. La Follette School of Public Affairs website, May 2013.

33. Richard Fry and Paul Taylor, "The Rise of Residential Segregation by Income," Pew Research Center Social and Demographic Trends website, August 1, 2012.
34. Mark Dixon, *Public Education Finances: 2012*, U.S. Census Bureau website, May 2014, p. xi.
35. See Michael Leachman and Chris Mai, "Most States Funding Schools Less Than Before the Recession," Center on Budget and Policy Priorities website, revised May 20, 2014.
36. See Andrew Ujifusa and Michele McNeil, "Analysis Points to Growth in Per-Pupil Spending—and Disparities," *Education Week*, January 22, 2014.
37. The Equity and Excellence Commission, *For Each and Every Child—A Strategy for Education Equity and Excellence*, U.S. Department of Education website, 2013, p. 18.
38. "Keeping Schools Local," *Wall Street Journal*, August 24, 1998.
39. Eduardo Porter, "In Public Education, Edge Still Goes to Rich," *New York Times*, November 5, 2013.
40. Ibid.
41. Ibid.

■   ■   ■

Reading as a Writer: Analyzing Rhetorical Choices

1. Reread the text, marking all the statistics in a new color. Your class might decide to work in pairs or groups and split up responsibility for different sections of the reading. Be ready to explain the significance of the numbers you are responsible for in relation to Reich's larger argument. Consider looking up some of the statistics to see if you can find more recent numbers (for example, on federal poverty guidelines or on minimum wage by state). Discuss your findings.

2. While Reich offers many facts and figures, he also makes an argument that these numbers tell a story of inequality that creates unfair disadvantages for many in our country. Mark the sentences in which Reich clearly advances his argument, and note where those sentences are in relationship to the facts he includes. Explain what you think are the strengths and weaknesses of his claims, and be ready to say why.

Writing as a Reader: Entering the Conversation of Ideas

1. Reich examines the historical context and policy decisions that have kept many people in the United States from moving up the economic ladder. Nikole Hannah-Jones (pp. 434–52 in Education) takes a similarly historical and policy-focused approach in her essay. Write an essay of your own in which you use examples from these readings to explain the impact of history and policies on individuals and families. What policy changes might you propose, and why?

2. Both Reich and Barbara Ehrenreich (pp. 482–85 in Sociology) focus on attitudes about the poor in the United States. How do assumptions about the poor help shape policies, and how do those policies affect people living in poverty? Compose an essay that uses examples and analysis from these readings to respond to these questions. Write yourself into this conversation, too (see Chapter 3), as you explain why understanding these concepts matters.

RICHARD H. THALER, CASS R. SUNSTEIN, AND JOHN P. BALZ

Choice Architecture

This reading is a condensed version of the argument Richard Thaler and Cass Sunstein make in their 2008 best-selling book *Nudge: Improving Decisions about Health, Wealth, and Happiness* (2008). These University of Chicago and Harvard professors, along with University of Chicago graduate (PhD in political science) John P. Balz, coined and popularized the term "choice architecture" to explain the ways small details—in consumer displays, software, fee structures, and more—can "nudge" us to make decisions in ways we may not notice. While the authors' expertise comes from business, law, and political science, their insights help us understand the broad implications of being the person who shapes others' choices and being the person whose choices are "nudged."

The authors offer an opening example to set up their inquiry—an easy-to-grasp experiment to gauge the effects of different cafeteria food arrangements on students' selections. In the paragraphs of analysis that follow, however, notice the authors' repeated use of the word "but" to signal deeper analysis of each of the options. (We recommend that you always circle the word "but" in analytical texts, since it usually signals an important refinement of an idea.) Even this seemingly easy example offers complex insights into the significant effects of small design differences. This is what they mean by "choice architecture."

As you read, pay attention to the key terms of the authors' argument. What do they mean by "paternalistic," for example (para. 2) and the related terms "Reflective System," "Automatic System," and "stimulus response compatibility" (paras. 7–9)? Be sure you can describe in your own words "the path of least resistance" or "default" (para. 16) and the concept of "mandated choice" (para. 23). Given their many examples, what other "nudges" have you experienced that you can now recognize and describe?

The implications of "choice architecture" are enormous, whether you are (or will one day be) such an architect or whether you are (we *all* are) someone who lives in a world shaped by this concept. Is it good or bad—or both—that we are nudged toward so many of the consumer choices we seem to make freely? These authors argue that we can learn a lot by noticing all the little "nudges" that can have a big impact on our lives, whether or not we are paying attention.

■ ■ ■

Consider the following hypothetical example: The director of food services for a large city school system runs a series of experiments that manipulate the way in which the food is displayed in cafeterias. Not surprisingly, she finds that what the children eat depends on such things as the order of the items. Foods displayed at the beginning or end of the line are more likely to be eaten than items in the middle, and foods at eye level are more likely to be consumed than those in less salient locations.

The question is: What use should the director make of this newfound knowledge?

Here are a few options to consider: *2*

1. Arrange the food to make the students best off, all things considered.
2. Choose the food order at random.
3. Try to arrange the food to get the kids to pick the same foods they would choose on their own.
4. Maximize the sales of the items from the suppliers that are willing to offer the largest bribes.
5. Maximize profits, period.

Option 1 has obvious appeal. Although there can be some controversies, few would argue with the premise that the kids would be better off eating more fruits and vegetables and fewer burgers, fries and sweets. Yes, this option might seem a bit intrusive, even paternalistic, but the alternatives are worse! Option 2, arranging the food at random, could be considered fair-minded and principled, and it is in one sense neutral. But from the perspective of a practical food service director does it make any sense to scatter the ingredients to a salad bar at random through the line, or separate the hamburgers from the buns? Also, if the orders are randomized across schools, then the children at some schools will have less healthy diets than those at other schools. Is this desirable?

Option 3 might seem to be an honorable attempt to avoid intrusion: *3*
try to mimic what the children would choose for themselves. Maybe this should be thought of as the objectively neutral choice, and maybe the director should neutrally follow people's wishes (at least where she is dealing with older students). But a little thought reveals that this is a difficult option to implement. The experiments prove that what kids choose depends on the order in which the items are displayed. What, then, are the true preferences of the children? What does it mean to try to devise a procedure for determining what the students would choose "on their own"? In a cafeteria, it is impossible to avoid some way of organizing food.

Option 4 might appeal to a corrupt cafeteria manager, and manipulat- *4*
ing the order of the food items would put yet another weapon in the arsenal of available methods to exploit power. But if the director is honorable and honest this would not have any appeal. Like Options 2 and 3, Option 5 has some appeal, especially to a trained economist or a food services director who is given incentives to follow this approach. But the school district must balance a range of priorities and requirements. Does it want its cafeterias to act as profit centers if the result is to make children less healthy?

In this example the director is what we call a *choice architect*. A choice *5*
architect has the responsibility for organizing the context in which people make decisions. Although this example is a figment of our imagination, many real people turn out to be choice architects, most without realizing it. Doctors describing the available treatments to patients, human resource

administrators creating and managing health care plan enrollment, marketers devising sales strategies, ballot designers deciding where to put candidate names on a page, parents explaining the educational options available to a teenager; these are just a few examples of choice architects.

As the school cafeteria shows, small and apparently insignificant 6 details can have major impacts on people's behavior. A good rule of thumb is to assume that "everything matters." Even something as seemingly insignificant as the shape of a door handle. Early in Thaler's career, he taught a class on managerial decision making to business school students. Students would sometimes leave class early to go for job interviews (or a golf game) and would try to sneak out of the room as surreptitiously as possible. Unfortunately for them, the only way out of the room was through a large double door in the front, in full view of the entire class (though not directly in Thaler's line of sight). The doors were equipped with large, handsome wood handles, vertically mounted cylindrical pulls about two feet in length.

When the students came to these doors, they were faced with two 7 competing instincts. One instinct says that to leave a room you push the door. This instinct is part of what psychologists call the Reflective System, a deliberate and self-conscious thought process by which humans use logic and reasoning to help them make decisions. The other instinct says, when faced with large wooden handles that are obviously designed to be grabbed, you pull. This instinct is part of what is called the Automatic System, a rapid, intuitive process that is not associated with what we would traditionally consider *thinking*.[1] It turns out that the latter instinct—the gut instinct—trumped the former—the conscious thought—and every student leaving the room began by pulling on the handle. Alas, the door opened outward.

At one point in the semester, Thaler pointed out this internal conflict 8 to the class, as one embarrassed student was pulling on the door handle while trying to escape the classroom. Thereafter, as a student got up to leave, the rest of the class would eagerly wait to see whether the student would push or pull. Amazingly, most still pulled! Their Automatic Systems triumphed; the signal emitted by that big wooden handle simply could not be screened out.

Those doors are examples of poor architecture because they violate 9 a simple psychological principle known as stimulus response compatibility, whereby the signal to be received (the stimulus) must be consistent with one's desired action. When signal and desire are in opposition, performance suffers and people blunder.

Consider, for example, the effect of a large, red, octagonal sign that 10 reads GO. The difficulties induced by such incompatibilities are easy to show experimentally. One of the most famous such demonstrations is the Stroop (1935) test. In the modern version of this experiment, people see words flashed on a computer screen and they have a very simple task. They press the right button if they see a word that is displayed in red, and press the left button if they see a word displayed in green. People find the task easy and can learn to do it very quickly with great accuracy. That is, until they are thrown a curve ball, in the form of the word GREEN displayed in red, or the word RED displayed in green. For these incompatible signals, response time slows and error rates increase. A key reason is that the Automatic System reads the word faster than the color naming system can decide the color of the text. See the word GREEN in red text and the nonthinking Automatic System rushes to press the left button, which is, of course, the wrong one.

Although we have never seen a green stop sign, doors such as the ones *11* described above are commonplace, and they violate the same principle. Flat plates say "push me" and big handles say "pull me," so don't expect people to push big handles! This is a failure of architecture to accommodate basic principles of human psychology. Life is full of products that suffer from such defects. Isn't it obvious that the largest buttons on a television remote control should be the power, channel, and volume controls? Yet how many remotes have the volume control the same size as the "input" control button (which if pressed accidentally can cause the picture to disappear)?

This sort of design question is not a typical one for economists to think *12* about because economists have a conception of human behavior that assumes, implicitly, that everyone relies completely on their reflective system, and a mighty good one at that! Economic agents are assumed to reason brilliantly, catalogue huge amounts information that they can access instantly from their memories, and exercise extraordinary will power. We call such creatures Econs. Plain old Humans make plenty of mistakes (even when they are consciously thinking!) and suffer all types of breakdowns in planning, self-control, and forecasting as documented in many of the other chapters in this book.

Since the world is made up of Humans, not Econs, both objects and *13* environments should be designed with Humans in mind. A great introduction to the topic of object design for humans [is] Don Norman's wonderful book *The Design of Everyday Things* (1990). One of Norman's best examples is the design of a basic four-burner stove. . . . Most such stoves have the burners in a symmetric arrangement . . . with the controls arranged in a linear fashion below. In this set-up, it is easy to get confused about which knob controls the front burner and which controls the back, and many pots and pans have been burned as a result. . . .

Norman's basic lesson is that designers need to keep in mind that *14* the users of their objects are Humans who are confronted every day with myriad choices and cues. The goal of this essay is to develop the same idea for people who create the environments in which we make decisions: *choice architects.* If you indirectly influence the choices other people make, you have earned the title. Consider the person who designs the menu in a restaurant. The chef will have decided what food will be served, but it is someone else's job to put those offerings on paper (or blackboard) and there are lots of ways to do this. Should hot starters be in a different category from cold ones? Are pasta dishes a separate category? Within categories, how should dishes be listed? Where should prices be listed? In a world of Econs, these details would not matter, but for Humans, nearly everything matters, so choice architects can have considerable power to influence choices. Or to use our preferred language, they can nudge.

Of course, choice architects do not always have the best interests *15* of the people they are influencing in mind. The menu designer may want to push profitable items or those about to spoil by printing them in bold print. Wily but malevolent nudgers like pushy mortgage brokers can have devastating effects on the people who are influenced by them. Conscientious choice architects, however, do have capability to self-consciously construct nudges in an attempt to move people in directions that will make their lives better. And since the choices these choice architects are influencing are going to be made by Humans, they will want their architecture to reflect a good understanding of how humans behave. . . .

Defaults: Padding the Path of Least Resistance

For reasons of laziness, fear, and distraction, many people will take what- *16* ever option requires the least effort, or the path of least resistance. All these forces imply that if, for a given choice, there is a default option—an option that will obtain if the chooser does nothing—then we can expect a large number of people to end up with that option, whether or not it is good for them. These behavioral tendencies toward doing nothing will be reinforced if the default option comes with some implicit or explicit suggestion that it represents the normal or even the recommended course of action.

Defaults are ubiquitous and powerful. They are also unavoidable in *17* the sense that for any node of a choice architecture system, there must be an associated rule that determines what happens to the decision maker if she does nothing. Of course, usually the answer is that if I do nothing, nothing changes; whatever is happening continues to happen. But not always. Some dangerous machines, such as chain saws and lawn mowers, are designed with "dead man switches," so that once a user lets go of the handle, the machine's blades stop. Some "big kid" slides at playgrounds are built with the first step about two feet off the ground to keep smaller kids from getting on and possibly hurting themselves.[2] When you leave a computer alone for a while to answer a phone call, nothing is likely to happen for a given period, after which the screen saver comes on. Neglect the computer long enough, and it may lock itself. Of course, a user can [decide] how long it takes before the screen saver comes on, but implementing that choice takes some action. Most computers come with a default time lag and a default screen saver. Chances are, those are the settings most people still have.

Downloading a new piece of software requires numerous choices, *18* the first of which is "regular" or "custom" installation. Normally, one of the boxes is already checked, indicating it is the default. Which boxes do the software suppliers check? Two different motives are readily apparent: helpful and self-serving. Making the regular installation the default would be in the helpful category if most users will have trouble with the custom installation. Sending unwanted promotional spam to the user's email account would be in the self-serving category. In our experience, most software comes with helpful defaults regarding the type of installation, but many come with self-serving defaults on other choices. Just like choice architects, notice that not all defaults are selected to make the chooser's life easier or better.

Many organizations, public and private, have discovered the immense *19* power of default options, big and small. Consider the idea of automatic renewal for magazine subscriptions? If renewal is automatic, many people will subscribe, for a long time, to magazines they don't read. Or the idea of automatically including seat reservations or travel insurance (for an extra charge, of course) when customers book train or airline tickets (Goldstein et al. 2008). Smart organizations have moved to double-sided printing as the default option. During the presidential campaign, Barack Obama's chief campaign advisor, David Plouffe, ordered all printers to be put on this setting, and the city of Tulsa, Oklahoma, estimates it will save more than $41,000 a year with double-sided printing (Simon 2008).

The choice of the default can be quite controversial. Here are two *20* examples. Faced with a budget crunch and the possible closing of some state parks because of the recent recession, Washington state legislators switched the default rule on state park fees that drivers pay when they renew their license plates. Before the recession, paying the $5 fee had been an option for drivers. The state switched from an [opt-in] to an opt-out arrangement where drivers are charged unless they ask not to pay it. For transparency, the state provides information to each driver explaining the reason behind the change. So far, the move has worked, though critics do not think it is a long-term solution to the state's financial problems.

In another example, an obscure portion of the No Child Left Behind *21* Act requires that school districts supply the names, addresses, and telephone numbers of students to the recruiting offices of branches of the armed forces. However, the law stipulates that "a secondary school student or the parent of the student may request that the student's name, address, and telephone listing not be released without prior written parental consent, and the local educational agency or private school shall notify parents of the option to make a request and shall comply with any request." Some school districts, such as Fairport, New York, interpreted this law as allowing them to implement an "opt-in" policy. That is, parents were notified that they could elect to make their children's contact information available, but if they did not do anything, this information would be withheld.

This reading of the law did not meet with the approval of then- 22 Secretary of Defense Donald Rumsfeld. The Defense and Education Departments sent a letter to school districts asserting that the law required an opt-out implementation. Only if parents actively requested that the contact information on their children be withheld would that option apply. In typical bureaucratic language, the departments contended that the relevant laws "do not permit LEA's [local educational agencies] to institute a policy of not providing the required information unless a parent has affirmatively agreed to provide the information."[3] Both the Defense Department and the school districts realized that opt-in and opt-out policies would lead to very different outcomes. Not surprisingly, much hue and cry ensued.

We have emphasized that default rules are inevitable—that private 23 institutions and the legal system cannot avoid choosing them. In some cases, though not all, there is an important qualification to this claim. The choice architect can force the choosers to make their own choice. We call this approach "required choice" or "mandated choice." In the software example, required choice would be implemented by leaving all the boxes unchecked, and by requiring that at every opportunity one of the boxes be checked in order for people to proceed. In the case of the provision of contact information to the military recruiters, one could imagine a system in which all students (or their parents) are required to fill out a form indicating whether they want to make their contact information available. For emotionally charged issues like this one, such a policy has considerable appeal, because people might not want to be defaulted into an option that they might hate (but fail to reject because of inertia, or real or apparent social pressure).

A good example where mandated choice has considerable appeal 24 is organ donation. As discussed by Johnson et al., some countries have adopted an opt-out approach to organ donation called "presumed consent." This approach clearly maximizes the number of people who (implicitly) agree to make their organs available. However, some people strenuously object to this policy, feeling that the government should not presume anything about their organs. An effective compromise is mandated choice. For example, in Illinois when drivers go to get their license renewed and a new photograph taken they are required to answer the question "do you wish to be an organ donor?" before they can get their license. This policy has produced a 60 percent sign up rate compared to the national average of 38 percent.[4] Furthermore, since the choice to be a donor was explicit rather than implicit, family members of deceased donors are less likely to object.

We believe that required choice, favored by many who like free- 25 dom, is sometimes the best way to go. But consider two points about the approach. First, Humans will often consider required choice to be a nuisance or worse, and would much prefer to have a good default. In the software example, it is helpful to know what the recommended settings are. Most users do not want to have to read an incomprehensible manual in order to determine which arcane setting to elect. When choice is complicated and difficult, people might greatly appreciate a sensible default. It is hardly clear that they should be forced to choose.

Second, required choosing is generally more appropriate for simple   26
yes-or-no decisions than for more complex choices. At a restaurant, the default option is to take the dish as the chef usually prepares it, with the option to substitute or remove certain ingredients. In the extreme, required choosing would imply that the diner has to give the chef the recipe for every dish she orders! When choices are highly complex, required choosing may not be a good idea; it might not even be feasible.

REFERENCES

Byrne, Michael D., and Susan Bovair. "A Working Memory Model of a Common Procedural Error." *Cognitive Science* 21 (1997): 31–61.

City of Tulsa. "City Hall's New Printing Policies Expected to Reduce Costs." City of Tulsa. March 2009. http://www.cityoftulsa.org/COTLegacy/Enews/2009/3-3/SAVINGS.ASP (accessed October 16, 2009).

Donate Life America. "National Donor Designation Report Card." Donate Life American web site (April 2009). http://www.donatelife.net/donante/DLA+Report+Card+2009 .pdf (accessed February 21, 2010).

Gawande, Atul. "The Checklist." *The New Yorker* 83, no. 39 (2007): 86–95.

Goldstein, Daniel G.; Johnson, Eric J.; Herrmann, Andreas; Heitmann, Mark. *Harvard Business Review* 86, no. 12 (2008): 99–105.

Norman, Donald. *The Design of Everyday Things*. Sydney: Currency, 1990.

Pronovost, Peter, Dale Needham, Sean Berenholtz, David Sinopoli, Haitao Chu, Sara Cosgrove, Bryan Sexton, Robert Hyzy, Robert Welsh, Gary Roth, Joseph Bander, John Kepros, and Christine Goeschel. "An Intervention to Decrease Catheter-Related Bloodstream Infections in the ICU." *New England Journal of Medicine* 355, no. 26 (2006): 2725–2732.

Thaler, Richard H., and Cass R. Sunstein. "Libertarian Paternalism," *American Economic Review* 93, no. 2 (2003): 175–79.

Simon, Roger. "Relentless: How Barack Obama Outsmarted Hillary Clinton." Politico.com. Washington, D.C. August 25, 2008. http://www.politico.com/relentless/ (accessed February 22, 2010).

Stroop, John R. "Studies of Interference in Serial Verbal Reactions." *Journal of Experimental Psychology* 12 (1935): 643–62.

Sunstein, Cass R., and Richard H. Thaler. "Libertarian Paternalism Is Not an Oxymoron." *University of Chicago Law Review* 70 (2003): 1159–1202.

Sunstein, Cass R. *Republic.com 2.0*. Princeton: Princeton University Press, 2007.

Tversky, Amos. "Elimination by Aspects: A Theory of Choice." *Psychological Review* 76 (1972): 31–48.

Van De Veer, Donald. *Paternalistic Intervention: The Moral Bounds on Benevolence*. Princeton: Princeton University Press, 1986.

Vicente, Kim J. *The Human Factor; Revolutionizing the Way People Live with Technology*. New York: Routledge, 2006.

Zeliadt, Steven B., Scott D. Ramsey, David F. Penson, Ingrid J. Hall, Donatus U. Ekwueme, Leonard Stroud, and Judith W. Lee. "Why Do Men Choose One Treatment over Another?" *Cancer* 106 (2006): 1865–74.

NOTES

0. This essay draws heavily on Thaler and Sunstein's book *Nudge* (2008) [and] other material that has appeared on the book's blog, which appears at (www.nudges.org) and is edited by Balz. This chapter was written well before Sunstein joined the Obama Administration as counselor to the Director of the Office of Management and Budget, later to be confirmed as Administrator of the Office of Information and Regulatory Affairs. It should go without saying that nothing said here represents an official position in any way. Thaler is a professor at the Booth School of Business, University of Chicago. Sunstein is a professor at the Harvard Law School. Balz is a Ph.D. student in the political science department at the University of Chicago.
1. In the psychology literature, these two systems are sometimes referred to as System 2 and System 1, respectively.
2. Thanks to a *Nudge* reader for this example.
3. Letter of July 2, 2003, to State School Officers signed by William Hanse, deputy secretary of education, and David Chu, undersecretary of defense.
4. Illinois's organ donation rate is compiled by Donate Life Illinois (http://www .donatelifeillinois.org/). For the national organ donor rate see (Donate Life America 2009).

■ ■ ■

Reading as a Writer: Analyzing Rhetorical Choices

1. Thaler, Sunstein, and Balz offer many examples as they illustrate their claims about the power of choice architecture. They describe the Stroop test (para. 10), which may be familiar to you. You can find online versions easily. Try one, and then discuss your experience in relation to this text. What differences—if any—did your peers experience, and what do you make of these differences?

2. In pairs or small groups, generate some additional examples of consumer nudges you have experienced online, in stores, on campus, or in other contexts. Explain your example in relation to the specific terms and claims of this reading.

Writing as a Reader: Entering the Conversation of Ideas

1. Thaler, Sunstein, and Balz's concept of choice architecture is interesting to apply to digital culture of the kind Evan Kindley describes in his essay "Quiz Mania" (pp. 507–14 in Media Studies). Compose an essay in which you apply the concept of choice architecture to some of the examples in Kindley's essay, and perhaps some examples from your own online experience. What aspects of digital culture are revealed through this lens, and what significance do you gather from your observations?

2. The idea of "default" settings as a way to "nudge" people into a decision can be applied to Andrew J. Hoffman's analysis of effective ways to persuade skeptics about climate change (pp. 693–701 in Sustainability and Environmental Studies). Write an essay in which you apply Thaler, Sunstein, and Balz's "default" and "nudge" theories to Hoffman's examples. Explain what you discover about effective argumentation and why you think it matters.

NAOMI KLEIN

From No Logo

Naomi Klein is a Canadian journalist who writes on a range of social issues, including feminism, militarism, and environmental injustices, but she is best known for her work on corporate abuses and the effects of globalization. She publishes frequently in newspapers and has written several books, including the best-seller *The Shock Doctrine: The Rise of Disaster Capitalism* (2008). This excerpt is taken from an earlier book, *No Logo* (2000, reissued in 2012), in which she lays out her critique of corporate greed. How have we, as well-meaning consumers, become complicit in that greed by allowing ourselves to become "branded," and with what effects?

Klein opens historically, observing in the mid-1980s a corporate shift from producing products to producing brands. Pay close attention to the way she analyzes this shift from manufacturing to marketing and how she distinguishes between advertising and branding, explained more fully in the section "The Beginning of the Brand." How and why did "brand essence" become more important to consumers than the products themselves? You might test your own responses to products like Kraft or Campbell's Soup or Quaker Oats—or other brands you name as a class—to consider the emotions those brands evoke that may have very little to do with the product itself. How do you—and Klein—account for these responses?

■ ■ ■

As a private person, I have a passion for landscape, and I have never seen one improved by a billboard. Where every prospect pleases, man is at his vilest when he erects a billboard. When I retire from Madison Avenue, I am going to start a secret society of masked vigilantes who will travel around the world on silent motor bicycles, chopping down posters at the dark of the moon. How many juries will convict us when we are caught in these acts of beneficent citizenship?

— David Ogilvy, founder of the Ogilvy & Mather
advertising agency, in *Confessions
of an Advertising Man*, 1963

The astronomical growth in the wealth and cultural influence of 1 multinational corporations over the last fifteen years can arguably be traced back to a single, seemingly innocuous idea developed by management theorists in the mid-1980s: that successful corporations must primarily produce brands, as opposed to products.

Until that time, although it was understood in the corporate world that 2 bolstering one's brand name was important, the primary concern of every solid manufacturer was the production of goods. This idea was the very gospel of the machine age. An editorial that appeared in *Fortune* magazine in 1938, for instance, argued that the reason the American economy had yet to recover from the Depression was that America had lost sight of the importance of making *things*.

> This is the proposition that the basic and irreversible function of an industrial economy is *the making of things*: that the more things it makes the bigger will be the income, whether dollar or real; and hence that the key to those lost recuperative powers lies . . . in the factory where the lathes and the drills and the fires and the hammers are. It is in the factory and on the land and under the land that purchasing power originates. [italics theirs]

And for the longest time, the making of things remained, at least in 3 principle, the heart of all industrialized economies. But by the eighties, pushed along by that decade's recession, some of the most powerful manufacturers in the world had begun to falter. A consensus emerged that corporations were bloated, oversized; they owned too much, employed too many people, and were weighed down with *too many things*. The very process of producing—running one's own factories, being responsible for tens of thousands of full-time permanent employees—began to look less like the route to success and more a clunky liability.

At around this same time a new kind of corporation began to rival the 4 traditional all-American manufacturers for market share; these were Nikes and Microsofts, and later, the Tommy Hilfigers and Intels. These pioneers made the claim that producing goods was only an incidental part of their operations, and that thanks to recent victories in trade liberalization and labor-law reform, they were able to have their products made for them by contractors, many of them overseas. What these companies produced primarily were not things they said, but *images* of their brands. Their real work lay not in manufacturing but in marketing. This formula, needless to say, has proved enormously profitable, and its success has companies competing in a race toward weightlessness: Whoever owns the least, has the fewest employees on the payroll and produces the most powerful images, as opposed to products, wins the race.

And so the wave of mergers in the corporate world over the last few 5 years is a deceptive phenomenon: It only *looks* as if the giants, by joining forces, are getting bigger and bigger. The true key to understanding these shifts is to realize that in several crucial ways—not their profits, of course—these merged companies are actually shrinking. Their apparent bigness is simply the most effective route toward their real goal: divestment of the world of things.

Since many of today's best-known manufacturers no longer produce 6 products and advertise them, but rather buy products and "brand" them, these companies are forever on the prowl for creative new ways to build and strengthen their brand images. Manufacturing products may require drills, furnaces, hammers, and the like, but creating a brand calls for a completely different set of tools and materials: It requires an endless parade of brand extensions, continuously renewed imagery for marketing, and, most of all, fresh new spaces to disseminate the brand's idea of itself.

In this section, I'll look at how, in ways both insidious and overt, this corporate obsession with brand identity is waging a war on public and individual space: on public institutions such as schools, on youthful identities, on the concept of nationality, and on the possibilities for unmarketed space.

The Beginning of the Brand

It's helpful to go back briefly and look at where the idea of branding first 7 began. Though the words are often used interchangeably, branding and advertising are not the same process. Advertising any given product is only one part of branding's grand plan, as are sponsorship and logo licensing. Think of the brand as the core meaning of the modern corporation, and of the advertisement as one vehicle used to convey that meaning to the world.

The first mass-marketing campaigns, starting in the second half of the 8 nineteenth century, had more to do with advertising than with branding as we understand it today. Faced with a range of recently invented products—the radio, phonograph, car, light bulb and so on—advertisers had more pressing tasks than creating a brand identity for any given corporation; first, they had to change the way people lived their lives. Ads had to inform consumers about the existence of some new invention, then convince them that their lives would be better if they used, for example, cars instead of wagons, telephones instead of mail, and electric light instead of oil lamps. Many of these new products bore brand names—some of which are still around today—but these were almost incidental. These products were themselves news; that was almost advertisement enough.

The first brand-based products appeared at around the same time as 9 the invention-based ads, largely because of another relatively recent innovation: the factory. When goods began to be produced in factories, not only were entirely new products being introduced but old products—even basic staples—were appearing in strikingly new forms. What made early branding efforts different from more straightforward salesmanship was that the market was now being flooded with uniform mass-produced products that were virtually indistinguishable from one another. Competitive branding became a necessity of the machine age—within a context of manufactured sameness, image based difference had to be manufactured along with the product.

So the role of advertising changed from delivering product news bulletins to building an image around a particular brand-name version of a product. The first task of branding was to bestow proper names on generic goods such as sugar, flour, soap, and cereal, which had previously been scooped out of barrels by local shopkeepers. In the 1880s, corporate logos were introduced to mass-produced products like Campbell's Soup, H.J. Heinz pickles and Quaker Oats cereal. As design historians and theorists Ellen Lupton and J. Abbott Miller note, logos were tailored to evoke familiarity and folksiness, in an effort to counteract the new and unsettling anonymity of packaged goods. "Familiar personalities such as Dr. Brown, Uncle Ben, Aunt Jemima, and Old Grand-Dad came to replace the shopkeeper, who was traditionally responsible for measuring bulk foods for customers and acting as an advocate for products . . . a nationwide vocabulary of brand names replaced the small local shopkeeper as the interface between consumer and product." After the product names and characters had been established, advertising gave them a venue to speak directly to would-be consumers. The corporate "personality," uniquely named, packaged and advertised, had arrived.

For the most part, the ad campaigns at the end of the nineteenth century and the start of the twentieth used a set of rigid, pseudoscientific formulas: Rivals were never mentioned, ad copy used declarative statements only, and headlines had to be large, with lots of white space—according to one turn-of-the-century adman, "an advertisement should be big enough to make an impression but not any bigger than the thing advertised." *11*

But there were those in the industry who understood that advertising wasn't just scientific; it was also spiritual: Brands could conjure a feeling—think of Aunt Jemima's comforting presence—but not only that, entire corporations could themselves embody a meaning of their own. In the early twenties, legendary adman Bruce Barton turned General Motors into a metaphor for the American family, "something personal, warm, and human," while GE was not so much the name of the faceless General Electric Company as, in Barton's words, "the initials of a friend." In 1923 Barton said that the role of advertising was to help corporations find their soul. The son of a preacher, he drew on his religious upbringing for uplifting messages: "I like to think of advertising as something big, something splendid, something which goes deep down into an institution and gets hold of the soul of it. . . . Institutions have souls just as men and nations have souls," he told GM president Pierre du Pont. General Motors ads began to tell about the people who drove its cars—the preacher, the pharmacist, or the country doctor who, thanks to his trusty GM, arrived "at the bedside of a dying child" just in time "to bring it back to life." *12*

By the end of the 1940s, there was a burgeoning awareness that a brand wasn't just a mascot or a catchphrase or a picture printed on the label of a company's product; the company as a whole could have a brand identity or a "corporate consciousness," as this ephemeral quality was termed at the time. As this idea evolved, the adman ceased to see himself as a pitchman and instead saw himself as "the philosopher-king of commercial culture," in the words of ad critic Randall Rothberg. The search for the true meaning of brands—or the "brand essence," as it is often called—gradually took the agencies away from individual products and their attributes and toward a psychological/anthropological examination of what brands mean to the culture and to people's lives. This was seen to be of crucial importance, since corporations may manufacture products, but what consumers buy are brands. *13*

It took several decades for the manufacturing world to adjust to this shift. It clung to the idea that its core business was still production and *14* that branding was an important add-on. Then came the brand equity mania of the eighties, the defining moment of which arrived in 1988 when Philip Morris purchased Kraft for $12.6 billion—six times what the company was worth on paper. The price difference, apparently, was the cost of the word "Kraft." Of course Wall Street was aware that decades of marketing and brand bolstering added value to a company over and above its assets and total annual sales. But with the Kraft purchase, a huge dollar value had been assigned to something that had previously been abstract and unquantifiable—a brand name. This was spectacular news for the ad world, which was now able to make the claim that advertising spending was more than just a sales strategy: It was an investment in cold hard equity. The more you spend, the more your company is worth. Not surprisingly, this led to a considerable increase in spending on advertising. More important, it sparked a renewed interest in puffing up brand identities, a project that involved far more than a few billboards and TV spots. It was about pushing the envelope in sponsorship deals, dreaming up new areas in which to "extend" the brand, as well as perpetually probing the Zeitgeist to ensure that the "essence" selected for one's brand would resonate karmically with its target market. For reasons that will be explored in the rest of this chapter, this radical shift in corporate philosophy has sent manufacturers on a cultural feeding frenzy as they seize upon every corner of unmarketed landscape in search of the oxygen needed to inflate their brands. In the process, virtually nothing has been left unbranded. That's quite an impressive feat, considering that as recently as 1993 Wall Street had pronounced the brand dead, or as good as dead.

The Brand's Death (Rumors of Which Had Been Greatly Exaggerated)

. . . On April 2, 1993, advertising itself was called into question by the very   *15* brands the industry had been building, in some cases, for over two centuries. That day is known in marketing circles as "Marlboro Friday," and it refers to a sudden announcement from Philip Morris that it would slash the price of Marlboro cigarettes by 20 percent in an attempt to compete with bargain brands that were eating into its market. The pundits went nuts, announcing in frenzied unison that not only was Marlboro dead, all brand names were dead. The reasoning was that if a "prestige" brand like Marlboro, whose image had been carefully groomed, preened, and enhanced with more than a billion advertising dollars, was desperate enough to compete with no-names, then clearly the whole concept of branding had lost its currency. The public had seen the advertising, and the public didn't care. The Marlboro Man, after all, was not any old campaign; launched in 1954, it was the longest-running ad campaign in history. It was a legend. If the Marlboro Man had crashed, well, then, brand equity had crashed as well. The implication that Americans were suddenly thinking for themselves en masse reverberated through Wall Street. The same day Philip Morris announced its price cut, stock prices nose-dived for all the household brands: Heinz, Quaker Oats, Coca-Cola, PepsiCo, Procter and Gamble, and RJR Nabisco. Philip Morris's own stock took the worst beating.

Bob Stanojev, national director of consumer products marketing for *16* Ernst and Young, explained the logic behind Wall Street's panic: "If one or two powerhouse consumer products companies start to cut prices for good, there's going to be an avalanche. Welcome to the value generation."

Yes, it was one of those moments of overstated instant consensus, but *17* it was not entirely without cause. Marlboro had always sold itself on the strength of its iconic image marketing, not on anything so prosaic as its price. As we now know, the Marlboro Man survived the price wars without sustaining too much damage. At the time, however, Wall Street saw Philip Morris's decision as symbolic of a sea change. The price cut was an admission that Marlboro's name was no longer sufficient to sustain the flagship position, which in a context where image is equity meant that Marlboro had blinked. And when Marlboro—one of the quintessential global brands—blinks, it raises questions about branding that reach beyond Wall Street, and way beyond Philip Morris.

The panic of Marlboro Friday was not a reaction to a single incident. *18* Rather, it was the culmination of years of escalating anxiety in the face of some rather dramatic shifts in consumer habits that were seen to be eroding the market share of household-name brands, from Tide to Kraft. Bargain-conscious shoppers, hit hard by the recession, were starting to pay more attention to price than to the prestige bestowed on their products by the yuppie ad campaigns of the 1980s. The public was suffering from a bad case of what is known in the industry as "brand blindness."

Study after study showed that baby boomers, blind to the alluring *19* images of advertising and deaf to the empty promises of celebrity spokespersons, were breaking their lifelong brand loyalties and choosing to feed their families with private-label brands from the supermarket—claiming, heretically, that they couldn't tell the difference. From the beginning of the recession to 1993, Loblaw's President's Choice line, Wal-Mart's Great Value, and Marks and Spencer's St. Michael prepared foods had nearly doubled their market share in North America and Europe. The computer market, meanwhile, was flooded by inexpensive clones, causing IBM to slash its prices and otherwise impale itself. It appeared to be a return to the proverbial shopkeeper dishing out generic goods from the barrel in a pre-branded era. . . .

The Brands Bounce Back

There were some brands that were watching from the sidelines as Wall *20* Street declared the death of the brand. Funny, they must have thought, we don't feel dead.

Just as the admen had predicted at the beginning of the recession, the   *21*
companies that exited the downturn running were the ones who opted
for marketing over value every time: Nike, Apple, the Body Shop, Calvin
Klein, Disney, Levi's, and Starbucks. Not only were these brands doing just
fine, thank you very much, but the act of branding was becoming a larger
and larger focus of their businesses. For these companies, the ostensible
product was mere filler for the real production: the brand. They integrated
the idea of branding into the very fabric of their companies. Their corporate cultures were so tight and cloistered that to outsiders they appeared to
be a cross between fraternity house, religious cult, and sanitarium. Everything was an ad for the brand: bizarre lexicons for describing employees (partners, baristas, team players, crew members), company chants,
superstar CEOs, fanatical attention to design consistency, a propensity
for monument-building, and New Age mission statements. Unlike classic
household brand names, such as Tide and Marlboro, these logos weren't
losing their currency; they were in the midst of breaking every barrier in
the marketing world—becoming cultural accessories and lifestyle philosophers. These companies didn't wear this image like a cheap shirt—their
image was so integrated with their business that other people wore it as
their shirt. And when the brands crashed, these companies didn't even
notice—they were branded to the bone.

So the real legacy of Marlboro Friday is that it simultaneously   *22*
brought the two most significant developments in nineties marketing and
consumerism into sharp focus: the deeply unhip big-box bargain stores
that provide the essentials of life and monopolize a disproportionate share
of the market (Wal-Mart *et al.*) and the extra-premium "attitude" brands
that provide the essentials of lifestyle and monopolize ever-expanding
stretches of cultural space (Nike *et al.*). The way these two tiers of consumerism developed would have a profound impact on the economy in
the years to come. When overall ad expenditures took a nosedive in 1991,
Nike and Reebok were busy playing advertising chicken, with each company increasing its budget to outspend the other. In 1991 alone, Reebok
upped its ad spending by 71.9 percent, while Nike pumped an extra 24.6
percent into its already soaring ad budget, bringing the company's total
spending on marketing to a staggering $250 million annually. Far from
worrying about competing on price, the sneaker pimps were designing
ever more intricate and pseudoscientific air pockets, and driving up prices
by signing star athletes to colossal sponsorship deals. The fetish strategy
seemed to be working fine: In the six years prior to 1993, Nike had gone
from a $750 million company to a $4 billion one and Phil Knight's Beaver-
ton, Oregon, company emerged from the recession with profits 900 percent higher than when it began.

Benetton and Calvin Klein, meanwhile, were also upping their spend-   *23*
ing on lifestyle marketing, using ads to associate their lines with risqué
art and progressive politics. Clothes barely appeared in these high-concept
advertisements, let alone prices. Even more abstract was Absolut Vodka,

which for some years now had been developing a marketing strategy in which its product disappeared and its brand was nothing but a blank bottle-shaped space that could be filled with whatever content a particular audience most wanted from its brands: intellectual in *Harper's*, futuristic in *Wired*, alternative in *Spin*, loud and proud in *Out*, and "Absolut Centerfold" in *Playboy*. The brand reinvented itself as a cultural sponge, soaking up and morphing to its surroundings.

Saturn, too, came out of nowhere in October 1990 when GM launched 24 a car built not out of steel and rubber but out of New Age spirituality and seventies feminism. After the car had been on the market a few years, the company held a "homecoming" weekend for Saturn owners, during which they could visit the auto plant and have a cookout with the people who made their cars. As the Saturn ads boasted at the time, "44,000 people spent their vacations with us, at a car plant." It was as if Aunt Jemima had come to life and invited you over to her house for dinner.

In 1993, the year the Marlboro Man was temporarily hobbled by 25 "brand-blind" consumers, Microsoft made its striking debut on *Advertising Age's* list of the top 200 ad spenders—the very same year that Apple computer increased its marketing budget by 30 percent after already making branding history with its Orwellian takeoff ad launch during the 1984 Super Bowl. Like Saturn, both companies were selling a hip new relationship to the machine that left Big Blue IBM looking as clunky and menacing as the now-dead Cold War.

And then there were the companies that had always understood 26 that they were selling brands before product. Coke, Pepsi, McDonald's, Burger King, and Disney weren't fazed by the brand crisis, opting instead to escalate the brand war, especially since they had their eyes firmly fixed on global expansion. They were joined in this project by a wave of sophisticated producer/retailers who hit full stride in the late eighties and early nineties. The Gap, Ikea, and the Body Shop were spreading like wildfire during this period, masterfully transforming the generic into the brand-specific, largely through bold, carefully branded packaging and the promotion of an "experiential" shopping environment. The Body Shop had been a presence in Britain since the seventies, but it wasn't until 1988 that it began sprouting like a green weed on every street corner in the United States. Even during the darkest years of the recession, the company opened between forty and fifty American stores a year. Most baffling of all to Wall Street, it pulled off the expansion without spending a dime on advertising. Who needed billboards and magazine ads when retail outlets were three-dimensional advertisements for an ethical and ecological approach to cosmetics? The Body Shop was all brand.

The Starbucks coffee chain, meanwhile, was also expanding during 27 this period without laying out much in advertising; instead, it was spinning off its name into a wide range of branded projects: Starbucks airline coffee, office coffee, coffee ice cream, coffee beer. Starbucks seemed to understand brand names at a level even deeper than Madison Avenue, incorporating marketing into every fiber of its corporate concept—from the chain's strategic association with books, blues, and jazz to its Euro-latte lingo. What the success of both the Body Shop and Starbucks showed was how far the branding project had come in moving beyond splashing one's logo on a billboard. Here were two companies that had fostered powerful identities by making their brand concept into a virus and sending it out into the culture via a variety of channels: cultural sponsorship, political controversy, the consumer experience, and brand extensions. Direct advertising, in this context, was viewed as a rather clumsy intrusion into a much more organic approach to image building.

Scott Bedbury, Starbucks' vice president of marketing, openly recognized that "consumers don't truly believe there's a huge difference between products," which is why brands must "establish emotional ties" with their customers through "the Starbucks Experience." The people who line up for Starbucks, writes CEO Howard Shultz, aren't just there for the coffee. "It's the romance of the coffee experience, the feeling of warmth and community people get in Starbucks stores." 28

Interestingly, before moving to Starbucks, Bedbury was head of marketing at Nike, where he oversaw the launch of the "Just Do It!" slogan, among other watershed branding moments. In the following passage, he explains the common techniques used to infuse the two very different brands with meaning: 29

> Nike, for example, is leveraging the deep emotional connection that people have with sports and fitness. With Starbucks, we see how coffee has woven itself into the fabric of people's lives, and that's our opportunity for emotional leverage . . . A great brand raises the bar—it adds a greater sense of purpose to the experience, whether it's the challenge to do your best in sports and fitness or the affirmation that the cup of coffee you're drinking really matters.

This was the secret, it seemed, of all the success stories of the late eighties and early nineties. The lesson of Marlboro Friday was that there never really was a brand crisis—only brands that had crises of confidence. The brands would be okay, Wall Street concluded, so long as they believed fervently in the principles of branding and never, ever blinked. Overnight, "Brands, not products!" became the rallying cry for a marketing renaissance led by a new breed of companies that saw themselves as "meaning brokers" instead of product producers. What was changing was the idea of what—in both advertising and branding—was being sold. The old paradigm had it that all marketing was selling a product. In the new model, however, the product always takes a back seat to the real product, the brand, and the selling of the brand acquired an extra component that can only be described as spiritual. Advertising is about hawking product. Branding, in its truest and most advanced incarnations, is about corporate transcendence. 30

It may sound flaky, but that's precisely the point. On Marlboro Friday, *31* a line was drawn in the sand between the lowly price slashers and the high-concept brand builders. The brand builders conquered, and a new consensus was born: The products that will flourish in the future will be the ones presented not as "commodities" but as concepts: the brand as experience, as lifestyle.

Ever since, a select group of corporations has been attempting to *32* free itself from the corporeal world of commodities, manufacturing, and products to exist on another plane. Anyone can manufacture a product, they reason (and as the success of private-label brands during the recession proved, anyone did). Such menial tasks, therefore, can and should be farmed out to contractors and subcontractors whose only concern is filling the order on time and under budget (ideally in the Third World, where labor is dirt cheap, laws are lax, and tax breaks come by the bushel). Headquarters, meanwhile, is free to focus on the real business at hand—creating a corporate mythology powerful enough to infuse meaning into these raw objects just by signing its name.

The corporate world has always had a deep New Age streak, fed—it *33* has become clear—by a profound need that could not be met simply by trading widgets for cash. But when branding captured the corporate imagination, New Age vision quests took center stage. As Nike CEO Phil Knight explains, "For years we thought of ourselves as a production-oriented company, meaning we put all our emphasis on designing and manufacturing the product. But now we understand that the most important thing we do is market the product. We've come around to saying that Nike is a marketing-oriented company, and the product is our most important marketing tool." This project has since been taken to an even more advanced level with the emergence of online corporate giants such as Amazon.com. It is online that the purest brands are being built: Liberated from the real-world burdens of stores and product manufacturing, these brands are free to soar, less as the disseminators of goods or services than as collective hallucinations.

Tom Peters, who has long coddled the inner flake in many a hard- *34* nosed CEO, latched on to the branding craze as the secret to financial success, separating the transcendental logos and the earthbound products into two distinct categories of companies. "The top half—Coca-Cola, Microsoft, Disney, and so on—are pure 'players' in brainware. The bottom half [Ford and GM] are still lumpy-object purveyors, though automobiles are much 'smarter' than they used to be," Peters writes in *The Circle of Innovation* (1997), an ode to the power of marketing over production.

When Levi's began to lose market share in the late nineties, the *35* trend was widely attributed to the company's failure—despite lavish ad spending—to transcend its products and become a free-standing meaning. "Maybe one of Levi's problems is that it has no Cola," speculated Jennifer Steinhauer in *The New York Times*. "It has no denim-toned house paint. Levi makes what is essentially a commodity: blue jeans. Its ads may evoke rugged outdoorsmanship, but Levi hasn't promoted any particular life style to sell other products."

In this high-stakes new context, the cutting-edge ad agencies no lon- 36 ger sold companies on individual campaigns but on their ability to act as "brand stewards": identifying, articulating, and protecting the corporate soul. Not surprisingly, this spelled good news for the U.S. advertising industry, which in 1994 saw a spending increase of 8.6 percent over the previous year. In one year, the ad industry went from a near crisis to another "best year yet." And that was only the beginning of triumphs to come. By 1997, corporate advertising, defined as "ads that position a corporation, its values, its personality and character," were up 18 percent from the year before.

With this wave of brand mania has come a new breed of businessman, 37 one who will proudly inform you that Brand X is not a product but a way of life, an attitude, a set of values, a look, an idea. And it sounds really great—way better than that Brand X is a screwdriver, or a hamburger chain, or a pair of jeans, or even a very successful line of running shoes. Nike, Phil Knight announced in the late eighties, is "a sports company"; its mission is not to sell shoes but to "enhance people's lives through sports and fitness" and to keep "the magic of sports alive." Company president-cum-sneaker-shaman Tom Clark explains that "the inspiration of sports allows us to rebirth ourselves constantly."

Reports of such "brand vision" epiphanies began surfacing from all 38 corners. "Polaroid's problem," diagnosed the chairman of its advertising agency, John Hegarty, "was that they kept thinking of themselves as a camera. But the '[brand] vision' process taught us something: Polaroid is not a camera—it's a social lubricant." IBM isn't selling computers; it's selling business "solutions." Swatch is not about watches; it is about the idea of time. At Diesel Jeans, owner Renzo Rosso told *Paper* magazine, "We don't sell a product, we sell a style of life. I think we have created a movement. . . . The Diesel concept is everything. It's the way to live, it's the way to wear, it's the way to do something." And as Body Shop founder Anita Roddick explained to me, her stores aren't about what they sell; they are the conveyers of a grand idea—a political philosophy about women, the environment and ethical business. "I just use the company that I surprisingly created as a success—it shouldn't have been like this, it wasn't meant to be like this—to stand on the products to shout out on these issues," Roddick says.

The famous late graphic designer Tibor Kalman summed up the 39 shifting role of the brand this way: "The original notion of the brand was quality, but now brand is a stylistic badge of courage."

The idea of selling the courageous message of a brand, as opposed 40 to a product, intoxicated these CEOs, providing as it did an opportunity for seemingly limitless expansion. After all, if a brand was not a product, it could be anything! And nobody embraced branding theory with more evangelical zeal than Richard Branson, whose Virgin Group has branded joint ventures in everything from music to bridal gowns to airlines to cola to financial services. Branson refers derisively to the "stilted Anglo-Saxon view of consumers," which holds that a name should be associated with a product like sneakers or soft drinks, and opts instead for "the Asian 'trick'" of the *keiretsus* (a Japanese term meaning a network of linked corporations). The idea, he explains, is to "build brands not around products but around reputation. The great Asian names imply quality, price and innovation rather than a specific item. I call these 'attribute' brands: They do not relate directly to one product—such as a Mars bar or a Coca-Cola—but instead to a set of values."

Tommy Hilfiger, meanwhile, is less in the business of manufacturing 41 clothes than he is in the business of signing his name. The company is run entirely through licensing agreements, with Hilfiger commissioning all its products from a group of other companies: Jockey International makes Hilfiger underwear, Pepe Jeans London makes Hilfiger jeans, Oxford Industries make Tommy shirts, the Stride Rite Corporation makes its footwear. What does Tommy Hilfiger manufacture? Nothing at all.

So passé had products become in the age of lifestyle branding that 42 by the late nineties newer companies like Lush cosmetics and Old Navy clothing began playing with the idea of old-style commodities as a source of retro marketing imagery. The Lush chain serves up its face masks and moisturizers out of refrigerated stainless-steel bowls, spooned into plastic containers with grocery-store labels. Old Navy showcases its shrink-wrapped T-shirts and sweatshirts in deli-style chrome refrigerators, as if they were meat or cheese. When you are a pure, concept-driven brand, the aesthetics of raw product can prove as "authentic" as loft living.

And lest the branding business be dismissed as the playground 43 of trendy consumer items such as sneakers, jeans, and New Age beverages, think again. Caterpillar, best known for building tractors and busting unions, has barreled into the branding business, launching the Cat accessories line: boots, back-packs, hats, and anything else calling out for a postindustrial *je ne sais quoi*. Intel Corp., which makes computer parts no one sees and few understand, transformed its processors into a fetish brand with TV ads featuring line workers in funky metallic space suits dancing to "Shake Your Groove Thing." The Intel mascots proved so popular that the company has sold hundreds of thousands of bean-filled dolls modeled on the shimmery dancing technicians. Little wonder, then, that when asked about the company's decision to diversify its products, the senior vice president for sales and marketing, Paul S. Otellini, replied that Intel is "like Coke. One brand, many different products."

And if Caterpillar and Intel can brand, surely anyone can. 44

There is, in fact, a new strain in marketing theory that holds that even 45
the lowliest natural resources, barely processed, can develop brand identities, thus giving way to hefty premium-price markups. In an essay appropriately titled "How to Brand Sand," advertising executives Sam Hill, Jack
McGrath and Sandeep Dayal team up to tell the corporate world that with
the right marketing plan, nobody has to stay stuck in the stuff business.
"Based on extensive research, we would argue that you can indeed brand
not only sand, but also wheat, beef, brick, metals, concrete, chemicals,
corn grits, and an endless variety of commodities traditionally considered
immune to the process."

Over the past six years, spooked by the near-death experience of Marl- 46
boro Friday, global corporations have leaped on the brand-wagon with
what can only be described as a religious fervor. Never again would the
corporate world stoop to praying at the altar of the commodity market.
From now on they would worship only graven media images. Or to quote
Tom Peters, the brand man himself: "Brand! Brand!! Brand!!! That's the
message . . . for the late '90s and beyond."

■   ■   ■

Reading as a Writer: Analyzing Rhetorical Choices

1. Try to summarize Klein's argument about how and why brands became
    more important than products starting in the mid-1980s. What is the dif-
    ference between advertising and branding according to Klein?

2. Divide into pairs/teams and look up the advertising costs and production
    information of a few popular brands, including some of your favorites.
    Also consult the costs of generic versions of these products. What conclu-
    sions can you draw using Klein's insights?

Writing as a Reader: Entering the Conversation of Ideas

1. How are Klein's ideas in conversation with Laura Pappano's analysis of
    the marketing of "big-time sports" on campuses (pp. 416–26 in Educa-
    tion)? Write an essay in which you use Klein's insights to analyze examples
    of athletic branding in Pappano's essay. Select at least one additional cam-
    pus athletic "brand" to analyze as you write yourself into this conversation
    about how campus athletic branding works and what you think about it.
    What does it have to do with education?

2. Klein's ideas about branding are interesting to consider in light of the ideas
    about marketing and "nature" found in Carolyn Merchant's essay "Eden
    Commodified" (pp. 732–39 in Sustainability and Environmental Studies).
    In an essay of your own that draws together insights and examples from
    Klein and Merchant, construct an argument about whether there can be
    an ethical approach to branding or marketing environmental products or
    issues. What are the possible hazards? What might be good about this kind
    of marketing? If you like, include an example of an environmental issue that
    could be marketed, keeping the cautionary ideas of these authors in mind.

ANN DUCILLE

From Multicultural Barbie and the Merchandising of Difference

Ann duCille has served as the chair and director of the Center for African American Studies at Wesleyan University. She has published widely on black women writers and on race and popular culture, particularly in her book *Skin Trade* (1996), which won the Myers Center Award for the Study of Human Rights in 1997. The essay here originally appeared in the Spring 1994 issue of *differences: A Journal of Feminist Cultural Studies*. In this piece about Barbie, you'll hear one of duCille's key interests in popular culture: the ways we all help establish cultural norms through producing and consuming goods and ideas.

A quick look through duCille's Works Cited list at the end of the essay shows that she draws on a range of academic conversations to frame her analysis of Barbie. She responds not only to scholars who write about Barbie but also to those who write about adolescent self-image, raising African American children, and various aspects of multiculturalism and diversity. As you read duCille's essay, keep track of when and how she draws on those she calls "Barbiologists" and those whose ideas give context to her broader analysis of culture. You will have to make similar moves in your own writing as you use various sources to help you build your own point.

While she draws on many other scholars' ideas to help her build her point, duCille also invites readers to identify with her personal experiences, particularly in the opening and closing sections of the essay. How effectively do these personal anecdotes—her own and others'—draw you into the piece? How might they shed new light on toys you played with as a child, toys you may have forgotten all about? Considering the way culture teaches us to pay attention to both race and physical appearance as we think about who "we" are, duCille ends her essay by asking, "Is Barbie bad?" Her answer: "Barbie is just a piece of plastic, but what she says about the economic base of our society—what she suggests about gender and race in our world—ain't good." DuCille should invite you to reconsider your own experiences with the "ideological work of child's play" (para. 5). If you ask the kinds of questions duCille asks of Barbie, you should discover similarly eye-opening answers.

■ ■ ■

The white missionaries who came to Saint Aug's from New England were darling to us. They gave Bessie and me these beautiful china dolls that probably were very expensive. Those dolls were white, of course. You couldn't get a colored doll like that in those days. Well, I loved mine, just the way it was, but do you know what Bessie did? She took an artist's palette they had also given us and sat down and mixed the paints until she came up with a shade of brown that matched her skin. Then she painted that white doll's face! None of the white missionaries ever said a word about it. Mama and Papa just smiled. (Sarah Delany)

This is my doll story (because every black journalist who writes about race gets around to it sometime). Back when I started playing with Barbie, there were no Christies (Barbie's black friend, born in 1968) or black Barbies (born in 1980, brown plastic poured into blond Barbie's mold). I had two blonds, which I bought with Christmas money from girls at school.

I cut off their hair and dressed them in African-print fabric. They lived together (polygamy, I guess) with a black G.I. Joe bartered from the Shepp boys, my downstairs neighbors. After an "incident" at school (where all of the girls looked like Barbie and none of them looked like me), I galloped down our stairs with one Barbie, her blond head hitting each spoke of the banister, thud, thud, thud. And galloped up the stairs, thud, thud, thud, until her head popped off, lost to the graveyard behind the stairwell. Then I tore off each limb, and sat on the stairs for a long time twirling the torso like a baton. (Lisa Jones)

Growing up in the 1950s, in the shadow of the second world war, it   *1* was natural for children—including little black children like my two brothers and me—to want to play war, to mimic what we heard on the radio, what we watched in black and white on our brand new floor model Motorola. In these war games, everyone wanted to be the Allied troops—the fearless, conquering white male heroes who had made the world safe for democracy, yet again, and saved us all from yellow peril. No one, of course, wanted to play the enemy—who most often was not the Germans or the Italians but the Japanese. So the enemy became or, more rightly, remained invisible, lurking in bushes we shot at with sticks we pretended were rifles and stabbed at with make-believe bayonets. "Take that," we shouted, liberally peppering our verbal assaults with racial epithets. "And that! And that!" It was all in fun—our venom and vigor. All's fair in wars of words. We understood little of what we said and nothing of how much our child's play reflected the sentiments of a nation that even in its finer, pre-war moments had not embraced as citizens its Asian immigrants or claimed as countrymen and women their American-born offspring.

However naively imitative, our diatribe was interrupted forever one   *2* summer afternoon by the angry voice of our mother, chastising us through the open window. "Stop that," she said. "Stop that this minute. It's not nice. You're talking about the Japanese. *Japanese*, do you understand? And don't let me ever hear you call them anything else." In the lecture that accompanied dinner that evening, we were made to understand not the history of Japanese-Americans, the injustice of internment, or the horror of Hiroshima, but simply that there were real people behind the names we called; that name-calling always hurts somebody, always undermines someone's humanity. Our young minds were led on the short journey from "Jap" to "nigger"; and if we were too young then to understand the origins and line points of all such pejoratives, we were old enough to know firsthand the pain of one of them.

I cannot claim that this early experience left me free of prejudice, but   *3* it did assist me in growing up at once aware of my own status as "different" and conscious of the exclusion of others so labeled. It is important to note, however, that my sense of my own difference was affirmed and confirmed not simply by parental intervention but also by the unrelenting sameness of the tiny, almost exclusively white town in which I was raised. There in the country confines of East Bridgewater, Massachusetts, the adults who surrounded me (except for my parents) were all white, as were the teachers who taught me, the authors who thrilled me (and instilled in me a love of literature), and the neighborhood children who called me nigger one moment and friend the next. And when my brothers and I went our separate ways into properly gendered spheres, the dolls I played with—like almost everything else about my environment—were also white: Betsy Wetsy, Tiny Tears, and Patty Play Pal.

It seems remarkable to me now, as I remember these childish things *4* long since put away, that, for all the daily reminders of my blackness, I did not take note of its absence among the rubber-skin pinkness of Betsy Wetsy, the bald-headed whiteness of Tiny Tears, and the blue-eyed blondness of Patty Play Pal. I was never tempted like Sarah Delany to paint the dolls I played with brown like me or to dress them in African-print fabric like Lisa Jones. (Indeed, I had no notion of such fabrics and little knowledge of the "dark continent" from which they came.) Caught up in fantasy, completely given over to the realm of make-believe, for most of my childhood I neither noticed nor cared that the dolls I played with did not look like me. The make-believe world to which I willingly surrendered more than just my disbelief was thoroughly and profoundly white. That is to say, the "me" I invented, the "I" I imagined, the Self I day-dreamed in technicolor fantasies was no more black like me than the dolls I played with. In the fifties and well into the sixties of my childhood, the black Other who was my Self, much like the enemy Other who was the foreign body of our war games, could only be imagined as faceless, far away, and utterly unfamiliar.

As suggested by my title, I am going to use the figure of multicultural *5* Barbie to talk about the commodification of race and gender difference. I wanted to back into the present topic, however, into what I have to say about Barbie as a gendered, racialized icon of contemporary commodity culture, by reaching into the past—into the admittedly contested terrain of the personal—to evoke the ideological work of child's play. More than simple instruments of pleasure and amusement, toys and games play crucial roles in helping children determine what is valuable in and around them. Dolls in particular invite children to replicate them, to imagine themselves in their dolls' images. What does it mean, then, when little girls are given dolls to play with that in no way resemble them? What did it mean for me that I was nowhere in the toys I played with?

If the Japan and the Africa of my youth were beyond the grasp (if not the *6* reach) of my imagination, children today are granted instant global gratification in their play—immediate, hands-on access to both Self and Other. Or so we are told by many of the leading fantasy manufacturers—Disney,

Hasbro, and Mattel, in particular—whose contributions to multicultural education include such play things as Aladdin (movie, video, and dolls), G.I. Joe (male "action figures" in black and white), and Barbie (now available in a variety of colors and ethnicities). Disneyland's river ride through different nations, like Mattel's Dolls of the World Collection, instructs us that "It's a Small World After All." Those once distant lands of Africa, Asia, Australia, and even the Arctic regions of the North Pole (yes, Virginia, there is an Eskimo Barbie) are now as close to home as the local Toys R Us and F.A.O. Schwarz. And lo and behold, the inhabitants of these foreign lands—from Disney's Princess Jasmine to Mattel's Jamaican Barbie—are just like us, dye-dipped versions of archetypal white American beauty. It is not only a small world after all, but, as the Grammy award-winning theme from *Aladdin* informs us, "it's a whole new world."

Many of the major toy manufacturers have taken on a global perspec-   7
tive, a kind of nearsightedness that constructs this whole new world as small and cultural difference as consumable. Perhaps nowhere is this universalizing myopia more conspicuous than in the production, marketing, and consumption of Barbie dolls. By Mattel's reckoning, Barbie enjoys 100 percent brand name recognition among girls ages three to ten, 96 percent of whom own at least one doll, with most owning an average of eight. Five years ago, as Barbie turned thirty, *Newsweek* noted that nearly 500 million Barbies had been sold, along with 200 million G.I. Joes—"enough for every man, woman, and child in the United States and Europe" (Kantrowitz 59–60). Those figures have increased dramatically in the past five years, bringing the current world-wide Barbie population to 800 million. In 1992 alone, $1 billion worth of Barbies and accessories were sold. Last year, Barbie dolls sold at an average of one million per week, with overall sales exceeding the $1 billion all-time high set the year before. As the *Boston Globe* reported on the occasion of Barbie's thirty-fifth birthday on March 9, 1994, nearly two Barbie dolls are sold every second somewhere in the world; about 50 percent of the dolls sold are purchased here in the United States (Dembner 16).

The current Barbie boom may be in part the result of new, multicul-   8
turally oriented developments both in the dolls and in their marketing. In the fall of 1990, Mattel, Inc. announced a new marketing strategy to boost its sales: the corporation would "go ethnic" in its advertising by launching an ad campaign for the black and Hispanic versions of the already popular doll. Despite the existence of black, Asian, and Latina Barbies, prior to the fall of 1990 Mattel's print and TV ads featured only white dolls. In what *Newsweek* described as an attempt to capitalize on ethnic spending power, Mattel began placing ads for multicultural Barbies in such Afrocentric publications as *Essence* magazine and on such Latin-oriented shows as *Pepe Plata* after market research revealed that most black and Hispanic consumers were unaware of the company's ethnic dolls. This targeted advertising was a smart move, according to the industry analysts cited by *Newsweek*, because "Hispanics buy about $170 billion worth of

goods each year, [and] blacks spend even more." Indeed, sales of black Barbie dolls reportedly doubled in the year following this new ethnically-oriented ad campaign.[1] But determined to present itself as politically correct as well as financially savvy, Mattel was quick to point out that ethnic audiences, who are now able to purchase dolls who look like them, also have profited from the corporation's new marketing priorities. Barbie is a role model for all of her owners, according to product manager Deborah Mitchell, herself an African American. "Barbie allows little girls to dream," she asserted—to which the *Newsweek* reporter added (seemingly without irony): "now, ethnic Barbie lovers will be able to dream in their own image" (Berkwitz 48).

Dream in their own image? The *Newsweek* columnist inadvertently 9 put his finger on precisely what is so troubling to many parents, feminist scholars, and cultural critics about Barbie and dolls like her. Such toys invite, inspire, and even demand a potentially damaging process not simply of imagining but of interpellation. When little girls fantasize themselves into the conspicuous consumption, glamour, perfection, and, some have argued, anorexia of Barbie's world, it is rarely, if ever, "in their own image that they dream."[2] Regardless of what color dyes the dolls are dipped in or what costumes they are adorned with, the image they present is of the same mythically thin, long-legged, luxuriously-haired, buxom beauty. And while Mattel and other toy manufacturers may claim to have the best interests of ethnic audiences in mind in peddling their integrated wares, one does not have to be a cynic to suggest that profit remains the motivating factor behind this merchandising of difference.[3]

Far from simply playing with the sixty or so dolls I have acquired in 10 the past year, then, I take them very seriously. In fact, I regard Barbie and similar dolls as Louis Althusser might have regarded them: as objects that do the dirty work of patriarchy and capitalism in the most insidious

---

[1] Mattel introduced the Shani doll—a black, Barbie-like doll—in 1991, which also may have contributed to the rise in sales, particularly since the company engaged the services of a PR firm that specializes in targeting ethnic audiences.

[2] Of course, the notion of "dreaming in one's own image" is always problematic since dreams, by definition, engage something other than the "real."

[3] Olmec Toys, a black-owned company headed by an African American woman named Yla Eason, markets a line of black and Latina Barbie-like dolls called the Imani Collection. Billed on their boxes as "African American Princess" and "Latin American Fantasy," these dolls are also presented as having been designed with the self images of black children in mind. "We've got one thing in mind with all our products," the blurbs on the Imani boxes read: "let's build self-esteem. Our children gain a sense of self importance through toys. So we make them look like them." Given their obvious resemblance to Barbie dolls—their long, straight hair and pencil-thin plastic bodies—Imani dolls look no more "like them," like "real" black children, than their prototype. Eason, who we are told was devastated by her son's announcement that he couldn't be a superhero because he wasn't white, may indeed want to give black children toys to play with that "look like them." Yet, in order to compete in a market long dominated by Mattel and Hasbro, her company, it seems, has little choice but to conform to the Barbie mold.

way—in the guise of child's play. But, as feminists have protested almost from the moment she hit the market, Barbie is not simply a child's toy or just a teenage fashion doll; she is an icon—perhaps *the* icon—of true white womanhood and femininity, a symbol of the far from innocent ideological stuff of which the (Miss) American dream and other mystiques of race and gender are made.

Invented by Ruth Handler, one of the founders of Mattel, and named   *11* after her daughter, Barbie dolls have been a very real force in the toy market since Mattel first introduced them at the American Toy Fair in 1959. In fact, despite the skepticism of toy store buyers—who at the time were primarily men—the first shipment of a half million dolls and a million costumes sold out immediately (Larcen A7). The first Barbies, which were modeled after a sexy German doll and comic strip character named Lilli, were all white, but in 1967 Mattel premiered a black version of the doll called "Colored Francie." "Colored Francie," like white "Francie Fairchild" introduced the year before, was supposed to be Barbie's "MODern" younger cousin. As a white doll modeled and marketed in the image of Hollywood's Gidget, white Francie had been an international sensation, but Colored Francie was not destined to duplicate her prototype's success. Although the "black is beautiful" theme of both the civil rights and black power movements may have suggested a ready market for a beautiful black doll, Colored Francie in fact did not sell well.

Evelyn Burkhalter, owner, operator, and curator of the Barbie Hall of   *12* Fame in Palo Alto, California—home to 16,000 Barbie dolls—attributes Colored Francie's commercial failure to the racial climate of the times. Doll purchasing patterns, it seems, reflected the same resistance to integration that was felt elsewhere in the nation. In her implied family ties to white Barbie, Colored Francie suggested more than simple integration. She implied miscegenation: a make-believe mixing of races that may have jeopardized the doll's real market value. Cynthia Roberts, author of Barbie: *Thirty Years of America's Doll* (1989), maintains that Colored Francie flopped because of her straight hair and Caucasian features (44), which seemingly were less acceptable then than now. No doubt Mattel's decision to call its first black Barbie "Colored Francie" also contributed to the doll's demise. The use of the outmoded, even racist term "colored" in the midst of civil rights and black power activism suggested that while Francie might be "MODern," Mattel was still in the dark(y) ages. In any case, neither black nor white audiences bought the idea of Barbie's colored relations, and Mattel promptly took the doll off the market, replacing her with a black doll called Christie in 1968.

While a number of other black dolls appeared throughout the late   *13* sixties and seventies—including the Julia doll, modeled after the TV character played by black singer and actress Diahann Carroll—it was not until 1980 that Mattel introduced black dolls that were called Barbie like their white counterparts. Today, Barbie dolls come in a virtual rainbow coalition of colors, races, ethnicities, and nationalities—most of which look remarkably like the prototypical white Barbie, modified only by a dash of color and a change of costume. It is these would-be multicultural "dolls of the world"—Jamaican Barbie, Nigerian and Kenyan Barbie, Malaysian Barbie, Chinese Barbie, Mexican, Spanish, and Brazilian Barbie, etcetera, etcetera, etcetera—that interest me. For me these dolls are at once a symbol and a symptom of what multiculturalism has become at the hands of contemporary commodity culture: an easy and immensely profitable way off the hook of Eurocentrism that gives us the face of cultural diversity without the particulars of racial difference.

If I could line up across the page the ninety "different" colors, cultures, and other incarnations in which Barbie currently exists, the fact of her unrelenting sameness (or at least similarity) would become immediately apparent. Even two dolls might do the trick: "My First Barbie" in white and "My First Barbie" in black, for example, or white "Western Fun Barbie" and black "Western Fun Barbie." Except for their dye jobs, the dolls are identical: the same body, size, shape, and apparel. Or perhaps I should say *nearly* identical because in some instances—with black and Asian dolls in particular—coloring and other subtle changes (stereotypically slanted eyes in the Asian dolls, thicker lips in the black dolls) suggest differently coded facial features. 14

In other instances, when Barbie moves across cultural as opposed to racial lines, it is costume rather than color that distinguishes one ethnic group or nation from another. Nigeria and Jamaica, for instance, are represented by the same basic brown body, dolled-up in different native garbs—or Mattel's interpretation thereof.[4] With other costume changes, this generic black body becomes Western Fun Barbie or Marine Barbie or Desert Storm Barbie, and even Presidential Candidate Barbie, who, by the way, comes with a Nancy Reagan-red taking-care-of-business suit as well as a red, white, and blue inaugural ball gown. Much the same is true of the generic Asian doll—sometimes called Kira—who reappears in a variety of different dress-defined ethnicities. In other words, where Barbie is concerned, clothes not only make the woman, they mark the racial and/or cultural difference. 15

Such difference is marked as well by the cultural history and language lessons that accompany each doll in Mattel's international collection. The back of Jamaican Barbie's box tells us, for example, *"How-you-du* (Hello) from the land of Jamaica, a tropical paradise known for its exotic fruit, sugar cane, breathtaking beaches, and reggae beat!" The box goes on to explain 16

---

[4]After many calls to the Jamaican Embassy in Washington, D.C., and to various cultural organizations in Jamaica, I have determined that Jamaican Barbie's costume—a floor-length granny-style dress with apron and headrag—bears some resemblance to what is considered the island's traditional folk costume. I am still left wondering about the decision-making process, however: why the doll representing Jamaica is figured as a maid, while the doll representing Great Britain, for example, is presented as a lady—a blonde, blue-eyed Barbie doll dressed in a fancy riding habit with boots and hat.

that most Jamaicans have ancestors from Africa. Therefore, "even though our official language is English, we speak patois, a kind of *'Jamaica Talk,'* filled with English and African words." The lesson ends with a brief glossary (eight words) and a few more examples of this "Jamaica Talk," complete with translations: *"A hope yu wi come-a Jamaica!* (I hope you will come to Jamaica!)" and *"Teck care a yusself, mi fren!* (Take care of yourself, my friend!)."* A nice idea, I suppose, but for me these quick-and-dirty ethnographies only enhance the extent to which these would-be multicultural dolls treat race and ethnic difference like collectibles, contributing more to commodity culture than to the intercultural awareness they claim to inspire.

Is the current fascination with the black or colored body—especially   *17* the female body—a contemporary version of the primitivism of the 1920s? Is multiculturalism to postmodernism what primitivism was to modernism? It was while on my way to a round table discussion on precisely this question that I bought my first black Barbie dolls in March of 1993. As carbon copies of an already problematic original, these colorized Mattel toys seemed to me the perfect tools with which to illustrate the point I wanted to make about the collapse of multiculturalism into an easy pluralism that simply adds what it constructs as the Other without upsetting the fundamental precepts and paradigms of Western culture or, in the case of Mattel, without changing the mold.

Not entirely immune to such critiques, Mattel sought expert advice   *18* from black parents and early childhood specialists in the development and marketing of its newest line of black Barbie dolls. Chief among the expert witnesses was clinical psychologist Darlene Powell Hopson, who coauthored with her husband Derek S. Hopson a study of racism and child development entitled *Different and Wonderful: Raising Black Children in a Race-Conscious Society* (1990). As part of their research for the book, the Hopsons repeated a ground-breaking study conducted by black psychologists Kenneth and Mamie Clark in the 1940s.

The Clarks used black and white dolls to demonstrate the negative   *19* effects of racism and segregation on black children. When given a choice between a white doll and a black doll, nearly 70 percent of the black children in the study chose the white doll. The Clarks' findings became an important factor in *Brown v. the Board of Education* in 1954. More recently, some scholars have called into question not necessarily the Clarks' findings but their interpretation: the assumption that, in the realm of make-believe, a black child's choosing a white doll necessarily reflects a negative self concept.[5] For the Hopsons, however, the Clarks' research remains

---

[5] See among others Morris Rosenberg's books Conceiving the Self (1979) and Society and the Adolescent Self-image (1989) and William E. Cross's Shades of Black: Diversity in African American Identity (1991), all of which challenge the Clarks' findings. Cross argues, for example, that the Clarks confounded or conflated two different issues: altitude toward race in general and attitude toward the self in particular. How one feels about race is not necessarily an index of one's self-esteem.

compelling. In 1985 they repeated the Clarks' doll test and found that an alarming 65 percent of the black children in their sample chose a white doll over a black one. Moreover, 76 percent of the children interviewed said that the black dolls "looked bad" to them (Hopson xix).

In addition to the clinical uses they make of dolls in their experiments, [20] the Hopsons also give considerable attention to what they call "doll play" in their book, specifically mentioning Barbie. "If your daughter likes 'Barbie' dolls, by all means get her Barbie," they advise black parents. "But also choose Black characters from the Barbie world. *You do not want your child to grow up thinking that only White dolls, and by extension White people, are attractive and nice*" (Hopsons 127, emphasis original). (Note that "Barbie," unmodified in the preceding passage, seems to mean white Barbie dolls.) The Hopsons suggest that parents should not only provide their children with black and other ethnic dolls but that they should get involved in their children's doll play. "Help them dress and groom the dolls while you compliment them both," they advise, offering the following suggested routine: "'This is a beautiful doll. It looks just like you. Look at her hair. It's just like yours. Did you know your nose is as pretty as your doll's?'" (119). They also suggest that parents use "complimentary words such as *lovely, pretty, or nice* so that [the] child will learn to associate them with his or her own image" (124).

Certainly it is important to help children feel good about themselves. [21] One might argue, however, that the "just like you" simile and the beautiful doll imagery so central to these suggestions for what the Hopsons call positive play run the risk of transmitting to the child a colorized version of the same old beauty myth. Like Barbie dolls themselves, they make beauty—and by implication worth—a matter of physical characteristics.

In spite of their own good intentions, the Hopsons, in linking play [22] with "beautiful" dolls to positive self-imagining, echoed Mattel's own marketing campaign. It is not surprising, then, that the Hopsons' findings and the interventional strategies they designed for using dolls to instill ethnic pride caught the attention of Mattel. In 1990 Darlene Hopson was asked to consult with the corporation's product manager Deborah Mitchell and designer Kitty Black-Perkins—both African Americans—in the development of a new line of "realistically sculpted" black fashion dolls. Hopson agreed and about a year later Shani and her friends Asha and Nichelle became the newest members of Barbie's ever-expanding family.

Shani means "marvelous" in Swahili, according to the dolls' press kit. [23] But as *Village Voice* columnist Lisa Jones has noted, the name has other meanings as well: "startling, a wonder, a novelty" (36). My own research indicates that while Shani is a Swahili female name meaning marvelous, the Kiswahili word "shani" translates as "an adventure, something unusual" (Stewart 120). So it seems that Mattel's new play thing is not just marvelous, too marvelous for words, but, as her name also suggests, she is difference incarnate—a novelty, a new enterprise, or, perhaps, as the black female Other so often is, an exotic. Mattel, it seems to me, both plays up

and plays on what it presents as the doll's exotic black-is-beautiful difference. As the back of her package reads:

> Shani means marvelous in the Swahili language . . . and marvelous she is!
> With her friends Asha and Nichelle, Shani brings to life the special style and
> beauty of the African American woman.
>
> Each one is beautiful in her own way, with her own lovely skin shade and
> unique facial features. Each has a different hair color and texture, perfect for
> braiding, twisting, and creating fabulous hair styles! Their clothes, too, reflect
> the vivid colors and ethnic accents that showcase their *exotic looks* and fash-
> ion flair!
>
> Shani, Asha, and Nichelle invite you into their glamorous world to share
> the fun and excitement of being a top model. Imagine appearing on magazine
> covers, starring in fashion shows, and going to Hollywood parties as you,
> Shani, Asha, and Nichelle live your dreams of beauty and success, loving every
> marvelous minute! (emphasis added)

While these words attempt to convey a message of black pride—after the
fashion of the Hopsons' recommendations for positive play—that message is clearly tied to bountiful hair, lavish and exotic clothes, and other
outward and visible signs not of brains but of beauty, wealth, and success.
Shani may be a top fashion model, but don't look for her (or, if Mattel's
own oft-articulated theory of Barbie as role model holds, yourself or your
child) at M.I.T.

Like any other proud, well-to-do parents of a debutante, Mattel gave   24
Shani her own coming out party at the International Toy Fair in February of 1991. This gala event included a tribute to black designers and an
appearance by En Vogue singing the Negro National Anthem, "Lift Every
Voice and Sing!"—evidently the song of choice of the doll Mattel describes
as "tomorrow's African American woman." Also making their debuts were
Shani's friends Asha and Nichelle, notable for the different hues in which
their black plastic skin comes—an innovation due in part to Darlene Hopson's influence. Shani, the signature doll of the line, is what we call in the
culture "brown-skinned"; Asha is honey-colored (some would say "high-
yella"); and Nichelle is deep mahogany. Their male friend Jamal, added in
1992, completes the collection.

For the un(make-)believing, the three-to-one ratio of the Shani   25
quartet—three black females to one black male—may be the most realistic thing about these dolls. In the eyes and the advertising of Mattel,
however, Shani and her friends are the most authentic black female thing
the mainstream toy market has yet produced. "Tomorrow's African American woman" (an appellation which, as Lisa Jones has noted, both riffs
and one-ups *Essence's* "Today's Black Woman") has broader hips, fuller
lips, and a broader nose, according to product manager Deborah Mitchell. Principal designer Kitty Black-Perkins, who has dressed black Barbies
since their birth in 1980, adds that the Shani dolls are also distinguished
by their unique, culturally-specific clothes in "spice tones, [and] ethnic

fabrics," rather than "fantasy colors like pink or lavender" (qtd. in Jones 36)—evidently the colors of the faint of skin.

The notion that fuller lips, broader noses, wider hips, and higher der- 26 riéres somehow make the Shani dolls more realistically African American raises many difficult questions about authenticity, truth, and the ever-problematic categories of the real and the symbolic, the typical and the stereotypical. Just what are we saying when we claim that a doll does or does not "look black"? How does black look? What would it take to make a doll look authentically African American? What preconceived, prescriptive ideals of legitimate blackness are inscribed in such claims of authenticity? How can doll manufacturers or any other image makers—the film indus-try, for example—attend to cultural, racial, and phenotypical differences without merely engaging the same simplistic big-lips/broad-hips stereo-types that make so many of us—blacks in particular—grit our (pearly white) teeth? What would it take to produce a line of dolls that more fully reflects the wide variety of sizes, shapes, colors, hair styles, occupations, abilities, and disabilities that African Americans—like all people—come in? In other words: what price difference? . . .

The Body Politic(s) of Barbie

> Barbie's body is a consumer object itself, a vehicle for the display of clothing and the spectacular trappings of a wealthy teenage fantasy life. Her extraor-dinary body exists not simply as an example of the fetishized female form typical of those offered up to the male gaze, but as a commodity vehicle itself whose form seduces the beholder and sells accessories, the real source of corporate profit. Like Lay's chips, no one can buy just one outfit for the doll. Barbie is the late capitalist girl incarnate. (McCombie)

In focusing thus far on the merchandising of racial, perhaps more so than 27 gender, difference, I do not mean to imply that racial and gender identi-ties are divisible, even in dolls. Nor, in observing that most if not all of Mattel's "dolls of the world" look remarkably like what the company calls the "traditional, blond, blue-eyed Barbie," do I mean to suggest that the seemingly endless recapitulation of the white prototype is the only way in which these dolls are problematic. In fact, the most alarming thing about Barbie may well be the extent to which she functions as what M. G. Lord calls a teaching tool for femininity, whatever her race or ethnicity. Lord, the author of *Forever Barbie: The Unauthorized Biography of a Real Doll*, due out later this year, describes Barbie as a "space-age fertility icon. She looks like a modern woman, but she's a very primitive totem of female power" (qtd. in Dembner 1).

Barbie has long had the eye and ire of feminists, who, for the most 28 part, have reviled her as another manifestation of the damaging myths of female beauty and the feminine body that patriarchy perpetuates through such vehicles as popular and commodity culture. A counter narrative also exists, however, one in which Barbie is not an empty-headed, material girl bimbo, for whom math class is tough, but a feminist heroine, who has been first in war (a soldier who served in the Gulf, she has worn the colors of her country as well as the United Colors of Benetton), first in peace (she held her own summit in 1990 and she's a long-time friend of UNICEF, who "loves all the children of the world"), and always first in the hearts of her country (Americans buy her at the rate of one doll every second). While time does not allow me to reiterate or to assess here all the known critiques and defenses of Barbie, I do want to discuss briefly some of the gender ideals that I think are encoded in and transmitted by this larger-than-life little woman and what Barbie's escalating popularity says about contemporary American culture.

In *Touching Liberty: Abolition, Feminism, and the Politics of the Body*   29
(1993), Karen Sanchez-Eppler argues that all dolls are intended to teach little girls about domesticity (133). If such tutelage is Barbie's not so secret mission, her methodology is far more complex and contradictory than that of the Betsy Welsy and Tiny Tears baby dolls I played with thirty-five years ago. Those dolls invoked and evoked the maternal, as they and the baby bottles and diapers with which they were packaged invited us to nestle, nurse, and nurture. Barbie's curvaceous, big-busted, almost fully female body, on the other hand, summons not the maternal but the sexual, not the nurturant mother but the sensuous woman. As Mel McCombie has argued, rather than rehearsing parenting, as a baby doll does, Barbie's adult body encourages children to dress and redress a fashion doll that yields lessons about sexuality, consumption, and teenage life (3). Put another way, we might say that Barbie is literally and figuratively a titillating toy.

Bodacious as they may be, however, Barbie's firm plastic breasts have   30
no nipples—nothing that might offend, nothing that might suggest her own pleasure. And if her protruding plastic mounds signify a simmering sensuality, what are we to make of her missing genitalia? McCombie suggests that Barbie's genital ambiguity can be read as an "homage to 'good taste'" and as a "reflection of the regnant mores for teenage girls—to be both sexy and adult yet remain virginal" (4). I agree that her body invites such readings, but it also seems to me that there is nothing ambiguous about Barbie's crotch. It's missing in inaction. While male dolls like Ken and Jamal have bumps "down there" and in some instances simulated underwear etched into the plastic, most Barbies come neither with drawers nor with even a hint of anything that needs covering, even as "it" is already covered or erased. As an icon of idealized femininity, then, Barbie is locked into a never-never land in which she must be always already sexual without the possibility of sex. Conspicuously sensual on top but definitively nonsexual below, her plastic body indeed has inscribed within it the very contradictory, whore/madonna messages with which patriarchy taunts and even traumatizes young women in particular.

This kind of speculation about Barbie's breasts has led the doll's cre-   31
ator, Ruth Handler, to chide adults for their nasty minds. "In my opinion

people make too much of breasts," Handler has complained. "They are just part of the body" (qtd. in BillyBoy 20). Mrs. Handler has a point (or maybe two). I feel more than just a little ridiculous myself as I sit here contemplating the body parts and sex life of a piece of plastic. What is fascinating, however, what I think is worth studying, what both invites and resists theorizing, is not the lump of molded plastic that is Barbie, but the imaginary life that is not—that is our invention. Barbie as a cultural artifact may be able to tell us more about ourselves and our society—more about society's attitudes toward its women—than anything we might say about the doll her or, rather, *itself*.

In the nineteenth century, Alexis de Tocqueville and others argued   *32* that you could judge the character, quality, and degree of advancement of a civilization by the status and treatment of its women. What is the status of women in soon to be twenty-first-century America, and can Barbie serve as a barometer for measuring that status? Barbie, it seems to me, is a key player in the process of socialization—of engendering and racialization—that begins in infancy and is furthered by almost everything about our society, including the books children read, the toys they play with, and the cartoons they watch on television.

While changing channels one Saturday morning, I happened upon a   *33* cartoon, just a glimpse of which impelled me to watch on. At the point that I tuned in, a big, gray, menacingly male bulldog was barking furiously at a pretty, petite, light-colored cat, who simply batted her long lashes, meowed coquettishly, and rubbed her tiny feline body against his huge canine leg in response. The more the dog barked and growled, the softer the cat meowed, using her slinky feline body and her feminine wiles to win the dog over. Her strategy worked; before my eyes—and, I imagine, the eyes of millions of children—the ferocious beast was transformed into a lovesick puppy dog, who followed the cat everywhere, repeatedly saving her from all manner of evil and danger. Time and time again, the bulldog rescued the helpless, accident-prone pussy from falling girders, oncoming traffic, and other hazards to which she, in her innocent frailty, was entirely oblivious. By the end, the once ferocious bulldog was completely domesticated, as his no longer menacing body became a kind of bed for the cat to nestle in.

There are, of course, a number of ways to read the gender and racial   *34* politics of this cartoon. I suppose that the same thought process that theorizes Barbie as a feminist heroine for whom men are mere accessories might claim the kitty cat, too, as a kind of feminist feline, who uses her feminine wiles to get her way. What resonates for me in the cartoon, however, are its beauty and the beast, light/dark, good/evil, female/male, race and gender codes: light, bright, cat-like femininity tames menacing black male bestiality. Make no mistake, however; it is not wit that wins out over barbarism but a mindless, can't-take-care-of-herself femininity.

Interestingly enough, these are the kinds of messages of which fairy   *35* tales and children's stories are often made. White knights rescue fair damsels in distress from dark, forbidding evils of one kind or another. As

Darlene and Derek Hopson argue: "Some of the most blatant and simplistic representations of white as good and black as evil are found in children's literature," where evil black witches and good white fairies—heroes in white and villains in black—abound (121).

What Barbie dolls, cartoons like the one outlined above, and even the 36 seemingly innocent fairy tales we read to our children seem to me to have in common are the mythologies of race and gender that are encoded in them. Jacqueline Urla and Alan Swedlund maintain that Barbie's body type constructs the bodies of other women as deviant and perpetuates an impossible standard of beauty. Attempting to live up to the Barbie ideal, others argue, fosters eating and shopping disorders in teenage girls—nightmares instead of dreams. BillyBoy, one of Barbie's most ardent supporters, defends his heroine against such charges by insisting that there is nothing abnormal about the proportions of Barbie's body. Rather, he asserts, "she has the ideal that Western culture has insisted upon since the 1920s: long legs, long arms, small waist, high round bosom, and long neck" (22). The irony is that BillyBoy may be right. "Unrealistic" or not, Barbie's weight and measurements (which if proportionate to those of a woman 5'6" tall would be something like 110 pounds and a top-heavy 39–18–33) are not much different from those of the beauty queens to whom Bert Parks used to sing "Here she is, Miss America. Here she is, our ideal."[6] If Barbie is a monster, she is our monster, our ideal.

"But is Barbie bad?" Someone asked me the other day if a black doll 37 that looks like a white doll isn't better than no black doll at all. I must admit that I have no ready answer for this and a number of other questions posed by my own critique. Although, as I acknowledged in the beginning, the dolls I played with as a child were white, I still remember the first time I saw a black doll. To me, she was the most beautiful thing I had ever seen; I wanted her desperately, and I was never again satisfied with white Betsy Wetsy and blonde, blue-eyed Patty Play Pal. She was something else, something *Other*, like me, and that, I imagine, was the source of her charm and my desire.

If I did not consciously note my own absence in the toys I played with, 38 that absence, I suspect, had a profound effect on me nevertheless. We have only to read Toni Morrison's chilling tale *The Bluest Eye* to see the effect of the white beauty myth on the black child. And while they were by no means as dire for me as for Morrison's character Pecola Breedlove, I was not exempt from the consequences of growing up black in a white world that barely acknowledged my existence. I grew up believing I was ugly: my

---

[6] In response to criticism from feminists in particular, the Miss America Pageant has attempted to transform itself from a beauty contest to a talent competition, whose real aim is to give college scholarships to smart, talented women (who just happen to look good in bathing suits and evening gowns). As part of its effort to appear more concerned with a woman's IQ than with her bra size, the pageant did away with its long-standing practice of broadcasting the chest, waist, and hip measurements, as well as the height and weight, of each contestant.

kinky hair, my big hips, the gap between my teeth. I have spent half my life smiling with my hand over my mouth to hide that gap, a habit I only began to get over in graduate school when a couple of Nigerian men told me that in their culture, where my body type is prized much more than Barbie's, such gaps are a sign of great beauty. I wonder what it would have meant for me as a child to see a black doll—or any doll—with big hips and a gap between her two front teeth.

Today, for $24.99, Mattel reaches halfway around the world and gives *39* little girls—black like me—Nigerian Barbies to play with. Through the wonders of plastic, dyes, and mass production, the company brings into the homes of African American children a Nigeria that I as a young child did not even know existed. The problem is that Mattel's Nigeria does not exist either. The would be ethnic dolls of the world Mattel sells, like their "traditional, blond, blue-eyed" all-American girl prototype, have no gaps, no big ears, no chubby thighs or other "imperfections." For a modest price, I can dream myself into Barbie's perfect world, so long as I dream myself in her image. It may be a small world, a whole new world, but there is still no place for me as *me* in it.

This, then, is my final doll story. Groucho Marx said that he wouldn't *40* want to belong to a club that would have him as a member. In that same vein, I am not so sure that most of us would want to buy a doll that "looked like us." Indeed, efforts to produce and market such truer-to-life dolls have not met with much commercial success. Cultural critics like me can throw theoretical stones at her all we want, but part of Barbie's infinite appeal is her very perfection, the extent to which she is both product and purveyor of the dominant white Western ideal of beauty.

And what of black beauty? If Colored Francie failed thirty years ago in *41* part because of her Caucasian features, what are we to make of the current popularity and commercial success of Black Barbie and Shani, straight hair and all? Have we progressed to a point where "difference" makes no difference? Or have we regressed to such a degree that "difference" is only conceivable as similarity—as a mediated text that no matter what its dye job ultimately must be readable as white. Listen to our language: we *"tolerate difference"*; we practice "racial tolerance." Through the compound fractures of interpellation and universalization, the Other is reproduced not in her own image but in ours. If we have gotten away from "Us" and "Them," it may be only because Them R Us.

Is Barbie bad? Barbie is just a piece of plastic, but what she says about *42* the economic base of our society—what she suggests about gender and race in our world—ain't good.

WORKS CITED

Berkwitz, David N. "Finally, Barbie Doll Ads Go Ethnic." *Newsweek* 13 Aug. 1990: 48.

BillyBoy. *Barbie: Her Life and Times.* New York: Crown, 1987.

Cross, William E., Jr. *Shades of Black: Diversity in African American Identity.* Philadelphia: Temple UP, 1991.

Delany, Sarah, and Delany, A. Elizabeth. *Having Our Say: The Delany Sisters' First 100 Years*. New York: Kodansha, 1993.

Dembner, Alice. "Thirty-five and Still a Doll." *Boston Globe* 9 Mar. 1994: 1+.

Jones, Lisa. "A Doll Is Born." *Village Voice* 26 Mar. 1991: 36.

Kantrowitz, Barbara. "Hot Date: Barbie and G.I. Joe." *Newsweek* 20 Feb. 1989: 59–60.

Hopson, Darlene Powell and Derek S. *Different and Wonderful: Raising Black Children in a Race-Conscious Society*. New York: Simon, 1990.

Larcen, Donna. "Barbie Bond Doesn't Diminish with Age." *Hartford Courant* 17 Aug. 1993: A6–7.

Lord, M. G. *Forever Barbie: The Unauthorized Biography of a Real Doll*. New York: Morrow, 1994.

McCombie, Mel. "Barbie: Toys Are Us." Unpublished essay.

Morrison, Toni. *The Bluest Eye*. New York: Washington Square, 1970.

Roberts, Cynthia. *Barbie: Thirty Years of America's Doll*. Chicago: Contemporary, 1989.

Rosenberg, Morris. *Conceiving the Self*. New York: Basic, 1979.

——. *Society and the Adolescent Self-image*. Middletown: Wesleyan UP, 1989.

Sanchez-Eppler, Karen. *Touching Liberty: Abolition, Feminism, and the Politics of the Body*. Berkeley: U of California P, 1993.

Stewart, Julia. African Names. New York: Carol, 1993.

Urla, Jacqueline, and Alan Swedlund. "The Anthropometry of Barbie: Unsettling Ideals of the Feminine in Popular Culture." *Deviant Bodies*. Ed. Jennifer Terry and Jacqueline Urla. Bloomington: Indiana UP, [1995].

■   ■   ■

Reading as a Writer: Analyzing Rhetorical Choices

1. List the key phrases duCille uses to build her argument in her early paragraphs (you might look in particular at paras. 5, 9, and 10), and be ready to explain them in your own words. Be sure you look up words that are new to you. For example, what do you think duCille means by "the commodification of race and gender difference" in paragraph 5? Work in pairs or groups to help make sense of some of these challenging phrases that are important to duCille's argument about Barbie.

2. Find two passages in which duCille uses a specific doll as an example to illustrate her larger argument. What words and phrases does she use to move between her detailed descriptions of the dolls and their packaging and her analysis of those details? How persuasive do you find her claims, based on the evidence in these passages? Explain your answer.

Writing as a Reader: Entering the Conversation of Ideas

1. While they examine different products, both duCille and coauthors Ken Gillam and Shannon R. Wooden (pp. 542–54 in Media Studies) are interested in marketing aimed at children. Given the market overlap between children's films and toys, there is a rich conversation you can enter with these authors. Select a children's film to analyze that has toys or children's products affiliated with it, and draw on these authors' ideas as you make an argument about the ways the film and its products depict gender and race. To what extent are stereotypes reinforced—or dismantled—in the film and products? What conclusions can you draw?

2. DuCille's emphasis on women's bodies and the marketplace intersects with Jean Kilbourne's concerns about the effects of advertising on girls and women (pp. 554–77 in Media Studies). Write an essay in which you use insights from duCille and Kilbourne to analyze a specific product (or product line) marketed toward girls or women. Draw on the visual rhetoric insights from Chapter 10 as you conduct your analysis. What do you conclude about the significance and effects of gendered marketing, based on your examples?

APPENDIX:
Citing and Documenting Sources

Y ou must provide a brief citation in the text of your paper for every quotation or idea taken from another writer, and you must list complete information at the end of your paper for the sources you use. This information is essential for readers who want to read the source to understand a quotation or an idea in its original context. How you cite sources in the body of your paper and document them at the end of your paper varies from discipline to discipline, so it is important to ask your instructor what documentation style he or she requires.

Even within academic disciplines, documentation styles can vary. Specific academic journals within disciplines will sometimes have their own set of style guidelines. The important thing is to adhere faithfully to your chosen (or assigned) style throughout your paper, observing all the rules prescribed by the style. You may have noticed small citation style differences among the examples in this text. That's because the examples are taken from the work of a variety of writers, both professionals and students, who had to conform to the documentation requirements of their publication venues or of their teachers.

Here we briefly introduce two common documentation styles that may be useful in your college career: the Modern Language Association (MLA) style, frequently used in the humanities, and the American Psychological Association (APA) style, often used in the social sciences. The information is basic, for use when you begin drafting your paper. In the final stages of writing, you should consult either the *MLA Handbook*, Eighth Edition, or the *Publication Manual of the American Psychological Association*, Sixth Edition.

Although you'll need the manuals or a handbook for complete style information, both the MLA (style.mla.org) and the APA (http://www .apastyle.org/learn/faqs/) maintain Web sites for frequently asked questions. Again, before you start your research, check with your instructor to find out whether you should use either of these styles or if there's another style he or she requires.

MLA and APA styles have many similarities. For example, both require short citations in the body of an essay linked to a list of sources at the end of the essay. But it is their differences, though subtle, that are crucial. To a great extent, these differences reflect the assumptions writers in the humanities and in the social sciences bring to working with sources. In particular, you should understand each style's treatment of the source's author, publication date, and page numbers in in-text citations, as well as verb use in referring to sources.

Author. MLA style prefers that you give the author's full name on first mention in your paper; APA style uses last names throughout. The humanities emphasize "the human element"—the individual as creative force—so MLA style uses the complete name at first mention to imply the author's importance. Because the social sciences emphasize the primacy of data in studies of human activity, in APA style last names are deemed sufficient for identifying the source.

Publication date. In-text citations using MLA style leave out the date of publication. The assumption is that the insights of the past may be as useful as those of the present. By contrast, APA in-text citations include the date of the study after the author's name, reflecting a belief in the progress of research, that recent findings may supersede earlier ones.

Verb use. MLA style uses the present tense of verbs ("the author claims") to introduce cited material, assuming the cited text's timelessness, whether written last week or centuries ago. By contrast, APA style acknowledges the "pastness" of research by requiring past-tense verbs for introducing cited material ("the author claimed" or "the author has claimed"); the underlying assumption is that new data may emerge to challenge older research.

Although it is useful to understand that different citation styles reflect different attitudes toward inquiry and research in different disciplines, for the purposes of your writing, it is mainly important to know the style you have to follow in your paper and to apply it consistently. Whenever you consult a source—even if you don't end up using it in your paper—write down complete citation information so that you can cite it fully and accurately if you need to. Doing so will help you be a responsible researcher and save you the trouble of having to hunt down citation information later. Table A.1 shows the basic information needed to cite books, chapters in books, journal articles, and online sources. You also should note any other

TABLE A.1   **Basic Information Needed for Citing Sources**

BOOKS	CHAPTERS IN BOOKS	JOURNAL ARTICLES	ONLINE SOURCES
Author(s) or editor(s)	Author(s)	Author(s)	Author(s)
Title and subtitle	Chapter title and subtitle	Article title and subtitle	Document title and subtitle
Edition information	Book editor(s)	Journal title	Print publication information, if any
Place of publication (APA only)	Book title	Volume and issue number	Site publisher or sponsor
Publisher	Edition information	Date of publication	Site title
Year of publication	Place of publication (APA only)	Page numbers	Date of publication or most recent update
	Publisher		URL or DOI
	Year of publication		Date accessed
	Page numbers		

information that could be relevant—a translator's name, for example, or a series title and editor. Being able to cite a source fully without having to go back to it to get more information saves you time.

THE BASICS OF MLA STYLE

In-text citations.   In MLA style, you must provide a brief citation in the body of your essay (1) when you quote directly from a source, (2) when you paraphrase or summarize what someone else has written, and (3) when you use an idea or a concept that originated with someone else.

In the excerpt that follows, the citation tells readers that the student writer's argument about the evolution of Ebonics is rooted in a well-established source of information. Because the writer does not mention the author in the paraphrase of her source in the text, she gives the author's name in the citation:

> The evolution of U.S. Ebonics can be traced from the year 1557 to the present day. In times of great oppression, such as the beginning of the slave codes in 1661, the language of the black community was at its most "ebonified" levels, whereas in times of racial progress, for example during the abolitionist movement, the language as a source of community identity was forsaken for greater assimilation (Smitherman 119).

The parenthetical citation refers to page 119 of Geneva Smitherman's book *Talkin and Testifyin: The Language of Black America* (1977). Smitherman is a recognized authority on Ebonics. Had the student mentioned Smitherman's name in her introduction to the paraphrase, she would not have had to repeat it in the citation. Notice that there is no punctuation within the parentheses and no *p.* before the page number. Also notice that the citation is considered part of the sentence in which it appears, so the period ending the sentence follows the closing parenthesis.

By contrast, in the example that follows, the student quotes directly from Richard Rodriguez's book *Hunger of Memory: The Education of Richard Rodriguez* (1982):

> Many minority cultures in today's society feel that it is more important to maintain cultural bonds than to extend themselves into the larger community. People who do not speak English may feel a similar sense of community and consequently lose some of the individuality and cultural ties that come with speaking their native or home language. This shared language within a home or community also adds to the unity of the community. Richard Rodriguez attests to this fact in his essay "Aria." He then goes on to say that "it is not healthy to distinguish public words from private sounds so easily" (183).

Because the student mentions Rodriguez in her text right before the quotation ("Richard Rodriguez attests"), she does not need to include his name in the parenthetical citation; the page number is sufficient.

Works cited.   At the end of your researched essay and starting on a new page, you must provide a list of works cited, a list of all the sources you have used (leaving out sources you consulted but decided not to use). Entries should be listed alphabetically by author's last name or by title if no author is identified. Figure A.1 (p. 804) is a sample Works Cited page in MLA style that illustrates a few of the basic types of documentation.

Steps to Compiling an MLA List of Works Cited

1 Begin your list of works cited on a new page at the end of your paper.

2 Put your last name and page number in the upper-right corner.

3 Double-space throughout.

4 Center the heading ("Works Cited") on the page.

5 Arrange the list of sources alphabetically by author's last name or by title if no author is identified.

6 Begin the first line of each source flush left; second and subsequent lines should be indented ½ inch.

7 Invert the author's name, last name first. In the case of multiple authors, only the first author's name is inverted.

8 Italicize the titles of books, journals, magazines, and newspapers. Put the titles of book chapters and articles in quotation marks. Capitalize each word in all titles except for articles (*a, an, the*), short prepositions (*in, at, of,* for example), and coordinating conjunctions (*and, but, for, so,* for example).

9　For books, list the name of the publisher and the year of publication. For chapters, list the editors of the book, the book title, and the publication information. For articles, list the title of the journal, magazine, or newspaper; the volume and issue numbers (for a journal); and the date of publication.

10　List the relevant page numbers for articles and selections from longer works.

The steps outlined here for compiling a list of works cited apply to printed sources. MLA formats for citing online sources vary, but this is an example of the basic format:

Author. "Title of Work." *Name of Site*, Publisher or Sponsor, publication date/most recent update date, DOI or URL.

Things to remember:

- Invert the author's name (or the first author's name only, when there are multiple authors).
- Italicize the name of the site.
- If the site publisher or sponsor — usually an institution or organization — isn't clear, check the copyright notice at the bottom of the Web page. If the name of the publisher or sponsor is identical to the name of the site, include only the Web site name in your citation.
- Give the publication date or the most recent update date. Use the day-month-year format for dates in the Works Cited list. Abbreviate all months except May, June, and July.
- Notice that there's a comma between the sponsor and the publication date.
- Include the DOI (if available) or URL for the source.
- If a source has no date, give the date of access at the end of the entry.

In addition to books, articles, and Web sites, you may need to cite sources such as films, recordings, television and radio programs, paintings, and photographs. For details on how to format these sources, consult a handbook (if your instructor has assigned one) or the *MLA Handbook*, Eighth Edition, or go to the MLA Style Center (style.mla.org).

Eck 10

Works Cited

For three or more authors, list the first author's name, followed by "et al." Gutiérrez, Kris D., et al. "English for the Children: The New Literacy of the Old World Order." *Bilingual Review Journal*, vol. 24, no. 1/2, Fall/Winter 2000, pp. 87-112.

Article in an online journal, no author "History of Bilingual Education." *Rethinking Schools,* vol. 12, no. 3, Spring 1998, www.rethinkingschools.org/restrict .asp?path=archive/12_03/langhst.shtml.

Article in a print journal Lanehart, Sonja L. "African American Vernacular English and Education." *Journal of English Linguistics*, vol. 26, no. 2, June 1998, pp. 122-36.

Article from a Web site Pompa, Delia. "Bilingual Success: Why Two-Language Education Is Critical for Latinos." *English for the Children*, One Nation/ One California, 1 Nov. 2000, www.onenation.org/article/ bilingual-success/.

Rawls, John. *Political Liberalism*. Columbia UP, 1993.

Essay in an edited collection; second source by same writer ---. "Social Unity and Primary Goods." *Utilitarianism and Beyond*, edited by Amartya Sen and Bernard Williams, Cambridge UP, 1982, pp. 159-85.

Rodriguez, Richard. "Aria." *Hunger of Memory: The Education of Richard Rodriguez*, Bantam Books, 1982, pp. 11-40.

Article in a magazine Schrag, Peter. "Language Barrier." *New Republic*, 9 Mar. 1998, pp. 14-15.

A book Smitherman, Geneva. *Talkin and Testifyin: The Language of Black America*. Wayne State UP, 1977.

Willis, Arlette Ingram. "Reading the World of School Literacy: Contextualizing the Experience of a Young American Male." *Harvard Educational Review*, vol. 65, no. 1, Spring 1995, pp. 30-49.

FIGURE A.1   Sample List of Works Cited, MLA Format

THE BASICS OF APA STYLE

In-text citations.   In APA style, in-text citations identify the author or authors of a source, page or paragraph numbers for the information cited, and the publication date. If the author or authors are mentioned in the text, provide the publication date immediately following the author's name:

> Feingold (1992) documented the fact that males perform much better than females in math and science and other stereotypically masculine areas (p. 92).

APA style does not explicitly require page or paragraph numbers to be included with paraphrased material. It does, however, recommend page or paragraph numbers for all in-text citations, particularly when readers might have trouble finding the material in the original source without that information. If the source is quoted directly, a page number must be included in parentheses following the quotation:

> Feingold (1992) argued that "men scored significantly higher than women in situations designed to test aptitude in mathematics and hard sciences" (p. 92).

APA style uses the abbreviation *p.* or *pp.* before page numbers, which MLA style does not. If the author is not introduced with a signal phrase, the name, year, and page number would be noted parenthetically after the quotation:

> One study found that "men scored significantly higher than women in situations designed to test aptitude in mathematics and hard sciences" (Feingold, 1992, p. 92).

Many studies in the social sciences have multiple authors. In a work with two authors, cite both authors every time:

> Dlugos and Friedlander (2000) wrote that "sustaining passionate commitment to work as a psychotherapist reflects passionate commitment in other areas of life" (p. 298).

Here, too, if you do not identify the authors in a signal phrase, include their names, the year the source was published, and the relevant page number parenthetically after the quotation—but use an ampersand (&) instead of the word *and* between the authors' names:

> Some believe that "sustaining passionate commitment to work as a psychotherapist reflects passionate commitment in other areas of life" (Dlugos & Friedlander, 2000, p. 298).

Use the same principles the first time you cite a work with three to five authors:

> Booth-Butterfield, Anderson, and Williams (2000) tested . . .
> (Booth-Butterfield, Anderson, & Williams, 2000, p. 5)

Thereafter, you can use the name of the first author followed by the abbreviation *et al.* (Latin for "and others") in roman type:

> Booth-Butterfield et al. (2000) tested . . .
> (Booth-Butterfield et al., 2000, p. 5)

For a work with six or more authors, use *et al.* from the first mention.

These are only some of the most basic examples of APA in-text citation. Consult the APA manual for other guidelines.

References.   APA style, like MLA style, requires a separate list of sources at the end of a research paper. In APA style, this list is called "References," not "Works Cited." The list of references starts on a new page at the end of your paper and lists sources alphabetically by author (or title if no author is identified). Figure A.2 shows a sample list of references with sources cited in APA style.

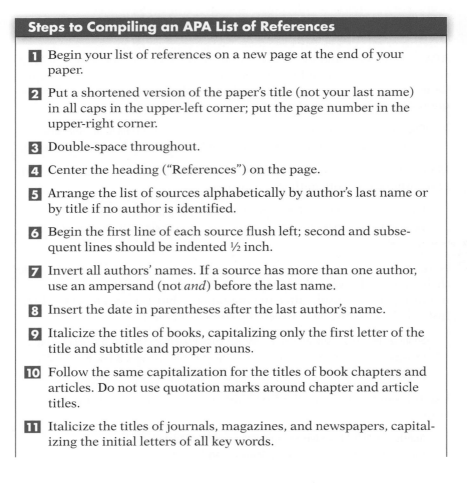

Steps to Compiling an APA List of References

1 Begin your list of references on a new page at the end of your paper.

2 Put a shortened version of the paper's title (not your last name) in all caps in the upper-left corner; put the page number in the upper-right corner.

3 Double-space throughout.

4 Center the heading ("References") on the page.

5 Arrange the list of sources alphabetically by author's last name or by title if no author is identified.

6 Begin the first line of each source flush left; second and subsequent lines should be indented ½ inch.

7 Invert all authors' names. If a source has more than one author, use an ampersand (not *and*) before the last name.

8 Insert the date in parentheses after the last author's name.

9 Italicize the titles of books, capitalizing only the first letter of the title and subtitle and proper nouns.

10 Follow the same capitalization for the titles of book chapters and articles. Do not use quotation marks around chapter and article titles.

11 Italicize the titles of journals, magazines, and newspapers, capitalizing the initial letters of all key words.

12 For books, list the place of publication and the name of the publisher. For chapters, list the book editor(s), the book title, the relevant page numbers, and the place of publication and the name of the publisher. For articles, list the journal title, the volume number, the issue number if each issue of the volume begins on page 1, the relevant pages, and the DOI (digital object identifier) if available. If you retrieve a journal article online and there is no DOI, include the URL of the journal's home page.

GENDER AND TEACHING   15

References

Journal article with no DOI

Campbell, R. J. (1969). Co-education: Attitudes and self-concepts of girls at three schools. *British Journal of Educational Psychology, 39,* 87.

Report, seven authors

Coleman, J., Campbell, E., Hobson, C., McPartland, J., Mood, A., Weinfeld, F., & York, R. (1966). *Equality of educational opportunity (The Coleman Report)*. Washington, DC: U.S. Government Printing Office.

Journal article with a DOI

Feingold, A. (1992). Sex differences in variability in intellectual abilities: A new look at an old controversy. *Review of Educational Research, 62,* 61–84. doi:10.3102/00346543062001061

Online source

Haag, P. (2003). *K–12 single-sex education: What does the research say?* Retrieved from http://www.ericdigests .org/2001-2/sex.html

Journal article retrieved online with no DOI

Hallinan, M. T. (1994). Tracking: From theory to practice. *Sociology of Education, 67,* 79–84. Retrieved from http:// www.asanet.org/journals/soe/

Hanson, S. L. (1994). Lost talent: Unrealized educational aspirations and expectations among U.S. youth. *Sociology of Education, 67,* 159–183. Retrieved from http://www .asanet.org/journals/soe/

Jovanovic, J., & King, S. S. (1998). Boys and girls in the performance-based science classroom: Who's doing the performing? *American Educational Research Journal, 35,* 477–496. doi:10.3102/00028312035003477

FIGURE A.2   Sample List of References, APA Format

Lee, V. E., & Marks, H. M. (1990). Sustained effects of the single-sex secondary school experience on attitudes, behaviors, and values in college. *Journal of Educational Psychology, 82*, 578–592.

Mickelson, R. A. (1989). Why does Jane read and write so well? The anomaly of women's achievement. *Sociology of Education, 62*, 47–63. Retrieved from http://www.asanet.org/journals/soe/

Scholarly book

Rosenberg, M. (1965). *Society and the adolescent self-image*. Princeton, NJ: Princeton University Press.

Schneider, F. W., & Coutts, L. M. (1982). The high school environment: A comparison of coeducational and single-sex schools. *Journal of Educational Psychology, 74*, 898–906.

Essay in an edited collection

Spade, J. Z. (2001). Gender education in the United States. In J. H. Ballantine & J. Z. Spade (Eds.), *Schools and society: A sociological approach to education* (pp. 270–278). Belmont, CA: Wadsworth/Thomson Learning.

Streitmatter, J. L. (1999). *For girls ONLY: Making a case for single-sex schooling*. Albany, NY: State University of New York Press.

Dissertation from a database

Winslow, M. A. (1995). *Where the boys are: The educational aspirations and future expectations of working-class girls in an all-female high school* (Doctoral dissertation). University of Arizona. Retrieved from ProQuest Dissertations and Theses database. (AAT 9622975)

The *APA Manual* is your best resource for formatting online sources, but here is an example of a basic reference to an online source:

Author. (Date posted/revised). *Document title*. Retrieved from URL

- Provide the author's name in inverted order: last name first. If no author is identified, alphabetize the entry by its title.
- Capitalize an online document title like an article title and italicize it; don't enclose it in quotation marks.
- Include a retrieval date after the word "Retrieved" only if the content is likely to change.

- Notice that there is no end punctuation after the DOI or URL.
- APA style asks you to break lengthy DOIs or URLs after a slash or before a period, being sure that your composing software doesn't insert a hyphen at the line break.

You should know that some sources you may rely on in your research in the social sciences—interviews and focus groups, for example—do not have to be included in your list of references. Instead, you would cite the person you interviewed or the focus group you conducted in the text of your paper. For example:

(J. Long, personal interview, April 7, 2017)

ACKNOWLEDGMENTS

Mary Aiken. "Designed to Addict." Excerpted from *The Cyber Effect: A Pioneering Cyberpsychologist Explains How Human Behavior Changes Online* by Mary Aiken. Copyright © 2016 by Cyber Matrix Limited. Used by permission of Spiegel & Grau, an imprint of Random House, a division of Penguin Random House LLC. All rights reserved. Any third party use of this material, outside of this publication, is prohibited. Interested third parties must apply directly to Penguin Random House LLC for permission.

Melissa Avdeeff. "Beyoncé and Social Media: Authenticity and the Presentation of Self." Excerpted from *The Beyoncé Effect: Essays on Sexuality, Race, and Feminism*, edited by Adrienne Trier-Bieniek. Copyright © 2016. Reprinted by permission of McFarland & Company, Inc.

Emily Badger. "Mapped: The Places Where Most Public School Children Are Poor." From the *Washington Post*, Wonkblog, May 13, 2015, https://www.washingtonpost.com/news/wonk/wp/2015/05/13/mapped-the-places-where-most-public-school-children-are-poor/?utm_term=.36097011ca12. Copyright © 2016 The Washington Post. All rights reserved. Used by permission and protected by the Copyright Laws of the United States. The printing, copying, redistribution, or retransmission of this Content without express written permission is prohibited.

Susan D. Blum. "The United States of (Non)Reading: The End of Civilization or a New Era?" From *HuffPost College*, October 8, 2013. Copyright © 2013 by Susan Blum. Reprinted with permission.

Rachel Carson. "A Fable for Tomorrow." From *Silent Spring* by Rachel Carson. Copyright © 1962 by Rachel L. Carson. Copyright © renewed 1990 by Roger Christie. Reprinted by permission of Houghton Mifflin Harcourt Publishing Company and Frances Collin, Trustee. All copying, including electronic, or redistribution of this text is expressly forbidden.

Ta-Nehisi Coates. "Between the World and Me." From *Between the World and Me* by Ta-Nehisi Coates. Copyright © 2015 by Ta-Nehisi Coates. Used by permission of Spiegel & Grau, an imprint of Random House, a division of Penguin Random House LLC. All rights reserved. Any third party use of this material, outside of this publication, is prohibited. Interested third parties must apply directly to Penguin Random House LLC for permission.

Anne Colby and Thomas Ehrlich, with Elizabeth Beaumont and Jason Stephens (the Carnegie Foundation for the Advancement of Teaching). Excerpt from "Undergraduate Education and the Development of Moral and Civic Responsibility." From *The Communitarian Network*, www2.gwu.edu/~ccps/Colby.html. Reprinted by permission of the Institute for Communitarian Policy Studies.

William Deresiewicz. "The End of Solitude." From the *Chronicle of Higher Education*, January 2009. Used with the permission of the *Chronicle of Higher Education*. Copyright © 2009. All rights reserved.

John Dickerson. "Don't Fear Twitter." From Nieman Reports, Summer 2008. Nieman Foundation for Journalism at Harvard. Reprinted by permission.

Ann duCille. Excerpt from "Dyes and Dolls: Multicultural Barbie and the Merchandising of Difference." From *differences: A Journal of Feminist Cultural Studies*, Spring 1994, Volume 6, No. 1, pp. 46–68. Copyright © 1994 Brown University and *differences: A Journal of Feminist Cultural Studies*. All rights reserved. Republished by permission of the copyright holder, and the present publisher, Duke University Press. www.dukeupress.edu.

Carol Dweck. "Chapter 1: The Mindsets." From *Mindset: The New Psychology of Success* by Carol S. Dweck, PhD. Copyright © 2006 by Carol S. Dweck. Used by permission of Random House, an imprint and division of Penguin Random House LLC. All rights reserved. Any third party use of this material, outside of this publication, is

with permission from John Wiley & Sons, Inc., from *Reading Research Quarterly* 36.1 (January/February/March 2001), pp. 8–26; permission conveyed through Copyright Clearance Center, Inc.

Laurie Ouellette. Excerpt from "Citizen Brand: ABC and the Do Good Turn in US Television." From *Commodity Activism: Cultural Resistance in Neoliberal Times*, edited by Roopali Mukherjee and Sarah Banet-Weiser. Copyright © 2012 New York University. Reprinted by permission.

Laura Pappano. "How Big-Time Sports Ate College Life." From the *New York Times*, January 22, 2012. Copyright © 2012 The New York Times. All rights reserved. Used by permission and protected by the Copyright Laws of the United States. The printing, copying, redistribution, or retransmission of this Content without express written permission is prohibited.

C. J. Pascoe. "'Dude, You're a Fag': Adolescent Masculinity and the Fag Discourse." From *Sexualities* 8.3 (2005), pp. 329–46. Copyright © 2005 by Sage Publications. Reprinted by permission of SAGE Publications, Ltd., London, Los Angeles, New Delhi, Singapore, and Washington, D.C.

William J. Peace. "Slippery Slopes: Media, Disability, and Adaptive Sports." From *The Body Reader: Essential Social and Cultural Readings*, edited by Mary Kosut and Lisa Jean Moore. Copyright © 2010 New York University. Reprinted by permission.

Michael Pollan. "Why Bother?" From the *New York Times Magazine*, April 20, 2008. Copyright © 2008 by Michael Pollan. Used by permission. All rights reserved.

William Powers. "Not So Busy," Chapter 12 from *Hamlet's Blackberry* by William Powers. Copyright © 2010 by William Powers. Reprinted by permission of HarperCollins Publishers.

Phil Primack. "Doesn't Anybody Get a C Anymore?" From the *Boston Globe*, October 5, 2008. Reprinted by permission.

Eugene F. Provenzo Jr. "Hirsch's Desire for a National Curriculum." Excerpt from *Critical Literacy: What Every American Ought to Know* by Eugene F. Provenzo Jr., pp. 53–55. Copyright © 2005 by Paradigm Publishers. Republished with permission of Taylor & Francis Group LLC Books; permission conveyed through Copyright Clearance Center, Inc.

Anna Quindlen. "Doing Nothing Is Something." From *Newsweek*, May 12, 2002. Copyright © 2002 by Anna Quindlen. Used by permission. All rights reserved.

Dana Radcliffe. "Dashed Hopes: Why Aren't Social Media Delivering Democracy?" From the *Huffington Post*, October 21, 2015, http://www.huffingtonpost.com/dana-radcliffe/dashed-hopes-why-arent-so_b_8343082.html. Copyright © 2015. Reprinted by permission of the author.

Claudia Rankine. "The Condition of Black Life Is One of Mourning." From *The Fire This Time: A New Generation Speaks about Race*, edited by Jesmyn Ward. Copyright © 2015 by Claudia Rankine and NYT Company. Reprinted with the permission of Scribner, a division of Simon & Schuster, Inc. All rights reserved. (First published in the *New York Times Magazine*, June 22, 2015.)

Sean F. Reardon, Jane Waldfogel, and Daphna Bassok. "The Good News about Educational Inequality." From the *New York Times*, August 28, 2016. Copyright © 2016 The New York Times. All rights reserved. Used by permission and protected by the Copyright Laws of the United States. The printing, copying, redistribution, or retransmission of this Content without express written permission is prohibited.

Robert B. Reich. "The Rise of the Working Poor." From *Saving Capitalism: For the Many, Not the Few* by Robert B. Reich. Copyright © 2015 by Robert B. Reich. Used by permission of Alfred A. Knopf, an imprint of the Knopf Doubleday Publishing Group, a division of Penguin Random House LLC. All rights reserved. Any third party use of this material, outside of this publication, is prohibited. Interested third parties must apply directly to Penguin Random House LLC for permission.

Richard Rodriguez. "Scholarship Boy." From *Hunger of Memory: The Education of Richard Rodriguez* by Richard Rodriguez. Copyright © 1982 by Richard Rodriguez. Reprinted by permission of David R. Godine, Publisher, Inc.

Stuart Rojstaczer. "Grade Inflation Gone Wild." From the *Christian Science Monitor*, March 24, 2009. Copyright © 2009 by Stuart Rojstaczer. Reprinted with permission.

Tom Standage. Excerpt from "History Retweets Itself," the epilogue to *Writing on the Wall: Social Media—The First 2,000 Years* by Tom Standage. Copyright © 2013. Reprinted by permission of Bloomsbury Publishing Inc.

Sandra Steingraber. "Despair Not." From *In These Times*, May 25, 2011, adapted from *Raising Elijah: Protecting Our Children in an Age of Environmental Crisis* by Sandra Steingraber. Copyright © 2011. Reprinted by permission of Da Capo Press, an imprint of Perseus Books LLC, a subsidiary of Hachette Book Group, Inc.

Richard H. Thaler, Cass R. Sunstein, and John P. Balz. Excerpt from "Choice Architecture" (April 2, 2010). Reprinted by permission.

Clive Thompson. "On the New Literacy." From *WIRED Magazine*, August 24, 2009. Copyright © 2009 Condé Nast. Reprinted with permission.

Sherry Turkle. "The Flight from Conversation." From the *New York Times Magazine*, April 22, 2012. Copyright © 2012 The New York Times. All rights reserved. Used by permission and protected by the Copyright Laws of the United States. The printing, copying, redistribution, or retransmission of this Content without express written permission is prohibited.

Sherry Turkle. "Growing Up Tethered." From *Alone Together: Why We Expect More from Technology and Less from Each Other* by Sherry Turkle. Copyright © 2011. Reprinted by permission of Basic Books, an imprint of Perseus Books LLC, a subsidiary of Hachette Book Group, Inc.

David Tyack. "Whither History Textbooks?" From *Seeking Common Ground: Public Schools in a Diverse Society* by David Tyack, Cambridge, Mass.: Harvard University Press. Copyright © 2003 by the President and Fellows of Harvard College. Reprinted by permission of the publisher.

Index of Authors, Titles, and Key Terms